ArtScroll Tanach Series®

A traditional commentary on the Books of the Bible

Rabbi Nosson Scherman/Rabbi Meir Zlotowitz
General Editors

Yechezkel

THE BOOK OF EZEKIEL / A NEW TRANSLATION WITH A COMMENTARY ANTHOLOGIZED FROM TALMUDIC, MIDRASHIC, AND RABBINIC SOURCES.

Published by

Mesorah Publications, ltd

ספר יחזקאל

Translation and Commentary by
Rabbi Moshe Eisemann

An Overview /
'Yechezkel — Dirge, Search and Rebirth'
by Rabbi Moshe Eisemann
in collaboration with
Rabbi Nosson Scherman

FIRST EDITION
First Impression . . . December 1977

SECOND EDITION
Revised and Corrected
First Impression . . . November 1979

THIRD EDITION
COMPLETE — 3 VOLUMES IN ONE
First Impression . . . November 1988
Second Impression . . . March 1994

Published and Distributed by
MESORAH PUBLICATIONS, Ltd.
4401 Second Avenue
Brooklyn, New York 11232

Distributed in Europe by
J. LEHMANN HEBREW BOOKSELLERS
20 Cambridge Terrace
Gateshead, Tyne and Wear
England NE8 1RP

Distributed in Israel by
SIFRIATI / A. GITLER—BOOKS
4 Bilu Street
P.O.B. 14075
Tel Aviv 61140

Distributed in Australia & New Zealand by
GOLD'S BOOK & GIFT CO.
36 William Street
Balaclava 3183, Vic., Australia

Distributed in South Africa by
KOLLEL BOOKSHOP
22 Muller Street
Yeoville 2198, Johannesburg, South Africa

YECHEZKEL / EZEKIEL — Three Volumes In One

ISBN
0-89906-085-4 (hard cover)
0-89906-086-2 (paperback)

Typography by CompuScribe at ArtScroll Studios, Ltd.
4401 Second Avenue / Brooklyn, N.Y. 11232 / (718) 921-9000

Printed in the United States of America by Moriah Offset
Bound by Sefercraft, Quality Bookbinders, Ltd. Brooklyn, N.Y.

Table of Contents

Table of Contents

List of Illustrations:

[*Appendices I-V appears in vol. 1; Appendix VI appears in vol. 2]

הסכמת מרן הגאון מהור״ר יעקב יצחק הלוי רודערמאן שליט״א
ראש ישיבת נר ישראל

ישיבת נר ישראל

NER ISRAEL RABBINICAL COLLEGE
400 MT. WILSON LANE
BALTIMORE, MARYLAND 21208

OFFICE OF THE PRESIDENT
RABBI JACOB I. RUDERMAN

כבוד ידידי הרה״ג הנעלה חכם ושלם
הרב משה אייזעמאן שליט״א.

באשר ידידי עומד להוציא לאור תרגום ופירוש על יחזקאל בלשון המדוברת לתועלת אלה שאינם מבינים לשון הקודש או שאין ביכלתם לעיין במקור הדברים, הנני לחזק את ידיו באשר שדעתי שהמפעל הזה להוציא ספרי קודש באנגלית לתועלת גדולה ובודאי שהרבה יהנו מזה.

ואף כי לא עיינתי בדבריו, כבר איתמחי גברא בספרו הראשון על עניני תפלה, ובודאי כמעשהו בראשון כך מעשהו בשני. ובטח שיוציא מתחת ידו דבר מתוקן.

ממני הדו״ש ושלום תורתו באהבה.

יעקב יצחק הלוי רודערמאן

הסכמת מרן הגאון מהור״ר יעקב קאמענצקי שליט״א
ראש ישיבת תורה ודעת

יעקב קאמענצקי
מאנסי, נוא יארק

RABBI J. KAMENTZKY
38 SADDLE RIVER RD.
MONSEY, NEW YORK 10952

בע״ה
יום ג׳ כ״ו כסלו תשל״ח פה מאנסי.
אל הו״כ ידידי הרב הגאון הנעלה איש המעלות והחמודות מוה״ר משה נ״י אייזמאן שלו׳ וכל טוב.

מה מאד שמחתי בראותי כי כבודו קיבל על עצמו לתרגם ספר יחזקאל באנגלית ולחבר פירוש על ספר זה, מיוסד על דברי חכמינו ז״ל ראשונים ואחרונים. הרבה עניינים בספר יחזקאל סתומים וחתומים הם ומעוררים תמיהות הדורשות יישוב, וכבר בקשו חכמים לגונזו מפני שמצאו בו דברים הסותרים לדברי תורה עד שדרשן חנני׳ בן חזקי׳, על אחת כמה וכמה שבדורנו זה קשה מאד להגיע לידי הבנת דברי הנביא. ולפיכך יישר כחו וחילו שעמל וטרח להראות דרך בלימוד הספר הזה ולהוציא את אוצרות התורה והמוסר הגנוזים בו. גם בגשתו אל הקודש פנימה, היינו במעשה המרכבה עשה יפה שכתב הקדמה כללית ובמקום פירוש מקיף ומפורש הביא רק תמצית דברי רבותינו הקדמונים. ובטח שיהי׳ רב התועלת למי שיהגה בו. והנני בזה לעודדו ולברכו שיזכה לגמור חיבורו ולהוציא לאור גם על החלק השני של ספר יחזקאל, לזכות את הרבים ולהגדיל את התורה ולהאדירה.

כעתירת ידידו המברכו מתוך הנפש בהוקרה

הסכמת מרן הגאון מהור״ר שניאור קוטלר שליט״א
ראש ישיבת בית מדרש גבוה

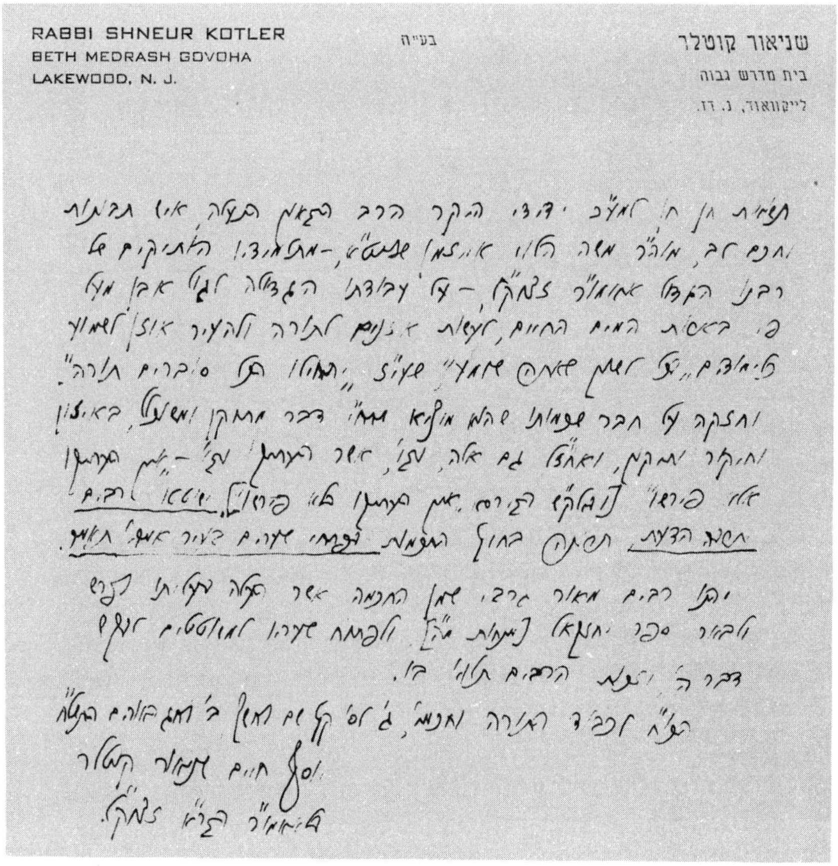

תשואות חן חן למע״כ ידידי היקר הרב הגאון הנעלה, איש תבונות וחכם לב, מוה״ר משה הלוי אייזמן שליט״א, — מתלמידיו הותיקים של רבינו הגדול אאמו״ר זצוק״ל, — על עבודתו הגדולה לגול אבן מעל פי בארות המים החיים, לעשות אזנים לתורה ולהעיר אוזן לשמוע כלימודים ,,בכל לשון שאתה שומע״, שעי״ז ,,יתחילו הכל סוברים תורה״. וחזקה על חבר שכמותו שהוא מוציא מתח״י דבר מתוקן ומשוכלל, באיזון וחיקור ותיקון, ואחז״ל גם אלה, וגו׳, אשר העתיקו, וגו׳ — ,,אין העתיקו אלא פירשו״ [ובילק״ש הגירסא ,,אין העתיקו בלא פירשו״]. **ישוטטו רבים ותרבה הדעת**, תרונה בחוץ החכמות **ובפתחי שערים בעיר אמרי׳ תאמר.**

יהנו רבים מאור גרבי שמן החכמה אשר העלה בעליתו לפרש ולבאר ספר יחזקאל [מנחות מ״ה], ולפתוח שעריו למשוטטים לבקש דבר ה׳, וזכות הרבים תלוי׳ בו.

הכו״ח לכבוד התורה וחכמי׳, ג׳ לס׳ קץ שם לחשך. ב׳ לחג האורים התשל״ח

יוסף חיים שניאור קוטלר
בלאאמו״ר הגר״א זצוק״ל

Preface

When the Editorial Board of Mesorah Publications asked me to contribute to their Tanach series I recognized an opportunity to put into practice ideas which had lain dormant within me for some time.

During my years of teaching Tanach to various groups I had come to discover in the Book of Ezekiel, *the stimulus to examine many concepts which became mainstays within my own* Hashkafah *framework.*

I found this interest reflected in the attitude of my students who seemed consistently to be inspired by the truths which we discovered together as we studied this Book.

Many years ago I started to keep notes on the Book of Ezekiel *in the hope that one day I might be able to share my thoughts with a wider public. This chance has now been granted me.*

Since much of the commentary developed from classroom experience its scope is somewhat different from that of most other books in the ArtScroll series. While in general it attempts to anthologize many of the classic commentators, there is also a great emphasis on the Hashkafah problems which were discussed as part of our learning. By their very nature these discussions reflect a subjective approach. I recognize that the same sources which lead me to certain conclusions might lend themselves just as well to different interpretations. Indeed, if the reader feels stimulated to research the wide range of topics which are touched upon in this work for his own ideas, I would feel richly rewarded.

It should also be noted that there is a relative lack of literature available on the Book of Ezekiel. *This in itself would have been enough to force the writer to range farther afield, beyond the immediate commentators, for the solution of many problems.*

In my search for an interpretation of the Book which would make its lessons viable to me, I was profoundly influenced by that school of Torah commentary which is associated with the name of Harav Samson Raphael Hirsch. Writers like Harav Joseph Carlebach in his Die Drei Grossen Propheten, *Dr. Yitzchak Breuer in his many works, and* להבחל״ח *Harav Joseph Breuer* שליט״א *in his* Das Buch Jecheskel *opened up vistas which made me understand for the first time why the Book of* Ezekiel *is indeed a* נְבוּאָה שֶׁהוּצְרְכָה לְדוֹרוֹת, a prophecy with lessons for every generation. *A cursory glance at the commentary will show the reader that I have drawn on many sources besides these. Nevertheless the thoughts of these men, and particularly those of Harav Joseph Breuer* שליט״א, *whose masterful commentary is quoted on almost every page, formed my basic approach to the whole Book.*

Thus, in a very real sense it is a personal book which I am presenting to the loyal readers of the ArtScroll series. It is my hope that the chords which the message of this prophet of exile and redemption have struck within me, are to a degree an echo of the song of yearning which is welling up in the collective soul of Knesses Israel, and that in turn, in whomever they may reach they will find a receptive ear and an understanding heart.

HASHEM's Name

W*herever the Hebrew Four-Letter Name of God appears, it is translated "HASHEM," i.e. 'The Name' — the Holy Name of God. Where the Hebrew has* Elokim, *the more general and less 'personal' Name of the Deity — it is translated 'God.' Although the Name of the Creator is generally written 'G-d' and not spelled out in its entirety, this Book is a portion of the Holy Scriptures and the full Four Letter Name of HASHEM appears in the Hebrew; it would have been ludicrous to abbreviate the spelling of the Name in English.*

Frequently found in Yechezkel is the expression אֲדֹנָי יֱהוִֹה i.e., a combination of the Name denoting Lordship with the Four Letter Name vocalized and pronounced as if it were written אֱלֹהִים. *Rather than attempt a translation we have rendered these Names: 'My Lord HASHEM/ELOHIM' in order to preserve the implied duality. The commentary to 2:4 discusses the meaning of this combination. Further elaboration is found in the ArtScroll commentary to* Genesis 15:8.

Transliteration

A cross between the Sephardi and Ashkenazi transliteration of Hebrew words was used: Ashkenazi consonants, so to speak, with Sephardi vowels: Thus Yonasan *not* Yonatan, *etc. Proper names that have become generally accepted have been retained; thus: Jeremiah, Jerusalem, Bethlehem, Zion were retained and not changed to conform to our method of transliteration. Although there are several inconsistencies, the style has generally been held throughout the work.*

אֶרֶץ יִשְׂרָאֵל, *was translated* Eretz Yisrael *(Land of Israel). Where the word 'Israel' is found, it refers to the Jewish people in general, not always specifically as distinct from the Tribe of Judah.*

The Letter Vav

The prefix ו, vav, *is an extremely versatile tool of the Hebrew language. Its use is by no means limited to the conjunction* 'and'. Ibn Janach *in the* Sefer Harikmah *isolates no fewer than seventeen instances* (Radak *in the* Michlol *has thirteen) in which the Hebrew language uses the* ו, vav, *but where English would require such participles as: so; as; when; with; but, and so on.*

Thus the translator has considerable freedom of choice and the monotony of a constantly repeated 'and' can be avoided. On the other hand this flexibility and freedom of choice imposes a great responsibility on him to choose correctly from among the many possible translations.

Ibn Janach *makes clear that the* וָו הַמְהַפֶּכֶת, the conversive ו *(that is, the* ו *which changes the tense of a verb from past to future, or from future to past) when* introducing *a subject,* is not *a conjunction and is not translated as* and. *Thus* וַיְהִי בִּשְׁלֹשִׁים שָׁנָה *at the beginning of Yechezkel is to be translated* 'It was in the thirtieth year' *rather than* 'And it was in the thirtieth year.' *However, where the form occurs in the course of a subject it serves a dual function: i.e., it is a conversive* ו *and also a conjunction. Thus:* וָאֶרְאֶה מַרְאוֹת אֱלֹהִים, 'And I saw visions of God.'

Acknowledgments

I owe a great debt of gratitude to RABBI NOSSON SCHERMAN *who has been a pillar of support and a patient and understanding source of encouragement throughout the writing of this volume. There is hardly a paragraph in the commentary which has not been improved by his perceptive editing. He kindly undertook the difficult task of writing the Overview, thereby lending the grace and eloquence of his masterful style to those thoughts which I felt were fundamental to the understanding of the Book. The smooth and pleasing flow of the translation must also be credited to him. I feel sure that this volume will join those others of the ArtScroll series which have earned him such a large following of grateful readers.*

To RABBI MEIR ZLOTOWITZ *must go the credit for the inspiration which led to the ArtScroll series of which this work is a part. When I undertook to work on this commentary I had no idea of the amount of work which it would require. But even then I feared that it would be beyond my capabilities, it was his gentle but firm prodding which launched me on this project which has proved to be a most rewarding experience. I am grateful to him for having had the vision and trust to encourage this endeavor.*

Everyone at ArtScroll has worked hard and lovingly at the many tasks needed to be done, which must often have been repetitive and tedious. The high technical standard and beauty of the book are the result of their very personal involvement with the project.

My profoundest gratitude goes to REB SHEA BRANDER, *who has once more outdone himself with a work of rare artistry. The nature of the book may be such as does not make for easy reading. Its pleasing appearance will surely help facilitate its study.*

My gratitude is also extended to the other members of the ArtScroll staff: SHIMON SHAMILZADEH *who cheerfully and efficiently supervised much of the technical work;* MISS ESTHER HARTMAN, MISS ROCHEL BRISMAN, *and* MRS. PEARL EIDLIS *who expertly set type despite the occasional difficulty of the manuscript and frequent corrections and additions; and* GOLDIE BORGER *who managed so much of the communication between Baltimore and New York with calm competence.*

RABBI AVIE GOLD *read the manuscript from beginning to end, checking all the sources and correcting the many mistakes which had crept into it. If text and commentary can make any claim to accuracy it is in no small measure due to his patience and erudition.*

NECHEMIAH DRILLMAN *and* BARNEA SELEVAN *read some of the galleys making corrections and valuable suggestions which I often incorporated into the commentary. I am grateful for their help and interest.*

A particular expression of thanks is due to MISS FEIGA ZYLBERMINC *of the Library of Congress. With unfailing patience and courtesy she filled the many, occasionally complicated, requests which I had to make in the course of this work. Many important parts of the commentary would have been missing without her help.*

Lastly, a word is in place concerning the two Yeshivos with which I have been associated during the last twenty years. The first uncertain steps in my teaching career were taken at the TALMUDICAL YESHIVAH OF PHILADELPHIA *and it was there that I first taught Tanach with the guidance and encouragement of the Roshei Hayeshiva,* HARAV ELYA SVEI שליט״א *and* HARAV SHMUEL KAMENETZKY שליט״א. *The commentary to Yechezkel began to take form during those years.*

For the past nine years it has been my privilege to be associated with YESHIVAS NER ISRAEL OF BALTIMORE, *where once more, over the years, I was able to continue teaching Tanach to many groups of interested talmidim. I am happy to be able to express my thanks to the Rosh Hayeshiva* מרן הגאון מורה״ר יעקב יצחק הלוי רודערמאן שליט״א *and to the Menahel,* HARAV NAFTOLI NEUBERGER שליט״א *for the wonderfully enriching years which I have spent there.*

Moshe Eisemann

לזכר נשמות אבי מורי החבר ר׳ חיים בן החבר ר׳ יחיאל הלוי ז״ל
ואמי מורתי האשה לאה בת ר׳ מאיר ע״ה,
ולזכר נשמות מורי חמי מוהר״ר חיים בן מוהר״ר אשר מיכאל הכהן ז״ל
וחמותי מורתי האשה ריקל בת ר׳ משה ע״ה.

An Overview
Yechezkel — Dirge, Search, and Rebirth

Twilight of the Monarchy
— A Historical Background

An Overview/ Yechezkel — Dirge, Search, and Rebirth

וּשְׁמַרְתֶּם וַעֲשִׂיתֶם כִּי הִוא חָכְמַתְכֶם וּבִינַתְכֶם לְעֵינֵי הָעַמִּים אֲשֶׁר יִשְׁמְעוּן אֵת כָּל הַחֻקִּים הָאֵלֶּה וְאָמְרוּ רַק עַם חָכָם וְנָבוֹן הַגּוֹי הַגָּדוֹל הַזֶּה. כִּי מִי גוֹי גָּדוֹל אֲשֶׁר לוֹ אֱלֹהִים קְרֹבִים אֵלָיו

Guard them [the commandments] and fulfill them for that is your wisdom and your understanding in the eyes of the nations, who will hear of all these decrees and say, 'Only a wise and understanding people is this great nation. For which nation is so great that it has God near it?' (Deut. 4:6-7).

וַתֶּמֶר אֶת מִשְׁפָּטַי לְרִשְׁעָה מִן הַגּוֹיִם וְאֶת חֻקּוֹתַי מִן הָאֲרָצוֹת אֲשֶׁר סְבִיבוֹתֶיהָ כִּי בְמִשְׁפָּטַי מָאָסוּ וְחֻקּוֹתַי לֹא הָלְכוּ בָהֶם

But she exchanged my ordinances for wickedness more than did the nations; and my decrees more than the lands around her; for My ordinances they spurned, and My decrees — they did not follow them (Ezekiel 5:6).

יחזקאל רישיה חורבנא וסיפיה נחמתא

Ezekiel's beginning [tells of] destruction and its conclusion [tells of] consolation (Bava Basra 14b).

I. Potential and Reality

What could have been

Moses portrayed what could have been; Yechezkel portrayed what was.

Israel could have been mankind's champion, its leader, the nation that demonstrated in its being the exaltation that could have been man's, the embodiment of the greatness for which Adam and his

descendants were created. Israel could have been the parchment upon which God's word was written, could have been a living, breathing Torah scroll, could have been the living example that true wisdom and understanding was the product of the fulfillment of God's word.

Israel could have been — had it but heeded the teachings and hearkened to the exhortations of Moses.

But Israel did not heed and did not hearken, and therefore it continued the process of redemption and exile until the final redemption with the coming of Messiah, may it be speedily in our days.

Because Israel was worthy, the Presence of God proudly rested upon the work of their hands.

Moses built a Tabernacle and Solomon built a Temple, and because Israel was worthy, the Presence of God proudly rested upon the work of their hands. So intense was the holiness of the *Shechinah*, God's Presence, as it rested in a cloud upon the Tabernacle that even Moses feared to enter *(Exodus* 40:34-35), and so total was its presence on the Temple that the priests could not enter *(I Kings* 8:11). But God's *Shechinah* rests ultimately on His people, not on their architecture. His purpose is Man, not man's temples. So, when Israel descended from the lofty heights of spiritual grandeur to the earthly depths of lust and iniquity, the *Shechinah* ascended from Israel's Temple which had become no more than a shell — beautiful but empty — and returned to the heavens where it had been before Israel fashioned earth into a habitation for God.

But God's Shechinah *rests ultimately on His people, not on their architecture.*

What Was — and Will Be

In ten agonizing stages, the Shechinah *slowly withdrew from the Holy City and the Holy Temple.*

It was the lot of Yechezkel to witness the tragedy which Israel had wrought — the departure of the *Shechinah* from its once hospitable abode because Israel no longer deserved its presence. In ten agonizing stages, the *Shechinah* slowly withdrew from the Holy City and the Holy Temple, leaving them naked to the onslaught of Nebuchadnezzar and his Babylonian hordes (see *Prefatory Remarks* to Ch. 1 and *comm.* to Ch. 10). All this Yechezkel saw and he cried out in hopeless despair.

אֲהָהּ אֲדֹנָי אֱלֹהִים הֲמַשְׁחִית אַתָּה אֵת כָּל שְׁאֵרִית יִשְׂרָאֵל בְּשָׁפְכְּךָ אֶת חֲמָתְךָ עַל יְרוּשָׁלָיִם

Alas God! Do you destroy the entire remnant of Israel in the outpouring of Your fury upon Jerusalem? (9:8).

But Yechezkel's visions were not all bleak.

But Yechezkel's visions were not all bleak. He was more than the prophet of destruction: he was the prophet to Jewish exiles in Babylon, those who would forge the new, uncorrupted Jewish nation which would become the human temples of the future. And he *saw* the future, the glorious future when the Temple — the Third and eternal one — would stand enveloped in a glory that would eclipse all which had gone before. Yechezkel had suffered the awful torment of hearing the angels describe God's withdrawal from the Temple saying, בָּרוּךְ כְּבוֹד ה׳ מִמְּקוֹמוֹ, *Blessed is the glory of God* [*as He departs*] *'from' His place* (3:12). He would exult with another vision as God transported him to Eretz Yisrael, and set him down on a high mountain overlooking Jerusalem (40:2). From there he would be taken to a gate facing eastward, once again to see glorious visions, like those with which he inaugurated his prophecies and which were the prelude to destruction as they showed the departure of holiness from the sullied Temple. But now, Yechezkel would see the glory of God borne on a chariot that was not drawing away from Zion — but was *returning* to it, never again to depart:

He would exult with another vision.

The glory of God borne on a chariot that was not drawing away from Zion — but was returning *to it, never again to depart.*

וּכְבוֹד ה׳ בָּא אֶל הַבָּיִת דֶּרֶךְ שַׁעַר אֲשֶׁר פָּנָיו דֶּרֶךְ הַקָּדִים

And the glory of God was coming to the House by way of the gate which faced eastward (43:4).

II. The Three Requisites

King

There were three commandments which Israel was to fulfill upon its arrival in Eretz Yisrael, three commandments with which the destiny of Israel was

inextricably bound: to appoint a king; to exterminate Amalek; and to build the *Bais HaMikdash.*

A king from the Davidic dynasty — as natural and indispensable to the fulfillment of Israel's purpose as is the natural order of night and day or the interaction and balance of the atom, solar system, and constellations to the physical universe.

A king from the Davidic dynasty — as natural and indispensable to the fulfillment of Israel's purpose as is the natural order of night and day or the interaction and balance of the atom, solar system, and constellations to the physical universe (see *Jeremiah* 30:8-9). The ultimate redemption would manifest itself in the appearance of *'a rod from the stem of Jesse ... who would judge the poor with righteousness, reprove the earth's humble with fairness, strike the land with the staff of his mouth, and with the spirit of his mouth put the wicked to death (Isaiah* 11:1,4). The king, the King Messiah, would be the proof and the culmination of redemption following the exile of seemingly endless centuries. (See *Overview* to The *Book of Ruth,* ArtScroll ed.)

Amalek

The king was charged with attaining perfection within the nation, but the Divine scheme called equally for obliterating the evil and corruption without. Israel was charged with the responsibility to turn this material world into a throne for the holy majesty of God, with inculcating the realization that His Name is One however it may manifest itself to myopic human eyes. But blocking the attainment of these goals stood the nation that is foremost in evil just as Israel is foremost in good.

But blocking the attainment of these goals stood the nation that is foremost in evil just as Israel is foremost in good.

רֵאשִׁית גּוֹיִם עֲמָלֵק, *Amalek is the leader of nations (Numbers* 24:20) in championing the cause of evil, the belief that all depends on the roll of the dice and that God's will is merely a challenge to be thwarted.

כִּי יָד עַל כֵּס יָהּ, *The hand of God is placed upon His throne (Exodus* 17:16) in an eternal oath to wage war against the nation that embodies evil and whose very existence imperils — no, *dooms!* — the performance of good. For The Holy One, blessed be He, swore that אֵין שְׁמוֹ שָׁלֵם וְאֵין כִּסְאוֹ שָׁלֵם, Israel's perception of His Name and of the majesty of His throne could never be complete until Amalek was erased from the

Israel's perception of His Name and of the majesty of His throne could never be complete until Amalek was erased from the face of the earth.

face of the earth *(Pesikta Rabbasi* 12; *Tanchuma, Tetze* 9).

Temple

The erection of the Holy Temple was the final step. In it *the place which HASHEM will choose there to make His Name rest (Deut.* 16:2), Israel could perceive as nowhere else the glory which exists everywhere.

In the time of Solomon, the formula was near completion — but Israel proved not to be equal to its potential for greatness.

In the time of Solomon, the formula was near completion. The Davidic dynasty was in place, the Temple was built, and Amalek was an insignificant vassal close to extinction. *Near* completion — but Israel proved not to be equal to its potential for greatness. It lost its monarchy, lost its sway over Amalek, the seed of Esau, and finally lost its Temple.

While the disintegration of Judea is commonly dated from the reign of Menashe (see section on *Twilight of the Monarchy*) the seeds of its destruction were planted much earlier. When Isaiah exhorted King Achaz that he must repent lest God punish Israel grievously for its sins, he prophesied:

יָבִיא ה׳ עָלֶיךָ וְעַל עַמְּךָ וְעַל בֵּית אָבִיךָ יָמִים אֲשֶׁר לֹא בָאוּ לְמִיּוֹם סוּר אֶפְרַיִם מֵעַל יְהוּדָה

HASHEM will bring upon you, your people, and your father's house days such as have not come from the day Ephraim turned away from Judah (Isaiah 7:17).

The Seed — Disunity

If one seeks the epitome of misfortune unequalled, he need look no further than the day the Ten Tribes led by Ephraim seceded from the kingdom of King Rechavam.

The implication is clear. If one seeks the epitome of misfortune unequalled, he need look no further than the day the Ten Tribes led by Ephraim seceded from the kingdom of King Rechavam, son of Solomon. It was not until Jacob's family, consisting of the twelve tribes, was complete that Jewish nationhood could begin; the unity of the twelve tribes was essential to the fulfillment of the nation; the High Priest bore the names of all twelve tribes on his breastplate as he performed the Temple service. But because David's successors did not maintain his lofty standard of conduct — the precondition for God's continued grace — they lost the privilege of ruling over the en-

Israel split — and when that happened, the nation began the descent.

tire nation. Israel split — and when that happened, the nation began the descent that culminated in the exile of Zidkiyahu more than three hundred years later.

The deficiencies of the Judean kings had effect beyond the borders of Eretz Yisrael.

The deficiencies of the Judean kings had effect beyond the borders of Eretz Yisrael, for it influenced the historic interaction between the nations of Jacob and Esau. The conflict between the two sons of Isaac and Rebeccah ran deep. Even before they were born, Rebeccah was prophetically informed וּלְאֹם מִלְאֹם יֶאֱמָץ וְרַב יַעֲבֹד צָעִיר, *one nation will be mightier than the other nation, and* [ultimately] *the older will serve the younger (Gen.* 25:23). Isaac promised Esau that וְהָיָה כַּאֲשֶׁר תָּרִיד וּפָרַקְתָּ עֻלּוֹ מֵעַל צַוָּארֶךָ, *it will be that when you bemoan* [the fact that Jacob is not loyal to the dictates of the Torah *(Targum; Rashi)*], *you will cast off his yoke from upon your neck (ibid.* 27:40).

There was a constant tension between Jacob and Esau. Only one could be dominant.

Thus, there was a constant tension between Jacob and Esau. Only one could be dominant. It was a spiritual see-saw: when Jacob was loyal to his spiritual calling, he was pre-eminent; when he lapsed, Esau would rise to dominate him. Never would both simultaneously be great.

Kings in Edom

וְאֵלֶּה הַמְּלָכִים אֲשֶׁר מָלְכוּ בְּאֶרֶץ אֱדוֹם לִפְנֵי מְלָךְ מֶלֶךְ לִבְנֵי יִשְׂרָאֵל

These are the kings who reigned in Edom [*the land of Esau*] *before a king reigned in Israel (ibid.* 36:31).

There were kings in Edom *before* there were kings in Israel. Those were the years when Jacob was exiled to the house of Laban and then to the land of Pharaoh, and when his children were enslaved. With Israel downtrodden, Esau was ascendant.

His family produced kings while Jacob's produced slaves. But when Israel entered its land, Edom dwindled to insignificance.

His family produced kings while Jacob's produced slaves. But when Israel entered its land and had its own righteous rulers, Edom dwindled to insignificance. During the reigns of Israel's first eight kings, Edom had no kings at all; it was a tributary state: וּמֶלֶךְ אֵין בֶּאֱדוֹם נִצָּב מֶלֶךְ, *There was no king in Edom, a deputy was king (I Kings* 22:48).

But then, in the days of King Yehoram of Judah, Edom rebelled and set up its own monarchy.

בְּיָמָיו פָּשַׁע אֱדוֹם מִתַּחַת יַד יְהוּדָה וַיַּמְלִכוּ עֲלֵיהֶם מֶלֶךְ

In his days Edom revolted from under the hand of Judah and appointed a king over themselves (II Kings 8:20).

That Edomite kingdom was reborn because Yehoram married the wicked Asaliah .

From that day onward, Edom would rise and Judah would fall. Many years would pass, but finally Edom, in the form of the Roman Empire would dominate the world and Israel would be led into captivity by it *(Bereishis Rabbah* 83:2). That Edomite kingdom was reborn because Yehoram married the wicked Asaliah, daughter of King Ahab and Queen Jezebel whose iniquities went beyond all bounds in Samaria. Thus, Israel's downfall began when its twelve tribes split asunder, Edom's ascendancy began when David's descendant fawned before the Samarian idolators. Israel does not live in isolation; its Edomite twin rises and falls according to Israel's spiritual ascent and descent *(Drashas HaRan II).*

So it was inevitable that the Temple would cease to exist as a building when it ceased to be a suitable resting place for the Shechinah

With the monarchy doomed and the Edomite nation — including its Amalekite offspring — growing in power, the third leg of Israel's national mission, the Holy Temple, could not long stand. God warned Solomon when he inaugurated the Temple that its existence, and, indeed the very survival of the nation in its Land, would depend on Israel's adherence to Torah *(I Kings* 9:2-9). So it was inevitable that the Temple would cease to exist as a building when it ceased to be a suitable resting place for the *Shechinah.*

The Future

If their deeds were perverse, then their sacrifices were an abomination.

Contrary to the delusions of the people in the generation of Yechezkel, the Temple was not their guarantee of national survival against Babylon, nor were the sacrifices an antidote to the spiritual poison afflicting them. The Temple and its service were reflections of the people. If the nation was empty, then the Temple was a shell; if their deeds were perverse, then their sacrifices were an abomination.

It is of major significance, however, that Yechezkel's prophecy concluded with a vision of the future return of God's glory. This vision placed his entire role in its proper perspective, for bleak though his immediate visions were and stark though his forecast for Jerusalem was, he remained a prophet of hope.

The cancer of the present had to be excised.

But Israel would remain God's chosen nation.

And the remnant in Babylon — were being groomed to blossom into the Torah nation that would succeed where its forebears had failed.

The cancer of the present had to be excised, the physical Jerusalem was doomed in order to reflect the spiritual disintegration of its people. *But Israel would remain God's chosen nation* and his *Shechinah* would yet return in a glory greater than Israel had ever known before. And the remnant in Babylon — reviled and derided by the self-proclaimed elite of Jerusalem — were being groomed by God and tutored by Yechezkel to blossom into the Torah nation that would succeed where its forebears had failed.

III. Yechezkel — Prophet to the Exile

Cause of Exile

So Yechezkel was the prophet whose primary mission was *away* from Eretz Yisrael — what is the mission of such a prophet? Clearly he must teach the unique lesson of exile and renew the perceptions of Israel's unique role — what is the lesson and what is the role?

וְאִם בְּזֹאת לֹא תִשְׁמְעוּ לִי וַהֲלַכְתֶּם עִמִּי בְּקֶרִי. וְהָלַכְתִּי עִמָּכֶם בַּחֲמַת קֶרִי

And if despite this you do not hearken to me, and go with me casually then I will proceed with you in a fury of casualness (Leviticus 26:27-28).

. . . וְאֶתְכֶם אֱזָרֶה בַגּוֹיִם . . .

And I will scatter you among the nations (ibid. v. 33).

The primary reason for the exile was that Israel treated God's service casually and His providence as coincidence.

The primary reason for the exile was that Israel treated God's service casually and His providence as coincidence. They failed to express in their lives the realization that the law of the Torah is no less a reality than the law of gravity; that He presides over the destiny of Israel and is intimately involved in its

vicissitudes. Instead they divorced their religious obligation from the perception that it had a decisive relationship to their everyday fortunes. An understanding of the fate of the nation, they thought, was to be found in the rules of statecraft or the vagaries of nature; what befell them, they thought, was a product of coincidence. The fortunes of Israel, they thought, were to be interpreted as one might interpret the fortunes of any other people or any other land — but they refused to realize that Israel is God's 'firstborn', or that its Land is the one 'upon which are God's eyes from beginning of the year until the end of the year' *(Deut.* 11:12).

An understanding of the fate of the nation, they thought, was to be found in the rules of statecraft or the vagaries of nature .

God punishes measure for measure; His response suits the sin. If Israel refuses to acknowledge that God's interest hovers over it offering Divine insulation from casual, meaningless coincidence, then God responds in kind. He removes His providence and allows His chosen nation to be scattered to countries from which the Divine gaze is averted. Israel is exiled from the fount of holiness and God lessens His providence over their fate. They thought their fate was determined by coincidence free from God's control; he responds by letting them be buffeted by the angry winds of coincidence.

God punishes measure for measure; His response suits the sin.

He Reigns Nonetheless

But even then — in the midst of His 'abandonment' — He does not forget that they are His .

But even then — in the midst of His 'abandonment' — He does not forget that they are His:

> 'It is beneficial to Israel that I [i.e. God personally, who remains with Israel] bring them to the land of their enemies. I do not abandon Israel so that they might say that they may as well imitate the deeds of the nations; instead, I appoint My prophets, to return them to goodness under My protecting wings. As it is written, *'What enters your thoughts — it shall not be! what you say "let us be like the nations and families of the earth." I swear, the words of my Lord, HASHEM / ELOHIM, with a strong hand, an outstretched arm,*

Against their will, God maintains His reign over them.

and outpoured wrath will I rule over you' (20:32-33). Against their will, God maintains His reign over Israel (*Sifra, Lev.* 26:41).

As God threatened Israel ... so He consoled them with the knowledge that He would never completely desert them, that His prophets would accompany them.

Thus, as God threatened Israel with the terrible punishment of removing His providence, so He consoled them with the knowledge that He would never completely desert them, that His prophets would accompany them. A prophet to the exile has the particular mission of bringing to fruition God's ringing declaration that *He will reign over Israel despite the nation's desire to imitate its hosts!* Let them approach Yechezkel with the classic impertinence: 'Does God have more claim on us now than has a man on the wife whom he has divorced? Do we bear any more responsibility to Him than does a slave toward a priest who has sold him to another master?' (*Sanhedrin* 105a). Yechezkel's task was to tell them, *'what enters your mind shall not be!'* And then Yechezkel was to take their hands, and reprovingly or lovingly lead them back under the wings of their once and still King.

Yechezkel was to take their hands, and reprovingly or lovingly lead them back under the wings of their once and still King.

Yechezkel's Mission

His awesome responsibility to bring God's message to an unresponsive audience.

'And the hand of HASHEM was upon me mightily' (3:14), Yechezkel exclaimed when thinking of his awesome responsibility to bring God's message to an unresponsive audience.

'When I came to destroy the city' (43:3) he lamented when thinking back to the time when the symbolism of his prophetic deeds portrayed Jerusalem's downfall.

'Come hear what is the word [of God] *... But they will not do it, for it has become like flute-music to them'* (33:31), God tells Yechezkel, warning him that his words may seem futile and pointless to the people, for so many of them will have no wish to listen.

But with it all, God tells him that *whether the people heed or whether they desist,* Yechezkel is to go to them *for they are 'your' people* (3:11). Yechezkel was to know that he must gird himself for his task not because he is assured the heady gratification of

He must neither fail them nor despair from them, because they are his. *Nor may he permit himself the luxury of despising these misguided masses.*

success — but because Israel is *his people.* He must neither fail them nor despair from them, because they are *his.* Nor may he permit himself the luxury of despising these misguided masses whose sins have caused the withdrawal of the *Shechinah* and the destruction of its abode, these brazen, hard-hearted people who mock the messenger of God. Yechezkel must still love them — for they are *his* people.

God commanded him to see the ruin and agony of his nation and act out his anguish.

And his feeling for *his* people was to be reflected in his person and his deeds. *'Pound with your hand and stamp with your foot and say "Alas!"'* God commanded him to see the ruin and agony of his nation and act out his anguish (6:11). More, He had Yechezkel undergo mortifying physical torment in order to enact upon himself the suffering and degradation of the people (Ch. 4).

How could they be made to believe that man's most beloved prize could be snatched away because of his sin?

But even that was not enough. How could Yechezkel teach the people of Jerusalem that their Temple would be taken from them? How could these mindless rebels against the word of God he convinced that the Temple was not their invincible guarantee against Nebuchadnezzar and his hordes? How could they be made to believe that man's most beloved prize could be snatched away because of his sin? That, too, Yechezkel had to demonstrate through the loss of the one who was most beloved to him — his wife. She would die in a plague, God told him. To Israel, the Temple was strength, joy, longing, delight, glory. Yechezkel's tragedy would be a sign for them that they, like he, could be bereaved. And for this, too, Yechezkel was ready — because they were *his* people.

How could a mortal man be so dedicated? Such dedication was the very essence of Yechezkel's mission.

Part of Him

Yechezkel was shown a scroll and *'it was inscribed within and without, and in it was inscribed lamentations, moaning, and woe* (2:10). God commanded

... אֱכוֹל אֶת הַמְּגִלָּה הַזֹּאת ... וָאֶפְתַּח אֶת פִּי
וַיַּאֲכִלֵנִי ... וַיֹּאמֶר אֵלַי בֶּן אָדָם בִּטְנְךָ תַאֲכֵל

וּמֵעֶיךָ תְמַלֵּא אֵת הַמְּגִלָּה הַזֹּאת . . . וָאֹכְלָה וַתְּהִי בְּפִי כִּדְבַשׁ לְמָתוֹק.

'Eat this scroll'. . . then I opened my mouth and He fed me. . . He said to me, 'Ben Adam feed your stomach and your innards fill with this scroll' . . . and I ate it and it was in my mouth as sweet as honey (3:1-3).

Yechezkel 'ate' his mission. He became one with it.

When someone eats, the food enters his body and becomes a part of it. So too, Yechezkel 'ate' his mission. He became one with it. To so great an extent did he submerge his private existence for the sake of his calling that his mission was not extraneous to his being — it *was* his being. Thus he willingly became a spectacle; a microcosm of their suffering, the fruits of their sin. The Book of Ezekiel is replete with Yechezkel's ordeals — all to teach his people what they had wrought, all to shock them into repentance and groom the new vine growing in Babylon into one fit to be transplanted to Jerusalem.

IV. Adam and Ben Adam

Retaining the Mission

Of all the prophets, God confers a unique title upon Yechezkel.

True, Yechezkel embodied the suffering of his generation, but he also embodied the greatness of their mission. Of all the prophets, God confers a unique title upon Yechezkel. Throughout the Book, he is called Ben Adam, and the nation of Israel is entitled Adam: אָדָם אַתֶּם, *You* [Israel] *are Adam* (34:31); אָדָם כָּל בֵּית יִשְׂרָאֵל כֻּלֹּה, *the Family of Israel in its entirety is Adam* (36:10). In expounding upon these verses, the Sages give us the famous dictum that is at once an inspiration and an unrelenting responsibility:

אתם קרואים אדם ואין אומות העולם קרואים אדם

You are called Adam, but the nations of the world are not called Adam (Yevamos 61a).

What is the implication of this title Adam? And why is Yechezkel called Ben Adam, son of Adam?

It was man himself who corrupted his deeds and thereby diminished his stature.

One small nation... refused to destroy its destiny and submerge its greatness.

It remained what it was created to be. They *withdrew* .

It was man himself who corrupted his deeds and thereby diminished his stature. When that diminution took place, there lived one small nation which survived the spiritual destruction because it refused to destroy its destiny and submerge its greatness before the idolatrous conflagration which devoured human hearts. Let mankind bow and prostrate itself to the world and its fullness; this nation would remain erect striving toward heaven with God's crown upon its head. Let them cast away their spiritual adornments and smash their crown into splinters; it would remain loyally and consistently under the reign of God. This nation did not depart from the others to ascend in a cloud and be covered by it, to become great and holy — it remained what it was created to be. *They* withdrew, descended to the dust and buried themselves in it, diminished and sullied themselves. They became a remnant, but it remained foremost, the first offering to the Rock of its life. Then it became apparent that all of creation from inception was worthwhile only for the sake of this nation: *For the sake of Israel which is called* רֵאשִׁית, *the foremost* — for all other nations shunned it, left it isolated in its status of holiness and purity. Intentionally they abandoned the mission that would have made *all* of them holy and pure; intentionally they abandoned the mission that would have made *all* of mankind *'foremost'* among the creatures of the universe; willfully they tore loose from their exalted status and became what they became *(Rabbi A.E. Kaplan, Torath HaAdam).*

What all mankind should have been, was realized by Abraham and henceforth became the exclusive legacy of Israel. 'You are called Adam'.

What the first man, Adam, should have been, became the goal of all mankind. What all mankind should have been, was realized by Abraham and henceforth became the exclusive legacy of Israel. *'You* are called Adam'. Once, it could have been *anyone,* should have been *everyone.* The first Adam was deserving of the title, so were the isolated righteous men of succeeding generations, and so was Noah. But generally speaking, the first twenty generations of human history were a wasteland devoid of Adam though it was increasingly populated with humans. Finally the title and challenge of Adam became vested in Israel. When Yechezkel's prophecy addressed the doomed nation as Adam, it was with a mixture of hope and despair.

When Yechezkel's prophecy addressed the doomed nation as Adam, it was with a mixture of hope and despair.

How could you — who should have been exalted Adam — become nothing more than a living clod fashioned from adamah, *the earth?*

You are Adam, the purpose of creation, the repository of Abraham's greatness, the seed from which future generations will grow to grace God's universe with people who will justify the existence of heaven and earth. *But how could you sink so low?* How could you — who should have been exalted Adam — become nothing more than a living clod fashioned from *adamah,* the earth?

The Implication of Adam

Man was intended as the footstool, the support and resting place of the Shechinah.

What is the implication of the title Adam with which man was crowned and by which he was challenged to make himself worthier than the angels? *Harav Samson Raphael Hirsch* (comm. to *Gen.* 1:26) derives the word from הֲדוֹם, a footstool. Man was intended as the footstool, the support and resting place of the *Shechinah.* Creation was meant to become an extension of God's holiness, but only man, by the proper use of his intelligence and his free-willed conquest of the animal within him, could make it so. No other element of creation would fashion the conditions for God's resting place — only man. He is, therefore, *Adam-Hadom,* the man who is the potential footstool of God's Presence. When man lives up to his calling, he earns the blessings of *Genesis:* that the earth and all its creatures become subservient to him, for they, by their very nature, exist only to

He is the potential footstool of God's Presence.

fulfill God's will; if he becomes what he was meant to be, then they realize their purpose only by serving him, the Adam who is God's footstool, and deputy. If, on the other hand, he demurs, preferring instead to be but a two-legged, articulate beast who is better able than they to define his lusts and seek ways to gratify them, then he must flee from the lion's roar and cringe before the earth's rumbling.

If he demurs, preferring instead to be but a two-legged, articulate beast, then he must flee from the lion's roar and cringe before the earth's rumbling.

For, *Hirsch* contends, the name Adam should not be taken as a reference to *adamah,* the earth; interpreting it as a reference to man's source. All land animals were created from the earth, and they emerged from it alive and fully functioning; if anything, it is *they* who should logically be named for the source from which they sprang. Man, however, did not emerge from the earth alive. What earth contributed to his existence was but his lifeless physical form, an inanimate statue. It did not become a living, functioning man until God breathed into it a soul, the power of life, imagination, and articulate speech. What logic is there in naming intelligent man after the earth which made but a partial — and ultimately inconsequential — contribution to his existence?

What logic is there in naming intelligent man after the earth which made but a partial — and ultimately inconsequential — contribution to his existence?

We may go further and venture to say that the name *Adamah* was conferred as a title of honor upon the earth because it was granted the privilege of participating in the fashioning of the very purpose of creation — Adam-man! Earth reached the zenith of its productivity when it was granted the role of becoming God's partner in the creation of His *'footstool.'*

Or, as *haKsav v'haKabballah, (Numbers* 23:19) interprets, Adam may well be derived from *adamah.* Nevertheless, Adam is the loftiest of all the nouns by which man is designated for it is his very derivation which constitutes his challenge. The abode of his soul is an earthy clod, the same substance that produced the lower forms of animal life and which represents the myriad lust to which he is subject. But he has the mission of conquering the *adamah* within

But he has the mission of conquering the adamah.

himself and turning it to the service of his soul. It is the highest expression of his potential that he is called upon — *expected* — to achieve this; the highest praise of his attainment of success is that he can be called *Adam:* the creature of the earth who conquered the earth (see *Gen.* 1:28).

Adam: *the creature of the earth who conquered the earth.*

This sublime mission had once been that of all mankind, but it was neglected and despised — until it was assumed by Abraham and his seed. Thus Israel became Adam, and no other member of the human family could aspire to that title.

It is in this sense that Yechezkel is called Ben Adam. *Though Israel failed it, he remained true to it.*

It is in this sense that Yechezkel is called *Ben Adam.* Uniquely, he represented Israel's mission of Adam. Though Israel failed it, he remained true to it.

> *It [the title Ben Adam for Yechezkel] is similar to a king whose wife and children were disloyal to him. He arose and evicted them from his home. Later, he sent for one of her sons and said to him: 'Son of that woman, come let me show you the house which I built for her and for you. Is there a flaw in my honor or in the house I built her?' So it was with Yechezkel ... The Holy One, blessed be He, said to him 'Ben Adam [in the sense that he is a son of the Adam nation] this is My honor, that I have raised you above all nations. Is there a flaw in My honor or in the House I built for you?' . . . (Tanna d'Bei Eliyahu 6).*

The Mission to Produce

If it fails to produce spiritual fruit, then it becomes a useless appendage.

Thus, Israel's mission is to represent not simple existence, but productivity. If it fails to produce spiritual fruit, then it becomes a useless appendage, serving no purpose on earth — a doomed fossil. This concept is represented by Yechezkel's analogy of vine and cedar (see Ch. 15 and 17). Other nations may be like a cedar which has utility as lumber even after it is cut down. Israel is a vine — while living it produces the fruit which gladdens God and man; when it withers, it is useless, entirely devoid of utility.

The title Adam and Ben Adam are used by Scripture for the very first time during the time of Yechezkel, the prophet of exile whose task was to rejuvenate Israel *away* from its home, and to accomplish in Babylon what had not been done in Jerusalem. In an era when sincere but puzzled Jews asked whether God could demand the allegiance of exiled Israel any more than a husband retained a claim over his divorced wife and a priest retained rights over his erstwhile slave, Yechezkel had to nurture the fledgling vine that was to become the future stronghold of a Torah nation. Foremost in his mission was to inculcate within them an awareness that they were still separate and charged with a higher mission: *they were still Adam,* and their role was the same whether the nearest mountain had atop it the *Bais HaMikdash,* or, להבדיל, Ba'al. They are still Adam with a unique mission, and they are not to assimilate themselves into whatever culture happens to be current in the particular country of this or that corner of the exile.

Yechezkel had to nurture the fledgling vine that was to become the future stronghold of a Torah nation.

The Seventh Year

Thus it is clear that Israel's purpose was to recognize the breath of God in every aspect of existence. They were exiled because they failed to do so. It is noteworthy that *Ramban (Lev.* 26:18) interprets the תּוֹכָחָה, *Admonition,* of *Leviticus* as bearing particularly on the conditions that led to the destruction of the First Temple and the exile at the hands of Babylon. The Torah indicates clearly that Israel's failure to observe the Sabbatical Year lay at the root of its suffering. Seventy times Israel ignored its obligation to let the soil rest, and, as a result, Eretz Yisrael would lay desolate for seventy years — until permission would be granted by Darius to return to Jerusalem and rebuild the Temple (see *ibid.* 26:34 and *Rashi*). The seventh year, the *Sabbath of the Earth,* represents the same concept as the seventh day of the week: that God created heaven and earth, and that man, by his forebearance, is witness to God's presence and majesty. Thus, when the earth is

The Torah indicates clearly that Israel's failure to observe the Sabbatical Year lay at the root of its suffering.

The seventh year, the Sabbath of the Earth, *represents the same concept as the seventh day of the week .*

permitted to lay fallow during the Sabbatical Year it reabsorbs the spiritual content it may have lost during the years when man's incessant labors could have led him to believe that his own endeavors — not God's largesse — produced his prosperity and success. Or, better said, when Israel desisted from its labors despite the normal human reaction that rest means starvation, it confirmed its status as God's Adam on earth. But when it failed to acknowledge God's guiding hand in man's destiny, it forfeited its right to the Land where His providence found its greatest expression. How natural and appropriate was God's choice of the nation that would impose exile and destruction upon Israel — Babylon. Nebuchadnezzar's kingdom was distinguished by its total submission to desire. Babylon was a lustful nation; its people were devoid of the control that raises man above the animal. When Israel failed to inject spirituality into its material existence, it was forced to endure its exile and strive for repentance among a nation of *adamah* people while its own Land demonstrated by its seventy years of rest that God's plan would be carried onward and His existence proven — if not by Israel's greatness, then by its degradation. (See *Michtav Me'Eliyahu* II p. 51.)

But when it failed to acknowledge God's guiding hand in man's destiny, it forfeited its right to the Land where His providence found its greatest expression.

When Israel failed to inject spirituality into its material existence, it was forced to endure its exile and strive for repentance among a nation of adamah *people.*

The Essential Israel

Independent nationhood is not a prerequisite for Israel's existence. The Land is important, but not decisive.

Only Torah is the indispensable essential, for Israel is defined either as a Torah nation or as no nation at all.

But Israel's rebirth during those years of exile attests to the essential nature of the nation. Independent nationhood is not a prerequisite for Israel's existence. The Land is important, but not decisive. Possession of its Land very often posed insuperable obstacles to Israel's fulfillment for it posed the temptation of 'let us be a nation like all the nations' as the tragic history of the First Temple demonstrated. Only Torah is the indispensable essential, for Israel is defined either as a Torah nation or as no nation at all. In Babylon, Torah greatness asserted itself once more as the period of exile became a period of national resuscitation under the aegis of the אַנְשֵׁי כְּנֶסֶת הַגְּדוֹלָה, *the Men of the Great Assembly,* who returned the crown to its glory of old, enveloping the

nation in the splendor of Torah greatness. Thus the exile taught another lesson. Faith in the omniscience of the Temple (see below) was futile, for the greatness of the nation was based not on its Temple, but on its Torah *(Yitzchak Breuer;* see *comm.* to 17:8 and *footnote* to 17:14).

V. Jerusalem and Exile

יְרוּשָׁלַיִם הַבְּנוּיָה כְּעִיר שֶׁחֻבְּרָה לָּהּ יַחְדָּו

Built-up Jerusalem, like a city that is compact together (Psalms 122:3).

When Solomon my son builds the Holy Temple in [Jerusalem's] midst, it will be built with the Shechinah, the Sanctuary, the Ark, and the Altar . . .

There is a Jerusalem built in heaven, and the Jerusalem below is destined to be just like it (Rashi).

Israel's Summit

The summit of Israel's achievement is in Jerusalem, the city which is earth's pinnacle of holiness, for, as indicated by *Rashi* above, the very essence of Jerusalem is that it unite within itself all symbols of holiness, and that it be a reflection on earth of the 'capital' of holiness in heaven. Its very name indicates its role. Shem, son of Noah, was its king; he called it שָׁלֵם, representing *peace* and *completion (Gen.* 14:18 see *Rashi).* Abraham, when he removed his son from the altar on Mount Moriah, called it ה' יִרְאֶה, *HASHEM will see (ibid.* 22:14). God combined both names in Jerusalem: City of Peace, City of Complete Fulfillment, City where Hashem Sees and Is Seen. So it is that the soaring prophecies of Isaiah revolve around the future glories of Jerusalem. And Yechezkel, too, concludes his prophecies with his vision of the future Jerusalem and the words וְשֵׁם הָעִיר מִיּוֹם ה' שָׁמָּה, *and the name of the city from that day on shall be: HASHEM Is There!* (48:35).

God combined both names in Jerusalem: City of Peace, City of Complete Fulfillment, City where Hashem Sees and Is Seen.

Israel's complete blessing can never be divorced from the sanctity of Zion from which Torah shall go forth.

It is surely true that Jerusalem without Torah is a sterile blessing (see above), but Israel's complete blessing can never be divorced from the sanctity of Zion from which Torah shall go forth.

All the more poignant and painful, therefore, was the contrast between the Jerusalem which would be and the Jerusalem that was. Therefore, all of Yechezkel's anguish was poured out upon Jerusalem, the City whose inhabitants had perverted its ideals of peace, completeness, and Godliness into strife, corruption, and idolatry. All the evil of his generation had concentrated itself upon Jerusalem, all its cruelty and licentiousness, its heresy and abomination. The city built parallel to the Jerusalem on High made a wall around itself, a wall to keep out not Nebuchadnezzar, but Hashem. In chastising the inhabitants of Jerusalem, Yechezkel repeated over and over the refrain that the sins were committed *within you* and *in your midst:*

The city built parallel to the Jerusalem on High made a wall around itself, a wall to keep out not Nebuchadnezzar, but Hashem.

> *Now you, Ben Adam, will you judge, will you judge the bloody city? — and then inform her of all her abominations! Then say, 'so said my Lord* HASHEM /ELOHIM, *the time has come for the city that spilled blood in her midst, and that made idols to render herself defiled. By your blood which you spilled are you guilty, and by your idols which you built are you defiled. Your days draw near and you have come to your years; therefore have I made you a reproach to the nations and a mockery to all the lands. Those near you and afar shall mock you — defiler of the Name, multiplier of tumult. Behold! the princes of Israel, each acting by force, were within you; in order to shed blood. Fathers and mothers have they made light of within you; with the stranger have they acted oppressively in your midst, orphan and widow have they afflicted within you. My holies have you despised and My Sabbaths*

desecrated. Slanderers were within you for the purpose of bloodshed, upon the mountains did they eat [idolatrous offerings] within you, adultery did they commit in your midst. The shame of a father have they revealed within you; the impurity of an unclean woman have they afflicted within you. A man with his neighbor's wife has committed abomination, and a man has defiled his daughter-in-law with lewdness, and a man has afflicted his sister, daughter of his father, within you. Bribery have they taken within you for the purpose of bloodshed; usury and interest have you taken and you have enriched your friends by oppression. And Me have you forgotten! — the words of my Lord, HASHEM/ELOHIM (22:2-12).

The Delusion

The sins are horrendous enough in themselves, but they are aggravated because they were committed in Jerusalem.

The people were obsessed with the delusion that Jerusalem and the Temple had an innate guarantee of survival.

The sins are horrendous enough in themselves, but they are aggravated because they were committed in *Jerusalem* — the Holy City, site of the Temple, repository of holiness, resting place of the *Shechinah*. Because Jerusalem was besmirched by them, the sins are more grave, less forgivable.

This degradation of Jerusalem is a primary theme of Yechezkel's prophecies, just as its future restoration is its triumphant conclusion. The people were obsessed with the delusion that Jerusalem and the Temple had an innate guarantee of survival against all outside aggression no matter what went on inside. Unheedful of their own role in its destiny, they polluted its greatness through their own baseness, erecting an 'iron wall' between themselves and the holiness of God which strove to emanate from the city into their hearts (see 5:5). All of Chapter 4 portrays Yechezkel 'at war' with the city which had become a repository of sin and which was now besieged by an 'enemy' that was truly nothing more than an accumulation of its people's centuries of sin. Yechezkel suffered with them, for them, seeking to

atone for them, shock them into repentance, hoping to save the Jerusalem that was and elevate it into the Jerusalem it would one day become. For Jerusalem *would* once more become the true Holy City. Tragically, Yechezkel was not to see the reality, only the vision of the future Jerusalem which still awaits fulfillment.

Tragically, Yechezkel was not to see the reality, only the vision of the future Jerusalem which still awaits fulfillment.

. . . וָאֱהִי לָהֶם לְמִקְדָּשׁ מְעַט בָּאֲרָצוֹת אֲשֶׁר בָּאוּ שָׁם

***Yet I have been for them a small sanctuary in the lands to which they came* (11:16).**

וִיהָבֵית לְהוֹן בָּתֵּי כְנִשְׁתָּא תִּנְיָן לְבֵית מַקְדְּשִׁי

I have given them synagogues, secondary to My Sanctuary (Targum).

Even the loss of the Temple was not complete, for a new concept was added to the life of the nation: the synagogue and study hall became miniature sanctuaries. There, the Jew could come to draw close to his Maker through prayer and Torah study. This new concept was of a piece with the changed nature of Israel. The nation had to revitalize itself without reliance on the centrality of Jerusalem and the Temple. In exile, Israel would build upon a foundation of Torah — its study and dedication to its commandments. And this would be the mission of each individual.

A new concept was added to the life of the nation: the synagogue and study hall became miniature sanctuaries.

The countless new sanctuaries of exile would enable every Jew to escape from his exile and find the *Shechinah*. When Jews join in a congregation of prayer or study, they tear themselves loose from the bonds of exile — they are redeemed from the exile awaiting them when they close their sacred books and return to their everyday concerns. Thus by providing Israel with these miniature sanctuaries even in the most distant corners of their dispersion, God provided the means by which they could insulate themselves from the corrosive effects of exile and raise themselves once again to the spiritual level which would return them to their earlier status of Adam — and even beyond, to the level of the 'End of Days' **(*Maharal, Ohr Chadash* 4:16. See 11:16).**

When Jews join in a congregation of prayer or study, they tear themselves loose from the bonds of exile.

VI. The Monarchy

Function of Monarchy

The Torah concept of a king is far from pomp, circumstance, self-indulgence, and power.

Monarchy is an integral part of Jewish nationhood, indeed, the appointment of a king is one of the six hundred thirteen commandments, and Jacob's final blessings included the designation of Judah as the regal tribe. But the Torah concept of a king is far from pomp, circumstance, self-indulgence, and power. In the Torah's vision, Israel's king is a man of righteousness and humility who leads the nation in the pursuit of wisdom, fear of God, and goodness. He is to be humble and shun arrogance, be merciful and considerate of even the lowliest, speak softly and be a servant of the people, endure their grievances and be their shepherd (*Hilchos Melachim* 2:6). Sadly, however, few of Israel's kings were of such lofty caliber. Those who were, led Israel to its zenith of spiritual greatness and — because Israel's status in this world is inextricably dependent on its spiritual stature — under those kings, the nation was secure and respected, even wealthy and powerful. David led it toward the summit that was achieved by Solomon — and all the civilized world vibrated to the call of wisdom and tranquility that rang forth from Jerusalem. Under the righteous Chizkiyahu, even young boys and girls were expert in the intricacies of the laws of purity and impurity — with the result that Sancherev's mighty army died in an instant. Jerusalem in Chizkiyahu's time was, indeed, impregnable because it was a fortress of learning and soul, not as the people of later generations deluded themselves, a city protected by its history and majestic Temple. (For a fuller discussion of the role and authority of the Monarchy, see *Overview* to *Ruth* ArtScroll ed.).

Jerusalem in Chizkiyahu's time was, indeed, impregnable because it was a fortress of learning and soul.

The natural order of Israel's existence is that its physical strength is a direct outgrowth of its spiritual health. When its study halls were filled, its soldiers

were mighty; when its hills were sprinkled with idolatrous altars, its arms were futile. Which it would be was in great measure the decision of the king. He could lead his people to spiritual heights or drag them down to depths. He could weakly allow evil to run its course or he could fight it.

Most of the kings, however, fell short — far short.

Most of the kings, however, fell short — far short. Some were weak and failed to prevent the incursions of idolatry. Others were wicked, and actively introduced the spiritual malignancy that led to destruction. There were isolated times when Israel was triumphant over its enemies even when it was spiritually degraded, but when that happened there was always a particular reason — to prevent desecration of the Name or to avoid intolerable suffering for Israel.

Menashe

The one held responsible for the eventual exile and destruction — was the son of one of the most righteous: Menashe ben Chizkiyahu.

Ironically, in the august line of Davidic kings the most wicked — the one held responsible for the eventual exile and destruction — was the son of one of the most righteous: Menashe ben Chizkiyahu.

> *Then HASHEM spoke through His servants the prophets saying: Because Menashe, king of Judah, did these abominations, doing evil beyond all that the Emori did before him and caused Judah to sin with his idols; therefore so said HASHEM, God of Israel, Behold! I bring evil upon Jerusalem and Judah, such that whoever hears of it — both his ears shall tingle! ... and I shall wipe out Jerusalem ... and I shall abandon the remnant of My inheritance and deliver them into the hand of their enemies (II Kings 21:10-14).*

At Yoshiyahu's death, Menashe's influence was still powerful though it was below the surface.

Of course the destruction came generations later, even after the reign of Menashe's righteous grandson Yoshiyahu who initiated an unprecedented degree of national repentance — but who died tragically at a young age before his work was complete. At Yoshiyahu's death, Menashe's influence was still

powerful though it was below the surface. With the strong and righteous ruler removed from the scene, Menashe's iniquitous legacy reasserted itself, and the Babylonian conquest was but a matter of time. So it was that Jeremiah, upon the threshhold of Judah's doom, heard the voice of God:

> *Even if Moses and Samuel were to stand before Me, My desire is not toward this people. Dispatch them from My sight and let them go ... such as are to death, to death; and such as are to the sword, to the sword; and such as are to famine, to famine; and such as are to captivity, to captivity ... because of Menashe, son of Yechizkiyahu, king of Judah, for what he did in Jerusalem! (Jeremiah* 15:1-4).

Menashe the individual *might repent, but Menashe the* king *could not undo the evil he had worked.*

So well had Menashe done his perfidious and corrosive work that, though his final decades were lived out in sincere and remorseful personal repentance, the inroads his evil had made on the spiritual life of the people were irreparable. Menashe the *individual* might repent, but Menashe the *king* could not undo the evil he had worked. When his great-grandson Yehoyakim sinned and, as a result, brought upon himself and his kingdom the army of Nebuchadnezzar and the armed bands of Chaldea and Aram, God's word bore witness that the evil of Yehoyakim and the misery that came in its wake were outgrowths of *'the sins of Menashe for all that he had done' (II Kings* 23:26).

But what of Menashe's grandson, the great and righteous Yoshiyahu?

> *And you, take up a lamentation for the princes of Israel. And say 'How was your mother a lioness, she crouched among the lions, among the young lions she raised her cubs. And she reared up one of her cubs ...* (19:1-3).

Like a lion, confident and unafraid Yoshiyahu crouched. Who would dare attack him?

With this powerful allegory, Yechezkel depicts the closing era of Judah's kingdom. Like a lion, confident and unafraid Yoshiyahu crouched. Who would

dare attack him? It was the fulfillment of Jacob's blessing to Judah, a blessing that conferred upon his power and bearing, dominion and ascendancy. How could he fall? How could the king lie fallen and maimed? The answer lies in another allegory of Yechezkel:

> *Ben Adam, what will become of the vine-tree from among all trees, the vine which was among the trees of the forest? Can wood be taken from it for productive use? Can a peg be taken from it ...? ... See! To fire was it given to devour ... could it be useful for work? See! When it was whole it could not be for productive use, surely when fire consumed it ...* (15:2-5).

Singe the vine, destroy its fruit-producing potential and what have you? — Nothing.

Singe the vine, destroy its fruit-producing potential and what have you? — Nothing. But let the vine do its work and it produces fruit that dwarfs all others in its potential. For from the vine comes wine that gladdens hearts and adorns God's altar. This is Israel: let it do its work and it is the grape which produces the wine of Torah and good deeds that are the very essence of creation.

Had the vine but been content to produce its sublime fruit! But it wasn't.

Had the vine but been content to produce its sublime fruit! But it wasn't. Yechezkel continues his allegory of Chapter 19 by telling how the lion of Judah chose to compete with other nations. It was not content to remain in its lofty isolation producing what only it could produce and, in the process, growing more powerful in every temporal way because — unlike other nations — Israel's body is nourished by its soul. Instead it encroached upon the other nations. For doing so, it was burned. And the vine, burned, is useless.

VII. A Lowly Kingdom

. . . the king of Babylon came to Jerusalem and took its king and its princes and brought them to him, to Babylon. Then he took from the seed of royalty and made a covenant with him and brought him into an oath, and took away the mighty of the Land. That he shall be a **מַמְלָכָה שְׁפָלָה lowly kingdom,** *that he might not be lifted up. That he should keep his covenant in order* ***that it might endure*** **(17:12-14).**

The Last Hope

Had they but accepted Yechezkel's entreaties that they consent to be a lowly kingdom, *Israel could have survived as an independent entity.*

Can it be that the destiny of the 'kingdom of priests and holy nation' is best served by servility and serfdom?

With this prophecy, a new element was introduced into Israel's destiny. Had they but accepted Yechezkel's entreaties that they consent to be a *lowly kingdom,* Israel could have survived as an independent entity until a spiritual resurgence entitled it to return to the level of Solomonic days and even beyond to the heights of the prophesied Messianic End of Days. But what was to be gained by acceptance of the inferior status of a vassal state? Why was lowliness preferable to grandeur? Can it be that the destiny of the 'kingdom of priests and holy nation' is best served by servility and serfdom?

Again we must return to the refrain that Israel's ultimate purpose — no! its *only* purpose — is to provide heaven and earth with spiritual content and meaning; to be the *Adam* of earth, the *grape-vine among the trees.* To do otherwise is to ignore the purpose of Israel and deprive the nations of their own need, little though they may recognize the validity and indispensability of that need. A child refuses to acknowledge his need for nutrition, schooling, and sufficient sleep, but that does not absolve his parents from guilt if they fail to provide them.

לֹא בְחַיִל וְלֹא בְכֹחַ כִּי אִם בְּרוּחִי אָמַר ה׳ צְבָאוֹת
Not by wealth and not by might, but by My spirit, said HASHEM of hosts (Zecharia 4:6).

David knew while he was crushing his enemies that his victories were gifts of God.

But such realizations are difficult.

How easy, how natural, how obvious, how imperative it is to think that one is at the helm of history instead of recognizing that he is merely an occasional wheel in the hands of the Helmsman.

Would the forest best be served if the vine tried to take the place of the redwood?

Only by living through the spirit of God can Israel be successful. David knew while he was crushing his enemies that his victories were gifts of God, and Solomon knew while all the world trooped to pay him tribute that he was but a conduit for the greatness of God. But such realizations are difficult for frail human beings when they are ensconced in positions of power. How easy, how natural, how obvious, how imperative it is to think that one is at the helm of history instead of recognizing that he is merely an occasional wheel in the hands of the Helmsman. Israel's role is to influence history through its allegiance to the Torah, thereby becoming the vibrant soul of the world. Should Israel meddle on the stage of world history when it had not yet perfected itself? Would not its entry into the arena of world powers distract its human and spiritual resources from their primary task? And would the forest best be served if the vine tried to take the place of the redwood?

Looking Inward

Israel could not afford the charade of prancing about with the lions of Babylon and Egypt as if it were indeed a world power capable of indulging in the sport of powerful monarchs.

No. Israel which had consistently ignored the lesson of the Sabbatical Year, which had within itself the cancerous legacy of Menashe — Israel could not afford the charade of prancing about with the lions of Babylon and Egypt as if it were indeed a world power capable of indulging in the sport of powerful monarchs. Better that it eschew that game. Let it remain under the suzerainty of a Nebuchadnezzar, freed from entanglement with the affairs of nations. Let it, instead, concentrate on itself and develop its spiritual majesty. When that happened, world power would flow as a natural consequence from spiritual grandeur. But the temptation is enormous to seek a role, to attempt to influence history, especially for a small country strategically situated at the crossroads of continents. Babylon, Egypt, Assyria, Persia, Rome — there were always major powers which sought dominion over the Land and it was only 'natural' for the rulers of Israel to seek influence by playing off one against the other or, even more 'natural', to take

up arms against major powers which sought to subjugate its land in the course of their empire-building, or to make it a highway for military forces plying the north-south battle route between Egypt and Babylon.

Of course this was the *natural* course — understandable and forgivable for any nation but Judah. Kings and rulers are accustomed to using military jingoism to enhance their own power and divert the attentions of their people from more serious concerns. The nation intent on external conquest forgets about its own poverty, disease, and ignorance. Its enemy is on the other side of its border and he invites hatred because he speaks a different language and has a different idol. The enemy within can wait for a better day. Judah, too, could easily be diverted by statecraft, political manipulation, and force of arms. Forgotten would be the mortal enemies which the likes of Menashe had infiltrated among them. When the vine is occupied with conquering the cedars it will not produce grapes.

The nation intent on external conquests forgets about its own ***poverty, disease,*** *and ignorance.*

When the vine is occupied with conquering the cedars it will not produce grapes.

But a *lowly kingdom* could relegate such matters where they belonged. Unable to influence events around it, it could concentrate on its own vineyard. A vanquished nation can develop within while allowing its conqueror to shoulder the burdens of raising armies to contend with adversaries and defend borders. Had Judah and its kings heeded the calls of Jeremiah and Yechezkel, the nation of Israel — still Adam even in its degradation — would have experienced a rebirth. Yoshiyahu's repentance and leadership would have been the first steps on the road leading back to the splendor of Chizkiyahu, Solomon, and David, — and eventually to Messiah, instead of the last brilliant flash of a dying fire.

Price of Refusal

The reluctance to accept such subservience was a misreading of Israel's true role. The essential Israel is the nation of Torah. All else flows from that central thesis. It became a nation in the wilderness, it blossomed again in Babylon, and it remained a nation in

exile. Israel is unique for it became and remained a people without the trappings of nationhood, and from the uniqueness flows its strength. The *lowly kingdom* concept was God's way of forcing Israel to return to its essentials and thereby achieve greatness once more. But Israel was appalled at a 'lowliness' it refused to countenance. It failed to realize that by accepting a status beneath its grandiose visions of itself, it could save its kingdom, Temple, and Jerusalem. Because it insisted on having all three *and* grandeur, it lost all.

By accepting a status beneath its grandiose visions of itself, it could save its kingdom, Temple, and Jerusalem. Because it insisted on having all three and *grandeur, it lost all.*

The result was that Israel became an even lowlier kingdom — disgraced, scattered, and enslaved. As it emerged from the trauma of its destruction, it entered a period of centuries when it was indeed a vassal nation. Even when the Second Temple was begun at the pleasure of Cyrus, and completed at the pleasure of Darius, true independence was something that Jews only read about in Tanach. Despite this — or *because* of it — the nation flowered and the study of the Oral Law reached new peaks.

Jeremiah told Zidkiyahu clearly:

> *So said HASHEM, Lord of Hosts, God of Israel: if you go out to the ministers of the king of Babylon you will save your own life, this city will not be consumed in fire, and you and your family will live. But if you do not go out to the ministers of the king of Babylon, then this city will be delivered in the hands of the Chaldeans and they will consume it in fire and you will not escape their hands (Jeremiah 38:17-18).*

The same counsel was offered by the Sages during the Roman siege of Jerusalem five centuries later. The Sages said, 'Let us make peace with Rome.' The militants refused and countered, 'Let us make war against them.' The Sages insisted, 'It will not succeed.' The militants had their way, and Jerusalem was razed, its pitiful survivors led westward to Rome on rivers of blood and tears, their anguish and

But Rabban Yochanan ben Zakkai capitulated to the emperor and in return was granted protection for the scholars of Yavneh.

degradation captured in the carvings on the Arch of Titus. But Rabban Yochanan ben Zakkai capitulated to the emperor and in return was granted protection for the scholars of Yavneh. His victory is measured in the eternity of the Torah that survived in Yavneh and produced the spiritual wealth that nurtures the nation to this day (Gittin 56 a-b).

But Zidkiyahu would not listen. He said:

> *I am afraid of the men of Judah who have deserted to the Chaldeans lest they deliver me into their hand and they torture me (Jeremiah 38:19).*
>
> *Then Zidkiyahu said to Jeremiah, 'Let no man know of these words and you shall not die. But if the ministers . . . . come to you . . . . then say to them I presented my supplication before the king' ... (ibid. vs.* 24-26).

VIII. Yehoyakim and Zidkiyahu

How tragic when leaders fear to lead. Especially when they are as truly great as Zidkiyahu was in his personal life.

Zidkiyahu, our Sages tell us, was a completely righteous man, but he was afraid. He feared his ministers and he feared his people and he let that fear blind him to the words of truth. How tragic when leaders fear to lead. Especially when they are as truly great as Zidkiyahu was in his personal life.

The Holy One, blessed be He, sought to return the entire world to desolation and void because of the generation of Zidkiyahu. He looked at Zidkiyahu [who was righteous] and His mind was set at ease.

> ביקש הקב״ה להחזיר את העולם כולו לתהו ובהו בשביל יהויקים נסתכל בדורו ונתקררה דעתו. בקש הקב״ה להחזיר את העולם כולו לתהו ובהו בשביל דורו של צדקיהו, נסתכל בצדקיהו ונתקררה דעתו. בצדקיהו נמי כתיב ויעש הרע בעיני ה׳? שהיה בידו למחות ולא מיחה
>
> *The Holy One, blessed be He, sought to return the entire world to desolation and void because of [the wickedness of] Yehoyakim [son of Yoshiyahu], but He looked at his generation [of righteous people] and His mind was set at ease. The*

Holy One, blessed be He, sought to return the entire world to desolation and void because of the generation of Zidkiyahu. He looked at Zidkiyahu [who was righteous] and His mind was set at ease. But concerning Zidkiyahu it is also written [just as it is about Yehoyakim] 'and he did evil in the eyes of HASHEM' [and if so why was his generation spared because of him? He was indeed righteous. His evil was] that he had the power to protest, but he did not protest (Sanhedrin 103a).

Kings and Generations

Yehoyakim's reign was distinguished primarily for the arrogance and impudence of the young king.

Yehoyakim's reign was distinguished primarily for the arrogance and impudence of the young king who was so different from his great father. The king actively sought to antagonize God, declaring that he was so self-sufficient that he had no need of the Creator (*Sanhedrin* 103b). God, in His forebearing mercy, presented Yehoyakim and his advisors with an opportunity to repent and save the kingdom and people (*Jeremiah* 36:1). Jeremiah was given the text of *Eichah*, the Book of Lamentations, and told to read it to Yehoyakim and his court. Could anyone listen to the elegy of woe and heartbreak knowing that it prophesied his own fate and that of the nation, hear it from an acknowledged prophet, and fail to be moved? Yes! Yehoyakim and his lackeys listened, tore the scroll from Jeremiah's hands, slashed it with a blade, and threw it into the fire. *And they feared not, and ripped not their clothes — the king and all his servants who heard these words (ibid. 36:24).*

Could anyone listen to the elegy of woe and heartbreak and fail to be moved? Yes! Yehoyakim and his lackeys.

They deserved destruction, but God looked at his generation and relented.

They deserved destruction, but God looked at his generation and relented. It was no ordinary generation. It included the ten thousand people whom Nebuchadnezzar exiled to Babylon eleven years before the destruction of the Temple. They were the most distinguished scholars and leaders of Judah, the *'carpenters and locksmiths'* (see *comm.* to 1:2) who established the community that was to become reborn Israel. But when Jerusalem was stripped of

them, nothing remained but a miserable remnant — a miserable remnant and the man who was to stand almost alone in his righteousness, the last tragic king of Judah, the noble but fearful Zidkiyahu who was great enough to save the world from annihilation, but too weak to save his Holy City and Temple from destruction.

Zidkiyahu who was great enough to save the world from annihilation, but too weak to save his Holy City and Temple from destruction.

Zidkiyahu's Eyes

תנו רבנן חמשה נבראו מעין דוגמא של מעלה וכולן לקו בהן ... צדקיה בעיניו

The Rabbis learned, Five were created in a supernatural likeness [with a characteristic that was beautiful far beyond the norm (Rashi)] and all were punished thereby .... Zidkiyahu with his eyes (Sot.h 10a).

Maharal (Aggados haShas) explains that, although every man is created in the 'likeness of God', there are infinite degrees to this likeness. Man's spiritual potential gives him some minute resemblance to His Creator, but it is plain that the degree of spirituality — and thus the degree of likeness to God — varies very widely from person to person. Surely, the 'likeness of God' found in Abraham, Isaac, and Jacob is light years beyond anything we have ever seen or can even imagine. As is the case with all Divine gifts, when a blessing is bestowed upon a human being, a commensurate responsibility comes with it to use the blessing wisely and properly. Man has a soul and intelligent, articulate thought; therefore he has the ability to raise the universe to the fulfillment of its purpose. If he does so his reward is great for, if one may so speak, he has given fulfillment to God Himself; if he falls short, he may be punished severely for he destroys the purpose of creation (*Avos* 5:1).

The degree of spirituality — and thus the degree of likeness to God — varies very widely from person to person.

If he falls short, he may be punished severely for he destroys the purpose of creation.

The greater one's gifts, therefore, the more difficult it is to be worthy of them. In the material sense, for example, the person who has enormous wealth and power and the authority to control the destiny of a nation can legitimately be held responsible for the shortcomings and failures of those under his sway. Simultaneously, however, the fact that he has so

much power over so many people makes his task immeasurably more difficult than if he were held accountable for himself alone. In the spiritual sense, too, it is a truly awesome gift to be created in the divine image to an extraordinary extent, but it calls for a concomitant degree of accomplishment and greatness that is enormously difficult to achieve, for it allows no missteps. Therefore, the generations between Adam and Noah fell so miserably — they were greater than they could bear. Descended from God's own handiwork, products of the couple that virtually witnessed creation, privy to the highest degrees of human perception of the divine — the standards expected of them were so exacting that they brooked no failure.

Therefore, the generations between Adam and Noah fell so miserably.

The standards expected of them were so exacting that they brooked no failure.

The five people who were granted supernatural spiritual beauty were expected to utilize their particular gifts to the maximum degree. The person with unusually acute eyesight who is assigned to lookout duty is not guilty if he fails to *hear* a faint sound, but it is inexcusable for him not to *see* something simply because a person with ordinary vision wouldn't have noticed. Those five people might have been excused for failures in realms other than their domains of greatness; but in those areas nothing less than maximum performance could be tolerated. Thus it was that their supernatural gifts proved their undoing.

Divine eyes see not only the physical object, but its essence as well.

Zidkiyahu was distinguished by his 'eyes.' Surely the Sages do not mean that he could sight a bird when it was barely a speck on the horizon. Divine eyes see not only the physical object, but its essence as well. The person who understands purpose, motive, and potential 'sees' much more than one who can merely describe the color and size of an object or human being. When the Sages tell us that Adam could see from one end of the world to the other, they mean that he had this spiritual vision as well as everything implied by the simple meaning of the words. In this sense, *Yalkut (II Kings* 252) tells us that Zidkiyahu's eyes were like Adam's eyes (see

footnote 12:12 and *Overview* to *Tehillim I* ArtScroll ed.).

Where He Failed

He lived in a pivotal period; he was king at a time when the future of the nation hung in the balance as it seldom has, before or since.

Thus we can place Zidkiyahu in his proper perspective. He was a great and righteous man; the Sages call him a צַדִּיק גָּמוּר, *a completely righteous person.* He lived in a pivotal period; he was king at a time when the future of the nation hung in the balance as it seldom has, before or since. The die had been cast by the iniquity of Menashe which had left deep, unhealed, still-festering scars on the national character, scars so deep that even the great Yoshiyahu could not cleanse them. Nevertheless, total destruction need not have been the fate of Jerusalem. The 'carpenters and locksmiths' were in Babylon planting the seed of a vine that would produce wondrous casks of wine and gladden hearts for millenia into the future. **Jerusalem's grandeur was doomed, but it and its Temple could have endured as a 'lowly** kingdom,' so to survive and regenerate. The knaves and fools in the City would not or could not see the truth, but Zidkiyahu had wondrous eyes. He knew. True, he was but an individual cast in a generation that merited annihilation. But he was great enough to save them *even as he was.* As he *could* have been, he was great enough to do more.

The knaves and fools in the City would not or could not see the truth, but Zidkiyahu had wondrous eyes. He knew.

He should have dismissed the objections of his officials and denied the rantings of the false prophets. No one could know better than he, could *see* more clearly than he, that the words of Jeremiah and Yechezkel were the words of God emanating from His prophets. When they counseled submission to Nebuchadnezzar, they urged not cowardice, but courage. **For it demanded courage and strength to fight the pressures of the present in order to build the** foundations of the future. No ruler likes to preside over a lowly kingdom. No king likes to overrule the demands of his ministers that he lead his people to great victories. No leader likes to tell his people that they must suffer humiliation and subjugation happily because it is their only way to strengthen their

For it demanded courage and strength to fight the pressures of the present in order to build the foundations of the future.

weakened inner fiber and go on to greatness in some undefined future time. And surely no king of Judah liked to tell the inhabitants of Jerusalem that the heart and soul of the people had shifted beyond the rivers of Babylon and that the magnificent building on Mount Moriah was barely a memory of what it had been in the days of Solomon.

He could see that Jerusalem was an empty mirage, that its hollowness could slowly be replenished only in lowliness, that the people had to relearn the ancient lesson that Israel's nationhood is not a geographical fact, but a spiritual reality.

Another king might have been deceived by 'reality', but Zidkiyahu 'saw' the *true* reality. He could see that Jerusalem was an empty mirage, that its hollowness could slowly be replenished only in lowliness, that the people had to relearn the ancient lesson that Israel's nationhood is not a geographical fact, but a spiritual reality. He *saw* — why did he not follow his eyes? And so he was doomed. Not because he was small, but because he was great. He and his family were captured. He was forced to watch the brutal execution of his children, and Nebuchadnezzar's soldiers cruelly pierced his eyes, over and over. The king who ignored his heavenly vision lived out his days in darkness. How poignant is the comment of the Sages.

The king who ignored his heavenly vision lived out his days in darkness.

וְאֶת עֵינֵי צִדְקִיָּהוּ עִוֵּר . . . זה משבעה שנדמו לאדם הראשון בעיניו, ונעצו לעיניו לונביות של ברזל ולא נתעוורו עד ששחטו את בניו לעיניו ובכה

And the eyes of Zidkiyahu, they blinded . . . He was one of the seven whose eyes were like Adam's. They pierced his eyes with spikes of iron, but they were not blinded until his children were slaughtered before him and he wept (II Kings, Yalkut 252).

His 'eyes' had a degree of vision like Adam's. Weapons could pierce them, but not blind their vision. But when he witnessed the extermination of his posterity and wept tears of realization of the extent of his failure, his vision left him.

A Fatal Weakness

The immediate cause of Zidkiyahu's downfall was his breach of faith with Nebuchadnezzar. Despite a pledge of allegiance to the conqueror, Zidkiyahu won freedom from the vow and mounted a revolt. But a deeper understanding of the affair dictates that even that episode was not a cause but an outgrowth. The *Prefatory Remarks* and *footnote* to Ch. 17 give a full review of the incident and its background, making clear that Zidkiyahu's perfidy was brought about by God to create the circumstances for a punishment that had already been dictated by the course of events. And even that rebellion was caused by the same weakness that caused Zidkiyahu's failure as king: he was too weak to overrule his ministers and do what he knew to be right. *They* demanded that he flout Nebuchadnezzar and he meekly complied (*Maharsha Sanhedrin* 103b).

Zidkiyahu's perfidy was brought about by God to create the circumstances for a punishment.

Indeed, we may find special significance in the means God chose to bring about his downfall. Not only does the punishment fit the crime, even the means to bring about the punishment correspond to the cause of the sin. Zidkiyahu failed to muster the strength to follow where his 'eyes' led him. His destruction, too, was caused by the same failure: the weakness of a leader unwilling to dominate his servants in the pursuit of righteousness.

Not only does the punishment fit the crime, even the means to bring about the punishment correspond to the cause of the sin.

The essential righteousness of Zidkiyahu, the complete Zaddik, remained. Despite his grievous suffering, he would live out his days in Babylon where he was respected as a great man. And he would live to see the death of his conqueror Nebuchadnezzar.

> *. . . . You shall not die by the sword; but you shall die in peace and like . . . the kings before you so will they lament you saying, 'Ah Master!' (Jeremiah* 34:4-5*).*

But his ministers — were they mad fools that they did not heed the word of God through His prophets? They saw that His words were not vain; why did they resist and thereby insure their own doom?

But his ministers saw that His words were not vain; why did they resist and thereby insure their own doom?

IX. The False Prophets

The Refusal to See

When the events of the Book of *Ezekiel* were taking place, Judah had already shrunk to little more than a city-state. The Ten Tribes of Samaria had long since been exiled. Already in the days of Chizkiyahu, the major portion of Judah had been conquered by Sancherev. Pharaoh and Nebuchadnezzar, in turn, had established uncontested domination over the remnant of the Jewish state, appointing and deposing kings at will (see section on *The Twilight of the Monarchy).* During Yehoyachin's reign, Nebuchadnezzar had exiled Jerusalem's most distinguished ten thousand to Babylon.

The remaining citizens of Jerusalem were convinced that their position was strong, even impregnable.

But human beings retain an almost unbounded capacity for self-deception, interpreting events to suit their own pre-conceived notions. The remaining citizens of Jerusalem, far from conceding that the hand of God was heavy upon them and that their only hope was to remain a 'lowly kingdom' were convinced that their position was strong, even impregnable:

— They had the Holy Temple in their midst. That they violated the very Torah whose laws conferred sanctity upon the Temple did not faze them. For, weren't they offering regular sacrifices upon its altar and wasn't the Temple Service enough to appease an angry God? Surely God would not allow His resting place on earth to go up in flames!

Surely God would not allow His resting place on earth to go up in flames!

— They, the remnant in Jerusalem, had been singled out to remain in the Holy City. The overwhelming portions of the Land had been conquered and their brethren had been dispersed by Sancherev, Pharaoh, and Nebuchadnezzar — *but they were left in place!* What more conclusive proof was possible of their worthiness? Surely they were the elite of the nation and God would not allow the brutish idol-worshipping king of Babylon to murder and exile them.

Surely they were the elite of the nation.

How logical it can be to believe what one wishes to believe.

How logical it can be to believe what one wishes to believe.

Jeremiah and Yechezkel? They claimed to be prophets — but there were other prophets who disputed them. There was an abundance of false prophets who suited their message to the desires of their listeners.

In the first year of Zidkiyahu's reign, Chananiah ben Azur, the 'prophet' of Gibeon stood in the Temple and proclaimed:

> *So says HASHEM of hosts, the God of Israel saying: I have broken the yoke of the king of Babylon. In two years more, I shall return to this place all the vessels of the House of HASHEM which Nebuchadnezzar, king of Babylon, took from this place and brought to Babylon. And Yechoniah [Yehoyachin] the king of Judah and all the exile of Judah which was brought to Babylon, I shall return to this place — the words of HASHEM. For I have broken the yoke of the king of Babylon (Jeremiah 28:2-4).*

How pleasant a prophecy. How enticing. How believable to people who were anxious to believe it.

How pleasant a prophecy. How enticing. How believable to people who were anxious to believe it.

And Shmaya of Chaleim sent messages to the people of Jerusalem and to the righteous High Priest Zephaniah ben Ma'asaiah and his fellow priests:

> *HASHEM made you priest ... to be responsible for the House of HASHEM, for every person who is insane and prophesies [to be imprisoned] ... and now why did you not shout at Jeremiah of Anasos who prophesies to you? ... (Jeremiah 29:26-27).*

The Crowning Calumny

In the crowning calumny, the false prophets dared berate the High Priest for even permitting Jeremiah to speak in the name of Hashem! And the people listened and believed, for the false prophets had learned well the art of talking what people wanted to hear and clothing it in high-sounding rhetoric. The

sum total of their falsehood was more than political division and the weakening of prophetic authority and royal will. They *cause My Name to be forgotten,* God said (*Jeremiah* 23:27) because God's Name on earth is the perception by the people that He exercises providence in their lives. His Name is HASHEM when they perceive His mercy, Elohim when they perceive His justice, Shaddai when they perceive His all-sufficing strength, and so on. But when false purveyors of 'prophecy' distort His word and throw up smokescreens of doubt about the veracity of His declarations, then His Name — i.e., the perception of His omnipresence and omniscience — becomes weakened and forgotten.

God's Name on earth is the perception by the people that He exercises providence in their lives.

Not surprisingly then, Yechezkel's prophecy lashes out vigorously against these purveyors of falsehood who bore a significant share of blame for the confusion of the people and the perfidy of the leaders. True, the ministers wanted to be misled, and could not honestly lay the blame for their treason at the mouths of Chananiah, Shmayah and their cohorts. But the prophets were the vehicles of slander, the *merkavah* of evil and betrayal.[1]

True, the ministers wanted to be misled, but the prophets were the vehicles of slander, the merkavah *of evil and betrayal.*

1. This particular culpability of the ministers, leaders, and prophets, and the resultant compliance of Zidkiyahu who was too weak to resist, is particularly relevant to the national mission as it manifested itself in those pivotal days. Harav Yitzchak Isaac Halevy *(Tekufas Hamikra)* comments that the sins and failures chronicled in the Books of *Kings* revolve exclusively around the royal households. The role of national independence places particular responsibility upon the leaders of the nation. As the executors of nationhood they determine the destiny of a sovereign people. The *general* population was left untouched by the shortcomings of the kings and their lackeys. This situation changed only with the reign of Menashe who brought corruption into the homes of the people — and it may be for this reason as much as for his wickedness that Menashe is singled out as the object of calumny (see above). Particularly during the last days of the Temple when the national mission became the acceptance of its new role as that of a 'lowly kingdom', the national leadership was the crucial segment of society.

X. The Book of Triumph

In one of Israel's most inspiring prophecies concerning the coming of Messiah at the End of Days, Yechezkel proclaims in the name of God:

> *Then shall I take you from the nations and gather you from among all the lands and bring you to your land. And I shall sprinkle upon you purifying waters and purify you from all your defilements, and from all your filth will I purify you. Then I will present you with a new heart, and a new spirit will I emplace within you, and I shall remove the stone heart from your flesh and give you a heart of flesh. My spirit will I emplace within you and I will bring about that you will walk in My decree and My ordinances will you keep and perform* (36:24-27).

This is the final fulfillment. It describes the time when Israel will become Adam, again and finally!

This is the final fulfillment. It describes the time when Israel will become Adam, again and finally! Surely Israel will strive mightily to earn that ultimate mercy when God's creation will attain its purpose through the vehicle of Israel. Yechezkel makes clear, however, in that very chapter and throughout his prophecy that the gift, as indeed every gift in Israel's history, will be granted for one sublime reason — the Sanctification of His Name.

> *Not for your sake do I do this, Family of Israel, but for the sake of My Holy Name which you have desecrated among the nations where you have come. And I will sanctify My great Name which was desecrated among the peoples which you have desecrated among them and the peoples will know that I am HASHEM ...* (36:22-23).

From the dawn of Israel's national history in Egypt, God declares (Ch. 20), Israel was chosen,

redeemed, and made great to sanctify His Name. There were other times — in Egypt, the desert, in Eretz Yisrael, and in exile — when Israel's iniquity merited destruction. Always it was forestalled in order to avoid Desecration of the Name. Redemption came in the past and will come in the future to sanctify It.

For this was the purpose of creation — that there be a universe peopled by a human race that could elevate it to approach God's sublime intention.

For this was the purpose of creation — that there be a universe peopled by a human race that could elevate it to approach God's sublime intention. With the passage of time, Abraham became the vehicle for the achievement of this purpose. Thus the entire existence of creation hinged upon the survival and success of Israel.

This small, scattered nation, whatever its temporary deficiencies, retained within itself the spark of Abraham, Isaac, and Jacob; the fire of Sinai; the seeds that would sprout into the 'vine' which would dwarf all the cedars and redwoods. It could sin grievously, but it remained the essence of God's will. And to preserve His purpose so that the universe would ultimately realize His will despite its stumbling and its flaws, Israel had to survive. God does not require man's offerings; whatever man can give Him is meaningless and inconsequential unless he can sanctify creation and thereby sanctify His Name.

For this Israel survived, survives, and will persevere. For this, He spares it and nurtures His spark and His seed within it.

For this Israel survived, survives, and will persevere. For this, He spares it and nurtures His spark and His seed within it.

The prophecies of Yechezkel, for all their starkness and terror, are truly visions of hope and comfort for their underlying motif, as well as their climactic visions, is that Israel will once again rise and be worthy of God's Temple and *Shechinah.* As the Book comes to its conclusion, Yechezkel is given the glorious vision of the 'dry bones' (Ch. 37).

Despair disappears; death turns to life; the 'corpse' of Israel becomes a vibrant new nation. Discordant Judah and Ephraim are once more united in a single nation.

Despair disappears; death turns to life; the 'corpse' of Israel becomes a vibrant new nation. Discordant Judah and Ephraim are once more united in a single nation. David is their king and Eretz Yisrael is their Land. A new covenant of peace is sealed between

God and Israel — an eternal covenant. He is their God and they are His people. All the world knows that *Israel* is sanctified because Hashem is their God — and the very sanctification of Israel becomes the most profound sanctification of the Name.

The Book of Ezekiel. A book of tragedy — surely. A book of despair — most assuredly not!

The Book of Ezekiel. A book of tragedy — surely. A book of despair — most assuredly not! For Israel may stumble and fall and be trampled. But it survives and rises and returns to Jerusalem which will assume a new and eternal name — ה׳ שָׁמָּה, *HASHEM is there* (48:35).

The Twilight of the Monarchy
— *A Historical Background**

Menashe Reigns — Decay Begins

With the ascension of Menashe to the throne of Jerusalem (3228), the sun began to set upon the era of the First Temple. For one hundred and ten more years, until the Babylonian conquest in the year 3338, some semblance of independence would continue. The hopes of averting the final tragedy would wax and wane with the fortunes of the various kings. But more and more, the soul of the Jewish people would crumble, eroded by the cankerous evil of the idol worship which Menashe planted among them. In the end, the physical destruction of Land and Temple would be no more than the outward manifestation of the inner decay to which the nation had gradually succumbed.

Chizkiyahu's Misgivings

Menashe's father, Chizkiyahu (3199-3228), had carried his people to a glorious zenith of spiritual attainment. He had been a 'Prince of Peace' (*Isaiah* 9:5) and had come tantalizingly close to becoming the מָשִׁיחַ, *Messiah (Sanhedrin* 94a). In his Divinely inspired vision, however, he saw that he would give birth to a son whose destructive wickedness would go beyond anything that had been known before — and this knowledge was the sorrow of his life. In desperation he decided not to marry so that the evil potential within his loins would not be realized. But the prophet Isaiah told him, בהדי כבשי דרחמנא למה לך מאי דמפקדת איבעי לך למעבד, ומה דניחא קמיה קוב״ה לעביד, *Why do you meddle in God's mysteries? You must do what you are commanded to do, and the Holy One, blessed be He, will do what pleases Him (Berachos* 10a).

* Dates are taken from *Toldos Am Olam.*

HASHEM's Verdict

His worst fears were confirmed. Although his son, Menashe, eventually repented *(II Chronicles* 33:12), the period of his wickedness was so destructive and the moral fiber of the people so thoroughly weakened, that the fate of Jerusalem was sealed *(II Kings* 21:10-15). The Land would be laid waste and the Temple would be destroyed, because of the *anger which Menashe had angered Him (ibid.* 23:26).

The darkness which Menashe cast over Jerusalem would not lift for fifty-seven long and painful years. His own reign of fifty-five years was followed by that of his son Ammon (3283-3285) whose wickedness exceeded even that of his father *(Sanhedrin* 103b).

Righteous Yoshiyahu

And then, just as a flame flickers most brightly just before it dies, hope shone once more in Jerusalem. Yoshiyahu, Ammon's son (3285-3316) rejected the heritage of evil which had come to him from his father and grandfather. With unprecedented energy *(II Kings* 23:25) Yoshiyahu set about to forge a renewed covenant between God and people *(ibid. v.* 3) and to cleanse the land of the idolatrous filth by which it had been inundated *(ibid. vs.* 4-20).

The Evil Residue

Yoshiyahu's death at the hands of the Egyptian Pharaoh *(ibid v.* 29), is a tragic burden which Israel carries on its road through history. Had he lived, the final holocaust might have been averted *(Eichah* 4:20). As it was, his life was extinguished before his task was completed. The people were not yet ready to answer his call to greatness. Outwardly they followed his lead, but their souls remained sick and their allegiance belonged to the familiar idols in whom Menashe and Ammon had taught them to seek comfort. (See *Ta'anis* 22b, and *footnote* to 8:3).

For twenty-two years more, the agony was to draw out. Yoshiyahu's son, Yehoachaz (3316), reigned for only three months. The Pharaoh who had killed his father deposed him and placed his brother, Yehoyakim (3316-3327) on his throne.

Yehoyakim The eleven turbulent years of Yehoyakim's rule witnessed the beginnings of the power struggle between the ascending might of Babylon and its firmly entrenched arch enemy, Egypt. After becoming a tributary of Nebuchadnezzar of Babylon *(II Kings* 24:1), Yehoyakim eventually died an ignominious death while a captive in Babylonian hands *(Vayikra Rabbah* 19:5).

Yehoyachin His son Yehoyachin, (3327) succeeded to the throne, but reigned for only three months (*II Kings* 24:8). He was taken to Babylon with the first great wave of exiles. These exiles comprised the elite of Jerusalem's people (*ibid. vs.* 14-16), in particular the חָרָשׁ וּמַסְגֵּר, *carpenters and locksmiths,* who included the great scholars and leaders of the period, including such men as Mordechai and Yechezkel who were to be the repository of Israel's future (see *comm.* to 1:2 and *footnote* to 4:14).

Zidkiyahu and Jeremiah Only the *lowly people of the Land (II Kings* 24:14) remained. Over them, Yehoyachin's uncle, Zidkiyahu (3327-3338) would reign for the final eleven years of Israel's travail. Jeremiah was the prophet in Jerusalem, exhorting the people until the very end to turn once more to God.

His message fell upon deaf ears. Israel's future lay not with the pitiful remnant which was left in Jerusalem, but with the vibrant exile community which was about to be established in Babylon.

Yechezkel Yechezkel ben Buzi, the Priest, would be prophet, guide, and mentor to this emerging community. Upon them, he would erect his fabulous visions of the glorious future which would be built upon the ruins of their tragic history.

The following is a brief synopsis of the passages in *II Kings* relating the monarchic history of the period which are relevant to a proper understanding of the *Book of Ezekiel.* The reader is urged to study the passages from which the synopsis is taken; obviously, what follows is no more than a summary of events.

20:21-21:7

Menashe

Menashe succeeds Chizkiyahu as king of Judah. He is evil, imitating the abominations of the idolatrous nations. Menashe introduces all manner of idol worship, altars, and pagan sacrifice. He even goes so far as to place an idol in the Temple.

21:10-26

In response to Menashe's wickedness, God informs His prophets that He will bring astonishing punishments upon Jerusalem and Judah, judgments comparable to those visited upon Samaria and the House of Ahab. In addition to his other abominations, Menashe is also guilty of much bloodshed. Upon his death, he is succeeded by his son, Ammon, who follows Menashe's evil footsteps until he is assassinated by his servants. Yoshiyahu becomes king.

22:1-13

Yoshiyahu

Only eight years old upon assuming the throne, Yoshiyahu is a righteous person who unswervingly follows the ways of his ancestor, David. His first major project is to appoint officials to supervise the repair of the Temple. Chilkiyahu, the High Priest, finds a Torah scroll in the Temple and has it read to the king. Yoshiyahu hears its contents and interprets it as a signal that he and the people will be sorely punished for the idolatry that is rampant in Judah. Filled with remorse and repentance, the king orders that the guidance of the prophets be sought.

23:1-20

The Repentance

Accompanied by the elders and the people, the king ascends to the Temple where he reads the scroll to the assemblage and pledges to comply with its contents. He has all idolatrous vessels removed from the Temple. He dispatches officials throughout the length and breadth of the Land to seek out and destroy all vestiges of idol worship, and to desecrate the graves of the idolators.

23:25-30

A repentance like Yoshiyahu's was unprecedented and unparalleled. Nevertheless, such roots had Menashe's iniquities struck, that God was unwilling to annul His decree against Judah. Yoshiyahu was killed in battle against Pharaoh Necho in Megiddo and was succeeded by his son Yehoachaz.

23:31-34

Rebirth of Sin

Yehoachaz returns to the evil ways of his grandfather and great-grandfather. After reigning for three months, he is deposed and imprisoned by Pharaoh Necho who levies a tax upon the Land. He appoints as king Eliyakim, son of Yoshiyahu and changes his name to Yehoyakim.

23:35-24:6

Nebuchadnezzar

Yehoyakim, too, is wicked. During his reign Nebuchadnezzar becomes ascendant and Yehoyakim becomes his vassal for three years; then he rebels. As part of His plan to destroy Judah, God sends bands of soldiers from surrounding nations to attack and harass the Land. Yehoyakim dies and is succeeded by his son Yehoyachin.

24:8-17

Yehoyachin, too, is an evil king. Nebuchadnezzar besieges Jerusalem and Yehoyachin capitulates. The Temple treasury and the royal treasury are looted by Nebuchadnezzar who exiles the most distinguished people of Jerusalem and the royal family to Babylon. He allows only the ordinary people to remain in Jerusalem. He appoints Mataniah to be king and renames him Zidkiyahu.

24:18-25:21

Zidkiyahu's Tragedy

Zidkiyahu is wicked [but see *Overview*] and it is still God's will to destroy Jerusalem. In the ninth year of Zidkiyahu's reign, Nebuchadnezzar lays siege to

Jerusalem. In the eleventh year of his reign, hunger is overpowering in the city and its fortifications are breached. Zidkiyahu flees but is taken captive and brought to Nebuchadnezzar who orders that he be forced to witness the slaughter of his children and then blinded. The Temple, the royal palace, and the entire city, are burned down by the Babylonian conquerors, and its wall destroyed. The remnant of the people is exiled by Nebuzaradan, the Babylonian commander. The vessels and copper pillars of the Temple are looted, and the leaders of the people executed in Rivlah by order of Nebuchadnezzar.

(See *Appendix II* for a time-line chart giving the chronology of the kings of Judah and Israel.)

יחזקאל

Some five years after the arrival in Babylon of the first wave of exiles who had been led into captivity by Nebuchadnezzar's hordes, Yechezkel ben Buzi, the priest, was granted a prophecy. As he stood on the banks of the river Kevar 'the heavens were opened' and he was shown 'the visions of God.'

These 'visions' are known in Talmudic literature as מֶרְכָּבָה, Merkavah, [lit. 'Chariot'] or מַעֲשֵׂה מֶרְכָּבָה, Ma'aseh Merkavah, [lit. 'the Work' or 'the Account' of the Chariot]

According to Rambam (Intro. to Moreh Nevuchim), Ma'aseh Merkavah is the name given to מַדָּעֵי הָאֱלֹהוּת, divine science or knowledge, which he defines (comm. to Mishnah, Chagigah 2:1) to include: 'the study concerning the totality of existence, the existence of the Creator, His knowledge, His attributes, the things that derive from Him, the angels, the soul, and the mind which is joined to man. Also that which comes after death.'

The Talmud (Chagigah 14b) recounts that Rabban Yochanan ben Zakkai, riding on a donkey, was accompanied by his student, Rabbi Elazar ben Aroch. Rabbi Elazar asked permission to recite something concerning Ma'aseh Merkavah: Immediately Rabban Yochanan ben Zakkai dismounted, sat on a stone under an olive tree, and covered his head.

Rabbi Elazar asked, 'My master! Why did you dismount from the donkey?'

Rabban Yochanan replied, 'Would it be right for me to ride on the donkey when you are reciting from the Ma'aseh Merkavah, [and therefore] the Divine Presence is with us, and the ministering angels are accompanying us?'

As soon as Rabbi Elazar ben Aroch began to recite from the Ma'aseh Merkavah, a fire descended from the heavens singeing all the trees in the field. The trees began to sing a song of jubilation. Rabban Yochanan ben Zakkai arose, kissed his student on the head, and said: 'Blessed be Hashem, the Lord of Israel, who has given Abraham our father a son who is able to understand, analyze, and explain the Ma'aseh Merkavah.'

In the light of this account we can readily understand why the Sages severely restricted the teaching of Ma'aseh Merkavah. 'We may not teach the Ma'aseh Merkavah even to a single student [i.e. privately] unless he is wise and can understand from within himself' (Chagigah 14b). This dictum is discussed by the Talmud (ad. loc.) and codified by Rambam (Yesodei haTorah 2:12). 'The Sages commanded

us not to expound upon these topics except to only one man at a time, provided he is wise and can understand from within himself; only then do we transmit to him "subject headings" and let him know a smattering of the matter. Then he must understand from within himself and know the conclusions of the matter and its depth.'

Rambam (ibid.) *continues: 'Concerning them Scripture says:* "Honey and milk beneath your tongue," (Shir haShirim *4:11) which the early Sages interpreted: 'Matters which are like* honey and milk [*i.e. the secrets of the Torah*] *shall remain* beneath your tongue [*i.e.: hidden from people who might be unable to cope adequately with the extreme depth and holiness of the subject.*]'

In consonance with this injunction of the Sages, we shall make no attempt to delve into the meaning and implications of Ma'aseh Merkavah *as we do in the commentary to the rest of the book. To do so would be presumptuous, unproductive — and even dangerous, for how can we hope to tread where even the greatest of our Sages hesitated to encroach?*

Nevertheless, it was the unanimous advice of the revered Roshei Hayeshivah שליט״א *that a translation and simple commentary be included. The Editorial Board of Mesorah Publications has therefore, prepared a translation and anthologized commentary on* Ma'aseh Merkavah. *Unlike the rest of this book, the* Merkavah *sections will scrupulously adhere only to the comments of such classic commentators as* Rashi, Ibn Ezra, Radak, *and* Metzudos. *There will be no attempt to fathom the unfathomable.*

Even to this limited approach to Ma'aseh Merkavah, *we must preface these words of extreme caution. The simple translation and the commentary are filled with references to such terms as wings, feet, faces, and animals. By no means can these be taken as literal descriptions of the heavens or of the angels. They are no more than expressions in this-worldly terms of supernatural concepts for which neither human language nor human intelligence are adequate. As an example, the Torah contains frequent references to* יַד ה׳ the hand of HASHEM. *Yet we know, and it is one of* Rambam's *cardinal principles, that God has no hand in the physical sense. The word 'hand' is a metaphorical reference to His power and guiding providence. Such uses of allegory are explained and clarified at length in the* Overview to Shir haShirim *pp. lvii-lxvi. In* Ma'aseh Merkavah *the reluctance of even the Sages to delve into it makes plain how inadequate we are even to attempt to read meaning into the narrative. Small wonder, therefore, that some of the commentators have refrained even from translation. However, the translation and commentary as offered provide a glimpse of the chapter's power. Surely the reader will realize that the treatment presented here contain but the faintest suggestion of the depths of meaning and sanctity inherent in* Ma'aseh Merkavah.

However, the Merkavah *visions are so basic to the prophecies of Yechezkel that certain introductory remarks are in order.*

Implicit in the term Merkavah, chariot, *is the idea of movement (*Kuzari *4:3). Yechezkel saw the heavenly throne, so to speak, in motion as its holiness left the Ark and its environs. His vision brought home to the exiles the full impact of the impending catastrophe in Jerusalem (*Radak).

The leitmotiv *of Yechezkel's prophecy is his apprehension of Israel as the bearers of the Divine Glory. God's Name is sanctified or desecrated by the ebb and flow of their fortunes (see* Pref. remarks *to Ch. 20 and* comm. *to v. 9* ibid.).

The Sages (Bereishis Rabbah 82:7) *express this thought with the phrase:* הָאָבוֹת הֵן הֵן הַמֶּרְכָּבָה, the forefathers themselves are the Merkavah.

In the gamut of Israel's experiences, exile is the Chilul Hashem, *Desecration of the Name, par excellence: 'And when they came to the nations to which they came, they desecrated My holy Name, in that* [*men*] *said of them: "These are the people of Hashem, and they are gone out from their land"* (36:20).'

Thus the Merkavah *vision taught that, during Israel's exile, God's glory was confined to the heavens. His earthly 'chariot', Knesses Israel, had failed Him. Instead of being the 'witnesses' to God's Presence on earth* (Isaiah *44:8) they had become a plaything for Nebuchadnezzar through whom he could boast of his own invincibility* (Isaiah *14:13 and 14. For an elaboration of this theme, see* comm. *to 10:1).*

Rosh Hashanah *31a depicts in heart-rending fashion how the Divine Presence withdrew gradually in ten stages from its place on the Ark in the Holy of Holies. God's intention had been that He might* 'dwell among them' (Exod. *25:8) by permitting His* Shechinah *to rest in the Temple. But, with the passage of centuries, Israel lost its perception of the Temple as the source of holiness within the nation. They came to look upon the Temple service as a means of appeasing God's anger at the theft, murder, and adultery which they practiced in their daily lives (*Jeremiah *7:9-11), rather than as a means to elevate themselves. The fatal attraction of the cult of idolatry had penetrated deep within the very Temple confines, where men and women groveled before graven images (Ch. 8). The Divine Presence could no longer find a place among so degraded a people.*

And so, slowly and gradually, from the Ark to the floor; from the floor to the courtyard; from the courtyard to the wall, the Shechinah *receded from its earthly habitation, casting, as it were, a last longing glance from the Mount of Olives before its final ascent to heaven by way of the wilderness. Behind it, to await the flames of Babylon, there remained only an empty shell, a* בֵּית הַמִּקְדָּשׁ, House of Holiness, *already gutted in all but its external features (*Shir haShirim Rabbah *3:3).*

But the recession of the Shechinah *did not end God's relationship to His beloved people. Poignantly human hands reach out from beneath the* Merkavah *(1:8, 8:3) beckoning to the penitent (*Pesachim *119a), hinting at God's 'longing' for a return. And at the very moment of departure, a stormy wind came from the north (1:4) to subjugate the world before Nebuchadnezzar, so that it might not be said that Israel fell before a lowly nation (*Chagigah *13b); even in their moment of utter disgrace, God safeguarded their honor.*

The Merkavah *vision can be seen from another perspective. The Zohar* (Exod. *2a) reads the entire vision as having the purpose of teaching the exiles that their ties to God had not been sundered: 'At that moment God called to His heavenly hosts and said to them: 'What are you doing here? When My beloved children are in the Babylonian exile should you be here? Arise all of you and go down to Babylon and I shall come with you ...'*

Thus, the tone is set for all the subsequent prophecies and exhortations of Yechezkel which have the purpose of assuring Israel of the continuation of their Divine destiny through the years of their exile.[1]

1. *Harav Joseph Carlebach* in his *Die Drei Grossen Propheten,* interprets the *Merkavah* vision as a reassurance to the exiles of the continuation of הַשְׁגָּחָה, *Divine Providence,* after the fall of Jerusalem. Until the very moment of the destruction, the people as a whole had refused to believe that Jerusalem and the Temple could ever fall. Lulled by the memory of Sancheriv's destruction at the gates of Jerusalem (*II Kings* 18-19) and their own mistaken conception of what made Jerusalem unique among the cities of the world, they found it inconceivable that Babylon could conquer them (see *Pref. Remarks* to Ch. 4 and *comm.* to 11:3). When, in fact, Nebuchadnezzar's hordes trampled on the Temple grounds, they could not imagine that the conqueror was a tool carrying out God's purpose. His triumph must have been perceived as a victory of brute force over God's providence; or they may have regarded it as proof that, as they put it, עָזַב ה׳ אֶת הָאָרֶץ, *God has forsaken the Land* (8:12 and 9:9). But the appearance of the Divine Presence in the heavens over Babylon taught them that the hand of God had never ceased directing Israel's destiny.

א 1 וַיְהִי | בִּשְׁלֹשִׁים שָׁנָה בָּרְבִיעִי בַּחֲמִשָּׁה
א לַחֹדֶשׁ וַאֲנִי בְתוֹךְ־הַגּוֹלָה עַל־נְהַר־כְּבָר

1. All prophetic books with the exception of this one begin by identifying the prophet — and often the time and place of his prophecy. The Book of Ezekiel, however, opens with the prophet's own words (which are then continued in *v.* 4). Verses 2 and 3, written in third person and supplying the missing information, must be regarded as parenthetical *(Rashi)*.

It is as though time, place and identity become insignificant in the face of the shattering impact of this revelation. We were in exile — and still the heavens opened! Time enough to fix this particular episode into its historical framework. The prophet's overriding message is the mere fact — timeless and unbounded in its implications — that God's *Merkavah* is revealed in the heavens of the Babylonian land of exile *(Harav Joseph Breuer.* See also *Pref. Remarks* to this chapter).[1]

וַיְהִי בִּשְׁלֹשִׁים שָׁנָה — *It happened in the thirtieth year.*

This statement takes on historical perspective in conjunction with *v.* 2. Computing backwards from the fifth year of Yehoyachin's exile, we reach the eighteenth year of Yoshiyahu's reign: five years for Yehoyachin, eleven years for Yehoyakim and the final fourteen years of Yoshiyahu's thirty-one year reign *(Rashi.* See chart attached to *Overview).*

This eighteenth year of Yoshiyahu's reign marked a major turning point in Israel's history. That the history of the *Jewish people* could be divorced from the history of the *Jewish land;* that the destruction of Jerusalem (*II Kings* 23:27), instead of dragging its people into oblivion, made possible a vibrant rebirth of Jewish nationhood in Babylon (see *Overview);* that the prophecy of the *Merkavah* was able to find receptive ears and hearts among the exiles — all of these can be traced directly to the events of that year.

For it was then that Chilkiyahu, the High Priest, found the Sefer Torah, *(II Kings* 23) a circumstance that stimulated a universal repentance of king and people. [It should be noted that not all the people repented sincerely. Some only went through the outward motions. See *Ta'anis* 22b and *comm.* to

1. The Sages (*Chagigah* 13b) comment on the thoroughness with which Yechezkel details his *Merkavah* vision. 'All that Yechezkel saw Isaiah [also] saw. [But] Yechezkel can be compared to a villager who saw the king, whereas Isaiah was like a city dweller who saw the king.'

According to *Rambam (Moreh Nevuchim* 3:6) the difference in approach between the two prophets can be traced to the audiences whom they addressed. Isaiah lived some two hundred years before Yechezkel. Then, the Temple stood in their midst in all its glory. Israel was familiar with the details of the *Merkavah,* as are city dwellers who daily see the king's chariot and need no description of it. The 'villagers' of Yechezkel's generation, steeped in the idolatrous abominations of Menashe (see *Overview)* for many decades, had, as it were, never seen the king, and every detail was new to them.

Alternately, *Rambam* suggests that the Talmudic simile may refer to the prophets themselves. Yechezkel, two hundred years after Isaiah, had not attained his predecessor's level of prophecy, and was startled by visions which Isaiah would have taken in stride.

When we consider that the thrust of this chapter, and indeed the whole Book, is to underline the fact of God's continued Presence in exile; then *Harav Breuer's* interpretation seems most apt. In his view it is the appearance of the king's chariot *in the village* which is startling. There is nothing astounding in meeting the king in the city. Similarly, Isaiah's vision of the Heavenly Throne in the Holy Temple did not inspire the same ecstacy as Yechezkel's vision by the banks of the River Kevar.

I *It happened in the thirtieth year in the fourth month*
1 *on the fifth of the month, as I was among the exile*

8:3]. Every vestige of idol worship was removed from the Land, and above all the people entered into a new covenant which was to bind them in loyal and loving adherence to the Torah (*II Kings* 23). The effects of the fifty-seven most destructive years of Jewish history — the combined reign of Menashe and Ammon — were nullified, and a spiritual rebirth of the nation was made possible.

Hence, the dating of the *Merkavah* vision as being in 'the thirtieth year'. To Yechezkel's contemporaries the meaning was obvious. Thirty years after the finding of the Sefer Torah (*Targum, Rashi* and *Metzudas David*), that event still bore fruit: the covenant had lasted. Exiled in an unclean land, Israel still perceived the *Shechinah*, the Divine Presence, in their midst.[1]

Rashi and *Radak* (see also *Ibn Ezra; Exodus* 12:40) based on *Seder Olam* 24, explain 'the thirtieth year' as being the thirtieth year of the *Yovel*, the fifty year cycle (*Lev.* 25:8).

This is computed on the basis of 40:1: *'In the twenty-fifth year of our exile, the beginning of the year on the tenth of the month.'* Our Sages teach that the start of the *Yovel* year is reckoned from the tenth of Tishrei, [i.e. *Yom Kippur*, as opposed to *Rosh Hashanah*]. Thus, if the twenty-fifth year from Yehoyachin's exile was a *Yovel* year, it follows that thirty years before the fifth year of that exile was also a *Yovel*.

This last *Yovel* year was also a significant historical landmark. The observance of *Yovel* (which is predicated on 'most inhabitants' (i.e. a majority of the nation's people) being on the land — (see *Arachin* 32b) had been abrogated with the exile of the Ten Tribes some two hundred years earlier. Nevertheless, Yoshiyahu had been able to celebrate it, because Jeremiah, the prophet, had 'gone to bring back the Ten Tribes and Yoshiyahu ruled over them' (*ibid.* 33a).

Thus, in that year there had been some hope that God might once more have mercy and that Israel would again return to the splendor of Solomonic times.

It was not to be. With Yoshiyahu's death at the hands of an Egyptian Pharaoh, there began a steady erosion of his repentance movement. Far from absorbing the lessons of the *Yovel: And the Land shall not be sold for permanent possession for the Land is Mine, for only strangers and sojourners are you with Me (Lev.* 25:23), Israel adopted the slogan: *It is ours! The Land has been given to us as an inheritance* (11:15). An added poignancy is thus achieved by dating the vision at Babylon's river to that final *Yovel* year whose great promise had been squandered.

וַאֲנִי בְתוֹךְ הַגּוֹלָה — *As I was among the exile.*

We find the word גּוֹלָה used to denote *exile (Amos* 1:15) and also to denote the individual people who are in exile (*Jeremiah* 29:4).

Rashi renders the word in the former manner, *Metzudas David*, in the latter. 3:11-15 implies that the *Merkavah* vision took place while Yechezkel was

1. We have no direct Midrashic or Talmudic sources which explain why the discovery of the Sefer Torah threw Yoshiyahu into such spiritual turmoil. *Radak (II Kings* 22:11) followed by many commentators, comments that the Sefer Torah was rolled to the passage in *Deuteronomy* which foretold the inevitable exile for king and nation, which would result from their sins. This was seen as an omen and a call for repentance [possibly because one would have expected it to be rolled to the beginning of *Genesis*]. While the *Talmud* does say that Yoshiyahu read that passage in the Torah *(Yerushalmi; Shakalim* 6), it does not mention the peculiarity of its having been rolled to that passage.

א ב־ג

נִפְתְּחוּ הַשָּׁמַיִם וָאֶרְאֶה מַרְאוֹת אֱלֹהִים:
ב בַּחֲמִשָּׁה לַחֹדֶשׁ הִיא הַשָּׁנָה הַחֲמִישִׁית
ג לְגָלוּת הַמֶּלֶךְ יוֹיָכִין: הָיֹה הָיָה דְבַר־
יְהוָה אֶל־יְחֶזְקֵאל בֶּן־בּוּזִי הַכֹּהֵן בְּאֶרֶץ

isolated from his people [confirming *Rashi*'s opinion].

עַל נְהַר כְּבָר — *By the River Kevar.*

Scripture would not have stressed this location unless it were significant. *Amos* (7:17, see also *Kesubos* 111a) teaches that, relative to the Land of Israel, all other places are אֲדָמָה טְמֵאָה, *unclean land.*

Holiness and purity, which are among the prerequisites for the gift of prophecy, are hardly possible in such surroundings. Indeed, the Sages *(Mechilta Bo* 12:1) teach that there is no prophecy outside Eretz Yisrael. Therefore, when exceptional circumstances required that prophecy be granted in Babylon, (see *comm. v.* 3), a ritually 'clean' place, such as a river bank was chosen (*Mechilta* ibid.).

Radak quotes a disagreement among the Sages as to whether the River Kevar is the Euphrates.

נִפְתְּחוּ הַשָּׁמַיִם — *The heavens opened.*

I commanded the heavens to open [in answer to] the voice of Yechezkel *(Bereishis Rabbah* 5:4). The implication is that the prophet prayed for this vision.

מַרְאוֹת אֱלֹהִים — *Visions of God.* [lit. *'divine visions'* or: *'great visions' (Radak)*].

Rashi explains the usage of the plural (מַרְאוֹת rather than מַרְאֶה) as indicating a blurred, inexact vision. This is in accordance with the dictum of the Sages that all the prophets, with the exception of Moses, apprehended their prophecy as if through an אִסְפַּקְלַרְיָא שֶׁאֵינָה מְאִירָה, *a speculum which is not lucid. Rambam (Moreh Nevuchim* 3:5) attributes the use of the plural to the fact that there were many different components to the *Merkavah,* with the result that Yechezkel saw a number of visions.

2. הַשָּׁנָה הַחֲמִישִׁית לְגָלוּת הַמֶּלֶךְ יוֹיָכִין — *The fifth year of the exile of King Yehoyachin.*

With the death of Yoshiyahu, the impetus of his great repentance movement (*comm. v.* 1) ebbed. He was succeeded by his son, Yehoachaz, who *'did evil in the eyes of HASHEM'* and was deposed by an Egyptian Pharaoh, after he had been king for only three months *(II Kings* 23).

He was followed by his brother Yehoyakim who also *'did evil in the eyes of HASHEM in all things as his fathers had done.'* The eleven years of his reign were plagued by Nebuchadnezzar's first interference in Judah's internal affairs (*ibid*); and the first wave of captives was exiled to Babylon in the third year of Yehoyakim's reign (*Daniel* 1:1).

His son Yehoyachin (Yoshiyahu's grandson) succeeded to the throne, but after only three months he, together with his family and court, was dragged into Babylonian exile as part of the first major *Galus.*

II Kings 24:14 reads: *And he* [Nebuchadnezzar] *exiled all of Jerusalem, and all the princes and all the warriors — ten thousand exiles — and all* הֶחָרָשׁ וְהַמַּסְגֵּר, *the carpenters and the locksmiths. None but the lowly people remained.*

It was over these 'lowly people' that Zidkiyahu, the last son of Yoshiyahu, reigned for the eleven final, tragic years of the Holy Temple's existence.

לְגָלוּת הַמֶּלֶךְ יוֹיָכִין, *King Yehoyachin's exile.* This was to be the nucleus from

by the River Kevar; the heavens opened and I saw visions of God.

2 *On the fifth of the month; it was the fifth year of the exile of King Yehoyachin.* 3 *The word of HASHEM had come to Yechezkel, the son of Buzi, the*

which a new, regenerated Israel would grow (see *Overview* and *comm.* to 11:15). Included in it were the best of Israel's sons.

The חָרָשׁ, *carpenters* and מַסְגֵּר, *locksmiths* mentioned in *II Kings* 24:14, were no ordinary workers. The Sages *(Sifri* to *Deut.* 32:25) identify them as the greatest תַּלְמִידֵי חֲכָמִים, *teachers of Torah*, in the nation. They silenced everyone who would want to argue with them (the root חרש denotes *silence* as well as *carpentry)* with their brilliance; and when they spoke everyone else would close his mouth (סגר, *to close*, hence also the root of *locksmith)* in order to listen.

Thus, it was the elite of Judah who first descended to Babylon, leaving the untutored masses behind.[1]

Scripture does not record Yechezkel's descent into captivity. However, since he refers to Yehoyachin's exile as גָּלוּתֵנוּ, *our exile*, (33:21, 40:1), it is assumed that he was among the 'carpenters and locksmiths' who came to Babylon together with Yehoyachin.

There is no hint in the book as to why his prophecy started in the fifth year and not before. *Seder Hadoros* (3,316), without citing a source reports that he spent the first five years in a Babylonian prison.

The fifth year of Yehoyachin's exile corresponds to the year 3332 from creation *(Toldos Am Olam).*

3. הָיֹה הָיָה — *Had come* [lit. 'was' or *'had been'; accentuated by the use of the infinitive* הָיֹה].

Rashi quotes *Mechilta d'Rabbi Shimon Ben Yochai* [see also *Targum*] that the prophecy recorded here was not Yechezkel's first. This is deduced from the doubling of the verb [i.e. this particular vision came to me after the gift of prophecy had already been given me previously]. This interpretation is further supported by the fact that the gift of prophecy rightfully belongs only in Eretz Yisrael (see *comm. v.* 1). It is assumed, therefore, that the mission of the prophet must have begun in the Holy Land. *Rashi* suggests that these unidentified earlier visions may be those recounted in either Ch. 2 or Ch. 17.

Kuzari (2:14) suggests that it may be that a prophecy *concerning* the Land of Israel might take place outside the Land, even if there were no prior visions. Alternately, the fact that Yechezkel spent his youth in the Land before he was exiled could have prepared him for his subsequent prophecy, even if none had actually been given him in Eretz Yisrael.

יְחֶזְקֵאל בֶּן בּוּזִי — *Yechezkel, the son of Buzi.*

1. The Sages *(Gittin* 88a) explain why God's providence decreed that the finest sons of Judah be exiled first. On the verse in *Daniel* 9:14: *'And God hastened the evil and brought it about — because He is righteous'*, they ask why it is deemed righteous to hasten evil. The answer is given: 'God acted charitably with Israel, in that Zidkiyahu's exile came about while Yehoyachin's exile was still in existence' [the ultimate destruction of the Holy Temple was pushed forward by two years, so that the masses of Zidkiyahu's exile would find an established Torah community in Babylon].

Thus, the *Galus Yechonya* (i.e. Yehoyachin) was the cornerstone of the great Jewish community which was to flourish in Babylon.

א
ד־ו

כַּשְׂדִּים עַל־נְהַר־כְּבָר וַתְּהִי עָלָיו שָׁם יַד־
ד יְהֹוָה׃ וָאֵרֶא וְהִנֵּה רוּחַ סְעָרָה בָּאָה מִן־
הַצָּפוֹן עָנָן גָּדוֹל וְאֵשׁ מִתְלַקַּחַת וְנֹגַהּ לוֹ
סָבִיב וּמִתּוֹכָהּ כְּעֵין הַחַשְׁמַל מִתּוֹךְ
ה הָאֵשׁ׃ וּמִתּוֹכָהּ דְּמוּת אַרְבַּע חַיּוֹת וְזֶה
ו מַרְאֵיהֶן דְּמוּת אָדָם לָהֵנָּה׃ וְאַרְבָּעָה

Eliyahu Rabba (6) derives בּוּזִי *Buzi* from the root בוז, *to shame*. Thus, *ben Buzi* is rendered: 'the son of men who allowed themselves to be shamed for the sake of My honor and the honor of Israel.'

יַד ה׳ — *The hand of HASHEM.*

This alludes to the shattering experience of prophecy, which throws the prophet into a trance *(Rashi)* [compare 3:14 *'And the hand of Hashem was upon me with force'*].

Ma'aseh Merkavah

In this vision, supernatural concepts are described in human terms. As explained in the *Prefatory Remarks,* they cannot be understood literally nor, in our spiritual poverty, are we equipped even to glimpse at their inner meaning.

4. וְהִנֵּה רוּחַ סְעָרָה — *And behold! A stormy wind.*

This is a prophetic idiom symbolizing the *Merkavah* of the *Shechinah's* Throne as the chapter elaborates further. Since it came in wrath to destroy Israel, it is represented as a stormy wind and cloud *(Rashi).*

בָּאָה — *Was coming.*

The word בָּאָה with the accent on the second syllable is in present tense. Had the accent been on the first syllable, it would have been past tense *(Rashi* to *Gen.* 29:6).

מִן הַצָּפוֹן — *From the north.*

Returning from the direction of Chaldea, [Babylon] to the north of Judah from where *'the evil* [i.e., the impending invasion of Judah by the Babylonians] *will break forth'* [*Jer.* 1:14] ...

The fierce northern storm went to conquer the entire world and subjugate it under the wicked Nebuchadnezzar, so that the nations might not say: Into the hand of a low people [viz. the Chaldeans (cf. *Isaiah* 23:13)] did God deliver His children *(Rashi;* cf. *Chagigah* 13b).

עָנָן גָּדוֹל — *A great cloud.*

I.e., he also saw a great cloud, portending impending calamity *(Metzudas David).*

וְאֵשׁ מִתְלַקַּחַת — *With a flashing fire.*

I.e. in the midst of the cloud *(Radak).*

The word מִתְלַקַּחַת, used to describe a flashing fire, is derived from the root לקח, *to take*: it is as if the fire seeks its freedom but is נִלְקָח, *grasped* or *held* by the burning object *(Metzudas Zion).* The fire symbolizes the impending burning of the Temple *(Metzudas David).*

וְנֹגַהּ לוֹ סָבִיב — *And a brilliance surrounding it.*

I.e. all of the above.

The *brilliance* alludes to the light of salvation which would ultimately envelop them after all their travail *(Rashi; Metzudas David).*

וּמִתּוֹכָהּ כְּעֵין הַחַשְׁמַל — [*And*] *from its midst came a semblance of Chashmal.*

The mysterious significance of this

I
4-6
priest, in the land of the Chaldeans by the River Kevar; and the hand of HASHEM was upon him, there.

4 *Then I looked and behold! A stormy wind was coming from the north, a great cloud with flashing fire and a brilliance surrounding it; and from its midst came a semblance of Chashmal from the midst of the fire;* 5 *and from its midst, a semblance of four Chayos. This was their appearance: they had the semblance of a man;* 6 *and four faces for each, and*

word is laden with esoteric connotation. It is a pure example of prophetic idiom, and beyond the realm of comprehension.

Rashi comments that *Chashmal* is the name of an angel, a semblance of whom Yechezkel envisioned from within the flames. Our Sages [*Chagigah* 13a] have taught that there was once a student who speculated upon the identity of *Chashmal*, whereupon a fire went forth from *Chashmal* and consumed him. Further, the word is an acrostic of the words חַיוֹת אֵשׁ מְמַלְלוֹת, *fiery Chayos speaking*. In an alternate interpretation, the Sages derive from the two words חַשׁ [=silent] and מְלַל [=speaking]. Thus, at times the angels are silent [חש], at times they speak [מל] i.e. praise Him. When the utterance goes forth from the Holy One, Blessed be He, they are silent, and when the utterance does not go forth from Him they speak. It is possible that *Chashmal* resembles the Essence of fire *(Rashi)*. [But none of the above explanations coincide with the context (*Rashi* next verse)].

It is the purest form of smokeless fire that the human senses can perceive ... The word is a compound of חַשׁ מַל [lit. *silent; speak*] for it is proper to be silent about its implications which defy human description *(Metzudas David)*.

5. וּמִתּוֹכָהּ — *And from its midst.*

I.e. the midst of the *fire* referred to above *(Rashi)*. Or, according to *Metzudas David*: of the *brightness* referred to above.

דְּמוּת אַרְבַּע חַיּוֹת — *A semblance of four Chayos.*

I.e. living beings *(Targum; Radak)*.

These were the bearers of the *Merkavah* which transported the King of Glory in exile *(Malbim)*.

וְזֶה מַרְאֵיהֶן — *This was their appearance,* [i.e of the Chayos.]

דְּמוּת אָדָם לָהֵנָּה — *They had the semblance of a man.*

Rashi 'marvels' at the implication that they had only a human face when *v.* 10 makes it clear that the angels' faces had the forms of animals as well. *Rashi* explains that the human form was preeminent and that the face is that of the Patriarch, Jacob.

According to *Metzudas David*, the reference was not to their *faces* [some of which resembled those of various animals] but to the form of their *bodies* which were human in form.[1]

1. [The above discussion concerning the 'faces' and 'forms' — like the rest of the simple comm. of this chapter — can be studied only in the context of the *Pref. Remarks* that a true understanding of the *Merkavah* is impossible for us.]

א
ז־י

פָנִים לְאֶחָת וְאַרְבַּע כְּנָפַיִם לְאַחַת לָהֶם׃
ז וְרַגְלֵיהֶם רֶגֶל יְשָׁרָה וְכַף רַגְלֵיהֶם כְּכַף
ח רֶגֶל עֵגֶל וְנֹצְצִים כְּעֵין נְחֹשֶׁת קָלָל׃ °וידו °וִידֵי ק׳
אָדָם מִתַּחַת כַּנְפֵיהֶם עַל אַרְבַּעַת
רִבְעֵיהֶם וּפְנֵיהֶם וְכַנְפֵיהֶם לְאַרְבַּעְתָּם׃
ט חֹבְרֹת אִשָּׁה אֶל־אֲחוֹתָהּ כַּנְפֵיהֶם לֹא־
יִסַּבּוּ בְלֶכְתָּן אִישׁ אֶל־עֵבֶר פָּנָיו יֵלֵכוּ׃
י וּדְמוּת פְּנֵיהֶם פְּנֵי אָדָם וּפְנֵי אַרְיֵה אֶל־

Ma'aseh Merkavah: In this vision, supernatural concepts are described in human terms. As explained in the *Prefatory Remarks,* they cannot be understood literally nor, in our spiritual poverty, are we equipped even to glimpse at their inner meaning.

6. וְאַרְבָּעָה פָּנִים לְאֶחָת — *And four faces for each.*

I.e. each of the four faces [i.e. man, lion, ox, and eagle as described in *v.* 10] appeared four times on each *Chayah,* once *in each direction,* making a total of sixteen faces for each *Chayah.* Each of the faces had four wings, so that each *Chayah* had sixty-four wings. The total for all four *Chayos* together were sixty-four faces and 256 wings *(Targum; Rashi).*[1]

7. וְרַגְלֵיהֶם רֶגֶל יְשָׁרָה — *Their legs were a straight leg.*

[The translation is literal and preserves the ambiguity]:

I.e., the legs were in proper position, close together *(Targum; Rashi).*[2]

Another interpretation: *Straight* means that they had no joints. These were unnecessary since, unlike other creatures, they had no need to sit or lie down *(Rashi; Metzudos).*

כְּכַף רֶגֶל עֵגֶל — *Like the sole of a rounded foot.*

The translation of עֵגֶל [=עָגֹל] as *rounded* follows *Targum* who renders סְגַלְגְלָן, round *(Rashi).*

Metzudos renders 'like the sole of a calf's foot.' *Rashi,* in *Isaiah* 6:2, notes this interpretation and adds that the angels covered these calf-like feet because they were reminiscent of Israel's sin of the Golden Calf.

וְנֹצְצִים — *And they glittered.*

The subject is the *legs* [not the *Chayos* as a whole] *(Metzudas David).*

כְּעֵין נְחֹשֶׁת קָלָל — *Like burnished bronze.*

Which sparkles brilliantly *(Metzudas David).*

1. It is forbidden to make a graven image containing the four faces of the *Chayos (Rosh Hashanah* 24b, *Yorah Deah* 141:4).

2. The Sages derive a *halachah* from this verse:

Rabbi Yose ben Rabbi Chaninah also said in the name of Rabbi Eliezer ben Yaakov: When one prays [Shemoneh Esrei], he should place his feet in proper position [i.e., close together *(Rashi)*], as it says: *And their feet were straight feet. (Berachos* 10b; cf. *Rambam Hil. Tefillah* 5:4; *Orach Chaim* 95:1). There is one opinion in *Yerushalmi (Berachos* 1:1), that during prayer the feet should be one directly in front of the other with the toes of the rear one touching the heel of the forward one.

four wings for each of them. 7 *Their legs were a*
straight leg; and the sole of their feet was like the sole
of a rounded foot, and they glittered like burnished
bronze. 8 *And human hands were under their wings*
on each of their four sides; and their faces and wings
were alike on the four of them. 9 *Joined to one*
another were their wings. They did not turn as they
moved, each went straight ahead. 10 *As for the*
semblance of their faces: the face of a man and the

8. וִידֵי אָדָם ... רִבְעֵיהֶם — *And human hands* [*were*] *under their wings on each of their four sides* [lit. *upon their four sides*].

Rashi, elaborating on *Targum,* comments that the *Chayos* were assigned to gather fiery coals and cast them upon Jerusalem to punish Israel. They *handed* the coals to one another so that they would become somewhat cooled in the process, thus mitigating the suffering (see *comm.* to 10:2). According to the Sages (*Yoma* 77a) had these coals not been cooled, Israel would have been exterminated, heaven forfend.

Radak notes that the כְּתִיב, *Masoretic spelling,* of the phrase is וְיָדוֹ אָדָם [lit. *and his hand is man.*] In this form, the phrase would be interpreted to mean וְיָדוֹ (יָדַי) אָדָם [lit. *his hand was human hands.*] Cf. the expression in *Song of Songs* 1:15 עֵינַיִךְ יוֹנִים [lit. *Your eyes are doves*] and which is interpreted to mean עֵינַיִךְ כְּעֵינֵי יוֹנִים [lit. *'Your eyes are like dove's eyes'*].

וּפְנֵיהֶם וְכַנְפֵיהֶם לְאַרְבַּעְתָּם — *And their faces and wings* [*were alike*] *on the four of them* (Following *Targum; Rashi*).

That is, the four *Chayos* resembled one another in the matter of their faces and wings (*Metzudas David*).

9. חֹבְרֹת אִשָּׁה אֶל אֲחוֹתָהּ כַּנְפֵיהֶם — *Joined to one to another* [lit. *'a woman to her sister'*], *were their wings.*

The wing of each would be spread to its neighbor on each side, until they were joined into a unit. Since the wings were extended upward and there were many wings on all sides of the *Chayos* [see *comm.* to *v.* 6], the outstretched wings covered their faces [see *v.* 11] (*Rashi*).

לֹא יִסַּבּוּ בְלֶכְתָּן — *They did not turn as they moved* [lit. *'walked'*].

They had no need to turn around to move in a particular direction, since each of the *Chayos* had faces on every side (*Rashi*).

אִישׁ אֶל עֵבֶר פָּנָיו יֵלֵכוּ — *Each went straight ahead* [lit. *'in the direction of his face'*].

Each went in the direction of the face which was toward its destination (*Rashi*); in whatever direction the *Chayos* were to go, they always moved forward since they had faces in every direction (*Metzudos David*).

10. [This verse describes the 'faces mentioned in *v.* 6]: Each of the four *Chayos* had the face of a *man* in front [the word לְאַרְבַּעְתָּם, *of the four of them* does not occur with reference to the face of *man* as it does in the other representations further in this verse because it was already noted in v. 6 that each of the four *Chayos* had a human appearance (*Malbim*)]. This was the case in each of the four directions of each *Chayah* [i.e., each *Chayah* had four human faces, one in each direction]. To the right *of each human face* there was

הַיָּמִין֙ לְאַרְבַּעְתָּ֔ם וּפְנֵי־שׁ֥וֹר מֵהַשְּׂמֹ֖אול
יא לְאַרְבַּעְתָּ֑ן וּפְנֵי־נֶ֖שֶׁר לְאַרְבַּעְתָּֽן׃ וּפְנֵיהֶ֕ם
וְכַנְפֵיהֶ֛ם פְּרֻד֖וֹת מִלְמָ֑עְלָה לְאִ֗ישׁ שְׁתַּ֙יִם֙
חֹבְר֣וֹת אִ֔ישׁ וּשְׁתַּ֣יִם מְכַסּ֔וֹת אֵ֖ת
יב גְּוִיֹתֵיהֶֽנָה׃ וְאִ֛ישׁ אֶל־עֵ֥בֶר פָּנָ֖יו יֵלֵ֑כוּ אֶ֣ל
אֲשֶׁ֣ר יִֽהְיֶה־שָׁ֩מָּה הָר֨וּחַ לָלֶ֜כֶת יֵלֵ֗כוּ לֹ֥א
יג יִסַּ֖בּוּ בְּלֶכְתָּֽן׃ וּדְמ֨וּת הַחַיּ֜וֹת מַרְאֵיהֶ֗ם
כְּגַחֲלֵי־אֵ֞שׁ בֹּעֲר֨וֹת כְּמַרְאֵ֣ה הַלַּפִּדִ֔ים
הִ֕יא מִתְהַלֶּ֖כֶת בֵּ֣ין הַחַיּ֑וֹת וְנֹ֣גַהּ לָאֵ֔שׁ
יד וּמִן־הָאֵ֖שׁ יוֹצֵ֥א בָרָֽק׃ וְהַחַיּ֖וֹת רָצ֣וֹא
טו וָשׁ֑וֹב כְּמַרְאֵ֖ה הַבָּזָֽק׃ וָאֵ֖רֶא הַחַיּ֑וֹת וְהִנֵּה֩
אוֹפַ֨ן אֶחָ֥ד בָּאָ֛רֶץ אֵ֥צֶל הַחַיּ֖וֹת לְאַרְבַּ֥עַת

Ma'aseh Merkavah: In this vision, supernatural concepts are described in human terms. As explained in the *Prefatory Remarks,* they cannot be understood literally nor, in our spiritual poverty, are we equipped even to glimpse at their inner meaning.

the face of a lion; to the left of each face, that of an ox; and to the back of each human face, that of an eagle *(Metzudas David).*

11. וּפְנֵיהֶם וְכַנְפֵיהֶם פְּרֻדוֹת מִלְמָעְלָה — *And as for their faces, their wings extended upward.*

The cantillation makes clear that וּפְנֵיהֶם, *their faces,* is an independent phrase. Thus the verse describes that the upward-stretching wings covered their faces *(Rashi).*

לְאִישׁ שְׁתַּיִם חֹבְרוֹת אִישׁ — *For each* [*face*] *two joined for each.*

I.e. the wings of one Chayah touched those of the next in order that the faces in between be covered *(Rashi).*

According to *Metzudas David,* each face had two wings attached. They were used to cover the faces.

וּשְׁתַּיִם מְכַסּוֹת אֵת גְּוִיֹתֵיהֶנָה — *And two covered their bodies.*

That is, with the two other wings [i.e. they had a total of four wings for each face], they covered their bodies *(Rashi).*

12. וְאִישׁ אֶל עֵבֶר פָּנָיו יֵלֵכוּ — *Each one went straight ahead* [lit. *'in the direction of his face'*].

[See *v.* 9.]

הָרוּחַ לָלֶכֶת — *The spirit to go.*

I.e. the desire to go *(Targum; Rashi).*

13. וּדְמוּת הַחַיּוֹת — *The appearance of the Chayos.*

The appearance of their *eyes* is referred to here; their *bodies* were already described above *(Radak).*

As the Sages explained it, this refers to the function they were about to perform, because incorporeal things defy description beyond their function. In this case, the *Chayos* were being charged with the mission of burning the Temple and the king's palace, therefore

face of a lion to the right of the four, the face of an ox to the left of the four; and the face of an eagle to the four. 11 *And as for their faces: their wings extended upward; for each face two joined for each, and two covered their bodies.* 12 *Each one went straight ahead, toward wherever there was the spirit to go — they went. They turned not as they went.* 13 *And as for the appearance of the Chayos: their appearance was like fiery coals, burning like the appearance of torches; it manifested itself among the Chayos. There was a brilliance to the fire, and from the fire went forth lightning.* 14 *And the Chayos ran to and fro like the appearance of Bazak.* 15 *When I saw the Chayos — behold! One Ofan was on the surface near the*

they are likened to *coals of fire (Malbim).*

הִיא מִתְהַלֶּכֶת בֵּין הַחַיּוֹת — *It manifested itself* [lit. *'walked about'*; see *Bereishis* 3:8] *among the Chayos.*

That is, the above appearance was shared by all the *Chayos (Rashi).*

According to *Radak* (following *Targum),* the specific subject is the *fire* which darted to and fro among the *Chayos.*

וְנֹגַהּ לָאֵשׁ — *There was a brilliance to the fire.*

Far more intense than that of a normal fire *(Rashi).*

Brightness illuminates but does not *consume;* so, too, Hashem indicated to him that His kindness had not ended: He would vent His wrath upon the 'wood and stones' but would not abandon His people. Eventually He would save them *(Malbim).*

14. וְהַחַיּוֹת רָצוֹא וָשׁוֹב — *And the Chayos ran to and fro* [lit. *'running and returning'*].

They were not stationary: each ran about and instantly returned to its position as quickly as lightning which flashes and withdraws at a speed beyond perception *(Metzudas David).*

כְּמַרְאֵה הַבָּזָק — *Like the appearance of Bazak.*

Bazak is a brilliant flash of light. *Rashi* gives four interpretations:
a) like the colorful light emanating from the fire of a crucible where gold is refined; b) like the quick flame from the highly flammable leftovers of olives in a pot; c) something quickly spreading out; d) like lightning.

Metzudas David cited above bases his comment on *Rashi*'s latter interpretation. In *Metzudas Zion* he explains that *bazak* is synonymous with *barak* [lightning] in the previous verse, since the letters *z* and *r* in Hebrew are occasionally interchanged.

15. אוֹפַן אֶחָד בָּאָרֶץ *One Ofan was on the surface* [lit. *'on the earth'*]

I.e. on the *'floor'* or *'surface'* of the expanse *(Rashi);* according to *Metzudas David* (following *Targum)* בָּאָרֶץ here

טז פָּנָיו׃ מַרְאֵה הָאוֹפַנִּים וּמַעֲשֵׂיהֶם כְּעֵין
תַּרְשִׁישׁ וּדְמוּת אֶחָד לְאַרְבַּעְתָּן
וּמַרְאֵיהֶם וּמַעֲשֵׂיהֶם כַּאֲשֶׁר יִהְיֶה הָאוֹפַן
יז בְּתוֹךְ הָאוֹפָן׃ עַל־אַרְבַּעַת רִבְעֵיהֶן
יח בְּלֶכְתָּם יֵלֵכוּ לֹא יִסַּבּוּ בְּלֶכְתָּן׃ וְגַבֵּיהֶן
וְגֹבַהּ לָהֶם וְיִרְאָה לָהֶם וְגַבֹּתָם מְלֵאֹת
יט עֵינַיִם סָבִיב לְאַרְבַּעְתָּן׃ וּבְלֶכֶת הַחַיּוֹת
יֵלְכוּ הָאוֹפַנִּים אֶצְלָם וּבְהִנָּשֵׂא הַחַיּוֹת
כ מֵעַל הָאָרֶץ יִנָּשְׂאוּ הָאוֹפַנִּים׃ עַל אֲשֶׁר
יִהְיֶה־שָּׁם הָרוּחַ לָלֶכֶת יֵלֵכוּ שָׁמָּה הָרוּחַ

Ma'aseh Merkavah: In this vision, supernatural concepts are described in human terms. As explained in the *Prefatory Remarks,* they cannot be understood literally nor, in our spiritual poverty, are we equipped even to glimpse at their inner meaning.

has the meaning of *below;* i.e., beneath the *Chayos.*

Ofan, [lit. *'wheel'*] is the name of one of the celestial angels.[1]

Yechezkel was shown the form of a *'wheel'* [*Ofan*] beneath each of the *Chayos (Metzudas David).* [Since *Ofan* is an angel which is inferior to *Chayah* (see *footnote),* it may be that each *Chayah* had a ministering *Ofan* 'below' it. As emphasized throughout the prefatory remarks, the prophet deals in idioms to which we are not privy. The significance of these idioms are among סִתְרֵי תוֹרָה, *the mysteries of Torah* which are infinitely beyond our capacity to fathom; therefore, we are forbidden even to conjecture about their true nature.]

אֵצֶל הַחַיּוֹת — *Near the Chayos.*

I.e. in the proximity of each of the *Chayos (Metzudas David).*

לְאַרְבַּעַת פָּנָיו — *By its four faces* [lit. *'to its four faces*].

Rashi in his primary interpretation, and *Metzudas David,* explain that one *Ofan* stood near each four-faced *Chayah;* not that there was one *Ofan* for each face. [Apparently *Rashi* refers to the four *main* faces of each *Chayah* as described in *v.* 6; the reference does not take into account that each *Chayah* had four of *each* face and hence a total of *sixteen.* Or, *Rashi* may refer to each of four 'directions' rather than each of its many faces.]

According to *Rashi*'s alternate interpretation, however, *its four faces* might refer to the *Ofanim* and thus imply that the *Ofanim* had four faces.

16. מַרְאֵה הָאוֹפַנִּים וּמַעֲשֵׂיהֶם כְּעֵין תַּרְשִׁישׁ — *The appearance of the Ofanim and their deeds were like Tarshish.*

[I.e., the physical representation assumed by the incorporeal *Ofanim* was in the prophetic idiom, similar to *Tarshish.*]

Tarshish is a brilliant transparent

1. There are ten levels of angels. Their names are Chayos, Ofanim, Er'elim, Chashmalim, Seraphim, Malachim, Elohim, B'nai Elohim, Cheruvim, and Ishim *(Rambam Yesodei haTorah* 2:7).

Chayos by its four faces. 16 *The appearance of the*
Ofanim and their deeds were like Tarshish with the
same semblance for the four; and their appearance
and their deeds were like an Ofan within an Ofan.
17 *Toward their four sides, whenever they went, they*
could go; they did not turn as they went. 18 *And they*
had backs and were tall and fearsome, and their
backs were full of eyes surrounding the four of them.
19 *As the Chayos move the Ofanim move by them*
and as the Chayos were lifted from upon the surface,
the Ofanim were lifted, 20 *wherever the spirit chose*
to go they went; there the spirit chose to go; the

gem [*Rashi* translates: 'crystal']. For the beauty of the *Ofanim* and the clarity of their workings, Yechezkel chose this brilliant, clear gem as a simile *(Metzudas David).*

הָאוֹפַן בְּתוֹךְ הָאוֹפָן — *An* [lit. *'the'*] *Ofan within an* [lit. *'the'*] *Ofan.*

In the physical representation, each *Ofan* was figuratively describable as one wheel being fixed crosswise into another wheel, so that the wheel could revolve unhampered in whatever direction the *Chayos* [who had complete mobility; see *v.* 12] desired to go *(Rashi).*

17. This verse explains why the *Ofanim* were as a *wheel within a wheel,* as stated in the previous verse: it was their function to provide complete mobility *(Metzudas David).*

18. וְגַבֵּיהֶן — *And they had backs:* [lit. *'and their backs'*].

The translation follows the cantillation, which separates this word from the rest of the phrase; [see *Radak.*]

וְגֹבַהּ לָהֶם וְיִרְאָה לָהֶם — *And they were tall and fearsome* [lit. *'and there was height to them and dread to them'*].

I.e. they were awesome in height, and inspired great fear. Others interpret וְיִרְאָה לָהֶם, *they stood in great reverence (Rashi).*

וְגַבֹּתָם מְלֵאֹת עֵינַיִם סָבִיב לְאַרְבַּעְתָּן — *And their backs were full of eyes surrounding the four of them.*

The translation follows *Radak* and *Metzudas Zion.* The purpose of *eyes surrounding* them was to afford full vision in every direction in order that the angels not swerve from their course *(Rashi).*

Metzudas David seems to perceive this verse as describing the rims of each of the four wheels, each rim having the power of vision.

19. וּבְלֶכֶת הַחַיּוֹת — *As the Chayos move.*

I.e. the *Ofanim* moved along with the *Chayos;* and when the *Chayos* ascended on high from the surface of the expanse, the *Ofanim* accompanied them *(Rashi; Targum);* the *Ofanim* having no independent capacity for movement. See next verse.

20. This verse elaborates on the statement of the previous verse *(Malbim):*

עַל אֲשֶׁר יִהְיֶה שָּׁם הָרוּחַ לָלֶכֶת יֵלֵכוּ — *Wherever* [lit. *'upon that which'*], *the*

לָלֶכֶת וְהָאוֹפַנִּים יִנָּשְׂאוּ לְעֻמָּתָם כִּי רוּחַ
כא הַחַיָּה בָּאוֹפַנִּים: בְּלֶכְתָּם יֵלֵכוּ וּבְעָמְדָם
יַעֲמֹדוּ וּבְהִנָּשְׂאָם מֵעַל הָאָרֶץ יִנָּשְׂאוּ
הָאוֹפַנִּים לְעֻמָּתָם כִּי רוּחַ הַחַיָּה
כב בָּאוֹפַנִּים: וּדְמוּת עַל־רָאשֵׁי הַחַיָּה רָקִיעַ
כְּעֵין הַקֶּרַח הַנּוֹרָא נָטוּי עַל־רָאשֵׁיהֶם
כג מִלְמָעְלָה: וְתַחַת הָרָקִיעַ כַּנְפֵיהֶם יְשָׁרוֹת
אִשָּׁה אֶל־אֲחוֹתָהּ לְאִישׁ שְׁתַּיִם מְכַסּוֹת
לָהֵנָּה וּלְאִישׁ שְׁתַּיִם מְכַסּוֹת לָהֵנָּה אֵת
כד גְּוִיֹּתֵיהֶם: וָאֶשְׁמַע אֶת־קוֹל כַּנְפֵיהֶם
כְּקוֹל מַיִם רַבִּים כְּקוֹל־שַׁדַּי בְּלֶכְתָּם קוֹל
הֲמֻלָּה כְּקוֹל מַחֲנֶה בְּעָמְדָם תְּרַפֶּינָה

Ma'aseh Merkavah: In this vision, supernatural concepts are described in human terms. As explained in the *Prefatory Remarks*, they cannot be understood literally nor, in our spiritual poverty, are we equipped even to glimpse at their inner meaning.

Spirit [i.e. Will of God *(Rashi)*] *chose* [lit. *'was'*] *to go, they went.*

I.e., in whatever direction the Will of God, Who was — if one may so express it — riding thereon [i.e. the *Merkavah*], wished to go, they went; for שָׁמָּה הָרוּחַ לָלֶכֶת, it was also the will of the *Chayos* to go there and thus they moved only as intended by God *(Metzudas David).*

Further, the *Chayos* did not have to be told which route to take, for the Spirit [i.e., Will] of God was in [i.e., known to] the *Chayos;* and the spirit [i.e., will] of the *Chayos* was in [i.e., known to] the *Ofanim.*

כִּי רוּחַ הַחַיָּה בָּאוֹפַנִּים — *For the spirit of the Chayah* [i.e. *Chayos*] *was in the Ofanim.*

The singular form is commonly used by Scripture in the collective sense as in *Chayah* in our verse. The definite article is sometimes generic, and denotes an indefinite member of a definite species.

That is, the will of each *Chayah* was ingrained within the *Ofanim* and they would therefore go in the direction willed by the *Chayah (Metzudas David).*

21. [This verse continues to elaborate on the coordination between the *Chayos* and *Ofanim.*]

בְּלֶכְתָּם יֵלֵכוּ וּבְעָמְדָם יַעֲמֹדוּ — *When they* [i.e. the *Chayos*] *moved, they* [i.e. both the *Chayos* and the *Ofanim*] *moved, and when they halted, they halted.*

I.e., when the *Chayos* moved, the *Ofanim* moved, and similarly, when the *Chayos* halted, the *Ofanim* halted [both in consonance with God's Will] *(Rashi).*

The thought is repeated in this verse to emphasize that it would never change *(Metzudas David).*

22. כְּעֵין הַקֶּרַח הַנּוֹרָא — [It] *resembled awesome ice.*

Awe-inspiring in its brilliance and whiteness *(Radak).*

[The *top* of this dome served as the

I
21-24

Ofanim were lifted opposite them for the spirit of the
Chayah was in the Ofanim. [21] *When they moved,*
they moved; and when they halted,they halted. And
when they were lifted from upon the surface, the
Ofanim were lifted opposite them, for the spirit of
the Chayah was in the Ofanim. [22] *And as for the*
semblance of the expanse above the heads of the
Chayos, it resembled awesome ice, spread out above
upon their heads. [23] *And beneath the expanse, their*
wings were even, one with the other: For each face
two covered them, and for each two covered them —
their bodies. [24] *Then I heard the sound of their wings*
like the sound of great waters, like the sound of
Shaddai as they moved, the sound of the words like
the sound of a company; when they halt they release

surface upon which rested the Throne described in *v.* 26.]

23. This verse further depicts their wings which were already mentioned in verses 8 and 9. They are described as being יְשָׁרוֹת [lit. *'straight'*] i.e., in line, corresponding *(Rashi)* to one another.

Thus, this verse indicates how the *wings* are the receptacles מִתַּחַת הָרָקִיעַ, *beneath the expanse,* in order to receive the שֶׁפַע, 'spiritual influence', through that expanse from the World above it.

24. וָאֶשְׁמַע אֶת קוֹל כַּנְפֵיהֶם — *Then I heard the sound of their wings.*

The translation follows *Metzudas David,* who explains it as *'the sound of their fluttering wings'.*

כְּקוֹל מַיִם רַבִּים — *Like the sound of great waters.*

I.e., torrential waters *(Metzudas David).*

כְּקוֹל שַׁדַּי — *Like the sound of Shaddai.*

This name of God indicates His might and His control of nature. The voice of God Who spoke with a mighty voice at Sinai [cf. *Deut.* 5:19] *(Metzudas David);* the voice which is described in Scriptures as *'The voice of HASHEM in strength! The voice of HASHEM in splendor! The voice of HASHEM breaks cedars ...'* [*Ps.* 29:4,5] *(Rashi).*

בְּלֶכְתָּם — *As they moved* [lit. *'went'*].

The reference is to the *sound of their wings* which he heard *as they moved (Metzudas David).*

קוֹל הֲמֻלָּה כְּקוֹל מַחֲנֶה — *The sound of the words, like the sound of a company.*

Their words of praise and blessing before God are like the loud sound of a large company of angels *(Rashi; Targum).*

קוֹל מַחֲנֶה, *The sound of a company,* i.e., the din of a crowd in an [armed] camp *(Metzudas David).*

בְּעָמְדָם תְּרַפֶּינָה כַנְפֵיהֶן — *When they halt they release their wings.*

I.e. dropping their wings to achieve silence *(Rashi).*

They halted in their place when the Word of God [beginning from 2:3] emanated resoundingly from above

כה כַנְפֵיהֶֽן׃ וַֽיְהִי־ק֔וֹל מֵעַ֕ל לָֽרָקִ֖יעַ אֲשֶׁ֣ר עַל־
כו רֹאשָׁ֑ם בְּעָמְדָ֖ם תְּרַפֶּ֥ינָה כַנְפֵיהֶֽן׃ וּמִמַּ֗עַל
לָרָקִ֙יעַ֙ אֲשֶׁ֣ר עַל־רֹאשָׁ֔ם כְּמַרְאֵ֥ה אֶֽבֶן־
סַפִּ֖יר דְּמ֣וּת כִּסֵּ֑א וְעַל֙ דְּמ֣וּת הַכִּסֵּ֔א
דְּמ֗וּת כְּמַרְאֵ֥ה אָדָ֛ם עָלָ֖יו מִלְמָֽעְלָה׃
כז וָאֵ֣רֶא ׀ כְּעֵ֣ין חַשְׁמַ֗ל כְּמַרְאֵה־אֵ֤שׁ בֵּית־לָהּ֙
סָבִ֔יב מִמַּרְאֵ֥ה מָתְנָ֖יו וּלְמָ֑עְלָה וּמִמַּרְאֵ֤ה
מָתְנָיו֙ וּלְמַ֔טָּה רָאִ֙יתִי֙ כְּמַרְאֵה־אֵ֔שׁ וְנֹ֥גַהּ
כח ל֖וֹ סָבִֽיב׃ כְּמַרְאֵ֣ה הַקֶּ֡שֶׁת אֲשֶׁר֩ יִהְיֶ֨ה
בֶעָנָ֜ן בְּי֣וֹם הַגֶּ֗שֶׁם כֵּ֣ן מַרְאֵ֤ה הַנֹּ֙גַהּ֙
סָבִ֔יב ה֕וּא מַרְאֵ֖ה דְּמ֣וּת כְּבוֹד־יהוָ֑ה
וָֽאֶרְאֶה֙ וָֽאֶפֹּ֣ל עַל־פָּנַ֔י וָֽאֶשְׁמַ֖ע ק֥וֹל

Ma'aseh Merkavah: In this vision, supernatural concepts are described in human terms. As explained in the *Prefatory Remarks,* they cannot be understood literally nor, in our spiritual poverty, are we equipped even to glimpse at their inner meaning.

their heads to address the prophet [as described in the next verse] *(Targum).*

Rashi continues, that according to the *Midrash,* the implication is that they halted their praises in deference to the *zaddikim* who have precedence in singing praise to God.

[Cf. *Chullin* 91b: Israel is dearer to God than the Ministering Angels ... For the Ministering Angels do not begin to sing praises in heaven until Israel has sung below. (Cf. also *Shir haShirim* 8:14 s.v. הַשְׁמִיעִינִי ArtScroll ed. p.203)].

25. This verse supplements the preceding verse and describes the circumstance by which the angels stood still in deference to the Voice of God which was about to be heard. When they halted, their wings dropped down and total silence prevailed *(Rashi; Metzudas David;* cf. *Malbim).*

The Divine Throne

26. כְּמַרְאֵה אֶבֶן סַפִּיר דְּמוּת כִּסֵּא — *Like the appearance of sapphire stone, in the likeness of a throne.*

That is, I perceived a luminous sapphire-like substance, and it was in the form of a throne. And on this throne-form, I perceived a form of human appearance, above the throne.

This is an allusion to the Blessed God. When saying 'a form with the appearance ...', Yechezkel surely implies that while God is totally devoid of form, he nonetheless employs the term 'form' to help make the image intelligible to the listener. He had perceived the departure of the *Shechinah* from the *Bais HaMikdash,* like a king astride his royal chariot *(Metzudas David).*

27. The verse continues that upon gazing further at the human likeness

I
25-28 *their wings.* [25] *So there was a sound from above the expanse which was upon their heads; when they halt, they release their wings.* [26] *And above the expanse which was above their heads was like the appearance of sapphire stone in the likeness of a throne; and upon the likeness of the throne a likeness like the appearance of a man upon it from above.* [27] *And I saw a semblance of Chashmal like the appearance of fire within it all around from the appearance of his loins and upward; and from the appearance of his loins and downward I saw as if the appearance of fire, and it had brilliance all around.* [28] *Like the appearance of the bow which shall be upon the cloud on a rainy day, so was the appearance of the brilliance all around. That was the appearance of the semblance of the glory of HASHEM!*

When I saw this, I threw myself upon my face and I heard a voice speaking.

upon the throne, he saw כְּעֵין חַשְׁמַל, *a semblance of Chashmal* (see *comm.* above on *v.* 4). The word *Chashmal* indicates that the Essence of God cannot be anthropomorphically perceived and is a combination of חַשׁ מַל, meaning that it is best to be silent as to its implications [חַשׁ=silent; מִלָּה=word] *(Metzudas David).*

Rashi offers no comment on *v.* 26, and on this verse, he comments merely: 'One is not permitted to reflect on this verse.'

Rambam in *Moreh Nevuchim* 3:7 offers the following: 'It is also noteworthy that the likeness of man above the throne is divided, the upper part being like the color of *Chashmal,* the lower part like the appearance of fire ... Now consider how the Sages clearly stated that the divided likeness of man does not represent God, Who is above the whole chariot, but represents a part of creation. The prophet likewise says [in the following verse]: *That was the appearance of the glory of HASHEM;* but *the glory of HASHEM* is different from *HASHEM* Himself. All the figures in this vision refer to the glory of the Lord, to the chariot, and not to Him Who rides upon the chariot; for God cannot be compared with anything.'

28. כְּמַרְאֵה הַקֶּשֶׁת — *Like the appearance of the bow.*

Yechezkel expressed his simile in these terms because, just as the colors of the rainbow are but the effect of the sunlight refracting through the atmosphere, so too, the Likeness of God's Glory which Yechezkel perceived is but the *effect* of His Intellectual Light [as distinguished from a physical light like that of the sun] the essence of which is indescribable in human terms *(Malbim).*

וָאֶרְאֶה וָאֶפֹּל עַל פָּנָי — *When I saw this, I threw myself* [lit. *'fell'*] *upon my face.*

ב
א־ג

א מְדַבֵּר׃ וַיֹּאמֶר אֵלַי בֶּן־
אָדָם עֲמֹד עַל־רַגְלֶיךָ וַאֲדַבֵּר אֹתָךְ׃
ב וַתָּבֹא בִי רוּחַ כַּאֲשֶׁר דִּבֶּר אֵלַי
וַתַּעֲמִדֵנִי עַל־רַגְלָי וָאֶשְׁמַע אֵת מִדַּבֵּר
ג אֵלָי׃ וַיֹּאמֶר אֵלַי בֶּן־אָדָם שׁוֹלֵחַ
אֲנִי אוֹתְךָ אֶל־בְּנֵי יִשְׂרָאֵל אֶל־גּוֹיִם
הַמּוֹרְדִים אֲשֶׁר מָרְדוּ־בִי הֵמָּה וַאֲבוֹתָם

In prostration before the Presence of God *(Metzudas David).*

Harav Joseph Breuer quotes *Hirsch's* comm. to *Gen.* 17:3: 'To throw yourself down' expresses the surrender of one's independence. When one throws himself down on his face, he ceases to see, and is able only to listen. He gives up his material and spiritual faculties entirely to the One before Whom one prostrates oneself. Thus, Yechezkel indicated his acceptance of the destiny to which the gift of the *Merkavah* vision had assigned him.

וָאֶשְׁמַע קוֹל מְדַבֵּר — *And I heard a voice speaking.*

And what the voice said, follows in the next chapter *(Rashi).*[1]

II

The Mission. *Yechezkel is to be the bearer of God's word to His people. Hardened by years of sin and rebellion, they are likely to ignore him. God exhorts him to be strong and unyielding in the face of this rejection. Yechezkel is to identify so completely with his task that there will be a total fusion of man and message.*

1. בֶּן אָדָם — *Ben Adam* [lit. *'son of man'*].

See *Overview (p. xxx)* for our conception of this mode of address. We leave the words untranslated since it is not clear whether בֶּן is to be taken as *son,* or as denoting a quality, as in בֶּן חַיִל, *warrior.*

Rashi and *Metzudas David* explain that Yechezkel was addressed with this name in order to stress to him that, despite the fact that he had been permitted to see the *Merkavah* vision (see Ch. 1), he was still but an ordinary mortal.

Eliyahu Rabbah (6) writes: [Ben] *Adam* is an expression of brotherhood, craving, and friendship. And thus did God speak to Yechezkel, the priest: *Ben Adam,* that is, son of good people, of righteous people, of people who allow themselves to be shamed all of their days for the sake of My honor and of Israel's.

עֲמֹד עַל רַגְלֶיךָ — *Stand on your feet.*

Yechezkel had prostrated himself after seeing the *Merkavah* (1:28). For the fulfillment of his mission he must rise and, as it were, stand firmly on the ground of reality, strong and upright as the bearer of God's truth (based on *Harav Breuer).*

[If this prophecy preceded the one in Ch. I (see *comm.* 1:3), then the exhortation to stand is not connected to the prostration in 1:28.]

1. *Radak* quotes the Sages who teach that when Israel received the Torah at Sinai, *every Jew* perceived the *Merkavah* to such an extent that even the simplest maidservant received a prophecy as great as this one of Yechezkel

*Then He said to me: Ben Adam, stand on your feet
and I shall speak to you.* 2 *Then a spirit entered
into me, as He spoke to me and stood me on my feet,
and I heard that by which He was addressing Himself
to me.*
3 *So He said to me: Ben Adam, I send you to the
children of Israel, to the rebellious nations that have
rebelled against Me; they and their fathers have*

2. וַתָּבֹא בִי רוּחַ — *Then a spirit entered into me.*

The preposition of our verse: בִּי, *'into me'* differs from that of 11:5 where Yechezkel says וַתִּפֹּל עָלַי רוּחַ ה׳, 'a spirit of HASHEM came *upon* me.' This indicates a basic difference between the *'spirit'* of our verse and that of 11:5. There, the word עָלַי, *'upon* me', indicates that the reference is to a spirit of *prophecy,* a divine gift which remains above man. He becomes its bearer and herald; it comes to him from *without* and raises him above the normal human level. He becomes the instrument through which God communicates with man. Our verse on the other hand, refers to a lower form of רוּחַ, *spirit,* as indicated by the word בִּי, *into* me; it is a form of prophecy that proceeds from within a person. It results in an intensification and enhancement of the person's own innate capacity. His words are *human* words and his deeds are *human* deeds, but they are borne and elevated by God's extraordinary gift of the *spirit* [*Hirsch, Bamidbar* 11:17. See below *comm.* to *v.* 5 on the concept of נָבִיא].

מִדַּבֵּר אֵלָי — *He was addressing Himself to me.*

The construction מִדַּבֵּר is equivalent to מִתְדַּבֵּר, the *Hispa'el* reflexive meaning *'He spoke to Himself'* [rather than lowering Himself to speak to mortal man]. This reflexive mood is used to minimize the apparent anthropomorphism inherent in God's addressing Himself directly to man (*Rashi*).[1]

3. גּוֹיִם הַמּוֹרְדִים אֲשֶׁר מָרְדוּ בִי — *The rebellious nations that have rebelled against Me.*

Although the word גּוֹי generally denotes a complete nation, Scripture occasionally uses it to describe the individual tribes of Israel [see *Gen.* 35:11]. Thus the tribes of Judah and Benjamin (who remained in *Eretz Yisrael* after the exile of the Ten Tribes) can be described in the plural as גּוֹיִם (*Rashi;Radak*). [The word גּוֹי is derived from גֵּו meaning *a body* or self-enclosed unit].

Radak conjectures that the plural גּוֹיִם may be used here because the בְּנֵי יִשְׂרָאֵל, *the children of Israel* had split them-

1. Throughout Scriptures, the direct *pi'el* form is used. [וַיְדַבֵּר ה׳ ...]. The exceptions are our verse, 43:6, and *Numbers* 7:89. Perhaps this can be explained by the fact that in all the three instances there is an element of wonder that God had deigned to speak to man. In *Numbers* the verse refers to the initial address from the Tabernacle which had just been dedicated. Israel's repentance of the sin of the Golden Calf had been accepted and God was actually revealing Himself to them from the Tabernacle which was their own handiwork! In our verse it is the first communication to a prophet in exile. And in Ch. 43 it heralds God's return to the future Temple. The reflexive voice in all these cases sets the tone of awe and wonder with which these manifestations of God's love were perceived.

ב
ד־ה

ד פָּשְׁעוּ בִי עַד־עֶצֶם הַיּוֹם הַזֶּה: וְהַבָּנִים
קְשֵׁי פָנִים וְחִזְקֵי־לֵב אֲנִי שׁוֹלֵחַ אוֹתְךָ
אֲלֵיהֶם וְאָמַרְתָּ אֲלֵיהֶם כֹּה אָמַר אֲדֹנָי
ה יֱהוִֹה: וְהֵמָּה אִם־יִשְׁמְעוּ וְאִם־יֶחְדָּלוּ כִּי

selves into a number of different 'nations', some worshipping the idols of *Moab*, some the idols of *Amon* and so on.

A particular poignancy is lent to the concept of גוֹיִם הַמּוֹרְדִים, *rebellious nations,* when we consider the term קְהַל גוֹיִם, *a community of nations (Gen.* 35:11) as it is interpreted by *Hirsch:* 'The people of Jacob form a model nation containing a great variety of characteristics. Among its tribes are martial, merchant, agricultural, scientific, and scholarly nations — the gamut of human endeavor. This was to demonstrate to the world that service of God and sanctification of His Name are the responsibility and within the competence of all manner of men, uniting into a single kingdom of God.'

Thus, the depth of God's anguish is expressed by referring to Israel as גוֹיִם. They had been blessed with a diversity of talents in order to demonstrate how every facet of human endeavour could be used in the service of God. Instead, in their wickedness, they had desecrated His Name.

פָּשְׁעוּ בִי — [Defiantly] *sinned against Me.*

The word פֶּשַׁע indicates a very serious order of sin because it involves a defiant intention to flout God's authority [see *Yomah* 36b].

Thus, *Targum* (in accordance with *Yomah* 36b) translates *'rebelled'.*[1]

4. וְהַבָּנִים קְשֵׁי פָנִים וְחִזְקֵי לֵב — *And the children are brazen of face and hard of heart.*

Eliezer of Beaugency renders קְשֵׁי פָנִים, *brazen faced,* as showing insolence against the people who rebuked them, and חִזְקֵי לֵב, *hard hearted,* as a refusal to submit. The intent of the verse is to contrast the children to the parents *(Rashi; Metzudas David; Malbim).* While the parents only sinned, the children had become unreceptive to rebuke, and even insolent.

Thus we read (33:32) that they viewed the words of the prophet ... *as a love song of one who has a pleasant voice and can play well on an instrument; so they hear your words, but they do not do them.*

1. Idol worship as practiced in antiquity was not a denial of God but at best a misconception of how best to serve Him (see *footnote* to 8:12) and at worst a rebellion *against* God. [See *Rashi Genesis* 10:9 for the concept: יוֹדֵעַ רִבּוֹנוֹ וּמִתְכַּוֵּן לִמְרוֹד בּוֹ, *one who knows his Master and consciously rebels against Him.* See also *Chidushei haRashba al Aggados haShas* on *Berachos* 6b for a detailed analysis of the philosophy which underlay this cult.]

The spirit of rebellion permeated the sins of this generation. Thus *Sanhedrin* 103b relates that King Ammon had incestuous relations with his mother. When she asked him: 'Can the source from which you came give you pleasure?' He answered her: 'Have I any intention besides angering my Creator?'

Later generations sinned against God because their belief in Him was too weak to help them withstand the blandishments of their baser selves. To fully recognize God's existence, and nonetheless to want to rebel against Him, is an experience unique to the earlier generations. Thus it precludes our full understanding of their sins.

This is illustrated by *Sanhedrin* 102a where it is related that Rav Ashi spoke disparagingly of King Menashe, because of the latter's idol worship. That night Menashe appeared to him in a dream and rebuked him, demonstrating how much greater his own knowledge of Torah had been than that of Rav Ashi. Thereupon Rav Ashi asked him: 'Since you were so wise, why did

defiantly sinned against Me up to this very day; 4 *and*
the children are brazen of face and hard of heart — I
send you to them. And you shall say to them: Thus
says my Lord HASHEM/ELOHIM. 5 *Now they,*
whether they will obey or whether they will desist —

[See *Overview (p.* lvi) for an explanation of this negative attitude.]

כֹּה אָמַר ... — *So says my Lord HASHEM / ELOHIM.*

Since nothing is said here about what Hashem said, *Metzudas David* interprets this phrase as advice to the prophet, not as a message which he is to convey. God tells him that whenever he talks to the people he should do so only in the name of God, since otherwise they will not listen to him. [See 3:25-27].

Malbim explains that Yechezkel is exhorted to relate his prophecies in God's name in order to comfort the people with the knowledge that even in their exile God continues His interest in them and that His providence is still extended over them. [See *v.* 5].

Harav Breuer sees the phrase as the complete message. The combination of the two names used here, אֲדֹנָי, [lit. *'my Master'*] together with the Tetragrammaton vocalized to read Elohim, is not unique to Yechezkel, but it is used very rarely in other books; in Yechezkel it appears constantly. *Hirsch (Deut.* 3:24) explains this combination thus: אֲדֹנָי: Because its literal meaning is *'my Master'* this Name of God denotes the prophet's gratitude that he has been found worthy to become the instrument for the accomplishment of God's will. The second Name, which combines the spelling of the Four-Letter Name with the vocalization and pronunciation of Elohim, represents *God's love showing itself in justice.* It conveys to us that even when God judges, denies, or punishes [i.e. אֱלֹהִים] He is still 'ה [i.e. the God of love and mercy].

This, then, is the spirit which is to permeate all the prophecies of this prophet of the exile: That the harshness of the judgments which God exercises over His people is no more than an outward manifestation of His abiding love for them. And this in itself is the total message of God. [See *comm.* to 20:33].[1]

you serve idols?' Menashe answered: 'If you had been there you would have lifted up your coat to run after me [i.e. to imitate me].'

Maharal explains Menashe's answer. Rav Ashi could not possibly comprehend that urge to worship idols because the urge had already disappeared before his time (see *Arachin* 32b). But, had he lived in the time when this desire was still rampant, he would have 'lifted up his coat' and run after Menashe to join him in his worship. The difference between a person who recognizes the enormity of his rebellion against God, but who cannot control the burning desire to sin, and one who is not wise enough to realize the full import of the horrendous act which he is committing, is evidenced in their reaction to an external condition which prevents them from sinning. The wise man will welcome this obstacle since it helps him to refrain from doing what he clearly wishes he had the power to avoid; the lesser man will resent the interruption and try to overcome the obstacle.

Thus Menashe told Rav Ashi not to talk disparagingly about his generation. Had Rav Ashi been there he would have 'picked up his coat' [i.e. sought to remove all obstacles] the better to run and serve the idol, since his recognition of God and the enormity of sinning against Him was infinitely smaller than that of Menashe.

1. Throughout the book *Harav Breuer* translates this combination of the two Names of God: "My Master Who reveals His love through justice." In this he goes beyond *Hirsch* who, while interpreting these names in this way, translates simply *Lord God.*

בֵּית מְרִי הֵמָּה וְיָדְעוּ כִּי נָבִיא הָיָה
בְתוֹכָם׃ ו וְאַתָּה בֶן־אָדָם אַל־
תִּירָא מֵהֶם וּמִדִּבְרֵיהֶם אַל־תִּירָא כִּי
סָרָבִים וְסַלּוֹנִים אוֹתָךְ וְאֶל־עַקְרַבִּים
אַתָּה יוֹשֵׁב מִדִּבְרֵיהֶם אַל־תִּירָא
וּמִפְּנֵיהֶם אַל־תֵּחָת כִּי בֵּית מְרִי הֵמָּה׃
ז וְדִבַּרְתָּ אֶת־דְּבָרַי אֲלֵיהֶם אִם־יִשְׁמְעוּ
ח וְאִם־יֶחְדָּלוּ כִּי מְרִי הֵמָּה׃ וְאַתָּה
בֶן־אָדָם שְׁמַע אֵת אֲשֶׁר־אֲנִי מְדַבֵּר אֵלֶיךָ
אַל־תְּהִי־מֶרִי כְּבֵית הַמֶּרִי פְּצֵה פִיךָ

5. אִם יִשְׁמְעוּ — *Whether they will obey* [lit. *'whether they will hear'*].

The root שמע is used often in the sense of *obeying*. (See for ex. *Exod.* 7:16). Thus *Targum,* too, translates יְקַבְּלוּן אוּלְפַן, *they will accept teaching.*

וְיָדְעוּ כִּי נָבִיא הָיָה בְתוֹכָם — *Yet they will know that a prophet has been among them.*

Even if they will not listen to your exhortations, a purpose will have been served — when punishment overtakes them, they will remember that they were warned, and will not be able to complain of an injustice (*Rashi; Metzudas David*).

Da'as Sofrim suggests: A purpose will have been served when they know that even in their exile a prophet was among them, although prophecy rightly belongs only in the Land of Israel. This will be a comfort to them, easing their bitterness, and also teaching them that exile has not released them from their obligations.[1]

6. כִּי סָרָבִים וְסַלּוֹנִים אוֹתָךְ — *Although they are thorn and thistle-like to you.*

If כִּי is translated in the usual way — *because,* the meaning of the verse is obscure. Why would the fact that they are as thorns and thistles be a reason not to be afraid? [See *Abarbanel*]. However כִּי can be used as *although* (11:16), and this is how *Malbim* takes it here.[2]

סָרָבִים — *Thorns.*

This translation follows *Dunash* quoted in *Rashi. Targum,* as well as *Rashi* and *Radak,* renders: *rebels.*

וְאֶל עַקְרַבִּים — *And among scorpions.*

1. This explanation is particularly apt when we consider the etymology of the word נָבִיא. The usual translation *'prophet'* [from *pro* — before and *phanai* — to speak] is not adequate because its connotation is merely the prediction of future events, a definition which does not exhaust the meaning of the word. *Rashi* [*Exod.* 7:1, based on *Menachem*] relates the word to ניב שְׂפָתָיִם, *(Isaiah* 57:19) denoting *speech.* [See also *Rashbam* ad. loc.]. *Ibn Ezra* [ad. loc.] however rejects this explanation based on the fact that נָבִיא derives from the root נבא while נִיב derives from ניב or נוב. [See *Gur Aryeh*]. *Ibn Ezra* relates נביא to revelation, i.e. God reveals His secrets to the prophet as indicated by כִּי אִם גָּלָה סוֹדוֹ אֶל עֲבָדָיו הַנְּבִיאִים, *unless He reveals His secret to His servants the prophets (Amos* 3:7).

Hirsch (Gen. 20:7) relates the root נבא to נבע, *to spring, flow forth,* or *well forth* and interprets: The source of God's word, the organ through which His spirit speaks to men. Hence, the form of the word is passive. This knowledge that a man capable of being God's organ was among them in spite of their exile, would be a source of enormous comfort to them.

II
6-8

for a rebellious family are they — yet they will know
that a prophet has been among them. 6 *And you, Ben*
Adam, fear them not, and of their words have no
fear, though they are thorn- and thistle-like to you,
and among scorpions do you dwell. Of their words be
not afraid and before them do not tremble, though a
rebellious family are they. 7 *And you shall speak My*
words to them whether they obey or whether they
desist — for 'Rebellion' are they!
8 *And you, Ben Adam, hear what I speak to you:*
Be not 'Rebellion' like the family of rebellion. Open

Targum renders A nation whose acts are like [the sting] of scorpions.

7. כִּי מְרִי הֵמָּה — *For 'Rebellion' are they.*

They are 'Rebellion' personified (*Radak*). [In Scripture a person is often identified with a quality, if this quality permeates his whole being. *Ps.* 109:4: וַאֲנִי תְפִלָּה, *and I am Prayer* [personified. (See also *Ramban Gen.* 25:28).

8. אַל תְּהִי מְרִי — *Be not 'Rebellion'.*

Do not rebel against Me by refusing to do My bidding (*Rashi*).

Eliezer of Beaugency suggests that Yechezkel might be provoked to refuse his role as prophet by the onerousness of the symbolic acts which he would be called upon to perform (see Ch. 4 and many subsequent passages). Indeed, in 4:14 we find him asking to be relieved of the obligation to eat meals which

2. The word כִּי is extremely versatile, and is used in Scripture in many different ways. *Reish Lakish* maintains that it can have four meanings: אִי, *if;* דִּילְמָא, *perhaps;* אֶלָּא, *but;* and דְּהָא, *since* (*Rosh Hashana* 3a; *Gittin* 90a; *Shavu'os* 49b, and *Ta'anis* 9a). Each of these four meanings has a variety of shadings (see *Rashi* to *Rosh Hashana, Gittin,* and *Shavu'os;* and *pseudo-Rashi* to *Ta'anis.* See also *Teshuvos Rashi* 251 in *Elfenbein's* ed.) so that a great number of nuances are obtained.

Thus, for example, *Metzudas David* to our verse, takes כִּי in its meaning of אִי, *if,* and translates: *Do not be afraid 'if' they are as thorns and thistles to you.*

However the meaning *'although'* which we have used here, seems not to fall under any of the four categories or subcategories as explained by *Rashi.* Since *Rashi* seems consistently to assume that there can be no meaning to כִּי except those attributed by *Reish Lakish,* it would seem that he would not agree to our rendering.

There are, however, many opinions that כִּי can be translated as *'although'.*

Thus *Ibn Janach* in his *Sefer haShorashim* states categorically that this translation is acceptable, and quotes many examples of its use (*Radak* in his *Sefer haShorashim* disagrees with *Ibn Janach*).

Me'iri in *Chibur haTeshuvah* (*Jerusalem* 5736) p.26 also quotes a number of instances where *'although'* would be the correct translation of כִּי.

Ibn Ezra to *Exod.* 13:17 quotes *Rabbi Moshe HaCohen* who takes כִּי as *although,* and disputes him. In *Exod.* 34:9 he quotes *Ibn Janach's* similar opinion, and in disagreeing, gives different interpretations of the vs. cited by *Ibn Janach.*

In the view of the *Tur, Ramban's* interpretation of *Exod.* 13:17, assumes a meaning of *'although'.*

ב ט וְאָכֹל אֵת אֲשֶׁר־אֲנִי נֹתֵן אֵלֶיךָ: וָאֶרְאֶה
ט־י וְהִנֵּה־יָד שְׁלוּחָה אֵלָי וְהִנֵּה־בוֹ מְגִלַּת־
י סֵפֶר: וַיִּפְרֹשׂ אוֹתָהּ לְפָנַי וְהִיא כְתוּבָה
פָּנִים וְאָחוֹר וְכָתוּב אֵלֶיהָ קִנִים וָהֶגֶה
ג א וָהִי: וַיֹּאמֶר אֵלַי בֶּן־אָדָם אֵת
א אֲשֶׁר־תִּמְצָא אֱכוֹל אֱכוֹל אֶת־הַמְּגִלָּה

were cooked with 'the dung which comes out of man' (4:12).

ఆ§ The 'eating' of the Scroll (2:8-3:3)

Eliezer of Beaugency points out that the passage which starts with the words 'open your mouth and eat' is a new section which does not follow directly from the foregoing.

Besides the possibility of taking this section literally, there is the option to view it metaphorically [i.e. 'eating' as a metaphor for careful consideration and absorption of the message] (*Rashi* and *Metzudas David*); or to assume that the whole sequence was seen by Yechezkel in a vision *(Radak).*

There is a wide divergence of opinion among the commentators as to when to assume symbolic acts to have actually taken place and when to consider them as having been seen in a vision. See *Rambam, Moreh Nevuchim* 2:46. We shall have occasion throughout this book to refer to this problem.

In any case, it is certain that 'eating' the Scroll implies a complete identification with its contents — a fusion between man and message.

פְּצֵה פִיךָ — *Open your mouth.*

In 3:2 we read וָאֶפְתַּח אֶת פִּי, *And I opened my mouth.* The root פצה always denotes an unwilling opening either with repugnance or by force *(Hirsch Gen.* 4:11). The prophet is told to absorb his message even if his whole being rebels against the task. Despite the extreme unpleasantness of the task, however, the prophet shoulders the burden lovingly (וָאֶפְתַּח not וָאֶפְצֶה) and finds the task *'sweet as honey'* (3:3).

9. וְהִנֵּה יָד שְׁלוּחָה אֵלָי וְהִנֵּה בוֹ ... — *And behold! a hand was outstretched to me! ... And behold! in it ...*

In Hebrew, the hand and all other parts of the body are usually in the feminine gender. This is true in our verse as seen from the feminine form of the verb שְׁלוּחָה. *Eliezer of Beaugency* explains the masculine form of the preposition בּוֹ by having it refer to the חֹפֶן יָד, *the palm of the hand,* which is masculine. However, *Rashi* simply points out that there are occasional exceptions to the above rule. (See *comm.* to 13:20).

10. פָּנִים וְאָחוֹר — *Within and without.* [lit. *face* and *back*].

If meant literally, this expression would simply convey that both sides of the Scroll were filled with writing. It would not tell us anything about the subject matter. We would then assume that the contents of the Scroll were the קִנִים וָהֶגֶה וָהִי, the various forms of lamentation mentioned at the end of the verse. It is difficult to reconcile this with 3:3 where the prophet reports that he found the Scroll *'sweet as honey to my mouth'.*

Rashi quotes *Targum* who interprets פָּנִים as *'that which occurred in the beginning'* and אָחוֹר as *'that which will occur in the end'.* Thus, the past and the future — the history and destiny of Israel. This would place the message which the prophet was to absorb in complete consonance with the whole book which is permeated by just this vision of the future built on the lessons

II
9-10

your mouth and eat what I give to you. [9] *Then I saw,*
and behold! a hand was outstretched to me! And
behold! in it was a scroll of a book. [10] *Then He spread*
it out before me — it was inscribed within and
without, and in it was inscribed lamentations, moaning, and woe.

III
1

He said to me: Ben Adam, that which you find — eat. Eat this scroll; and go speak to the Family of Israel!

of the past. (See particularly Chs. 16 and 20).

In this interpretation the word אֵלֶיהָ, would be translated *in addition to* (as in *Lev.* 18:18) rather than *in it* or *on it* as *Radak* and *Metzudas David* take it. The meaning would be that קִנִים וָהֶגֶה וָהִי were written on the scroll *in addition* to its other contents. (See *Da'as Sofrim).* These words are taken by most commentators as various forms of lamentations.

The translation of קִנָה as lamentation needs no elaboration. הֶגֶה is used in a similar sense in *Job* 37:2. הִי does not recur again in Scripture. *Eliezer of Beaugency* reads it as an expression of woe, similar to הָהּ (30:2). We find this use in *Sanhedrin* 11a. *Rabbi Eliezer Hakalir* seems to interpret our verse in this way in his *Kina* אֵיכָה אַשְׁפָּתוֹ פָּתוּחַ in which one verse reads מִמָּרוֹם מְגִלָּה כָּתַב בְּנֶהִי קִנִים וָהֶגֶה וָהִי מִי זֶה אָמַר וַתֶּהִי — *with wailing He wrote a scroll from heaven, lamentations moaning and woe: Who has commanded and it came to pass (if not the Lord)?* — an obvious reference to our verse. Indeed some commentators consider הִי as a contraction of נֶהִי, a more common expression of lament.

The words can also be understood differently. While קִנִים certainly means *lamentations,* the root הגה also has the meaning of *thought* (as in *Ps.* 1:2). *Hirsch (Gesammelte Schriften* III p.249) translates הִי as a derivative combined from הָיָה, *was* and יִהְיֶה, *will be,* thus: *developing being.* Our sentence can thus be translated: *And it was inscribed with history and destiny. In addition to which were written: Lamentations, analysis, and developing being.*

Thus Yechezkel was told to absorb the complete panorama of Jewish history, together with the lesson that — upon reflection and analysis — the earthly travail visited upon Israel can be recognized as no more than a way station on the road leading to the future. This is a succinct statement of the totality of Yechezkel's visions. Small wonder that he found it sweet and needed no 'prying open of the mouth' when called upon to 'swallow' it (see *comm.* to *v.* 8).

Targum renders קִנִים וָהֶגֶה וָהִי in the following manner: *If Israel transgresses the Torah, the nations will rule over her. But if they keep the Torah, then all manner of lamentations will be removed from them.* [See *footnote* to 14:4 on *Targum's* propensity to read comfort into passages which seem to be intended as rebukes.]

III

1. אֵת אֲשֶׁר תִּמְצָא — *That which you find.*

Metzudas David interprets the phrase symbolically. Yechezkel is to eat

ג

ב־ו

הַזֹּאת וְלֵךְ דַּבֵּר אֶל־בֵּית יִשְׂרָאֵל׃
ב וָאֶפְתַּח אֶת־פִּי וַיַּאֲכִלֵנִי אֵת הַמְּגִלָּה
ג הַזֹּאת׃ וַיֹּאמֶר אֵלַי בֶּן־אָדָם בִּטְנְךָ תַאֲכֵל
וּמֵעֶיךָ תְמַלֵּא אֵת הַמְּגִלָּה הַזֹּאת אֲשֶׁר
אֲנִי נֹתֵן אֵלֶיךָ וָאֹכְלָה וַתְּהִי בְּפִי כִּדְבַשׁ
ד לְמָתוֹק׃ וַיֹּאמֶר אֵלָי בֶּן־אָדָם לֶךְ־
בֹּא אֶל־בֵּית יִשְׂרָאֵל וְדִבַּרְתָּ בִדְבָרַי
ה אֲלֵיהֶם׃ כִּי לֹא אֶל־עַם עִמְקֵי שָׂפָה
וְכִבְדֵי לָשׁוֹן אַתָּה שָׁלוּחַ אֶל־בֵּית
ו יִשְׂרָאֵל׃ לֹא | אֶל־עַמִּים רַבִּים עִמְקֵי
שָׂפָה וְכִבְדֵי לָשׁוֹן אֲשֶׁר לֹא־תִשְׁמַע
דִּבְרֵיהֶם אִם־לֹא אֲלֵיהֶם שְׁלַחְתִּיךָ הֵמָּה

— i..e study and accept — that which he *finds* written within the scroll and without.

בֵּית יִשְׂרָאֵל — *The Family of Israel.*

It is the duty of the prophet to discover that the בֵּית מְרִי, *the rebellious family* of 2:5, is really the *Family of Israel.* Their rebellion is only on the surface and does not erode the inner core of sanctity which is their essence (based on *Harav Breuer).*[1]

2. וַיַּאֲכִלֵנִי — *And He fed me.*

God's support was needed to help him bear the enormity of his mission.

3. See *comm.* to 2:8 and 10.

כִּדְבַשׁ לְמָתוֹק — *As sweet as honey* [lit. *'as honey for sweetness'*].

5. עִמְקֵי שָׂפָה וְכִבְדֵי לָשׁוֹן — *Incoherent speech* [lit. *'deep of speech'*] *and heavy tongue.*

To a person who had identified with his message as completely as Yechezkel had done through 'consuming' the scroll (see Ch. 2), the truths contained therein would seem to be self-evident. He would be inclined to ascribe his hearer's obstinate refusal to accept his words to a lack of eloquence on his own part. He would tend to feel that if only the familiar idiom or the persuasive phrase would not elude him, he could surely convince his listeners of the truth of his message.

Yechezkel is told that the problem is not one of communication. After all, the exile was not yet five years old and the

1. The idea that Israel's sins do not alter the essential holiness which is its soul is one of the great themes of Aggadic literature. It finds its classic expression in *Bereishis Rabbah* 65:15: *'And I am a smooth man' (Gen.* 27:11) ... Rabbi Levi said: '[This is comparable] to a hairy person and a bald man who were standing by the threshing floor. The chaff rose and became entangled in the hair of the hirsute man [and became difficult or impossible to remove]. The chaff rose and rested on the head of the bald man; he wiped his head with his hand and removed it. Thus Esau [the hairy man, representing the non-Jewish nations] becomes filthied with sin throughout the year and has no means of atonement, but Jacob [Israel, the smooth-skinned man] becomes filthied with sin throughout the year and Yom Kippur comes and he has the possibility of atonement.'

See also 1:5 ArtScroll ed.of *Shir haShirim, comm.* to 1:5.

[2] *So I opened my mouth, and He fed me this scroll.*
[3] *Then He said to me: Ben Adam, cause your stomach to eat, and fill your innards with this scroll which I give you.*

And I ate it; and it was in my mouth as sweet as honey.

[4] *And He said to me: Ben Adam go! Come to the Family of Israel, and speak with My words to them.*
[5] *For you are not sent to a people of incoherent speech and heavy tongue, but to the Family of Israel;*
[6] *not to numerous peoples of incoherent speech and heavy tongue whose words you cannot understand. Had I sent you to them they would have heeded you.*

ears of the people would still be attuned to the finest nuances of their mother tongue. Moreover, as *v.* 6 teaches, a receptive audience would not be deterred even by the absence of a common language.

The problem then must lie at a deeper level; and that is stated in *v.* 7.

6-7. אִם לֹא אֲלֵיהֶם שְׁלַחְתִּיךָ — *Had I sent you to them* [lit. *'Had I not sent you to them*].

The translation follows *Targum,* which does not, however, account for the לֹא, *not,* in the phrase (אִם 'לֹא' אֲלֵיהֶם).

Rashi inverts the words in the sentence, as though the לֹא were written later. Thus: אֲלֵיהֶם שְׁלַחְתִּיךָ, *had I sent you to them,* אִם לֹא, *I swear that,* הֵמָּה יִשְׁמְעוּ אֵלֶיךָ, *they would have listened to you.* Thus the phrase אִם לֹא is taken as an oath.

Radak and *Metzudas David* accomplish the same idea, without inverting the words. In this interpretation the oath comes at the beginning of the phrase: *I swear that if I had sent you to them that they would have listened to you.*

Harav Joseph Breuer renders: *While I did not send you to them directly, they will still listen to your message* [*when they hear about it*].

According to all the interpretations the meaning is the same: Language would never prove a barrier between prophet and people. A nation which is predisposed to accept the prophet's exhortations would understand them. But Israel, *strong of forehead and hard of heart,* will not.[1]

1. The theme that Israel in its degradation, sinks to lower depths, and is less inclined to repentance than the nations of the world, runs through the whole book. *'The daughters of the Philistines that are ashamed of your lewd way'* (16:27), which *Targum (ad. loc.)* translates: Had I sent prophets to them they would have subjugated themselves, but you did not repent of your sinful ways.

In 16:33 we read: *'To all harlots gifts are given; but you have given gifts to all your lovers, and have bribed them to come to you from all around, in your harlotries.'*

The Sages explain Yonah's flight from God [to avoid chastising Nineveh] in the same terms. '[I will flee] because the gentiles are predisposed to repentance. [I do not want] to show Israel in a bad light' *(Yalkut Yonah* 1).

The explanation for this strange phenomenon must be seen in the quality of עַזּוּת,

ז יִשְׁמְעוּ אֵלֶיךָ: וּבֵית יִשְׂרָאֵל לֹא יֹאבוּ
לִשְׁמֹעַ אֵלֶיךָ כִּי־אֵינָם אֹבִים לִשְׁמֹעַ אֵלָי
כִּי כָּל־בֵּית יִשְׂרָאֵל חִזְקֵי־מֵצַח וּקְשֵׁי־לֵב
ח הֵמָּה: הִנֵּה נָתַתִּי אֶת־פָּנֶיךָ חֲזָקִים לְעֻמַּת
פְּנֵיהֶם וְאֶת־מִצְחֲךָ חָזָק לְעֻמַּת מִצְחָם:
ט כְּשָׁמִיר חָזָק מִצֹּר נָתַתִּי מִצְחֶךָ לֹא־תִירָא
אוֹתָם וְלֹא־תֵחַת מִפְּנֵיהֶם כִּי בֵּית מְרִי
י הֵמָּה: וַיֹּאמֶר אֵלָי בֶּן־אָדָם אֶת־
כָּל־דְּבָרַי אֲשֶׁר אֲדַבֵּר אֵלֶיךָ קַח בִּלְבָבְךָ
יא וּבְאָזְנֶיךָ שְׁמָע: וְלֵךְ בֹּא אֶל־הַגּוֹלָה אֶל־
בְּנֵי עַמֶּךָ וְדִבַּרְתָּ אֲלֵיהֶם וְאָמַרְתָּ אֲלֵיהֶם
כֹּה אָמַר אֲדֹנָי יֱהֹוִה אִם־יִשְׁמְעוּ וְאִם־

7. כִּי אֵינָם אֹבִים לִשְׁמֹעַ אֵלָי — *For they do not wish to obey* [lit. *'listen to'*] *Me.*

Since God did not speak to them directly, it seems likely that לִשְׁמֹעַ is to be taken in the sense of *obeying* rather than listening (see *Exod.* 7:16).

חִזְקֵי מֵצַח וּקְשֵׁי לֵב — *Strong of forehead and hard of heart.*

I.e. brazen or impudent, and stubborn.

8. The prophet is promised the moral strength necessary to stand up against their insolence.

וְאֶת מִצְחֲךָ חָזָק — *And your forehead hard.*

This is explained in the next verse.

9. כְּשָׁמִיר חָזָק מִצֹּר — Shamir-*like, stronger than flint.*

We follow *Targum* and *Breuer* in leaving the obscure word שָׁמִיר untranslated.

Possible meanings are:

— A particularly hard kind of rock *(Rashi);*

— Iron which is harder than rock (*Radak* and *Metzudas David).*

Based on the tradition of the Sages (also quoted by *Rashi)* that *Shamir* was a worm which possessed the miraculous ability to cut rocks, *Malbim* suggests that the meaning of the verse is: Just as the *Shamir* worm, which is really soft, is endowed with the miraculous quality of strength greater than rock, so also your *aggressive, vehement strength,* which the *Talmud (Beitza* 25b) ascribes to Israel: Why was the Torah given to Israel [and not to the other nations]? Because they are עַזִּין, *aggressively strong* [and they need the Torah to curb the excesses to which this vehemence could lead them more than any other nation]. Had the Torah not been given to Israel no nation could have stood up against them. For *Reish Lakish* said: There are three עַזִּין, *aggressive ones:* Israel among the nations, the dog among the animals, and the rooster among the birds.

While the quality of עַזּוּת is an admirable one in its rightful place — *be* עַז *like a leopard ... to do the will of your Father in heaven (Avos* 5:20) — it is nevertheless a quality which can lead a person to disaster when misused. Thus, עַז פָּנִים לְגֵהִינּוֹם, *the insolent person is destined for Gehhinom (ibid.).*

7 *But the Family of Israel will not wish to heed you, for they do not wish to obey Me, for the Family of Israel are strong of forehead and hard of heart.*

8 *Behold! I have made your face hard against their face, and your forehead hard against their forehead.*
9 Shamir-*like, stronger than flint have I made your forehead. Fear them not nor be dismayed before them though a rebellious family are they.*

10 *Then He said to me: Ben Adam, all My words which I shall speak to you take into your heart and with your ears hearken;* 11 *and go! Come to the exile, to the children of your people and speak to them; and say to them: Thus says My Lord* HASHEM/ELOHIM *— whether they listen or whether they desist.*

forehead, — a familiar metaphor for fortitude — which by nature would be soft and pliant, will be endowed with supernatural strength to fortify you in your confrontations.

וְלֹא תֵחַת — *Nor be dismayed.*

Hirsch (Deut. 1:21) demonstrates (from *I Samuel* 2:4) that חתת means to be broken — thus: to lose courage, to be afraid.

10. קַח בִּלְבָבְךָ וּבְאָזְנֶיךָ שְׁמָע — *Take into your heart and hearken with your ears.*

Yechezkel was destined to hear many things against which his ears would certainly rebel, had not the ideas behind them previously found an abiding understanding in his heart. Therefore the 'taking into the heart' must precede the 'listening with the ears' *(Harav Breuer).*

11. בֹּא אֶל הַגּוֹלָה — *Come to the exile.*

In 1:1 we saw that גּוֹלָה could refer to either the state of exile or to the people who are in exile. In this verse, the latter meaning is intended.

Da'as Sofrim suggests that the singular form גּוֹלָה (as opposed to גּוֹלִים) is used to point out that even in exile the Jews formed one solid and cohesive community, untorn by factional strife. This together with the use of בְּנֵי עַמֶּךָ, *the children of your people,* combines to bring home to the prophet the need to remember Israel's greatness, even while rebuking them for their shortcomings.

Until this point Yechezkel might still have supposed that the field of his prophecy would be in the Land of Israel, whose people might well have been described by the harsh terms used by God. After all they had not yet been exposed to the softening experience of exile. With this verse the prophet is told that the exiles themselves had not benefited from their heart-rending experience. They are the rebels and the sinners to whom his prophecy is to be mainly directed *(Harav Breuer).*

וְדִבַּרְתָּ אֲלֵיהֶם וְאָמַרְתָּ אֲלֵיהֶם — *And speak to them; and say to them.*

Whereas דבר is the concise expression of a thought, אמר refers to the articulation of the thought to the

יב יְחַדֵּלוּ: וַתִּשָּׂאֵנִי רוּחַ וָאֶשְׁמַע אַחֲרַי קוֹל
רַעַשׁ גָּדוֹל בָּרוּךְ כְּבוֹד־יהוה מִמְּקוֹמוֹ:
יג וְקוֹל | כַּנְפֵי הַחַיּוֹת מַשִּׁיקוֹת אִשָּׁה אֶל־
אֲחוֹתָהּ וְקוֹל הָאוֹפַנִּים לְעֻמָּתָם וְקוֹל
יד רַעַשׁ גָּדוֹל: וְרוּחַ נְשָׂאַתְנִי וַתִּקָּחֵנִי וָאֵלֵךְ

mind and feelings of another person, the complete explanation and development of a thought (*Hirsch* to *Lev.*21:1). The prophet is exhorted not to satisfy himself with a dry, formal statement of his message, but to explain it persuasively to his listeners (*Harav Breuer*).

[According to *Sifri* (*Deut.* 1) דבר denotes a harsh manner of speech while אמר, according to *Mechilta* (*Exod.* 19:3) is a soft and understanding manner of speech. Accordingly we may interpret this verse as an exhortation to the prophet to use any possible ways to communicate with the people.]

12. וַתִּשָּׂאֵנִי רוּחַ — *And a wind lifted me up.*

Imbued with a deep understanding of the difficulties which he would encounter, but also with a guarantee of divine help in the execution of his task, Yechezkel must now enter upon his mission. While still isolated from his people, he had been shown the Merkavah and apprised of his destiny. The time had now come to join them.

After He ended His words, He commanded the wind to carry him to the place of the exiles (*Rashi*). [In 2:2 as in our chapter, *v.* 24, רוּחַ is used as 'spirit.' However, in this verse — as in 8:3 — it must be rendered 'wind' (see *Isaiah* 41:16).]

Through 'eating' the scroll, Yechezkel had become identified with his destiny as 'Ben Adam', the symbolic personification of his people. He had become a passive tool in the hands of a divine plan. Now he shoulders his mission, not of his own volition, but because the Divine wind carries him there. [This is the implication even according to *Radak*, who surmises that Yechezkel was not actually carried by the wind, but experienced this sensation only in a prophetic vision.]

וָאֶשְׁמַע אַחֲרַי — *And I heard behind me.*

From the vantage point of the prophet, who was leaving one place to go to another, אַחֲרַי would connote the place which he had just left (*Radak*). *Eliezer of Beaugency* goes so far as to read מִמְּקוֹמוֹ together with this phrase, as though it were written וָאֶשְׁמַע אַחֲרַי (מִמְּקוֹמוֹ) בָּרוּךְ כְּבוֹד הַשֵּׁם, *and I heard behind me from His place* ...

On the other hand, since Yechezkel had been lifted from the earth and was now held suspended above it by the wind — אַחֲרַי, *behind me*, might connote the entire earth (*Hirsch, Siddur*), which would mean that the song of glory emanates from the whole earth.

[*Bereishis Rabbah* (65:21) which interprets אַחֲרַי as *after me* (i.e., in time rather than place), seems to take בָּרוּךְ כְּבוֹד ה׳ מִמְּקוֹמוֹ in a different sense from that indicated by the simple meaning of this verse. See *footnote*.][1]

1. In context, the interpretations of *Radak* and *Metzudas David* seem most apt. The recognition of the fact that the increase of God's glory is not bounded by location, and that exile is as fertile a ground for His glorification as any other situation, is in consonance with the tenor of the entire *Merkavah* vision. However, it seems likely that the central place which this phrase occupies in our prayers assumes a meaning which goes beyond the immediate contextual implications. Thus in the *Kedushah* the phrase לְעֻמָּתָם בָּרוּךְ יֹאמֵרוּ, *Facing one another they say 'Blessed — '*, implies that this proclamation is said by the heavenly hosts in answer to the קָדוֹשׁ

12 *And a wind lifted me up; and I heard behind me the sound of a great noise: Blessed be HASHEM from His place;* 13 *and the sound of the wings of the 'Chayos' touching one another, and the sound of the 'Ofanim' opposite them; and the sound of a great noise.*

14 *Then a wind lifted me and took me. And I went*

בָּרוּךְ כְּבוֹד ה׳ מִמְּקוֹמוֹ — *Blessed be HASHEM from His place.*

Rambam (Moreh Nevuchim 1:64) states that כְּבוֹד ה׳ could be a synonym for HASHEM Himself. Thus we translate כְּבוֹד ה׳ as *HASHEM.*

However, *Metzudas David,* interprets the entire statement as meaning that the glory of HASHEM is not diminished in exile. Although Israel's apprehension of God is reduced as their distance from Him increases, He (i.e., His glory) remains inviolate.

In *Radak's* view the verse teaches that God's glory is *increased* (ברך, *to increase* as in בְּרֵיכָה, *a well* — see *Overview* in ArtScroll ed. of *Bircas Hamazon)* by His departure. He will no longer be offended by the *'jealousy-provoking image'* (see Ch. 8) which had been erected in the Temple.

According to both these meanings, the correct translation would be: *'The glory of HASHEM'.*

13. וְקוֹל — *And the sound.*

I.e. in addition to hearing the above praise of God, Yechezkel heard the following sounds.

מַשִּׁיקוֹת — *Touching* [lit. *'kissing'*].

I heard the sound of the angelic wings touching one another, creating a new song of praise (*Rashi*); or signaling the withdrawal of the *Shechinah* upon its *Merkavah-chariot (Metzudas David).*

14. וְרוּחַ נְשָׂאַתְנִי וַתִּקָּחֵנִי — *And a wind lifted me and took me.*

קָדוֹשׁ קָדוֹשׁ, *Holy, Holy, Holy,* of *Isaiah* 6:3. (The אָז בְּקוֹל רַעַשׁ גָּדוֹל of Shabbos morning, is based on our verse and אָז, *then,* means 'in answer to').

Indeed we find meanings ascribed to this phrase which seem to lift it beyond the confines of contextual continuity. In *Shemos Rabbah* 23:15 we read: 'The *Chayos* who carry the throne do not recognize the 'likeness' and when their turn comes to say the hymn they say: In which place is He? We do not know whether here or in a different place. But, wherever He is — בָּרוּךְ כְּבוֹד ה׳ מִמְּקוֹמוֹ!'

Rambam (Moreh Nevuchim 1:8) explains that the word מָקוֹם *place,* is used in a borrowed sense, to describe a person's or being's level of accomplishment or perfection. He translates our phrase as signifying: 'Blessed be HASHEM in accordance with His degree of perfection [i.e. totally and without limit]. Not even the angels can grasp the essential nature of God. Therefore His praise is couched in words that can incorporate an infinite range of meaning. Our recitation of these words implies that whatever His true degree of perfection may be, let it be expressed in these words with which we praise Him.

Rabbi Chayim of Volozhin (Nefesh haChayim Sha'ar 3) interprets מִמְּקוֹמוֹ 'From His place (outwards),' meaning that the phrase conveys the thought that the actual 'place' of HASHEM cannot be known *(Chagigah* 13b). We can never grasp His essence — only His way of relating to us.

Bereishis Rabbah 65:21, which interprets אַחֲרַי, as *after me* [i.e. the praise which the angels sing to HASHEM must await the completion of man's praises] surely also agrees with one of the above interpretations.

מַר בַּחֲמַת רוּחִי וְיַד־יהוָה עָלַי חָזָקָה׃
טו וָאָבוֹא אֶל־הַגּוֹלָה תֵּל אָבִיב הַיֹּשְׁבִים
אֶל־נְהַר־כְּבָר °ואשר הֵמָּה יוֹשְׁבִים
שָׁם וָאֵשֵׁב שָׁם שִׁבְעַת יָמִים מַשְׁמִים
טז בְּתוֹכָם׃ וַיְהִי מִקְצֵה שִׁבְעַת
יָמִים וַיְהִי דְבַר־יהוָה אֵלַי
יז לֵאמֹר׃ בֶּן־אָדָם צֹפֶה נְתַתִּיךָ לְבֵית
יִשְׂרָאֵל וְשָׁמַעְתָּ מִפִּי דָּבָר וְהִזְהַרְתָּ
יח אוֹתָם מִמֶּנִּי׃ בְּאָמְרִי לָרָשָׁע מוֹת תָּמוּת
וְלֹא הִזְהַרְתּוֹ וְלֹא דִבַּרְתָּ לְהַזְהִיר רָשָׁע
מִדַּרְכּוֹ הָרְשָׁעָה לְחַיֹּתוֹ הוּא רָשָׁע בַּעֲוֺנוֹ
יט יָמוּת וְדָמוֹ מִיָּדְךָ אֲבַקֵּשׁ׃ וְאַתָּה כִּי־

°וָאֵשֵׁב ק׳

According to *Radak* this is a repetition of *v.* 12, necessitated by the interruption of *v.* 13. *Malbim* explains that in *v.* 12 he was simply lifted up and suspended in the air. In this verse the wind takes him to his destination.

וָאֵלֵךְ מַר בַּחֲמַת רוּחִי — *And I went in bitterness in the anger* [or *heat*] *of my spirit.*

It was unpleasant for me to chide my people *(Rashi). Metzudas David* thinks that his sorrow was caused by the knowledge, imparted to him in the *Merkavah* vision, that the Holy Presence was leaving the Temple.

וְיַד ה׳ עָלַי חָזָקָה — *And the hand of HASHEM was upon me mightily.*

The scroll which Yechezkel had been fed had tasted sweet as honey to him. He had joyously made himself an instrument of God's intentions. Now that he was about to embark upon the realization of his destiny as a prophet of God, the heavy responsibility weighed upon him.

15. וָאֵשֵׁב הֵמָּה יוֹשְׁבִים שָׁם — *And I dwelt where they were dwelling.*

The translation follows the קְרִי, *the Masoretic reading,* as opposed to the כְּתִיב, *the spelling of the text* which reads ואשר (a ר instead of a ב). The meaning of this word as it is spelled is obscure.

Radak renders it וַאֲשֶׁר: *And when I saw them* sitting there I sat there among them ....

מַשְׁמִים — *Desolate,* or *silent (Targum).*

Malbim adduces his silence to the fact that he had not been given a specific message to convey to them.

Abarbanel on the other hand sees *v.* 17 as a rebuke to Yechezkel for not sharing his vision with the people. He had been appointed a צֹפֶה, a *sentinel* and had the obligation not to remain silent. In this view we must explain the silence as *Da'as Sofrim* does; he simply did not have the courage to hurt the people by describing to them what he had been shown and by explaining its full import to them.

17-21. These vs. delineate the responsibilities of a sentinel towards his people. Both *Eliezer of Beaugency* and *Abarbanel* explain this section as a rebuke to Yechezkel for having kept

in bitterness in the anger of my spirit. And the hand
of HASHEM was upon me mightily. 15 *Then I came to*
the exiles — to Tel Aviv — who were dwelling by the
River Kevar and I dwelt where they were dwelling.
And I sat there seven days, desolate among them.
16 *It happened at the end of seven days that the*
word of HASHEM came to me saying: 17 *Ben Adam: A*
sentinel have I appointed you for the Family of
Israel; and — when you hear a matter from My
mouth — warn them on My behalf.
18 *When I say of the wicked one: 'You shall surely*
die' — and you did not warn him and did not speak
up to warn the wicked one concerning his evil way,
to save his life! He, the wicked one, shall die for his
sin, but I shall demand his blood from you. 19 *But*

silent for the seven days during which he *sat desolate among them. Eliezer of Beaugency* adds the specific criticism that the prophet should have made the people aware of God's anger, as evinced by the *Merkavah* vision. This would have spurred them to repent (*v.* 18).

These instructions were to lie dormant in Yechezkel's heart for six years. Vs. 25-27 deny him the role of the 'reprover' since the people's obduracy would neutralize his efforts. Not until the twelfth year of the exile (33:21) was his 'mouth opened' (*ibid.* 22) and the freedom granted him to move among the people, who, shattered by the catastrophic events in Jerusalem, would finally be receptive to his teachings.

Indeed 33:1*ff* elaborates upon the 'sentinel' metaphor, repeating and expanding upon much of what the prophet was told here. At that point the time had come to put these instructions into practice.

We can only surmise the reason for telling Yechezkel these matters so long before they could be actively applied. Perhaps the knowledge that so much of the evil that was going on about him could have been prevented if only a path could be found to the people's hearts would imbue his symbolic activities (Ch. 4 and onwards) with greater immediacy and urgency.

18. בְּאָמְרִי לָרָשָׁע — *When I say of* [lit. *'to'*] *the wicked one.*

By sending the prophet to tell the wicked person of his impending doom, it is as though God talks to him directly (*Radak*). *Eliezer of Beaugency takes the root* אמר in the sense of 'intending' (see *Exod.* 2:14), and translates: When I decide [concerning] the wicked one.

וְלֹא דִבַּרְתָּ לְהַזְהִיר רָשָׁע ... לְחַיֹּתוֹ — *And you did not speak up to warn the wicked one ... to save his life.*

To avoid the apparent redundancy [the verse already said: וְלֹא הִזְהַרְתּוֹ] *Abarbanel* renders the verse: וְלֹא הִזְהַרְתּוֹ, *You did not warn him that he would die,* וְלֹא דִבַּרְתָּ ... לְחַיֹּתוֹ, *and you did not even warn him [without mentioning the death penalty] in order to save his life.*

וְדָמוֹ מִיָּדְךָ אֲבַקֵּשׁ — *But I shall demand his blood from you.*

If you had conveyed My message to him he would have repented. By with-

הִזְהַרְתָּ רָשָׁע וְלֹא־שָׁב מֵרִשְׁעוֹ וּמִדַּרְכּוֹ
הָרְשָׁעָה הוּא בַּעֲוֺנוֹ יָמוּת וְאַתָּה אֶת־
כ נַפְשְׁךָ הִצַּלְתָּ׃ וּבְשׁוּב צַדִּיק
מִצִּדְקוֹ וְעָשָׂה עָוֶל וְנָתַתִּי מִכְשׁוֹל לְפָנָיו
הוּא יָמוּת כִּי לֹא הִזְהַרְתּוֹ בְּחַטָּאתוֹ
יָמוּת וְלֹא תִזָּכַרְןָ צִדְקָתוֹ אֲשֶׁר עָשָׂה
כא וְדָמוֹ מִיָּדְךָ אֲבַקֵּשׁ׃ וְאַתָּה כִּי הִזְהַרְתּוֹ
צַדִּיק לְבִלְתִּי חֲטֹא צַדִּיק וְהוּא לֹא־חָטָא
חָיוֹ יִחְיֶה כִּי נִזְהָר וְאַתָּה אֶת־נַפְשְׁךָ
כב הִצַּלְתָּ׃ וַתְּהִי עָלַי שָׁם יַד־יְהוָה
וַיֹּאמֶר אֵלַי קוּם צֵא אֶל־הַבִּקְעָה וְשָׁם

holding this chance from him, you are guilty of his death *(Radak).*[1]

20. The responsibility of the prophet is not confined to exhorting wicked people to repent. A צַדִּיק, *a good person,* can also falter in his path of righteousness. When this occurs, the true spiritual leaders of the people will know where the blame lies: כִּי לֹא הִזְהַרְתּוֹ, *because* you did not warn him! Whatever the prophet may have done was evidently not sufficient *(Harav Breuer).*

וְנָתַתִּי מִכְשׁוֹל לְפָנָיו — *I shall place a stumbling block before him.*

This is to be taken together with the next two words: הוּא יָמוּת. The meaning is that I will bring about an occurrence through which he will die *(Radak, Metzudas David).*

1. *Eliyahu Rabba* (Ch. 11) explains his guilt in terms of the dictum of the Sages that: כָּל יִשְׂרָאֵל עֲרֵבִים זֶה בָּזֶה, *All [the people of] Israel are responsible for each other (Shevuos* 39a). *Yalkut* (1:802) expresses the same thought with the words: ... this teaches us that the sins of Israel are upon the heads of their judges.

The obligation to rebuke, and the severe guilt which attaches to one who fails to do so, is often stressed by the Sages in connection with the generations immediately preceding the destruction of Jerusalem and the Temple:

— Zidkiyahu, the last king of Judah, was a righteous man. He is described as 'evil' because he had the ability to stop people from sinning and did not do so *(Sanhedrin* 103a).

— Although they had previously been marked to be saved, the 'holy ones' (9:6) were the first ones to be killed in the city because they could have protested the sins but did not do so *(Shabbos* 55a).

— Jerusalem was destroyed because they did not rebuke one another *(Shabbos* 119b).

The concept of עֲרֵבוּת, *mutual responsibility,* rests upon a unique perception of nationhood. Only when the whole nation is perceived as 'one body' can this idea be maintained. (See *Maharal Nesivos Olam Nesiv Hatochacha* 2). Thus, according to *Rabbi Nechemia*'s view *(Sanhedrin* 43b) עֲרֵבוּת did not begin until the Israelites had crossed the Jordan and entered into their own land. (See *Appendix* III).

At the moment when the exile was about to start and the outward bonds of nationhood were about to be destroyed, it was necessary to teach that the inner cohesion of the nation was indestructible and that their mutual responsibility had not been abrogated.

you, if you did warn the wicked one, and he did not
turn away from his wickedness and his wicked way,
he will die in his sin — but you have saved your soul.
20 *And when a righteous person turns from his*
righteousness and commits iniquity. I shall place a
stumbling block before him — he shall die! Since you
did not warn him he shall die in his sin, and his
righteous deeds which he did will not be remembered
— and I shall demand his blood from your hand.
21 *But you — if you warned the righteous man, that*
the righteous should not sin, and he did not sin; he
shall surely live because he took heed. And as for you
— you have saved your soul.
22 *The hand of HASHEM was upon me: Get up! go*
out to the valley, and there will I speak with you.

Rashi (based on *Talmud Yomah* 86b) interprets the verse as referring to a formerly righteous person who has begun to sin in secret. If he will be punished for these sins it will seem unjust to people who still look upon him as a Zaddik. Therefore, God will cause him to sin in public so that everyone will know about his duplicity.

וְלֹא תִזָּכַרְןָ צִדְקֹתָו אֲשֶׁר עָשָׂה — *And his righteous deeds which he did will not be remembered.*

They will not be able to save him from the sentence of death *(Metzudas David).*

In this interpretation there is no implication that his earlier good deeds will go unrewarded. All that is said is that they will not save him from his just punishment.

There are however, situations in which good deeds are completely 'forgotten' and remain unrewarded, such as when the person who performed them is a תּוֹהֶא עַל הָרִאשׁוֹנוֹת, *regrets having done them. Rashi* (based on *Kiddushin* 40b) interprets our verse in this way, although the *Talmud* quotes 33:12 rather than our verse, as its source.

22. צֵא אֶל הַבִּקְעָה — *Go out to the valley.*

In preparation for another *Merkavah* vision, the prophet is told to isolate himself once more from the people and to go to a valley — a comparatively 'clean' place, more suitable for visions which would normally have been possible only in Eretz Yisrael *(Radak).*

The use of the definite article (הַבִּקְעָה) indicates that a particular valley is meant. *Radak* identifies it as the valley of the 'mixing of the languages' where the Babylonian nation was born *(Gen.* 11:9). This would be the ideal location for the *Merkavah* (the manifestation of God's Providence — see *Prefatory Remarks* to ch. 1) to find its resting place in exile.[1]

1. Babylon is the first of the 'four kingdoms' (Babylon, Media-Persia, Greece, and Rome) who were destined to subjugate Israel. In innumerable passages in Talmudic and Midrashic sources

ג כג אֲדַבֵּר אוֹתָךְ׃ וָאָקוּם וָאֵצֵא אֶל־הַבִּקְעָה
כג־כז וְהִנֵּה־שָׁם כְּבוֹד־יהוה עֹמֵד כַּכָּבוֹד אֲשֶׁר
רָאִיתִי עַל־נְהַר־כְּבָר וָאֶפֹּל עַל־פָּנָי׃
כד וַתָּבֹא־בִי רוּחַ וַתַּעֲמִדֵנִי עַל־רַגְלָי וַיְדַבֵּר
אֹתִי וַיֹּאמֶר אֵלַי בֹּא הִסָּגֵר בְּתוֹךְ
כה בֵּיתֶךָ׃ וְאַתָּה בֶן־אָדָם הִנֵּה נָתְנוּ
עָלֶיךָ עֲבוֹתִים וַאֲסָרוּךָ בָּהֶם וְלֹא תֵצֵא
כו בְּתוֹכָם׃ וּלְשׁוֹנְךָ אַדְבִּיק אֶל־חִכֶּךָ
וְנֶאֱלַמְתָּ וְלֹא־תִהְיֶה לָהֶם לְאִישׁ מוֹכִיחַ
כז כִּי בֵּית מְרִי הֵמָּה׃ וּבְדַבְּרִי אוֹתְךָ אֶפְתַּח
אֶת־פִּיךָ וְאָמַרְתָּ אֲלֵיהֶם כֹּה אָמַר אֲדֹנָי
יֱהֹוִה הַשֹּׁמֵעַ ׀ יִשְׁמָע וְהֶחָדֵל ׀ יֶחְדָּל כִּי
ד א בֵּית מְרִי הֵמָּה׃ וְאַתָּה בֶן־אָדָם
א קַח־לְךָ לְבֵנָה וְנָתַתָּה אוֹתָהּ לְפָנֶיךָ

23. כְּבוֹד ה׳ עֹמֵד — *The glory of HASHEM stood.*

Radak explains that another *Merkavah* vision was needed to teach Yechezkel the exact nature of God's Providence.

Da'as Sofrim, however, based on the verb עוֹמֵד, *standing,* suggests that this second vision revealed the *Merkavah* as having *come to rest* in Babylon, as opposed to the previous vision which depicted the *Merkavah* in motion — *leaving the Temple.*

For the meaning of כְּבוֹד ה׳, see *comm. v.* 12.

24-27. The obduracy of the people would not permit Yechezkel to shoulder the task of the צוֹפֶה, *sentinel (v.* 17), directly. The possibility that the Temple might really be destroyed was simply unacceptable to a people nurtured on the experience of constant Divine intervention. Finding an echo in the hearts of the exiles and drowning out the words of the prophet was the message of the false prophets who maintained that the collapse of Babylon and the return to Zion was only a matter of time.

For the moment then, the medium of his communication would be his actions (Ch. 4-5). In horrifyingly graphic detail, more eloquent than words, Yechezkel, the BEN ADAM — the true son of Israel,

these four 'kingdoms' are depicted as the antitheses of Godliness. Israel — itself the *Merkavah* — the bearer of God's glory becomes subjugated to them, when it does not live up to its high destiny.

The idea of one nation being chosen to carry the divine message in a world hostile to Godliness, was born in the דוֹר הַפְּלָגָה, *the Generation of Division (Gen.* 11:1-9) from which the 'seventy nations' of history emerged. Prior to that mankind was one unified family and would have remained so had that generation not rebelled against God.

This valley from which sprang the origins of Israel's greatness, was now to see the results which flow from Israel's flouting of its calling.

III
23-27

[23] *So I arose and went out to the valley; and see there!*
the glory of HASHEM *stood, like the glory which I*
saw by the River Kevar. And I threw myself upon
my face.

[24] *Then a spirit came into me and stood me up*
upon my feet. And He spoke to me and said to me:
Come seal yourself within your house. [25] *And you*
Ben Adam! see, they have put ropes upon you and
bound you with them; and you shall not go out
among them. [26] *And I will make your tongue cleave*
to the roof of your mouth, and you shall become
mute, and not be for them a reprover — for they are a
rebellious family. [27] *But when I speak to you, I will*
open your mouth. And you shall say to them: Thus
says my Lord HASHEM/ELOHIM. *He who heeds will*
obey and he who desists will desist — for they are a
rebellious family.

IV
1

***N**ow you, Ben Adam, take yourself a brick, put it before you, and inscribe on it a city — Jerusalem!*

would live through, symbolically, the terrors of the destruction and exile. Perhaps in this way a path could be found to the hearts of the people.

Oral communication would be reserved for וּבְדַבְּרִי אוֹתְךָ, *when I speak to you* (*v.* 27), i.e., formal messages from God to His people.

Yechezkel's 'dumbness', the prohibition against speaking directly to his people as an אִישׁ מוֹכִיחַ, *a reprover* (*v.* 26), would be lifted only when the catastrophe of undeniable historical experience would have opened the hearts of the people to his words (24:26-27 and 33:21-22).

IV

God commands Yechezkel to act out the forthcoming siege of Jerusalem.

Jeremiah had vainly tried to warn the people that it was only a matter of time before Jerusalem would fall. His prophecies had been ignored because his listeners would not accept the idea that their city was vulnerable. They felt that the presence of the Temple in their midst was a guarantee that God's providence would protect them. In their distorted view, it was possible to lead lives of violence and immorality as long as they continued their ritual devotions in the Temple (*Jeremiah* 7:8-11).

They are now to learn that Temple and City are inviolable only so long as they serve as the conduit through which God's presence finds a welcome in the peoples' hearts. When God's word is banished from the city, when His prophet is excluded and kept behind an iron wall (*v.* 3), then Jerusalem, no less than any other city, can be destroyed.

ד
ב־ה

ב וְחַקּוֹתָ עָלֶיהָ עִיר אֶת־יְרוּשָׁלִָם: וְנָתַתָּה
עָלֶיהָ מָצוֹר וּבָנִיתָ עָלֶיהָ דָּיֵק וְשָׁפַכְתָּ
עָלֶיהָ סֹלְלָה וְנָתַתָּה עָלֶיהָ מַחֲנוֹת וְשִׂים־
ג עָלֶיהָ כָּרִים סָבִיב: וְאַתָּה קַח־לְךָ מַחֲבַת
בַּרְזֶל וְנָתַתָּה אוֹתָהּ קִיר בַּרְזֶל בֵּינְךָ וּבֵין
הָעִיר וַהֲכִינֹתָה אֶת־פָּנֶיךָ אֵלֶיהָ וְהָיְתָה
בַמָּצוֹר וְצַרְתָּ עָלֶיהָ אוֹת הִיא לְבֵית
ד יִשְׂרָאֵל: וְאַתָּה שְׁכַב עַל־צִדְּךָ
הַשְּׂמָאלִי וְשַׂמְתָּ אֶת־עֲוֺן בֵּית־יִשְׂרָאֵל
עָלָיו מִסְפַּר הַיָּמִים אֲשֶׁר תִּשְׁכַּב עָלָיו
ה תִּשָּׂא אֶת־עֲוֺנָם: וַאֲנִי נָתַתִּי לְךָ אֶת־שְׁנֵי

2. וְנָתַתָּה עָלֶיהָ מָצוֹר — *Then lay siege against it.*

Yechezkel was to complete the picture of the city by inscribing upon the brick all the appurtenances of a siege.

דָּיֵק — *Fort.*

The translation follows *Radak* and *Metzudas Zion* who render דָּיֵק as 'tower', one major aspect of a siege. *Targum* renders כַּרְקוֹם which has a wider range of meaning, encompassing the whole of the siege. Thus *Onkelos* translates מָצוֹר (*Deut.* 20:20) as כַּרְקוֹמִין. (See *Aruch* כַּרְקוֹם who quotes *Yerushalmi Gittin* 3:4 'What is כַּרְקוֹם? Bells, chains, dogs, chickens, and armies surrounding a city.' See also *Gittin* 28b 'A city surrounded by a כַּרְקוֹם').

כָּרִים — *Commanders.*

Whose function it is to prevent people from entering or leaving the city *(Rashi). Radak* and others translate : *battering rams.*

[*Radak* in *Sefer haShorashim* points out that the literal meaning of כָּרִים is *fat sheep.* The word is used here in a derisive borrowed sense for *commanders.*]

3. מַחֲבַת — *Pan.*

Sifra (to *Vayikra* 2:7) defines מַחֲבַת, as a flat, shallow pan, as opposed to מַרְחֶשֶׁת which is a deep pan.

קִיר בַּרְזֶל בֵּינְךָ וּבֵין הָעִיר — *An iron wall between yourself and the city.*

The iron wall might symbolize the wall of the city *(Rashi* and *Metzudas David).* Then Yechezkel, lying on the other side of the 'wall' with 'uncovered arm' *('As a man making war': Rashi v.* 7), would be cast in the role of the besieging Nebuchadnezzar *(Rashi).* By having the prophet himself act this part, God brought home to the people that the conquering hordes of Babylon carry out His decree, no less than the man of God. Thus, in a sense, even the enemy soldiers are נְבִיאֵי ה׳, *the ones in whom God's message issues.* (See comm. to 2:5).[1]

No other symbol could have more

1. That the despoilers of Israel are only tools in the hands of Divine Providence is a constantly recurring theme in Scriptures. Thus Jeremiah (25:9 and other places) refers to Nebuchadnezzar as *'My servant'.* In Isaiah the same point is constantly stressed regarding Sancheriv and the Assyrian armies. (See especially 10:5-15).

*2 Then lay siege against it and build a fort against it;
cast a mound against it; set up camps against it, and
appoint commanders around it. 3 As for you, take
yourself an iron pan, and emplace it as an iron wall
between yourself and the city. Concentrate your face
toward it — so it shall be besieged and you shall lay
siege to it. It is a sign to the Family of Israel.*

*4 As for you, lie upon your left side, and place the
iniquity of the Family of Israel upon it. According to
the number of days which you shall lie upon it, shall
you carry their sin. 5 For I have given for your sake*

unambiguously shattered the false doctrine that Jersualem, as the City of God, was inviolable. Not only would God's protective presence not shield the city; on the contrary, it would itself become the instrument of destruction, the witness of Jerusalem's inner decay.

Metzudas David does not go so far as to identify the prophet with Nebuchadnezzar, as does *Rashi*. He limits the teaching of the symbolism to a statement that: Besides the enemy, God was also fighting against the city.

However the *Talmud (Berachos* 32b) uses this verse as the source for Rabbi Elazar's statement: From the day that the Temple was destroyed, an iron wall separates Israel from their Father in heaven. The *iron pan* is not the wall of Jerusalem, but a symbol of the rupture between city and soul, between the 'upper' and 'nether' Jerusalem *(Ta'anis* 5a). The prophet is symbolically excluded from the city, the word of God finds no echo in the hearts of its inhabitants — and Jerusalem lies exposed to Babylon's military might.

Thus the prophet himself, cut off from any meaningful communication with his people; lying 'shackled' and weighed down by their sins (*comm. v.* 4), is revealed as the true 'besieger' of the city (וְצַרְתָּ עָלֶיהָ), the mute accuser who guarantees its downfall. (based on *Harav Breuer).*

4. וְאַתָּה שְׁכַב עַל צִדְּךָ הַשְּׂמָאלִי — *As for you, lie upon your left side.*

A person facing east would have the north to his left and the south to his right. *Rashi* explains that the left or northern side symbolizes the Northern Kingdom — Samaria, and the right or southern side (*v.* 6), the Kingdom of Judah. Thus בֵּית יִשְׂרָאֵל, *the Family of Israel,* in our verse refers not to the whole of Knesses Yisrael, but to the Ten Tribes of Samaria.

וְשַׂמְתָּ אֶת עֲוֹן בֵּית יִשְׂרָאֵל עָלָיו — *And place the iniquity of the Family of Israel upon it.*

It is the sins of Israel which turn the prophet into an 'enemy' (see *comm.* to *v.*3) who besieges the city. Thus the duration of the siege is determined by the number of years during which Israel sinned against God (see below).

תִּשָּׂא אֶת עֲוֹנָם — *Shall you carry their sin.*

The pain and suffering which the prophet would endure in the course of 390 days of immobility (*vs.* 5 and 8) would 'atone' for the sins of the people *(Rashi).* This comment interprets the verb נשא (the root of תִּשָּׂא in our verse)

ד עֲוֹנָם לְמִסְפַּר יָמִים שְׁלֹשׁ־מֵאוֹת
ו וְתִשְׁעִים יוֹם וְנָשָׂאתָ עֲוֺן בֵּית־יִשְׂרָאֵל׃
ו וְכִלִּיתָ אֶת־אֵלֶּה וְשָׁכַבְתָּ עַל־צִדְּךָ
°הימיני שֵׁנִית וְנָשָׂאתָ אֶת־עֲוֺן בֵּית־ °הַיְמָנִי ק׳
יְהוּדָה אַרְבָּעִים יוֹם יוֹם לַשָּׁנָה יוֹם לַשָּׁנָה

as 'to forgive'. Indeed we find such usage in other parts of the Bible (see especially *Exod.* 34:7).

It is obvious that complete forgiveness is not contemplated here, since the siege continued and Jerusalem ultimately fell. But even granting the limited nature of the forgiveness, it is still difficult to understand how the prophet's suffering could bring about any atonement.

Perhaps the ordeal which symbolized Yechezkel's love for his people [... 'to tell you that as long as Israel is suffering so the righteous people are with them in their suffering' *(Vayikra Rabbah* 28:6)], combined with his role as 'Nebuchadnezzar the conquerer', served to bring home to the people how even in the moment that God punishes Israel, His love for them remains unchanged. This realization would have generated some thoughts of repentance which would attain a degree of atonement for them. (See Appendix III).

Radak however renders תִּשָּׂא not as relating to forgiving, but as 'bearing the guilt of a sin' (*Exod.* 28:42-43). The 'sign' for the Family of Israel (*v.* 3) would be that the years of their sinning would bring untold suffering upon them.

Harav Breuer interprets the root נשא in its original sense of 'carrying' — being weighed down by something. The sins of Israel 'weigh down' the prophet and immobilize him (3:25), forcing his prophecy to take the form of bizarre symbolism rather than the more normal method of oral communication.[1]

[For a further discussion of the concept that the suffering of a righteous man can atone for the community, see Appendix III).

5. וַאֲנִי נָתַתִּי לְךָ אֶת שְׁנֵי עֲוֹנָם לְמִסְפַּר יָמִים *— For I have given for your sake the years of their iniquity as a number of days.*

The symbolism would have been impossible if a full year of 'siege' had been needed for every year of sin. Hence, *Metzudas David* renders the apparently redundant וְנָשָׂאתָ עֲוֹן בֵּית יִשְׂרָאֵל, [lit. *'and you will bear the sin of the House of Israel'*] as *'and thus'* [because I will reckon only a single day for each year] *you will be 'able'* ... Therefore, one day is to be considered as symbolizing a full year.

שְׁלֹשׁ מֵאוֹת וְתִשְׁעִים יוֹם *— Three hundred and ninety days.*

Since we have seen *(comm.* to *v.* 4) that the left side symbolizes the Northern Kingdom, these 390 days would seem to be associated with the kings and people of Samaria. However, from Jeroboam's reign until the Assyrian exile, there were no more than approximately 240 years. The balance represents years of sin during the times of the Judges.

1. So bizarre do these symbolic actions seem, that *Rambam (Moreh Nevuchim* 2:46) writes· 'God forbid that God should expose His prophets to the laughter and raillery of fools.' His opinion, and also *Radak's,* is that none of the actions recorded here did in fact take place, but that Yechezkel saw himself doing them, in a prophetic vision.

However, *Seder Olam* 26 (see *comm.* to 8:1) assumes all these occurrences to have happened literally.

the years of their iniquity as a number of days; three hundred and ninety days, so you can bear the iniquity of the Family of Israel.

6 *When you shall complete these, then lie again upon your right side a second time; and bear the iniquity of the Family of Judah for forty days; a day for a year, a day for a year have I assigned it to you,* 7 *and*

[The period of the Judges is counted from the death of Joshua until the beginning of the reign of King Saul.]

[The Northern Kingdom, whose first king was Jeroboam, came into being during the reign of Solomon's son, Rechavom.]

[For the kings of Judah and Israel see Appendix, Table I.]

Rashi computes the years of the Samarian monarchy as follows: Jeroboam, 22; Nadav, 2; Ba'asha, 24; Elah, 2; Omri, 12; Achav, 22; Achaziahu, 2; Yehoram, 12; Yehu, 28; Yehoachaz, 16; Yehoash, 16; Jeroboam, 41; Menachem, 10; Pekachyahu, 2; Pekach, 20; Hoshea, 9; for a total of 240 years. For the period of the Judges, the sinful years are those during which Israel was subjugated by foreign kings: Cushan, 8; Eglon, 18; Sisera, 20; Midian, 7; Amon, 18; Philistia, 40; yielding a sub-total of 111 years which, together with the 240 years, comes to 351. *Rashi* adds the forty years from Micha, who set up an institutionalized idol until the Ark was captured in Eli's time. This gives a total of 391 years. *Rashi* explains that the final year of *Hoshea ben Eila*'s reign is not counted since the exile took place in that year. *Biur Hagrah* to *Seder Olam* 26 fills the gap from 351 years to 390 years with the 39 years of Eli.

Seder Olam 26 reads: 'This teaches us that Israel angered God for 390 years from the time they entered the Land, until they left it.'

[According to this method of computation the symbolism of the left side and the 390 days are not in accord with each other. The left side symbolized the Northern Kingdom, but 150 days of sinning took place before Samaria even came into existence! Apparently the meaning is that the 240 years of Samaria's sins are seen as the *culmination* of the previous 150 years. *Together* they brought about the Assyrian exile.]

Abarbanel (followed by *Malbim)* suggests that the 390 years might be reckoned from the reign of Rechavam the son of Solomon, until the destruction of Jerusalem.

[It is customary in Scripture to count as a full year any part of a calendar year during which a monarch reigned. Thus, if a king died in *Tammuz* and his successor died in *Cheshvan*, the twelve-month period would be reckoned as three years because it was divided among the reigns of three kings. Thus, although a computation of the various reigns from Rechavam's time comes to more than 390 years, by counting overlapping years only once, the sum of all the reigns amount to exactly 390 years.]

Therefore, because this computation involves only the Judean kings, *Abarbanel* abandons the idea that the left side symbolizes Samaria. He suggests that the left side of a person, where the heart is located, is particularly symbolic of the contemplation which occupied the prophet during this whole period (see below for the explanation of the 40 years of *v.* 6).

6. וְשָׁכַבְתָּ עַל צִדְּךָ הַיְמָנִי — *Then lie again upon your right side.*

To teach us that the family of Judah (the 'right' or Southern Kingdom) angered God for forty years, from the time that the ten tribes were exiled until Jerusalem was destroyed *(Seder Olam* Ch. 26).

Rashi computes: Menashe, 22 [the Sages deduce that he sinned for only 22 of the 55

ד
ז־יא

ז נְתַתִּיו לָךְ: וְאֶל־מְצוֹר יְרוּשָׁלִַם תָּכִין
ח פָּנֶיךָ וּזְרֹעֲךָ חֲשׂוּפָה וְנִבֵּאתָ עָלֶיהָ: וְהִנֵּה
נָתַתִּי עָלֶיךָ עֲבוֹתִים וְלֹא־תֵהָפֵךְ מִצִּדְּךָ
ט אֶל־צִדֶּךָ עַד־כַּלּוֹתְךָ יְמֵי מְצוּרֶךָ: וְאַתָּה
קַח־לְךָ חִטִּין וּשְׂעֹרִים וּפוֹל וַעֲדָשִׁים
וְדֹחַן וְכֻסְּמִים וְנָתַתָּה אוֹתָם בִּכְלִי אֶחָד
וְעָשִׂיתָ אוֹתָם לְךָ לְלָחֶם מִסְפַּר הַיָּמִים
אֲשֶׁר־אַתָּה | שׁוֹכֵב עַל־צִדְּךָ שְׁלֹשׁ־
י מֵאוֹת וְתִשְׁעִים יוֹם תֹּאכְלֶנּוּ: וּמַאֲכָלְךָ
אֲשֶׁר תֹּאכְלֶנּוּ בְּמִשְׁקוֹל עֶשְׂרִים שֶׁקֶל
יא לַיּוֹם מֵעֵת עַד־עֵת תֹּאכְלֶנּוּ: וּמַיִם

years he reigned]:Ammon, 2;Yehoyakim, 11; and the first five years of Zidkiyahu's reign. The events recorded here took place in the fifth year of his reign (1:2).

If the 390 days of the previous verse are to be computed until the destruction of Jerusalem (see *Abarbanel* above), then the final forty years were already included in the large total; thus Yechezkel had already suffered for these forty years. The additional 'besieging' prescribed in our verse must then be seen as indicating that the sins of the final forty years were of a more serious nature because the people willfully ignored the lessons which they should have learned from the exile of the Northern Kingdom.

Malbim, in line with this thinking, computes the forty years from the thirteenth year of King Yoshiyahu's reign. That was when Jeremiah started to prophesy. By ignoring his message, the people sealed their own doom.

That the forty days indicate the final years before the destruction, seems to be shown by the fact that during those concluding days of his ordeal, even the meager food permitted the prophet during the 390 days, was apparently withheld (see *comm.* to *v.* 9).

7. וּזְרֹעֲךָ חֲשׂוּפָה — *And your arm shall be bared.*

Like a man who wages war *(Rashi).*

וְנִבֵּאתָ עָלֶיהָ — *You shall prophesy against it.*

Since Yechezkel was not allowed to speak to the people unless he had a specific message from God (3:26-27), the 'prophesying' referred to in this verse would be through his symbolic actions *(Harav Breuer).*

8. וְהִנֵּה נָתַתִּי עָלֶיךָ עֲבוֹתִים — *See! I have placed ropes upon you.*

The people, by their obduracy, had 'placed ropes' upon him (3:25), preventing him from effectively fulfilling his role during his many years as a reprover. Now it was God's turn to 'place ropes' upon him. They would tie him down securely to show that no change would be permitted in the fate presaged by his 'lying'.

9-13. Although Yechezkel was a 'besieger' during the 430 days, he became one because previously he, the bearer of God's word, had been 'exiled' from Jerusalem by the refusal of the people to heed his message. This was the symbolism of the iron wall (see

IV
8-11

to the siege of Jerusalem shall you concentrate your face, and your arm shall be bared. You shall prophesy against it.

8 *See! I placed ropes upon you that you shall not turn from side to side until you have completed the days of your siege.*

9 *Now you, take for yourself wheat, barley, beans, lentils, millet, and spelt; put them in one vessel and prepare them for yourself for food. According to the number of days which you lie on your side — three hundred and ninety days — are you to eat it.*

10 *Now your food which you are to eat shall be by weight, twenty shekels a day; from one time to the other are you to eat it.* 11 *And water by measure shall*

comm. to *v.* 3). However, throughout the 'siege' he was to bear himself, not as a conquerer, but as an exile, eating food unaesthetically prepared, in minute quantities, 'which they had prepared for dogs — who refused to touch it' *(Vayikra Rabbah* 28:6). This was designed to bring home to the people the horrors of exile, and to show them that whenever Israel suffers, the צַדִּיקִים, *'the righteous ones'* suffer with them *(Vayikra Rabbah* ad. loc.).

9. בִּכְלִי אֶחָד — *In one vessel.*

In normal times a person separates the wheat from the inferior grains. During a siege, or while captive in exile, he would not have the time nor the inclination to concern himself with the unappetizing nature of this mixture.

לְלָחֶם — *For food* [lit. *'bread'*].

The translation follows *Targum* who translates לְמֵיכַל. This translation seems to assume that the 'cake of barley' mentioned in *v.* 12 was eaten in addition to the cereal mentioned in our verse *(Metzudas David)* [i.e. Yechezkel's diet consisted not only of bread]. Most commentators, however, take the meaning of לֶחֶם in our verse as *bread* and offer various interpretations to *v.* 12 (see below).

שְׁלֹשׁ מֵאוֹת וְתִשְׁעִים יוֹם — *Three hundred and ninety days.*

Metzudas David assumes that the diet of the forty days would be the same as that permitted during the 390 days. No specific mention is made because it is considered as self-evident. *Eliezer of Beaugency,* however, sees the forty days as symbolizing the final disintegration of normal life in the city. During this time not even these sorry rations were to be allowed (see below *v.* 16).

10. בְּמִשְׁקוֹל — *By weight.*

During a siege, a severe rationing system must be imposed to prevent the available food from being used up too quickly *(Rashi).*

מֵעֵת עַד עֵת — *From one time to the other.*

I.e. a twenty-four hour period.

בִּמְשׂוּרָה תִּשְׁתֶּה שִׁשִּׁית הַהִין מֵעֵת
יב עַד־עֵת תִּשְׁתֶּה: וְעֻגַת שְׂעֹרִים תֹּאכְלֶנָּה
וְהִיא בְּגֶלְלֵי צֵאַת הָאָדָם תְּעֻגֶנָה
יג לְעֵינֵיהֶם: וַיֹּאמֶר יהוה
כָּכָה יֹאכְלוּ בְנֵי־יִשְׂרָאֵל אֶת־לַחְמָם
טָמֵא בַּגּוֹיִם אֲשֶׁר אַדִּיחֵם שָׁם:
יד וָאֹמַר אֲהָהּ אֲדֹנָי יֱהוִה הִנֵּה נַפְשִׁי
לֹא מְטֻמָּאָה וּנְבֵלָה וּטְרֵפָה לֹא־אָכַלְתִּי
מִנְּעוּרַי וְעַד־עַתָּה וְלֹא־בָא בְּפִי בְּשַׂר
טו פִּגּוּל: וַיֹּאמֶר אֵלַי רְאֵה

12. וְעֻגַת שְׂעֹרִים — *As barley cake.*

Metzudas David (following *Targum* — see *comm. v.* 9) explains that this loaf of bread was permitted in addition to the mixed cereal mentioned in *v.* 8. However, other commentators read our verse as referring to the food mentioned above and offer various explanations:

— *Rashi:* Prepared unappetizingly as one prepares a cake of barley. Not as one would prepare a cake of wheat *(Eruvin* 81a).

— *Radak:* Although a mixture of many cereals is difficult to eat, you should consider it as though it were made only of barley, which, while not as good as wheat, can nevertheless be eaten more readily than the mixture.

— *Eliezer of Beaugency:* The main ingredient in the mixture is to be barley.

This latter interpretation agrees with *Vayikra Rabbah* 28:6. The *Midrash* explains that barley was to be the main ingredient because of its laxative qualities, thus increasing the discomfort of the prophet.

Alternately, the *Midrash* suggests that barley is specified in order to stress that the little food available to them, was granted in the merit of the *Omer* sacrifice *(Lev.* 23:9-14) which was made of barley.

בְּגֶלְלֵי צֵאַת הָאָדָם — *Dung excreted by man.*

Of all the terrible requirements which were imposed upon the prophet, this was the only one from which he recoiled in horror (*v.* 14). *Harav Breuer* explains that this abhorrence goes beyond the natural disgust which anyone might have been expected to feel. Human excretion is symbolic of the physical, animal-like aspect of man's being; therefore the holiness of the Israelite camp and God's Presence among them were predicated upon the absence of such dung (*Deut.* 23:13-15). Its use in the preparation of Yechezkel's food was an eloquent statement of the depths to which Israel had sunk.

לְעֵינֵיהֶם — *In their sight.*

Through observing the prophet in every detail of his travail, the people would come to realize the seriousness of their plight.

13. טָמֵא — *Unclean.*

In a disgusting and unappetizing way [i.e. the word טָמֵא here refers not to ritual unsuitability, but to the unedible nature of the food] *(Rashi). Eliezer of Beaugency* suggests that ritually unclean food might be meant. In exile, the conquerors might expect their

IV 12-14

you drink: one sixth part of a hin, from one time to the other shall you drink. 12 *Now you shall eat it as barley cake, and you shall bake it with the dung excreted by man, in their sight.*

13 *HASHEM said: Thus will the children of Israel eat their food: unclean; among the nations, whither I will repulse them.*

14 *And I said: Woe my Lord HASHEM/ELOHIM! See, my soul has not been defiled, I have not eaten that which died by itself or was torn, from my youth until now, nor has loathsome meat come into my mouth.*

captives to transgress the laws of their religion.

14. נַפְשִׁי לֹא מְטֻמָּאָה וּנְבֵלָה וּטְרֵפָה לֹא אָכַלְתִּי ... וְלֹא בָא בְּפִי בְּשַׂר פִּגּוּל — *My soul has not been defiled, I have not eaten that which died by itself or was torn ... nor has loathsome meat come into my mouth.*

All the terms in this phrase have halachic significance: טֻמְאָה is a state of ritual uncleanliness; נְבֵלָה is an animal which died without שְׁחִיטָה, *ritual slaughter;* טְרֵפָה is an animal which was ritually slaughtered but had previously been 'torn' and rendered halachically unfit to eat; and פִּגּוּל is a sacrifice which was rendered unfit because the Kohen or the owner intended to perform some of the requirements after the halachically allotted time.

The problem arises, why Yechezkel found it necessary to stress that he had not eaten forbidden foods.[1]

The Sages *(Chullin* 37b) read into this passage the anguished cry of a man who had guarded his טַהֲרָה, *'his moral purity'* by meticulously avoiding any semblance of the forbidden even when no halachic sanctions existed. Thus: נַפְשִׁי לֹא מְטֻמָּאָה, I did not think provocative thoughts by day and thus did not have unclean emissions at night.

וּנְבֵלָה וּטְרֵפָה לֹא אָכַלְתִּי, I never ate meat from an animal which was ill before it was slaughtered.

בְּשַׂר פִּגּוּל, I have not eaten meat whose permissibility was in doubt even though a Sage ruled that it was indeed permitted.

15. Yechezkel's cry is answered. The ultimate degradation against which his soul had rebelled, would not be required of him.

Eliezer of Beaugency stays closer to the literal meaning of the verse but interprets the terms in a non-halachic

1. Although most commentators hold that Yechezkel came to Babylon among הֶחָרָשׁ וְהַמַּסְגֵּר, *'the carpenters and the locksmiths'* of Yehoyachin's exile (see *comm.* 1:2) there is an absence of conclusive proof for this thesis. It has been suggested that he may have been among the youths who were taken some years earlier (*Daniel* 1:3-4) to act as chamberlains in the court of the king. As we know from the story of Daniel, Chanania, Mishael, and Azariah *(ibid)* these youths were indeed exposed to severe pressure to eat non-kosher food *(Daniel* 1:8-16). It would then be natural for Yechezkel to stress that he had not succumbed to these pressures.

ד נָתַתִּי לְךָ אֶת־°צפועי הַבָּקָר תַּחַת °צְפִיעֵי ק׳
טז־יז גֶּלְלֵי הָאָדָם וְעָשִׂיתָ אֶת־לַחְמְךָ
טז עֲלֵיהֶם: וַיֹּאמֶר אֵלַי בֶּן־
אָדָם הִנְנִי שֹׁבֵר מַטֵּה־לֶחֶם בִּירוּשָׁלַ͏ִם
וְאָכְלוּ־לֶחֶם בְּמִשְׁקָל וּבִדְאָגָה וּמַיִם
יז בִּמְשׂוּרָה וּבְשִׁמָּמוֹן יִשְׁתּוּ: לְמַעַן יַחְסְרוּ
לֶחֶם וָמָיִם וְנָשַׁמּוּ אִישׁ וְאָחִיו וְנָמַקּוּ
ה א בַּעֲוֺנָם: וְאַתָּה בֶן־אָדָם קַח־לְךָ |
א חֶרֶב חַדָּה תַּעַר הַגַּלָּבִים תִּקָּחֶנָּה לָּךְ

sense. [He does not offer an explanation for נְבֵלָה וּטְרֵפָה לֹא אָכַלְתִּי].

נַפְשִׁי לֹא מְטֻמָּאָה, Yechezkel as befits a priest had been fastidious in his habits, and not eaten anything offensive to the aesthetic.

בְּשַׂר פִּגּוּל, meat which is three days old and therefore not palatable. [This explanation is based on the literal translation of *Lev.* 19:7. The *Halachah* interprets the Torah's interdiction differently (see *comm.* above).

16-17. These verses contain the explanation of the symbolic acts described above.

הִנְנִי שֹׁבֵר מַטֵּה לֶחֶם — *Behold I break the staff of bread.*

This phrase and וְנָמַקּוּ בַּעֲוֺנָם (*v.* 17) are taken from the תּוֹכָחָה, *the Admonition* recorded in *Lev.* 26. *Ramban (ibid.* 26:16) shows that the prophecies contained in the Admonition refer to the history of the destruction of the First Temple, while those contained in the Admonition of *Deut.* 28 foretell the events of the destruction of the Second Temple.

It is natural that Yechezkel would draw upon this Torah source to find the words which would convey a sense of urgency to his people.

[See Appendix citing *Rabbi David Zvi Hoffman's* list of expressions of blessing and curse drawn by Yechezkel from the admonition of *Lev.* 26.]

17. לְמַעַן — *For.*

This translation follows the standard commentators. It is a rare use of the word which is usually translated: *'in order that'.*

Harav Breuer takes its meaning in this way. Verses 16 and 17 refer to the two stages of the siege mentioned above (*v.* 9). *V.* 16 describes the first part of the siege during which food would still be available, albeit in small and measured quantities. This, however, would lead to the ultimate horror of the final stages [depicted in *v.* 17, and symbolized by the forty days during which Yechezkel would be denied even that meager diet — *comm.* above] when there would be no food available at all.

וְנָמַקּוּ בַּעֲוֺנָם — *And they will pine away in their sin.*

Rashi to *Lev.* 26:39 explains the root מקק as implying a 'melting away'. According to *Ibn Janach* and *Radak* its meaning is closer to 'rotting' or 'wasting away'.

IV 15-17

15 *He said to me: 'Look! I have permitted you the dung of cattle instead of the excrement of man. And you shall prepare your food upon them.'*

16 *Then He said to me: 'Ben Adam! Behold I break the staff of bread in Jerusalem, and they shall eat bread by weight and with dread, and water by measure and in desolation shall they drink;* 17 *for they will lack bread and water, and they will be desolate each man and his brother, and they will pine away in their sin.*

V 1

You, Ben Adam, take yourself a sharp sword; a barber's razor take yourself and pass it over your

V

1-4. The 'siege' of Jerusalem is complete, and the fate of its inhabitants is now to be depicted. In an act of shocking disfigurement and debasement *(Carlebach)* the prophet is told to shave his head and beard, and to use the hairs to symbolize in various ways what is to become of Jerusalem's people.

We have previously referred to the conflicting views of the major commentators as to whether all the symbolic acts demanded of the prophets were actually performed or whether they took place only in 'prophetic visions' (see *comm.* to 2:8 and *footnote* to 4:4).

In this case a new dimension is added to the problem in that shaving the beard with a razor is in violation of the law *(Lev.* 19:27). Although prophets were told to *refrain* from obeying certain commands of the Torah on occasion, [Yechezkel was forbidden to follow the customs of mourning upon the death of his wife (24:16-17), Jeremiah was not to take a wife and beget children (16:2), and was not to comfort a mourner or rejoice at a wedding *ibid.* 16:5-8], there is no other instance where God commanded a prophet to transgress Torah law.

The strongest proponent of the view that in general the symbolisms are to be taken literally, is *Abarbanel,* who, in unusually sharp terms, takes issue with *Rambam* and *Ibn Ezra* who hold that the command that *Hosea* take a *'wife of harlotry and children of harlotry' (Hosea* 1) happened only in a prophetic vision.

Nevertheless, even Abarbanel agrees that, because of the transgressions it would have involved, the command to Yechezkel to shave with a razor must be taken allegorically.

There are various approaches among the commentators to explain the choice of this particular act. *Radak,* because the Torah describes the use of the razor as הַשְׁחָתָה, *destroying completely (Lev.* 19:27), sees the act of shaving as a fitting symbol of the destruction to which the people were to be exposed.

Malbim, because shaving severs the connection between the hair and the body, surmises that it symbolizes the break that was to occur in the close relationship between God and Israel.

Harav Breuer, based on *Hirsch's* understanding of hair as an insulating force guarding the body against outside influences (*Lev.* 14:8), suggests that the

ה והעברת על־ראשך ועל־זקנך ולקחת
ב לך מאזני משקל וחלקתם: שלשית ב
באור תבעיר בתוך העיר כמלאת ימי
המצור ולקחת את־השלשית תכה
בחרב סביבותיה והשלשית תזרה לרוח

shaving might symbolize the exposure of Jerusalem to the surrounding armies.

[If we recall that the term Ben Adam, is treated as the incarnation of *Knesses Israel* in this book (see *Overview* p. xxxii) another possibility is suggested. Hairs and nails are impermanent, dispensable and replaceable parts of the body which are least basic to the health and well-being of the whole (see *Rabbi Zadok HaKohen, Yisroel Kedoshim* p. 15). Thus, in the 'body' of *Knesses Israel,* hair would symbolize the least significant and most dispensable part of the population. Taking Yechezkel, the man, as symbolic of *eternal Knesses Israel,* his hair would represent a single generation whose acts condemn it to the fates, which Yechezkel was to act out, but whose 'cutting off' would not impair the essential nature of *Knesses Israel.*

This symbolism would be entirely in consonance with the rest of the Book which stresses again and again that the *essential* closeness between God and His people could not be breached by the *incidental* sins and exile of one generation].

תער הגלבים — *A barber's razor.*

This expression does not recur in Scripture. Therefore, its exact meaning must be sought in its context. *Rashi* suggests either the razor of leather workers, or the razor of barbers. *Targum* in a number of places (some quoted in *Radak)* uses the root גלב to denote shaving. This would support *Rashi's* second interpretation.

1. חרב חדה תער הגלבים — *A sharp sword, a barber's razor.*

While most commentators explain תער הגלבים as explanatory of חרב חדה [i.e. *'sharp sword'* is to be understood as *'a barber's razor.'*] *Malbim* intensifies the gruesome symbolism by explaining that a *'sharp sword'* is here to be used *in place* of a *'barber's razor'* [i.e. the shaving is to be done with a sword (see *Rashi).*]

על ראשך ועל זקנך — *Over your head and beard.*

Malbim suggests that the hair of the head tends to disfigure a person when it is allowed to grow too long, while the beard lends dignity and beauty to the face. The former would symbolize the wicked people; the latter, the righteous ones. The lesson would be that both righteous and wicked people would be lost in the downfall of Jerusalem (see 9:6).

מאזני משקל — *A balance scale.*

It was to be Divine Providence (as symbolized by the scales) rather than chance, which would lead the population to their respective fates *(Harav Breuer).*

וחלקתם — *And divide them.*

Use the scales to weigh and divide the hair exactly, as specified in the next verse.

2. The symbolism contained in this verse is graphically detailed in *v.*12. The fire raging in the city is the plague and famine which will be rampant there; the sword stands for the slaughter to be wreaked upon its fleeing inhabitants, and the hairs which are to be thrown to the winds are the exiles who are destined to be scattered in all directions.

V
2

head and beard. And take yourself a balance scale
and divide them. 2 *A third shall you ignite in the fire*
in the city, upon completion of the days of the siege;
take a third and strike it with a sword around her;
and a third shall you scatter to the wind, and I will

(*Metzudas David* renders רוּחַ in *v.* 2 as *wind* and in *v.* 12 as *direction.)*

בָּאוּר תַּבְעִיר — *You shall ignite* [lit. *'burn'*] *in the fire.*

The raging, plague-induced fever which resulted from the terrible famine (see above).

Megillas Eichah describes in vivid detail the state of the city in those terrifying times. We quote from *Toldos Am Olam:* And bread was becoming steadily scarcer, and the city fell prey to famine, thirst and destitution. *'All her people were sighing searching for bread. They traded their treasures for food to keep alive' (Eichah* 1:11). *'The tongue of the suckling cleaves to its palate for thirst; young children beg for bread, no one extends it to them ... Those who feasted extravagantly lay destitute in the streets; those who were brought up in scarlet clothing wallow in garbage' (ibid.* 4:4-5).

And the daughters of Zion would meet and see each other in the streets. One would say to the other: 'Why have you come out into the street, you who, in your modesty, have never before come out into the street?' And she would answer her: 'Can I dissemble before you — the pangs of famine are too powerful for me; I cannot bear them.' And they would hold each other and go begging in the streets without finding support. And they would fall upon the pillars and die upon them. Concerning these does it say *'like corpses in the streets of the city (ibid.* 2:12).

בְּתוֹךְ הָעִיר — *In* [lit: — *in the midst of*] *the city.*

The 'city' engraved upon the brick (*Rashi* and other commentators).

כִּמְלֹאת יְמֵי הַמָּצוֹר — *Upon completion of* [lit. — *when ... are fulfilled*] *the days of the siege.*

Rashi and some commentators seem to take this as meaning the period after the 430 days of the 'siege' are completed. However, *Eliezer of Beaugency* places this action in the final forty days.

תַּכֶּה בַחֶרֶב — *Strike* [*it*] *with a sword.*

An idea of the slaughter which accompanied the fall of Jerusalem can be gleaned from the Talmud (*Gittin* 57b): Rabbi Joshua ben Karcha said: An old man of Jerusalem told me, in this valley Nebuzaradan the 'chief butcher' killed 211 myriads (2,110,000) and in Jerusalem he killed 94 myriads (940,000) on one stone.

סְבִיבוֹתֶיהָ — *around her,* i.e., around the city.

The word סְבִיבוֹתֶיהָ, *round about her,* implies a particular slaughter *outside* the city walls. *Rashi* explains that this refers to the people who were caught while fleeing the city. *Radak* reads in it a specific reference to King Zidkiyahu and his court who were captured by the Babylonians while attempting to escape through a cave under the walls of the city (*II Kings* 25:5-6).

וְהַשְּׁלִשִׁית תִּזְרֶה לָרוּחַ — *And a third part shall you scatter to the wind.*

This could be a general reference to all the exiles who would be scattered in many directions *(Metzudas David* and *Eliezer of Beaugency).*

However, the phrase, וְחֶרֶב אָרִיק אַחֲרֵיהֶם, *and I will unsheathe a sword*

ה
ג־ה

ג וְחֶרֶב אָרִיק אַחֲרֵיהֶם: וְלָקַחְתָּ מִשָּׁם
מְעַט בְּמִסְפָּר וְצַרְתָּ אוֹתָם בִּכְנָפֶיךָ:
ד וּמֵהֶם עוֹד תִּקָּח וְהִשְׁלַכְתָּ אוֹתָם אֶל־תּוֹךְ
הָאֵשׁ וְשָׂרַפְתָּ אֹתָם בָּאֵשׁ מִמֶּנּוּ תֵצֵא־
ה אֵשׁ אֶל־כָּל־בֵּית יִשְׂרָאֵל: כֹּה
אָמַר אֲדֹנָי יֱהוִה זֹאת יְרוּשָׁלַםִ בְּתוֹךְ
הַגּוֹיִם שַׂמְתִּיהָ וּסְבִיבוֹתֶיהָ אֲרָצוֹת:

after them, creates an association with the story of the pitiful remnant of Jews who had been allowed to remain in the Land of Israel after the exile; and who, against the direct advice of Jeremiah (*Jeremiah* 42-43), fled to Egypt after the assassination of Gedalya ben Achikom. Thinking that by fleeing they would escape the fury of *Nebuchadnezzar,* they, in their abject fear, did not hesitate to leave the Land in complete desolation. To them Jeremiah called out (*Jeremiah* Ch. 42:16): *'And the sword of which you are afraid; there in the land of Egypt will it overtake you!'*

Because of this association [although the actual formulation is taken from *Lev.* 26:33, see *Appendix*] *Rashi* and *Radak* see our verse as a reference to that episode.

3. וְלָקַחְתָּ מִשָּׁם — *Take from there.*

A relatively small number of the population will be favored with God's special love and protection. *Eliezer of Beaugency,* alone among the major commentators, understands this *'taking'* to happen before the final, third part of the people is to be scattered to the winds of exile. Thus, it refers to the few people who remained in the Land after the final captivity (*II Kings* 25:22). However, *Rashi, Radak,* and *Metzudas David* see it as a reference to the exiles who were taken to Babylon [rather than those who were scattered to the many neighboring countries — see *Jer.* 40:11] and who, under special Divine Providence and protection, were to form the nucleus of a revitalized nation that would flourish during the period of the Second Temple.

4. וּמֵהֶם עוֹד תִּקָּח — *Then take from them again.*

Even this tiny remnant will not go unscathed. Fire will take its toll from them also.

While *Rashi* and *Radak* see this as a reference to the two false prophets *Ahab* and *Zidkiyahu* who were burned by *Nebuchadnezzar (Jeremiah* 29:21-22), *Metzudas David* and *Eliezer of Beaugency* interpret the symbolism more broadly:

Rampaging fires were to be a constant in Jewish history. Whether in the form of the famine and plague which followed in the wake of Rome's victorious legions *(Metzudas David),* or of the fires and tortures which would be the lot of Jewish martyrs through centuries of suffering and oppression deriving from the corrosive, and destructive influence of the Nazarene and other divisive sects *(Eliezer of Beaugency).*

Either way, מִמֶּנּוּ, *from these historic events* onwards, fire would be the constant companion of the Jewish people along their road of history.

Rashi and *Radak,* seeing a less sweeping symbolism in this final act, [see above] render מִמֶּנּוּ, from the fire which Yechezkel was to kindle in the engraved

unsheathe a sword after them. [3] *Take from there a*
numbered few, and bind them in the ends of your
garment. [4] *Then take from them again. Throw them into the fire's midst and burn them in the fire. From it a fire will go forth to the entire Family of Israel.*
[5] *Thus says my Lord HASHEM/ELOHIM: This is Jerusalem! Among the nations have I placed her; and*

city. These flames would 'grow' into the consuming fire of Israel's fate.

5. זאת יְרוּשָׁלַיִם — *This is Jerusalem!*

God's cry of anguish. This caricature of a city, pounded by enemies without and famine within; this city, separated by an iron wall from its Father in Heaven (4:3); this is what has become of Jerusalem!

[Perhaps this particular expression זאת יְרוּשָׁלַיִם is God's answer to the derisive cry recorded in *Eichah* 2:15: *All who pass along the way clap hands at you; they hiss and wag their head at the daughter of Jerusalem: 'Could this be the city* (הֲזֹאת הָעִיר) *that was called perfect in Beauty, Joy of all the Earth?'.* God answers: 'Yes! (זאת יְרוּשָׁלַיִם) this is indeed what has happened to Jerusalem.'] [1]

Throughout the Book it is the degradation of Jerusalem which occupies the prophet. It was to be the repository of all that is meta-historical in Israel's experience — the city whose soul יְרוּשָׁלַיִם שֶׁל מַעֲלָה, *the higher, spiritual Jerusalem* could be glimpsed through its stones. It was to be the tangible fulfillment of its name's implication [*Bereishis Rabbah* 56:16 explains the name to be a combination of Abraham's insight: בְּהַר ה׳ יֵרָאֶה, *the mountain on which HASHEM becomes visible to His people (Bereishis* 22:14 and *Rashi)* [the numerical value of יְרוּ, 216 equals that of יֵרָאֶה] and שָׁלֵם, *the city of peace,* the manner in which it was perceived by Shem, son of Noah (*Bereishis* 14:18 and *Rashi).*] The city which God's Presence turns into a place of peace.

At the culmination of his prophecies, the final sentence in the Book, Yechezkel celebrates the ultimate restoration of Jerusalem to its rightful place: *And the name of the city from that day shall be:* ה׳ שָׁמָּה, *HASHEM is there.*

בְּתוֹךְ הַגּוֹיִם שַׂמְתִּיהָ וּסְבִיבוֹתֶיהָ אֲרָצוֹת — *Among the nations have I placed her; and lands are around her.*

Her baseness is all the more reprehensible since I placed her in the center of the inhabited earth under ideal political and climatic conditions *(Radak; Rashi* and *Metzudas David).*

However, Israel's central position also carries implications concerning her destiny. Both Isaiah (2:3) and Micah (4:2) see the אַחֲרִית הַיָּמִים, *the mil-*

1. *Vayikra Rabbah* 21:5 lists all those meritorious symbols which 'accompanied' the High Priest into the Holy of Holies on *Yom Kippur.* Based on the phrase *(Lev.* 16:3) בְּזֹאת יָבֹא אַהֲרֹן, *with* 'זאת' [i.e. things which are referred to as זאת, *'this'*] *shall Aaron come.* The *Midrash* goes on to list those things which Scripture introduces with the word זאת, *'this'.* Among them is Jerusalem, for our verse says, זאת יְרוּשָׁלַיִם. Thus, this expression is taken as one of love and endearment. Although, in context, it comes as the introductory phrase of a bitter denunciation of Jerusalem, the very sharpness of the structure is in itself a proof of the underlying love. See *Amos* 3:2: *Only you have I loved among all the families of the earth; therefore I will visit your sins upon you.*

ה
ו־ח

ו וַתֶּמֶר אֶת־מִשְׁפָּטַי לְרִשְׁעָה מִן־הַגּוֹיִם
וְאֶת־חֻקּוֹתַי מִן־הָאֲרָצוֹת אֲשֶׁר
סְבִיבוֹתֶיהָ כִּי בְמִשְׁפָּטַי מָאָסוּ וְחֻקּוֹתַי
ז לֹא־הָלְכוּ בָהֶם: לָכֵן כֹּה־
אָמַר | אֲדֹנָי יֱהוִֹה יַעַן הֲמָנְכֶם מִן־
הַגּוֹיִם אֲשֶׁר סְבִיבוֹתֵיכֶם בְּחֻקּוֹתַי לֹא
הֲלַכְתֶּם וְאֶת־מִשְׁפָּטַי לֹא עֲשִׂיתֶם
וְכְמִשְׁפְּטֵי הַגּוֹיִם אֲשֶׁר סְבִיבוֹתֵיכֶם לֹא
ח עֲשִׂיתֶם: לָכֵן כֹּה אָמַר אֲדֹנָי

lennium, as a time when the nations of the world will say: *'Come, let us go up to the mountain of HASHEM, to the House of Jacob's God, that He may teach us of His ways, that we may walk in His paths; for Torah emanates from Zion and the word of HASHEM from Jerusalem'.* All of them will see Jerusalem as the focus of their aspirations, and the source of their inspiration. This was God's purpose in placing Jerusalem among the nations *(Malbim);* and had Jerusalem chosen greatness instead of degradation it need not have waited until the millennium for its ultimate fulfillment *(Harav Breuer).*

All the more poignant then, is the remark of *Eliezer of Beaugency:* 'I have placed her among the nations — and she learned from their deeds'. Far from excercising her function as a light to the nations, she had allowed herself to be dragged down into the mire of their depravity.

6. וַתֶּמֶר אֶת מִשְׁפָּטַי — *But she exchanged My ordinances.*

While *Radak* renders וַתֶּמֶר as 'she rebelled' (from מרה), *Rashi* and *Metzudas David* identify it as a form of מור, *to exchange.*

[חֻקִּים are generally interpreted to be Divine laws for which no reason is given and which are beyond the realm of human comprehension. By use of the translation *decree,* we have attempted to convey this concept. *Hirsch* translates מִשְׁפָּטִים as *social laws,* a concept we follow by our translation *'ordinances.'* This implies laws that are necessary for the order and fair functioning of society.]

In Ch. 20 Yechezkel repeats several times the purpose of God's חֻקִּים and מִשְׁפָּטִים, *His decrees and ordinances: 'that man may perform them and live by them'. Targum* (ad. loc.) augments: 'live by them in eternal life'. Israel exchanged these life-giving laws for decadent practices, more virulent than those of the surrounding nations.

This translation would be in consonance with 16:34: *And 'the contrary' was in you from other women, in that you solicited harlotry and were not solicited; and in that you gave hire and no hire was given to you. And you were contrary!* (See *footnote* to 3:6-7).

Rashi suggests that special blame might attach to Israel who flouted the laws of the Torah, although they had originally accepted it. The nations are less at fault since they had never accepted the Torah.

7. לָכֵן — *Therefore.*

Again and again the לָכֵן is repeated (here and in *vs.* 8, 10, and 11) to bring

V
6-8

lands are around her. [6] *But she exchanged My ordinances for wickedness more than did the nations; and My decrees more than the lands around her; for My ordinances they spurned, and My decrees — they did not follow them.*

[7] *Therefore, thus says my Lord HASHEM/ELOHIM: Because you readied yourselves more than the nations around you; in My decrees you did not walk, and My ordinances you did not fulfill; even like the laws of the nations around you have you not done.*

[8] *Therefore thus says my Lord HASHEM/ELOHIM:*

home that the tragedies about to overtake them are not chance occurrences, but a direct result of their perfidy.

יַעַן הֲמָנְכֶם — *Because you readied yourselves,* i.e., *for degradation.*

The translation follows *Rashi* who traces this obscure word to the root ימן meaning *to prepare* (as in *Jonah* 2:1).

Radak and *Metzudas David* derive the word from the word הָמוֹן meaning *a multitude,* and render the verse thus: [Just because] I have *'multiplied you'* into a great nation, have you rebelled against Me. My very love for you has brought about your obduracy [i.e. My blessings for you have been so abundant that you have taken them for granted and forgotten their source]. An analogy is suggested from *Deut.* 32:15, *And Yeshurun became fat and kicked* [i.e. rebelled].

Yet a third alternative, that of *Menachem ben Saruk* quoted by *Rashi,* is that the expression belongs to the root המה, *tumult.* The meaning of the verse would then be: *Because you have acted more tumultuously than the nations ...*

Eliezer of Beaugency, in agreement with the derivation of *Radak,* renders: *Because your sins have been multitudinous ...*

Harav Breuer bases his interpretation on *Hirsch's* commentary to *Gen.* 17:5: כִּי אַב הֲמוֹן גּוֹיִם נְתַתִּיךָ, *for as a father of the swaying masses of nations have I appointed you. Hirsch* writes: Without Abraham's spirit the masses of the nations are a הָמוֹן a *confused, swaying throng,* no one knows their origin, no one knows their destiny. Their movement lacks direction and purpose. They are not צָבָא, *a multitude of people organized into a cohesive group around a central directing force for a common purpose,* but a הָמוֹן, a disorderly muddled mass. Abraham, because he brings a centralizing spirit to them, becomes their spiritual father.

At the inception of their nationhood, Israel was contrasted to the purposeless, directionless throng of the other nations. But in their degradation, Israel, which should have been the צְבָא ה׳, *the 'army' of HASHEM* had become even more directionless than the nations which surrounded them.

וּכְמִשְׁפְּטֵי הַגּוֹיִם אֲשֶׁר סְבִיבוֹתֵיכֶם לֹא עֲשִׂיתֶם — *Even like the laws of the nations around you have you not done.*

The nations were not disloyal to their duties, false though they be, but you have exchanged My Honor for worthlessness *(Rashi).*

The Talmud (*Sanhedrin* 39b) points to an apparent contradiction between our verse (And you *have not* [even]

ה יְהֹוִה הִנְנִי עָלַיִךְ גַּם־אָנִי וְעָשִׂיתִי
ט־י בְתוֹכֵךְ מִשְׁפָּטִים לְעֵינֵי הַגּוֹיִם׃
ט וְעָשִׂיתִי בָךְ אֵת אֲשֶׁר לֹא־עָשִׂיתִי וְאֵת
אֲשֶׁר־לֹא־אֶעֱשֶׂה כָמֹהוּ עוֹד יַעַן כָּל־
י תּוֹעֲבֹתָיִךְ׃ לָכֵן אָבוֹת יֹאכְלוּ
בָנִים בְּתוֹכֵךְ וּבָנִים יֹאכְלוּ אֲבוֹתָם
וְעָשִׂיתִי בָךְ שְׁפָטִים וְזֵרִיתִי אֶת־כָּל־

done etc.), and 11:12 which reads: *And you have done in accordance with the laws of the nations which are round about you.*

The answer is given: You *have* done like the worst among them [*Rashi:* As for example *Meisha* king of *Moab* who sacrificed his son to idols (*II Kings* 3:27)]; you *have not* done like the best among them [*Rashi:* As for example *Eglon* the king of *Moab* who gave honor to God by standing up at the mention of God's Name — *(Judges* 3:20)].

8. גַּם אָנִי — *I, too.*

You have dealt falsely against Me, so I will be against you *(Rashi).*

Da'as Soferim points out the similarity of the גַּם אָנִי, *I, too,* of our verse, with the constantly repeated אַף אָנִי and גַּם אָנִי in the 'Admonition' of *Lev.* 26 (see *Appendix*).

The 'Admonition' identifies Israel's unwillingness to keep the laws of the Torah with an abrogation of the בְּרִית, the *covenant,* between God and it (*ibid.* 26:15). When a covenant is broken by one party, neither side remains bound by its provisions. Hence as a result of Israel's betrayal of its trust, God will also be against them *(Sforno, Lev.* 26:16).

Various commentators read other connotations into the use of the אַף אָנִי in the passage in *Lev.*, all of them equally applicable to the גַּם אָנִי in our verse. *Ohr Hachayim* identifies the word אָנִי with God's Attribute of Mercy. The meaning of the passage would then be, that even God's mercy supports the strictures and curses contained in the 'Admonition' (see the discussion of the Tetragrammaton vocalized as Elohim in 2:4 where this concept is elaborated).

Sefer haBahir quoted by *Ramban* renders: My role will not be limited solely to passing judgment [i.e. while leaving its execution to an intermediary, such as God did in the case of Sancheriv, whose forces were smitten by an angel, but not directly by God]. I will involve myself in the actual punishment as well.

9. אֵת אֲשֶׁר לֹא עָשִׂיתִי וְאֵת אֲשֶׁר לֹא אֶעֱשֶׂה כָמֹהוּ עוֹד — *What I have never done and the like of which, I will nevermore do.*

Radak compares this to the expression in the 'Admonition' (*Deut.* 28:59) וְהִפְלָא ה׳ אֶת מַכֹּתְךָ, *HASHEM will make your suffering extraordinary* (lit. *'wondrous').*

Still, extraordinarily severe though these sufferings were, it seems unlikely that there were no tragedies to compare with them during the two millennia of bloodshed, massacre, pogrom and holocaust of our *galus* experience.

Da'as Sofrim suggests that the uniqueness of these 'judgments' lay not in their severity, but in the change they brought about in the national character of Israel.

Until the ultimate redemption, Israel

Behold, I too am against you, and I will execute judgment in your midst in the sight of the nations. [9] And I will do with you what I have never done, and the like of which I will nevermore do — because of all your abominations.

[10] Therefore, fathers shall eat sons in your midst, and sons will eat their fathers, and I shall execute judgments among you, and scatter your entire remnant in every direction.

would never again be the nation of God in its own land, with God's Temple in its midst — a potential 'light' unto the nations. Its history would unfold in quite different dimensions; almost always by the tolerance of conquering nations. Even its brief period of independence would be only a shadow of its former glory. Therefore, no future fall would be as painful as the one which ended the period of its greatest potential.[1]

10. וּבָנִים יֹאכְלוּ אֲבוֹתָם — *And sons will eat their fathers.*

Lev. 26:29 foretells the horror of parents cannibalizing their children in the unbearable pangs of their hunger. However, that chapter does not state explicitly that children would do the same to their parents. According to *Yalkut* and *Vilna Gaon,* it is indicated there only by a redundant word. Our verse is cited as conclusive proof (*Toras Kohanim* ad. loc.).

וְעָשִׂיתִי בָךְ שְׁפָטִים — *And I shall execute judgments among you.*

Eliezer of Beaugency explains this phrase as referring to the striking of the sword which was threatened in *v.* 2.

Thus, the three different fates which had been symbolized by Yechezkel's hairs (*v.* 2), are incorporated by our verse as follows:
Fathers shall eat sons (*v.* 10): *A third shall you ignite* (*v.* 2). [See *comm.* above, that this refers to the famine]. *I shall execute judgments* [i.e. the sword] (*v.* 10): *take a third and strike it with the sword* (*v.* 2). *I shall scatter all your entire remnant in every direction* (*v.* 10): *And a third shall you scatter to the wind* (*v.* 2).

This phrase is almost identical to that in *v.* 8: וְעָשִׂיתִי בְתוֹכֵךְ מִשְׁפָּטִים *I will execute judgments in your midst.* The inference would thus be that there, too, the reference is to the sword. This lends weight to the opinion of *Sforno* (quoted above) that גַּם אָנִי, *also I (in v.* 8), is used because the abrogation of the Covenant on the part of Israel cleared the way for God to execute reciprocal judgments against them. The *'sword'* is the instrument of such judgment as indicated by *Lev.* 26:25 which describes the *'sword'* which will come against them as: חֶרֶב נֹקֶמֶת נְקַם בְּרִית, *the avenging sword, vengeance of the covenant,* i.e. specifically identifying the sword as the instrument of God's vengeance for the abrogation of the Covenant (see below *v.* 17).

וְזֵרִיתִי אֶת כָּל שְׁאֵרִיתֵךְ — *And I shall scatter your entire remnant.*

1. An analogy to this is found in *Exodus* 34:10. After forgiveness had been attained for the sin of the Golden Calf, God says to Moses: *'Behold I make a covenant: in the presence of all your people I will do miracles, such as have not been done in all the world, nor in all the nations; all the people in whose midst you are, shall see the work of God, how awe-inspiring it*

יא שְׁאֵרִיתֵךְ לְכָל־רוּחַ: לָכֵן חַי־אָנִי נְאֻם
אֲדֹנָי יֱהֹוִה אִם־לֹא יַעַן אֶת־מִקְדָּשִׁי
טִמֵּאת בְּכָל־שִׁקּוּצַיִךְ וּבְכָל־תּוֹעֲבֹתָיִךְ
וְגַם־אֲנִי אֶגְרַע וְלֹא־תָחוֹס עֵינִי וְגַם־אֲנִי
יב לֹא אֶחְמוֹל: שְׁלִשִׁתַיִךְ בַּדֶּבֶר יָמוּתוּ
וּבָרָעָב יִכְלוּ בְתוֹכֵךְ וְהַשְּׁלִשִׁית בַּחֶרֶב
יִפְּלוּ סְבִיבוֹתָיִךְ וְהַשְּׁלִישִׁית לְכָל־רוּחַ
יג אֱזָרֶה וְחֶרֶב אָרִיק אַחֲרֵיהֶם: וְכָלָה אַפִּי
וַהֲנִחוֹתִי חֲמָתִי בָּם וְהִנֶּחָמְתִּי וְיָדְעוּ כִּי־

On *Lev.* 26:33: וְאֶתְכֶם אֱזָרֶה בַגּוֹיִם, *and I shall scatter you among the nations, Toras Kohanim* comments: 'This is a harsh judgment against Israel. For when people from one place are all exiled to the same location, they can see each other and find comfort. You, however, are different. I will scatter you among the nations like a man winnowing barley so that no kernel cleaves to another ...!'

11. חַי אָנִי ... אִם לֹא — *As I live ... surely* [lit. 'As I live ... if not'].

This is the typical form of a Hebrew oath. It has no parallel idiom in English.

אֶת מִקְדָּשִׁי טִמֵּאת בְּכָל שִׁקּוּצַיִךְ — *You have defiled My Sanctuary with all your detestations.*

This refers to the idol which King Menashe placed on the Temple grounds [*II Kings* 21:7] *(Radak).*

However, when we consider that the end of our verse: *And I will be pitiless as well* describes God's reaction to the pitiless child sacrifice which seems to have been rampant in Israel *(Metzudas David),* it is reasonable to assume that יַעַן אֶת מִקְדָּשִׁי טִמֵּאת is an echo of: לְמַעַן טַמֵּא אֶת־מִקְדָּשִׁי, *in order to defile My Sanctuary (Lev.* 20:3), where the expression refers to child sacrifice. *Rashi* (ad. loc.) explains that מִקְדָּשִׁי, *My Sanctuary,* does not refer to the Temple (which would not be defiled by child sacrifices brought outside its confines), but to *'Knesses Israel which is sanctified (or set aside) for Me'.* (For a detailed treatment of this concept see *comm.* to 20:26).

וְגַם אֲנִי אֶגְרַע — *Also I will diminish.*

Even as you diminished My Honor when you placed idols in My House, so I will diminish your honor, and you will be unworthy in the eyes of strangers and they will execute judgments against you *(Radak).*

Da'as Sofrim compares the word אֶגְרַע to מִגְעֶרֶת in *Deut.* 28:20. This word can be derived from the root גער, to *rebuke harshly* in which case our phrase would mean: 'I will rebuke

is, that I shall do with you'. Ramban (v. 9) points out that this cannot be interpreted as a promise of greater miracles in the future than had occurred in the past. There is no record of anything more miraculous than the Ten Plagues or the Splitting of the Sea. The promise of *'miracles such as have not been done in all the world'* refers to the revealed Presence of God *(Shechinah)* in their midst.

Just as the advent of this *Shechinah* is described as a greater miracle than any that had gone before it, so Its departure, in the form of the destruction of the Temple, is described by Yechezkel as a *'judgment'* the like of which will never recur.

V
11-13

11 *Therefore as I live, says my Lord* HASHEM/
ELOHIM: *Surely, because you have defiled My Sanctuary with all your detestations and all your abominations, also I will diminish you; My eye will not spare and I will be pitiless, as well.*
12 *One third of you shall die by the plague, and with famine will they be consumed in your midst; a third by the sword will fall around you; and a third will I scatter to every direction, and unsheathe a sword after them.*
13 *My anger will be spent, I will put My fury to rest against them and so find consolation. Then they*

harshly'. However as *Harav David Tzvi Hoffman* to *Deut.* demonstrates, מְגַעֶרֶת, by an interchange of letters can be derived from גרע, *to diminish.* It would then be the opposite of בְּרָכָה, *blessing.* Our phrase would then mean: *'And I also will diminish* [*your honor*] *(Radak).*

וְגַם אֲנִי לֹא אֶחְמוֹל — *And I will be pitiless as well.*

Even as you had no compassion for My Honor *(Radak).*

Metzudas David (see above) comments that Israel's lack of compassion expressed itself in the cruel practice of child sacrifice.

12. This verse spells out in detail the meaning of the symbolic acts described at the beginning of the chapter.

יִכְלוּ בְתוֹכֵךְ — *Will they be consumed in your midst* (lit. *'they will be finished').*

13. וְכָלָה אַפִּי וַהֲנִיחֹתִי חֲמָתִי בָּם וְהִנֶּחָמְתִּי — *My anger will be spent, I will put My fury to rest against them and so find consolation.*

Each of the key verbs in this phrase, כלה, נוח, and נחם, lend themselves to various interpretations, which can influence the entire tenor of the verse.

כלה — The basic meaning is related to כל, *complete.* Thus: *to complete or use up (Gen.* 21:15)· or *to attain a preordained purpose* [i.e. to attain completion] *(Gen.* 2:1 — *Hirsch);* or *to disappear* [i.e. to be gone completely] (Job 7:9).

נוח — This verb's basic meaning is *'to rest'.* In our verse, its construction is in the הִפְעִיל, the *causative.* Thus it can mean *to place* (37:1); or *to allow to come to rest (Deut.* 3:20).

נחם — This can mean *to comfort (Isaiah* 12:1); or *to change one's mind;* or *strike a new direction (Num.* 23:19) (see *Hirsch* to *Gen.* 5:30 and 6:6).

Thus the sentence can be rendered: 'And I will use up My anger (*Radak,* based on *Deut.* 32:23) and place My fury upon them *(Metzudas David),* and find comfort (for all the evil that they have done to Me)' *(Rashi).*

In this rendering the tone of the verse is one of unrelieved 'anger', in consonance with the entire passage.

However, the verse can also be seen as injecting a note of comfort, and is taken thus by *Harav Breuer.* He renders: 'And My anger will disappear, [in accordance with the tenor of comfort and appeasement which his rendering yields, we might also translate: And My anger will reach its preordained conclusion — see below on וְיָדְעוּ כִּי אֲנִי ה'] and I will allow My fury to come to rest — through having been directed against them, thus being able to strike a new

אֲנִי יהוה דִּבַּרְתִּי בְּקִנְאָתִי בְּכַלּוֹתִי חֲמָתִי
יד בָּם: וְאֶתְּנֵךְ לְחָרְבָּה וּלְחֶרְפָּה בַּגּוֹיִם
טו אֲשֶׁר סְבִיבוֹתָיִךְ לְעֵינֵי כָּל־עוֹבֵר: וְהָיְתָה
חֶרְפָּה וּגְדוּפָה מוּסָר וּמְשַׁמָּה לַגּוֹיִם
אֲשֶׁר סְבִיבוֹתָיִךְ בַּעֲשׂוֹתִי בָךְ שְׁפָטִים
בְּאַף וּבְחֵמָה וּבְתֹכְחוֹת חֵמָה אֲנִי יהוה
טז דִּבַּרְתִּי: בְּשַׁלְּחִי אֶת־חִצֵּי הָרָעָב הָרָעִים
בָּהֶם אֲשֶׁר הָיוּ לְמַשְׁחִית אֲשֶׁר־אֲשַׁלַּח
אוֹתָם לְשַׁחֶתְכֶם וְרָעָב אֹסֵף עֲלֵיכֶם
יז וְשָׁבַרְתִּי לָכֶם מַטֵּה־לָחֶם: וְשִׁלַּחְתִּי

direction [in My relationship to them.]' The implication is that even during the exercise of *'judgments'* God waits eagerly for the time when He will be able to lay aside that fury which is only a tool of correction in His hand.

וְיָדְעוּ כִּי אֲנִי ה׳ דִּבַּרְתִּי — *And they shall know that I, HASHEM, have spoken.*

Once the time comes when God can lay aside *'anger'* and *'fury'* as the means of revealing Himself to His people, they will realize that it was *HASHEM* — God in His all-encompassing mercy — Who had revealed Himself to them during the years of their exile and deprivation (see *comm.* to 2:4).

בְּקִנְאָתִי — *In My passion.*

Hirsch (Exod. 20:5) explains the root קנא to mean: to demand something as a matter of right, or to stand up in defense of one's own or someone else's rights which have been violated.

14-17. Twice more (vs. 15 and 17) is the refrain: אֲנִי ה׳ דִּבַּרְתִּי, *I HASHEM, have spoken,* taken up from *v.* 13; providing the *leitmotif* for the whole passage.

V. 13 which looks forward to the time when God's anger will have come to rest, proclaims: וְיָדְעוּ כִּי אֲנִי ה׳ דִּבַּרְתִּי, *they shall know ...,* because with hind sight, God's merciful Providence will be obvious to everyone. However, the prophet spells out that even while God's educating anger rages in all its fury, blinding its victims to anything but the experience of His uncompromising justice, it is nevertheless an emanation of Hashem, *the God of mercy.*

And thus, the displays of desolation and suffering in the very place where Jerusalem had flaunted its erstwhile pride and beauty — these scenes are not sterile punishments; they are instruments of תּוֹכָחָה and מוּסָר, of *rebuke* and *instruction,* and therefore of regeneration.

Because they are intended to be instruments of education and regeneration, the gruesome messengers of death will never destroy them completely. The *'arrows of famine'* which are sent against them, אֲשֶׁר הָיוּ לְמַשְׁחִית, *would,* (under normal circumstances) *have been for destruction.* Ordinarily they would surely have destroyed, but as *Deut.* 32:23 foretells: חִצַּי אֲכַלֶּה בָּם, *My arrows I will use up against them,* on which *Sifri* comments: My arrows will be used up, but they [Israel] will not be destroyed.

shall know that I, HASHEM, have spoken in My passion, when I spend My wrath upon them.

14 *And I shall make you into a desolation and a reproach among the nations that are around, in the sight of every passerby.* 15 *And she shall be a reproach and a taunt, an instruction and an astonishment to the nations that are around you; when I shall execute judgments on you in anger, fury, and with furious rebukes. I, HASHEM, have spoken.*

16 *When I dispatch upon them the evil arrows of famine, which should have caused destruction, which I shall send to destroy you, then I will increase famine upon you and I will break your staff of bread;*

Thus, not even in the moment when it fell to Yechezkel's lot to spell out in graphic and ghastly detail, the fate which would overtake Jerusalem, did he allow them to lose sight of the inviolability of their eternal relationship to God (based on *Harav Breuer).*

14. לְחָרְבָּה וּלְחֶרְפָּה — *A desolation and a reproach.*

Your Land will be *destroyed,* and this will cause you *embarrassment* in the presence of the nations whose lands will remain inhabited while yours is desolate *(Radak).*

15. גְּדוּפָה — *A taunt.*

Malbim here points out that the word is invariably used when an insult is directed against something holy. Thus, the word suggests the taunting of the nations directed against Israel's self image as a holy nation. (See 20:27, for a full analysis of the verb גדף).

מוּסָר — *Instruction.*

The translation follows *Radak* and most commentators. *Rashi* renders: *suffering.*

וּמְשַׁמָּה — *Astonishment.*

See *I Kings* 9:8.

16. *Harav Breuer* points out the accelerating severity of the famine. First the *'arrows of hunger'* then the *'hunger increased upon them',* until finally the *'staff of bread'* is completely broken.

אֲשֶׁר הָיוּ לְמַשְׁחִית — *Which should have caused destruction.* (lit. *'which were for destruction').*

Normally so severe a famine would have wiped out the entire nation. But Israel carries with it the guarantee of its ultimate survival and vindication, despite the horrors of its deprivation *(Harav Breuer).*

אֲשֶׁר אֲשַׁלַּח אוֹתָם לְשַׁחֶתְכֶם — *Which I shall send to destroy you.*

As explained above, the purpose of the famine was not to destroy Israel, hence the verse must be understood as expressing the viewpoint of the nations. They consider the purpose of this famine to be the destruction of Israel. In reality, however, Israel will outlive them *(Harav Breuer).*

ו עֲלֵיכֶם רָעָב וְחַיָּה רָעָה וְשִׁכְּלֻךְ וְדֶבֶר
א־ד וָדָם יַעֲבָר־בָּךְ וְחֶרֶב אָבִיא עָלַיִךְ אֲנִי
א יהוָה דִּבַּרְתִּי: וַיְהִי דְבַר־
ב יהוָה אֵלַי לֵאמֹר: בֶּן־אָדָם שִׂים פָּנֶיךָ
ג אֶל־הָרֵי יִשְׂרָאֵל וְהִנָּבֵא אֲלֵיהֶם: וְאָמַרְתָּ
הָרֵי יִשְׂרָאֵל שִׁמְעוּ דְּבַר־אֲדֹנָי יֱהוִה כֹּה־
אָמַר אֲדֹנָי יֱהוִה לֶהָרִים וְלַגְּבָעוֹת
וְלַגֵּאָיוֹת ק׳ לָאֲפִיקִים °ולגאות הִנְנִי אֲנִי מֵבִיא
ד עֲלֵיכֶם חֶרֶב וְאִבַּדְתִּי בָּמוֹתֵיכֶם: וְנָשַׁמּוּ

17. In this verse a fourth messenger of death is added to the three with which the chapter has dealt previously. The 'evil beasts' were not mentioned before. However, in 14:21, God speaks of the 'four evil judgments' which He sent against Jerusalem. They are: the sword; famine; evil beasts; and plague.

Concerning these four 'judgments' *Rabbi David Tzvi Hoffman* writes in *Lev.*: *'The sword of the enemy'* is the curse resulting from the abrogation of the Covenant (as seen in *Lev.* 26:25). Because of this Covenant, Israel was chosen from among the nations as סְגוּלַּת ה׳, *the special love of God*, whom its enemies cannot harm without being punished. If, however, Israel abrogates the Covenant, they will fall before the sword of the enemy.

Famine comes because of the desecration of the holiness of the Land which was given to them with the express understanding that they would hallow it. If they do not abide by this condition, the Land will not produce its fruits. (See *Avos* 5:8).

Evil beasts overpower man when he forgets his destiny and destroys the צֶלֶם אֱלקים, *'image of God'* which privileges him to rule over the beasts. (See *Rashi* to *Gen.* 1:28).

Finally, the *plague* enters the Land whose inhabitants rebel against God. Because of their disobedience to Him, they are punished by death just as Adam was punished. [See *Avos* 5:8,9 for a listing of sins which are punished by these same four judgments.]

VI

Ch. 5 dealt with the destruction of Jerusalem. Yechezkel's audience in Babylon would experience this only vicariously. By contrast גָּלוּת, *exile*, was the all pervasive reality of their existence. It is to the problem of *galus* that Ch. 6 addresses itself.

In Ch. 5 the repetition of the phrase: אֲנִי ה׳ דִּבַּרְתִּי taught the people that the horrors of famine, plague, sword, and explusion were to be understood as being מוּסָר, *an instruction*, and תּוֹכָחָה, *a rebuke*, paving the way to a נֶחָמָה, *a change of direction*, in God s relation to them (see above).

In Ch. 6 the refrain וִידַעְתֶּם כִּי אֲנִי ה׳, *and they shall know that I am* HASHEM, repeated four times (*vs.* 7,10,13,14) serves a similar purpose. Idolatry, with all its pernicious influence, had so saturated the Land that a complete liquidation of existing conditions had become necessary. Only from the fresh perspective made possible by exile would Israel be able to return to its true destiny — 'knowledge of God'.

V
17

17 *I shall send upon you famine and evil beasts that*
they should bereave you, plague and blood shall pass
among you; and the sword will I bring against you. I,
HASHEM, have spoken.

VI
1-4

And the word of HASHEM came to me saying:
2 *Ben Adam, set your face toward the mountains*
of Israel; and prophesy to them, 3 *and say: Moun-*
tains of Israel, hear the word of my Lord HASHEM/
ELOHIM. Thus says the Lord HASHEM/ELOHIM to
the mountains and to the hills, to the ravines and to
the valleys. Behold! I, even I will bring a sword upon
you and destroy your high places. 4 *Desolate shall*

2. שִׂים פָּנֶיךָ אֶל הָרֵי יִשְׂרָאֵל — *Set your face toward the mountains of Israel.*

The mountains (plural) of *Israel* not the mountain (singular) of *HASHEM*. The mountain of God, envisioned throughout Scripture as the focus of mankind's spiritual striving, was to be the source from which *'Torah'* and *'the word of HASHEM'* were to emanate, enabling the nations to walk the paths of God (*Isaiah* 2:3). Instead of this one center, with its single unambiguous message, Israel had chosen to convert its mountains, hills, ravines, and valleys, into so many small places of worship bringing about the inevitable erosion and adulteration of their spiritual orientation [see *footnote* to next verse] *(Harav Breuer).*

3. וְאִבַּדְתִּי בָּמוֹתֵיכֶם — *And I will destroy your 'high places'.*

The 'high places' [i.e. altars] which were erected for idol worship and which stood in all the places mentioned *(Metzudas David).* This interpretation of *Bamah* as an idolatrous altar is based on the similarity between our passage and *Lev.* 26:30-31, which employs the phrase וְהִשְׁמַדְתִּי אֶת בָּמֹתֵיכֶם, *and I will destroy your 'Bamos'*, with this meaning. Throughout the Pentateuch, *Bamah* is never used in any other sense. However, starting from *I Samuel* (9:12-25) we find the word used to describe places of worship where sacrifices were brought to Hashem, both when such sites were permitted, and also subsequently, after they became forbidden.[1]

Harav Breuer, favors the interpretation that *Bamos* in our verse, refers to those altars which were used for divine worship. The pernicious

1. A short survey of the *Halachah* and history of the *Bamah*, as a means of serving God, (rather than for the purpose of idol-worship), is in place.

Deut. 12:8-14 states the prohibition of sacrificial service anywhere other than in one central Sanctuary to be chosen by God. However, the passage indicates that there were times when such service would be acceptable anywhere. *Mishnah Zevachim* 112b traces the history of the *Bamah* in these words: Until the Tabernacle [in the desert] was erected, *Bamos* were permitted ... once the Tabernacle was erected *Bamos* were forbidden ... When they [Israel] came to *Gilgal, Bamos* were once more permitted ... when they came to *Shiloh* they [*Bamos*] were forbidden ... When they came to *Nov* and *Giv'on* they were once more permitted ... When

ו מִזְבְּחוֹתֵיכֶם וְנִשְׁבְּרוּ חַמָּנֵיכֶם וְהִפַּלְתִּי
ה־ו ה חַלְלֵיכֶם לִפְנֵי גִּלּוּלֵיכֶם׃ וְנָתַתִּי אֶת־פִּגְרֵי
בְּנֵי יִשְׂרָאֵל לִפְנֵי גִּלּוּלֵיהֶם וְזֵרִיתִי אֶת־
ו עַצְמוֹתֵיכֶם סְבִיבוֹת מִזְבְּחוֹתֵיכֶם׃ בְּכֹל

influence which these *Bamos* had on the spiritual orientation of the people is described in the *footnote.* It would be natural for God's avenging fury to be directed against them. When we consider the active form of the verb

they came to *Jerusalem* the *Bamos* were forbidden, never to be permitted again, for this was the נַחֲלָה, *the inheritance* [i.e. the single Sanctuary referred to in *Deut.* 12:9).

In short, when the central Sanctuary had a permanent nature (*Shiloh* and *Jerusalem*), *Bamos* were forbidden.

[The factor which determined the status of a Sanctuary was the presence of the *Ark* with the *Luchos, the Tablets of Stone.* In *Shiloh,* and *Jerusalem* they were in the Sanctuary; hence all *Bamos* were forbidden. In the other places of communal worship, such as *Nov* and *Giv'on,* the Ark was absent (see *Yerushalmi Megillah* 1:12) and *Bamos* were therefore permitted.]

Even after King Solomon built the Temple in Jerusalem, *Bamos* were still widely used for sacrifice, even during the reigns of righteous kings. The reason for this widespread flouting of the *halacha* is a matter of conjecture. It is possible that the people found it difficult to tear themselves away from a mode of worship that had been perfectly acceptable for many years *(Maharitz Chayos; Darkei Moshe);* or perhaps, *Jeroboam ben Nevat* cast doubt as to whether Solomon's Temple was indeed that final 'inheritance' which *Deut.* mentioned as the point at which *Bamos* would be finally and permanently outlawed. After all, Jerusalem was not identified by name in that passage *(ibid.).*

Whatever the explanation, *Bamos* flourished until the reign of *Chizkiyahu,* who banished them from the Land (*II Kings* 18:4).

Chizkiyahu's son Menashe introduced the most virulent forms of idol worship in Jerusalem. He also rebuilt the *Bamos* which Chizkiyahu had destroyed (*II Kings* 21:3). While in context it might be argued that these *Bamos* were erected for idol worship and thus did not have the nature of the *Bamos* under discussion, *Da'as Sofrim* (ad. loc.) suggests that they may have been designed for divine worship — which had been their purpose in the past — and that Menashe used them as an opening to pry the still-righteous people away from the central worship in Jerusalem.

In the major eradication of idol worship instigated by Yoshiyahu (*II Kings* 23:4-15) all traces of the idolatrous altars and images which Menashe had introduced were removed. However, as far as the *Bamos* are concerned, no destruction is mentioned. The term used is: טמא, *that Yoshiyahu made them unclean.* (ad. loc. *v.* 8 and *v.* 13). However the forbidden use of *Bamos* must certainly have stopped at that time.

No mention is made in *Kings* of a reintroduction of idol worship, or a return to the use of the *Bamos* between Yoshiyahu's death and the Babylonian conquest. However, from our chapter and various other references in Yechezkel (see particularly Chs. 8, 9, 17, and Ch. 20:29, 31 where the words עַד הַיּוֹם, *until this day* are used) it would seem that both idolatrous practices and the *Bamah* cult, had begun to proliferate once more.

Hirsch (Deut. 12:9) explains the underlying philosophy for the prohibition against *Bamah* service. Worship at the central Sanctuary, the repository of Torah, would always be defined and disciplined both through the Ark in the Holy of Holies, and in Torah's living embodiment, the *Sanhedrin,* which had its seat in the Temple courtyard. *Bamah* worship, which did not have the restraining influence of a 'Torah-presence' to guide it, would be an invitation to subjective individual caprice which could degenerate into a service that might come to exist side by side with idolatrous altars and images.

History bore out this fear. The degeneration of the spiritual orientation of Israel, which ultimately led to the destruction of Temple and Jerusalem, is constantly traced in the Book of Kings to the proliferation of the *Bamos* (see *comm.).*

your altars become and broken shall your sun-images become and I will cast down your corpses before your idols. 5 *I will set the carcasses of the Children of Israel before their idols and I will scatter your bones around your altars.* 6 *In all your habitations the cities*

וְאִבַּדְתִּי, *and I will destroy,* in our verse, as contrasted to the *passive* form of וְנָשַׁמּוּ, *and they shall become desolate,* and וְנִשְׁבְּרוּ, *and they shall be broken,* in the next verse, the meaning appears as follows. God will 'destroy' the *Bamos.* Without the supportive base of this seemingly legitimate expression of worship, the truly idolatrous altars and images would erode and disappear of themselves.

4. חַמָּנֵיכֶם — *Your sun-images.*

Certain idol-images, placed on the roofs, to the sun *(Rashi);* for they served the sun *(Metzudas David).*

It must not be supposed that the sun was ever looked upon as an independent deity. *Halevi (Doros haRishonim, Tekufas haMikra* Ch. 7) proves conclusively that the service to the מְלֶאכֶת שָׁמַיִם, *the heavenly rulership,* was prompted by the thought that these heavenly bodies were delegated by the true God, to grant or withhold favors — but always in a subservient role. This is borne out by *Toras Kohanim, Lev.* 26:30, which identifies חַמָּנִים as *magicians.* They used to track the heavenly bodies to ascertain the positions at which it would be propitious to extract favors from them *(Malbim).*

וְהִפַּלְתִּי חַלְלֵיכֶם לִפְנֵי גִּלּוּלֵיכֶם — *And I shall cast down your corpses before your idols* [lit. *'dung'*].

A reference to *Lev.* 26:30: *'And I shall set your carcasses on the carcasses of your idols'. Rashbam* and *Ibn Ezra* (ad. loc.) explain that the people would be killed while worshiping in the houses of idolatry.[1]

The word גָּלָל, *dung,* is a derisive term for idols which is intended to graphically portray their spiritual filth. [See *comm.* to 20:7 for an elaboration].

5. וְנָתַתִּי אֶת פִּגְרֵי בְּנֵי יִשְׂרָאֵל לִפְנֵי גִּלּוּלֵיהֶם — *And I will set the carcasses of the Children of Israel before their idols.*

In death they cease to be חַלְלֵיכֶם, *your corpses* [i.e. those whose allegiance belonged to the mountains of Israel, who stand 'accused' in this chapter] but those of the *Children of Israel.* Once the fatal bonds to the idols are cut loose, atonement is achieved and the love of God is regained *(Harav Breuer).*

Metzudas David does away with the apparent redundancy of this sentence by explaining not only will the people be killed in front of their idols (וְהִפַּלְתִּי,

1. The Talmud (*Sanhedrin* 63b) uses this verse to illustrate how deeply the people became attached to idol worship: Eliyahu, the Righteous One, was searching out the people dying of famine in Jerusalem. Once he found a child bloated with hunger, lying in a dung heap. He asked him: 'To which family do you belong?'

He said to him: 'Such and such a one.'

He asked him: 'Is anyone left from this family?'

He answered him: 'There are none besides me'.

He asked him: 'If I were to teach you one thing by which you could live, would you learn it?'

He said to him: 'Yes'.

He said to him: 'Say every day: "Hear O Israel, HASHEM our God, HASHEM is one".'

The child said to him: 'Far be it from me to mention the name of Hashem, which my parents did not teach me.' Immediately he took his idol out of his bosom, embraced it and kissed it. Then his abdomen split open and his idol fell upon the ground, and he fell on top of it, in accordance with the verse which reads: *And I shall set your carcasses upon the carcasses of your idols.*

מוֹשְׁבוֹתֵיכֶם הֶעָרִים תֶּחֱרַבְנָה וְהַבָּמוֹת
תִּישָׁמְנָה לְמַעַן יֶחֶרְבוּ וְיֶאְשְׁמוּ
מִזְבְּחוֹתֵיכֶם וְנִשְׁבְּרוּ וְנִשְׁבְּתוּ גִּלּוּלֵיכֶם
ז וְנִגְדְּעוּ חַמָּנֵיכֶם וְנִמְחוּ מַעֲשֵׂיכֶם: וְנָפַל
חָלָל בְּתוֹכְכֶם וִידַעְתֶּם כִּי־אֲנִי יהוה:
ח וְהוֹתַרְתִּי בִּהְיוֹת לָכֶם פְּלִיטֵי חֶרֶב בַּגּוֹיִם
ט בְּהִזָּרוֹתֵיכֶם בָּאֲרָצוֹת: וְזָכְרוּ פְלִיטֵיכֶם
אוֹתִי בַּגּוֹיִם אֲשֶׁר נִשְׁבּוּ־שָׁם אֲשֶׁר
נִשְׁבַּרְתִּי אֶת־לִבָּם הַזּוֹנֶה אֲשֶׁר־סָר מֵעָלַי

v. 4) but they will remain there, unburied.

6. *Verse.* 6 bears out *Harav Breuer's* understanding of *vs.* 3 and 4 (see *comm.).* Once the *Bamos* are laid desolate, the destruction of the idolatrous altars, idols, and sun-images follows automatically. This is the simple implication of the word לְמַעַן. As *Metzudas David* explains: The destruction will be so great, incorporating whole cities, *in order that* all the altars etc. will be wiped out.

וְיֶאְשְׁמוּ מִזְבְּחוֹתֵיכֶם — *your altars may be desolated.*

The translation follows *Targum, Radak,* and *Metzudas David.* It does not however account for the added א, which is not found in the root שמם, *desolate. Rashi* renders: Your altars will become recognized in their *sinfulness* (אָשָׁם, *sin).*

וְנִמְחוּ מַעֲשֵׂיכֶם — *And your deeds [be] erased.*

Once the idols and images are destroyed, it will be obvious that they were never more than *'your deeds'.* No power or holiness ever attached to them *(Harav Breuer).*

7. וִידַעְתֶּם כִּי אֲנִי ה׳ — *And so you shall know that I am HASHEM.*

This phrase is the key to the entire chapter [see *Prefatory Remarks*]. Once every reminder of the idolatrous cult will have been wiped out, Israel will once more find its way back to the truth which had become hidden and distorted in their minds under the weight of the alien culture which had permeated their land. With the slate wiped clean, and from the perspective of exile (*v.* 8) this knowledge of God (*v.* 10) will once more be revitalized (based on *Harav Breuer).*

8-9. וְהוֹתַרְתִּי ... פְּלִיטֵי חֶרֶב ... פְּלִיטֵיכֶם — *But I shall leave remnants ... some who escape the sword ... your survivors.*

With superb pedagogical insight, the prophet had painted the pictures of the awesome destruction which was to overtake Jerusalem, in the familiar phrases of the *Tochachah* in *Leviticus* 26 [see Appendix IV] *(Harav Breuer).* It was necessary to make the people understand that the tragedies which had overtaken them, did not result from some capricious political and military happenstance, but were the considered and necessary fulfillment of the prophecy which they had carried in their national conscience from even before they had entered the land.[1]

In Ch. 20, we find the Elders of Israel arguing that the reality of exile had relieved them of the need to keep the Torah (see *comm.* to 20:1). This was based on an erroneous conception of the nature of exile.

VI
7-9

will be destroyed and the high places made desolate so that your altars may be destroyed and desolated, your idols may be broken and terminated, your sun-images cut down, and your deeds be erased. 7 *And the corpses will fall in your midst and so you shall know that I am HASHEM.* 8 *But I shall leave remnants that you shall have some that escape the sword among the nations when you are scattered among the lands.* 9 *So your survivors will remember Me among the nations where they were taken captive, how I was anguished by their straying heart which turned away*

Yechezkel leads them through the highlights of their history and shows them how, from the very beginning, exile had been predetermined as an indispensible tool in their evolution towards the realization of their destiny. (*Comm.* ad. loc. *v.* 32).

The choice of words in this and the foregoing chapters, has the same purpose.

As our chapter turns to the verses of comfort, where exile is depicted as the opportunity for repentance and regeneration, the same range of associations is aroused by the thrice reiterated concept of the 'remnant' ('I will leave over', 'those that escape' etc.).

Alive in their minds from the days of Isaiah was the idea of the pure, repentant remnant — the indestructible 'trunk' of the tree of Israel which will stand replete with holy seed even after it had been denuded of its leaves (*Isaiah* 6:13). Isaiah had called his own son שְׁאָר יָשׁוּב, *'The remnant shall return'* (*ibid.* 7:3) to symbolize that שְׁאָר — that 'remnant' which would one day find its way back to the Mighty God (*ibid.* 10:21).

But already eight hundred years earlier (*Lev.* 26:39-41) it was the 'נִשְׁאָרִים', *the remnant,* who, while pining away in the lands of their enemies (*v.* 39), would reach a stage at which *'their unyielding heart will bow itself, and they will satisfy the debt of their iniquity'* (*v.* 41), thus fulfilling the purpose of their dispersion (*Ibn Ezra v.* 41).

9. אֲשֶׁר נִשְׁבַּרְתִּי —*How I was anguished* [lit. *'how I was broken*]. The translation follows *Metzudas Zion.*

1. *Yitzchak Breuer (Der Neue Kusari)* demonstrates how the unmatched historical miracle of Israel's survival in exile is foretold in the passage in *Lev.* It would be *their* Land which lies desolate in *their* absence, *their* cities which would remain in ruin (*v.* 33). Eagerly longing for their return, the Land would reject any attempts by Israel's enemies to settle it (*v.* 32); and they would ever remain uniquely 'Israel' while in the land of their 'enemies' (*vs.* 36,38,41,44). No total assimilation would ever make it possible for them to fuse into their surroundings, thereby losing their identity; no historical evolution would ever sever the ties between people and country.

Surely, these associations would find an echo in the hearts of Yechezkel's listeners. Perhaps they were familiar with Yirmiyahu's prophecy (*Jeremiah* 31:34-35) that just as surely as God's iron laws of nature forced sun, moon, and stars into their unchanging courses, so Israel's essential nature as *'a nation before Me'* was an immutable law of world history *'all the days'* (*v.* 35) — including their years in exile (*Yitzchak Breuer, Moriah*). And they would find comfort in the knowledge that the horrendous contemporary realities which were about to overtake them, far from implying rejection by God, were in fact the concomitant and inevitable result of the eternal Covenant forged so many years ago at Sinai (*Lev.* 26:46).

וְאֵת עֵינֵיהֶם הַזֹּנוֹת אַחֲרֵי גִּלּוּלֵיהֶם
וְנָקֹטּוּ בִּפְנֵיהֶם אֶל־הָרָעוֹת אֲשֶׁר עָשׂוּ
י לְכֹל תּוֹעֲבֹתֵיהֶם׃ וְיָדְעוּ כִּי־אֲנִי יְהוָה לֹא
אֶל־חִנָּם דִּבַּרְתִּי לַעֲשׂוֹת לָהֶם הָרָעָה
יא הַזֹּאת׃ כֹּה־אָמַר אֲדֹנָי יֱהוִה
הַכֵּה בְכַפְּךָ וּרְקַע בְּרַגְלְךָ וֶאֱמָר־אָח אֶל
כָּל־תּוֹעֲבוֹת רָעוֹת בֵּית יִשְׂרָאֵל אֲשֶׁר
יב בַּחֶרֶב בָּרָעָב וּבַדֶּבֶר יִפֹּלוּ׃ הָרָחוֹק בַּדֶּבֶר
יָמוּת וְהַקָּרוֹב בַּחֶרֶב יִפּוֹל וְהַנִּשְׁאָר
וְהַנָּצוּר בָּרָעָב יָמוּת וְכִלֵּיתִי חֲמָתִי בָּם׃
יג וִידַעְתֶּם כִּי־אֲנִי יְהוָה בִּהְיוֹת חַלְלֵיהֶם
בְּתוֹךְ גִּלּוּלֵיהֶם סְבִיבוֹת מִזְבְּחוֹתֵיהֶם אֶל
כָּל־גִּבְעָה רָמָה בְּכֹל | רָאשֵׁי הֶהָרִים
וְתַחַת כָּל־עֵץ רַעֲנָן וְתַחַת כָּל־אֵלָה
עֲבֻתָּה מְקוֹם אֲשֶׁר נָתְנוּ־שָׁם רֵיחַ נִיחֹחַ
יד לְכֹל גִּלּוּלֵיהֶם׃ וְנָטִיתִי אֶת־יָדִי עֲלֵיהֶם
וְנָתַתִּי אֶת־הָאָרֶץ שְׁמָמָה וּמְשַׁמָּה

וְנָקֹטּוּ בִּפְנֵיהֶם — *And they shall consider themselves loathsome.*

This form of the root קוט is found only in *Ezekiel. Rashi* derives it from קטט, *quarreling.* Thus: You shall quarrel with yourselves [i.e. regret your former actions]. *Targum* uses דנק with which he also renders נֶאֱנָחִים, *the ones who sob* (9:4) and הֵאָנֵק, *sigh* (24:17). Thus: sob to yourselves. *Radak* interprets as 'cutting off'. Thus: consider yourselves worthy of being cut off. *Ibn Ezra (Ps.* 95:10) translates אָקוּט בְּדוֹר as *'I was disgusted with* . . . understanding the root as similar to קוץ, *to be disgusted.*

We translate 'loathsome' in which most of these meanings seem indicated.

10. לֹא אֶל חִנָּם דִּבַּרְתִּי — *Not in vain have I spoken.*

What I have spoken will come about *(Radak).* It is not without cause but a direct result of your actions *(Metzudas David).*

In the context of the foregoing, it could be suggested that since the exile and destruction will have stimulated them to shame and repentance, their suffering will not have been in vain *(Harav Breuer).*

11. הַכֵּה בְכַפְּךָ וּרְקַע בְּרַגְלְךָ — *Pound with your hand and stamp with your foot.*

Signs of distress and mourning (*Rashi* and *Metzudas David). Eliezer of*

from Me and by their eyes which strayed after their
idols. Then they shall consider themselves loathsome
for the evils they did in all their abominations.
10 *Then shall they know that I am* HASHEM, *not in*
vain have I spoken to do to them this evil thing.
11 *Thus says my Lord* HASHEM/ELOHIM: *Pound with*
your hand and stamp with your foot and say, Alas!
because of all the evil abominations of the Family of
Israel who will fall by the sword, by famine, and by
plague. 12 *He who is afar will die by the plague and he*
who is near will fall by the sword, he that remains
and is besieged will die by famine; and I shall spend
My fury upon them. 13 *And you shall know that I am*
HASHEM *when their corpses will be among their idols*
surrounding their altars; on every high hill in all the
mountaintops and under every green tree and under
every thick terebinth — the place where they gave the
savor of satisfaction to all their idols. 14 *And I shall*
stretch out My hand over them and lay the Land
waste and desolate from the wilderness of Diblah

Beaugency comments that these outward signs would help to impress the seriousness of the message upon the people. [Perhaps, the listeners would be more likely to accept the prophet's harsh predictions, when they see how distressed he himself is by them].

The same actions (i.e. pounding of the hands and stamping of the feet) are used in 25:6, to denote rejoicing. While it may be that these actions can be interpreted only in the context of the circumstances that cause them, [that is that they can be stimulated either by joy or by distress, depending on the circumstances] *Harav Breuer* suggests that they may have had a dual function: Overtly they were surely signs of mourning for the terrible catastrophe that was to overtake his people. However, underlying them was a sense of jubilation that in the harshness of the punishment lay the seed of repentance and rejuvenation (compare *Isaiah* 12:1).

12. וְכִלֵּיתִי חֲמָתִי בָּם — *And I shall spend my fury upon them.*

See 5:13 and *comm.*

13. עֲבֻתָּה — *Thick* i.e., with thick foliage, following *Rashi.*

14. שְׁמָמָה וּמְשַׁמָּה — *Waste and desolate.*

The translation follows *Radak. Rashi* and *Metzudas David* render מְשַׁמָּה, *surprising.*

ז מִמִּדְבַּר דִּבְלָתָה בְּכֹל מוֹשְׁבוֹתֵיהֶם וְיָדְעוּ
א־ג א כִּי־אֲנִי יהוה: וַיְהִי דְבַר־יהוה
ב אֵלַי לֵאמֹר: וְאַתָּה בֶן־אָדָם כֹּה־אָמַר
אֲדֹנָי יֱהֹוִה לְאַדְמַת יִשְׂרָאֵל קֵץ בָּא הַקֵּץ
אַרְבַּע ק׳ ג עַל־°ארבעת כַּנְפוֹת הָאָרֶץ: עַתָּה הַקֵּץ

מִמִּדְבַּר דִּבְלָתָה — *from the wilderness of Diblah.*

Radak suggests that the letter *'daleth'* in דִּבְלָתָה might be a substitution for a *'resh'*. The place would then be identical with רִבְלָה where Nebuchadnezzar was encamped and where Zidkiyahu was blinded and his sons slain (*II Kings* 25:6). The destruction could thus be said to have started from there.

וְיָדְעוּ כִּי אֲנִי ה׳ — *So shall they know that I am HASHEM.*

The prophecy had come to Yechezkel with the Name HASHEM/ELOHIM (*v.*11) (the Tetragrammaton, vocalized to read *Elohim* — i.e. mercy clothed in justice [see *comm.* to 2:4]). The immediate experience of what was to come, would be felt as a manifestation of God's stern and uncompromising justice. The first phrase in this verse וְנָטִיתִי אֶת יָדִי, *And I will stretch out My hand,* casts God in the role of the executor of Jerusalem's fate. However, the end result would be that from the ruins of a ravaged land would arise a new and purer knowledge of the God of mercy.[That is the meaning of the phrase that: *So shall they know that I am HASHEM.*]

VII

In this chapter we learn something new concerning the causes of Jerusalem's destruction. It is not only God, Who in His *anger* and *fury* (*vs.* 3 and 8) will *judge* and *punish* (*vs.* 3,4,8 and 9). It is the people who by their actions become their own executioners; their *'violence'* turns into a *'punishing rod'*, (*v.* 11) which will smite everything in its path.

When the קֵץ, *the end* will come upon them, it will be recognized as a הַקָּצָה, an *'awakening'* (*v.* 6). The people will realize that their wickedness brought about conditions which contained within them the seeds of destruction. Jerusalem would fall to the enemy even without God's active intervention; the city's destruction requires nothing more than a *'turning away of God's face'* (*v.* 22), a removal of His divine protection, for the flood-gates to be opened.

God intervened on the side of Israel's enemies, not because it was necessary, but as an outgrowth of Israel's perfidy in abrogating their covenant with Him. (See *comm.* to 5:8 with particular attention to the view of *Sefer haBahir* as quoted by *Ramban; Toras Kohanim* to *Lev.* 26:16). If He had not done so, they still would have been lost. Having become untrue to God, the people lost His protection; thus their downfall was inevitable.

It is a constantly recurring theme in Scriptures that whereas God tends the acts of the righteous, and nurtures them to full fruition, the wickedness of the wicked contains the seeds of their own erosion and destruction, results that come about without direct intervention from God.

Ps. 1:6 states: כִּי יוֹדֵעַ ה׳ דֶּרֶךְ צַדִּיקִים וְדֶרֶךְ רְשָׁעִים תֹּאבֵד, *For HASHEM recognizes the way of the righteous, while the way of the wicked is doomed,* i.e. it is the *'way'* of the wicked which leads to doom [in and of itself]. (See *Hirsch* ad loc.). Other instances can be found in: *Ps.* 31:18-21; 34:20,22; 37:17,38-40; and *I Samuel* 2:9.

Israel had related to God בְּקֶרִי, *casually (Lev.* 26:21, 23, 27, 40), ascribing the gathering clouds of threatening misfortune to natural causes growing out of the political and military realities of the time *(Rambam, Hilchas Ta'anis* 1:3).

[Although *Ibn Ezra* (ad loc.) suggests that קֶרִי might mean strength or arrogance, we follow *Rambam's* view, shared by most commentators (including *Ibn Ezra* in his second rendering),

throughout all their habitations. So shall they know that I am HASHEM.

The word of HASHEM, came to me, saying:
2 As for you Ben Adam, thus says my Lord
HASHEM/ELOHIM: 'To the soil of Israel, an end!
The end has come upon the four corners of the earth.

that it is related to the word מִקְרֶה, *a chance occurrence.* This is borne out by *Toras Kohanim* which reads: אַתֶּם עֲשִׂיתֶם אֶת דִּינַי עֲרָאִי בָּעוֹלָם אַף אֲנִי אֶעֱשֶׂה אֶתְכֶם עֲרָאִי בָּעוֹלָם, You have considered My judgments to be 'casual' (i.e. undirected, chance occurrences), (therefore) I, too, will make (your fate) 'casual' i.e. I will abandon you to the vagaries of an undirected historical process. See *Hirsch* to *Lev.* 26:23,24.]

Because of this attitude they had forfeited their expectations of a special protective Providence: God would 'walk with them' בְּקֶרִי *(ibid.* 24,28).

A small, relatively weak, strategically important nation, unprotected by God's shielding hand, would quite naturally fall prey to the overwhelming strength of Nebuchadnezzar's mighty forces. When Jerusalem falls, the people will 'awaken' to the loss which they had long since sustained when they chose to turn away from God.

2. לְאַדְמַת יִשְׂרָאֵל קֵץ בָּא הַקֵּץ עַל אַרְבַּע כַּנְפוֹת הָאָרֶץ — *To the soil of Israel an end! The end has come upon the four corners of the earth.*

The word קֵץ, *an end,* from the root קצץ (repeated five times in *vs.* 2, 3, and 6) is used in order that the similarity between it and הֵקִיץ, *to awake,* from the root קוץ or יקץ, should create an association with the idea of an 'awakening'. (See *Pref. Remarks* and *comm. v.* 6).

Such a patterned use of words with similar sounds (לָשׁוֹן נוֹפֵל עַל לָשׁוֹן, see *Rashi, Gen.* 3:15 and *Num.* 21:8 and 9) is common in Scriptures. *Ibn Ezra (Gen.* 3:1) and *Ramban (Exod.* 3:2) regard it as צַחוּת הַלָּשׁוֹן, a *splendor* or *beautification* of the language.[1]

Our translation follows the cantillation which includes the words לְאַדְמַת יִשְׂרָאֵל, *to the soil of Israel,* as part of the message to the people, i.e., an end is coming to the Land. An alternative would have been to interpret the phrase as a salutation, i.e., that the message was addressed to the אַדְמַת יִשְׂרָאֵל [parallel to the הָרֵי יִשְׂרָאֵל of Ch. 6], telling the Land that קֵץ בָּא, an end was at hand.

In contrast to קֵץ *end,* (without the definite article) in the first part of the sentence, the הַקֵּץ, *'the* end' of the second part, implies a specific, known 'end'. The verses, *When you shall beget children and children's children and you will have become old* [וְנוֹשַׁנְתֶּם] *in the Land and will practice depravity and*

1. A word is in place concerning the use of tools of rhetoric in Scriptures, particularly as it applies to those parts which are written in poetic form. (Our chapter is at the very least a prose-poem, i.e. there is a certain regularity of rhythm [see particularly *vs.* 6 and 10] and a patterned structure [a constant repetition of certain words: קֵץ (2,3,6); בָּא (2,5,6,7,10,12); תּוֹעֵבָה, דֶּרֶךְ, שָׁפַט, נָתַן (3,8); חוּס, חָמַל (4,9); צְפִירָה (7,10); אַף (3,8); עַתָּה (3,8); הָמוֹן (11,12,13); and conspicuous use of paronomasia (לָשׁוֹן נוֹפֵל עַל לָשׁוֹן), such as מֵהֶם, מֵהֲמוֹנָם, מֵהֱמֵהֶם in *v.* 11, and תָּקְעוּ בַתָּקוֹעַ, in v.14] which differentiates it from the patterns of everyday speech. That Yechezkel was viewed as a poet by many of his listeners is evident from a number of passages in the book, particularly 33:32: *And you are to them as a love song of one who has a pleasant voice and can play well on an instrument, so they hear your words but do not do them.*

Maharal (Nesivos Olam, Nesiv Ha'avodah 12) ascribes the use of שִׁירָה *(poetic form)* in the description of events, to a reaction to the profundity of the event. The more moving or signifi-

ז עָלַיִךְ וְשִׁלַּחְתִּי אַפִּי בָךְ וּשְׁפַטְתִּיךְ
ג כִּדְרָכָיִךְ וְנָתַתִּי עָלַיִךְ אֵת כָּל־תּוֹעֲבוֹתָיִךְ׃

make an image, the representation of anything at all, and will do that which is evil in the eyes of HASHEM your God, to provoke him to anger. I call heaven and earth to witness against you this day that you will be lost, quickly lost, from the Land to which you cross the Jordan to take it into possession (Deut. 4:25-26) are interpreted by the Sages *(Sanhedrin* 38a) as alluding to the exile which would take place 852 (the numerical value of וְנוֹשַׁנְתֶּם) years after the arrival of Israel into the Land. *Rashi* interprets the definite article in our verse, to refer to that particular, predetermined 'end'.[1]

In *Rashi*'s view (concurred with by *Metzudas David)* the *'four corners of the earth'* in the last part of the sentence, also refer to *Eretz Yisrael.* It is an amplification of the earlier statement that an end will come to the Land: an end will come to all four corners of the Land — none will escape the fury of God.

However, the idiom normally symbolizes the entire world, and *Malbim* and *Harav Breuer* take it in that sense. The meaning of the verse would then be that the 'end' which was to come upon the Land of Israel, would also be an *'end'* for all countries of the earth.

This recalls *Chagigah* 13b (see *Pref. Remarks* to Ch. 1.) which explains the *'stormy wind'* (1:4) as coming to subjugate the nations of the world to Nebuchadnezzar's dominion, so that it might not be said that Israel fell to a lowly nation (see also *Jeremiah* 25:15-29).

Thus we see that the fall of Jerusalem is presented as part of a world conquest by Babylon. It differs from other nations, only in that it will be the first to fall. Even at the moment of its destruction, Jerusalem remains the focus of God's Providence.

3. עַתָּה — *Now.*

The 'end' is to come very soon *(Metzudas David).*

וְשִׁלַּחְתִּי אַפִּי בָךְ — *And I will send My anger against you.*

The simple meaning, as we have translated it, indicates that God will send forth His punishments against Israel and the *Pi'el* voice [as opposed to

cant the occurrence, the more unusual in its makeup or ramifications, the greater the need to express its description in a heightened, less simple style.

Radak points out the use of *paronomasia* (לָשׁוֹן נוֹפֵל עַל לָשׁוֹן) (and also of *rhyme* — see 16:50) in many places. 'It is the custom of singers and mourners to speak their dirges, poems, and words in a beautiful way (דֶּרֶךְ צַחוּת) *(Michah* 1:10). However, just as a word may be chosen because of its similarity to other words in the sentence, it may occasionally be changed in order to avoid monotony (see *Radak* to *Ps.* 36:5 and 6).

Malbim (Intro. to *Isaiah*), cautions that we must not view the use of the tools of rhetoric in Scriptures as aesthetic dressing. Each God-given and God-inspired word must have a significance beyond mere beauty of expression. (For an analysis of the essential agreement of *Radak* with this opinion. See *Wolf, Nevi'ei Ha'emes* 3:3).

It is obvious that the prophets did make use of such tools, in cases where they would add dimensions to the message which would not otherwise have been attainable. Thus *Ramban (Exod.* 15:1) explains the occasional switch in tenses found in prophecy (i.e. that the prophet speaks of future events in the past or present tense, or vice versa) as a tool by which the prophet conveys the unambiguous certainty with which the events are to be accepted.

It is in this sense that some of the poetic forms of our chapter (described above) are to be understood. They were tools by which Yechezkel conveyed the urgency and immediacy of the catastrophe, which was about to overtake Jerusalem.

VII
3

3 *Now the end is upon you, and I will send My anger against you and punish you according to your ways, and I will place upon you all your abominations;*

the *Kal* [וְשִׁלַּחְתִּי] indicates the severity of the action (see Appendix V).

The use of the *Pi'el,* however, can have a different significance. The root שלח in the *Pi'el* often has the meaning *'to let loose', 'to free from restraint',* rather than to actively send. [See *Exod.* 22:4 for this use in connection with a person who allows his animals to wander freely into another's field, and *Gen.* 30:25 as one example of many, where the term is used in connection with freeing a servant.] If this is the intention with which the term is used here, the correct translation would be: *'And I will unleash My anger against you'.* The 'anger' of God, would, as it were, come against them automatically without God's direct intervention. (See *Pref. Remarks*).

We cannot be certain, however, that this is the meaning, since the *Pi'el* form of שלח is occasionally used in place of an ordinary *Kal* (see for example *Gen.* 28:6). (For comparable uses of the *Pi'el* form in Yechezkel, see 14:19, and 28:23).

כִּדְרָכַיִךְ ... תּוֹעֲבוֹתָיִךְ — *According to your ways ... your abominations.*

According to *Malbim,* 'ways' are the inner qualities of a person from which his actions — in this case, 'abominations' — derive. The meaning of the phrase is that since God would judge them in accordance with their 'ways' [i.e. He would find that they had made wicked tendencies part and parcel of their being], He would punish them for all their 'abominations' and not excuse their deeds as unavoidable outgrowths of inborn characteristics.

וְנָתַתִּי עָלַיִךְ אֵת כָּל תּוֹעֲבוֹתָיִךְ — *And I will place upon you all your abominations.*

The root נתן is often used as a synonym for the *giving* of reward or punishment *(I Kings* 8:39, *Jeremiah* 17:10, 32:19, *Ps.* 28:4). However in all these cases the object of the verb is the reward or punishment to be given. The use of the sin itself as the object (*I will place ... your abominations*) is, with one exception (*I Kings* 8:32), found exclusively in *Ezekiel.* (Three times in our chapter [3,4,8]; 9:10; 11:21; 16:43).

An analogous use of נתן is found in *Lev.* 16:21, where the sins of the children of Israel are to be symbolically *'placed'* on the head of the שָׂעִיר לַעֲזָאזֵל, the goat which was pushed to its death from a mountain top as part of the atonement process of *Yom Kippur.* The goat is then to 'carry' these sins upon itself to a rocky cliff.

While the meaning in that passage is symbolic (see *Ibn Ezra* ad loc., and also to *Deut.* 11:29 where he draws an analogy to the sentence: *'And you shall place the blessing on Mount Gerizim and the curse on Mount Eival'. Hirsch* and *Hoffman* make the same comparison in their commentaries to *Lev.),* the implication intended is clearly an identification between the goat and the sin. The meaning of our verse would be, that, having judged Israel according to its *'ways',* God sees them as identified and fused with their abominations. This would make its meaning identical to the phrase in the next sentence: *'And your abominations will be in your midst.'* This would place the idea expressed in our verse in consonance with those other verses in our chapter, which view the downfall of the wicked as a natural outgrowth of their evil, even without the direct interference of God. (See Pref. Remarks).

1. In fact, the exile occurred only 850 years after Israel entered the Land, two years before the prescribed time. The *Talmud* describes this as an act of mercy on the part of God *(Sanhedrin* 38a) because, had He waited the two years, the sins of Israel would have accumulated to the point where the punishment would have been more than the people could bear — a fulfillment of the dire prophecy, *You will be completely destroyed (Deut.* 4:26).

ז
ד־ז

ד וְלֹא־תָחוֹס עֵינִי עָלַיִךְ וְלֹא אֶחְמוֹל כִּי
דְרָכַיִךְ עָלַיִךְ אֶתֵּן וְתוֹעֲבוֹתַיִךְ בְּתוֹכֵךְ
ה תִּהְיֶיןָ וִידַעְתֶּם כִּי־אֲנִי יהוה: כֹּה
אָמַר אֲדֹנָי יֱהוִה רָעָה אַחַת רָעָה הִנֵּה
ו בָאָה: קֵץ בָּא בָּא הַקֵּץ הֵקִיץ אֵלָיִךְ הִנֵּה
ז בָּאָה: בָּאָה הַצְּפִירָה אֵלֶיךָ יוֹשֵׁב הָאָרֶץ
בָּא הָעֵת קָרוֹב הַיּוֹם מְהוּמָה וְלֹא־הֵד

4. לֹא תָחוֹס ... וְלֹא אֶחְמוֹל — [*My eye*] *will not spare ... nor will I pity.*

Malbim demonstrates that חוס is always used to convey the idea that something should not be destroyed because it is too useful to be wasted. Where pity is awakened because of the innate goodness of the object, the word חמל is used.

וְתוֹעֲבוֹתַיִךְ בְּתוֹכֵךְ תִּהְיֶיןָ — *And your abominations will be in your midst.*

You will be identified with your abominations (see *comm.* to *v. 3).*

וִידַעְתֶּם כִּי אֲנִי ה׳ — *Then you shall know that I am HASHEM.*

Not in spite of, but *because* of the severity of the punishment, you will experience an extraordinary closeness to God *(Harav Breuer).*

It is with those closest to Him, that God deals most strictly. Thus, Israel's closeness is reflected as much in its suffering as in its times of glory.[1]

5. רָעָה אַחַת רָעָה — *An evil, a singular evil.*

A complete evil, unique and greater than any other evil — the destruction of the Temple *(Rashi).*

The Sages view the destruction of the Temple as a greater evil than the oppression to which the Jewish people were often exposed. *Sanhedrin* 96b, tells how the descendants of many of their enemies, including Haman's, eventually became Jewish and shook off the heritage of evil left them by their ancestors. The Talmud goes on to say: God also wanted to bring descendants of this wicked person [Nebuchadnezzar] under the wings of the *Shechinah.* The ministering angels said to Him: 'Master of the World, he destroyed Your house and burned Your halls, would You bring him under the wings of the *Shechinah?'* Referring to this it is written: *'I [wanted to] cure Babylon, but she would not be cured' (Jeremiah* 51:9).

הִנֵּה בָאָה — *See! it comes.*

The accent is on the second letter (א) and indicates the present tense. (*Rashi,* see also *Rashi* to *Gen.* 29:6).

6. הֵקִיץ אֵלָיִךְ — *It is wakened against you.*

The word קֵץ, meaning *an end,* derives from the root קצץ, while הֵקִיץ, *is awakened,* derives from the root קיץ. The play on words (paronomasia) sure-

1. One of the miracles in the Temple centered on the *Cheruvim,* the two child-like figures which were part of the *Kapores,* the *cover* of the Ark. *Bava Basra* 99a relates that when Israel did God's will, the two *Cheruvim* faced each other; when Israel did not do God's will they turned away from each other. [See footnote to 9:3.]

Commentators ask how this statement can agree with *Yoma* 54b which tells that when the nations entered the Holy of Holies at the fall of Jerusalem, they found the *Cheruvim* in each other's embrace. Surely the time of the destruction would be described as one at which Israel did not do God's will! (See *Ri Migash* ad. loc.).

4 *My eye will not spare you nor will I pity; for your ways will I place upon you and your abominations will be in your midst. Then you shall know that I am HASHEM.*

5 *Thus says my Lord HASHEM/ELOHIM: An evil, a singular evil, see! it comes.*

6 *An end is come, it has come — the end!, It is wakened against you. See! it comes.*

7 *The dawn has come against you, dweller of the Land. The time is come, close is the day of confusion — not the shouting of the mountains.*

ly has the purpose of hinting at the association of ideas, namely that *'the end'* merely spells *'an awakening'* to the condition which brought about the present disasters. (See *Pref. Remarks* and *footnote* to v. 2). Among the major commentators, only *Eliezer* of *Beaugency* seems to read הֵקִיץ, not as a derivative of קיץ, *to awaken* but as a new verb, meaning *to bring about an end,* formed from the noun קֵץ.

Some commentators take הֵקִיץ as a transitive verb, i.e. He [God] has 'woken up' the 'end' against you. However this interpretation seems unlikely, since, although קיץ is used transitively in post Biblical Hebrew, it is used in Scripture as an intransitive verb only *(Radak, Michlol Hape'olim).*

הִנֵּה בָּאָה — *See! it comes.*

The 'evil' mentioned in *v.* 5 *(Radak).* It cannot refer to קֵץ in our verse, since קֵץ is masculine and בָּאָה is feminine.

7. בָּאָה הַצְּפִירָה — *The dawn* [or *morning*] *has come.*

In contrast to *vs.* 5,6 בָּאָה is accentuated on the first syllable and is in the past tense *(Rashi).*

צְפִירָה — *Dawn.*

Rashi and *Metzudas David* trace this word to the Aramaic root צפר, *dawn* or *morning.* (See also in *Judges* 7:3).

The word recurs only in *Isaiah* 28:5 where all commentators (with the exception of *Eliezer of Beaugency,* see below) render it as a synonym of עֲטָרָה, *a crown,* namely a *diadem.* Based on that rendering, *Targum* on our verse translates: *'Kingship has come'* — referring to the conquest of *Nebuchadnezzar.*

Radak suggests that the basic meaning of the root צפר is to *surround.* Thus the use of צְפִירָה in *Isaiah* as a *diadem,* i.e. that which encircles. The same association by which סִיבָּה, a *cause* is derived from סבב, *to surround,* would also give צְפִירָה the meaning of *cause.* He translates: *That which is happening to you is* [*by*] *the providence of God.*

Eliezer of Beaugency renders the word both here and in *Isaiah* as *strength* or *might.* Thus בָּאָה הַצְּפִירָה would mean *'Force has overtaken you'.*

וְלֹא הֵד הָרִים — *(And) not the shouting of the mountains.*

One of the answers which has been suggested is that the closeness which caused the *Cheruvim* to embrace when Israel was doing God's will is derived from the same source as the love for Israel which God demonstrated in the severity of their suffering at the Destruction.

We do not say *Tachanun* on *Tishah B'Av* because it is referred to as מוֹעֵד, *a time of meeting with God (Eichah* 1:15) *(Orach Chaim* 559:4). The late Telsher Rav, *Rabbi Avraham Yitzchok Bloch,* explains this custom in the spirit of the above. Israel can 'meet' God in pain as well as in joy. *Tishah B'Av* is a מוֹעֵד, *a meeting,* as surely as Israel's Holidays.

ז
ח־יא

ח הָרִים׃ עַתָּה מִקָּרוֹב אֶשְׁפּוֹךְ חֲמָתִי עָלַיִךְ
וְכִלֵּיתִי אַפִּי בָּךְ וּשְׁפַטְתִּיךְ כִּדְרָכָיִךְ
ט וְנָתַתִּי עָלַיִךְ אֵת כָּל־תּוֹעֲבוֹתָיִךְ׃ וְלֹא־
תָחוֹס עֵינִי וְלֹא אֶחְמוֹל כִּדְרָכַיִךְ עָלַיִךְ
אֶתֵּן וְתוֹעֲבוֹתַיִךְ בְּתוֹכֵךְ תִּהְיֶיןָ וִידַעְתֶּם
י כִּי אֲנִי יהוה מַכֶּה׃ הִנֵּה הַיּוֹם הִנֵּה בָאָה
יָצְאָה הַצְּפִרָה צָץ הַמַּטֶּה פָּרַח הַזָּדוֹן׃
יא הֶחָמָס קָם לְמַטֵּה־רֶשַׁע לֹא־מֵהֶם וְלֹא

Targum renders: And there will be none who will escape to the strongholds of the mountains. *Rashi* explains that *Targum* arrives at this meaning by identifying the word הֵד with הֵידָד, *the cry* or *shout of encouragement,* mentioned in *Isaiah* 16:9 and in *Jeremiah* 25:30. The literal meaning of the verse would then be: *There will be no* [*encouraging*] *shouts* [*urging that people seek the protection*] *of the mountains.*

Radak sees the same relationship to הֵידָד but renders it as *'echo'*. The meaning of the phrase is that the sound coming from the mountains will come from a real enemy; it will not be an echo which is a sound without a tangible source.

Metzudas David traces the word to הוד, *beauty* or *splendor.* The mountains will lose their usual beauty and instead they will be ugly and filthy due to the blood of corpses lying on them.

8. עַתָּה מִקָּרוֹב — *Now, speedily.*

The translation follows *Rashi. Malbim,* in order to avoid the apparent redundancy, translates מִקָּרוֹב, *from nearby.* Their fate is not far removed, either in time or space.

וְכִלֵּיתִי אַפִּי בָּךְ — *(And I will) spend my anger against you.*

See *comm.* to 5:13.

וּשְׁפַטְתִּיךְ כִּדְרָכַיִךְ וְנָתַתִּי עָלַיִךְ אֵת כָּל תּוֹעֲבוֹתָיִךְ — See *comm.* to *v.* 3 above.

9. See *comm.* to *v.*4.

10. יָצְאָה הַצְּפִרָה — See *comm.*to *v.* 7 above.

צָץ הַמַּטֶּה פָּרַח הַזָּדוֹן — *The rod has blossomed, arrogance has budded.*

The rod with which you are to be beaten [the Babylonians] has blossomed [it will shortly bear fruit, i.e. the punishment which it will inflict]. Arrogance, [i.e. Nebuchadnezzar, the man of arrogance] has budded [has been uncovered just like buds break through their protective covering,] and will speedily bear fruit *(Rashi; Metzudas David).*

Radak suggests that מַטֶּה might be taken as a derivative of the root נטה, *to bend* or *to pervert.* He renders the verse: *'The perversion of justice which you practiced has blossomed* [*i.e. will bear fruit*] *your arrogance has budded.'* The meaning would then be that the catastrophe which was about to overtake them is to be the outgrowth of their own acts. This would give our verse the same meaning as *v.*11. See below. (And see *Prefatory Remarks).*

11. הֶחָמָס — *Injustice.*

The word חָמָס appears in Scripture as a term denoting general injustice and violence (e.g. *Gen.* 6:11,13), and also as a specific reference to theft or stolen objects (e.g. *Jonah* 3:8), since property

8 *Now, speedily, I will pour out My fury upon you, spend My anger against you, and judge you according to your ways; and I shall place upon you all your abominations.*

9 *And My eye will not spare nor will I pity. In accordance with your ways will I place upon you, and your abominations will be in your midst. Then you shall know that I, HASHEM, strike.*

10 *See the day! see it comes! the dawn has come
forth. The rod has blossomed, arrogance has budded.*
11 *Injustice has arisen into a rod of wickedness; not*

gained through theft has been obtained violently or unjustly.

The use of חָמָס in our sentence, and especially the term מָלְאָה חָמָס in *v.* 23, creates an association with *Gen.* 6:9*ff* where God brings the Deluge upon mankind because the land was מָלְאָה חָמָס, *filled with injustice. Sanhedrin* 108a points to the connection: Rabbi Yochanan said: Come and see how great is the power of חָמָס for the 'generation of the Flood' transgressed every law, but were finally condemned only when they started to steal, as it says: *For the land was full of* חָמָס *and see! I will destroy them with the land.*

And it is written: *Injustice has arisen into a rod of wickedness* (our verse). Rabbi Elazar said: This teaches us that חָמָס raised itself up like a staff and accused them before God.

Hirsch (*Gen.* 6:11) thinks that חָמָס [as opposed to גָזֵל, *robbery,* and as used in the Bible rather than in the technical terminology of the *Talmud* — see *Bava Kama* 62a] denotes the kind of wrongdoing for which there is no legal recourse, because each individual act of חָמָס is too petty to have a standing in court.[1]

Society can protect itself from thievery. It can impose sanctions to prevent such criminal acts from unraveling its social fabric. But חָמָס — the injustice and dishonesty that evades legal stricture — erodes the moral standing of a people and will eventually rise up to accuse them of such inner decay that the eradication of their social structure becomes an historical and moral imperative, if the people are to be permitted to regenerate and rediscover their essential Godliness.

קָם — *Has arisen.*

The root קום can be used to denote a change of status, not necessarily connected with *rising up.* See *Genesis* 23:17, and *Lev.* 27:19.

לְמַטֵּה רֶשַׁע — *Into a rod of wickedness.*

The injustice, i.e. stolen property, which is in your hands has risen up against you as a rod of wickedness to destroy you *(Rashi).*

1. *Bereishis Rabbah* 31:5 describes חָמָס practiced by the 'generation of the Flood' in the following way: חָמָס is the theft of less than a *perutah* (the legal minimum value for a court case), and this is what the people of the 'generation of the Flood' used to do. One man would bring out a box full of lupines [to sell]. All the people would come and taste a lupine worth less than a *perutah* in order that they would not be legally liable for payment. In this way they would be stealing from the seller [since they had no intention of buying his wares] in such a way that he had no legal recourse to protect himself.

יב מֵהֲמוֹנָם וְלֹא מֶהֱמֵהֶם וְלֹא־נֹהַּ בָּהֶם: בָּא
הָעֵת הִגִּיעַ הַיּוֹם הַקּוֹנֶה אַל־יִשְׂמָח
וְהַמּוֹכֵר אַל־יִתְאַבָּל כִּי חָרוֹן אֶל־כָּל־
יג הֲמוֹנָהּ: כִּי הַמּוֹכֵר אֶל־הַמִּמְכָּר לֹא יָשׁוּב
וְעוֹד בַּחַיִּים חַיָּתָם כִּי־חָזוֹן אֶל־כָּל־
הֲמוֹנָהּ לֹא יָשׁוּב וְאִישׁ בַּעֲוֺנוֹ חַיָּתוֹ לֹא־
יד יִתְחַזָּקוּ: תָּקְעוּ בַתָּקוֹעַ וְהָכִין הַכֹּל וְאֵין
הֹלֵךְ לַמִּלְחָמָה כִּי חֲרוֹנִי אֶל־כָּל־הֲמוֹנָהּ:

According to *Metzudas David* רֶשַׁע describes the cruelty with which Nebuchadnezzar (הֶחָמָס=אִישׁ הֶחָמָס) who has become God's מַטֶּה, *rod,* will strike the people.

Harav Breuer, noting that the Babylonians are described as רִשְׁעֵי הָאָרֶץ *the wicked of the land* (*v.*21), suggests that מַטֵּה רֶשַׁע might mean *the rod of the wicked.* It is the moral decay of Jerusalem's society (הֶחָמָס) which has put into the Babylonian hands a degree of power which they would never have found from within themselves (see below).

לֹא מֵהֶם וְלֹא מֵהֲמוֹנָם וְלֹא מֶהֱמֵהֶם וְלֹא נֹהַּ בָּהֶם — *Not from them, nor from their multitudes nor from their children. For there is not one who seeks among them.*

Both the place of this phrase in the context of the sentence and the meaning of the individual words מֶהֱמֵהֶם and נֹהַּ present great difficulties. The following are among the solutions offered:

— *Rashi* takes מֶהֱמֵהֶם as *children.* (He does not make clear how he arrives at this meaning). [*Radak* who also translates *children* adduces two possible explanations: Either the word is formed from a dual מֵהֶם, *from them* (i.e. מֵהֶם + מֵהֶם), and means anything at all of theirs — including their children. Or it comes from the root: המה, *to long for something* and means that which a person longs for — namely his children.] He derives נֹהַּ, from the root נהה in the sense of longing after someone.

The phrase is addressed to Israel's enemies: *'Do not spare any of the wicked people of Israel, not them, nor their multitudes nor their children, since there is none among them who longs for God.'*

— *Radak* renders הָמוֹן as wealth, מֶהֱמֵהֶם as children (see above) and traces נֹהַּ to the root נהה in its meaning of moaning or sighing.

The phrase is a prophecy and means, 'None shall escape the exile, not the people, nor their wealth, nor their children. The suffering will be so great and all pervasive that people will not even mourn their losses anymore.'

— *Metzudas David* renders מֶהֱמֵהֶם as deriving from המה, the roaring noise of battle, and נֹהַּ, as does *Radak* — from נהה meaning to groan.

The phrase follows directly upon the first part of the sentence. Nebuchadnezzar has become a rod striking cruelly at the people. However his success cannot be ascribed to his military might, nor to the multitudes who are with him, nor to the roaring noise of his forces. [They are but tools in the hand of God]. Therefore no mourning should take place over them [i.e. they should not be punished] since their actions were not of their own volition.

— *Harav Breuer*'s rendering is iden-

*from them, nor from their multitudes nor from their
children. For there is not one who seeks among them.*
12 *The time has come, the day has drawn near. Let
the buyer not be glad nor let the seller mourn; for
wrath is upon her entire multitude.* 13 *For the seller —
to that which is sold he shall not return, even were
they yet alive. For a vision is upon her entire multitude — it will not return. Each man — with his sin, his very being; they can find no strength.*
14 *They have blown the horn and prepared
everything — but none goes to war. For My anger is*

tical with that of *Metzudas David* except that he translates לֹא נֹהַּ בָּהֶם as in consonance with the rest of the phrase — 'the sorrowing [in Jerusalem] is not to be attributed to them.'

12. Normally a person forced to sell his field would be sad at losing his property, while the buyer would be happy. With the knowledge of an imminent exile upon them, however, the sale would have no real significance to either of them.

13. כִּי הַמּוֹכֵר ... לֹא יָשׁוּב — *For the seller ... shall not return.*

Once exiled, the seller will never see his field in another's hands, therefore there is no reason for him to mourn *(Rashi).*

Radak detects an association between the wording of our phrase and *Lev.* 25:13, where the law of the *Yovel* (the fiftieth year, when fields are returned to their sellers) is expressed in the words: בִּשְׁנַת הַיּוֹבֵל הַזֹּאת תָּשֻׁבוּ אִישׁ אֶל אֲחֻזָּתוֹ, and interprets our verse: Even when the *Yovel* year comes, the seller will not return to his field.

וְעוֹד בַּחַיִּים חַיָּתָם — [Even] *were they yet alive.*

We have translated according to *Radak. Rashi* renders: Throughout their lifetime.

חַיָּה is used in Scripture as a synonym for soul (*Ps.* 143:3). The literal translation of בַּחַיִּים חַיָּתָם is *while their souls are still alive.*

כִּי חָזוֹן אֶל כָּל הֲמוֹנָהּ לֹא יָשׁוּב — *For a vision is upon her entire multitude — it will not return.*

Rashi follows *Targum* who renders: For prophets have constantly called upon her multitudes [to repent] but they will not repent.

וְאִישׁ בַּעֲוֹנוֹ חַיָּתוֹ — *Each man — with his sin, his very being.*

Each one of them, his life and his soul, cleaves to his sin *(Rashi).*

לֹא יִתְחַזָּקוּ — *They can find no strength.*

To control their evil inclination *(Rashi).* Or, *(Metzudas David),* They will not be able to come back to their land to take possession (יִתְחַזָּקוּ) of it.

14. תָּקְעוּ בַתָּקוֹעַ — *They have blown the horn.*

To urge the people to make ready for war. However, the fear of the enemy will be so overwhelming that no one will have the courage to fight. *(Rashi* and *Metzudas David).*

According to *Radak* the horn is blown to warn the people to come into the protected environs of the city.

תָּקוֹעַ is never used in Scriptures. It is

טו הַחֶרֶב בַּחוּץ וְהַדֶּבֶר וְהָרָעָב מִבָּיִת אֲשֶׁר
בַּשָּׂדֶה בַּחֶרֶב יָמוּת וַאֲשֶׁר בָּעִיר רָעָב
טז וָדֶבֶר יֹאכְלֶנּוּ׃ וּפָלְטוּ פְּלִיטֵיהֶם וְהָיוּ אֶל־
הֶהָרִים כְּיוֹנֵי הַגֵּאָיוֹת כֻּלָּם הֹמוֹת אִישׁ
יז בַּעֲוֺנוֹ׃ כָּל־הַיָּדַיִם תִּרְפֶּינָה וְכָל־בִּרְכַּיִם
יח תֵּלַכְנָה מָּיִם׃ וְחָגְרוּ שַׂקִּים וְכִסְּתָה אוֹתָם
פַלָּצוּת וְאֶל כָּל־פָּנִים בּוּשָׁה וּבְכָל־
יט רָאשֵׁיהֶם קָרְחָה׃ כַּסְפָּם בַּחוּצוֹת יַשְׁלִיכוּ
וּזְהָבָם לְנִדָּה יִהְיֶה כַּסְפָּם וּזְהָבָם לֹא־יוּכַל
לְהַצִּילָם בְּיוֹם עֶבְרַת יהוה נַפְשָׁם לֹא
יְשַׂבֵּעוּ וּמֵעֵיהֶם לֹא יְמַלֵּאוּ כִּי־מִכְשׁוֹל
כ עֲוֺנָם הָיָה׃ וּצְבִי עֶדְיוֹ לְגָאוֹן שָׂמָהוּ

a word, coined for this particular phrase and is used as לָשׁוֹן נֹפֵל עַל לָשׁוֹן *paronomasia.* See *footnote* to *v.* 2.

16. כְּיוֹנֵי הַגֵּאָיוֹת — *Like the doves of the valleys.*

Who are not usually found in the mountains, and moan because they are homeless *(Malbim).*

כֻּלָּם הֹמוֹת — *All of them moaning.*

Radak thinks that they moan as part of their repentance (אִישׁ בַּעֲוֺנוֹ).

Alternately the meaning could be that they moan in their misery, knowing that their sins brought them to their sad plight.

17. וְכָל בִּרְכַּיִם תֵּלַכְנָה מָּיִם — *And all the knees will flow water.*

The perspiration of fear *(Rashi).*

Radak takes מַיִם, *water,* literally and inserts the word 'like'. *And all their knees will melt like water.*

Metzudas David combines the two interpretations, and renders: The sweat of fear will cause their knees to appear as though they were melting.

18. וְחָגְרוּ שַׂקִּים — *And they shall gird themselves in sacks.*

A symbol of mourning and suffering *(Metzudas David).*

19. כַּסְפָּם ... וּזְהָבָם — *Their silver ... their gold.*

This could refer either to their idols of silver and gold, or to their wealth *(Radak).* Neither can save them on the day of Hashem's anger. Then, the enemy will be the famine which is raging in the streets of Jerusalem, and money will be useless since no food will be available.

לְנִדָּה — *Fit for discarding.*

The word derives from נדד or נדה which has the meaning of *wandering* or *moving away.* Thus נִדָּה would represent something from which one should keep his distance. This is the meaning ascribed by *Radak* and *Metzudas Zion.*

Rashi renders the word as *'an object of disgust.'* The word (in a borrowed sense) is occasionally used in this sense in Scriptures (e.g. *Ezra* 9:11).

VII 15-20

upon all her multitude. 15 *The sword without, and*
plague and famine within. He that is in the field will
die by the sword, and he that is in the city — famine
and plague will consume him. 16 *And their fugitives*
will flee, and be upon the mountains like the doves of
the valleys, all of them moaning, each in his sin. 17 *All*
the hands will be slack, and all the knees will flow
water. 18 *And they shall gird themselves in sacks, and*
trembling will cover them. On every face will be
shame, and on all their heads, baldness.

19 *Their silver they will throw in the streets and*
their gold will be fit for discarding. Their silver and
gold will be unable to save them on the day of
HASHEM's anger. They shall not satisfy their souls
nor fill their bowels, for it was the stumbling block of
their sins. 20 *And the beauty of their ornament — for*
majesty had He placed it — the images of their

It is of interest that *Rashi (Eichah* 1:8) translates נִידָה as *wanderer.*

כִּי מִכְשׁוֹל עֲוֹנָם הָיָה — *For it was the stumbling block of their sins.*

Their suffering which had become a stumbling block for them, came about because of their sins *(Metzudas David).*

According to *Eliezer of Beaugency,* מִכְשׁוֹל refers back to כַּסְפָּם וּזְהָבָם: *their silver and their gold.* These had been the stumbling block which caused them to sin.

20. וּצְבִי עֶדְיוֹ — *And the beauty of their ornament.*

Rashi, Radak, and *Metzudas David* agree that this phrase refers to the Temple which God had placed in their midst as a symbol of majesty (לְגָאוֹן שָׂמָהוּ). It was the source of their pride (גָּאוֹן) because God's Presence was manifest in it *(Radak).*

They had defiled it by placing their idols within its sacred confines. Therefore God *presented* the Temple (נְתַתִּיו, lit. *'I gave it')* as something to be discarded, i.e. he placed a distance between Himself and the Temple, delivering it into the hands of the enemy *(Metzudas David).*

A totally different translation is suggested by *Eliezer of Beaugency.* צְבִי עֶדְיוֹ refers to the *silver and gold* of the previous verse and is to be translated: *Their wealth.* In addition there is a play on words because עֲדִי, an *ornament* (derived from עדה) has a sound association with עֵדוּת, *testimony* (derived from עוד). The sentence is to be rendered thus: *Their wealth which had been given to them as testimony* [of God's love] *they placed upon themselves as a sign of majesty to be a source of pride to themselves* [i.e., fruit of their own accomplishment]. *Also they fashioned their idols from it. Therefore God forced them to discard it.*

In this interpretation, the phrase נְתַתִּיו ... לְנִדָּה has the same meaning as וּזְהָבָם לְנִדָּה יִהְיֶה of the previous verse.

וְצַלְמֵי תוֹעֲבֹתָם שִׁקּוּצֵיהֶם עָשׂוּ בוֹ עַל־
כא כֵּן נְתַתִּיו לָהֶם לְנִדָּה: וּנְתַתִּיו בְּיַד־הַזָּרִים
לָבַז וּלְרִשְׁעֵי הָאָרֶץ לְשָׁלָל וְחִלְּלוּהָ:
כב וַהֲסִבֹּתִי פָנַי מֵהֶם וְחִלְּלוּ אֶת־צְפוּנִי
כג וּבָאוּ־בָהּ פָּרִיצִים וְחִלְּלוּהָ: עֲשֵׂה
הָרַתּוֹק כִּי הָאָרֶץ מָלְאָה מִשְׁפַּט דָּמִים
כד וְהָעִיר מָלְאָה חָמָס: וְהֵבֵאתִי רָעֵי גוֹיִם
וְיָרְשׁוּ אֶת־בָּתֵּיהֶם וְהִשְׁבַּתִּי גְּאוֹן עַזִּים

21. If *v.* 20 referred to the Temple (see *comm.* to *v.* 20), then *vs.* 21 and 22 continue the description of its profanation: If the subject of *v.* 20 was the gold and silver of Jerusalem, then *v.* 21 continues with this theme, and the profanation of the Temple (צְפוּנִי, *my hidden place*) is dealt with in *v.* 22.

וְחִלְּלוּהוּ — *And they shall profane it.*

Radak points out that the כְּתִיב *the spelling* of this word differs from the קְרִי, *the pronunciation.* In the spelling the object is feminine and refers to the *Shechinah.* In the pronunciation the object is masculine and refers to the Temple.

[It can be shown that in most cases where a קְרִי־כְּתִיב occurs, the spelling, being more 'remote' from the reader than the pronunciation, describes the inner essential meaning, while the pronunciation deals with the outer, more tangible realities. This is completely borne out in the example dealt with here. The destruction of the Temple is the outer manifestation of the 'profaning of the *Shechinah.*' (See *Pref. Remarks* to Ch. 1.). [For a partial examination of קְרִי and כְּתִיב in Scripture, see *Wolf, Nevi'ei Ha'emes* 2:6. See also *Radak II Sam.* 15:21].

If this verse refers to the silver and gold of *v.* 20 *(Eliezer of Beaugency),* the *profanation* would consist of the use of this treasure which had been given to Israel to aid them in their role as God's witnesses (see *comm.* to *v.* 20) for profane purposes.

22. וַהֲסִבֹּתִי פָּנַי מֵהֶם — *And I shall turn My face away from them.*

And I shall remove My שְׁכִינָה, *Divine Presence,* from among them *(Targum).* The hand of the enemy can profane the holy Temple only once the Divine Presence has been withdrawn from it. (See *Pref. Remarks* to Ch. 1).

It is significant that the *Shechinah* will not be withdrawn from the Temple buildings but מֵהֶם, *from them.* God's Presence had never been localized within the Temple confines. Rather it was the people themselves, elevated by the Temple in their midst to be worthy bearers of sanctity, in whom the *Shechinah* had dwelt *(Exod.* 25:8 and 29:43-46). The Divine Presence would be withdrawn from them — and the Temple buildings would crumble in ruins.

צְפוּנִי — *My hiding place.*

The place in which I was hidden among them, i.e. the Temple *(Rashi). Metzudas David* renders *'My hidden place',* i.e. the private place which was hidden from prying eyes — the Holy of Holies.

וְחִלְּלוּ אֶת צְפוּנִי — *And they will profane My hiding place.*

For the Temple to lie at the mercy of the conquerer God need but *'turn His face away.'* No direct intervention of God is required (see *Pref. Remarks).*

abominations and their detestations they made in it. Therefore I have presented it to them as fit for discarding. 21 *And I will present it in the hands of the strangers for a prey, and to the wicked of the earth for a spoil, and they shall profane it.* 22 *And I shall turn My face away from them and they will profane My hiding place and into it will come the brazen and profane it.*

23 *Make the chain! For the Land is full of bloodguilt, and the city is full of injustice.* 24 *And I shall bring the most wicked of the nations and they will inherit their houses. And I shall put an end to the pride of the mighty; and that which should have hallowed them will be defiled.*

23. עֲשֵׂה הָרַתּוֹק — *Make the chain!*

Symbolizing the captivity of the exiles *(Rashi).*

It is not clear whether this command is addressed to Yechezkel, who had previously played the role of the aggressor (see 4:3); or whether God is calling out to the Babylonians to prepare themselves for their triumph *(Harav Breuer).*

וְהָעִיר מָלְאָה חָמָס — *And the city is full of injustice.*

See *comm.* to *v.* 11.

Radak stresses that once the city is filled with חָמָס, *injustice,* it cannot possibly continue to exist as a social unity (see *comm.* ad. loc.). In this interpretation the verse presents the dual cause of the city's doom, which we have traced throughout the chapter. The *'bloodguilt'* calls for punishment and demands God's intervention. The injustice guarantees a natural disintegration.

24. גְּאוֹן עַזִּים — *The pride of the mighty.*

The Temple had been placed in their midst as a symbol of their גְּאוֹן, *their majesty (v.* 20). By using that same word to describe the conceit of the mighty ones in Israel, Scripture draws our attention to the pitiful exchange which they had made; they had bartered true majesty for a semblance of power which now lay at the mercy of the *most wicked of the nations.*

מְקַדְשֵׁיהֶם — *That which should have hallowed them,* i.e. what should have hallowed the *people* (not מִקְדְּשֵׁיהֶם *their Sanctuary).*

The Temple long since lost its true holiness with the withdrawal of the שְׁכִינָה. All that is left is the memory of what might have been *(Harav Breuer).* See *comm.* to *v.* 22.

25-27. The tragedy of the time will be that even in the moment when the predictable end will come upon them, the people will still be certain that peace is to be found.

The false prophets to whom they now turn in vain *(v.* 26) had for so long lulled them into a sense of security based on an erronous conception of the function of the Temple in their midst (see *comm.* to 3:24-27), that even in the face of the holocaust they could not

ז
כה־כד

כה וְנִחֲלוּ מְקַדְשֵׁיהֶם׃ קְפָדָה־בָא וּבִקְשׁוּ
כו שָׁלוֹם וָאָיִן׃ הֹוָה עַל־הֹוָה תָּבוֹא
וּשְׁמֻעָה אֶל־שְׁמוּעָה תִּהְיֶה וּבִקְשׁוּ חָזוֹן
מִנָּבִיא וְתוֹרָה תֹּאבַד מִכֹּהֵן וְעֵצָה
כז מִזְּקֵנִים׃ הַמֶּלֶךְ יִתְאַבָּל וְנָשִׂיא יִלְבַּשׁ
שְׁמָמָה וִידֵי עַם־הָאָרֶץ תִּבָּהַלְנָה מִדַּרְכָּם
אֶעֱשֶׂה אוֹתָם וּבְמִשְׁפְּטֵיהֶם אֶשְׁפְּטֵם
ח
א
א וְיָדְעוּ כִּי־אֲנִי יהוה׃ וַיְהִי | בַּשָּׁנָה
הַשִּׁשִּׁית בַּשִּׁשִּׁי בַּחֲמִשָּׁה לַחֹדֶשׁ אֲנִי

come to grips with the reality of the Temple's purpose.

Only after the complete collapse of all the pillars of their social structure — prophet, priest, elders, king, prince, and finally the people themselves (*vs.* 26-27), would they finally come to know the true implications of their relations with Hashem (*v.* 27) (based on *Harav Breuer.* See also *Isaiah* 3:1-6).

25. קְפָדָה בָא — *A cutting off has come.*

This expression is used in contrast to קֵץ בָּא, *an end has come* (*v.* 6) to indicate a considered, planned, and predictable end [as in the word מַקְפִּיד in Talmudic usage] *(Harav Breuer).*

26. הֹוָה עַל הֹוָה — *Happening shall come upon happening.*

This translation follows *Rashi. Targum* and most commentators, render: Breaking upon breaking.

וּבִקְשׁוּ חָזוֹן מִנָּבִיא — *Then they shall seek vision from a prophet.*

But will not find it *(Radak; Metzudas David).*

וְתוֹרָה תֹּאבַד מִכֹּהֵן — *But teaching shall be lost from the priest.*

Whose function it was to instruct the people [*Malachi* 2:7] *(Rashi).*

27. הַמֶּלֶךְ ... וְנָשִׂיא —*King ... prince.*

Most commentators view the second phrase as meaning essentially the same as the first and the word מֶלֶךְ and נָשִׂיא both refer to the governor, Gedalya ben Achikom, who was appointed by Nebuchadnezzar after the destruction.

מִדַּרְכָּם ... וּבְמִשְׁפְּטֵיהֶם — *According to their ways ... and by their own judgments* [lit. *'according to their laws'*] i.e., as they deserve.

God would impose on them exactly the fate which they had forged for themselves by their actions.

VIII

In a prophetic vision, Yechezkel is transported to Jerusalem.

For six more years, the doomed city would struggle on under the illusion of its indestructability. But, unbeknown to its inhabitants, the preparations for the end were already under way.

Even within the confines of the Bais HaMikdash, the cankerous lust for idol worship was eroding the last vestiges of holiness. Silent messengers of death were speeding through the streets of the city, and stage by stage the *Shechinah* was withdrawing from Its resting place.

VII 25-27

[25] *A cutting off has come — and they shall seek peace and it is not there.* [26] *Happening shall come upon happening, and news shall be upon news. Then they shall seek vision from a prophet, but teaching shall be lost from the priest, and counsel from the elders.* [27] *The king shall mourn and the prince will be clothed with appallment, and the hands of the people of the Land will be confused. Of their own ways shall I do to them, and by their own judgments shall I judge them. And they shall know that I am* HASHEM.

VIII 1

It was in the sixth year, in the sixth month on the fifth of the month, as I sat in my house with the

As these and other metaphysical events unfolded before the prophet's eyes, he would learn God's verdict; that the city was indeed to be destroyed and that the future of Israel would lie with the exiled communities of Babylon.

All this Yechezkel will tell to the exiles (11:25), that is, the elders of Judah who had gathered in his house (8:1). They will have been exposed to the full impact of the knowledge that it was their destiny to be the repository of Israel's future.

During the next four chapters, Yechezkel will trace the spread of the spiritual cancer that will end with destruction and exile:

Ch. 8 — Idol worship in the Bais HaMikdash.

Ch. 9 — Beginning of the withdrawal of the Shechinah; the messengers of death.

Ch. 10 — Continued withdrawal of the Shechinah. The fire of destruction is ready to be hurled against the city.

Ch. 11 — The fate of the city's inhabitants is sealed. The future lies with the exiles. The Shechinah completes Its withdrawal from Jerusalem.

1. בַּשָּׁנָה הַשִּׁשִּׁית — *In the sixth year.*

I.e. the sixth year since the beginning of Yehoyachin's exile (see *comm.* to 1:2).

בַּשִּׁשִּׁי בַּחֲמִשָּׁה לַחֹדֶשׁ — *In the sixth [month] on the fifth [day] of the month.*

From 1:1-2 we learn that Yechezkel's first vision took place on the fifth of the fourth month (5 *Tammuz*) of the fifth year. That vision ends in 3:14. Vs. 15-16 (*ibid.*) date his second vision seven days later (12 *Tammuz*). In that vision he was commanded to lie immobilized in his house for 430 days [390 days lying on his left side — forty days lying on his right side (4:4-6)]. But our verse is dated in the fifth day of the sixth month (5 Elul) of the sixth year and only 406 days have elapsed of the 430 day period. But אֲנִי יוֹשֵׁב בְּבֵיתִי, I was sitting in my house contradicts the וְאַתָּה שְׁכַב עַל צִדְּךָ, *lie on your side,* of 4:4. *Seder Olam* 26, therefore, deduces that between *Tammuz* of the fifth year and *Elul* of the sixth year there must have been an extra *Adar,* thus adding another 30 days. *Radak* points out that this deduction is valid only if we assume that the symbolic actions of Ch. 4 actually took

יוֹשֵׁב בְּבֵיתִי וְזִקְנֵי יְהוּדָה יוֹשְׁבִים לְפָנָי
ב וַתִּפֹּל עָלַי שָׁם יַד אֲדֹנָי יֱהֹוִה׃ וָאֶרְאֶה
וְהִנֵּה דְמוּת כְּמַרְאֵה־אֵשׁ מִמַּרְאֵה מָתְנָיו
וּלְמַטָּה אֵשׁ וּמִמָּתְנָיו וּלְמַעְלָה כְּמַרְאֵה־
ג זֹהַר כְּעֵין הַחַשְׁמַלָה׃ וַיִּשְׁלַח תַּבְנִית יָד
וַיִּקָּחֵנִי בְּצִיצִת רֹאשִׁי וַתִּשָּׂא אֹתִי רוּחַ |
בֵּין־הָאָרֶץ וּבֵין הַשָּׁמַיִם וַתָּבֵא אֹתִי
יְרוּשָׁלַמָה בְּמַרְאוֹת אֱלֹהִים אֶל־פֶּתַח
שַׁעַר הַפְּנִימִית הַפּוֹנֶה צָפוֹנָה אֲשֶׁר־שָׁם
ד מוֹשַׁב סֵמֶל הַקִּנְאָה הַמַּקְנֶה׃ וְהִנֵּה־שָׁם

place. If, however, they were seen by Yechezkel only in prophetic vision (see *footnote* to 4:4) no difficulty exists.

וְזִקְנֵי יְהוּדָה — *With the elders of Judah.*

Who had come to Babylon with Yehoyachin's exile *(Radak).*

Nothing is told about these elders. We do not know why they came, nor does it appear that Yechezkel's vision came in reaction to any question of theirs.

This stands in marked contrast to the two accounts (Chs. 14 and 20) of the *'elders of Israel'* who *'came'* to *'seek an answer'* (14:3 and 20:1) from God. In both instances their seeking grew out of impure motives which are revealed and condemned in God's answer.

These elders do not 'seek' any answers and the vision in our chapter is not in response to their questions. They do not 'come' to the prophet, but are there because they are prompted by an inner need to share the horrors of his long confinement *(Harav Breuer).* They — the *'carpenters and locksmiths'* (see *comm.* to 1:2) — know that the lessons to be derived from Yechezkel's agony are addressed to them because they are to be the builders of a regenerated nation *(Harav Breuer)* (see *Pref. Remarks).*

Ma'aseh Merkavah

In this vision, supernatural concepts are described in human terms. As explained in the *Prefatory Remarks,* they cannot be understood literally nor, in our spiritual poverty, are we equipped even to glimpse at their inner meaning.

2. In this verse we find idioms similar to those of *Ma'aseh Merkavah* in Ch. 1. The cautionary notes found in the *Pref. Remarks* there apply here as well.

וָאֶרְאֶה — *And I saw.*

[Cf. *comm.* to 1:27 for similar vision.]

Rashi notes, as he does in his *comm.* to 1:27, that 'one is not permitted to reflect on this verse.'

3. וַיִּקָּחֵנִי בְּצִיצִת רֹאשִׁי — *And took me by a lock of my head.*

There would be another time when Yechezkel's prophetic vision would transport him to Jerusalem (40:1-2). He would be shown the vision of Israel's future, the *Bais HaMikdash* rebuilt in its former glory. God would carry him with love and consideration placing him softly upon a 'high mountain.' In our

elders of Judah sitting before me, and the hand of my Lord HASHEM/ELOHIM fell upon me there.
2 And I saw: And behold his likeness like the appearance of fire; from the appearance of his loins and downward fire; from the appearance of his loins and upward like the appearance of a radiance like a semblace of Chashmal.
3 Then he put forth the form of a hand and took me by a lock of my head; and a wind lifted me up between the earth and the heaven and brought me to Jerusalem in visions of God, to the door of the inner gate which faces northward where was the seat of the image of jealousy which provokes

chapter Yechezkel is to witness Israel's degeneration. He is 'dragged by the hairs of the head' as a master drags his slave to prison *(Radak).*

בְּמַרְאוֹת אֱלֹהִים — *In a vision of the Lord.*

Only *Eliezer of Beaugency* thinks that Yechezkel was physically transported to Jerusalem during a prophetic experience (מַרְאוֹת אֱלֹהִים in contrast to מַרְאוֹת הַלַּיְלָה, *visions of the night,* [i.e. a dream], which would have implied that he was not actually taken). Most commentators interpret מַרְאוֹת אֱלֹהִים as indicating that he only visualized his journey, but did not actually experience it.

שַׁעַר הַפְּנִימִית הַפּוֹנֶה צָפוֹנָה — *The inner gate which faces northward.*

The inner gate is the gate of the Temple courtyard (עֲזָרָה). It is referred to as *inner* (see *I Kings* 6:36) in contrast to the Temple Mount (הַר הַבַּיִת) which is called הַחִיצֹנָה, *outer* (10:5) *(Radak).*

The courtyard had gates on all its four sides. Yechezkel was taken to the northern gate.

אֲשֶׁר שָׁם מוֹשַׁב סֵמֶל הַקִּנְאָה הַמַּקְנֶה — *Where was the seat of the image of jealousy which provokes jealousy.*

The image of jealousy was an idol that had been emplaced there in earlier times. Yechezkel saw *'the seat of the image'*, but not the idol itself. Together with all vestiges of idol worship, it was destroyed during Yoshiyahu's cleansing of the Land and Temple (*II Kings* 23:6). In the books of *Kings* and *Jeremiah* no mention is found of any restoration of idol worship. Therefore we must assume that, although Yoshiyahu's descendants *'did evil in the eyes of HASHEM'*, they nevertheless did not reinstate the public desecrations which had proliferated during the reigns of Menashe and Ammon *(Harav Joseph Breuer.* See also *Malbim).*[1]

1. Both Scripture and *Talmud* reinforce the position that the public idol worship, rampant during the reigns of Menashe and Ammon did not reappear in the years prior to the destruction. Scripture makes no mention of a reinstatement of idol worship in either *Kings* or *Jeremiah* (unless *II Kings* 23:37 which states that Yehoyakim: *'did evil ... in all things as his fathers had done'* can be seen as a reference to idol worship. See also *II Chron.* 36:14). For the teaching of the *Talmud* see *Yomah* 9b and *Sanhedrin* 103b which derive from *Isaiah* 28:20 that the idolatry imposed by Kings Menashe and Ammon were prime factors in the destruc-

ח כְּבוֹד אֱלֹהֵי יִשְׂרָאֵל כַּמַּרְאֶה אֲשֶׁר
ה ה רָאִיתִי בַּבִּקְעָה׃ וַיֹּאמֶר אֵלַי בֶּן־אָדָם

Ma'aseh Merkavah: In this vision, supernatural concepts are described in human terms. As explained in the *Prefatory Remarks*, they cannot be understood literally nor, in our spiritual poverty, are we equipped even to glimpse at their inner meaning.

During the last few years of Jerusalem's travail, however, when the onslaught of shattering realities blurred memories of Yoshiyahu's reforms and led some people to distortedly think that: *'God has forsaken the Land' (v.* 12), it is, of course, possible that a new idol was made to replace that of Menashe.

It is also possible, as *Da'as Sofrim* suggests, that an image may have existed, but that it was so small and well hidden, that it was known only to an initiated few. Thus it would have been protected from the populace who would not have tolerated an idol in their midst.

If the purpose of the image was to educate the people to a veneration of the powers of nature as being the source of their well being (see *comm. v.* 12 and 16), no better location than the northern part of the courtyard could have been chosen. It was there that the major sacrifices were slaughtered [*Lev.* 1:11] *(Eliezer of Beaugency)*; and it was in the northern section of the sanctuary that the שֻׁלְחָן, *table,* of the show-bread — symbol of Israel's wealth and material prosperity was placed *(Exod.* 40:22). As *Hirsch (Lev.* 1:11, and various other places in his commentary) demonstrates it is in the north, that Israel is to sublimate the *material-sensual* aspects of its existence to divine service. The *'image of jealousy'* (see below) spoke eloquently of the 'futility' of such a sublimation *(Harav Breuer).*

סֶמֶל הַקִּנְאָה הַמַּקְנֶה — *The image of jealousy which provokes jealousy.*

Rashi indicates two sources of jealousy, thus explaining the apparent redundancy. The image itself, apart from its location, was designed to be a challenge to God and its location in particular provoked another jealousy.

Not satisfied with erecting an ordinary idol, Menashe had given it four

tion. Scripture stresses repeatedly *(II Kings* 21:11-17, 24:3; *Jeremiah* 15:4) that it was because of Menashe's sins that city and Temple were doomed.

It follows, that after the death of Ammon, (Menashe's son who intensified the sin of his father), there was no idolatry blatant enough to bring about Israel's downfall. [*Eichah Rabbasi* (Intro. 22) which describes the constant acceleration of idol worship in Judah, could well be referring to the reigns of Menashe and Ammon.] Indeed Menashe's grandson Yoshiyahu initiated a general repentance and cleansing during which every last remnant of the idolatrous cult was destroyed, including the idol which his grandfather had brought into the Temple *(II Kings* 23:6).

Commentators grapple with the difficult question, of how God could have brought about the final destruction because of Menashe's sins, since Menashe himself repented in the latter part of his reign *(II Chron.* 33:12-13), and in view of the general repentance during Yoshiyahu's reign. *(Kli Yakar* on *Kings* quotes *Ralbag* and *Abarbanel* and adds some interpretations of his own. See also *Malbim* to *Jeremiah* 15 and *II Kings* 23. See *comm.* to 18:2 for an exhaustive treatment of this problem). The common thread running through the various solutions is based on the assumption that in spite of Yoshiyahu's efforts, the reforms which he initiated did not succeed in breaking the people's deeply cherished attachment to idol worship [see *Ta'anis* 22b].

Jeremiah, in a prophecy received during Yoshiyahu's reign (*Jeremiah* 3:6, 10) reports that: *'In spite of all,* [Israel's] *false sister Judah did not repent with all her heart; but falsely.' Rashi*

jealousy. 4 *And see there! the Glory of the God of Israel, like the vision which I had seen in the valley.*
5 *And He said to me: 'Ben Adam, please lift up*

faces *(Sanhedrin* 103b), one facing in each direction, so that from wherever a person entered the Sanctuary he could not avoid being confronted by it. *Devarim Rabbah* 2:13 teaches that the four faces were identical with those figures which were represented in the *Merkavah* (Ch. 1). Thus with unparalleled impudence, Menashe threw a challenge to God, by usurping the very symbols with which He allowed Himself to be apprehended by man! Thus it was a סֵמֶל הַקִּנְאָה, *an image of jealousy*

But it was also הַמַּקְנֶה; it provoked jealousy by its location. [The word is an irregular form. The root is קנא and its causative form would normally be הַמַּקְנִיא.]

II Kings 21:7 stresses that Menashe placed his idol *in the House concerning which HASHEM had said ... 'I will place My Name* [*there*] *forever.'* Now, in the Temple there could be no room for two masters (see *Yomah* 9b). Thus Menashe must have intended to drive God, as it were, from His Sanctuary *(Kli Yakar* ad. loc.). *Eichah Rabbasi* (Intro. 22) intimates such an intention when it reads בַּבִּאָה *(v.* 5 lit. *'in the entry')* as an expression of woe: בַּיְיה בַּיְיה, *'Alas! Alas! The stranger is driving out the Owner of the House.' Rashi's* interpretation לְרָחֳקָה מֵעַל מִקְדָּשִׁי, *to drive* [*Me*] *away from My Sanctuary,* [*v.* 6] indicates the same thought, also based on *Eichah Rabbasi.* Scripture here substitutes a ה, *he,* for the א, *aleph,* in the root, and conjugates accordingly. We may assume that this is the second jealousy-provoking aspect of the image.

4. ... וְהִנֵּה – *And see!*

Menashe had hoped to drive God out of His Sanctuary (see above) and yet, the *Shechinah* still lingered on. The vision was identical with the one in the valley (Ch. 3). It was a *Merkavah* with its connotation of movement (see *Pref. Remarks* to Ch. 1). However, it was only *prepared* to move. The withdrawal which would presage the final destruction had not yet begun.

God would not leave His Sanctuary without first revealing to His prophet how His plans had been thwarted. This would be the purpose of the visions which were now to be shown to Yechezkel.

(ad. loc.) comments: The generation of Yoshiyahu pretended to be righteous but were in fact wicked. They would paint idolatrous pictures on the inside of their doors, on two separate panels. Upon the arrival of the people charged with destroying idols, the people would open the door [thus concealing the idols] making it impossible to detect the idols.

Thus we see that in secret or at the very least in their thoughts and attitudes the people continued to adhere to the cult which the youthful Menashe imposed on them and which, through thought patterns ingrained through years of usage, could not be shaken loose.

Thus it was Menashe's sin which finally destroyed Israel. The shackles of habit which bound the people had been forged by him; their beliefs and actions were the bitter fruit of the seeds which he had sown.

Alternately, it has been suggested, that it was literally Menashe's sin which caused the destruction. It was to him that God sent His servants, the prophets *(II Kings* 21:11) to apprise him of the fact that his actions had doomed Israel. Even after the pronouncement of this verdict, God suspended its execution in the hope that the people might be galvanized into a true inner repentance. When it became evident that they remained essentially unmoved, even after Yoshiyahu's efforts, the original verdict pronounced over Menashe's sins went into effect.

The sources make evident that it is extremely unlikely that there was a public idol at the gates of the Temple courtyard in Yechezkel's time.

ח ו שָׂא־נָא עֵינֶיךָ דֶּרֶךְ צָפוֹנָה וָאֶשָּׂא עֵינַי
דֶּרֶךְ צָפוֹנָה וְהִנֵּה מִצָּפוֹן לְשַׁעַר הַמִּזְבֵּחַ
ו סֶמֶל הַקִּנְאָה הַזֶּה בַּבִּאָה: וַיֹּאמֶר אֵלַי בֶּן־
מָה הֵם ק׳ אָדָם הֲרֹאֶה אַתָּה °מֵהֵם עֹשִׂים תּוֹעֵבוֹת
גְּדֹלוֹת אֲשֶׁר בֵּית־יִשְׂרָאֵל | עֹשִׂים פֹּה
לְרָחֳקָה מֵעַל מִקְדָּשִׁי וְעוֹד תָּשׁוּב תִּרְאֶה

5. שָׂא נָא עֵינֶיךָ — *Please lift up your eyes.*

In *v.* 3 we demonstrated the probability that there was no actual idol at the northern gate. The import of our verse would then be that the prophet was shown *the inner truth* rather than *the outer form (Malbim).* Even if no actual idol could be seen by the physical eye, the penetrating *prophetic* eye of Yechezkel saw the essential situation. In the hearts of the people the idol really 'was' there. (The expression *'lift up your eyes'* need not be construed as pertaining only to physical sight. See for example *Ps.* 121:1, and *Jeremiah* 3:2).[1]

This would be completely in consonance with the other visions which Yechezkel was shown in this and the subsequent three chapters. Certainly the messengers of death in Ch. 9 were not discernible to the physical eye, nor could anybody but the prophet have seen the gradual withdrawal of the *Merkavah.* The thoughts of the people (11:5) were as important to the prophet's understanding (see also 14:3) of their fate as were their actions, and the fire of 10:2 was not a physical one.

דֶּרֶךְ צָפוֹנָה — *Northward* (lit. *'the way to north').*

Someone looking northward from the northern gate would be looking outward to the Temple Mount. This would indicate that the idol was not in the Temple proper *(Rashi).* It is difficult to reconcile this with *Sanhedrin* 103b according to which Menashe's idol was in the Sanctuary (or from Ammon's time, in the Holy of Holies). It would seem that if a new idol were made it would not be returned to the same location where it had stood in Menashe's day. [See however *Eichah Rabbasi* (Introduction 22) which places the image mentioned in our verse into the Holy of Holies].

לְשַׁעַר הַמִּזְבֵּחַ — *Of the altar gate.*

The gate in the northern wall which was exactly in line with the altar *(Rashi).*

סֶמֶל הַקִּנְאָה הַזֶּה — *This image of jealousy.*

The article הַזֶּה, *this,* is usually appropriate only when referring to an actual object (see *Rashi Exod.* 12:2). Its use favors those opinions which hold that there existed an actual image (see above).

בַּבִּאָה — *In the entry* (lit. *'where one comes'* from בוא).

The word does not recur in Scripture. It is perhaps for that reason that *Eichah Rabbasi* (loc. cit.) takes the word out of context and reads בַּיָּיה בַּיָּיה, *Alas! alas ...* (see above).[2]

6. הֲרֹאֶה אַתָּה מָה הֵם עֹשִׂים — *Do you see what they do?*

[ראה in various forms to describe the prophet's visions is repeated no less

1. For treatment of the idea that the Torah addresses itself to essential truths rather than to overt manifestations, see *Michtav Me'Eliyahu I* p. 161 ff. (But see also *Maharal Chidushei Aggadah* to *Avodah Zarah* 10b and Introduction I to *Gevuros Hashem).*

your eyes northward.' So I lifted up my eyes northward and behold! north of the altar gate was this image of jealousy in the entry. 6 *Then He said to me: 'Ben Adam, do you see what they do? The great abominations which the Family of Israel do here to drive Me away from My Sanctuary? But turn again — you will see great abominations.'*

than ten times in the thirteen remaining verses of our chapter. It is difficult to escape the conclusion that it is used to intensify the realization of the abject folly of the people who (*v.* 12) based their perfidy on the patently ridiculous idea, that אֵין ה׳ רֹאֶה, *HASHEM does not see.*]

In *v.* 12 we shall see that ראה is used, not so much in the sense of *'seeing'* as in the sense of *'considering'* (see below). The meaning of our verse would then be: 'Do you realize what the real intentions of the people are?' (i.e. that their purpose is to drive Me away). [The question is, of course, rhetorical. See *Rashi* to *Isaiah* 27:7].

מָה הֵם — *What they.*

The כְּתִיב, *the masoretic spelling* is מֵהֵם (the two words are written as one).

Harav Breuer (based on *Hirsch's* commentary to *Exodus* 4:2) suggests that this spelling directs the reader's attention to the הם rather than the מה. It is not so much what is being done, as who is doing it which is so inexplicable. It is בֵּית יִשְׂרָאֵל who are bowing abjectly in front of graven images!

פֹּה — *Here.*

The very place which was to be the source of Israel's holiness, became the witness of their depravity; this intensifies the stricture. (Compare the use of the word שָׁם in 20:28 [see *comm.* ad. loc. *v.* 40.] A similar effect is achieved in Ch. 22 by the constant repetition of the word בָּךְ).

לְרָחֳקָה מֵעַל מִקְדָּשִׁי — *To drive* [*Me*] *away from My Sanctuary?*

The translation follows *Rashi.* The verse could equally well be rendered: *To sunder (themselves) from My Sanctuary (Harav Breuer.* See also *Targum).*

[Perhaps the reason for the ambiguity is that the two ideas are essentially one. Only when *both* God and Israel are 'in' the Sanctuary, does it retain meaning. God's own holiness is, of course, independent of both the Sanctuary and Israel. But in order for the Temple to be truly sacred, it must be made worthy of God's Presence by the fitness of Israel. The presence of the First is contingent upon the worthiness of the second. The Beis HaMikdash is described as both God's and Israel's house].

7-12. In Ch. 3 (see *footnote* to *v.* 6) we learned how Israel, in its degradation, sinks to lower depths than any other nation. In 5:7 we saw this confirmed in the bitter accusation, that their actions were such as could not be compared favorably with those of their more God-fearing neighbors. And in footnote to 20:23 we trace Israel's fatal attraction to the most depraved forms of idol worship, forms

2. As noted, the *Midrash* uses this verse to indicate that the image was placed in the Holy of Holies. ('Alas! alas! the stranger is driving out the Owner of the House'). How can this be reconciled with the beginning of the verse: *'Lift up your eyes northward ... '?* Again the solution suggests itself that its *factual,* overt location was to the north, but essentially in the people's minds (and thus in terms of *'prophetic reality')* it 'was' in the Holy of Holies.

ח
ז־י

ז תּוֹעֵבוֹת גְּדֹלוֹת׃ וַיָּבֵא אֹתִי אֶל־פֶּתַח
הֶחָצֵר וָאֶרְאֶה וְהִנֵּה חֹר־אֶחָד בַּקִּיר׃
ח וַיֹּאמֶר אֵלַי בֶּן־אָדָם חֲתָר־נָא בַקִּיר
ט וָאֶחְתֹּר בַּקִּיר וְהִנֵּה פֶּתַח אֶחָד׃ וַיֹּאמֶר
אֵלַי בֹּא וּרְאֵה אֶת־הַתּוֹעֵבוֹת הָרָעוֹת
י אֲשֶׁר הֵם עֹשִׂים פֹּה׃ וָאָבוֹא וָאֶרְאֶה
וְהִנֵּה כָל־תַּבְנִית רֶמֶשׂ וּבְהֵמָה שֶׁקֶץ
וְכָל־גִּלּוּלֵי בֵּית יִשְׂרָאֵל מְחֻקֶּה עַל־הַקִּיר

from which a decent-minded person would recoil in horror.

If a single scene could depict all these truths in ghastly clarity, it would be one in which seventy elders of Israel — perhaps the actual *Sanhedrin (Radak),* grovel and burn incense in front of pictures of vermin and livestock engraved upon their Temple walls.

Could this really have happened? Certain it is that, if indeed it did occur, it was not generally known. Jeremiah, who throughout *Kings* and the book of *Jeremiah* is depicted as having free access to the Temple, apparently knew nothing of such a desecration. Zidkiyahu, who was *completely righteous (Sanhedrin* 103a. See *Overview)* would surely not have tolerated such flagrant flaunting of the idolatrous cult *(Da'as Sofrim).*

Three solutions suggest themselves. It is possible that the Temple contained a secret chamber known only to the initiated. And while it is unlikely that its constant use by seventy people could remain undetected, the possibility exists (suggested by *Da'as Sofrim)* that the ceremony witnessed by Yechezkel, was an isolated occurrence.

Abarbanel holds that the wall and the hole (*v.* 7) were not a part of the Temple. Yechezkel was shown a wall, told to excavate a hole in it to symbolize his penetration of the innermost secrets of the population, and shown what the people were doing in the privacy of their own homes (*v.* 12). According to *Abarbanel,* Yechezkel was not shown a scene of seventy men serving the engraved idols in the Temple confines.

[A third alternative is possible. In a wider and deeper sense, God's Sanctuary is *Knesses Israel,* the people themselves. (Compare *Lev.* 20:3 and *Rashi* ad. loc.) The Temple is only the conduit through which God dwells among *them.* If seventy men, each in his private room (*v.* 12) are engaged in hideous fetishism, then this desecration truly takes place in God's Sanctuary — His people. (In exactly the same way as a person who offers his son to the fire-belching Molech [*Lev. loc. cit.*] *'defiles My sanctuary'* even though the service was not performed in the Temple confines). The scene which Yechezkel was allowed to witness with his prophetic eye 'occurred' within the perspective of prophecy as surely as the prophetic eye discerned the *'image of jealousy'* on its ostensibly empty pedestal. (see *comm. v.* 3).]

7. פֶּתַח הֶחָצֵר — *The door of the courtyard.*

— I.e. The door of the 'northern gate' mentioned in *v.* 3 *(Rashi).* Up to now Yechezkel had been some distance from the gate. Now he was brought close.

8. וְהִנֵּה פֶּתַח אֶחָד — *And see! a single door.*

[7] *And He brought me to the door of the courtyard; I looked — and see! a hole in the wall.* [8] *Then He said to me: 'Ben Adam, please excavate the wall.' So I excavated in the wall, and see! a single door.* [9] *Then He said to me: 'Enter and see the evil abominations which they do here.'*

[10] *So I entered and I looked; and see! every form of creeping thing and animal of detestation and every manner of idol of the Family of Israel; carved into*

As he excavated the hole, a secret door became visible *(Rashi);* or the enlarged hole itself may have served as a door *(Radak).*

The term *'a single* door' shows that this was the only means of access. This would help to preserve the secrecy of the hidden chamber *(Da'as Sofrim).*

9. בֹּא — *Enter.*

The root בוא is occasionally used in the sense of *'to enter'* rather than *'to come'*. See for example *Gen.* 7:13 and 41:21.

פֹּה — *Here.*

See *comm.* to *v.* 6. The word is used once more in *v.* 17.

10. כָּל תַּבְנִית רֶמֶשׂ וּבְהֵמָה שֶׁקֶץ — *Every form of creeping thing and animal of detestation.*

Ch. 11:15 tells us how the inhabitants of Jerusalem looked upon themselves. In grandiose self-delusion they saw themselves as the true 'inheritors of the land' in contrast to their exiled brethren, who, in their view, had been driven out of the Land because they were undeserving of it. Yet, from our verse we see that their pride, which goaded them into ignoring the gathering clouds of catastrophe, did not prevent them from groveling in front of the vermin of the earth!

Isaiah 2:20 describes the 'End of Days' as the time when: *Man will throw away the idols of his silver and the idols of his gold which had caused him to bow down to moles and bats.* Once God's Providence is denied (see *comm.* to *v.* 12) man is in fact subservient to the smallest of God's messengers on earth. The teeth of the mole can indeed gnaw away at the very foundations of his wealth. *(Hirsch, Gesammelte Schriften II* p. 189. See also *Midrash* to *Koheles* 5:8 and commentary to ArtScroll edition). If man does not bow to God he bows down to the lowliest gnat.

וְכָל גִּלּוּלֵי בֵּית יִשְׂרָאֵל — *And every [manner] of idol of the Family of Israel.*

The inclusion of *manner* in the translation follows *Harav Breuer.* Obviously, not all the idols of Israel were in the chamber.

Da'as Sofrim notes how, although only small numbers of people were involved in the desecrations witnessed by Yechezkel, the prophet's strictures seem directed to the entire *'family of Israel'.* Scripture teaches that even if only a few people actually succumb to their evil inclinations, the climate making it possible was a national malaise; therefore, it is within the nation as a whole that the source of individual perfidy must be sought. (For a full treatment of this concept: See *Halevi's Doros Horishonim, Tekufas Hamikra* and *Michtav Me'eliyahu I,* p. 162. See also introductory remarks to Ch. 16).

ח
יא־יג

יא סָבִיב | סָבִיב׃ וְשִׁבְעִים אִישׁ מִזִּקְנֵי
בֵית־יִשְׂרָאֵל וְיַאֲזַנְיָהוּ בֶן־שָׁפָן עֹמֵד
בְּתוֹכָם עֹמְדִים לִפְנֵיהֶם וְאִישׁ מִקְטַרְתּוֹ
יב בְּיָדוֹ וַעֲתַר עֲנַן־הַקְּטֹרֶת עֹלֶה׃ וַיֹּאמֶר
אֵלַי הֲרָאִיתָ בֶן־אָדָם אֲשֶׁר זִקְנֵי בֵית־
יִשְׂרָאֵל עֹשִׂים בַּחֹשֶׁךְ אִישׁ בְּחַדְרֵי
מַשְׂכִּיתוֹ כִּי אֹמְרִים אֵין יהוה רֹאֶה אֹתָנוּ
יג עָזַב יהוה אֶת־הָאָרֶץ׃ וַיֹּאמֶר אֵלַי עוֹד

11. וְשִׁבְעִים אִישׁ מִזִּקְנֵי בֵית יִשְׂרָאֵל — *And seventy men of the elders of the Family of Israel.*

A fulfillment of Isaiah's (3:12) prediction: *'My people! Your guides lead astray.'* The Sanhedrin to whom the people looked for examples, were the worst offenders *(Radak).*

We do not know who Ya'aznayahu ben Shafan was. The special mention of his name marks him as the most important — and therefore the most culpable — among them.

12. See intro. remarks to *vs.* 7-12 for some possible ways of explaining this verse. In *Metzudas David's* interpretation, it does not refer to Yechezkel's vision. He renders: *You have not even seen* [the even greater abominations] *which they perpetrate in their* [private] *paved chambers.* [Had you seen that, you would have been even more astounded.]

בַּחֹשֶׁךְ — *In the darkness.*

[If *darkness* refers to night — as could be inferred from *Targum* to the next phrase, see below — it could be that the night was especially suited to this particular fetishism for it is then that the כֹּחוֹת הַטּוּמְאָה, *the forces of evil* are rampant in the world. (See *Luzzato, Derech Hashem* IV:6).

בְּחַדְרֵי מַשְׂכִּיתוֹ — *His paved rooms.*

The translation follows *Rashi* who traces מַשְׂכִּית to the root שכה *to spread out* or *over.* (See *Lev.* 26:1 and *Toras Kohanim* ad loc., and *Num.* 33:52. In both places *Targum Onkelos,* who renders אֶבֶן מַשְׂכִּית as a *'stone for prostration'*, seems to concur.) A person who prostrates himself is 'spread over' the ground. On our verse, however, *Targum renders: Bedroom.* In this he is followed by *Eliezer of Beaugency* who renders our phrase: 'a private room *closed off from prying eyes'.* [The root, according to this translation, may be סכה, *to see,* thus a room where outsiders are not to see.]

Radak in *Sefer HaShorashim* relates the word to שְׂכִיּוֹת הַחֶמְדָּה *(Isaiah* 2:16) where it represents the idea of ornamentation. Thus חַדְרֵי מַשְׂכִּיתוֹ would be 'his ornamented room.' This would aptly fit the context of the previous verse which describes the room as having pictures engraved upon its walls. This interpretation assumes the meaning *'to look at'* for the root שכה. An ornament is described as an object which people look at and admire.

אֵין ה׳ רֹאֶה אֹתָנוּ — *HASHEM does not see us.*

The root ראה in Scripture can mean not only *'to see'*, but also *'to consider'*, or *'to take an interest'. (See Ibn Ezra* and *Ramban* to *Gen. 1:4).* This is its meaning in our verse. It was not God's *ability* which was in question, but His *involvement.* The sinners contended that God was so far removed from human af-

VIII
11-13

the wall, all around. 11 *And seventy men of the elders*
of the Family of Israel, with Ya'azanyahu ben Shafan standing among them, were standing before them, each man with his censer in his hand; and a thick cloud of incense rose up.

12 *Then He said to me: 'Have you seen, Ben Adam, what the elders of the Family of Israel do in the darkness, each man in his paved rooms? For they say: "HASHEM does not see us. HASHEM has forsaken the Land."'*
13 *And He said to me: 'Turn*

עָזַב ה׳ אֶת הָאָרֶץ — *HASHEM has forsaken the Land.*

fairs, that it was pointless to turn to Him in prayer *(Radak).*[1]

1. It is tragic when man, in his foolish pride, becomes convinced of his invincibility; it is even more tragic when he is so small in his own eyes that he cannot apprehend his own greatness. Steeped in the pernicious beliefs of the idol cult, thinking themselves at the mercy of cosmic forces which controlled their destiny, the people had become desensitized to their innate Godliness. God had introduced Himself to them at the dawn of their history as אֶהְיֶה אֲשֶׁר אֶהְיֶה, *I shall be* [*with them*] *during this oppression as I will be* [*with them*] *during all subsequent oppressions (Rashi, Exod.* 3:14), But in their present perception of Him, He had changed into a cold, impersonal, remote deity, uninvolved with them and inaccessible to them.

[*Rambam Hilchos Teshuvah* 3:7, enumerates five of the most serious forms of מִינוּת, *heresy.* The first four deal with misconceptions concerning the nature of God: His existence; His uniqueness; His incorporeality; and His eternity. The fifth kind of heretic is one who solicits celestial bodies to act as intermediaries between himself and God, thus implying that man is incapable of praying directly to God. Man's inability to apprehend his own Godliness, is no less a heresy than his inability to know God as He wishes Himself to be known.]

Thus it came about that men, reared in the philosophy of the idolators, considered it sinful and disrespectful to turn to God for their own mundane and seemingly insignificant needs *(D'rashos haRan, Drush* 9).

Radak (II Kings 17:27) demonstrates that even in the worst times Israel never forgot its true heritage. They always remembered the God of their fathers. Their mistake was that they thought Him too far removed from mundane affairs, and that He could be approached only through an intermediary. Thus, incidents like the following became possible.

— Ravshake, the Assyrian general, found a receptive and sympathetic audience, when he argued (*Isaiah* 36:7) that Israel could not expect God's help and intervention because Chizkiyahu had offended Him by removing the (idolatrous) *'high places and altars'* from the land.

— The people said: *'Abraham was one and he inherited the Land; but we are many, the Land is given to us for inheritance'* (33:24). *Tosefta Sota* (6:5), explains: If Abraham who served only one God inherited the Land, we who serve many gods should surely inherit the Land. If Abraham who sacrificed only one son inherited the Land, we who sacrifice our sons and daughters should surely inherit the Land.

— Jeremiah (*Jeremiah* Ch. 44) rebukes the pitiful remnant of Jews, who fled to Egypt after the holocaust, for worshiping the heavenly hosts. They defy him with the argument that precisely such worship had always ensured Israel's well being. Only after idolatry was eradicated [presumably referring to Yoshiyahu's reforms] had troubles and exile overtaken the country.

To such depths had Israel fallen! It is against the background of these beliefs that our verse must be understood.

ח תָּשׁוּב תִּרְאֶה תּוֹעֵבוֹת גְּדֹלוֹת אֲשֶׁר־
יד־טז יד הֵמָּה עֹשִׂים׃ וַיָּבֵא אֹתִי אֶל־פֶּתַח שַׁעַר
בֵּית־יהוה אֲשֶׁר אֶל־הַצָּפוֹנָה וְהִנֵּה־
שָׁם הַנָּשִׁים יֹשְׁבוֹת מְבַכּוֹת אֶת־
טו הַתַּמּוּז׃ וַיֹּאמֶר אֵלַי הֲרָאִיתָ בֶן־
אָדָם עוֹד תָּשׁוּב תִּרְאֶה תּוֹעֵבוֹת גְּדֹלוֹת
טז מֵאֵלֶּה׃ וַיָּבֵא אֹתִי אֶל־חֲצַר בֵּית־יהוה
הַפְּנִימִית וְהִנֵּה־פֶתַח הֵיכַל יהוה בֵּין
הָאוּלָם וּבֵין הַמִּזְבֵּחַ כְּעֶשְׂרִים וַחֲמִשָּׁה
אִישׁ אֲחֹרֵיהֶם אֶל־הֵיכַל יהוה וּפְנֵיהֶם

An explanatory phrase. *HASHEM* does not see *because* He has forsaken the Land (Metzudas David).

14. פֶּתַח שַׁעַר בֵּית ה׳ אֲשֶׁר אֶל הַצָּפוֹנָה — *The door of the northern gate of the House of HASHEM.*

He was brought into the courtyard proper, to a gate which led into the northern wall of the הֵיכָל, *Temple building (Rashi).*

מְבַכּוֹת אֶת הַתַּמּוּז — *Causing the Tammuz to cry.*

The translation follows Rashi, who, (with *Radak* and *Metzudas David)* comments that the *Tammuz* was an idol that was made in such a way that it could appear to *cry,* as if begging for sacrifices. Its eyes were made of soft lead. When a fire was kindled inside the idol, the eyes melted, giving the appearance of tears rolling down its face.

Other explanations of the passage, however, avoid the implication of such flagrant desecration of the Temple courtyard.

— *Rambam (Moreh Nevuchim* 3:29) tells of a heathen custom that the first day of the month of Tammuz was observed as a day of mourning to commemorate the death of a 'prophet' named Tammuz who had been executed for advocating the worship of constellations. *Rambam* makes special mention of the fact that the mourning was done by women. (See *Moreh Nevuchim* ed. Kapach, Jerusalem 1972, p.333, *footnote* 74.) [Since *v.* 1 dates Yechezkel's visions in the sixth month, (i.e. Elul) we must assume that he was shown events which were not actually taking place at that moment. This would be another example of prophetic vision dealing with essentials rather than with actualities as discussed above.]

— *Radak* in one explanation takes *Tammuz* not as the name of an idol, but as a noun meaning 'burning'. The women mourned the many children who were burned as sacrifices to idols.

— *Harav Breuer,* takes note of modern research which identifies the *Tammuz* as the pagan idol of rebirth and growth. He was said to be born every spring when nature regenerated itself, and to die with the advent of summer when the burning heat of the sun destroyed much of spring's rebirth. The custom was to mourn his annual 'death'.

15. תּוֹעֵבוֹת גְּדֹלוֹת מֵאֵלֶּה — *Greater abominations than these.*

The three previous desecrations had been described as תּוֹעֵבוֹת גְּדֹלוֹת, *great abominations.* There was no indication

again — you will see great abominations which they do.'

14 So He brought me to the door of the northern gate of the House of HASHEM and see there! the women sit causing the Tammuz to cry. 15 And He said to me: 'Did you see, Ben Adam? Turn again — you will see greater abominations than these.'

16 Then He brought me to the inner courtyard of the House of HASHEM, and see! at the door of HASHEM's Temple, between the entrance-hall and the altar were some twenty-five men, their backs to HASHEM's Temple and their faces eastwards, and

that any one of them was worse than the others. The prophet will now be shown horrors exceeding all previous ones.

Indeed the shame to be described seared a lasting mark upon Israel's conscience. Of all the sins committed during the tragic closing years of the First Temple, it was this one which was singled out for remembrance during the period of the Second Temple.

The *Mishnah* in *Succa* (51b) describes how the שִׂמְחַת בֵּית הַשּׁוֹאֵבָה, *the Rejoicing Attending the Drawing of Water* was performed during *Succos*: '... when they reached the gate which leads out to the east they turned their faces from east to west and said: 'Our fathers who were in this place stood with their backs toward the Temple of the Lord and their faces towards the east, and they worshipped the sun towards the east; but as for us, our eyes are turned to the Lord.' Rabbi Judah said: They used to repeat the phrase and say: "We are the Lord's and our eyes are turned to the Lord".'

16. אֶל חֲצַר בֵּית ה׳ הַפְּנִימִית — *To the inner courtyard of the House of HASHEM*.

Yechezkel, who was already in the courtyard (*v.*14), was now moved from the northern site, to the east. [The Temple entrance was to the east. The Holy of Holies (and therefore the שְׁכִינָה, *the Divine Presence*) was in the west.]. The prophet was brought between the altar and the entrance-hall leading into the Temple building.

כְּעֶשְׂרִים וַחֲמִשָּׁה אִישׁ — *Some twenty-five men.*

We meet these twenty-five men once more in 11:1. There they are, *'twenty-five men'*, not *'some twenty-five men'*. At this point their number is approximated because it is less significant to identify them accurately than to recognize the enormity of their act. In Ch. 11, however, their opinions are discussed; in that context each is important as an individual *(Harav Breuer)*.

אֲחֹרֵיהֶם אֶל הֵיכַל ה׳ וּפְנֵיהֶם קֵדְמָה — *Their backs to HASHEM's Temple and their faces eastwards.*

The end of the verse tells why they faced eastwards. They were worshiping the sun. Why was it necessary to relate that their backs were towards God's Temple? In the seemingly superfluous phrase, *Yoma 77a* detects an indication of how these people had finally dredged the depths of obscene insolence: 'This teaches us that they uncovered

ח
יז

קִדְמָה וְהֵמָּה מִשְׁתַּחֲוִיתֶם קֵדְמָה לַשָּׁמֶשׁ׃
יז וַיֹּאמֶר אֵלַי הֲרָאִיתָ בֶן־אָדָם הֲנָקֵל לְבֵית
יְהוּדָה מֵעֲשׂוֹת אֶת־הַתּוֹעֵבוֹת אֲשֶׁר עָשׂוּ
פֹה כִּי־מָלְאוּ אֶת־הָאָרֶץ חָמָס וַיָּשֻׁבוּ
לְהַכְעִיסֵנִי וְהִנָּם שֹׁלְחִים אֶת־הַזְּמוֹרָה

themselves and evacuated downwards'. The hideously degrading Pe'or worship (see comm. to 20:23) had finally found its way into God's Temple.

וְהֵמָּה מִשְׁתַּחֲוִיתֶם — *And they destructively bow.*

A combination of two roots: שחה*, to bow* and שחת*, to destroy.* As they bowed down to the sun, they were destroying the Temple *(Rashi)* (or perhaps themselves, see below *comm.* to *v.* 17).

לַשָּׁמֶשׁ — *To the sun.*

Life on earth is supported by, and dependent upon, the sun. Its iron laws bind earth to an unchanging orbit, dictating times and seasons, warmth and light, growth and decay. God called the sun and its attendant solar system, *rulers* of day and night *(Gen.* 1:16); תַּחַת הַשָּׁמֶשׁ*, beneath the sun,* is the all-inclusive phrase used by Scripture to describe the whole of physical existence (e.g. *Koheles* 1:3) *(Maharal, Tif'eres Yisrael* 4).

Time is the great challenger to the concept of a finite world, begun by God's free untrammeled will and ending with the withdrawal of God's favor. Determined by the inexorable, undeviating motion of celestial bodies around the sun with no apparent beginning and no discernable end, time functions without revealing the hand of God which ordains it. God 'hid' Himself behind a veil of 'natural law' when He made the world; this sun-determined time, more than any other factor, seems to challenge His Providence (based on *Harav Yitzchak Hutner's Pachad Yitzchak, Rosh Hashana* 27).

Thus the *Shechinah* in the west, and the sun in the east are the two seemingly irreconcilable poles upon the axis of human experience. In fact, however, they are not diametrically opposite poles at all; that time itself can be sanctified is the subject of God's first command to Knesses Yisrael (*Ex.* 12:2. *Pachad Yitzchak* loc. cit.). The people had not learned that lesson. By turning their backs to the *Shechinah* and bowing to the sun, they proclaimed their belief in a blind determinism from which God's Providence was excluded.

17. הֲנָקֵל לְבֵית יְהוּדָה — *Is it too trivial for the Family of Judah.*

The syntax is extremely difficult.

Rashi and *Metzudas David* render: Are the evils which they have done outside the Temple (i.e. filling the Land with injustice) not enough for them, that they also come into the Temple to anger me? In this rendering וַיָּשֻׁבוּ לְהַכְעִיסֵנִי describes all four abominations mentioned in the chapter, [the idol at the entrance gate; the elders in their paved rooms, the women bemoaning the Tammuz; and the twenty-five men bowing to the sun] and וְהִנָּם שֹׁלְחִים ... is a new thought.

Eliezer of Beaugency and *Malbim* have original ways of rendering וְהִנָּם שֹׁלְחִים ... (see below) and in their translation the verse speaks with that thought: Is it not enough that they have committed so many sins, i.e. desecrated My House and in addition filled the Land with injustice that now they also שֹׁלְחִים אֶת הַזְּמוֹרָה ... ?

In *Harav Breuer*'s view this verse addresses itself to the obscene horror

they destructively bow eastward to the sun.
17 *He said to me: 'Did you see, Ben Adam? Is it too trivial to the Family of Judah to prevent their doing the abominations that they have committed here — that they have filled the land with injustice, and they yet return to anger Me? See them! they hurl their*

described in the previous verse. God cries out to the prophet: 'Were the previous three abominations [the idol at the Temple entrance; the elders groveling in front of the graven images; the women bemoaning the Tammuz] not enough? These acts alone would guarantee the collapse of Jerusalem's social structures. [כִּי מָלְאוּ אֶת הָאָרֶץ חָמָס, *for they have filled the land with injustice.* (See *comm.* to 7:11). The idea is the same one as expressed in *Gen.* 6:11: *'And the earth was corrupt before God and the earth was filled with injustice'.* *Hirsch* comments: When the world is corrupt before God all the human institutions and laws of society cannot prevent society in general from going to ruin. The erosion of this social structure is guaranteed with the absence of sanctions imposed by a life oriented towards the striving for holiness]. Why then do My people continue to anger Me with this ultimate degradation? Why do they allow their humanity to be destroyed (see above *v.* 16 on מִשְׁתַּחֲוִיתֶם) by sinking to the levels of an animal?

כִּי מָלְאוּ אֶת הָאָרֶץ חָמָס — *That they have filled the land with injustice.*

See Commentary to 7:11.

וְהִנָּם שֹׁלְחִים אֶת הַזְּמוֹרָה אֶל אַפָּם — *See them! they hurl their shame against their face.*

Targum's rendering of זְמוֹרָה as בַּהֲתָא, *shame,* is not literal *(Radak).* He uses it to avoid explicating the obscenity of the actual meaning.

That the phrase has an unusually offensive connotation can be seen from the *Mesorah* which lists the word אַפָּם, *their face* as one of the eighteen תִּקּוּנֵי סוֹפְרִים, *emendations of the scribes. Sifre* (to *Num.* 10:35) states that the true meaning of the word would be אַפִּי, *My face,* meaning the face of God. However, to safeguard God's honor, the word was changed to אַפָּם, *'their* face', so that the offensive connotation not refer directly to God.[1]

Targum also changes the singular form אַפָּם to the plural אַפֵּיהוֹן, thus altering the meaning from *nose* to *face.* (Scripture invariably uses the plural אַפַּיִם for *face,* while the singular אַף means *nose*). This change from *nose* to *face* was made necessary because of *Targum's* insertion of the word *shame,* a condition which is registered on the *face,* not on the *nose.*

Literally then the connotation would be: 'And see! they hurl the זְמוֹרָה against My nose.'

What is זְמוֹרָה?

Rashi traces the word to the root זמר, *to sing.* In *v.*16 we saw that the people had 'uncovered themselves and were evacuating downwards towards the west. זְמוֹרָה is the sound and ugly smell which is part of 'breaking the wind' [See *Aruch* on תרז]. So also *Metzudas David.*

Radak also translates זְמוֹרָה as an evil smell (without explaining the etymology) and explains that the whole phrase is used to describe the 'evil smelling' [because of its idolatrous source] incense which the people were offering up (*v.* 11).

1. For an examination of the concept of תִּקּוּן סוֹפְרִים *(Megillah* 25b) see *Chumash Mechokekey Yehudah, Karney Ohr* 22 to *Gen.* 18:13.

ח
יח

יח אֶל־אַפָּם: וְגַם־אֲנִי אֶעֱשֶׂה בְחֵמָה לֹא־
תָחוֹס עֵינִי וְלֹא אֶחְמֹל וְקָרְאוּ בְאָזְנַי קוֹל
א גָּדוֹל וְלֹא אֶשְׁמַע אוֹתָם: וַיִּקְרָא בְאָזְנַי
קוֹל גָּדוֹל לֵאמֹר קָרְבוּ פְּקֻדּוֹת הָעִיר
ב וְאִישׁ כְּלִי מַשְׁחֵתוֹ בְּיָדוֹ: וְהִנֵּה שִׁשָּׁה

ט
א־ב

A number of liturgical poems (פִּיוּטִים) to *Parshas Zachor*, identify זְמוֹרָה as the *phallus*. [See *Zera Ephraim* to *Pesikta Rabbasi, Parshas Zachor* 117, quoting *Ra'avan*]. *Yerushalmi Avoda Zara* 3:6 records that the *Ba'al*, who seems to have been the idol most popular among the Canaanite heathens, was made in the shape of a phallus. Thus, in this view, not only the service of the *Pe'or* was brought into *God's* Temple (see above *comm.* to *v.* 16) but also that of the *Ba'al* [*Harav Breuer*].

The word זְמוֹרָה also means *a branch*. *Eliezer of Beaugency* understands its use in our verse in that sense. He translates: *They allow the [evil] branches of their vineyard to grow with abandon (שֹׁלְחִים) in their presence.* Instead of ridding themselves of their evil practices, they retain them and allow them to flourish.

Malbim traces זְמוֹרָה to the root זמר, *to cut off*. The verse refers to the internecine slaughter which was taking place within the city: 'And see! they are permitting slaughter (זְמוֹרָה) to rampage (שֹׁלְחִים) in the city, to their own aggravation (אַפָּם meaning *anger*).

18. וְגַם אֲנִי — *Also I.*

The prophet is given to understand that the impending destruction cannot be avoided. God cannot remain silent in the face of the provocations displayed to Yechezkel.

IX

Even as the people, locked in a fool's paradise of delusion concerning their invincibility (11:3), continue their normal lives, God's messengers spread through the city, marking it for death and destruction.

The daily Temple service continues; indeed, to the people, the existence of the Temple in their midst is an ironclad guarantee against disaster (Jeremiah 7:4). But silently, unbeknown to them, the very nature of the Temple is changing. Its soul, the *Shechinah*, the Divine Presence, begins to withdraw, leaving it a lifeless hulk of wood and stone, ready for defilement *(v.* 7) and destruction.

1. וַיִּקְרָא בְאָזְנַי — *He called in my ears.*

Because this chapter is a direct continuation of the previous one, there is no need to identify God as the One Who *'called'*.

קוֹל גָּדוֹל — *A loud voice.* See below.

קָרְבוּ פְּקֻדּוֹת הָעִיר — *Bring near those appointed over the city.*

The word קָרְבוּ can be taken as the third person plural past tense, *Kal*, in which case the phrase would be translated: 'Those who are appointed over the city *have drawn near*; or the word may be understood as the imperative in the *Pi'el*, thus: *'Bring near (Rashi)* or *draw near (Metzudas David)*, those who are appointed over the city.'

[Perhaps the commentators felt that the *Pi'el*, a construction that implies a more intense act was indicated by the words קוֹל גָּדוֹל, a *loud voice*.] According to this interpretation, Yechezkel was permitted to listen to the heavenly voice which instructed the angels to proceed on their way. God's messengers (or angels) do His bidding by *listening to the 'voice' of His speech (Ps.* 103:20).

VIII
18

shame in their own face. 18 *I, too, will react with fury. My eye will not spare nor pity. Though they will cry in My ears with loud voice — yet I will not hear them.'*

IX
1-2

He called in my ears with a loud voice, saying: 'Bring near those appointed over the city, each with his weapon of destruction in his hand.'

2 *And see! six men coming from the way of the up-*

[See *Luzzatto, Likkutei Adir Bamorom, Yalkut Yedi'os Ha'emes* p. 34l.]

פְּקֻדּוֹת הָעִיר — *Those who are appointed over the city.*

The word פְּקֻדָּה can have the meaning of *fate* or *visitation* (as in *Numbers* 16:29); or an *appointed official* (as in 44:11). The commentators assume the latter meaning [presumably because of the next phrase, *Each one with his weapon* ...]. However *Eichah Rabbasi* 2:4 probably had the first meaning in mind. The *Midrash* reads into the use of the word פְּקֻדּוֹת, a hint that the catastrophe about to overtake Jerusalem was tied to the sin of the Golden Calf *(Exod.* 32), concerning which Moses was told: וּבְיוֹם פָּקְדִי וּפָקַדְתִּי עֲלֵיהֶם חַטָּאתָם *'And on the day of My vengeance I will visit upon them, their sin' (ibid. v.* 34). Thus the *'fate'* (פְּקוּדָה) which is now overtaking Jerusalem, is that *visitation* to which they had been destined from the very beginning.[1]

Who are the *'appointed ones'* who are summoned to the city?

The *Talmud (Shabbos* 55a) identifies them as the six expressions of God's fury (see below, v. 2) — destroying messengers or angels of God, sent to execute judgment over the condemned population.

Radak identifies them as the Babylonian generals mentioned in *Jeremiah* 39:3. *Radak* notes that although *eight* generals are mentioned there, one of them may have been the supreme commander, and not directly involved in the fighting. The eighth would be the 'man clothed in linen.'

[Since the prophet is shown the inner, essential truth, rather than the outward, tangible occurrence (see *comm.* 8:3), the two interpretations are not mutually exclusive. Certainly no Babylonian general could have conquered Jerusalem if he did not personify God's own fury.]

2. וְהִנֵּה שִׁשָּׁה אֲנָשִׁים — *And see! Six men.*

Who are these six men? Said *Rav Chisdah:* קֶצֶף, אַף, וְחֵמָה, וּמַשְׁחִית, וּמְשַׁבֵּר, וּמְכַלֶּה, *(Shabbos* 55a). [It is difficult if not impossible, to find exact English

1. While the worship of the Golden Calf was not idolatry in its grossest form (see *Ramban* ad. loc.), it is nevertheless certain that aspects of idol worship were involved (see *Yoma* 66b and *Rashi* on *Exod.* 32:20).

In 20:23 (see also *footnote* to 6:8-9) we trace the *Midrashic* idea that the Babylonian exile had been predestined from the earliest days of Israel's national existence. Because both the first and second generations in the wilderness proved unable to rid themselves of their attachment to idol worship, it became inevitable that the foundations of their future kingdom, would not be strong enough to withstand the buffeting of the surrounding cultures.

In this sense the destruction of the Temple and the exile of the people were indeed *'visitations'* of the sin of the Golden Calf.

ט אֲנָשִׁים בָּאִים ׀ מִדֶּרֶךְ־שַׁעַר הָעֶלְיוֹן אֲשֶׁר ׀
ב מָפְנֶה צָפוֹנָה וְאִישׁ כְּלִי מַפָּצוֹ בְּיָדוֹ
וְאִישׁ־אֶחָד בְּתוֹכָם לָבֻשׁ בַּדִּים וְקֶסֶת

equivalents for these six terms. The first three denote forms of Divine *anger,* the other three, forms of Divine *destruction.* All are assumed to be *Divine messengers or angels* in Talmudic literature. For detailed source material see *Reuven Margalioth: Malachei Elyon, Mossad Harav Kook,* Jerusalem 1964.]

שַׁעַר הָעֶלְיוֹן — *The upper gate.*

The name of a Temple gate facing northeast, [*II Kings* 15:35] the direction of Babylon *(Radak).* It was from Babylon that the destruction of the Temple was to come [compare *Jer.* 1:13-14].

כְּלִי מַפָּצוֹ — *His sledgehammer* [lit. *'His weapon of shattering*]

I.e. a more exact description of the *'weapon of destruction'* of *v.* 1.

וְאִישׁ אֶחָד בְּתוֹכָם לבוּשׁ בַּדִּים — *One man among them was clothed in linen.*

Rabbi Yochanan said: This is the angel Gabriel, as it is written: *And one man was among them clothed in linen. (Eichah Rabbasi* 2:4). [In the book of *Daniel,* Gabriel is described as being dressed in linen] *(Radak.* See also *Rashi, Yoma* 77a). Therefore, the *Midrash* and all other Talmudic sources assume the 'man clothed in linen' to be the angel Gabriel. [But see *Yalkut Yechezkel* 349].

Since the *six men* were identified by name (see above) it would seem that the *man clothed in linen* was a seventh man *(Radak).*

However, *Eichah Rabbasi* (ibid.) and *Yalkut* (ibid.) assume him to have been among the six: Rabbi Yochanan said this refers to Gabriel, the fiercest angel among them. [However, *Yalkut* reads: This refers to the angel of mercy among them, who is Michael] .

Since Gabriel was among the *'six men',* he must also have come armed with weapons of destruction and shattering *(vs.* 1 and 2). Nevertheless, it is clear that his mission was also one of mercy, for he is charged with marking the righteous people to be spared (*v.* 4), and with guaranteeing that the consuming fire will not be completely destructive (see below *comm.* to 10:2,7).

See also *Mechilta* to *Bo* (referring to *v.* 11 of our chapter): 'They who were commanded to do 'bad' did not report that their mission had been accomplished. He, who was commanded to do 'good' reported that his mission had been accomplished.

Eichah Rabbasi takes note of this dual role: This angel functioned in three different capacities: Scribe, executioner, and High Priest. [He was clothed in linen, the garment worn by the High Priest on Yom Kippur.] Certainly the High Priest functions at the pole opposite to that of the executioner.[1]

That both functions are vested in one messenger can best be understood in the light of *Pesachim* 118b which relates that when Nebuchadnezzar ordered Chananyah, Mishael and Azaryah thrown into the fiery furnace, Yurkami the angel of hail offered to go down to cool the fire. Gabriel said to him: 'This

1. Gabriel is the angel of *fire (Pesachim* 118a, *Yoma* 21b). It is he who was sent to destroy Sodom in Abraham's time *(Bava Metzia* 86b) and it was he who burned the Assyrian army at the gates of Jerusalem *(Sanhedrin* 95b). This is the capacity (i.e. as a bearer of destroying fire) in which the Sages interpret his role in our chapter. (See *Tanchuma Tazria* 9: 'And so you find, when those five angels of destruction came to destroy Jerusalem ... Gabriel was sent with them ... (and) God said to Gabriel: Fill your hands with burning coals ... and throw them upon the city ...'). Nevertheless, throughout history, it was Gabriel who intervened when Israel was in danger (*Sanhedrin* 26a; also *Pesachim* 118a).

IX 2 *per gate which faces northward, each man with his sledgehammer in his hand. One man among them was clothed in linen with the slate of the scribe at his*

would not be a fitting proof of God's might, for you are the angel of hail and everyone knows that water can extinguish fire. But if I, the angel of fire, go down and cool the inside of the furnace, it will be a *miracle within a miracle'*. So God said to Gabriel 'Go down!'

Thus, a salvation derived from the very agency of 'destruction', is imbued with a special miraculous dimension. It is a *'miracle within a miracle'*.

Throughout this and the next two chapters, we perceive a tension between God's uncompromising justice, which demands complete destruction, and a merciful counterforce which moderates the implementation of those demands.

— The city's entire population including the righteous people, (see *comm.* to *v.* 6) is condemned to die — yet thousands were eventually spared.

— Gabriel is commanded to hurl burning coals upon the city — but they are allowed to 'cool' in his hands for many years, in order that the total destruction implicit in the original command, might not take place (*comm.* Ch. 10:2,7).

— In *v.* 8, Yechezkel reads the unfolding events as implying the total destruction of *'all* the remnant of Israel'. In His answer *(vs.* 9-10) God does not deny that this is indeed what is about to occur. Not until 11:15ff is the prophet told that Israel *does* have a future — vested in the communities of the exile.

That God's mercy is allowed to temper His justice is a 'miracle'. That the very agent of God's justice becomes the instrument of His mercy — is a *'miracle within a miracle'*. It is a statement that *Knesses Israel* by its very nature 'rejects' destruction. Its eternal existence is a 'law of nature', as immutable as the rising and setting of the sun *(Jeremiah* 33:25-26).

Shabbos 55a identifies one of God's six messengers as חֵמָה (see *comm.*). *Tosafos* ad. loc. notes that *Avodah Zarah* 4b, interprets the verse in *Isaiah* 27:4, חֵמָה אֵין לִי, *I have no fury* as meaning that God will never have חֵמָה, *fury*, towards Israel. How then could 'fury' have been one of His six avenging angels?

The answer would seem to lie in the tension which we have recognized. The objective, uncompromising quality of God's justice may indeed demand that He invoke His all-consuming fury. However, Israel's intrinsic 'oneness' with God (see *comm.* below) guarantees its eternal survival preventing God's fury from wreaking complete destruction.

This truth finds its most eloquent expression in *Eichah Rabbasi* where the roles 'executioner' and 'high priest' are fused in the person of Gabriel. When the high priest enters the Holy of Holies on Yom Kippur clothed in white linen garments, he personifies that inner purity of *Knesses Israel* which makes atonement possible because it prevents sin from leaving a permanent mark (see *Maharal, D'rush Na'eh l'Shabbos Teshuva; footnote* to 3:1; and *comm.* to 5:1). It is at this point of essential holiness that an unbreakable דְּבֵקוּת, *a cleaving*, between God and Israel takes place. Israel must survive, because it is 'one' with God! *(Maharal* loc. cit.). [By combining his role of 'executioner' with that of High Priest there is a built-in guarantee that even as 'executioner' he will never destroy completely.] [1]

1. According to *Megillah* 31b, the permeance of the bond between Israel and its Land was the subject of the exchange between God and Abraham at the בְּרִית בֵּין הַבְּתָרִים, the *'Covenant between the Pieces' (Gen.* 15:8-9). God promised the Land to Abraham. Abraham asked (*v.* 8): *'By what may I know that I will inherit it?* God answers (*v.* 9): *'Take for Me a calf ... '*

Recognizing that Abraham could not have doubted God's promise, the Sages comment that

ט ג־ד

הַסֹּפֵר בְּמָתְנָיו וַיָּבֹאוּ וַיַּעַמְדוּ אֵצֶל
ג מִזְבַּח הַנְּחֹשֶׁת׃ וּכְבוֹד | אֱלֹהֵי יִשְׂרָאֵל
נַעֲלָה מֵעַל הַכְּרוּב אֲשֶׁר הָיָה עָלָיו
אֶל מִפְתַּן הַבָּיִת וַיִּקְרָא אֶל־הָאִישׁ
הַלָּבֻשׁ הַבַּדִּים אֲשֶׁר קֶסֶת הַסֹּפֵר
ד בְּמָתְנָיו׃ וַיֹּאמֶר יהוה אֵלָו עֲבֹר

וְקֶסֶת הַסֹּפֵר — *With the slate of the scribe.*

In addition to his roles as 'executioner' and 'high priest' (see above), Gabriel also functions as a scribe. *Radak* points out that this activity would express itself in the 'marks' to be made on the foreheads of the men (*v.* 4). Presumably, then, *the slate of the scribe* is representative of all other scribal implements, including the pen, which would also have been hanging at his hips.

מִזְבַּח הַנְּחֹשֶׁת — *The copper altar.*

Shabbos 55a points out that in Yechezkel's time the altar in the Temple courtyard was made not of copper but of stone. (The copper altar of Moses had been 'hidden' by Solomon when it proved too small and been replaced by a huge stone altar. *Rashi* ad. loc.). The allusion to copper, then, refers to the copper musical instruments with which the Levites accompanied the sacrificial service. These Levites were to be the first victims (*Rashi* ad. loc.).

Yalkut suggests that special mention is made of the altar, in order to 'recall the sin of King Achaz.' Impressed by the heathen altar which he had seen in Damascus, Achaz ordered that a replica be placed in the Temple Courtyard (*II Kings* 16:10). It was to serve as the main altar while Solomon's altar became secondary, — or possibly, may have been rendered unfit for use.

[Perhaps the Sages mean to suggest that this craven mimicry of heathen worship was an underlying cause of all that happened later.]

3. וּכְבוֹד אֱלֹהֵי יִשְׂרָאֵל נַעֲלָה מֵעַל הַכְּרוּב — *Then the Glory of the God of Israel rose up from the Cheruv.*

From upon the lid [of the Ark] where the *Shechinah* had rested up to now; it began a gradual, ten-stage withdrawal from the Temple. This is the first stage [of withdrawal]: from the Cheruv to the threshold of the Holy of Holies *(Rashi)*. [See *Pref. Remarks* to Ch. 1].

Rashi interprets the word כְּרוּב as symbolic of the entire *Kapores*. [The *Kapores*, the lid of the ark had two *Cheruvim*, childlike figures (*Chagiga* 13b) fashioned from its two ends. They stood facing each other across the ark, with wings stretched upwards covering the *Kapores* (*Exod.* 25:18-20)].

[The use of the singular word *Cheruv* as a collective noun, denoting the two *Cheruvim*, is unique. Perhaps it was chosen to reflect the

Abraham questioned only the *permanence* of the gift (see *Maharal Gevuras Hashem* 8). How could he know that his children would never sin so grievously as to lose their right to the Land? God answered: *'In the merit of the sacrifices'*. *Maharal* (loc. cit.) explains God's answer. Sin does not become an integral part of Israel's being, for if it did, sacrifices could never achieve atonement. Sin cannot besmirch the essential core of Israel's purity. Thus, they will never sink to a level at which their ties to the Land would be permanently sundered.

The events recorded in Chs. 8-12, which show that even in the face of God's raging fury Israel will survive, are the fulfillment of that prophecy.

hips. And they came and stood by the copper altar.
3 *Then the glory of the God of Israel rose up from*
atop the cheruv on which it had been to the threshold
of the House; and He called to the man clothed in
linen, on whose hips was the slate of the scribe. 4 *And*
HASHEM said to him: 'Pass in the midst of the city, in

tradition, (*Yoma* 54b) that 'when the gentiles entered the Temple they found the *Cheruvim* locked in each other's embrace', (see *footnote* to 7:4 for an elaboration of this theme) thus forming a complete unity, which symbolized the essential oneness of God and Israel] [1]

1. Not all commentators agree that the *Cheruvim* which embraced one another were those that were above the Ark. Reference could be to the כְּרוּבִים דְצוּרְתָא, the *Cheruvim* painted on the Temple walls. (See *Ritva* to *Bava Basra* 99a, and *Rashi, Yoma* loc. cit.)

The Talmud (*Rosh Hashanah* 31a) details the ten stages of the withdrawal. However, there are a number of variant readings of the passage in *Rosh Hashanah* (which is paralleled in Avos d'Rabbi Nosson 34:6), see commentators to both places and *Dikdukei Sofrim*. *Rashi's* reading is as follows:

Rav Yehudah bar Idi said in the name of Rabbi Yochanan: . . . The *Shechinah* travelled [in] ten stages as shown by Scriptures from the *Kapores* to the *Cheruv;* from the *Cheruv* to the *Miftan* (threshold); from the *Miftan* to the *Chatzer* (courtyard) ...

There, the Talmud quotes our verse to illustrate the *second* of the ten stages (i.e. from the *Cheruv* to the *Miftan*, — see *Rashi*, there). This does not accord with *Rashi* on our verse which states that our verse describes the *first* of the ten stages.

In another discrepancy with his commentary to our verse, *Rashi* there (*Rosh Hashanah* loc. cit.) explains *Cheruvim* as one of the two *Cheruvim* which *King Solomon* had made (*I Kings* 6:23), rather than the *Cheruvim* of the *Kapores.*

According to *Rashi* in *Rosh Hashanah* then, the sequence of events was as follows: The *Shechinah* was originally ensconced on the *Kapores* between the two *Cheruvim (Exodus* 25:22). At some time, it moved onto one of Solomon's *Cheruvim.* From there it moved to the threshold of the Holy of Holies, and it was this *second* move which is described in our chapter.

The sequence of events described by *Rashi* in *Rosh Hashanah,* seems to be borne out by our tradition concerning the fate of the Ark.

Although it is certain that there was no ark in the Holy of Holies of the Second Temple (*Yoma* 21b), there is a difference of opinion concerning the fate of the Ark during the twilight years of the First Temple (*Yoma* 53b). According to one opinion it was buried by King Yoshiyahu (ibid. 52b) in anticipation of the destruction; according to another, it was carried to Babylon together with Yehoyachin's exile.

Thus, at the time of Yechezkel's vision (the sixth year of Yehoyachin's exile — 8:1) the Ark was no longer in the Temple, and Yechezkel could not have seen the *Shechinah* withdraw from it.

[*Rashi* on Yechezkel, according to whom the prophet saw the withdrawal from the *Kapores* (see *comm.)* would include this vision with those symbolic ones which in their *external* form, were no longer true in Yechezkel's time. — See *comm.* to 8:5. Alternately, it might be suggested that *Rashi* may have known of opinions not recorded in the *Talmud* — perhaps *Midrashic* — according to whom, the Ark was still in the Temple at that time].

The sequence of events which suggests itself is thus as follows:

Either in Yoshiyahu's reign through burial, or later through exile (when the gentiles saw the *Cheruvim* embracing — see *comm.*) the Ark was removed from the Holy of Holies. This was the moment at which the *Shechinah* left its seat on the *Kapores* and came to rest upon one of Solomon's *Cheruvim.*

In our chapter, Yechezkel was shown how the *Shechinah* withdrew from that *Cheruv* some five years before the final destruction.

ט
ד
בְּתוֹךְ הָעִיר בְּתוֹךְ יְרוּשָׁלָ͏ִם וְהִתְוִיתָ תָּו עַל־מִצְחוֹת הָאֲנָשִׁים הַנֶּאֱנָחִים וְהַנֶּאֱנָקִים עַל כָּל־הַתּוֹעֵבוֹת הַנַּעֲשׂוֹת

4. בְּתוֹךְ הָעִיר בְּתוֹךְ יְרוּשָׁלָ͏ִם — *In the midst of the city, in the midst of Jerusalem.*

Radak notes the apparent redundancy. Although we know that the 'city' is Jerusalem, the prophet stresses it in order to highlight the sadness of the fact that the very city which God had chosen as the dwelling place of His *Shechinah*, was to suffer destruction. (See *comm.* to 8:6).

וְהִתְוִיתָ תָּו — *And mark a sign.*

The root תוה is only found once more in Scripture (*I Samuel* 21:14). Its meaning is to make a mark or sign. [We discount *Job* 31:35 which many commentators trace to a different root.]

The Sages (*Shabbos* 55a) interpret the word תָּו in our verse as a proper noun — the last letter of the *Aleph Beis*, meaning that the sign with which the people were marked was the letter *tav*.

The passage in *Shabbos* reads: Why a *tav?* [Note that the *Talmud* assumes that both the righteous and the sinners were marked with a *tav*, the former in ink, and the latter in blood. The following explanations must be understood within that framework.]

— *Rav* said: *Tav* — You shall live, *tav* — You shall die (i.e. the letter *tav*, ת, used as a prefix indicates the second person future tense. Thus, תִּחְיֶה, *you shall live*, תָּמוּת, *you shall die.* The differentiation between the signs of death and that of life was indicated by the use of blood and ink respectively (see below).

— *Shmuel* said: תַּמָּה זְכוּת אָבוֹת, *the merit of the Fathers has been used up,* i.e. the salvation of the righteous must be deserved in their own merit, since זְכוּת אָבוֹת, *the merit of the fathers*, was no longer available. The wicked who had no personal merit would, therefore, be destroyed *(Maharsha* — but see *footnote*).[1]

1. [For treatment of the problems arising from the concept that the זְכוּת אָבוֹת may have been used up, see: *Tosafos* (ad. loc.); *Maharsha, Chidushei Aggadah* (ad. loc., to מִימוֹת הוֹשֵׁעַ בֶּן בְּאֵרִי); *Sefas Emes (Exodus* for the year 5645); *Michtav Me'Eliyahu v.* 1. p. 14 *(London* 5715); *Pachad Yitzchak, Pesach* 65.]

Maharsha leaves unexplained why Shmuel deems the *tav* an apt sign. Why would the righteous people be marked with a sign which symbolizes what would not save them (merit of the fathers), rather than their own merit which was in fact the basis of their salvation?

Rashi on the *Torah* may yield a different interpretation.

As an introduction to the *'Thirteen Attributes of Mercy'*, which Moses was taught after having obtained forgiveness for the sin of the Golden Calf, God said to him (*Exodus* 33:19): *'I shall cause all My goodness to pass before you'*. To this *Rashi* comments: '... for when you needed to implore Me to have mercy on Israel, you mentioned the merit of the fathers thinking that *if the merit of the fathers is used up*, there is no more hope. Now I will pass the complete attribute of My goodness before you ... to teach you the order of prayer, *even if the merit of the fathers is finished* ... for My mercies never cease'.

In *Deut.* 32:35 a time is foretold when God will punish Israel when *'their foot slips'* i.e. when the merit of the fathers, upon which they rely, will have ceased' (*Rashi*).

In *v.* 36 the Torah goes on to say, how, after this occurrence God will see Israel's helplessness and 'repent' on their destruction.

Thus, both passages demonstrate the special relationship between God and Israel guaranteeing the unchanging mercy and love of God even when Israel will have sunk so low that even the merit of the fathers is of no avail.

This, then, would be the meaning of the *Tav* in Shmuel's opinion. With the imprint of the *Tav* upon their forehead, God testifies that despite the unhappy fact that the merit of the fathers was תַּמָּה, *come to an end*, His undying love would result in their salvation.

IX 4 *the midst of Jerusalem, and mark a sign on the foreheads of the men who sigh and groan for all the abominations that are done within it.'*

— *Rabbi Yochanan* said: תָּחוֹן זְכוּת אָבוֹת, *Let the merit of the Fathers cause favor,* i.e. to be saved in the merit of Abraham, Isaac, and Jacob, one's actions must indicate that he is indeed their descendant. Thus, the righteous people, who could be looked upon as true descendants of the Patriarchs, would be saved; but not the wicked *(Maharsha).*

— *Reish Lakish* says: *Tav* is the last letter of God's seal. [God's seal is said to be אֱמֶת, *truth*]. The implication is that the letter *Tav* in ink or blood, would testify to the justice of the people's fate.

— *Rabbi Shmuel ben Nachmani* said: These are the people who kept the Torah from *Aleph* to *Tav* (i.e. from the beginning to the end). The implication for the wicked people is that they desecrated that same Torah from the beginning to the end *(Maharsha).*

הָאֲנָשִׁים הַנֶּאֱנָחִים וְהַנֶּאֱנָקִים — *The men who sigh and groan.*

God said to Gabriel: Go and mark the foreheads of the righteous men with a *tav* of ink so that the messengers of destruction shall not have power over them; and the foreheads of the wicked people with a *tav* of blood, so that the messengers of destruction shall have power over them.

The simple meaning of the verse is that the righteous men were to be marked for salvation, but there is no mention of marking the wicked men for destruction. The Sages apparently base their interpretation on the redundancy of the second word, נֶאֱנָקִים. It is taken as referring to the death throes of the wicked people — as in 26:15 and *Jeremiah* 51:52. (See *Tosafos* and *Maharsha* ad. loc.).

God's 'Attribute of Justice' said to Him: 'Master of the world! Why are these different from those?' He answered: 'These are completely righteous people and those completely wicked'. So *Justice* said: 'Were they [the righteous] not able to protest?' God answered: 'It is clear to Me that their protests would have been ignored'. *Justice* said: 'Master of the world! If it was clear to You, was it clear to them? (*Shabbos* 55a).

This passage provides the background for our understanding of this section. There were people in Jerusalem who were 'completely righteous', and God intended that they should be spared. The accuser (in the form of God's attribute of Divine Justice) would not relent in his charge that even the 'completely righteous' had forfeited their claim to special protection by having failed to protest against evil.[1]

The *Talmud* goes on to relate that God acceded to this argument: Rav Achah ben Chaninah said: 'Never [except in this unique instance] did God utter a good intention, and then recant.' He ordered the messengers to begin the slaughter with the righteous people (based on *v.* 6, see *comm.* ad loc.).

It is significant that the original intention to spare these 'completely righteous people' was not based on the blamelessness of their lives, but because they *'sighed and groaned because of all the abominations'.* Furthermore, it seems that the inadequacy of this very 'sighing and groaning' was the object of the accusers criticism. The disapproval remained internal; it did not express itself in actual protest against the abominations.

The explanation for this must be sought in the words of *Vilna Gaon* in

1. According to *Avodah Zarah* 4a, their failure to protest put them into a category of צַדִּיק שֶׁאֵינוֹ גָּמוּר, *a zaddik who is not completely righteous.* A צַדִּיק גָּמוּר, *a completely righteous person,* will never be included even in a communal decree. This explains Abraham's intercession for the righteous people of Sodom.

ט ה בְּתוֹכָהּ: וּלְאֵלֶּה אָמַר בְּאָזְנַי עִבְרוּ בָעִיר
ה־ו אַל|עֵינְכֶם ק׳ אַחֲרָיו וְהַכּוּ °עַל־תָּחֹס °עֵינֵיכֶם וְאַל־
ו תַּחְמֹלוּ: זָקֵן בָּחוּר וּבְתוּלָה וְטַף וְנָשִׁים
תַּהַרְגוּ לְמַשְׁחִית וְעַל־כָּל־אִישׁ אֲשֶׁר־
עָלָיו הַתָּו אַל־תִּגַּשׁוּ וּמִמִּקְדָּשִׁי תָּחֵלּוּ
וַיָּחֵלּוּ בָּאֲנָשִׁים הַזְּקֵנִים אֲשֶׁר לִפְנֵי

Even Shleimah, that when God's decree is directed against the total *community*, then even its righteous members will be included in the decree (see below *v.* 6, see also *Bava Kamma* 60a).

For an elaboration of this far reaching concept, see *Rabbi Elchanan Wasserman* in *Kovetz Ma'amarim (Jerusalem* 5723, p. 37). Further references are: *Bava Kama* 60a; *Tosafos* and *Ran* to *Ta'anis* 21b (see *Shulchan Aruch, Orech Chayim* 576:3); *Sifri* to *Deut.* 32:25; *Shabbos* 32a; *Sforno* to *Exodus* 12:13.

Righteous people are considered a part of the community and thus, liable to its common fate, unless they separate themselves from it. Originally, it was deemed sufficient that they 'sighed and groaned,' thus demonstrating disapproval. *Justice* claimed, however, that as long as they failed to protest actively, they remained part of the community — and thus were culpable together with the sinners.

5. וּלְאֵלֶּה אָמַר — *Then to these He said.*

Gabriel, in his capacity as scribe had marked all the people with the appropriate sign. The other six (or five — see above) messengers were told to pass through the city and execute the judgments without mercy.

אַל תָּחוֹס עֵינְכֶם — *Let your eyes neither spare.*

This is another example of קְרִי־כְּתִיב. That is that the word is spelled one way (עַל — meaning: *'on'*) and pronounced another (אַל — meaning: *'do not'*). In *comm.* to 7:21 we discussed the idea that the כְּתִיב, *the written word*, being more 'remote' from the reader would tend to describe the inner meaning, while the קְרִי would deal with the actual occurrence. *Radak*'s rendering of our verse bears out this interpretation: He explains the spelling עַל as implying ... smite those *on* whom you would ordinarily have mercy — and certainly those who truly deserve their fate. The meaning of the pronunciation is: Do not have mercy. Thus, the spelling describes the inner feeling of the messengers, while the pronunciation describes the deed they were called upon to perform.

6. זָקֵן בָּחוּר וּבְתוּלָה וְטַף וְנָשִׁים — *Old man, young man and maiden, children and women.*

See *comm.* to *v.* 4. The decree had been issued against the community rather than against individuals. Therefore, even innocent people were to be included, unless they had specifically removed themselves from the sinful community.

[An analogous passage may be found in *Deut.* 32:25: *Outside, the sword bereaves; indoors, terror — the young man and the maiden, the suckling and the aged.*

Sifri (ad. loc.) remarks: 'גַּם בָּחוּר — You have caused Me to send forth My [punishing] hands against My chosen ones. (בָּחוּר, *a young man*, is read as בְּחִיר, *a chosen one.)* ...

גַּם בְּתוּלָה, these are the ones who are blameless, like a maiden who has never sinned.

יוֹנֵק, they drink the words of the Torah, as a suckling drinks at his mother's breast.

עִם אִישׁ שֵׂיבָה, do not read שֵׂיבָה, *the aged,*

[5]Then to these He said in my hearing: 'Follow him through the city and strike. Let your eye neither spare nor show mercy. [6] Old man, young man and maiden, children and women, massacre to utter destruction. But any man upon whom is the sign do not approach. And begin from My Sanctuary'; so they began with the old men who were in front of the House.

but יְשִׁיבָה, *Yeshivah.* This teaches us that they sat in the Yeshivah (i.e. to teach Torah).

Thus, we see that destruction which is decreed upon a community will sweep up the innocent together with the guilty.]

וְעַל כָּל אִישׁ אֲשֶׁר עָלָיו הַתָּו אַל תִּגַּשׁוּ — *But any man upon whom is the sign — do not approach.*

The people who had 'sighed and groaned' about the abominations, thus excluding themselves from the community of sinners, are to be spared.

וּמִמִּקְדָּשִׁי תָּחֵלּוּ — *And begin from My Sanctuary.*

The people who served idols within the Temple confines (Ch. 8) created the greatest חִלּוּל הַשֵּׁם, *desecration of God's Name,* and are therefore to be killed first *(Radak).*

Eliezer of Beaugency, according to the simple meaning of the verse, sees a parallel between this verse and *Exod.* 21:14 which reads: *'From My altar you shall take him* [the murderer] *to die'.* The altar does not provide a sanctuary from punishment. Thus, too, our verse teaches, that the idol worshippers are to be killed *even though* they were in the *Bais Hamikdash.*

However, the Sages (*Shabbos* 55a) read this phrase as the point at which God accedes to the argument of the Attribute of Justice (see above) and agrees that even the צַדִּיקִים גְּמוּרִים, *the completely righteous people,* should not be spared, because, although they had 'sighed and groaned', they had not protested.

Rav Yoseph taught: 'Do not read מִקְדָּשִׁי, *My Sanctuary,* but מְקוּדָּשַׁי, *My holy ones.* These are the men who kept the whole Torah from *aleph* to *tav.* [Perhaps Rav Yoseph based '' e need to reinterpret the word on the unexpected sequence of the phrases. Were וּמִמִּקְדָּשִׁי תָּחֵלּוּ to be understood in its simple meaning (see above), then it should have appeared earlier in the verse immediately after the command to kill the old men. It seems incongruous that it is placed only after the declaration that the righteous bearers of the *'sign'* be spared. Therefore, *Rav Yoseph* interprets it as a 'change of heart', calling for punishment to be visited even upon those righteous people who failed to protest the sins of the community.]

Thus, even the צַדִּיקִים גְּמוּרִים are to be killed, and in fact they are to be the very first victims of the slaughter [see *Bava Kama* 60a: *Rabbi Yonasan* said: 'Punishments come to the world only because of the wicked, but they accost the righteous people first'. *Maharal, Chidushei Aggadah, Shabbos* ad. loc. discusses this concept].

וַיָּחֵלּוּ בָּאֲנָשִׁים הַזְּקֵנִים אֲשֶׁר לִפְנֵי הַבָּיִת — *So they began with the old men who were in front of the house.*

Radak and *Metzudas David* identify these 'old men' as the seventy men mentioned in 8:11.

If מִמִּקְדָּשִׁי is to be understood as Rav Yoseph takes it (see above), then the זְקֵנִים אֲשֶׁר לִפְנֵי הַבָּיִת, are the elders of the *Sanhedrin,* the High Court, which had

ז הַבָּיִת׃ וַיֹּאמֶר אֲלֵיהֶם טַמְּאוּ אֶת־הַבַּיִת
וּמַלְאוּ אֶת־הַחֲצֵרוֹת חֲלָלִים צֵאוּ וְיָצְאוּ
ח וְהִכּוּ בָעִיר׃ וַיְהִי כְּהַכּוֹתָם וְנֵאשֲׁאַר אָנִי
וָאֶפְּלָה עַל־פָּנַי וָאֶזְעַק וָאֹמַר אֲהָהּ אֲדֹנָי
יֱהֹוִה הַמַשְׁחִית אַתָּה אֵת כָּל־שְׁאֵרִית
יִשְׂרָאֵל בְּשָׁפְכְּךָ אֶת־חֲמָתְךָ עַל־
ט יְרוּשָׁלִָם׃ וַיֹּאמֶר אֵלַי עֲוֺן בֵּית־יִשְׂרָאֵל
וִיהוּדָה גָּדוֹל בִּמְאֹד מְאֹד וַתִּמָּלֵא הָאָרֶץ
דָּמִים וְהָעִיר מָלְאָה מֻטֶּה כִּי אָמְרוּ עָזַב

its seat in the Temple *(Maharsha Shabbos* ad. loc.).

7. טַמְּאוּ אֶת הַבַּיִת — *Defile the House.*

Do not allow concern for the defilement of the Temple to deter you from killing people even in the Temple confines; it has already been defiled by the idol worship which had taken place there *(Radak).*

וּמַלְאוּ אֶת הַחֲצֵרוֹת חֲלָלִים — *And fill the courtyards with slain men.*

I.e., the various courtyards which comprised the Temple grounds *(Radak).*

8. וַיְהִי כְּהַכּוֹתָם וְנֵאשֲׁאַר אָנִי — *It was while they slew and I* [alone] *was left.*

Radak reads וְנֵאשֲׁאַר as a combination of two forms. וְאֶשָּׁאַר — *And I remained (Kal,* first person, future) and וְנִשְׁאַר — *And he was left (Nif'al,* passive voice, third person, past). The fusion of the two forms conveys a dual message: He remained in the courtyard of the Temple after the divine messengers had left (as they were told to do in the previous verse); he was the only person in the courtyard who was left alive. Only he had been marked with the saving *tav mark.* (This seems the implication of the *Nif'al* form).

וָאֶפְּלָה — *And I threw myself.*

The translation indicates a purposeful preparation for prayer. This interpretation follows *Ramban* to *Gen.* 17:3. (See *comm., ArtScroll* ed. there).

אֲהָהּ — *Alas! Targum* renders it as a request: 'Accept my prayer'.

אֲהָהּ אֲדֹנָי ה׳ הֲמַשְׁחִית אַתָּה אֵת כָּל שְׁאֵרִית יִשְׂרָאֵל — *Alas! my Lord, HASHEM/ELOHIM, are You destroying the entire remnant of Israel?*

How can it be Your intention to destroy the entire remnant of Israel, when even Your Justice is only an outward manifestation of Your Mercy? *(Harav Breuer)* [This is the meaning of the Four-Letter Name, vocalized to read *Elohim* — see *comm.* to 2:4).

אֵת כָּל שְׁאֵרִית יִשְׂרָאֵל — *The entire remnant of Israel.*

Although only the fate of Jerusalem was depicted in Yechezkel's vision, the inhabitants of Jerusalem were in fact the 'whole remnant of Israel' since all the rest of the people had either been killed or exiled *(Radak).*

Da'as Sofrim suggests that Yechezkel may have thought that with Jerusalem's downfall, the exiled community in Babylon would also disintegrate. Indeed the miraculous regenerative power of exile (see *comm.* to 6:7-9) was not verbalized to the prophet until 11:14-16. Until Yechezkel had learned that lesson, there was every reason for him to think that the exiled community could survive

*[7]So He said to them: 'Defile the House and fill the
courtyards with slain men. Get out!' So they went
out and slayed in the city.*
*[8] It was while they slew and I alone was left, that I
threw myself down upon my face and I cried and
said: 'Alas, my Lord HASHEM/ELOHIM are You
destroying the entire remnant of Israel as You pour
out Your anger on Jerusalem?'*
*[9] Then He said to me: 'The iniquity of the Family
of Israel and Judah is exceedingly great: the Land was
filled with bloodshed, and the city was filled with in-*

only as long as it had ties to a vibrant, living national entity in its homeland.

Thus, the downfall of Jerusalem seemed to presage the obliteration of Israel as a nation.

9-10. In response to Yechezkel's anguished cry, God answers that He cannot have mercy on them, nor spare them, because their sin was exceedingly great, their land was filled with bloodshed, and Jerusalem with injustice.

In context, we would have expected God's answer to center on the flagrant idol worship which Yechezkel had been brought to Jerusalem to witness (see previous chapter). Nowhere was it hinted that God's wrath was directed to the interpersonal relationships of the people.

The passage recalls *Bereishis Rabbah* 38:6, where the Sages explain that the דוֹר הַפְּלָגָה, the *Generation of the Dispersion,* which built the Tower of Babel, were not punished as severely as the דוֹר הַמַּבּוּל, *the Generation of the Flood,* because the former lived in peace with one another while the latter fought among themselves. The *Midrash* reads: '*Rebbi* said: Great is peace! For even when Israel serves idols, if they are at peace with one another, God says: I cannot rule over (punish) them ...'

God's answer to Yechezkel would thus be, that the bloodshed and injustice in Jerusalem precluded the exercise of mercy. Therefore, they would be punished in full measure for the idol worship in their midst.

If our understanding of this passage is correct, then special significance attaches to the *Midrash* in *Eichah Rabbasi* 4:9 (quoted in *Yalkut*). The *Midrash* remarks that our verse contains a more severe stricture גָּדוֹל בִּמְאֹד מְאֹד — *exceedingly great* — than that recorded concerning the sins of Sodom (וְחַטָּאתָם כִּי כָבְדָה מְאֹד). Why then was Sodom punished with complete destruction while a remnant was saved from Jerusalem? The *Midrash* answers that the people of Jerusalem even during the worst horrors of starvation, remained sensitive to one another's needs. When they were reduced to cannibalism, in the final throes of the siege, they would share their dreadful meal with others [see *Rashi* to *Sanhedrin* 104b.]

Thus, while it was their fighting and quarreling which had brought disaster upon them, nevertheless, in the worst moments their innate love for one another asserted itself.

9. וַתִּמָּלֵא הָאָרֶץ דָּמִים — *The Land was filled with bloodshed.*

The meaning is that it was filled with

ט יהוה אֶת־הָאָרֶץ וְאֵין יהוה רֹאֶה׃

י־יא י וְגַם־אֲנִי לֹא־תָחוֹס עֵינִי וְלֹא אֶחְמֹל
יא דַּרְכָּם בְּרֹאשָׁם נָתָתִּי׃ וְהִנֵּה הָאִישׁ |
לְבֻשׁ הַבַּדִּים אֲשֶׁר הַקֶּסֶת בְּמָתְנָיו
מֵשִׁיב דָּבָר לֵאמֹר עָשִׂיתִי °כְּאשֶׁר כְּכֹל אֲשֶׁר ק׳
צִוִּיתָנִי׃

י א וָאֶרְאֶה וְהִנֵּה אֶל־

א־ב הָרָקִיעַ אֲשֶׁר עַל־רֹאשׁ הַכְּרֻבִים כְּאֶבֶן
סַפִּיר כְּמַרְאֵה דְּמוּת כִּסֵּא נִרְאָה עֲלֵיהֶם׃
ב וַיֹּאמֶר אֶל־הָאִישׁ | לְבֻשׁ הַבַּדִּים וַיֹּאמֶר

murderers. [דָּמִים = שׁוֹפְכֵי דָמִים, *shedders of blood*] *(Radak).*

מֻטֶּה — *Injustice.*

A unique form of the verb נטה, *to incline.*

כִּי אָמְרוּ עָזַב ה׳ אֶת הָאָרֶץ — *For they said: HASHEM has forsaken the Land.*

See *comm.* to 8:12.

10. וְגַם אֲנִי לֹא תָחוֹס עֵינִי — *And I, too — My eye will not spare.*

Just as they did not pity one another, so I will not pity them *(Radak).*

דַּרְכָּם בְּרֹאשָׁם נָתָתִּי — *I have placed their way upon their head.*

I.e., I have brought them to account for their misdeeds. See *comm.* to 7:3.

11. עָשִׂיתִי כְּכֹל אֲשֶׁר צִוִּיתָנִי — *I have done as all You commanded me.*

I have marked the people who were to be marked *(Radak).*

In the קְרִי, *reading of the text*, the word כְּכֹל, *as all*, is added — עָשִׂיתִי כְּכֹל אֲשֶׁר צִוִּיתָנִי, *I have done as all You have commanded me.* [Perhaps the dual form hints at the tradition of the Sages (*v.* 6) that the marked people were also to be killed because they had not protested. The כְּתִיב, *the written form* does not include כְּכֹל and means: 'I have done as You have commanded', that is I have marked the people. The קְרִי adds that subsequently even those people were killed.]

X

Once more the prophet is shown the ineffable Glory of God in a *Merkavah* vision, and once again (see *Pref. Remarks* to Ch. 1), we must leave the details of that vision shrouded in the secrecy enjoined upon us by the dictum *(Proverbs* 25:2): *It is the glory of God to conceal a thing.*

However, as Harav Breuer points out, the few verses in this chapter which we can understand in a modest way, are sufficient to imbue us with the overwhelming sense of pathos which is evoked by the final departure of the *Shechinah* from its beloved resting place.

This is compared to a king who was leaving his palace and was kissing the walls and embracing the pillars saying: 'Alas [what will become of] the peace of my house and my sanctuary; alas [what will become of] my precious house for the peace which is gone [from here]?' *(Pesiktah* quoted in *Yalkut).*

However, as we shall see, an element of comfort and reconciliation will not be missing, even from this tragic picture.

IX 10-11

justice. For they said: "HASHEM has forsaken the
Land, and HASHEM sees not." 10 And I, too — My eye
will not spare nor will I have mercy. I have placed
their way upon their head.'

11 But behold! The man clothed in linen, with the
slate upon his hips, brings back an answer, saying: 'I
have done as all You commanded me.'

X 1-2

I looked and see! By the expanse which is above
the heads of the Cheruvim something like a
sapphire stone, like the appearance of the form
of a throne; appeared over them.

2 Then He said to the man clothed in linen, and he

1. 8:4 already states that *Yechezkel* apprehended a *Merkavah* vision upon entering the Temple. Therefore our chapter assumes the presence of the *Merkavah* and proceeds with the description.

הָרָקִיעַ אֲשֶׁר עַל רֹאשׁ הַכְּרֻבִים — *The expanse which is above the heads of the Cheruvim.*

We translate רָקִיעַ as *'expanse'* since the most basic meaning of the root רקע is, *'to spread out' (Ps.* 136:6). [This is in contrast to *Genesis* where the translation 'firmament' is clearly in order since there the word refers to the heavens.] Whatever other meaning the word may have in our context, must remain part of the *Merkavah* mystery.

Our verse has the רָקִיעַ over the heads of *Cheruvim.* In 1:22 the רָקִיעַ is described as being over the heads of a *chayah.* The implication (borne out by *v.* 20: *'And I knew that they were Cheruvim')* is, that the *chayos* of Ch. 1, are here depicted as *Cheruvim.*

[*Rambam, Yesodei haTorah* 2:1 places *Chayah* first, and *Cheruv* ninth in the ten levels of the hierarchy of God's messengers; see *footnote* to 1:15.]

Cheruvim may be interpreted as *'bearers of God's Glory'* (an idea developed by *Hirsch* and *Hoffmann* in their *comm.* to *Gen.* 3:24. See *Ps.* 18:11). Accordingly, the implication would be that God had now chosen the heavenly *Merkavah* as the new *'bearers of His Glory'* in place of the Cheruvim who had been on the Holy Ark. While Israel had been worthy to have the *Shechinah* in their midst, His Presence rested upon the earthly Cheruvim. With the destruction of the Temple and Israel's dispersion among the nations, however, God must find the bearers of His Glory outside the human sphere.

Thus the shattering implication of סִלּוּק הַשְּׁכִינָה, *the withdrawal of the Shechinah,* is brought out in vivid clarity by referring to the *Chayos* of the *Merkavah* as *Cheruvim (Harav Breuer).*

2. וַיֹּאמֶר אֶל הָאִישׁ לְבֻשׁ הַבַּדִּים — *Then He said to the man clothed in linen.*

Gabriel, the שַׂר הָאֵשׁ, *the angel of fire* (see *footnote* to 9:2), is now delegated to hurl the divine fire upon the doomed city.

וַיֹּאמֶר אֶל הָאִישׁ ... וַיֹּאמֶר — *Then He said to the man ... and he said.*

Rashi points out the apparent redun-

י
ג־ה

בֹּא אֶל־בֵּינוֹת לַגַּלְגַּל אֶל־תַּחַת לַכְּרוּב
וּמַלֵּא חָפְנֶיךָ גַחֲלֵי־אֵשׁ מִבֵּינוֹת לַכְּרֻבִים
ג וּזְרֹק עַל־הָעִיר וַיָּבֹא לְעֵינָי: וְהַכְּרֻבִים
עֹמְדִים מִימִין לַבַּיִת בְּבֹאוֹ הָאִישׁ וְהֶעָנָן
ד מָלֵא אֶת־הֶחָצֵר הַפְּנִימִית: וַיָּרָם כְּבוֹד־
יהוה מֵעַל הַכְּרוּב עַל מִפְתַּן הַבָּיִת
וַיִּמָּלֵא הַבַּיִת אֶת־הֶעָנָן וְהֶחָצֵר מָלְאָה
ה אֶת־נֹגַהּ כְּבוֹד יהוה: וְקוֹל כַּנְפֵי
הַכְּרוּבִים נִשְׁמַע עַד־הֶחָצֵר הַחִיצֹנָה

dancy of the second וַיֹּאמֶר, *and he said.* The Sages say that although Gabriel had been told to take the fire himself, he asked [i.e. the second *and he said*] one of the *Cheruvim* to hand it to him, so that the coal might be 'cooled' in the hands of the *Cheruv* in order that the city not be destroyed completely *(Yoma* 77a). Therefore, the first *He,* refers to God and is in upper case, while the second *he,* in lower case, refers to Gabriel. See *v.* 7 below.

בֹּא אֶל בֵּינוֹת לַגַּלְגַּל אֶל תַּחַת לַכְּרוּב — *Go in between the Galgal, beneath the Cheruv.*

The *Galgalim* are synonymous with the *Ofanim (Rashi).*

The singular is used in the collective sense: i.e., go in between the *Galgalim,* beneath the *Cheruvim; Galgalim* are of a lower order than the *Cheruvim (Radak).*

וּמַלֵּא חָפְנֶיךָ גַחֲלֵי אֵשׁ מִבֵּינוֹת לַכְּרוּבִים — *And fill your hands with fire-coals from among the Cheruvim.*

Jerusalem would be consumed by a divine fire. The city later destroyed by Nebuchadnezzar's hordes would be one whose inner life had already been extinguished by the divine wrath *(Shir HaShirim Rabbah* 3:3).

[If indeed the *Cheruvim* are to be seen as bearers of the Divine Glory (see *comm.* to *v.* 1), then the command that the fire issue from *'among the Cheruvim',* was meant to imply that the destruction of the beloved — but unfaithful — city was demanded in vindication of God's Glory. There is another message implicit in the verse, however. Since the same Cheruv cooperates in 'cooling' the coal *(v.* 7), it is clear that that same glory of God demands that Jerusalem shall not be utterly destroyed, but that the potential for its ultimate regeneration shall remain. See *comm.* to 9:2.]

3. מִימִין לַבַּיִת — *To the south* [lit. *right*] *of the House.*

The translation of יָמִין as *south* follows *Rashi.* In Scriptural usage, east is frequently referred to as פָּנִים [lit. *face*] and קֶדֶם [lit. *front* or *before*]. When one faces eastward, the south will be to his right.

The *Merkavah* had been by the gate (8:3-4), but had now moved inward to the Sanctuary, to be ready to receive the *Shechinah (Eliezer of Beaugency).* It came to the south of the Sanctuary rather than to its north, in order to avoid the side where the abominations were committed (see *comm.* to 8:3) *(Radak).*

4. וַיָּרָם כְּבוֹד ה׳ מֵעַל הַכְּרוּב — *Then up*

said: 'Go in between the Galgal, beneath the Cheruv, and fill your hands with fire-coals from among the Cheruvim, and throw them upon the city!' So he came before my eyes.

3 *And the Cheruvim stand to the south of the House, as the man came; and the cloud filled the inner courtyard.* 4 *Then up rose the Glory of HASHEM from upon the Cheruv, to the threshold of the House and the House was filled by the cloud. And the courtyard was filled with the glow of the Glory of HASHEM.* 5 *And the sound of the wings of the Cheruvim was heard up to the outer courtyard as the*

rose the Glory of HASHEM from upon the Cheruv.

The withdrawal of the *Shechinah* from the *Cheruv* to the threshold has already been described in 9:3. Our verse repeats it *(Rashi)* in order to complete the detailed account of the ultimate and full withdrawal from the Sanctuary which is about to take place (*v.* 19 and 11:22-23).

Alternately, as *Metzudas David* suggests, it could be that the *Shechinah* had returned after having left the *Cheruv* for the threshold (9:3). Our verse describes the second withdrawal. God was likened to a king who 'kissed the walls and embraced the pillars' on being forced to leave his palace (see *Pref. Remarks*). This would account for his returning to the palace which he had already vacated for a last glimpse before his final departure *(Harav Breuer).*

5. עַד הֶחָצֵר הַחִיצֹנָה – *Up to the outer courtyard.*

— I.e., the Temple Mount. One might think [that it was not heard beyond the Temple Mount] because the voice was low? Therefore it says *'Like the voice of El Shaddai when He speaks'* [at *Sinai* where it says '... *with a great voice'* *(Deut.* 5:19) *(Metzudas David).*] But when it reached the outer courtyard it [the voice] was cut off *(Rashi.* See also *Rashi* to *Lev.* 1:1).

[*Ramban* (Intr. to *Terumah, Exod.* 25) explains the presence of the *Shechinah* in the Sanctuary, as being meant to perpetuate, in a tangible form, the Sinaitic revelation in Israel's midst. That very *Shechinah* which had revealed Itself to Moses on Sinai, was henceforth to be ensconced between the *Cheruvim,* upon the Holy Ark. Thus as the *Shechinah* withdraws from the Sanctuary, an epoch in Israel's history comes to a close as the Sinaitic revelation ceases to be a tangible reality within them.

One recalls the dictum of the Sages *(Kesubos* 17a) that the withdrawal of Torah should be accompanied by the same circumstances as its giving. Thus the *'great voice'* of Sinai is heard as the *Shechinah* finally withdraws. Indeed, it might be said that God's withdrawal from the Sanctuary held a lesson as significant as that taught at Sinai when His *Shechinah* first came to dwell in the human sphere: That Israel's degeneration can cause סִלּוּק הַשְּׁכִינָה, *the withdrawal of the Shechinah,* indicates their uniqueness — עַם סְגֻלָּה, [God's] *treasured nation,* a title they won at

ו כְּקוֹל אֵל־שַׁדַּי בְּדַבְּרוֹ׃ וַיְהִי בְּצַוֹּתוֹ אֶת־
הָאִישׁ לְבֻשׁ־הַבַּדִּים לֵאמֹר קַח אֵשׁ
מִבֵּינוֹת לַגַּלְגַּל מִבֵּינוֹת לַכְּרוּבִים וַיָּבֹא
ז וַיַּעֲמֹד אֵצֶל הָאוֹפָן׃ וַיִּשְׁלַח הַכְּרוּב אֶת־
יָדוֹ מִבֵּינוֹת לַכְּרוּבִים אֶל־הָאֵשׁ אֲשֶׁר
בֵּינוֹת הַכְּרֻבִים וַיִּשָּׂא וַיִּתֵּן אֶל־חָפְנֵי
ח לְבֻשׁ הַבַּדִּים וַיִּקַּח וַיֵּצֵא׃ וַיֵּרָא לַכְּרֻבִים
ט תַּבְנִית יַד־אָדָם תַּחַת כַּנְפֵיהֶם׃ וָאֶרְאֶה
וְהִנֵּה אַרְבָּעָה אוֹפַנִּים אֵצֶל הַכְּרוּבִים
אוֹפַן אֶחָד אֵצֶל הַכְּרוּב אֶחָד וְאוֹפַן אֶחָד
אֵצֶל הַכְּרוּב אֶחָד וּמַרְאֵה הָאוֹפַנִּים כְּעֵין
י אֶבֶן תַּרְשִׁישׁ׃ וּמַרְאֵיהֶם דְּמוּת אֶחָד
לְאַרְבַּעְתָּם כַּאֲשֶׁר יִהְיֶה הָאוֹפַן בְּתוֹךְ
יא הָאוֹפָן׃ בְּלֶכְתָּם אֶל־אַרְבַּעַת רִבְעֵיהֶם
יֵלֵכוּ לֹא יִסַּבּוּ בְּלֶכְתָּם כִּי הַמָּקוֹם אֲשֶׁר־
יִפְנֶה הָרֹאשׁ אַחֲרָיו יֵלֵכוּ לֹא יִסַּבּוּ

Sinai (Exod. 19:5) — no less than their initial preparadness to accept the *Shechinah* in their midst.

For now, however, this teaching was confined to the Temple limits *(Rashi,* above). The people outside the Temple were blithely unaware of their great loss.]

אֵל שַׁדָּי — *El Shaddai.*

This is a Name of God which is variously interpreted by the commentators. It is fully discussed in the *comm.* to *Gen.* 17:1, ArtScroll ed. Its general connotation is that God dominates and changes the laws of nature at will; that He is all-sufficient; or that He sets boundaries to human suffering or to the expansion of the universe.

6. וַיְהִי בְּצַוֹּתוֹ — *Then it happened, as He commanded.*

The narrative is now continued from the end of *v.* 2 *(Radak).*

7. וַיִּשְׁלַח הַכְּרוּב אֶת יָדוֹ — *So the Cheruv stretched out his hand.*

See *comm.* to *v.* 2.

וַיִּשָּׂא וַיִּתֵּן — *And he lifted and gave* [*it*] — I.e. the fire from among the *Cheruvim (Metzudas David).*

וַיִּקַּח וַיֵּצֵא — *Then he took* [*it*] *and went out.*

Rashi and *Radak* (based on *Midrash Tanchuma Emor* 3) point out that Gabriel did not throw the coals upon Jerusalem immediately. For another six years [the vision took place in the sixth year (8:1)], the coals would 'dim' in his hands as he waited vainly for Israel to repent.

The *Midrash* continues: 'When he

voice of El Shaddai when He speaks.
6 *Then it happened, as He commanded the man*
clothed in linen saying: 'Take fire from among the
Galgal, from among the Cheruvim'. And he came and
stood near the Ofan. 7 *So the Cheruv stretched out*
his hand from among the Cheruvim to the fire which
is among the Cheruvim, and he lifted and gave it into
the hands of the one clothed in linen. Then he took it
and went out.
8 *And there appeared under the wings of the*
Cheruvim the form of a man's hand. 9 *Then I looked*
and see! Four Ofanim were beside the Cheruvim, a
single Ofan beside a single Cheruv, and a single Ofan
beside a single Cheruv; and the appearance of the
Ofanim was like Tarshish stone. 10 *And as for their*
appearance, the same semblance was for all four; as if
the Ofan were to be within the Ofan. 11 *When they*
went, they went toward their four sides. They turned
not as they went; for after whatever place the head
inclined, they went. They turned not as they went.

saw that they did not [repent] he wanted to throw [the fire] and to stamp them [Israel] out completely. God said to him: 'Gabriel, Gabriel do not do it. There are people among them who are charitable with one another.'

Ma'aseh Merkavah: In this vision, supernatural concepts are described in human terms. As explained in the *Prefatory Remarks*, they cannot be understood literally nor, in our spiritual poverty, are we equipped even to glimpse at their inner meaning.

8. וַיֵּרָא לַכְּרֻבִים תַּבְנִית יַד אָדָם תַּחַת כַּנְפֵיהֶם — *And there appeared under the wings of* [lit. *'to'*] *the Cheruvim the form of a man's hand,* [cf. 1:8].

This verse thus explains the reference to *'hand'* in the previous verse *(Metzudas David).*

Radak comments that the expressions וַיֵּרָא, *there appeared,* and תַּבְנִית, *form,* are meant to convey how all these various manifestations appeared to him in the prophetic vision. This does not suggest that the *Cheruvim* actually have *'hands', 'feet',* or *'wings'.* Further, although the phrase *man's hand* is in singular, it is in the collective sense and refers to hands appearing under *each* of the wings.

9-10. [This *Merkavah* description essentially parallels 1:15, 16. See *comm.* there.]

9. אוֹפָן אֶחָד אֵצֶל הַכְּרוּב אֶחָד — *A single Ofan beside a single Cheruv.*

I.e. beside each *Cheruv* there was one *Ofan,* etc. *(Metzudas David).*

י
יב־יח

בְּלֶכְתָּם׃ יב וְכָל־בְּשָׂרָם וְגַבֵּהֶם וִידֵיהֶם
וְכַנְפֵיהֶם וְהָאוֹפַנִּים מְלֵאִים עֵינַיִם סָבִיב
יג לְאַרְבַּעְתָּם אוֹפַנֵּיהֶם׃ לָאוֹפַנִּים לָהֶם
יד קוֹרָא הַגַּלְגַּל בְּאָזְנָי׃ וְאַרְבָּעָה פָּנִים
לְאֶחָד פְּנֵי הָאֶחָד פְּנֵי הַכְּרוּב וּפְנֵי הַשֵּׁנִי
פְּנֵי אָדָם וְהַשְּׁלִישִׁי פְּנֵי אַרְיֵה וְהָרְבִיעִי
טו פְּנֵי־נָשֶׁר׃ וַיֵּרֹמּוּ הַכְּרוּבִים הִיא הַחַיָּה
טז אֲשֶׁר רָאִיתִי בִּנְהַר־כְּבָר׃ וּבְלֶכֶת
הַכְּרוּבִים יֵלְכוּ הָאוֹפַנִּים אֶצְלָם וּבִשְׂאֵת
הַכְּרוּבִים אֶת־כַּנְפֵיהֶם לָרוּם מֵעַל הָאָרֶץ
לֹא־יִסַּבּוּ הָאוֹפַנִּים גַּם־הֵם מֵאֶצְלָם׃
יז בְּעָמְדָם יַעֲמֹדוּ וּבְרוֹמָם יֵרוֹמּוּ אוֹתָם כִּי
יח רוּחַ הַחַיָּה בָּהֶם׃ וַיֵּצֵא כְּבוֹד יהוה מֵעַל

Ma'aseh Merkavah: In this vision, supernatural concepts are described in human terms. As explained in the *Prefatory Remarks*, they cannot be understood literally nor, in our spiritual poverty, are we equipped even to glimpse at their inner meaning.

11. [Cf. *comm.* to 1:17].

12. וְכָל בְּשָׂרָם ... — *And their whole body* [following *Metzudas David*; lit. *'their whole flesh'*] ...

According to *Rashi* and *Radak*, the verse describes the *Ofanim;* i.e. in the physical representation it refers to the parts of the wheels and their rims which were surrounded with *'eyes'* to afford them full vision as described in 1:18. *Radak* remarks that the esoteric literature explains why the term בָּשָׂר, *body* or *flesh*, is used with reference only to the *Ofanim*, but not the *Cheruvim*.

According to *Metzudas David*, the imagery of *'flesh'*, back, hands and wings applies to the *Cheruvim* as well.

The 'eyes' surrounding the *Ofanim* echoes 1:18.

לְאַרְבַּעְתָּם אוֹפַנֵּיהֶם — *For the four of them their Ofanim.*

I.e., to the four *Ofanim* of each of the *Chayos (Rashi; Metzudas David).*

13. לָהֶם קוֹרָא הַגַּלְגַּל בְּאָזְנָי — *They were called* [by the term *(Metzudas David)*] *'The Galgal'* [collective for Galgalim] *in my earshot* [lit. *my ears*], i.e. while I heard, or in my hearing *(Targum).*

That is, I overheard that the angel referred to the *Ofan* as *Galgal (Rashi).*

Radak comments that it is not the intent of the verse to state the fact that the *Ofan* was called *Galgal;* since the two words are synonyms, such a statement would be redundant. Rather the verse says that whatever the *Galgalim* did was upon a specific command.

14. פְּנֵי הַכְּרוּב — *The face of a Cheruv.*

This verse portrays a marked dif-

X
12-18

[12] *And their whole body, their back, their hands, and their wings, and their Ofanim were full of eyes all around for the four of them their Ofanim.* [13] *As for the Ofanim, they were called 'The Galgal' in my earshot.* [14] *And each had four faces: the first face was the face of a Cheruv; the second face, the face of a man; the third, the face of a lion; and the fourth, the face of an eagle.* [15] *When the Cheruvim were lifted up — it was the Chayah which I saw at the River Kevar.* [16] *And as the Cheruvim move, the Ofanim move beside them; and as the Cheruvim lift their wings to rise from upon the surface, neither did the Ofanim turn away from beside them.* [17] *When they stood, they stood; when they rose, they rose with them; for the spirit of the Chayah was within them.* [18] *So the Glory of God went out from upon the*

ference between the *Merkavah* vision here and in Ch. 1 in that here, instead of the face of an ox [1:10] we have the face of a *Cheruv*.

Rashi notes that [the vision is the same]; the face of the ox had changed to that of a *Cheruv*.

This is based on *Chagigah* 13b:

Resh Lakish, noting that the ox is not mentioned here, said: Yechezkel entreated, and God changed the ox into a *Cheruv*, for Yechezkel said 'Lord of the Universe! Shall the accuser [i.e., the ox which was a reminder of Israel's sin with the golden calf] be an advocate?' [since the chariot interceded on behalf of Israel (see *Rashi* ad. loc.).]

Furthermore, the *Talmud ibid.* explains that the *Cheruvim* had a human likeness. Therefore what is the difference between the *face of the Cheruv* and the *face of the man?* — The face of the man is of an adult; the *Cheruv* that of a boy. [See *Rashi* ad loc. and *Exod.* 25:18].

15. This verse emphasizes that the *Merkavah* vision of our chapter is no different from the one he had experienced at the River Kevar, in Ch. 1. The sole exception is that the manifestation of the ox was now replaced by a *Cheruv (Metzudas David).*

[*Rashi* and *Metzudas David* hold that the change from *Chayah* to *Cheruv*, which is noted in *vs.* 1,15 and 20, was occasioned by the elimination of the ox in favor of the *Cheruv (v.* 14). *Radak*, however, sees the two things as unrelated. Two things change in this chapter. The *Chayos* are referred to as *Cheruvim*, and the ox changes into a *Cheruv*. Our *comm.* to *vs.* 1 and 20, is based on *Radak*'s understanding.]

וַיֵּרֹמּוּ הַכְּרוּבִים — *When the Cheruvim were lifted up.*

The verb וַיֵּרֹמּוּ, *lifted up*, parallels the verb נשא, *lifted up*, used in reference to the *Chayos* in 1:19-21; the difference can be explained only esoterically *(Radak)*.

16-17. See *comm.* to 1:19-21.

יט מִפְתַּן הַבָּיִת וַיַּעֲמֹד עַל־הַכְּרוּבִים: וַיִּשְׂאוּ
הַכְּרוּבִים אֶת־כַּנְפֵיהֶם וַיֵּרוֹמּוּ מִן־הָאָרֶץ
לְעֵינַי בְּצֵאתָם וְהָאוֹפַנִּים לְעֻמָּתָם וַיַּעֲמֹד
פֶּתַח שַׁעַר בֵּית־יהוה הַקַּדְמוֹנִי וּכְבוֹד
כ אֱלֹהֵי־יִשְׂרָאֵל עֲלֵיהֶם מִלְמָעְלָה: הִיא
הַחַיָּה אֲשֶׁר רָאִיתִי תַּחַת אֱלֹהֵי־יִשְׂרָאֵל
בִּנְהַר־כְּבָר וָאֵדַע כִּי כְרוּבִים הֵמָּה:
כא אַרְבָּעָה אַרְבָּעָה פָנִים לְאֶחָד וְאַרְבַּע
כְּנָפַיִם לְאֶחָד וּדְמוּת יְדֵי אָדָם תַּחַת
כב כַּנְפֵיהֶם: וּדְמוּת פְּנֵיהֶם הֵמָּה הַפָּנִים
אֲשֶׁר רָאִיתִי עַל־נְהַר־כְּבָר מַרְאֵיהֶם יא
א וְאוֹתָם אִישׁ אֶל־עֵבֶר פָּנָיו יֵלֵכוּ: וַתִּשָּׂא א

18-19. [The next of the ten stages of withdrawal is described.]

18. מֵעַל מִפְתַּן הַבָּיִת — *From upon the threshold of the House.*

Where It had been stationed [see on 9:3] *(Metzudas David).*

19. וְהָאוֹפַנִּים לְעֻמָּתָם — *And the Ofanim were opposite them.*

I.e. the *Ofanim* were coordinated with every movement of the *Cheruvim* [see 1:19-21] *(Metzudas David).*

וַיַּעֲמֹד — *And it stood.*

I.e., the entire *Merkavah:* collectively, including the *Ofanim (Radak; Metzudas David).*

פֶּתַח שַׁעַר בֵּית ה׳ הַקַּדְמוֹנִי — *The eastern gate of the House of HASHEM.*

I.e. of the Temple, which represented the second stage of the withdrawal from the Holy of Holies to the Temple Court *(Rashi).*

20. הִיא הַחַיָּה ... וָאֵדַע כִּי כְרוּבִים הֵמָּה — *This is the Chayah ... And I knew that they were Cheruvim.*

Yechezkel's despondency is relieved by a sudden ray of light. It is true that Israel's God has chosen new *Cheruvim,* new *bearers of His Glory* (see above *comm.* to *v.* 1). But the new 'bearer' is the very *Chayah* which Yechezkel saw in his first *Merkavah* vision at the banks of the river Kevar. Thus God's Glory would not be carried away from His people. It would descend with them into the Babylonian exile. (See *Pref. Remarks* to Ch. 1). The bond which binds Israel to Him and Him to His people will never be broken.

It is 'The God of Israel' Who mounted the *Merkavah (v.* 19), and He continues to be Israel's God in the country of their exile *(v.* 20). (Based on *Harav Breuer).*

וָאֵדַע כִּי כְרוּבִים הֵמָּה — *And I knew, that they were Cheruvim.*

I.e., since in every respect — except for the *Cheruvim* — this *Merkavah* vision resembled that which I had seen at the River Kevar, I knew of a certainty that the *Cheruvim* I now saw were identical with the *Chayos* I saw previously,

threshold of the House, and stood above the
Cheruvim. 19 *And the Cheruvim lifted their wings*
and rose up from the Land in my sight as they went
out, and the Ofanim were opposite them and it stood
at the entrance of the eastern gate of the House of
HASHEM. And the Glory of Israel's God was upon
them, above. 20 *This is the Chayah which I saw*
beneath the God of Israel at the River Kevar. And I
knew that they were Cheruvim. 21 *Four faces each for*
every one and four wings for every one, and the form
of human hands beneath their wings. 22 *And as for*
the likeness of their face, they were the faces which I
saw by the River Kevar — their appearances and
them — each one moving straight ahead.

although they now had the face of a *Cheruv* in place of the ox (*Rashi; Metzudas David).*

21-22. By further paralleling the description of the *Cheruvim* with what he already saw of the *Chayos* in 1:4-8, the prophet closes the description by reaffirming his belief that the vision which he was now experiencing was indeed the same *Merkavah* he had envisioned in Ch. 1.

XI

Ramban (lev. 20:3) teaches that the *Shechinah,* God's Presence, dwells in Israel only to the degree that it is perceived and treasured. If it is ignored, or even worse, actively rejected, then the *Shechinah* withdraws.

In Ch. 8, Yechezkel had been shown a people in rebellion against the *Shechinah* in their midst. This rebellion was unambiguously expressed by the 'jealousy-provoking image' *(v.* 3) raised at the entrance of the Temple grounds (see *comm.* ad. loc). In prostrating themselves before the basest forms of animal life *(v.* 10), before the forces that control the ebb and flow of the seasons (*v.* 14), and before the life-supporting, all-powerful sun (*v.* 16), the people projected their self-image as a nation forsaken by God *(v.* 12) and attempted to make peace with the cosmic forces which seemed to control their destiny.

How would people who considered themselves to be thrown entirely upon their own resources, assess their chances against the mighty Babylonian army.

It is with this question that the first half of our chapter grapples.

In previous chapters (Ch. 1: *Pref. Remarks, comm.* to 3:24-27; and 4:1-3) we discussed the attitude of people who thought themselves invincible *because* of Jerusalem's transcendental character, predicated on God's eternal presence there. This is in sharp contrast to the attitudes discussed here.

These conflicting ideas need not be reconciled. In the confusion reigning in these final years, a wide range of views was found among the people. It was the duty of the prophets to react to each of them.

יא
ב־ד

אֹתִי רוּחַ וַתָּבֵא אֹתִי אֶל־שַׁעַר בֵּית־יְהוָה
הַקַּדְמוֹנִי הַפּוֹנֶה קָדִימָה וְהִנֵּה בְּפֶתַח
הַשַּׁעַר עֶשְׂרִים וַחֲמִשָּׁה אִישׁ וָאֶרְאֶה
בְתוֹכָם אֶת־יַאֲזַנְיָה בֶן־עַזֻּר וְאֶת־פְּלַטְיָהוּ
ב בֶן־בְּנָיָהוּ שָׂרֵי הָעָם׃ וַיֹּאמֶר אֵלָי
בֶּן־אָדָם אֵלֶּה הָאֲנָשִׁים הַחֹשְׁבִים אָוֶן
וְהַיֹּעֲצִים עֲצַת־רָע בָּעִיר הַזֹּאת׃
ג הָאֹמְרִים לֹא בְקָרוֹב בְּנוֹת בָּתִּים הִיא
ד הַסִּיר וַאֲנַחְנוּ הַבָּשָׂר׃ לָכֵן

1. שַׁעַר בֵּית ה׳ הַקַּדְמוֹנִי — *The east gate of the House of HASHEM.*

Rashi comments that these twenty-five men are identical with those mentioned in 8:16. [*Malbim* points out that previously Yechezkel had seen them only from behind. Only now did he see them clearly enough to identify them.] The verse there tells that these men bowed to the sun: *'At the door of HASHEM's Temple, between the entrance hall and the altar.'* Because this location is identical to that mentioned here, *Radak* holds that our verse refers back to Yechezkel's original coming (i.e., A wind *had* lifted me up, etc.).

Malbim interprets our *gate* to be the one leading onto the הַר הַבַּיִת, the *Temple Mount.* In that case Yechezkel was now taken there.

עֶשְׂרִים וַחֲמִשָּׁה אִישׁ — *Twenty-five men.*

Not כְּעֶשְׂרִים וַחֲמִשָּׁה, *approximately twenty-five* as in 8:16. See *comm.* there.

יַאֲזַנְיָה בֶן עַזּוּר, פְּלַטְיָהוּ בֶן־בְּנָיָהוּ — *Ya'azaniah ... Pelatiahu.*

These names must have been meaningful to Yechezkel's listeners. About Ya'azaniah we know nothing at all. Concerning Pelatiahu there are conflicting traditions as to whether or not he was righteous. (See *comm.* to *v.* 13).

2. וְהַיֹּעֲצִים עֲצַת רָע בָּעִיר הַזֹּאת — *Who give evil counsel in this city.*

Because they were princes and prominent among the people, the prevalent attitudes in the city were derived from their thinking *(Radak).*

3. לֹא בְקָרוֹב בְּנוֹת בָּתִּים — *[Our doom] is not near — build houses!*

The translation follows *Rashi, Radak,* and *Metzudas David.*

The 'iniquitous connivings and evil counsels' of these men must be understood against the background of events described in *Jeremiah* 26-29.

The mood of the people spurred on by false prophets, was one of unbounded confidence and national pride. Many people branded Jeremiah a traitor for his prophecies that God had granted world-dominion to Babylon and that Israel must make peace with this situation and repent of the evil ways which had caused it. So angered were the people that Jeremiah's very life was endangered. Spurious prophecies abounded, which claimed that even that section of the nation which had already been exiled would soon return and that King Yehoyachin, who was wasting away in Babylonian prisons, would be reinstated as king.

To counteract this mood, Jeremiah composed a *'book'*, or letter which he sent to the elders of the people who were already in Babylon. It exhorted them to see their exile as a long lasting

A wind lifted me up and brought me to the east gate of the House of HASHEM, which faces eastward. And see! at the door of the gate — twenty-five men; in their midst I saw Ya'azaniah the son of Azzur and Pelatiahu the son of Benayahu, princes of the people.
2 Then He said to me: 'Ben Adam, these are the men who connive iniquity, and who give evil counsel in this city, 3 who say: "Our doom is not near — build houses! It is the caldron and we are the flesh."

one, and to settle down in the country which was to be their home for seventy years. And it excoriated as charlatans the prophets, sorcerers, and dreamers who predicted a quick return.

The first sentence of this *'book'* reads: *'Build houses and dwell, plant gardens and eat their produce' (Jeremiah* 29:5).

The prophet's opponents in Jerusalem couched their heretical message in identical idiom: 'Our fate is not about to overtake us. Far from building houses in Babylon, it is here in Jerusalem that our future must be seen. It is here that houses must be built' *(Harav Joseph Breuer).*

הִיא הַסִּיר וַאֲנַחְנוּ הַבָּשָׂר — *It is the caldron and we are the flesh.*

The false prophets likened Jerusalem to a pot in which meat is being cooked. Just as the meat is not removed from the pot until it is fully cooked, so we shall not be forced to leave Jerusalem before our time. We will stay there until we die a natural death! *(Rashi; Radak; Metzudas David).*

This then is the answer to the question which we posed in the *Pref. Remarks* to this chapter. Even though these men 'knew' God to have forsaken the Land (9:9), even though they had affirmed that 'knowledge' by prostrating themselves to the sun and negating Divine providence with the crassest obscenity (8:16 see *comm.)* they still had no doubts about their ability to hold their own against mighty Babylon.

This self-confidence recalls *Beitza* 25b (see *footnote* to 3:6-7): 'Had the Torah not been given to Israel, no nation would be able to stand up against them.' This is so because the people of Israel are עַזִּים, *aggressively and vehemently strong,* or as *Rashi* explains there: 'Difficult to conquer.' The sanctifying and disciplining bonds of the Torah were needed to temper their vehemence.[1]

Eliezer of Beaugency reads our verse in an entirely different way: The Jews of Jerusalem said: 'It is not common to build a house for a short time.' When a person builds a house he does not build it for ten or twenty years, but for a

1. Our history is replete with examples of this עַזּוּת. *Yerushalmi Ta'anis* 4:5 tells of Bar Koziva's army of two hundred thousand soldiers, each missing a finger. (In order to prove his unflinching strength and courage each recruit had to bite off a finger.) The Sages sent to him and said: 'How long will you maim the men of Israel?' Bar Koziva asked them: 'How then will I test them?'

They replied: 'Admit no man to your ranks who is unable to uproot a cedar tree from the Lebanon while riding his horse.' He then had two hundred thousand of these, and two

ה הִנָּבֵא עֲלֵיהֶם הִנָּבֵא בֶּן־אָדָם: וַתִּפֹּל
עָלַי רוּחַ יהוה וַיֹּאמֶר אֵלַי אֱמֹר כֹּה־
אָמַר יהוה כֵּן אֲמַרְתֶּם בֵּית יִשְׂרָאֵל
ו וּמַעֲלוֹת רוּחֲכֶם אֲנִי יְדַעְתִּיהָ: הִרְבֵּיתֶם
חַלְלֵיכֶם בָּעִיר הַזֹּאת וּמִלֵּאתֶם חוּצֹתֶיהָ
ז חָלָל: לָכֵן כֹּה־אָמַר אֲדֹנָי יֱהוִֹה
חַלְלֵיכֶם אֲשֶׁר שַׂמְתֶּם בְּתוֹכָהּ הֵמָּה
הַבָּשָׂר וְהִיא הַסִּיר וְאֶתְכֶם הוֹצִיא
ח מִתּוֹכָהּ: חֶרֶב יְרֵאתֶם וְחֶרֶב אָבִיא
ט עֲלֵיכֶם נְאֻם אֲדֹנָי יֱהוִֹה: וְהוֹצֵאתִי אֶתְכֶם

hundred years or more — a firm and permanent structure. But we are destined to be killed shortly. Our houses will be our graves even as flesh in a pot is destined to be consumed. We have no choice but to slaughter cattle and sheep, to eat and to drink, for tomorrow we shall die.'

4. לָכֵן — *Therefore.*

Because they have such completely false ideas, it is necessary for you to prophesy in order to contradict them *(Metzudas David).*

5. כֵּן אֲמַרְתֶּם בֵּית יִשְׂרָאֵל — *Thus have you said, Family of Israel.*

I know that you have been saying that Jerusalem is like a caldron and you are like the flesh. I tell you, however, that it will indeed be a caldron for the corpses which you have placed in it — for they came to an end in it. But as for you, it will not contain you like a caldron until the day of your death — for I shall drive you out from it *(Rashi).*

[See Ch. 24, where the parable of the caldron and the flesh is used against the inhabitants of Jerusalem.]

וּמַעֲלוֹת רוּחֲכֶם אֲנִי יְדַעְתִּיהָ — *And as for what comes into your mind, I know it.*

Not only your open speech is known to Me. Every detail of your thoughts is also clear to Me *(Metzudas David).*

6. הִרְבֵּיתֶם חַלְלֵיכֶם בָּעִיר הַזֹּאת — *You have multiplied your slain in this city.*

hundred thousand of those. And when he went out to war he would say: 'Master of the world! Do not help us [i.e., we do not need Your help to be victorious] but also do not hinder us.'

We recall the zealots in Jerusalem in the waning days of the Second Temple who were willing to pit their puny numbers against the mighty hordes of Rome.

And in our own days *Rabbi E.E. Dessler* in *Michtav Me'Eliyahu v.3* p.195 notes: 'Truly, even in our own generation we see a quality of inner strength and equanimity in *Eretz Yisrael,* more than in any other land. We have seen with our own eyes that at a time when in recent years throughout the lands there was fear of another world war, God forbid, and people fled from country to country, to places considered safe ... No one fled from *Eretz Yisrael* for fear of war. No fear reigned in *Eretz Yisrael,* and this seemed miraculous for surely there was more to fear there than anywhere else.

And we see another wondrous thing. In *Eretz Yisrael* they rely on miracles, that they can stand up against even the multitude of our enemies — even those among us who have not been blessed with the light of faith [in God] and are non-believers. Where then did they acquire this trust? This can only derive from the blessings with which God has blessed the land.'

4 *Therefore prophesy against them, prophesy Ben Adam.'*

5 *Then the spirit of HASHEM descended upon me and He said to me: Say! 'Thus says HASHEM: Thus have you said, Family of Israel, and as for what comes into your mind, I know it.*
6 *You have multiplied your slain in this city; and filled its streets with the slain.*
7 *Therefore, thus says my Lord HASHEM/ELOHIM: Your slain which you have placed within it — they are the flesh, and it is the caldron. But I will withdraw you from within it.*
8 *You have feared the sword, but the sword I shall bring against you. The words of my Lord HASHEM/ELOHIM.*
9 *So I*

Because of your words and your thoughts that you will not be exiled, you continue to do evil. Thereby you multiply the corpses in this city and fill the streets with them *(Metzudas David).*

[We have seen the unbounded confidence of the people in their ability to survive; perhaps they could indeed have withstood the onslaughts of Babylon by itself. But because God, Himself, would join the ranks of their enemies (see *comm.* to 5:8), they were doomed.

Nevertheless they could have saved themselves. Jeremiah had expressly told King Zidkiyahu that if he would *'bring his neck under the yoke of Babylon's king',* he and his whole nation would be spared *(Jeremiah* 27:12). But the people refused to listen and it was their obduracy which brought about the war. The corpses littering the streets of Jerusalem were 'their' corpses — caused by their own stubbornness. But for them, the slaughter could have been averted.]

7. The parable of the caldron is turned against them. Jerusalem will indeed be a caldron — but only for the corpses within it. You, the living, who feel so secure within its walls, will be driven out of it.

'In vain have you built your houses (*v.* 3). Fathers and sons will go into exile and there will be no one to inherit the houses' *(Rashi).*

8. חֶרֶב יְרֵאתֶם — *You have feared the sword.*

When you turned for help to the king of Egypt, as it is written (17:15) concerning Zidkiyahu: 'And he rebelled against him [against Nebuchadnezzar, who had instated him as king and exacted an oath of loyalty from him] sending his messengers to Egypt [to ask Pharaoh] to give him horses and many men' *(Rashi).*

[Zidkiyahu's violation of his oath is repeatedly dealt with in Scripture (see *comm.* to Ch. 17). In our chapter the issue is not his perfidy, but the motives which prompted it. As occurred many times before, Israel had fallen into the trap of relying on a military alliance rather than on God's providence. The very sword which they had sought to avert with Pharaoh's help, was brought

יא
י־יג

מִתּוֹכָהּ וְנָתַתִּי אֶתְכֶם בְּיַד־זָרִים וְעָשִׂיתִי
י בָכֶם שְׁפָטִים: בַּחֶרֶב תִּפֹּלוּ עַל־גְּבוּל
יִשְׂרָאֵל אֶשְׁפּוֹט אֶתְכֶם וִידַעְתֶּם כִּי־אֲנִי
יא יהוה: הִיא לֹא־תִהְיֶה לָכֶם לְסִיר וְאַתֶּם
תִּהְיוּ בְתוֹכָהּ לְבָשָׂר אֶל־גְּבוּל יִשְׂרָאֵל
יב אֶשְׁפֹּט אֶתְכֶם: וִידַעְתֶּם כִּי־אֲנִי יהוה
אֲשֶׁר בְּחֻקַּי לֹא הֲלַכְתֶּם וּמִשְׁפָּטַי לֹא
עֲשִׂיתֶם וּכְמִשְׁפְּטֵי הַגּוֹיִם אֲשֶׁר
יג סְבִיבוֹתֵיכֶם עֲשִׂיתֶם: וַיְהִי כְּהִנָּבְאִי
וּפְלַטְיָהוּ בֶן־בְּנָיָה מֵת וָאֶפֹּל עַל־פָּנַי
וָאֶזְעַק | קוֹל גָּדוֹל וָאֹמַר אֲהָהּ אֲדֹנָי

against them by God Himself (אָבִיא, *I will bring*).]

10. עַל גְּבוּל יִשְׂרָאֵל אֶשְׁפּוֹט אֶתְכֶם — *At the border of Israel shall I punish you.*

II Kings 25:6 relates how Zidkiyahu was captured during his flight from Jerusalem and taken to Ribla. There, Nebuchadnezzar had Zidkiyahu's children slaughtered, and the king himself blinded.

Rashi and *Radak* read our verse as referring to that incident because Ribla is in the land of Chamos *(II Kings* 25:21), which lay at Israel's boundary *(Num.* 34:8).

אֶשְׁפּוֹט אֶתְכֶם — *Shall I punish you.*

The root שפט is generally translated as, *to judge.* However the meaning often seems closer to, *to punish* (see for ex. *I Sam.* 3:13), and would seem to be the better translation in our context.

11. הִיא לֹא־תִהְיֶה לָכֶם לְסִיר — *It shall not be a caldron for you.*

Jerusalem will not protect you in the sense that a caldron protects the flesh within it *(Rashi).*

וְאַתֶּם תִּהְיוּ בְּתוֹכָהּ לְבָשָׂר — *But you shall become flesh within it.*

Although it will not protect you from outside enemies as does a caldron (hence the end of the verse: *At the borders of Israel* ...), still you will be scorched and broken in it just as meat is scorched and broken up in a caldron (see 24:3-6).

12. וִידַעְתֶּם כִּי־אֲנִי ה׳ — *Then you shall know that I am HASHEM.*

Rashi (Exod. 6:3) points out that the Four Letter Name, represents God in His capacity of 'Truth': as fulfilling His promise. It is in this sense that *Radak* and *Metzudas David* read our verse. You shall know that I am HASHEM when I bring about the fate which I have threatened.

Harav Breuer sees the phrase as an answer to the people's false idea that God had forsaken the earth (see 8:12). 'It is not as you had thought. You shall know that every detail of the fate which will overtake you is from the hand of God.'

[Perhaps the next phrase: *For you did not walk in My laws* etc., would be a logical extension of this thought. The reason you felt that God had forsaken the Land was because of your own failure to perceive Him. By ignoring

*shall withdraw you from within it and deliver you
into the hands of strangers; and I shall execute judgments upon you.* 10 *By the sword shall you fall. At
the border of Israel shall I punish you that you
should know that I am* HASHEM. 11 *It shall not be a
caldron for you, but you shall become flesh within it.
At the borders of Israel shall I punish you.* 12 *Then
you shall know that I am* HASHEM, *for in My decrees
you did not walk and My ordinances you did not perform, but according to the ordinances of the nations
around you, you did act.'* 13 *It was as I prophesied
that Pelatiahu the son of Benayahu died. So I threw
myself down upon my face, cried in a great voice,
and said: 'Alas, my Lord* HASHEM/ELOHIM, *do You*

those laws of the Torah whose purpose it is to sanctify a person and to help him perceive the Divine Presence you became insensitive to His Presence.]

וּכְמִשְׁפְּטֵי הַגּוֹיִם אֲשֶׁר סְבִיבוֹתֵיכֶם עֲשִׂיתֶם — *But according to the ordinances of the nations around you, you did act.*

See *comm.* to 5:7.

13. Although Yechezkel had seen (9:6) that every inhabitant of Jerusalem was marked for death, he had assumed that some time would elapse before their fate would be realized, thus giving them time to repent *(Radak).* When he saw his prophetic word felling Pelatiahu directly, he feared that the whole populace would die in the same way *(Metzudas David).* The fate had been pronounced against [*'old man, young man, maiden, child and women'*] (9:6). Since Pelatiahu belonged to the elders *('old man')* it was reasonable to assume that death, having started from the elders, would now spread to the others who had been mentioned *(Mahari Kara).*

These commentaries embody what *Mahari Kara* calls: פְּשׁוּטוֹ, *the simple meaning* of the verse. The Sages *(Kidushin* 72b) paint a different picture.

Rav and Shmuel disagree. One comments that Yechezkel was horrified at Pelatiahu's death, because subsequently, during the Babylonian exile, he rendered an important service to the Jews. (In this view, Pelatiahu died many years later and Yechezkel saw into the future.) Why would a man with such great merits die in the bloom of life? The other interprets Yechezkel's reaction as being prompted by Pelatiahu's wickedness. He had been among the twenty-five people who had bowed to the sun (see above). Why would such a wicked man die 'upon his bed' rather than by violence?

According to either interpretation the question remains why this matter is raised in the context of our chapter. The answer may be found in *Maharal (Chidushei Aggadah* ad. loc.) who asks, according to the interpretation that Pelatiahu was wicked, why should Yechezkel have cried out: 'Alas, my Lord, HASHEM/*ELOHIM, do You make a termination of the remnant of Israel?'*

יֶהוִֹה כָּלָה֙ אַתָּ֣ה עֹשֶׂ֔ה אֵ֖ת שְׁאֵרִ֥ית
יד יִשְׂרָאֵֽל׃ וַיְהִ֥י דְבַר־יְהוִ֖ה
טו אֵלַ֥י לֵאמֹֽר׃ בֶּן־אָדָ֗ם אַחֶ֤יךָ אַחֶ֙יךָ֙ אַנְשֵׁ֣י
גְאֻלָּתֶ֔ךָ וְכָל־בֵּ֥ית יִשְׂרָאֵ֖ל כֻּלֹּ֑ה אֲשֶׁ֨ר
אָמְר֜וּ לָהֶ֗ם יֹשְׁבֵ֤י יְרֽוּשָׁלִַ֙ם֙ רַֽחֲקוּ֙
מֵעַ֣ל יְהוָ֔ה לָ֥נוּ הִ֛יא נִתְּנָ֥ה הָאָ֖רֶץ

Maharal explains that it seemed to Yechezkel that Pelatiahu's peaceful death could be understood only if God had removed His הַשְׁגָחָה, *His Providence,* from Israel. Otherwise a more severe punishment would surely have been meted out to him. Thus Pelatiahu's death confirmed Yechezkel's worst fears; God seemed indeed to have forsaken the Land [and this would guarantee the ultimate destruction of Israel].

[While *Maharal* discusses only that opinion which sees Pelatiahu as a wicked man, his explanation could serve to justify the presence of this passage in our chapter according to both opinions. According to either view, the apparent miscarriage of justice, whether the punishment was too severe or too lenient, seems to point to the absence of God's Providence over His people.]

14-21. At last, we come to the climax of all that Yechezkel had been shown in the past four chapters. In Jerusalem he had seen a corrupt society stubbornly clinging to the outer trappings of a national existence which had long since lost its inner vitality. He had equated this society with שְׁאֵרִית יִשְׂרָאֵל, *the remnant of Israel* (see *comm.* to 6:8). Its disintegration represented for him the complete end of Israel.

Now the truth unfolds before his prophetic eye. Jerusalem is *not* the *'remnant of Israel.'* It is the people in exile who are the *'remnant'* whose *'heart of stone'* will one day turn into a receptive *'heart of flesh'*, into whose being a *'new spirit'* will penetrate *(v.* 19) and who will be the true builders of Israel's future in Israel's Land *(v.* 17). In defiance of every law of history (see *comm.* to 6:8) they will flourish towards a spiritual regeneration even while scattered to the remotest ends of a hostile world *(v.* 16). The *Shechinah* which has left its dwelling place in the Temple will accompany them and make Its Presence felt in their *'small sanctuaries' (v.* 16) — their synagogues and study houses.

It is they who will be God's nation. It is to them that He will be God.

15. Yechezkel's true brothers [אַח from אחה *to unite* — hence used also for one who shares feelings and attitudes, see *Prov.* 17:17] are his fellow exiles in Babylon. In preceding chapters the prophet was a passive spectator witnessing actions of people whose destiny he did not share. His lot was with the exiles, denigrated and scorned by Jerusalem's inhabitants, but harboring within themselves the seeds for a new Jerusalem.

אַחֶיךָ אַחֶיךָ אַנְשֵׁי גְאֻלָּתֶךָ — *Your brothers, your brothers, men of your kinship.*

The translation of אַנְשֵׁי גְאֻלָּתֶךָ as *men of your kinship* follows *Targum. Mahari Kara* draws a parallel with *Lev.* 25:25.

The triple expression *(Your brothers, your brothers, men of your kinship)* alludes to the three waves of exiles who had been driven from the Land. [*Yehoyachin*'s exile to Babylon had been preceded by the two-stage dispersion of the Northern Kingdom: first the two tribes on the eastern bank of the

XI 14-15

make a termination of the remnant of Israel?' 14 *Then the word of HASHEM came to me, saying:* 15 *'Ben Adam! Your brothers, your brothers, men of your kinship, and all the Family of Israel, all of it, about whom the inhabitants of Jerusalem had said: "Get far from HASHEM, to us the Land is given for an*

River Jordan (*II Kings* 15:29-30) and then the remainder of the ten tribes (*II Kings* 17:6)] (*Radak*).

וְכָל בֵּית יִשְׂרָאֵל כֻּלֹּה — *And all the Family of Israel, all of it.*

After alluding to three separate exiles, the prophet now describes them all together (*Radak*). [Perhaps he means to stress that despite their dispersion through many countries, they still form one essential unity — they are the true *Family of Israel.*] [1]

The apparently redundant word כֻּלֹּה, might be translated: *'in its totality'*, that is, not merely the remaining individual members of that *'family'*, but *'in its totality'* referring to all factors and conditions requisite to complete, flawless redemption. (See *Gen.* 24:1 for the use of the word כֹּל in this sense. God did not bless Abraham with 'everything'. Rather Abraham's blessed state was complete. He lacked nothing which would have contributed to his good fortune).

יֹשְׁבֵי יְרוּשָׁלַיִם — *The inhabitants of Jerusalem.*

This hitherto unused expression seems to set aside the *'inhabitants of Jerusalem'* from the people described in this and the previous three chapters, who had been intent upon driving God from His Sanctuary (see Ch. 8 and *Pref. Remarks* to this chapter). The general population, however,(the *'inhabitants of Jerusalem')* seem to have held the opposite view. They felt protected from Babylonian attack by their closeness to God, Whose Sanctuary stood in their midst. The slogan which they hurled derisively (*Rashi*) against their exiled brothers: *'Get far away from HASHEM, to us the Land is given for an inheritance'* is the eloquent expression of the false doctrine of Jerusalem's impenetrability.

To these people Jeremiah had called out (*Jeremiah* 7:4): *'Do not put your trust in the falsehoods which declare:* הֵיכַל ה׳ הֵיכַל ה׳ *The Sanctuary of God, the Sanctuary of God'* [for] הֵיכַל ה׳ הֵמָּה, it is they themselves — the people — who are [or should be] the true sanctuary of God (based on *Hirsch*).

These people had not seen God upon His *Merkavah*, had not seen the *Shechinah* in motion as it gradually departed Jerusalem. In their minds Solomon's Temple was God's eternal resting place (*Ps.* 132:15), and they were not shaken by Jeremiah's threat (*Jer.* 7:12) that the Temple was no more inviolable than *Shiloh* had been.

The truth, however, as told to them by Jeremiah, and as demonstrated so

1. Yechezkel sees the return of the ten tribes as an integral part of Israel's future. See 37:15-28 (and *Gur Aryeh* to *Gen.* 45:14).

Much has been written on this subject. *Rabbi Akiba* (*Sanhedrin* 110b) taught that the 'ten tribes are not destined to return.' *Rashi* (ad. loc.) in one version, writes that this refers only to the original exiles — but their descendants would indeed come back and be united with the rest of Israel. *Rashi* cites another interpretation of *Rabbi Akiba*'s view that even the descendants of the 'ten tribes' would never return. In Ch. 37 we shall discuss *Rabbi Akiba's* opinion in the light of many Scriptural sources quoted by *Ramban* (*Sefer haGeulah*) which support the assertion that the ten tribes will return.

יא
טז־יז

טז לְמוֹרָשָׁה: לָכֵן אֱמֹר כֹּה
אָמַר אֲדֹנָי יֱהוִה כִּי הִרְחַקְתִּים בַּגּוֹיִם
וְכִי הֲפִיצוֹתִים בָּאֲרָצוֹת וָאֱהִי לָהֶם
לְמִקְדָּשׁ מְעַט בָּאֲרָצוֹת אֲשֶׁר־בָּאוּ
יז שָׁם: לָכֵן אֱמֹר כֹּה־אָמַר אֲדֹנָי
יֱהוִה וְקִבַּצְתִּי אֶתְכֶם מִן־הָעַמִּים וְאָסַפְתִּי
אֶתְכֶם מִן־הָאֲרָצוֹת אֲשֶׁר נְפֹצוֹתֶם בָּהֶם

graphically in Yechezkel's *Merkavah* visions was very different. God does not rest within a building, but within a people. The beautiful building in their midst had ceased to be a Sanctuary the moment the *Shechinah* began Its departure.

Henceforth there would be a multitude of sanctuaries, as described in the next verse.

16. לָכֵן אֱמֹר — *Therefore say.*

The implication is that the message is directed to the exiles (see *Metzudas David).*

[The danger was ever present that the derisive attitude of Jerusalem's people would leave its mark on the exiles. They might think of themselves as being rejected by Him (see 33:10 and 37:11) *Therefore* they are to be apprised of their place in God's plan].

כִּי הִרְחַקְתִּים ... וָאֱהִי לָהֶם — *Though I have removed them far off ... yet I have been for them.*

[Throughout the book, the verb זרה *'scatter'* is used as a parallel to הפיץ, *'disperse'* (12:15, 20:23, 22:15, 36:19). It is only here that הרחק, *'removed far off'* is used together with הפיץ. This seems to echo the slight which the dwellers of Jerusalem hurled against the exiles (*v.* 15): רַחֲקוּ מֵעַל ה׳, *Get far from HASHEM.* God's answer is that they may indeed be distant, but that it was He who placed them at a distance to further the fulfillment of His plan.]

Although I have indeed exiled them among the nations, they are destined to be gathered from among them and to be brought back to Israel *(v.* 17). *Therefore* I have taken care not to forsake them even in their captivity. My *Shechinah* has accompanied them. They can find It in their small sanctuaries.

לְמִקְדָּשׁ מְעַט — *A small sanctuary.*

'I have given them *houses of gathering* (synagogues) which are second to My Temple' *(Targum* quoted by most commentators).

Even in the darkest exile, the Jew can find the *Shechinah* through תְּפִלַּת הַצִּבּוּר the communal prayer in the synagogue.[1]

17-20. Since the entire exiled community (including the ten tribes) was the butt of Jerusalem's derision (*v.* 15), it follows that the forthcoming promise of reconciliation includes them all.

1. Indeed, the synagogue affords the Jew the opportunity to tear himself loose from the bonds of exile. As a צבור, *a community* within which the *Shechinah* rests, Jewish individuals form a unity joined to God which thereby transcends the shackles of space and escapes the confines of its physical location.

God said: 'Everyone who studies *Torah,* busies himself with kindness, and takes part in communal prayer, is considered by Me as though he had redeemed Me and My children from among the nations' (*Berachos* 8a).

inheritance."
16 *Therefore say: Thus says my Lord HASHEM/ELOHIM: Though I have removed them far off among the nations, and though I have scattered them among the countries, yet I have been for them a small sanctuary in the countries where they came.*
17 *Therefore say: Thus says my Lord HASHEM/ELOHIM, I shall assemble you from the nations, and gather you in from the countries where*

God's promise here is couched in the same terms as that recorded in *Deut.* Here, He says: וְקִבַּצְתִּי אֶתְכֶם מִן הָעַמִּים, *and I will assemble you from the nations.* There, in promising God's ultimate redemption, Moses said וְקִבֶּצְךָ מִכָּל הָעַמִּים ... מִשָּׁם יְקַבֶּצְךָ, *'and He will assemble you from among all the nations ... from there shall He assemble you (Deut.* 30:3-4).

The implication then is, that the subject of Yechezkel's prophecy in this passage is the complete redemption associated with Messianic times. [The theme of the לֵב בָּשָׂר, *the heart of flesh (v.* 19), is repeated and elaborated upon in 36:26, which manifestly deals with Messianic times. See *Ramban, Deut.* 30:6].

It is equally clear in context, however, that Yechezkel's prophecy must have been understood by his listeners as referring to their own plight and their own return to Jerusalem. In view of the fact that the return from the Babylonian exile fell painfully short of a total redemption, this would seem to present a difficulty. [See *Ramban, Sefer haGeulah* (Ed. Chavel, Jerusalem 5723, pp. 270-274) for a detailed analysis of which of Yechezkel's prophecies were not fulfilled during the return from Babylon and must therefore be construed as referring to the final Messianic redemption.]

Ramban (Sefer haGeulah loc. cit. p. רעז*)* provides the answer. He deals with a similar problem regarding some prophecies of Isaiah. They have the ring of describing Messianic times, but according to the tradition of the Sages, referred to events and personalities which existed during the reign of King Chizkiyahu.

Ramban explains that prophecies contain a wide range of potential which can be actualized at many levels. Had Chizkiyahu and his generation risen to the challenge of their time and attained the required heights of spiritual perfection, then Isaiah's prophecies would have come true in the full grandeur and range of their potential. But the people fell short of this perfection and therefore the prophecies were realized on a much smaller scale than they would have been otherwise. Their full potential was left for Messianic times.

The same tensions exist within Yechezkel's prophecies. Had the people risen to a true *teshuva,* an unreserved turning to God and the Torah, the

Maharal (Ohr Chadash) comments: '... for the *Shechinah* is with Israel in the exile ... [and] when they gather together 'to' God, as for example during communal prayer, that is considered a 'gathering in' of the dispersion which is Israel's lot among the nations, and it can be viewed as a redemption from among the nations. Know then, that Israel among the nations, even when a thousand of them are in one place, are considered 'scattered.' But while they pray they are as one community, gathered in and drawn to God. And through this they leave [their exile] among the nations and rise up from among them *(Ohr Chadash* to *Esther* 4:16).

יח וְנָתַתִּי לָכֶם אֶת־אַדְמַת יִשְׂרָאֵל׃ וּבָאוּ־
שָׁמָּה וְהֵסִירוּ אֶת־כָּל־שִׁקּוּצֶיהָ וְאֶת־כָּל־
יט תּוֹעֲבוֹתֶיהָ מִמֶּנָּה׃ וְנָתַתִּי לָהֶם לֵב אֶחָד
וְרוּחַ חֲדָשָׁה אֶתֵּן בְּקִרְבְּכֶם וַהֲסִרֹתִי לֵב
הָאֶבֶן מִבְּשָׂרָם וְנָתַתִּי לָהֶם לֵב בָּשָׂר׃
כ לְמַעַן בְּחֻקֹּתַי יֵלֵכוּ וְאֶת־מִשְׁפָּטַי יִשְׁמְרוּ
וְעָשׂוּ אֹתָם וְהָיוּ־לִי לְעָם וַאֲנִי אֶהְיֶה
כא לָהֶם לֵאלֹהִים׃ וְאֶל־לֵב שִׁקּוּצֵיהֶם
וְתוֹעֲבוֹתֵיהֶם לִבָּם הֹלֵךְ דַּרְכָּם בְּרֹאשָׁם
כב נָתַתִּי נְאֻם אֲדֹנָי יֱהֹוִה׃ וַיִּשְׂאוּ הַכְּרוּבִים
אֶת־כַּנְפֵיהֶם וְהָאוֹפַנִּים לְעֻמָּתָם וּכְבוֹד

return from Babylon would have signalled the Messianic era. (See *Berachos* 4a and *Sanhedrin* 98b: 'Israel might have been granted the same miracles in Ezra's time as they were granted in the days of Joshua. But sin prevented it.' See *Rashi* on this passage at *Yechezkel* 43:10. [The explanation of this passage is a later addition to *Rashi*, but must certainly have been based on a *Midrashic* source.] See also *Malbim*'s introductory remarks to *Chaggai* 1:1).

Once more the opportunity was missed. The שִׁיבַת צִיּוֹן, *the return to Jerusalem* did come about, many of the exiles resettled in Eretz Yisrael (including also some of the ten tribes — *Ramban* loc. cit. pp. 272-273), and the Temple was rebuilt. However, the redemption was but a pale shadow of what might have been. Yechezkel's vision in its fullest sense, will be fulfilled only in the days of Messiah.

17. וְקִבַּצְתִּי ... וְאָסַפְתִּי — *I shall assemble you ... and gather you in.*

The verb אסף, *gather in*, is not used again in conjunction with *assemble* (we find וְהֵבֵאתִי, *and I will bring* 36:24 and 37:21).

[Perhaps אסף is used here because it has the additional connotation of 'to bring inside' (see for ex. *Deut.* 22:2). Thus, its use would imply that, far from having been rejected by Jerusalem (as the *'dwellers of Jerusalem'* had derisively claimed), the exiles would one day be brought back inside the Holy City.]

18. וְהֵסִירוּ אֶת כָּל שִׁקּוּצֶיהָ — *And* [*they*] *shall take away* [*from it*] *all its detestations.*

I.e. the *'detestable things'* which had been there since before the exile *(Eliezer of Beaugency)*, or which were placed there by the conquerors *(Radak)*.

Metzudas David takes הֵסִיר in the sense of 'to withhold' (see *II Sam.* 7:15). They will refrain from doing the *'detestable acts'* which were now taking place.

19. לֵב אֶחָד — *A single* [lit. *one*] *heart.*

Targum renders: *'a fearing heart'* (see *Minchas Shai).*

The expression לֵב אֶחָד is found in Scripture in the sense of *unanimous.* (See *I Chron.* 12:39, and *II* 30:12) and is used by the Sages in that sense *(Mechilta* to *Exod.* 19:2 quoted by *Rashi).* The sense would then be that the whole nation would be as one in the

XI
18-22

you have been scattered, and give you the Land of
Israel. 18 *Then they shall come there and take away*
from it all its detestations and all its abominations.
19 *Then I shall give them a single heart, and a new*
spirit shall I emplace in you; I shall remove the stony
heart from their flesh and give them a heart of flesh,
20 *so that they may walk in My decrees and guard My*
ordinances and perform them. Then they shall be for
Me a nation, and I shall be for them, God.
21 *But for their heart which follows the heart of*
their detestations and abominations, I have placed
their way upon their head. The words of my Lord
HASHEM/ELOHIM.'
22 *Then the Cheruvim raised their wings and the*

service of God. This theme is frequently found in the description of Messianic times (see for ex. *Zephaniah* 3:9).

Metzudas David takes אֶחָד as meaning *'undivided'*. (See for ex. *Exod.* 26:11 for this usage). The people's heart will no longer be burdened by doubt. They will single-mindedly turn to God.

לֵב הָאֶבֶן — *The stony heart.*

A heart unwilling to accept reproof *(Radak).* The Jews had been described (2:4 see *comm.)* as being חִזְקֵי לֵב, *hard of heart.*

לֵב בָּשָׂר — *A heart of flesh.*

Soft and ready to submit *(Rashi).*

20. לְמַעַן — *So that.*

At the very dawn of their existence, Israel had been exhorted to adhere to God's חֻקִּים and מִשְׁפָּטִים, *His decrees and ordinances,* as the sole guaranty of both temporal and spiritual life. *(Lev.* 18:5; see *comm.* to 20:11). The single minded *'heart of flesh'* and *'new spirit'* which God would grant them *(v.* 19) would help them to walk in these ways and to guard them.

וְהָיוּ לִי לְעָם — *Then they shall be for Me a nation.*

To believe in Me and to observe My commandments *(Metzudas David).*

וַאֲנִי אֶהְיֶה לָהֶם לֵאלֹהִים — *And I shall be for them, God.*

To save them and to help them *(Metzudas David).*

21. לֵב שִׁקּוּצֵיהֶם וְתוֹעֲבוֹתֵיהֶם — *The heart of their detestations and abominations.*

The translation follows *Radak.* It was as though the heart of the people of Jerusalem was split in two. One part inclined towards idol worship (the *'stony heart'* of *v.* 19, according to *Harav Breuer),* and their heart of hearts (לִבָּם) which intuitively perceived its truth. But the *'stony heart'* was the mightier of the two, and dragged their whole heart after it.

Metzudas David translates לֵב שִׁקּוּצֵיהֶם as the 'inner' meaning of idol worship. The word לֵב, then is taken in the same sense as in *Exod.* 15:8.

דַּרְכָּם בְּרֹאשָׁם נָתַתִּי — *I have placed their way upon their head.*

See *comm.* to 7:3.

22-23. The *Shechinah* finally leaves the Temple completely.

יא
כג־כה

כג אֱלֹהֵי־יִשְׂרָאֵל עֲלֵיהֶם מִלְמָעְלָה׃ וַיַּעַל
כְּבוֹד יהוה מֵעַל תּוֹךְ הָעִיר וַיַּעֲמֹד עַל־
כד הָהָר אֲשֶׁר מִקֶּדֶם לָעִיר׃ וְרוּחַ נְשָׂאַתְנִי
וַתְּבִאֵנִי כַשְׂדִּימָה אֶל־הַגּוֹלָה בַּמַּרְאֶה
בְּרוּחַ אֱלֹהִים וַיַּעַל מֵעָלַי הַמַּרְאֶה אֲשֶׁר
כה רָאִיתִי׃ וָאֲדַבֵּר אֶל־הַגּוֹלָה אֵת כָּל־דִּבְרֵי

יב
א־ג

א יהוה אֲשֶׁר הֶרְאָנִי׃ וַיְהִי
ב דְבַר־יהוה אֵלַי לֵאמֹר׃ בֶּן־אָדָם
בְּתוֹךְ בֵּית־הַמֶּרִי אַתָּה יֹשֵׁב אֲשֶׁר
עֵינַיִם לָהֶם לִרְאוֹת וְלֹא רָאוּ אָזְנַיִם
לָהֶם לִשְׁמֹעַ וְלֹא שָׁמֵעוּ כִּי בֵּית מְרִי
ג הֵם׃ וְאַתָּה בֶן־אָדָם
עֲשֵׂה לְךָ כְּלֵי גוֹלָה וּגְלֵה יוֹמָם לְעֵינֵיהֶם

24-25. *Yechezkel's* vision is completed. His brothers (*v.* 15), the people of the exile, will now be told of their destiny.

XII

From the very beginning of his mission, Yechezkel had known that his fellow exiles would not be receptive to his message (2:3-7, 3:25-27).

Ch. 4 tells how he willingly lived through 430 days of suffering and deprivation, in the hope that he might reach the people's heart by graphically depicting Jerusalem's travail. In Ch. 5, with the symbolism of the hair he represented the fate of famine, pestilence, murder, and exile which was hanging over Jerusalem's inhabitants. None of this had availed. They had eyes to see — but they did not see *(v. 2)*.

In Chs. 6-7 he had spelled out in brutal and unsparing detail the inevitable results of Jerusalem's continuing obduracy. We can only guess at the eloquence with which he conveyed the horrors which he had been shown in Chs. 8-11. Nothing helped. They had ears to hear — but they did not hear *(ibid)*.

And so, the prophet is commanded to embark upon another series of symbolic acts. This time he would draw on the exiles' own experience of being dragged into captivity, to help them to recognize and appreciate Jerusalem's plight.

2. בֵּית הַמֶּרִי — *The family of rebellion.*

The definite article (הַמֶּרִי) indicates something known from before. Already in 2:5, in his very first vision, Yechezkel had been warned that Israel was a בֵּית מְרִי, *a rebellious family*. His own experiences have now confirmed it *(Harav Breuer)*.

אֲשֶׁר עֵינַיִם לָהֶם לִרְאוֹת ... — *Who have eyes to see, ...*

See *Pref. Remarks* to this chapter.

3-6. To avoid the difficulty of some seeming redundancies, and the apparent contradiction between what was done *'by day'* and what *'by night'*, we follow

XI 23-25

Ophanim opposite them, and the glory of the God of
Israel was upon them, above.
23 *So HASHEM rose*
from within the city, and stood upon the mountain
which is east of the city.
24 *and a wind lifted me and*
brought me to Chaldea to the exile — in a vision by
the spirit of God. And the vision which I had seen
rose up from me.
25 *Then I spoke to the exile all the*
words of HASHEM which He had shown me.

XII 1-3

1 *The word of HASHEM came to me, saying:*
2 *Ben Adam! You dwell amid the family of rebellion, who have eyes to see, but did not see; they have ears to hear, but did not hear. For a family of rebellion are they.*
3 *And you, Ben Adam make yourself implements*
for exile, and go into exile by day before their eyes,

Harav Breuer (based on *Malbim).* Four different events will be portrayed — two past and two future: First would come the exile of the ten tribes and Yehoyachin's exile, both of them awakening painful memories of the past. These associations would then prepare the people to understand the two other symbols: Those standing for the impending exile of Jerusalem's inhabitants, and Zidkiyahu's abortive attempt to escape.

3. עֲשֵׂה לְךָ כְּלֵי גוֹלָה — *Make yourself implements for exile.*

That is: a light, a dish, and a mat [upon which to eat *(Ran)*] *(Nedarim* 40b).

If the people had taken Yechezkel's action to heart and prepared such articles for themselves, they would have been able to alleviate the discomforts of the exile in some small way. But they ignored the prophet's message and suffered the consequences. We quote *Eichah Rabbasi,* 1:22:

What are 'implements for exile'? ... a bag, a mat, and a dish. And each one can be used for two purposes. The bag can contain flour and be used as a pillow. The dish can be used to eat and to drink from; the mat to sit on and to sleep on ... But they did not listen. When they embarked on their exile they tried to knead their dough and did not know how. They dug in the earth to make a hole in which to knead, and the pebbles got stuck in the dough. When they began to eat, their teeth were blunted, as it is written: *He ground my teeth on gravel (Eichah* 3:16).

Certainly the purpose of these symbolic acts was to convince the people of the imminence of their exile. But, in His love for them, God simultaneously wanted to advise the people how to cope with the rigors of the journey.

יוֹמָם — *By day.*

The translation follows *Targum* i.e., enact your exile in broad daylight so that the people can see you and draw

וְגָלִיתָ מִמְּקוֹמְךָ אֶל־מָקוֹם אַחֵר לְעֵינֵיהֶם
ד אוּלַי יִרְאוּ כִּי בֵּית מְרִי הֵמָּה: וְהוֹצֵאתָ
כֵלֶיךָ כִּכְלֵי גוֹלָה יוֹמָם לְעֵינֵיהֶם וְאַתָּה
תֵּצֵא בָעֶרֶב לְעֵינֵיהֶם כְּמוֹצָאֵי גּוֹלָה:
ה לְעֵינֵיהֶם חֲתָר־לְךָ בַקִּיר וְהוֹצֵאתָ בּוֹ:
ו לְעֵינֵיהֶם עַל־כָּתֵף תִּשָּׂא בָּעֲלָטָה תוֹצִיא
פָּנֶיךָ תְכַסֶּה וְלֹא תִרְאֶה אֶת־הָאָרֶץ כִּי־

the proper lesson from your deed.

Rashi translates: 'over a period of days', commenting: 'Day by day. Repeat this for two or three days, like a person readying himself for exile, so that the exiles [in Babylon] will see and ask you what you are doing. And you will tell them that it is a symbol for Zidkiyahu and his people, so that they [the exiles] may send their messengers to them [to Jerusalem] to inform their brothers and relatives who are there of all the things they hear from you.'

וגלה יומם לְעֵינֵיהֶם וְגָלִיתָ מִמְּקוֹמְךָ אֶל מָקוֹם אַחֵר לְעֵינֵיהֶם — *And go into exile by day before their eyes, then move away from your place to another place before their eyes.*

He was to depict two different exiles. The first portrayed aimless wandering without indication of a specific destination, even as the Northern Kingdom (the Ten Tribes) had been dragged away to unknown places leaving no trace of communal life.

The depiction of the second exile was to be from one place to another, like Yehoyachin's exile — of which Yechezkel's listeners were the victims — which had been from Jerusalem to Babylon.

Both events were rooted firmly in the national consciousness. They were undeniable. Perhaps this would ready Israel for the next symbol.

לְעֵינֵיהֶם — *Before their eyes.*

That this phrase is repeated no less than six times in these three verses is surely meant to echo the expression: '... *who have eyes to see but did not see*' of *v.* 2. With these graphic pictures unfolding before the people's eyes, perhaps their eyes could be made to see.

4. וְהוֹצֵאתָ כֵלֶיךָ כִּכְלֵי גוֹלָה — *And you shall bring out your implements, like implements of exile.*

In the two previous 'exiles' only the 'implements of exile' were used. They were only reminders of what had passed. Now that the impending exile is about to be enacted, a greater realism is necessary. Yechezkel is to take 'his implements — as many as he can carry on his shoulder *(v.* 6) — and ready them together with the 'implements of exile' *(v.* 3) in preparation for the evening's flight.

וְאַתָּה תֵּצֵא בָעֶרֶב לְעֵינֵיהֶם — *And go out in the evening before their eyes.*

The actual flight is to take place in the evening, in order to symbolize *Zidkiyahu*'s evening escape.

כְּמוֹצָאֵי גּוֹלָה — *As an exile exiting.*

מוֹצָא denotes the 'breaking of camp' and preparation for a journey *(Num.* 33:2). *Metzudas David* translates: 'as those who go out into exile.'

5. חֲתָר לְךָ בַקִּיר — *Dig through the wall.*

Make for yourself an excavation in the wall of the house and through this

XII
4-6

then move away from your place to another place
before their eyes. Perhaps they will perceive, for a
rebellious family are they. 4 *And you shall bring out*
your implements, like implements of exile, by day
before their eyes. And go out in the evening before
their eyes, as an exile exiting. 5 *Before their eyes, dig*
through the wall, and bring forth through it. 6 *Before*
their eyes, on the shoulder carry, in the darkness
bring forth; cover your face that you should not see

you should escape. This alludes to *Zidkiyahu* who would escape from the city through a cave *(Metzudas David).*

See *comm.* to *v.* 10-14 below, where we quote the passage from *Jeremiah* which describes Zidkiyahu's flight.

No mention is made there of an excavation. [*Radak* points out that this omission presents no difficulty. Scriptures frequently relate an occurrence, and describes its details elsewhere. It should be noted that no mention is made in any of the three sources quoted below of anything being carried on the shoulder or of the fact that Zidkiyahu covered his face.][1]

In fact, the account states that he left from the 'gate between the walls.' We must assume then, that it was in the garden that the excavation took place. Unable to leave by the front door of his palace, he had to find an alternate way through the garden *(Radak* to *v.* 7).

6. עַל כָּתֵף תִּשָּׂא — *On the shoulder carry.*

Every detail is to be true to life. He is to carry his few belongings on the shoulder, just as a fugitive is unable to take along anything but the bare necessities.

בָּעֲלָטָה תוֹצִיא — *In the darkness bring forth.*

A fugitive would be afraid to carry a light for fear it might lead to his discovery *(Metzudas David).*

פָּנֶיךָ תְכַסֶּה — *Cover your face.*

Like one who is ashamed and fearful of being recognized *(Metzudas David).* Certainly King Zidkiyahu would have wanted to disguise himself during his flight. He would cover his face so completely that he would be unable to see the ground.

1. *Ramban (Gen.* 42:21) notes that Joseph's plea to his brothers for mercy is mentioned not in Ch. 37, where the account of the sale is given, but in Ch. 42 where the conscience of the brothers is stirred by the memory of his cries.

Ramban states: 'It is the way of Scripture to be brief in one place but to expand in another.' He does not offer an explanation for this practice.

It has been suggested that the significance of Joseph's ignored pleading is emphasized by placing it in the later chapter. The narrative in Ch. 37 is little affected by the omission of Joseph's pleading, but its insertion in Ch. 42 explains the brothers' frame of mind as they stood before Pharaoh's viceroy [Joseph], endangered and at his mercy.

Similarly the details of Zidkiyahu's flight do not matter when the actual event is reported in Scripture; significant is that he fled and that a terrible fate overtook him.

The ignominious details of the flight, the pathetic picture of a mighty prince tunneling under a garden wall, weighed down by the burden of his pitifully few belongings attempting to hide his shame behind a cloth covering his face, belong in Yechezkel's presentation to the people, its impact strengthened by the vividness of the detail.

יב
ז־יב

ז מוֹפֵת נְתַתִּיךָ לְבֵית יִשְׂרָאֵל׃ וָאַעַשׂ כֵּן
כַּאֲשֶׁר צֻוֵּיתִי כֵּלַי הוֹצֵאתִי כִּכְלֵי גוֹלָה
יוֹמָם וּבָעֶרֶב חָתַרְתִּי־לִי בַקִּיר בְּיָד
בָּעֲלָטָה הוֹצֵאתִי עַל־כָּתֵף נָשָׂאתִי
ח לְעֵינֵיהֶם׃ וַיְהִי דְבַר־יְהוָה אֵלַי
ט בַּבֹּקֶר לֵאמֹר׃ בֶּן־אָדָם הֲלֹא אָמְרוּ אֵלֶיךָ
בֵּית יִשְׂרָאֵל בֵּית הַמֶּרִי מָה אַתָּה עֹשֶׂה׃
י אֱמֹר אֲלֵיהֶם כֹּה אָמַר אֲדֹנָי יֱהֹוִה
הַנָּשִׂיא הַמַּשָּׂא הַזֶּה בִּירוּשָׁלִַם וְכָל־בֵּית
יא יִשְׂרָאֵל אֲשֶׁר־הֵמָּה בְתוֹכָם׃ אֱמֹר אֲנִי
מוֹפֶתְכֶם כַּאֲשֶׁר עָשִׂיתִי כֵּן יֵעָשֶׂה לָהֶם
יב בַּגּוֹלָה בַשְּׁבִי יֵלֵכוּ׃ וְהַנָּשִׂיא אֲשֶׁר־
בְּתוֹכָם אֶל־כָּתֵף יִשָּׂא בָּעֲלָטָה וְיֵצֵא

כִּי מוֹפֵת נְתַתִּיךָ לְבֵית יִשְׂרָאֵל — *For as a sign have I appointed you to the Family of Israel.*

Yechezkel's destiny was to be a symbol for his people. He was to constitute a microcosm of Israel's fate. This symbolism would reach its peak in 24:15-27 when, as a מוֹפֵת, *a symbol,* he would have to lose 'the desire of his eyes' — his wife, to symbolize the destruction of the Temple.

7. חָתַרְתִּי לִי בַקִּיר בְּיָד — *I dug through the wall by hand.*

Another detail of added realism. A fugitive would not have the correct tools for digging, and in any case, he would be afraid of making any noise. Yechezkel therefore excavated the wall by hand.

10-14. Scripture describes Zidkiyahu's aborted attempt to escape in three places (*II Kings* 25, *Jeremiah* 39 and 52). The most detailed account is in *Jeremiah* 39:3-7: *'And all the officers of the Babylonian king came and sat at the middle gate ... When Zidkiyahu the king of Judah and all the soldiers saw them, they fled and went out of the city at night through the king's garden, through the gate between the walls, and they went through the valley. The army of the Chaldeans pursued them and they overtook Zidkiyahu in the plains of Jericho; and they took him and brought him to Nebuchadnezzar, King of Babylon, to Ribla in the land of Chamos and he spoke harshly to him. The King of Babylon slaughtered Zidkiyahu's sons in his sight in Ribla, and all the princes of Judah did the King of Babylon slaughter. And the eyes of Zidkiyahu he blinded, and he shackled him in irons to bring him to Babylon'* [*Jeremiah* 52:11 adds: *'And they put him in prison until the day of his death'.*]

10. הַנָּשִׂיא הַמַּשָּׂא הַזֶּה בִּירוּשָׁלִָם — *This prophecy concerns the Prince in Jerusalem.*

The translation follows *Metzudas David.* The 'Prince' is King Zidkiyahu. The prophecy concerns him and the

the ground, for as a sign have I appointed you to the Family of Israel.'

7 *And I did as I was commanded, I brought out my implements as implements of exile, by day; and in the evening I dug through the wall by hand; I brought out in the darkness, I carried on my shoulder; in their sight.*

8 *The word of HASHEM came to me in the morning,
saying:* 9 *'Ben Adam, have not the Family of Israel, the rebellious family, said to you: "What are you doing?"*

10 *Say to them: "Thus says my Lord HASHEM/ELOHIM, This prophecy concerns the Prince in Jerusalem, and all the Family of Israel, in
whose midst they are."* 11 *Say: "I am your sign. As I have done so shall be done to them: into exile, into
captivity shall they go.* 12 *And the Prince who is among them, shall shoulder in the darkness and*

house of Israel, all of whom live in Jerusalem.

The expression מַשָּׂא, to denote prophecy is not used again in the Book of Ezekiel, although it occurs frequently in other Prophets (*Nahum* 1:1, *Habbakuk* 1:1; *Malachi* 1:1). According to *Radak (Jeremiah* 23:36) מַשָּׂא means prophecy because it denotes the spoken word, as in *Ps.* 16:4.

[It seems likely that the word is used here because of its assonance with the word נָשִׂיא. (See remarks on לָשׁוֹן נוֹפֵל עַל לָשׁוֹן, *paronomasia,* in *footnote* to 7:2). In addition to נָשִׂיא we also have the repeated use of יִשָּׂא, which is also phonetically related.

Perhaps it is used to stimulate another association. The word מַשָּׂא also means *'burden'*. The awesome responsibility of prophecy lay heavily upon Yechezkel (see 3:11). Certainly the tragedy which he was now called upon to enact must have been a heavy burden upon him. Zidkiyahu was a צַדִּיק גָּמוּר, *a wholly righteous person* (see *Overview),* and yet, because of the sins of his generation he was to come to such a tragic end. The term מַשָּׂא is indeed apt for such a prophecy.]

אֲשֶׁר הֵמָּה בְתוֹכָם — *In whose midst they are.*

'They' refers to Yechezkel's listeners. Although great distance separated them from their brothers in Jerusalem, they were nevertheless *'in their midst',* because their thoughts were constantly in Jerusalem *(Harav Breuer).*

Metzudas David however renders they [the people] are in the midst of them [i.e. the streets of Jerusalem].

12. אֶל כָּתֵף יִשָּׂא — *Shall shoulder* [lit. *'shall carry upon the shoulder'*] i.e., Zidkiyahu shall carry the vessels of exile.

בַּקִּיר יַחְתְּרוּ לְהוֹצִיא בוֹ פָּנָיו יְכַסֶּה יַעַן
אֲשֶׁר לֹא־יִרְאֶה לַעַיִן הוּא אֶת־הָאָרֶץ:
יג וּפָרַשְׂתִּי אֶת־רִשְׁתִּי עָלָיו וְנִתְפַּשׂ
בִּמְצוּדָתִי וְהֵבֵאתִי אֹתוֹ בָבֶלָה אֶרֶץ
כַּשְׂדִּים וְאוֹתָהּ לֹא־יִרְאֶה וְשָׁם יָמוּת:
יד וְכֹל אֲשֶׁר סְבִיבֹתָיו עֶזְרֹה וְכָל־אֲגַפָּיו
אֱזָרֶה לְכָל־רוּחַ וְחֶרֶב אָרִיק אַחֲרֵיהֶם:
טו וְיָדְעוּ כִּי־אֲנִי יהוה בַּהֲפִיצִי אוֹתָם בַּגּוֹיִם
טז וְזֵרִיתִי אוֹתָם בָּאֲרָצוֹת: וְהוֹתַרְתִּי מֵהֶם

בַּקִּיר יַחְתְּרוּ — *In the wall shall they excavate.*

The plural form, יַחְתְּרוּ, is probably attributable to the fact that Zidkiyahu was initially accompanied by soldiers who deserted him later on — see *II Kings* Ch. 25, and *Jeremiah* Ch. 52. It is significant that in spite of this he carried his own belongings.

פָּנָיו יְכַסֶּה — *His face shall he cover.*

For shame that he is fleeing the city by night *(Rashi)*.[1]

13. וּפָרַשְׂתִּי אֶת רִשְׁתִּי עָלָיו — *And I shall spread My net upon him.*

He had a cave running from his house to the plains of Jericho and fled through that cave. What did God do? He brought a deer in front of the Chaldean army. It ran from them over the top of the cave, and they pursued it. When Zidkiyahu left the cave in the plains of Jericho they saw him coming out and captured him *(Rashi)*.

וְאוֹתָהּ לֹא יִרְאֶה — *But it shall he not see.*

Zidkiyahu never saw Babylon, the land of his captivity, for in Ribla in the land of Chamos he [Nebuchadnezzar] spoke harshly to him and blinded his eyes and then brought him to Babylon *(Rashi)*.

וְשָׁם יָמוּת — *And there will he die.*

Jeremiah 34:4-5 predicts that Zidkiyahu would not die by the sword but in peace and full royal honors would be accorded him at his funeral. The Sages state that Nebuchadnezzar died during Zidkiyahu's lifetime [thus he died 'in peace' because he lived to know of his tormentor's punishment.] Thereafter Zidkiyahu was released from prison, but died immediately.

Mo'ed Katan 28b ascribes the honor done him at his death, to the merit of his

1. In *v.* 6 Yechezkel had been told to cover his face. As a result, he would be prevented from seeing the ground. There is no conclusive indication that he was told to cover his face to make it *impossible* for him to see the ground. Nevertheless the word יַעַן in our verse indicates just that: he will cover his face in order that he will not see the Land (its use in the sense *'in order that'* is unique).

Zidkiyahu's were no ordinary eyes. *Sotah* 10a teaches that they were created in the Divine image. *Yalkut, II Kings*:252 states that they were like the eyes of Adam (see *Overview* and *Overview* to *Tehillim I ArtScroll* ed.).

[*Rashi* to *Sotah* (ad. loc.) comments that he knows no source from which the Sages derived this. It may be that they concluded this from the constant reference in Scripture to Zidkiyahu's seeing or not seeing. For example: 12:12, 13; *Jeremiah* 22:10-12 (see *Rashi*), 32:4, 34:3.]

Divine eyes see not only the physical object, but also apprehend its essence. When Moses was told that he could not enter the Land of Israel, he was nevertheless permitted to see it, as

leave. In the wall shall they excavate to bring out
through it. His face shall he cover so as not to see the
earth with his eyes. 13 *And I shall spread My net*
upon him and he will be caught in My snare. Then I
shall bring him to Babylon, the land of the Chal-
deans, but it shall he not see and there will he die.
14 *Then everyone around him — his aides and all his*
officers — I will scatter to every direction, and the
sword will I unsheath after them. 15 *And they shall*
know that I am HASHEM *when I scatter them among*
the nations and disperse them among the countries.
16 *But I will leave over from them a few men, from*

having rescued Jeremiah from the pit into which he had been thrown by the non-believers who wished to silence his prophecies (see *Jeremiah* 38:6-10).

14. וְכֹל אֲשֶׁר סְבִיבֹתָיו עֶזְרֹה וְכָל אֲגַפָּיו — *Then everyone* [lit. *'all who are'*] *around him — his aides and all his officers.*

Zidkiyahu had surrounded himself with fighting men to help him escape. This was in defiance of Jeremiah's advice (*Jeremiah* 38:17) that if he would submit to the Babylonians, his life and the city of Jerusalem would be spared.

עֶזְרֹה — *His aides.*

The irregular feminine ending (עֶזְרֹה instead of עֶזְרוֹ) indicates the weakness and futility of these 'helpers' *(Harav Breuer)*.

אֲגַפָּיו — *His officers.*

The translation follows *Rashi*. *Targum* renders: *'his camp'*. *Radak* (supported by *Menachem* quoted by *Rashi*) comments that the word is related to גַּף, *wing*. Thus it would denote a 'wing' or detachment of an army.

אֱזָרֶה לְכָל רוּחַ — *I will scatter to every direction.*

Rashi and *Radak* read this as referring to the small remnant which remained in Jerusalem after the destruction with Yochanan ben Koreach. These people fled to Egypt, and eventually fell victim to Nebuchadnezzar's sword (*Jeremiah* 43).

15. See *comm.* to 6:8-10.

16. וְהוֹתַרְתִּי מֵהֶם אַנְשֵׁי מִסְפָּר — *But I will leave over from them a few men.*

In spite of the similarity between our verse and 5:3, the idea expressed is quite different. There the מְעַט בְּמִסְפָּר, *the few in number* are to be set aside from the third of the people who were destined to be exiled *(ibid. v.* 2). Hence, that refer-

Abraham before him had been shown the Land *(Gen.* 13:14). *Sifri* to *Numbers* comments: Rabbi Akiba said: Scripture tells us that God showed Moses all the inner chambers of the Land of Israel. Rabbi Eliezer said: [He] gave the eyes of Moses strength so that he could see from one end of the world to the other. *Sifri* goes on to compare Moses' 'seeing' to that of Abraham. (See also *Targum Yonasan* to *Deut.* 34:1-3).

It would have been normal for Zidkiyahu to have wanted to carry the memory of the Land with him into exile. By casting a last, longing look, he could have locked the Land into his heart, as Moses had done from the distant banks of the Jordan.

By refusing even to see the Land as he left, Zidkiyahu seems to be testifying that his tie to its inner holiness had been severed. His averted eyes marked him as the true exile.

אַנְשֵׁי מִסְפָּר מֵחֶרֶב מֵרָעָב וּמִדָּבֶר לְמַעַן
יְסַפְּרוּ אֶת־כָּל־תּוֹעֲבוֹתֵיהֶם בַּגּוֹיִם אֲשֶׁר־
יז בָּאוּ שָׁם וְיָדְעוּ כִּי־אֲנִי יהוה: וַיְהִי
יח דְבַר־יהוה אֵלַי לֵאמֹר: בֶּן־אָדָם לַחְמְךָ
בְּרַעַשׁ תֹּאכֵל וּמֵימֶיךָ בְּרָגְזָה וּבִדְאָגָה
יט תִּשְׁתֶּה: וְאָמַרְתָּ אֶל־עַם הָאָרֶץ כֹּה־
אָמַר אֲדֹנָי יֱהֹוִה לְיוֹשְׁבֵי יְרוּשָׁלַםִ אֶל־
אַדְמַת יִשְׂרָאֵל לַחְמָם בִּדְאָגָה יֹאכֵלוּ
וּמֵימֵיהֶם בְּשִׁמָּמוֹן יִשְׁתּוּ לְמַעַן תֵּשַׁם
אַרְצָהּ מִמְּלֹאָהּ מֵחֲמַס כָּל־הַיֹּשְׁבִים
כ בָּהּ: וְהֶעָרִים הַנּוֹשָׁבוֹת תֶּחֱרַבְנָה וְהָאָרֶץ
שְׁמָמָה תִהְיֶה וִידַעְתֶּם כִּי־אֲנִי

ence is to an elite minority who were to form the 'repentant remnant' discussed at 6:8-9.

In our verse however, the אַנְשֵׁי מִסְפָּר, the *few men*, are to be saved from *'sword, famine, and plague.'* Reference is thus to the entire population which was to be exiled. Not all belonged to the righteous few, mentioned in Chs. 5 and 6. Some were among the very sinners who had caused Jerusalem's destruction and their exile had a special purpose.

36:20 notes the possibility that exile may bring about a חִלּוּל הַשֵּׁם, *a desecration of God's Name.* Inevitably, as God's people wander among the nations, the question will arise, why God permitted this to happen. Would this not imply a weakness on the part of God? How else could His people lose His land?

Our verse provides the solution to this problem. There would be those among the exiles who by their bearing and actions (see 14:22-23) would proclaim to the wide world the depths to which Israel had sunk. Upon seeing them, everybody would recognize the justice of God's actions. God had permitted Jerusalem to be destroyed, nay, had Himself joined in its destruction (*comm.* to 5:8) not because He is weak, but because He is just.

This realization will not only neutralize the potential חִלּוּל הַשֵּׁם, *desecration of God's Name,* caused by the exile but will actually provide *'comfort'* to Israel's remnants (14:22). No greater desecration of God's Name exists, than the fact of God's people living a life of degradation in God's own land. When this occurs, exile becomes a historical imperative, on the road to universal recognition of God.

17-20. The fearful deprivation which was to reign during the siege of Jerusalem, had already been depicted by Yechezkel in the symbolic actions described in Ch. 4. It would seem superfluous to demonstrate it once more. Because of this *Harav Breuer* holds that the prophet was now called upon to describe the situation of the pitiful remnant which would remain in Jerusalem under Gedalya *after* the destruction of

XII 17-20

the sword, from the famine, and from the plague; that they may relate all their abominations among the nations where they came, and they shall know that I am HASHEM." '

17 *The word of HASHEM came to me, saying,* 18 *'Ben Adam, your bread — with quaking shall you eat; and your water — with trembling and anxiety shall you drink;* 19 *and say to the people of the Land: "Thus says my Lord HASHEM/ELOHIM concerning the dwellers of Jerusalem, on the soil of Israel: Their bread, with anxiety will they eat, and their water in desolation will they drink, because its Land will be desolate of its fullness, because of the injustice of all who dwell in it.* 20 *Then the inhabited cities shall be laid waste, and the Land will be a desolation. And you shall know*

the Temple, and *after* the bulk of the population had been dragged into captivity *(II Kings* 25:22, and *Jeremiah* Ch. 40). From *Jeremiah* 42:14 we learn that the fear of hunger did in fact stalk this small community.

[No difficulty is posed by the use of the term יֹשְׁבֵי יְרוּשָׁלַיִם, *the dwellers of Jerusalem,* to describe this remnant rather than the term יֹשְׁבֵי הֶחֳרָבוֹת הָאֵלֶּה, *the dwellers of these ruins,* as used in 33:24. In Ch. 33 Yechezkel points out the folly of their misplaced optimism and therefore stresses the ruin of the Land. In our chapter, because the significant point is the unsettled conditions of life in Jerusalem, there is no need to underline the city's state of ruin.]

The *desolation* described in *v.* 20 וְהָאָרֶץ שְׁמָמָה תִהְיֶה, *and the Land will be a desolation,* would then refer to the total devestation of the Land after the last inhabitants had left for Egypt.

19. וְאָמַרְתָּ אֶל עַם הָאָרֶץ — *And say to the people of the Land.*

In the Book of Ezekiel as in the rest of Scripture, the term עַם הָאָרֶץ, *the people of the Land,* usually underlines the contrast between the common people and other groups in the population. Thus in 7:26-27 the term is used in conjunction with prophet, priest, elder, king, and prince; and in 22:23-29, together with prophets, priests, and officers.

In our verse the expression refers to Yechezkel's fellow exiles *(Radak; Metzudas David)* but it is not clear why this particular term is used to describe them.

Toras Kohanim to *Lev.* 20:2 interprets עַם הָאָרֶץ as עַם שֶׁבִּגְינוֹ נִבְרֵאת הָאָרֶץ, *the people for whose sake the earth was created.* Perhaps the absolute and total break with the Land (see above) achieves added poignancy when the listeners are called עַם הָאָרֶץ.

אַרְצָהּ — *Its Land.*

I.e. Jerusalem's Land *(Radak).*

מֵחֲמַס — *Because of the injustice.*

See *comm.* to 7:11.

20. וְהָאָרֶץ שְׁמָמָה תִהְיֶה — *And the Land will be a desolation.*

See above.

כא יהוה: וַיְהִי דְבַר־יְהוָה
כב אֵלַי לֵאמֹר: בֶּן־אָדָם מָה־הַמָּשָׁל הַזֶּה
לָכֶם עַל־אַדְמַת יִשְׂרָאֵל לֵאמֹר יַאַרְכוּ
כג הַיָּמִים וְאָבַד כָּל־חָזוֹן: לָכֵן אֱמֹר אֲלֵיהֶם
כֹּה־אָמַר אֲדֹנָי יֱהוִה הִשְׁבַּתִּי אֶת־הַמָּשָׁל
הַזֶּה וְלֹא־יִמְשְׁלוּ אֹתוֹ עוֹד בְּיִשְׂרָאֵל כִּי
אִם־דַּבֵּר אֲלֵיהֶם קָרְבוּ הַיָּמִים וּדְבַר כָּל־
כד חָזוֹן: כִּי לֹא יִהְיֶה עוֹד כָּל־חֲזוֹן שָׁוְא
כה וּמִקְסַם חָלָק בְּתוֹךְ בֵּית יִשְׂרָאֵל: כִּי |

וִידַעְתֶּם כִּי אֲנִי ה׳ — *And you shall know that I am HASHEM.*

See *v.* 15 and *comm.* to 6:7-10.

21-25. In the same way that grease will make an arrow slide harmlessly off a shield, לֵיצָנוּת, *ridicule* will make a person impervious to instruction and guidance *(Mesillas Yesharim).*

Often a pithy, well-turned phrase designed to make light of the prophet's message — a taunting מָשָׁל, *proverb* — can neutralize his words, robbing them of their sting more effectively than open defiance.

When just such a proverb was bandied about in Jerusalem, Isaiah (28:22) implored the people of his generation: *'And now do not indulge in mockery, for your punishment will be great.'* If he warned them of impending doom, they would answer: *'We have made a covenant with death, and an agreement with the grave.'* The Sages *(Avodah Zarah* 18b) spell out the results of this attitude: Rabbi Elazar said: Mockery is hard. Its beginnings are suffering, its end is destruction.

Yechezkel was forced to contend with the same problem. In 11:3-13, he contended with a saying which the people used to buttress their defiance of the Babylonians, and again in 18:2, he was faced with mockery of the fairness of God's justice.

The following passage deals with another such proverb, this one having no less a purpose than to deny the efficacy of prophecy itself.

22. מָה הַמָּשָׁל הַזֶּה — *What is this proverb?*

The word generally used for *a pithy saying or proverb* is מְלִיצָה rather than מָשָׁל which means a *parable* (from משל, *to control* i.e the means by which an abstract idea is made comprehensible). Our verse uses the term מָשָׁל because this idea was expressed so frequently that it entered the category of commonly used parables. [Apparently a parable is a more frequently used figure of speech] *(Radak).*

לָכֶם — *Of yours.*

Yechezkel seems to be included in the criticism. *Radak* compares this to *Exod.* 16:28 where Moses was included in God's stricture concerning the people who attempted to collect the *manna* on Shabbos. [The idea would seem to be that the leader is also considered at fault when the people do wrong (see *comm.* and *Appendix* III).] Alternatively, *Radak* suggests that these were the precise words with which Yechezkel was to address the dwellers of Jerusalem, then לָכֶם, *of yours,* would refer only to the people.

יַאַרְכוּ הַיָּמִים וְאָבַד כָּל חָזוֹן — *The days will*

that I am HASHEM".'
[21] *The word of HASHEM came to me, saying:* [22] *'Ben
Adam: What is this proverb of yours in the Land of
Israel, saying: "The days will draw out and every vision will disappear."* [23] *Therefore say to them: "Thus
says my Lord HASHEM/ELOHIM: I will put an end to
this proverb and they will no longer express it in
Israel." But say to them: "The days are near and the
word of every vision.* [24] *For there shall no more be
any vain vision, nor smooth divination, within the
Family of Israel.* [25]*For, I am HASHEM — I shall speak*

draw out and every vision will disappear.

The days will draw out and the punishment will not come. Meanwhile, the evil prophecies which the prophets say about us will be lost, forgotten, and annulled *(Rashi).*

Prophecies concerning the destruction of Jerusalem had been made for many years, but the city still stood. Surely conditions would continue as they had in the past *(Eliezer of Beaugency).*

[ארך, *drawing out* in the *Kal* with 'days' as the subject occurs only once more in Scripture. After the *'days had drawn out'* Abimelech the king of the Philistines observed Isaac disporting himself in the manner of a husband with Rebecca. *Rashi* comments: Isaac said, 'From now on, since they have not seized her yet, I have nothing more to fear.' Thus the idiom seems to imply a time lapse which lulls a person into a false sense of security. This is the precise meaning in our context.]

The translation of אָבַד as *'disappear'* seems most apt in our context. [*Targum* translates תְּבַטֵּל, *annulled.*] אבד is used in that sense in 19:5, and many other places.

23. וְלֹא יִמְשְׁלוּ אֹתוֹ עוֹד — *And they will no longer express it.*

Events will insure that never again will there be any doubts about a prophecy not coming about. They will see that a lapse of time never implies that the prophecy might be forgotten *(Harav Breuer).*

קָרְבוּ הַיָּמִים — *The days are near.*

Not יִקְרְבוּ in the future tense, which would have been the exact parallel to יַאַרְכוּ *'will' draw out* in *v.* 22, but קָרְבוּ, in the past tense to stress the certainty. It is as though the days had already come.

[It is conceivable that הַיָּמִים, *the days* in the mouth of the prophet had a different meaning than that intended by the same word in the proverb — undefined future days that will never come. It may be that the prophet had specific days in mind (see 7:7, 10, 12). The days of punishment are at hand.]

וּדְבַר כָּל חָזוֹן — *And the word of every vision.*

Harav Breuer suggests that the construct form of דְּבַר indicates an implied word. The meaning is וּדְבַר ה׳ כָּל חָזוֹן. *All these visions are the word of God,* and will therefore surely come about.

24. The constant assurances which the false prophets gave the people that Jerusalem would not fall (see next chapter), created the background against which these pernicious proverbs could develop. Once history will have

יב
כו־כח

אֲנִי יהוה אֲדַבֵּר אֵת אֲשֶׁר אֲדַבֵּר דָּבָר
וְיֵעָשֶׂה לֹא תִמָּשֵׁךְ עוֹד כִּי בִימֵיכֶם
בֵּית הַמֶּרִי אֲדַבֵּר דָּבָר וַעֲשִׂיתִיו נְאֻם
כו אֲדֹנָי יֱהֹוִה: וַיְהִי
כז דְבַר־יהוה אֵלַי לֵאמֹר: בֶּן־אָדָם הִנֵּה
בֵית־יִשְׂרָאֵל אֹמְרִים הֶחָזוֹן אֲשֶׁר־הוּא
חֹזֶה לְיָמִים רַבִּים וּלְעִתִּים רְחוֹקוֹת הוּא
כח נִבָּא: לָכֵן אֱמֹר אֲלֵיהֶם כֹּה אָמַר
אֲדֹנָי יֱהֹוִה לֹא־תִמָּשֵׁךְ עוֹד כָּל־דְּבָרָי
אֲשֶׁר אֲדַבֵּר דָּבָר וְיֵעָשֶׂה נְאֻם אֲדֹנָי

יג
א־ב

א יֱהֹוִה: וַיְהִי דְבַר־יהוה אֵלַי
ב לֵאמֹר: בֶּן־אָדָם הִנָּבֵא אֶל־נְבִיאֵי יִשְׂרָאֵל
הַנִּבָּאִים וְאָמַרְתָּ לִנְבִיאֵי מִלִּבָּם שִׁמְעוּ

unambiguously clarified God's true intentions, the false prophets would lose their power over the people's mind.

25. אֲנִי ה' אֲדַבֵּר ... וְיֵעָשֶׂה ... אֲדַבֵּר דָּבָר וַעֲשִׂיתִיו — *For I am HASHEM, I shall speak ... and it will be done ... I shall speak a word and I will have done it.*

We quote from *Harav Yitzchak Hutner, Pachad Yitzchak* to *Rosh Hashanah* Ch. 8:

At the beginning of (the *sidrah) Vo'eirah: 'And My Name HASHEM, I did not make known to them.' Rashi* explains: 'I have not revealed Myself to them in My quality of *Truth,* for I promised and did not [yet] fulfill.' From this we see that in the ineffable Name of God, lies the quality of His Truth.

The meaning is as follows. Doubt concerning the fulfillment of promises are possible only because these promises are for the future; because of the time lapse between promise and fulfillment, certainty does not [yet] exist.

But the nature of the ineffable Name is the combination of 'He was', 'He is', and 'He will be', in one totality (הָיָה הֹוֶה, וְיִהְיֶה), transcending all differences between past, present, and future. Within this frame, the future is as real and true as the past.

This is *Rashi*'s intent in saying that when the ineffable Name had not been revealed, the quality of God's truth had not been revealed.

Thus our verse, introduced by the words: אֲנִי ה' (God's ineffable Name) sees that which shall be done (וְיֵעָשֶׂה) as the equal of that which shall have been done (וַעֲשִׂיתִיו).

There is no place for the proverb which the people had been saying.

27-28. The proverb of the previous passage referred to prophecy as a whole. We now turn to the attitude which the people expressed concerning Yechezkel's specific warnings. As in 11:3, the tendency of the people was to see the fulfillment of his prophecies in the distant future. It would not concern them personally.

The prophet is told to assure them that, on the contrary, the prophecies

XII 26-28

that which I shall speak, a word and it will be done. It shall be delayed no longer; for in your days, O family of rebellion, I shall speak a word and I will have done it. The words of my Lord HASHEM/ELOHIM*".'* 26 *The word of* HASHEM *came to me saying:* 27 *'Ben Adam! See the Family of Israel is saying: "The vision which he sees is many days off and concerning distant times does he prophesy."* 28 *Therefore say to them: "Thus says my Lord* HASHEM/ELOHIM*: No longer delayed will be any word of Mine, but the word that I shall speak shall be done. The words of my Lord* HASHEM/ELOHIM*".'*

XIII 1-2

The word of HASHEM *came to me, saying:* 2 *'Ben Adam, prophesy against the prophets of Israel who prophesy; and say to those that prophesy*

would come true in the immediate future (compare 7:3, 6-8, 10).

28. לא תִמָּשֵׁךְ עוֹד — *No longer delayed.*

With the masculine דָּבָר as subject, we would have expected the masculine יִמָּשֵׁךְ. However the feminine form was chosen to underline the weakness of a message which loses its effectiveness when the time lapse before its fulfillment is too long *(Harav Breuer).*

XIII

Ten measures of sycophancy (חֲנוּפָּה) are in the world — nine in Jerusalem and one in the rest of the world. This is the meaning of the verse: *'For from the prophets of Jerusalem sycophancy went out to all the Land'* [*Jeremiah* 23:15] (*Esther Rabbah* 1:17).

From the earliest days of the monarchy, prophets of God had to face the opposition of unscrupulous charlatans who did not hesitate to invoke God's Name in order to authenticate so called 'prophecies' which had no other purpose than to play on the peoples' desire to believe the best, and to be lulled into a false sense of security. (See *I Kings* Ch. 22).

This was true in earlier days when less was at stake; as the clouds of the final destruction of Jerusalem were gathering it was bound to occur all the more. The people sought out prophets to reinforce their desperate hopes that this danger would pass as had all previous ones, instead of exposing them to the ruthlessly probing and unforgiving light of self-examination demanded by God's prophets.

While these false prophets claimed to speak in the Name of God, the result of their activities was nevertheless to *'cause My Name to be forgotten'* (*Jeremiah* 23:27) because God's true *'Name'* is His people's perception of His exercise of providence in their lives. By directing the people away from the introspection which might have led to a true repentance, the false prophets were instrumental in encouraging the gradual erosion of the national character which made inevitable the destruction of the city and Temple.

Yechezkel's prophecy is now directed against these prophets (see *Overview IX).*

2. נְבִיאֵי יִשְׂרָאֵל הַנִּבָּאִים — *The prophets of Israel who prophesy.*

That *false* prophets are meant is clear from the end of the verse: לִנְבִיאֵי מִלִּבָּם,

יג
ג־ה

ג דְּבַר־יהוָה: כֹּה אָמַר אֲדֹנָי יֱהוִה הוֹי
עַל־הַנְּבִיאִים הַנְּבָלִים אֲשֶׁר הֹלְכִים
ד אַחַר רוּחָם וּלְבִלְתִּי רָאוּ: כְּשֻׁעָלִים
ה בֶּחֳרָבוֹת נְבִיאֶיךָ יִשְׂרָאֵל הָיוּ: לֹא

that prophesy out of their own heart. The opening phrase, however, makes no mention of this. Yechezkel is told simply to address himself to *'the prophets of Israel that prophesy.'*

Ramban (Deut. 13:2) explores the use of the term נָבִיא for a false prophet [i.e. an apparent contradiction in terms because the word נָבִיא, by definition, means one who *speaks* the word of God (see *comm.* and *footnote* to 2:5).] Perhaps it is used in a borrowed sense; he is described as a prophet because he *claims* to be one, not because he *is* one. On the other hand, it has been observed that some people seem to possess the faculty of clairvoyancy; they accurately foretell events, without knowing the source of their inspiration. Scripture refers to them as נָבִיא because they bear a partial similarity to true prophets in that they can foretell the future.

In ch. 2 (*footnote* to *v.* 5) we found that the root נבא was related to נבע, *to spring or well forth.* The prophet is the organ through which inspiration *wells forth* and is communicated to his audience. Israel's pride is that God Himself is the source of their prophetic inspiration *(Deut.* 18:9-18. See also *Rambam, Moreh Nevuchim* 1:15 who demonstrates that נְבִיאִים, *prophets,* are also called מַלְאָכִים, *messengers).* True prophecy, because it is God's message to His people, comes from outside the prophet's being (see *comm.* to 2:2).

When the prophet looks only within his own heart (לִנְבִיאֵי מִלִּבָּם) for inspiration, when he follows only the whim which moves him (הֹלְכִים אַחַר רוּחָם), then he cannot be guide and mentor to his people. He is himself part of the nation, and by looking only within himself, he merely gives expression to the very thoughts and feelings which are cause and symptom of the national malady.

3. הַנְּבִיאִים הַנְּבָלִים — *The foolish prophets.*

The translation follows *Targum* and *Rashi.*

It is difficult to trace a consistent treatment of the word נָבָל in the *Targum* of *Nevi'im* and *Kesuvim.*

There are instances where the denotation is *'folly'* (טִפְּשָׁא, שָׁטְיָא), *'wickedness'* (רִשְׁעָיָא) and *'shame'* (קְלָנָא). There are also cases where *Targum* does not translate at all, but renders with the Hebrew word נָבָל.

The following is a list of fifteen of the times the word is mentioned:

Twice in *II Sam.*: (3:33) *Targum* renders רְשִׁיעִין; (13:13) שָׁטְיָא.

Twice in *Isaiah*: (32:5 and 6). Both are rendered רַשִׁיעָיָא.

Once in *Jeremiah*: (17:11). *Targum* renders רַשִׁיעָיָא.

In our verse (13:3). *Targum* renders דְמִשְׁתַּטָן.

Four times in *Ps.*: (14:1) שָׁטְיָא; (53:2) נָבָל; (74:18,22) טִפְּשָׁא.

Three times in *Prov.*: (17:7,21, and 30:22). Each time *Targum* renders טַפְּשָׁא.

Twice in *Job* (2:10) קְלָנָא, (30:8) נָבָל.

The process by which נבל (lit. to *'wither'* or *'fall away')* becomes an expression denoting *'folly'* is traced by *Ramban* to *Deut.* 32:6. He refers to *Exod.* 18:18 where נָבֹל תִּבֹּל means *'you will become exhausted' (Targum* renders מִלְאָה תִלְאֶה). Thus a person who is too tired or exhausted to pursue knowledge is a נָבָל, *a foolish person.*

Ramban to *Deut.* 32:6 defines נָבָל as an *ingrate.* Perhaps there is no better adjective to describe the false prophets.

out of their own hearts: "Hear the word of HASHEM!
3 *Thus says my Lord HASHEM/ELOHIM: Woe unto the foolish prophets, who follow their own whim, and things which they have not seen.*
4 *Like foxes among the ruins, so your prophets, O Israel, have*

Prophecy is the greatest gift which God bestows on man, and is the highest level of existence to which a person can aspire *(Rambam, Moreh Nevuchim* 2:36). To abuse this gift by falsely labeling their own imaginations as a communication from God, is the basest form of ingratitude.

[Another alternative suggests itself for the choice of נְבָלִים to describe the false prophets. In Rabbinic literature the word נוֹבֵל is used to describe a spurious variant of something. Thus *Bereishis Rabbah* 17:7 speaks of three נוֹבְלוֹת, three spurious variants. (Sleep is a נוֹבֵל of death; a dream is a נוֹבֵל of prophecy; Shabbos is a נוֹבֵל of *Olam Habah,* the World to Come).

The prophets who substitute their own thoughts and desires for God's word as the source of their inspiration are thus נְבִיאִים נְבָלִים. [For evidence that the root נבל can have this meaning in Scriptural Hebrew also, see *Nesinah la'Ger* to *Deut.* 32:6.]

The usual meaning of נָבָל, is a *'low, base person' (Radak* to our verse. See also *Radak* to Isaiah 32:5). *Jeremiah* 23:14 and 29:23 reports that the *prophets of Jerusalem* were immoral, committed adultery, lied, and supported the wicked in their wickedness. (29:23 describes them as having done a נְבָלָה בְּיִשְׂרָאֵל). It is perhaps for that reason that the description נְבָלִים is chosen in our verse.

It seems unlikely that these sins were committed openly. *Rambam (Hilchos Yesodei haTorah* 7:7) describes in detail the level of holiness required of someone who aspires to prophecy. He describes the דַּרְכֵי הַנְּבוּאָה, *the ways of prophecy* as ways of *holiness* and *abstinence.* It is inconceivable that people who lived openly immoral lives could lay claim to the title of prophecy. In fact, *Rambam (Avoda Zara* 5:9) warns against an inclination to deal leniently with a false prophet: because of his high standing, since he walks in דַּרְכֵי הַנְּבוּאָה, *the paths of prophecy.*

The term נָבָל would then also imply a criticism of these false prophets as hypocrites.

4. כְּשֻׁעָלִים בָּחֳרָבוֹת — *Like foxes among the ruins.*

When a man enters one of the openings in the wall of the ruins, the fox will run out by another opening. He will not stand in the opening to fight *(Rashi).*

Thus *Rashi* sees the metaphor of the foxes, as being directed to the *cowardice* of the false prophets. [The courage required of a true prophet in those difficult times is described in 2:6.]

Radak (based on *Shir HaShirim* 2:15) sees the foxes as destroyers of the vineyard to which *Knesses Israel* is compared. The false prophets, by capturing the minds of the weaker people in Israel, hastened its destruction.

Eliezer of Beaugency paints a picture of foxes gaining entry into the ruins through holes in the walls, and through their play, breaking new holes in the walls. (Compare *Nehemiah* 3:35). The prophets might have taken a lesson from the previous 'breaches' in Israel's wall. The Northern Kingdom was no more; Yehoyachin had already been exiled, and the people who had gone with him were in Babylon. Nebuchadnezzar's grip on Jerusalem was tightening. By right, the prophets should have been concerned with protecting the people against further ravages. Instead they encouraged defiance, thus ensuring new breaches in the national existence.

יג
ו־ט

עֲלִיתֶם בַּפְּרָצוֹת וַתִּגְדְּרוּ גָדֵר עַל־בֵּית
יִשְׂרָאֵל לַעֲמֹד בַּמִּלְחָמָה בְּיוֹם יְהוָה׃
ו חָזוּ שָׁוְא וְקֶסֶם כָּזָב הָאֹמְרִים נְאֻם־
יְהוָה וַיהוָה לֹא שְׁלָחָם וְיִחֲלוּ לְקַיֵּם
ז דָּבָר׃ הֲלוֹא מַחֲזֵה־שָׁוְא חֲזִיתֶם וּמִקְסַם
כָּזָב אֲמַרְתֶּם וְאֹמְרִים נְאֻם־יְהוָה וַאֲנִי
ח לֹא דִבַּרְתִּי׃ לָכֵן כֹּה אָמַר אֲדֹנָי יֱהוִה
יַעַן דַּבֶּרְכֶם שָׁוְא וַחֲזִיתֶם כָּזָב לָכֵן הִנְנִי
ט אֲלֵיכֶם נְאֻם אֲדֹנָי יֱהוִה׃ וְהָיְתָה יָדִי אֶל־
הַנְּבִיאִים הַחֹזִים שָׁוְא וְהַקֹּסְמִים כָּזָב
בְּסוֹד עַמִּי לֹא־יִהְיוּ וּבִכְתָב בֵּית־יִשְׂרָאֵל

5. לֹא עֲלִיתֶם בַּפְּרָצוֹת — *You have not ascended into the breaches.*

You did not perform good deeds which could have prevented the evil from coming *(Rashi).*

Rashi does not offer an explanation for וַתִּגְדְּרוּ גָדֵר. *Radak* and *Metzudas David* render the two phrases as two distinct activities. When a wall is breached during a war two things must be done. First the breach must be manned to prevent the enemy from rushing in. Then, it must be repaired.

You have not ascended into the breaches to prevent the enemy from entering, either through protesting the abuses that were taking place in the city *(Radak)*; or through prayer *(Metzudas David).* (From *Jeremiah* 27:18 it can be seen that a true prophet will pray for his people).

וַתִּגְדְּרוּ גָדֵר — *Nor built a fence.*

By repenting and doing good deeds *(Radak);* or by inspiring the people to repent *(Metzudas David).*

לַעֲמֹד בַּמִּלְחָמָה — *To stand firm in the battle.*

In order that they should be able to stand in battle against the enemy when God's punishment will come about.

6. חָזוּ שָׁוְא וְקֶסֶם כָּזָב — *They have seen vanity and false divination.*

The dual activities of *vision* and *divination* have already been mentioned in 12:24, and will be repeated in our chapter in *vs.* 7 and 9.

Two different activities are indicated (see *Radak).* Firstly, they had *visions,* but they were vain because they were not inspired by God.

In addition to their spurious 'visions' the prophets also sank to the level of magic rites and divinations in a desperate attempt to discover what the future held in store. [A tragic erosion of the proud standing which Israel had in the past. *Bala'am* sang their praise for having no need for such activities because God reveals their future to them *(Numbers* 23:23).]

But these divinations would prove to be כָּזָב. They would end in delusion. כָּזָב means falseness in the sense of frustrated expectations. (See *Isaiah* 58:11).

וְיִחֲלוּ — *Yet they hoped.*

Metzudas David treats the word as though it were in the הִפְעִיל, *causative* voice. They caused Israel to expect the fulfillment of their prophecy.

been. 5 *You have not ascended into the breaches nor*
built a fence for the Family of Israel, to stand firm in
the battle on the day of HASHEM. 6 *They have seen*
vanity and false divination, those who say: 'The
words of HASHEM!' *But* HASHEM *did not send them*
— yet they hoped that the word would be confirmed.
7 *Have you not seen a vain vision and a false divina-*
tion have you not said? Yet you say, 'The word of
HASHEM' *— and I have not spoken!*
8 *Therefore, thus says my Lord* HASHEM/
ELOHIM: *'Because you have spoken vanity, and*
have seen falsehood, therefore see! I am against
you.' The words of my Lord HASHEM/ELOHIM; 9 *and*
My hand will be against the prophets who see vanity
and who divine falsehood. They shall not be in the
counsel of My people, and in the roll of the Family of

It is also possible that the subject of וְיִחֲלוּ is the *House of Israel* of the previous verse. Israel hopes for the fulfillment of the false prophecies.

Malbim reads the phrase as a rhetorical question. How can they [the prophets] expect their false prophecies to come true?

9. בְּסוֹד עַמִּי לֹא יִהְיוּ — *They shall not be in the counsel of My people.*

Three threats are made against the false prophets: they will not be in the people's counsel, they will not be inscribed in the roll of Israel, and they will not enter the Land.

Of the three threats, only the third one presents no difficulty. They will not be among those who will be privileged to return to Israel, when the Babylonian exile will have been completed.

What is meant by סוֹד עַמִּי?

The word סוֹד is used in Scripture in two ways. It can mean a group of people with a common interest, which brings them intimately together (see for ex. *Jeremiah* 6:11 and 15:17). Or it can be a secret, as in *Proverbs* 11:13.

Metzudas David assumes the former meaning. By their perfidy, these prophets have excluded themselves from the community of Israel — a community which has no room for people whose every activity serves only to undermine it.

Translating the word as 'secret' allows for a variety of interpretations. *Targum* (also *Radak)* reads the verse as excluding the prophets from 'the good *hidden things* which God has secreted for His people.'

Mahari Kara renders 'secret' here as a synonym for prophecy. True prophecy is God's *secret* which he imparts to His servants, the prophets *(Amos* 3:7). The false prophets will forever be excluded from sharing these secrets. God will never choose them as His prophets.

וּבִכְתָב בֵּית יִשְׂרָאֵל לֹא יִכָּתֵבוּ — *And in the roll of the Family of Israel shall they not be written.*

Both *Radak* and *Metzudas David* follow the *Targum.* They render: And in the writing for eternal life which is recorded for the righteous ones of

לֹא יִכָּתֵבוּ וְאֶל־אַדְמַת יִשְׂרָאֵל לֹא יָבֹאוּ
י וִידַעְתֶּם כִּי־אֲנִי אֲדֹנָי יֱהֹוִה: יַעַן וּבְיַעַן
הִטְעוּ אֶת־עַמִּי לֵאמֹר שָׁלוֹם וְאֵין שָׁלוֹם
וְהוּא בֹּנֶה חַיִץ וְהִנָּם טָחִים אֹתוֹ תָּפֵל:
יא אֱמֹר אֶל־טָחֵי תָפֵל וְיִפֹּל הָיָה | גֶּשֶׁם
שׁוֹטֵף וְאַתֵּנָה אַבְנֵי אֶלְגָּבִישׁ תִּפֹּלְנָה
יב וְרוּחַ סְעָרוֹת תְּבַקֵּעַ: וְהִנֵּה נָפַל הַקִּיר
הֲלוֹא יֵאָמֵר אֲלֵיכֶם אַיֵּה הַטִּיחַ אֲשֶׁר
יג טַחְתֶּם: לָכֵן כֹּה אָמַר אֲדֹנָי יֱהֹוִה
וּבִקַּעְתִּי רוּחַ־סְעָרוֹת בַּחֲמָתִי וְגֶשֶׁם שֹׁטֵף
בְּאַפִּי יִהְיֶה וְאַבְנֵי אֶלְגָּבִישׁ בְּחֵמָה לְכָלָה:

Israel, they will not be entered. *Metzudas David*, finding a parallel in *Isaiah* 4:3 comments further that the expression *'to be written in the roll'* is apt for describing someone destined for life in the World to Come.

Harav Breuer referring to *Hirsch*'s comm. to *Exod.* 32:32, suggests that the *'roll of the family of Israel'* might mean that *'book'* mentioned throughout Scripture, which serves as the metaphor for God's Providence over His people. When *Moses* asked to be erased *'from Your book which You have written' (ibid.)* he had in mind that 'roll'. The false prophets will never be able to legitimize themselves as part of that nation of Israel over which God extends His special Providence.

10. יַעַן וּבְיַעַן — *Because, and again because.*

Radak and *Metzudas David* take the double expression as a means of stressing the justice of the impending punishment.

Developing this concept further, *Harav Breuer* quotes *Hirsch* to *Lev.* 26:43 who demonstrates that the double expression is used in cases where the projected punishment is in the category of מִדָּה כְּנֶגֶד מִדָּה, *a measure for a measure*, i.e., is exactly suited to the crime (see *Targum Yerushalmi* to *Lev.* 26:43; Introduction to *Eichah Rabbasi* 21; *Bereishis Rabbah* 94, and *Midrash Sh'muel* to *II Sam* 24:6). In our case, *v.* 14 tells how the prophets themselves will be buried under the wall of deception which they had helped to erect (see below). Their life-work will spell their own ruin.

Targum attaches separate meanings to the two words. *Targum* is consistent throughout Scripture in treating such double expressions as two separate thoughts. (Examples from *Ezekiel* are: 16:6-8,23; 36:3. See also 16:28). He renders: *Because* you prophesied falsely, and *because* you misled My people.

בֹּנֶה חַיִץ — *He builds a partition.*

According to *Yerushalmi Shevi'is* 3:6 חַיִץ denotes a partition made from stones arrayed on top of one another, but without any form of mortar to bind them together. Thus it is a very weak wall. To cover it with a thin veneer of plaster will ill-serve the builder, for the wall will still be fragile despite its illu-

XIII 10-13

Israel shall they not be written, and to the Land of Israel shall they not enter. Then you shall know that I am the Lord HASHEM/ELOHIM.

10 *Because, and again because, they led My people astray, saying: 'Peace!' But there is no peace. And when he builds a partition, they smear it with daub.*
11 *Say to those who smear with daub: 'It will collapse. There will be a deluge.' And as for you, O great hailstones — you are to fall! And O stormy wind — you are to break forth!* 12 *And see! When the wall will have fallen, will it not be said to you: 'Where is the daub which you smeared?'* 13 *Therefore so says my Lord HASHEM/ELOHIM: I will break out a stormy wind in My fury, and a deluge in My anger will there be and great hailstones in My fury to consume.*

sion of permanence. When the elements finally break it down, it will be too late to correct the mistake.

Jerusalem's inhabitants had thrown up a wall of illusions behind which they thought themselves securely protected. Had they not been reinforced in their fallacious thinking by the false prophets who promised peace where there was no peace, they would surely have come to realize the truth as it was presented to them by Jeremiah and Yechezkel. However, they were blinded by the veneer of hope with which the false prophets glossed over their wall of illusions.

וְהִנָּם טָחִים אֹתוֹ תָּפֵל — *They smear it with daub.*

Rashi interprets: 'Earth which looks like plaster but cannot withstand rain.'

In Biblical Hebrew the word תָּפֵל is used to describe things which are inferior or tasteless. It is in this sense that *Radak* and *Metzudas David* take the word. [*Radak* also quotes his father who translated תָּפֵל as bricks which had not been fired in a kiln.]

Targum renders: *Plain cement without straw.* This may be based on *Talmudic* literature where תָּפֵל is used in the sense of paste or cement (see *Aruch haShalem* תפל = תְּפִילָה) and it is possible that the *Targum* took it in that sense.

[It is also possible that a dual meaning was intended. The word is used to convey both its meanings. The prophets daubed the partition with תָּפֵל (cement) which was תָּפֵל (inferior and inadequate to the task).]

11-16. As the elements lashing against an inferior wall will ultimately smash it to the ground, so will the impending events tear apart the fabrications which nation and prophets erected in their unseeing and unfounded optimism.

11. וְאַתֵּנָה — *And as for you.*

The translation follows *Radak* who interprets that God addresses the hailstorms and wind, ordering them to strike at the people.

Metzudas David, however, renders '*I will assign* [lit. *give*] the hailstones and wind.'

יד וְהָרַסְתִּי אֶת־הַקִּיר אֲשֶׁר־טַחְתֶּם תָּפֵל
וְהִגַּעְתִּיהוּ אֶל־הָאָרֶץ וְנִגְלָה יְסֹדוֹ וְנָפְלָה
וּכְלִיתֶם בְּתוֹכָהּ וִידַעְתֶּם כִּי־אֲנִי יְהוָה:
טו וְכִלֵּיתִי אֶת־חֲמָתִי בַּקִּיר וּבַטָּחִים אֹתוֹ
תָּפֵל וְאֹמַר לָכֶם אֵין הַקִּיר וְאֵין הַטָּחִים
טז אֹתוֹ: נְבִיאֵי יִשְׂרָאֵל הַנִּבְּאִים אֶל־
יְרוּשָׁלַם וְהַחֹזִים לָהּ חֲזוֹן שָׁלֹם וְאֵין
יז שָׁלֹם נְאֻם אֲדֹנָי יֱהוִה: וְאַתָּה
בֶן־אָדָם שִׂים פָּנֶיךָ אֶל־בְּנוֹת עַמְּךָ
הַמִּתְנַבְּאוֹת מִלִּבְּהֶן וְהִנָּבֵא עֲלֵיהֶן:
יח וְאָמַרְתָּ כֹּה־אָמַר | אֲדֹנָי יֱהוִה הוֹי
לִמְתַפְּרוֹת כְּסָתוֹת עַל | כָּל־אַצִּילֵי יָדַי
וְעֹשׂוֹת הַמִּסְפָּחוֹת עַל־רֹאשׁ כָּל־קוֹמָה

14. וּכְלִיתֶם בְּתוֹכָהּ — *And you are consumed in it.*

See *comm.* to *v.* 10.

15. וְכִלֵּיתִי אֶת חֲמָתִי — *Thus shall I spend My fury.*

See *comm.* to 5:13.

17-23. We cannot know the exact nature of the sorcery described in these verses. However, a picture unfolds of a people harried by superstitious fears, seeking solace (and willingly paying for it) in magical rites practiced by wily women who exerted a petrifying hold over their clients. These treacherous sorceresses were a far cry indeed from the נָשִׁים צִדְקָנִיּוֹת, *the righteous women,* who, by their steadfast belief in God's providence were instrumental in bringing about the redemption from Egypt (*Sota* 11b).

In contrast to the false prophets whose prophecies were directed to the broad issues facing the nation, the sorceresses seem to have catered only to individual needs. They promised life, or threatened death to those who sought their advice.

17. בְּנוֹת עַמְּךָ — *The daughters of your people.*

The expressions בְּנֵי עַמְּךָ (3:11; 33:2, 12, 17, 30; 37:18) and בְּנוֹת עַמְּךָ (here) are unique to the book of *Ezekiel.*

For purposes of this discussion we can exclude *Lev.* 19:18, where the expression has a halachic connotation (*Sifri* ad. loc.).

I have not found any discussion among the classical commentators, as to the exact connotation of the term בְּנֵי (בְּנוֹת) עַמְּךָ.

There is at least one passage in the *Torah,* in which the inflection of the noun עם is of the greatest significance. In the account of the sin of the Golden Calf (*Exod.* 32), the tensions in the relationship between God and His people, are indicated by these inflections.

In *v.* 7 God tells Moses: 'Go down for עַמְּךָ, *your* people, have sinned.' In *v.* 11 Moses prays to God asking Him: 'Why, My God, should Your anger be kindled against *Your* people?' In *v.* 14 we read that God retracted the evil which He had said to do to *His people'* (*see Yalkut Shimoni* 79 ad. loc. and *Rashi* to *v.* 7 and 33:13 *ibid*).

Thus, we find two different connotations to the inflection: עַמְּךָ. In *v.* 7, God, as it were, excludes Himself; they are Moses' people but not His, meaning that they are unworthy of divine mercy to mitigate the enormity of

[14] *Then shall I break down the wall which you*
smeared with daub, and bring it down to the ground,
so that its foundation shall be bared. When it falls
and you are consumed in it, then shall you know that
I am HASHEM. [15] *Thus shall I spend My fury upon*
the wall and upon those who smear it with daub, and
I shall say to you: 'There is neither wall, nor those
who smear it.'
[16] *Prophets of Israel that prophesy concerning*
Jerusalem, and who see for it a vision of peace — and
there is no peace. The words of my Lord
HASHEM/ELOHIM.*"*
[17] *And as for you, Ben Adam, set your face against*
the daughters of your people who prophesy out of
their own heart; and prophesy against them. [18] *And*
say: "So says my Lord HASHEM/ELOHIM: *Woe to*
those who sew cushions upon all armpits, and make
wraps for the head of all people to trap souls. Would

their sin. Moses, on the other hand, uses the term to stress that the nation, himself included, is God's people and deserving of His forgiveness despite the gravity of their lapse.

In our verse both meanings seem possible. Yechezkel is told to turn his face to the daughters of *his* [Yechezkel's] people — indicating that because of their perfidy, they are not to be regarded as God's people.

Alternately, the expression might have been used to arouse Yechezkel's love and consideration for the poor, misguided women. God exhorts the prophet not to forget that whatever their depravity, they are still daughters of *his* people.

18. הוֹי — *Woe.*

Yechezkel reserves this particular expression of anguish for the leaders of Israel who misuse their positions and betray their trust (*v.* 3 above, and 34:2).

כְּסָתוֹת are *cushions.* מִסְפָּחוֹת are a kind of *wrap* or *veil* (from ספח, *to cleave to,* because they are constantly worn. See *Radak* in *Sefer HaShorashim* to ספח. See also *Metzudas Zion).* These cushions were tied to the armpits of either the clients or the women (see *comm.* to *v.* 20) and the veils or wraps were draped over the heads of the clients. These were then used in some form of divination. As *Rashi* points out, we have no way of knowing exactly what transpired at these sessions or how these objects were used.

אַצִּילֵי יָדַי — *Armpits.*

The translation follows *Rashi* based on *Targum,* who identifies אָצִיל with מַרְפֵּק (see *Rashi, Arachin* 19b) which he defines as armpit *(Rashi* to *Mishnah, Shabbos* 92a, see *Tosaphos* ad. loc.) *Tosaphos* disagrees and defines both אָצִיל and מַרְפֵּק as *elbow.*

The form יָדַי [lit. *my hands* or *arms*] for יָדַיִם, *hands* or *arms* is irregular, but does occasionally appear. See *Isaiah* 19:9 *(Radak).*

כָּל קוֹמָה — *All people.*

Metzudas David interprets that

לְצוֹדֵד נְפָשׁוֹת הַנְּפָשׁוֹת תְּצוֹדֵדְנָה לְעַמִּי
יט וּנְפָשׁוֹת לָכֶנָה תְחַיֶּינָה: וַתְּחַלֶּלְנָה אֹתִי
אֶל־עַמִּי בְּשַׁעֲלֵי שְׂעֹרִים וּבִפְתוֹתֵי לֶחֶם
לְהָמִית נְפָשׁוֹת אֲשֶׁר לֹא־תְמוּתֶנָה
וּלְחַיּוֹת נְפָשׁוֹת אֲשֶׁר לֹא־תִחְיֶינָה
כ בְּכַזֶּבְכֶם לְעַמִּי שֹׁמְעֵי כָזָב: לָכֵן
כֹּה־אָמַר | אֲדֹנָי יֱהֹוִה הִנְנִי אֶל־
כִּסְּתוֹתֵיכֶנָה אֲשֶׁר אַתֵּנָה מְצֹדְדוֹת שָׁם
אֶת־הַנְּפָשׁוֹת לְפֹרְחוֹת וְקָרַעְתִּי אֹתָם
מֵעַל זְרוֹעֹתֵיכֶם וְשִׁלַּחְתִּי אֶת־הַנְּפָשׁוֹת
אֲשֶׁר אַתֶּם מְצֹדְדוֹת אֶת־נְפָשִׁים
כא לְפֹרְחֹת: וְקָרַעְתִּי אֶת־מִסְפְּחֹתֵיכֶם
וְהִצַּלְתִּי אֶת־עַמִּי מִיֶּדְכֶן וְלֹא־יִהְיוּ עוֹד

קוֹמָה [lit. *'that which stands'*] describes human beings since, among all creatures, only they stand erect.

Radak explains the use of the word in that the clients were forced to stand while the divination was taking place.

לְצוֹדֵד נְפָשׁוֹת — *To trap souls.*

They trap souls for *Gehinnom,* by encouraging the wicked in that they divine peace for them, and weaken the righteous by warning them that evil will befall them *(Rashi).*

וּנְפָשׁוֹת לָכֶנָה תְחַיֶּינָה — *Souls for your own livelihood?*

The women took payment for their services (see *v.* 19) *(Rashi).* Thus for their own gain they unscrupulously tampered with people's lives.

19. וַתְּחַלֶּלְנָה אֹתִי אֶל עַמִּי — *And you have profaned Me among My people.*

You caused a desecration of God's Name by causing people to turn their trust away from God, and, instead, feel themselves at the mercy of these fetishes *(Radak* and *Metzudas David).*

בְּשַׁעֲלֵי שְׂעֹרִים וּבִפְתוֹתֵי לֶחֶם — *For handfuls of barley and for morsels of bread.*

For such pathetically small payment (see *Eruvin* 64b), they ruined the lives of their clients.

לְהָמִית ... וּלְחַיּוֹת — *to slay ... to preserve.*

By their false predictions it was as though they slew innocent lives, and as though they preserved guilty ones *(Metzudas David).*

לְעַמִּי שֹׁמְעֵי כָזָב — *My people who listen to lies.*

[Perhaps the word עַמִּי, *'My' people* is used to accentuate the contrast to בְּנוֹת עַמְּךָ of *v.* 17. (See *comm.* there). The pathos of the situation is heightened when God's own people sinks to a level at which they consider their lives to be governed by sorcery.]

20. אֶת הַנְּפָשׁוֹת לְפֹרְחוֹת — *The souls to make them fly.*

Rashi following *Targum,* renders this

you trap souls of My people? Souls for your own
livelihood? 19 *And you have profaned Me among My*
people for handfuls of barley and for morsels of
bread, to slay souls that should not die, and to
preserve souls that should not live; when you lied to
My people, who listen to lies.
20 *Therefore, thus says my Lord*
HASHEM/ELOHIM: See! I turn against your cushions
with which you trap the souls to make them fly, and I
will tear them from your arms. And I will set free the
souls which you trap, the souls which you cause to
fly; 21 *and I will tear your wraps and I will save My*
people from your clutches and they will no longer be

extremely obscure phrase: The souls which you [through your sorcery] cause to fly to *Gehinnom.*

These souls will be saved when God tears the cushions 'into' which these souls had been trapped from the arms to which they were attached.

Rashi does not interpret the almost identical phrase at the end of the verse: אֶת נְפָשִׁים לְפֹרְחֹת.

Metzudas David (with *Targum)* render it identically, and sees it as an extension of the earlier word נְפָשׁוֹת, *souls.*

The full meaning of the final phrase would then be: And I will set free the souls which you entrap — these souls which you caused to fly to *Gehinnom.*

No explanation is given for the unique form of the plural of נֶפֶשׁ as נְפָשִׁים.

Harav Breuer, avoiding the seeming redundancy of the last three words of the sentence and also accounting for the masculine ending of נְפָשִׁים, suggests a different translation. While the first פֹּרְחוֹת is to be translated as 'flying from the body' in the sense of *Targum* and *Rashi,* the second one could be taken as 'flying to freedom.' Thus the complete phrase would read: And I will send out the souls which you trap, allowing those [newly freed souls] to fly to freedom.

The masculine form נְפָשִׁים is used to suggest the strength gained through the new freedom from the sorceresses.

[A word is in place concerning the occasional, seemingly arbitrary, changes from masculine to feminine and vice versa which occur in Scripture (another example occurs in our verse: זְרוֹעֹתֵיכֶם (i.e. masc.) instead of the expected זְרוֹעֹתֵיכֶן (i.e. fem.) and in the next one: מִסְפְּחֹתֵיכֶם (i.e. masc.) instead of the expected מִסְפְּחֹתֵיכֶן (i.e. fem.)

Occasionally an explanation is possible, such as *Harav Breuer*'s treatment of נְפָשִׁים. In the same way he explains the masculine forms quoted above as indicating the strong (masc.) control which the women exercised over their clients. See also his treatment of the feminine form of עֶזְרָה at 12:14.]

זְרוֹעֹתֵיכֶם — *Your arms.*

The simple meaning of the verse seems to imply that the cushions were worn by the women rather than by their clients. Alternately the clients' arms might be seen as belonging to the women since these arms were under their control *(Radak).*

כב בְּיֶדְכֶן לִמְצֻדָה וִידַעְתֶּן כִּי־אֲנִי יהוה: יַעַן
הַכְאוֹת לֶב־צַדִּיק שֶׁקֶר וַאֲנִי לֹא
הִכְאַבְתִּיו וּלְחַזֵּק יְדֵי רָשָׁע לְבִלְתִּי־שׁוּב
כג מִדַּרְכּוֹ הָרָע לְהַחֲיֹתוֹ: לָכֵן שָׁוְא לֹא
תֶחֱזֶינָה וְקֶסֶם לֹא־תִקְסַמְנָה עוֹד
וְהִצַּלְתִּי אֶת־עַמִּי מִיֶּדְכֶן וִידַעְתֶּן כִּי־אֲנִי

א יהוה: וַיָּבוֹא אֵלַי אֲנָשִׁים מִזִּקְנֵי יִשְׂרָאֵל
ב וַיֵּשְׁבוּ לְפָנָי: וַיְהִי דְבַר־
ג יהוה אֵלַי לֵאמֹר: בֶּן־אָדָם הָאֲנָשִׁים
הָאֵלֶּה הֶעֱלוּ גִלּוּלֵיהֶם עַל־לִבָּם וּמִכְשׁוֹל
עֲוֺנָם נָתְנוּ נֹכַח פְּנֵיהֶם הַאִדָּרֹשׁ אִדָּרֵשׁ
ד לָהֶם: לָכֵן דַּבֵּר־אוֹתָם וְאָמַרְתָּ אֲלֵיהֶם

22. יַעַן הַכְאוֹת — *Because you have cowed.*

The righteous people would become depressed at the thought that they are destined to die in spite of their righteousness *(Rashi)*. Similarly, as we learn in the last part of the verse, the wicked people would feel encouraged by an optimistic divination.

XIV

Some of the elders of Israel came and sat before the prophet. *Radak* stresses that this occurred after the prophecies of the previous chapter. Perhaps he means to indicate that they came in reaction to Yechezkel's words: If, as Yechezkel declared, their self-proclaimed 'prophets' were not trustworthy, then they would seek guidance from him.

In seeking out a new guide, however, they had not changed their basic attitudes. In their hearts they were still tied to those beliefs which had been both cause and result of their idolatrous practices. In fact they sought to 'deceive' God *(Eliezer of Beaugency* to *v.* 8), by feigning a desire to search Him out, while using His true prophet, Yechezkel, as they had used the false prophets before him *(Harav Breuer)*.

The first part of the chapter addresses itself to these people.

1. וַיָּבוֹא אֵלַי — *Then came to me* [lit. *'and he came'*].

The singular וַיָּבוֹא is used (instead of the plural וַיָּבוֹאוּ) to teach that they came single-mindedly, as a united group (*Rashi* and *Radak*). [According to the *Mesorah* there are eight places where the singular וַיָּבוֹא is used instead of the contextually required plural form. In each case an explanation is needed. As an example — see *Rashi* to *Num.* 13:22]

2. God reveals their secret thoughts to the prophet.

3. הֶעֱלוּ גִלּוּלֵיהֶם עַל לִבָּם — *Have brought up their idols upon their heart.*

With the intention of serving them *(Rashi)*.

Radak (v. 5) points out that idol worship was no longer practiced by the exiles. [Thus he cannot agree with *Rashi*.]

XIII 22-23

in your clutches to be trapped. Then shall you know
that I am HASHEM. [22] *Because you have cowed the*
heart of the righteous with lies though I have not
pained him; and strengthened the hands of the
wicked that he might not repent from his evil way,
that his life might be preserved.
[23] *Therefore vanity shall you not see, nor divina-*
tions divine any longer. Thus shall I save My people
from your hand. Then shall you know that I am
HASHEM."'

XIV 1-4

Then came to me men from the elders of Israel,
and they sat before me.
[2] *And the word of HASHEM came to me saying:*
[3] *'Ben Adam, these men have brought up their idols*
upon their heart, and the stumbling block of their sin
have they placed before their faces. Shall I make
Myself accessible to them? [4] *Therefore speak with*
them and say to them: "Thus says my Lord

In attempting to trace the exact meaning of the idiom מַעֲלֶה עַל לֵב, we find that in various places in Scripture, *Targum* uses a number of different translations. The particular rendering which *Targum* uses here: ... אַסִּיקוּ עַל לִבְּהוֹן, is adopted by him when the phrase מַעֲלֶה עַל לֵב indicates *remembering (Isaiah* 65:17 and *Jeremiah* 3:16). *Targum* uses the same translation for עוֹלָה עַל רוּחַ, which seems to have the meaning of a *secret aspiration* as in 11:5 and 20:32. The meaning of the idiom would then approximate: While they no longer worship idols, they *'remember them* (with longing)' or *'secretly aspire'* to their return.

וּמִכְשׁוֹל עֲוֹנָם נָתְנוּ נֹכַח פְּנֵיהֶם — *And the stumbling block of their sins have they placed before their faces.*

They constantly view idols as gods to be feared *(Rashi).*

Because the idiom נָתַן נֹכַח הַפָּנִים is not found elsewhere in Scripture, it is difficult to define its exact usage. *Metzudas David* renders it as emphasizing the sin of the previous phrase: Not only are their thoughts oriented towards idol worship — they even *practice* it! Once more this seems to contradict *Radak's* assertion that the exiles did not worship idols.

הַאִדָּרֹשׁ אִדָּרֵשׁ לָהֶם — *Shall I make Myself accessible to them?*

דרש, *to seek* in the *Nif'al,* passive has the meaning: *to make oneself accessible* (see *Isaiah* 65:1).

God's rhetorical question implies that the people had indeed requested that God become accessible to them, although such a request is not explicitly mentioned. But, because of their secret longing for idols, God will not make Himself accessible to their questioning.

כֹּה־אָמַר ׀ אֲדֹנָי יֱהֹוִה אִישׁ אִישׁ
מִבֵּית יִשְׂרָאֵל אֲשֶׁר יַעֲלֶה אֶת־גִּלּוּלָיו
אֶל־לִבּוֹ וּמִכְשׁוֹל עֲוֺנוֹ יָשִׂים נֹכַח פָּנָיו
וּבָא אֶל־הַנָּבִיא אֲנִי יהוה נַעֲנֵיתִי לוֹ
ה בָה בְּרֹב גִּלּוּלָיו: לְמַעַן תְּפֹשׂ אֶת־ — בָּא ק׳
בֵּית־יִשְׂרָאֵל בְּלִבָּם אֲשֶׁר נָזֹרוּ מֵעָלַי
ו בְּגִלּוּלֵיהֶם כֻּלָּם: לָכֵן
אֱמֹר ׀ אֶל־בֵּית יִשְׂרָאֵל כֹּה אָמַר אֲדֹנָי
יֱהֹוִה שׁוּבוּ וְהָשִׁיבוּ מֵעַל גִּלּוּלֵיכֶם
ז וּמֵעַל כָּל־תּוֹעֲבֹתֵיכֶם הָשִׁיבוּ פְנֵיכֶם: כִּי

However He will 'respond' (נַעֲנֵיתִי, *v.*4 see below) in a way suited to the occasion *(Radak).*

4. אִישׁ אִישׁ מִבֵּית יִשְׂרָאֵל — *Every man from the Family of Israel.*

We have already noted that many of Yechezkel's expressions are taken from *Leviticus.* (See *Appendix IV.)* The expression אִישׁ אִישׁ מִבֵּית יִשְׂרָאֵל of our verse, and the same expresson with the addition of וּמִהַגֵּר אֲשֶׁר יָגוּר בְּיִשְׂרָאֵל, *'and from the stranger who dwells in Israel'* (*v.* 7) recurs repeatedly in *Lev.* and is also combined there with וְנָתַתִּי פָנַי בָּאִישׁ הַהוּא (*v.* 8) indicating the punishment of כָּרֵת, *being 'cut off' from the nation.*

For a more detailed analysis, see Sefer Vayikra by *Rabbi David Zvi Hoffman* to Ch. 17 (p. 329 of *Vol.* 1).

The overall effect of this formulation would be, to express the idea that such people have no need *to seek an answer* (לִדְרֹשׁ) from God. Their 'answer' has already been given in the *Torah.* A heart, rooted in idol worship, is effectively *'cut off'* from the nation of Israel (based on *Harav Breuer*).

נַעֲנֵיתִי לוֹ — *I will respond to him.*

The word is in the *Nif'al* (passive) voice thus meaning literally *'to be answered'.* This cannot be the meaning in our case, because God is not being answered, rather He answers.

Radak and *Metzudas David* solve the problem by taking ענה to mean *'to declare',* as in *Deut.* 26:5. The meaning of the passive form would be *'to take note'* or *'accept'* a declaration *(Metzudas David);* or *to be stimulated or goaded into a response* to a declaration *(Radak).*

However, *Targum* renders מִשְׁתְּאֵיל לֵיהּ, similar to the translation he offers for אִדָּרֵשׁ אִדָּרֵשׁ in *v.* 3. It means *'will allow Myself to be inquired of'.* Thus, *Targum* would seem to attach the same meaning to the passive form of *to answer* in our verse: That is, *'I will allow myself to be stimulated into answering'.*

בָא בְּרֹב גִּלּוּלָיו — [Though] *he comes with the multitude of his idols.*

Although the spelling is בה [lit. *'in it'*], it is read בָא, *'he came'.* (See 7:21 for an analysis of קְרִי and כְּתִיב, the variation between pronunciation and spelling). *Harav Breuer* comments that the spelling of our verse, בה might mean that really the answer to this man lies *'in it',* in his own inability to tear himself loose from the loyalties to his idolatrous cult.

The exact meaning of the phrase depends on how we understand לְמַעַן

XIV
5-6

HASHEM/ELOHIM: Every man from the Family of Israel who will bring up his idols to his heart, and place the stumbling block of his sin opposite his face, yet he comes to the prophet — I, HASHEM, will respond to him, though he comes with the multitude of his idols; [5] *so as to take hold of the Family of Israel in their heart because they have withdrawn themselves from Me with their idols, all of them."*

[6] *Therefore say to the Family of Israel: "Thus says my Lord HASHEM/ELOHIM: Return and bring back from your idols and from all your abominations, bring back your faces.*

תְּפֹשׂ אֶת בֵּית יִשְׂרָאֵל בְּלִבָּם, of the next verse.

From this verse the Sages *(Kidushin* 39b, *Chulin* 142a) derive that not only the act but even the intention to worship idols is punishable [i.e. תפש is taken in the sense: *to catch* or *find guilty*]. In the case of other sins, however, a person is liable only for the deed. The Sages read this verse as part of God's rebuke.

However *Targum* renders: In order to bring the family of Israel close, to place repentance in their hearts [i.e. תפש is taken in the sense: *to seize and bring close*].

Mahari Kara points out that *Targum*'s rendering is not the simple meaning of the verb תפש, and therefore he prefers the earlier rendering.

However, throughout Scripture there is a tendency in the *Targum* to read a comforting meaning into verses, which, in context, seem obviously to intend rebuke. Some examples from the Book of *Ezekiel* are: 2:5, 7, 10; 3:11; 21:8, 9.

Thus the entire sequence can be understood in two ways:

Targum renders: I, HASHEM, will permit Myself to be inquired of since he comes to seek teaching from Me, *in spite of the fact* that mixed up in him is his idol worship. [I lower Myself to do] this, in order to bring the family of Israel close to repentance in their heart.

Rashi agrees with *Targum*.

Radak renders: I, HASHEM, will respond to him, *because* he comes with the multitude of his idols. This, in order to uncover the secret thoughts which he harbors in his heart.

5. לְמַעַן תְּפֹשׂ — *So as to take hold.*

See above *(v.* 4).

6. שׁוּבוּ וְהָשִׁיבוּ — *Return and bring back.*

I.e. bring back your errant hearts *(Rashi).*

Although הָשִׁיבוּ is in the *Hiph'il* voice (causative, i.e. causing another to commit an act), its normal meaning is as a call to an individual *to repent*, rather than to cause others to do so (18:32). However, when it comes together with שׁוּבוּ, *repent*, the usual translation would create an obvious redundancy. Thus *Rashi* to 18:30 renders שׁוּבוּ, *repent* and הָשִׁיבוּ, *cause others to repent*. *Rashi* does not follow that course in our verse, however, because of the context.

Since the last two words הָשִׁיבוּ פְּנֵיכֶם, would seem to refer to the *'stumbling blocks'* which they had put *'opposite their faces'* (vs. 3 and 4), [פְּנֵיכֶם of our verse parallel to פְּנֵיהֶם of *v.* 3 and 4],

יד
ח־ט

אִישׁ אִישׁ מִבֵּית יִשְׂרָאֵל וּמֵהַגֵּר אֲשֶׁר־
יָגוּר בְּיִשְׂרָאֵל וְיִנָּזֵר מֵאַחֲרַי וְיַעַל
גִּלּוּלָיו אֶל־לִבּוֹ וּמִכְשׁוֹל עֲוֹנוֹ יָשִׂים
נֹכַח פָּנָיו וּבָא אֶל־הַנָּבִיא לִדְרָשׁ־לוֹ בִי
ח אֲנִי יהוה נַעֲנֶה־לּוֹ בִּי: וְנָתַתִּי פָנַי
בָּאִישׁ הַהוּא וַהֲשִׁמֹתִיהוּ לְאוֹת
וְלִמְשָׁלִים וְהִכְרַתִּיו מִתּוֹךְ עַמִּי וִידַעְתֶּם
ט כִּי־אֲנִי יהוה: וְהַנָּבִיא

Rashi interprets הָשִׁיבוּ as *'bring back'*, referring to לִבָּם, *the hearts* upon which the idols had been *brought up* (v. 3 and 4). Thus a call for repentance goes out both to the heart and to the face, but both calls are addressed to the individuals acting upon themselves.

7. אִישׁ אִישׁ מִבֵּית יִשְׂרָאֵל וּמֵהַגֵּר ... — *For every man from the family of Israel and from the stranger ...*

Radak infers from the mention of the גֵּר, *the stranger* or *proselyte*, that many Babylonians probably attached themselves to the Jewish faith when they saw the truth and justice of God, as attested to by Israel's exile.

לִדְרָשׁ לוֹ בִי — *Through him to seek an answer of Me.*

Although לִדְרָשׁ אֶת is the more common usage, we do occasionally find the verb used with the prefix ...בּ. (See *I Chron.* 10:14, and *II* 34:26).

אֲנִי ה׳ נַעֲנֶה לוֹ בִּי — *I, HASHEM, will respond to him for My sake.* [lit. *'through Me'*].

The translation follows *Radak's* rendering of this difficult phrase.

Once more *Radak* points to the change in the verb used. The people came לִדְרשׁ, *to seek an answer (v.* 3). This is refused them. However, HASHEM allows Himself to be moved, נַעֲנֶה, to a response, in order to reveal the secrets of their heart.

8. וְנָתַתִּי פָּנַי בָּאִישׁ הַהוּא — *And I will set My face against that man.*

Targum translates: And I will set My *anger* ... *Radak* and *Metzudas David* quote various places in Scripture where פָּנִים is used as a synonym for anger, because a person's anger is reflected in his face.

Rashi (Lev. 17:10, based on *Toras Kohanim* ad loc. see also *Rashi Sotah* 9a) renders פָּנַי, *face* as פְּנַאי, *spare time.* The phrase means that God will turn His full attention to the punishment of this man. *Mizrachi* and *Gur Aryeh* (ad loc.) explain that the Sages prefer this translation because the expression God *'turns His face'* is generally used to denote that God shows favor. Therefore God's *face* cannot be meant here.

וְנָתַתִּי פָּנַי — *And I will set My face.*

Afterwards — if he does not listen to the words of the prophet *(Rashi).* This comment is based on *Rashi's* agreement with the *Targum* that נַעֲנֶה, *will respond,* in *vs.* 4 and 7 was with the purpose of influencing the man to repent. Hence this threat can only be understood in the light of a refusal to heed the call to repentance. *Radak* and *Metzudas David* who explained נַעֲנֶה as a response designed to uncover the people's perfidy, have no problem with this verse, because the previous verses presume a need for punishment. Thus

[7] *For every man from the Family of Israel and from
the stranger who sojourns in Israel who withdraws
himself from Me and brings up his idols to his heart,
and the stumbling block of his sin does he set opposite his face; yet he comes to the prophet through
him to seek an answer of Me. I* HASHEM *will respond
to him for My sake,* [8] *and I will set My face against
that man and make him a sign and parables, and I
shall cut him off from amid My people. Then shall
you know that I am* HASHEM. [9] *When the prophet is*

they do not require the caveat stated by *Rashi*.

וַהֲשִׂמוֹתִיהוּ לְאוֹת וְלִמְשָׁלִים — *And I will make him a sign and parables.*

This translation follows *Targum* and *Rashi* who read the word with a שׂ, *Sin*, and treat it as coming from the root שׂים, *to put*. *Metzudas David* reads וַהֲשְׁמוֹתִיהוּ (with a שׁ [*Shin*]), in which case the word derives from שמם *to be desolate*. The meaning, then, is: *And I will make him desolate* [*so that he shall be*] *a sign and parables.*[1]

וְהִכְרַתִּיו מִתּוֹךְ עַמִּי — *And I will cut him off from amid* [lit. 'the midst of'] *My people.*

The verse seems to imply the punishment of כָּרֵת, a penalty mentioned in the Torah for a variety of specific sins. Since the sin of seeking out God's word from a prophet, while harboring thoughts of idol worship, is not mentioned in the Torah, the question arises as to how the 'cutting off of the soul' can be exacted as punishment. We must classify this punishment as כָּרֵת מִדִּבְרֵי קַבָּלָה, a heavenly punishment the source of which is in the Prophets (rather than in the Torah).

We do not know the exact nature of the particular כָּרֵת mentioned here. *Ramban (Lev.* 18:29) reasons that when אִישׁ, *man* is used in connection with כָּרֵת instead of נֶפֶשׁ, *soul*, then the punishment is directed against the sinners physical life and does not effect the life of his soul after death. In our context, וְהִכְרַתִּיו, *I will cut him off*, (the punishment of the person who asks the prophet) seems to be parallel to וְהִשְׁמַדְתִּיו, *I will destroy him*, of the following verse (the punishment of the prophet). Throughout Scripture, הַשְׁמָדָה, *destruction*, seems to deal with physical existence, hence we may assume that the 'cutting off' also refers to physical rather than spiritual life.

There is an additional implication to וְהִשְׁמַדְתִּיו based on *Deut.* 9:20, where *Rashi* explains לְהַשְׁמִידוֹ as indicating כִּלּוּי בָּנִים, *dying without children* (or at

1. The system by which we differentiate between the שׁ *(sh)* and the שׂ *(s)* sounds by placing a dot over the right or left side of the letter respectively, is an innovation that was not used when Scripture was written, nor was it yet established in the Talmudic period. Therefore, it is not uncommon to find the *'shin'* and *'sin'* sounds interchanged. For example, acrostics are formed without regard to the pronounciation of the ש (see: *Psalms* 111:10; 119:161-168; *Lamentations* 3:61-63). The Talmudic Sages switch freely from one pronunciation to the other. For one example among many, see *Sotah* 3a where תִשְׂטֶה (שׂ as in *s*) yields שְׁטוּת (שׁ as in *sh*). For this reason we must not be surprised to find divergent opinions about the correct rendering of this word.

כִּי־יְפֻתֶּה וְדִבֶּר דָּבָר אֲנִי יהוה פִּתֵּיתִי
אֵת הַנָּבִיא הַהוּא וְנָטִיתִי אֶת־יָדִי
עָלָיו וְהִשְׁמַדְתִּיו מִתּוֹךְ עַמִּי יִשְׂרָאֵל:
י וְנָשְׂאוּ עֲוֺנָם כַּעֲוֺן הַדֹּרֵשׁ כַּעֲוֺן הַנָּבִיא
יא יִהְיֶה: לְמַעַן לֹא־יִתְעוּ עוֹד בֵּית־יִשְׂרָאֵל
מֵאַחֲרַי וְלֹא־יִטַּמְּאוּ עוֹד בְּכָל־פִּשְׁעֵיהֶם
וְהָיוּ־לִי לְעָם וַאֲנִי אֶהְיֶה לָהֶם לֵאלֹהִים
יב נְאֻם אֲדֹנָי יֱהֹוִה: וַיְהִי דְבַר־יהוה

least without grandchildren — see *Gur Aryeh* ad loc.). It seems likely that the word would have the same meaning in our context.

9. וְהַנָּבִיא כִי יְפֻתֶּה — [*And*] *when the prophet is enticed.*

Rashi to *Exod.* 22:15 renders יְפַתֶּה *(Pi'el)* to persuade, hence the *(Pu'al)* form (passive construction) means: *To be persuaded* or *enticed.*

To the word פִּתֵּיתִי, *Rashi* explains: I have opened a door for him facing in whichever direction he may want. And this would seem to indicate that 'He who wants to defile himself — the doors are opened for him' *(Shabbos* 104a).

[It is unlikely that *Rashi* here (in contrast to *Rashi* in *Exodus)* understands the word as *persuaded.* The expression *the doors are opened for him* does not imply a positive act of persuasion; rather, that no obstacle is placed in the path of one who wants to sin. It is more likely that *Rashi* here interprets the word as *to open* (פתח = פתה); or as *'straying'* or *'being mistaken'* as does *Ramban* in *Exod.* loc. cit. In either case God does not *persuade* the prophet to deceive; He merely *permits* him to go his way.']

Who, then, (if we assume *Rashi*'s opinion to *Exodus)* persuades the false prophet to prophesy? The answer is given in the second part of our verse: אֲנִי ה׳ פִּתֵּיתִי, *I, HASHEM, led* [*the prophet*] *astray.*

Why would God lead the prophet astray?

Radak provides the answer. In 13:3 we recognized that many of the false prophets projected themselves as God-fearing people, while secretly living immoral and sinful lives. God will send them spurious inspiration to prophesy so that when their predictions are shown to be false, their wickedness will be revealed to all.

10. וְנָשְׂאוּ עֲוֺנָם — *And they will* [*both*] *bear their sin.*

The one who inquires and the false prophet are equally culpable.

כַּעֲוֺן הַדֹּרֵשׁ — *Like the sin of the inquirer.*

I.e. the person who insincerely seeks the counsel of a true prophet, but refuses to follow his teaching *(Targum; Rashi; Radak).*

Or, he who inquires of the false prophets *(Metzudas David).*

12-20. Superficially, this passage presents great difficulties. It seems to deny the tenet that a righteous man has the power to protect the community in which he lives — a tenet which, according to *Sanhedrin* 99b is so basic to Judaism, that one who denies it is said to lose his portion in the world to come.

Further, it seems to call into question the doctrine of זְכוּת אָבוֹת, *the merit of fathers,* by which mercy can be shown to children for their fathers' sakes.

*enticed and speaks a word, I, HASHEM, have enticed
that prophet, and I will stretch out My hand upon
him, and destroy him from amid My people, Israel.*
10 *And they will both bear their sin: like the sin of the
inquirer, like the sin of the prophet shall it be;* 11 *so
that they should no longer make the Family of Israel
stray from Me, and no longer be defiled by all their
sins. And they shall be considered My people and I
shall be for them a God. The words of my Lord
HASHEM/ELOHIM." '*
12 *And the word of HASHEM came to me, saying:*

These difficulties can be resolved if we do not view the passage in isolation, but in context with other prophecies uttered by Yechezkel and Jeremiah at that time.[1]

22:30 reads: *And I sought for a man among them that should put up a fence and stand in the breach before Me, for the Land that I should not destroy it. But I could not find* [*one.*]

The implication is that a righteous man could indeed have averted the threatening tragedy, provided that he גֹּדֵר גָּדֵר, *built a fence,* וְעֹמֵד בַּפֶּרֶץ, *and stood in the breach. Radak* followed by *Metzudas David,* equates עֹמֵד בַּפֶּרֶץ with prayer. This is based on *Psalms* 106:23. Thus it would seem that prayer would have helped. If *Jeremiah* 15:1 states unequivocally that even the prayers of a Moses or a Samuel would not have helped, the answer must lie in the precondition of גֹּדֵר גָּדֵר, *putting up a fence,* implying that prayer alone, without an accompanying fence, would be insufficient even if the prayer was to come from a Moses or a Samuel. *Metzudas David* (22:30) identifies this 'builder of fences' with one who stimulates the people towards תְּשׁוּבָה, *repentance.* This very same thought is expressed by *Rashi* to *Jeremiah* (loc. cit.).

Thus we learn that the prayers of a righteous person can indeed help his community, provided they are part of a more general effort to bring about the reform of the abuses practiced by that community.

Again, we read in *Jeremiah* 5:1: *Roam through the open places of Jerusalem; and look, I pray you, and know, and search her streets, if you (can) find a man, if there is one who does justice, and pursues faith — I will forgive her.* Once more we see that a single good man could have swayed the balance. And yet we know *(Psalms:* 79:2, but see *Rashi)* that among the victims were, also, righteous people *(Radak).*

In solution, *Radak* suggests that in

1. Our תּוֹרָה שֶׁבִּכְתָב, our *Written Torah* (comprising *Torah, Prophets,* and *Hagiographa)* is an organic whole. Since no contradiction can exist in such a systematic whole, a legitimate means of determining פְּשַׁט, *the textual meaning* of a given passage, will be to see that it does not contradict another passage.

Thus, for example, even though, the *Torah* makes the *unqualified* statement that: *He visits the sins of the fathers upon the children (Exod.* 20:5; 34:7; *Num.* 14:18; *Deut.* 5:9), the Sages, limit its application to a case in which the children continue in the evil ways of the parents. This qualification avoids contradiction with the statement that: *Children will not die for the sins of their parents (Deut.* 24:16). (See *Berachos* 7a, and *Sanhedrin* 27b).

It is by this same method that we must determine the meaning of our passage.

יג אֵלַי לֵאמֹר: בֶּן־אָדָם אֶרֶץ כִּי תֶחֱטָא־לִי
לִמְעָל־מַעַל וְנָטִיתִי יָדִי עָלֶיהָ וְשָׁבַרְתִּי
לָהּ מַטֵּה־לָחֶם וְהִשְׁלַחְתִּי־בָהּ רָעָב
יד וְהִכְרַתִּי מִמֶּנָּה אָדָם וּבְהֵמָה: וְהָיוּ
שְׁלֹשֶׁת הָאֲנָשִׁים הָאֵלֶּה בְּתוֹכָהּ נֹחַ דָּנִאֵל
וְאִיּוֹב הֵמָּה בְצִדְקָתָם יְנַצְּלוּ נַפְשָׁם נְאֻם
טו אֲדֹנָי יֱהֹוִה: לוּ־חַיָּה רָעָה אַעֲבִיר בָּאָרֶץ
וְשִׁכְּלָתָּה וְהָיְתָה שְׁמָמָה מִבְּלִי עוֹבֵר
טז מִפְּנֵי הַחַיָּה: שְׁלֹשֶׁת הָאֲנָשִׁים הָאֵלֶּה
בְּתוֹכָהּ חַי־אָנִי נְאֻם אֲדֹנָי יֱהֹוִה אִם־בָּנִים
וְאִם־בָּנוֹת יַצִּילוּ הֵמָּה לְבַדָּם יִנָּצֵלוּ

order for the righteous person to be able to influence the fate of his city, he must be in its *'open places'*, in its *'streets'*, part and parcel of the city's life and activity (Compare *Hirsch* to *Gen.* 18:24). In Jerusalem, the righteous people were confined to their homes; society had banished them from its midst, and so their merit was unavailing.

A rounded picture now emerges. If a community can be moved to repentance by the good people among it, if it allows them to be part of its communal life, then it benefits from the efficacy of their prayers, and the merit of their presence. Jerusalem had effectively isolated itself from these life-giving influences, and therefore could no longer be helped, even by a Noah, Daniel, or, Job in their midst.

(For a discussion of the problem of זְכוּת אָבוֹת, *merit of the fathers*, see below, *v.* 16).

13. The passage deals with four *'evil judgments' (v.* 21) which are: famine, wild beasts, sword, and plague. (See *comm.* to 5:17). All of them are foretold in the *Tochachah, the Admonition* of *Lev.* 26.

לִמְעָל מַעַל — *Committing treachery.*

The term מְעִילָה is used to describe an act of perfidy whereby something is used for a purpose other than the one for which it was intended. [E.g. the adultery of a married woman *(Num.* 5:12), or the use of sacred property for secular purposes (*Lev.* 5:15).]

Where the gift of a land is misused, God sends 'messengers' to wrest it from its inhabitants.

מַטֵּה לָחֶם — [*Its*] *staff of bread.*

Same as 5:16, above. The expression is based on *Lev.* 26:26.

וְהִכְרַתִּי מִמֶּנָּה אָדָם וּבְהֵמָה — *And cut off from it man and beast.*

The beasts will die as a punishment for the people *(Radak).*

14. נֹחַ דָּנִאֵל וְאִיּוֹב — *Noah, Daniel, and Job.*

Even if such great men as these three were to live in the city, their merit would only be sufficient to save their own lives, but not the general population.

The righteousness of Noah, Daniel, and Job had stood up in the face of overwhelming pressures (*Radak).* Noah remained pure, while surrounded on all sides by a completely corrupt society. Daniel remained steadfast even in the

XIV
13-16

13 'Ben Adam, when a land sins against Me, committing treachery and I stretch out My hand upon it, and break its staff of bread, and I dispatch famine against it, and cut off from it man and beast.
14 Though such three men be in its midst, Noah, Daniel and Job, they, by their righteousness will save their own soul. The words of My Lord HASHEM/ELOHIM.

15 If I cause evil beasts to traverse the Land and bereave it, and it be desolate without wayfarer because of the beasts. 16 These three men in its midst — as I live, the words of my Lord HASHEM/ELOHIM, they will save neither sons nor daughters. They alone

lions' den *(Radak)* and against the blandishments of the royal court of Babylon *(Harav Breuer).* Job did not bow under the terrible pressure of his suffering *(Radak),* nor lose his purity in a generation which, according to the Sages was 'drowning in immorality' *(Harav Breuer).*

Again, each of them witnessed the collapse of the matrix of the society within which they had lived *(Radak):* Noah of a whole world, Daniel of his country, and Job, of his family *(Abarbanel).*

In their travail each of these three men had also been exposed to some of the four 'evil judgments' enumerated in this passage, and had escaped them unscathed.

Such qualities would make these three men the ideal prototype of the צַדִּיק, *the righteous man* who, having withstood the pressures of Jerusalem's corrupt society, would escape its collapse and be saved from the four terrible messengers of death which would converge upon the city.

16. אִם בָּנִים וְאִם בָּנוֹת יַצִּילוּ — *They will neither save sons nor daughters.*

Radak points out that בָּנִים and בָּנוֹת need not necessarily mean sons and daughters. It is also used to denote *children* in general (See *Exod.* 21:31). The meaning of the phrase is that they will not even save the innocent members of the community, but this does not preclude the ability of the righteous to save their own children. See *comm.* to 9:4-6.

However, the Sages *(Midrash Aggados Bereishis* 10) interpret the verse as referring to their own sons and daughters — even they cannot be saved.

There is another source which shows that a father will not always be able to save his children. *Deut.* 32:39 reads: *And there is none who can save from My hand. Sifri* remarks: 'Fathers cannot save sons. Abraham cannot, save Ishmael, Isaac cannot save Esau.' How can we reconcile this with the doctrine of זְכוּת אָבוֹת, *the merit of the father,* which helps their children?

The continuation of the *Sifri* seems to contain the key to the understanding of our problem: We have learned that fathers cannot save sons, but maybe brothers can save brothers? Therefore it is written *(Psalms* 49:8): *'A brother can surely not redeem a man.'* And even if he were to give all the money in the world, still he is not given atonement ...

The subject of *Sifri* is obviously not

יז וְהָאָרֶץ תִּהְיֶה שְׁמָמָה׃ אוֹ חֶרֶב אָבִיא
עַל־הָאָרֶץ הַהִיא וְאָמַרְתִּי חֶרֶב תַּעֲבֹר
בָּאָרֶץ וְהִכְרַתִּי מִמֶּנָּה אָדָם וּבְהֵמָה׃
יח וּשְׁלֹשֶׁת הָאֲנָשִׁים הָאֵלֶּה בְּתוֹכָהּ חַי־אָנִי
נְאֻם אֲדֹנָי יֱהֹוִה לֹא יַצִּילוּ בָּנִים וּבָנוֹת כִּי
יט הֵם לְבַדָּם יִנָּצֵלוּ׃ אוֹ דֶּבֶר אֲשַׁלַּח אֶל־
הָאָרֶץ הַהִיא וְשָׁפַכְתִּי חֲמָתִי עָלֶיהָ בְּדָם
כ לְהַכְרִית מִמֶּנָּה אָדָם וּבְהֵמָה׃ וְנֹחַ דָּנִאֵל
וְאִיּוֹב בְּתוֹכָהּ חַי־אָנִי נְאֻם אֲדֹנָי יֱהֹוִה
אִם־בֵּן אִם־בַּת יַצִּילוּ הֵמָּה בְצִדְקָתָם
כא יַצִּילוּ נַפְשָׁם׃ כִּי כֹה
אָמַר אֲדֹנָי יֱהֹוִה אַף כִּי־אַרְבַּעַת שְׁפָטַי ׀
הָרָעִים חֶרֶב וְרָעָב וְחַיָּה רָעָה וָדֶבֶר
שִׁלַּחְתִּי אֶל־יְרוּשָׁלִָם לְהַכְרִית מִמֶּנָּה
כב אָדָם וּבְהֵמָה׃ וְהִנֵּה נוֹתְרָה־בָּהּ פְּלֵטָה

זְכוּת אָבוֹת, *the merit of the fathers,* a doctrine which asserts that a righteous father can attain a standard of holiness and spiritual perfection which will be implanted in his descendants to such an extent that even if they subsequently sin, the potential for holiness still remains with them. This serves as a compelling reason to hope that they can once more work themselves up to its demand. Therefore God gives them time and assistance toward repentance. (See *Michtav Me'Eliyahu v.*1 pp. 10-14).

Within the scope of such a זְכוּת אָבוֹת, there would be no reason to believe that brothers could save brothers any more than that a father could save his son. Certainly such a זְכוּת אָבוֹת could not be compared to bribery, where atonement is attained in exchange for money.

This form of זְכוּת אָבוֹת never involves the *saving* of a son. *'Saving'* implies that the son deserves a given punishment but is *'saved'* as a favor to the father. This, indeed, would be analogous to bribery, and might well be done to favor a brother or other relative.

זְכוּת אָבוֹת, on the other hand, postulates that a son who has retained the potential for holiness which was implanted in him by his father, does *not* deserve the punishment , for he has an inner strength which stamps his sin as an aberration.

A righteous man can *save* only himself. He can never *save* his children. If the children have retained the spark of holiness implanted in them by the father, they will merit God's favor *in their own right.*

But Jerusalem's children, even those of righteous parents, had blotted out their own potential for holiness. Their parents will not be able to save them.[1]

shall be saved, but the Land shall be desolate.
17 *Or if a sword will I bring upon that Land, and say: 'Let the sword traverse the Land,' and I cut off from it man and beast,* 18 *and these three men are in its midst — as I live, the words of my Lord HASHEM/ELOHIM, they will not save sons or daughters, for they alone will be saved.*
19 *Or if pestilence will I send to that Land, and I pour My fury upon it in blood, to cut off from it man and beast,* 20 *and Noah, Daniel, and Job are in it — as I live, the words of my Lord HASHEM/ELOHIM, they shall save neither son nor daughter. They in their righteousness shall save their own souls.'*
21 *For thus says my Lord HASHEM/ELOHIM: 'How much more when I send My four evil judgments — sword, hunger, evil beasts, and plague — against Jerusalem, to cut off from it man and beast.* 22 *But see! a surviving remnant is left in it who are*

17. וְאָמַרְתִּי חֶרֶב תַּעֲבֹר בָּאָרֶץ — *And (I) say: 'Let the sword traverse the land.'*

There is no parallel to this phrase concerning the other three of the four 'evil judgments.' *Radak* explains that reference is to the talk of the travelers who see the approaching armies. Since God sends the armies and stimulates their talk, it is as though He is speaking.

Harav Breuer suggests that only regarding the sword, is it necessary to stress that it is God who sends the armies — that without realizing it, they are His messengers. The natural phenomena are obviously sent only by God's will, and there is no need to state so specifically.

21. אַף כִּי — *How much more.*

Any one of the four evil messengers is sufficient to annihilate an entire country. Certainly in the case of Jerusalem where God sent all four, complete destruction should have resulted. However, לְהַכְרִית מִמֶּנָּה אָדָם וּבְהֵמָה, means only that it would have been *sufficient* to destroy both man and beast. In actual fact God will not allow this to happen and, as the following verse goes on to say, there will be a remnant *(Rashi* and *Radak).*

1. *Radak* to *v.* 14, quotes this *Sifri* in connection with our chapter, and we have attempted an explanation which would help to throw a light upon the problem implicit in the doctrine of זְכוּת אָבוֹת.

However other ways of interpreting the *Sifri* are possible, and then it would have no connection with our chapter.

Thus *Rashba (Teshuvos haRashba* 5:49 and see *Rachamim Le'Chayim* there) interprets the *Sifri* as referring only to reward and punishment in the World to Come. זְכוּת אָבוֹת can help in This World, but not in the World to Come.

For further references see *Margalis haYom* by *Rabbi Re'uven Margolis* to *Sanhedrin* 104a and by the same author *Chasdei Olam,* p. 592 in the *Sefer Chasidim* which he published.

הַמּוּצָאִים בָּנִים וּבָנוֹת הִנָּם יוֹצְאִים יד
אֲלֵיכֶם וּרְאִיתֶם אֶת־דַּרְכָּם וְאֶת־ כג
עֲלִילוֹתָם וְנִחַמְתֶּם עַל־הָרָעָה אֲשֶׁר
הֵבֵאתִי עַל־יְרוּשָׁלַםִ אֵת כָּל־אֲשֶׁר
כג הֵבֵאתִי עָלֶיהָ: וְנִחֲמוּ אֶתְכֶם כִּי־תִרְאוּ
אֶת־דַּרְכָּם וְאֶת־עֲלִילוֹתָם וִידַעְתֶּם כִּי
לֹא חִנָּם עָשִׂיתִי אֵת כָּל־אֲשֶׁר־עָשִׂיתִי בָהּ
א נְאֻם אֲדֹנָי יֱהוִה: וַיְהִי דְבַר־יְהוָה טו
ב אֵלַי לֵאמֹר: בֶּן־אָדָם מַה־יִּהְיֶה עֵץ־הַגֶּפֶן א־ה
מִכָּל־עֵץ הַזְּמוֹרָה אֲשֶׁר הָיָה בַּעֲצֵי הַיָּעַר:
ג הֲיֻקַּח מִמֶּנּוּ עֵץ לַעֲשׂוֹת לִמְלָאכָה אִם־
יִקְחוּ מִמֶּנּוּ יָתֵד לִתְלוֹת עָלָיו כָּל־כֶּלִי:
ד הִנֵּה לָאֵשׁ נִתַּן לְאָכְלָה אֵת שְׁנֵי קְצוֹתָיו
אָכְלָה הָאֵשׁ וְתוֹכוֹ נָחָר הֲיִצְלַח
ה לִמְלָאכָה: הִנֵּה בִּהְיוֹתוֹ תָמִים לֹא יֵעָשֶׂה

22. פְּלֵטָה הַמּוּצָאִים בָּנִים וּבָנוֹת — *A* [surviving] *remnant ... who are brought out, sons and daughters.*

'Sons and daughters' does not seem a good description of the remnant. It is obviously used to heighten the sense of the unexpected, by contrast to the earlier verses where it was said that *'sons and daughters'* would not be saved. However the *'surviving remnant'* surely consisted of all kinds of people, both young and old.

The Sages read the phrase as though the passive הַמּוּצָאִים was written in the active form: הַמּוֹצִאִים. It is to be understood as an explanation of why this remnant will be saved. It is because their descendants will be worthy. They are to be spared for their children's sake.

אֶת דַּרְכָּם וְאֶת עֲלִילוֹתָם — *Their way and their deeds.*

According to *Malbim,* דֶּרֶךְ describes a person's traits and character, while עֲלִילָה is the action which derives from these traits.

וְנִחַמְתֶּם עַל הָרָעָה — *And you will be consoled for the evil.*

See *comm.* to 12:16.

XV

Israel is the 'vine' which God uprooted from Egypt and planted in His Holy Land *(Ps.* 80:9). Over the vineyard in which He planted it, God expended love and care in the hope that it would produce the luscious grapes for which it had such rich potential *(Isaiah* 5:1-3).

Its failure to produce those grapes *(ibid.)* constitutes the story of Israel's tragedy.

The vine is unique among fruit-bearing trees. All others have a value independent of their fruit. Their wood is strong and pliant and can be put to many uses. The vine alone stands or

XIV brought out, sons and daughters! See they come
23 forth to you, and you shall see their way and their
deeds; and you will be consoled for the evil which I
brought upon Jerusalem, all that I brought upon it.
23 Then they will comfort you, when you see their
way and their deeds. And you shall know that not in
vain did I do all that I did in it. The words of my Lord
HASHEM/ELOHIM.'

XV The word of HASHEM came to me, saying:
1-5 2 'Ben Adam! What will become of the vine-tree,
from among all trees, the branch which grew among
the trees of the forest? 3 Can wood be taken from it
for productive use? Could they take from it a peg
upon which to hang any vessel? 4 See! it was
presented to the fire for fuel, its two ends the fire consumed, and its inner part was charred — is it useful
for work? 5 See! When it was whole it could not be

falls by the harvest which it produces. Its fruits are the noblest of all, but if they fail, there is nothing left. Its wood is unsuitable for any purpose.

For Israel, there can be no secular existence. Its body is doomed to destruction unless it produces the fruits of holiness.

That Israel's existence is not, and never can be, grounded in the natural order of things, is a theme that runs like a thread throughout the *Torah*.

It begins when *Isaac* was born miraculously from a mother, who by nature was sterile (*Yevamos* 64b); and continues until the destruction of the second Temple when *Rabban Yochanan ben Zakai* exclaimed in a moment of profound ecstacy: 'Happy are you Israel! when you do God's will no nation can rule over you, but when you do not do God's will, then He gives you into the hands of the lowliest nation, and not only to the lowliest nation but to their animals' (*Kesubos* 66b).

Even an animal, no matter how lowly, deserves a place in a physical world. But an Israel which does not do God's will, has no place at all.

2. אֲשֶׁר הָיָה בַּעֲצֵי הַיָּעַר — *Which grew* [lit. *was*] *among the trees of the forest.*

Rashi and *Radak* take this part of the verse as a modifier of the earlier reference to the *vine-tree*. I.e., the question: What will become of the vine-tree ... does not refer to vines flourishing in a vineyard, but to the lone vine branch which grows fruitless among the other barren trees of the forest.

3. הֲיֻקַּח מִמֶּנּוּ עֵץ — *Can wood be taken from it?*

The wood of the vine is unsuitable for use as lumber. This verse establishes that a vine without fruit serves no useful purpose.

לַעֲשׂוֹת לִמְלָאכָה — *For productive use.*

מְלָאכָה does not only mean the act of working, but also describes the thing

טו לַמְּלָאכָה אַף כִּי־אֵשׁ אֲכָלַתְהוּ וַיֵּחָר
ו־ח ו וְנַעֲשָׂה עוֹד לִמְלָאכָה׃ לָכֵן כֹּה
אָמַר אֲדֹנָי יֱהֹוִה כַּאֲשֶׁר עֵץ־הַגֶּפֶן בְּעֵץ
הַיַּעַר אֲשֶׁר־נְתַתִּיו לָאֵשׁ לְאָכְלָה כֵּן
ז נָתַתִּי אֶת־יֹשְׁבֵי יְרוּשָׁלָם׃ וְנָתַתִּי אֶת־פָּנַי
בָּהֶם מֵהָאֵשׁ יָצָאוּ וְהָאֵשׁ תֹּאכְלֵם
וִידַעְתֶּם כִּי־אֲנִי יהוה בְּשׂוּמִי אֶת־פָּנַי
טז ח בָּהֶם׃ וְנָתַתִּי אֶת־הָאָרֶץ שְׁמָמָה יַעַן
א א מָעֲלוּ מַעַל נְאֻם אֲדֹנָי יֱהֹוִה׃ וַיְהִי

that is being made. (See *Lev.* 13:48. See also *Ibn Ezra* to *Gen.* 33:14).

4-5. Verse 4 develops *v.* 3. If, as *v.* 3 testifies, a barren vine-tree is unsuited for any productive use; how much more useless would it be once it had been committed to flames, had its two ends burned, and its whole being singed and charred?

This reasoning is spelled out in *v.* 5.

5. וְנַעֲשָׂה עוֹד לִמְלָאכָה — *Can it be put to* [lit. *used*] *for productive use?*

This vine which was virtually valueless to begin with and was then mutilated and disfigured — surely it can serve no useful purpose.

6. כֵּן נָתַתִּי אֶת יֹשְׁבֵי יְרוּשָׁלָיִם — *So have I presented the dwellers of Jerusalem.*

Jerusalem had also been exposed to fire. Its two extremes had been 'burned' off in the form of two exiles which had been dragged to Babylon — Yehoyakim with much of the royal family *(Daniel* 1:2), and then Yehoyachin, with the 'carpenters and locksmiths' *(II Kings* 24:14).

The 'middle of the vine' — the pitiful remnant which remained in Jerusalem with Zidkiyahu — had also been 'singed' — its destiny sealed by the glowing coals which Gabriel had been ordered to hurl upon them (10:2).

How blind, then, is the optimism of Jerusalem's dwellers (11:3,15)! How could they hope to survive in such a reduced situation, when even in the best of times a secular, Godless life is unthinkable for Israel? *(Rashi).*

While *Rashi* interprets the two burned 'ends' as the exiles of Yehoyakim and Yehoyachin, *Radak* suggests that one might refer to the Assyrian exile of the Northern Kingdom, while the other would symbolize the tribulations which had come upon the Kingdom of Judah.

7. מֵהָאֵשׁ יָצָאוּ וְהָאֵשׁ תֹּאכְלֵם — *From the fire have they come forth and fire will consume them.*

The simple meaning of the verse is to complete the comparison of Jerusalem to the vine. Once the vine is removed from the fire which had already consumed it in part, it must be returned to the fire for it is useless. So, too, Jerusalem can expect no other fate, than to be consigned to the flames of destruction.

However, *Targum* reads a new thought into the phrase. He renders: They have transgressed the words of the Torah which had been given from within a fire; and they will be destroyed by nations which are as fierce as fire.

[*Bava Basra* 79a reads: Rav Yehuda said

productive for work, surely when fire consumed it and it was charred — can it be put to productive use?
6 *Therefore, thus says my Lord* HASHEM/ELOHIM: *like the vine-tree among the trees of the forest, which I have presented to the fire for fuel, so have I presented the dwellers of Jerusalem.* 7 *And I will set My face against them. From the fire have they come forth, and fire will consume them. And you shall know that I am* HASHEM, *when I set My face against them.* 8 *And I will render the Land desolate, because you have dealt treacherously. The words of My Lord* HASHEM/ELOHIM.'

in the name of Rav: Whoever separates himself from Torah will be consumed by fire. As it is written: *And I shall turn My face against them. From the fire have they come forth and fire will consume them.*

Harav Shlomo Wolbe in *Ali Shur (Be'er Yaakov* 5725) p. 218 explains: The so-called 'fire' inherent in Torah is similar to temporal fire whose flames constantly strive upward. It is a spiritual force so powerful that, as a result of its influence, even bodily drives and urges strive for spiritual purpose. This was David's meaning when he said ecstatically כָּמַהּ לְךָ בְשָׂרִי, *my flesh longs for You (Ps.* 63:2).

As the Sages said: The very body of a Torah scholar is transformed into this spiritual fire *(Chagigah* 27a). He who withdraws himself from the Torah's fire, however, is consumed by fire. In place of the holy fire that sanctifies but does not consume, another fire comes, a fire that consumes and destroys to the very foundation; for physical lust and bodily drives are themselves like a spiritual fire. But they destroy the man who chooses them.]

XVI

This chapter is referred to in *Shabbos* 129b as פָּרָשַׁת תּוֹכֵחָה, *a chapter of rebuke.* In it Yechezkel castigates the sinners of Israel with uncompromising severity. From a superficial reading one would suppose that his entire generation was caught up in sins of the most grievous nature.

And yet, the historical truth may have been quite different. The sins described may have been committed by a relatively small part of the populace.

In the view of *Halevi (Doros HaRishonim, Tekufas Hamikra), hyperbole* is permitted to the prophet, whose object is not to give a historical account, but to chastise his listeners, and to point out to them the depths of evil into which it is possible to sink. Again and again we find prophets speaking in a way which seems to convey the picture of a universal breakdown of values, when a careful study of the sources shows that the transgressions were limited to a compartively small number of people. For example, upon careful reading of the sources, it can be seen that the Ba'al worshippers of Yehu's time were so few that they were all able to fit into a single building (see *II Kings* 10:18-28), although a casual reading of the relevant parts of *II Kings* yields the impression that the greater part of the nation was involved. Again, in *Joshua* Ch. 7 the whole of Israel is blamed for transgressing the ban, when in fact only one man, Achan, had done so.

[See however *Igros Chazon Ish* 1:209].

Halevi (ibid.) agrees that in the long years of Menashe's reign, a great part of the nation joined in the sins which previously had been largely centered around the royal household, and

ב דְּבַר־יְהוָה אֵלַי לֵאמֹר: בֶּן־אָדָם הוֹדַע
ג אֶת־יְרוּשָׁלַ͏ִם אֶת־תּוֹעֲבֹתֶיהָ: וְאָמַרְתָּ
כֹּה־אָמַר אֲדֹנָי יֱהֹוִה לִירוּשָׁלַ͏ִם מְכֹרֹתַיִךְ
וּמֹלְדֹתַיִךְ מֵאֶרֶץ הַכְּנַעֲנִי אָבִיךְ הָאֱמֹרִי
ד וְאִמֵּךְ חִתִּית: וּמוֹלְדוֹתַיִךְ בְּיוֹם הוּלֶּדֶת

it is conceivable, therefore, that the picture painted in our chapter does reflect the true conditions of the time. Nevertheless, it must be understood that this need not necessarily be so. It is quite possible that the actual number of people who would fit the descriptions of our chapter, was comparatively small.

[We have translated תּוֹכֵחָה as *rebuke* because it is in that sense that it is generally used, and because *Targum* translates it with the same word that he uses for מוּסָר, *ethical teaching* (See *Targum* to *Ps.* 39:12 and 50:17).

However, *Rashi* to *Shabbos* (loc. cit.) renders פָּרָשַׁת תּוֹכֵחָה as an expression denoting *demonstrative argument;* i.e. *making known* which of two parties had wronged the other. This rendering imbues our chapter with a subtly different slant.]

The rebuke, leveled against Jerusalem in our chapter, is so fierce, that according to Rabbi Eliezer *(Mishnah, Megillah* 4:10) it is forbidden to select it as a Haftorah, the portion from Prophets read in the Synagogue.[1]

As is often the case when Scripture speaks in parables, *Targum* does not translate literally, but concentrates completely on the inner meaning. In the commentary, we shall begin by quoting *Targum* on verses where it deviates significantly from the simple meaning, and then make such comments as seem to be indicated.

2. הוֹדַע אֶת יְרוּשָׁלַיִם — *Inform* [lit. *'make known to'*] *Jerusalem.*

Targum renders: To the *dwellers of Jerusalem.*

3. *Targum:* And you shall say: Thus says HASHEM, God, to the dwellers of Jerusalem: Your dwelling places were from the Land of Canaan, there I appeared to your father Abraham at the 'Covenant between the Pieces' and made known to him that you will go down to Egypt, and that I would redeem you with an outstretched arm. And by the merit of your father I will expel the Emorites from before you, and destroy the Hittites.

מְכֹרֹתַיִךְ — *Your dwelling place.*

An obscure term. *Targum* and those commentators who read *'dwelling place'* assume that the כ is in place of a ג and it is as though the word were written מְגֹרֹתַיִךְ *(Ramban* to *Gen.* 41:47 brings many examples of an interchange between these two letters. *Metzudas Zion* writes that the letters גיכ״ק are interchangeable).

[The phrase מְכֹרֹתַיִךְ ... מֵאֶרֶץ הַכְּנַעֲנִי is not quite clear according to this rendering. We would expect a dwelling place to be 'in' a land (בְּאֶרֶץ), not 'from' a land (מֵאֶרֶץ).]

Menachem, quoted by *Rashi,* interprets the word as תּוֹלָדָה, *birth* or *family connections* (see also *Rashbam* to *Gen.* 49:5). In a similar vein *Mahari Kara* renders 'neighbors' (as in *II Kings* 12:6). The meaning would be: You were

1. *Megillah* 25b relates that someone selected this chapter as a *Haftorah* in the presence of Rabbi Eliezer. Rabbi Eliezer said to him: 'Rather than examining [and exposing] the abominations of Jerusalem, [you should] examine the abominations of your own mother.' They did, and found the man to be a *Mamzer,* born of an illicit marriage.

Because of the extreme gravity which Rabbi Eliezer attached to this, it has become the custom to eliminate this chapter from the *Haftoros.* Although the *Halachah* lies with the Sages who permit its selection (and indeed *Rambam, Mishneh Torah, Seder Tefillos Kol Hashanah* indicates it as the *Haftorah* of *Shemos),* in practice it is not used *(Levush haChur* 493).

XVI
1-4

The word of HASHEM came to me, saying: [2] *'Ben Adam! Inform Jerusalem of her abominations,*
[3] *and say: "Thus says my Lord HASHEM/ELOHIM to Jerusalem. Your dwelling place and your birthplace are of the Land of Canaan. Your father is the Emorite, and your mother a Hittite.*
[4] *And as for your birth, on the day that you were*

influenced by your family connections or neighbors in the Land of Canaan.

Harav Breuer, and others, derive the word from the root כור, *to dig* or *tunnel out.* Hence, the place from which you were brought forth, your origin. (The idiom would be identical with *Isaiah* 51:1).

אָבִיךְ הָאֱמֹרִי וְאִמֵּךְ חִתִּית — *Your father is the Emorite, and your mother, a Hittite.*

This difficult phrase can be interpreted in two ways. It may be describing the parents, or it may be telling us something about the child.

Rashi writes: Abraham and Sarah took their greatness from there (the land of the Emorites) and the sons of Ches (the Hittites) gave her, (Sarah), a grave.

This seems, in some form, to be a criticism of Abraham and Sarah. *Sanhedrin* 44b bears this out: When God said to Yechezkel, go and tell Israel: 'Your father is the *Emorite* and your mother a *Hittite',* the Attribute of Justice said to God: 'Master of the world! If Abraham and Sarah were to come and stand before You, would You say this to them and shame them?'

In addition, the prohibition against using this passage as *Haftorah* (see above) is also based on this interpretation. The mere fact that Israel's sins are recounted, would not disqualify this passage more than any of the numerous *Haftoros* which deal with Israel's shortcomings. It is only because aspersions are cast upon Israel's ancestors that it is different (*Tosafos Yom Tov* to *Megillah* 4:10. See also *Levush haChur* loc. cit).

However, most commentators see our verse as a criticism of the children, rather than the parents.

— In your actions you appear as a product of Canaanite upbringing, as though you had been born and lived there. You act *as though* your father were an *Emorite* and your mother a *Hittite (Radak).*

— Your actions make it seem as though your father who lived in *Emorite* country, was in fact an *Emorite* and your mother was in fact a *Hitite* (like the people among whom they dwelt) *(Eliezer of Beaugency).*

[This introductory sentence sums up Jerusalem's tragedy. There is nothing which distinguishes it from any Canaanite city. It is as though eight hundred years of history had been wiped away. Seven Canaanite nations had been driven out of the Land, to be replaced by a people who came to resemble them in every aspect of their degeneracy.

The pathos of this historical tragedy is spelled out in unforgiving detail in the following parable. For the sake of greater clarity, we have divided the parable into four sections: *vs.* 4-8; 9-14; 15-34; and 35-42. This division follows the logic of the chapter's context, and it is useful in helping clarify the prophet's messages.]

4-8. *The first part of the parable:* An infant girl, abandoned by her parents at birth, lies in the open field with no one to show her any compassion. Filthy and neglected [she faces seemingly certain death]. The narrator passes by, sees the child wallowing in its blood, and, far

טז אוֹתָךְ לֹא־כָרַּת שָׁרֵּךְ וּבְמַיִם לֹא־רֻחַצְתְּ
ה לְמִשְׁעִי וְהָמְלֵחַ לֹא הֻמְלַחַתְּ וְהָחְתֵּל לֹא
חֻתָּלְתְּ: ה לֹא־חָסָה עָלַיִךְ עַיִן לַעֲשׂוֹת לָךְ

from being repulsed by its appearance, he promises that she will live.

Still on her own, the child grows to womanhood in the fields, dirty and unattended. Once more her benefactor passes by, sees her beauty [hidden beneath the grime] and takes her for his wife.[1]

In graphic strokes, the parable draws a picture of Israel's life in Egypt, and of its redemption. It forms the basis of many insights which the Sages recognized concerning these events. Much of our understanding will be based on *Sifri* (to *Bo* 12:6). [It will be noted that *Sifri* takes the verses out of order for the purpose of its interpretation. In the commentary we shall explain the verses in the order in which they come.]

Rabbi Massiah ben Cheresh used to say: It is written *(v. 8)*: *And I passed by you and I saw you and see! Your time was the time of love.* The [time had come for the] oath which God had sworn to Abraham that He would redeem his sons, but they had no *mitzvos* with which to busy themselves in order to [merit] redemption. As it is written: *Your bosom was developed, and your hair was grown long, but you were naked and bare (v. 7)* — naked of commandments. So God gave them two commandments, the blood of the Passover offering and the blood of circumcision with which they would busy themselves so that they should be redeemed. As it is written *(v. 6)*: *And I passed by you and I saw you downtrodden in your blood* ... and it is also written *(Zechariah 9:11)*: *As for you also, I sent out your captives from the pit by*

1. As developed in the commentary, the parable is, of course, the story of Israel's nascence as a people.

We have bracketed two phrases, both of which are *implied* but not explicated in the text. Both are of great import to the meaning of the parable, and deserve at least a cursory analysis.

1) The foundling would have died without the help of her benefactor. This makes her subsequent infidelity doubly reprehensible. Israel is God's special *creation (Ps.* 102:19). It could never have existed as a distinct nation without God's direct intervention in its history. Its attempt to lose its identity, becoming indistinguishable from all other nations by means of idol worship (20:32) is a negation of the very soul of its being. It is perfidy of the lowest order.

This idea must be understood in context of the parable which describes Israel as having been abandoned by its parents. What does this mean?

All nations are 'children' of historical imperatives. Their 'parents' are those beginnings from which, under the immutable law of causality, they must develop. Israel knows no physical cause for its existence (see *footnote* to *Pref. Remarks* Ch. 15); its being is predicated entirely on God's Providence. (See *Midrash Shemos Rabbah* 15:8, and *Maharal, Netzach Yisroel* 13).

An Israel divorced from God is a historical paradox from which disaster must flow.

2) The benefactor did not allow himself to be repelled by the surface grime. His eyes pierced the outer layer and enabled him to apprehend the inner core of beauty.

Yalkut Va'eschanan 828 describes Israel's existence in Egypt. On the surface they were quite indistinguishable from the Egyptians. Both were uncircumcized, both wore their hair plaited. Indeed it was difficult to justify Israel's miraculous redemption. Only God recognized that inviolable core of holiness, from which His nation would grow.

When Israel seeks satisfaction from the surface rewards of assimilation, it forgets how transitory such values are. It ignores its essential being upon which its whole existence is predicated.

XVI born, your navel was not cut, nor were you washed
5 with water for cleansing. You were not salted nor
were you swaddled. 5 No eye pitied you to do for you

the blood of your covenant. Therefore, Scripture commanded that the Passover Lamb be taken four days prior to its slaughter, for reward comes only as a result of actions.[1]

We now turn to the individual verses:

4. *Targum:* And also when your fathers went down to Egypt, strangers in a land they did not own, the Congregation of Israel was enslaved and oppressed, just like a child forsaken on the open field, whose umbilical cord had not been cut, who had not been washed in water, who had not been salted with salt and who had not been swaddled in clothes.

... לֹא כָרַּת שָׁרֵּךְ — *Your navel was not cut ...*

The four activities mentioned in our verse were considered essential to the well-being of a new born child, and, because no Biblical prohibition (מְלָאכָה דְאוֹרַיְתָא) was involved, they were permitted even on the Sabbath (*Shabbos* 129b and *Tosafos* ad. loc.).

The cutting of the cord and the washing are self-explanatory. The custom of salting the child had the purpose of firming up his flesh (*Rashi*) and the swaddling clothes were used to straighten the limbs (*Metzudas David*).

While most commentators are content to see the verse as a general description of a neglected child, and do not assign a specific meaning to each of the four activities, *Malbim* treats each one separately.

The cutting of the umbilical cord is the point in the baby's life when it ceases to take nourishment directly from the mother and gains its independence from her. A new-born nation will have been bound by social and cultural ties to the people among whom it matured to nationhood. Its self-assertion and adherence to principles of its own, would be the cutting of its 'umblilical cord.'

Then the child is cleaned. The blood and other fluids which sullied it at birth, are washed away. The new nation will cleanse itself of old clinging habits and legislate laws which will produce a harmonious and just society.

The flesh must then be strengthened and the limbs straightened out. The individual people must be given independence and self-reliance; and the body-politic, the community, must be

1. The *Midrash* in *Shemos Rabbah* 23:9 relates: When Israel was in Egypt and one of the daughters of Israel was ready to bear a child, she would go out to the field and bear the child there. Once the child was born, she would forsake it and give it to the Holy One Blessed be He, saying: 'Master of the World! I have done my part. Now You do Yours!'

Rabbi Yochanan said: Immediately God, in His glory, would 'descend' and cut the umbilical cord, and wash and anoint them. And this is as Yechezkel says: *And you were thrown out upon the open field in your loathsomeness (v.* 5). And it is written: *And as for your birth, on the day when your were born, your navel was not cut (v.* 4) ... And He would put two rocks in his hand, one would feed him oil; and one, honey. As it says: *And he made him suckle honey from the rock (Deut.* 32:13). And they grew up in the field as it says: *I made you thrive like the plants of the field (v.* 7). And when they grew up they would go home to their parents who would ask them: Who looked after you? And they would answer: A young man handsome and good, came down and filled all our needs. As it is written: *My beloved is clear skinned and ruddy, pre-eminent above ten-thousand (Shir haShirim* 5:10). And when Israel came to the sea, these youngsters were there and they saw the Holy One Blessed be He at the sea. And they said to their parents: This is He, who did these things to us when we were in Egypt. As it is written: *This is my God and I will beautify Him (Exod.* 15:2).

טז אַחַת מֵאֵלֶּה לְחֻמְלָה עָלַיִךְ וַתֻּשְׁלְכִי אֶל־
ו פְּנֵי הַשָּׂדֶה בְּגֹעַל נַפְשֵׁךְ בְּיוֹם הֻלֶּדֶת
ו אֹתָךְ׃ וָאֶעֱבֹר עָלַיִךְ וָאֶרְאֵךְ מִתְבּוֹסֶסֶת
בְּדָמָיִךְ וָאֹמַר לָךְ בְּדָמַיִךְ חֲיִי וָאֹמַר לָךְ

enabled to stand straight by appointing teachers and judges to support its structures.

Israel in Egypt had none of these qualities.

5. *Targum:* The eye of Pharaoh did not have compassion upon you to do you even one favor, to allow you relief from your labors, and to have mercy on you. And he passed laws of annihilation concerning you to throw your male children into the river, to destroy you during the time that you were in Egypt.

6. *Targum:* And the memory of the covenant with your fathers came before Me, and I revealed Myself to redeem you. For I knew that you were being caused to suffer in your slavery. And I said to you: Through the blood of circumcision will I have compassion for you, and through the blood of the Passover lamb will I redeem you.

וָאֶעֱבֹר עָלַיִךְ — *Then I passed by you.*

According to the *Targum* (above): *I revealed Myself to redeem you.* This rendering places the verse at the end of the Egyptian exile. God reveals Himself to His people and helps them deserve redemption by allowing them to perform the two commandments, *Pesach* and *Milah.*

[As with the *Sifri* which we quoted above, this interpretation ignores the sequence of the verses. *Targum* explains *v.* 8 as referring to Moses' vision at the burning bush.]

Radak offers an alternative to the *Targum,* and interprets the passage in a manner which retains the correct chronology of events.

In his system, verses 4-6 describe conditions immediately following the death of Joseph. When the *new king who did not know Joseph (Exod.* 1:8) arose, he took advantage of Israel's friendlessness and helplessness and forced them — with all manner of cruelty — into slave labor. He drove them out into the fields (וַתֻּשְׁלְכִי אֶל פְּנֵי הַשָּׂדֶה of *v.* 5 corresponds to וּבְכָל עֲבֹדָה בַּשָּׂדֶה, *to all labor in the field* of *Exod.* 1:14) to work, and, also, so that the Egyptians would not be offended by the close proximity of the Jews (see *Gen.* 43:32).

V. 6 describes God's messages to His people during this period. Aaron, Miriam, and later Moses exhorted the people not to succumb to idol worship (see *comm.* to 20:7) and to retain their identity. The people, depressed by the filth which covered them because of the mud and clay used to make bricks, were encouraged to know that in spite of their filth (בְּדָמַיִךְ, *your blood,* in the parable, symbolizes the mud and clay) they would, in the end, be redeemed.

The revelations in connection with the actual redemption, are described in *v.* 8.

מִתְבּוֹסֶסֶת — *Downtrodden.*

Follows *Rashi.*

בוס in the *Kal* does indeed mean *'to tread'* [for one example among many see *Isaiah* 14:25] and the *Nif'al* (passive) should then mean *to be trodden upon.* This is how *Rashi* renders the word.

However, since the word appears here in the *Hispa'el* (reflexive) mood, *Radak* and *Metzudos* translate it as *wallowing.*

XVI
6

any of these, to have compassion on you. And you were cast out upon the open field in your loathsomeness, on the day you were born. [6] *Then I passed by you and saw you downtrodden in your blood. And I said to you: "In your blood, live." And I said to you: "In your blood, live."*

וָאֹמַר לָךְ בְּדָמַיִךְ חֲיִי וָאֹמַר לָךְ בְּדָמַיִךְ חֲיִי — *And I said to you: 'In your blood live.' And I said to you: 'In your blood live.'*

In spite of your filth, you shall live *(Rashi).*

According to *Radak* (above) we are dealing with the filth of mud and clay and the state of slavery which is implicit in it. The message is that in spite of the seemingly unending slavery, redemption would surely come in the end. The sentence is repeated to stress the absolute certainty of this promise.

However, as seen from *Sifri* and *Targum,* the Sages interpret the verse as referring to the blood of the *Pesach* offering and the blood of circumcision.[1]

[*Rashi* here explains that this interpretation derives from the repetition of the phrase referring to blood. *Rashi* to *Exod.* 12:6 derives it from the plural form, דָמַיִךְ lit. *'your bloods.'*]

The Sages attach great significance to these two sets of blood. [*Pirkei D'Rav Elazar* Ch. 29, writes that not only the redemption from Egypt, but also the future redemption will come in the merit of these two commandments.] References to them abound in *Midrashic* literature. [For example *Shemos Rabbah* 19:6 reports that God kissed and blessed each one of the people as the blood of their circumcision mingled with the blood of the *Pesach* offerings.]

The combination of the two commandments is explained by *Maharal, Gur Aryeh* (to *Exod.* 12:6). *Milah* is the sign on a Jew's body that he is God's servant — His עֶבֶד. (A slave used to carry a seal upon himself attesting to his owner.) The act of bringing the *Pesach* offering is called עֲבוֹדָה, *service (Exod.* 13:5).

[In *Pachad Yitzchak* to *Pesach* Ch. 42, *Harav Yitzchak Hutner* explains why just this particular command is referred to as עֲבוֹדָה. (All *Mitzvos* are acts of עֲבוֹדָה, *service of God,* but *Pesach* is unique in that the *Torah* specifically calls it עֲבוֹדָה).]

Neither would be complete without the other. It is not enough to *be* an עֶבֶד, *a servant* if no עֲבוֹדָה, *service* is performed. On the other hand עֲבוֹדָה done by someone who is not an עֶבֶד cannot be defined as true 'service', for it is essentially voluntary. Together the two commandments combine to produce true עַבְדוּת, servitude.

[Through *Maharal*'s explanation we gain a better understanding of *Targum:* Through the blood of the circumcision *will I have compassion upon you* and through the blood of the Passover lamb *will I redeem you* (see *comm.* to 13:10 where we note the tendency of *Targum* to ascribe separate meanings to double expressions): compassion because of *Milah,* because *Milah* marks Israel as His own; redemption because of *Pesach,* as a reward for the service done.]

1. Since the Torah prohibits an עָרֵל, *an uncircumcised person* from eating the *Pesach* offering *(Exod.* 12:48) it was necessary for all the people who had been lax in this matter, to circumcise themselves on this occasion.

In accordance with the interpretation of *Sifri* and *Targum* that our verse refers to *Pesach* and circumcision, it has become the custom to quote this verse at a *Brith Milah.*

ז בְּדָמַיִךְ חֲיִי׃ רְבָבָה כְּצֶמַח הַשָּׂדֶה נְתַתִּיךְ
וַתִּרְבִּי וַתִּגְדְּלִי וַתָּבֹאִי בַּעֲדִי עֲדָיִים שָׁדַיִם
נָכֹנוּ וּשְׂעָרֵךְ צִמֵּחַ וְאַתְּ עֵרֹם וְעֶרְיָה׃
ח וָאֶעֱבֹר עָלַיִךְ וָאֶרְאֵךְ וְהִנֵּה עִתֵּךְ עֵת
דֹּדִים וָאֶפְרֹשׂ כְּנָפִי עָלַיִךְ וָאֲכַסֶּה עֶרְוָתֵךְ

7. *Targum:* Manifold, like the plants of the field, have I made you. And you increased and became strong, and grew into families and tribes. And because of the good deeds of your fathers, the time approached for your community to be redeemed, for you were enslaved and oppressed.

רְבָבָה כְּצֶמַח הַשָּׂדֶה נְתַתִּיךְ — *To thrive like the plants of the field did I cause you.*

As it is written: *And the children of Israel were fruitful and increased abundantly and multiplied (Exod.* 1:7) *(Rashi).*

When applied to Israel's history, this is certainly the meaning of the verse, as is also attested in the *Haggadah,* where our verse is brought to illustrate the meaning of the word רָב, *many (Deut.* 26:5).

However, in the parable, the foundling did not increase in number.

Metzudas David solves this problem by reading this phrase as part of the previous verse. The benefactor tells the foundling that she will live, and also promises her that she will have many children.

The root רבב from which רְבָבָה is formed, has the meaning to *grow big,* besides its more frequent meaning, *to increase* (see *Gen.* 18:20, and *Isaiah* 6:12 as examples). Thus רְבָבָה might also indicate the thriving of an individual. (See *Rabbeinu Tam* in *Teshuvas Dunash* p.82).

כְּצֶמַח הַשָּׂדֶה — *Like the plants of the field,* which thrive without any attention *(Eliezer of Beaugency).*

According to *Ritva (Haggadah)* the simile hints at the miraculous increase of the Jews, which came in direct proportion to the degree of suffering to which they were exposed. *('The more they afflicted them, the more they multiplied') (Exod.* 1:12). The Jews are likened to grass; the more it is cut, the more it tends to grow.

וַתִּרְבִּי וַתִּגְדְּלִי — *And you increased and grew.*

Radak translates the one expression as denoting an increase in number; the other an increase in size.

Again, this presents a difficulty in the parable (as opposed to the inner meaning), since the foundling did not increase in number. *Metzudas David* renders וַתִּרְבִּי as, *'being brought up': You were brought up and grew big.*

וַתָּבֹאִי בַּעֲדִי עֲדָיִים — *And came to have great charm.*

Follows *Rashi* who renders עֲדִי as a synonym of מִכְלוֹל which means *'beauty'* (see 38:4).

Rashi quotes *Dunash* who renders עֲדִי as *'ornament'* which is also *Radak*'s view. Since the foundling is still *'naked and bare'* it surely cannot mean that she was wearing ornaments. The implication would have to be that she had come of an age at which she was ready to be adorned by them. Another possibility would be to interpret 'ornaments' as those parts of the body which are the indications of approaching maturity *(Radak).*

If we are to find a specific symbolism in this part of the parable, then the ornaments for which Israel was ready are the laws of the Torah *(Radak).*

Menachem, quoted by *Rashi* interprets עֲדִי as a *time lapse. Rabbeinu*

[7] *To thrive like the plants of the field did I cause you; and you increased and grew, and came to have great charm, bosom developed and your hair grown long, but you were naked and bare.*

[8] *And I passed by you and saw you, and see! Your time was the time of love. And I spread My skirt over you and covered your nakedness, swore to you and*

Tam (loc. cit.) presents *Menachem's* rendering in the following way: וַתִּרְבִּי וַתִּגְדְּלִי וַתָּבֹאִי בַּעֲדִי עֲדָיִים, *'One year passed, another year passed, then many years passed'* [*until you reached the stage of maturity.*]

שָׁדַיִם נָכֹנוּ וּשְׂעָרֵךְ צִמֵּחַ — *Bosom developed and your hair grown long.*

Signs of maturity *(Rashi).*

Radak comments that the two breasts symbolize the Written and Oral Law, from which Israel was to draw spiritual sustenance in the same way that an infant nurses.

In the growing hair, signs of change from minority to full responsibility, he sees a reference to those among the Jews who attained a spiritual maturity and were able to tear themselves loose from the confining shackles of the barren religious life which they had led up to that point.

וְאַתְּ עֵרֹם וְעֶרְיָה — *You were naked and bare.*

This need not describe complete nakedness (see *Isaiah* 20:2), but could refer to the pitiful rags with which a slave would cover himself *(Radak).*

We have noted the *Sifri* which renders: Naked and bare of *mitzvos.* If liberation from Pharaoh's slavery is to have any meaning, then they must show themselves willing to become 'slaves' to God. *Milah* and *Pesach* would express this willingness (see above).

The masculine form of עֵרֹם (instead of עֲרוּמָּה) is unexpected. *Radak* explains that Israel is occasionally looked upon as עַם, *nation,* (male), and sometimes as כְּנֶסֶת, *gathering,* (female). Consequently, either form is acceptable.

8. *Targum:* And I revealed Myself to Moses at the burning bush, for I knew that the time for your redemption had come, and I protected you, and caused your sins to pass away. And I swore by My words to redeem you as I had sworn to your parents, said the Lord God, that you might be a nation serving before Me.

וָאֶעֱבֹר עָלַיִךְ וָאֶרְאֵךְ וְהִנֵּה עִתֵּךְ עֵת דֹּדִים — *And I passed by you, and saw you, and see! your time was the time of love.*

I revealed Myself to Moses at the burning bush, and he did signs and wonders at My command, and I showed that the time of love had come so that I fought for you against Egypt, until I brought you out from there with a strong hand. *(Radak).*

Thus *Radak* takes the second 'passing by' as the revelation at the burning bush, while the first one (*v.* 6) had been the prophecies in Egypt exhorting them to forsake the idol-cult (see above).

עֵת דֹּדִים — *The time of love.*

The moment to which all of creation had been directed (see *Rashi* to *Gen.* 1:31) had at last come. And it was a time of love! At last man had wrested himself from every impure and ignoble impulse (*Yevamos* 103b) and had become a suitable resting place for the *Shechinah,* the Divine Presence (*Exod.* 20:21). At last the time for a mutually obligating covenant had come; a time when, if God

טז וָאֶשָּׁבַע לָךְ וָאָבוֹא בִבְרִית אֹתָךְ נְאֻם
ט אֲדֹנָי יֱהוִֹה וַתִּהְיִי־לִי׃ ט וָאֶרְחָצֵךְ בַּמַּיִם
וָאֶשְׁטֹף דָּמַיִךְ מֵעָלָיִךְ וָאֲסֻכֵךְ בַּשָּׁמֶן׃

would take them to Himself as a people, He would be for them a God *(Exod.* 6:7). Reference is to the moment when Israel stood at Mt. Sinai.

Perhaps it is the high drama of this moment which brings about the injection of God's Name — *'The words of my Lord HASHEM/ELOHIM'* — unexpectedly into the parable (based on *Harav Breuer).*

וָאֶפְרֹשׂ כְּנָפִי עָלַיִךְ — *And I spread My skirt over you.*

This connotes a *'taking to oneself'* as in *Ruth* 3:9. It is identical with God's statement: *'And I will take you to Me as a nation'* [Exod. 6:7] *(Radak).*

וָאֲכַסֶּה עֶרְוָתֵךְ — *And covered your nakedness.*

In terms of the parable this is self-explanatory.

As far as Israel is concerned, the meaning is; that by teaching them the right way, and by showing them wonders and signs, God turned them to true faith and removed the shame of 'nakedness' from them *(Radak).*

וָאֶשָּׁבַע לָךְ — *Swore to you.*

That I would not be disloyal to you *(Metzudas David).* This, in terms of the parable.

For Israel, reference is to the oath which God swore to them (implied by the word: לָכֵן, *therefore,* at *Exod.* 6:6, see also *comm.* to 20:6) *(Rashi),* that He would redeem them from Egypt and take them to Himself as a nation.

וָאָבוֹא בִבְרִית אֹתָךְ — *And entered a covenant with you.*

To reinforce the above oath *(Metzudas David).*

For Israel, it is the covenant at Mt. Sinai *(Exod.* 24:8) which is meant. *(Rashi* and *Radak).* It was that covenant which was to bind them to their acceptance of the Torah. (See *Ramban* to *Exod.* 24:1, and *Lev.* 25:1).

וַתִּהְיִי לִי — *And you became Mine.*

The foundling became the benefactor's wife.

For Israel, this is the great moment, when, at the end of forty years of wandering in the desert, Moses finally declared to them: *This day you have become a nation to HASHEM, your God (Deut.* 27:9).

9-14. *The second part of the parable.* This section describes the love which the benefactor lavishes on his bride. He showers her with every conceivable garment and ornament which might help to enhance her natural beauty. She, in turn, uses them to the best advantage, and by her regal bearing and nature, becomes famous among all the nations.

It is impossible to do justice to the wealth of *Midrashic* literature describing how each of the gifts enumerated here was replete with God's love and longing for Israel.

[See for example *Shemos Rabbah* 25:6: Human usage is that the slave washes the master, but God is not so, as it is written: *And I washed you with water.* Human usage is that the slave dresses his master ... puts the shoes on for his master ... but God is not so ...]

As one representative *Midrash* we shall quote from *Yalkut,* which deals with the entire passage as one unit. We shall not repeat the allusions in the individual verses, and will limit the commentary to quoting the *Targum* and commenting on the more obscure expressions.

Rabbi Tanchum said: When Israel

XVI entered a covenant with you — the words of my Lord
9 *HASHEM/ELOHIM — and you became Mine.* 9 *Then I
washed you with water and cleansed away your
blood from you, and I anointed you with oil;*

left Egypt, God decked them with thirteen ornaments.[1]

[There is some conflict about how the number thirteen is arrived at in our chapter. The *Midrash,* quoted in the commentary, starts the count at *v.* 9, which contains three favors: 1) I washed you with water; 2) I cleaned off your blood; and 3) I anointed you with oil.

Some *Midrashim* start the count at *v.* 10 and substitute: 1) fine flour; 2) honey; and 3) oil (*v.* 13) for the first three in our list.]

1) *I washed you with water* — from the filth of idol worship. 2) *I cleaned your blood off you* — i.e., the blood of the *Pesach* and of the *Milah.* 3) *I anointed you with oil* — That is the שֶׁמֶן הַמִּשְׁחָה, *the oil of anointing* (with which the *Kohanim,* the priests, and the *Mishkan,* the Tabernacle with all its vessels, were anointed. See *Exod.* 30:26-28). 4) *And I clothed you with embroidered garments* — when (Israel) said: נַעֲשֶׂה וְנִשְׁמַע, *We will do and we will listen (ibid.* 24:7), sixty myriads of angels came down and clothed them. Alternately, this refers to the [curtains of the] Tabernacle which were embroidered. (See *ibid.* 26:36). 5) *And I shod you with Tachash leather,* a cover made from the skin of the *Tachash,* [for the *Mishkan*]. (See *ibid. v.* 14). 6) *And I bound you with linen* — i.e. the clothes of the *Kohanim. (See ibid.* 28:39). 7) *And I covered you with silk* — God said to Israel: I have made you significant in the world (a play on the words, מֶשִׁי, *silk,* = מַמָּשׁ: *significant)* ... Alternately, these are the pillars of cloud concerning which it is written: *'The pillar of cloud will not move ...' (ibid.* 13:22) (a play on the words, מֶשִׁי, *silk,* = יָמִישׁ, *to move*). 8) *And I decked you with ornaments* — For God decked them with all manner of ornaments. 9) *And I put bracelets on your hands* — i.e. the two tablets of the covenant. 10) *And a necklace on your neck* — i.e. the *Sefer Torah.* 11) *And I placed a nose ring on your nose* — *Your nose is like a tower in the Lebanon (Shir haShirim* 7:5). (See ArtScroll ed. of *Shir haShirim* p. 181, *footnote* 1). 12) *And earrings on your ears* — These are the ten commandments which implanted themselves in Israel's ears. 13) *And a crown of beauty on your head* — That is the שְׁכִינָה, *the Divine Glory,* as it is written: *And their King passed before them, and HASHEM was at their head' (Michah* 2:13).

9. *Targum:* And I redeemed you from the slavery of the Egyptians, and I removed strong ownership from you and led you into freedom.

1. *Midrashim* attach great significance to the number *thirteen,* mentioned here. The *thirteen* gifts which the Jews were called upon to donate to the *Mishkan (Exod.* 25:3-7), were actually a moral obligation upon them in view of the thirteen favors they had received at the Exodus. Nevertheless, God views them as a voluntary donation, and will reward them with *thirteen* signs of protective love, in Messianic times *(Isaiah* 4:5-6).

[*Maharal* points out that the numerical value of אֶחָד, *one,* is *thirteen* (1+8+4). For this reason *thirteen* covenants were established concerning the בְּרִית מִילָה, *the covenant of circumcision (Nedarim* 31b). Since a בְּרִית, *a covenant* has the purpose of fusing the interests of the two contracting parties (that is to make *'one'* out of them) the number *thirteen* is particularly suited to the concept of covenant.

We may assume that the same idea underlies the triad of *'thirteens'* in the *Midrash* which we have quoted.]

י וְאַלְבִּשֵׁךְ רִקְמָה וָאֶנְעֲלֵךְ תָּחַשׁ וָאֶחְבְּשֵׁךְ
יא בַשֵּׁשׁ וַאֲכַסֵּךְ מֶשִׁי: וָאֶעְדֵּךְ עֶדִי וָאֶתְּנָה
יב צְמִידִים עַל־יָדַיִךְ וְרָבִיד עַל־גְּרוֹנֵךְ: וָאֶתֵּן
נֶזֶם עַל־אַפֵּךְ וַעֲגִילִים עַל־אָזְנָיִךְ וַעֲטֶרֶת
יג תִּפְאֶרֶת בְּרֹאשֵׁךְ: וַתַּעְדִּי זָהָב וָכֶסֶף
וּמַלְבּוּשֵׁךְ °ששי וָמֶשִׁי וְרִקְמָה סֹלֶת °שֵׁשׁ ק׳
וּדְבַשׁ וָשֶׁמֶן °אכלתי וַתִּיפִי בִּמְאֹד מְאֹד °אָכָלְתְּ ק׳
יד וַתִּצְלְחִי לִמְלוּכָה: וַיֵּצֵא לָךְ שֵׁם בַּגּוֹיִם
בְּיָפְיֵךְ כִּי | כָּלִיל הוּא בַּהֲדָרִי אֲשֶׁר־שַׂמְתִּי

10. *Targum:* And I clothed you in embroidered garments from the treasures of your enemies, and I placed precious shoes upon your feet, and I hallowed *Kohanim* from among you to serve before Me, and the High Priest with colored clothes.

וָאַלְבִּשֵׁךְ רִקְמָה — *And I clothed you in embroidered garments.*

See *Rashi* to *Exod.* 26:36.

וָאֶנְעֲלֵךְ תָּחַשׁ — *And shod you in tachash leather.*

We have not translated תַּחַשׁ. This in accordance with *Shabbos* 28b that the *tachash* whose skin was used to make covers for the *Mishkan* was a unique creation which was made available to Moses for that purpose and then disappeared forever.

[*Mizrachi* notes the difficulty that if the תַּחַשׁ promptly became extinct, how was it available for shoes? One of his suggested solutions is, that its temporary existence lasted throughout the forty years that Israel wandered in the desert.]

וָאֶחְבְּשֵׁךְ בַּשֵּׁשׁ — *And I bound you with linen.*

The verb חבש is used mostly in connection with head covering (24:17; also *Exod.* 29:9; *Jonah* 2:6). However, its literal meaning is *to wind around* or *to tie up.* The borrowed usage for the covering of the head is due to the ancient practice of winding a length of material around the head in the fashion of a turban. (See *Ibn Ezra* to *Exod.* 29:9, who relates it to חוֹבֵשׁ, *one who imprisons. Radak* in *Sefer haShorashim* also compares 34:4, *the binding* or *tying up of a wound).*

Thus *Metzudas David* suggests as the meaning of our phrase: *I have tied a linen sash about you.*

11. *Targum:* And I established you firmly with the words of the Torah written on two tablets of stone, and I gave them through Moses. And I hallowed you with the holiness of My great Name.

וָאֶעְדֵּךְ עֶדִי — *Decked you with ornaments.*

Even *Menachem* who did not translate בַּעֲדִי עֲדָיִים of *v.* 7 as 'ornaments', will agree to this translation. In *v.* 7 he considered this translation impossible since the foundling was still naked *(Rabbeinu Tam* in *Teshuvas Dunash).* Here, however, the literal translation fits the context of the verse.

וְרָבִיד עַל גְּרוֹנֵךְ — *And a necklace on your neck.*

Rashi to *Gen.* 41:42 translates רָבִיד as 'necklace'. The root רבד means to *join* or *link something together.*

Rashbam (ibid.) holds that the root

[10] *clothed you in embroidered garments, and shod you in tachash leather; bound you with linen, and covered you with silk;* [11] *decked you with ornaments; put bracelets on your hands and a necklace on your neck;* [12] *placed a ring on your nose, and earrings on your ears and a crown of beauty on your head.*

[13] *And you decked yourself with gold and silver, and your garments were linen, silk, and embroidery. Fine flour, honey, and oil did you eat; you became exceedingly beautiful, fit for royalty.* [14] *Your fame went forth among the nations for your beauty, for it was perfect through My splendor which I placed upon*

רבד means *to spread out* or *cover.* In his view a רָבִיד would be a kind of cloak.

12. *Targum:* And I placed the ark of My covenant among you, and the clouds of My Glory provided shade over you, and an Angel, sent from before Me, leading at your front.

13. *Targum:* And I placed My Tabernacle among you, fashioned from gold and silver and curtains of linen, colored and decorated [and goodly portions like fine flour, like honey and like oil did you eat], and you became wealthy and exceedingly strong. And you became fit and ruled over all kingdoms.

וַתַּעְדִּי זָהָב וָכֶסֶף — *And you decked yourself with gold and silver.*

Israel reacts joyously to God's gifts. She has only one wish — to appear beautiful to Him. She willingly accepts the implications of a dwelling place for the *Shechinah* in her midst, and recognizes that the source of her sustenance is the offerings which she brings *(Harav Breuer).*

וַתִּצְלְחִי לִמְלוּכָה — *Fit for royalty.*

Hirsch (Gen. 24:21) defines צלח as success which was won against difficult odds. By your striving you achieved a regal nature *(Harav Breuer).*

[For the Torah concept of *'royalty',* see *Ibn Ezrah* to *Num.* 6:7. The *Nazirite* has the *'crown of his God on his head'. Ibn Ezra* remarks: Know then, that all men are 'servants' to earthly desires. The king who carries the crown of true royalty on his head, is he who is free from (physical) desires.

Israel, having received the *Torah* and having welcomed the *Shechinah* into its midst, had attained this true royalty].

14. *Targum:* And the fame of [you] *Knesses Israel* went out among the nations, in your beauty, because it was perfect — the glory which I placed upon you, said the Lord God.

In *Radak*'s view the וַתִּצְלְחִי לִמְלוּכָה of the previous verse, and the account of Israel's fame in this verse, refer to the reigns of David and Solomon. Prior to the secession of the Ten Tribes during the reign of Rechavam, Israel had indeed achieved universal acclaim.

15-34. *The third part of the parable:* This describes the infidelity of the foundling. With reckless abandon and unparalleled promiscuity she not only makes herself available, but actively solicits the attentions of every passerby. Unmindful of the fact that it is her husband who has given her precious jewels and luxurious garments, she uses his

טז טו עָלַיִךְ נְאֻם אֲדֹנָי יֱהוִֹה: וַתִּבְטְחִי בְיָפְיֵךְ
טו־טז וַתִּזְנִי עַל־שְׁמֵךְ וַתִּשְׁפְּכִי אֶת־תַּזְנוּתַיִךְ
טז עַל־כָּל־עוֹבֵר לוֹ־יֶהִי: וַתִּקְחִי מִבְּגָדַיִךְ
וַתַּעֲשִׂי־לָךְ בָּמוֹת טְלֻאוֹת וַתִּזְנִי עֲלֵיהֶם

very gifts as blandishments with which to seduce her lovers.

We have had occasion to discuss Israel's lust for 'other gods' (See *comm.* to 6:4 and 8:3).[1]

It is impossible for us to conceptualize this craving, because we have never experienced its like. From the nature of the parable (with its elaboration in Ch. 23), we must assume that in its essence it was an urge to betray God.

[*Harav Yitzchak Hutner* contrasts the urge to worship idols, with that of מִינוּת, *denial of God.* The former is the drive to *'shoulder a yoke of falsehood'*, the latter to *'throw off the yoke of truth'*. *Ramban* loc. cit. points out that the expression that God is קַנָּא, *jealous,* is unique to the sin of idol worship. God is 'jealous' of him *'who gives My glory to another, and My praise to graven images' (Isaiah* 42:8).]

In the annals of Israel's history, the evil inclination towards idol worship is unique, in that it disappeared, not as a result of human energies, but because of prayer for divine intervention.

Sanhedrin 64a relates that this prayer was offered after the building of the Second Temple:

Woe, woe, this [tempter] is the one who destroyed the Temple, burnt the Holy Hall, killed the righteous ones, and sent Israel into exile from their Land. He is still dancing among us. Did You not give him to us that (for conquering him) we should receive reward? We want neither him nor the reward for overcoming him.

The *Talmud* goes on to recount that the prayer was answered and the inclination towards idolatry finally disappeared from Israel.

From *Arachin* 32b it appears that 'conquest by prayer' was not a coincidence. Joshuah is blamed for not having prayed for the removal of this terrible urge in his time. Moses would have done so if only he had been admitted to the Land of Israel.

[Perhaps, by the insight we gain from the comparison of idol-worship to adultery, we can understand why its elimination had to come through prayer and God's direct intervention. If the sin of idol worship is the urge to break

1. We use the literal translation *'other gods'* with reluctance. *Rashi (Exod.* 20:3 based on *Mechilta)* refrains from translating אֱלֹהִים אֲחֵרִים in that manner because it constitutes an implied insult indicating that חַס וְחָלִילָה there are other gods in addition to Hashem. Therefore, *Rashi* there translates, gods who are strange and unresponsive to those who serve them, or whom other people (אֲחֵרִים) call gods.

However, in the context of our chapter, it seems justified to adopt (with *Ramban ibid.)* the literal translation. A wife's faithlessness presupposes the existence of a lover other than her husband.

The cosmic forces which were the focus of original unadulterated idol worship (see *Rambam Mishneh Torah Avodah Zarah* Ch. 1) are the facade behind which God 'hides' Himself from us. From the locus of human perception it is they who control the destiny of man. (See *comm.* to 8:16). In terms of human perception, they seem indeed to be 'other gods'. That they were viewed as such by the people can be seen from *Sanhedrin* 64a which relates that when the lust for idol worship was finally exorcised from Israel, it burst out 'like a flaming lion' from the *Holy of Holies.* It would seem that in the people's minds their idols occupied a place as prominent as that of the true God.

you. The words of my Lord HASHEM/ELOHIM. 15 *But*
you trusted in your beauty, and philandered because
of your fame. And you poured your harlotries upon
every passerby. It was his! 16 *So you took of your*
garments and made yourself harlequin platforms,
and philandered upon them. This should not have

loose from our dependence on God's providence, then the only true repentance is the complete and unreserved affirmation of that dependence. This was indicated by declaring in fervent prayer that only He could free us from the shackles of idolatry. (See *Arachin* loc. cit. where the elimination of idol worship is compared to dwelling in a *Succah*, i.e. in entering the booth where one is totally enveloped by the holiness of the commandment, one acknowledges the benevolent all encompassing providence of God and our complete dependence upon it.)]

15. וַתִּבְטְחִי בְיָפְיֵךְ — *But you trusted in your beauty.*

Most commentators see this phrase as analagous to *Deut.* 32:15: *And Yeshurun became fat and rebelled. (Radak, Eliezer of Beaugency).* According to them וַתִּבְטְחִי would better be translated *you were confident* or *self-assured* (because of your beauty), as in *Proverbs* 28:1.

However, *Metzudas David* suggests: You put your trust in your spiritual beauty. You were sure that because of your beauty, i.e. your goodness and uniqueness, God would not forsake you in spite of your infidelity. This interpretation would place the allusion in consonance with the many other passages which we have recognized, which explained the obduracy of Jerusalem's dwellers as based on what they thought was a special relationship to God. (See *footnote* to *Pref. Remarks* Ch. 11).

וַתִּשְׁפְּכִי אֶת תַּזְנוּתַיִךְ — *And you poured your harlotries.*

You showed your beauty to all passersby, until the desire for your harlotry prevailed upon them to ravish you *(Rashi).*

Radak explains even more graphically: As a vessel runs over when it is filled so your harlotry was so great, that it poured over and engulfed others.

לוֹ יֶהִי — *It was his* [lit. *'to him it will be'*]

Whoever requested your harlotry was granted his wish *(Rashi).*

זְנוּת; *licentiousness* is feminine, hence the verb should have been לוֹ תֶּהִי, *to him it* (fem.) *shall be. Radak* avoids the difficulty by interpolating the implied masc. word חֵשֶׁק, *desire.* Your desire was extended to him.

Targum renders: *This was not a good thing to do.* That is, he reads לוֹ as though it were spelled לֹא, *not.*

The allusion is to the worship of the Golden Calf and the idolatry which, in the tradition of the Sages, was practiced by the tribe of *Dan* even in the desert *(Rashi).*

16. בָּמוֹת טְלֻאוֹת — *Harlequin platforms.*

I.e. platforms of widely diverse colors.

טלא means to patch.[The travelers in *Joshua* 9:5 wore נְעָלוֹת מְטֻלָּאוֹת, which as interpreted by *Berachos* 43b means *patched shoes.*] Since patches often have various colors, a dappled, variegated effect, is described in Scripture as טָלוּא. Hence, the dappled sheep of *Gen.* 30:32.

The harlot covered her platform with (or as *Radak* comments, built up her platform from) many gaily colored patches of cloth, in order to attract men by its pleasing appearance.

יז לֹא בָאוֹת וְלֹא יִהְיֶה: וַתִּקְחִי כְּלֵי
תִפְאַרְתֵּךְ מִזְּהָבִי וּמִכַּסְפִּי אֲשֶׁר נָתַתִּי לָךְ
יח וַתַּעֲשִׂי־לָךְ צַלְמֵי זָכָר וַתִּזְנִי־בָם: וַתִּקְחִי
אֶת־בִּגְדֵי רִקְמָתֵךְ וַתְּכַסִּים וְשַׁמְנִי
יט וּקְטָרְתִּי °נתתי לִפְנֵיהֶם: וְלַחְמִי אֲשֶׁר־
נָתַתִּי לָךְ סֹלֶת וָשֶׁמֶן וּדְבַשׁ הֶאֱכַלְתִּיךְ
וּנְתַתִּיהוּ לִפְנֵיהֶם לְרֵיחַ נִיחֹחַ וַיֶּהִי נְאֻם
כ אֲדֹנָי יֱהֹוִה: וַתִּקְחִי אֶת־בָּנַיִךְ וְאֶת־
בְּנוֹתַיִךְ אֲשֶׁר יָלַדְתְּ לִי וַתִּזְבָּחִים לָהֶם

°נָתַתְּ ק׳

The allusion is to the wide variety of altars which were built and to the many deities which were worshipped *(Radak).*

לֹא בָאוֹת — *This should not have been.*

The translation follows *Rashi. Radak* renders: *This shall never come about* (synonymous with וְלֹא יִהְיֶה) while *Metzudas David* translates: It had never been so.

The intent, according to all versions, is that the profusion of idols to which Jerusalem proclaimed allegiance was unique. Never before nor ever again would it be duplicated.

17. צַלְמֵי זָכָר — *Images of man.*

Statues of the male figure through which she could satisfy her carnal cravings *(Metzudas David)* (compare *Rashi* to *I Kings* 15:13).

The unnaturally raging lust for idolatrous practices knew no barriers of propriety.

And all this with זְהָבִי and כַּסְפִּי, *My gold and My silver* (compare Hoshea 2:10). God Himself had given them the riches which they now turned against Him.

19. וְלַחְמִי אֲשֶׁר נָתַתִּי לָךְ — *And My bread which I gave you.*

As above, the betrayal is the more shocking because God's own gifts are used to propitiate the false deities to whom the people prostrated themselves.

Rashi quotes the *Midrash* that reference is to the heavenly מָן, *manna,* which was placed in worship before the Golden Calf.

According to the *Midrash,* the verses in *Nehemiah* 9:18-19 refer to this outrage and express amazement that, in spite of their flagrant profanation, God continued to send the *manna,* and did not forsake His people.[1]

וַיֶּהִי — *And so it was.*

You cannot deny it, for I, God, know

1. The use of the *manna* for the idol worship is perfidy at its most heinous. *Manna* is the tangible form of זִיו הַשְּׁכִינָה, the *'Shine of Divine Glory'* and expresses the height of spiritual perfection to which Israel rose at the banks of the Sea of Reeds *(Ramban* to *Exod.* 16:6).

Using it as a sacrifice to the Golden Calf, symbolized a brutal repudiation of Israel's holiness, in favor of subjugation to the gross materialism represented by the idol.

That God continued to allow the *manna* to fall from heaven and at the very moment of their infidelity continued to shield them lovingly within the עַנְנֵי כָבוֹד the *'clouds of glory'* (see *Nehemiah* loc. cit.), is an example of His boundless loving-kindness, which sustains the sinner even at the very moment of his sin. (For treatment of this theme, see *Tomer Devorah* by *Rabbi Moshe Kordovero* Ch. 1).

XVI been, *and shall not be.* [17] *Then you took your*
17-20 *beautiful objects, from My gold and My silver which*
I gave you, and made yourself images of man, and
philandered with them; [18] *took your embroidered*
garments and covered them, and My oil and My in-
cense you placed before them; [19] *My bread which I*
gave you — fine flour, oil, and honey did I feed you —
and placed it before them for a pleasant savor. And
so it was. The words of my Lord HASHEM / ELOHIM.
[20] *Then you took your sons and daughters whom*
you begot for Me, and these you slaughtered to them,

it and testify that it was so *(Metzudas David).*

20. וַתִּקְחִי אֶת בָּנַיִךְ וְאֶת בְּנוֹתַיִךְ — *Then you took your sons and daughters.*

The children are not spared. In the frenzy of her lust, their mother will slaughter even them to appease the voracious appetite of her lovers. But in doing so, her infamy extends beyond her own infidelity — הַמְעַט מִתַּזְנוּתָיִךְ, *was your harlotry so trivial?* She is tampering with the future. They may be *her children,* but they were *'born to Me',* they are the seed from which a future of holiness is destined to grow *(Targum).*

An individual, even an entire generation, may be dispensable in the context of the 'body' of a nation whose existence spans eternity. (See *comm.* to 5:1, for a discussion of this theme based on *Yisroel Kedoshim* by *Rabbi Zadok HaKohen).* But when the parent-child relationship is violated, the act transpires within the dimensions of eternity. It takes on a significance beyond that of the individual for it implies a disdain for the institution that assures survival of the nation. (Compare *Ramban's* remarks to the prohibition of slaughtering the mother animal and her offspring on the same day, and the prohibition against taking the mother bird together with the chicks or the eggs [*Deut.* 22:6] In his view these acts offend the מִין, the *species,* rather than the individual animal.)

[This verse acknowledges that children can be considered as their mother's, (in contrast to the clothes, ornaments and food of the previous verses which had come wholly from the husband), for it was she who bore them. The father's claim is valid only in that the children are the potential of his future.

The next verse takes the argument further. They are really בָּנַי, *My children.* Because the children are vital to his ultimate survival, the father has as real a claim to them as the mother. And God had already proclaimed: *'You are the children of HASHEM your God' (Deut.* 14:1).]

(For another aspect of the sin of child sacrifice see *comm.* to 20:26).

אֲשֶׁר יָלַדְתְּ לִי — *Whom you begot for Me.*

If a man had five sons he would raise four of them for idol worship, and he would send one to study Torah. If he then decided to sacrifice one of them to the *Molech,* he would choose the son who was studying Torah. (*Rashi* quoting *Midrash Tanchumah* to explain the term *'borne to Me.').*

Rashi himself holds that the term

כא לֶאֱכוֹל הַמְעַט °מתזנותך: וַתִּשְׁחֲטִי אֶת־
כב בָּנַי וַתִּתְּנִים בְּהַעֲבִיר אוֹתָם לָהֶם: וְאֵת
כָּל־תּוֹעֲבֹתַיִךְ וְתַזְנֻתַיִךְ לֹא °זכרתי אֶת־
יְמֵי נְעוּרָיִךְ בִּהְיוֹתֵךְ עֵרֹם וְעֶרְיָה
כג מִתְבּוֹסֶסֶת בְּדָמֵךְ הָיִית: וַיְהִי אַחֲרֵי כָּל־
רָעָתֵךְ אוֹי אוֹי לָךְ נְאֻם אֲדֹנָי יֱהֹוִה:
כד וַתִּבְנִי־לָךְ גֶּב וַתַּעֲשִׂי־לָךְ רָמָה בְּכָל־
כה רְחוֹב: אֶל־כָּל־רֹאשׁ דֶּרֶךְ בָּנִית רָמָתֵךְ
וַתְּתַעֲבִי אֶת־יָפְיֵךְ וַתְּפַשְּׂקִי אֶת־רַגְלַיִךְ
כו לְכָל־עוֹבֵר וַתַּרְבִּי אֶת־°תזנותך: וַתִּזְנִי
אֶל־בְּנֵי־מִצְרַיִם שְׁכֵנַיִךְ גִּדְלֵי בָשָׂר וַתַּרְבִּי
כז אֶת־תַּזְנֻתֵךְ לְהַכְעִיסֵנִי: וְהִנֵּה נָטִיתִי יָדִי

°מִתַּזְנוּתַיִךְ ק׳
°זָכַרְתְּ ק׳
°תַּזְנוּתַיִךְ ק׳

refers to the first-born sons, who would normally be sanctified for God (*Exodus* 13:2).

הַמְעַט מִתַּזְנוּתָיִךְ — *Was your harlotry so trivial?*

Have you not sinned against Me enough without perpetrating this infamy? *(Metzudas David)*

21. בְּהַעֲבִיר אוֹתָם לָהֶם — *By causing them [the children] to pass for them* i.e. the idols..

For a discussion of the word בְּהַעֲבִיר in this connection, see *comm.* to 20:26.

22. וְאֵת כָּל תּוֹעֲבֹתַיִךְ — *And with all your abominations* ...

אֵת can have the meaning, *'with'* as well as simply denoting the accusative case (as it does in the next phrase: אֵת יְמֵי נְעוּרָיִךְ).

The intent is, that, even at the depth of her depravity, she might have been able to pull herself out of the downward spiral of iniquity. If only she had allowed her mind to reflect for a moment on her past; if she had but realized that, in her lowliness it had not been *Ba'al* or *Molech* who had stood by her! *(Harav Breuer)*

Malbim translates: *'Through your abominations.'* Because she was so involved in harlotry, she came to forget her antecedents.

לֹא זָכַרְתְּ אֶת יְמֵי נְעוּרָיִךְ — *You remembered not the days of your youth.*

The kindness which I did you while you were still a young nation in Egypt *(Rashi)*.

זָכַרְתִּי is spelled with an extra י as though it were pronounced לֹא זָכַרְתִּי, *'I' did not remember. Radak* explains that this alludes to the fact that when God poured out His kindness to Israel in its youth He chose not to *'remember'*, or consider that there would come a day when they would be disloyal to him.

[For the doctrine, that God does kindness without reference to the future wickedness of the recipient, see *Rosh Hashanah* 16b.]

23. וַיְהִי אַחֲרֵי כָּל רָעָתֵךְ — *What should have been after all your wickedness?*

The translation follows *Targum*.

XVI
21-26

to devour! Was your harlotry so trivial 21 *that you*
slew My children and offered them by causing them
to pass for them? 22 *And with all your abominations*
and harlotries you remembered not the days of your
youth, when you were naked and bare, downtrodden
in your blood were you.

23 *What should have been after all your*
wickedness? Woe, woe to you! The words of my
Lord HASHEM/ELOHIM.

24 *And you built yourself an eminent place; and*
made yourself a lofty place in every street. 25 *At the*
head of every road you built your lofty places, and
you have made an abomination of your beauty, and
opened your legs to every passerby and multiplied
your licentiousness; 26 *and philandered with the*
Egyptians, your neighbors, great of flesh; and mul-
tiplied your harlotries to provoke Me.

'What shall be your end after all your wickedness?'

Radak renders: *And it was* [so] *after all your wickedness* i.e. because you were disloyal to Me, you once again became as naked and forsaken as you were then in the days of your earliest youth.

אוֹי אוֹי לָךְ — *Woe, woe to you.*

Targum, who usually assigns separate meanings to dual expressions (see above *v.* 6 and 13:10) renders: 'Woe that you sinned and woe that you did not repent.'

24. גַּב ... רָמָה — *An eminent place ... a lofty place.*

The eminent and lofty places are to be used for the practice of harlotry (*v.* 16). At the same time, of course, these 'places' allude to the proliferating idolatrous altars which were generally set up on hills and mountains.

25. וַתְּתַעֲבִי אֶת יָפְיֵךְ — *And you have made an abomination of your beauty.*

'You desecrated your holiness' (*Targum*).

וַתְּפַשְּׂקִי אֶת רַגְלַיִךְ — *And opened your legs.*

[The unsparing explication reflects the shameless abandon, with which Israel flaunted her lust for the idols. Compare *footnote* to 20:23.]

26. גִּדְלֵי בָשָׂר — *Great of flesh.*

Targum renders מְסַרְבְּלֵי בְּסַר which simply means *'fleshy'* and indicates a sensous, self-indulgent nature (*Avodah Zarah* 2b).

However, *Rashi, Radak*, and *Metzudas David* all see בָּשָׂר as a euphemism for the male organ of generation, as in *Leviticus* 15:3.

לְהַכְעִיסֵנִי — *To provoke Me.*

The multitude of your infidelities was so great, that it could not have been caused only by carnal desire. Your intention must also have been to provoke Me (*Metzudas David*).

טז עָלַיִךְ וָאֶגְרַע חֻקֵּךְ וָאֶתְּנֵךְ בְּנֶפֶשׁ
כח־לב שֹׂנְאוֹתַיִךְ בְּנוֹת פְּלִשְׁתִּים הַנִּכְלָמוֹת
כח מִדַּרְכֵּךְ זִמָּה: וַתִּזְנִי אֶל־בְּנֵי אַשּׁוּר
מִבִּלְתִּי שָׂבְעָתֵךְ וַתִּזְנִים וְגַם לֹא שָׂבָעַתְּ:
כט וַתַּרְבִּי אֶת־תַּזְנוּתֵךְ אֶל־אֶרֶץ כְּנַעַן
ל כַּשְׂדִּימָה וְגַם־בְּזֹאת לֹא שָׂבָעַתְּ: מָה
אֲמֻלָה לִבָּתֵךְ נְאֻם אֲדֹנָי יֱהֹוִה בַּעֲשׂוֹתֵךְ
אֶת־כָּל־אֵלֶּה מַעֲשֵׂה אִשָּׁה זוֹנָה שַׁלָּטֶת:
לא בִּבְנוֹתַיִךְ גַּבֵּךְ בְּרֹאשׁ כָּל־דֶּרֶךְ וְרָמָתֵךְ
°עשׂיתי בְּכָל־רְחוֹב וְלֹא־°הייתי כַּזּוֹנָה °עָשִׂית °הָיִית ק׳
לב לְקַלֵּס אֶתְנָן: הָאִשָּׁה הַמְּנָאָפֶת תַּחַת

27. וָאֶגְרַע חֻקֵּךְ — *(And I have) diminished your allotment.*

(See *Genesis* 47:22. Also *Ramban* to *Exodus* 15:25).

Reference is to the famine in the days of the Judges [*Ruth* 1:1] *(Rashi).*

בְּנוֹת פְּלִשְׁתִּים הַנִּכְלָמוֹת מִדַּרְכֵּךְ זִמָּה — *The daughters of the Philistines who are ashamed of your lewd ways.*

Had I sent prophets to them they would have humbled themselves. But you did not repent from your sinful ways *(Targum).*

[For an elaboration of the theme that Israel in its degradation sinks to lower depths than other nations, see footnote to 3:6. See also *comm.* to 5:7 and 8:7-12.]

Sifri to *Deut.* 32:17 reports, that Israel was the supplier of idols to the whole world. If a gentile came across an unfamiliar idol, he would say: 'This is an idol of the Jews'.

28. מִבִּלְתִּי שָׂבְעָתֵךְ — *Because you were insatiable.*

Because your licentiousness with Egypt (*v.* 26) did not satisfy you *(Rashi).*

Targum renders the verse: And you strayed after the Assyrians because you did not know the Torah, and you strayed with them, *and knew no repentance.*

29. אֶל אֶרֶץ כְּנַעַן כַּשְׂדִּימָה — *With the land of the peddlers, towards Chaldea.*

With *Rashi* and *Metzudas David* we have translated אֶרֶץ כְּנַעַן as *land of the peddlers* (as in *Proverbs* 31:24. See also *Rashi* to *Gen.* 38:2) in order to solve the difficulty of the seemingly incongruous equating of the lands of Canaan and Chaldea.

Radak reads: You have increased your licentiousness by [seeking inspiration from] the land of Canaan [as it had been before Joshua's conquest, and, not satisfied with that, you turned] to Chaldea [for further inspiration].

Eliezer of Beaugency seeks a solution by comparing our verse to 23:14-17. There Yechezkel tells how Israel, while still in its own land, cast longing glances towards Chaldea, lusting after the variety of their gods; how she sent messengers inviting Chaldea to come and share her bed of love.

The meaning would then be: You increased your licentiousness within the

[27] *Now see! I stretched out My hand against you,
diminished your allotment, delivered you to the
whim of those that hate you, the daughters of the
Philistines who are ashamed of your lewd way.*
[28] *And you philandered with the Assyrians, because
you were insatiable; and you philandered with them,
but you were still not sated.* [29] *Then you increased
your harlotry with the land of the peddlers — towards
Chaldea. But even with this you were unsated.*
[30] *How corrupt is your heart!, the words of my Lord
HASHEM/ELOHIM, when you do all these, the deeds
of a domineering, philandering woman.* [31] *When you
build your eminent place at the head of every road,
and your lofty place have you made in every street,
and been unlike a harlot, praising hire.* [32] *Adulterous*

land of Canaan [not called the Land of Israel because they had degraded it to the level of its former depravity] by looking towards the Chaldeans.

30. מָה אֲמֻלָה לִבָּתֵךְ — *How corrupt is your heart!*

The translation follows *Rashi.* In the same vein *Targum* renders: How great is the wickedness of your heart!

Radak and *Metzudas Zion* translate: How your heart is cut off [from sensitivity to the evil of your ways]. *Radak* comments that the unusual feminine form of לֵב, is intended to underline its ineffectiveness.

Menachem and *Radak* in *Sefer haShorashim* translate: How weak is your heart!

אִשָּׁה זוֹנָה שַׁלָּטֶת — *A domineering, philandering woman.*

The translation follows *Targum* who renders: A harlot who rules over herself, i.e. she is answerable only to herself (see also *Metzudas David).*

Rashi interprets the word, as if in the passive mood. A harlot ruled by her evil inclination (or her passion).

31. וְלֹא הָיִית כַּזּוֹנָה לְקַלֵּס אֶתְנָן — *And (you have) been unlike a harlot, praising hire.*

A typical harlot will rejoice in a beautiful gift given her as her hire. To you the gift was of secondary importance. It was the act of licentiousness itself which attracted you *(Rashi).*

Radak and *Metzudas David* take קלס in the opposite meaning: To *'talk disparagingly', to 'denigrate'.* A normal harlot will play down the gift which she is given, in order that she might obtain a better one. In the heat of your desire you make do with anything.

אֶתְנַן, *Rashi* explains the root (either תנה or תנן) to mean: *to hire.* In Scripture it is used exclusively as the payment made to a harlot.

Radak (Sefer haShorashim) traces the word to the root תנה meaning *to stipulate* or *make a condition.* The payment to the harlot is an אֶתְנַן, because it was stipulated that it be given to her.

32. הָאִשָּׁה הַמְנָאֶפֶת — [*The*] *adulterous wife* [lit. *'woman'*]

According to *Rashi,* this verse ad-

לג אִישָׁהּ תִּקַּח אֶת־זָרִים׃ לְכָל־זֹנוֹת יִתְּנוּ־
נֵדֶה וְאַתְּ נָתַתְּ אֶת־נְדָנַיִךְ לְכָל־מְאַהֲבַיִךְ
וַתִּשְׁחֳדִי אוֹתָם לָבוֹא אֵלַיִךְ מִסָּבִיב
לד בְּתַזְנוּתָיִךְ׃ וַיְהִי־בָךְ הֶפֶךְ מִן־הַנָּשִׁים
בְּתַזְנוּתַיִךְ וְאַחֲרַיִךְ לֹא זוּנָּה וּבְתִתֵּךְ
אֶתְנָן וְאֶתְנַן לֹא נִתַּן־לָךְ וַתְּהִי לְהֶפֶךְ׃
לה-לו לָכֵן זוֹנָה שִׁמְעִי דְּבַר־יהוה׃ כֹּה־
אָמַר אֲדֹנָי יֱהוִה יַעַן הִשָּׁפֵךְ נְחֻשְׁתֵּךְ
וַתִּגָּלֶה עֶרְוָתֵךְ בְּתַזְנוּתַיִךְ עַל־מְאַהֲבָיִךְ
וְעַל כָּל־גִּלּוּלֵי תוֹעֲבוֹתַיִךְ וְכִדְמֵי בָנַיִךְ

dresses Israel directly. You, Israel, are like an adulterous wife, who seeks satisfaction from strangers, even though she is married [and would presumably have her physical needs filled by her husband] *(Metzudas David).*

33-34. These verses continue the thought begun in *v.* 31. In this harlot's eyes the hire is unimportant. [Israel serves idols without making her allegiance to them dependent on whether she benefits from them]. She will forego her hire completely, and even pay lovers to come to her. [Normally a people would be expected to be loyal to their own God, and denigrate the gods of foreign nations. Israel, in marked contrast to the norm, lusted for the strange gods] *(Radak).*

33. נֵדֶה is synonymous with אֶתְנָן. It is not found elsewhere in Scripture.

34. וַיְהִי בָךְ הֶפֶךְ מִן הַנָּשִׁים — *So in you was the opposite of other women.*

Once more, the stress is on Israel's depravity, contrasting it unfavorably with that of the nations. See *comm.* to *v.* 27.

35-42. The fourth part of the parable describes the vengeance which the wronged husband exacts from his faithless wife. Her lovers will turn against her as he reveals her disgrace to them. In this way her licentious behavior will finally cease. The husband's anger will have been spent, and the stage set for a reconciliation.

Israel will be reconciled with God when she grasps the nature of her uniqueness. When Balaam unwillingly blessed the Jewish people he said *(Numbers* 23:9) הֶן עָם לְבָדָד יִשְׁכֹּן, *See this people dwells alone. Shemos Rabbah* 15:8 remarks on the word הֶן (the letters of which have the numerical value of 5, and 50 respectively), that it denotes uniqueness. All other numbers have partners. For ex., 1+9=10, as do 2+8, 3+7 and so on. So too, 10+90=100 and so on. The only exceptions are 5 and 50; they combine with no other number. Thus, the letters הן (5 and 50) stand alone and are, therefore, the fitting paean to Israel's solitude.

Maharal (Netzach Yisrael 13) sees this as the reason why the letter נ, *nun,* is left out of the acrostic formed by the initial letters of the twenty-one verses of *Ps.* 145 *(Ashrei). Talmud Berachos* 4b explains the omission because נ is the initial letter of the verse *(Amos* 5:2): *She has fallen* (נָפְלָה) *and will not rise again, the virgin of Israel. Maharal* explains that the association of the letter נ with נְפִילָה *falling* is not coincidental but

wife, who under her husband takes strangers! 33 *To*
all harlots are given gifts, but you have given your
gifts to all your lovers, and bribed them to come to
you from all around, with your harlotries. 34 *So in*
you was the opposite of other women in your
harlotries, and after you will be no such harlotry — in
that you gave hire, but hire was not given to you.
Thus you have become the opposite.
35 *Therefore O harlot! Hear the word of* HASHEM.
36 *So says my Lord* HASHEM/ELOHIM: *Since*
outpoured was your shame and revealed was your
nakedness, in your harlotries with your lovers, and
because of all the idols of your abominations, and in
accordance with the blood of your children, which

essential. נ stands alone (see above) and therefore must fall. The *Talmud* (loc. cit.) goes on to say that in the following verse of *Ashrei (Ps.* 145:14): סוֹמֵךְ ה׳ לְכָל הַנֹּפְלִים, *God supports all those who fall,* the antidote to Israel's helplessness is given. Without God the *'virgin of Israel'* must stumble. Supported by God, she stands straight.

This is the truth which Israel will learn. She has no real friends. *All the nations hate Israel (Bereishis Rabbah* 63:9). The strangers whom she had thought of as her lovers turn against her with a ferocious hatred, leaving her naked and bare as she had been in her youth.

God's anger will have been dissipated in the moment of truth, when — amid the burning ruins of the Temple, laid waste by the very Chaldeans to whom she had turned with such longing glances *(v.* 29) — Israel turns once more to Him. At that moment the *Cheruvim* on the Holy Ark, will once more be locked in loving embrace, symbolizing the love between God and Israel. (See *footnote* to 7:4).

35. לָכֵן זוֹנָה — *Therefore, O harlot.*

Targum softens the uncompromising severity of this salutation. He renders: Therefore, *Knesses Israel* whose actions are like those of a harlot. (See *footnote* to 14:4).

36. יַעַן הִשָּׁפֵךְ נְחֻשְׁתֵּךְ — *Since outpoured was your shame.*

We have followed *Targum*'s euphemism. Almost all commentators comment that נְחֹשֶׁת in our verse, is used to describe the lower part of the female body, just as the term is used in *Mishnaic* Hebrew to describe the base of a stove. The phrase is assumed to parallel וַתִּגָּלֶה עֶרְוָתֵךְ.

The verb הִשָּׁפֵךְ, *has been poured out* is used in *Rashi*'s view to describe the flow issuing from the woman's body from frequent cohabitation, while *Radak* and *Metzudas David* see it simply as a synonym for תִּגָּלֶה, *revealed,* i.e. a thing is open and revealed while it is being poured out.

Eliezer of Beaugency is almost alone in translating נְחֻשְׁתֵּךְ as *your copper.* You have publicized your lustful heart and licentious spirit by your promiscuity, even as copper and impurities pour out in full sight when subjected to a fire.

וְכִדְמֵי בָנַיִךְ — *And in accordance with the blood of your children.*

The punishment to be meted out to

לז אֲשֶׁר נָתַתְּ לָהֶם: לָכֵן הִנְנִי מְקַבֵּץ אֶת־
כָּל־מְאַהֲבַיִךְ אֲשֶׁר עָרַבְתְּ עֲלֵיהֶם וְאֵת
כָּל־אֲשֶׁר אָהַבְתְּ עַל כָּל־אֲשֶׁר שָׂנֵאת
וְקִבַּצְתִּי אֹתָם עָלַיִךְ מִסָּבִיב וְגִלֵּיתִי
עֶרְוָתֵךְ אֲלֵהֶם וְרָאוּ אֶת־כָּל־עֶרְוָתֵךְ:
לח וּשְׁפַטְתִּיךְ מִשְׁפְּטֵי נֹאֲפוֹת וְשֹׁפְכֹת דָּם
לט וּנְתַתִּיךְ דַּם חֵמָה וְקִנְאָה: וְנָתַתִּי אֹתָךְ
בְּיָדָם וְהָרְסוּ גַבֵּךְ וְנִתְּצוּ רָמֹתַיִךְ
וְהִפְשִׁיטוּ אוֹתָךְ בְּגָדַיִךְ וְלָקְחוּ כְּלֵי
מ תִפְאַרְתֵּךְ וְהִנִּיחוּךְ עֵירֹם וְעֶרְיָה: וְהֶעֱלוּ
עָלַיִךְ קָהָל וְרָגְמוּ אוֹתָךְ בָּאָבֶן וּבִתְּקוּךְ
מא בְּחַרְבוֹתָם: וְשָׂרְפוּ בָתַּיִךְ בָּאֵשׁ וְעָשׂוּ־בָךְ
שְׁפָטִים לְעֵינֵי נָשִׁים רַבּוֹת וְהִשְׁבַּתִּיךְ
מב מִזּוֹנָה וְגַם־אֶתְנַן לֹא תִתְּנִי־עוֹד: וַהֲנִחֹתִי
חֲמָתִי בָּךְ וְסָרָה קִנְאָתִי מִמֵּךְ וְשָׁקַטְתִּי
מג וְלֹא אֶכְעַס עוֹד: יַעַן אֲשֶׁר לֹא־°זכרתי

°זָכַרְתְּ ק׳

her is מִדָּה כְּנֶגֶד מִדָּה, *a measure for a measure.* Her blood will be shed even as she had shed the blood of her children, to appease her lovers *(Radak).*

Rashi interprets כִּדְמֵי as though it were written בִּדְמֵי, *And because of the blood ...* See *Ramban Gen* 25:31, for the use of the prefix כ in this manner.

37. אֲשֶׁר עָרַבְתְּ עֲלֵיהֶם — *To whom you have been pleasant.*

This translation follows *Radak* and *Metzudas David,* who take ערב in its meaning of *sweetness* or *pleasantness.*

Eliezer of Beaugency takes the root in its meaning of *pledging, taking on an obligation.* You guaranteed your loyalty to them.

וְאֵת כָּל אֲשֶׁר אָהַבְתְּ עַל כָּל אֲשֶׁר שָׂנֵאת — *All whom you loved with all whom you hated.*

All the nations will join in the plunder of Jerusalem; former allies, such as Egypt, Assyria, and the Chaldeans, together with constant enemies, such as the Philistines *(Mahari Kara).*

וְגִלֵּיתִי עֶרְוָתֵךְ אֲלֵהֶם — *And uncover your nakedness to them.*

Just as a harlot is punished by makeing her stand unclothed in public, so Israel will be exposed to attack without protection *(Metzudas David).*

38. וּשְׁפַטְתִּיךְ מִשְׁפְּטֵי נֹאֲפוֹת — *And I will punish you with the punishments of adultresses.*

See *comm.* to **11:10**, for the meaning of שפט.

וּנְתַתִּיךְ דַּם חֵמָה וְקִנְאָה — *And emplace you for a bloody death of anger and jealousy.*

you gave them; 37 therefore see! I will gather all your
lovers to whom you have been pleasant — all whom
you loved with all whom you hated — gather them
against you from around, and uncover your
nakedness to them. Then they will see all your
nakedness. 38 And I will punish you with the punishments of adultresses and murderesses, and emplace
you for a bloody death of anger and jealousy. 39 Then
I shall place you in their hands, and they will destroy
your eminent places and break down your lofty
places, strip you of your clothes and take your
beautiful vessels, and leave you naked and bare.
40 And they will raise up against you an assemblage
and pelt you with a stone and pierce you with their
sword; 41 they will burn your houses with fire, and
execute punishments against you before the eyes of
many women. And I will make you stop being a
harlot, and also hire will you give no more.
42 And I shall relieve My fury in you, and My
jealousy shall turn away from you. Then shall I rest
and be angry nevermore.
43 Because you did not remember the days of your

The translation follows *Targum* and commentators.

39. גַּב and רָמָה are the platforms mentioned in *v.* 24. In the parable they are set aside for use in acts of licentiousness. Allusion is to the altars which were used for idol worship.

Having misused the gifts which God had given her, and having therefore lost them, Israel remains once more bare and naked as she had been before God took her to Himself.

40. וְרָגְמוּ...וּבִתְּקוּךְ — *Pelt...and pierce.*

Radak comments that the stoning and the piercing by the sword could not have been meant to kill the harlot since *v.* 41 obviously assumes her to be still alive. They must have been means of punishing and disgracing her.

41. וְהִשְׁבַּתִּיךְ — *And I will stop you* [lit. *'and I will cause you to cease'*]

Having endured the tortures mentioned above, she will cease to be a harlot. Even if she wanted to offer herself to a lover (*v.* 34), a disgraced woman would not be acceptable.

42. See *comm.* to 5:13.

[This verse tells of the husband's appeasement. The subsequent passages can easily be viewed as the interpretation of the parable. As noted above, our division of the parable into four parts was done with the sole purpose of reducing the unwieldiness of the commentary to this extremely long chapter.]

43. לֹא זָכַרְתְּ אֶת יְמֵי נְעוּרָיִךְ — *You did not remember the days of your youth.*

The kindness which I did you at the

טז
מד־מו

°עָשִׂית ק׳

אֶת־יְמֵי נְעוּרַיִךְ וַתִּרְגְּזִי־לִי בְּכָל־אֵלֶּה
וְגַם־אֲנִי הֵא דַּרְכֵּךְ | בְּרֹאשׁ נָתַתִּי נְאֻם
אֲדֹנָי יֱהוִה וְלֹא °עשיתי אֶת־הַזִּמָּה עַל
מד כָּל־תּוֹעֲבֹתָיִךְ: הִנֵּה כָּל־הַמֹּשֵׁל עָלַיִךְ
מה יִמְשֹׁל לֵאמֹר כְּאִמָּה בִּתָּהּ: בַּת־אִמֵּךְ אַתְּ
גֹּעֶלֶת אִישָׁהּ וּבָנֶיהָ וַאֲחוֹת אֲחוֹתֵךְ אַתְּ
אֲשֶׁר גָּעֲלוּ אַנְשֵׁיהֶן וּבְנֵיהֶן אִמְּכֶן חִתִּית
מו וַאֲבִיכֶן אֱמֹרִי: וַאֲחוֹתֵךְ הַגְּדוֹלָה שֹׁמְרוֹן

dawn of your nationhood *(Radak* and *Metzudas David).*

The full fury of God's anger is released against Israel because of her wanton disregard of the obligations which a sense of gratitude would have imposed on her.[1]

God had said: זָכַרְתִּי לָךְ חֶסֶד נְעוּרַיִךְ *(Jeremiah* 2:2), *I remember for you the kindness of your youth.*

He kept His love awake, even after Israel's betrayal of Him. But Israel has not remembered.

הֵא is a contraction of the word הִנֵּה, See!

וְלֹא עָשִׂית אֶת הַזִּמָּה — *But you did not consider this.* [lit. *'you did not do the plan'*].

The translation follows *Targum* who renders: *'You did not make a plan to repent for all your abominations.' Rashi* supports this interpretation, stating: The word זִמָּה in Scripture is always a *plan*, sometimes with good intentions and sometimes with bad.

Radak translates: You did not consider this, while you were committing all your abominations.

Metzudas David takes זִמָּה as a *'shameful act'* and reads the phrase as a rhetorical question: 'Have you not committed this lewdness in addition to all your abominations?'

44. כְּאִמָּה בִּתָּהּ — *Like mother, like daughter* [lit. *'is her daughter'*]

A מָשָׁל, *pithy saying,* which compares Israel, the daughter, to the land of *Canaan,* the mother.

Nothing has changed since Israel came to Canaan and God's Land is once more plunged into the abominations which had marked it as a symbol of depravity before they came.

45. בַּת אִמֵּךְ אַתְּ — *Your mother's daughter are you.*

You are typical of the people who have lived on this Land.

גֹּעֶלֶת אִישָׁהּ וּבָנֶיהָ — *Spewing forth her husband and her children.*

The translation follows *Rashi* and other commentators who take געל in *Kal* (usually: *'to loathe')* in our verse, to have the meaning of *Hiph'il, the causative: 'to vomit out'* or to reject.

In accordance with its unique character, as the Land of God's particular providence, Eretz Yisrael will not tolerate sin within its boundaries (*Ramban, Lev.* 18:25). Israel had been warned that if it would not live a life of holiness in accordance with the dictates of the Torah, it would be *'vomited out' (ibid.* ·*v.* 28) in the same way as the Canaanites had been rejected, before them *(ibid. v.* 25).

1. A sense of gratitude is the moral imperative upon which our service of God is to be based. For elaborations on this theme see: *Chovos Halevovos, Sha'ar Avodas Ho'Elohim,* and *Ramban* to *Exod.* 20:17. This *Ramban* is discussed by *Harav Yitzchak Hutner* in *Pachad Yitzchak* to *Shavu'os, Ma'amar* 7.

youth, but have angered Me with all these, see! Also I
— your way upon your head will I place, the words of
my Lord HASHEM/ELOHIM. But you did not consider
this, concerning all your abominations. 44 *See! Every*
user of a proverb will use this proverb against you,
saying: Like mother, like daughter. 45 *Your mother's*
daughter are you, spewing forth her husband and
children, and sister of your sister are you, who
spewed forth their husbands and children. Your
mother was a Hittite, and your father, an Emorite.
46 *And your bigger sister is Samaria, she and her*

In this interpretation, אִישָׁהּ וּבָנֶיהָ, *her husband and her children* would be her king and people. This would explain the use of male symbols, in place of the feminine metaphors which are usual when *Knesses Israel* is described. Here, the entire community of *Knesses Israel* is not meant, but the individual components, king and people, of which the community is composed *(Radak).*

Abarbanel suggests that the subject of גֹּעֶלֶת, *spewing forth,* is not אִמֵּךְ, *your mother* [i.e. the Land] (as in the previous interpretation), but בַּת, *daughter.* Israel, the daughter, shows a *loathing* to her 'husband' [God] and her 'children' [the individuals who make up the nation]. By being disloyal to her destiny of holiness, she rejects God. By sacrificing her children, she shows her 'loathing' of them.

וַאֲחוֹת אֲחוֹתֵךְ אַתְּ — *And sister of your sister are you.*

The land of Canaan is Israel's 'mother' because she grew up in its bosom. *Sodom* and *Amorah,* Canaan's southern inhabitants are described as 'sisters' *(Radak).*

The sins of Sodom and Amorah — nations which are viewed as the very prototype of depravity — were intolerable, only because they took place within the confines of the Holy Land *(Ramban, Genesis* 19:5). They were destroyed as the Canaanites would one day be destroyed.

אִמְּכֶן חִתִּית וַאֲבִיכֶן אֱמֹרִי — *Your mother was a Hittite, your father an Emorite.*

Radak and *Metzudas David* render in the same way as in *v.* 3. (See *comm.* there).

Targum reads the whole verse as God's plaint to His people: 'Why have you behaved as though you were a true daughter of Canaan? ... Did not your mother Sarah live among the Hittites, and your father Abraham among the Emorites, without being influenced by them?'

46-52. Judah is compared unfavorably with both Samaria and Sodom. Depraved as these kingdoms had been, Judah was more blameworthy.

[Judah is more to blame than Samaria because it should have learned a lesson from Samaria's downfall, but Samaria had no such example to follow. *(Rashi* to *Jeremiah* 3:11). *Radak* (ad. loc.) suggests that Judah's transgressions were more heinous, because the idols were actually brought into God's Temple (Ch. 8).

Sodom had not stood at Mount Sinai, had not seen a David or a Solomon, had never had God's Temple in its midst. Though it reached the very lowest depths of depravity, it had never been lifted to the glorious heights which were part of Judah's national consciousness.]

46. וַאֲחוֹתֵךְ הַגְּדוֹלָה — *And your bigger sister.*

טז
מז־נא

הִיא וּבְנוֹתֶיהָ הַיּוֹשֶׁבֶת עַל־שְׂמֹאולֵךְ
וַאֲחוֹתֵךְ הַקְּטַנָּה מִמֵּךְ הַיּוֹשֶׁבֶת מִֽימִינֵךְ
מז סְדֹם וּבְנוֹתֶיהָ׃ וְלֹא בְדַרְכֵיהֶן הָלַכְתְּ
וּכְתוֹעֲבוֹתֵיהֶן °עשׂיתי כִּמְעַט קָט — °עָשִׂית ק׳
מח וַתַּשְׁחִתִי מֵהֵן בְּכָל־דְּרָכָיִךְ׃ חַי־אָנִי נְאֻם
אֲדֹנָי יֱהוִה אִם־עָשְׂתָה סְדֹם אֲחוֹתֵךְ הִיא
וּבְנוֹתֶיהָ כַּאֲשֶׁר עָשִׂית אַתְּ וּבְנוֹתָיִךְ׃
מט הִנֵּה־זֶה הָיָה עֲוֹן סְדֹם אֲחוֹתֵךְ
גָּאוֹן שִׂבְעַת־לֶחֶם וְשַׁלְוַת הַשְׁקֵט
הָיָה לָהּ וְלִבְנוֹתֶיהָ וְיַד־עָנִי וְאֶבְיוֹן
נ לֹא הֶחֱזִיקָה׃ וַתִּגְבְּהֶינָה וַתַּעֲשֶׂינָה
תוֹעֵבָה לְפָנָי וָאָסִיר אֶתְהֶן כַּאֲשֶׁר
נא רָאִיתִי׃ וְשֹׁמְרוֹן כַּחֲצִי חַטֹּאתַיִךְ
לֹא חָטָאָה וַתַּרְבִּי אֶת־תּוֹעֲבוֹתַיִךְ מֵהֵנָּה

Bigger, because the northern kingdom comprised ten tribes while Judah consisted of only two *(Radak).*

וּבְנוֹתֶיהָ — *And her daughters.*
Suburbs *(Num.* 21:25).

עַל שְׂמֹאלֵךְ — *On your left.*
When one faces east, the north is to his left and the south to his right (see 4:4).

וַאֲחוֹתֵךְ הַקְּטַנָּה מִמֵּךְ — *And your sister who is smaller than you.*
Sodom had fewer inhabitants than Judah. It was situated towards the south (מִימִינֵךְ).

47. וְלֹא בְּדַרְכֵיהֶן הָלַכְתְּ — *If only you had walked in their ways.*
The translation follows *Rashi,* who indicates other places where לֹא has this meaning (see *II Kings* 5:17). The word וְלֹא seems to mean: [would it] not [be better if].

כִּמְעַט קָט — *A trifle!*
קָט is a contraction of קָטָן, *small* and כִּמְעַט קָט means *very small!* (see *Metzudas Zion).* In *Rashi*'s (and *Targum*'s) rendering the meaning is that if Israel had not sinned more than Samaria or Sodom, it would have been a small matter. However, they were even more corrupt.

Metzudas David takes the sentence as a statement of fact: You did not learn from them to limit your evil-doing to the comparatively low level of their sins. You went beyond them in your corruption.

48. אִם עָשְׂתָה ... כַּאֲשֶׁר עָשִׂית — *Have not done as did you ...*
They did not exchange their 'god' — as you exchanged yours — for an empty shell *(Radak).*

49. הִנֵּה זֶה הָיָה עֲוֹן סְדֹם אֲחוֹתֵךְ — *See! This was the sin of Sodom, your sister.*
Only this was their sin. They did not go beyond this *(Metzudas David).*

גָּאוֹן שִׂבְעַת לֶחֶם וְשַׁלְוַת הַשְׁקֵט — *Pride, surfeit of bread, and undisturbed peace.*

daughters who dwell on your left, and your sister
who is smaller than you, who dwells on your right —
Sodom and her daughters. 47 *If only in their ways had*
you gone, and like their abominations had you acted.
A trifle! But you were more corrupt than they in all
your ways. 48 *As I live! The words of my Lord*
HASHEM/ELOHIM: Sodom, your sister, she and her
daughters have not done as did you and your
daughters. 49 *See! This was the sin of Sodom, your*
sister: pride, surfeit of bread, and undisturbed peace
were hers and her daughter's but the hand of the
poor and the needy did she not support. 50 *And they*
were haughty and committed abomination before
Me, so I removed them when I perceived it.
51 *And as for Samaria, like half your sins, has she*
not sinned, but you increased your abominations

She was proud because of her wealth and security. In her pride she overlooked the needs of the poor *(Metzudas David)*.[1]

50. וַתִּגְבְּהֶינָה — *And they were haughty.*

Rashi refers to *Sanhedrin* 109a, where Sodom's well-being is described. Their fertile fields yielded virtually unlimited food and rich veins of gold and precious stones ran beneath the earth.

Their uncontrolled access to all this material wealth stimulated habits of self-indulgence, which resulted in תּוֹעֵבָה, *abomination*, the sexual perversions with which we are familiar from the account of Sodom and Amorah in Genesis.

51. וְשֹׁמְרוֹן כַּחֲצִי חַטֹּאתַיִךְ לֹא חָטָאָה — *And as for Samaria, like half your sins, has she not sinned.*

See *Intro.* to *vs.* 46-52.

1. We know from *Sanhedrin* 109a and b (see also *Rashi* to *Gen.* 18:21) how every humane instinct, every charitable thought was supressed and tortured out of existence in *Sodom*. The perversion of social justice and responsibility which was the norm within their society, and the rampant misanthropy which governed their relations toward strangers are castigated throughout Scripture, the *Talmud* and *Midrash*.

If Yechezkel in this passage seems intent on minimizing Sodom's sin, it is only within the context of his strictures of Jerusalem. Judged against Jerusalem's greater culpability, there might even be a 'justification' for Sodom's actions *(vs.* 51 and 52).

[No sin can ever be judged by a single objective standard. From different points of view, the perspective may vary:

— The brothers were wrong in selling Joseph and were deserving of punishment in God's judgment *(Amos* 2:6). Nevertheless from Joseph's point of view, it was God, and not they, who had caused him to be sold *(Gen.* 45:8).

— Shimi ben Gerah cursed King David and Solomon was given the duty to punish him *(I Kings* 2:9). David, however, refused to be involved in his punishment because, from his perspective, God had inspired the curse *(II Samuel* 16:11).

— When David initiated a census of Israel without resorting to the counting of shekalim,

וַתְּצַדְּקִי אֶת־°אחותך בְּכָל־תּוֹעֲבֹתַיִךְ °אֲחוֹתַיִךְ ק׳
נב אֲשֶׁר °עשיתי׃ גַּם־אַתְּ | שְׂאִי כְלִמָּתֵךְ
אֲשֶׁר פִּלַּלְתְּ לַאֲחוֹתֵךְ בְּחַטֹּאתַיִךְ אֲשֶׁר־ °עָשִׂית ק׳
הִתְעַבְתְּ מֵהֵן תִּצְדַּקְנָה מִמֵּךְ וְגַם־אַתְּ
בּוֹשִׁי וּשְׂאִי כְלִמָּתֵךְ בְּצַדֶּקְתֵּךְ אַחְיוֹתֵךְ׃
נג וְשַׁבְתִּי אֶת־שְׁבִיתְהֶן אֶת־°שבית סְדֹם °שְׁבוּת ק׳
וּבְנוֹתֶיהָ וְאֶת־°שבית שֹׁמְרוֹן וּבְנוֹתֶיהָ °שְׁבוּת ק׳
נד °ושבית שְׁבִיתַיִךְ בְּתוֹכָהְנָה׃ לְמַעַן °וּשְׁבוּת ק׳
תִּשְׂאִי כְלִמָּתֵךְ וְנִכְלַמְתְּ מִכֹּל אֲשֶׁר
נה עָשִׂית בְּנַחֲמֵךְ אֹתָן׃ וַאֲחוֹתַיִךְ סְדֹם
וּבְנוֹתֶיהָ תָּשֹׁבְןָ לְקַדְמָתָן וְשֹׁמְרוֹן
וּבְנוֹתֶיהָ תָּשֹׁבְןָ לְקַדְמָתָן וְאַתְּ וּבְנוֹתַיִךְ
נו תְּשֻׁבֶינָה לְקַדְמַתְכֶן׃ וְלוֹא הָיְתָה סְדֹם
אֲחוֹתֵךְ לִשְׁמוּעָה בְּפִיךְ בְּיוֹם גְּאוֹנָיִךְ׃

וַתְּצַדְּקִי אֶת אֲחוֹתַיִךְ — *And justified your sisters.*

The sins that they have committed seem less blameworthy when compared to yours. Relative to you Sodom and Samaria seem righteous *(Radak).*

52. אֲשֶׁר פִּלַּלְתְּ לַאֲחוֹתֵךְ — *In that you judged your sister.*

Before her own moral collapse, Jerusalem had self righteously presumed to judge Samaria. She had judged her sister to be deserving of punishment *(Rashi).*

53. וְשַׁבְתִּי ... אֶת שְׁבוּת סְדֹם — *And I will return ... the captivity of Sodom.*

We do not know of any 'return' of the 'captives' of Sodom. A future date must be envisaged *(Radak),* specifically the Messianic age *(Metzudas David).*

Since Judah did 'return' after the seventy years of the Babylonian exile, we must assume that this passage refers to a complete return of all Israel's people. This, of course, never happened and will come true only in Messianic times.

Rashi explains the 'return' of Sodom as meaning the revitalization of her land, which had been rendered unproductive by the sulphur and brimstone which had been showered upon it.

Ramban (comm. to *Job* 42:10) demonstrates that שׁוּב does not necessarily mean 'to return'. It can also mean *'to replace'.* [God did not 'return' Job's losses (וה׳ שָׁב אֶת שְׁבוּת אִיּוֹב) — his dead sons did not return to life — but He *replaced* them]. Thus, our verse means that the lands vacated by Sodom's

the people were also culpable for cooperating *(Ramban Num.* 16:21). Nevertheless, David, in his prayer *(II Sam.* 24:17) argues that he alone is to blame because he had taken the initiative.

Jerusalem is called upon to see the extenuating factors in Sodom's actions in order to increase its own feeling of guilt.]

XVI *beyond them, and justified your sisters by all the*
52-57 *abominations which you committed.* 52 *Also you,*
bear your shame in that you judged your sister.
Through your sins by which you acted more
abominably than they, they became more righteous
than you. Also you, feel ashamed and bear your
humiliation as you justify your sisters.
53 *And I will return their captivity, the captivity of*
Sodom and her daughters, and the captivity of
Samaria and her daughters and the captivity of your
captives in their midst, 54 *so that you shall carry your*
humiliation, and be humiliated for all you have done,
in comforting them. 55 *And your sisters Sodom and*
her daughters will return to their beginnings, and
Samaria and her daughters will return to their begin-
nings, and you and your daughters will return to
your beginning.
56 *And was not your sister Sodom a 'report' in your*
mouth, on the day of your pride? 57 *Before your*

destruction would once more be settled, by Israel.

וּשְׁבוּת שְׁבִיתַיִךְ בְּתוֹכָהְנָה — *And the captivity of your captives in their midst.*

But not at an earlier date, since you are no more deserving than they *(Metzudas David).* This thought is repeated in *v.* 55.

54. לְמַעַן תִּשְׂאִי כְלִמָּתֵךְ — *So that you shall carry your humiliation.*

The length of your exile has the purpose of shaming you for your behavior which served as a 'comfort' for your sisters. They were able to find self-justification because of the more aggravated degree of your wickedness *(Metzudas David).*

Rashi suggests an alternative meaning for בְּנַחֲמֵךְ אֹתָן. They will feel companionship and therefore, comfort in their own misfortune, as you suffer with them.

55. See *comm.* to *v.* 53.

56. וְלוֹא הָיְתָה ... — *And was not ... ?*

Rashi and *Metzudas David* treat the verse as a rhetorical question: During the days of her pride, Israel would hold up Sodom as an example of the fate which would overtake sinners. If so, why did Israel herself not heed the message?

Radak reads the verse as a statement: During the days of her pride, Israel never once considered Sodom's fate as a warning of her own impending doom.

לִשְׁמוּעָה — *A* [lit. *for a*] *report.*

A fresh report which was now heard for the first time, and consequently of great interest *(Rashi).*

נז בְּטֶרֶם תִּגָּלֶה רָעָתֵךְ כְּמוֹ עֵת חֶרְפַּת
בְּנוֹת־אֲרָם וְכָל־סְבִיבוֹתֶיהָ בְּנוֹת
נח פְּלִשְׁתִּים הַשָּׁאטוֹת אוֹתָךְ מִסָּבִיב: אֶת־
זִמָּתֵךְ וְאֶת־תּוֹעֲבוֹתַיִךְ אַתְּ נְשָׂאתִים נְאֻם
נט יְהוָֹה: כִּי כֹה אָמַר אֲדֹנָי יֱהוִֹה
וְעָשִׂית אוֹתָךְ כַּאֲשֶׁר עָשִׂית אֲשֶׁר־בָּזִית
ס אָלָה לְהָפֵר בְּרִית: וְזָכַרְתִּי אֲנִי אֶת־
בְּרִיתִי אוֹתָךְ בִּימֵי נְעוּרָיִךְ וַהֲקִימוֹתִי לָךְ
סא בְּרִית עוֹלָם: וְזָכַרְתְּ אֶת־דְּרָכַיִךְ וְנִכְלַמְתְּ

57. בְּטֶרֶם תִּגָּלֶה רָעָתֵךְ — *Before your wickedness was revealed.*

Metzudas David reads this phrase as part of the previous verse: *'On the day of your pride, before your wickedness was revealed.'*

כְּמוֹ עֵת חֶרְפַּת בְּנוֹת אֲרָם ... בְּנוֹת פְּלִשְׁתִּים — *As at the time of the taunt of the daughters of Aram ... the daughters of the Philistines.*

Reference is to the reign of Achaz, when Judah was subjected to attacks and conquests by both Aram and the Philistines *(II Kings* 16, and *II Chron.* 28).

For the first time in Judah's history, flagrant and shameless idol worship spread throughout the land (תִּגָּלֶה רָעָתֵךְ). The king himself passed his son through fire in idolatrous extravagance *(ibid.).* Until then, even those kings who had sinned, had, at least outwardly retained some measure of propriety *(Metzudas David).*

In a sense the wars which Aram, in alliance with Samaria's Pekach ben Remalyahu waged against Judah, spelled the beginning of the end. In his despair, Achaz turned to Assyria for help *(ibid.).* Instead of coming to Achaz's aid, the Assyrians used the opportunity to gain a foothold in Israel from which, in a short while, they launched the campaigns which resulted in the destruction of the Northern Kingdom, and of a large part of Judah.

If Achaz and his people had taken the lessons of Sodom to heart, even at that late moment, tragedy could have been averted. But they did not. Instead they embarked on the road which, some 140 years later, was to lead to total destruction.

הַשָּׁאטוֹת אוֹתָךְ — *Who disdain you.*

The translation is based on *Targum* (דְּבָזוּ יָתִיךְ). The root is unique to *Yechezkel.* In 28:24, 26 where the word is used precisely as it is in our verse, *Targum* also renders בזה. In 25:6, 15, and 36:5, where the word comes as an adjective of נֶפֶשׁ, *soul, Targum* renders צְפוּחַ נְפַשׁ, which means *'rashness'* or *'recklessness'.* (See *Rashi* to 25:6, where he first interprets the term as one of *'derision'.* He continues: And I say, that it is an expression denoting שטף, *flooding.* This latter would agree with the idea of rashness or recklessness. However, some read שאף, *to swallow* in *Rashi* instead of שטף).

The root שוט in Aramaic, means *'to despise'* and occurs often in the *Targumim.* See for ex. *Targum* to *Gen.* 25:34. See also *Bava Basra* 16b.

Radak renders: *Who despoil you. (Radak* in *Sefer haShorashim* שאט, explains that just as בזה has two meanings, i.e. to despise and to despoil, so

XVI
58-61

wickedness was revealed, as at the time of the taunt of the daughter of Aram and all its surroundings, the daughters of the Philistines who disdain you from all around.
58 Your harlotry and your abominations, you have borne them. The words of my Lord HASHEM/ELOHIM.
59 For thus says my Lord HASHEM/ELOHIM: I shall deal with you as you have done, that you have despised the oath in breaking the covenant.

60 But I will remember My covenant with you in the days of your youth, and I will establish for you an everlasting covenant.
61 Then shall you remember your ways and be humiliated, as you take your sisters

also שאט. When used with נֶפֶשׁ, it means *to despise,* but when used alone it means *to despoil).*

58. אַתְּ נְשָׂאתִים — *You have borne them.*

You have been punished *(Radak)*; or are going to be punished *(Metzudas David)* for your lewdness and abominations.

59. וְעָשִׂיתְ אוֹתָךְ כַּאֲשֶׁר עָשִׂית — *I shall deal with you, as you have done.*

I have punished you in accordance with your actions in violating the oath and covenant which you made with Me at Sinai *(Rashi).*

Radak points out that the word וְעָשִׂיתְ, *And I shall deal* is spelled without the final *yud,* which is pronounced in the reading. The written form וְעָשִׂית means *you* have done, while the spoken form וְעָשִׂיתִי means *I* have done which becomes 'I will do' by means of the conversive *vav.* The written form (כְּתִיב) implies: '*You* have done that which you have done' meaning it is your fault. Combined with the spoken form, וְעָשִׂיתִי, the implication is: your doing (וְעָשִׂית), caused My doing (וְעָשִׂיתִי). (See *comm.* to 7:21).

60. וְזָכַרְתִּי אֲנִי אֶת בְּרִיתִי אוֹתָךְ — *But I will remember My covenant with you.*

In contrast to you who have been false to your commitment, I, God, will be true to Mine *(Rashi; Radak).*

בִּימֵי נְעוּרָיִךְ — *In the days of your youth.*

The days of Israel's 'youth' are the years between the Exodus and the entry into Eretz Yisrael *(Radak).*

The same term is used by *Jeremiah* 2:2. [It may be that, within the context of the chapter, the reference is to the covenant mentioned in *v.* 8, and the *days of your youth* are those described at the beginning of the parable.]

בְּרִית עוֹלָם — *An everlasting covenant.*

Israel's commitment had been *'for us and our children, to eternity' (Deut.* 29:28).

This is the covenant which God promises to establish *(Radak).*

[The outpouring of love expressed in this verse qualified it as one of the ten vs. of 'remembering' (זִכְרוֹנוֹת) in the *Musaf* prayer of *Rosh Hashanah.*]

61. וְזָכַרְתְּ אֶת דְּרָכַיִךְ — *Then shall you remember your ways.*

Eliezer of Beaugency renders: When

טז סב־סג בְּקַחְתֵּךְ אֶת־אֲחוֹתַיִךְ הַגְּדֹלוֹת מִמֵּךְ אֶל־
הַקְּטַנּוֹת מִמֵּךְ וְנָתַתִּי אֶתְהֶן לָךְ לְבָנוֹת
סב וְלֹא מִבְּרִיתֵךְ׃ וַהֲקִימוֹתִי אֲנִי אֶת־בְּרִיתִי
סג אִתָּךְ וְיָדַעַתְּ כִּי־אֲנִי יהוה׃ לְמַעַן תִּזְכְּרִי
וָבֹשְׁתְּ וְלֹא יִהְיֶה־לָּךְ עוֹד פִּתְחוֹן פֶּה
יז מִפְּנֵי כְּלִמָּתֵךְ בְּכַפְּרִי־לָךְ לְכָל־אֲשֶׁר
א א עָשִׂית נְאֻם אֲדֹנָי יֱהֹוִה׃ וַיְהִי

בְּקַחְתֵּךְ אֶת אֲחוֹתַיִךְ הַגְּדֹלוֹת מִמֵּךְ אֶל הַקְּטַנּוֹת מִמֵּךְ — *As you take your sisters who are bigger than you, together [with those who are] smaller than you.*

Samaria and Sodom were not the only sisters. (אֲחוֹתַיִךְ is in the plural). Israel had made itself 'sister' to many nations, some bigger and some smaller than she. In the glorious future depicted here, all these sisters would become her children — her daughters. She would no longer lower herself to their level, but on the contrary, become guide and mentor to all of them *(Harav Breuer).*

Rashi and *Radak* take בָנוֹת in the sense that it has been used in the rest of the chapter — as suburbs. The subject of the verse is the expanded boundaries which Israel will one day control. Among the neighbors, both big and small, who would eventually become part of a greater Israel, would be some וְלֹא מִבְּרִיתֵךְ, not necessarily Jewish *(Radak);* or perhaps even some not originally envisaged in the בְּרִית בֵּין הַבְּתָרִים, *the Covenant between the Pieces,* in which *Eretz Yisrael* was promised to Abraham *(Rashi* quoting *Tanchumah).*

וְלֹא מִבְּרִיתֵךְ — *But not because of your covenant.*

The translation follows *Targum.* (See above for two other possibilities). I, God, will establish My covenant with you *(v.* 62) but it will not be a result of your loyalty to your commitments.

you, Israel, will have remembered your ways and been ashamed ... .

A precondition to the establishment of God's eternal covenant is Israel's repentance as expressed in her shame.

The term וְנִכְלַמְתְּ in this verse and כְּלִמָּתֵךְ in *v.* 63, must not be confused with the *'bearing of shame'* which is mentioned in *vs.* 52 and 54 and (by implication) in *v.* 58. Throughout *Yechezkel* the term נְשִׂיאַת כְּלִמָּה, *the bearing of shame* has the connotation of a punishment (see 32:24,25,30; 34:29; 36:6,7,15; 39:26; 44:13). But in a context such as our verse the term refers to shame which is a positive and integral part of the process of תְּשׁוּבָה, *repentance.* (See *Sha'arei Teshuvah* of *R' Yonah* 1:6, and *comm.* to 20:43).

That shame will be stimulated by Israel's realization that she is the recipient of God's favors in spite of her wickedness *(Rashi).*

The classical example of this cleansing kind of shame is 43:10,11. There Yechezkel is told that he may pass on the details of the future Temple to Israel only if they show a feeling of shame for their past sins.

Eliezer of Beaugency comments that only an expression of shame would guarantee that there would be no return to the sins of the past. He draws a parallel to the passage in *Exod.* 33:6 where as a precondition for the return of the Divine Presence, the people had to demonstrate the sincerity of their repentance by divesting themselves of the 'ornaments' with which they had bedecked themselves at Sinai.

who are bigger than you with those who are smaller than you and I will give them to you for daughters — but not because of your covenant. [62] *Then shall I establish My covenant with you, and you shall know that I am* HASHEM. [63] *That you may remember and feel shame and have no more excuse because of your humiliation, when I have forgiven you all that you have done. The words of my Lord* HASHEM/ELOHIM."

Ultimately, God's love for Israel will surmount all barriers, even those thrown up by His people. (See *comm.* to 9:2 and *footnote* on תַּמָּה זְכוּת אָבוֹת *ibid. v.* 4).

62. See above.

63. לְמַעַן תִּזְכְּרִי וָבֹשְׁתְּ — *That you may remember and feel shame,* the overwhelming shame of the true penitent (see *footnote* to *v.* 61).

פִּתְחוֹן פֶּה — *An excuse* [lit. *'an opening of the mouth'*].

While you were still in exile, you might have felt that your suffering was sufficient to cancel the debt which your wickedness had placed upon you. No such 'excuse' will exist when one day God will shower His goodness upon you *(Radak).*

בְּכַפְּרִי לָךְ — *When I have forgiven you* [lit. *'when I have cleansed you'*]

[See *Ramban* to *Gen.* 32:21].

XVII

In 12:5 (see also *footnote* ad. loc.) we noted that details omitted by Scripture from the original account of an event, will occasionally be given elsewhere.

Our chapter, by means of a parable, gives a full description of Zidkiyahu's rebellion against Nebuchadnezzar. In contrast to *II Kings* 24:20 and *Jeremiah* 52:3 which simply state that the rebellion took place, (וַיִּמְרֹד צִדְקִיָּהוּ בְּמֶלֶךְ בָּבֶל), Yechezkel describes its full background, including Zidkiyahu's request for help to the Egyptian Pharaoh (which is alluded to, but not expressed in *Jeremiah* 37:5-7).

In the *Overview* we noted the Sages' assessment of Zidkiyahu as a צַדִּיק גָּמוּר, *a completely righteous person,* and we examined the general outline of his tragic reign. At this point, it is appropriate to discuss his rebellion, in greater detail.

The picture, emerging from the perspective of the Sages, is quite different from that yielded by a superficial reading of the Scriptural sources.

From our chapter it is abundantly clear that: Zidkiyahu was bound by oath and covenant to be loyal to Nebuchadnezzar; that in seeking an Egyptian alliance he broke his word; and that he was severely castigated for this.

Nedarim 65a tells a different story. In this account Zidkiyahu observed Nebuchadnezzar in an unseemly act — he was eating a live (or raw) rabbit. Nebuchadnezzar was embarrassed and exacted an oath from Zidkiyahu that he would never tell anyone about this. Zidkiyahu had the oath annulled by the Sanhedrin thus contravening the spirit, if not the letter of the oath. The *Talmud* offers this account as an explanation of a passage in *II Chronicles.*

A careful analysis of the passage in *Chronicles* will, in fact, yield the *Talmud*'s source. We

יז ב דְּבַר־יְהוִה אֵלַי לֵאמֹר: בֶּן־אָדָם חוּד
ב־ד חִידָה וּמְשֹׁל מָשָׁל אֶל־בֵּית יִשְׂרָאֵל:
ג וְאָמַרְתָּ כֹּה־אָמַר | אֲדֹנָי יֱהוִה הַנֶּשֶׁר
הַגָּדוֹל גְּדוֹל הַכְּנָפַיִם אֶרֶךְ הָאֵבֶר מָלֵא
הַנּוֹצָה אֲשֶׁר־לוֹ הָרִקְמָה בָּא אֶל־הַלְּבָנוֹן
ד וַיִּקַּח אֶת־צַמֶּרֶת הָאָרֶז: אֵת רֹאשׁ
יְנִיקוֹתָיו קָטָף וַיְבִיאֵהוּ אֶל־אֶרֶץ כְּנַעַן

can best get a clear picture by comparing that passage with the passages in *II Kings* and *Jeremiah* (which are essentially identical).

1. *Jeremiah* 52:2-3

... וַיַּעַשׂ הָרַע בְּעֵינֵי ה׳ כְּכֹל אֲשֶׁר עָשָׂה יְהוֹיָקִם

And he did evil in the eyes of HASHEM, like all that Yehoyakim did.

כִּי עַל אַף ה׳ הָיְתָה בִּירוּשָׁלַיִם וִיהוּדָה עַד הִשְׁלִיכוֹ אוֹתָם מֵעַל פָּנָיו וַיִּמְרֹד צִדְקִיָּהוּ בְּמֶלֶךְ בָּבֶל.

For through the anger of HASHEM it happened in Jerusalem and Judah until He cast them from before Him. And Zidkiyahu rebelled against the King of Babylon.

2. *II Chronicles* 36:12-13

וַיַּעַשׂ הָרַע בְּעֵינֵי ה׳ אֱלֹהָיו לֹא נִכְנַע מִלִּפְנֵי יִרְמְיָהוּ הַנָּבִיא מִפִּי ה׳

And he did evil in the eyes of HASHEM his God, and did not humble himself before Jeremiah the prophet from the mouth of HASHEM

וְגַם בַּמֶּלֶךְ נְבוּכַדְנֶאצַּר מָרָד אֲשֶׁר הִשְׁבִּיעוֹ בֵּאלֹהִים ...

Also against King Nebuchadnezzar did he rebel, who caused him to swear by God.

An analysis of 1. yields the following conclusions: a. The first verse has no bearing on the rebellion. The *'evil'* is that he continued in Yehoyakim's ways, and, according to *Sanhedrin* 103a, it means only that he did not prevent others from sinning. He personally was blameless.

b. The second verse deals with the rebellion and according to *Rashi* (ad. loc.), teaches, that God Himself goaded Zidkiyahu to rebel, in order to bring about the downfall of Jerusalem.

The passage does not indicate what means God used to cause Zidkiyahu to rebel.

Let us turn to an analysis of 2.

a. In contrast to 1. where the 'evil' is unrelated to the rebellion (and was in fact not committed by Zidkiyahu at all — see above), the 'evil' in 2. is identified as his refusal to humble himself to Jeremiah. *This can refer only to the rebellion,* because a careful study of Jeremiah reveals no other matter in which Zidkiyahu defied the prophet.

b. Therefore the 'rebellion' mentioned in the second verse (מָרָד) must be a *different* one, since the second verse is introduced with וְגַם, *also.* When we add to this that in the second verse the king's proper name is used, in contrast to 1. where he is called only מֶלֶךְ בָּבֶל, *King of Babylon,* we have the source for the Talmud's story. There was a second 'rebellion', one that was directed against the *man* rather than against the *king.*

We also note that in the first verse of 2., (which we have shown to deal with the main rebellion) no mention is made that it was inspired by God (in contrast to 1. — see above).

We may conjecture that the incident described in the Talmud was the tool by which God goaded Zidkiyahu to rebellion.

The following sequence is suggested:

In order to bring about Jersualem's downfall, God causes Zidkiyahu to rebel 1. Zidkiyahu the perfect zaddik would not do so under normal circumstances; he had bound himself by an oath of loyalty. Therefore, he is exposed to an occurrence at which Nebuchadnezzar is degraded in his eyes. [*Tanchumah (Buber) Vo'eira* 18 has a variant reading: '... (Zidkiyahu) saw Nebuchadnezzar eating with saliva drooling on his beard. ... He said: 'Is this the man to

XVII
1-4

And the word of HASHEM came to me, saying:
2 Ben Adam! Pose a riddle and describe with a parable to the Family of Israel.

3 And you shall say: 'So says my Lord HASHEM/ELOHIM: The great eagle — great of wing, long of pinion, full of plumage — who has many colors, came to the Lebanon, and took the crown of the cedar.
4 The top of the young twigs he cropped, and brought it to the land of the peddler. In the city of the

whom the whole world should be subjugated?]. Having lost his respect for the king, Zidkiyahu wins annulment of his oath of secrecy and talks disparagingly about Nebuchadnezzar (*Talmud* based on 2.).

Two things have now happened (by Divine Providence): Zidkiyahu feels that he ought not to be subservient to Nebuchadnezzar whom he deems unworthy; and he has violated the spirit of his oath to the Babylonian king.

Under the circumstances, it became easier for him to submit to the pressures within his kingdom (see *Overview*) to break his oath of loyalty and to seek an Egyptian alliance against Babylon.

God had not placed this thought directly in his mind. Providence had been limited to creating the background against which it became possible. Zidkiyahu should, in fact, have remained loyal, in spite of everything. Yechezkel castigates him severely for his perfidy.

2. חוּד חִידָה וּמְשֹׁל מָשָׁל — *Pose a riddle and describe with a parable.*

Vilna Gaon to *Prov.* 1:6, defines a מָשָׁל as something that can be understood independently, without reference to the concept it illustrates. It is a מָשָׁל, *a parable,* only because it is being used to illustrate something else; otherwise it would simply be a story.

A חִידָה, *riddle,* is also a parable in the sense that it is used to illustrate another thing. But, in contrast to a מָשָׁל it cannot stand alone. If that to which it alludes is unknown, it cannot be understood.

Hence, the parable in this chapter, which ascribes human qualities to eagles and trees, is a חִידָה as well as a מָשָׁל, for without knowledge of the story alluded to, the listener cannot fathom it.

3. הַנֶּשֶׁר הַגָּדוֹל ... אֲשֶׁר לוֹ הָרִקְמָה — *The great eagle ... who has many colors.*

The eagle flies higher than any other bird, an apt simile for Nebuchadnezzar, the world conquerer *(Radak).*

רִקְמָה, see *comm.* to 16:10. Since רִקְמָה literally is *embroidery,* the term is used for anything that is colorful. Hence the variegated plumage of an eagle.

הַלְּבָנוֹן — *The Lebanon.*

The mighty forest, with its cedars, standing higher than any other trees, is a symbol for the entire land of Israel, which is 'higher' than all other lands *(Radak).*

צַמֶּרֶת הָאָרֶז — *The crown of the cedar.*

The cedar is the highest tree in the Lebanon, therefore it stands for Jerusalem. Its 'crown' would be Mount Zion, the royal residence *(Radak).*

4. אֵת רֹאשׁ יְנִיקוֹתָיו קָטָף — *The top of the young twigs he cropped.*

The young twigs at the top of the cedar, would be the children of the royal household, their 'head' the young King Yehoyachin who was exiled at the age of eighteen (*II Kings* 24:8) *(Radak).*[1]

1. We have followed *Radak* in identifying the exiled king as Yehoyachin since it was he who

ה בְּעִיר רֹכְלִים שָׂמוֹ: וַיִּקַּח מִזֶּרַע הָאָרֶץ
וַיִּתְּנֵהוּ בִּשְׂדֵה־זָרַע קָח עַל־מַיִם רַבִּים
ו צַפְצָפָה שָׂמוֹ: וַיִּצְמַח וַיְהִי לְגֶפֶן סֹרַחַת
שִׁפְלַת קוֹמָה לִפְנוֹת דָּלִיּוֹתָיו אֵלָיו
וְשָׁרָשָׁיו תַּחְתָּיו יִהְיוּ וַתְּהִי לְגֶפֶן וַתַּעַשׂ

אֶל אֶרֶץ כְּנַעַן — *To the land of the peddler.*

Used here to describe Babylon, as in 16:29. See above.

5. וַיִּקַּח מִזֶּרַע הָאָרֶץ — *And he took from the seed of the land.*

This refers to Zidkiyahu *(Rashi)*. Nebuchadnezzar did not import a foreign king. He realized that, in the same way that a field will reject a plant for which soil and climate are not suitable, so Jerusalem could not flourish under a king whose values were not those of the people *(Radak)*.

וַיִּתְּנֵהוּ בִּשְׂדֵה זָרַע — *And placed it in a fertile field.* [lit. *'a field of seeds'*]

There was every expectation that the seed which was indigenous to the land, would flourish, given the optimum conditions for growth.

קָח עַל מַיִם רַבִּים — *He planted it by abundant waters.*

This follows *Rashi,* who together with *Menachem (Machberes,* קח) and *Mahari Kara* ascribes a meaning of *growth* or *planting* or *taking root.*

Others take קָח as a contraction of לָקַח, *he took.* He took it to a location which was close to water.

With a constant supply of water, the tree can be expected to grow strong, and to cast a dark shadow. *Mahari Kara* sees this as a reference to the tradition of the Sages *(Eichah Rabbasi* 2:18, based on *Jeremiah* 27:3) that Nebuchadnezzar gave Zidkiyahu dominion over the kings of Edom, Moab, Amon, Tyre and Sidon. Thus, Nebuchadnezzar placed Zidkiyahu in a position where his power could grow.

צַפְצָפָה שָׂמוֹ — *A mountain willow did he make it.*

Succah 34a defines a צַפְצָפָה as a *willow* which grows on the mountain, as opposed to one which grows by the river [עֲרָבָה].

For the meaning in terms of the con-

was exiled to Babylon, and was succeeded by Zidkiyahu, as our chapter goes on to describe.

Rashi, alone among the commentators identifies the exiled king as Yehoyakim. In view of the following, it is difficult to see why *Rashi* chooses Yehoyakim rather than Yehoyachin:

1. Yehoyakim was not succeeded by Zidkiyahu, as is assumed by our chapter, but by Yehoyachin.

2. There is no clear evidence anywhere that Yehoyakim was ever exiled to Babylon. (See: *Seder Olam* Ch. 25; *Arachin* 12a and *Rashi* ad. loc.; *Vayikra Rabbah* 19:6; *Sifri* to *Deut.* 11:17, *Rashi* to *II Kings* 24:6).

Briefly these sources yield that:

a. In the fourth year of Yehoyakim's reign, the Babylonian armies under Nebuchadnezzar subjugated the land of Israel, but took no captives (*Rashi, Arachin* loc. cit.).

b. Three years later Yehoyakim began a three-year rebellion against Babylonian rule.

c. At the end of those three years (that is, the eleventh and last year of Yehoyakim's reign), Nebuchadnezzar returned and shackled Yehoyakim with the intention of taking him captive to Babylon. However, before this could be done, Yehoyakim died within *Eretz Yisrael.*

[*Rashi* in *Arachin* loc. cit. seems to indicate at one point that Yehoyakim was, in fact, exiled at the end of his reign. But the sources quoted above seem to contradict this.] (See further in *comm.* to 19:5-9).

traders he placed it.

5 *And he took from the seed of the land and placed it in a fertile field, he planted it by abundant waters; a mountain willow did he make it.* 6 *So it sprouted and became a spreading vine, low of stature, that its tendrils might turn to it and its roots be under it. And it became a vine and brought forth*

text, several explanations are offered.

— *Targum* renders: He [Nebuchadnezzar] made it like a *planted* vine. *Radak* explains the *Targum*: A tree will grow much faster from a shoot, than from a seed. Although here, a seed was sown (*v.* 5), it was placed so advantageously that it was as though a shoot had been planted.

— *Rashi:* A kind of tree with many branches.

— *Eliezer of Beaugency* and *Mahari Kara* interpret צַפְצָפָה from the root צפה, *to overflow* or *flood.* Thus, a plant which is constantly inundated with water, and will therefore grow well.

None of these commentators take into account that *Succah* (loc. cit.) defines צַפְצָפָה as a poor, stunted plant.

The *Talmud*'s interpretation of the verse, takes it out of context. It reads: The Holy One, Blessed be He, said: I had said that Israel should be to Me like something planted on many waters, like an עֲרָבָה, but they converted themselves into a צַפְצָפָה, *a mountain willow.* i.e. God wanted Israel to be like a luxuriant plant, but, by its sins, it denied itself this blessing.

Harav Breuer offers this interpretation: Although Nebuchadnezzar planted the seed in good and fertile ground, it was his intention that it should grow into nothing more than a mountain willow. The nation which Zidkiyahu was to govern, was to be small and stunted, without independence or strength.[1]

6. וַיִּצְמַח — *So it sprouted.*

Zidkiyahu's reign was blessed with success. Until his rebellion [in the fifth year of his reign (*Radak*)] he was a strong king, to whom his neighbors were subservient [see above] (*Radak*).

לְגֶפֶן סֹרַחַת — *A spreading vine.*

See above. The root סרח denotes *overlapping* or *hanging free* as in *Exod.* 26:12.

שִׁפְלַת קוֹמָה — *Low of stature.*

To serve the Babylonian king (*Rashi*).

The former rulers of Judah had been compared to the cedar (*vs.* 3 and 4), a tall and strong tree. It was Nebuchadnezzar's intention that from then on the royal house should be like a low vine whose branches would not spread out from its trunk, but on the contrary, would turn inwards (לִפְנוֹת דָּלִיּוֹתָיו אֵלָיו). It was to be a *'lowly kingdom'* [*v.* 14] (*Metzudas David*).

לִפְנוֹת דָּלִיּוֹתָיו אֵלָיו — *That its tendrils might turn to it.*

Towards the Babylonian king (*Rashi*).

וְשָׁרָשָׁיו תַּחְתָּיו — *And its roots be under it.*

The tendency of the vine's roots is to

1. We shall see in the course of the chapter, that in God's plan, this was to be an advantage to Israel. However, although Nebuchadnezzar was the tool through which God chose to implement His plans, the king never saw himself as God's agent. He was always limited to his own selfish perceptions. (For a development of this theme see *Ramban* to *Genesis* 15:14).

ז בַּדִּים וַתְּשַׁלַּח פֹּארוֹת: וַיְהִי נֶשֶׁר־אֶחָד
גָּדוֹל גְּדוֹל כְּנָפַיִם וְרַב נוֹצָה וְהִנֵּה הַגֶּפֶן
הַזֹּאת כָּפְנָה שָׁרָשֶׁיהָ עָלָיו וְדָלִיּוֹתָיו
שִׁלְחָה־לּוֹ לְהַשְׁקוֹת אוֹתָהּ מֵעֲרֻגוֹת
ח מַטָּעָהּ: אֶל־שָׂדֶה טּוֹב אֶל־מַיִם רַבִּים
הִיא שְׁתוּלָה לַעֲשׂוֹת עָנָף וְלָשֵׂאת פֶּרִי
ט לִהְיוֹת לְגֶפֶן אַדָּרֶת: אֱמֹר כֹּה אָמַר אֲדֹנָי
יֱהוִה תִּצְלָח הֲלוֹא אֶת־שָׁרָשֶׁיהָ יְנַתֵּק
וְאֶת־פִּרְיָהּ | יְקוֹסֵס וְיָבֵשׁ כָּל־טַרְפֵּי

grow downwards, rather than to spread out *(Metzudas David).*

Rashi, explains that it was intended that the roots should be *'under'* the Babylonian king.

וַתַּעַשׂ בַּדִּים וַתְּשַׁלַּח פֹּארוֹת — *And brought forth branches and sent out boughs.*

Symbolic of Zidkiyahu's success before the rebellion *(Radak).*

Radak points out that *fruits* are not mentioned. Since Zidkiyahu was destined to have his sons slaughtered before his eyes *(II Kings* 25:7) he cannot be said to have borne fruit.

7. וַיְהִי נֶשֶׁר אֶחָד גָּדוֹל — *And there was another great eagle* [lit. *'one great eagle'*]

In his attempt to gain independence from Babylon, Zidkiyahu turned to the Egyptian Pharaoh for help. This is never stated in so many words (except in *v.* 15 below — see *Pref. Remarks* to this chapter), but it is indicated in *Jeremiah* 37:5-7 where we learn that Pharaoh actually left Egypt to come to Israel's aid, but that Jeremiah foretold that he would return without having helped.[1]

כָּפְנָה שָׁרָשֶׁיהָ עָלָיו — *Its roots hungered toward him.*

The translation follows Rashi who relates the word to the Aramaic כְּפַן, *hunger* (see *Machberes* כפן).

1. According to the Sages quoted by *Rashi,* God caused the sea to throw up some of the flotsam left over from the time when the Egyptians drowned in the Sea of Reeds. When the Egyptians saw this and remembered that their ancestors had died because of the Jewish people, they decided to turn back.

[Throughout Israel's history, Egypt proved itself to be an unreliable ally. Assyria attacked the Northern Kingdom *(II Kings* 17:4) when Israel stopped paying its annual tribute, in the hope of gaining independence through an alliance with *Suh,* the king of Egypt. With reference to this, Hoshea (7:11) called the Northern Kingdom *a gullible pigeon* running confusedly between Egypt and Assyria, instead of turning to God.

Isaiah (30:2-3) blamed Judah for seeking an Egyptian alliance against Sancherev, and prophesied that their reliance on Egypt would yet prove to be a shame and embarrassment to them. Indeed when the Assyrian general Ravshakeh stood at Jerusalem's gates *(II Kings* 18:21-24), he mocked them for their vain hope that Egypt might help them. They had relied on a staff which was a *broken stick.* If a person leans on it, far from lending support, it pierces his hand.

Yechezkel himself will return to this same metaphor when he castigates Egypt for its treachery (29:6-7). He prophesies that never more will Egypt tempt Israel away from God, by attracting false hopes of help. After Egypt's decline, Israel will once more turn to God in its distress.]

branches, and sent out boughs.[7] *And there was another great eagle, great of wing and abundant of plumage. And see! This vine — its roots hungered toward him, its tendrils it extended toward him from the bed of its planting, that he might water it.* [8] *In a fertile field, by abundant waters, was it planted, to produce branches and bear fruit, to become a stately vine."*

[9] *Say: "So says my Lord HASHEM/ELOHIM: Shall it prosper? Will he not tear out its roots and cut off its fruits that it may wither, all its sprouting leaves*

However, *Targum* renders; *'bent'* or *'inclined'*. *Rashi* and *Radak* suggest that the root may have acquired its meaning in a roundabout way. כפן may be the same as כנף (the letters are inverted). [This is common in Hebrew, e.g. כֶּבֶשׂ = כֶּשֶׂב. See also *comm.* to *v.* 21]. In Talmudic literature, כנף means *to gather in.* Since we occasionally find words which are used to describe opposites (סקל, can mean *to stone,* and *to remove stones),* כפן may become: *to turn towards.*

מֵעֲרֻגוֹת מַטָּעָהּ — *From the bed of its planting.*

Nebuchadnezzar had given Zidkiyahu sufficient scope to establish a viable kingdom. (See *comm.* to *v.* 5). Yet, for help in establishing the very kingdom which Nebuchadnezzar had given him, Zidkiyahu turned to Pharaoh.

8. אֶל שָׂדֶה טוֹב אֶל מַיִם רַבִּים הִיא שְׁתוּלָה — *In a fertile field, by abundant waters, was it planted.*

There was no need to turn to Pharaoh. Israel had everything she needed, even while she was under Babylon's dominion *(Rashi).*

[Except independence! But independence was never a *sine qua non* of Israel's nationhood. Other nations may indeed require land, language, and social institutions *(Gen.* ch.10) to qualify them as a separate people. To Israel, however, born and sustained miraculously among alien people and in the desert, nationhood is a fact even without those conditions. They are cherished gifts which God grants if they are deserved and if they can help Israel in the achievement of her destiny. When these gifts become impediments, they are taken away until they are once more earned — but their absence can never spell the dissolution of Israel's peoplehood. God's people can function as a satellite to a Babylonian empire as well as they can function as an independent nation. (See *Pref. Remarks* and *footnotes* to Ch. 15 and *Introd. Remarks* to 16:35-42)].

לְגֶפֶן אַדֶּרֶת — *A stately vine.*

Rashi quotes *Targum: A strong vine.*

9. תִּצְלָח — *Shall it prosper?*

This is an implied question, as though preceded by the letter ה which denotes interrogation: הֲתִצְלָח, *Can it prosper?*

The first eagle will surely come to uproot the ungrateful and disloyal vine and cause it to dry up.

וְאֶת פִּרְיָהּ יְקוֹסֵס — *And cut off its fruits.*

This refers to the sons of Zidkiyahu who were slaughtered in his presence *(Rashi.* See *Radak* quoted in *comm.* to *v.* 6).

יז צִמְחָהּ תִּיבָשׁ וְלֹא־בִזְרֹעַ גְּדוֹלָה וּבְעַם רָב
י־יד י לְמַשְׂאוֹת אוֹתָהּ מִשָּׁרָשֶׁיהָ׃ וְהִנֵּה
שְׁתוּלָה הֲתִצְלָח הֲלֹא כְּגַעַת בָּהּ רוּחַ
הַקָּדִים תִּיבַשׁ יָבֹשׁ עַל־עֲרֻגֹת צִמְחָהּ
יא תִּיבָשׁ׃ וַיְהִי דְבַר־יְהוָה אֵלַי
יב לֵאמֹר׃ אֱמָר־נָא לְבֵית הַמֶּרִי הֲלֹא
יְדַעְתֶּם מָה־אֵלֶּה אֱמֹר הִנֵּה־בָא מֶלֶךְ־
בָּבֶל יְרוּשָׁלַםִ וַיִּקַּח אֶת־מַלְכָּהּ וְאֶת־
יג שָׂרֶיהָ וַיָּבֵא אוֹתָם אֵלָיו בָּבֶלָה׃ וַיִּקַּח
מִזֶּרַע הַמְּלוּכָה וַיִּכְרֹת אִתּוֹ בְּרִית וַיָּבֵא
אֹתוֹ בְּאָלָה וְאֶת־אֵילֵי הָאָרֶץ לָקָח׃
יד לִהְיוֹת מַמְלָכָה שְׁפָלָה לְבִלְתִּי הִתְנַשֵּׂא

וְלֹא בִזְרֹעַ גְּדוֹלָה וּבְעַם רָב — *No great power, nor many people.*

The second eagle, or Pharaoh, will not honor his commitment. His legions will not come to your defense. (See *comm.* to *v.* 7) *(Rashi).*

לְמַשְׂאוֹת — *Ripping out.*

This denotes *movement* or *uprooting* as in *Micah* 2:2 *(Metzudas Zion).*

Targum explains the entire phrase as referring to Nebuchadnezzar. He will not require *great power* and *many people* to uproot Israel. It is true that the siege was a long one, but Nebuchadnezzar himself did not find it necessary to be there the whole time *(Radak).*

10. וְהִנֵּה שְׁתוּלָה הֲתִצְלָח — *Now see! It is planted — can it prosper?*

Various translations are offered.

— *Rashi:* See! Now it is planted well. Can it hope to prosper if it becomes disloyal to him who planted it originally?

— *Radak:* See! She thinks herself firmly planted, i.e., Zidkiyahu thinks that he can be independent of Babylon. Can she hope to prosper? i.e., How can Zidkiyahu delude himself, in view of his perfidy in breaking the covenant?

— *Metzudas David:* (Continuing from the previous verse, which assumed that the first eagle would uproot the vine). See! Let us assume that he does not uproot it, and it continues to grow. Nevertheless, can it hope to prosper?

רוּחַ הַקָּדִים — *The east wind.*

The east wind is dry and destructive *(Hoshea* 13:15). In addition, Babylon lies northeast of the Land of Israel *(Radak).* [See *Rashi* to *Exod.* 14:21].

12. אֱמָר נָא — *Say now.*

Targum invariably translates נָא as כְּעַן, *now.* (So, also *Radak, Sefer haShorashim* נא).There are, however, instances, where the Sages point out specifically that נָא is an expression of *entreaty* (cf. *Talmud Berachos* 9a, *Sifri Num.* 12:6). It would seem that the expression denotes general exhortation; sometimes as entreaty, sometimes as encouragement and urgency.

[However *Ibn Ezra* to *Gen.* 12:11, where, in context, the word surely implies *'entreaty'*, still stresses that its true meaning is *'now'* (inverted from

might wither? No great power, nor many people will
prevent its ripping out by the roots. 10 *Now see! It is*
planted — can it prosper? When the east wind
touches will it not wither utterly? In the very bed of
its sprouting, shall it wither".'
11 *And the word of HASHEM came to me saying:*
12 *'Say now to the Family of Rebellion: "Do you not*
know what these are?" Say: "See! The king of Baby-
lon came to Jerusalem, took its king and princes, and
brought them to him to Babylon. 13 *Then he took*
from the seed of royalty and sealed a covenant with
him; brought him under an oath and the mighty of
the Land he took away; 14 *to be a lowly kingdom that*
might not be elevated; that he should keep his cove-

the Arabic אן), and cites examples (*Gen.* 27:2, *Lamentations* 5:16) where it can have no other meaning.]

In our verse there seems no special purpose for an entreaty; *'now'*, however, is apt. The time has come to turn from the parable and to identify its meaning.

אֶת מַלְכָּהּ וְאֶת שָׂרֶיהָ — *Its king and (its) princes.*

The 'crown of the cedar' (*v.* 3), Yehoyakim, and his princes (*Rashi*). (See *footnote* to *v.* 4).

13. וַיִּקַּח מִזֶּרַע הַמְּלוּכָה — *Then he took from the seed of royalty.*

Refers to Zidkiyahu (*Rashi*).

וַיִּכְרֹת אִתּוֹ בְּרִית וַיָּבֵא אֹתוֹ בְּאָלָה — *And sealed a covenant with him; brought him under an oath.*

Zidkiyahu's true name was Matanyah. Nebuchadnezzar changed the name to Zidkiyahu (צדק = *righteous* [of] יָהו = God) to remind him of God's full righteousness and justice, if he breaks the covenant and the oath (*Krisus* 5b).

בְּאָלָה — *An oath.*

Follows *Targum* and *Nedarim* 65a. Occasionally the word is used to denote *'curse'* (See for example, *Deut.* 29:19 where *Targum* renders לְוָטַיָא, *curses.* For a discussion, see *Shavu'os* 35b and 36a).

וְאֶת אֵילֵי הָאָרֶץ לָקָח — *And the mighty of the Land he took away.*

The princes (*Rashi*). In addition to exacting a covenant and an oath, Nebuchadnezzar carried off many of the most important people as hostages against a rebellion (*Radak*).

14. לִהְיוֹת מַמְלָכָה שְׁפָלָה לְבִלְתִּי הִתְנַשֵּׂא — *To be a lowly kingdom that might not be elevated.*

[*Jeremiah* 25:9, refers to Nebuchadnezzar as God's *'servant.'* In 30:25, the sword which the Babylonian king wields against Egypt is described as *'My (God's) sword.'* Nebuchadnezzar, like other world conquerers before him, is seen by Scripture as God's instrument for the fulfillment of His purpose in history.

God, as Creator of the world and as Master of its history, had willed that all the countries on earth should bow to Babylonian rule (*Jeremiah* 27:5-8). Jeremiah addressed a special message to

יז טו־יט

טו לִשְׁמֹר אֶת־בְּרִיתוֹ לְעָמְדָהּ׃ וַיִּמְרָד־בּוֹ
לִשְׁלֹחַ מַלְאָכָיו מִצְרַיִם לָתֶת־לוֹ סוּסִים
וְעַם־רָב הֲיִצְלָח הֲיִמָּלֵט הָעֹשֵׂה אֵלֶּה
טז וְהֵפֵר בְּרִית וְנִמְלָט׃ חַי־אָנִי נְאֻם אֲדֹנָי
יֱהוִה אִם־לֹא בִּמְקוֹם הַמֶּלֶךְ הַמַּמְלִיךְ
אֹתוֹ אֲשֶׁר בָּזָה אֶת־אָלָתוֹ וַאֲשֶׁר הֵפֵר
יז אֶת־בְּרִיתוֹ אִתּוֹ בְתוֹךְ־בָּבֶל יָמוּת׃ וְלֹא
בְחַיִל גָּדוֹל וּבְקָהָל רָב יַעֲשֶׂה אוֹתוֹ
פַרְעֹה בַּמִּלְחָמָה בִּשְׁפֹּךְ סֹלְלָה וּבִבְנוֹת
יח דָּיֵק לְהַכְרִית נְפָשׁוֹת רַבּוֹת׃ וּבָזָה אָלָה
לְהָפֵר בְּרִית וְהִנֵּה נָתַן יָדוֹ וְכָל־אֵלֶּה
יט עָשָׂה לֹא יִמָּלֵט׃ לָכֵן כֹּה־אָמַר
אֲדֹנָי יֱהוִה חַי־אָנִי אִם־לֹא אָלָתִי אֲשֶׁר
בָּזָה וּבְרִיתִי אֲשֶׁר הֵפִיר וּנְתַתִּיו בְּרֹאשׁוֹ׃

Zidkiyahu: *'Bring your necks under the yoke of the Babylonian king and serve him and his people — and live. Why should you die, you and your people by sword, in famine and in plague, as God had threatened for such nations as would not serve the Babylonian king' (ibid. v.. 12-13).*

Thus the idea of the מַמְלָכָה שְׁפָלָה, *the lowly kingdom,* which Nebuchadnezzar wanted to impose upon Jerusalem, was God's direct wish for His people.

Had Zidkiyahu accepted the destiny imposed upon him, tragedy would have been averted. His refusal to submit and the events which resulted from it, make up the story of the destruction of the Temple and the Babylonian exile.] [1]

לְעָמְדָהּ — *That it might endure.*

This could refer either to the מַמְלָכָה שְׁפָלָה, that the kingdom might endure; or to the בְּרִית, that the covenant might be kept (see *Metzudas David).*

15. וַיִּמְרָד בּוֹ — *But he rebelled against him.*

See *Pref. Remarks.*

1. In *comm.* to *v.* 8, we touched upon the role of independent nationhood in Israel's destiny.
In his עִקְבְתָא דִמְשִׁיחָא, *Messianic Footfalls, Yitzchak Breuer* discusses the concept of the 'lowly' nation from a historical persepective.
Independent nationhod was never an undiluted blessing for the Jewish people. Israel's essential being as God's own people — unbounded because it is unsupported by historical 'imperatives', living in and solely dependent upon the rarefied atmosphere of God's direct providence — is put to its severest test in the crucible of independent nationhood.
The urge to *'be like the nations, like the families of the earth'* (20:32) is well-nigh irrepressible, as the tragic story of Jewish history throughout the First Temple eloquently attests.

XVII
15-19

nant that it might endure. 15 *But he rebelled against*
him by sending his agents to Egypt, to give him
horses and numerous people. Shall he prosper? Shall
he escape who does such things? Shall he break a
covenant and yet escape? 16 *As I live, the words of*
my Lord, HASHEM/ELOHIM, surely in the place of the
king who made him reign, whose oath he despised
and whose covenant he broke; with him, in the midst
of Babylon, shall he die. 17 *But not with a large army*
or a great multitude will Pharaoh aid him in the war,
with pouring of mounds and building of forts, to cut
off many souls. 18 *And as for him that despised an*
oath to break a covenant — now see! he had given his
hand, yet did all of these — he shall not escape.
19 *Therefore so says my Lord HASHEM/ELOHIM: As I*
live, surely My oath which he has despised, and My
covenant which he has broken I shall place it on his

16. For Zidkiyahu's death in Babylon, see *Jeremiah* 34:5. See also 12:13 and *comm.* there.

17. For דָּיֵק, see *comm.* to 4:2. For Pharaoh's perfidy, see *comm.* to *v.* 7.

18. וְהִנֵּה נָתַן יָדוֹ — *Now see! he had given his hand.*

Giving the hand implies a promise and commitment *(Radak; Metzudas David).*

19. אָלָתִי ... וּבְרִיתִי — *My oath ... and My covenant.*

Zidkiyahu invoked God's Name when he made his oath. It is therefore considered God's oath and His covenant *(Radak; Metzudas David).*

Vayikra Rabbah 6:5 takes בְּרִיתִי, *My covenant* as referring to Israel's covenant with God at Mt. Sinai. Zidkiyahu could never have been false to his commitment to Nebuchadnezzar had he not previously shaken off the bonds of Sinai's covenant *(Harav Joseph Breuer).*

וּנְתַתִּיו בְּרֹאשׁוֹ — *I shall place it on his head.*

This refers to the blinding of Zidkiyahu *(II Kings* 25:7). *(Rashi* based on *Vayikra Rabbah* loc. cit.).

Israel reached the peaks of its spiritual attainments (אַנְשֵׁי כְּנֶסֶת הַגְּדוֹלָה, *The Men of the Great Assembly,* reaction of the *Mishnah,* etc.) when it was undistracted by the demands and tests of independent nationhood — when, as a subject nation, it was thrown upon the one essential and unchanging postulant of its national existence, the *Torah,* for national identity.

As a satellite nation in Babylonia's empire, Israel could have looked inward and rediscovered itself as the עַם סְגוּלָה, *the peculiar treasure* of God.

Because Zidkiyahu broke his covenant, and refused to humble himself, that discovery had to take place on the banks of Babylon's rivers.

כ וּפָרַשְׂתִּי עָלָיו רִשְׁתִּי וְנִתְפַּשׂ בִּמְצוּדָתִי
וַהֲבִיאוֹתִיהוּ בָבֶלָה וְנִשְׁפַּטְתִּי אִתּוֹ שָׁם
כא מַעֲלוֹ אֲשֶׁר מָעַל־בִּי׃ וְאֵת כָּל־מִבְרָחָו
בְּכָל־אֲגַפָּיו בַּחֶרֶב יִפֹּלוּ וְהַנִּשְׁאָרִים
לְכָל־רוּחַ יִפָּרֵשׂוּ וִידַעְתֶּם כִּי אֲנִי יְהוָה
כב דִּבַּרְתִּי׃ כֹּה אָמַר אֲדֹנָי יֱהוִה
וְלָקַחְתִּי אָנִי מִצַּמֶּרֶת הָאֶרֶז הָרָמָה
וְנָתָתִּי מֵרֹאשׁ יֹנְקוֹתָיו רַךְ אֶקְטֹף
כג וְשָׁתַלְתִּי אָנִי עַל הַר־גָּבֹהַּ וְתָלוּל׃ בְּהַר

20. וּפָרַשְׂתִּי עָלָיו רִשְׁתִּי — *So I will spread My net over him.*

Rashi refers back to 12:13. See *comm.* there.

וְנִשְׁפַּטְתִּי אִתּוֹ — *And I will wrangle with him.*

Metzudas David translates אֶתְוַכַּח, *I will argue* (see also *Rashi* to 20:4). However, since *Targum* translates: *I will punish* and *Radak* renders: *I will demonstrate your perfidy,* we translate *wrangle* as denoting something stronger than *argue* (see *comm.* to 20:25).

21. וְאֵת כָּל מִבְרָחָיו — *And all his fugitives.*

Targum renders: *'All his mighty warriors,'* as though the word were written מִבְחָרָיו (as in 23:7), *'his chosen ones'* (see *Rashi).* [See *comm.* to *v. 7*].

Harav Breuer suggests that this might be a play on words. His *'chosen ones'* turn out to be *'his fugitives'* those that flee with him, and even desert him (see *II Kings* 25:5). (See *comm.* to the feminine form עֶזְרֹה in 12:14 which we explain as connoting the impotence of the bodyguard).

בְּכָל אֲגַפָּיו — *With all his officers.*

See *comm.* to 12:14.

וְהַנִּשְׁאָרִים לְכָל רוּחַ יִפָּרֵשׂוּ — *And the remaining ones, to every direction will be spread out.*

This is a milder form of אֱזָרֶה לְכָל רוּחַ (12:14). *Harav Breuer,* referring to *Avodah Zarah* 10b explains that this would suggest the positive function which גָּלוּת, *exile,* has in God's plans. The Jews will be *'spread out'* in every direction because: Even as it is impossible for the world to exist without winds (רוּחַ), so it is impossible for the world to exist without Israel.

Through exile every people of the earth will have contact with Israel — *spread out* among them.

22-24. The Babylonian eagle had planted a lowly vine *(v.* 5) in Jerusalem. In time he would return to smash and uproot it *(v.* 9), leaving the fertile field *(v.* 5) of Israel a smoldering ruin, empty and desolate, to wait seventy long years for the return of its children.

What came of the *'top of the young twigs' (v.* 4), the youthful king Yehoyachin whom he had ignominiously dragged into captivity after only three months as king? *(II Kings* 24:8).

Concerning this Yehoyachin, Jeremiah had said: *For if Kenayahu* (i.e., Yehoyachin) *the son of Yehoyakim the king of Judah were to be a signet ring on My right hand — from there I would tear him off ... Thus says Hashem: Condemn this man to childlessness, a man who will see no success in his days.*

head. [20] *So I will spread My net over him, and he will*
be caught in My trap, and I will bring him to
Babylon, and I will wrangle with him there for the
treachery which he has committed against Me.
[21] *And all his fugitives, together with all his officers,*
will fall by the sword; and the remaining ones, to
every direction will be spread out. Then shall you
know that I, HASHEM, have spoken.

[22] *So says my Lord HASHEM/ELOHIM: I will take*
from the crown of the high cedar and place it. From
the head of the young twigs, I will crop a tender one,
and plant it on a high and eminent mountain. [23] *On*

For none of his seed shall ever sit on David's throne or again rule over Judah (*Jeremiah* 22:24,30).

And yet, in Chaggai's prophecy concerning the return to Zion, it is just a grandson of this very Yehoyachin, whom we saw condemned to childless ignominy, who is God's chosen one, and is placed as a signet-ring upon His hand: *On that day, the word of HASHEM of Hosts, I will take you, Zerubavel ben She'alti'el My servant, the words of HASHEM, and I shall place you as a signet-ring. For you, I have chosen. The words of HASHEM of Hosts* (*Chaggai* 2:23).

The bridge between these seemingly irreconcilable passages lies in the regeneration which *Teshuvah*, repentance, makes possible. 'Great is Teshuvah, *Rambam* writes (*Mishnah Torah, Hilchos Teshuvah* 7); for it is the means by which a man can change his whole being'.

And it is Yehoyachin, whom *Rambam (ibid.)* holds up as the prime example of the efficacy of *Teshuvah*.

[For a full account of Yehoyachin's *Teshuvah* see *Vayikra Rabbah* 19:6. See also *Sanhedrin* 27b and 38a.]

David's royal dynasty מַלְכוּת בֵּית דָּוִד, the lineage from which one day Messiah will come, was perpetuated through Yehoyachin (see *Vayikra Rabbah* loc. cit.).

Thus the *'Top of the young twigs'* which, to mortal eyes, seemed condemned to a barren exile in Babylon, was really the young shoot, which God Himself was planting in order to produce the stately cedar, which would one day cast its shade over the whole of mankind (based on *Harav Breuer*).

22. וְלָקַחְתִּי אָנִי מִצַּמֶּרֶת הָאֶרֶז הָרָמָה — *I will take from the crown of the high cedar.*

And I shall draw near, from the royal house of David, which is compared to a high cedar, and I shall establish from his descendants ... *(Targum).*

Rashi identifies the subject of the verse as the מֶלֶךְ הַמָּשִׁיחַ, Messiah. *Radak* explains that it refers to Zerubavel, the grandson of Yehoyachin, the leader of the people who would return to Israel at the end of the Babylonian exile *(Chaggai 2:23).*

Essentially the two explanations are identical. Zerubavel is the progenitor of the Messiah.

הַר גָּבֹהַּ וְתָלוּל — *A high and eminent mountain.*

תֵּל is a hillock, so תָּלוּל (the doubled form) describes a high mountain.

יז מְרוֹם יִשְׂרָאֵל אֶשְׁתֳּלֶנּוּ וְנָשָׂא עָנָף וְעָשָׂה
כד פֶרִי וְהָיָה לְאֶרֶז אַדִּיר וְשָׁכְנוּ תַחְתָּיו כֹּל
צִפּוֹר כָּל־כָּנָף בְּצֵל דָּלִיּוֹתָיו תִּשְׁכֹּנָּה׃
כד וְיָדְעוּ כָּל־עֲצֵי הַשָּׂדֶה כִּי אֲנִי יְהוָה
הִשְׁפַּלְתִּי | עֵץ גָּבֹהַּ הִגְבַּהְתִּי עֵץ שָׁפָל
הוֹבַשְׁתִּי עֵץ לָח וְהִפְרַחְתִּי עֵץ יָבֵשׁ אֲנִי
יח א יְהוָה דִּבַּרְתִּי וְעָשִׂיתִי׃ וַיְהִי דְבַר־
א־ב ב יְהוָה אֵלַי לֵאמֹר׃ מַה־לָּכֶם אַתֶּם מֹשְׁלִים
אֶת־הַמָּשָׁל הַזֶּה עַל־אַדְמַת יִשְׂרָאֵל
לֵאמֹר אָבוֹת יֹאכְלוּ בֹסֶר וְשִׁנֵּי הַבָּנִים

Yechezkel reaffirms Isaiah's vision (*Isaiah* 2:2) in which the house of God will be established upon a high mountain to which all nations will flock to learn the ways of God.

In the same sense *v.* 23 envisages David's progeny as a strong cedar, whose branches are both fruitful and shady under which all birds [כֹּל צִפּוֹר, *the clean birds,* כָּל כָּנָף, *the unclean ones* as well (*Chullin* 139b)] can find protection from the burning sun. [See *comm.* to 8:16, for a discussion of the sun as symbol of the challenge to God's Providence.]

24. הִשְׁפַּלְתִּי עֵץ גָּבֹהַּ — *I have lowered a high tree.*

The Chaldeans who ruled over Israel (*Rashi*).

הוֹבַשְׁתִּי עֵץ לָח — *I have dried a moist tree.*

Zidkiyahu and his descendants (*Rashi*).

וְהִפְרַחְתִּי עֵץ יָבֵשׁ — *And made blossom a dry tree.*

Yehoyachin who was exiled without children, will bear Zerubavel in Babylon, and he will be prince of Judah to rule over it (*Rashi*).

So the chapter ends with the assurance that in the very moment of what seemed to be the final dissolution of the Jewish nation, God sows and protects the seed from which the future will develop.

XVIII

In 12:21-25, we noted the prophet's battle against מְשָׁלִים, *the short pithy sayings,* which capsulated the people's attitudes, and served as slogans around which to rally opposition to God's message.

The all-pervasive reality which permeated every facet of existence during Jerusalem's final few years was the impending holocaust. Faced with the certainty of destruction, people were forced to consider its implications for God's justice and providence.

They knew themselves to be sinners; but they also knew that their sins were not greater than those of earlier generations. At best they saw themselves beset by a cumulative guilt for which they were only partially responsible. At worst, they were innocent victims of their parents' sins which were being visited upon them.

In their minds the very justice of God was called into question as they grappled with these

XVII the mountain of the height of Israel will I plant it,
24 and it shall bear branches and produce fruit, and it
shall become a stately cedar, and under it shall dwell
all birds and all winged things, in the shade of its
tendrils shall they dwell. 24 And all the trees of the
field shall know that I, HASHEM, have lowered a high
tree, and raised a low tree; I have dried a moist tree
and made blossom a dry tree. I, HASHEM, have
spoken and have done.'' '

XVIII The word of HASHEM came to me, saying:
1-2 2 What do you want, you who use this proverb
on the soil of Israel, saying: "The fathers eat unripe
grapes, and the sons' teeth become blunt."

problems. And this questioning would have a profound effect upon their actions and attitudes.

They formulated their probings into the מָשָׁל, *the proverb,* with which this chapter deals.

2. מֹשְׁלִים אֶת הַמָּשָׁל הַזֶּה — *Who use this proverb.*

For the use of the word מָשָׁל in this connection, see 12:22. The saying in our chapter would seem to combine the elements of both parable (metaphor) and proverb.

עַל אַדְמַת יִשְׂרָאֵל — *On the soil of Israel.*

Radak reads: *Concerning* the Land of Israel.

That the proverb was actually used in Jerusalem is attested by *Jeremiah* 31:28.

בֹּסֶר — *Unripe grapes.*

Pesachim 53a defines the term: בֹּסֶר is a grape which has reached the size of a white bean.

תִּקְהֶינָה — *Become blunt.*

Koheles 10:10 uses קֵהָה to describe a *blunt* knife.

Menachem (Machberes קה) combines our word with יקהה *(Proverbs* 30:17) and translates both as *weakness.* [So also *Metzudas Zion,* here]. Thus: the teeth were too weak to cut the food. [*Radak* in *Sefer haShorashim* lists the two roots separately. He defines יקה as *obedience,* and קהה as *a weakness in cutting,* i.e. blunt.]

אָבוֹת יֹאכְלוּ בֹסֶר וְשִׁנֵּי הַבָּנִים תִּקְהֶינָה — *The fathers eat unripe grapes and the sons' teeth become blunt.*

The generation of Yechezkel proclaimed: 'This is God's way, the fathers sin and the sons are punished. After all, the kings of Israel sinned for many years before they were exiled. We too shall not fear that we will be punished for our sins [i.e. God will wait, and the punishment will eventually befall future generations]' *(Rashi).*

In *Rashi*'s view this proverb is essentially the same as the one mentioned in 12:22. The difficulties in understanding the ways of God's providence lulled the people into a sense of security. God's punishment would either not come at all (Ch. 12, *ibid.)* or would come after their lifetime.

God's answer comes in *v.* 4. The son is as much *'His'* as is the father; he would not be punished for the sins of his father.

The rest of the chapter goes on to

describe God's justice, but does not address itself to the source of the confusion. We are not told why exile did not overtake the Northern Kingdom until so late in their history, nor is a solution offered to the immediate problem (implied though not stated by *Rashi)* as to why this particular generation should suffer for wrongs not solely of its own doing.

In *Radak*'s view, this problem is the subject of the proverb. It is a cry of anguish, at the seeming injustice of their fate. Again and again they had been told that *Menashe*'s sins had made the destruction inevitable — but why should they be punished for the sins of an earlier generation? (See *comm.* and *footnote* to 8:3, for a discussion of this problem. See further, *footnote,* below).

The answer is contained in *v.* 19, which reiterates the lesson of *Exod.* 20:5 and 34:7, that God will indeed visit the father's sins upon the children, where these later continue in his evil ways. As the Sages teach in *Sanhedrin* 27b: כְּשֶׁאוֹחֲזִין מַעֲשֵׂה אֲבוֹתֵיהֶן בִּידֵיהֶן, *when they grasp the deed of their fathers in their own hands.* [The *Talmud* provides this modification in order to avoid a contradiction from *Deut.* 24:16 which states that: *children will not die for (the sins of) their fathers.* For other ways to eliminate this apparent contradiction, see *Bamidbar Rabbah* 19:33, and *Midrash Tana'im Deut.* 24:16.] By continuing the practices of their sinful parents the children express their own approval of the earlier sins, and thus render themselves equally culpable. The generation of the destruction could have avoided its fate if it had struck a new path instead of aping its parents.

Harav Breuer sees the proverb as an expression of the stark fatalism which grew out of their perceptions.If they were being victimized for sins which were not of their own doing, then what point could there be in trying to better themselves? Was God's divine gift of תְּשׁוּבָה, *repentance,* viable in a system which punished one man for another's transgressions?

Again the answer is that, of course the road of repentance is open to them — God visits the guilt of parents only upon unregenerate descendants.[1]

1. Rabbinic sources contradict these attempts to harmonize the conclusions of this chapter with the doctrine of פֹּקֵד עֲוֹן אָבֹת עַל בָּנִים, *He recalls the sin of fathers upon children (Exod.* 20:5), by applying the modification of *Sanhedrin* 27b (see comm.).

Makkos 24a, states explicitly that this doctrine was *'annulled'* by Yechezkel, when he said in our chapter *(v.* 4): *'Whichever soul sins, it shall die'* (implying that children will never be punished for their fathers). In this view no harmonization is needed, since the earlier doctrine was no longer operative. [Some commentators (see *Aruch La'Ner* ad. loc.) maintain that this 'annulment' is, in reality, only an explanation of the dictum of the Torah (i.e. that *'Whichever soul sins, it shall die'* is true only when the children are righteous, but that when they continue in their father's ways they will be punished for their father's sin also.) However, this is contradicted by *Agados Bereishis* Ch. 10 (see *comm.* to 14:16) which states clearly that with Yechezkel's statement *(v.* 4) a change was inaugurated in God's Providence.]

The following is an attempt to explain the people's dilemma as expressed by the proverb, while interpreting Yechezkel's answer to mean that an annulment of Moses' doctrine did, in fact, take place.

Some general remarks should preface this discussion:

— *a.* True, the destruction occurs in a generation which is only partly, and perhaps, hardly at all responsible, for the sins which caused the downfall. But this fact should not be seen as a result of the doctrine of *'visiting-the-sins-of-the-fathers-upon-the-children'* (פֹּקֵד עֲוֹן אָבֹת עַל בָּנִים).

In 9:4 we discussed the decree which is issued against the *community* rather than the individual. We noted that such a decree would involve the innocent as well as the guilty *as long as they form part of the same community.* This concept of *community* spans the generations, and survives the deaths of individuals. (אֵין הַצִּיבּוּר מֵתִים, *A community does not die* [*Temurah* 15b]). The people who lived during the reign of Zidkiyahu are members of the same *community* as the people who lived in the reign of Menashe. *Knesses Israel is one eternal, unchanging entity!* Just as we understand that a decree issued against the *community* will cause

the innocent to suffer together with the wicked, so the fact that the decree will be actualized at a time when all the people are *innocent* will not surprise us. The decree is addressed to the *community*, not the man. Consequently the proverb was not aimed at any apparent injustice involved with the destruction of Temple and country; the people understood the concept of joint communal responsibility. However their status as individuals did trouble the people as we shall see further.

– *b*. The doctrine: פֹּקֵד עֲוֹן אָבֹת עַל בָּנִים, *He recalls the sin of fathers upon children*, should not be understood simply to mean that children will be punished for their parents' guilt, given the proper circumstances.

In the Torah the doctrine is stated in conjunction with the associated idea that: *'He does kindness to thousands'* [of generations]. That doctrine does *not* assert that the reward earned by the righteous man is given instead to his children, but that *part of his reward* is that God will be kind to his descendants. So, too, the wicked man is punished *partly* in that God will withhold His kindness from his descendants. The kindness and favors which God shows to every individual in helping him in his struggle for purity and goodness, will be withheld from someone who obdurately clings to the evil ways of his father, thereby strengthening his own propensity towards evil.

This was the basis for the anguish which the people articulated in the proverb! They themselves had not been responsible for the conditions into which, and the attitudes with which they had been born. They felt that the tendency to sinfulness was deeply ingrained within themselves. Their fathers had eaten the unripe fruits. They had been born into homes where idol worship was the norm, where all the abominations which, tragically had become part of life in Jerusalem, were practiced.

If their father's sins were to be recalled upon them, if God's support in their spiritual struggle were to be withheld from them, their teeth would indeed be blunted. What hope could they have of being able to change that which had been part of their being from earliest childhood?

God's answer is to be found in His annulment of Moses' dictum, through Yechezkel's prophecy.

– *c*. To understand the strange notion that a later prophet would be able to *annul* what Moses had said in the Torah, two possibilities suggest themselves.

Maharal in *Makkos* suggests that Moses is the ideal אִישׁ הָאֱלֹהִים, *the Man of God* (Elohim denoting God as *Judge)*, in whose world-view absolute and uncompromising justice is axiomatic. Moses' frame of reference was perfection; within that high standard, the shortcomings of parents might be deemed grievous enough to affect succeeding generations. However, Moses himself was aware that other leaders would arise in Israel, whose lesser degree of perfection would permit of a more flexible and compromising mode of justice, and in whose purview, Moses' doctrine would be 'annulled'.

In his deeply perceptive essay on *The Book of Ezekiel*, in *Die Drei Grossen Propheten*, *Rabbi Joseph Carlebach* demonstrates another possibility.

The destruction of the Temple was to bring about a profound and far-reaching change in the relationship between God and sinning man. By means of the Temple Service – particularly on *Yom Kippur* – the relationship to God had been a *communal* one. The High Priest brought *communal* sacrifices which would atone for each *individual* who was a component of the community. Particularly the שְׂעִיר הַמִּשְׁתַּלֵּחַ, *the goat which was sent to be thrown off the rocks (Leviticus* 16:21-22), had the property of achieving atonement for all members of the community – in some cases even if the individual had not repented (See *Rambam Hilchos Teshuvah* 1:2).

[As *Maharal* points out, the assumption (of *Pirkei Avos* 1:12) that Aaron loved peace is not based on any particular verse, but rather on the very nature of the *communal* service which he performed, a service which had the effect of uniting all the individuals in the community into one loving unit (*Derech Chaim* to loc. cit.).]

The destruction of the Temple, which brought with it the elimination of the Temple service, changed the entire picture Suddenly each individual, laden with his own sins, faced his Creator alone. The support which had once been drawn from the community was no more.

These altered circumstances, asserts *Rabbi Carlebach*, contained the seeds for the annulment of Moses' decree. Before the destruction, when each *son* was a part of the supportive *whole* of the community, the sins of the father, himself a member of that same community, could well be visited upon him. After the destruction, as each individual stands alone before God, he could be judged only with reference to himself.

Thus the time had come when Israel needed a Yechezkel rather than a Moses; a leader

יח
ג־ו

ג תִּקְהֶינָה: חַי־אָנִי נְאֻם אֲדֹנָי יֱהֹוִה אִם־
יִהְיֶה לָכֶם עוֹד מְשֹׁל הַמָּשָׁל הַזֶּה
ד בְּיִשְׂרָאֵל: הֵן כָּל־הַנְּפָשׁוֹת לִי הֵנָּה כְּנֶפֶשׁ
הָאָב וּכְנֶפֶשׁ הַבֵּן לִי־הֵנָּה הַנֶּפֶשׁ הַחֹטֵאת
ה הִיא תָמוּת: וְאִישׁ כִּי־יִהְיֶה צַדִּיק
ו וְעָשָׂה מִשְׁפָּט וּצְדָקָה: אֶל־הֶהָרִים לֹא
אָכָל וְעֵינָיו לֹא נָשָׂא אֶל־גִּלּוּלֵי בֵּית

3-4. We quote *Radak:* 'I shall let you know My justice and My ways, so that you shall no longer misunderstand them. Consider, and you shall see that it is so. All souls are Mine, and I placed them in the body in order that they might lead it to follow Me, and I wish them to live, not to die, for they are Mine, a part of Me, both father and son! How can you possibly imagine that I would punish a soul that committed no sin. Far be it from Me!'

4. הַנֶּפֶשׁ הַחֹטֵאת הִיא תָמוּת — *Whichever soul sins, it shall die.*

And shall not suffer for the sins of another. This 'annuls' the *Torah* doctrine of פֹּקֵד עֲוֹן אָבֹת עַל בָּנִים *(Makkos* 24a). (See *footnote* to *v.* 2 for an analysis of this concept).

הִיא תָמוּת — *It shall die.*

Radak points out that the verbs *to live* and *to die* as used in our chapter, are not to be taken only in their literal sense. *Living* is a metaphor for all good things that can happen to a person, *dying* stands for all bad things. [This does not accord with *Rav Sa'adiah Gaon* who interprets the life and death of our chapter as being in *Olam Haba,* the World to Come. (See *Me'iri Chibur haTeshuva Jerusalem* 5736 p. 35).]

5-9. These verses contain the description of the צַדִּיק, *the righteous man,* who shall live [but who will not shield his wicked son (*vs.* 10-13) from punishment].

[If we take the question, implied in the proverb, as dealing only with the problem of *transferred guilt,* this passage would seem to be redundant. We are told nothing of this *zaddik*'s parents therefore the question of *transferred guilt* does not arise. He is not part of the problem decried in the parable.That the fully righteous person does not suffer for the sins of his wicked father is asserted in *vs.* 14-20. If, however, with *Rabbi Joseph Carlebach* (see *footnote* to *v.* 2) we can see the exile as tearing away the supportive matrix of communal Temple service, then we understand why the prophet was so anxious to demonstrate how an individual, in whichever circumstances he finds himself, can attain 'life'.]

It is not easy to determine why the prophet chose just these examples to illustrate a righteous life. *Radak* isolates five categories within which they fall. 1. *Idol worship,* a transgression בֵּין אָדָם לַמָּקוֹם *between man and God,* and the greatest of all sins; 2. *Business relationships,* as being constantly ap-

through whom the Torah's absolute concept of pure justice could be tempered by a greater readiness for merciful compromise, to suit the altered circumstances.

This was the prophet's answer: *'Whichever soul sins, it shall die.'* As they stood before God as individuals, so God would judge them as indivduals. For the new circumstances, in a situation where the perfection of a Moses was no longer to be expected, a new, more merciful, understanding awaited them.

XVIII
3-6

[3] *As I live, the words of my Lord HASHEM/*
ELOHIM, there will no longer be among you those
who use this proverb in Israel. [4] *See! All souls are*
Mine, like the soul of the father, so the soul of the
son, they are Mine. Whichever soul sins, it shall die.
[5] *But if a man be righteous and practice justice and*
righteousness: [6] *upon the mountains did he not eat;*
his eyes did he not lift to the idols of the Family of

plicable in daily life; 3. *Moral behavior,* an area of constant temptation (incestuous relationships need not be mentioned since most people would not be attracted to them); 4. *Positive commands,* of which charity is among the most important; 5. *Communal relationships,* as being fundamental to normal life. (See further in *comm.* to *v.* 6.)

5. מִשְׁפָּט וּצְדָקָה — *Justice and righteousness.*

This combination occurs frequently in Scripture. While the meaning of מִשְׁפָּט, *justice,* is clear, the word צְדָקָה is less easy to define.

Following, is a partial list of definitions, found in the classical commentators.

[According to the early lexicographers *(Menachem, Ibn Janach* and also *Radak),* the masculine צֶדֶק and the feminine צְדָקָה are completely synonymous. However, *Ibn Ezra* to *Deut.* 24:13 writes that צֶדֶק is synonymous with מִשְׁפָּט, *justice;* while the feminine form צְדָקָה could have a different meaning. (See *Sanhedrin* 6b).]

Rambam, (Moreh Nevuchim 3:53) writes that צְדָקָה is related to צֶדֶק which he defines *(ibid.* 2:39) as a state in which seemingly conflicting claims are resolved by being perfectly balanced one with another. Thus צְדָקָה is an action through which *all* legitimate claims are satisfied. A person's soul has a 'claim' upon him. It wishes to control his actions, causing him to act in an ethical way even when there is no legal obligation upon him. Thus if a person is good or helpful to another, where the law does not require it of him, his action is considered צְדָקָה since he is giving his soul its due.

Ramban (Lev. 20:17) equates צְדָקָה with חֶסֶד, *kindness.* The terms are: 'twins which are always mentioned [together].'

Rabbeinu Yonah (Prov. 1:3) defines צֶדֶק (and presumably צְדָקָה) as an act which goes: לִפְנִים מִשּׁוּרַת הַדִּין, *beyond the requirements of the law.*

Malbim (Isaiah 1:27) writes that מִשְׁפָּט refers to relations with one's fellow-man, while צְדָקָה describes his relations to God.

[For another, exhaustive analysis of צְדָקָה, see *Hirsch*'s commentary to *Genesis* 15:6].

6. אֶל הֶהָרִים לֹא אָכָל — *Upon the mountains did he not eat.*

He did not serve idols by eating idolatrous sacrifices upon the mountains [where it was the custom to practice idolatry] *(Targum* and *Rashi).*

The אֶל is to be understood like עַל, *upon (Radak).*

וְעֵינָיו לֹא נָשָׂא — *His eyes did he not lift.*

Not only did he not worship idols, he never even inclined his mind towards them *(Radak).*

The verse contains the first four prohibitions which one must observe to be considered a *zaddik,* a righteous person. The requirements do not appear

יִשְׂרָאֵל וְאֶת־אֵשֶׁת רֵעֵהוּ לֹא טִמֵּא וְאֶל־
ז אִשָּׁה נִדָּה לֹא יִקְרָב: וְאִישׁ לֹא יוֹנֶה
חֲבֹלָתוֹ חוֹב יָשִׁיב גְּזֵלָה לֹא יִגְזֹל לַחְמוֹ
ח לְרָעֵב יִתֵּן וְעֵירֹם יְכַסֶּה־בָּגֶד: בַּנֶּשֶׁךְ לֹא־
יִתֵּן וְתַרְבִּית לֹא יִקָּח מֵעָוֶל יָשִׁיב יָדוֹ

to be stringent. Surely a person would have to go beyond these simple requirements to be considered a true *zaddik*.

Sanhedrin 81a paints an entirely different picture. The man who does not *'eat upon the mountains'*, is one who is so completely good that he can stand completely upon his own merits, without drawing upon זְכוּת אָבוֹת, *the merit of the fathers.*

He who does not *'lift up his eyes to the idols'* is the man who goes about in a modest and becoming manner, and does not project himself with an arrogant קוֹמָה זְקוּפָה, *an exaggeratedly erect stance.*

Defiling *'his neighbor's wife'*, is projected as interfering in his livelihood.

And approaching *'a woman in her impurity'*, is the description of permitting oneself to be supported by charity.

Thus our verse postulates a very high moral standard for the person who is to be considered a *zaddik*.[1]

7-8. These verses seem to present the same difficulty as *v.* 6. Some of the sins mentioned are so gross that a person could not be described as a *zaddik* simply because he refrains from committing them. However, no attempt is made by the Sages, to explain these verses as having any other than their ordinary meaning.

Maharsha (ad. loc.) suggests a solution. He points out that the qualities mentioned here could be subsumed under מִשְׁפָּט וּצְדָקָה of *v.* 5. That they are mentioned separately indicates that a man is being described who goes well beyond the halachic boundaries of these sins. We shall indicate *Maharsha*'s thinking, in each case.

וְאִישׁ לֹא יוֹנֶה — *No man will he oppress.*

The injunction in the Torah וְלֹא תוֹנוּ אִישׁ אֶת עֲמִיתוֹ, *None of you may oppress his comrade (Lev.* 25:17) would apply only to a fellow Jew. The *zaddik,*

1. The passage in *Sanhedrin* is introduced by the words דָּרַשׁ רַב אַחָא בְּרִ׳ חֲנִינָא, *Rav Acha ben Rabbi Chanina interpreted. Rashi* ad. loc. points out that this דָּרַשׁ, this *interpretation* is לָאו כְּמַשְׁמָעוּתֵיהּ, *not in accordance with the simple meaning.* [In *Rashi*'s terminology, דרש is not something *opposed* to the simple meaning, but rather an explanation or development of it. Occasionally the דָּרַשׁ is in accordance with the מַשְׁמָעוּת, *the simple meaning* (see *Rashi Sanhedrin* 70a) and sometimes it goes beyond the simple meaning, as in our case. (See *Yonah Frankel, Darko Shel Rashi Be'feirusho Le'Talmud Bavli, Jerusalem* 5735, pp. 58 and 142).]

In *Rashi*'s view, Rav Acha was forced to develop the interpretation of the verse beyond its simple meaning because of the problem raised in the commentary. The sins mentioned are so gross that no man could be considered a *zaddik* merely for avoiding these particular transgressions.

The question however remains. What basis did Rav Acha have for his seemingly farfetched interpretation?

Rav Acha's assumption must be that a *zaddik* would not only avoid a given sin in its crassest form, but would refrain even from such actions which are outgrowths of the same basic character flaws which, when aggravated and unfettered, result in the gross transgressions mentioned in the text. Thus, while interfering with another's livelihood is a far cry from defiling his wife, both grow out of a disregard for the legitimate rights of another human being.

a. Idol worship draws upon the pernicious doctrine that man needs an intermediary between himself and God. (See *footnote* to 8:12). That man is furthest removed from this,

Israel; his neighbor's wife did he not defile; and an impure woman did he not approach; [7] *no man will he oppress; a pledge for a debt will he return; loot will he not rob; his bread will he give to the hungry; the naked will he cover with a garment;* [8] *for interest will he not lend; any increase will he not take; from iniquity will he withhold his hand; true justice will he*

however, will not oppress any man.

חֲבֹלָתוֹ חוֹב יָשִׁיב — *A pledge for a debt will he return.*

Rashi and *Radak* explain that he complied with the Torah's requirement that when his debtor needs the use of the pledge, the lender will return it to him.

According to *Maharsha,* he goes beyond the Torah's requirement. In the event that he forgot to return the pledge one night, he will voluntarily give it up completely and carry the debt without collateral.

גְּזֵלָה לֹא יִגְזֹל — *Loot will he not rob.*

Even in a situation where his neighbors had robbed him and he might be legally and morally entitled to take something back, he will not do so.

לַחְמוֹ לְרָעֵב יִתֵּן — *His bread will he give to the hungry.*

He would prefer to give up *his own meal,* rather than fulfill his charitable obligations with inferior food.

וְעֵירֹם יְכַסֶּה בָּגֶד — *The naked will he cover with a garment.*

And not just with a piece of cloth, which would have sufficed according to the strict letter of the law.

8. בַּנֶּשֶׁךְ לֹא יִתֵּן וְתַרְבִּית לֹא יִקָּח — *For interest will he not lend; any increase will he not take.*

Even in a situation where only the *lending* or the *payment,* but not both, involved interest. [If a person lends a hundred bushels with the understanding that the payment will consist of one hundred and twenty, that loan was made with an *interest* agreement. If the price goes down and a hundred and twenty bushels are worth as much as the original one hundred, then the *payment* does not involve interest. The converse is true when the prices rise.]

מֵעָוֶל יָשִׁיב יָדוֹ — *From iniquity will he withhold his hand.*

He has refused any kind of bribery. [This is an area in which it is easy to go

who stands alone before his Creator and does not even draw upon the merit of the fathers. Nothing is permitted to intrude upon the immediacy of his relationship with God.

b. The man who walks with a haughty, arrogant bearing offends the idea that *'the whole world is filled with His glory' (Kidushin* 31a). In its more aggravated form, such a denial of the omnipresence of God could lead to the idea that there are other potent forces in the world to whom one might turn.

c. The best way to avoid interference with his neighbor's most precious and intimate possession, would be to hold his neighbor's every possession sacrosanct. A person who cannot bring himself to damage his neighbor in even a casual indirect way will have insured himself against the temptation to do him more direct harm.

d. The Torah prohibits relations with a woman during the period of her impurity. To approach her at such a time would imply that the person who does so is at the mercy of his needs, and will fill them in an unacceptable manner. A person strong enough to refuse charitable help because of a taint of shamefulness is the disciplined person who will control temptation where more serious transgressions are at stake.

[Some of the above, is based loosely on *Maharal Chidushei Aggadah,* to *Sanhedrin.* See also *Maharsha* ad. loc.]

מִשְׁפַּט אֱמֶת יַעֲשֶׂה בֵּין אִישׁ לְאִישׁ׃
ט בְּחֻקּוֹתַי יְהַלֵּךְ וּמִשְׁפָּטַי שָׁמַר לַעֲשׂוֹת
אֱמֶת צַדִּיק הוּא חָיֹה יִחְיֶה נְאֻם אֲדֹנָי
י יֱהֹוִה׃ וְהוֹלִיד בֶּן־פָּרִיץ שֹׁפֵךְ דָּם וְעָשָׂה
יא אָח מֵאַחַד מֵאֵלֶּה׃ וְהוּא אֶת־כָּל־אֵלֶּה
לֹא עָשָׂה כִּי גַם אֶל־הֶהָרִים אָכַל וְאֶת־
יב אֵשֶׁת רֵעֵהוּ טִמֵּא׃ עָנִי וְאֶבְיוֹן הוֹנָה
גְּזֵלוֹת גָּזָל חֲבֹל לֹא יָשִׁיב וְאֶל־הַגִּלּוּלִים

beyond the halachic requirements. Where the halachah would forbid only direct payment of a bribe, the *zaddik* might disqualify himself from judging, even if he had received unconnected, even trivial, favors from one of the litigants.]

מִשְׁפַּט אֱמֶת יַעֲשֶׂה — *True justice did he execute.*

Da'as Sofrim points out that *true* justice is extremely rare in the sense that its truth is apparent to all. More often than not, one or another, or perhaps both of the parties will feel that the decision was not fair. Great integrity is required of the judge in weighing all the many details which may effect judgment, so exactly that the decision will really be *true* in everyone's eyes.

9. צַדִּיק הוּא חָיֹה יִחְיֶה — *He is a righteous man; he shall surely live.*

V. 11 describes the *'violent son'* as one who: אֶת כָּל אֵלֶּה לֹא עָשָׂה, *he did not do all these.* The implication is that total compliance is required; hence only one who complies with every one of the high moral standards enumerated here, can be considered a *zaddik.* When he came to this passage Rabban Gamliel used to cry, 'How could anyone hope to live? Rabbi Akiva comforted him. The verse is to be translated: *He did not do* any *of these. One who transgresses all of them is called a 'violent son'* (see *v.* 10). But if a person falls short of some of the standards in this passage, he might still be considered a *zaddik* (*Sanhedrin* loc. cit.).

חָיֹה יִחְיֶה — *He shall surely live.*

In *v.* 4 we pointed out that *death* and *life* as used in this passage are metaphorical.

The promise of *life* comes for walking in God's decrees and guarding the ordinances. We have an almost identical passage in *Lev.* 18:4-5. *Ramban* (ad. loc.) comments on why the promise is made in such general terms. He explains that the type of *life* granted a person as a reward for doing his duty, depends on his attitude in doing it. He enumerates the following categories.

a. A person who serves God for the purpose of obtaining a temporal reward. The *life* granted him is temporal; a long, pleasant, life in This World.

b. If a person does good out of fear of God, knowing that sin brings punishment in the World to Come, he will be granted eternal *life,* free from punishment and savoring the good of that world.

c. If a person serves God out of love, his *life* will span both worlds. His temporal life will be happy and content and his reward will be complete in the World to Come.

d. The highest attainable level of service, is that in which the person denigrates all worldly considerations, and lives only in the presence of his

execute between man and man; 9 in My decrees will
he go; My ordinances did he observe to practice
truth. He is a righteous man; he shall surely live! The
words of my Lord, HASHEM / ELOHIM.
10 But he begot a violent son who sheds blood, and
he does to his brother any of these. 11 And all these
did he not do, for even upon the mountains did he
eat; and his neighbor's wife did he defile; 12 the poor
and the needy did he oppress; loot did he rob; a
pledge did he not return; and to the idols did he lift

God, as though he had no bodily needs at all. Such a one will live eternally, even his body attaining immortality as happened to Chanoch and Elijah.

See further in *comm.* to 20:11.

We have now learned that a *zaddik* can attain *life* by dint of his own efforts (see *comm.* above *vs.* 5-9). The prophet now turns to the problem of *transferred* merit.

10. וְהוֹלִיד בֵּן פָּרִיץ — *But he begot a violent son.*

פרץ, means *to break through.* Thus a פָּרִיץ is one who 'breaks through' the barriers of propriety *(Metzudas Zion),* or the barriers which his father had erected to protect his righteousness *(Harav Breuer).*

וְעָשָׂה אָח מֵאַחַד מֵאֵלֶּה — *And he does to his brother, any of these.*

The translation follows *Targum,* with whom most commentators concur (as seems borne out from *v.* 18) in spite of the obvious difficulty in syntax — for, according to his interpretation, the verse should have read לְאָחִיו, 'to *his* brother', instead of אָח, '*a* brother'.

Radak in *Sefer haShorashim* points out that, in our context *'brother'* is used in a wider sense, and means *'fellow man'.*

[The problem of how *'shedding blood'* enters into this litany of sins, which, in other respects, parallels the examples contained in *vs.* 5-9, is solved by *Harav Breuer* with the following translation: *'Who is considered as if shedding blood by doing even one of these things to his brother'.*]

Radak suggests that אָח could be an abbreviation of אֶחָד, *one.* The translation would be: *And he does one of these things.*

Ibn Ezra (Sfas Yeser 134) attaches a new meaning from the context. He translates אָח as, *'whichever one'.*

11. וְהוּא אֶת כָּל אֵלֶּה לֹא עָשָׂה — *And all these did he not do.*

He did not perform any of the good acts, described in the passage dealing with the *zaddik (Rashi).* See *comm.* to *v.* 9.

כִּי גַם ... — *For even* [lit. *also*].

Not only did he refrain from doing good, he actively did evil *(Metzudas David).*

12. עָנִי וְאֶבְיוֹן הוֹנָה — *The poor and the needy, did he oppress.*

The poor are used as examples, as being easiest to oppress *(Radak).*

עָנִי וְאֶבְיוֹן — *The poor and the needy.*

According to *Bava Metzia* 111b an אֶבְיוֹן is more needy than an עָנִי. The former has nothing at all [*Rashi* ad. loc. derives the word from the root אבה, *to desire,* hence: One who desires everything] and has lost all sense of shame. An עָנִי [from ענה, *to afflict (Radak, Sefer haShorashim* under ענה)]

יג נָשָׂא עֵינָיו תּוֹעֵבָה עָשָׂה: בַּנֶּשֶׁךְ נָתַן
וְתַרְבִּית לָקַח וָחָי לֹא יִחְיֶה אֵת כָּל־
הַתּוֹעֵבוֹת הָאֵלֶּה עָשָׂה מוֹת יוּמָת דָּמָיו
יד בּוֹ יִהְיֶה: וְהִנֵּה הוֹלִיד בֵּן וַיַּרְא אֶת־כָּל־
חַטֹּאת אָבִיו אֲשֶׁר עָשָׂה וַיִּרְאֶ וְלֹא יַעֲשֶׂה
טו כָּהֵן: עַל־הֶהָרִים לֹא אָכָל וְעֵינָיו לֹא
נָשָׂא אֶל־גִּלּוּלֵי בֵּית יִשְׂרָאֵל אֶת־אֵשֶׁת
טז רֵעֵהוּ לֹא טִמֵּא: וְאִישׁ לֹא הוֹנָה חֲבֹל לֹא
חָבָל וּגְזֵלָה לֹא גָזָל לַחְמוֹ לְרָעֵב נָתָן
יז וְעֵרוֹם כִּסָּה־בָגֶד: מֵעָנִי הֵשִׁיב יָדוֹ נֶשֶׁךְ
וְתַרְבִּית לֹא לָקָח מִשְׁפָּטַי עָשָׂה בְּחֻקּוֹתַי
הָלָךְ הוּא לֹא יָמוּת בַּעֲוֹן אָבִיו חָיֹה יִחְיֶה:
יח אָבִיו כִּי־עָשַׁק עֹשֶׁק גָּזַל גֵּזֶל אָח וַאֲשֶׁר
לֹא־טוֹב עָשָׂה בְּתוֹךְ עַמָּיו וְהִנֵּה־מֵת
יט בַּעֲוֹנוֹ: וַאֲמַרְתֶּם מַדֻּעַ לֹא־נָשָׂא הַבֵּן בַּעֲוֹן

on the other hand, is poor and afflicted, but has retained some sense of personal pride.

תּוֹעֵבָה עָשָׂה — *Abomination did he commit.*

Rashi (presumably based on *Lev.* 18:22) explains this as referring to homosexual perversion.

Seeking a parallel to the previous passage *(vs.* 5-9), *Radak* interprets that the intent is having relations with a woman during the period of her impurity.

13. וָחָי — *Should he live?*

Is in the form of an incredulous query *(Radak).*

מוֹת יוּמָת דָּמָיו בּוֹ יִהְיֶה — *He shall surely die and his blood will be upon himself.*

His own responsibility for his 'death' is stressed. The father will not be punished for his son's sin *(Eliezer of Beaugency.* See also below, *v.* 20).

It has now been taught, that the merits of the righteous father will not save his wicked son (see *comm.* to 14:16). The prophet now turns to the problem of the righteous son, born of a wicked father.

14. וַיִּרְאֶה וְלֹא יַעֲשֶׂה כָּהֵן — *And he saw and did not imitate them* [lit. *do like them*].

He realized *(saw* in his heart) that it was not good to act in this way *(Rashi).*

15-17. See *comm.* to *vs.* 6-8 above.

17. מֵעָנִי הֵשִׁיב יָדוֹ — *From the poor did he withhold his hand* i.e., from harming the poor *(Rashi).*

This quality seems to have no parallel among the qualities listed in *vs.* 6-8. However, a careful pairing of the two lists shows that מֵעָוֶל יָשִׁיב יָדוֹ, *He has withheld his hand from iniquity (v.* 8) has no apparent parallel in *vs.* 15-17. We therefore conclude that although

his eyes; abomination did he commit; [13] *for interest*
did he lend; and increase did he take — should he
live? He shall not live! He has done all these
abominations; he shall surely die and his blood will
be upon himself.

[14] *And see! He begot a son who saw all the sins of*
his father that he had done. And he saw, and did not
imitate them [15] *Upon the mountains he did not eat;*
his eyes did he not lift to the idols of the Family of
Israel; his neighbor's wife did he not defile; [16] *no*
man did he oppress; a pledge did he not take; loot
did he not rob; his bread to the hungry did he give;
and the naked did he cover with a garment; [17] *from*
the poor did he withhold his hand; neither interest
nor increase did he take; My ordinances did he per-
form; and in My decrees did he go. He shall not die
for his father's sin. He shall surely live.

[18] *His father, because he cruelly oppressed, robbed*
loot of a brother, and did what is not good among his
people, see! He died for his sin. [19] *Yet you ask: Why*
did the son not bear the sin of the father? But the son

they occupy different positions in the respective lists, these two phrases are nevertheless intended to parallel each other.

18. בְּתוֹךְ עַמָּיו — *Among his people.*

The wicked father practiced his evil in public. He was not embarrassed by being observed while sinning *(Radak).*

19-20. According to *Radak,* these verses contain the answer to the original question posed by the proverb (see *comm.* to *v.* 2). God's justice will not permit anyone to be rewarded or punished for actions which are not his. The sole exception to this is the son who אוֹחֵז מַעֲשֵׂה אֲבוֹתָיו בְּיָדוֹ, *continues in the evil ways of his parents.* He is culpable under the doctrine of פֹּקֵד עֲוֹן אָבֹת עַל בָּנִים, *He recalls the sin of fathers upon children, (Exod.* 20:5) and this doctrine justifies the pending destruction, which will come *'because of the sins of Menashe'* (see *comm.* and *footnote* to *v.* 2).

[According to *Makkos* 24a, *Aggados Bereishis* Ch. 10, and our explanation, (based upon *Rabbi Joseph Carlebach* see *footnote* to *v.* 2), these verses delineate the new usage which will come about in the wake of the changed circumstances to be inaugurated by the destruction of the Temple.]

19. וַאֲמַרְתֶּם מַדֻּעַ לֹא נָשָׂא הַבֵּן בַּעֲוֹן הָאָב — *Yet you ask: Why did the son not bear the sin of the father?*

This question is prompted by their own experiences. They are to be

הָאָב וְהַבֵּן מִשְׁפָּט וּצְדָקָה עָשָׂה אֵת כָּל־
חֻקּוֹתַי שָׁמַר וַיַּעֲשֶׂה אֹתָם חָיֹה יִחְיֶה׃
כ הַנֶּפֶשׁ הַחֹטֵאת הִיא תָמוּת בֵּן לֹא־יִשָּׂא
בַּעֲוֺן הָאָב וְאָב לֹא יִשָּׂא בַּעֲוֺן הַבֵּן צִדְקַת
הַצַּדִּיק עָלָיו תִּהְיֶה וְרִשְׁעַת °רשע   °הָרָשָׁע ק׳
כא עָלָיו תִּהְיֶה׃ וְהָרָשָׁע
כִּי יָשׁוּב מִכָּל־חַטֹּאתָו אֲשֶׁר עָשָׂה
וְשָׁמַר אֶת־כָּל־חֻקּוֹתַי וְעָשָׂה מִשְׁפָּט
כב וּצְדָקָה חָיֹה יִחְיֶה לֹא יָמוּת׃ כָּל־פְּשָׁעָיו
אֲשֶׁר עָשָׂה לֹא יִזָּכְרוּ לוֹ בְּצִדְקָתוֹ
כג אֲשֶׁר־עָשָׂה יִחְיֶה׃ הֶחָפֹץ אֶחְפֹּץ מוֹת
רָשָׁע נְאֻם אֲדֹנָי יֱהֹוִה הֲלוֹא בְּשׁוּבוֹ
כד מִדְּרָכָיו וְחָיָה׃ וּבְשׁוּב
צַדִּיק מִצִּדְקָתוֹ וְעָשָׂה עָוֶל כְּכֹל
הַתּוֹעֵבוֹת אֲשֶׁר־עָשָׂה הָרָשָׁע יַעֲשֶׂה וָחָי

destroyed because of *Menashe*'s sins. Why should the hypothetical son be saved? *(Radak)*

21-23. The prophet calls out a ringing affirmation for the possibility of תשובה, *repentance*.

In *Harav Breuer*'s view that the proverb had the purpose of denying the efficiacy of repentance, (see *comm. v.* 2), these verses, combined with *v.* 19, contain the answer. Repentance would indeed be meaningless if a man were punished for sins which he did not commit. But since the son is punished only when he continues in his father's evil ways, the opportunity to repent is always available to him.

According to *Radak*, these verses are meant to reinforce the doctrine stated in *v.* 20, that no man can be made to suffer for another's sin. If even the sinner can avoid punishment by changing his ways, then certainly one who never sinned, will not be punished (see *Shemos Rabbah* 31:6).

21-22. וְהָרָשָׁע כִּי יָשׁוּב ... כָּל פְּשָׁעָיו ... לֹא יִזָּכְרוּ — *As for the wicked man, if he should turn away ... All his transgressions ... will not be remembered.*

The beauty of the concept of *Teshuvah, repentance,* in all its grandeur (see *comm.* to *v.* 24) is expressed by the Sages at *Shir HaShirim* 5:16. *Solomon* sings of the *'sweetness'* of God's words, and that sweetness is nowhere more pronounced than in the voice which beckons a sinner, prostrate by the weight of his guilt, to rid himself of the burdens of his past. [*Yalkut ibid.* See ArtScroll edition of *Shir HaShirim. Rashi* ad. loc., who adds that the past is not only annulled, but converted to merit, is based on *Yomah* 86b. There,

justice and righteousness did he do, all My decrees
did he safeguard and perform them. He shall surely
live. 20 *Whichever soul sins, it shall die! The son shall*
not bear for the sin of the father, nor the father bear
for the sin of the son. The righteousness of the
righteous person shall be upon him, and the
wickedness of the wicked person shall be upon him.
21 *As for the wicked man, if he should turn away*
from all his sins which he did, and safeguard all My
decrees, and do justice and righteousness; he shall
surely live. He will not die. 22 *All his transgressions*
which he committed will not be remembered against
him. For the righteousness which he did, he shall live.
23 *Do I desire at all the death of the wicked man — the*
words of my Lord HASHEM/ELOHIM *— is it not ra-*
ther his return from his ways, that he might live?
24 *Now when a righteous man turns away from his*
righteousness, and does iniquity like all the abomina-
tions which the wicked man did; shall he do them

the Sages derive from 33:19, that a תְּשׁוּבָה מֵאַהֲבָה, *a repentance born from love* rather than from fear of punishment will bring about the conversion of sins to merit. For a discussion of this concept see *Maharal, Nesivos Olam, Nesiv Hateshuva* Ch. 2].

23. The love and yearning expressed in this verse have earned it a place in the *Neilah* prayer of *Yom Kippur*, together with *v.* 32 and 33:11.

See further below, *comm.* to *v.* 24.

24. See *comm.* to 3:20. Once more, the prophet teaches that a situation may arise in which, a *zaddik* who becomes wicked, will lose the merits of his former righteousness. *Rashi* (based on *Kiddushin* 40b) limits this to a case in which he *regrets* the good deeds which he had done in the past.

[This doctrine raises a problem concerning the concept of repentance. The sages view it as a unique, God-given mercy (see *Yalkut* here, that neither *wisdom, prophecy,* nor *Torah* could conceive of *Teshuvah*. Only God Himself granted it. *Rabbeinu Yonah,* begins his *Sha'arei Teshuvah* by defining *Teshuvah* as a special favor of God). In the light of the lesson taught in our verse, this seems suspect. If a person can wipe out his former merits by regretting them, why is it so revolutionary a concept that one has the ability to nullify his past sins?

Harav Yitzchak Hutner offers the following solution. The Torah equates *good* with *life,* and *evil* with *death* (see *Deut.* 30:15). When a person performs a good deed, he gains *life,* when he sins he *dies.* There is a basic difference

כָּל־צִדְקֹתָו אֲשֶׁר־עָשָׂה לֹא תִזָּכַרְנָה
בְּמַעֲלוֹ אֲשֶׁר־מָעַל וּבְחַטָּאתוֹ אֲשֶׁר־חָטָא
כה בָּם יָמוּת׃ וַאֲמַרְתֶּם לֹא יִתָּכֵן דֶּרֶךְ אֲדֹנָי
שִׁמְעוּ־נָא בֵּית יִשְׂרָאֵל הֲדַרְכִּי לֹא יִתָּכֵן
כו הֲלֹא דַרְכֵיכֶם לֹא יִתָּכֵנוּ׃ בְּשׁוּב־צַדִּיק
מִצִּדְקָתוֹ וְעָשָׂה עָוֶל וּמֵת עֲלֵיהֶם בְּעַוְלוֹ
כז אֲשֶׁר־עָשָׂה יָמוּת׃ וּבְשׁוּב רָשָׁע
מֵרִשְׁעָתוֹ אֲשֶׁר עָשָׂה וַיַּעַשׂ מִשְׁפָּט
כח וּצְדָקָה הוּא אֶת־נַפְשׁוֹ יְחַיֶּה׃ וַיִּרְאֶה
°וישוב מִכָּל־פְּשָׁעָיו אֲשֶׁר עָשָׂה חָיוֹ

°וַיָּשָׁב ק׳

between life and death: life cannot endure without sustenance; bereft of food, life ceases. But death is absolute; nothing is needed to sustain it, and nothing in nature can reverse it. When a person appreciates and clings to the spiritual values of the life-level which he has attained, he thereby provides the spiritual sustenance needed to maintain his higher life. But if he regrets his good deeds he witholds the sustenance required by his spiritual life, with the result that it withers and dies. *'His merits are not remembered'*; this is a natural phenomenon, for one cut off from the source of life cannot live.

But the sinner has already 'died'. For him to commence upon a regimen of repentance and good deeds would logically resemble feeding and medicating a corpse. That repentance *does* achieve spiritual resurrection is a gift of God that is truly unique.]

25. וַאֲמַרְתֶּם לֹא יִתָּכֵן דֶּרֶךְ ה׳ — *And when you say: 'Incorrect is the way of the Lord.'*

תכן means, to *regulate, measure,* or *estimate.* Therefore in the *Nif'al* (passive) it conveys the idea of measuring up to a standard. God's *way* seems not to be measurable by an absolute standard of justice. There seemed no reason why a person's former deeds, whether good or bad, should be wiped out by a change in his attitude. If a *zaddik* became wicked, he should still be rewarded for his earlier good deeds, even though he now regretted them. If a wicked man repented he should still be punished for his earlier sins. [That both problems disturbed them is indicated by the repetition of this question in *v.* 29.]

God answers that, on the contrary, their *ways* [i.e. those inner drives which control a person's actions — see *comm.* to 7:3] do not 'measure up' to the standards of His expectations.

[It seems likely that the people's distorted perception was rooted in their corrupted understanding of *reward* and *punishment.* God's 'ways' are eminently logical if, as discussed above, reward is equated with *'life'*, and punishment with *'death'*. That is, reward and punishment are not external, not an arbitrary *quid pro quo,* but natural outgrowths — indeed, they are manifestations — of a person's inner growth or decay.

A people who would sacrifice their children to a fiery *Molech,* (20:26,31) or grovel before the earth's vermin (ch. 8), in order to beg favors or appease some unreasoning anger, would be unlikely to view reward and punishment from

and live? All his righteousness which he had done
will not be remembered in the treachery with which
he betrays and in his sin which he sins. For them he
shall die.
25 *And when you say: "Incorrect is the way of the*
Lord." Listen, now, Family of Israel! Is My way incor-
rect? Are not your ways incorrect? 26 *When the*
righteous man turns away from his righteousness,
and does iniquity, then he will die for them. For the
iniquity which he did, he shall die. 27 *And if the*
wicked man turns away from his wickedness which
he did, and does justice and righteousness, his own
soul will he cause to live. 28 *Because he sees and turns*
away from all his transgressions which he did, he

that perspective. In their understanding, reward is payment for a service performed, punishment is revenge for a rebellious act; neither are seen as reflections of their own level of spiritual attainment.

Because they fell so far short of a true understanding of God's service, they failed to perceive the total righteousness of God's justice.]

26. וּמֵת עֲלֵיהֶם — *Then he will die for them.*

For regretting his good deeds and for the evil which he is now doing *(Radak).*

[In *comm.* to *vs.* 21-23 we noted *Yomah* 86b that if a person repents because of his *love* for God, his sins are turned into merits. This is based on 33:19 which reads: וּבְשׁוּב רָשָׁע מֵרִשְׁעָתוֹ וְעָשָׂה מִשְׁפָּט וּצְדָקָה עֲלֵיהֶם הוּא יִחְיֶה — *Now if a wicked person repents of his wickedness, and does justice and righteousness; for them he will live.* The word עֲלֵיהֶם is taken to refer to the sins which he committed before his repentance. Even they contribute to his reward of *life* because they become transformed into merits.

On the same basis, the word עֲלֵיהֶם in our verse would indicate that his former good deeds contribute to the punishment he now suffers. For this, however, we find no justification in the Talmud. Perhaps the explanation is that his former righteousness makes his present lapse more reprehensible. After learning how pleasant are the paths of goodness, he chose to desert them for evil.]

וּמֵת עֲלֵיהֶם — *Then he will die for them*

Metzudas David sees this as part of the answer to the people's question (in *v.* 25). That the *zaddik* who has become a sinner should die is good. His death prevents him from sinking into further degradation.

27-28. *Metzudas David* continues to see these verses as answers to the people's question. There is every reason to permit the repentant sinner to go on living (חָיוֹ יִחְיֶה לֹא יָמוּת). Because, as he begins to do God's will (וַיַּעַשׂ מִשְׁפָּט וּצְדָקָה) he will begin to reflect on his past and bring about a regeneration of his soul (הוּא אֶת נַפְשׁוֹ יְחַיֶּה). This will be accomplished as he sees just how bad his ways have been (וַיִּרְאֶה וַיָּשָׁב מִכָּל פְּשָׁעָיו).

יח
כט־לב

כט יִחְיֶה לֹא יָמוּת: וְאָמְרוּ בֵּית יִשְׂרָאֵל לֹא
יִתָּכֵן דֶּרֶךְ אֲדֹנָי הַדְּרָכַי לֹא יִתָּכְנוּ בֵּית
ל יִשְׂרָאֵל הֲלֹא דַרְכֵיכֶם לֹא יִתָּכֵן: לָכֵן
אִישׁ כִּדְרָכָיו אֶשְׁפֹּט אֶתְכֶם בֵּית יִשְׂרָאֵל
נְאֻם אֲדֹנָי יֱהֹוִה שׁוּבוּ וְהָשִׁיבוּ מִכָּל־
פִּשְׁעֵיכֶם וְלֹא־יִהְיֶה לָכֶם לְמִכְשׁוֹל עָוֹן:
לא הַשְׁלִיכוּ מֵעֲלֵיכֶם אֶת־כָּל־פִּשְׁעֵיכֶם אֲשֶׁר
פְּשַׁעְתֶּם בָּם וַעֲשׂוּ לָכֶם לֵב חָדָשׁ וְרוּחַ
לב חֲדָשָׁה וְלָמָּה תָמֻתוּ בֵּית יִשְׂרָאֵל: כִּי לֹא
אֶחְפֹּץ בְּמוֹת הַמֵּת נְאֻם אֲדֹנָי יֱהֹוִה
יט
א־ב
א וְהָשִׁיבוּ וִחְיוּ: וְאַתָּה שָׂא קִינָה
ב אֶל־נְשִׂיאֵי יִשְׂרָאֵל: וְאָמַרְתָּ מָה אִמְּךָ

29. See above, *comm.* to *v.* 25.

30. לָכֵן אִישׁ כִּדְרָכָיו אֶשְׁפֹּט אֶתְכֶם — *Therefore each man according to his ways shall I judge you.*

I.e., your present ways. Your past will have been wiped out *(Metzudas David).*

שׁוּבוּ וְהָשִׁיבוּ — *Return and bring back.* (See *comm.* to 14:6).

Targum renders: שׁוּבוּ *Return to My service,* וְהָשִׁיבוּ *and cast away idol-worship from yourselves.*

31. וַעֲשׂוּ לָכֶם לֵב חָדָשׁ — *And make for yourselves a new heart.*

This verse affirms once more the sinner's ability to regenerate himself. The sterile fatalism expressed in the proverb *(comm. v.* 2) has no basis in reality.

32. See *comm.* to *v.* 23.

Targum here renders וְהָשִׁיבוּ as *Return to My srevice* (in contrast to his rendering in *v.* 30. There the appeal to return to God's service was expressed with the word שׁוּבוּ. Therefore, *Targum* sought another meaning for הָשִׁיבוּ, rendering it as a remonstrance to desist from idolatry).

XIX

Yechezkel is to sing a קִינָה, a dirge, for the princes of Israel.

In quick succession the reigns of Yoshiyahu's two sons and grandson had ended in disaster, as they languished in exile, or died a cruel death.

Yehoachaz and Yehoyachin had been dragged to Egypt and Babylon respectively. Yehoyakim's body had been torn limb from limb by the Babylonians. (See *Vayikra Rabbah* 19:5).

In a few short years Zidkiyahu was to be ignominiously captured and the final agony of the Land would be ended. [For historical background, see *Twilight of the Monarchy* p. lxii].

And so, Yechezkel is to mourn Yoshiyahu's royal house *(Metzudas David* — see below).[1]

1. שָׂא קִינָה — *Take up a lamentation.* [The identical command is given to Yechezkel in 27:2 and 28:12 concerning Tyre and its king; and in 32:2 concern-

XVIII 29-32 *shall surely live. He shall not die.* 29 *Yet the Family of*
Israel says: "Incorrect are the ways of the Lord." Is it
My ways that are incorrect, Family of Israel? Are not
your ways incorrect? 30 *Therefore, each man ac-*
cording to his ways, shall I judge you Family of Israel
— the words of my Lord HASHEM/ELOHIM — return
and bring back from all your transgressions that they
be not for you a stumbling block of iniquity.

31 *Cast away from yourselves all your transgres-*
sions by which you transgressed, and make for
yourselves a new heart and a new spirit. Why should
you die, Family of Israel? 32 *For I desire not the death*
of him that dies, the words of my Lord HASHEM/
ELOHIM. Repent and live!'

XIX 1-2 *And you, take up a lamentation for the princes of*
Israel. 2 *And say: 'Alas — your mother was a*

ing Pharaoh, the king of Egypt.]

אֶל נְשִׂיאֵי יִשְׂרָאֵל — *For the princes of Israel.*

The אֶל [lit. *'to'*] is to be understood as עַל, *for (Radak).*

There is considerable disagreement among the commentators as to which of the four *'princes of Israel'* belonging to the house of Yoshiyahu are referred to in this *kinnah.* We shall note the various opinions at the appropriate

1. This *kinnah* (dirge) is only one of a series of *kinnos* inspired by the tragedy of this righteous king.

— In the greatest of all lamentations, *Megillas Eichah,* (written by Jeremiah to mourn Jerusalem's destruction), all of Ch. 4 is descriptive of Yoshiyahu *(Eichah Rabbasi* 4:1 and *Malbim* to *II Chron.* 35:25). It tells of his great potential and mourns his premature death.

— *Amos* predicts a time when Israel's sun will set at midday and its songs will be changed to dirges *(Amos* 8:9-10). The Sages *(Mo'ed Katan* 25b) interpret the passage as likening Yoshiyahu's untimely death at an early age to the setting of the sun at midday.

— Indeed *Targum* and *Rashi* to *Chron.* (loc. cit.) assert that for every sorrow over which Israel would ever have to sing a dirge — mention should also be made of Yoshiyahu's tragedy. [It is thus placed in a category comparable to the sin of the *Golden Calf* — see *Exod.* 32:34 and *Rashi.*] In the order of *kinnos* which we recite on *Tish'ah B'Av,* אֵיכָה אֱלִי קוֹנְנוּ מֵאִילָיו, is devoted to this theme.

There is a reason why so much sadness attaches to the tragedy of this great *zaddik.* With his death on the bloodstained battleground of Meggidoh, there died the last hope of averting the final Destruction. From *Eichah* 4:20 we know that Israel's hope had depended on Yoshiyahu. The *lowly kingdom* which was needed in order to achieve Israel's regeneration (see *Overview p. xlv,* and *comm.* and *footnote* to 17:14) could have flourished under him, and in the long run, his *Teshuvah* movement would have taken root. As events unfolded, his call to repentance had not succeeded in penetrating all layers of society (see *footnote* to 8:3) and his eventual successor, the righteous Zidkiyahu, could not accept the concept of a *lowly kingdom.*

As it was, all was lost, and the long dark night of exile was to fall.

לְבִיָּא בֵּין אֲרָיוֹת רָבָצָה בְּתוֹךְ כְּפִרִים
ג רִבְּתָה גוּרֶיהָ׃ וַתַּעַל אֶחָד מִגֻּרֶיהָ כְּפִיר
הָיָה וַיִּלְמַד לִטְרָף־טֶרֶף אָדָם אָכָל׃
ד וַיִּשְׁמְעוּ אֵלָיו גּוֹיִם בְּשַׁחְתָּם נִתְפָּשׂ
ה וַיְבִאֻהוּ בַחַחִים אֶל־אֶרֶץ מִצְרָיִם׃ וַתֵּרֶא

verses, and summarize at the end of the chapter.

2. מָה אִמְּךָ לְבִיָּא — *Alas — your mother was a lioness!*

The translation follows *Radak* who interprets מָה, as denoting *'wailing'* or *'lamentation'* as opposed to its usual meaning of *'what'*.

Rashi, however, renders *What was your mother — a lioness!* i.e., your mother was great, strong, and fearless.

The 'mother' of the parable is either *Knesses Israel (Rashi* and *Radak),* or the royal house of Yoshiyahu *(Metzudas David).*

בֵּין אֲרָיוֹת רָבָצָה — *Among lions she crouched.*

When Israel's kings were righteous, they were able to live in strength and peace among their dangerous neighbors. [*Radak* identifies אֲרָיוֹת, *lions,* as the Babylonians]. She was able to rear her cubs, without any worry. [גור is the baby lion who does not yet go out on the hunt, כְּפִיר is the young lion who hunts and kills, but has not yet reached the maturity of the אֲרִי, the full-grown lion].

It is no coincidence that Israel's kings are compared to *lions.* It was Jacob himself who promised kingship to Judah's descendants with the words גוּר אַרְיֵה יְהוּדָה, *A young lion is Judah (Gen.* 49:9).

Hirsch's translation of that phrase reads: *'A young-old lion is Judah',* and he comments: 'You combine the courage of youth (גּוּר) with the prudence of age (אַרְיֵה).' Thus the כְּפִיר, the young killer lion, who in his new found skill at the hunt, is wild and blood-thirsty, is never an apt metaphor for Israel's kings.

Harav Breuer uses this insight to explain the second phrase in our verse. She raised her cubs (גּוּר) *as* cubs (training them not to lust after blood) among the young (blood-thirsty) lions (the gentile kings) (כְּפִרִים). Israel's kings are brought up in strength tempered by a tradition of prudence and a love of peace.

3. וַתַּעַל — *And she reared up.*

The verb is in the הִפְעִיל, *the causative* voice. *Harav Breuer* (in line with his interpretation of the previous verse) comments: The mother became untrue to her own principles by raising this one cub to be a כְּפִיר, a young (blood-thirsty) lion, and thereby mortally wounded an אָדָם, *man, Israel* whose very essence is to be אָדָם (see *comm.* to 34:31 and *Overview),* the human — and humane — peak of God's creative work.

Reference in this and the next verse, is obviously to *Yehoachaz* the first son to succeed *Yoshiyahu.* He was deposed *(II Kings* 23:33) and dragged into Egyptian captivity after only three months of rule, as described in *v.* 4 *(ibid. v.* 31).

אָדָם אָכָל — *Man did he devour.*

He stole from Israel who are called אָדָם [34:31] *(Rashi).* [This would be another example of the phenomenon discussed at 12:5, that occasionally Scripture will record an event, but leave its details for some other place. *II Kings* 23:32 states only that *'he did evil in the eyes of HASHEM',* without specifying a particular area of wickedness. It is only

lioness! Among lions she crouched, amidst young
lions did she rear her cubs. 3 *And she reared up one*
of her cubs; he became a young lion, and he learned
to tear prey, man did he devour. 4 *So against him*
were gathered nations, in their pit he was caught; and
they brought him with hooks to the land of Egypt.

here that we discover that he was an oppressive king.]

Radak explains that Yehoachaz is described as a 'young lion' because his kingship was of a very limited nature. Much of the Land had already been destroyed. His defiance of Pharaoh is described as an attack on אָדָם, *a man,* in contrast to the animals which would be a lion's usual prey. It was unreasonable for a puny king like Yehoachaz to fight the mighty Pharaoh.

4. וַיִּשְׁמְעוּ אֵלָיו גּוֹיִם — *So against him were gathered nations.*

The Egyptian forces who heard that he was rebelling against them (this is implied though not stated in the relevant passages in *Kings* and *Chronicles)* gathered against him *(Radak).*

The translation follows *Metzudas David.* The literal translation would be: *'And the nations heard towards him'.* This becomes *'gathered'* because armies *'listen'* to orders when they are mustered.

[See *I Sam.* 15:4 where וַיְשַׁמַּע has the meaning: *and he gathered.*]

בְּשַׁחְתָּם נִתְפָּשׂ — *In their pit was he caught.*

The openings of pits were camouflaged with straw, so that animals might fall into them *(Rashi).*

בַּחַחִים — *With hooks.*

The iron ring which is inserted in the animal's nose so that it may be pulled along *(Rashi).*

Reference is to *II Kings* 23:33.

5-9. *Rashi, Radak, Metzudas David,* and *Ibn Ezra* (to *Daniel* 1:1) all interpret the passage to refer to Yehoyakim. *V.* 8, which tells of nations gathering against him, is seen as a reference to *II Kings* 24:2 where God sends the hordes of Chaldea, Aram, Mo'ab, and Amon against Judah during Yehoyakim's reign. That interpretation raises a difficulty, for *v.* 9 speaks of an exile to Babylon implying that Yehoyakim was brought there.

In *footnote* to 17:4, we discussed the question of whether Yehoyakim was actually exiled to Babylon. We concluded that the sources do not conclusively establish this. On the basis of our passage (see *comm.* above, *v.* 3 based on *comm.* to 12:5) we would be forced to conclude that there was, at least, a temporary exile (see below).

Abarbanel points out that this would not remove the difficulty, since, *v.* 9 states that the captivity took place in order that *'his voice be no longer heard',* which would not be true if he was in Babylon for only a short time. *Abarbanel* therefore suggests that only *v.* 8 refers to Yehoyakim. The first part of *v.* 9 refers to Yehoyachin and the last part, to Zidkiyahu both of whom were indeed exiled to Babylon (see below).

Eliezer of Beaugency comments that כְּפִיר שָׂמָתְהוּ, *she made him into a young lion, of v.* 5, refers to all three kings (Yehoyakim, Yehoyachin and Zidkiyahu) since 'It is the way of Scripture to include all the kings of a nation in one single description'. The references to a Babylonian exile, however, would be to Yehoyachin and Zidkiyahu only.

כִּי נֽוֹחֲלָה אָֽבְדָה תִּקְוָתָהּ וַתִּקַּח אֶחָד
ו מִגֻּרֶיהָ כְּפִיר שָׂמָתְהוּ׃ וַיִּתְהַלֵּךְ בְּתוֹךְ־
אֲרָיוֹת כְּפִיר הָיָה וַיִּלְמַד לִטְרָף־טֶרֶף
ז אָדָם אָכָל׃ וַיֵּדַע אַלְמְנוֹתָיו וְעָרֵיהֶם
הֶחֱרִיב וַתֵּשַׁם אֶרֶץ וּמְלֹאָהּ מִקּוֹל
ח שַׁאֲגָתוֹ׃ וַיִּתְּנוּ עָלָיו גּוֹיִם סָבִיב מִמְּדִינוֹת
וַיִּפְרְשׂוּ עָלָיו רִשְׁתָּם בְּשַׁחְתָּם נִתְפָּשׂ׃
ט וַיִּתְּנֻהוּ בַסּוּגַר בַּֽחַחִים וַיְבִאֻהוּ אֶל־מֶלֶךְ

5. וַתֵּרֶא כִּי נוֹחֲלָה — *And she saw herself disillusioned.*

תּוֹחֶלֶת from the root יחל, is *'hope'*. The root in the נִפְעַל, *passive* voice used here, suggests disappointment (i.e., she was made to hope) the hope was drawn out for a long time and left unfulfilled *(Radak).*

Rashi traces the word to חלה, *to be sick.* The loss of hope made her sick.

וַתִּקַּח אֶחָד מִגֻּרֶיהָ — *And she took one of her cubs* i.e., Yehoyakim (See above).

כְּפִיר שָׂמָתְהוּ — *Into a young lion did she make him.*

Radak points to the problem, that Yehoyakim was not made king by the 'mother', (Knesses Israel) but by Pharaoh *(II Kings* 23:34). He solves this by saying that Pharaoh appointed him king with the approval of the populace.

6. וַיִּתְהַלֵּךְ בְּתוֹךְ אֲרָיוֹת — *And he roamed among the lions.*

The use of the הִתְפָּעֵל, *the reflexive* voice, implies a going back and forth.

Radak explains this as a description of his fluctuating loyalties. Sometimes he would be true to Nebuchadnezzar, at other times, as when he rebelled against Babylon *(II Kings* 24:1), — he went to Pharaoh for aid.

Harav Breuer explains the use of the reflexive, as indicating Yehoyakim's free roaming, undirected by the expressed wishes of God, and following only his own whims.

כְּפִיר הָיָה — *A young lion was he.*

He never attained the status of a full grown lion. His rule did not leave the country stronger than it was before he became king *(Radak).*

According to *Harav Breuer* (see *comm.* to *v.* 2), the meaning is that he did not achieve the inhibiting prudence of old age. His power made him wild and blood-thirsty.

אָדָם אָכָל — *Man did he eat.*

As in *v.* 3, *Radak* explains that he challenged adversaries who would normally have been beyond his strength. In this case it would refer to the armies of Chaldea and other countries, which were mightier than he. (See Introductory Remarks to *vs.* 5-9).

Alternately *Radak* suggests that the phrase might refer to the innocent blood which Yehoyakim shed throughout his kingdom, as attested to by *II Kings* 24:4.

7. וַיֵּדַע אַלְמְנוֹתָיו — *And he destroyed their palaces.*

The translation follows *Targum,* although it presents great difficulty. Firstly, the root ידע which usually means *'to know'* must be rendered *'to destroy'.* *Radak* and *Metzudas David* refer to the same usage in *Judges* 8:16. *(Sefer haShorashim* of *Radak,* after discussing this possibility, and suggesting various other verses where the root might have

XIX
5-9

[5] *And she saw herself disillusioned, lost was her*
hope. So she took another of her cubs; into a young
lion did she make him. [6] *And he roamed among the*
lions; a young lion was he. And he learned to tear
prey; man did he eat. [7] *And he destroyed their*
palaces and their cities he laid waste; then, desolate
became the land and its fullness through the noise of
his roar. [8] *So against him gathered the nations, on*
every side, from the provinces, and they spread their
net over him; in their pits was he caught. [9] *Then they*
put him in a neck-stock with hooks, and brought him

such a meaning, prefers to translate all of them on the basis of the more usual meaning: *'to know'.)* Secondly, אַלְמְנוֹתָיו must be interpreted as though it were written אַרְמְנוֹתָיו, meaning *palaces* (substituting a ר, *resh*, for the ל, *lamed*). *Metzudas David* shows that such exchanges of letters are found occasionally in Scripture.

The alternative is to translate literally. *He knew (or violated) his widows*, i.e., after having killed many men in his kingdom, he violated their widows.

The first alternative would seem to have the advantage of providing a more apt parallel to the second phrase: וְעָרֵיהֶם הֶחֱרִיב, *and laid waste their cities.*

However, *Radak* in *Sefer haShorashim (ibid.)* suggests a solution (see also *Radak*, here). The destruction of the cities is a *result* of his actions. By killing people and violating their widows, he *'destroyed'* the cities, for he caused the disintegration of the society within them.

וְעָרֵיהֶם הֶחֱרִיב — *And their cities he laid waste.*

See above. *Rashi* suggests that Yehoyakim ruined the cities by imposing unbearable taxes upon them, to satisfy his obligations to Pharaoh *(II Kings* 23:33).

וַתֵּשַׁם אֶרֶץ וּמְלֹאָהּ מִקּוֹל שַׁאֲגָתוֹ — *Desolate became the land and its fullness through the noise of his roar.*

The land of Judah became desolate because he terrified his subjects. The expression *'through the noise of his roar'* is consistent with the metaphor of the lion.

8. וַיִּתְּנוּ עָלָיו גּוֹיִם — *So against him gathered the nations.*

Based on *II Kings* 24:2. See above.

The translation follows *Targum.* An analagous use is at *Nehemiah* 5:7. See *Rashi* ad. loc.

Radak renders our verse as though the word בְּקוֹל, *with a loud voice,* were implied. Thus: ויתנו עָלָיו גוים [בקול] — *The nations roared against him.*

The idiom נָתַן עַל ... בְּקוֹל, as *making a tumult against someone* is found in Scripture *(*for example, *Jeremiah* 12:8).

In the same way that *Radak* sees an implied בְּקוֹל, *Metzudas David* sees an implied מוֹקֵשׁ, *stumbling block: they* [the nations] *placed a stumbling block in front of him.*

9. וַיִּתְּנֻהוּ בַסּוּגַר — *And they put him in a neck-stock.*

Targum renders קוֹלָרִין, the band or chain placed on a prisoner's neck. (See also *Radak, Sefer haShorashim* at סגר.)

בָּבֶל יְבִאֻהוּ בַּמְּצֹדוֹת לְמַעַן לֹא־יִשָּׁמַע
י קוֹלוֹ עוֹד אֶל־הָרֵי יִשְׂרָאֵל׃ אִמְּךָ
כַגֶּפֶן בְּדָמְךָ עַל־מַיִם שְׁתוּלָה פֹּרִיָּה
יא וַעֲנֵפָה הָיְתָה מִמַּיִם רַבִּים׃ וַיִּהְיוּ־לָהּ
מַטּוֹת עֹז אֶל־שִׁבְטֵי מֹשְׁלִים וַתִּגְבַּהּ

וַיְבִאֻהוּ אֶל מֶלֶךְ בָּבֶל — *And brought him to the king of Babylon.*

In the *Intro. Remarks* to *vs.* 5-9, we noted the problem of whether Yehoyakim was, in fact, ever taken to Babylon.

Ibn Ezra to *Daniel* 1:1-2 holds that the text in Daniel offers incontrovertible evidence that Yehoyakim was, in fact, exiled to Babylon. In order to accommodate Jeremiah's prophecy (*Jeremiah* 22:19) that Yehoyakim's body would be thrown out at the gates of Jerusalem. *Ibn Ezra* suggests that in the third year of his reign he was taken to Babylon, chained in a fortress for about a year, and then returned to Israel where he was eventually killed and his body violated. Our passage refers to his temporary exile.

This view is shared by *Radak*. The difficulty lies in viewing a temporary exile as fulfilling the prophecy: *'that his voice be no longer heard ... '* (We noted above that this was *Abarbanel's* objection). *Radak* solves this problem by saying that the original plan was to imprison him permanently. It was a change of heart on the part of Nebuchadnezzar which allowed him to return. (See further, concerning *Radak*'s interpretation of this verse, in the concluding remarks to this chapter).

Metzudas David, based on the future tense of יְבִאֻהוּ בַּמְּצֹדוֹת, *'that they might bring him into strongholds'*, which implies an *intention*, rather than an action, explains: They brought him to the Babylonian king with the intention of having him taken to Babylon in captivity. In actual fact, however, he was never taken, because he died before his sentence could be executed. (See *footnote* to 17:4).

Eliezer of Beaugency has the passage refer only to Yehoyachin and Zidkiyahu (see above, introductory remarks to *vs.* 5-9).

Abarbanel, as mentioned above, thinks that *v.* 8 was the last verse to deal with Yehoyakim. The first part of *v.* 9 (וַיִּתְּנֻהוּ בַסּוּגַר בַּחַחִים) refers to Yehoyachin, and the next phrase (וַיְבִאֻהוּ אֶל מֶלֶךְ בָּבֶל) refers to Zidkiyahu. Thus all four kings are mentioned in this *Kinnah*. (See below).

לְמַעַן לֹא יִשָּׁמַע קוֹלוֹ עוֹד — *That his voice be no longer heard.*

This is consistent with the use of the same metaphor מִקּוֹל שַׁאֲגָתוֹ, in *v.* 7. (*Radak*).

10-14. The *kinna* continues (*Rashi*) but the metaphor changes. The *'mother'* now becomes a fruitful vine, with many branches, planted in fertile, well-tilled ground.

We have already noted (*comm.* to *v.* 2), that the part of the *kinna* which compares the royal house to a pride of lions, is aptly based on Jacob's blessing in which he called his son Judah a *'young lion'*. It has been suggested that the comparison to the vine is based on the same blessing, in which Jacob also promised Judah an abundance of vines and wine (*Harav Breuer*). [See *Gen.* 49:9, 11].

10. אִמְּךָ כַגֶּפֶן בְּדָמְךָ — *Like one whose mother was a vine, are you likened.*

Most commentators follow *Targum* in translating the unusual form בְּדָמְךָ

to the king of Babylon, that they might bring him into fortresses in order that his voice be no longer heard upon the mountains of Israel.

10 *Like one whose mother was a vine are you likened, by waters planted, fruitful and full-branched it was, from abundant waters.* 11 *And it had strong rods for scepters of sovereigns, and high grew*

(instead of בְּדְמוּתְךָ) as deriving from the root דמה, *to be similar.*

Targum renders: *'Knesses Israel when it does the will of the Torah, is like a vine ...'*

Radak explains *Targum* as referring to the reigns of David, Solomon, and the other righteous kings during which the royal house was blessed with all manner of success.[1]

פֹּרִיָּה וַעֲנֵפָה — *Fruitful and full-branched.*

This describes the flourishing reigns of the early kings, according to *Targum* and *Radak.*

In the view of *Eliezer of Beaugency* (see *footnote*) it describes what might have been in the reigns of Yehoyakim and Zidkiyahu. They had been given every opportunity to flourish within the boundaries placed upon them by the realities of their situation.

11. וַיִּהְיוּ לָהּ מַטּוֹת עֹז אֶל שִׁבְטֵי מֹשְׁלִים — *And it had strong rods for scepters of sovereigns.*

Targum (quoted by *Rashi)* renders: *'And she (Knesses Israel) had strong rulers, mighty kings.'* See *Ramban* to *Gen.* 49:10, that שֵׁבֶט always refers to the scepter of the ruler.[2]

1. Although the vine is often used in Scripture to describe Israel in positive terms (see for example: *Ps.* 80:9 and 15), this usage is not consistent with Yechezkel's symbolism. On the two other occasions where he used the vine as a metaphor, it was in negative terms. In Ch. 15, the wood of the vine was declared worthless for anything but fuel, and in Ch. 17 it was contrasted disadvantageously to the lordly cedar.

Eliezer of Beaugency interprets the metaphor in a manner which is consistent with the earlier symbolism, and at the same time offers a different solution to the difficult בְּדָמְךָ. He renders: *Your mother was sentenced to be a lowly vine, because of the blood which had been shed (*בְּדָמְךָ from דָּם, *blood,* the correct grammatical form), *but nevertheless* [within the framework of her lowly state] *she was given an abundance of water which could have helped her to flourish.*

2. Once more the problem arises (see *footnote* above) that the branches of the vine are not notably strong. On the contrary, Ch. 15 depicts them as weak and useless. The glory of the vine lies in its fruit, not in its utility. When we recall (introductory remarks to *vs.* 10-14) the possibility that Yechezkel borrows his symbolism from Jacob's blessing of Judah, a solution is suggested.

On the verse: אֹסְרִי לַגֶּפֶן עִירֹה *(Gen.* 49:11), *He binds his foal to the vine, Hirsch* comments: If one can tie an animal, and especially an עַיִר, the lively mettlesome young donkey to a vine, it is a sign of an infinitely increased development in nature (the vine stem growing as strong and sturdy as that of a tree), and of immense prosperity and abundance.

Thus we recognize a symbolism wherein the lowly vine is endowed with a strength which it would not normally have.

The idea is duplicated in *Ps.* 80:11, where the vine which symbolizes Israel is described as having *'branches like the cedars of God.'* A *vine* with branches like *cedars!*

We now see a development of the theme which we recognized in the *Pref. Remarks* to Ch. 15. Inherently Israel is a vine. Its purpose is to produce fruits of holiness. Its physical ex-

קוֹמָתוֹ עַל־בֵּין עֲבֹתִים וַיֵּרָא בְגָבְהוֹ בְּרֹב
יב דָּלִיֹּתָיו׃ וַתֻּתַּשׁ בְּחֵמָה לָאָרֶץ הֻשְׁלָכָה
וְרוּחַ הַקָּדִים הוֹבִישׁ פִּרְיָהּ הִתְפָּרְקוּ
יג וְיָבֵשׁוּ מַטֵּה עֻזָּהּ אֵשׁ אֲכָלָתְהוּ׃ וְעַתָּה
יד שְׁתוּלָה בַמִּדְבָּר בְּאֶרֶץ צִיָּה וְצָמָא׃ וַתֵּצֵא
אֵשׁ מִמַּטֵּה בַדֶּיהָ פִּרְיָהּ אָכָלָה וְלֹא־הָיָה
בָהּ מַטֵּה עֹז שֵׁבֶט לִמְשׁוֹל קִינָה הִיא
וַתְּהִי לְקִינָה׃

וַתִּגְבַּהּ קוֹמָתוֹ — *And high grew its stature.*

Throughout the passage there is a constant change from the masculine to the feminine forms. *Radak* points this out, but offers no explanation. To avoid confusion we have used the neutral *'it'* in the translation. [We have discussed this stylistic phenomenon in the *comm.* to 13:20.]

עַל בֵּין עֲבֹתִים — *To between the interwoven branches.*

See *Rashi* to *Lev.* 23:40 where he translates עֲבֹת as *interwoven. Rashi* here, renders: Trees whose branches are many.

Radak, consistent with his opinion that the passage describes the glorious reigns of David and Solomon (*comm.* to *v.* 10), interprets the verse as depicting Israel's eminence among the nations. All of them paid tribute to the mighty empire which had grown up through God's providence to His people.

Eliezer of Beaugency who comments that the 'lowly' reigns of Yehoyakim and Zidkiyahu are the subject of the parable, writes: 'The height of its tendrils *thin as they were,* grew beyond the branches of the other trees. For this is the nature of the vine, that its tendrils spread out to the heights of trees.' The meaning is that the lowly vine in its own way, could have achieved great eminence.

12. וַתֻּתַּשׁ בְּחֵמָה — *Then it was scattered in fury.*

The translation follows *Rashi. Targum* and *Metzudas David* render: *It was plucked up.*

Radak hears an echo, in our verse, of the prophecy in *Deut.* 29:27: *'And HASHEM uprooted them from their land in wrath and in anger and in great indignation and sent them out to another land, as this day.'* From its highest and mightiest estate among the nations, Israel becomes the lowliest and most despised.

Ibn Ezra to *Dan.* 1:1-2 [in whose system of interpretation only Yehoachaz and Yehoyakim have been mentioned; see *intro. remarks* to *vs.* 5-9], reads this verse as a reference to Yehoyachin.

[It is significant that neither motive nor executioner are mentioned; this in contrast to 17:9, which, in describing the destruction of the vine, mentions both the agent of the uprooting (Nebuchadnezzar, the first eagle) and his motive (Zidkiyahu's betrayal). The east wind causes the tree to wither, its branches to fall away, fire consumes it,

istence has no meaning. Its wood is useless. If, in God's providence, it is granted physical strength and dominion, it does not change into a *cedar,* whose strength lies within itself; it remains the *vine* which retains its essential nature, but is imbued with supernatural cedar-like strength. When God's help is withdrawn, its wood reverts to its vine-like impotence.

its stature to between the interwoven branches, and it
was seen in its height, by its many tendrils. 12 *Then it*
was scattered in fury, to the ground cast down, and
the east wind withered its fruit, dismembered and
withered were its strong rods; fire devoured it. 13 *And*
now it is planted in the desert, in ground dry and
thirsty. 14 *And fire went forth from the rods of its*
branches, devouring its fruit. No longer in it was a
strong rod, a scepter to rule.

It is a lamentation and became a lamentation.'

all without any apparent extraneous cause.

It is as though Israel will crash down under the weight of its own greatness. Israel's fattening carries the roots of its own destruction within it *(Deut.* 32:15. Compare *footnote* to 17:14).]

וְרוּחַ הַקָּדִים — *The east-wind.*

See *comm.* to 17:10. *Rashi* comments: This refers to Nebuchadnezzar.

הוֹבִישׁ פִּרְיָהּ — *Withered its fruit.*

He slaughtered Zidkiyahu's sons *(Rashi.* See *II Kings* 25:7).

וְיָבֵשׁוּ מַטֵּה עֻזָּהּ — *Withered, were its strong rods.*

A reference to King Zidkiyahu *(Radak).*

אֵשׁ אֲכָלָתְהוּ — *Fire devoured it.*

[Up to this point individual kings had been exiled *(vs.* 4 and 9), but the royal house continued. Now finally, everything is consumed. The Davidic line seems ended, and awaits its regeneration through Yehoyachin's repentance (see *comm.* to 17:22-24).]

13. וְעַתָּה שְׁתוּלָה בַמִּדְבָּר — *And now it is planted in the desert.*

In exile, which is like a parched desert to Israel *(Radak).*

[But it is *planted!* It is true that, bereft of the *'many waters'* its growth will be stunted and it will not be able to produce either many fruits, or very strong branches; but its life will be sustained and the seed of a vibrant future will be safeguarded within itself (see *comm.* to 6:8).]

14. וַתֵּצֵא אֵשׁ מִמַּטֵּה בַדֶּיהָ — *And fire went forth from the rods of its branches.*

The fire breaks out from within itself. *Targum* renders: *Nations, mighty like fire, came because of the evil sins of her people.*

This refers to Zidkiyahu, who caused the destruction, and after whom the ruling scepter was no more. This completes the mention of all four kings *(Radak.* See also *Ibn Ezra* to *Dan.* 1:1,2).

קִינָה הִיא וַתְּהִי לְקִינָה — *It is a lamentation and became a lamentation.*

It was a *kinnah* when Yechezkel prophesied it, and turned into a true *kinnah* when the prophecies became realities *(Radak).*

In the *footnote* to Ch. 7:2 we discussed the use of poetic forms in Scripture. We learned from *Maharal (Nesivos Olam, Nesiv Ho'Avodah* 12) that poetry is used when the events described are of such a profound or moving nature, that a heightened form of expression is needed, to lift the impact of the account beyond the realm of the ordinary.

Such an event is the disintegration of the Davidic dynasty. The royal line from which, in Jacob's vision, the Messianic age was to blossom, had shown itself to be unequal to its destiny.

כ
א־ב

א וַיְהִי | בַּשָּׁנָה הַשְּׁבִיעִית בַּחֲמִישִׁי בֶּעָשׂוֹר
לַחֹדֶשׁ בָּאוּ אֲנָשִׁים מִזִּקְנֵי יִשְׂרָאֵל לִדְרֹשׁ
ב אֶת־יְהוָה וַיֵּשְׁבוּ לְפָנָי: וַיְהִי

In the twenty-two years following Yoshiyahu's death, four kings had betrayed the lofty standards which their father and grandfather Yoshiyahu had bequeathed to them. Their inadequacy had guaranteed that the doom which had threatened since Menashe's reign (see *footnote* to Ch. 8:3) would not be averted.

It need not have been. The mighty lion need not have been dragged, cowering and subdued into captivity. The stately and bountiful vine could have continued to dispense its blessings instead of having to wither in an arid and hostile desert.

The hot tears of the prophet are shed over the abysmal gap which lay between the infamy of the realities and the glory of what might have been.

The poetic form, makes it difficult to identify with certainty, which people or events are being described. [*Maharal* (loc. cit.) points out that among the properties of the poem — which comes not to *instruct* but to *elevate* — are a lack of attention to the niceties of grammar and to historical or logical sequence]. The many and varied opinions of the commentators have complicated the Commentary to this Chapter, and a short summary of the opinions is in order.

Targum, beyond identifying the 'mother' as *Knesses Israel,* does not mention any individual person or event.

Rashi, thinks that the *kinnah* is addressed to Zidkiyahu, *(v.* 2) but that it describes only Yehoachaz (*v.* 3) and Yehoyakim (*v.* 5). In *v.* 12 there is a reference to the slaughter of Zidkiyahu's sons, but nothing is interpreted as a description of either Zidkiyahu himself or to events of his reign or fate. Yehoyachin is not mentioned at all.

Radak (v. 1) states that the *kinnah* deals with three kings: Yehoachaz, Yehoyakim and Zidkiyahu. The first two are dealt with in the same way as in *Rashi*'s system. *Radak* goes beyond *Rashi* in identifying Zidkiyahu as the subject of *v.* 14. In addition, because of the historical problems raised by *v.* 9 (see *comm.),* he conjectures that that passage might be referring to Zidkiyahu, although his conclusion (as quoted in the *comm.)* is that it does, indeed refer to Yehoyakim.

Metzudas David (v. 1) mentions only Yehoachaz and Yehoyakim. No other names or events are identified in the *kinnah.*

Both *Eliezer of Beaugency* and *Abarbanel,* though differing on the specifics, interpret the *kinnah* to include a mention of all four kings.

[We can only guess at the reason for the omission of Yehoyachin and Zidkiyahu in some of the systems. It is possible that the *kinnah* was said before the final destruction, which might explain why Zidkiyahu is not mentioned. Yehoyachin's absence presents the greater problem. Perhaps, since he repented, and the royal house was indeed destined to continue through him (see *comm.* to Ch. 17, *Introductory Remarks* to *vs.* 22-24), he was not included in a *kinnah* which mourns the destruction of the royal house.]

XX

In this chapter God reveals to Yechezkel that the underlying factor and prime mover in the history of כְּנֶסֶת יִשְׂרָאֵל, *the Community of Israel,* is the imperative of קִדּוּשׁ שֵׁם שָׁמַיִם, *the Sanctification of God's Name.* [See *comm.* to *v.* 9 for an elaboration of this concept]. Israel's ability to achieve this goal is traced through three different situations, each with its own challenge:

In Egypt, Israel lacked the status of separate nationhood. They were the slaves of the host people.

In the Wilderness these conditions were reversed. In splendid isolation, they were separated from any contact with the outside world, knowing only the tangible presence of God in their midst.

In Eretz Yisrael they were independent, within their own borders. Nevertheless, they were a Nation among the Nations, exposed to the temptations inherent in that condition.

In each of these situations, Israel failed to lift itself above the prevailing culture. But even when they failed in the tasks set out for them by God, and succumbed to the blandishments of

XX 1 *It happened in the seventh year, in the fifth month on the tenth of the month that men from among the Elders of Israel came to seek an answer from HASHEM, and they sat in front of me.*

a universally practiced cult of idol worship, God did not destroy them, for only through their history could the truths which mankind must learn be made known (see *comm.* to *v.* 9), and God's Name be sanctified.

Knesses Israel, as sole bearer of the Divine truth cannot escape its destiny. It will continue its travail in the crucible of the מִדְבַּר הָעַמִּים, *the Wilderness of the Nations* (see *comm.* to *v.* 35), until, with its ultimate return to *Eretz Yisrael,* the lessons of history will have been learned.

1. וַיְהִי בַּשָּׁנָה הַשְּׁבִיעִית — *It happened in the seventh year.*

The seventh of the eleven years which elapsed between the exile of Yehoyachin and the destruction of the Temple [See 1:2 above] *(Radak).*

בַּחֲמִשִׁי בֶּעָשׂוֹר לַחֹדֶשׁ — *In the fifth [month] on the tenth of the month.*

The date is specified in order to emphasize that it was by direct הַשְׁגָּחָה, *God's providence,* that the Elders of Israel came on that particular day and were shown the inexorable path to disaster being followed by the people. On that very date, the tenth of Av, the destruction was destined to take place in exactly four more years *(Radak).* [Although the Holy Temple was desecrated and set afire on the afternoon of *Tisha b'Av,* the Ninth of Av, it was on the tenth that the destruction actually took place *(Ta'anis* 29a).]

אֲנָשִׁים מִזִּקְנֵי יִשְׂרָאֵל — *Men from among the Elders of Israel.*

These men remain anonymous, perhaps because they represented an attitude of an entire generation (see further commentary to this verse). Commentators cite *Seder Olam* (missing from our editions) identifying them as Chananiah, Mishael, and Azariah. (See *footnote* below).

לִדְרֹשׁ אֶת ה׳ — *To seek [an answer] from HASHEM.*

Targum, translates, לְמִתְבַּע אוּלְפַן, *to demand teaching.* [i.e. seek an explanation.] This accords with *Midrash Tanchuma* on *Deut.* 29:11, paraphrased here by *Rashi,* which reads: When, in Yechezkel's days [the Jews] wanted to throw off the yoke of [Hashem's] oath ... they said to him [Yechezkel]: 'If a slave is bought by a Kohen, *a priest,* is he permitted to eat תְּרוּמָה, *the Priestly tithe,* that is forbidden to an Israelite?' He answered them: 'He may eat.' They said to him: 'If [the priest] then sells him to an Israelite, doesn't he [the slave] leave his [the Kohen's] control [and thus lose the privilege of eating the tithes]?' He said to them: 'Yes'. They said to him: 'We, too, have left His [Hashem's] control. Let us be like all the nations' *(v.* 32).

Thus the *Midrash* interprets לִדְרֹשׁ אֶת ה׳, as the groping of a people, bewildered by their first Galus experience, for an explanation and perhaps a reassurance concerning their continuing relationship to Hashem.[1]

1. When Nebuchadnezzar erected a statue and demanded that everyone bow to it, Chananiah, Mishael, and Azariah resolved not to comply. They sought advice from Daniel who refused to answer them and sent them to Yechezkel. He in turn told them that he had learned from his teacher Isaiah that in time of God's anger it was best not to aggravate the rulers under whom they had to live. Chananiah, Mishael, and Azariah refused to accept this answer, and asked Yechezkel *(v.* 1) to inquire from God whether He would help them if they defied the edict. The answer *(v.* 3) was that God would not help.

The *Midrash* goes on to relate how Chananiah, Mishael, and Azariah left Yechezkel's house

כ
ג־ו

ג דְּבַר־יְהוָה אֵלַי לֵאמֹר: בֶּן־אָדָם דַּבֵּר
אֶת־זִקְנֵי יִשְׂרָאֵל וְאָמַרְתָּ אֲלֵהֶם כֹּה
אָמַר אֲדֹנָי יֱהוִה הֲלִדְרֹשׁ אֹתִי אַתֶּם
בָּאִים חַי־אָנִי אִם־אִדָּרֵשׁ לָכֶם נְאֻם אֲדֹנָי
ד יֱהוִה: הֲתִשְׁפֹּט אֹתָם הֲתִשְׁפּוֹט בֶּן־אָדָם
ה אֶת־תּוֹעֲבֹת אֲבוֹתָם הוֹדִיעֵם: וְאָמַרְתָּ
אֲלֵיהֶם כֹּה־אָמַר אֲדֹנָי יֱהוִה בְּיוֹם בָּחֳרִי
בְיִשְׂרָאֵל וָאֶשָּׂא יָדִי לְזֶרַע בֵּית יַעֲקֹב
וָאִוָּדַע לָהֶם בְּאֶרֶץ מִצְרָיִם וָאֶשָּׂא יָדִי
ו לָהֶם לֵאמֹר אֲנִי יְהוָה אֱלֹהֵיכֶם: בַּיּוֹם
הַהוּא נָשָׂאתִי יָדִי לָהֶם לְהוֹצִיאָם מֵאֶרֶץ
מִצְרָיִם אֶל־אֶרֶץ אֲשֶׁר־תַּרְתִּי לָהֶם זָבַת

Ramban (Gen. 25:22) comments that whenever Scripture uses the word לִדְרֹשׁ in connection with God, it means to *pray.* Many commentators understand our verse in this way, and see the rest of the chapter as an explanation of why God refused to listen to their prayer.

Perhaps the true meaning of the words is indeed, *to pray.* But the Sages identified the inner questionings recorded in the above *Midrash* (see also *footnote),* as being the stimulant which was behind the urge to pray.

3. חַי אָנִי — *As I live* [lit. *'I am alive'*] [See *comm.* to 5:11].

אִם אִדָּרֵשׁ לָכֶם — *I will not make Myself accessible to you* [lit. *'If I will ...'*]

With these words God rejects the *seeking* of the elders. See *comm.* to *v.* 1.

4. הֲתִשְׁפֹּט אֹתָם — *Would you rebuke them?*

Rashi interprets הֲתִשְׁפֹּט as לְשׁוֹן וִכּוּחַ. While it is not clear whether *Rashi* uses this term to denote *discussion* or *admonition* [it was used both ways in the Middle Ages], the use of the prepositional form אֹתָם, *'to* them', rather than עִמָּם, *'with* them' indicates that they are to be the object of, not equal partners in the discussion. Therefore, we assume that *Rashi* had in mind the stronger term *rebuke.* This is also the opinion of *Targum.*

5. בְּיוֹם בָּחֳרִי — *On the day of My choice.*

Although Israel's uniqueness was predestined from the times of the forefathers, the actual *choice* (in a practical sense) took place after they had already become a Nation. See *Deut.* 4:37: *And because He loved your fathers and chose 'his' seed after him* [i.e. although the fathers were already

determined to lay down their lives in spite of this rejection. Subsequently, HASHEM appeared to Yechezkel telling him that He would surely help them, but that He wanted them to show their willingness to sacrifice their lives with תְּמִימוּת, *perfect belief,* that love of God which will express itself even when God Himself seems to spurn it. The *Midrash* interprets לִדְרֹשׁ אֶת ה׳ of our verse as a reference to the quest for an answer by the three men whose deep inner conviction of what must be HASHEM's will had been refuted by Wisdom (Daniel) and Prophecy (Yechezkel) and who were nevertheless certain of the correctness of their instinct. They came to HASHEM demanding that their love be confirmed *(Shir haShirim Rabbah* 7:13).

2 *Then the word of HASHEM came to me, saying.*
3 *'Ben Adam, speak to the Elders of Israel and say to them: "Thus spoke my Lord HASHEM/ELOHIM: Is it to seek of Me that you come? As I live I will not make Myself accessible to you. The words of my Lord HASHEM/ELOHIM."*

4 *Would you rebuke them, would you rebuke, Ben Adam? Of the abominations of their fathers inform them.*

5 *And say to them:*

"So said my Lord HASHEM/ELOHIM: On the day of My choice of Israel when I swore to the seed of Jacob's family and made Myself known to them in Egypt, then I swore to them saying I am HASHEM,
your God. 6 *On that day I swore to them to take them*
out from the land of Egypt, to the Land which I had

beloved, the 'seed' is 'chosen'].

Targum Yonasan on that verse reads: 'And because He loved your fathers Abraham, Isaac, and Jacob and chose *Jacob's sons* after him.' This reflects the use of the singular in the verse — 'and chose *his* seed after *him*.'

Ibn Ezra, ad. loc., explains that the Torah used the singular form in order to stress that the choice was limited to Jacob's descendants, not the B'nei Ketura *(Gen.* 25:1-4) or the family of Ishmael *(ibid.* 12-15). [Although they were physical descendants of Abraham, they were not considered his 'seed' in terms of his covenant with God.] This would explain the use of לְזֶרַע בֵּית יַעֲקֹב — *'the descendants of Jacob's family'* in our verse.

וָאֶשָּׂא יָדִי — *When I swore* [lit. *'I lifted up My hand.'*]

Although Scripture does not explicitly mention an oath in its account of the Egyptian exile, *Yalkut (Deut.* 828) explains that the word לָכֵן, *therefore, (Exod.* 6:6) implies an oath.

Rashi (based on *Vayikra Rabbah)* points out that God's 'hatred' at Israel's infidelity in Egypt was suppressed for over nine hundred years because of His love for them. It was only because they were again so blatantly rebellious that this early transgression is recalled.

6. אֶל אֶרֶץ אֲשֶׁר תַּרְתִּי לָהֶם — *To the land which I had sought out for them.*

God had sought out for them the land which from earliest antiquity, had been the focus of man's spiritual striving. Cain killed Abel in order that it might be his, Ishmael hated Isaac because of it, and Esau's undying enmity for Jacob came because Isaac had passed on the gift of the Land to Jacob *(Kuzari* 2:14).

Long before Israel came out of Egypt, it was known as the ideal location for divine service. Malki-Zedek — whom the Sages identify with Shem, son of Noah — had come to Jerusalem while it was still in Canaanite hands, because he knew that only there would he be able to achieve close proximity to God *(Ramban, Gen.* 14:18).

The עִנְיָן הָאֱלֹהִי, the *divine destiny*

כ
ז־ח

חָלָב֙ וּדְבַ֔שׁ צְבִ֥י הִ֖יא לְכָל־הָאֲרָצֽוֹת׃
ז וָאֹמַ֣ר אֲלֵהֶ֗ם אִ֣ישׁ שִׁקּוּצֵ֤י עֵינָיו֙ הַשְׁלִ֔יכוּ
וּבְגִלּוּלֵ֥י מִצְרַ֖יִם אַל־תִּטַּמָּ֑אוּ אֲנִ֖י יְהוָ֥ה
ח אֱלֹהֵיכֶֽם׃ וַיַּמְרוּ־בִי֮ וְלֹ֣א אָב֣וּ לִשְׁמֹ֣עַ אֵלַי֒
אִ֣ישׁ אֶת־שִׁקּוּצֵ֤י עֵֽינֵיהֶם֙ לֹ֣א הִשְׁלִ֔יכוּ
וְאֶת־גִּלּוּלֵ֥י מִצְרַ֖יִם לֹ֣א עָזָ֑בוּ וָאֹמַ֞ר

which it is Israel's historic mission to realize, can flourish only in Eretz Yisrael, just as a vine of even the noblest strain needs ideal soil and climactic conditions in order to develop *(Kuzari* 2:12).

Indeed, the very climate of the Land turns people's hearts towards God. In contrast to Egypt where the annual inundation of the Nile valley seems to make it independent of God's providence, Eretz Yisrael must have rain if it is to yield its bounties *(Ramban, Deut.* 11:10). God exercises His providence over it more directly than over any other land *(Ramban, Lev.* 18:25). Because His Presence is there more than in any other place *(Ramban, Gen.* 33:20), the commandments which are performed there are of an entirely different qualitative order than those performed outside its boundaries *(Ramban, Lev.* loc. cit.). In fact, relative to a person living in the Land, one who is not there can be considered like one who has no God *(Kesubos* 110b).

It is the 'choicest of all inhabited lands' *(Ramban, Gen.* 1:1), 'the center of the earth, the portion of God, unique to Him' *(Ramban, Drasha to Koheles).* Its inhabitants can aspire to prophecy, it is just one level below the Garden of Eden *(Kuzari* 2:14).

The Elders feared that the impending exile implied that God was about to reject His people *(v.* 1). But the truth was quite different. This uniquely holy land does not tolerate sin within its boundaries *(Ramban Lev.* loc. cit.) and it was about to spew them out as it had spewed out the Canaanites before them *(Lev.* 18:28). Cleansed of their sins by the purifying *galus* experience (see *comm.* and *footnote* to 6:8-9), they would one day return to the Land *(v.* 40) which in the meantime would lie desolate, awaiting their return *(Lev.* 26:32).

זָבַת חָלָב וּדְבַשׁ צְבִי הִיא לְכָל הָאֲרָצוֹת — *Flowing with milk and honey, a splendor for all the lands.*

God showered physical as well as spiritual gifts upon this Land. Its rich pastures supported healthy cattle which produced an abundance of milk. Its climate encouraged the growth of trees which yielded large and luscious fruits whose plentiful syrup oozed out making the land flow with honey.

It is full of all of God's goodness: grain, wine, oil and cattle. Truly it is a splendor for all the lands' *(Ramban, Exod.* 3:8).

7. וָאֹמַר אֲלֵהֶם — *And I said to them.*

God's message to the people was delivered through Aaron. According to the *Midrash,* eighty years before Moses had the vision at the burning bush, Aaron was already a prophet in Egypt, exhorting the people to remain true to their holy destiny *(Rashi).*

שִׁקּוּצֵי עֵינָיו ... וּבְגִלּוּלֵי מִצְרַיִם — *The idols of his eyes ... and with the idols of Egypt.*

שִׁקּוּץ and גִלּוּל are used interchangeably in Scripture to denote idols. These names were chosen because of their connotation of something detestable and disgusting.

Hirsch (Vayikra 11:10) traces the meaning of שֶׁקֶץ. It refers exclusively to

XX
7-8

sought out for them, flowing with milk and honey, a splendor for all the lands.

7 *And I said to them: Every man, cast away the idols of his eyes and with the idols of Egypt do not defile yourselves! I am* HASHEM, *your God.*

8 *And they rebelled against Me and did not want to listen to Me. No man! — the idols of their eyes they did not cast out and the idols of Egypt, they did not*

spiritual and mental disgust. Just as the eating of certain animals is forbidden with the words וְאֶת נִבְלָתָם תְּשַׁקֵּצוּ — *and their carcasses shall you hold in abomination,* so, too, the term שַׁקֵּץ תְּשַׁקְּצֶנּוּ *you shall utterly detest it (Deut.* 7:26), is used to refer to all forms of idol worship.

In both cases, that which is enjoined is foreign to Israel's spiritual nature and must be utterly rejected. שֶׁקֶץ הֵם לָכֶם וְשֶׁקֶץ יִהְיוּ לָכֶם, [By their nature] *they are abominable to you and* [therefore] *you are to treat them as abomination (Lev.* 11:10,11).

There is much uncertainty among linguists as to the root of the word גִּלּוּל. However *Rashi (Deut.* 29:16) writes: That they were evil smelling and disgusting like גָּלָל, *body wastes* (see below).

שִׁקּוּצֵי עֵינָיו — *The idols of his eyes.*

While the word שִׁקּוּץ is often used in Scripture to denote idols, it is only here that it is used in connection with the eyes. *Malbim* explains that certain types of idol worship are associated with the eye because they involve visually erotic behavior.

[The stress on the 'eye' is particularly appropriate in view of the time and place at which this prophecy was said. It was during Egyptian slavery when for the first time the family of Jacob was about to forget the truths which they had learned from their fathers and to assimilate into the host culture. Aaron meant to stress that the ostensible attractions of the idols, appealed only to the eye. Their true essence, however, was in complete contradiction to the spiritual calling of the Jewish people.

This also explains the interpretation of גלול=גָּלָל as body waste and the use of this word as a title for idols. Just as food has many forms of nourishment, so also in man's striving for the divine there are many acceptable forms of worship. But just as there are components of food which the body must eliminate because it cannot assimilate them, so, too, the idolatrous cult of Egypt had to be utterly rejected for it had no redeeming value. (See *Ramban Deut.* 12:22 that the pre-eminent cult in Egypt was blood-centered and was directed towards establishing communication with demons). Thus, in the very first prophecy against idol worship — given in Egypt through Aaron — these terms were coined; subsequently they were always used to describe the grossness and coarseness of idolatry.]

8. *Rashi* points out that while some of the people always remained loyal to their heritage, huge segments of the community succumbed to idol worship. These were the ones who died during the plague of חֹשֶׁךְ, *darkness.*

The state of Knesses Israel in Egypt is described by the *Midrash (Yalkut Va'eschanan* 828) in this way: *'A nation from the midst of a nation:* This teaches us that these [the Jews] were uncircumcised and these [the Egyptians] were uncircumcised, these wore their hair

כ
ט־יא

לִשְׁפֹּ֤ךְ חֲמָתִי֙ עֲלֵיהֶ֔ם לְכַלּ֤וֹת אַפִּי֙ בָּהֶ֔ם
ט בְּת֖וֹךְ אֶ֥רֶץ מִצְרָֽיִם׃ וָאַ֙עַשׂ֙ לְמַ֣עַן שְׁמִ֔י
לְבִלְתִּ֥י הֵחֵ֖ל לְעֵינֵ֣י הַגּוֹיִ֑ם אֲשֶׁר־הֵ֣מָּה
בְתוֹכָ֔ם אֲשֶׁ֨ר נוֹדַ֤עְתִּי אֲלֵיהֶם֙ לְעֵ֣ינֵיהֶ֔ם
י לְהוֹצִיאָ֖ם מֵאֶ֥רֶץ מִצְרָֽיִם׃ וָאוֹצִיאֵ֖ם
יא מֵאֶ֣רֶץ מִצְרָ֑יִם וָאֲבִאֵ֖ם אֶל־הַמִּדְבָּֽר׃ וָאֶתֵּ֤ן

plaited and these wore their hair plaited. If so, in justice Israel should not have been redeemed from Egypt. Rav Shmuel bar Nachman said: Had God not obliged himself by an oath, Israel would never have been redeemed from Egypt.

וָאֹמַר לִשְׁפֹּךְ חֲמָתִי עֲלֵיהֶם לְכַלּוֹת אַפִּי בָּהֶם — *And I intended to pour My fury upon them, to spend My anger on them.*

At one point during the Egyptian exile God had wanted to destroy His people. We do not know when this was. *Radak (v. 9)* suggests that the people's spiritual level took a turn for the better when Moses came to Egypt. They believed his message *(Exod.* 4:31) and cast aside their evil ways. In this view the episode referred to in our verse must have happened earlier.

The Sages have a different tradition in this matter. *Mechilta* to *Exod.* 12:6 quotes an opinion that clearly indicates that even immediately prior to the Exodus, the cult of idolatry still had a powerful hold on Israel. In this view, the purpose of preparing a lamb for the Passover sacrifice four days in advance *(ibid.)* was so that the people would have time to shake themselves loose from idolatry.

Be that as it may, our verse tells us that God would have destroyed Israel at some time during their Egyptian exile. That He did not do so was in order to avoid חִלּוּל הַשֵּׁם, *the desecration of God's Name* which would have resulted from such a move (see below).

9. וָאַעַשׂ לְמַעַן שְׁמִי לְבִלְתִּי הֵחֵל לְעֵינֵי הַגּוֹיִם *— But I acted for the sake of My Name, that it not be desecrated in the eyes of the nations.*

God failed to destroy His people purely to avoid a חִלּוּל הַשֵּׁם, *a desecration of His Name.*[1]

10. וָאֲבִאֵם אֶל הַמִּדְבָּר — *And [I] brought them to the Wilderness.*

God swore (*v.* 6) that he would take them out of Egypt and bring them to the

1. This verse seems to imply that there were no positive reasons for Israel's redemption; זְכוּת אָבוֹת, *the merit of the Forefathers,* and the covenants which God had made with them seem to play no role at all. Indeed as we have seen in *comm.* and *footnote* to 9:4 and 14:16, it is possible for children so completely to renounce the spiritual heritage of their fathers, that תַּמָּה זְכוּת אָבוֹת, *the merit of the fathers ceases.* Such a point seems, in fact, to have been reached in Egypt, where, as *Rambam* writes *(Hilchos Avodah Zarah* 1:3): 'The plant which Abraham had planted was almost uprooted and the family of Jacob went back to the mistakes and gropings of the rest of the world.'

Nevertheless, it should be plain that this is far from a complete portrayal of the state of Israel. At the very beginning of the story of Israel's redemption the Torah tells us: *'And God heard their cries and God remembered His covenant with Abraham, Isaac and Jacob. And God saw the Children of Israel, and God took note' (Exod.* 2:24,25).

It would seem that Israel's redemption came as a result of their cries, which stimulated God to remember His covenant with the Patriarchs. (See also *Yerushalmi Ta'anis* 1:1 and ArtScroll *Haggadah* p. 116).

How can we reconcile these two seemingly contradictory accounts?

We shall let *Ramban* guide us to an understanding of the very fundamental concepts with

*forsake. And I intended to pour My fury upon them,
to spend My anger on them, in the midst of the land
of Egypt.* 9 *But I acted for the sake of My Name, that
it not be desecrated in the eyes of the nations midst
which they are; in whose sight I had made Myself
known to them to remove them from the land of
Egypt.*

10 *And I took them out of the land of Egypt and
brought them to the Wilderness;* 11 *and gave them*

Land which He had sought out for them. Instead of taking them to *Eretz Yisrael* by the shortest route, they were guided through the desert (*Exod.* 13:17). Apparently the road to the Land must lead through the Wilderness just as the path of redemption from the final exile lies through the "Wilderness of the Nations" (see *v.* 35 and commentary there).

which we are dealing.

The idea that Israel is permitted to survive in order to avoid Desecration of the Name does not start with Yechezkel. *Numbers* 14:13-20 teaches that it was just such an argument offered by Moses, which caused God to forgive the people for the sin of the spies; and *Deut.* 32:26 teaches the same concept.

Ramban (Deut. ibid.) explains:

It is not because *He wishes to demonstrate His might to His enemies.* God has no need to do this. But, *God created man ... so that* [*man*] *should be able to apprehend the Divine.* God's purpose was thwarted by all the nations. They all became mired in sin and denied Him. *Only this* [*one*] *nation* [*Israel*] *remained loyal to Him, and through their history He made known His omnipotence and thus became recognized by the nations of the world once more.* If it were conceivable that Israel would ever be lost, God's link to mankind would be severed, and the whole purpose of creation would come to naught. *Therefore that same will of God with which He willed the creation, must guarantee the eternal existence of this People for they are the closest to Him and know Him better than anyone.*

God's withholding of anger from Israel, is no grudging support given to a nation which is innerly bankrupt, but whose outer and empty shell must be preserved to make a show for the nations. Rather it is in recognition of the fact that God's design and Israel's fate are intertwined; that the Jewish People are the bearers of Divine Glory on earth, and that therefore, there must be within them an indestructible core of holiness which sin can never destroy. (See *comm.* and *footnote* to 9:2).

This recognition, in turn, opens the flood-gates of God's love for His people. *Ramban* continues: *This is the meaning of the verse (Isaiah* 63:8): *For they are My nation, sons who will never be false.* Surely it is *Ramban*'s intention that we take that verse in its context. It continues: ... *therefore He was a Savior to them. In all their sorrows He suffers with them* (this follows the קְרִי, *the reading).* Nowhere is there a more eloquent statement of the essential oneness of God and Israel.

We are now able to solve our problem. In *vs.* 8 and 9 Yechezkel declares that Israel had sinned so grievously that only its unique character (see above) prevented its destruction. It was not destroyed because Israel must be eternal so that God's relationship with mankind can be maintained.

With this, the stage is set for the account in *Exodus.* These people, these bearers of God's Glory, must have their prayers answered. And as God hears their prayers, the memory of their beloved father rises up before Him and triggers an unprecedented outpouring of love and mercy. (See *Ramban, Exod.* 2:25 and *Da'as Chochmah Umussar* by *Rabbi Yerucham Levovitz,* New York 5727, Ch. 11).

לָהֶם אֶת־חֻקּוֹתַי וְאֶת־מִשְׁפָּטַי הוֹדַעְתִּי
אוֹתָם אֲשֶׁר יַעֲשֶׂה אוֹתָם הָאָדָם וָחַי
יב בָּהֶם: וְגַם אֶת־שַׁבְּתוֹתַי נָתַתִּי לָהֶם
לִהְיוֹת לְאוֹת בֵּינִי וּבֵינֵיהֶם לָדַעַת כִּי אֲנִי
יג יְהֹוָה מְקַדְּשָׁם: וַיַּמְרוּ־בִי בֵית־יִשְׂרָאֵל
בַּמִּדְבָּר בְּחֻקּוֹתַי לֹא־הָלָכוּ וְאֶת־מִשְׁפָּטַי
מָאָסוּ אֲשֶׁר יַעֲשֶׂה אֹתָם הָאָדָם וָחַי בָּהֶם
וְאֶת־שַׁבְּתֹתַי חִלְּלוּ מְאֹד וָאֹמַר לִשְׁפֹּךְ

God's special relationship with Abraham was expressed with the words כִּי יְדַעְתִּיו — *For I have given him My special care (Bereishis* 18:19, *Hirsch* trans.). This same expression is repeated in connection with Knesses Israel: אֲנִי יְדַעְתִּיךָ בַּמִּדְבָּר, *I gave you My special care in the Wilderness (Hoshea* 13:5). God's special relationship with Israel was established in the Wilderness. There was a purpose in this. In contradistinction to the other people of the world whose nationhood is predicated upon land and language (see *Gen.* 10:5), Knesses Israel became God's nation in a situation in which none of the usual conditions of nationhood existed. This established that Israel's existence depends on no condition other than the will of God (based on *Moriah* by *Yitzchok Breuer* 2:2).

11. וְאֶת מִשְׁפָּטַי — *And My ordinances.*

The translation follows the sense of *Hirsch* who translates מִשְׁפָּטִים as *social laws.* It is based on the *Toras Kohanim* which defines מִשְׁפָּטִים as such laws which one would have known about even if they had not been expressly ordained by the Torah. See below.

אֲשֶׁר יַעֲשֶׂה אוֹתָם הָאָדָם וָחַי בָּהֶם — *Which, if a man performs them he shall live through them.*

These words are from *Lev.* 18:5. [This is one of the very many passages in which Yechezkel — more than any other prophet — quotes directly from the Torah. (See *Appendix IV*).

Ramban (Lev. 18:5), mindful of the fact that מִשְׁפָּטִים are social laws, interprets וָחַי בָּהֶם in a temporal sense. If we adhere to the מִשְׁפָּטִים, *the ordinances* of the Torah, then our society will be a peaceful and stable one. This is the 'life' which is promised here. [In contrast, חֻקִּים, *decrees,* control man's relationship to God and nature *(Hirsch).*]

However *Toras Kohanim* (reflected in *Targum* here) explains the 'life' promised in these verses as referring to life after death, the life in the World to Come. All the laws of the Torah, including the 'social' ones, address themselves to our souls more than to our physical existence, because physical existence is itself no more than a preparation for the ultimate life in the Hereafter (see *Mesillas Yesharim Ch.*1).

In this sense, *Ramban (Deut.* 14:1) sees the promise of immortality as being inherent in Israel's role of an עַם קָדוֹשׁ, *a holy nation.* The concept of sanctity makes it impossible to view life on earth as an end in itself.

This interpretation is particularly apt for our chapter whose theme is the unbreakable bond between God and Israel — that Nation of Priests — who, contrary to the ideas of the elders (see *comm.* to *v.* 1), can never shake themselves loose from the bonds of their holiness.

12. אֶת שַׁבְּתוֹתַי נָתַתִּי לָהֶם — *My Sabbaths have I given them.*

Of all the laws of the Torah, only the

XX
12-13

My decrees, and My ordinances I made known to them, which, if a man performs them, he shall live through them. 12 *And also My Sabbaths have I given them, to be a sign between Me and them; that it be known that I am HASHEM Who sanctifies them.*

13 *But the Family of Israel rebelled against Me in the Wilderness; in My decrees they did not walk, and My ordinances they spurned, which, if a man performs them he shall live through them; and they desecrated My Sabbaths exceedingly. So I intended*

Sabbath is singled out for special mention in our chapter. This is not an isolated instance. In *Nechemiah,* 9:14 (a chapter strikingly similar to ours in many ways) we find the same phenomenon.

The *Midrashim* take note of this, and deduce that the Sabbath is as 'weighty' as all the other laws of the Torah combined.

After Israel left Egypt, the very first of the Torah laws which they were called upon to practice, was the Sabbath law (*Exod.* 16:23). [The laws of Marah were given for study, not for practice — see *Rashi* and *Ramban Exod.* 15:25. See also *Tosafos, Shabbos* 87b].

This is no coincidence. The Sabbath, that eternal sign between God and Israel *(Exod.* 31:13 and 17) has always served as the litmus test of Israel's loyalty to its destiny as the bearer of God's Presence on earth. No other law in the Torah stands in such direct opposition to the pernicious doctrines of the cult of idolatry.

In the weekly observance of its Sabbath laws, Israel testifies unambiguously to God's mastery over the universe. The mighty forces of nature, before whom idolatrous man trembled and whose symbols he worshipped, held no terrors for a people who knew the world and its fullness to be God's. No other law could have prepared them as well for their travels in the terrifying desolation of the wilderness.

13. בְּחֻקּוֹתַי לֹא הָלָכוּ — *In My decrees they did not walk.*

They tested Me with the golden calf, in Refidim where they hesitated to accept the Torah, and by keeping some of the Manna overnight in violation of God's command *(Rashi).*

וְאֶת שַׁבְּתֹתַי חִלְּלוּ מְאֹד — *And they desecrated My Sabbaths exceedingly.*

Some of the people went out on the Sabbath to gather Manna (*Rashi).*

Thus, according to *Rashi,* the verse refers to specific instances when the people rebelled against God's will. *Radak* and *Metzudas David* agree and add that the word מְאֹד, *exceedingly,* alludes to the fact that those who went to gather Manna on the Sabbath, were desecrating the very first Sabbath ever given *(Shabbos* 118b). *Metzudas David* adds that the story of the *wood gatherer (Numbers* 15:32) happened on the very next Sabbath (see *Tosafos, Bava Basra* 119b and *Malbim, Emor* 237).

However in *v.* 21 we find the בָּנִים, the second generation in the wilderness, accused of desecrating the Sabbath although Scripture does not record such occurrences explicitly.

[*Rashi* assumes that if actual desecration of the Sabbath is implied by our verse, then reference is to specific instances which are recorded in the Torah. However *N'tziv (Ha'amek Davar, Numbers* 15:32) deduces from our verse that desecration of the Sab-

יד חֲמָתִי עֲלֵיהֶם בַּמִּדְבָּר לְכַלּוֹתָם: וָאֶעֱשֶׂה
לְמַעַן שְׁמִי לְבִלְתִּי הֵחֵל לְעֵינֵי הַגּוֹיִם
טו אֲשֶׁר הוֹצֵאתִים לְעֵינֵיהֶם: וְגַם־אֲנִי
נָשָׂאתִי יָדִי לָהֶם בַּמִּדְבָּר לְבִלְתִּי הָבִיא
אוֹתָם אֶל־הָאָרֶץ אֲשֶׁר־נָתַתִּי זָבַת חָלָב
טז וּדְבַשׁ צְבִי הִיא לְכָל־הָאֲרָצוֹת: יַעַן
בְּמִשְׁפָּטַי מָאָסוּ וְאֶת־חֻקּוֹתַי לֹא־הָלְכוּ
בָהֶם וְאֶת־שַׁבְּתוֹתַי חִלֵּלוּ כִּי אַחֲרֵי
יז גִלּוּלֵיהֶם לִבָּם הֹלֵךְ: וַתָּחָס עֵינִי עֲלֵיהֶם
מִשַּׁחֲתָם וְלֹא־עָשִׂיתִי אוֹתָם כָּלָה
יח בַּמִּדְבָּר: וָאֹמַר אֶל־בְּנֵיהֶם בַּמִּדְבָּר

bath was rampant in the Wilderness and that many unrecorded instances occurred.]

Another interpretation seems possible when we consider that in *v.* 16 we are told the underlying cause of all this rebellion; כי אַחֲרי גלוליהם לִבָּם הלך, *because their heart goes after their idols.* This is one of the most poignant sentences in Yechezkel's rebuke. The *idols of Egypt* of *v.* 7 had suddenly become *'their idols.'* In Egypt there had been the possibility of interpreting their idol worship as simply an aping of the prevailing culture, which did not penetrate beneath the surface to enter their inner being. Now, in the wilderness away from any alien influence, it became evident that, to a significant extent, Egyptian idol worship had become part of their own being making them unable to submit completely to the implications of their destiny.

Bearing in mind the lessons of the previous verse concerning the Sabbath, it is possible that the *desecration* mentioned in this verse does not refer to any specific act of desecration, but rather to a spurning of the lessons of the Sabbath.

[In the same way *Ps.* 95:8-11 teaches that worse than the actual sins committed in Masah and Merivah (*Exod.* 17:1-7), the attitude underlying these sins caused God to swear that Israel would not enter the Land. Similarly in *Ps.* 78:22, the desert generation is faulted: *For they did not believe in God and did not trust His salvation.* (See also *Ps.* 106).]

If we see our chapter against the denigration of the Sabbath, we perceive a generation whose years of bondage left their mark and made it impossible for them to rise to the heights that were expected from them.[1] This is the 'desecration of the Sabbath' of which they were guilty.

14, וָאֶעֱשֶׂה לְמַעַן שְׁמִי – *But I acted for the sake of My Name.*

In *Numbers* 14:20, God announced His forgiveness for the sin of the מְרַגְּלִים, *spies,* with the words: סָלַחְתִּי כִּדְבָרֶךָ, *I have forgiven in accordance*

1. Any discussion of the sins of the דוֹר הַמִּדְבָּר, *Generation of the Wilderness*, must take into account the fact that the *Midrash (Vayikra Rabbah* 9:1) calls this generation דור שכולו דֵעָה, *a generation whose entire essence was one of closeness to God.* An exhaustive analysis of how to understand the sins of these great people, based on *Michtav Me'Eliyahu* is given in the *Overview* of the Artscroll ed. of *Megillas Ruth.*

XX
14-18

to pour My fury on them in the Wilderness — to make an end of them.

14 But I acted for the sake of My Name that it should not be desecrated in the eyes of the nations, in front of whom I had taken them out. 15 And also I swore to them in the Wilderness not to bring them to the land which I had given, flowing with milk and honey. It is a splendor for all the lands. 16 Because My ordinances they spurned; and as for My decrees, they did not walk in them; My Sabbaths they desecrated because after their idols goes their heart.

17 And My eye pitied them rather than destroy them, and I did not put an end to them in the Wilderness.

18 And I said to their children in the Wilderness: In

with your words. Moses had argued that if God were to destroy Israel in the Wilderness, the nations of the world would claim that He lacked the power to take them to the Promised Land *(ibid. v.* 13-16). Then he prayed, basing his entreaty on some of God's attributes of mercy *(v.* 18). *Rashi (ibid. v.* 20) underscores the fact that כִּדְבָרֶךָ, *in accordance with your words,* refers to the argument; *not* to the prayer. A point had been reached at which prayer was without potency, and only the need to avoid Desecration of the Name made forgiveness possible. [See *footnote* to *v.* 9].

15. [See *comm.* to *v.* 6].

16. כִּי אַחֲרֵי גִלּוּלֵיהֶם לִבָּם הֹלֵךְ — *Because after their idols goes their heart.*

The idols which they had served in Egypt *(Metzudas David).* [See *comm.* to *v.* 13].

17. וַתָּחָס עֵינִי עֲלֵיהֶם — *And My eye pitied them.*

The root חוס is used many times in Scripture both in connection with the word עַיִן, *eye,* and without it. The two forms seem identical in meaning.

וְלֹא עָשִׂיתִי אוֹתָם כָּלָה — *And I did not put an end to them.*

They deserved to be completely wiped out, but I spared them *(Metzudas David).* [See *footnote* to *v.* 9.]

18. וָאֹמַר אֶל בְּנֵיהֶם בַּמִּדְבָּר — *And I said to their children in the Wilderness.*

The challenges and failures of the fathers are repeated in the generation of the sons.

The division between the two generations is not an artificial one. Rather it points to perhaps the most pivotal change in our history.

Bereishis Rabbah 3:5 reads: *And God made a division between the light and the darkness (Gen.* 1:4) — this refers to the Book of *Numbers* which differentiates between the generation that went out of Egypt, and the generation which entered the Land.

The generation which left Egypt was

בְּחוּקֵּי אֲבוֹתֵיכֶם אַל־תֵּלֵכוּ וְאֶת־
מִשְׁפְּטֵיהֶם אַל־תִּשְׁמֹרוּ וּבְגִלּוּלֵיהֶם אַל־
יט תִּטַּמָּאוּ׃ אֲנִי יְהֹוָה אֱלֹהֵיכֶם בְּחֻקּוֹתַי לֵכוּ
כ וְאֶת־מִשְׁפָּטַי שִׁמְרוּ וַעֲשׂוּ אוֹתָם׃ וְאֶת־
שַׁבְּתוֹתַי קַדֵּשׁוּ וְהָיוּ לְאוֹת בֵּינִי וּבֵינֵיכֶם
כא לָדַעַת כִּי אֲנִי יְהֹוָה אֱלֹהֵיכֶם׃ וַיַּמְרוּ־בִי
הַבָּנִים בְּחֻקּוֹתַי לֹא־הָלָכוּ וְאֶת־מִשְׁפָּטַי
לֹא־שָׁמְרוּ לַעֲשׂוֹת אוֹתָם אֲשֶׁר יַעֲשֶׂה
אוֹתָם הָאָדָם וָחַי בָּהֶם אֶת־שַׁבְּתוֹתַי
חִלֵּלוּ וָאֹמַר לִשְׁפֹּךְ חֲמָתִי עֲלֵיהֶם לְכַלּוֹת
כב אַפִּי בָּם בַּמִּדְבָּר׃ וַהֲשִׁבֹתִי אֶת־יָדִי וָאַעַשׂ
לְמַעַן שְׁמִי לְבִלְתִּי הֵחֵל לְעֵינֵי הַגּוֹיִם
כג אֲשֶׁר־הוֹצֵאתִי אֹתָם לְעֵינֵיהֶם׃ גַּם־אֲנִי

the generation of 'light.' God related to them with miracles, uninhibited by any natural limitations. If this generation had entered the land of Israel, no wars would have been necessary (*Rashi, Deut.* 1:8). The life of the Wilderness with its tangible manifestations of God's presence in their midst would have entered the Land of Israel with them.

The sin of the מְרַגְּלִים, *the spies,* changed all this. In choosing to follow the 'normal' procedures for conquering a land, Knesses Israel showed itself unable to live a life completely divorced from any natural bounds. They became the generation of 'darkness', a people for whom the הַשְׁגָּחָה, *God's Providence,* would have to be in a more hidden manner, disguised behind a screen of nature (based on Intro. to *Numbers, Ha'amek Davar).*

Thus, when God addressed Himself to the 'sons,' the implication is: Your fathers failed Me at the level of *their* existence and duties. Do you now, in your capacity as בָּאֵי הָאָרֶץ, *those who will come to the Land,* with the duty of living a holy life in a *natural way,* not fail as they had done.

בְּחוּקֵי אֲבוֹתֵיכֶם אַל תֵּלֵכוּ — *In the decrees of your fathers do not walk.*

The meaning of this sentence is obscure. *Metzudas David* explains: The laws which your fathers made up from their own minds, which God did not command. But Scripture does not record any 'laws' which would come under this category. *Rashi* and other commentators are silent on the subject.

Perhaps the key to a different understanding can be found in *Psalm* 95 which finds one basic criticism that sufficed to condemn the whole generation. *Do not harden your hearts as you did in Merivah, as you did on the day of Masah in the wilderness. Where your fathers challenged Me, they tested Me though they saw My deeds (Ps.* 95:8-9) [referring to the events recorded in *Exod.* 17:1-7. In desperation at not finding

the decrees of your fathers do not walk, and their ordinances do not observe, and with their idols do not defile yourselves.
19 *I am HASHEM your God. In My decrees walk; and My ordinances, observe; and perform them.*
20 *My Sabbaths sanctify, and the will be a sign between Me and you; to know that I am HASHEM your God.*
21 *But the children rebelled against Me. In My decrees they did not walk; My ordinances, they did not observe to perform them, which, if a man performs them he would live through them; My Sabbaths they desecrated, and I intended to pour out My fury on them, to spend My anger on them in the*
22 *Wilderness. Yet I refrained from doing so, and I acted for the sake of My Name, that it not be desecrated in the eyes of the nations before whom I had taken them out.*

any water to drink they asked: *Is HASHEM in our midst or not?*] It is this challenging and testing which the psalmist condemns, and which indeed provided the background for one of the prohibitions of the Torah. *Do not challenge HASHEM your God as you challenged Him in Masah (Deut.* 6:16).

Ramban (ibid.) explains this prohibition: 'You should not say that we will keep the Torah only if Hashem is in our midst to do miracles for us, or if we have food and live well.... This is considered a great sin, for it is not right to serve Hashem for the sake of receiving a reward.'

A person who obeys the laws of the Torah only because they seem to guarantee the fulfillment of his needs turns the laws of God into *his* laws, because he obeys them only as long as they suit him. It is not surprising that the Psalmist saw just this sin as the most fundamental, since it subverted the very purpose of their redemption: *My servants are they whom I have taken out from the land of Egypt (Lev.* 25:55).

This then would be God's exhortation to the second generation. Do not subvert the purpose of the laws of the Torah by treating them as *your* laws. Keep them because they are *My* decrees and *My* ordinances (*v.* 19).

21. וַיַּמְרוּ בִי הַבָּנִים — *But the children rebelled against Me.*

These are the ones who cleaved to the Ba'al Pe'or (*Metzudas David).* (See *Numbers* 25:1-9) [and see further in *comm.* to *v.* 23].

22. וַהֲשִׁבֹתִי אֶת יָדִי — *Yet I refrained* [lit. *'I held back My hand'*] *from doing so.*

The *Targum* in line with his constant concern to eliminate any anthropomorphism, translates: And I held back the striking of My strength. [We find the same idiom above in 18:17, and there *Targum* takes יָדִי literally.]

נָשָׂאתִי אֶת־יָדִי לָהֶם בַּמִּדְבָּר לְהָפִיץ
כד אֹתָם בַּגּוֹיִם וּלְזָרוֹת אוֹתָם בָּאֲרָצוֹת: יַעַן
מִשְׁפָּטַי לֹא־עָשׂוּ וְחֻקּוֹתַי מָאָסוּ וְאֶת־
שַׁבְּתוֹתַי חִלֵּלוּ וְאַחֲרֵי גִּלּוּלֵי אֲבוֹתָם הָיוּ
כה עֵינֵיהֶם: וְגַם־אֲנִי נָתַתִּי לָהֶם חֻקִּים לֹא
כו טוֹבִים וּמִשְׁפָּטִים לֹא יִחְיוּ בָּהֶם: וָאֲטַמֵּא
אוֹתָם בְּמַתְּנוֹתָם בְּהַעֲבִיר כָּל־פֶּטֶר רָחַם

23. נָשָׂאתִי אֶת יָדִי — *I swore* [lit. *'I raised My hand'*]

Rashi and *Radak* identify the oath in this verse with the passage in *Deut.* 4:25, which foretells that they would speedily lose the Land when they succumbed to the idol worship of Canaan. It is significant that the passage closes with the sentence: *And you shall search from there for HASHEM, your God, and you will find, when you search with all your heart and with all your soul ... because HASHEM your God is a merciful God (ibid. v.* 29,31).

Thus in the very passage in which the inevitable exile was predicted, the return and reconciliation with God are mentioned.

This then is the answer to the *Elders* in *v.* 1 (see *comm.)* There is no question of a *selling* in your situation. When a Kohen sells his slave, no ties remain between them and the slave can certainly no longer eat the priestly tithe. Your exile, far from being a break in the ties which bind you to God, has been part of your destiny from the first dawn of nationhood, and is only a step along the path which leads to the ultimate fulfillment of God's purpose.

לְהָפִיץ אֹתָם בַּגּוֹיִם — *To scatter them among the nations.*

In *v.* 21 (see *comm.)* we learned that the rebellion of the second generation was their *cleaving to the Ba'al Pe'or* and as our verse makes clear that sin guaranteed an eventual exile from the Land of Israel.[1]

24. וְאֶת שַׁבְּתוֹתַי חִלֵּלוּ — *And My Sabbaths they desecrated.*

See *comm.* on *v.*13 which discusses

1. To better understand the nature of this rebellion, we quote from *Sanhedrin* 64a: There was a gentile woman who was exceedingly ill. She swore that if she recovered she would serve every idol in the world. She recovered and did as she had sworn. When she came to the Pe'or she asked the priests: How does one serve this idol. They said to her: One eats beets and drinks strong wine and evacuates in front of it. So she said: It were better that I should become sick once more and not serve an idol in this way. But you Israel are different: [in connection with the Pe'or] it says הַנִּצְמָדִים, *those that cleave* [but in connection with God it says] *You who are joined to HASHEM your God (Deut.* 4:4) [being 'joined' implies a lesser relationship than 'cleaving'.]

Thus the service of the Pe'or, which involved such disgusting acts that even a heathen woman was revolted by them, exerted a magnetic attraction which, in a sense, was stronger than their ties to God.

Today we have no understanding for this terrible urge to worship idols; we live in a time when this יֵצֶר הָרַע, *evil inclination* has been taken away from us. [See *footnote* to 2:3]. But apparently for the generation of the בָּאֵי הָאָרֶץ, *those who entered the land,* the drive was so strong that they were willing to sacrifice their high attainments of holiness on its altars.

A people so strongly oriented towards idol worship would not be able to withstand the constant pressures to conform, to which they would be exposed in Eretz Yisrael, and the ultimate exile became a foregone conclusion.

[23] *Also, I swore to them in the Wilderness to scatter them among the nations and to disperse them among the lands,* [24] *because My ordinances they did not perform, and My decrees they spurned, and My Sabbaths they desecrated, and after the idols of their fathers were their eyes.* [25] *So I too gave them decrees which were not good, and ordinances through which they could not live.* [26] *And I defiled them through their own gifts, when causing each firstborn to pass;*

the desecration of the Sabbaths mentioned in this verse.

25. וְגַם אֲנִי נָתַתִּי לָהֶם חֻקִּים לֹא טוֹבִים — *So I too gave them decrees which are not good.*

'I gave them into the hands of their evil inclination, that they might stumble through their sins.' (*Rashi* based on *Targum*). Thus it was not God who gave them *bad laws,* but their own impulses which mastered them and laid down boundaries within which they were forced to act.

Rashi avoids the problem of how God could cause a person to sin by explaining that God *gave them into the hands of the evil inclination,* from which the sins then followed as a matter of course. This seems to go further than *Rambam* in *Hilchos Teshuvah* 6:3, who says only that sometimes justice will demand that a sinner be prevented from repenting his sins, thereby leaving himself open to punishment. *Rambam* stops short of saying that God would deliver a person into the hands of his evil inclination.

Radak (borne out by *Midrash Tanchuma, Mishpatim* 3) explains that as a result of rebelling against God, Israel would be subjugated by foreign conquerers who would impose *decrees which would not be good,* and *ordinances which would not lead to life;* in contrast to God's laws, which they had rejected.

Thus the *bad laws* can be said to come from God, since it is He who allowed Israel to be conquered by the alien nations. (See *comm.* on next verse).

26. וָאֲטַמֵּא אוֹתָם בְּמַתְּנוֹתָם — *And I defiled them through their own gifts.*

The *gifts* are the firstborn sons whom I commanded Israel to sanctify to Me (*Exod.* 13:2). I gave these gifts into the hands of their evil inclination to cause them to pass to the Molech, the idol whose service entailed child sacrifice through fire (*Lev.* 18:21). These are the laws which are not good (*Rashi*).

Rashi sees our verse as an example of the חֻקִּים לֹא טוֹבִים of the previous verse. Left to their own impulses, the people degraded the command of sanctifying the firstborn, into a superstitious rite designed to placate some morally blind, grasping natural force — from whom, so the thinking went, one could win favors by catering to its lusts (see *Hirsch comm.* on *Lev.* 18:21).[1]

בְּהַעֲבִיר כָּל פֶּטֶר רָחַם — *When causing each firstborn to pass.*

The root עבר in the הִפְעִיל, *the*

1. That this particularly dreadful distortion of one of the Torah's holy commands was chosen as an example of *bad laws* is no coincidence.

The opening words of our verse are an echo of the passage (*Vayikra* 20:3) which condemns a person who gives his son to the Molech because in doing so טַמֵּא אֶת מִקְדָּשִׁי וּלְחַלֵּל אֶת שֵׁם קָדְשִׁי, *He defiles My Sanctuary, and desecrates My holy Name.* Now the *sanctuary* mentioned in this verse cannot mean the Holy Temple, since the service of the Molech did not take place

לְמַ֣עַן אֲשַׁמֵּ֔ם לְמַ֙עַן֙ אֲשֶׁ֣ר יֵדְע֔וּ אֲשֶׁ֖ר אֲנִ֥י
כז יְהוָֽה׃ לָכֵ֞ן דַּבֵּ֗ר
אֶל־בֵּ֤ית יִשְׂרָאֵל֙ בֶּן־אָדָ֔ם וְאָמַרְתָּ֣
אֲלֵיהֶ֔ם כֹּ֥ה אָמַ֖ר אֲדֹנָ֣י יֱהֹוִ֑ה ע֗וֹד זֹ֚את
גִּדְּפ֤וּ אוֹתִי֙ אֲב֣וֹתֵיכֶ֔ם בְּמַֽעֲלָ֥ם בִּ֖י מָֽעַל׃
כח וָאֲבִיאֵם֙ אֶל־הָאָ֔רֶץ אֲשֶׁ֤ר נָשָׂ֙אתִי֙ אֶת־
יָדִ֔י לָתֵ֥ת אוֹתָ֖הּ לָהֶ֑ם וַיִּרְאוּ֩ כָל־גִּבְעָ֨ה
רָמָ֜ה וְכָל־עֵ֣ץ עָבֹ֗ת וַיִּזְבְּחוּ־שָׁ֞ם אֶת־
זִבְחֵיהֶ֗ם וַיִּתְּנוּ־שָׁם֙ כַּ֣עַס קָרְבָּנָ֔ם וַיָּשִׂ֤ימוּ
שָׁם֙ רֵ֣יחַ נִיחוֹחֵיהֶ֔ם וַיַּסִּ֥יכוּ שָׁ֖ם אֶת־

causative is used in the Torah, both when discussing the command to sanctify the first born *(Exod.* 13:12), and in connection with giving one's son to the Molech *(Leviticus* 18:21).

In both cases the word could have the same meaning: the passing from one state to another *(Ibn Ezra).* In the former case the meaning would be that we are commanded to sanctify our first born, by passing him from a neutral state into a state of holiness. In the latter case it refers to making one's child into an abomination.

However *Rashi* (based on *Midrashim)* translates וְהַעֲבַרְתָּ in *Exod.* as 'separate', and in *Leviticus* he explains that לְהַעֲבִיר refers to the 'passing through' the fire which was the service of the Molech.

Rashi on our verse takes בְּהַעֲבִיר in this latter sense. *Radak,* however, ex-

in the Temple and had no connection to it. Because of this *Rashi* explains that it is Knesses Israel which is described here as the 'sanctuary' of God. Knesses Israel will become *unclean* if one of its members delivers his son to the Molech.

Ramban raises the question: How can the nation become unclean because of the acts of a single man? He explains this with reference to the dictum *(Berachos* 35b) that if a person uses something from this world without reciting the required blessing, he is stealing from Knesses Israel. The explanation for this is ... because [God's] purpose in creating the world was that people should have opportunities to bless His great Name for it is this which gives the world meaning. If not [if people do not make the blessing] He, with His holy Name will rise and the Divine Presence will disappear from Israel. Now certainly if he takes the fruit and gives it over to the Molech! ...

The Divine Presence is with us only to the degree that we recognize its closeness. We do this by seeing every gift which HASHEM gives us as presenting us with the opportunity of blessing and thanking Him. If we choose to ignore this, and enjoy our possessions without a blessing and certainly when we offer them up to propitiate the Molech — the very antithesis of holiness — then the Divine Presence leaves us, and we remain טָמֵא, *unclean.*

This is the meaning of the 'desolation' mentioned in our verse. When we cause our children *to pass to the Molech,* leaving ourselves 'defiled' and bereft of the Divine Presence, then we are truly desolate.

But this desolation will lead to the recognition that *I am HASHEM,* and thus it carries within itself the seeds of salvation.

According to *Radak* in *v.* 25 (see *comm.),* we can now see the two verses as complementing each other. The rebellion of Israel causes the desolation which comes from the departure of the Divine Presence, leaving them open to conquest by foreign armies who will impose evil, death-dealing laws.

that I may lay them desolate, in order that they should know that I am HASHEM."
27 *Therefore, speak to the Family of Israel, Ben Adam, and say to them: "Thus says my Lord HASHEM/ELOHIM: Even this: your fathers blasphemed Me by betraying Me with treachery.*
28 *But I brought them to the Land which I had sworn to give them; and they saw every high hill and every thick tree, and they slaughtered there their sacrifices, and they offered there the provocation of their offerings, placed there their savor of satisfaction, and*

plains the word in the same way as *Ibn Ezra:* The sin consists of taking the child out of the sanctity of God and passing him into the purview of the Molech.

We translate *when causing ... to pass* to accomodate both opinions.

27. דַּבֵּר אֶל בֵּית יִשְׂרָאֵל – *Speak to the Family of Israel.*

At this point the answer to the Elders of Israel (see *comm. v.* 1) has been completed. It has been fully explained why God refuses to make Himself accessible to them *(v.* 3). The prophet now turns to the entire Family of Israel *(Harav Breuer).*

עוֹד זֹאת – *Even this* [lit. *'also this'*]

What follows is even worse than the evils recounted up to now *(Rashi).*

גִּדְּפוּ אוֹתִי אֲבוֹתֵיכֶם – *Your fathers blasphemed Me.*

The term גִּדּוּף indicates a blasphemous denial of God's power to control events. That this is its definition is evident from *II Kings* 19:6-22 with reference to the declarations of Sancheriv's messengers that God was powerless to save Jerusalem from the attacks of the Assyrian army *(Hirsch, Num.* 15:30).

The Land of Israel is of such a nature that the thoughts of its inhabitants should be constantly turned towards God *(Deut.* 11:10 and *Ramban ibid.).* It was the Land which God had chosen to be *His portion* under His direct control, as opposed to all other lands which were governed through intermediaries *(Ramban; Lev.* 18:25). [See *comm.* to *v.* 6]. But by using every hill and every tree in the Land for idol worship (*v.* 28), they subverted its unique character and God's relationship to it, degrading Him in their minds to the level of the idols of the neighboring nations.

This גִּידּוּף, *blasphemy,* is even worse than the worship of the Molech mentioned in *v.* 26. It constitutes the misreading of the very essence of their being.

בְּמַעֲלָם בִּי מָעַל – *By betraying Me with treachery.*

The particular disloyalty connoted by the verb מעל in *Tanach,* is an act whereby something is treacherously used for a purpose other than that for which it was meant. (Thus the adultery of a married woman [*Num.* 5:12], or the use of sacred property for secular purposes [*Lev.* 5:15]). Using God's own Land for idolatrous purposes, is an act of מְעִילָה *(Harav Breuer).*

28. רֵיחַ נִיחוֹחֵיהֶם – [*Their offerings which would provide*] *their savor of satisfaction.*

Based on *Rashi (Lev.* 1:9).

כט נִסְכֵּיהֶם׃ וָאֹמַר אֲלֵהֶם מָה הַבָּמָה אֲשֶׁר־
אַתֶּם הַבָּאִים שָׁם וַיִּקָּרֵא שְׁמָהּ בָּמָה
ל עַד הַיּוֹם הַזֶּה׃ לָכֵן אֱמֹר |
אֶל־בֵּית יִשְׂרָאֵל כֹּה אָמַר אֲדֹנָי יֱהוִה
הַבְדֶרֶךְ אֲבוֹתֵיכֶם אַתֶּם נִטְמְאִים וְאַחֲרֵי
לא שִׁקּוּצֵיהֶם אַתֶּם זֹנִים׃ וּבִשְׂאֵת מַתְּנֹתֵיכֶם
בְּהַעֲבִיר בְּנֵיכֶם בָּאֵשׁ אַתֶּם נִטְמְאִים
לְכָל־גִּלּוּלֵיכֶם עַד־הַיּוֹם וַאֲנִי אִדָּרֵשׁ לָכֶם
בֵּית יִשְׂרָאֵל חַי־אָנִי נְאֻם אֲדֹנָי יֱהוִה אִם־
לב אִדָּרֵשׁ לָכֶם׃ וְהָעֹלָה עַל־רוּחֲכֶם הָיוֹ לֹא
תִהְיֶה אֲשֶׁר | אַתֶּם אֹמְרִים נִהְיֶה כַגּוֹיִם
כְּמִשְׁפְּחוֹת הָאֲרָצוֹת לְשָׁרֵת עֵץ וָאָבֶן׃
לג חַי־אָנִי נְאֻם אֲדֹנָי יֱהוִה אִם־לֹא בְּיָד

29. מָה הַבָּמָה — *What is this Bamah?*

The word בָּמָה connotes *height.* However its usage as a description of an altar was based not on its physical height, but on its function of attracting the אֵשׁ שֶׁל מַעֲלָה, the heavenly fire (*Abarbanel* and *Metzudas Zion);* or of stimulating the worshiper to elevate himself spiritually to the service of God.

God asks the people: By what right do you give the name *Bamah* to the altars which you erected for the purpose of idol worship? Certainly no spiritual heights are attained by the people who prostrate themselves there, and no heavenly fires descend upon them.

אֲשֶׁר אַתֶּם הַבָּאִים שָׁם — *To which it is* [*only*] *you who come?*

Only you come there, not God Who promised (*Exod.* 20:21) to 'come' to an altar erected in His Name (*Harav Breuer*).

וַיִּקָּרֵא שְׁמָהּ בָּמָה עַד הַיּוֹם הַזֶּה — *Yet it was called Bamah until this day.*

The people were not ashamed of this distortion, and continued calling their altars *Bamah.*

31. חַי אָנִי ... אִם אִדָּרֵשׁ לָכֶם — *As I live ... I will not make Myself accessible to you.*

In *v.* 3 God refused to make Himself accessible to the Elders of Israel who had come to 'seek an answer' from Him. In this verse, the rejection is expanded to include the entire Family of Israel (see *comm. v.* 27).

It is, of course, inconceivable that such a rejection should be permanent. [See *footnote* to *v.* 9]. Indeed in 36:37 Yechezkel himself recorded God's comforting reversal: *Thus said my Lord HASHEM / ELOHIM: Furthermore I will make Myself accessible to the family of Israel. Midrash Tanchuma (Vo'eira* 13, quoted by *Rashi v.* 3) quotes this as one of the instances where we find that God will reverse Himself and not fulfill a threatened punishment, saying: 'I am not like a human being who threatens evil and then prides himself in doing it.'

32. וְהָעֹלָה עַל רוּחֲכֶם — *What enters your thoughts.*

This verse and the next, bring to a climax the answer to the Elders (see

poured out there their drink offerings. 29 *Then I said*
to them: What is this Bamah to which it is only you,
who come? Yet it was called Bamah until this day.'
30 *Therefore, say to the Family of Israel: "Thus*
said my Lord HASHEM/ELOHIM*: In the way of your*
fathers do you defile yourselves?! And after their
abominations do you go astray?! 31 *And in giving*
your gifts, in passing your sons through fire, you
defile yourselves for your idols to this day; yet I
should make Myself accessible to you, Family of
Israel! As I live — the words of my Lord HASHEM/
ELOHIM *— I will not make Myself accessible to you.*
32 *What enters your thoughts — it shall not be!*
What you say: Let us be like the nations, like the
families of the lands, to serve wood and stone. 33 *As I*
live — the words of my Lord HASHEM/ELOHIM *—*

comm. v. 1). What is said here is the logical conclusion of everything that went before. Israel has a destiny (*vs.* 5 and 6) which binds it permanently to God *(footnote v.* 9). Far from breaking this relationship, the exile to which they were now exposed, is an integral part in allowing God's plans *(ibid.)* to reach their fulfillment (*comm. v.* 33). It was predicted centuries earlier *(comm. v.* 23) and was an inevitable result of their inability to shake themselves loose from the spiritual bonds which tied them to Egypt even after their physical redemption (*comm. v.* 13).

Therefore, הָיוֹ לֹא תִהְיֶה, *It* [your thoughts] *shall not be.*

[The verb לֹא תִהְיֶה is preceded by the infinitive הָיוֹ for emphasis].

נִהְיֶה כַגּוֹיִם — *Let us be like the nations.*

'Let us throw off His yoke from our necks, since He has driven us away' *(Rashi)*[1]

כְּמִשְׁפְּחוֹת הָאֲרָצוֹת לְשָׁרֵת עֵץ וָאָבֶן — *Like the families of the lands, to serve wood and stone.*

The plural form of אֶרֶץ, *land*, always means countries *(Targum).* Thus מִשְׁפְּחוֹת הָאֲרָצוֹת means people who live in other countries. [*Rabbi Joseph Carlebach* in *Die Drei Grossen Propheten* translates 'country-bound' families — see *comm. v.* 10].

1. In his *Ikv'sah di'M'shichah (Kovetz Ma'amorim Jerusalem* 5723), written shortly before World War II, Rabbi Elchonon Wasserman traces the thrust towards assimilation which engulfed Jewry of his day and which seemed to be so accurately foretold in this passage. He writes that the three descriptions of God's anger contained in the next verse: 1) the strong hand, 2) the outstretched arm, and 3) the outpoured fury, would surely come about as well. Prophetically he points out that there was no way of knowing which of these three stages had been reached at the time of his writing, but that surely the immediate future would tell. We are witnesses to the 'poured out fury' which swept him away together with a large part of Europe's Jews.

כ
לד-לו

חֲזָקָה וּבִזְרוֹעַ נְטוּיָה וּבְחֵמָה שְׁפוּכָה
לד אֶמְלוֹךְ עֲלֵיכֶם: וְהוֹצֵאתִי אֶתְכֶם מִן־
הָעַמִּים וְקִבַּצְתִּי אֶתְכֶם מִן־הָאֲרָצוֹת
אֲשֶׁר נְפוֹצוֹתֶם בָּם בְּיָד חֲזָקָה וּבִזְרוֹעַ
לה נְטוּיָה וּבְחֵמָה שְׁפוּכָה: וְהֵבֵאתִי אֶתְכֶם
אֶל־מִדְבַּר הָעַמִּים וְנִשְׁפַּטְתִּי אִתְּכֶם שָׁם
לו פָּנִים אֶל־פָּנִים: כַּאֲשֶׁר נִשְׁפַּטְתִּי אֶת־

33. בְּיָד חֲזָקָה וּבִזְרוֹעַ נְטוּיָה — *With a strong hand and an outstretched arm.*

The very same *strong hand and outstretched arm* with which God had shown His love for them in Egypt by punishing the nation which enslaved Israel, will continue to be with them in their exile. It is the same loving God Who, because of their sins, must now deal with them with *outpoured fury (Harav Breuer).*

That this *fury* is only an outward appearance, but that its motivation is God's abiding love is expressed throughout Yechezkel by the use of the Four-Letter Name denoting God's love, vocalized to read *Elohim,* the Name denoting God's justice. *Harav Breuer* translates this as: *He whose loving kindness is revealed through justice.* [See *comm.* and *footnote* to 2:4].

Thus the import of this verse is that God's plans remain unchanged. However, what could have been brought about through manifestations of His lovingkindness, must now, because of Israel's sins, come about through the manifestation of His stern justice.

An exhaustive treatment of how God's purpose will be brought about either through kindness or justice, dependent only on Israel's actions, can be found in the opening paragraphs of *Rabbi Moshe Chaim Luzzato's Da'as Tevunos.*

34-38. These five verses are interpreted in two different ways. The divergent opinions derive from a disagreement concerning the meaning of מִדְבַּר הָעַמִּים, *the Wilderness of the Nations,* in *v.* 35. *Rashi* and others translate the word מִדְבָּר, *desert,* literally and hold this group of verses to describe the gathering-in of the exiles, whose path will lead through a wilderness just as it did for our fathers in Egypt.

Abarbanel and others interpret מִדְבַּר הָעַמִּים to be a metaphor for גָּלוּת, *exile,* and see the passage as a description of Israel's *Galus* experience.

34. וְהוֹצֵאתִי אֶתְכֶם מִן הָעַמִּים — *And I shall take you out from the nations.*

Rashi leaves this verse unexplained, because, according to his understanding of *v.* 35 (see above) it presents no difficulties. The meaning of חֵמָה שְׁפוּכָה, *outpoured anger,* is obscure in this context, and *Metzudas David* explains that God's fury will be poured onto the nations causing them to drive Israel from their lands by force. There is no indication whether the description refers to the return from the Babylonian exile or to the ultimate redemption of Israel.

If the Wilderness of the Nations is a metaphor for exile *(Abarbanel, Malbim, Harav Breuer)* the question must be asked: from which lands and nations will God gather them — to send them into exile? *Malbim* and *Harav Breuer* solve the problem by interpreting this verse as looking ahead. The sequence must be read as follows: I will ultimately take you out from the nations ..., but *first* I will bring you into the wilderness of the nations.

with a strong hand and an outstretched arm and with outpoured fury will I rule over you.

34 *And I shall take you out from the nations, and gather you from the lands into which you were scattered, with a strong hand and an outstretched arm and with outpoured fury.* 35 *And I will bring you to the 'Wilderness of the Nations' and I will wrangle with you there, face to face.* 36 *As I wrangled with*

Abarbanel however, explains that the 'nations' and 'lands' refer to the original countries in which the exiles had settled. The meaning then would be: Do not think that you can be absorbed by these countries and lose your identity in them by assimilation. They are only אֶרֶץ מְגוּרֵיהֶם, *the land of their sojournings* (*v.* 38), not your permanent homes and you will have to leave them and wander all over the world before you can return to your true home.[1]

[In this context the choice of the verbs וְהוֹצֵאתִי and וְקִבַּצְתִּי is perhaps intended to provide a sharp contrast with *v.* 41, where these very same verbs denote the ultimate gathering in of the exiles.]

35. מִדְבַּר הָעַמִּים — *The Wilderness of the Nations.*

Rashi identifies this with the desert which Israel traversed on its way out of Egypt. It is called the Wilderness of the Nations because it borders on a number of lands (see *Rashi, Num.* 34:3). However we do find exile described as a wilderness *(Hosea* 2:16 and *Rashi)* and this justifies the alternate explanation, that the Wilderness of Nations is a metaphor for the Galus experience *(Malbim).* Just as only the hand of God made existence possible in the wilderness where no natural power could have sustained their nationhood; so also, Israel, scattered among the nations of the world could not for a moment have survived in defiance of the laws of history were it not for God's sustaining hand.

וְנִשְׁפַּטְתִּי אִתְּכֶם שָׁם — *And I will wrangle with you there.*

Metzudas David translates: אֶתְוַכַּח, *I will argue.* However the Hebrew word has a stronger connotation than the English 'argue'. It is more in the nature of a demonstration of justification (see *I Sam.* 12:7). *Radak* translates: I will let you know your evil deeds. In addition to this, *Targum* translates our verse: *I will punish.* We therefore translate *wrangle* as being closest to the real meaning.

פָּנִים אֶל פָּנִים — *Face to face.*

Israel's tragic history in exile was as much 'face to face' with God, as their triumphant forty years in the wilderness. Bereft of every tie which could bind a nation together without common language or territory, they travel the road of *Galus* in the presence of God! God is not indifferent to Jewish experience. He smiles and frowns, rewards and punishes because Israel's spiritual status is vital to His plan of creation. Thus, the suffering of *Galus* is no less the product of His hand than the caress of constant miracles in the wilderness (based on *Dr. Yitzchak Breuer* in *Moriah).*

1. *Abarbanel* explains the whole passage as relating to the situation in Spain, where many Jews saw the acceptance — at least outwardly — of another religion as the best way to avoid the persecutions of the Inquisition.

אֲבוֹתֵיכֶם בְּמִדְבַּר אֶרֶץ מִצְרָיִם כֵּן
אִשָּׁפֵט אִתְּכֶם נְאֻם אֲדֹנָי יֱהוִֹה׃
לז וְהַעֲבַרְתִּי אֶתְכֶם תַּחַת הַשָּׁבֶט וְהֵבֵאתִי
לח אֶתְכֶם בְּמָסֹרֶת הַבְּרִית׃ וּבָרוֹתִי מִכֶּם
הַמֹּרְדִים וְהַפּוֹשְׁעִים בִּי מֵאֶרֶץ מְגוּרֵיהֶם
אוֹצִיא אוֹתָם וְאֶל־אַדְמַת יִשְׂרָאֵל לֹא
לט יָבוֹא וִידַעְתֶּם כִּי־אֲנִי יהוה׃ וְאַתֶּם בֵּית־
יִשְׂרָאֵל כֹּה־אָמַר | אֲדֹנָי יֱהוִֹה אִישׁ
גִּלּוּלָיו לְכוּ עֲבֹדוּ וְאַחַר אִם־אֵינְכֶם
שֹׁמְעִים אֵלָי וְאֶת־שֵׁם קָדְשִׁי לֹא תְחַלְּלוּ־
מ עוֹד בְּמַתְּנוֹתֵיכֶם וּבְגִלּוּלֵיכֶם׃ כִּי בְהַר־
קָדְשִׁי בְּהַר | מְרוֹם יִשְׂרָאֵל נְאֻם אֲדֹנָי

36. כַּאֲשֶׁר נִשְׁפַּטְתִּי ... בְּמִדְבַּר אֶרֶץ מִצְרָיִם — *As I wrangled ... in the Wilderness of the land of Egypt.*

This refers to the people who died in the wilderness because their sins showed them to be unworthy of entering *Eretz Yisrael.*

37. וְהַעֲבַרְתִּי אֶתְכֶם תַּחַת הַשָּׁבֶט — *And I will make you pass under the rod.*

Most commentators interpret this as a metaphor for counting, in the same sense as it is used in *Lev.* 27:32.

[The sheep pass single-file under the shepherd's crook in order that he may count them and separate the tenth one as a tithe. Interpreted thus, this 'passing' is a prelude to the 'separation' of the next verse.]

Rashi, however, explains: 'So that you should be submitted to My chastisement.' This accords with the usual connotation of the word שֵׁבֶט, *rod,* as symbolizing a means of punishment (see *Prov.* 22:15).

[*Rashi* may have ignored the similarity of the idiom to that used in *Leviticus* because here the הִפְעִיל, the *causative* (וְהַעֲבַרְתִּי *will cause to pass)* is used, instead of the *Kal.* In this sense it is possible that the expression וְהַעֲבַרְתִּי is used intentionally to remind the people of the sins which had caused these punishments בְּהַעֲבִיר כָּל פֶּטֶר רָחַם, *when causing each first born to pass* (*v.* 26). Because you 'passed' your children to the *Molech,* I will 'pass' you under the rod of My punishment.]

בְּמָסֹרֶת הַבְּרִית — *Into the bond of the covenant.*

This is the only place in Scripture where the word מָסֹרֶת is used. *Rashi* translates it in the sense that it is used in Rabbinic literature — a giving over, i.e., the transmission of the covenant from generation to generation. *Radak* however traces it to the root אָסַר, to tie and reads it as though the word were מַאֲסֹרֶת, *a bond.*

38. וּבָרוֹתִי מִכֶּם — *And (I will) separate from among you.*

Whether this 'separation' will come about by means of some final testing in a future wilderness *(Rashi);* or in the crucible of the *Galus (Abarbanel),* the rebels and the sinners will be weeded out and not be permitted to make a breach in כָּל בֵּית יִשְׂרָאֵל, *the whole Fami-*

your fathers in the Wilderness of the land of Egypt so
I will wrangle with you — the words of my Lord
HASHEM/ELOHIM — 37 *and I will make you pass un-*
der the rod, and bring you into the bond of the cove-
nant, 38 *and separate from among you those who rebel*
and those who transgress against Me; from the land
of their sojourning will I take them out but to the soil
of Israel none shall come. Then shall you know that I
am HASHEM.
39 *And you, Family of Israel, thus said my Lord*
HASHEM/ELOHIM: Each of you, go serve his idols —
since you do not listen to Me. But My holy Name,
desecrate no longer with your gifts and your idols.
40 *But on My holy mountain, on the mountain of*
the height of Israel — the words of my Lord

ly of Israel (*v.* 40) who are destined to serve God and be worthy of His good will *(ibid.).*

לֹא יָבוֹא — *None shall come.*

The singular form, יָבוֹא is used instead of the plural יָבוֹאוּ which would have better fit the syntax of the verse. The usage indicates that not a single one of the rebels or sinners will come to the Land of Israel *(Harav Breuer).*

39. אִישׁ גִּלּוּלָיו לְכוּ עֲבֹדוּ — *Each of you go serve his idols.*

Rashi comments that there is less חִלּוּל הַשֵּׁם, *desecration of God's Name,* if you serve idols exclusively, and do not continue to serve God at the same time. The people had increased their affront to God by sacrificing to the Molech their first-born sons, those very children who had been sanctified to God.

Abarbanel (based on *Radak)* reads this passage as a warning couched in a challenge: *Go and serve your idols and see what will happen to you!* The next part of the verse is then explained as though the *vavs* were eliminated: [וְ]אַחַר אִם אֵינְכֶם שֹׁמְעִים אֵלַי [וְ]אֶת שֵׁם קָדְשִׁי לֹא תְחַלְּלוּ עוֹד — *If you do not listen to Me* [*you will not have the opportunity*] *of further desecrating My Name,* because you will not be among those (*v.* 40) who will eventually serve Me in the Land of Israel.

40. כִּי — *But (Metzudas David).*

The harshness of God's rejection in the previous verse is tempered by the vision of the ultimate return to the Land of Israel. The rule imposed with outpoured fury (*v.* 33) becomes a rule of love. The Tetragrammaton, the Name representing God's mercy, will shine forth unobscured by the vocalization which hid it in a cloak of uncompromising justice (see *comm. v.* 33): And you shall know that I am *Hashem* (*v.* 42).

בְּהַר מְרוֹם יִשְׂרָאֵל — *On the mountain of the height of Israel.*

The Temple Mount is higher than the rest of Eretz Yisrael, and Eretz Yisrael is higher than the rest of the world *(Radak).*

יְהוָה שָׁם יַעַבְדֻנִי כָּל־בֵּית יִשְׂרָאֵל כֻּלֹּה
בָּאָרֶץ שָׁם אֶרְצֵם וְשָׁם אֶדְרוֹשׁ אֶת־
תְּרוּמֹתֵיכֶם וְאֶת־רֵאשִׁית מַשְׂאוֹתֵיכֶם
מא בְּכָל־קָדְשֵׁיכֶם: בְּרֵיחַ נִיחֹחַ אֶרְצֶה אֶתְכֶם
בְּהוֹצִיאִי אֶתְכֶם מִן־הָעַמִּים וְקִבַּצְתִּי
אֶתְכֶם מִן־הָאֲרָצוֹת אֲשֶׁר נְפֹצֹתֶם בָּם
מב וְנִקְדַּשְׁתִּי בָכֶם לְעֵינֵי הַגּוֹיִם: וִידַעְתֶּם כִּי־
אֲנִי יהוה בַּהֲבִיאִי אֶתְכֶם אֶל־אַדְמַת
יִשְׂרָאֵל אֶל־הָאָרֶץ אֲשֶׁר נָשָׂאתִי אֶת־יָדִי

In *Isaiah* (2:3) the height of the Temple Mount is described as a point towards which the nations of the world will flock saying: *'Let us go and climb to the Mountain of HASHEM, to the House of Jacob's God that He may teach us of His ways, and that we may walk in His paths.'*

Thus the implication here is that the קִדּוּשׁ הַשֵּׁם, *the sanctification of God's Name,* the ultimate point towards which the flow of history is directed (see Introduction to this chapter), will come about in the end of days.

וְשָׁם ... שָׁם ... שָׁם — *There.*

The constant repetition of this word highlights the contrast with *v.* 28 where it was also used repetitively in order to put into sharp relief the staggering implication of just *where* the offerings were being brought *(Harav Breuer).*

כָּל בֵּית יִשְׂרָאֵל כֻּלֹּה — *All the Family of Israel, all of it.*

This repetition [כָּל and כֻּלֹּה] is to emphasize that *all* their tribes (i.e. including the ten lost tribes) are included in this prophecy *(Ramban, Sefer Hag'eulah, Sha'ar I).*

[See 37:15-28, and *comm.* and *footnote* to 11:15].

Radak explains the emphasis as a contrast to *v.* 35 where the rebels and the evil doers are to be weeded out (see *comm.* there). בָּאָרֶץ *in the Land,* is in contrast to מִדְבַּר הָעַמִּים, *the Wilderness of the Nations* in *v.* 35-38. Those who will come to the Land will remain whole. None of them need ever be lost.

אֶרְצֵם — *I will find pleasure in them.* [lit. *'I will want them'*].

תְּרוּמֹתֵיכֶם — *Your Terumos* [lit. *'those of your possessions which are to be lifted up'*].

This describes some of the gifts which every Jew had to give the priest from his produce. We follow *Hirsch* in his translation of the Torah who leaves this word untranslated for want of an exact equivalent in the vernacular.

רֵאשִׁית — *The finest* [lit. *'the first'*].

Scripture often uses this word to denote quality. (See *Exod. 30:23 and Shir haShirim* 4:14).

מַשְׂאוֹתֵיכֶם — *Your gifts.*

This translation follows *Metzudas David. Rashi* renders the word *food.* In either case it describes the sacrifices which are the food for the altar. [This is in contrast to the perversion of the רֵיחַ נִיחֹחַ, *the savor of satisfaction* of *v.* 28.]

41. בְּרֵיחַ נִיחֹחַ אֶרְצֶה אֶתְכֶם — *Through the savor of satisfaction I will find pleasure in you.*

Through the savoring [smell] of the קְטוֹרֶת, *the incense* [offered twice daily in the Temple service] which provides one with satisfaction *(Metzudas David).*

Malbim notes that the רִצּוּי, *the*

HASHEM/ELOHIM — there, all the Family of Israel, all of it, shall serve Me in the Land, there I will find pleasure in them, and there I will long for your Terumos and the finest of your gifts from all your holy things. 41 *Through the savor of satisfaction I will find pleasure in you; when I bring you forth from the nations and gather you from the lands in which you were scattered. And I will be hallowed through you in the eyes of the nations.* 42 *And you will know that I am HASHEM when I bring you to the soil of Israel, to the Land which I swore to give it to*

finding of pleasure is in *you,* in the people, not in the sacrifices.

In the previous verse we saw that a purposeful repetition of the word שָׁם, *there,* was used to serve as a contrast to *v.* 28. It is probable that the רֵיחַ נִיחֹחַ, *the savor of satisfaction* mentioned here is also to stress how *on My holy mountain* [in contrast to the perversion of רֵיחַ נִיחֹחַ of *v.* 28] the sacrificial service will once more find pleasure in God's eyes.

It is also possible that this expression is used, with *Lev.* 26:31 in mind. There, Israel was told that once the Temple was destroyed, God would no longer find pleasure in sacrifices [*Ibn Ezra, ibid.*] The verse reads: לֹא אָרִיחַ בְּרֵיחַ נִיחֹחֲכֶם, *I shall not find pleasure in the savor of satisfaction* [*which you bring*]. The return to the Temple Mount will inaugurate a time when God will once more find pleasure in their service.

וְנִקְדַּשְׁתִּי בָכֶם לְעֵינֵי הַגּוֹיִם — *And I will be hallowed through you in the eyes of the nations.*

They will see in *your good deeds* My strength and ability and providence *(Malbim).* The Sages teach that קִידּוּשׁ הַשֵּׁם, the sanctification of God's Name is brought about by our good deeds *(Yoma* 86a).

However the formulation ... נִקְדַּשׁ בְּ in Yechezkel, usually means that God's Name will be hallowed through His deeds (see 28:22, also *Rashi, Bamidbar* 20:13). Thus the meaning would be that God's name will be hallowed when the nations of the world see the ingathering of the exiles (see *Rashi* 36:23).

At this point history will have run its course. God's forbearance (*v.* 9, 14, 22) in order to avoid a חִלּוּל הַשֵּׁם, *a desecration of His Name,* will have borne fruit and the *Galus* experience will fall into perspective — a dream (*Ps.* 126:1) with no reality of its own.

This thought pervades Yechezkel's prophecy (28:25, 36:23), and with it he concludes his teachings (39:27-29) before embarking on the vision of the third and final Holy Temple.

42. וִידַעְתֶּם כִּי אֲנִי ה׳ — *And you will know that I am HASHEM.*

Almighty God takes pleasure in His creatures only to the extent that man *knows* and praises his Maker *(Ramban, Exod.* 13:16). The knowledge of God is the purpose of creation, and will be achieved with the return to *Eretz Yisrael.*

כִּי אֲנִי ה׳ — *That I am HASHEM.*

[See *comm. v.* 40].

מג לָתֵ֥ת אוֹתָ֖הּ לַאֲבוֹתֵיכֶֽם׃ וּזְכַרְתֶּם־שָׁ֗ם
אֶת־דַּרְכֵיכֶם֙ וְאֵת֙ כָּל־עֲלִילֽוֹתֵיכֶ֔ם אֲשֶׁ֥ר
נִטְמֵאתֶ֖ם בָּ֑ם וּנְקֹֽטֹתֶם֙ בִּפְנֵיכֶ֔ם בְּכָל־
מד רָעוֹתֵיכֶ֖ם אֲשֶׁ֥ר עֲשִׂיתֶֽם׃ וִֽידַעְתֶּם֙ כִּֽי־אֲנִ֣י
יהוָ֔ה בַּעֲשׂוֹתִ֥י אִתְּכֶ֖ם לְמַ֣עַן שְׁמִ֑י לֹ֩א
כְדַרְכֵיכֶ֨ם הָֽרָעִ֜ים וְכַעֲלִילֽוֹתֵיכֶם֙
הַנִּשְׁחָת֔וֹת בֵּ֣ית יִשְׂרָאֵ֔ל נְאֻ֖ם אֲדֹנָ֥י יֱהוִֽה׃

43. וּזְכַרְתֶּם שָׁם ... וּנְקֹטֹתֶם — *And you shall remember there ... and you shall loathe yourselves.*

Verse 40, שָׁם אֶרְצֵם, *there I will find pleasure in them* as well as countless other parts of Yechezkel, leaves no doubt about the love of God for His people in the Messianic era. Thus this verse and similar passages in Ch.36, should not be interpreted as implying a grudging attitude on the part of God.

Rather the constant admonition that they remember their wickedness, must be understood as a part of the repentance, which according to the Sages (*Sanhedrin* 97b) is a precondition to the ultimate redemption.

As taught by *Rabbeinu Yonah* [*Sha'arei Teshuva, (Sha'ar I) Ikarim* 1, 3, and 6], integral parts of repentance are: חֲרָטָה, *regret,* יָגוֹן, *anguish,* and בּוּשָׁה, *shame.* Under the heading of 'shame' he quotes Yechezkel 16:63, a passage similar to ours, thereby indicating the context in which it must be understood.

Knesses Israel, in Messianic times, will be a nation of בַּעֲלֵי תְשׁוּבָה, *sinners returned to God.*

your fathers.
43 *And you shall remember there your ways and all
your deeds by which you became defiled; and you
shall loathe yourselves in your own sight for all your
evils which you have done.* 44 *Then shall you know
that I am HASHEM, when I do with you for My
Name's sake; not in accord with your evil ways and
your corrupt deeds, O Family of Israel. The words of
my Lord HASHEM/ELOHIM." '*

וּנְקֹטֹתֶם בִּפְנֵיכֶם — *And you shall loathe yourselves.*

[See *comm.* to 6:9].

44. וִידַעְתֶּם כִּי אֲנִי ה׳ — *Then shall you know that I am HASHEM.*

Who can be trusted to fulfill His promise *(Metzudas David).*

The Four-Letter Name is the one by which God reveals Himself as trustworthy in the fulfillment of His promise. (See *Rashi, Exod.* 6:3. See also *Harav Yitzchok Hutner, Pachad Yitzchak, Sha'ar Yerach Ha'Eisonim* 8:5 and 6, for an elaboration of this concept).

When the final redemption will have come, Israel will recognize that its whole history is no more than a fulfillment of the destiny which God had mapped out for them in the dawn of their history.

לְמַעַן שְׁמִי — *For My Name's sake.*

For the honor of My Name *(Metzudas David).*

A final repetition of the *leitmotiv* of this chapter. All history is no more than the revelation of God's Glory. [See *footnote* to *v.* 9].

כא
א־ב

א־ב וַיְהִי דְבַר־יְהוָה אֵלַי לֵאמֹר: בֶּן־אָדָם שִׂים פָּנֶיךָ דֶּרֶךְ תֵּימָנָה וְהַטֵּף אֶל־דָּרוֹם

XXI

This chapter contains a number of prophecies concerning the sword of Nebuchadnezzar. We see it burnished and sharpened in preparation for the slaughter and are shown the final havoc which it will wreak in Jerusalem. We are even permitted a glimpse of Nebuchadnezzar as he practices the magic rites which are to help him lay his plans for the war.

The stage for the true understanding of these events is set in the first of the prophecies (vs. 1-12) and particularly in v. 8: And say to Israel's soil: Thus says HASHEM: Behold! I am against you. I shall draw My sword from its scabbard and cut off from among you righteous and wicked alike. *It is not really Nebuchadnezzar's sword at all. He is no more than a tool in God's hand (see footnote 4:3;* comm. *14:17;* Habbakuk *1:12), and the sword which he wields is God's sword (30:24). His path to Jerusalem had been mapped out for him long before he stood at the crossroads (v. 26) attempting to divine his future (see* Ramban, Exodus *14:4).*

We do not know for certain why this particular series of prophecies follows immediately upon the last chapter. Perhaps the reference to God's outstretched arm (20:33) created the association with the sword (based on Sifri *to* Deut. *26:8, quoted in the* Haggadah*), which is then expanded in our chapter. Perhaps there is a more direct and fundamental connection. The lesson which the elders of Israel had been taught in chapter 20 was that the impending conquest and destruction were not the result of chance circumstances, but had always been an integral part of God's plan for His people. The natural outgrowth of this lesson is the understanding that the mighty Nebuchadnezzar is no more than a puppet whom God uses for the furtherance of His design.*

1-4. Jerusalem is compared to a forest in which God will kindle an all-consuming fire. The forest will be totally destroyed, everything in its vicinity singed, and God's punishing fury universally recognized.

2. שִׂים פָּנֶיךָ — *Set your face.*

This idiom, which seems to be synonymous with הַטֵּף and הִנָּבֵא, *prophesy* (see *Targum* who renders *accept prophecy)* is unique to Yechezkel. No other prophet is ever charged to prophesy with these words, but in the Book of *Ezekiel* they occur nine times (6:2; 13:17; 21:2; 21:7; 25:2; 28:21; 29:2; 35:2; 38:2).

It is not easy to define the exact meaning of this idiom since it occurs rarely in Scripture, and then usually in a completely different context. Thus *Genesis* 31:21 which tells that Jacob set his face towards Mount Gilead, will not help since the meaning there is obviously that he turned to travel in that *direction.*

A comparison can be found in *Jeremiah* 21:10, where God says *for I have set My face against this city for evil but not for good. Rashi* there (following *Targum)* translates ...*My anger* [but see *comm.* 14:8]. The word פָּנִים, *face,* can have this meaning since emotions are reflected in the face (see *Radak, Metzudos* 14:8). The idiom would then convey an angry prophecy.

The word פָּנִים, *face,* is used occasionally as a synonym for the person himself. (See *Ibn Ezra, Exodus* 33:14). This is true not only when the subject is God (as in *Exodus* 33:14), but also when a human is meant (see *II Samuel* 17:11). Thus the idiom שִׂים פָּנֶיךָ would mean that the prophet is to concentrate his entire being upon the object of his prophecy.

This might explain why only Yechezkel was charged with this particular

21
1-2

The word of HASHEM came to me saying. 2 *Ben Adam, set your face in the direction of the south and let your words flow southward; prophesy*

mode of address. He, more than any other prophet, became completely identified with his prophecy (see *Overview* p. xviii ff.; *comm.* 2:8, 12:6) and he, particularly, was the man whose whole essence was involved in his prophetic task.

תֵּימָנָה...דָּרוֹם...נֶגֶב — *South.*

All three expressions denote south.

Daas Sofrim quotes *Tosafos* to *Bava Metzia* 60b which states the preference of Scripture for using diverse expressions where possible in order to beautify the language.

For the etymology of תֵּימָן, *Radak* in *Sefer HaShorashim* offers the root ימן which indicates *the right-hand side.* The south lies to the right of someone facing east. (See *comm.* 4:4). For נֶגֶב, *Sefer HaShorashim* suggests the root נגב, meaning *parched* or *unsettled.* The southern part of *Eretz Yisrael* is warmer and more sparsely inhabited than the north where the climate is less harsh. For דָּרוֹם no explanation is offered.

[It should be noted that in Hebrew the frame of reference for directions is that the speaker faces eastward. Thus, the south is to his right, the north to his left and so on. This orientation occasionally causes difficulty for Westerners who are trained to think of north as the primary direction.]

Against which south is Yechezkel to prophesy?

Yechezkel's prophetic parable is given in verses 2-4, while its interpretation is found below in verses 7-10.[1] A comparison of our verse with verse 7, which contains the interpretation of our verse (see below), yields the following meanings: תֵּימָנָה represents *Jerusalem;* דָּרוֹם, *sanctuaries*; and נֶגֶב, *soil of Israel.* (However *Rashi, Radak,* and *Metzudos* identify יַעַר הַשָּׂדֶה נֶגֶב of our verse as Jerusalem.)

All these places are referred to as *south,* relative to Yechezkel, who was in Babylon, which is north of *Eretz Yisrael* *(Rashi; Radak; Metzudos).*

However, *Eliezer of Beaugency* and *Mahari Karo* write that south is used because Jerusalem and the Land of Judah are in the southern part of *Eretz Yisrael* (i.e., south is used not relative to Babylon but relative to the northern section of *Eretz Yisrael*; but see *comm.* below).

Why is the southern location of Jerusalem so important to the message of the prophet?

Perhaps the answer lies in Jeremiah's prophecy concerning the Babylonian conquest: *From the north will the evil begin (Jeremiah* 1:14). The Torah uses symbolism drawn from many aspects of the physical world, and the cardinal points of the compass are prominent among them. (See *Cardinal Points and Color Shemes in Jewish Symbolism, Dr. Paul Forcheimer,* Breuer Jubilee Volume, New York 1962). The north is considered to be the repository of the evil forces which God created in nature (see *Pirkei d'Rabbi Eliezer* ch. 3), while the south is associated with learning and wisdom , the raw material for holiness. (Therefore the *Menorah* [*candelabrum*], symbolizing spirituality and wisdom was in the southern part of the Temple while the Table, symbolizing material

1. Following is a phrase by phrase comparison of the parable (*vs.* 1-4) and its interpretation (*vs.* 7-10).

2. בֶּן־אָדָם שִׂים פָּנֶיךָ דֶּרֶךְ תֵּימָנָה *Ben Adam, set your face in the direction of the south*	7. בֶּן־אָדָם שִׂים פָּנֶיךָ אֶל־יְרוּשָׁלַיִם *Ben Adam, set your face toward Jerusalem,*
וְהַטֵּף אֶל־דָּרוֹם *and let your words flow southward;*	וְהַטֵּף אֶל־מִקְדָּשִׁים *and let your words flow toward the Sanctuaries;*

ג וְהִנָּבֵא אֶל־יַעַר הַשָּׂדֶה נֶגֶב: וְאָמַרְתָּ
לְיַעַר הַנֶּגֶב שְׁמַע דְּבַר־יהוה כֹּה־אָמַר
אֲדֹנָי יֱהוִֹה הִנְנִי מַצִּית־בְּךָ | אֵשׁ וְאָכְלָה
בְךָ כָל־עֵץ־לַח וְכָל־עֵץ יָבֵשׁ לֹא־תִכְבֶּה
לַהֶבֶת שַׁלְהֶבֶת וְנִצְרְבוּ־בָהּ כָּל־פָּנִים

acquisition, was in the northern part. See *Bava Basra* 25b.) The north-south axis is the location of the tension between the materialistic and the sublime. (See also 38:6, 15; 39:2.)

Jeremiah was taught that Babylon's ascendancy had implications far beyond political or military circumstances. The world was about to be subjugated by a northern force; a materialism which would not be capable of sublimation (see *comm.* 7:5). In contrast to other enemies of Israel, Nebuchadnezzar, who now stood poised to crush mankind, had no descendants who became גֵּרִים, *proselytes,* an indication of his utter lack of spiritual content.

Yechezkel was taught the same lesson from the opposite perspective. He was shown that the southern repository of the spirit was about to fall.

וְהַטֵּף — *And let* [*your words*] *flow.*

This is the הִפְעִיל, *causative,* of the root נטף, *to flow.* It describes a flow of words.

וְהִנָּבֵא — *And prophesy.*

The root נבא, *to prophesy,* is always used in the passive. The prophet is no more than the passive instrument through whom God reveals His will. (See footnote to 2:5).

יַעַר הַשָּׂדֶה נֶגֶב — *The forest-field of the south.*

Radak and *Metzudos* see the phrase as a description of Jerusalem, which was filled with both righteous and wicked people just as a forest is filled with different types of trees.

However, *Rashi* interprets the symbolism as referring to the holy Temple which was destined to be like a forest and a field: It would be plowed like a field, and foxes would roam in its ruins as in a forest.

וְהִנָּבֵא אֶל־יַעַר הַשָּׂדֶה נֶגֶב:
and prophesy against the forest-field of the south.

3. וְאָמַרְתָּ לְיַעַר הַנֶּגֶב
And say to the forest-field:

שְׁמַע דְּבַר־ה׳
Hear the word of H*ASHEM.*

כֹּה־אָמַר אֲדֹנָי ה׳
Thus says My Lord H*ASHEM*/E*LOHIM:*

הִנְנִי מַצִּית־בְּךָ אֵשׁ
Behold! I kindle within you a fire

וְאָכְלָה בְךָ כָל־עֵץ־לַח וְכָל־עֵץ יָבֵשׁ
that will consume within you every fresh tree and every dry tree.

לֹא־תִכְבֶּה לַהֶבֶת שַׁלְהֶבֶת
An inextinguishable intense flame

וְהִנָּבֵא אֶל־אַדְמַת יִשְׂרָאֵל:
and prophesy against the soil of Israel.

8. וְאָמַרְתָּ לְאַדְמַת יִשְׂרָאֵל
And say to Israel's soil:

כֹּה אָמַר ה׳
Thus says H*ASHEM:*

הִנְנִי אֵלַיִךְ וְהוֹצֵאתִי חַרְבִּי מִתַּעְרָהּ
Behold! I am against you. I shall draw My sword from its scabbard.

וְהִכְרַתִּי מִמֵּךְ צַדִּיק וְרָשָׁע:
and cut off from among you righteous and wicked.

9. יַעַן אֲשֶׁר־הִכְרַתִּי מִמֵּךְ צַדִּיק וְרָשָׁע
Because I have cut off from among you righteous and wicked,

לָכֵן תֵּצֵא חַרְבִּי מִתַּעְרָהּ
therefore, my sword shall leave its scabbard

3

against the forest-field of the south. 3 *And say to the forest-field: Hear the word of HASHEM. Thus says my Lord HASHEM/ELOHIM: Behold! I kindle within you a fire that will consume within you every fresh tree and every dry tree, an intense flame that will not be extinguished, and every face from the south of the*

A comparison with verse 7 (see footnote) indicates that this phrase refers to אַדְמַת יִשְׂרָאֵל, *soil of Israel* (and not the Temple in Jerusalem).

R' Eliezer of Beaugency explains the comparison to a forest by pointing out that the Land of Judah was filled with rulers and princes in the same way as a forest is filled with mighty cedars. *Mahari MiTrani* writes that just as a forest is filled with trees, so the Land of Judah was filled with cities.

[The expression יַעַר הַשָּׂדֶה, *forest-field,* is very difficult since the two words describe contradictory conditions. Although usually translated as *forest,* יַעַר is also used in Scripture as a symbol of desolation (see *Hosea* 2:14; *Micah* 3:12; *Jeremiah* 26:18). (It has been suggested that it could describe any area with densely planted vegetation or, indeed, any desolate and uninhabitable space.) שָׂדֶה, besides its meaning as a *field* upon which produce is sown, is also used to denote countryside (see *Exodus* 9:19; *Deut.* 22:25, 28:3). In any event, we do not find the two terms in conjunction with each other.

[In view of the unique combination יַעַר הַשָּׂדֶה, the following interpretation is possible. The only other place in Scripture where these two words are combined is in *Psalms* 132:6, where King David's search for the Holy Temple is described. He found it in שְׂדֵי יָעַר, which, according to *Mahari MiTrani* (there) is a proper noun — the name of the place where the Temple was ultimately built.]

[In referring to the Temple's ultimate destruction, Yechezkel may have intended a play on words, based on the place name (see *Zephaniah* 2:4 for comparable usage). The Temple that was built at שְׂדֵי יָעַר would indeed turn into field and forest (as in *Rashi* above). After its destruction, no trace of it would remain as though nothing had ever disturbed the original pastoral setting. [In this intepretation, the sequence of the words is inverted, i.e., יַעַר הַשָּׂדֶה instead of שְׂדֵי יָעַר, to make clear that the expression is not used as a proper noun.]

3. הִנְנִי מַצִּית־בְּךָ אֵשׁ — *Behold! I kindle within you a fire.*

Verse 8 interprets this part of the parable to refer to God's sword, which He will extract from its scabbard. There, as throughout Scripture, the 'sword' symbolizes wholesale murder. Previously, Yechezkel has used fire as a symbol of famine and plague (5:2, 12), but not of the sword. Moreover, the simile of the sword would have been more accurately described by having the trees of the forest cut (as in *Isaiah* 14:8) rather than burned down.

It seems likely that the symbol of fire is used because of the indiscriminate destruction which it causes. When trees are cut down, they are condemned as individuals. When a fire sweeps through a forest, the totality of the forest is consumed. God's judgment against Jerusalem was addressed to the community rather than the individual (see Appendix III *comm.* 9:4), and for such a judgment the fire is the most apt metaphor.

It is unambiguously God Himself who kindles the fire (הִנְנִי מַצִּית; see also *v.* 4). It is not natural happenstance but the expression of Divine justice (see pref.).

כָּל־עֵץ־לַח וְכָל־עֵץ יָבֵשׁ — *Every fresh tree and every dry tree.*

According to *v.* 8, this means that both *the righteous and the wicked* will be destroyed.

לַהֶבֶת שַׁלְהֶבֶת — *An intense flame* [lit. *the flame of the flame*].

The term לַהֶבֶת שַׁלְהֶבֶת is difficult since the words have identical mean-

ד מִנֶּגֶב צָפוֹנָה: וְרָאוּ כָּל־בָּשָׂר כִּי אֲנִי יהוה
ה בִּעַרְתִּיהָ לֹא תִּכְבֶּה: וָאֹמַר אֲהָהּ אֲדֹנָי
יֱהוִה הֵמָּה אֹמְרִים לִי הֲלֹא מְמַשֵּׁל
ו מְשָׁלִים הוּא: וַיְהִי דְבַר־יהוה

ings. In fact, *Targum* uses שַׁלְהֶבֶת as a translation of לַהֶבֶת (see *Targum Exodus* 3:2).

[שַׁלְהֶבֶת is a noun formed from the verb שַׁלְהֵב belonging to the שַׁפְעֵל voice, in which the letter ש is put before the root and indicates a הִפְעִיל, *causative voice*. This form is found frequently in post-Biblical Hebrew, such as שַׁעְבֵּד, *to enslave*, (from עבד) or שַׁחְרֵר, *to free* (from חרר). The verb שַׁלְהֵב, *to kindle*, is not found in Scripture but occurs in *Midrashim* (see *Koheles Rabbah* 1).]

Radak views the doubling of the word as an intensification. This agrees with *Targum*, who renders *the all consuming flame. R' Breuer* (based on *Hirsch, Exodus* 29:37) believes that לַהֶבֶת שַׁלְהֶבֶת, *means flame caused by another flame*. The flames that sweep through the forest are only the outward result of an *inner* decay which is the true destroyer of the trees. In this interpretation, the phrase expresses the thought taught by the Sages in *Shir HaShirim Rabbah* 3:3 (see also pref. ch. 1): Nebuchadnezzar burned a Temple which in reality had been gutted long before he set fire to it. Its protective soul had departed as soon as Israel proved itself unequal to the Divine Presence in its midst.

וְנִצְרְבוּ־בָהּ כָּל־פָּנִים — *And every face ... shall be singed by it.*

צרב describes the scarring of the skin, as in *Leviticus* 13:23.

מִנֶּגֶב צָפוֹנָה — *From the south of the North.*

The translation follows *Rashi, Radak*, and *Metzudos*, who, based on the interpretation of our verse in *v.* 9, render: *All faces* [including those of the gentile nations] *which lie to the south of the Northern kingdom* [Babylon] *will be singed in the fire* (see *comm., v.* 9). Judah was not the only kingdom which was to be crushed by the northern power (see *comm., v.* 2). Babylon had been granted dominion over many other nations as well (see ch. 1; *comm.* 7:2 for a discussion based on *Chagigah* 13b). All would succumb to Babylon's southward thrust.

4. וְרָאוּ כָּל־בָּשָׂר כִּי אֲנִי ה׳ בִּעַרְתִּיהָ — *Thus all flesh shall see that I, HASHEM, have kindled it.*

It will be obvious to everyone that God Himself is destroying His beloved city. (See pref.; *Overview; comm.* 4:3, 5:8). The use of the word וְרָאוּ, *and they shall see*, instead of the more usual וְיָדְעוּ, *and they shall know*, is noteworthy, particularly since *v.* 10, in the interpretation of the parable, uses the latter. From *Leviticus* 5:1 we can judge the nuances of the two words: ראה indicates an actual observation; ידע, a deduction (see *Shavuos* 33b). In *comm.* to 14:17, we noted how much easier it is to detect the hand of God in a

וְנִצְרְבוּ־בָהּ כָּל־פָּנִים מִנֶּגֶב צָפוֹנָה: *and every face from the south of the north will be singed by it.*	אֶל־כָּל־בָּשָׂר מִנֶּגֶב צָפוֹן: *against all flesh from the south of the north.*
4. וְרָאוּ כָּל־בָּשָׂר *Thus all flesh shall see*	**10.** וְיָדְעוּ כָּל־בָּשָׂר *Thus all flesh shall know*
כִּי אֲנִי ה׳ בִּעַרְתִּיהָ *that I, HASHEM, have kindled it.*	כִּי אֲנִי ה׳ הוֹצֵאתִי חַרְבִּי מִתַּעְרָהּ *that I, HASHEM, have drawn my sword from its scabbard.*
לֹא תִּכְבֶּה: *It shall not be extinguished.*	לֹא תָשׁוּב עוֹד: *It shall nevermore return.*

north shall be singed by it. ⁴ *Thus all flesh shall see that I, HASHEM, have kindled it. It shall not be extinguished.*

⁵ *I said: Ah! my Lord HASHEM/ELOHIM, they say about me: Is he not an inventor of fables?*

⁶ *So the word of HASHEM came to me, saying:*

natural phenomenon than in a human activity. Yechezkel had to stress that not only famine, pestilence and wild beasts were the expression of God's will, but the invading armies were also His messengers. This could explain the usage in our verse. At the level of the parable when forest and fire are used metaphorically, it is easy enough to 'see' the hand of God. In verse 10, when the actual events, which were enacted by human agency, are spelled out, God's direction of the fortunes of war is less obvious. It must be deduced; it is not to be observed.

5. הֲלֹא מְמַשֵּׁל מְשָׁלִים הוּא — *Is he not an inventor of fables?*

They will think that I am simply showing off my skills as a storyteller (see 33:31-32) and will not believe that the parable is a metaphor for a Divine message *(Radak).*

Metzudos explains that the very ambiguity of a parable would give the people leeway to interpret it in any way they saw fit, even to the extent of obscuring the intended message.

[*Radak* and *Metzudos* touch on the two points which are both the strength and weakness of a metaphor. It must tolerate a sufficiently wide range of interpretation if it is to fulfill its primary educational purpose which, according to *Rambam,* (Introduction to *Moreh Nevuchim*), is to present a message in such a way that both scholar and layman can absorb it at a level appropriate to their respective understanding. However, the very multifaceted nature of its range of potential meaning creates the danger that a completely spurious interpretation might be attempted.

An example is the metaphor contained in the first four verses of our chapter. Three possible (and in themselves correct) understandings could be suggested. It might simply be the story of a raging forest fire. It might symbolize the destruction of the Holy Temple, which in itself is really only a symbol for Israel, the true Sanctuary of the Divine Presence on earth (see footnote 20:26). People intoxicated by the sense of their own superiority and considering themselves to be the sole and true heirs of Israel's greatness (11:15) might distort the message completely and think the metaphor 'forest-field' inappropriate for them, and therefore assume that the message is not addressed to them at all, but is directed against other, lesser nations who lived to the south of Babylon.

Rambam (there) also makes the point that a metaphor must have a beauty of its own if it is to be effective (see footnote). However, the greater the dramatic tension of the metaphor itself, the greater the danger that it might detract from the impact of the message.

For either or both of these reasons Yechezkel asks that he be given the message without benefit of the metaphor.[1]

1. An apt metaphor can certainly add new dimensions to the understanding. (See footnote 7:2 for an examination of the prophet's use of tools of rhetoric).

The metaphor has been compared to a stereoscope which takes two flat pictures and fuses them together to create a third image which projects a completely new view. In the same way a metaphor brings together a subject with its description, and the two interact to convey new nuances.

Proverbs 25:11 speaks of the skillfully wrought metaphor as being like *golden apples*

כא
ז־י

ז אֵלַי לֵאמֹר: בֶּן־אָדָם שִׂים פָּנֶיךָ אֶל־
יְרוּשָׁלַ͏ִם וְהַטֵּף אֶל־מִקְדָּשִׁים וְהִנָּבֵא אֶל־
ח אַדְמַת יִשְׂרָאֵל: וְאָמַרְתָּ לְאַדְמַת יִשְׂרָאֵל
כֹּה אָמַר יהוה הִנְנִי אֵלַיִךְ וְהוֹצֵאתִי
חַרְבִּי מִתַּעְרָהּ וְהִכְרַתִּי מִמֵּךְ צַדִּיק
ט וְרָשָׁע: יַעַן אֲשֶׁר־הִכְרַתִּי מִמֵּךְ צַדִּיק
וְרָשָׁע לָכֵן תֵּצֵא חַרְבִּי מִתַּעְרָהּ אֶל־כָּל־
י בָּשָׂר מִנֶּגֶב צָפוֹן: וְיָדְעוּ כָּל־בָּשָׂר כִּי אֲנִי

7. God accedes to Yechezkel's request and proclaims the message in explicit terms.

וְהַטֵּף אֶל־מִקְדָּשִׁים — *And let* [*your words*] *flow to the Sanctuaries.*

The plural form of מִקְדָּשׁ, *Sanctuaries*, is surprising. *Rashi* writes that it hints at the destruction of both the first and the second Temples.

According to *Radak* and *Metzudos*, the plural alludes to the many parts of the Temple courtyards and buildings — all of them destined to be destroyed.

[דָּרוֹם, *south*, which in *v.* 2 was the metaphor for מִקְדָּשִׁים, *Sanctuaries*, is symbolic of the potential for holiness which is inherent in man (see *comm., v.* 2). Perhaps the plural form hints at that other *Sanctuary — the Family of Israel* — which was also addressed by Yechezkel's prophecy.]

8. וְהוֹצֵאתִי חַרְבִּי מִתַּעְרָהּ — *I shall draw My sword from its scabbard.*

[This phrase is also a מָשָׁל, *parable*, since God does not actually draw a sword from His scabbard. This is strange since the specific purpose of these verses is to avoid the use of metaphor.

Perhaps חַרְבִּי refers to the sword of Nebuchadnezzar, which is called *God's sword* in 30:24 (see *pref.*), since the king acts only as God's agent. Our phrase would mean that God will cause Nebuchadnezzar to draw his sword (which in reality is God's sword) from its scabbard.]

וְהִכְרַתִּי מִמֵּךְ צַדִּיק וְרָשָׁע — *And (I shall) cut off from among you righteous and wicked* [*alike*].

The righteous and the wicked were symbolized by the fresh tree and dry tree of verse 3.

The order of their mention implies, surprisingly, that the fresh tree will burn before the dry one, and the righteous will be cut down before the wicked. *Bava Kama* 60a states that in a situation in which the righteous are to

covered with a filigree of silver. The golden apple's value far exceeds that of the silver filigree, but it is enhanced by the silver covering. The filigree, on the other hand, is beautified by the golden apple glittering within it. The careless observer may think that it is merely a silver ornament, but upon close examination, the gold can be seen through the mesh *(Rambam).*

By describing the impending destruction as a forest fire, the prophet would achieve vividness and dramatic tension. The metaphor touched the sense of hearing (the crackling roar of the fire); of smell (the burning, smoking debris); and of sight (the images of fleeing animals). All this would have imparted a sense of realism to people who surely had witnessed fires, but had never experienced siege and surrender. On the other hand, the knowledge that the prophet was describing the destruction of the holy Temple would have made the destruction of the forest-field far more poignant.

The message would have been greatly enriched had Yechezkel used God's metaphor as he had done at other times (see ch. 17). On this occasion, Yechezkel feared that its disadvantages outweighed its gains and asked that he be granted the prophecy in explicit terms.

7 Ben Adam, set your face toward Jerusalem, and let
your words flow to the Sanctuaries and prophesy
against the soil of Israel. 8 And say to Israel's soil:
Thus says HASHEM: Behold! I am against you. I shall
draw My sword from its scabbard and cut off from
among you righteous and wicked alike. 9 Because I
have cut off from among you righteous and wicked
alike, therefore My sword will leave its scabbard
against all flesh from the south of the north. 10 Thus

be punished together with the wicked (see Appendix III, references there), the righteous ones will be wiped out first in order to spare them the sight of the complete destruction.

According to *Avodah Zarah* 4a, the צַדִּיק, *righteous man,* mentioned in our verse can only be צַדִּיק שֶׁאֵינוֹ גָמוּר, *less than completely righteous.* [This avoids a contradiction from Abraham's intercession for the righteous people in Sodom. Abraham held it improper for the righteous to be included in the general destruction; he referred to *completely* righteous people.]

Even a righteous man would be caught up in the common fate of his community for failing to disassociate himself from them by protesting their misdeeds. The man who is completely good should have set himself apart from the sinning town and thereby not be considered part of them. Only the less than completely righteous, or those who are completely righteous but did not attempt to dissuade their fellow citizens from sinning, can be considered part of the community and be destined to share its fate.]

According to *Targum,* וְהִכְרַתִּי, *I will cut off,* has two meanings. For the righteous, it spells exile; for the wicked, death. Thus *Targum* translates the phrase: I shall exile the righteous people from among you so that I may destroy the wicked.

9. יַעַן ... לָכֵן — *Because ... therefore*

This verse introduces a cause and effect relationship which is missing in the parable of verse 3. God's sword is to be drawn against *all flesh of the south* [corresponding to *all the faces* which are to be singed], that is, the gentile nations which lie to the south of Babylon, *because* God is cutting off from Israel the righteous with the wicked.

A punishment which is introduced with the word יַעַן, is one which is מִדָּה כְּנֶגֶד מִדָּה, *measure for measure,* exactly suited to the crime (see *comm.* 13:10).

Why does one follow from the other? *Rashi, Radak,* and *Metzudos* answer that the gentile nations rejoiced at Israel's calamity. Because the destruction was so complete, the nations felt elated. As a punishment, they fell victim to Nebuchadnezzar's sword.

This thought will be encountered repeatedly in Yechezkel's prophecies against the gentile nations (chs. 25-32) and discussed there. Here, it is analyzed in the context of the parable and its message.

What is so very evil about the nations' exultation?

'Woe to the idol worshipers. They have lost but do not realize what they have lost [with the destruction of the Temple]. When the Temple stood, the altar would atone for them. Now who will atone for them?' (*Succah* 65b).

R' Yehoshua ben Levi said, 'If the nations had known how beneficial the Temple was for them, they would have surrounded it with sentries to guard it, for it was more beneficial for them than for Israel' (*Bamidbar Rabbah* 1:3).

In place of my love they hated me (Psalms 109:4). On Succos, Israel

יְהוָה הוֹצֵאתִי חַרְבִּי מִתַּעְרָהּ לֹא תָשׁוּב
יא עוֹד׃ וְאַתָּה בֶן־אָדָם
הֵאָנַח בְּשִׁבְרוֹן מָתְנַיִם וּבִמְרִירוּת תֵּאָנַח
יב לְעֵינֵיהֶם׃ וְהָיָה כִּי־יֹאמְרוּ אֵלֶיךָ עַל־מָה
אַתָּה נֶאֱנָח וְאָמַרְתָּ אֶל־שְׁמוּעָה כִי־בָאָה
וְנָמֵס כָּל־לֵב וְרָפוּ כָל־יָדַיִם וְכִהֲתָה כָל־
רוּחַ וְכָל־בִּרְכַּיִם תֵּלַכְנָה מַּיִם הִנֵּה בָאָה
יג וְנִהְיָתָה נְאֻם אֲדֹנָי יֱהוִה׃ וַיְהִי
יד דְבַר־יְהוָה אֵלַי לֵאמֹר׃ בֶּן־אָדָם הִנָּבֵא

would bring seventy bullocks for the seventy nations ... Israel said, 'Master of the World, see, we bring seventy bullocks for them and they should have loved us. Instead, they hated us (*Bamidbar Rabbah* 1:2).

The gentile nations also have an inner core of holiness. If they had only realized it, the Divine Presence of God in the Temple could have been the focus of their own spiritual strivings. More than for Israel who, through their Torah, are themselves a sanctuary for the Divine, the Temple was an indispensable condition for the spiritual development of the gentile nations. Instead they exulted at its destruction, thereby showing themselves to be divested of any spiritual core. They had driven all understanding of the Divine from their hearts. They too fell victim to the powers of the north (see *comm. v.* 2).

10. לֹא תָשׁוּב עוֹד — *It shall nevermore return.*

The sword shall not return to its scabbard until every nation singled out by the prophets is subjugated *(Radak; Metzudos).*

This relates to the beginning of the sentence as follows. The very thoroughness with which the sword will do its work will prove that it is God, Who is wielding it. Were it merely an accident of history, there would not be such undeviating consistency *(Metzudos).*

11. הֵאָנַח בְּשִׁבְרוֹן מָתְנַיִם — *Groan with breaking loins.*

One who groans because of a terrible tragedy feels as if his loins are breaking *(Radak).*

Scripture depicts the loins as the seat of a person's strength (*Job* 40:16; *Nachum* 2:2). Therefore any blow that

1. *Berachos* 58b and *Kesubos* 52a deduce from our verse that a groan shatters half the body of a person (since the loins are in the center of the body) or (based on *v.* 12) the whole body.

The Sages' point seems to be that total personal involvement in Jerusalem's tragedy was expected of the exiles. (See 24:15-24, Overview, p. XXIX.)

Yechezkel had a difficult task as guide and mentor to the exiles. On the one hand, he was to uplift their spirits and reinforce their self-confidence so that they would not be discouraged by the disdain of the remnant in Jerusalem (see 11:14-20; *comm., v.* 16; 33:10; 37:11). He had to train them that they would not succumb with the destruction of the Temple, but on the contrary, would carry God's Sanctuary with them into exile (*v.* 16, *comm.* and footnote).

However, this could have caused the exiles to consider themselves self-sufficient and to regard Jerusalem's impending destruction with dispassion. They might have felt it was not their concern. Nebuchadnezzar's armies were leveling artifacts of a decadent past, for they, the exiles, harbored within themselves the seeds of a vibrant future. Yechezkel's task was to dispel such thoughts and impress upon the exiles the dimensions of their immense loss.

21
11-13

all flesh shall know that I, HASHEM, have drawn My
sword from its scabbard. It shall nevermore return.
11 Now you, Ben Adam, groan with breaking loins
and with bitterness, groan in their sight. 12 And it
shall be when they say to you: For what do you
groan? Then say: Because of the approaching tidings,
when every heart will melt, all hands weaken, every
spirit grow faint and all knees be watery. Behold! It
comes and has happened! The words of my Lord
HASHEM/ELOHIM.
13 The word of my HASHEM came to me, saying:

threatens them (*Deuteronomy* 33:11) or trembling that seizes them (*Isaiah* 21:3; *Nachum* 2:11) spells the erosion of human strength.

The prophet's agony is to shatter him completely.

לְעֵינֵיהֶם — *In their sight.*

This was just one of the many actions which Yechezkel was commanded to do לְעֵינֵיהֶם, *in their sight* (see 4:12; 12:3-7; 24:24; *comm.* 12:3), in his capacity as מוֹפֵת, *a sign* of instruction for his fellow exiles (see *comm.*, 12:6; Overview pp. xxviii-xxxix).

12. אֶל־שְׁמוּעָה כִּי־בָאָה — *Because of* [lit. *to*] *the approaching* [lit. *coming*] *tidings.*

The word בָּאָה, *come,* is accented on the last syllable, which makes it in the present tense (see *comm.* 7:5,7). The present tense is used to describe a future event in order to underline the absolute certainty that it will occur. (See *Ramban, Exodus* 15:1; footnote 7:2).

וְנָמֵס כָּל־לֵב ... וְכָל־בִּרְכַּיִם תֵּלַכְנָה מַּיִם — *When every heart will melt ... and all knees be watery* [lit. *will flow water*].

See *comm.* to 7:17.

This verse describes the 'breaking of the whole body' mentioned in *Berachos* 58b and *Kesubos* 52a (see footnote above). The impact of the actual events foretold will be shattering.[1]

הִנֵּה בָאָה וְנִהְיָתָה — *Behold! It comes and has happened.*

The tidings will come soon (הִנֵּה בָאָה), and the events which they describe will indeed have happened (וְנִהְיָתָה) *(Radak).*

R' Breuer renders וְנִהְיָתָה, *it has already happened.* In the prophet's mind the future destruction has long since taken place (see ch. 9). The Babylonian army will only destroy the outer hulk of what had once been.

13-18. These verses, in poetic form, contain a dirge concerning the sword which God is about to unleash against His people. It is evident from the context that it is God Himself Who is lamenting.

1. *Koheles Rabbasi* 12:8 describes in heartrending fashion the meeting between the two exiles: When Zidkiyahu's exile came [to Babylon], Yehoyachin's exile came out to meet them. Underneath [their clothing] they wore sackcloth [for mourning], but on the outside they wore white garments [as citizens of Babylon who had to outwardly rejoice at Nebuchadnezzar's victory]. The old exiles asked them, 'What has become of my father? What has become of my mother [left behind eleven years earlier]?'

[The new exiles] answered, 'They have been killed.'

With one hand they would mourn [their dead], and with the other hand they would wave [in honor of Nebuchadnezzar's victory].

וְאָמַרְתָּ כֹּה אָמַר אֲדֹנָי אֱמֹר חֶרֶב חֶרֶב
טו הוּחַדָּה וְגַם־מְרוּטָה: לְמַעַן טְבֹחַ טֶבַח
הוּחַדָּה לְמַעַן־הֱיֵה־לָהּ בָּרָק מֹרָטָּה אוֹ
טז נָשִׂישׂ שֵׁבֶט בְּנִי מֹאֶסֶת כָּל־עֵץ: וַיִּתֵּן
אֹתָהּ לְמָרְטָה לִתְפֹּשׂ בַּכָּף הִיא־הוּחַדָּה
חֶרֶב וְהִיא מֹרָטָּה לָתֵת אוֹתָהּ בְּיַד־הוֹרֵג:

14. חֶרֶב חֶרֶב — *A sword, a sword.*

Radak writes that this dirge continues the previous prophecies and refers to the *sword* of *vs.* 9 and 10. The word is doubled for effect (see *footnote* 7:2).

Targum, in accordance with his system of rendering double expressions with different meanings (see *comm.* 13:10) translates: the sword of the Babylonian king [Nebuchadnezzar] and the sword of the people of Ammon. The latter refers to Ishmael ben Nesaniah *(Rashi)* who was sent by the Ammonite king to assassinate Gedaliah ben Achikom, whom Nebuchadnezzar appointed governor of Judah after the exile of Zidkiyahu (*Jeremiah* 40,41).

15. אוֹ נָשִׂישׂ שֵׁבֶט בְּנִי מֹאֶסֶת כָּל־עֵץ — *Or should we rejoice? My son's staff scorns every wood.*

The commentators offer various interpretations for this very obscure phrase.

— *Rashi:* Could one possibly think that it is still a time for rejoicing? The rod with which I chastised My son is harder than any other rod and scorns the blows of any rod or wood, which are like nothing compared to it.

— *Radak:* Shall we perhaps rejoice [in assuming that this sword is meant for other people but not for ourselves? This we cannot do for it is destined to cut down only] My son's *scepter.* It *spurns* [the cutting down of] any other tree.

— *Metzudos* interprets שֵׁבֶט בְּנִי as *tribe* [i.e., populace] *of my son.*]

— *Eliezer of Beaugency:* Is it perhaps coming to give others pleasure as their enemy falls [i.e., it is not destined to come against Israel, but to interfere in the quarrels of two other nations]? No! for it is melting [מאס, *to spurn* turns into מסס, *to melt*] the scepter of My son. [It is turned against] every tree [both moist and dry as in *v.* 3], representing the righteous as well as the wicked.

[According to *Rashi* and *Radak* the subject of נָשִׂישׂ, *should we rejoice,* is Israel. This introduces a jarring note since the speaker of the rest of the sentence is, as we have seen, God Himself (בְּנִי, *My son). Eliezer of Beaugency* does not explain the use of the first person plural (נָשִׂישׂ) which seems inapt in his rendering.

A glance at *v.* 16 shows it to be a smooth continuation of the first part of *v.* 15. The impression is that the whole phrase אוֹ נָשִׂישׂ שֵׁבֶט בְּנִי מֹאֶסֶת כָּל־עֵץ is an interjection in the middle of the dirge, but not part of it.

We have called this obviously poetic passage a dirge, because its whole tenor seems to express God's sorrow at the calamity about to overtake His children.

But in *Deuteronomy* 28:63 we read: *And even as HASHEM rejoiced* (שָׂשׂ) *over you to benefit you and to increase you; so HASHEM will rejoice* (יָשִׂישׂ) *over you to make you lost and to destroy you.*

There is an element of joy in the punishments which God inflicts on Israel for through its suffering Israel will eventually turn back to God. (*Hirsch* and *Hoffman* ad. loc. **See Appendix VI).**

As the dirge mourns the destruction which the sharpened and burnished sword will bring about, the mood turns to the prophecy in the Torah which deals with the impending destruction. And in the middle of the dirge the question suddenly impinges upon the mind: Perhaps a dirge is out of place; should We (the royal plural) perhaps rejoice at the eventual repentance? (Compare comm. to 6:11.)

If indeed this is the view taken of the events which are about to take place, then

21
14-16

14 *Ben Adam, prophesy and say: Thus says my Lord: Say:*

A sword, a sword —
sharpened and even burnished.
15 *That it may make a slaughter —*
has it been sharpened;
That it may flash —
has it been burnished.
Or should we rejoice?
My son's staff scorns every wood.
16 *Then He had it burnished —*
to make it fit the hand.
It has been sharpened — a sword —
and it has been burnished,
to place it in the killer's hand.

Nebuchadnezzar takes the form of God's שֵׁבֶט, His *educating rod.* (As in *Proverbs* 13:24. See also comm. to 20:37. Compare this usage with *Isaiah* 10:5.) The rod would normally be made out of wood; when a metal rod is meant it is explicated as in *Psalms* 2:9. An ineffective rod is one which cannot do its work because it is only made out of wood; it needs the strength of metal in order to impress. Such a rod, because it is ineffective would take on the female gender (מֹאֶסֶת) as we have seen in comm. to 12:14 and 13:20.

This then would be the answer to the question that perhaps joy is in place instead of a dirge. I cannot stop mourning because the amount of punishment required is overwhelming. The שֵׁבֶט, the *educating rod,* which is to be used against My son is weak and ineffective as long as it is made of wood [i.e., a limited punishment will not have the desired result]. The nature of the need is such that it scorns wood and must be made out of metal, i.e., become a sword (see *Rashi* to *Psalms* 2:9. See also *Rashi* here to *v.* 16). Therefore the destruction will be so great that it drowns out the thought of the ultimate benefit. The immediate need is to mourn and not to rejoice. And so the dirge continues. [See further in *comm.* to *v.* 18.]

16. וַיִּתֵּן — *Then He had* ... [lit. *gave it*].

Rashi and *Radak* assume God to be the subject. This also seems to be the interpretation of *Targum,* who renders *And He permitted punishment to be given into the hands of the Babylonian king.*

By contrast, *Metzudos* reads the subject as the enemy: *And the enemy gave the sword to be burnished ...*

אֹתָהּ — *It.*

According to *Rashi* this refers to the שֵׁבֶט, *rod,* of the previous verse. God gave over this rod to be made into a sword.

Radak and *Metzudos* who interpreted שֵׁבֶט בְּנִי differently from Rashi (see above) learn that our verse refers to the sword mentioned in the previous two verses.

לְמָרְטָה לִתְפֹּשׂ בַּכָּף — *Burnished — to make it fit the hand.*

Rashi points out that these three words are to be read together as in our translation.

הִיא־הוּחַדָּה חֶרֶב — *It has been sharpened — a sword.*

The rod of *v.*15 is really a sword. It is to be sharpened so that it might be placed in Nebuchadnezzar's hands *(Rashi).*

Radak suggests that the words should be translated as though they were

יז זְעַק וְהֵילֵל בֶּן־אָדָם כִּי־הִיא הָיְתָה בְעַמִּי
הִיא בְּכָל־נְשִׂיאֵי יִשְׂרָאֵל מְגוּרֵי אֶל־חֶרֶב
יח הָיוּ אֶת־עַמִּי לָכֵן סְפֹק אֶל־יָרֵךְ: כִּי בֹחַן
וּמָה אִם־גַּם־שֵׁבֶט מֹאֶסֶת לֹא יִהְיֶה נְאֻם
יט אֲדֹנָי יֱהֹוִה: וְאַתָּה בֶן־אָדָם

inverted: הִיא חֶרֶב הוּחַדָּה, *this sword was sharpened.*

17. כִּי־הִיא הָיְתָה בְעַמִּי — *For it will be against My people.*

Rashi translates: It (the sword) will come against My people. He understands the use of the past tense as prophetic usage which speaks of future events as though they had already occured. (See *Ramban, Exodus* 15:1, and footnote to 7:2.)

According to *Radak,* reference is to events which had already occured. Yoshiyahu and Yehoyakim had already been killed and the exiles had been dragged away by the power of the sword. [*Radak* also mentions the slaughter of Zidkiyahu's sons (II *Kings* 25:7) which at the time of this prophecy still lay in the future.]

מְגוּרֵי אֶל־חֶרֶב הָיוּ אֶת־עַמִּי — *Gathered around the sword they came against* [lit. *were*] *My people.*

This translation follows *Rashi* who traces מְגוּרֵי to the root אגר, *together. Radak* thinks that the root is גור, *to be afraid* and translates: Fearers of the sword were My people (even before it came against them. See 11:8).

[*Radak* points out the unexpected construct form of מְגוּרֵי (instead of מְגוּרִים) which is usually used to indicate the genitive or possessive case. He brings examples where we find a similar usage. (This is true mostly in poetic passages. Parallels from *Ezekiel* are 13:2 and 38:11).]

18. כִּי בֹחַן — *Because — a test!*

A measure of the obscurity of this sentence can be taken from the fact that Rashi attempts no fewer than three explanations, *Targum's* and two of his own. Our translation follows *Rashi's* first personal interpretation. Many others are offered by the commentators.

[Note that בֹּחַן can either be a verb, in which case it is in the third person, past, tense, *Pu'al* passive voice: *He was tested* (see *Ibn Janach, Sefer haSheroshim*) or it could be a noun meaning: *test (Radak, Sefer haShorashim).*]

We present some of the interpretations:

Targum's explanation is based on his understanding of the related phrase in verse 15. There he renders: אוֹ נָשִׂישׂ שֵׁבֶט בְּנִי, *the tribe of My son* (Judah and Benjamin) *rejoiced* [at the exile of the ten tribes of the Northern Kingdom. Those tribes were exiled because they worshiped idols, a practice that was not imitated by Judah and Benjamin. מֹאֶסֶת כָּל־עֵץ, *they scorned all idols* (עֵץ, *wood* is a reference to idols made by man). But now, even Judah and Benjamin worship idols.]

In this vein he renders our verse as follows (see *Rashi):* [For prophets prophesied against them and they did not repent, therefore] כִּי בֹחַן, *it is a tested truth* [that they will not repent]! וּמָה, *and what* [will be their end] אִם גַּם שֵׁבֶט מֹאֶסֶת, *if even the tribe* (Judah and Benjamin) *who scorned* [the ten tribes for serving idols and for being exiled as a result] לֹא יִהְיֶה, *will cease to exist?*

Rashi offers two interpretations. Either: כִּי בֹחַן, *for they have been tried* [with all kinds of suffering] וּמָה, *and what* [will happen to them] אִם גַּם שֵׁבֶט מֹאֶסֶת, *if even this rod which scorns* [all other wood as being too soft (see comm. to *v.* 15) will come upon it]? לֹא יִהְיֶה, *they can surely no longer exist.*

Or: An explanation based on a different understanding of verse 15. In this rendering verse 15 is to be translated as follows: אוֹ נָשִׂישׂ, *shall we*

17 *Cry out and wail, Ben Adam!*
For it will be against My people.
It will be against all princes of Israel.
Gathered around the sword
they came against My people.
Therefore smite upon your thigh.
18 *Because — a test!*
And what if even this scorning rod?
He shall not survive!
The words of my Lord HASHEM/ELOHIM.

perhaps rejoice [that the sword is not destined to come against us, since] שֵׁבֶט בְּנִי מֹאֶסֶת כָּל עֵץ, *My son's tribe* [Judah] *scorns all idols?* A hope is expressed that perhaps Judah's innate rejection of idol worship might yet save him.

Now, verse 18 reads thus: כִּי בֹחַן [The sword is after all destined to come against them (*v.* 17)] *because it is clear* [to Me that they will not experience a true repentance]. וּמָה, *And what* [purpose is there in waiting any longer for their repentance], אִם גַּם שֵׁבֶט מֹאֶסֶת, *even if* [they bring themselves once more to be] *a tribe which scorns* [idol worship]. לֹא יִהְיֶה, *It will not survive* [this repentance will not be lasting.]

Our translation follows *Rashi* as cited above. *Radak* suggests the following: כִּי בֹחַן, [The sword has been taken from its scabbard; sharpened and burnished] *for a testing* [of Israel in order that through it they shall repent]. וּמָה אִם גַּם שֵׁבֶט מֹאֶסֶת לֹא יִהְיֶה, *And what will have been the purpose* [of these preparations] *if it spurns* [the cutting down of] *My son's scepter* [just as it spurns all other wood]?

Among the major commentators, only *Mahari MiTrani* sees בֹּחַן as deriving not from the root meaning *to test,* but as *a tower* as in *Isaiah* 23:13. He renders: כִּי בֹחַן, *For the tower* [for the purpose of besieging Jerusalem has been built] וּמָה, *and what* [purpose will it serve]. אִם גַּם שֵׁבֶט מֹאֶסֶת לֹא יִהְיֶה, *if it will not be a destroying rod?* [In *v.* 15 *Mahari MiTrani* translates שֵׁבֶט בְּנִי מֹאֶסֶת כָּל עֵץ as, *the rod* (i.e., the sword) *which strikes My son destroys* (see *Jeremiah* 36:22) *all wood*].

[In our interpretation of *v.* 15 we thought it possible that God refused to 'rejoice' at the positive aspects of the destruction because the 'educating rod' was unable to be effective without turning into a sword. The destruction was thus so great that it drowned out any thought of the regenerative force of suffering.

In this view we might suggest the following interpretation:

V. 17 had called upon Yechezkel to *cry out and wail* because of the sword that was to come upon God's people. Once more this suggests the question (implied here, though explicated in verse 15) that perhaps a dirge is not appropriate because of the positive aspects of the suffering to which they were to be exposed. To this verse 18 answers: כִּי בֹחַן, *for they have been tested* (and failed) וּמָה אִם גַּם שֵׁבֶט מֹאֶסֶת לֹא יִהְיֶה, *What (*would be the difference) *if the educating rod had not scorned* (wood)? I.e., even if the educating rod would have been strong and not betrayed weakness by scorning wood. This interpretation is implied by the differing genders of יִהְיֶה (masculine) and מֹאֶסֶת (feminine).

The meaning is that in contrast to what was said in verse 15 it is not the overwhelming harshness of the punishment which blots out any feeling of joy. Even if the punishment had been less severe there would have been ample reason to mourn, not for the suffering but for the failure (כִּי בֹחַן) which brought it about.]

[After all attempts to explain the dirge of the sword much obscurity still

הִנָּבֵא וְהַךְ כַּף אֶל־כָּף וְתִכָּפֵל חֶרֶב
שְׁלִישִׁתָה חֶרֶב חֲלָלִים הִיא חֶרֶב חָלָל
כ הַגָּדוֹל הַחֹדֶרֶת לָהֶם: לְמַעַן | לָמוּג לֵב
וְהַרְבֵּה הַמִּכְשֹׁלִים עַל כָּל־שַׁעֲרֵיהֶם
נָתַתִּי אִבְחַת־חָרֶב אָח עֲשׂוּיָה לְבָרָק

remains. Space has not permitted the anthologizing of every opinion. The reader is advised to seek further on his own. *Malbim* has an entirely original approach to the whole section which is too involved to anthologize but which goes very far in solving some of the textual problems which remain].

19-22. These verses contain another dirge concerning the sword. That they are not simply a continuation of the previous one can be seen from the fact that in verse 19 the prophet is called upon to prophesy. In the masoretic text, this section is divided from the earlier one [a פָּרָשָׁה סְתוּמָה].

19. וְהַךְ כַּף אֶל־כָּף — *Pound hand upon hand.*

In the manner of mourners *(Rashi)*. The prophet's anguish reflects God's own sorrow (*v.* 22). [See 6:11 and comm. there.]

וְתִכָּפֵל חֶרֶב שְׁלִישִׁתָה חֶרֶב חֲלָלִים הִיא חֶרֶב חָלָל הַגָּדוֹל — *For the third sword will be magnified* [lit. *doubled*] *over the sword of the slain. This is the sword of the great massacre* [lit. *corpse or corpses*].

Our translation follows *Rashi's* rendering of this difficult verse. Two swords had been mentioned above (*v.* 14). *Targum* had identified them as: The sword of the Babylonian king, Nebuchadnezzar, and the sword of Ammon which, through the hands of Ishmael ben Nesaniah, assassinated Gedalyah ben Achikom (see comm. to *v.* 14). Now there is to be a *third sword* which is much worse than these other two. They were described only as *sword of the slain,* while this third sword is described as *sword of the great massacre.* The latter term is considered stronger, either because of the added adjective הַגָּדוֹל, *the great,* or because the use of the generic חָלָל indicates a dense mass of corpses in which the individual victim is insignificant.

[The word חָלָל, literally *a corpse,* is also used generically (as in 6:7, 28:3, and *Nahum* 3:3) to mean a large number of corpses. To indicate this connotation of our verse, we have translated *massacre.*]

This third sword symbolizes the final campaigns of Nebuchadnezzar, which carried his armies to every corner of the inhabited world and finally wiped out every remnant of the Jewish people except that which had been led captive to Babylon. Foremost among these victims was the small community of Jews who had remained in Judah under the leadership of Gedaliah ben Achikom and fled to Egypt after his assassination (see *Jeremiah* 43, 44). Egypt finally fell to Nebuchadnezzar, and these fugitives were slaughtered.

Radak and *Metzudos* differ slightly with *Rashi. Radak* suggests that שְׁלִישִׁתָה, does not mean third but great [as in שָׁלִישׁ, *a high official (Exodus* 14:7)], and the verse would mean: *and double a great sword.*

Metzudos does not take חָלָל as a generic term but translates חָלָל הַגָּדוֹל, *the great slain one,* referring to King Zidkiyahu, who was conquered by this sword.

Eliezer of Beaugency offers a different translation. In 5:2, Yechezkel divided his hair (see *comm.* 5:1-4) into three equal parts. One third was to be smitten by the sword, one third was to be burned, and one third was to be scattered to the wind and *I will unsheathe a sword after them.* Thus, the sword controlled two of the three thirds.

21
19-20

[19] *And you Ben Adam, prophesy and pound hand upon hand:*

For the third sword will be magnified
over the sword of the slain.
This is the sword of the great massacre
which penetrates to them.
[20] *So that the heart may melt*
and stumbling-blocks increase
in all their gates,
I have caused the scream of the sword —
Alas!
It is ready to flash;

Hence: *The sword will be doubled upon an extra third.*

וְתִכָּפֵל — *Will be magnified* [lit. *doubled*].

We may surmise that וְתִכָּפֵל, *will be doubled* is in the נִפְעַל, *passive voice* in order to stress that Nebuchadnezzar's sword is not an independent agent. It is forced by God to do what it does.

הַחֹדֶרֶת לָהֶם — *Which penetrates to them.*

The root חדר does not recur in Scripture as a verb. The commentators assume that it is related to חֶדֶר, *room.* Wherever you flee, the sword will pursue you to your innermost chambers *(Mahari Karo).*

Eliezer of Beaugency compares *Deuteronomy* 32:25: *Outside, the sword will bereave; inside* [וּמֵחֲדָרִים], *there is fear,* which he interprets to mean that the fear of the bereaving sword will penetrate the houses (but see *Rashi* there.)

An alternative is suggested by *Radak* and *Metzudos:* the sword was stored in a room [in preparation for the slaughter].

20. אִבְחַת־חָרֶב — *The scream of the sword.*

The translation follows *Rashi* who suggests that אִבְחַת, which does not recur in Scripture, is derived from נבח, *to bark (Isaiah* 56:10).

Other suggestions are that the א in אִבְחַת, might be a substitute for a ט and the phrase means טִבְחַת חֶרֶב, *the slaughter of the sword (Radak).*

[The justification for this substitution is based on a rule frequently invoked by the commentators. The alphabet as we know it (א, ב, ג ...) is not the only way of arranging the letters. The Talmud and Midrash know of many other possible combinations (see *Shabbas* 104). Letters which combine in some of these variant systems can be substituted for each other. An example of this substitution is the word שֵׁשַׁךְ which Jeremiah uses to describe Babylon (*Jeremiah* 25:26, 51:41). The word is based on the substitution of ש, for ב and כ for ל in the word בָּבֶל. This is justified because in the alphabet which combines the first and last letters, the second and the penultimate and so on (את, בש, גר ...) the ב and the ש come together as do also the כ and the ל.

Another system combines the units with each other in a different way (אט, בח, גז ...). Accordingly א and ט become interchangeable and אִבְחַת can be understood as though it were written טִבְחַת.]

Menachem, quoted by *Rashi,* deduces from the context that the meaning is: *the fear of the sword.*

אָח עֲשׂוּיָה לְבָרָק — *Alas! It is ready to flash.*

אָח, *Alas!* is an expression of woe.

כא מְעֻטָּה לְטָבַח: הִתְאַחֲדִי הֵימִינִי הָשִׂימִי
כב הַשְׂמִילִי אָנָה פָּנַיִךְ מֻעָדוֹת: וְגַם־אֲנִי
אַכֶּה כַפִּי אֶל־כַּפִּי וַהֲנִחֹתִי חֲמָתִי אֲנִי
כג יהוה דִּבַּרְתִּי: וַיְהִי
כד דְבַר־יהוה אֵלַי לֵאמֹר: וְאַתָּה בֶן־אָדָם

מְעֻטָּה לְטָבַח — *It is sheathed until the slaughter.*

Most commentators follow *Rashi,* who relates it to עטה, *to cover.* The sword is to be sheathed until it is needed, in order to retain its sharpness and brightness. *Menachem* (quoted by *Rashi)* relates the word to עֵיטָה (*Daniel* 2:14) *a plan,* and renders: *It is intended for slaughter.*

21. הִתְאַחֲדִי — *Concentrate.*

Except for *Mahari Karo* who understands this word in its Aramaic sense (see *Targum* 19:4): *to take hold,* the commentators assume it to be related to אֶחָד, *one.* Therefore we have rendered it *concentrate,* attempting to express the idea that people should hew to a single philosophy.

[It is the sword which is being addressed since the verbs are in the feminine gender].

Rashi comments: Hold yourself to one direction, either the right or the left. He does not explain what message is being given to the sword.

It could be that he understands the phrase like *Mahari Karo* who renders: Take hold of the right or the left direction [as long as you keep away from Jerusalem.] Or, he might interpret as does *Eliezer of Beaugency:* Stay [consistently] to the right or to the left. [Do not waver from either direction until you have destroyed completely what is there.]

Radak and *Metzudos* interpret the verse as referring to Nebuchadnezzar's dilemma, depicted in *v.* 24 ff. As he travels southward from Babylon, Nebuchadnezzar is in doubt whether to turn to his right to Jerusalem — or to his left — to Rabbah, the capital of Ammon. (See *comm.* below.) Our verse calls upon him to make his decision and turn either right or left.

22. וְגַם־אֲנִי אַכֶּה כַפִּי אֶל־כַּפִּי — *I too shall pound My hand upon My hand.*

God Himself joins in the signs of sorrow which He had enjoined upon the prophet [*v.* 19] *(Rashi).* He mourns because he knows that Nebuchadnezzar's choice will fall on Jerusalem and not upon Ammon [see above] *(Radak).*

Targum renders: I shall bring punishment upon punishment.

[*Rambam* in *Moreh Nevuchim* 1:27 discusses *Targum's* system of translating all apparent anthropomorphisms in such a way as to remove any taint of corporeality from God. This system is followed by *Onkelos* in the Torah and *Targum Yonasan* in Prophets. See, for example, 9:9 and 43:2. This explains why *Targum* here prefers *punishment* to the literal *hand.* It is, however, difficult to find a consistent treatment of this problem. For example, see 20:33, where no attempt is made to use any kind of circumlocution. For a detailed analysis, see *Ramban, Genesis* 46:1.]

וַהֲנִחֹתִי חֲמָתִי — *And I shall put My fury to rest.*

See *comm.* 5:13 for different ways of understanding this phrase. *Rashi's* rendering here is not quite clear. In contrast to 5:13 where he translates: *My anger will not trouble Me any more,* he seems to imply in our verse that the meaning is: *I will place My anger.* [Although I mourn, My anger demands vindication.]

In contrast, *Metzudos* renders here: *My anger will rest,* although in 5:13 he renders: *I will place My anger.*

אֲנִי ה׳ דִּבַּרְתִּי — *I, HASHEM, have spoken.*

I am able to make sure that My words

it is sheathed until the slaughter.
21 Concentrate — to the right —
set yourself — to the left —
wherever your face is destined.
22 I too shall pound My hand upon My hand, and I
shall put My fury to rest. I, HASHEM, have spoken.
23 The word of HASHEM came to me saying:
24 Now you, Ben Adam, set yourself two roads for

come true *(Radak)*. And so it shall be *(Metzudos)*. [See *comm.* 11:12; 12:25.]

24-27. Nebuchadnezzar, the man, has been entirely absent from Yechezkel's prophecies. The prophet had seen all too clearly that a destroying sword was to come over his people, bringing terrible suffering and deprivation; but the agency through which God was to bring about the calamity had remained nebulous, without form or identity. (The king of Babylon has been mentioned only twice, 17:12 and 19:9, in verses dealing with events which had already taken place.) Now in this vision the prophet is suddenly face-to-face with the enemy. It is Nebuchadnezzar, king of Babylon, who is being driven inexorably to Jerusalem — and with this identification the event is placed firmly in its true cosmic perspective.

The people of Israel are the bearers of God's Glory on earth (see Overview p. xxx ff.; footnote 20:9). In the Torah view of history, the implacable foes of the Divine are the אַרְבַּע מַלְכֻיּוֹת, *Four Kingdoms* (Babylon, Media-Persia, Greece, and Rome; see footnote 3:22), who, each in its own way and from its own perspective (see *Maharal, Ner Mitzvah)*, were to subjugate Israel — and attempt to banish God's Presence from earth.

We say *cosmic perspective* because the *Midrash* teaches us that as surely as this struggle animates and directs Israel's historic destiny, so it also lies at the very core of universal creation.

Israel's destiny was forged at the בְּרִית בֵּין הַבְּתָרִים, *Covenant of the Parts,* when God revealed its future to Abraham. On the verse: *And see! a dread, great darkness falls upon him (Genesis* 15:12), the *Midrash* remarks:

אֵימָה, *dread,* refers to Babylon; חֲשֵׁכָה, *darkness,* refers to Media; גְּדֹלָה, *great,* refers to Greece; נֹפֶלֶת עָלָיו, *falls upon him,* refers to Edom.

Thus, even before Israel existed as a nation, its future is depicted against the background of a world shrouded in the awesome darkness of the Four Kingdoms. (For an analysis of the relationship between the Egyptian exile which was explicated at the *Covenant of the Parts,* and the Four Kingdoms which are only hinted at there, see *Pachad Yitzchak, Pesach* 21:1, 53:7. See also ArtScroll *Zemiroth,* pp. 170-184.) God will dispel that darkness through the light which Israel will cast upon the stage of world history.

But long before Abraham, at the very dawn of existence, the Torah hints at a world of chaos and darkness which awaits redemption by the Spirit of God. *When the earth was astonishingly empty, with darkness upon the surface of the deep, and the Divine Presence hovered upon the surface of the waters (Genesis* 1:2). The Midrash (*Bereishis Rabbah* 2:4) comments:

... תֹהוּ, *astonishingly,* refers to Babylon; וָבֹהוּ, *empty,* refers to Media; וְחֹשֶׁךְ, *with darkness,* refers to Greece; עַל פְּנֵי תְהוֹם, *upon the surface of the deep,* refers to the wicked kingdom (Edom-Rome); וְרוּחַ אֱלֹהִים, *and the Divine Presence,* refers to the spirit of the מָשִׁיחַ, *Messiah.*

The moment of the destruction of the Temple is the moment that the world is

שִׂים־לְךָ | שְׁנַיִם דְּרָכִים לָבוֹא חֶרֶב מֶלֶךְ־
בָּבֶל מֵאֶרֶץ אֶחָד יֵצְאוּ שְׁנֵיהֶם וְיָד בָּרֵא
כה בְּרֹאשׁ דֶּרֶךְ־עִיר בָּרֵא: דֶּרֶךְ תָּשִׂים לָבוֹא
חֶרֶב אֵת רַבַּת בְּנֵי־עַמּוֹן וְאֶת־יְהוּדָה
כו בִירוּשָׁלִַם בְּצוּרָה: כִּי־עָמַד מֶלֶךְ־בָּבֶל

to be plunged into this cosmic darkness, and Nebuchadnezzar is God's agent at this cataclysmic point in history.

Nebuchadnezzar had been richly endowed with the qualities of kingship. In his heyday he was absolute ruler of the whole physical world (*Daniel* 2:38). He was capable of soaring to spiritual heights beyond anything which we can imagine (*Daniel* 3:33; *Sanhedrin* 92b). In his dream of the Four Kingdoms, which he saw in the form of a human statue (*Daniel* 2:31 ff.) he was the *head of gold (Daniel* 2:38), mightier by far than the subsequent nations (which are depicted as silver, copper, and iron, respectively). In Daniel's dream (*Daniel* 7:2 ff.), in which the Four Kingdoms appeared as wild animals, it was Nebuchadnezzar who appeared as the lion — undisputed king of the animal world.[1]

All these gifts were harnessed in service of the fulfillment of his destiny. His kingship was to be the one that would replace that of God. He was the one who would plunge the world into a darkness from which it will not be released until the advent of the Messiah.

He realized the enormity of what he was about to do. Depraved as he was, he hesitated to take the steps which would reverse human history for centuries to come. This passage portrays that hesitation, and the irrevocable hand of God driving him relentlessly to the Destruction.

24. שִׂים־לְךָ שְׁנַיִם דְּרָכִים — *Set yourself two roads.*

Yechezkel is to act out the king's indecision as he stands at the crossroad attempting to divine whether indeed it is he who will execute God's judgment. According to the tradition of the Sages (*Sanhedrin* 95b), Nebuchadnezzar was one of the five survivors of the fire which consumed Sennacherib's army when the latter attempted to capture Jerusalem in Chizkiyahu's days (*II Kings* 19:35). He knew (as a Roman general was to know at the destruction of the second Temple — see *Gittin* 56a) that God's anger would be directed against anyone who raised his hand against Jerusalem (*Pesikta Rabbasi* 26:54); and he was afraid. So terrified, was he that even at the moment the Temple was burning in front of him, he could not bring himself to enter it. God sent the Angel, Michael, who dragged Nebuchadnezzar's horse into the Holy of Holies (*Yalkut Koheles* 999).

God's Providence had prepared the way. *The heart of a king is like a split stream in the hands of God. He directs it to whichever way He wants (Proverbs* 21:1). The mightiest king is no more than a puppet in God's hands (*Rabbeinu Yonah, Proverbs* 21:1

1. *Maharal* in *Ner Mitzvah* points out the profound significance of the fact that in Daniel's dream the Four Kingdoms appeared as animals, while Nebuchadnezzar saw them in human form. In the Torah perspective (Daniel's dream), the Four Kingdoms, in their negation of all that is Godly, fall short indeed of the Adam ideal of Creation (see Overview IV p.xxx ff.). They, as truly as the actual animal world, exist only to serve true Adam's needs. It is a measure of Nebuchadnezzar's depravity that he, in contrast, saw just these Four Kingdoms as Man, the fulfillment of Creation's purpose rather than its servant. In his purview, it is not Israel who is Adam (*Yevamos* 61a) — mainstay and focus of creation — but the Four Kingdoms in their rejection of the Divine who are the true Man.

21
25-26

the sword of the Babylonian king to come. From one land they shall both diverge. And clear a place! Clear it at the head of a city-road. 25 *Prepare a road for the sword to come to Rabbah, the Ammonite capital, and to Judah, fortified in Jerusalem.* 26 *For the king of*

explains that specifically kings whose decisions affect multitudes of people are exceptions to the general rule of free choice; with regard to their role as leaders of nations God directs their decisions); and God had decided that Nebuchadnezzar was to destroy the Temple.[1]

For eighteen years a בַּת קוֹל, *heavenly voice*, was heard in the palace of Nebuchadnezzar saying, 'Evil slave! Go and destroy your Master's house, for his sons do not listen to Him.' [So] he stood at a crossroads. One path led to the wilderness, the other to Jerusalem ... He began to divine with his arrows (*v.* 26). He shot an arrow towards Rome, it did not fly true; towards Alexandria, it did not fly true; towards Jerusalem — and it flew true. He sowed seeds and planted shoots; for Rome, they did not blossom; for Alexandria, they did not blossom; for Jerusalem, they blossomed. He lit lights and lamps ... He launched ships (according to *Koheles Rabbah*) ... He inquired of fetishes. He examined livers ... and all pointed toward Jerusalem (*Eichah Rabbasi, Pesichta* 23).

As the people saw Yechezkel enact these scenes, they would learn that Jerusalem was indeed doomed. The ascendancy of the Four Kingdoms was about to begin. [In *Radak's* view Yechezkel did not actually act out these scenes. He saw them in prophetic vision. See *comm.* 2:8, 5:1-4.)

חֶרֶב מֶלֶךְ־בָּבֶל — *The sword of the Babylonian king.*

This is the second sword, concerning which God had said (*v.* 10); *I shall take out My sword from its scabbard* (*Radak*). The tenor of the whole chapter is that Nebuchadnezzar is no more than a tool in God's hand. His sword is really God's sword.

מֵאֶרֶץ אֶחָד יֵצְאוּ שְׁנֵיהֶם — *From one land they shall both diverge.*

That land is Babylon (*Radak; Metzudos*).

וְיָד בָּרֵא — *And clear a place.*

יָד is taken as *place* (as in *Deuteronomy* 23:13). בָּרֵא is an imperative (*Radak*) and can mean *clear* (*Rashi*) or *choose* (*Radak; Metzudos*).

דֶּרֶךְ־עִיר — *A city-road.*

This is a road leading to the city (*Radak*).

25. Even as his campaign begins, Nebuchadnezzar's decision is not yet made. Perhaps he will take the road to Rabbah (see *II Samuel* 11:1), capital of Ammon, and the battle will be just another in the long chain of conquests which have made Babylon great. Perhaps the time has not yet come to heed the heavenly voice which has been echoing through his palace for the past eighteen years (see *comm. v.* 24).

יְהוּדָה בִירוּשָׁלַיִם בְּצוּרָה — *Judah, fortified in Jerusalem.*

The translation is literal. *Metzudos* translates *Judah,* which dwells *in fortified Jerusalem. Radak* adds: and feels safe there. The implication is that the whole of Judah feels safe and impregnable because Jerusalem is in its midst. This was indeed true in happier

1. For a practical application of this doctrine, see *Ramban* to *Exodus* 14:4. In his view, the greatest miracle during Israel's deliverance from Egypt was the fact that Pharaoh followed the Jews through the split sea. He had suffered the plagues; he had seen the miraculous parting of the waters. Surely logic would have told him that it was dangerous to carry the pursuit into the sea; but the decision was not his. God had decreed that the Egyptians should drown.

אֶל־אֵם הַדֶּרֶךְ בְּרֹאשׁ שְׁנֵי הַדְּרָכִים
לִקְסָם־קָסֶם קִלְקַל בַּחִצִּים שָׁאַל בַּתְּרָפִים
כז רָאָה בַּכָּבֵד: בִּימִינוֹ הָיָה | הַקֶּסֶם יְרוּשָׁלִַם
לָשׂוּם כָּרִים לִפְתֹּחַ פֶּה בְּרֶצַח לְהָרִים
קוֹל בִּתְרוּעָה לָשׂוּם כָּרִים עַל־שְׁעָרִים
כח לִשְׁפֹּךְ סֹלְלָה לִבְנוֹת דָּיֵק: וְהָיָה לָהֶם
°כִּקְסָם־ ק׳ °בקסום־שָׁוְא בְּעֵינֵיהֶם שְׁבֻעֵי שְׁבֻעוֹת
כט לָהֶם וְהוּא־מַזְכִּיר עָוֺן לְהִתָּפֵשׂ: לָכֵן

times (see *Psalms* 46), but Jerusalem had lost its splendor (see ch. 22) and would fall as easily as any other city.

26. אֵם הַדֶּרֶךְ — *Crossroads* [lit. *mother of the road*].

The two roads turn towards the point from which they diverge as children turn towards their mother *(Radak)*. The term **אֵם**, *mother*, is also used for an important city (*II Samuel* 20:19) because it is like a mother to the smaller cities which surround it *(Radak, Sefer HaShorashim)*.

קִלְקַל בַּחִצִּים — *He flashed with the arrows.*

Rashi (in accord with *Targum)* writes that the arrows were shot (causing them to flash), and the divination was accomplished by observing the direction in which they flew.

Radak writes that they were burnished brightly and served as a mirror in which the sorcerer would find images to guide him.

Ibn Janach (Sefer HaShorashim) translates: *He shook the arrows. Mahari MiTrani* explains that he wrote the names Jerusalem and Ammon on two arrows and rolled them like dice.

תְּרָפִים — *Teraphim.*

We leave the term untranslated since it is not clear what type of fetishes these were. They are not idols. *Metzudos* writes that they had human form and could be made to tell the future. (See *Ibn Ezra, Genesis* 31:19).

For extensive treatment of *Teraphim* see ArtScroll *Bereishis* 31:19.

רָאָה בַּכָּבֵד — *Examined the liver.*

As it is taken out of an animal, the liver glistens. This glistening is used for divination *(Metzudos)*.

27. בִּימִינוֹ הָיָה הַקֶּסֶם יְרוּשָׁלִַם — *In his right hand the sorcery indicated Jerusalem.*

Traveling south from Babylon, Jerusalem lies to the right (west) and the Ammonite Rabbah to the left (east).

כָּרִים ... סֹלְלָה ... דָּיֵק — *Commanders ... mound ... fort.*

See *comm.* to 4:2.

28. וְהָיָה לָהֶם כִּקְסָם־שָׁוְא בְּעֵינֵיהֶם — *But it was as a vain divination in their eyes.*

The people in Judah attached no importance to the result of Nebuchadnezzar's divinations. Although the results had repeatedly pointed to Jerusalem, they felt themselves safe.

שְׁבֻעֵי שְׁבֻעוֹת לָהֶם וְהוּא מַזְכִּיר עָוֺן לְהִתָּפֵשׂ — *Oaths upon oaths were theirs — this recalling sin so that they might be conquered.*

They felt as safe as though the Babylonians had sworn not to attack them. Their hypocritical reliance on the imagined oath of the Babylonians would recall how unreliable their own oaths were. Zidkiyahu had sworn allegiance to Nebuchadnezzar and broken his oath (ch. 17). By what right, therefore, could Israel expect others to honor oaths made

Babylon stood at the crossroads at the head of the two roads to practice divination. He flashed with the arrows, inquired of the Teraphim, examined the liver. 27 *In his right hand the sorcery indicated Jerusalem — to appoint commanders, to urge on to murder, to raise his voice in trumpeting, to place commanders at the gates, to pour out a mound, to build a fort.* 28 *But it was as a vain divination in their eyes. Oaths upon oaths were theirs — this recalling sin so that they might be conquered.*

to them, even if such oaths had been made? *(Radak).*

R' Breuer's rendering of the verse is laden with bitter irony. The people ignored the results of Nebuchadnezzar's divinations because they declared themselves immune from the influences of magic forces. They considered themselves to be the direct charges of God Himself, because שְׁבֻעֵי שְׁבֻעוֹת לָהֶם, *He had sworn to them that they were His,* beyond the power of magic.

But these same people had indulged in every kind of sorcery when they craved support for their rejection of the warnings addressed to them by God's prophets (ch. 13). With wanton disregard of their people's pride that *Jacob knows no sorcery nor Israel divination (Numbers* 23:23), they had groveled before any false prophet who would pander to their illusions of invincibility.

Now that the forces of magic seemed to confirm their worst fears, they swung to the other extreme. They were God's direct concern and need not fear the heathen divinations. וְהוּא מַזְכִּיר עָוֹן לְהִתָּפֵשׂ, their hypocritical vacillations would recall their former reliance on sorcery and hasten their doom.

Rashi (as does *Targum*) translates שְׁבֻעֵי שְׁבֻעוֹת as *seven times seven.* In this he follows the Midrash (*Eichah Rabbasi, Pesichta* 23; see above *v.* 24).

Yechezkel said to Israel: You could have had the merit of delving into the Torah which has forty-nine (seven times seven) facets. Now that you did not deserve this, Nebuchadnezzar came and made forty-nine divinations against you, as it is written שְׁבֻעֵי שְׁבֻעוֹת לָהֶם.

[We have not followed the usual practice of quoting *Targum* and *Rashi* at the beginning of the *commentary* because it seems that their rendering is not meant as פְּשַׁט, *the simple meaning,* but rather as something additional hinted in the verse. See Appendix VI for an elaboration of the point.]

The *Midrash* proceeds to interpret the next phrase in the verse: וְהוּא מַזְכִּיר עָוֹן לְהִתָּפֵשׂ, *recalling sin so that they may be conquered.* This refers to the murder of the prophet Zechariah ben Yehoyadah who, in the time of Yehoash, king of Judah, was killed on orders of the king for attempting to stop the blatant idol worship upon which the people were about to embark (*II Chronicles* 24:20). According to the tradition of the Sages, the blood of this *priest and prophet* (see *Eichah* 2:20; *comm.*) seethed on the ground of the Temple for 252 years, until the destruction (*Koheles Rabbah* 3:16) and precluded any possibility of תְּשׁוּבָה, *repentance (Sanhedrin* 7a). The people's disregard of Nebuchadnezzar's divinations recalled this sin and hastened the destruction.[1]

1. The murder of Zechariah occupies a central place in the Aggadah surrounding the destruction of the Temple. *Gittin* 57b and *Sanhedrin* 96b tell in detail how Nebuchadnezzar's

כא
ל-לא

כֹּה־אָמַר אֲדֹנָי יֱהוִה יַעַן הַזְכַּרְכֶם עֲוֺנְכֶם
בְּהִגָּלוֹת פִּשְׁעֵיכֶם לְהֵרָאוֹת חַטֹּאותֵיכֶם
בְּכֹל עֲלִילוֹתֵיכֶם יַעַן הִזָּכֶרְכֶם בַּכַּף
ל תִּתָּפֵשׂוּ׃ וְאַתָּה חָלָל רָשָׁע
נְשִׂיא יִשְׂרָאֵל אֲשֶׁר־בָּא יוֹמוֹ בְּעֵת עֲוֺן
לא קֵץ׃ כֹּה אָמַר אֲדֹנָי

29. יַעַן הַזְכַּרְכֶם עֲוֺנְכֶם — *Since you cause your sin to be remembered.*

You constantly commit new sins, and these cause your old ones to be remembered *(Rashi).*

בְּהִגָּלוֹת פִּשְׁעֵיכֶם לְהֵרָאוֹת חַטֹּאתֵיכֶם — *As your rebellions are revealed to show your transgressions.*

As your new rebellions come into the open, they cause your old transgressions to be seen *(Rashi).*

יַעַן הִזָּכֶרְכֶם — *Because you are recalled.*

You are recalled by Me, as sinners *(Rashi).*

בַּכַּף תִּתָּפֵשׂוּ — *You will be grasped in the hand.*

You will be given over into the hands

general Nebuzaradan slaughtered thousands of people in order to appease the seething blood, but nothing helped until he appealed to the slain Zechariah to demand no more killings lest the whole nation be slaughtered. At that point the blood stopped seething. Nebuzaradan, shocked into a realization of the enormity of all the murders he had committed when even one soul was so dear to God, deserted his position and became a Jew. (This story is in the *kinnah* of the Ninth of Av: בְּיוֹם אַכְּפִי הִכְבַּדְתִּי.)

The *Talmud* and *Midrashim* do not explain why just this particular sin remained with the people for so many generations and found no atonement until the destruction of the Temple. A hint may be found in *Sanhedrin* 7a, where the Sages explain Aaron's decision to cooperate with the people's demands in the matter of the Golden Calf. He reasoned that if he were to defy them and they killed him, they would have murdered *priest and prophet,* just as they would one day murder Zechariah, and for this there could never be any atonement — as evidenced by that story. Aaron preferred to make the Golden Calf. Idol worship is a terrible sin, but can be wiped out with repentance.

We deduce that the Sages understand the particular heinousness of this sin to have been caused by the fact that *priest and prophet* were killed. For such a sin, no repentance is possible.

The explanation of this could be as follows: תְּשׁוּבָה, *repentance,* assumes an inner core of purity and holiness which sin can never erode. (See footnote 3:1, 9:2.) The conduits through which this inner core of holiness is reinforced in Israel are priest and prophet. The *kohen,* through the Temple service, brings the Divine Presence to dwell among Israel (*Exodus* 25:8, 29:46), and the prophet, through the great personal purity which he attains (*Rambam, Mishneh Torah, Yesodei HaTorah* ch. 7) provides the means by which God communicates with His people (see footnote 2:5).

The wanton murder of priest and prophet (particularly in defense of idol worship) constitutes a repudiation of this inner core of holiness. Once that inner core has been eradicated, no repentance is possible. For 252 years the seething blood of the slain priest and prophet mutely pointed to that fatal erosion which had taken place in Israel's soul. From that moment on Israel lost that purity of perception of itself and its role in God's plan which would have made repentance possible.

We can now see how the *Midrash's* explanation is extremely apt for our verse. The people had not been afraid of Nebuchadnezzar's divinations. They thought of themselves as God's special charges beyond the control of natural forces [see *comm.*]. This attitude would surely recall the assassination of Zechariah. Had they themselves not repudiated that very call of holiness with which they now prided themselves?

[29] *Therefore, thus says my Lord HASHEM/ELOHIM: Since you cause your sin to be remembered, as your rebellions are revealed to show your transgressions in all your deeds; because you are recalled, you will be grasped in the hand.* [30] *Now you:*

Corpse of wickedness, prince of Israel.
whose day has come
at the time of the concluding sin.

[31] *Thus says my Lord HASHEM/ELOHIM:*

of the Babylonian king (*Targum*, quoted in *Rashi*).

[In verse 29, we translated the similar word לְהִתָּפֵשׂ as *to be conquered*. The connotation of both words is essentially the same.]

Our verse reinforces what was taught in the previous one. Their present attitudes could only serve to recall their past transgressions, the broken oath of Zidkiyahu (*Radak*) and the murder of Zechariah at the hands of Yehoash's servants (*Midrash*).

30-32. In these verses the prophet castigates Zidkiyahu unmercifully for his failure as king. The Davidic crown has finally been lost and rulership is to pass to Nebuchadnezzar (*Rashi; Radak*) not to be restored to David's descendants until Messianic times (*Metzudos*).

30. חֲלַל רָשָׁע — *Corpse of wickedness.*

You, Zidkiyahu, prince of Israel, deserve to be killed because of your wickedness (*Rashi*, based on *Targum*).

In this interpretation, Zidkiyahu is referred to as חָלָל, *a corpse*, because he is destined to die (עַל שֵׁם סוֹפוֹ) as in 18:32 (see *Radak* there).

However, the Sages (*Berachos* 18b) read the verse as describing Zidkiyahu's present state. He is in the category of רְשָׁעִים בְּחַיֵּיהֶן קְרוּיִין מֵתִים, *the wicked are considered dead even during their lifetime.*

How can such a description be used for Zidkiyahu, who, in *Sanhedrin* 103a is described as צַדִּיק גָּמוּר, *a completely righteous man*, whose merit saved his whole generation? The description in our verse must apply to him not as an individual but as the king (this is evidenced by the context; see below), and in that capacity he was indeed wicked and a failure. (See Overview VIII and Appendix I, *Why the Double Identity.*)[1]

Radak and *Metzudos* suggest that חָלָל may derive from the root meaning *to profane*. The meaning of our phrase would then be: *You wicked one who are profaned* [from any pretense to holiness].

אֲשֶׁר־בָּא יוֹמוֹ — *Whose day has come.*

The day has come to remove the kingship from him (*Radak*). בָּא could also be understood in the sense of the setting sun. His day (or sun) has set (*Metzudos*).

עֲוֹן קֵץ — *The climactic sin.*

This sin is the one which fills the measure [for which he will finally be punished] (*Rashi; Metzudos*).

Radak translates: *the sin which will bring about the king's end.*

1. Although Zidkiyahu is being castigated as the king rather than as an individual, the description still seems extremely harsh. Did he really deserve to be called a *corpse* in his lifetime? Were there no redeeming features?

Perhaps the explanation can be found in a dictum which the Sages taught concerning

כא יְהוִה הָסִיר֙ הַמִּצְנֶ֔פֶת וְהָרֵ֖ים הָֽעֲטָרָ֑ה
לב זֹ֣את לֹא־זֹ֔את הַשָּׁפָ֣לָה הַגְבֵּ֔הַ וְהַגָּבֹ֖הַ
לב הַשְׁפִּֽיל׃ עַוָּ֥ה עַוָּ֛ה עַוָּ֖ה אֲשִׂימֶ֑נָּה גַּם־
זֹאת֙ לֹ֣א הָיָ֔ה עַד־בֹּ֞א אֲשֶׁר־ל֧וֹ הַמִּשְׁפָּ֛ט

31-32. In these verses God pours out the full force of His fury against the king.

All the phrases in these verses are obscure and many different interpretations are offered. In order to maintain the integrity of the various interpretations, we shall take the verses as a whole instead of treating them phrase by phrase.

It should be noted that a complicating factor is the difficulty which surrounds the word מִצְנֶפֶת, *turban*. In the Torah this term is used exclusively for the headgear of the כֹּהֵן גָּדוֹל, *High Priest.* Nevertheless some commentators *(Radak; Metzudos; Ramban, Exodus* 28:2) feel that in our verse it is used with the king in mind and is to be understood as a synonym for עֲטָרָה, *crown.* In this case, the whole phrase: הָסִיר הַמִּצְנֶפֶת וְהָרִים הָעֲטָרָה, *Remove the turban! take off the crown!* is a call to Zidkiyahu to give up his rulership.

However the Sages seem to take the phrase הָסִיר הַמִּצְנֶפֶת as referring to the high priest's turban. If this is so, there could be two different relationships between the phrases הָסִיר הַמִּצְנֶפֶת and הָרִים הָעֲטָרָה.

Both relationships are considered in the Talmud (*Gittin* 7a) and a true understanding requires a short glance at the relevant passage.

Along with many other things which the Sages enjoined זֵכֶר לְחוּרְבָּן, *in memory of the destruction of the Temple* (see *Orach Chayim* 560), they forbade bridegrooms to wear the crowns which it had been customary to put on at weddings. At issue in the Talmud (ibid.) is the source of this prohibition. Rav Chisda thinks that it derives from our verse. הָרִים הָעֲטָרָה, *take off the crown,* because הָסִיר הַמִּצְנֶפֶת, *the turban had been removed* from the High Priest; [i.e., the relationship between the two phrases is causal. Since the Temple is no more, the wearing of a crown is offensive.] Rav Huna, on the other hand, holds that the prohibition against the bridegroom's crown was not based on any verse in Scripture. The Sages had forbidden it without scriptural sanction. Our verse is simply a call to both High Priest and king to divest themselves of the symbols of their authority; [i.e., the relationship is *not* causal. Although Rav Huna agrees with Rav Chisda that מִצְנֶפֶת refers to the *Kohen Gadol's* turban, he holds that this injunction

Joseph. R' Yehudah said in Rav's name: Why was Joseph called *bones* during his own lifetime? [In *Genesis* 50:25 Joseph asked his brother to carry his *bones* out of Egypt when God would redeem them from there], because he did not protest for his father's honor. His brothers repeatedly referred to their father as *your servant our father,* yet he said nothing to them (*Sotah* 13b). *Maharal* (there) explains: to have his father called *your servant* to his face, repeatedly, should have galvanized him to some sort of action. If Joseph could listen to these words with equanimity, he was really *bones.* Some of a living person's sensitivity seems to have been missing in him.

Zidkiyahu's failure as king, and his description in Scripture as רָשָׁע, *an evil person,* came about because he did not rebuke his people for their sins (*Sanhedrin* 103a; see Overview VIII). He was 'dead' to the implications of their actions. He should have been shocked into the realization that it was in his hands to save or lose the future. He kept silent and all was lost. He was a *corpse* even though he was alive.

Our explanation is borne out by *Midrash Tanchuma, Zos HaBerachah* 7, which explains why the wicked are considered dead in their own lifetime: For he sees the sun shining and does not bless God for it. He sees it setting and does not make the blessing. He eats and drinks and does not bless.

The Sages are evidently pointing out that the death ascribed to the living רָשָׁע means an insensitivity to the impression which would normally evoke a response.

21
32

Remove the turban!
Lift off the crown!
Neither this nor that —
exalt the degraded
and degrade the exalted.
32 *Desolate, desolate, desolate*
will I make it.
This too shall not be
until the advent of the master of justice —

is entirely unrelated to the command that the king remove his crown.

Rambam (Hilchos Ta'anis 5:15) and *Shulchan Aruch, (Orach Chayim* 560) reflect Rav Chisda's opinion.

We shall consider the meaning of our verses according to both opinions.

31. *Rashi* (in accordance with *Targum*) translates as follows: הָסִיר הַמִּצְנֶפֶת וְהָרִים הָעֲטָרָה, *I shall tear off the turban* [of Serayah the High Priest] *and annul the crown* [from Zidkiyahu's head]. [The phrases are taken in Rav Huna's sense.] זֹאת לֹא זֹאת, *Neither of them* [will remain in the land]. הַשָּׁפָלָה הַגְבֵּהַ, *the lowly are to be lifted* [Gedalyah ben Achikam who is now lowly will become Governor of Judah], וְהַגָּבֹהַ הַשְׁפִּיל, *and the high one will be degraded* [Zidkiyahu who is now the rightful king will lose his position].

32. עַוָּה עַוָּה עַוָּה אֲשִׂימֶנָּה, *Desolate, desolate, desolate will I make it.*

[Kingship had been taken from Yechonyah (Yehoyachin) and given to Zidkiyahu, then it was taken from Zidkiyahu and given to Gedalyah ben Achikom (these are two of the three desolations)] גַּם זֹאת לֹא הָיָה, *but that also will not last* [Gedalyah's rulership will also be of short duration] עַד בֹּא אֲשֶׁר לוֹ הַמִּשְׁפָּט, *until he who will administer justice will come* [for Gedalyah will be assassinated by Ishmael ben Nesanyah (this is the third desolation)], וּנְתַתִּיו, *and I shall put him* [Gedalyah into his (Ishmael's) hand].

Radak and *Metzudos* agree that מִצְנֶפֶת is not the turban of the High Priest, but a synonym for עֲטָרָה, *the crown.* The first two phrases announce that Zidkiyahu is to lose his kingdom. [The relationship of the two phrases is in accord with the opinion of Rav Hunah.] In the interpretations of the rest of the verses they differ slightly:

Radak: זֹאת לֹא זֹאת, *This* [crown] *will not* [as Zidkiyahu thinks] *be like this* [i.e., his (Zidkiyahu's) permanently]. [But] הַשָּׁפָלָה הַגְבֵּהַ, [Yehoyachin who is presently in exile and is therefore] *the low one, will be exalted* [since his descendant Zerubavel was destined to lead the return to Zion]. וְהַגָּבֹהַ הַשְׁפִּיל, *And* [*Zidkiyahu who is now*] *the elevated person will be thrown down.* עַוָּה עַוָּה עַוָּה אֲשִׂימֶנָּה, [This crown] *I will bend out of shape* [for three generations. This is indicated by the thrice repeated עַוָּה and refers to the three generations which elapsed before Zerubavel returned to Judah] גַּם זֹאת לֹא הָיָה, [But] *this* [bending out of shape] *had not happened before* [because although the individual kings had sinned the crown had never passed from the Davidic line], עַד בֹּא אֲשֶׁר לוֹ הַמִּשְׁפָּט, *until* [Nebuchadnezzar] *whose task it was to administer justice came,* וּנְתַתִּיו, *and I put that* [justice into his hands].

Metzudos: זֹאת, *this* [evil] which is befalling Zidkiyahu, that none of his children were to succeed to his throne] לֹא זֹאת, *is not like* [i.e., it is worse than] *this* [the sorrows which had befallen Yehoyakim and Yehoyachin who had at least been succeeded by close family]. (For the rest of the sentence his

לג וּנְתַתִּיו: וְאַתָּה בֶן־אָדָם
הִנָּבֵא וְאָמַרְתָּ כֹּה אָמַר אֲדֹנָי יֱהֹוִה אֶל־
בְּנֵי עַמּוֹן וְאֶל־חֶרְפָּתָם וְאָמַרְתָּ חֶרֶב
חֶרֶב פְּתוּחָה לְטֶבַח מְרוּטָה לְהָכִיל לְמַעַן
לד בָּרָק: בַּחֲזוֹת לָךְ שָׁוְא בִּקְסָם־לָךְ כָּזָב
לָתֵת אוֹתָךְ אֶל־צַוְּארֵי חַלְלֵי רְשָׁעִים
לה אֲשֶׁר־בָּא יוֹמָם בְּעֵת עֲוֹן קֵץ: הָשֵׁב

interpretation is the same as that of Radak.) עַוָּה עַוָּה עַוָּה אֲשִׂימֶנָּה, *I will twist* [Zidkiyahu's kingship] *out of shape* [none of his descendants will ever rule]. גַּם זֹאת לֹא הָיָה, [But] *also this* [the elevation referred to in the previous verse; that the lowly Yehoyachin would one day shine in Zerubavel's governership] *will not last* [for Zerubavel's rulership will also never be complete] עַד בֹּא אֲשֶׁר לוֹ הַמִּשְׁפָּט, *until* [the messiah] *to whom it rightfully belongs will come.* וּנְתַתִּיו, [and to him] *I shall give it.*

Finally we shall offer *Harav Breuer's* interpretation as an example of how the first two phrases can be interpreted in Rav Chisda's view that they have a causal relationship to one another. הָסִיר הַמִּצְנֶפֶת וְהָרִים הָעֲטָרָה, *Since the High Priest has ceased to function* [i.e., the Temple service has been denuded of any meaning] *royalty must also fall.* זֹאת, *when the one* [the erosion of the Temple service] *has happened* לֹא זֹאת *then the other* [royalty] *cannot exist.* [Israel's kings are to rule over a holy nation who are bearers of God's Glory]. הַשָּׁפָלָה הַגְבֵּהַ וְהַגָּבֹהַ הַשְׁפִּיל, [there has been an absolute upheaval of values] *important issues become secondary, the senseless becomes central.* עַוָּה עַוָּה אֲשִׂימֶנָּה, *I shall destroy it utterly,* גַּם זֹאת לֹא הָיָה, *absolutely nothing may remain,* עַד בֹּא אֲשֶׁר לוֹ הַמִּשְׁפָּט, *until the deserving one* [the Messiah] *comes,* וּנְתַתִּיו, *and to him I shall give it over.*[1]

33-37. The prophet turns to Ammon, which had earned a reprieve when Nebuchadnezzar's divination led him towards Jerusalem (*v.* 24). Chapter 25 depicts the vicious joy which these old and bitter enemies of Israel felt at Jerusalem's downfall. But even before that time, it was they who had encouraged Nebuchadnezzar to overcome his fears (see *comm. v.* 24) and attack the Jews *(Sanhedrin* 96b).

This prophecy assures them that their relief was only temporary. They too would one day day fall to the sword.

[The commentary on this prophecy follows *Radak*, who is closest to the consensus of commentators. For other approaches, see *Rashi's* second interpretation, *Eliezer of Beaugency,* and *Malbim* among others.]

33. אֶל־בְּנֵי עַמּוֹן וְאֶל־חֶרְפָּתָם — *To the children of Ammon and their taunting.*

Chapter 25 describes in detail how the people of Ammon mocked Jerusalem in her travail. *Rashi* here adds that the Ammonites considered their reprieve (see above) as a vindication of their deity. It seemed to them that their god was stronger than Israel's God, since Nebuchadnezzar had chosen to attack Jerusalem rather than Ammon's Rabbah.

1. The Talmud (*Gittin* 7a) offers another explanation for the phrase זֹאת לֹא זֹאת. When God told Israel: *Remove the turban! Take off the crown,* the ministering angels asked God: Master of the World, זֹאת? Should *this* happen to Israel who accepted the Torah unquestioningly at Sinai? So He answered them: לֹא, *No,* זֹאת, *This* is to happen to Israel who *lowered the high and raised the low* and erected an idol in the Temple.

21
33-34

and him I shall emplace.

33 *Now you, Ben Adam, prophesy and say: Thus says my Lord HASHEM/ELOHIM to the children of Ammon and their taunting. And you shall say:*

A sword, an open sword
burnished for slaughter
to encompass and in order to flash.

34 *While vanity is envisioned for you;*
While falsehood is divined for you;
To place you with the necks
of the slain wicked ones
whose day has come
at the time of the climactic sin.

חֶרֶב חֶרֶב פְּתוּחָה *A sword, an open sword.*

[The translation in accordance with *Radak* follows the cantillation, which divides the phrases as follows: חֶרֶב חֶרֶב פְּתוּחָה—לְטֶבַח מְרוּטָה—לְהָכִיל לְמַעַן בָּרָק. The translation would differ slightly (and in some ways would be more logical) according to the division of *Metzudos:* פְּתוּחָה לְטֶבַח—מְרוּטָה לְהָכִיל—לְמַעַן בָּרָק, *open for slaughter, burnished to encompass, in order to flash.*

This call to the sword is almost identical with that which spurred it on against Israel *(v.* 14). However, our verse introduces the idea of the *open* unsheathed sword. In *Radak's* view, this implies that the sword will remain unsheathed even after Nebuchadnezzar will have disappeared from the stage of history. According to 25:4, Ammon would fall to the *children of the East,* rather than to Babylon (but see *comm.* there; *Josephus, Kadmonios* 10:7 reports that Nebuchadnezzar subdued Ammon and Moab). Although the conquerors are different, the sword is the same. It remains unsheathed until God's plan will have been accomplished.

לְהָכִיל לְמַעַן בָּרָק – *To encompass* [*and*] *in order to flash.*

Radak reads this phrase as though it were written (ו)לְמַעַן בָּרָק. The sword was burnished for slaughter (לְטֶבַח מְרוּטָה) so that the slaughter might be all-encompassing. A second purpose was that it might flash like lightning. [*Metzudos'* spacing of the words (see above) would make the injection of the conjunction unnecessary.]

34. בַּחֲזוֹת לָךְ שָׁוְא – *While vanity is envisioned for you.*

This phrase is addressed to Ammon as a nation; hence the feminine form לָךְ. The prophet tells the Ammonites that while their soothsayers were lulling them with *vanity* and *falsehood,* describing to them a future of peace and security, their fate would be quite the opposite ... *(Radak).*

לָתֵת אוֹתָךְ אֶל־צַוְּארֵי חַלְלֵי רְשָׁעִים – *To place you with* [lit. *to*] *the necks of the slain wicked ones.*

By lulling their people into a fake sense of security, the soothsayers had caused the Ammonites to be placed in a position similar to that of the *necks of the slain, wicked* Judeans, who had finally been overtaken by their sins, which had exceeded the limit *(Radak).*

At first glance, it appears that the sword is being addressed. However, it would be awkward for *you* to refer to two different indirect objects in the same sentence. Hence,

כא
לו־לז

אֶל־תַּעְרָהּ בִּמְקוֹם אֲשֶׁר־נִבְרֵאת בְּאֶרֶץ
לו מְכֻרוֹתַיִךְ אֶשְׁפֹּט אֹתָךְ׃ וְשָׁפַכְתִּי עָלַיִךְ
זַעְמִי בְּאֵשׁ עֶבְרָתִי אָפִיחַ עָלָיִךְ וּנְתַתִּיךְ
בְּיַד אֲנָשִׁים בֹּעֲרִים חָרָשֵׁי מַשְׁחִית׃
לז לָאֵשׁ תִּהְיֶה לְאָכְלָה דָּמֵךְ יִהְיֶה בְּתוֹךְ
הָאָרֶץ לֹא תִזָּכֵרִי כִּי אֲנִי יְהוָה
א דִּבַּרְתִּי׃ וַיְהִי דְבַר יְהוָה אֵלַי
ב לֵאמֹר׃ וְאַתָּה בֶן־אָדָם הֲתִשְׁפֹּט הֲתִשְׁפֹּט
אֶת־עִיר הַדָּמִים וְהוֹדַעְתָּהּ אֵת כָּל־

כב
א־ב

most commentators learn that the whole sentence is addressed to Ammon.

עֲוֹן קֵץ — *The concluding sin.*
See *comm. v.* 30.

35. הָשֵׁב אֶל־תַּעְרָהּ — *Returned to its scabbard?*

Do you really think that the sword is about to be returned to its scabbard? *(Radak; Metzudos).*

[In a context in which the sword was described as open and burnished for slaughter, it is incongruous to take this phrase as a definite statement. The awkwardness might perhaps be avoided according to *Radak* in *v.* 33. If indeed it would not be Babylon but the Children of the East before whom Ammon would fall, then the verse might be saying: Even though the Babylonian sword will be sheathed, a sword will nevertheless overtake you eventually.]

Eliezer of Beaugency considers our verse a continuation of verse 33. The sword will be returned to its scabbard with its sharpness unimpaired. Ordinarily, so much killing would have blunted the blade; but this sword will be so sharp that nothing will dull it.

בִּמְקוֹם אֲשֶׁר־נִבְרֵאת בְּאֶרֶץ מְכֻרוֹתַיִךְ — *In the place where you originated* [lit. *were created*], *in the land of your dwelling.*

The Ammonites were so sure that they would be safe that they did not take the precaution of fleeing to another place. Nebuchadnezzar's sword would overtake them on their home ground *(Radak).*

אֶרֶץ מְכֻרוֹתַיִךְ — *The land of your dwelling.*
See 16:13.

אֶשְׁפֹּט אֹתָךְ — *I shall punish you.*
See *comm.* 11:10.

36. אָפִיחַ — *I shall blow.*

In my anger, I will blow upon the flames to make them more intense *(Rashi, Metzudos).*

אֲנָשִׁים בֹּעֲרִים — *Brutish men.*

Radak comments that the word בֹּעֲרִים derives from the root בער, which can mean either *to be foolish* or *brutish,* or *to burn.* Thus אֲנָשִׁים בֹּעֲרִים means either *brutish men* or *men who are burned.*

[The choice of the term בֹּעֲרִים fits well with the beginning of the verse: *with the fire of my fury.*] It is possible that a play on words is intended and that both meanings are implied *(R' Breuer).*

חָרָשֵׁי מַשְׁחִית — *Artisans of destruction.*

חָרָשׁ is often used in Scripture as an *artisan* (see *Exodus* 35:35); hence, *a skilled person.*

37. דָּמֵךְ יִהְיֶה בְּתוֹךְ הָאָרֶץ לֹא תִזָּכֵרִי — *Your blood shall sink into the ground. You shall be unremembered.*

When Scripture calls for vengeance for blood that was shed unjustly, the expression is: *Ground! do not cover my blood (Job* 16:18). Here the earth will swallow the blood, and no one will

21
35-37
[35] *Returned to its scabbard?*
In the place where you originated,
in the land of your dwelling,
I shall punish you!
[36] *And I shall pour My anger*
upon you.
With the fire of My fury
I shall blow upon you;
I shall place you in the hand
of brutish men,
artisans of destruction.
[37] *For the fire you shall be fuel;*
Your blood shall sink into the ground;
You shall be unremembered.
For I HASHEM have spoken.

22
1-2
The word of HASHEM came to me saying: [2] *Now*
you Ben Adam, will you rebuke, will you rebuke
the city of bloodshed and let her know all her

remember to avenge the Ammonites' death *(Radak).*

The implication is that Ammon will be completely wiped out and no trace will remain. Yet, even this utter desolation will not remain without its ray of hope. See *comm.* 25:7 *(R' Breuer).*

XXII

The bitter denunciation of Jerusalem in this chapter is unparalleled in Scripture. Many are the passages in Tanach which describe Jerusalem's degradation and bemoan its deafness to the call for greatness, but none approach the severity and unsparing explications which Yechezkel poured out upon it.

The greatest falls occur from the greatest heights. Throughout the Book we have learned how Israel, when it loses touch with its soul, sinks to depths undreamed of by the gentile nations (see 3:6-7; 16:33-34; fn. 20:23). The same is true of Jerusalem — particularly, the Jerusalem of Yechezkel's vision.

The heights to which Jerusalem can aspire are evident in the names by which the prophets called the Jerusalem of the future, such names as City of Righteousness, Faithful City, City of HASHEM and others (see: Isaiah *1:26; 60:14; 62:24;* Jeremiah *3:17; 33:16;* Zecharyah *8:3). None of these compare with the grandeur of Yechezkel's vision. As the climax of the picture which he paints of a rebuilt and regenerated Jerusalem, indeed as the apex of his entire prophecy, he calls Jerusalem* ה׳ שָׁמָּה, HASHEM is There *(48:35). The Sages teach (*Bava Basrah *75b): Do not read* ה׳ שָׁמָּה, HASHEM Is There, but ה׳ שְׁמָהּ, HASHEM Is its Name. *Its name — its essential being — will be identified with HASHEM. Not the city which God loves,*

ג תּוֹעֲבוֹתֶיהָ: וְאָמַרְתָּ כֹּה אָמַר אֲדֹנָי יֱהֹוִה
עִיר שֹׁפֶכֶת דָּם בְּתוֹכָהּ לָבוֹא עִתָּהּ

seeks, or blesses, but the one with which HASHEM's Shechinah is fused in complete unison. It will be at one with the Divine.

This affinity to Godliness is ground and justification for its existence. It is located upon earth, but is not of the earth. It is within the human sphere only for the purpose that through its portals man may enter the יְרוּשָׁלַיִם שֶׁל מַעְלָה (Ta'anis *5a), the Celestial Jerusalem, the city of God's aspirations (*Ta'anis *5a) to which the earthly Jerusalem is as a body to a soul (see* Overview *V).*

The יֵצֶר הָרַע, inclination to evil, *invariably focuses on that which is best and purest. It ignores the gentile nations and concentrates only on Israel, most of all the Sages of Israel. The greater the man, the greater is his evil inclination (*Succah *52a; see* Maharal, Tiferes Yisrael *48;* Nesivos Olam, Nesiv Ko'ach Hayetzer *2). By controlling the evil inclination, its intended victim can spur himself to even greater heights; but if he permits himself to succumb to its blandishments, he is denuded of his soul (*Bava Basrah *16a).*

Jerusalem had succumbed. Body and soul had been torn asunder. Bereft of its essence, Jerusalem crashed to the lowest depths (see Pref. *ch. 15). Yechezkel, who was granted the exalted vision of its potential, had to mourn its fall.*

*There is no middle ground for Jerusalem. If it does not reach the apex of its potential, it sinks far below the norm of other cities. This is true of the people of Israel as well (*Pref. *ch. 15).*

*The laws of the Torah are Israel's wisdom in the eyes of the nations (*Deut. *4:6-9). Through these laws, Israel is considered wise in the eyes of the nations; but (*v. *9) if the people distort the laws through forgetfulness, they will be considered fools* (Rashi).

*The wisest or the most foolish! There is no middle ground. Man, endowed with intellect, is the noblest of God's creatures. The human infant, with its undeveloped intellectual ability, is less capable of fending for itself than any animal young. Israel, impregnated by the Torah's holiness, is the crown of mankind. Denuded of holiness, the people of Israel become the dregs of human society (*R' Yerucham Levovitz, *ch. 56,* Daas Chochmah Umussar v. *2).*

Ramban, *describing his visit to* Eretz Yisrael, *wrote* (Letter to his son Nachman): *'What shall I tell you concerning the Land! Its forsakeness is great; its desolation terrible. The rule is whichever is holier is more desolate: Jerusalem worst of all, Judah more than Galilee. However, in spite of the destruction, it is exceedingly good ... '*

2. הֲתִשְׁפֹּט — *Will you rebuke.*

Our translation follows *Rashi* as explained in the *commentary* to 20:4.

R' Breuer suggests a different translation for הֲתִשְׁפֹּט.

The root שפט can also mean *to take someone's part, to ensure that he gets his due* [e.g., שִׁפְטוּ יָתוֹם, *protect the orphan's legal rights (Isaiah* 1:17)]. It is Israel's right to be stopped short on its headlong rush to catastrophe. If Yechezkel truly loves his people, he will shoulder the difficult and thankless task (conveyed by the double הֲתִשְׁפֹּט) of helping them to remake their lives. This can only be done by confronting them with the full horror of their ways. Accordingly, הֲתִשְׁפֹּט would be rendered *will you not take their part.*

The shattering visions of the previous chapter which described Nebuchadnezzar's merciless sword decimating Jerusalem's inhabitants would surely have awakened God's mercy rather than His anger. The suffering of His people inspires God's compassion. (See *Isaiah* 63:9.)

עִיר הַדָּמִים — *This city of bloodshed.*

22 *abominations?* [3] *And say: Thus says my Lord*
3 *HASHEM/ELOHIM: O city, shedding blood in her*
midst to hasten her time, and which fashioned filth

This uncompromisingly harsh expression had been used by *Nahum* (3:1) to describe Nineveh, the capital of Assyria, the arch enemy who had exiled the northern kingdom. Used here, it awakens that association. Jerusalem had sunk to the moral level of Nineveh.

Could murder have been rampant in Jerusalem? One recalls the story (*Nedarim* 22a) that as Ullah was traveling to *Eretz Yisrael* from Babylon, two of his companions had a quarrel and one of them killed the other. Rabbi Yochanan refused to believe that such a thing could have happened within *Eretz Yisrael.* Ullah assured him that at that moment they had not yet crossed the boundary. The murder had taken place outside the holy borders.

The Sages believed that the holiness of the Land would help a person to control his rage. It is inconceivable that murder could happen in *Eretz Yisrael.*

The possibility, of course, exists that the matter is relative. In Rabbi Yochanan's time, the tangible presence of the *Shechinah* was more evident than in the terrible years preceding the destruction of the first Temple (see *Michtav MeEliyahu,* vol. 3 p. 195).

Another view is that the bloodshed referred to throughout the chapter does not mean actual murder. *Isaiah* 1:15 and 21 also uses terms such as דָּמִים, *blood,* and רְצִיחָה, *murder,* in connection with Jerusalem, but it is evident from the context that these terms refer to the distortions of justice within the city. Where princes and judges are corrupt and view their positions as means for eliciting bribes and gifts from the populace (*Isaiah* 1:23), the suffering borne by the people is described as bloodshed in the kind of hyperbole permissible in prophecy (see *pref.,* ch. 16). This is the nature of the bloodshed mentioned in our chapter *(R' Breuer).*

Psalms 106:38 hints at another possible solution: *They shed innocent blood, the blood of their sons and daughters whom they slaughtered before Canaan's gods. Then the earth was made false through the blood.*[1] The bloodshed is not murder through quarrels or for gain, but the slaughter of children for idol worship.

3. בְּתוֹכָהּ — *In her midst.*

Blood is shed openly within the city; people do not bother to hide their crimes. In addition, the city is polluted by the blood shed within it (see *II Kings* 21:16) *(Radak).*

לָבוֹא עִתָּהּ — *To hasten her time.*

This phrase is a continuation of כֹּה אָמַר אֲדֹנָי ה׳, *Thus says my Lord HASHEM/ELOHIM.* God has decreed that Jerusalem's time has come because

1. We have translated וַתֶּחֱנַף הָאָרֶץ, *then the earth was made false (Psalms* 106:38) in contrast to *Targum* and *Metzudos* who translate: *then the earth was made guilty,* in accordance with *Ramban* to *Numbers* 35:33, where the same expression is used to describe what happens when murder is committed in the Land of Israel. *Ramban* explains that חֲנוּפָה describes any act that deceives the eye, hiding the true nature of what is taking place. According to *Ramban,* reference is to the curses in *Deuteronomy* 28:38-42, in which the land produces fruits which the people will not be permitted to enjoy. Thus the land will 'deceive' the people as a result of the cardinal sins: idol worship, adultery, and murder.

Why is חֲנוּפַת הָאָרֶץ, *the falseness of the land,* an apt punishment for murder?

Maharal (Drush al haTorah) asks why murder is referred to as שְׁפִיכַת דָּמִים, *bloodshed,* in view of the many ways of killing a person without touching his blood. He answers that in accordance with Scriptural usage which equates דָּם, *blood,* with נֶפֶשׁ, *soul,* (cf. *Leviticus* 17:11), *bloodshed* means not killing, but *separating* body and soul. *R' Hutner* uses this insight of the *Maharal* to explain why the term *bloodshed* is never used for the killing of an animal (*Pachad Yitzchak, Shavuos* 8:15).

The sin is accurately reflected in a situation in which the land produces its fruits but does

ד וְעָשְׂתָה גִלּוּלִים עָלֶיהָ לְטָמְאָה: בְּדָמֵךְ
אֲשֶׁר־שָׁפַכְתְּ אָשַׁמְתְּ וּבְגִלּוּלַיִךְ אֲשֶׁר־
עָשִׂית טָמֵאת וַתַּקְרִיבִי יָמַיִךְ וַתָּבוֹא
עַד־שְׁנוֹתָיִךְ עַל־כֵּן נְתַתִּיךְ חֶרְפָּה
ה לַגּוֹיִם וְקַלָּסָה לְכָל־הָאֲרָצוֹת: הַקְּרֹבוֹת
וְהָרְחֹקוֹת מִמֵּךְ יִתְקַלְּסוּ־בָךְ טְמֵאַת
ו הַשֵּׁם רַבַּת הַמְּהוּמָה: הִנֵּה נְשִׂיאֵי

of the blatant bloodshed within the city *(Rashi).*

וְעָשְׂתָה גִלּוּלִים — *And* [*which*] *fashioned filth* [lit. *made excretions*].

Throughout the book, Yechezkel has used the term גִלּוּלִים, to denote idols (see commentary to 20:7). But in this verse, *Metzudos* translates גִלּוּלִים, *disgusting activities, without reference to idol* worship. Perhaps he did so because of the combination of the verb עשה with גִלּוּלִים, which is unique to this verse and the next. עשה, *to do,* is not an apt term for idol worship.

[Although the verb also occurs with the meaning *to make* (as in *Exodus* 25:8) the context makes it unlikely that the prophet is bemoaning the *manufacture* of idols. Even *Targum,* who does interpret גִלּוּלִים in its usual sense of idols, translates: *Who serve idols within it* rather than *Who make idols.*]

Targum and *Radak* translate the phrase as a description of idol worship.

The combination of murder and idol worship in the same verse is significant. Idolatry can flourish only in a culture in which the worth of the individual person is degraded (see fn, 8:12). Where self-worth is eroded because of the pernicious doctrines of the supremacy of the natural forces, a person is unable to perceive the צֶלֶם אֱלֹהִים, *the Divine image,* of his fellow man. Murder is not far behind. (Based on *R' Breuer.* See further below).

וְעָשְׂתָה גִלּוּלִים — *And* [*which*] *fashioned filth.*

The phrase assumes an injected 'which' *(Rashi).*

עָלֶיהָ — *Within herself.*

The translation follows *Targum.* The use of עַל, *on,* to mean *within* is unusual.

לְטָמְאָה — *For contamination.*

[From *Numbers* 35:33 we learn that murder 'defiles the land. *Ramban* (see *fn. v.* 2) identifies this defilement with סלוק הַשְּׁכִינָה, *the departure of the Divine Presence,* which results from the shedding of blood. This is the contamination meant here.]

Radak explains the טֻמְאָה, *contamination,* of our phrase as a טֻמְאַת הַנֶּפֶשׁ, *contamination of the soul,* rather than of the land.

The sins mentioned in our chapter parallel those mentioned in the Sidrah *Kedoshim (Lev.* ch. 19 and 20) as being the antitheses of קְדוּשָׁה, *holiness. Radak* notes that the prohibition against idol worship (*Lev.* 19:4) follows almost

not deliver them. The land grants its bounty to its inhabitants as reward for their Divine service (see *Deut.* 11:13-17; *Rambam, Hilchos Teshuvah* 9:1). Through bloodshed, the land loses its 'soul' — the *Shechinah* [*Divine Presence*] departs (see *Ramban, Numbers* 35:33). Then the land no longer yields its gifts to its people. If it simply stopped producing fruit, no lesson would be taught. Barrenness can have physical causes. However, when the land is healthy and produces crops, but withholds them from its people, it is clear that the Divine Presence has departed. While physical functions remain unimpaired, meaningful life has fled.

The term עִיר הַדָּמִים, *city of bloodshed,* takes on new dimensions in light of the *Maharal's* definition of bloodshed. עִיר הַדָּמִים is *the city from which the soul is banished.*

22
4-6

within herself for contamination. 4 *Through your*
blood which you shed you became guilty and
through your filth which you fashioned you became
contaminated. Thus you brought your days near and
reached the limit of your years. Therefore, have I
made you a mockery to the nations, and a conversa-
tion piece for all the lands. 5 *Those who are near and*
those who are far from you will mock you: Con-
taminated of name! Great of confusion! 6 *Behold the*

immediately upon the exhortation to be holy [*Leviticus* 19:2], implying that the sin of idolatry defiles the soul, which we are obliged to hallow.

4. וַתַּקְרִיבִי יָמַיִךְ וַתָּבוֹא עַד־שְׁנוֹתָיִךְ — *Thus you brought your days near and reached the limit of your years* [lit. *and you came until your years*].

Jerusalem has brought about its own end. This point is repeated in different words for the sake of emphasis *(Radak; Metzudos). Rashi* adds that *your years* hints at the period of 852 or 850 years which are derived from the word וְנוֹשַׁנְתֶּם *(Deut.* 4:25) as the time which Israel would occupy the land before the exile (See *comm., fn.* 7:12).

In accordance with his conviction that Scripture does not contain repetition merely for the sake of emphasis, *Malbim* offers the following interpretation.

The two words: אָשַׁמְתְּ, *became guilty,* and טָמֵאת, *became contaminated,* in the first part of the sentence describe two aspects of every transgression against God's will. In addition to the sin itself (אָשַׁמְתְּ), there is also the residue of impurity which defiles the sinner. The latter remains even if the act of transgression has been atoned (see *Shaarei Teshuvah* of *Rabbeinu Yonah, Shaar* 1:9).

Malbim further demonstrates that יָמִים, *days,* usually means a continuum of time and denotes a pleasant period, while שָׁנִים, *years (*from שנה, *to change)* refers to the changing life cycles which are rung in by the new years, often bringing trouble and sorrow in their wake.

In his view the meaning of the phrase is as follows: The end of *your* pleasant *days is coming close* — the punishment for your sins is about to overtake you. After that, *you will come to the years of changing life cycles* which will bring suffering upon you because of the residual uncleanliness which will not be removed by the initial punishment for the sin.

חֶרְפָּה ... קַלָּסָה — *A mockery ... a conversation piece.*

Although קלס and חרף are used in the identical way here, we have chosen to translate קַלָּסָה as *conversation piece* in accordance with *Rashi (Sotah* 27a), who writes that its real meaning is שְׂפַת יֶתֶר, *extravagant talk,* which is why it is used both as mockery and as praise. (See *comm.* 16:31.)

נְתַתִּיךְ חֶרְפָּה ... וְקַלָּסָה — *Have I made you a mockery ... and a conversation piece.*

The nations mock you and talk about you freely. They do not fear you because נְתַתִּיךְ, *I have placed you;* I have allowed them to rule over you. This is in contrast to the position which Israel should ideally occupy among the nations (*Deut.* 28:10): *All the nations of the earth will see that the Name of HASHEM is upon you and they will fear you (Radak).*

5. טְמֵאַת הַשֵּׁם — *Contaminated of name.*

You were once called עַם קָדוֹשׁ, *a holy*

יִשְׂרָאֵל אִישׁ לִזְרֹעוֹ הָיוּ בָךְ לְמַעַן
ז שְׁפָךְ־דָּם: אָב וָאֵם הֵקַלּוּ בָךְ לַגֵּר עָשׂוּ
בַעֹשֶׁק בְּתוֹכֵךְ יָתוֹם וְאַלְמָנָה הוֹנוּ בָךְ:
ח־ט קָדָשַׁי בָּזִית וְאֶת־שַׁבְּתֹתַי חִלָּלְתְּ: אַנְשֵׁי

nation (Deut. 14:2). This name has been defiled. Now people call you עַם טְמֵא שְׂפָתַיִם, *a people with contaminated lips (Isaiah* 6:5; *Rashi).*

רַבַּת הַמְּהוּמָה — *Great of confusion.*

You are subject to tremendous upheavals caused by famine, sword, and plague *(Radak). Metzudos* renders: *The cries* [of the oppressed] *create a din* (see 7:7).

6. נְשִׂיאֵי יִשְׂרָאֵל אִישׁ לִזְרֹעוֹ — *The princes of Israel, every man for his own power.*

The picture of Israel's princes forgetting their duty towards the people in the mindless pursuit of their own gain, is particularly poignant when we consider the etymology of the word נָשִׂיא.

It connotes נָשִׂיא *that which is exalted* (from נשא) and therefore denotes a *prince* exalted above his people, or a *cloud* high above the earth (as in *Jeremiah* 10:13, 51:16; *Psalms* 135:7; *Proverbs* 25:14).

Hirsch explains that the identity of terms is no coincidence. The cloud draws its sustenance from below as the earth's water rises, but subsequently returns that water to the earth in the form of blessed rain. This is the Torah's perception of a prince. He should be exalted by the people, but only so that he may return the wealth and power which he gets from them by ruling justly and caring for the needs and aspirations of his subjects (see *Rambam, Hilchos Melachim* 2:6).

A *nassi* who pursues only his own interests and drains the strength of his people without returning it to them makes a mockery of his title.

The transgressions of Jerusalem's inhabitants are specified in the following verses. Not the heinousness of the sins torments the prophet, but that they were committed in Jerusalem. Over and over the prophet laments, *within you,* the Holy City, were these abominations perpetrated!

Rashi points out that almost all the sins listed are found in the *Sidrah Kedoshim (Lev.* 19, 20). (The *comm.* traces each sin to its source in the Torah.) *Leviticus* 19:2 is a call to Israel to express its innate Godliness in a sanctity which is akin to God's holiness: *Be holy; for holy am I, HASHEM, your God.* This is followed by prohibitions which by their nature are inimical to that sanctity. By transgressing those very commands, Jerusalem's people were flouting the call to greatness. They rejected holiness at the very source from which it is to emanate to the world — in Jerusalem, from which the word of God is to go forth (*Isaiah* 2:3).

7. אָב וָאֵם הֵקַלּוּ בָךְ — *Father and mother have they slighted within you.*

The honoring of father and mother is so central to the concept of holiness that the command to fear them follows immediately upon the commandment that Israel is to be holy (Lev. 19:2-3).

The first indictment hurled against Jerusalem is that parents were slighted there. Having lost their self-image as Adam, they could no longer be host to the *Shechinah.*[1]

לַגֵּר עָשׂוּ בַעֹשֶׁק בְּתוֹכֵךְ — *Toward the stranger they acted oppressively in your midst.*

Leviticus 19:33 prohibits oppression of the stranger. The severity of the sin

1. Man can rise above the pettiness of every day existence and achieve the purity inherent in his essential Godliness only if he recognizes that he is a unique being, created and shaped lovingly by the triad of God, father, and mother (*Kiddushin* 30b). His individuality cannot be

22
7-8

*princes of Israel, every man for his own power were
they within you, for the sake of bloodshed. 7 Father
and mother have they slighted within you; toward
the stranger they acted oppressively in your midst;
orphan and widow they wronged within you. 8 My
sanctities you spurned, My Sabbaths you desecrated.*

of oppressing the stranger can be gauged by noting that the Torah repeats this prohibition no less than thirty-six times (*Bava Metziah* 59b).

In Jerusalem there is even less excuse than in any other place for mistreating the stranger. The whole of *Eretz Yisrael* is God's land, and its inhabitants merely strangers and sojourners (*Lev.* 25:23). If this is true of those parts of the land which were divided among the tribes, then certainly in Jerusalem, which had not been divided (*Rambam, Hilchos Beis Habechirah* 7:14), all the inhabitants were merely strangers and visitors in God's sanctuary. If they mistreated the real strangers, obviously they considered themselves owners of Jerusalem. They had forgotten Jerusalem's sanctity, and considered her the same as any other city.[1]

יָתוֹם וְאַלְמָנָה הוֹנוּ בָךְ — *Orphan and widow they wronged within you.*

The specific reference to orphan and widow derives from *Exodus* 22:21. However, the types of defenseless people subject to such wrongs are by no means limited to these two. *Leviticus* 19 is replete with exhortations to defend the rights of those who are economically or socially disadvantaged.

God is the *father of the orphans, the defender of the widows (Psalms* 68:6). A society which is insensitive to the sufferings of these unfortunates has rejected God's special charges and, by implication, shown its disdain for His presence in their midst.

8. קָדָשַׁי בָּזִית — *My sanctities you spurned* [lit. *you treated with contempt*].

Leviticus 19:5 teaches that sacrifices are to be brought לִרְצוֹנְכֶם, *to bring about God's good will towards you (Ramban, Lev.* 19:2). You have controverted this exhortation *(Rashi).*

submerged by the myriad of other beings, for just as the universe was created by God, so too is man a product of God and his parents (see *Maharal, Tif. Yis.* 41 on the repeated juxtaposition of the laws of honoring parents with the laws of the Sabbath).

Through this partnership with God (*Kiddushin* 30b), the parents themselves are elevated to the level of creators (*Maharal; Kiddushin* 31b: When Rav Yosef heard his mother approach he would say, 'I will rise before the approaching *Shechinah* [*Divine Presence*]'*)*. Their child is not the result of a chance meeting of two people, of a seed left haphazardly to live or die as the vagaries of nature determine. He is Adam, a footstool for the Divine on earth (see *Overview* IV, *The Implication of Adam)* equipped to sublimate his existence to something akin to the Divine.

When a man is unkind to his parents, God says, 'I have done well not to dwell among them; had I dwelt among them they would have caused Me to suffer also' (*Kiddushin* 31b).

No man who slights his parents can be a bearer of the *Shechinah*. If he does not understand the partnership between them and God, then he cannot see himself as God's creature.

1. There is another way in which the Jerusalemites' insensitivity to the stranger's vulnerability showed that their ties to the Divine had been severed.

In *Shemoneh Esrei,* we pray God to extend His mercy to the צַדִּיקִים, *righteous ones;* חֲסִידִים, *devoted ones;* זְקֵנִים, *elders,* סוֹפְרִים, *scribes,* and גֵּרִים, *strangers.* The inclusion of גרים in the list of Israel's spiritual leaders is unexpected.

Maharal (Gevuros H*ASHEM* 9) explains that in a very real sense the elders of Israel and its spiritual leaders are themselves גֵּרִים, *strangers,* in the physical world in which they function. Their essence is their שֵׂכֶל, *mind,* whose real place is with the spiritual rather than the physical.

כב רָכִיל הָיוּ בָךְ לְמַעַן שְׁפָךְ־דָּם וְאֶל־
י הֶהָרִים אָכְלוּ בָךְ זִמָּה עָשׂוּ בְתוֹכֵךְ:
י עֶרְוַת־אָב גִּלָּה־בָךְ טְמֵאַת הַנִּדָּה עִנּוּ־בָךְ:

Radak writes that contempt was shown by bringing sick or wounded animals for sacrifices (based on *Malachi* 1:6-8; see *Temurah* 7a). There are many other forms of treating קָדָשִׁים, *holy things,* with contempt: covering the hands to avoid touching the blood of the sacrifice (*Kerisus* 28b); delaying the sacrificial services for an animal which is ready (*Zevachim* 90b, *Rashi, Tosaphos);* allowing a sacrifice to lie unskinned (*Shabbos* 16b). Any of these could be meant here.

The classic case of treating holy things with contempt is the account of Eli's sons (*I Samuel* 2:12-18) forcefully taking their parts of the sacrifice before the fats had been offered upon the altar. Because of these misdeeds, terrible punishments were prophesied against Eli's family (*I Samuel* 2:30-36). *Sifri (Numbers* 18:1) combines our verse with that account: We find that the verdict was sealed against Eli only because they treated the sacrifice with contempt; in the same way, the verdict against Jerusalem's inhabitants was sealed for the same reason, as it is written: *You have treated my holy things with contempt.*

When Eli was castigated for his son's transgressions, the prophet told him (*I Samuel* 2:30): *Those that honor Me I will honor, but those that disdain Me shall be shamed.* Contempt for the sacrifices was seen as contempt for Him who had shown that through them He could be approached. If the *Kohanim* grabbed the parts to be eaten before the fats were yielded to the altar, then obviously they did not see themselves as eating from God's table (*Chullin* 120a). They considered their part of the offering as their due, perhaps as payment for their efforts.

Such a distortion of the nature of Divine service could not be tolerated. Eli's family lost its claim to the High Priesthood, and Jerusalem's dwellers lost their Temple. Service in it had lost all meaningful value.

וְאֶת־שַׁבְּתֹתַי חִלָּלְתְּ — *My Sabbaths you desecrated.*

See *comm.* 20:12-13.

Sabbath observance is listed among the laws of holiness in *Lev.* 19:3. As *Exodus* 31:13 teaches, the Sabbath is a *sign* between God and Hs people. Thus, desecration of the Sabbath implied a renunciation of that special bond.

9. אַנְשֵׁי רָכִיל הָיוּ בָךְ — *Talebearers were among you.*

Talebearing is prohibited by *Leviticus* 19:16. For the etymology of רָכִיל, see *Rashi* and *Ramban* there.

Yechezkel lists talebearing among the causes of the *Shechinah's* departure, which precipitated Jerusalem's downfall, because the Sages declare that nothing can tear asunder the fabric of society as effectively as talebearing. To act as host to the *Shechinah,* Israel must be כְּאִישׁ אֶחָד בְּלֵב אֶחָד, *as one man with a single heart (Rashi, Exodus* 19:2). The prevalence of talebearing among them will surely drive away the *Shechinah.*

Ahab's armies were victorious, although they were idolators, while David's forces sometimes suffered defeat, although they were on a high spiritual level. In David's Israel there was strife and discord, while Ahab ruled over a people who lived in peace with one another (*Vayikrah Rabbah* 26:2).

When David saw the discord among

A feeling of being truly at home in the physical world testifies to spiritual bankruptcy. (Cf. *Maharal, Derashah for Shabbos Teshuvah,* that the numerical value of עֵשָׂו, *Esau,* equals שָׁלוֹם, *peace:* Esau is of this world; consequently he is at peace and in harmony with his surroundings.)

9 *Talebearers were among you — for the sake of
bloodshed; upon the mountains they ate among you;
evil plans did they lay in your midst.* 10 *A father's
nakedness he uncovered within you; women in im-*

his people, he asked, 'What is the *Shechinah* doing among us?' (*Vayikrah Rabbah* 26:2).

וְאֶל־הֶהָרִים אָכְלוּ בָךְ — *Upon the mountains they ate among you.*

This refers to idol worship, which was customarily done on mountains and high places (see *comm.* 18:6). It is prohibited by *Leviticus* 19:4.

זִמָּה עָשׂוּ בְתוֹכֵךְ — *Evil plans did they lay in your midst.*

The word זִמָּה from the root זמם, can mean an evil plot (as in *Isaiah* 32:7). It is understood here in this sense by *Targum* and *Rashi*. *Scripture* uses it also to describe the lewdness and forbidden relations between the sexes (as in *Judges* 20:6). This is how *Radak* understands it in our verse. In his view it introduces the next two verses.

If we examine the structure of verses 9-12 we notice that a series of transgressions בֵּין אָדָם לַמָּקוֹם, *between man and God* (e.g., idol worship and incest) are bracketed among the transgressions בֵּין אָדָם לַחֲבֵרוֹ, *between man and man.* To *R' Breuer*, this juxtaposition is intended to stress the point that one's obligations to God and to his fellow man cannot exist independently of each other. A society cannot be viable if it ignores man's spiritual obligations. Mutual respect, the *sine qua non* of a beneficient society, will be eroded unless man views himself and, by extension, his fellow man, as the *Adam-Hadom*, the footstool of the Divine (see *Overview* IV).[1]

10-11 The Torah introduces the prohibitions against forbidden sexual relations with the exhortation not to follow in the ways of Egypt and Canaan (*Lev.* 18:3). The Canaanites had lived in a state of deep moral turpitude. This immorality had finally defiled the land and brought about the expulsion of its populace (*Lev.* 18:25).

The inhabitants of Jerusalem sank to the same level of perversity. They were about to lose the land, as the Torah had predicted. There was nothing to distinguish them from the nations who had been driven out before them. (See *Leviticus* 18:28).

The sordid pictures painted in the following passages do not necessarily reflect the actual conditions. Only a small portion of the people may have committed the sins enumerated in our chapter, but the prophet laments as though there were a universal lapse of values in order to impress his listeners with the gravity of the situation. (See *pref.*, ch. 16, where the use of hyperbole in prophetic discourse is discussed.) Besides, the fact that the majority tolerated the sins of the minority makes them all guilty in the eyes of the prophet (see fn. 3:18; *Appendix* III).

10. עֶרְוַת־אָב גִּלָּה־בָךְ — *A father's nakedness he uncovered within you.*

This refers to adultery committed

1. This idea was expressed by Ben Azai (*Toras Kohanim, Lev.* 19:18). Rabbi Akivah said that *You shall love your neighbor as yourself* is the all encompassing rule of Torah. Ben Azai retorted that *Genesis* 5:1 states an even greater rule, for there it is written that Man was formed in the image of God. (See commentators to *Toras Kohanim.*) The former dictum could have been interpreted simply as a guide to social conduct; the latter places social conduct in the framework of Divine relations.

Harav David Kronglass pointed out that the Mishnah (*Avos* 4:1) *Who is worthy of honor? He who honors others,* bases its lesson on the verse: *For those that honor Me, I will honor* (*I Samuel* 2:30). The Mishnah speaks of honoring man, the verse speaks of honoring God, how can the one be offered as proof of the other? In honoring man we honor God, for it is the Divine essence of man which is the object of our respect.

יא וְאִישׁ | אֶת־אֵשֶׁת רֵעֵהוּ עָשָׂה תּוֹעֵבָה
וְאִישׁ אֶת־כַּלָּתוֹ טִמֵּא בְזִמָּה וְאִישׁ אֶת־
יב אֲחֹתוֹ בַת־אָבִיו עִנָּה־בָךְ: שֹׁחַד לָקְחוּ־בָךְ
לְמַעַן שְׁפָךְ־דָּם נֶשֶׁךְ וְתַרְבִּית לָקַחַתְּ
וַתְּבַצְּעִי רֵעַיִךְ בַּעֹשֶׁק וְאֹתִי שָׁכַחַתְּ נְאֻם
יג אֲדֹנָי יֱהוִה: וְהִנֵּה הִכֵּיתִי כַפִּי אֶל־
בִּצְעֵךְ אֲשֶׁר עָשִׂית וְעַל־דָּמֵךְ אֲשֶׁר הָיוּ
יד בְּתוֹכֵךְ: הֲיַעֲמֹד לִבֵּךְ אִם־תֶּחֱזַקְנָה יָדַיִךְ

with one's father's wife, as *Leviticus* 20:11 teaches: *A man who has lain with his father's wife has uncovered his father's nakedness; both of them shall surely be put to death.*

Although the prophet delivers the rest of the accusations in the plural, the singular is used here (גִּלָּה rather than גִּלּוּ).

Radak thinks that it was used to allude to the specific case of King Ammon who, according to *Sanhedrin* 103b had incestuous relations with his mother. (See footnote to 2:3).

טְמֵאַת הַנִּדָּה עִנּוּ־בָךְ — *Women in impurity* [lit. *contaminated by menstruation*] *they afflicted within you.*

This act is forbidden by *Leviticus* 20:18: *A man who has lain with a women in flow and has uncovered her nakedness ...*

11. וְאִישׁ אֶת־אֵשֶׁת רֵעֵהוּ עָשָׂה תּוֹעֵבָה — *A man against his neighbor's wife would commit abomination.*

Leviticus 20:10 teaches: *A man who has had illicit relations with a married woman ...*

וְאִישׁ אֶת־כַּלָּתוֹ טִמֵּא בְזִמָּה — *And a man would defile his daughter-in-law with lewdness.*

A man who has lain with his daughter-in-law, both of them shall surely be put to death ... (Lev. 20:12).

וְאִישׁ אֶת־אֲחֹתוֹ בַת־אָבִיו עִנָּה־בָךְ — *And a man would afflict his sister — his father's daughter — within you.*

This is based on *Leviticus* 20:17: — *A man who takes his sister, his father's daughter or his mother's daughter, and he sees her nakedness ...*

12. שֹׁחַד לָקְחוּ־בָךְ — *Bribery they took within you.*

This particular formulation comes from *Deuteronomy* (27:25). Sidrah Kedoshim, however, contains a variety of exhortations designed to ensure that justice will not be distorted (e.g., *Lev.* 19:15).

God's rulership over Israel is predicated upon a just and fair society. [Compare the eleventh blessing in *Shemoneh Esrei,* where the prayer for God's Kingship is preceded by the prayer that God restore judges to Israel. *Isaiah* (11:3-5) envisages the Messiah's most exalted task to be the inauguration of an era of absolute justice and fairness. Man can only give God His due when he has learned not to cheat his fellow man. [Cf. *Rashi, Shabbos* 31a: Hillel's dictum *What is hateful to you do not do to others* includes also an admonition against treating God in a manner which one would find hateful if applied against himself.]

Ramban (Deut. 1:17) goes so far as to say that the whole purpose of creation was the establishment of a just society in which no one would be oppressed. Elsewhere, *Ramban* (especially *Exodus* 13:16) states that the purpose of creation is for man to become aware of and praise his Creator. The two statements do not contradict one another. True awareness of God can

purity they afflicted within you. 11 *A man against his*
neighbor's wife would commit abomination; and a
man would defiled his daughter-in-law with
lewdness; and a man would afflict his sister — his
father's daughter — within you. 12 *Bribery they took*
within you, for the sake of bloodshed; interest and
increase have you taken, and enriched your friends
with loot — but Me you have forgotten. The words of
my Lord HASHEM/ELOHIM.

13 *Now behold! I have pounded My hand because*
of your robbery which you committed, and because
of your bloodshed which was in your midst. 14 *Can*
your courage endure or your hands be strong in the

flourish only in a society where justice, consideration, and fairness prevail.

It is for this reason that Jerusalem is above all called the city *filled with justice, where righteousness rests* (*Isaiah* 1:21).

When bribery, with its attendant distortion of justice, becomes rampant in Jerusalem, the city must fall. It can no longer claim to be God's resting place.

נֶשֶׁךְ וְתַרְבִּית לָקַחַתְּ — *Interest and increase have you taken.*

The formulation is taken from *Leviticus* 25:36. The taking of interest and increase (see *Radak* that the terms are interchangeable) runs contrary to the responsibility for the poor (e.g., *Leviticus* 19:10).

וַתְּבַצְּעִי — *And (you have) enriched.*

The princes of Israel used the wealth which they wrung out of the populace to pay neighboring nations such as Egypt and Assyria to be their military allies. In doing this, they forgot that Israel's true protection lies only in God's hands (*Radak; Metzudos*).

13. וְהִנֵּה הִכֵּיתִי כַפִּי אֶל־בִּצְעֵךְ — *Now behold! I have pounded My hand because of your robbery.*

The pounding of God's hand is a reference to 21:22 where God says: *I will also pound My hand upon My hand ....*

We have translated the root בצע as *enrichment* in *v.* 12 and as *robbery* in our verse. The word can have both meanings (as an example of the former see *Exodus* 18:21, *Psalms* 119:36; for the latter see *Jeremiah* 6:13). We have followed the commentators in *v.* 12 and the Sages in our verse.

The Sages remark that Yechezkel enumerated twenty-four sins, and left robbery for last, indicating that it is the worst. Rabbi Shimon ben Abba said in Rabbi Yochanan's name, 'In a bagful of sins, robbery will be the first to accuse' (*Vayikrah Rabbah* 33:6). The same Rabbi Yochanan also said that although the דּוֹר הַמַּבּוּל, *the generation of the Deluge,* violated various prohibitions, its fate was sealed only because of robbery (*Sanhedrin* 108a; *comm.* 7:11; *Meshech Chochmah, Exodus* 15:29; *comm., v.* 9).

In contrast to other sins which do not extend beyond the moment of transgression, robbery is a sin that continues as long as the stolen property remains in the thief's possession. A society which condones robbery is rife with sin (*Chiddushei Aggadah, Sanhedrin*).

14. הֲיַעֲמֹד לִבֵּךְ — *Can your courage*

כב
טו־כ

לַיָּמִים אֲשֶׁר אֲנִי עֹשֶׂה אוֹתָךְ אֲנִי יהוָה
טו דִּבַּרְתִּי וְעָשִׂיתִי׃ וַהֲפִיצוֹתִי אוֹתָךְ בַּגּוֹיִם
וְזֵרִיתִיךְ בָּאֲרָצוֹת וַהֲתִמֹּתִי טֻמְאָתֵךְ
טז מִמֵּךְ׃ וְנִחַלְתְּ בָּךְ לְעֵינֵי גוֹיִם וְיָדַעַתְּ
יז כִּי־אֲנִי יהוָה׃ וַיְהִי דְבַר־יהוָה
יח אֵלַי לֵאמֹר׃ בֶּן־אָדָם הָיוּ־לִי בֵית־יִשְׂרָאֵל
°לְסִיג ק׳ °לסוּג כֻּלָּם נְחֹשֶׁת וּבְדִיל וּבַרְזֶל וְעוֹפֶרֶת
יט בְּתוֹךְ כּוּר סִגִים כֶּסֶף הָיוּ׃ לָכֵן
כֹּה אָמַר אֲדֹנָי יֱהוִה יַעַן הֱיוֹת כֻּלְּכֶם
לְסִגִים לָכֵן הִנְנִי קֹבֵץ אֶתְכֶם אֶל־תּוֹךְ
כ יְרוּשָׁלָםִ׃ קְבֻצַת כֶּסֶף וּנְחֹשֶׁת וּבַרְזֶל

endure? [lit. *Can your heart stand?*].

The heart is described as the seat of courage as *his heart is the lions' heart* (*II Samuel* 17:10).

אִם תֶּחֱזַקְנָה יָדַיִךְ — *Or can your hands be strong?*

[We may conjecture that when Zecharyah used the same term תֶּחֱזַקְנָה יְדֵיכֶם to encourage the returned exiles to build the Second Temple (*Zechariah* 8:9), he had our verse in mind. Israel had indeed been weak in war; but they would be strong in peace as they rebuild the ruins of their past.]

דִּבַּרְתִּי וְעָשִׂיתִי — *I ... have spoken and* [*I have*] *done.*

The past tense is used in place of the future to emphasize the certainty of what was about to happen (see *fn.*, 7:2).

16. וְנִחַלְתְּ בָּךְ — *And you shall* [*be brought to*] *tremble within yourself.*

Three possible roots are offered for this difficult word. *Rashi* derives it from חלחל, *to tremble,* and we have followed his interpretation in the translation.

Metzudos (and one interpretation of *Radak*) derives the word from חלל, *to desecrate. You will be desecrated because of yourself.*

Radak also suggest that the word derives from נחל, *to inherit.* They had been God's inheritance; but they will now become their own, because God has rejected them.

R' Breuer also derives the word from נחל, but in line with his approach to the whole chapter (see *comm. v.* 2), he translates in a positive manner: Because of the cleansing effect of the exile (*v.* 15), *you will control your own destiny.* You will have found yourself once more.

18-22 *Radak* and *Metzudos* read the following verses as one more description of the terrible fate which is to overtake the inhabitants of Jerusalem, while *R' Breuer* reads the passage as a promise of hope and vindication for God's people.

R' Breuer notes in this sequence of verses which uses the parable of silver being purged of its impurities, that there is a progressive increase in the quantity of silver among the impurities. At first Israel seems to contain only dross כֻּלָּם נְחֹשֶׁת וּבְדִיל וּבַרְזֶל וְעוֹפֶרֶת, *all of them are copper, tin, iron and lead* (*v.* 18), with only a hint of the potential silver. There is some silver waiting to be salvaged from among the base metals, but only fierce fires will release it. God exposes the mixture to the merciless heat of the furnace, sure of the presence

22
15-20 *days when I shall deal with you? I, HASHEM, have*
spoken and done. 15 *Then I shall scatter you among*
the nations and disperse you among the lands and
make an end of your contamination from you.
16 *Then you shall be brought to tremble within*
yourself in the sight of the nations — and you shall
know that I am HASHEM.
17 *The word of HASHEM came to me saying:* 18 *Ben*
Adam, the Family of Israel have become dross to Me;
all of them are copper, tin, iron, and lead in the midst
of a furnace. Dross were they which had been silver.
19 *Therefore, so says my Lord HASHEM/ELOHIM:*
Since all of you have turned into dross, therefore see!
I collect you into the midst of Jerusalem, 20 *a collec-*
tion of silver, copper, iron, lead, and tin into the

of silver: קְבֻצַת כֶּסֶף וּנְחֹשֶׁת וּבַרְזֶל וְעֹפֶרֶת וּבְדִיל אֶל־תּוֹךְ כּוּר, *a collection of silver, copper, iron, lead and tin into the midst of a furnace (v.* 20). Then, the sterling essence of Israel (see *comm., fn.,* 3:1) emerges from the holocaust: כְּהִתּוּךְ כֶּסֶף בְּתוֹךְ כּוּר, *like the melting down of silver in the midst of a furnace (v.* 22). The dross has been entirely eliminated.

Israel, seeing itself once more in its pristine purity, realizes that salvation emerged from the suffering imposed by a merciful God, Who, out of love for His people, had exposed them to the cleansing flames: וִידַעְתֶּם כִּי־אֲנִי ה׳ שָׁפַכְתִּי חֲמָתִי עֲלֵיכֶם, *Then you shall know that I, HASHEM, have poured out My fury upon You (v.* 22).

18. הָיוּ־לִי בֵית־יִשְׂרָאֵל לְסִיג — *The family of Israel have become dross to Me.*

When they came out of Egypt they were like silver, but after entering the land — the furnace of their testing — they became debased by acting wickedly *(Metzudos).*

[The word pronounced סִיג is written **סוג**, *to turn away,* implying that Israel became *dross* when they turned away from God *(R' Breuer).* In *comm.* 7:21 the interpretation of קְרִי וּכְתִיב, *differing spelling and pronunciation* is discussed.]

כֻּלָּם נְחֹשֶׁת וּבְדִיל וּבַרְזֶל וְעוֹפֶרֶת — *All of them are copper, tin, iron, and lead.*

The furnace proved them all to be less than silver. Not all of them sank to the lowest depths; there were many different levels among them. Nevertheless, all fell short of the silver which they had once seemed to be. Similarly, Israel, which entered *Eretz Yisrael* on such a high spiritual plateau, fell to much lower levels upon being tested in the crucible of life *(Metzudos).*

סִיגִים כֶּסֶף הָיוּ — *Dross were they which had been silver* [lit., *dross of silver were they*].

The translation follows *Radak* who reads the phrase as though it were written with the addition of a *vav: They are* [*now*] *dross* [*but*] *had once been silver.*

19-20 אֶל־תּוֹךְ יְרוּשָׁלָיִם...אֶל־תּוֹךְ כּוּר — *Into the midst of Jerusalem... into the midst of a furnace.*

Jerusalem is to be the furnace in which the base metals are melted down

וְעוֹפֶרֶת וּבְדִיל אֶל־תּוֹךְ כּוּר לָפַחַת־עָלָיו
אֵשׁ לְהַנְתִּיךְ כֵּן אֶקְבֹּץ בְּאַפִּי וּבַחֲמָתִי
כא וְהִנַּחְתִּי וְהִתַּכְתִּי אֶתְכֶם׃ וְכִנַּסְתִּי אֶתְכֶם
וְנָפַחְתִּי עֲלֵיכֶם בְּאֵשׁ עֶבְרָתִי וְנִתַּכְתֶּם
כב בְּתוֹכָהּ׃ כְּהִתּוּךְ כֶּסֶף בְּתוֹךְ כּוּר כֵּן תֻּתְּכוּ
בְתוֹכָהּ וִידַעְתֶּם כִּי־אֲנִי יהוה שָׁפַכְתִּי
כג חֲמָתִי עֲלֵיכֶם׃ וַיְהִי דְבַר־
כד יהוה אֵלַי לֵאמֹר׃ בֶּן־אָדָם אֱמָר־לָהּ אַתְּ
אֶרֶץ לֹא מְטֹהָרָה הִיא לֹא גֻשְׁמָהּ בְּיוֹם
כה זָעַם׃ קֶשֶׁר נְבִיאֶיהָ בְּתוֹכָהּ כַּאֲרִי שׁוֹאֵג

until they become unrecognizable. Sword, famine, plague, and exile are to be the flames which will leave the people irrevocably changed *(Radak).*

לְהַנְתִּיךְ — *To melt ... down.*

The root is נתך. The initial *nun* of a root is normally dropped in the *Hiphil* (e.g., לְהַפִּיל, *to throw down,* from נפל, rather than לְהַנְפִּיל). While the retention of the *nun* is not unique (e.g., *Judges* 20:31), it is certainly rare, and especially striking in our verse where the regular וְהִתַּכְתִּי also occurs. The *nun* is retained to indicate the full difficulty involved in the purification process *(R' Breuer).*

וְהִנַּחְתִּי וְהִתַּכְתִּי — *And I shall emplace you and melt you down.*

I shall place you into the furnace [city] in order to melt you down [punish you] *(Radak; Metzudos).*

Alternatively, וְהִנַּחְתִּי can be translated, *I will leave you* [*to your fate*] *(Radak).*

21. וְנָפַחְתִּי עֲלֵיכֶם — *And (I shall) blow upon you.*

This verse adds that God will fan the flames of His anger *against you* (עֲלֵיכֶם).

The previous verse speaks of fanning the flames upon the furnace *(Radak).*

According to *Metzudos* the word נָפַחְתִּי, *I shall blow,* indicates that the suffering will continually intensify.

22. כְּהִתּוּךְ כֶּסֶף — *Like the melting down of silver.*

Silver is the most difficult of all the metals to purify. The suffering will last a long time just as the processing of silver takes a long time *(Radak).*

23-31 All the pillars which normally support a viable society have crumbled. Prophets, priests, princes, and finally the whole populace have completely lost their bearings; not a single person remains upon whom God's hopes might be pinned. No option remains but to put an end to this unclean city.

24. אֱמָר־לָהּ — *Say to her.*

To Jerusalem *(Radak).*

אַתְּ אֶרֶץ לֹא מְטֹהָרָה הִיא — *You are a land that has not been cleansed.*

This refers back to the appellation hurled at Jerusalem in verse 5 where she was described *as contaminated of name.* By calling her *a land that has not been cleansed* in our verse, Yechezkel alludes to the earlier description. An alternative meaning is: You have made no effort through repentance to cleanse your defiled name *(Radak).*

לֹא גֻשְׁמָהּ בְּיוֹם זָעַם — *She had not been rained upon on the day of fury.*

Drought is the punishment predicted in *Deuteronomy* (11:17) for not listening to God's command *(Radak).*

22
21-25

midst of a furnace, to blow fire upon it to melt it
down. So I shall collect you in My anger and in My
fury, and I shall emplace you and melt you down. 21 *I*
shall gather you in a blow upon you with the fire of
My wrath, then you shall be melted down within it.
22 *Like the melting down of silver in the midst of a*
furnace so shall you be melted down in her midst.
Then you shall know that I, HASHEM, have poured
out My fury upon you.

23 *The word of HASHEM came to me, saying.* 24 *Ben*
Adam, say to her: You are a land that has not been
cleansed; she had not been rained upon on the day of
fury. 25 *A conspiracy of her prophets is in her midst;*
like a roaring lion tearing prey, souls have they

Rashi (with *Targum*) takes the two phrases together. *You are a land which has not been cleansed by purifying rains.* Rain is a metaphor for the good deeds which might have protected the land from the impending destruction.

The *Talmud* learns from our verse that the Land of Israel was not innundated by the flood in Noah's time. The *day of anger* refers to the day of the Flood (*Zevachim* 113a; also see *Rabbeinu Bachya, Genesis* 8:11 for an explanation of the earlier part of the verse according to this view).

While Aggadic interpretations such as this do not necessarily take the context of the verse into account, and the simple meaning of the entire passage may ignore this reference to the Deluge, *R' Breuer* uses this view of the Sages in his interpretation. The Land of Israel had been spared the cleansing fury of the Deluge. Now it had sunk to a level where it could achieve regeneration only through a deluge of fire (*v.* 31).

25. קֶשֶׁר נְבִיאֶיהָ בְּתוֹכָהּ — *A conspiracy of her prophets is in her midst.*

Jerusalem's false prophets were unanimous in their evil plans *(Rashi)* to lull the people into a sense of security based on the false assumption that Jerusalem could never fall *(Radak).* (See *Overview IX, The False Prophets; comm.* ch. 13.)

R' Breuer finds it difficult to interpret our verse as referring to the false prophets. In the list of Israel's leaders who had failed in their task, the prophets are mentioned in *v.* 28, after priests (*v.* 26) and princes (*v.* 27). Why should they be listed twice?

(*Radak* to *v.* 28 explains that the repetition is for emphasis. Responsibility for the total disintegration of Jerusalem's society rested mainly with the false prophets.)

R' Breuer suggests that our verse refers to Israel's kings. They are described as a *conspiracy of her prophets* because their failure to perform their duties was a direct result of the prophets' conspiracy to prevent Jerusalem from apprehending the seriousness of her situation. The list of leaders castigated in our passage would then be: kings, priests, princes, prophets, and finally the people themselves. This structure is paralleled in *Zephaniah* 3:3-4.

כַּאֲרִי שׁוֹאֵג טֹרֵף טָרֶף נֶפֶשׁ אָכָלוּ — *Like a roaring lion tearing prey, souls have they devoured.*

טֹרֵף טָרֶף נֶפֶשׁ אָכָלוּ חֹסֶן וִיקָר יִקָּחוּ
כו אַלְמְנוֹתֶיהָ הִרְבּוּ בְתוֹכָהּ׃ כֹּהֲנֶיהָ חָמְסוּ
תוֹרָתִי וַיְחַלְּלוּ קָדָשַׁי בֵּין־קֹדֶשׁ לְחֹל לֹא
הִבְדִּילוּ וּבֵין־הַטָּמֵא לְטָהוֹר לֹא הוֹדִיעוּ
וּמִשַּׁבְּתוֹתַי הֶעְלִימוּ עֵינֵיהֶם וָאֵחַל
כז בְּתוֹכָם׃ שָׂרֶיהָ בְקִרְבָּהּ כִּזְאֵבִים טֹרְפֵי
טָרֶף לִשְׁפָּךְ־דָּם לְאַבֵּד נְפָשׁוֹת לְמַעַן
כח בְּצֹעַ בָּצַע׃ וּנְבִיאֶיהָ טָחוּ לָהֶם תָּפֵל חֹזִים
שָׁוְא וְקֹסְמִים לָהֶם כָּזָב אֹמְרִים כֹּה אָמַר
כט אֲדֹנָי יֱהוִה וַיהוָה לֹא דִבֵּר׃ עַם הָאָרֶץ
עָשְׁקוּ עֹשֶׁק וְגָזְלוּ גָּזֵל וְעָנִי וְאֶבְיוֹן הוֹנוּ
ל וְאֶת־הַגֵּר עָשְׁקוּ בְּלֹא מִשְׁפָּט׃ וָאֲבַקֵּשׁ
מֵהֶם אִישׁ גֹּדֵר־גָּדֵר וְעֹמֵד בַּפֶּרֶץ לְפָנַי
בְּעַד הָאָרֶץ לְבִלְתִּי שַׁחֲתָהּ וְלֹא מָצָאתִי׃
לא וָאֶשְׁפֹּךְ עֲלֵיהֶם זַעְמִי בְּאֵשׁ עֶבְרָתִי
כִּלִּיתִים דַּרְכָּם בְּרֹאשָׁם נָתַתִּי נְאֻם אֲדֹנָי

[The simile is more apt for kings than for prophets, as in *Zephaniah* 3:3-4 (see above).]

Applied to prophets, the meaning would be that just as a lion confuses his prey by roaring, these prophets confused the people with their declamations, thereby bringing about their destruction *(Radak).*

חֹסֶן וִיקָר יִקָּחוּ — *Strength and beauty have they taken.*

By encouraging the people to cleave to their evil ways, the false prophets caused the destruction of the city. When the enemy broke in, taking the city's ornaments, it was as though the false prophets themselves were perpetrating the plunder *(Radak).*

אַלְמְנוֹתֶיהָ הִרְבּוּ בְתוֹכָהּ — *Her widows have they increased in her midst.*

When the enemy slays men in battle, widowing their wives, it is as though the false prophets are the killers because they are responsible for the killing *(Radak).*

26. כֹּהֲנֶיהָ חָמְסוּ תוֹרָתִי — *Her Priests have robbed My Torah.*

The *kohanim, priests,* are charged with teaching Torah to the people (*Deut.* 33:10). By withholding their teaching, they are robbing the people of their rightful heritage *(Rashi).*

The obligation of the priests to teach the difference *between holy and profane, between clean and unclean* is taught in *Leviticus* 10:10-11.

28. וּנְבִיאֶיהָ טָחוּ לָהֶם תָּפֵל — *And her prophets smeared daub for them.*

The same expression is found in 13:10 and explained there. *Rashi* interprets: imitation plaster which cannot withstand rain. *Radak* interprets: something inferior and tasteless. See 13:10.

The role of the false prophets dis-

devoured. Strength and beauty have they taken. Her
widows have they increased in her midst. 26 *Her*
priests have robbed My Torah and desecrated My
sanctities. Between holy and profane they made no
distinction, and between contaminated and purified
they did not make known. From My Sabbaths they
hid their eyes and I became profaned among them.
27 *Her princes are within her like wolves tearing prey;*
to shed blood, to destroy lives in order to reap
plunder. 28 *And her prophets smeared daub for them,*
saw vanity and divined falsehood for them. They
say: 'So says my Lord HASHEM/ELOHIM,*' but*
HASHEM *did not speak.*

29 *The people of the land have perpetuated oppres*
sion and robbed spoils. The poor and the needy they
have wronged and oppressed the stranger unjustly.
30 *So I sought among them a man who would build a*
fence and stand in the breach before Me for the sake
of the Land that it might not be destroyed. But I
found not. 31 *So I will pour My fury over them. With*
the fire of My wrath I have consumed them. I have
placed their way upon their head. The words of my
Lord HASHEM/ELOHIM.

cussed in *Overview* IX, is the theme of ch. 13.

29. עַם הָאָרֶץ – *The people of the Land.*

I.e., the common people.

For further explanation, see *comm.* 12:19.

עָנִי וְאֶבְיוֹן – *The poor and the needy.*

The *poor* are those with little property, but a semblance of self respect. The *needy* are totally destitute and desirous of everything they see with little remnant of shame.

See *comm.* 18:12 for further discussion of these terms.

30. וָאֲבַקֵּשׁ מֵהֶם אִישׁ גֹּדֵר־גָּדֵר וְעֹמֵד בַּפֶּרֶץ – *So I sought among them a man who would build a fence and stand in the breach.*

Building a fence is a metaphor for arousing the people to repentance; and standing in the breach means praying for their salvation. Such a man could have saved the city (*Metzudos; see comm.* 14:12-20).

31. וָאֶשְׁפֹּךְ עֲלֵיהֶם זַעְמִי – *So I will pour My fury over them.*

This refers to the flood of fire, discussed in *comm., v.* 24.

דַּרְכָּם בְּרֹאשָׁם נָתַתִּי – *I have placed their way upon their head.*

See *comm.* 7:3 for a discussion of this concept.

א יְהוָה: וַיְהִי דְבַר־
ב יְהוָה אֵלַי לֵאמֹר: בֶּן־אָדָם שְׁתַּיִם נָשִׁים
ג בְּנוֹת אֵם־אַחַת הָיוּ: וַתִּזְנֶינָה בְמִצְרַיִם
בִּנְעוּרֵיהֶן זָנוּ שָׁמָּה מֹעֲכוּ שְׁדֵיהֶן וְשָׁם
ד עִשּׂוּ דַּדֵּי בְּתוּלֵיהֶן: וּשְׁמוֹתָן אָהֳלָה
הַגְּדוֹלָה וְאָהֳלִיבָה אֲחוֹתָהּ וַתִּהְיֶינָה לִי
וַתֵּלַדְנָה בָּנִים וּבָנוֹת וּשְׁמוֹתָן שֹׁמְרוֹן
ה אָהֳלָה וִירוּשָׁלַםִ אָהֳלִיבָה: וַתִּזֶן אָהֳלָה

XXIII

This chapter is similar to chapter 16 in many ways. Once more the vehicle which the prophet chooses for his mussar, castigation, *is the parable of the faithless wife who seeks fulfillment of her unnatural lust through numerous lovers. And once more we are shocked by the unsparing explication of the crassest forms of lewdness for which we have not been prepared by our previous exposure to the language of Scripture,* לשון הַקֹּדֶשׁ, the holy language, *which is usually so careful to avoid any contact with the unclean and impure (see* Pesachim *3a, and* Moreh Nevuchim *3:8). It is as though the prophet understood that a time had come in which the only hope of reaching the people lay in tearing aside the cushioning layers of acceptable language and exposing them brutally to the depths of their degradation* (R' Joseph Breuer).

Our chapter differs from chapter 16 in that there are two protagonists instead of one. There we have one orphan girl whom the benefactor takes as his wife; here we have two sisters, Oholah and Oholivah, who are married to one man.

These sisters are identified as Shomron and Jerusalem, the capitals of the northern and southern kingdoms respectively, and their tragic fate provides the historical background of the parable.

In the course of the commentary we shall have occasion to analyze the significance of an Israel divided into two sister states. We shall try to fathom their nature and destiny as they appear through the perspective of Yechezkel's description.

We shall allow the prophet to lead us back to the earliest dawn of Israel's nationhood in Egypt and we shall glance back even further to the days of the Patriarchs when the seeds of this division were first sown. Finally, we shall catch a glimpse of the grandeur of Yechezkel's vision of the Messianic age (Ch. 37) when the bitter divisions of the past will have been forgotten at last, and a גוי אחד, a unified nation, *will dwell in peace on Israel's hills never to be separated again; rising to the heights of its destiny under Davidic kingship, a fitting abode for God's Presence on earth.*

2. שְׁתַּיִם נָשִׁים — *Two women.*

Two states which are comparable to two women (*Targum* quoted by *Rashi*).

בנות אם אַחַת הָיוּ — *Daughters of one mother were they.*

These two states developed from one unified congregation, in Rehaboam's days (*Rashi*).

For the account of the division and the events which led to it, see *I Kings* 12.

3. וַתִּזְנֶינָה במצרים — *Now they indulged in promiscuity in Egypt.*

We have recognized (16:15-34) that Scripture uses sexual lust as a metaphor for Israel's lust for idol worship. *Radak* finds a similar meaning in our chapter

23
1-4

The word of HASHEM came to me, saying: [2] Ben
Adam, two women, daughters of one mother were
they. [3] Now they indulged in promiscuity in Egypt,
in their youth they were promiscuous. There, their
bosoms were pressed and there they squeezed their
virgin breasts. [4] And their names were: Oholah, the
larger one, and Oholivah her sister. They became
Mine and bore sons and daughters. Now their true
names: Shomron was Oholah and Jerusalem,
Oholivah.

also (However *Rambam, Igeres HaShmad* 2, interprets our verse literally, deriving from it that Israel had loose morals in Egypt.)

Israel's attraction to the Egyptian idol worship is dealt with in 20:7-8; see *comm.* 20:13.[1]

מִעֲכוּ שְׁדֵיהֶן ... עִשּׂוּ דַּדֵּי בְּתוּלֵיהֶן — *Their bosoms were pressed ... they squeezed their virgin breasts.*

The use of a metaphor, describing limited licentiousness which falls short of actual intercourse, is intentional. The idol worship in Egypt was not as depraved as that which was to be practiced later *(Metzudos).*

4. וּשְׁמוֹתָן אָהֳלָה הַגְּדוֹלָה וְאָהֳלִיבָה אֲחוֹתָהּ — *And their names were: Oholah, the larger one, and her sister, Oholivah.*

The northern kingdom is called Shomron after the name of its capital city. This, although Shomron was built by Omri some fifty years after the establishment of the kingdom *(Rashi).* The southern kingdom is referred to as Jerusalem, after its capital.

In the prophetic vision, these two sister states are given the names:

1. It is particularly striking that our verse is in the plural, implying that even in Egypt, Israel was divided into two nations ('Now *they* indulged in promiscuity'). Historically, of course, the division into two kingdoms occurred in Rehaboam's reign and indeed verse 2 above seems to stress that point by identifying the two sisters as being daughters of one mother. How then are we to understand our verse which traces the division back to Egypt?

The quest for a solution to this problem will lead us back to the days of the Patriarchs and Jacob's marriage to the two sisters, Leah and Rachel. At that time two disparate streams were formed in Israel which would leave their distinct marks on the nation's entire history, even up to the very end of days when, according to the tradition of our Sages (*Succah* 52a; see *Ramban, Exodus* 17:9), the Davidic Messiah who will be descended from Leah's son, Judah, will be preceded by a Messiah from Rachel's son, Joseph.

Bereishis Rabbah to *Genesis* 29:16, after describing the respective descendants of these two sisters as: 'two bolts traversing world history from one end to the other', shows how these two families duplicated each other's accomplishments throughout the ages. Indeed, the history of Israel upon its land is divided by *Psalms* (78:67) between the period of 'Joseph's tent' (pre-Davidic times when the Tabernacle was mostly at Shiloh, the portion of Joseph's son, Ephraim) and the period in which Joseph was rejected in favor of Judah (the Davidic era when the monarchy was vested in Judah's descendants and the Temple stood in Jerusalem.)

The division of the nation into the northern and southern kingdoms in Rehaboam's reign, is also seen by Scripture as an extension of the division between two families. The northern kingdom is usually referred to as Ephraim (as in the whole book of *Hosea* — a prophet of the northern kingdom; Jeroboam ben Nevat, founder of the northern kingdom was descendant of Ephraim), while the southern kingdom is called Judah. Indeed, Yechezkel's Messianic vision of the ultimate unity of Israel (ch. 37) is a joining together of the Tree of Judah with the Tree of Ephraim.

In this same vein *Bereishis Rabbah (Genesis* 44:18) interprets the confrontation between

תַּחְתָּי וַתַּעְגַּב עַל־מְאַהֲבֶיהָ אֶל־אַשּׁוּר

Oholah and Oholivah. Both names are formed from אֹהֶל, a *tent* or *dwelling place*. These names are familiar from the קִינָה, *lamentation*, for the night of Tishah B'Av which starts with the words שׁוֹמְרוֹן קוֹל תִּתֵּן.

Oholah (אָהֳלָה) means *'her' tent*, because God had no part in the tabernacles of Shomron. They were dedicated to the golden calves which Jeroboam ben Nevat had erected (see *I Kings* 12:28). Oholivah (אָהֳלִיבָה) means *My tent is within her*. This name places Judah, in which God's Temple stood, in sharp contrast to Shomron.

The assigning of special names to Shomron and Jerusalem is significant. The parable could well have stood without them in the same way that chapter 16 describes Jerusalem and its infidelity, together with that of Shomron and Sodom, by means of a similar parable, without attaching special names.

A name serves to identify the exact nature of a person or object. [שֵׁם, *name*, seems related to שָׁם, *there*. (See *Sefer haShorashim* of both *Ibn Janach* and *Radak*.) By means of a name man expresses his impression of things. Thereby he indicates their *place* in his world (*Hirsch, Genesis* 2:19).] We must assume that these names are to tell us something about Shomrom and Jerusalem which we would not have known without them.

R' Joseph Breuer weaves the names Oholah and Oholivah into the parable [in contrast to the other commentators in whose view (see above) the significance of the two names *(her tent* and *My tent is in her)* seems limited to Shomron and Jerusalem proper]. These two sisters were married to one man, yet Oholah maintained her own separate tent. It was her tragic mistake to think that she could remain loyal to her husband even while maintaining herself apart from him and his bed. As more and more lovers began to visit her tent, the fallacy of her thinking was revealed. Oholivah, on the other hand, was the wife who initially focused all her strivings upon her husband's tent. He thought of her as 'My tent' which was *within her*. Nevertheless, she also eventually succumbed to the blandishments of other lovers.

Moving now from the parable to the historical realities which it describes, we may say that the name Oholah which was given to Shomron points unambiguously to the inner decay which brought about its ultimate downfall: an unwillingness to subordinate itself to Judah in its Divine worship of God.

Judah and Joseph over the matter of the stolen cup as transcending the two personalities involved, and focusing instead upon these two strands in Jewish history.

Thus, even though the division into two kingdoms came comparatively late in Jewish history, the duality reflected in this division can be said to have existed much before that. Seen in this perspective, Israel's lack of fidelity to God in Egypt can, indeed, be ascribed to *two* sisters, symbolizing both strains of the nation.

(For the significance of this duality, see *Michtav MeEliyahu* vol. 2, p.218; comm. v. 4.)

Although the verb זנה, *to be promiscuous* or *commit harlotry*, is used to describe both the idol worship which took place in Egypt and the subsequent transgressions which led to the destruction of the Temple, it should be noted that there is a difference in the severity of the sins.

Midrash Rabbah (Exodus 32:11) teaches that Moses' purpose in breaking the Tablets of the Law when he found the people worshiping the golden calf, was comparable to a messenger sent by a king to betroth a woman to him. Upon discovering that the woman had been unfaithful, the messenger tore up the marriage contract [*kesubah*] so that her transgression should be that of an unmarried rather than a married woman. Idol worship after the covenant at Sinai is comparable to the infidelity of a married woman, while the Egyptian idol worship can at the most be described as the promiscuity of an unmarried person.

This comparative minimizing of the guilt of Israel in Egypt is shown in the description that follows.

⁵ *Now Oholah was promiscuous under Me and she lusted for her lovers — for nearby Assyria —* ⁶ *clothed*

[See *Doros HoRishonim, Tekufas Hamikrah,* ch. 5 for an exhaustive analysis of Jeroboam ben Nevat's golden calves. He shows conclusively that they were not meant for idol worship, but were simply symbols which he offered the people in their service to God so that they should not feel the need to go to Jerusalem and worship at the Temple. The Torah prohibits such symbols, but they are not idols.]

An insight into the dual roles of Leah's and Rachel's descendants is offered in *Michtav MeEliyahu* (vol. 2, p.218). It is the destiny of Rachel's descendants to prepare the way for Leah's descendants to serve God in the ideal manner, in much the way that the Josephic Messiah [מָשִׁיחַ בֶּן יוֹסֵף] is to prepare the way for the Davidic Messiah [מָשִׁיחַ בֶּן דָּוִד]. It had been God's will that the northern kingdom would serve as a testing ground for the development of a Torah-true nation, and that the lessons gleaned from the experience could then be refined into producing the kind of ideal kingship which Judah was destined to produce.

Thus, the Oholah nature of the northern kingdom, its refusal to be subordinate, is not a coincidental fault, but one that by its very nature made a mockery of God's plan. Ephraim's role, by definition, is to be subordinate to Judah, and if he balks at that destiny, he is doomed.

The Sages express this same truth in Aggadic terms (*Sanhedrin* 102a). R' Abba taught: God held on to Jeroboam's garment (in supplication) and said to him, 'Repent! and I and you and Jesse's son (David) will roam together in the Garden of Eden.'

Jeroboam asked Him, 'Who will go first?'

So He answered, 'Jesse's son will go first.'

Jeroboam said, 'If so, I will not come.

In this Aggadah the whole tragedy of the northern kingdom is encapsulated.

אָהֳלָה הַגְּדוֹלָה — *Oholah, the larger one.*

Oholah is called larger, because the northern kingdom was made up of ten tribes as opposed to the southern one which was composed of only Judah and Benjamin.

[The word גְּדוֹלָה often means *older,* a translation which is inappropriate here since Jerusalem was older than Shomron.]

5-10 Assyria played a decisive role in the destinies of both the northern and the southern kingdoms. Assyrian kings exiled the ten tribes of the northern kingdom (*II Kings* 5:29-30, 17:6; *I Chronicles* 5:26; see also *Isaiah* 8:23, *Rashi*), and Sennacherib, king of Assyria, conquered the greater part of Judah (*II Kings* 18:13; *Isaiah* 8:8) until Divine intervention finally destroyed him at the very gates of Jerusalem (see *II Kings* 18:13 — 19:37; *Isaiah* chs. 36, 37). Both kingdoms brought this scourge upon themselves by inviting Assyria to interfere in their internal affairs. (For the northern kingdom's political ties with Assyria, see below and *II Kings* 15:17-20; ch. 16.) It is this dangerous flirtation with their mortal enemy which the prophet castigates in our chapter *(Rashi).* (For background, see *II Kings* ch. 16-19.)

וַתַּעְגַּב עַל מְאַהֲבֶיהָ אֶל אַשּׁוּר קְרוֹבִים — *And she lusted for her lovers — for nearby Assyria.*

The translation *nearby* follows *Rashi. Radak* and *Metzudos* translate קְרוֹבִים as *relatives.* She considered Assyria as close to herself as a relative.

In *R' Breuer's* view, קְרוֹבִים describes the affinity which Shomron felt towards Assyria and its lifestyle (see *vs.* 6-7 below). The northern kingdom had never quite committed itself to the demanding standards of God's service. It was inconceivable to her that such standards were in fact the kernel from which unbounded joy and satisfaction could grow (see *Hosea* 2:7). Assyria

ו קְרוֹבִים׃ לְבֻשֵׁי תְכֵלֶת פַּחוֹת וּסְגָנִים
בַּחוּרֵי חֶמֶד כֻּלָּם פָּרָשִׁים רֹכְבֵי סוּסִים׃
ז וַתִּתֵּן תַּזְנוּתֶיהָ עֲלֵיהֶם מִבְחַר בְּנֵי־אַשּׁוּר
כֻּלָּם וּבְכֹל אֲשֶׁר־עָגְבָה בְּכָל־גִּלּוּלֵיהֶם
ח נִטְמָאָה׃ וְאֶת־תַּזְנוּתֶיהָ מִמִּצְרַיִם לֹא
עָזָבָה כִּי אוֹתָהּ שָׁכְבוּ בִנְעוּרֶיהָ וְהֵמָּה
עִשּׂוּ דַּדֵּי בְתוּלֶיהָ וַיִּשְׁפְּכוּ תַזְנוּתָם עָלֶיהָ׃
ט לָכֵן נְתַתִּיהָ בְּיַד־מְאַהֲבֶיהָ בְּיַד בְּנֵי אַשּׁוּר

seemed to contain the promise of a fulfilled life.

The lusting refers to the wooing of the Assyrian king, Pul, by Menachem ben Godi (*II Kings* 15:17-20; *Rashi; pref.* to *vs.* 5-10).

6. לְבֻשֵׁי תְכֵלֶת — *Clothed in blue wool.*

The ostentatious wealth of the Assyrian nobles quickened Oholah's interest. Forgotten was the task of Rachel's descendants to sublimate the temporal (see *Michtav MeEliyahu* vol. 2, p. 218). The unfettered indulgence of Assyria found an echo in her heart.

7. וַתִּתֵּן תַּזְנוּתֶיהָ עֲלֵיהֶם — *And she bestowed her promiscuity upon them.*

Immediately she used all her wiles to become attractive to them. Mindless of the horrendous degradation which would result from the unthinking pursuit of bodily gratification, she allowed her lust to lead her into the filth of their defilement.

8. וְאֶת תַּזְנוּתֶיהָ מִמִּצְרַיִם לֹא עָזָבָה — *Nor did she forgo her promiscuity with Egypt.*

Assyria, the former ally, turned into a mortal enemy. Then Israel, under Hoshea ben Elah, turned to Egypt for help. (See *Hosea* 7:11: *Ephraim became a gullible dove with no mind. To Egypt they called; to Assyria they went.*) The messengers which this last king of Shomron sent to Soh, the king of Egypt, precipitated the final Assyrian campaign against the northern kingdom (*II Kings* 17:4-7). According to *Rashi*, our verse refers to this incident. *Rashi* does not explain how Israel's earlier association with Egypt caused Hoshea ben Elah to seek Soh's assistance.

[*Comm.* to *v.* 5 and this verse follows *Rashi* in interpreting the lust which Israel displayed as the seeking of alliances with Assyria and Egypt. This interpretation uses a mixed metaphor since infidelity is the usual symbol of idol worship, and was so used in *v.*3 (see *comm.*). In our verses, promiscuity symbolizes the misguided, politically motivated steps which Israel took in its internal and external struggles, for had they trusted in God, they would not have needed the Assyrian kings (*Rashi, v.* 5).][1]

To *Radak* and *Metzudos*, the entire chapter deals with an attraction to As-

1. An analysis of the Torah's prohibition against returning to Egypt will help to provide insight into our verse.

Rambam (Hilchos Melachim 5:7-8) writes: It is permitted to live anywhere in the world except in Egypt...because her actions are more depraved than those of other lands. (The Biblical prohibition is mentioned in *Succah* 51b. However, while *Talmud Bavli* mentions only one prohibition, *Yerushalmi, Succah* 5:1 and *Mechilta, Exodus* 14:13 mention three separate prohibitions in the Torah. *Rambam* in *Sefer HaMitzvos* bases *Lo Sa'aseh* 46 on the later sources.)

Rambam and *Ramban (Deut.* 17:16) give Egypt's depraved actions as a reason for the

*in blue wool, governors and rulers, pleasant young
men all of them, horsemen riding steeds.* 7 *And she
bestowed her promiscuity upon them, all of them the
choicest of Assyria's sons. And for whomever she
lusted — in all their filth she became defiled.* 8 *Nor did
she forgo her promiscuity with Egypt, for with her
they lay in her youth, they squeezed her virgin
breasts and they poured their philanderings upon
her.* 9 *Therefore, I have put her in the hands of her
lovers, in the hand of Assyria's sons for whom she*

syrian and Egyptian idol worship. According to these commentators, the use of the metaphor is consistent. This verse explains Israel's promiscuity with Egypt as resulting from the earlier association with that country (אוֹתָהּ שָׁכְבוּ בִנְעוּרֶיהָ כִּי). Israel became acquainted with Egypt's idols during her years of bondage there (see ch. 20), and remembered them in later years.

9. לָכֵן ... — *Therefore.*

God gave over the northern kingdom into Sennacherib's hands *(Rashi), because* it had placed its trust in Assyria.

This is an aspect of God's justice which expresses itself in the form of מִדָּה כְּנֶגֶד מִדָּה, *punishment that fits the crime.*

[The fall of Israel into the very same human hands in which it places its trust is a recurring theme in Aggadic literature, e.g., *Bereishis Rabbah (Genesis* 21:27). Abraham made a pact with the Philistine Abimelech, for which he had set aside seven sheep. To this the Midrash comments: [God said] You have given him seven sheep without My authorization; [therefore] I swear that [his people] will kill seven righteous men from among your descendants [and] his descendants will lay seven of your tabernacles waste.

prohibition, although the sources do not state this expressly.

However, *Mechilta* and *Yerushalmi* point out that Israel transgressed these prohibitions on three separate occasions and were punished each time. The first of these three occasions is in the days of Sennacherib, for it says: *Woe to those who descend to Egypt for help (Isaiah* 31:1). This refers to the debacle which occurred when Hoshea ben Elah sent messengers to Soh, the king of Egypt *(Rashi).*

Thus, the Torah's prohibition against returning to Egypt is not limited to living there, but includes seeking an alliance with them. [Although the *halachah* expressly permits business relationships *(Rambam),* an alliance, which subjects Israel to some degree of Egyptian dominion, is included in the prohibition.

Egypt's depraved behavior can explain the prohibition against living there, but why is there danger of emulating her ways in making a political or military alliance with her?

It would seem that Israel's stay in Egypt created ties between the two people which were not easily forgotten. Memories of the suffering in Egypt were short, as evidenced by the incidents which took place while Israel was still wandering in the desert. Many times they felt the urge to return to Egypt rather than face the rigors of their difficult destiny. God commanded His people to sunder all ties to Egypt, for Israel's affinity for Egypt could have proved a serious obstacle to Israel's achieving its destiny of being the people of God alone.

History bore this out. Again and again Israel turned to Egypt for help — never remembering the many disappointments it had suffered (see footnote 17:7; ch.29).

This, then, would be the meaning of our verse. Israel turned to Egypt for help because of the feeling of kinship which remained from the time that, as slaves, they had absorbed Egyptian culture.

י אֲשֶׁר עָגְבָה עֲלֵיהֶם: הֵמָּה גִּלּוּ עֶרְוָתָהּ
בָּנֶיהָ וּבְנוֹתֶיהָ לָקָחוּ וְאוֹתָהּ בַּחֶרֶב
הָרָגוּ וַתְּהִי־שֵׁם לַנָּשִׁים וּשְׁפוּטִים עָשׂוּ
יא בָהּ: וַתֵּרֶא אֲחוֹתָהּ אָהֳלִיבָה
וַתַּשְׁחֵת עַגְבָתָהּ מִמֶּנָּה וְאֶת־תַּזְנוּתֶיהָ
יב מִזְּנוּנֵי אֲחוֹתָהּ: אֶל־בְּנֵי אַשּׁוּר עָגָבָה
פַּחוֹת וּסְגָנִים קְרֹבִים לְבֻשֵׁי מִכְלוֹל
פָּרָשִׁים רֹכְבֵי סוּסִים בַּחוּרֵי חֶמֶד כֻּלָּם:
יג וָאֵרֶא כִּי נִטְמָאָה דֶּרֶךְ אֶחָד לִשְׁתֵּיהֶן:

10. הֵמָּה גִּלּוּ עֶרְוָתָהּ — *They uncovered her nakedness.*

A harlot used to be punished by undressing her and parading her in public. In the same way, Assyria dragged its captives into exile in a manner calculated to cause them great embarrassment *(Metzudos).*

בָּנֶיהָ וּבְנוֹתֶיהָ לָקָחוּ וְאוֹתָהּ בַּחֶרֶב הָרָגוּ — *Her sons and daughters they took, and her they slaughtered with the sword.*

The Assyrian exile took place in three waves (*II Kings* 15:29-30; 17:6; *Chronicles* 5:26). First the tribes on the eastern shore of the Jordan (Reuven and Gad) were taken, then Naftali and Zevulun, and finally the rest of the nation. *Metzudos* writes that *sons and daughters* refers to these first two exiles, who are considered the children of Shomron. The third exile *(and her they slaughtered)* refers to the destruction of Shomron and the exile of the remaining six tribes of the northern kingdom.

וַתְּהִי שֵׁם לַנָּשִׁים — *Thus she became a byword among the women.*

She served as an example whereby all women would know the penalty for harlotry. They would say: See what fate overtook this one because of her promiscuity *(Rashi).*

11. זְנוּנֵי אֲחוֹתָהּ — *The harlotries of her sister.*

See comm., v. 29.

Oholah's fate had been meant as a warning to all other women (see *v.* 10). Certainly her sister Oholivah should have taken the implied lesson to heart. That she did not do so vastly exacerbated her culpability (see *Jeremiah* 3:6-12; *comm.* 16:46-52).[1]

1. The time immediately following the exile of the northern kingdom was a portentous one in Israel's history. With one blow, the nation had been truncated by the loss of ten tribes. For the very first time in Israel's history, a foreign power had succeeded in substantially decimating its numbers. Moreover, since twelve tribes constitute the essential structure of the nation (see *Ramban, Deuteronomy* 33:6), Israel's integrity as bearers of God's Glory on earth had been eroded as well.

Israel lay broken before Sennacherib's hordes. Not satiated by his victory over Shomron, he sent his armies against Judah (*II Kings* 18:13). His camp was identical in size and form to the armies with which the four kings of *Genesis* 14:1-16 fought against Abraham, and to the hordes which, in the End of Days will accompany Gog, king of Magog, in his campaign against Israel (*Sanhedrin* 95b; see chs. 38, 39).

Maharal (Chiddushei Aggadah, Sanhedrin 95b) explains that each of these three wars occurs at a turning point in the relationship between Israel and the nations. In Abraham's time Israel came into being, posing the first challenge to a mankind oblivious of its spiritual destiny. The nations rose up against Israel to vindicate their existence. Again, in the End of Days, when the choice of Israel becomes final, the nations will rise up in a last futile attempt to

23
10-13

lusted. [10] *They uncovered her nakedness, her sons*
and daughters they took, and her they slaughtered
with the sword. Thus she became a byword among
the women and they executed punishments upon her.
[11] *Now her sister Oholivah observed, but was even*
more corrupt in her lusting than she, and her
promiscuity than the harlotries of her sister. [12] *For*
Assyria's sons she lusted — neighboring governors
and rulers, gorgeously clothed, horsemen riding
upon steeds, pleasant young men all of them. [13] *Now*
I saw that she was defiled. Both had gone the same
way.

12. אֶל בְּנֵי אַשּׁוּר עָגְבָה — *For Assyria's sons she lusted.*

This refers to Achaz, who sent messengers to the Assyrian king to ask his help *(Rashi).*[1]

13. דֶּרֶךְ אֶחָד לִשְׁתֵּיהֶן — *Both had gone the same* [lit. *one*] *way.*

The expectation had been that Oholivah, the sister in whose life God's tent played the major role, would be less

reverse the climax towards which history had flowed.

In Sennacherib's time, the nations were aroused by the exile of the ten tribes. Suddenly, Israel was shattered and, it appeared, could be dealt a death blow. Indeed, by any natural law, Israel would have succumbed. Judah's fortified cities had been smashed, its territory overrun, and only Jerusalem remained. Nothing could save it — except God's direct intervention. God willed that the Jewish people should live, and destroyed the beseiging armies with a heavenly fire (*II Kings* 19:35).

This portentous confrontation between Sennacherib and Chizkiyahu could have been the cataclysm from which Messianic times emerge. 'God wanted to make Chizkiyahu the Messiah and Sennacherib, Gog and Magog. At the last moment, Chizkiyahu fell short of this call to greatness (*Sanhedrin* 94a), and the tragic erosion of Israel's glory continued unchecked until it ended in the destruction.

Chizkiyahu faltered because the lessons of the northern kingdom's downfall were not learned. Shomron fell because it would not place its complete trust in God alone. A Messiah must be able to lift himself above the influences of the thinking and reactions of ordinary men. He must stand before God completely free of any worldly considerations. (See *Maharal, Sanhedrin* 94a, for the explanation of the statement that Chizkiyahu did not become the Messiah because he failed to say *Shirah, a song of jubilation,* upon Sennacherib's downfall. See also Overview to ArtScroll *Shir HaShirim.)*

Chizkiyahu was not able to shake off the shackles of ordinariness. The Sages criticize him for stripping the Temple gates to obtain gold for a bribe to Assyria (*II Kings* 18:16; see *Berachos* 10b), and for his eagerness to curry favor with the Babylonians (*II Kings* 20:13; see *Pirkei d'Rabbi Eliezer* 52; *Bereishis Rabbah* 19:11).

Because they prevented Chizkiyahu from becoming the Messiah, these failures lie at the root of some of the great tragedies of Jewish history. The vehemence of Yechezkel's criticism in our verses must be understood against this background.

1. With Achaz's reign, difficult days began for Judah. With reckless abandon, Achaz encouraged the spread of idol worship throughout the land (*II Kings* 16:3-4), forbade study of the Torah (*Sanhedrin* 103b), and systematically suspended the entire educational system of the country to ensure that a generation would grow up devoid of any contact with holiness (*Yerushalmi Sanhedrin* 10:2).

In the face of such defiance, God exposed Judah to the attacks of its enemies (*II Chronicles*

יד וַתּוֹסֶף אֶל־תַּזְנוּתֶיהָ וַתֵּרֶא אַנְשֵׁי מְחֻקֶּה
עַל־הַקִּיר צַלְמֵי °כשדיים חֲקֻקִים
טו בַּשָּׁשַׁר׃ חֲגוֹרֵי אֵזוֹר בְּמָתְנֵיהֶם סְרוּחֵי
טְבוּלִים בְּרָאשֵׁיהֶם מַרְאֵה שָׁלִישִׁים כֻּלָּם
דְּמוּת בְּנֵי־בָבֶל כַּשְׂדִּים אֶרֶץ מוֹלַדְתָּם׃

°כַּשְׂדִּים ק׳

prone to take lovers than Oholah. These hopes were disappointed. Exposed to similar pressures, Judah failed as miserably as Shomron.

14-19 From his castigation of the wicked Achaz, the prophet turns to a review of Chizkiyahu's failings.

Chizkiyahu was one of the greatest kings (see *comm., v.* 11). In a time pregnant with Messsianic potential, he seemed to be the *Prince of Peace (Isaiah* 9:5; *Rashi),* in whom the aspirations of mankind could be realized. In contrast to his father Achaz, who had sought to undermine Israel's loyalty to the Torah by dismantling the entire educational system, Chizkiyahu, with unprecedented vigor, spread the knowledge of Torah among all layers of society (*Sanhedrin* 94b). He helped his people to recognize that their real strength lay in their loyalty to God. The Sages in *Sanhedrin* 94 find this fact alluded to by the king's name: חִזְקִיָּה, *strength of God.*

This king, above all others, should have been free from any taint of blame for the eventual Babylonian exile. Yet, in the unsparing prophetic eyes of Isaiah, he carried a major responsibility for it.

The tragic account of how this man, whose potential had been so great, failed in one of the most important challenges of his life is told in *II Kings* 20:12-19 (*Pirkei de'Rabbi Eliezer* 52; *Bereishis Rabbah* 19:11).

He had been fatally ill and miraculously cured. Upon his recovery, the Babylonian king Berodach Baladon sent him messages of congratulations. Impressed by the distance which the king's emissaries had traveled to visit him, he, in turn, wanted to impress them. He opened his treasure houses for their inspection and went so far as to open the Holy Ark in the Temple for their edification *(Yalkut Shimoni, Genesis,* 77). God sent Isaiah to tell him that as a result of his actions, his descendants would one day be servants in the Babylonian king's household.

Sanhedrin 104a ascribes the punishment of exile to the fact that not only

28:19). Edomites and Philistines swooped down upon the weakened land to snatch what they could of its territory (*II Chronicles* 28:17-19).

Worst of all, his excesses brought about a revolution among his subjects against the whole Davidic dynasty (*Isaiah* 8:6; see *Rashi*). Abetted by this internal rebellion, Pekach ben Remalyahu, king of Shomron, and Retzin, king of Aram, made an alliance to destroy Achaz and his whole family, and establish a new royal line (*II Kings* 16:5; see *Isaiah* 7:6).

This king, rootless and helpless in the face of those disasters, trembled like a tree in a gale at the prospect of this invasion (*Isaiah* 7:2). His fears were fully justified, because the combined Shomronite and Aramean armies did indeed smash through his defenses and wreak untold suffering, death, and captivity among his people (*II Chronicles* 28:5-8).

In abject terror, Achaz now sacrificed to the gods of Damascus (capital of Aram) in the vain hope of appeasing the Arameans by this flattery (*II Chronicles* 25:23; see *Sanhedrin* 103a; *Doros HaRishonim, Tekufas Hamikrah* ch. 7).

Finally, in desperation, he turned to Tiglas Pileser, king of Assyria, for aid to prop his crumbling throne (*II Kings* 16:7-9). This alliance precipitated the northern kingdom's destruction and won him a temporary respite. But, predictably, this alliance also ended in disaster. As soon as he was free from his campaign against the north, Tiglas Pileser turned against Achaz (*II Chronicles* 28:20) and eventually conquered the greater part of Judah.

14 *Now she added to her promiscuity seeing men engraved upon the wall, images of Chaldeans engraved in color.* 15 *Girded with belts upon their hips, hanging turbans upon their heads. All of them looked like officers. They looked like Babylon's children, Chaldeans, land of their birth.* 16 *And she*

did the Babylonian emissaries sit at his table, but he and his wife personally served them. *Maharal* (there) explains that his personal service constituted a voluntary subservience to an alien power, akin to the exile experience.

In *Rashi's* view, our passage refers to this incident. The individual verses offer a new perspective on this sad episode.[1]

14. וַתּוֹסֶף אֶל תַּזְנוּתֶיהָ — *Now she added to her promiscuity.*

The increase was that she lusted after people whom she had never seen in person. Merely seeing their images engraved upon the walls (see below) was enough to stimulate her desire for them *(Rashi; Metzudos).*

Rashi explains this as a criticism of Chizkiyahu for attempting to curry favor with the Babylonians after seeing them only once, on the occasion of their visit after his sickness (see above). There were no real ties between the two countries which would have justified his eagerness to generate good relations with them.

Radak explains that *she added to her promiscuity* was accomplished by decorating her walls with the images mentioned at the end of this verse. Oholivah engraved the images upon her walls because of her great lust for these foreign idols. *Radak* associates this with the verse in *Psalms* 106:35: *They were scattered among the nations and were influenced by their deeds.* (See *Vayikrah Rabbah* 33:6 for support of *Radak's* view.)

אַנְשֵׁי מְחֻקֶּה עַל־הַקִּיר — *Men engraved upon the wall.*

אַנְשֵׁי in the construct [סמיכות] form [instead of אֲנָשִׁים in the plural] is irregular, but not unique (see *Radak* for examples).

מְחֻקֶּה comes from the root חקה which has the same meaning as לחקק, *to engrave.* The former root was used by Yechezkel in 8:10, the latter, in the next part of the verse.

צַלְמֵי כַשְׂדִּיים — *Images of Chaldeans.*

These generated interest because of their unusual clothing *(Rashi).*

בַּשָּׁשַׁר — *In color.*

The translation follows *Radak* and *Metzudos. Rashi* translates *types of pictures.*

15. This verse describes the strange clothes worn by the Babylonians engraved upon the wall *(Rashi v.* 11).

The description (as in *v.* 6) is of men whom the faithless wives might find attractive. *Rambam* points out in *Moreh Nevuchim* that we need not find a particular significance in every detail of a parable. The significance lies in the total picture, not in its component parts.

סְרוּחֵי טְבוּלִים — *Hanging turbans.*

סרח is used to describe a superfluous length of cloth (e.g., *Exodus* 26:12). טָבוּל, which does not recur in Scripture as a noun, is judged by context to be a

1. The Sages teach that Nebuchadnezzar was one of the few survivors of the holocaust at Jerusalem's gates when the Assyrian army was burned *(Sanhedrin* 95b). The difficulty with interpreting this *Aggadah* literally is not the great age which this would assign to Nebuchadnezzar at the time of the Destruction (140 years later), since this is consistent with other *Aggados.* The difficulty lies rather in the assumption that the Babylonian Nebuchadnezzar was part of the Assyrian army and in the significance of his survival.

Interpreting the *Aggadah* figuratively, the Sages are teaching us that even the great miracle

טז וַתַּעְגְּבָ עֲלֵיהֶם לְמַרְאֵה עֵינֶיהָ וַתִּשְׁלַח
יז מַלְאָכִים אֲלֵיהֶם כַּשְׂדִּימָה: וַיָּבֹאוּ אֵלֶיהָ
בְנֵי־בָבֶל לְמִשְׁכַּב דֹּדִים וַיְטַמְּאוּ אוֹתָהּ
בְּתַזְנוּתָם וַתִּטְמָא־בָם וַתֵּקַע נַפְשָׁהּ מֵהֶם:
יח וַתְּגַל תַּזְנוּתֶיהָ וַתְּגַל אֶת־עֶרְוָתָהּ וַתֵּקַע
נַפְשִׁי מֵעָלֶיהָ כַּאֲשֶׁר נָקְעָה נַפְשִׁי מֵעַל
יט אֲחוֹתָהּ: וַתַּרְבֶּה אֶת־תַּזְנוּתֶיהָ לִזְכֹּר
אֶת־יְמֵי נְעוּרֶיהָ אֲשֶׁר זָנְתָה בְּאֶרֶץ
כ מִצְרָיִם: וַתַּעְגְּבָה עַל פִּלַגְשֵׁיהֶם אֲשֶׁר

head covering or turban. The meaning would then be *a turban,* part of which hangs down (*Rashi's* first interpretation). *Rashi* further suggests that טבולים is derived from the root טבל, *to dip* or *submerge,* and describes a cloth which has been dipped in dye.

דְּמוּת בְּנֵי־בָבֶל כַּשְׂדִּים אֶרֶץ מוֹלַדְתָּם — *They looked like Babylon's children, Chaldeans, land of their birth.*

The Babylonians wore their native garb with pride. They did not lust after strange and foreign customs as the Judeans were doing *(Radak).*

16. וַתַּעְגְּבָה עֲלֵיהֶם לְמַרְאֵה עֵינֶיהָ — *And she lusted for them because of what she had seen.*

The pictures engraved on the wall in *v.* 14 *(Rashi).*

וַתִּשְׁלַח מַלְאָכִים אֲלֵיהֶם כַּשְׂדִּימָה — *Sending them emissaries, to Chaldea.*

There is no previous mention in Scripture of these messengers. The allusion must have been clear to Yechezkel's listeners. *Daas Sofrim* suggests that Chizkiyahu sent messengers to the Babylonian king to reciprocate for the emissaries who came to him when he recovered from his illness.

17. וַיָּבֹאוּ אֵלֶיהָ בְנֵי־בָבֶל — *Then Babylon's sons came to her.*

To *Rashi,* the flirtation of this verse refers to the messengers which Berodach Baladon sent to Chizkiyahu.

[However, that incident, and the attraction which the Chaldeans subsequently held for Judah, are described in the previous verses. This verse must refer to cordial relations between the two countries which grew out of their initial contact with Chizkiyahu and lasted for decades, until Babylon's dreams of empire led to the conquest of Judah during Yehoyakim's reign *(II Kings* 24:1).]

וַתֵּקַע נַפְשָׁהּ מֵהֶם — *But she tore herself away from them.*

Both *Rashi* and *Metzudos* compare תקע to the expression which describes the *dislocation* of Jacob's thigh bone *(Genesis* 32:25). However, instead of translating נַפְשָׁהּ in its more common sense as we have, *Metzudos* demonstrates that נֶפֶשׁ is used in Scripture to describe desire (e.g., *Genesis* 23:8). Ac-

at Jerusalem's gates did not completely eradicate those weaknesses in Israel's character which had brought on the Assyrian menace. The seeds from which the eventual destruction was to grow remained untouched. Chizkiyahu's dealings with Assyria, his original submission to ransom demands, and his subsequent failure to say *Shirah,* a song of jubilation, concerning the miracle (see *comm. v.* 11), showed that the basic flaw remained.

This was borne out by Chizkiyahu's relations with his Babylonian visitors in an episode which contributed to the eventual Destruction.

In this sense, Nebuchadnezzar 'survived' the holocaust.

23
17-19

lusted for them because of what she had seen,
sending them emissaries, to Chaldea. 17 *Then*
Babylon's sons came to her for a bed of love, defiling
her with their philandering. Now she became defiled
through them, but she tore herself away from them.
18 *So she revealed her promiscuity, she revealed her*
nakedness. So I tore Myself away from her as I was
torn away from her sister.
19 *Now she increased her promiscuity, remember-*

cordingly he renders *her desire was torn from them.*

According to *Rashi* and numerous other commentators, this verse refers to the rebellions of Yehoyakim *(II Kings* 24:1) and Zidkiyahu *(II Chronicles* 36:13; see *pref.* ch. 17).

The high hopes that were generated in Chizkiyahu's reign are finally dashed to the ground. As Judah flaunts her harlotry, God at last turns away. Jerusalem has spurned His love as Shomron had done before.

19-21 The prophet reserves his most searing contempt for Judah's lusting after Egypt. No other passage in Scripture paints Israel's degradation in more graphic, loathsome lines than these that describe her as lusting for concubinage with a people with whom cohabitation is tantamount to living with donkeys and horses (*v.* 20).[1]

19. לִזְכֹּר אֶת יְמֵי נְעוּרֶיהָ אֲשֶׁר זָנְתָה בְּאֶרֶץ מִצְרָיִם — *Remembering the days of her youth when she debauched in the land of Egypt.*

See *comm., v.* 8.

In *Rashi's* view, the phrase refers to Zidkiyahu's abortive attempt to forge an alliance with Egypt against Babylon. (See 17:15; *comm.,* footnote 17:17).

20. וַתַּעְגְּבָה עַל פִּלַגְשֵׁיהֶם — *Lusting for their concubinage.*

The translation follows *Rashi* and many other commentators. Israel was so enamored of Egypt that she was willing to cleave him under any circumstances, even to be only a concubine.

1. *Maharal* teaches that in Scripture, the donkey symbolizes physicality in contrast to spirituality (see *Gevuros Hashem* 29). [Although the Hebrew word for חֲמוֹר, *donkey,* is strikingly similar to the word חֹמֶר, *matter,* as used by *Maharal,* it is unlikely that he bases his analysis on this similarity since the use of חֹמֶר to mean *matter* began in the Middle Ages and is not found in Scripture.]

Based on the description of Egypt as חֲמוֹר in *v.* 20, the Sages see Egypt as the prototype of physicality among the nations (see *Maharal,*ch. 4). For that very reason, God's Providence ordained that Israel — the prototype of pure spirituality among the nations, the antithesis of Egypt — should grow to nationhood in Egypt. (Darkness sets off the beauty of light. Crass sensuality stimulates a striving for undefiled holiness *(Maharal).)*

God's redemption of Israel from Egypt is described by the Sages as being 'like a shepherd who reached into the animal's womb to remove a fetus' *(Midrash Shochar Tov;* see *Maharal,* ch. 3). During its bondage, Israel had become so enmeshed in Egyptian life that it and its host people seemed like one organism. The absolute contrast between Israel and Egypt would come about only with Israel's maturity, but in the initial stages of its development, Israel was to Egypt as a fetus to its mother.

As Israel leaves God, the old Egyptian heritage makes its presence felt, and the horrific picture emerges of an Israel craving the concubinage of an Egypt with its donkey-like flesh and horse-like issue.

It is small wonder that the prophet could not contain himself in the face of such a cosmic disaster.

בְּשַׂר־חֲמוֹרִים בְּשָׂרָם וְזִרְמַת סוּסִים
כא זִרְמָתָם׃ וַתִּפְקְדִי אֵת זִמַּת נְעוּרָיִךְ
בַּעְשׂוֹת מִמִּצְרַיִם דַּדַּיִךְ לְמַעַן שְׁדֵי
כב נְעוּרָיִךְ׃ לָכֵן אָהֳלִיבָה כֹּה־
אָמַר אֲדֹנָי יֱהוִה הִנְנִי מֵעִיר אֶת־
מְאַהֲבַיִךְ עָלַיִךְ אֵת אֲשֶׁר־נָקְעָה נַפְשֵׁךְ
כג מֵהֶם וַהֲבֵאתִים עָלַיִךְ מִסָּבִיב׃ בְּנֵי בָבֶל
וְכָל־כַּשְׂדִּים פְּקוֹד וְשׁוֹעַ וְקוֹעַ כָּל־בְּנֵי
אַשּׁוּר אוֹתָם בַּחוּרֵי חֶמֶד פַּחוֹת וּסְגָנִים
כֻּלָּם שָׁלִשִׁים וּקְרוּאִים רֹכְבֵי סוּסִים
כד כֻּלָּם׃ וּבָאוּ עָלַיִךְ הֹצֶן רֶכֶב וְגַלְגַּל
וּבִקְהַל עַמִּים צִנָּה וּמָגֵן וְקוֹבַע יָשִׂימוּ
עָלַיִךְ סָבִיב וְנָתַתִּי לִפְנֵיהֶם מִשְׁפָּט
כה וּשְׁפָטוּךְ בְּמִשְׁפְּטֵיהֶם׃ וְנָתַתִּי קִנְאָתִי בָּךְ

According to this translation, the formulation עַל פִּלַגְשֵׁיהֶם, lit. *on their concubines*, is awkward.

Mahari MiTrani offers: Israel was not only attracted to Egypt, but also to Egypt's concubines — the nations subservient to Egypt.

בְּשַׂר חֲמוֹרִים בְּשָׂרָם — *Whose flesh is the flesh of donkeys.*

The allusion is to the male organ of the Egyptians. (For a comparable use of בָּשָׂר, see 16:26, *comm.*).

וְזִרְמַת סוּסִים זִרְמָתָם — *And whose issue is the issue of horses.*

The allusion is to the seminal issue of the Egyptians. זֶרֶם is usually an outpouring of rain as in *Habbakuk* 3:10 *(Rashi).*

21. וַתִּפְקְדִי אֵת זִמַּת נְעוּרָיִךְ — *And you remembered the promiscuity of your youth.*

The verb לפקד occurs with many meanings, among them *to remember* (e.g., *Genesis* 2:1).

See *comm.*, footnote *v.* 8; footnote *v.* 20.

22. לָכֵן — *Therefore.*

See *comm., v.* 9.

23. פְּקוֹד וְשׁוֹעַ וְקוֹעַ — *Pekod, Shoa, and Koa.*

The Babylonian army will be made up not only of Chaldeans, but also of the armies of satellite nations. This is according to *Targum* and many commentators who write that פְּקוֹד שׁוֹעַ וקוֹעַ are place names.

Radak comments that the three words describe various kinds of officers. פקד means *to appoint* (as in *Genesis* 40:4; פָּקִיד is someone appointed to do a job, as in *Genesis* 41:34). שׁוֹעַ means *a mighty person* (as in *Job* 34:19). קוֹעַ does not recur in Scripture and can be interpreted only from the context.

בַּחוּרֵי חֶמֶד — *Pleasant young men.*

This echoes the description of the characteristics which had first attracted Israel to Assyria (*v.* 6). To *R' Breuer*, the intention is to be sarcastic: Does Israel still think of the Assyrians as pleasant?

The description קְרוֹבִים, *neighboring,* from *v.* 5 is missing here. The time had

ing the days of her youth when she debauched in the
land of Egypt, 20 Lusting for their concubinage, those
whose flesh is the flesh of donkeys and whose issue
is the issue of horses. 21 And you remembered the
promiscuity of your youth, when squeezed by Egypt
were your breasts, for the sake of your youthful
bosom.

22 Therefore Ohilovah! thus says my Lord
HASHEM/ELOHIM: See I shall arouse your lovers
against you, those from whom you were torn away;
and shall bring them against you from round about.
23 Babylon's children and all Chaldeans, P'kod, Sho'a
and Ko'a, all Assyria's sons with them, pleasant
young men, governors and rulers all of them. Officers and appointees, horsemen all. 24 Against you
will come encircling camps, chariots and wheels, and
with a company of nations, buckle, shield, and
helmet will they place against you round about. I will
assign punishment to them and they will punish you
according to their laws. 25 And I will set My jealousy

long past that Israel could have a feeling of affinity for the Assyrians (see *comm., v.* 5).

קְרוּאִים — *Appointees* [lit. *those who are called or summoned*].

A similar expression in *Numbers* 16:2 means *those that are called* by the congregation to give counsel — the important people in the community. In this sense, *Radak* interprets the word in our verse.

R' Breuer translates *ones who were invited* by God, for the purpose of destruction. A similar expression in *Zephaniah* 1:7, has this meaning.

24. הֹצֶן — *Encircling camps.*

The translation of this obscure word follows *Rashi. Targum* suggests *weapons* and translates as though the text were בְּהֹצֶן, *with weapons. Radak* translates *war chariot.*

וְנָתַתִּי לִפְנֵיהֶם מִשְׁפָּט — *And I will assign punishment to them.*

I will make them My representatives to administer the judgments which are incumbent upon Me to execute *(Rashi)*. The Babylonian army is no more than a tool in God's hands to administer punishment to His people (*Rashi; Radak, Metzudos;* see fn. 4:3; *comm.* 14:17; *pref.*, ch. 21; *comm.* 24:8, 24-27).

וּשְׁפָטוּךְ בְּמִשְׁפְּטֵיהֶם — *And they will punish you according to their laws.*

Radak and *Metzudos* interpret these words together with the foregoing ones: I shall place your judgment in their hands, and they will administer it according to their laws.

Rashi learns a new thought from these words. The Babylonians had been delegated by God to become the executors of His judgment. They went

וְעָשׂוּ אוֹתָךְ בְּחֵמָה אַפֵּךְ וְאָזְנַיִךְ
יָסִירוּ וְאַחֲרִיתֵךְ בַּחֶרֶב תִּפּוֹל הֵמָּה
בָּנַיִךְ וּבְנוֹתַיִךְ יִקָּחוּ וְאַחֲרִיתֵךְ תֵּאָכֵל
כו בָּאֵשׁ: וְהִפְשִׁיטוּךְ אֶת־בְּגָדַיִךְ וְלָקְחוּ
כז כְּלֵי תִפְאַרְתֵּךְ: וְהִשְׁבַּתִּי זִמָּתֵךְ מִמֵּךְ
וְאֶת־זְנוּתֵךְ מֵאֶרֶץ מִצְרָיִם וְלֹא־תִשְׂאִי
עֵינַיִךְ אֲלֵיהֶם וּמִצְרַיִם לֹא תִזְכְּרִי־
כח עוֹד: כִּי כֹה אָמַר אֲדֹנָי יֱהֹוִה
הִנְנִי נֹתְנָךְ בְּיַד אֲשֶׁר שָׂנֵאת בְּיַד אֲשֶׁר־

beyond their mandate, inflicting suffering *according to their laws* which had not been intended by God. This refers in particular to the blinding of Zidkiyahu (*II Kings* 25:7).[1]

25. אַפֵּךְ וְאָזְנַיִךְ יָסִירוּ — *Your nose and your ears they will remove.*

Married women who took lovers were punished by having their faces disfigured. Nose and ears are the distinctive features which lend a face grace and beauty *(Radak)*. [This should not be misconstrued as Torah law. Clearly it refers back to the words *and they will punish you according to their laws* of *v.* 24.]

Rashi and *Radak* point out that the nose and ears in our verse symbolize royalty and priesthood. Both are to be removed from Israel. The nose, the most prominent feature of the face, stands for the king, the most exalted person in the nation. The ears symbolize the High Priest whose movements were heard because of the golden bells attached to his vestments. [2]

וְאַחֲרִיתֵךְ — *And your residue* [lit. *those at your back*].

1. This idea is discussed by *Ramban* to *Genesis* 15:14.

At the Covenant between the Parts, God foretold that Abraham's descendants would be enslaved in a foreign country, but eventually they would be freed and their oppressors punished.

Ramban analyzes this passage in the light of the doctrine of free will. If it was God's will that Pharaoh should enslave the Jews, why was he punished for it?

One of *Ramban's* answers is that Pharaoh's treatment of the Jews was much harsher than was required for the fulfillment of God's wishes. He illustrates this with the case of Nebuchadnezzar. He, too, knew of his destiny to be God's tool in the destruction of the land and Temple (*Jeremiah* 25:9; 32:28-29; 26:6; 40:23). Nevertheless, the Babylonians were eventually severely punished for their role in these events. In *Ramban's* view the answer lies in the excesses which he practiced: *I was angered at My people; I desecrated My inheritance and gave them into your hands; but you showed no mercy.* [*Even*] *upon the aged did you impose your yoke (Isaiah* 47:6).

2. מַלְכוּת and כְּהוּנָּה, *kingship* and *priesthood,* are essential components in the totality of Knesses Israel, *the Congregation of Israel.*

Zecharyah (4:2-14) saw Israel, God's light to the nations (*Isaiah* 60:1), in the form of a golden candelabrum flanked by two olive trees pouring oil into it. Upon enquiring as to the meaning of this symbolism, he is told that these are the two בְּנֵי הַיִּצְהָר (lit. *sons of oil).* The meaning, according to *Rashi,* is that the trees represent kingship and priesthood *(both of which used oil for anointing), which help the candelabrum of Israel to shed the best possible light.*

23
26-28

against you and they will act upon you with fury. Your nose and your ears they will remove, and your residue will fall by the sword. They will take your sons and daughters, and your residue will be consumed by fire. 26 *And they will strip you of your clothes and take the objects of your splendor.* 27 *And I will cause you to cease your lewdness and your promiscuity from the land of Egypt. You shall no more lift your eyes to them, nor any longer remember Egypt.*

28 *For thus says my Lord* HASHEM/ELOHIM: *Behold! I place you in to the hand of those whom you hated; in the hand of those from whom you were*

The ordinary people (*Targum* renders *your nation*) are described as *residue* in contrast to king and priest who are symbolized by nose and ears, which are at the front part of the head (*Radak*).

וְאַחֲרִיתֵךְ — *And your residue.*

This second *residue* is translated by *Targum* as *the best of your property,* i.e., the fields and houses which will remain after the exiles have departed (*Radak*).

26. וְהִפְשִׁיטוּךְ אֶת־בְּגָדָיִךְ — *And they will strip you of your clothes.*

They will remove the priestly vestments (*Rashi*).

וְלָקְחוּ כְּלֵי תִפְאַרְתֵּךְ — *And take the objects of your splendor.*

They will take the vessels used in the Temple service (*Radak*).

Alternatively *Radak* suggests that the whole verse refers to all the plunder taken from the city.

27. וְהִשְׁבַּתִּי זִמָּתֵךְ מִמֵּךְ — *And I will cause you to cease your lewdness.*

The exiles no longer lusted after idol worship (*Radak*). This opinion of *Radak* is discussed in *comm.* 14:3. *Rashi* there does not share this view. The tradition of the Sages (*Sanhedrin* 64a; *Arachin* 32b) is that the urge for idol worship was eradicated by Ezra, towards the end of the Exile rather than at its beginning.

[It is possible to reconcile these seemingly conflicting opinions. *Metzudos,* who agrees with *Radak* in his interpretation of our verse, explains that idol worship among the exiles disappeared because through their suffering, they came to recognize the folly of their ways. However, the Talmudic tradition is that this urge was eliminated through God's direct intervention, in answer to Israel's prayer (see sources quoted above; *comm.* 16:15-34). We may surmise that the people did, indeed, relinquish their old practices in the suffering of the exile. However, in anticipation of the return to Israel, Ezra found it necessary to pray that the evil inclination toward idolatry would once and for all be eradicated. Had this not been done, there was a danger that when their condition was eased, the people would once more revert to idolatry.]

וּמִצְרַיִם לֹא תִזְכְּרִי עוֹד — *Nor any longer remember Egypt.*

Israel was never again to place its trust in Egypt. (See *comm.* 29:16 and footnote 23:8.)

28. בְּיַד אֲשֶׁר שָׂנֵאת — *Into the hands of those whom you hated.*

The Chaldeans against whom you rebelled (*Rashi*). See *comm. v.* 17.

כט נָקְעָה נַפְשֵׁךְ מֵהֶם: וְעָשׂוּ אוֹתָךְ בְּשִׂנְאָה
וְלָקְחוּ כָּל־יְגִיעֵךְ וַעֲזָבוּךְ עֵרֹם וְעֶרְיָה
וְנִגְלָה עֶרְוַת זְנוּנַיִךְ וְזִמָּתֵךְ וְתַזְנוּתָיִךְ:
ל עָשֹׂה אֵלֶּה לָךְ בִּזְנוֹתֵךְ אַחֲרֵי גוֹיִם עַל
לא אֲשֶׁר־נִטְמֵאת בְּגִלּוּלֵיהֶם: בְּדֶרֶךְ אֲחוֹתֵךְ
לב הָלָכְתְּ וְנָתַתִּי כוֹסָהּ בְּיָדֵךְ: כֹּה
אָמַר אֲדֹנָי יֱהֹוִה כּוֹס אֲחוֹתֵךְ תִּשְׁתִּי
הָעֲמֻקָּה וְהָרְחָבָה תִּהְיֶה לִצְחֹק וּלְלַעַג
לג מִרְבָּה לְהָכִיל: שִׁכָּרוֹן וְיָגוֹן תִּמָּלֵאִי כּוֹס
שַׁמָּה וּשְׁמָמָה כּוֹס אֲחוֹתֵךְ שֹׁמְרוֹן:
לד וְשָׁתִית אוֹתָהּ וּמָצִית וְאֶת־חֲרָשֶׂיהָ
תְּגָרֵמִי וְשָׁדַיִךְ תְּנַתֵּקִי כִּי אֲנִי דִבַּרְתִּי נְאֻם
לה אֲדֹנָי יֱהֹוִה: לָכֵן כֹּה אָמַר

29. וְעָשׂוּ אוֹתָךְ בְּשִׂנְאָה — *And they will act toward you with hatred.*

See *Ramban* quoted in footnote *v.* 24.

וַעֲזָבוּךְ עֵרֹם וְעֶרְיָה — *And forsake you naked and bare.*

Perhaps the prophet had 16:7 in mind. After the destruction it will be as though the history of centuries were wiped out. You will be as *naked and bare* as you were before the redemption from Egypt.

וְנִגְלָה עֶרְוַת זְנוּנַיִךְ — *That the shame of your harlotry will be uncovered.*

We have followed *Metzudos* in translating עֶרְוָה as *shame.* We translate זְנוּנַיִךְ (from זנן rather then the usual form from זנה) as *harlotry* in order to differentiate it from תַּזְנוּתַיִךְ at the end of the verse. (See also *v.* 11; cf. 16:37.)

30. עָשֹׂה אֵלֶּה לָךְ — *These things are done to you.*

The infinitive is occasionally used to indicate that the act is done constantly. See *Rashi* to Exodus 20:8.

בִּזְנוֹתֵךְ אַחֲרֵי גוֹיִם — *For your promiscuity in pursuit of the nations.*

See *comm., v.* 9.

31. וְנָתַתִּי כוֹסָהּ בְּיָדֵךְ — *Therefore I placed her cup in your hand.*

The 'cup of bitterness' occurs frequently in Scripture as a metaphor for suffering. See *Jeremiah* 25:15 ff. for a detailed use of this figure of speech in connection with Nebuchadnezzar's conquests.

32. הָעֲמֻקָּה וְהָרְחָבָה — *The deep and wide one.*

The cup of verse 31 is both wide and deep. It can hold much suffering.

תִּהְיֶה לִצְחֹק וּלְלַעַג — *It will be a cause of scorn and derision.*

The translation follows *Radak.* The 'cup', representing your suffering, will evoke the *scorn and derision* of your enemies. According to *Metzudos,* Israel *will be an object of scorn and derision.*

מִרְבָּה לְהָכִיל — *Ample enough to contain.*

The cup has ample room for all the punishment it must contain *(Radak).*

According to *Metzudos,* the derision of the nations will be *too much to bear.*

33. שִׁכָּרוֹן וְיָגוֹן תִּמָּלֵאִי — *With*

torn away; [29] *and they will act toward you with*
hatred and take away all your labors and forsake you
naked and bare, that the shame of your harlotry will
be uncovered, your lewdness and your promiscuity.
[30] *These things are done to you for your promiscuity*
in pursuit of the nations, because you became defiled
in their filth. [31] *You followed the path of your sister,*
therefore I placed her cup in your hand. [32] *Thus says*
my Lord HASHEM/ELOHIM: Your sister's cup you
shall drink, the deep and wide one! It will be a cause
of scorn and derision; ample enough to contain!
[33] *With drunkenness and sadness you shall be filled,*
a cup of astonishment and desolation, your sister
Shomron's cup. [34] *You shall drink it and suck it out,*
smash its shards, and tear at your bosom — for I have
spoken. The words of my Lord HASHEM/ELOHIM.
[35] *Therefore, thus says my Lord HASHEM/*

drunkenness and sadness you shall be filled.

Usually a drunk person is confused but happy. The bitter drink from this cup will bring nothing but sorrow *(Metzudos).*

כּוֹס שַׁמָּה וּשְׁמָמָה — *A cup of astonishment and desolation.*

שַׁמָּה and שְׁמָמָה are both derived from שמם, meaning *to be desolate* (as in 33:28) and *to be shocked* or *appalled* (as in 26:16). שַׁמָּה is used in both senses. *Deuteronomy* 28:37 uses it as *astonishment* and *Jeremiah* 44:22, as *desolation.* שְׁמָמָה usually means *desolation* (as in *Isaiah* 1:7) but is also occasionally used as *astonishment* (see 7:27).

Our translation attempts to avoid redundancy.

34. To *Radak* and *Metzudos,* this verse describes the depths of degradation to which Oholivah will sink in her drunken frenzy. To *Rashi* and *R' Breuer,* the verse contains the hope for an ultimate end to all of Israel's suffering.

וְשָׁתִית אוֹתָהּ וּמָצִית וְאֶת חֲרָשֶׂיהָ תְּגָרֵמִי — *You shall drink it and suck it out, smash its shards.*

The picture is of a insatiable drunk, sucking on the cup long after the wine is gone, even smashing it so as not to lose a single drop of the liquid.

גֶּרֶם is a *bone* (*Genesis* 49:14); hence גרם means *to break bones* (*Numbers* 24:8). Here it is used in a borrowed sense for breaking an earthenware vessel into shards.

וְשָׁדַיִךְ תְּנַתֵּקִי — *And tear at your bosom.*

In her drunken stupor, she is unaware that she is wounding herself.

In line with his interpretation of 16:7 (see *comm.* there), *Radak* writes that the two breasts symbolize the Written and Oral Law. When Oholivah tears at her breasts, she is cutting herself off from the sources of her spiritual sustenance.

[This interpretation is similar to *Shir HaShirim* 4:5 where שְׁנֵי שָׁדַיִךְ, (lit., *your two breasts)* is interpreted by *Rashi* as Moses and Aaron, your two sources of *spiritual* nourishment.]

Yalkut Shimoni (quoted by *Rashi*)

אֲדֹנָי יֱהֹוִה יַעַן שָׁכַחַתְּ אוֹתִי וַתַּשְׁלִיכִי
אוֹתִי אַחֲרֵי גַוֵּךְ וְגַם־אַתְּ שְׂאִי זִמָּתֵךְ
לו וְאֶת־תַּזְנוּתָיִךְ׃ וַיֹּאמֶר יהוה
אֵלַי בֶּן־אָדָם הֲתִשְׁפּוֹט אֶת־אָהֳלָה וְאֶת־
אָהֳלִיבָה וְהַגֵּד לָהֶן אֵת תּוֹעֲבוֹתֵיהֶן׃
לז כִּי נִאֵפוּ וְדָם בִּידֵיהֶן וְאֶת־גִּלּוּלֵיהֶן
נִאֵפוּ וְגַם אֶת־בְּנֵיהֶן אֲשֶׁר יָלְדוּ־לִי
לח הֶעֱבִירוּ לָהֶם לְאָכְלָה׃ עוֹד זֹאת עָשׂוּ
לִי טִמְּאוּ אֶת־מִקְדָּשִׁי בַּיּוֹם הַהוּא וְאֶת־
לט שַׁבְּתוֹתַי חִלֵּלוּ׃ וּבְשַׁחֲטָם אֶת־בְּנֵיהֶם
לְגִלּוּלֵיהֶם וַיָּבֹאוּ אֶל־מִקְדָּשִׁי בַּיּוֹם הַהוּא
מ לְחַלְּלוֹ וְהִנֵּה־כֹה עָשׂוּ בְּתוֹךְ בֵּיתִי׃ וְאַף

takes a different view. Indeed, Israel will have drunk and sucked out the dregs of bitterness. (שָׁתִית ... מָצִית), but once this has happened, the cup of bitterness will finally be smashed beyond repair. [This is in contrast to the cup of punishment which God plans for the nations (*Jeremiah* 51:7) which will be made of gold and will therefore never be broken. (See *Isaiah* 51:17-23: After Israel has drained the bitter cup of its last drops, God takes it away. It has served its purpose.)] The prophet never allows his audience to forget that the suffering is not an end in itself; it will surely lead to regeneration.

R' Breuer interprets the tearing of the breasts in this same vein. Oholivah's breasts had been desecrated by the lewd advances of the Egyptians (vs. 3, 8, 21). When she is finally purified by her suffering, she will want to tear away these reminders of her tainted past, so that her pure heart may once more be revealed *(R' Breuer).*

35. וַתַּשְׁלִיכִי אוֹתִי אַחֲרֵי גַוֵּךְ — *And thrown Me behind your back.*

This obscure idiom occurs three times in Scripture. *Targum* here translates *you have removed fear of Me from before your eyes.* In *I Kings* 14:9, *Targum* renders *My service have you removed from your eyes.* To *Nechemiah* 9:26 we have no *Targum.*

36. הֲתִשְׁפּוֹט — *Will you rebuke?*

See *comm.* 20:4; 22:2.

אֶת־אָהֳלָה וְאֶת־אָהֳלִיבָה — *Oholah and Oholivah.*

Why does Yechezkel reprove Oholah — Shomron — who had disappeared from the stage of history some 180 years earlier?

R' Breuer explains this in the same way that he explains Yechezkel's suffering for Shomron's atonement in 4:4 (see *comm.* there). Each part of Israel lives in every other part. The two tribes of the southern kingdom bear the sins of the lost ten tribes, and are the guarantors of the latter's eventual return. (See *comm.*, footnote 9:15; 37:15-28). Oholah lives in Oholivah.

37. כִּי נִאֵפוּ — *For they committed adultery.*

In this litany of sins, *adultery* is to be taken literally. It is not a metaphor for idol worship since that is mentioned separately later *(Radak; Metzudos;* see 22:10-11, *comm.* there).

ELOHIM: Because you have forgotten Me and thrown
Me behind your back, therefore you shall bear your
lewdness and your promiscuity. 36 *HASHEM said to*
me: Ben Adam, will you rebuke Oholah and
Oholivah and tell them of their abominations? 37 *For*
they committed adultery and blood is in their hands.
They committed adultery with their filth and even
their children whom they had born to Me did they
pass before them that they may be consumed. 38
Moreover this they have done to Me: they defiled
My Sanctuary on that day, and My Sabbaths they
desecrated. 39 *And while slaughtering their children*
for their idols, they would come to My Sanctuary on
that very day to defile it. Behold — so have they done
in My house!

וְדָם בִּידֵיהֶן — *And blood is in their hands.*

Radak recalls 22:2, where Jerusalem is called עִיר הַדָּמִים, *blood city* (see *comm.*, footnote there).

וְאֶת גִּלּוּלֵיהֶן נִאֵפוּ — *They committed adultery with their filth.*

Here, *adultery* refers to idol worship and *filth* is Yechezkel's consistently used term of contempt for idols *(Metzudos).*

וְגַם אֶת בְּנֵיהֶן אֲשֶׁר יָלְדוּ לִי — *Even their children whom they had borne to Me.*

They had circumcised these children on the eighth day, giving them, as it were, to God (*whom they had born to Me*). Still they sacrificed them to the Molech *(Radak;* see 20:26, *comm.*, footnote).

The *comm.* has followed *Radak* and *Metzudos*, who write that four separate transgressions are mentioned: adultery, murder, idolatry, and child sacrifice. In *Rashi's* view, however, only two transgressions are listed; the second half of the sentence is the explanation of the first. The *adultery* is with idols, the *blood* is that of the slaughtered children (see *comm.* 22:2).

38. טִמְּאוּ אֶת מִקְדָּשִׁי בַּיּוֹם הַהוּא — *They defiled My Sanctuary on that day.*

On the very day that they sacrificed their children to the Molech, they would come to God's Sanctuary, thereby committing further abominations *(Rashi).* Under such circumstances the very sacrifices which they brought to God were an abomination *(Radak).*

(See footnote 20:26 for another explanation of this verse.)

וְאֶת שַׁבְּתוֹתַי חִלֵּלוּ — *And My Sabbaths they desecrated.*

They slaughtered their children on the Sabbath *(Rashi).* (See 22:8; *comm.* 20:12-13).

39. Once more, Yechezkel laments the particular evil of continuing to serve God at the very same time that they desecrated His Name with the slaughter of their children (see *comm.* 20:39; *Isaiah* 1:12-13; *Rashi, v.* 13).

עָשׂוּ בְּתוֹךְ בֵּיתִי — *So have they done in My house!*

They have come to My house after committing these abominations *(Rashi, v.* 38).

Radak suggests an alternative in-

כִּי תִשְׁלַחְנָה לַאֲנָשִׁים בָּאִים מִמֶּרְחָק
אֲשֶׁר מַלְאָךְ שָׁלוּחַ אֲלֵיהֶם וְהִנֵּה־בָאוּ
לַאֲשֶׁר רָחַצְתְּ כָּחַלְתְּ עֵינַיִךְ וְעָדִית עֶדִי׃
מא וְיָשַׁבְתְּ עַל־מִטָּה כְבוּדָּה וְשֻׁלְחָן עָרוּךְ
לְפָנֶיהָ וּקְטָרְתִּי וְשַׁמְנִי שַׂמְתְּ עָלֶיהָ׃
מב וְקוֹל הָמוֹן שָׁלֵו בָהּ וְאֶל־אֲנָשִׁים מֵרֹב
°סָבָאִים ק׳ אָדָם מוּבָאִים °סובאים מִמִּדְבָּר וַיִּתְּנוּ

terpretation. They have even brought their idol worship into My house. In front of images which had been engraved upon the Temple walls, the Elders of Israel burned incense, as described in 8:11 (see *comm.* there).

40-44 Two different ideas can be traced in the bitter denunciation contained in this passage.

In the view of *Rashi, Radak,* and *Metzudos,* there is something worse than the dreadful list of sins enumerated in the previous verses. It is the shamelessness with which Israel attempts to curry favor with the surrounding nations.

When crowds of people descend upon Jerusalem, not in war but in peace *(v.* 42), because Israel has sought their friendship through all kinds of messengers *(v.* 40), and through the wiles of a promiscuous woman trying to win the attention of her lovers *(vs.* 40, 41), then we know that Israel has lost that inner strength which was once its pride. Abraham was called the Ivri (from עבר, *side; Genesis* 14:13) because all the world was on one side, and he on the other *(Bereishis Rabbah* 42:13). The ways of the Torah were never understood by the nations of the world *(Sifri, Deut.* 33:2); Israel's greatness lies in its isolation *(Deut.* 32:12, see *comm.* 16:35-42), not in its integration.

Isaiah (2:6 ff.) had already traced the disintegration of a Torah society to a situation in which people found fulfillment in יַלְדֵי נָכְרִים, *foreign values,* instead of in their own holy and unique essence. And now Yechezkel, through whose mouth God taught the unique Adam-status of Israel (34:31; *Yevamos* 62a; Overview IV) teaches that the spineless eagerness with which Israel seeks to ingratiate itself with the neighboring people is more damaging than its individual sins.[1]

A second possible approach is offered by *R' Breuer.* He interprets the passage as a condemnation of the foreign alliances which Israel sought. It felt secure and at peace once these pacts had been concluded *(v.* 42). Israel had driven the Divine Presence from its midst to free itself from the demands of holiness only to find itself shackled by its dependence on the whims of its neighbors.

The picture of the promiscuous harlot painted in chapter 16 is repeated here; but whereas there she put on make-up and ornaments to make herself attractive to the foreign *idols,* she wears them here to attract foreign *people.*

A nation cut adrift from its roots perceives its allies as the source of its security and feels it must appease them

1. Individual sins can find atonement, but the distortion of the self-image which Israel must have leads to its decay in the long run.

In Egypt, there had been a complete breakdown in Israel's adherence to the most fundamental laws (ch. 20). Nevertheless, as the Sages teach us, they merited redemption because of a stubborn clinging to the outward trappings of their unique nationhood *(Mechilta;* see *Meshech Chochmah, Exodus* 12:22).

40 *Now all the more since they send for men who*
come from afar, for whom a messenger had been sent
— and behold they came! — Those for whom you
washed, daubed your eyes and donned ornaments.
41 *You sat on a stately couch with a table prepared*
before it, and My incense and My oil you set upon it.
42 *The voice of a multitude — at peace — within it,*
and of men, many people, neighbors brought from

as if they were gods.

In the end those very arms which were once held out lovingly to God so that He might place His bracelets upon them (16:11), the very head upon which God once placed a crown of beauty (16:12), are, in an act of ultimate debasement, offered to these new lovers (*v.* 42).

We shall trace these two ideas as we comment on the individual verses.

40. וְאַף כִּי — *Now all the more.*

The opening words אַף כִּי, *now all the more,* indicate an escalation of evil (*Rashi;* other commentators).

[Yechezkel uses אַף כִּי in this sense at 14:21 and 15:5. However, other meanings are possible. See e.g., *Genesis* 3:1.]

The cantillation divides the following description into three parts, thus giving the sentence a distinct rhythm. תְּשַׁלַּחְנָה לַאֲנָשִׁים, *they send for men;* בָּאִים מִמֶּרְחָק, *who come from afar;* אֲשֶׁר מַלְאָךְ שָׁלוּחַ אֲלֵיהֶם וְהִנֵּה בָאוּ, *for whom a messenger had been sent and behold! they came.*

The rhythm helps to convey the feeling of outrage. Again and again, Yechezkel returns to the unbelievable degradation in the scene unfolding before his prophetic eye. (See footnote 7:2 for the prophet's use of rhythm as an aid in conveying his message.)

לַאֲשֶׁר — *For whom.*

The men thus summoned are the ones *for whom* you made the preparations described below.

41. וּקְטָרְתִּי וְשַׁמְנִי — *My incense and My oil.*

Her crime was all the more heinous because she offered her lovers the food that came to her from God (cf. 16:17-18).

42. וְקוֹל הָמוֹן שָׁלֵו בָהּ — *The voice of a multitude — at peace — within it.*

We expect nations with designs for war to descend upon Jerusalem. When they come *at peace* we must be suspicious *(Rashi).*

In line with his interpretation *R' Breuer* translates: *Because of the multitudes descending upon her,* [*she feels*] *peace within herself.* Her alliances give her a sense of security.

וְאֶל אֲנָשִׁים — *And of* [lit. *to*] *men.*

Lest we think that the tumult came from a multitude of animals, the verse stresses that it was a multitude of men *(Rashi).*

סָבָאִים — *Neighbors.*

The translation follows *Rashi,* based on *Targum. Radak* and *Metzudos* favor rendering this word as a proper noun referring to Seva, the son of Kush (*Genesis* 10:7). Thus *even the nation of Seva came from the wilderness.*

R' Breuer renders *drunkards* as in *Deuteronomy* 21:20. In his view, this phrase is connected to תְּשַׁלַּחְנָה, *they have sent for,* in verse 40: *She sends for men, any one of a multitude of men. Even drunkards are brought from the wilderness.* The initial feeling of safety is soon dissipated. As she recognizes the weakness of her position, she struggles more and more desperately for support. She makes alliances with completely unsuitable nations.

צְמִידִים אֶל־יְדֵיהֶן וַעֲטֶרֶת תִּפְאֶרֶת עַל־
מג רָאשֵׁיהֶן: וָאֹמַר לַבָּלָה נִאוּפִים עַתָּ °יזנה
מד תַזְנוּתֶיהָ וָהִיא: וַיָּבוֹא אֵלֶיהָ כְּבוֹא
אֶל־אִשָּׁה זוֹנָה כֵּן בָּאוּ אֶל־אָהֳלָה וְאֶל־
מה אָהֳלִיבָה אִשֹּׁת הַזִּמָּה: וַאֲנָשִׁים צַדִּיקִם
הֵמָּה יִשְׁפְּטוּ אוֹתְהֶם מִשְׁפַּט נֹאֲפוֹת
וּמִשְׁפַּט שֹׁפְכוֹת דָּם כִּי נֹאֲפֹת הֵנָּה וְדָם
מו בִּידֵיהֶן: כִּי כֹה אָמַר
אֲדֹנָי יֱהֹוִה הַעֲלֵה עֲלֵיהֶם קָהָל וְנָתֹן
מז אֶתְהֶן לְזַעֲוָה וָלָבַז: וְרָגְמוּ עֲלֵיהֶן אֶבֶן
קָהָל וּבָרֵא אוֹתְהֶן בְּחַרְבוֹתָם בְּנֵיהֶם
וּבְנוֹתֵיהֶם יַהֲרֹגוּ וּבָתֵּיהֶן בָּאֵשׁ יִשְׂרֹפוּ:
מח וְהִשְׁבַּתִּי זִמָּה מִן־הָאָרֶץ וְנִוַּסְּרוּ כָּל־

°יזנו ק׳

וַיִּתְּנוּ צְמִידִים אֶל יְדֵיהֶן — *They placed bracelets on their hands.*

In *Rashi's* view Oholah and Oholivah are the subject. They put ornaments upon their hands in order to appear attractive to their neighbors. The letter ו, *vav*, in וַיִּתְּנוּ is superfluous, so that the whole sentence reads *for the sake of many men, neighbors brought in from the wilderness, do they put bracelets on their hands ... (Rashi).*

In *R' Breuer's* view, Israel's new allies are the subject. [The masculine form of וַיִּתְּנוּ favors this interpretation.] Israel accepts bracelets and diadems from her neighbors in place of the beautiful ornaments she had once received from God.

43. וָאֹמַר לַבָּלָה נִאוּפִים — *And I said of this one who was worn out by adultery.*

The root בלה means *to be worn out* (as in *Deut.* 29:4). Hence the noun בָּלָה means something old and no longer fit for use. In a borrowed sense it has been used to describe a woman past the age of childbirth *(Genesis* 18:12) or a person worn out by overwork (*Exodus* 18:18). Here, according to *Rashi* and many other commentators it describes a woman aged before her time by her promiscuity.

Eliezer of Beaugency renders *I thought she was tired of adultery,* i.e., that adultery had lost its charm for her.

עַתָּה יִזְנֶה תַזְנוּתֶיהָ — *Now surely her promiscuity will depart from her!*

The word זוֹנָה, *harlot,* is rendered by *Targum* נַפְּקַת בְּרָא, *one who goes out.* It follows that the verb לזנה can also mean *to go out* or *to leave.* יִזְנֶה תַזְנוּתֶיהָ is thus a play on words, meaning *her promiscuity will depart from her.*

וָהִיא — *But she* [*stayed the same*].

God's expectations were disappointed. She remained the same harlot *(Rashi).*

Eliezer of Beaugency arrives at the same meaning through a different translation: *And she* to whom it is no new experience, is as much and as enthusiastically involved (וָהִיא) as they who have never prostituted themselves before.

44. וַיָּבוֹא אֵלֶיהָ — *And each of them came* [lit. *he came*] *to her.*

the wilderness. They placed bracelets on their hands
and splendid crowns upon their heads. 43 *And I said*
of this one who was worn out by adultery: Now
surely her promiscuity will depart from her! But she
stayed the same. 44 *And each of them came to her as*
one approaches a harlot; so they came to Oholah and
Oholivah, women of lewdness. 45 *Righteous men —*
they shall punish them with the punishment of
adulteresses and the punishment of murderers; for
adulteresses are they, and blood is on their hands.
46 *For thus says my Lord HASHEM/ELOHIM: Let there*
be brought up a company against them and let them
be placed for horror and spoil. 47 *And the company*
shall pelt them with stones and slash them with their
swords. Their sons and daughters they will slaughter
and their houses burn in fire. 48 *Then will I have*
caused lewdness to cease from the land, and all the

The Masoretes note the unexpected singular form וַיָּבוֹא, *he came.* (See *Minchas Shai.*) Perhaps the singular is used to stress that each lover who came to her was treated as an individual. Although she had known so many, she still gave each one her complete attention. (See *Radak; Metzudos.)*

אִשֹּׁת הַזִּמָּה — *Women of lewdness.*

The unique plural form אִשֹּׁת (normally נָשִׁים), *women,* is used to express disgust. These are no normal women *(Radak).*

45. וַאֲנָשִׁים צַדִּיקִים — *Righteous men.*

The Babylonians and Assyrians who are the executors of God's judgment (see *comm., vs.* 23, 24) are considered righteous when compared to the two sisters. (See 16:51, 52; and *comm.* there.)

הֵמָּה יִשְׁפְּטוּ אוֹתְהֶם — *They shall punish them.*

The punishment is described below *(Rashi).* See *vs.* 23, 24. [For translation of יִשְׁפְּטוּ as *punish,* see *comm.* 11:10.]

46. הַעֲלֵה ... וְנָתֹן — *Let there be brought up ... and let them be placed* [lit. *and place*] ...

These verbs, which are in the infinitive form, are used in place of the jussive (let there be). [For other examples of this usage, see *Leviticus* 6:7; *Numbers* 6:5].

47. The two categories of punishment in this verse fit the two crimes in verse 45. The children are to be killed and the houses burned because of the adultery which the mothers committed, thereby undermining family life. They themselves are to be slain by sword because of the blood they had shed *(Rashi).*

48. וְהִשְׁבַּתִּי זִמָּה מִן הָאָרֶץ — *Then will I have caused lewdness to cease from the land.*

Idolatry will no longer be practiced *(Radak).* (See comm., *v.* 27.)

כג מט הַנָּשִׁים וְלֹא תַעֲשֶׂינָה כְּזִמַּתְכֶנָה: וְנָתְנוּ
מט זִמַּתְכֶנָה עֲלֵיכֶן וַחֲטָאֵי גִלּוּלֵיכֶן תִּשֶּׂאינָה
כד א וִידַעְתֶּם כִּי אֲנִי אֲדֹנָי יֱהֹוִה: וַיְהִי°
א־ב דְבַר־יהוה אֵלַי בַּשָּׁנָה הַתְּשִׁיעִית בַּחֹדֶשׁ
ב הָעֲשִׂירִי בֶּעָשׂוֹר לַחֹדֶשׁ לֵאמֹר: בֶּן־אָדָם
°כְּתָב־ ק׳ °כתוב־לְךָ אֶת־שֵׁם הַיּוֹם אֶת־עֶצֶם הַיּוֹם

וְנִוַּסְּרוּ כָּל הַנָּשִׁים — *And all the women will have been chastised.*

The surrounding nations will learn a lesson from Israel's downfall *(Radak).*

וְלֹא תַעֲשֶׂינָה כְּזִמַּתְכֶנָה — *Not to imitate* [lit. *commit*] *your lewdness.*

Even if they continue to serve idols, it will not be with a profligacy like yours (see *comm.*, 16:27), nor will they be disloyal to their own particular idol (see *comm.* 16:33-34) *(Radak).*[1]

49. וְנָתְנוּ זִמַּתְכֶנָה עֲלֵיכֶן — *And they shall place your lewdness upon you.*

Your judges (*v.* 45) will place the punishment of your lewdness upon your head *(Rashi).*

XXIV

At last the day had come which was to bring Yechezkel's prophecies of destruction to their gruesome climax.

Bava Basra *14b describes the Book of Ezekiel:* רישיה חורבנא וסיפיה נחמתא, its beginning [*tells of*] destruction and its conclusion [*tells of*] consolation.

*Without exact guidance from the Sages as to where this break in the Book occurs, we are inclined to see this chapter as the conclusion of the first section (*R' Breuer *points out that* v. *3 is the last time in the Book that Israel is referred to as* בֵּית הַמֶּרִי, a family of rebellion.)

We would then assume that Chapts. 25-32, containing the prophecies directed against the neighboring nations, form the bridge between the early part of the Book, with its message of Israel's destruction, and the conclusion of the Book which describes the future consolation. The consolation of the second section is hinted at through these chapters which foretell the destruction of Israel's enemies (see pref. chs. 25-32).

It is thus logical to begin chapter 33 with a renewed exhortation to the prophet concerning his duties as צֹפֶה, sentinel *(33:7), over and above that which he was told in 3:17-21, since the whole thrust of his prophecy was about to change.*

[*The last part of ch. 33 (23-33) seems to contradict this division, since it appears to belong among the prophecies of destruction contained in the first part of the Book. However, if, as* Metzudos *interprets that section, it is addresseed to the remnant left in Jerusalem with Gedaliah* after *the final exile (see* comm. *there) then this poses no problem.*]

The date of the Tenth of Teves is to be seared indelibly upon Israel's consciousness. It is to become the first of the four fast days which Israel accepted by prophetic decree (see Zechariah *8:19;* Rosh HaShanah *18a, and b) and which would accompany them through the dark years of exile and suffering about to begin.*

Since the purpose of these fast days is 'to awaken hearts to be receptive to the

1. *Sotah* 8b uses our verse to derive the obligation of women to be present when a *sotah,* [*a woman suspected of adultery,*] is examined in the Temple. In the event she is guilty, they are to learn a lesson from her disgrace not to act as she had.

23
49

women will have been chastised not to imitate your
lewdness. 49 *And they shall place your lewdness*
upon you and the sins of your filth you shall bear,
and you shall know that I am my Lord
HASHEM/ELOHIM.

24
1-2

The word of HASHEM came to me in the ninth year,
in the tenth month, on the tenth of the month,
saying: 2 *Ben Adam, write for yourself the name of*

paths of repentance, [they] remind us of the evils which caused ... these sorrows [so that] in remembering [them] we can be helped to repent and improve' (Rambam, Hilchos Taanis *5:1), this date will endure in significance for Israel even after the final redemption. Then, in accordance with Zechariah's vision, these fast days will be turned into days of happiness and rejoicing, for their darkness will have generated the light of understanding.*

Both great communities of Israel — those who were still in Jerusalem and those who had already set out on the long trek through the wilderness of the nations *(see* comm. *20:35) — had good cause to remember this day.*

In Jerusalem, the long-dreaded siege of the city became a reality. It was only a matter of time before the city would fall.

In the exile, Yechezkel was called upon to perform two final symbols of exquisite drama, which once and for all would shatter the comfortable assumptions which, even at this late date, seemed to delude the people into equanimity concerning the fate of their beloved homeland.

Throughout his life as a prophet, Yechezkel had to fight two pernicious misconceptions. The first of these was the belief of the people in their own physical prowess. Jerusalem's inhabitants had no doubts at all that in a final showdown with the Babylonian army they would emerge victorious. We have encountered and discussed this עַזּוּת, fierce vehemence, *in footnote 3:6-7; and particularly in the* comm., *and footnote 11:3 where we first heard the parable of the caldron and the flesh. The first part of our chapter addresses itself to uncovering the fallacy of this thinking.*

Even more distorted was Israel's conception of the function of God's Temple in their midst. They thought that its presence would protect them irrespective of their own moral standing. (See footnote to pref., ch. 1; 11:15.) Yechezkel's heartrending loss in the second half of our chapter would teach the people how wrong they were. Even their beloved Temple could be destroyed just as Yechezkel's wife was struck down suddenly by the plague.

The two halves of the chapter are directed against these two false assumptions (Abarbanel).

1. בַּשָּׁנָה הַתְּשִׁיעִית — *In the ninth year.*

This is the ninth year of Yehoyachin's exile and Zidkiyahu's reign *(Metzudos).*

בַּחֹדֶשׁ הָעֲשִׂירִי — *In the tenth month.*

The significant dates concerning the destruction of the Temple are clustered around the winter and summer solstices (in Teves and Tammuz), while Nissan and Tishri, the times of the equinoxes, are seasons during which Israel achieves its greatest moments. This idea is discussed by *Maharal* in *Netzach Yisrael,* ch. 5.

2. כְּתָב־לְךָ — *Write for yourself.*

This translation is literal although the

הַזֶּה סָמַךְ מֶלֶךְ־בָּבֶל אֶל־יְרוּשָׁלַםִ בְּעֶצֶם
ג הַיּוֹם הַזֶּה׃ וּמְשֹׁל אֶל־בֵּית־הַמֶּרִי מָשָׁל
וְאָמַרְתָּ אֲלֵיהֶם כֹּה אָמַר אֲדֹנָי יֱהֹוִה
ד שְׁפֹת הַסִּיר שְׁפֹת וְגַם־יְצֹק בּוֹ מָיִם׃ אֱסֹף
נְתָחֶיהָ אֵלֶיהָ כָּל־נֵתַח טוֹב יָרֵךְ וְכָתֵף

word לְךָ, *for yourself*, would seem to be superfluous. If the word is idiomatic, the translation of the complete phrase would be simply *write*. For a discussion of the opinions of *Rashi* and *Ramban* regarding the use of לְךָ in similar phrases, see ArtScroll *Bereishis 12:1*.

אֶת שֵׁם הַיּוֹם אֶת עֶצֶם הַיּוֹם הַזֶּה — *The name of this day — this very day.*

Most commentators assume a literal meaning. Yechezkel is to write down two things: the *name of this day*, meaning the day of the week, and the *very day*, meaning the day of the month.

We are not told where this is to be written nor the reason for this command. The commentators explain that the prophet was to put these dates into writing so that when the news of the siege would reach the exiles in Babylon they would find the prophet's prediction borne out exactly, thus enhancing his position among them.

The rendering of שֵׁם הַיּוֹם, *the name of this day*, as the day of the week is problematic. Nowhere in our tradition is any significance attached to the particular day of the week on which this event occurred, nor is it clear why the day of the week should be called *the 'name' of this day*, since the days do not have any particular name, only numbers (counted from the Sabbath). Why was an exact record of the day of the week necessary to reinforce the position of the prophet? Would not the recorded date of the month be sufficient to accomplish this?

The expression שֵׁם הַיּוֹם, *the name of this day*, does not recur in Scripture. Therefore, any rendering must be based on conjecture and judged entirely by the context.

Perhaps the whole phrase כְּתָב לְךָ אֶת שֵׁם הַיּוֹם is idiomatic and should not be translated literally.

The word שֵׁם means not only *name* but also *reputation* or *fame* (see *Genesis* 11:4, 12:2). Yechezkel himself uses the word in that sense in 16:14, 34:24, and 39:13.

The root כתב is not limited to actual writing. When Jeremiah (22:30) decreed that Yehoyachin would be childless with the words: כִּתְבוּ אֶת הָאִישׁ הַזֶּה עֲרִירִי, *write this man as childless*, nothing was actually written (see *Radak* there); rather, it was an admonition that the decree be recorded in the minds of the people. (See also *Ezekiel* 13:9.)

The meaning of the idiom would then be: *Record the significance of this day.*

This rendering fits well with the next phrase, אֶת עֶצֶם הַיּוֹם הַזֶּה, *this very day*. This phrase occurs often in Scripture and requires careful definition.

The root עצם means *to be strong. Ramban (Leviticus* 23:28) writes that עֶצֶם הַיּוֹם means the *essential inner power of the day*. A day is called עֶצֶם הַיּוֹם when by its essential nature it is particularly suited to the role assigned to it.[1]

Ramban bases this interpretation on *Targum* who renders עֶצֶם הַיּוֹם as כְּרַן יוֹמָא. We know no meaning for כְּרַן but *Ramban* testifies that he saw texts in which the spelling was קְרַן, and therefore assumes that the כ of כְּרַן is a substitute for the ק. קֶרֶן is the

1. *Maharal* (in *Netzach Yisrael;* see *comm., v.* 1) discusses the significance of the number ten (the tenth day of the tenth month) relative to the concept of destruction. There is something in the essence of the day that suits it particularly to destruction.

The description of the tenth of Teves as עֶצֶם הַיּוֹם finds an expression in *halachah* according to some opinions.

According to our present arrangement of the Jewish calendar, the Tenth of Teves is the only fast day which can fall on a Friday, but never on the Sabbath *(Orach Chaim* 428:2). *Orach Chaim* 550:3 rules that no Rabbinically instituted fast day may be observed on the Sabbath,

this day — this very day. The king of Babylon
besieged Jerusalem on this very day. 3 *Now compose*
a parable for the rebellious family and say to them:
Thus said my Lord HASHEM/ELOHIM: Set the
caldron, set it and also pour water into it. 4 *Gather its*
cuts into it, every good cut; thigh and shoulder. With

horn of an animal; the seat of its strength. Hence עֶצֶם הַיּוֹם describes the inner power of the day.

The whole phrase is to be rendered: *Record the significance of this day, its inner suitability for the events which happened on it (R' Breuer).*

3. וּמְשֹׁל אֶל־בֵּית־הַמֶּרִי מָשָׁל — *Now compose a parable for the rebellious family.*

In 21:5, Yechezkel objected that if he were to talk in parables, he would be considered simply a storyteller and his message would have little impact. Here he raises no such objection. The time of fearing that his message would not be taken seriously had long passed. The events in Jerusalem confirmed only too bitterly that his prophecies had been very accurate indeed (*R' Breuer;* but see 33:31-32).

In 11:3, the inhabitants of Jerusalem confidently flung the parable of the caldron and the meat in the face of the prophet. As surely as meat is not removed from the pot until it is done, so they would not be ejected prematurely from Jerusalem. They were safe and would remain there until their dying day. The time had now come that in bitter irony both meat and caldron will be scorched by the searing flames of destruction.

שְׁפֹת הַסִּיר שְׁפֹת — *Set the caldron, set it.*

The root שפת means *to arrange* something or *to set* it upon its place. (See *Sefer HaShorashim* of *Ibn Janach* and *Radak*). שְׁפַתַּיִם (40:43) is the object upon which things are arranged. (See commentators, especially *Radak,* 40:43).

וְגַם־יְצֹק בּוֹ מָיִם — *And also pour water into it.*

Water is needed for the cooking process *(Metzudos)* and symbolizes the appurtenances of the siege *(Rashi).* In *Radak's* view, the function of water in the pot is to slow down the heating. Without water the heat would be so intense that the meat would be burned. Pouring the water symbolizes the length of time which the siege took [from the ninth (*v.* 1) till the twelfth year (33:21)]. This was part of God's punishment so that famine, plague, and sword would have time to do their work.

4. כָּל־נֵתַח טוֹב — *Every good cut.*

All the choicest cuts are to be gathered into the caldron. This symbolizes the gathering into Jerusalem of all the best and mightiest people (*Rashi;* see *Targum).* All came to the city to seek refuge because they could not remain outside the city during the siege.

and any fast days which fall on it are delayed till Sunday or, in the case of the Fast of Esther, moved up to Thursday. In theory, at least, this rule would apply to the Tenth of Teves if it could fall on the Sabbath.

However, *Bais Yosef* to *Orach Chaim* (550:3) quotes opinions that this fast day is an exception to the rule. If it could fall on the Sabbath, one would have to fast on that day just as in the case of Yom Kippur. This is derived from the expression עֶצֶם הַיּוֹם הַזֶּה, *this very day,* which is used both in connection with Yom Kippur and with the Tenth of Teves. (See *Chiddushei HaGriz* for a discussion.)

כד
ה־ז

ה מִבְחַר עֲצָמִים מַלֵּא: מִבְחַר הַצֹּאן לָקוֹחַ
וְגַם דּוּר הָעֲצָמִים תַּחְתֶּיהָ רַתַּח רְתָחֶיהָ
ו גַּם־בָּשְׁלוּ עֲצָמֶיהָ בְּתוֹכָהּ: לָכֵן
כֹּה־אָמַר | אֲדֹנָי יֱהֹוִה אוֹי עִיר הַדָּמִים
סִיר אֲשֶׁר חֶלְאָתָה בָהּ וְחֶלְאָתָהּ לֹא
יָצְאָה מִמֶּנָּה לִנְתָחֶיהָ לִנְתָחֶיהָ הוֹצִיאָהּ
לֹא־נָפַל עָלֶיהָ גּוֹרָל: כִּי דָמָהּ בְּתוֹכָהּ
הָיָה עַל־צְחִיחַ סֶלַע שָׂמָתְהוּ לֹא
שְׁפָכַתְהוּ עַל־הָאָרֶץ לְכַסּוֹת עָלָיו עָפָר:

עֲצָמִים — *Bones.*

This refers to the cuts of meat which generally follow the contours of the bones *(Radak).*

5. מִבְחַר הַצֹּאן לָקוֹחַ — *Take the choicest of the flock.*

The best of Israel are to be found in Jerusalem. (*Targum* translates: Nebuchadnezzar collects the choicest soldiers against Jerusalem. *Rashi* rejects this rendering as it does not fit the parable.)

וְגַם דּוּר הָעֲצָמִים תַּחְתֶּיהָ — *And also arrange the bones beneath it.*

Rashi writes that דור means *to arrange* (as in *Isaiah* 29:3; see *Rashi* there). Within the caldron, the bones are to be arranged beneath the more meaty parts. (However, תַּחְתֶּיהָ, *beneath it,* is singular.) *Mahari Karo* explains that this was the custom when cooking meat so that the more important people, who are served first, would receive the more desirable portions. The symbolism suggests that the weaker people (the meaty joints) are to be supported by the mighty warriors (the bones).

Others write that דור means *to ignite* (מְדוּרָה in *v.* 9 is *a large fire).* The bones are to be placed *beneath* the caldron and ignited to be used as fuel (the singular תַּחְתֶּיהָ, *beneath it,* is apt).

Why are bones to be used as fuel? *Radak* thinks that reference is to the bones of the murdered of Jerusalem (see *v.* 6: עִיר הַדָּמִים; *comm.* 22:2). The bones of these victims feed the fire which is to burn Jerusalem. [*Radak* is not disturbed by the dual usage of the metaphor. In *v.* 4 *bones* symbolized the people of Jerusalem who are to be burned in the caldron.]

Perhaps, after all, the bones on the outside of the caldron are the same as those on the inside. Is not the evil of the people itself the cause of their destruction? (See pref., ch. 7.)

רַתַּח רְתָחֶיהָ וְגַם בָּשְׁלוּ עֲצָמֶיהָ בְּתוֹכָהּ — *Seethe its boilings, so that even its bones shall have been cooked within it.*

The heat is to be so intense that even the hard bones will be softened. Even the mightiest warriors will fall before the ferocity of Babylon's attack *(Radak).*

6. עִיר הַדָּמִים — *Blood-city.*

See *comm.* 22:2.

סִיר אֲשֶׁר חֶלְאָתָה בָהּ — *Caldron whose filth is within it.*

Normally the fatty, inedible part of the soup would be removed. Here it had remained inside. Jerusalem's sinners *(Rashi)* or sins *(Radak; Metzudos)* were still within her. Nothing had changed.

Our translation of חֶלְאָתָה in the possessive, *'whose'* filth is indicated by *Targum, Rashi,* and *Radak.* However, this possessive form should be indicated by a מַפִּיק ה׳, a *dagesh* in the suffixial *hay;* but the *dagesh* is absent in this

the choicest bones fill it. ⁵ *Take the choicest of the*
flock and also arrange the bones beneath it. Seethe its
boilings, so that even its bones shall have been
cooked within it. ⁶ *Therefore, thus says my Lord*
HASHEM/ELOHIM: Woe, O blood-city, caldron
whose filth is within it and whose filth has not left;
cut by cut — empty it, no lot was cast over it. ⁷ *For*
her blood remained within her, she placed it upon a
smooth rock. She did not pour it upon the ground to
cover it with dust. ⁸ *That it might generate fury, that*

phrase although it does appear when the word appears later in the verse.

The absence of the מַפִּיק ה (חֶלְאָתָה, rather than חֶלְאָתָהּ) is particularly noteworthy since two words later the spelling is as expected. This irregularity causes *R' Breuer* to offer a different interpretation. חֶלְאָתָה is not *its* filth but *filth.* The phrase is to be translated: *a caldron containing filth.* All the succulent and meaty joints in the pot are only so much filth in God's eyes. וְחֶלְאָתָהּ לֹא יָצְאָה מִמֶּנָּה, *its filth* (that is, the filth which had become part of its being because it had been there for so long) *has not left it.*

לִנְתָחֶיהָ לִנְתָחֶיהָ הוֹצִיאָהּ — *Cut by cut — empty it.*

One group after another went out to surrender to the Chaldeans *(Radak).*

לֹא־נָפַל עָלֶיהָ גּוֹרָל — *No lot was cast over it.*

The usual way to divide the meat in a pot is to take out all of the meat and then to draw lots to decide who receives each portion. Jerusalem's inhabitants were to surrender piecemeal, each group seeking the best terms it could get *(Rashi).*

In the original parable (ch. 11), the caldron represented the protecting wall which ensured that the people would not be driven out of Jerusalem. Here, as in 11:17, the prophet stresses that all of them would, in fact, be lost, unlike the occasional instance of a threatening enemy who can be placated by the surrender of a few individuals. In such a case the people would cast lots to determine which among them would be sacrificed. Here no such lot would be cast *(R' Breuer).*

7. כִּי דָמָהּ בְּתוֹכָהּ הָיָה — *For her blood remained within her.*

The murders committed in Jerusalem were done so brazenly that no effort was made to conceal the blood, so to speak. Had they allowed the blood to flow out onto the earth, it would have been absorbed and hidden; but, as the verse continues, they allowed the blood, i.e., their crimes, to remain open to public view.

עַל־צְחִיחַ סֶלַע — *Upon a smooth rock.*

The fate of עִיר הַדָּמִים, *the blood-city* (see *comm.* 22:2) is sealed by wanton, openly committed murder.

צְחִיחַ סֶלַע is a smooth *(Rashi)* or *dry (Metzudas David) rock* which does not absorb blood, thus the blood lies there in the open; or the *pinnacle of the rock (Radak)* which makes it too high and awkward to cover up. In all opinions, it describes the freedom with which murder is committed since no attempt is made to hide it (see *comm.* 22:3).

The Sages in the *Midrash* interpret this section as referring to the murder of Zechariah, prophet and priest in the time of King Yehoash (some 252 years earlier). According to tradition, his blood lay seething on the Temple

ח לְהַעֲלוֹת חֵמָה֙ לִנְקֹ֣ם נָקָ֔ם נָתַ֥תִּי אֶת־דָּמָ֖הּ
ט עַל־צְחִ֣יחַ סָ֑לַע לְבִלְתִּ֖י הִכָּסֽוֹת׃ לָכֵ֗ן
כֹּ֤ה אָמַר֙ אֲדֹנָ֣י יֱהֹוִ֔ה א֖וֹי עִ֣יר הַדָּמִ֑ים גַּם־
י אֲנִ֖י אַגְדִּ֥יל הַמְּדוּרָֽה׃ הַרְבֵּ֤ה הָֽעֵצִים֙
הַדְלֵ֣ק הָאֵ֔שׁ הָתֵ֖ם הַבָּשָׂ֑ר וְהַרְקַח֙
יא הַמֶּרְקָחָ֔ה וְהָעֲצָמ֖וֹת יֵחָֽרוּ׃ וְהַעֲמִידֶ֥הָ
עַל־גֶּחָלֶ֖יהָ רֵקָ֑ה לְמַ֨עַן תֵּחַ֜ם וְחָ֣רָה
נְחֻשְׁתָּ֗הּ וְנִתְּכָ֤ה בְתוֹכָהּ֙ טֻמְאָתָ֔הּ תִּתֹּ֖ם
יב חֶלְאָתָֽהּ׃ תְּאֻנִ֖ים הֶלְאָ֑ת וְלֹֽא־תֵצֵ֨א מִמֶּ֜נָּה֙
יג רַבַּ֣ת חֶלְאָתָ֔הּ בְּאֵ֖שׁ חֶלְאָתָֽהּ׃ בְּטֻמְאָתֵ֖ךְ
זִמָּ֑ה יַ֤עַן טִֽהַרְתִּיךְ֙ וְלֹ֣א טָהַ֔רְתְּ מִטֻּמְאָתֵ֖ךְ
לֹ֣א תִטְהֲרִי־ע֔וֹד עַד־הֲנִיחִ֥י אֶת־חֲמָתִ֖י

grounds where it had been shed, acting as a constant reminder of the depths to which Israel had sunk. They had not even covered his blood with earth (לֹא שְׁפָכַתְהוּ עַל־הָאָרֶץ לְכַסּוֹת עָלָיו עָפָר) as the *halachah* required when even certain animals are slaughtered (*Lev.* 17:13). [This crime and the central position which it occupies in the *Aggadah* surrounding the Destruction are discussed in *comm.* footnote 21:28.]

8. In the spirit of justice based on מִדָּה כְּנֶגֶד מִדָּה, *measure for measure,* God agrees that the blood of the innocent victims should not be absorbed by the earth. It will continue to lie on the צְחִיחַ סֶלַע, *smooth rock,* but for a different reason: לְהַעֲלוֹת חֵמָה לִנְקֹם נָקָם, *that it might generate fury, that vengeance may be taken.* It will remain there, reminding God to vent His fury upon the defilers of His beloved city.

9. לָכֵן — *Therefore.*

Because the blood lies upon, it will not be forgotten. *Therefore, woe* to the *blood-city (Metzudas David).*

Our verse leads back to the parable. God Himself will increase the fire under the caldron. (See *comm.* 5:8.)

10. הַרְבֵּה הָעֵצִים הַדְלֵק הָאֵשׁ הָתֵם הַבָּשָׂר — *Piling up the faggots, kindling the fire, consuming the meat.*

All the verbs are in the infinitive, as this verse is a continuation of the previous one. God will increase the fire by doing what is described here *(Metzudos).*

וְהַרְקַח הַמֶּרְקָחָה — *Then adding the spice mixture.*

It is customary to add spices to the dish after the meat has shriveled *(Metzudos).*

The translation follows *Metzudos,* who divides the words according to the cantillation which separates הָתֵם הַבָּשָׂר, *consuming the meat,* from וְהַרְקַח הַמֶּרְקָחָה, *adding the spice mixture. Rashi* reads the two phrases together: *As the meat shrivels, stir it as one would a mixture of spices.*

וְהָעֲצָמוֹת יֵחָרוּ — *And the bones shall be scorched.*

Even the bones will be scorched by the great heat *(Metzudos).*

11. וְהַעֲמִידֶהָ עַל־גֶּחָלֶיהָ רֵקָה — *Standing it empty upon the coals.*

God continues the description of

vengeance might be taken, I have placed her blood
upon a smooth rock that it might not be covered.
[9] *Therefore, thus said my Lord HASHEM/ELOHIM:*
Woe, O blood-city; even I shall build up the fire —
[10] *piling up the faggots, kindling the fire, consuming*
the meat; then adding the spice mixture, and the
bones shall be scorched, [11] *standing it empty upon*
the coals. Thereby will its bottom be heated and
scorched, and its contamination be melted into it — its
filth being consumed. [12] *Falsehood having weakened,*
here abundant filth cannot leave here except by fire,
her filth. [13] *Because of your contamination, lewd-*
ness! Because I tried to cleanse you but you would
not be cleansed, you will not be cleansed again of
your contamination, until I place My fury upon you.

what He will do. When all the food in the caldron is burnt, He will stand the caldron empty upon the coals, לְמַעַן תֵּחַם וְחָרָה נְחֻשְׁתָּהּ, *thereby will its bottom be heated and scorched.* (For נְחֻשְׁתָּהּ, see *comm.* 16:35). This is in order that וְנִתְּכָה בְתוֹכָהּ טֻמְאָתָהּ, *its contamination be melted into it,* i.e., the contamination, which had caked and stuck to the walls of the pot, will melt, and flow down to the caldron's bottom — so that תִּתֹּם חֶלְאָתָהּ, *its filth will be consumed.* Once it has been exuded from the walls into the pot, the filth will be burned as the food was burned before it. The pot will be clean. Nothing will remain as a reminder of its past *(Metzudos).*

12. תְּאֻנִים הֶלְאָת — *Falsehood having weakened.*

The root און can be *falsehood* and לאה means *to be tired* or *weak.* From these premises *Rashi* renders: *She has tired out* the poor people in her midst *through falsehood. Radak* and *Metzudas David* translate: *She has weakened herself by falsehood.*

R' Breuer takes און in its meaning of *strength* and translates: *All power has been weakened.*

בָּאֵשׁ חֶלְאָתָהּ — *Except by fire, her filth.*

Because of all her sins, the filth within her has become very great. There is no way to rid her of it, except through fire.

13. בְּטֻמְאָתֵךְ זִמָּה — *Because of your contamination, lewdness.*

Because of your contamination, which took the form of *lewdness,* you will be lost *(Rashi).*

יַעַן טִהַרְתִּיךְ וְלֹא טָהַרְתְּ — *Because I tried to cleanse you, but you would not be cleansed.*

I sent prophets to exhort you to repent, but you would not listen *(Rashi).*

מִטֻּמְאָתֵךְ לֹא תִטְהֲרִי־עוֹד — *You will not be cleansed again of your contamination.*

Metzudos renders this as an assessment, not as a threat. *You will surely not be cleansed, until I place My fury upon you.*

יד בָּךְ: אֲנִי יהוה דִּבַּרְתִּי בָּאָה וְעָשִׂיתִי לֹא־
אֶפְרַע וְלֹא־אָחוּס וְלֹא אֶנָּחֵם כִּדְרָכַיִךְ
וְכַעֲלִילוֹתַיִךְ שְׁפָטוּךְ נְאֻם אֲדֹנָי
טו יֱהוִה: וַיְהִי דְבַר־יהוה אֵלַי לֵאמֹר:

14. בָּאָה וְעָשִׂיתִי — *It has come and I have accomplished.*

What I warned is being accomplished. The siege has already started *(Metzudos).*

לֹא אֶפְרַע ... וְלֹא אֶנָּחֵם *I shall not frustrate ... nor recant.*

פרע is the *frustration* of a plan, נחם is to *reconsider* a decision.

15-25. Yechezkel was introduced as a מוֹפֵת, *sign*, for his people in 12:6.

The word is so basic to an understanding of Yechezkel's precise function (see also Overview II, Yechezkel's Mission), that it is essential to define its meaning exactly. The etymology of the word is obscure. *Ibn Janach* and *Radak*, each in his *Sefer HaShorashim*, assume its root to be יפת (which does not recur in any other form) and (purely from context) define the word as *symbol.*

Hirsch to *Exodus* 4:21 agrees that it derives from that root, but he maintains that it is the *hiphil* of יפת which has the same meaning as פתה, *to be open* to an impression or a teaching. In the *hiphil*, it would mean to make someone responsive to a teaching.

However, *Ramban* to *Deuteronomy* 13:2 suggests that the word is a shortened form of מוּפְלַאַת (that is, with the ל and א removed; *(Ramban* shows that words in Scripture are occasionally formed in this way) and therefore derives from the root פלא, something *supernatural* or *wonderful.* Yechezkel is a מוֹפֵת to his people because he acts in a way that arouses wonder in those who observe him.

Yechezkel was destined to be a microcosm of their fate. God now apprises him of the greatest sacrifice[1] which his מוֹפֵת, *destiny*, was to entail. In one dreadful moment his wife, focus of his love and yearning, would be

1. It is true that the general usage of the term 'sacrifice' implies a free-willed offering, a concept that does not fit the circumstance of Yechezkel and his wife, neither of whom were given a choice in the matter. In this instance the 'sacrifice' element of Yechezkel's loss revolves around the unquestioning submission with which he accepted God's decree. He had been able to fuse his private life so completely with Israel's destiny that even this most difficult of God's demands seemed no more than natural to him.

The focus of the narrative is Yechezkel's bereavement. We can appreciate his shattering sense of loss, but at the same time, we recall that he had happily shouldered his מוֹפֵת-destiny. He had willingly *swallowed* the scroll which was to fuse his life with that of his people, and found it sweet as honey (2:8-3:3, see *comm.;* Overview II, *Part of Him).*

What of Yechezkel's wife who offers the supreme sacrifice as part of her husband's mission? Did she know of her fate? Did she shoulder it willingly? Given the fact that her death and Yechezkel's acceptance of it were meant to symbolize Israel's national mission, exactly what was the ordeal intended to represent to the nation? The last of these questions is discussed in the *commentary.* Scripture is silent on the earlier ones, and nowhere in the literature is the matter examined from her perspective.

Rambam in *Moreh Nevuchim* 3:24 addresses himself to the question of the נִסָּיוֹן, *test,* to which God occasionally subjects an individual or a whole people. He suggests that sometimes the purpose of these tests is to demonstrate to the nations of the world what true loyalty to God demands — to what lengths a servant of God will go in the fulfillment of His will.

In *Rambam's* view, then, the need to educate the nations is good and sufficient reason to expose people to great mental and physical suffering. Perhaps this is part of the destiny of the people of Israel as the bearers of God's glory on earth (for a discussion see footnote to 20:9). If they are to teach all mankind, then their personal claim to life must be subordinate to that duty.

The need to instruct Israel is not less than the need to teach the nations. Yechezkel's wife truly died עַל קִדּוּשׁ הַשֵּׁם, *for the sanctification of God's Name.*

[14] *I HASHEM have spoken, it has come and I have accomplished. I shall not frustrate, pity, nor recant. According to your ways and deeds have they punished you. The words of my Lord HASHEM/ELOHIM.*

[15] *The word of HASHEM came to me, saying:*

taken from him by the plague and he would be left to mourn a void which would replace his partnership with her — to mourn, but without the supporting catharsis of the practices which the *halachah* imposes on the mourner. As the archetypal mourner of Israel's past splendor, the practices of an individual mourner would be inappropriate for him. Their purpose is to allow the mourner to singularize himself and give outward expression to the sorrow that separates him from his friends and neighbors. In the universal bereavement of a destroyed Temple, no mourning symbols would be in place.

Based on our narrative, R' Yochanan teaches in *Sanhedrin* 22a: If a man loses his first wife, it is as though the Temple had been destroyed in his lifetime. *Sotah* 17a teaches that the terms אִישׁ and אִשָּׁה *(man and woman) between them contain God's Name (the* י of אִישׁ and the ה of אִשָּׁה). If they act as they should, God's Presence rests upon them jointly. If they do not, fire (the אֵשׁ which is left in each word when the י and ה are removed) consumes them. Thus, the union of man and wife provides a resting place for God's Presence on earth.

When his wife dies, that union can be no more. God is bereft of a locus for His *Shechinah*. In a small way, a temple has been destroyed *(Maharal, Chiddushei Aggadah, Sanhedrin* 22a).[1]

16-17. The directions given to Yechezkel concerning his mourning for his wife are the blueprint for his people's reaction to the destruction of the Temple (*v.* 22). They are to be our guide in understanding this catastrophe which is unique (see *comm.* 5:9, 7:5) in the annals of Israel's history.

The prophet is allowed no release for the grief that rends his heart. Not a single tear (דִּמְעָתֶךָ, *your tear*, is in the singular) may escape him, and if, in spite of himself, a groan wells up within him, he must release it in silence (*Ibn Janach's* interpretation of הֵאָנֵק דֹּם). His private grief is to be shared with no one.

The mourning practices prescribed by the Torah effect a sensitive balance of relief and control for the bereaved. On one side, the balm of tears is encouraged to soften the edge of pain. On the other side an intellectual acceptance of the immortality of the soul, and thus an avoidance of excessive anguish is required (see *Ramban, Deuteronomy* 14:1.)

Our passage guided the Sages in identifying those practices which are appropriate to the Torah's view of mourning. Those outlets which Yechezkel was commanded to deny himself are the ones which are ordained under ordinary circumstances (see *Moed Katan* 15a, b).

For *underlying* ideas of the individual practices, see *Abarbanel* here and *Hirsch, Chorev* 42.

Other mourners may not don the symbol of their majesty (*tefillin*, see *Yoreh Deah* 388), or wear shoes (symbol of independence and self sufficiency, see *Chorev* 42; *Orach Chayim* 46:1; *Mishneh Berurah* 554:31; *Yoreh Deah* 382). Yechezkel was called upon to act as usual.

Other mourners must hide their face

1. See *Kiddushin* 30b: (There are three partners in [the creation of] man); *Yerushalmi Berachos* 9:1: (Man needs woman; woman needs man; both need the Divine Presence); *Rashi* to *Shir HaShirim* 1:16; *Kiddushin* 31b (When R' Yosef heard his mother's footsteps he said, 'The *Shechinah* approaches) *Maharal, Tiferes Yisrael* 41; *Sanhedrin* 22a; *Kesubos* 5a.

טז בֶּן־אָדָם הִנְנִי לֹקֵחַ מִמְּךָ אֶת־מַחְמַד
עֵינֶיךָ בְּמַגֵּפָה וְלֹא תִסְפֹּד וְלֹא תִבְכֶּה
יז וְלוֹא תָבוֹא דִּמְעָתֶךָ: הֵאָנֵק | דֹּם מֵתִים
אֵבֶל לֹא־תַעֲשֶׂה פְּאֵרְךָ חֲבוֹשׁ עָלֶיךָ
וּנְעָלֶיךָ תָּשִׂים בְּרַגְלֶיךָ וְלֹא תַעְטֶה עַל־

behind a veil (*Yoreh Deah* 386; see commentators for an analysis of why this practice has been discontinued) in overt recognition of their withdrawal from society (*Chorev* 42) and must receive their first meal, after burying their dead (סְעוּדַת הַבְרָאָה) from neighbors rather than partake of their own food (*Yoreh Deah* 378) as part of a gradual easing back into society (*Chorev*, 42; *Abarbanel* writes that the rationale is to relieve the mourner of the bother of preparing his own meal). Yechezkel was denied such expressions of his inner turmoil.

In only one area was Yechezkel treated like other mourners. The obligation of silence — silence from the sound of Torah learning (*Yoreh Deah* 344) and from greetings between him and his fellow man (*Yoreh Deah* 345) — was incumbent on him also.

Why does Israel not mourn overtly for its Temple? Why, if most expressions are denied them, must they nevertheless conform to the requirement of silence? (See *Tosafos; Moed Katan* 15a).

The commentators suggest that the mourning symbols are appropriate only where other people are in a position to offer comfort. When the Temple is destroyed, mourning is universal, and the symbols are meaningless.

R' Breuer divides the mourning practices into three categories, reflecting different psychological needs. Those governing contact between mourner and society (עֲטִיפַת הָרֹאשׁ, *covering the face*, and סְעוּדַת הַבְרָאָה, *the meal after the burial*) would be meaningless following the destruction of the Temple, since the potential comforters, the neighboring nations, are not only indifferent to Israel's suffering but even revel in it and jubilate because of it (chs. 25-33).

[Perhaps there was to be no display of mourning because in its relation to the nations of the world, nothing had really changed for Israel. Its purpose is to educate them toward a knowledge of God (see footnote 20:9). That lesson can be taught in adversity as well as in success (see *comm.* 20:33). In fact, the moment of the Destruction was the moment in which God turned once more to His people, with the full and unstinting outpouring of His love (see footnote 7:4). It is only in the depth of its own heart that Israel knows the loss it has sustained with the destruction of the Temple. While facing the world bravely in its new and as yet untried role, the void in its heart expresses itself in silence.]

To avoid attracting the sneers of these neighbors it is best to avoid the outward signs of mourning, the unadorned head and the bare feet. Better to appear as usual than to suffer such humiliation!

Finally, the right to lament and weep is denied to those who callously brought about their own bereavement. Had it not been their own sins which drove God from their midst and made the Destruction possible? That the silence of mourning was nonetheless imposed on him, demonstrating to all the shattering impact of his sorrow, made the absence of the other symbols all the more poignant.

16. מַחְמַד עֵינֶיךָ — *The darling of your eyes.*

This refers to his wife, as evidenced by *v.* 18. He loved her very much (*Metzudos*).

וְלֹא תִסְפֹּד וְלֹא תִבְכֶּה וְלוֹא תָבוֹא דִּמְעָתֶךָ — *You may not lament, nor weep, nor may*

24
16-17

16 *'Ben Adam, see I shall take from you the darling of your eyes, by the plague. You may not lament, nor weep, nor may you shed your tear.* 17 *Silence your groan; do not practice mourning rites; don your majesty, and put your shoes upon your feet; do not*

you shed your tear.

R' Breuer notes the escalation. Not only should you not air her praise in public (ספד); you should not even weep privately. Not only an outpouring of grief is forbidden; even a single tear may not be shed.

Literally, the words לוֹא תָבוֹא דִּמְעָתֶךָ mean *let your tears not come. Radak* augments: *upon your cheek.*

17. הֵאָנֵק דֹּם – *Silence your groan* [lit. *from groaning be silent*].

This translation follows *Turgum* and most commentators. It has the same general sense as the three exhortations of the previous verse.

Ibn Janach (Sefer HaShorashim) suggests: *Sigh in silence.* It is an exhortation to keep his sorrow to himself.

Rashi offers: *Pine away in silence.*

(*Rashi* uses הִתְמַקְמֵק which means *to rot* or, in a borrowed sense, *to pine away.* See *Taanis* 25b. Our translation does not follow *Rashi* since it is not clear why he takes the root אנק out of its more common usage, *to sigh* or groan.)

The Sages take the two words separately. Each teaches a separate lesson: הֵאָנֵק, *groan!* From here we see that it is correct to bemoan the dead (*Yerushalmi Moed Katan* 3:5); דֹּם, *silence!* A mourner is forbidden שְׁאֵילַת שָׁלוֹם, *greetings,* and תַּלְמוּד תּוֹרָה, *the study of Torah.* Yechezkel, himself, is included in these exhortations (see above).

מֵתִים אֵבֶל לֹא תַעֲשֶׂה – *Do not practice mourning rites.*

The words מֵתִים אֵבֶל are inverted. The expected form would have been אֵבֶל מֵתִים, *mourning the dead. Radak* points out that such inversions are not infrequent.

From the four exhortations which follow, (discussed in pref., *vs.* 16-17), *Moed Katan* 15a, b deduces the correct conduct for a mourner. Whichever practices Yechezkel was denied are normally required. Why is the same reasoning not applied to the first part of the verse? Yechezkel was told to keep silent. By inference, other mourners should be excused from silence.

Many solutions are offered. (See commentaries to *Moed Katan* 15a, b and *Ramban, Toras HaAdam*). *Ritva* answers that logically we should assume Yechezkel to have been an exception only where he was told not to perform certain practices. Whatever he was told that he must do is certainly standard for other mourners.

פְּאֵרְךָ חֲבוֹשׁ עָלֶיךָ – *Don your majesty.*

פְּאֵר is used throughout Scripture as *headgear.* The root פאר means *grace* or *splendor* and is therefore appropriate for a hat, which lends grace to a person's appearance. (*Radak; Metzudos*).

חבש means *to bind* and is the term favored by Scripture for donning a hat (see *comm.* 16:10).

A mourner would generally be required to remove his hat and to cover his head with a veil instead. Yechezkel was told to dispense with this requirement (*Radak*).

In the tradition of the Sages (*Moed Katan* 15a), our verse refers to *tefillin.* Yechezkel was to wear his *tefillin,* although other mourners would not be allowed do so on the first day of mourning (see *Yoreh Deah* 388).

Mahari Kara explains the expression פְּאֵר, *majesty,* in connection with *tefillin.* The Sages interpret the verse (*Deuteronomy* 28:10): *All the nations of the world will see that the name of HASHEM is called upon you and fear you,* as a reference to the *tefillin* of the head. They lend majesty and awe to Israel in the eyes of the nations.

יח שָׂפָם וְלֶחֶם אֲנָשִׁים לֹא תֹאכֵל: וָאֲדַבֵּר
אֶל־הָעָם בַּבֹּקֶר וַתָּמָת אִשְׁתִּי בָּעָרֶב
יט וָאַעַשׂ בַּבֹּקֶר כַּאֲשֶׁר צֻוֵּיתִי: וַיֹּאמְרוּ אֵלַי
הָעָם הֲלֹא־תַגִּיד לָנוּ מָה־אֵלֶּה לָּנוּ כִּי
כ אַתָּה עֹשֶׂה: וָאֹמַר אֲלֵיהֶם דְּבַר־יהוֹה
כא הָיָה אֵלַי לֵאמֹר: אֱמֹר | לְבֵית יִשְׂרָאֵל
כֹּה־אָמַר אֲדֹנָי יֱהוִֹה הִנְנִי מְחַלֵּל אֶת־
מִקְדָּשִׁי גְּאוֹן עֻזְּכֶם מַחְמַד עֵינֵיכֶם
וּמַחְמַל נַפְשְׁכֶם וּבְנֵיכֶם וּבְנוֹתֵיכֶם אֲשֶׁר
כב עֲזַבְתֶּם בַּחֶרֶב יִפֹּלוּ: וַעֲשִׂיתֶם כַּאֲשֶׁר
עָשִׂיתִי עַל־שָׂפָם לֹא תַעְטוּ וְלֶחֶם אֲנָשִׁים
כג לֹא תֹאכֵלוּ: וּפְאֵרֵכֶם עַל־רָאשֵׁיכֶם

That majesty is to be retained by Yechezkel.

18. וָאֲדַבֵּר אֶל־הָעָם בַּבֹּקֶר — *Now I spoke to the people in the morning.*

The prophet shared his prophecy with the people on the morning of the 10th of *Tevet.* In the evening his wife had died, and as he buried her the next morning *(Mahari MiTrani),* he proceeded to act in the way that had been prescribed for him.

19. The people were intrigued because he did not modify his behavior as befits a mourner. They realized that there must be a lesson in his actions for them.

21. הִנְנִי מְחַלֵּל אֶת־מִקְדָּשִׁי — *Behold! I shall profane My Sanctuary.*

Previously (7:21, 22) the prophet spoke of *strangers* and the *wicked of the earth* who would profane the Sanctuary. In our verse the disguise is dropped. It is God Himself Who profanes the Sanctuary (see 5:8). The others are only tools in His hand *(Radak).*

גְּאוֹן עֻזְּכֶם — *The pride of your strength.*

What a source of pride the בֵּית הַמִּקְדָּשׁ, *Temple,* locus of Divine Presence on earth, could have been! (See *comm.* 7:20.) What a fount of strength, to direct and inspire Israel's aspirations. Both pride and strength had been degraded (*comm.* 7:24). Even as applied to the Temple their meaning had become distorted. The people's pride in the Temple was the unthinking arrogance through which they assumed that the Temple would protect them in spite of their sins *(R' Eliezer of Beaugency).*

מַחְמַד עֵינֵיכֶם — *The darling of your eyes.*

The Temple was very beautiful *(Radak).*

וּמַחְמַל נַפְשְׁכֶם — *And the yearning of your soul.*

The false prophets, who buoyed up the people's spirits with promises of an early return to Jerusalem [see *Overview* IX; 13:1-17], had an ally in the intense sense of yearning which the people felt for the Temple they had left behind *(Radak).* Psalm 137 portrays the fervor with which the memory of Zion was kept alive at the banks of Babylon's rivers.

veil yourself to the lips nor eat the bread of other people.

18 *Now I spoke to the people in the morning and
my wife died in the evening, and in the morning I did
as I had been commanded.* 19 *Now the people said to
me, 'Will you not tell us what these are to us — what
you are doing?'*

20 *And I said to them, 'The word of HASHEM came
to me, saying:* 21 *'Say to the family of Israel: "Thus
says my Lord HASHEM/ELOHIM: Behold! I shall
profane My Sanctuary, the pride of your strength,
the darling of your eyes, and the yearning of your
soul. Also your sons and your daughters, whom you
have forsaken, will fall by the sword.* 22 *And you are
to do as I did. Do not veil yourselves to the lip nor eat
the bread of other people.* 23 *Have your majesty upon*

חמל can also mean *mercy. Eliezer of Beaugency* translates this phrase in a negative way. The Temple was the means by which the people hoped to elicit mercy from God. In their distorted view, it had become a bargaining chip with which to negotiate with God.

וּבְנֵיכֶם וּבְנוֹתֵיכֶם — *Also your sons and your daughters.*

In reading this phrase together with the next sentence, it is clear that the mourning practices were not to be applied even to the people who would lose sons and daughters in the impending holocaust. Just as Israel had been to blame for the loss of the Temple and had thus forfeited its right to lament it (pref., 16-17), so these parents who had been instrumental in bringing about their children's doom forfeited their right to mourn for their children *(R' Breuer).*

22. עַל-שָׂפָם לֹא תַעְטוּ וְלֶחֶם אֲנָשִׁים לֹא תֹאכֵלוּ — *Do not veil yourselves to the lip nor eat the bread of other people.*

Do not observe mourning practices because there is none to comfort you. There is none among you who will not be a mourner, and mourning practices make sense only when there are comforters *(Rashi).*

In *R' Breuer's* opinion, the two practices mentioned in this verse reflect the mourner's relation to society (see pref., *vs.* 16-17). In this case they would govern the contact between Israel and its neighbors; but these neighbors, far from comforting Israel in its travail, actively rejoiced in it.

23. וּפְאֵרְכֶם עַל-רָאשֵׁיכֶם ... — *Have your majesty upon your heads ...*

Rashi refers to the *Midrash (Yalkut II* 364):

When Nebuchadnezzar came down from Jerusalem with the exiles who accompanied Zidkiyahu, they were greeted by the exiles who had come with Yehoyachin [to Babylon eleven years earlier]. The welcomers came, wearing black [mourning] clothes underneath and white [festive] clothes on top, as though celebrating Nebuchadnezzar's victory. They were jubilating in front of

וְנַעֲלֵיכֶם בְּרַגְלֵיכֶם לֹא תִסְפְּדוּ וְלֹא
תִבְכּוּ וּנְמַקֹּתֶם בַּעֲוֺנֹתֵיכֶם וּנְהַמְתֶּם אִישׁ
כד אֶל־אָחִיו: וְהָיָה יְחֶזְקֵאל לָכֶם לְמוֹפֵת
כְּכֹל אֲשֶׁר־עָשָׂה תַּעֲשׂוּ בְּבֹאָהּ וִידַעְתֶּם
כה כִּי אֲנִי אֲדֹנָי יֱהֹוִה: וְאַתָּה בֶן־אָדָם
הֲלוֹא בְּיוֹם קַחְתִּי מֵהֶם אֶת־מָעֻזָּם מְשׂוֹשׂ
תִּפְאַרְתָּם אֶת־מַחְמַד עֵינֵיהֶם וְאֶת־מַשָּׂא
כו נַפְשָׁם בְּנֵיהֶם וּבְנוֹתֵיהֶם: בַּיּוֹם הַהוּא
יָבוֹא הַפָּלִיט אֵלֶיךָ לְהַשְׁמָעוּת אָזְנָיִם:
כז בַּיּוֹם הַהוּא יִפָּתַח פִּיךָ אֶת־הַפָּלִיט
וּתְדַבֵּר וְלֹא תֵאָלֵם עוֹד וְהָיִיתָ לָהֶם
כה
א לְמוֹפֵת וְיָדְעוּ כִּי־אֲנִי יהוה: וַיְהִי

Nebuchadnezzar ... while anxiously asking: 'What has become of my father ... my son ... my brother ...?'

It is to this tragic charade that our verse refers.

וּנְמַקֹּתֶם בַּעֲוֺנֹתֵיכֶם — *Pine away because of your sins.*

This punishment is foretold in *Leviticus* 26:39. See Appendix IV.

24. בְּבֹאָהּ — *When it comes to pass.*

When the punishment comes about, then you shall do as I have done *(Metzudos).*

25. אֶת־מַחְמַד עֵינֵיהֶם — *The darling of their eyes.*

In *v.* 21, this expression referred to the Temple. Here, according to the cantillation, the phrase refers to the children mentioned at the end of the verse.

מַשָּׂא נַפְשָׁם — *The desire* [lit. *the uplifting of their soul*].

The translation follows *Rashi.* In *Radak's* view the phrase is a synonym for *longing.*

26-27. The coming of the fugitive, the bearer of the dread news of Jerusalem's destruction, is the turning point in Yechezkel's career. In 3:24-27 the people's obduracy had placed shackles upon his hands, making it impossible for him to circulate among them in order to reprove them. They could not come to grips with the idea that Jerusalem might really be destroyed. With the coming of the fugitive all this would be changed. Faced with the realities which they had so long denied, they would at last open their hearts to the mentor who had tried so hard to prevent the catastrophe.

26. בַּיּוֹם הַהוּא — *During that time* [lit. *on that day*].

33:21 reports that the fugitive came to the exiles on the fifth day of Teves in the 12th year (reporting the Destruction that had occurred from the seventeenth of Tammuz until the Ninth of Av in the previous year). Therefore, בַּיּוֹם הַהוּא cannot mean the day on which the destruction took place. *Radak* suggests that יוֹם can indicate a period of time. בַּיּוֹם הַהוּא is then translated: *during that time.*

24
24-27 *your heads, and your shoes upon your feet. Do not
lament or weep. Pine away because of your sins and
moan toward one another.* 24 *Let Yechezkel be a sign
for you, like everything he has done, you are to do.
When it comes to pass, you shall know that I am the
Lord* HASHEM/ELOHIM.*"*

25 *'And you Ben Adam, will that not be on the day
that I take their strength from them, the joy of their
glory, the darling of their eyes, and the desire of their
soul — their sons and daughters!* 26 *During that
time, the fugitive will come to you, to make your ears
hear.* 27 *On that day, your mouth will be opened with
the fugitive's, and you shall speak and no longer be
dumb. Then you shall be a wondrous man to them,
and they shall know that I am* HASHEM.*'*

יָבוֹא הַפָּלִיט — *The fugitive will come.*

The definite article (הַפָּלִיט) indicates that the fugitive is known to us. (Compare *Genesis* 14:13; *Midrashim, Rashi).* According to *Pirkei Eliezer* 27, it is the angel Michael who came to break the terrible news to Yechezkel.[1]

27. אֶת־הַפָּלִיט — *With the fugitive.*

The translation follows *Rashi.*

וְהָיִיתָ לָהֶם לְמוֹפֵת — *Then you shall be a wondrous man to them.*

Once they have become receptive to your message (*vs.* 26-27) your מוֹפֵת status will change. You will be transformed from a *sign* of destruction into *an object of wonderment* because of the accuracy of your prophecies *(R' Breuer).*

1. According to the *Midrash,* Michael is called פָּלִיט, *a fugitive,* because of the following event. After the angel Samael had successfully caused Adam and Eve to sin, God cast him and his cohorts down from the level of sanctity which he had enjoyed. In falling, Samael tried to grab Michael and would have pulled him down as well if God had not saved him from this fate. Thus Michael is a פָּלִיט, *fugitive.*

[We suggest the following interpretation: Samael had been delegated to tempt Adam into sinning. Had Adam remained impervious to his blandishments, Samael would have been firmly entrenched among God's holy angels, as an instrument for the sanctification of God's Name.

Because Adam sinned, thus reducing the exalted spiritual level of mankind, sin and evil, as represented by Samael, became integral parts of human existence. Samael, the satanic evil inclination, was 'cast down' to do his work on earth.

In falling, he tried to drag the angel Michael along, wanting the evil of sin to envelop even the protecting angel of Israel.

God prevented this from happening. The essence of Israel is inviolable by sin. It can never fall with Samael's fall (see footnote to 3:1).

This inner core of Israel's holiness was also saved from the holocaust in Jerusalem. The fugitive was Michael, who could not be destroyed in the fire which burned the Temple.]

⁂ Prefatory Remarks to Chapters 25-32

The following seven chapters, which deal with prophecies concerning Israel's neighbors and seem to form a cohesive unit, might well be the bridge between the first section of the Book of Yechezkel *which deals with destruction and the latter part which deals with consolation (see footnote to pref. to ch. 24). Although other chapters in* Yechezkel *(35, 38-39) also deal with the nations, they are interspersed among sections which obviously deal with consolation. These seven chapters, however, would seem to constitute a separate section.*

Although there is no overt mention of consolation in them, they nevertheless have such a connotation by the mere fact that they foretell the destruction of Israel's enemies. [Eliezer of Beaugency *thinks that those prophecies belong here because most of the nations mentioned joined in the siege of Jerusalem spoken of in the last chapter.*] *A more general discussion of the function of such prophecies against the nations in Scripture in general and in* Yechezkel *in particular will yield additional insights.*

Apart from certain prophetic books which are concerned almpst exclusively with a foreign nation (Yonah *and* Nahum) *large sections of the three major prophets* (Isaiah, Jeremiah *and* Yechezkel) *and portions of some minor prophets likewise deal with the nations. Jeremiah was even called a* נָבִיא לַגּוֹיִם, a prophet to the nations (Jeremiah *1:5), and some of his prophecies* (Jeremiah *46:1) are introduced as being the* word of HASHEM עַל הַגּוֹיִם, against the nations.[1]

We must pose the broad question of how these prophecies belong in Scripture. There is rarely any mention of Israel benefiting directly from the punishment which will overtake her neighbors, we must, therefore, exclude the possibility that these prophecies are directly a consolation for Israel.

It is suggested by some commentators that these sections are meant to educate Israel in the ways of God and are therefore not addressed to the nations at all. This interpretation is most difficult, however, since some of these prophecies are written in the second person (as for example the section dealing with Ammon in ch. 25) and are therefore manifestly addressed to nations other than Israel. On the other hand, it is hard to see how the nations could have been instructed by these prophecies since, with the exception of Jonah, *Scripture contains no account of attempts to communicate these messages to the nations.*

---

1. Our discussion of prophecies 'to the nations' should take place against the background of the following clarification.

Moses told Israel, *A prophet from among you, from your brothers as I am, will HASHEM your God establish for you (Det.* 18:15). *Sifri* deduces: *'For you,* but not for the idol-worshipers. How then was Jeremiah called a 'prophet for the nations'? — [It means for Israel] who acts like the nations.' Thus *Sifri* understands Jeremiah's title, נָבִיא לַגּוֹיִם, *prophet of the nations,* as referring to Israel rather than to the gentile nations.

Clearly, however, the interpretation of *Sifri* is difficult to reconcile with the verses cited above and with *Jeremiah* 1:10: *See I have appointed you this day over the nations* (עַל הַגּוֹיִם) *and over the Kingdoms. ...* Therefore, we are inclined to understand *Sifri's* interpretation in a narrower sense.

R' Yitzchak Hutner finds two distinct sources for the concept of prophecy in Scripture. The first is *Deuteronomy* 18:15 which we have quoted above. It refers to the general concept of prophecy, by means of which God communicates with the people. The second, derives from *Exodus* 24:12 where God says to Moses: *Come up to Me to the mountain and I shall give to you the stone tablets, the Torah and commandments which I have written to teach them. Talmud Berachos* 5a attaches separate meanings to each section of this verse, and the words *which I have written* (אֲשֶׁר כָּתַבְתִּי) are interpreted as a reference to Prophets and Hagiographa.

Thus we have prophecy in general based on the verse in *Deuteronomy*, and כִּתְבֵי הַקֹּדֶשׁ, *Scriptural writings,* based on the verse in *Exodus*.

We conclude, therefore, that in God's eyes Israel is the repository of all Divine truth, even that which is meant for the other nations. The obligation lies upon the nations to recognize this condition and avail themselves of the opportunity to inquire of Israel and learn what God wishes of them. In much the same way, God commanded that the Torah be inscribed in seventy languages upon stones which were to be erected at the border of Israel, so that all the nations might come and learn it from them (see Deut. *27:1-8 and* Sotah *35b). For not availing themselves of that opportunity, the nations deserved destruction (*Sotah ibid.)

If we are correct in this thought, then, indeed these prophecies are a fitting part of the consolation prophecies of Yechezkel. [We are not here concerned with the function of this type of prophecy in the other Prophets.] In spite of Jerusalem's destruction, Israel had not lost its primacy among the nations (see comm. *to 1:4). It was still to Israel that God turned when He wanted to address mankind.*

XXV

This chapter contains a group of four prophecies directed against some of Israel's neighbors. The nations are dealt with in a logical geographical pattern, that is, from north to south and then west. The sequence is Ammon, Moab, Edom and Philistia.

The date of these prophecies is not indicated. However, since they tell of the punishments merited by these nations for rejoicing in Israel's agony, they clearly refer to events which took place after the Destruction. According to Seder Olam *26:18, Nebuchadnezzar 'swamped'* [שטף] *the Jews in Ammon and Moab in the twenty-third year of his reign, which is some four years after the Destruction (see* II Kings *28:8). This indicates that at that time these two nations had already been subjugated by him.*

If indeed it is Babylon which is to destroy these countries (see comm. *to* Children of the East *in* v. *4), then the events described would be a fulfillment of Jeremiah's prophecy (*Jeremiah *25, 27) that all these nations were to be conquered by Babylon (see* Chagigah 23b; comm. *1:4).*

* * * * * *

In this and subsequent chapters which address themselves to the fate of the foreign nations, a constantly recurring theme is that they are to be punished because of their malicious exultation at Israel's destruction.

Why should such terrible suffering be imposed on nations in punishment for

---

We suggest that when *Sifri* deduces from *Deuteronomy* that prophecy will be limited to Israel, the restriction applies only to the type of prophecy discussed in that particular passage — not the form of prophecy contained in Scripture.

A careful study of the verse in *Deuteronomy* reveals that God promises Israel a substitute for the magicians and star gazers which were common among the Canaanite nations and which were prohibited to Israel. [See *Rambam* in his Introduction to *Mishnah*, and *Vilna Gaon* to *Proverbs* 16:4, that it was customary to consult the prophets on all kinds of personal matters. (But see *Ha'amek Davar* and *R' Hirsch* to *Deuteronomy* 18:15).] This kind of prophecy is indeed to be limited to Israel. Only with them is God so close that he will bestow the gift of prophecy for even the private needs of an individual.

But prophecy which has universal application, such as that found in Scripture (derived from *Exodus)*, is not denied the nations. [For confirmation of this thesis see *Midrash Tanchuma, Balak* 1.]

According to this assumption, *Sifri's* description of Jeremiah as a prophet to Israel 'who act like the nations' can be understood in a narrow sense. *Sifri* does *not* contradict the simple statement that Jeremiah is indeed to prophesy to the nations. *Sifri* intends to point out, however, that Jeremiah is *not* to be a prophet to the nations in *every* aspect of prophecy, including the individual, personal sense, but only in the general, universal sense.

ב דְבַר־יְהוָה אֵלַי לֵאמֹר: בֶּן־אָדָם שִׂים
פָּנֶיךָ אֶל־בְּנֵי עַמּוֹן וְהִנָּבֵא עֲלֵיהֶם:
ג וְאָמַרְתָּ לִבְנֵי עַמּוֹן שִׁמְעוּ דְּבַר־אֲדֹנָי
יֱהֹוִה כֹּה־אָמַר אֲדֹנָי יֱהֹוִה יַעַן אָמְרֵךְ
הֶאָח אֶל־מִקְדָּשִׁי כִי־נִחָל וְאֶל־אַדְמַת
יִשְׂרָאֵל כִּי נָשַׁמָּה וְאֶל־בֵּית יְהוּדָה כִּי
ד הָלְכוּ בַּגּוֹלָה: לָכֵן הִנְנִי נֹתְנָךְ לִבְנֵי־קֶדֶם

what seems to imply an ethical shortcoming? Their glee, blameworthy and reprehensible as it was, did not contravene any of the seven Noachic laws. Why then, should the punishment be so severe?

This question calls into focus the very essence of the Torah's perception of the gentile nations and their relationship to God and Israel.

The Torah stresses repeatedly that no special expectations of reward set Israel apart from the other nations. The promise of life *for walking in God's statutes is to* man *in general (*Leviticus *18:5), not to Israel in particular; Heaven's gates are exhorted to open for any* nation of enduring loyalty (Isaiah *26:2). All righteous people will enter God's gates (*Psalms *33:1). Nor will God's kindness be bestowed upon Israel exclusively. All* who are good and straightforward in their hearts (Psalms *125:4) will merit it (*Yalkut, Leviticus *591).*

Israel is distinguished not in privileges but in responsibilities. (See comm. *5:5). It is to be the* מַמְלֶכֶת כֹּהֲנִים, kingdom of priests (Exodus *19:6), who (*Sforno *there) are to lead the whole of mankind to God just as a* kohen *within Israel is assigned to strengthen the bond between God and His people.*

Since God's lofty purpose for the nations of the world can be realized only by their willingness to be led by Israel, their right to existence must depend on the degree to which they are willing to learn from Israel and her fate. Indeed, the one nation which will obstinately and unbendingly refuse to accede to Israel's role — Amalek (see Yalkut, Exodus *268) —* is for that reason *condemned to ultimate, total destruction. (See* Pachad Yitzchak *to Purim, ch. 1).*

The destruction of Temple and land had been planned as a lesson to mankind. Deuteronomy *29:23 describes how the nations were to realize that Israel's terrible fate resulted from its forsaking of God and His covenant. Had the nations learned this lesson and related to Israel and her situation according to God's plan, they would thereby have justified their existence.*

However, Israel's neighbors were far from being sobered by the holocaust. Instead, they mindlessly rejoiced at the downfall of their enemy. They were condemned to destruction, therefore — not in punishment for their unethical reaction, but because their attitude revealed that they could never fulfill the purpose of their existence. Thus, they forfeited their right to exist.

2-11. Ammon and Moab had always harbored a particularly virulent hatred of Israel. As children of Lot, the nephew of Abraham (*Genesis* 19:31-38), they might have been expected to have feelings of gratitude and good will towards Abraham's descendants. Instead, in an outpouring of malicious spite, they refused Israel the most basic human needs — food and drink — while it was traveling through the desert, and as a result, their male descendants were forever barred from marrying into the Jewish people (*Deut.* 23:4-8). Their un-

25
1-4

The word of HASHEM came to me saying: 2 Ben
Adam, set your face towards the children of Am-
mon and prophecy against them. 3 And say to the
children of Ammon: Hear the word of my Lord
HASHEM/ELOHIM. Thus says my Lord
HASHEM/ELOHIM: Because you said 'Hurrah!' of My
Sanctuary when it was desecrated and of the land of
Israel when it was laid waste and of the family of
Judah when they went into exile, 4 therefore, behold!
I present you to the sons of the East as a possession,

reasoned hatred continued, and *Sanhedrin* 96b relates how they relentlessly urged Nebuchadnezzar to wage his campaign against Jerusalem at a time when he was still hesitant. When the Temple finally fell, they paid no heed to the plunder upon which all the other armies fell. They were eager to lay hands upon the *Sefer Torah* so that they might expurgate from it the verse in *Deuteronomy* which condemned them eternally for their ethical bankruptcy (*Eichah Rabbasi* 1:40; see ArtScroll *Eichah* 1:10 and *Midrash* there for a fuller account of their depravity and how Yechezkel's prophecy against them resulted from it). It is to these שִׁיבְהֵי בִישִׁי, *bad neighbors (Sanhedrin* 96b) that Yechezkel now turns.

3. הֶאָח — *Hurrah!*

All commentators view this term as an expression of joy. *Targum* translates: חֶדְוָא, which means *happiness.*

We have discussed the folly of this joy in *commentary* 21:9. Little did the Ammonites realize how much Israel's loss was also their own.

אֶל־מִקְדָּשִׁי כִּי־נִחָל — *Of My Sanctuary when it was desecrated.*

Our translation follows *Targum* who traces נחל to חלל, *to desecrate. Rashi* traces it to נחל, *to inherit,* and translates: *My Sanctuary which was taken over [by strangers].*

Ammon's malicious delight seems to have had three separate causes: the destruction of the Temple, the laying waste of Israel's land, and the exiling of her people.

The latter two are understandable enough, in view of their hatred for the people, and one can well imagine that a deserted land seemed to offer the opportunity for territorial expansion into the deserted land *(Mahari Kara).* Why was there joy at the destruction of the Temple?

Perhaps it was just a malevolent satisfaction that Israel's pride and majesty (see *comm.* 7:20, 24:21) had been ravaged. It is also possible that in this irrational hatred there was an innate revulsion for the Divine. The *Shechinah* serves as witness to the depravity of an Ammon or a Moab. What a relief they must have felt in thinking that the crumbling walls of the Temple presaged an end to the moral demands implicit in the Divine Presence!

4. לִבְנֵי קֶדֶם — *To the sons of the East.*

Who are the *sons of the East? Rashi* writes that it means Babylonians who dwelt to the east (that is, northeast) of Jerusalem.

However Babylon is not referred to as *the sons of the East* anywhere else; instead we find Babylon described as the enemy to the north *(Jeremiah* 1:14). (Although, as mentioned in *comm.* 21:33, *Josephus* in *Kadmonios* 10:7 does report that Ammon and Moab were subdued by Nebuchadnezzar.)

Radak and *Metzudos* write that the

לְמוֹרָשָׁה וְיִשְּׁבוּ טִירוֹתֵיהֶם בָּךְ וְנָתְנוּ בָךְ
מִשְׁכְּנֵיהֶם הֵמָּה יֹאכְלוּ פִרְיֵךְ וְהֵמָּה
ה יִשְׁתּוּ חֲלָבֵךְ׃ וְנָתַתִּי אֶת־רַבָּה לִנְוֵה
גְמַלִּים וְאֶת־בְּנֵי עַמּוֹן לְמִרְבַּץ־צֹאן
ו וִידַעְתֶּם כִּי־אֲנִי יהוה׃ כִּי כֹה
אָמַר אֲדֹנָי יֱהוִה יַעַן מַחְאֲךָ יָד וְרַקְעֲךָ
בְּרָגֶל וַתִּשְׂמַח בְּכָל־שָׁאטְךָ בְּנֶפֶשׁ אֶל־
ז אַדְמַת יִשְׂרָאֵל׃ לָכֵן הִנְנִי נָטִיתִי אֶת־
יָדִי עָלֶיךָ וּנְתַתִּיךָ °לבג לַגּוֹיִם וְהִכְרַתִּיךָ °לְבַז ק׳
מִן־הָעַמִּים וְהַאֲבַדְתִּיךָ מִן־הָאֲרָצוֹת
ח אַשְׁמִידְךָ וְיָדַעְתָּ כִּי־אֲנִי יהוה׃ כֹּה

Medianites and Persians are meant. Although Ammon and Moab would not fall victim to Babylon, they would eventually be conquered by the Persians. (See *comm.* 21:33 for a discussion of this opinion.)

R' Breuer points out that in *Jeremiah* 49:28, *sons of the East* is used to describe tribes of nomads, tent-dwellers, who followed flocks of sheep and camels. Mighty Ammon was to lie at the mercy of nomadic tribes who, under normal circumstances, should have been much too weak for such a conquest. Nevertheless, they would become masters of Ammon, setting up their encampments and harvesting freely the produce of the land. Ammon's proud cities would become grazing grounds for the nomads' flocks. In a true sense, the land which had been given to Ammon as יְרֻשָּׁה, *an inheritance* (*Deuteronomy* 2:19), would now be a מוֹרָשָׁה, *possession,* for their conquerers. This conquest by *sons of the East* would only be temporary. In the end, mighty Babylon was to come and engulf Ammon together with the rest of the nations (*v.* 7).

טִירוֹתֵיהֶם — *Their palaces.*

If *the sons of the East* are nomadic tent dwellers (see above), one would not expect them to build palaces. *R' Breuer* suggests that the ease with which they took Ammon encouraged them to try settling there, against their usual custom. *R' Eliezer of Beaugency* simply translates טִירוֹתֵיהֶם as *their tents.*

According to *Radak* who understands *sons of the East* as an allusion to the Persian conquerors, they would not destroy the land and then move on. They, as the land's new masters, would settle it by building their own cities there.

5. רַבָּה...בְּנֵי עַמּוֹן — *Rabbah ... sons of Ammon.*

Rabbah was the capital of Ammon. By *sons of Ammon,* the verse means the other important cities of the Ammonites. The conquerors would pillage the cities contemptuously by using them for their flocks *(Metzudos).*

6. יַעַן מַחְאֲךָ יָד וְרַקְעֲךָ בְּרָגֶל — *Because you pounded your hand and stamped your foot.*

Thereby, you displayed your joy at the tragedy of Israel. These same acts, however, are also used to express grief as in 6:11 *(Rashi;* see *comm.* to 6:11).

בְּכָל שָׁאטְךָ בְּנֶפֶשׁ — *With all the rashness of your soul.*

The translation follows *Targum* and

25
5-7

and they shall establish their palaces within you,and place their encampments within you. They shall eat your fruits, and they shall drink your milk.
[5] *And I shall make Rabbah a pasture for camels and the sons of Ammon a resting place for flocks, so you shall know that I am* HASHEM.

[6] *For thus says my Lord,* HASHEM/ELOHIM*: Because you pounded your hand and stamped your foot and rejoiced with all the rashness of your soul about the land of Israel —*
[7] *therefore I have extended My hand against you and presented you as spoils to the nations, and cut you off from the peoples and made you perish from among the lands. I shall destroy you — then you shall know that I am* HASHEM.

Rashi's second comment. See *commentary* to 16:57 for a fuller discussion.

Radak and *Metzudos* follow *Rashi's* alternative rendering. שאט is an expression of disdain: *with all the disdain of which your soul is capable.* Israel seemed utterly lost; Ammon felt invincible.

7. This verse turns to the Babylonian conquest which was indicated at 21:33 (see above). Until now they had only suffered the indignity of having the eastern nomads use their land as their own. Now they faced annihilation at Nebuchadnezzar's hands.

וּנְתַתִּיךָ לְבַז לְגוֹיִם — *And presented you as spoils to the nations.*

The fact that בַּז, *spoils,* is written בַּג, *food* (see *Daniel* 1:5), indicates the ridiculous ease with which the conqueror was able to do whatever he wanted. Ammon was like a meal spread before him.

וְיָדַעְתָּ כִּי אֲנִי הַשֵּׁם — *Then you shall know that I am* HASHEM.

The suffering of Ammon, no less than that of Israel, has as its ultimate goal the knowledge of God. Moreover, that knowledge will bear fruit. *Jeremiah* 49:6 talks of an eventual return of Ammon's captives *(R' Breuer).*

1. *R' Breuer's* idea of two separate conquests described in *vs.* 3-5, and *vs.* 6-7, respectively, was used as the basis for the *commentary* because of the advantages which it offers from a textual standpoint.

Verses 6-7 seem to be separate from verses 3-5, for the following considerations. First, both have separate, almost identical introductions (שִׁמְעוּ דְּבַר אֲדֹנָי ה׳ in *v.* 3, and כֹּה אָמַר אֲדֹנָי ה׳ in *v.* 6) and endings (וִידַעְתֶּם כִּי אֲנִי ה׳ in *v.* 5 and וְיָדַעְתָּ כִּי אֲנִי ה׳ in *v.* 7). Second, the earlier section addresses Ammon in the feminine gender, while the latter uses the masculine. Third, according to the Masorah, vs. 6 and 7 form a complete paragraph.

The separate introductions and conclusions are reasonably explained by separate conquests. The switch from the feminine to the masculine forms also presents no difficulty: Ammon is projected as feminine, that is, weak (see *comm.* 12:14) only when it lies at the mercy of the militarily insignificant nomadic tribes of the sons of the East, but to fall before the Babylon might is certainly no indication of weakness. In that section, Ammon is referred to in the masculine.

כה
ט־יב

אָמַר אֲדֹנָי יֱהֹוִה יַעַן אֲמֹר מוֹאָב וְשֵׂעִיר
ט הִנֵּה כְּכָל־הַגּוֹיִם בֵּית יְהוּדָה: לָכֵן הִנְנִי
פֹתֵחַ אֶת־כֶּתֶף מוֹאָב מֵהֶעָרִים מֵעָרָיו
מִקָּצֵהוּ צְבִי אֶרֶץ בֵּית הַיְשִׁימוֹת בַּעַל
°וְקִרְיָתָיְמָה ק׳ י מְעוֹן °וקריתמה: לִבְנֵי־קֶדֶם עַל־בְּנֵי
עַמּוֹן וּנְתַתִּיהָ לְמוֹרָשָׁה לְמַעַן לֹא־תִזָּכֵר
יא בְּנֵי־עַמּוֹן בַּגּוֹיִם: וּבְמוֹאָב אֶעֱשֶׂה שְׁפָטִים
יב וְיָדְעוּ כִּי־אֲנִי יהוה: כֹּה
אָמַר אֲדֹנָי יֱהֹוִה יַעַן עֲשׂוֹת אֱדוֹם

8-14. The prophet turns his attention to Moab and Seir (Edom). They are mentioned together in verse 8 and then treated separately: Moab in verses 9-11, and Edom in verses 12-14.

Radak explains that they are mentioned together because they were neighbors and they both rejoiced at Israel's downfall. The question of why Ammon is mentioned only separately (*v.* 10) can be answered by *Malbim's* deduction from *Jeremiah* 49:1 that Ammon actually annexed some of Israel's lands while Moab and Edom did not.

8. הִנֵּה כְּכָל הַגּוֹיִם בֵּית יְהוּדָה — *Behold! the family of Judah is like all the nations.*

They have lost God's special love. They are at Nebuchadnezzar's mercy, just like all other nations *(Rashi).*

When, at the last moment, Jerusalem was saved from Sennacherib's onslaught and not exiled together with the ten tribes of Israel, its neighbors suspected that there might be something special about this people in whose midst God had chosen to dwell. Now they saw that there was nothing to separate Judah from the other nations *(Radak).* It did not enjoy God's special protection, but lay at the mercy of natural forces *(Metzudos).*

When the enemy entered Jerusalem, Ammon and Moab entered with them ... they entered the Holy of Holies and found the two *cherubim* (winged, childlike figures on the covering of the ark). They took them and paraded with them through the streets of Jerusalem and declared: Was it not said that this nation does not serve idols? See what we have found and what they were serving. Everybody is the same! ... See! the family of Judah is like all the nations (*Eichah Rabbasi* 9).

Rashi quotes a different tradition, according to which they took the *cherubim* which were in each other's embrace (see footnote 7:4) and paraded them through the streets to deride Israel which had prided itself on its modesty. In the holiest place it kept symbols which appeared erotic to Moabite eyes.

9. כֶּתֶף מוֹאָב מֵהֶעָרִים — *The flank of Moab from the cities.*

כָּתֵף, *a shoulder,* is used here in a borrowed sense to describe the fortified cities at Moab's borders (מֵעָרָיו מִקָּצֵהוּ, *from the ends of its cities)* which were designed to keep out the enemy. Moab prided itself on these cities. They were צְבִי אֶרֶץ, *the beauty of the land.* These would be opened, leaving the land vulnerable *(Metzudos).*

בֵּית הַיְשִׁימוֹת בַּעַל מְעוֹן וְקִרְיָתָיְמָה — *Beis HaYeshimos, Baal Meon, and Kiryasayma.*

Beis HaYeshimos was in the Plains of Moab (*Numbers* 33:49) but was conquered by Israel and subsequently became part of Reuven's portion of the

25
8-12

[8] *Thus says my Lord HASHEM/ELOHIM: Because
Moab and Seir say, 'Behold! The family of Judah is
like all the nations,'* [9] *therefore behold! I will expose
the flank of Moab from the cities, from its cities at its
border, the beauty of the land — Beis HaYeshimos,
Baal Meon, and Kiryasayma,* [10] *for the children of the
East against the children of Ammon, and I have
presented it as an inheritance so that the children of
Ammon will not be remembered among the nations.*
[11] *And against Moab I shall execute punishments,
and they shall know that I am HASHEM.*
[12] *Thus says my Lord HASHEM/ELOHIM: Since
Edom acted in wreaking vengeance against the family*

Land of Israel (*Joshua* 13:20). *Baal Meon* was, according to *Numbers* 32:38, built up by Reuven and, if it is identical with בֵּית בַּעַל מְעוֹן (*Joshua* 13:17), Moses confirmed their ownership of it. *Kiryasayma* was also built by Reuven (*Numbers* 32:37) and given to that tribe by Moses (*Joshua* 13:19).

[One must assume that at some later date Moab recaptured these cities, and that they then became a vital factor in Moab's own system of fortifications.]

10. לִבְנֵי קֶדֶם עַל־בְּנֵי עַמּוֹן — *For the children of the East, against the children of Ammon.*

Moab's territory was to be opened in order to allow the children of the East (see *v.* 4), access in their campaign against Ammon *(Rashi).*

[Moab is not threatened with a loss of land as Ammon had been. The children of the East will travel through Moab, but will not annex any part of it. Perhaps the justice of מִדָּה כְּנֶגֶד מִדָּה, *measure for measure,* demanded this. Ammon had annexed part of Israel (*Jeremiah* 49:1; see *comm., vs.* 8-14) and was punished by having its land taken away. There is no report that Moab took Israel's land.]

לְמַעַן לֹא תִזָּכֵר בְּנֵי־עַמּוֹן בַּגּוֹיִם — *So that the children of Ammon may not be remembered among the nations.*

This recalls 21:37. See *comm.* there.

12-14. In chapter 24 there is a much longer and more detailed prophecy against Edom. There, the unique place which Edom occupies among Israel's enemies is discussed. In this chapter, however, and particularly verse 8, which brackets Edom together with Moab, Edom is not treated distinctly but as one among Israel's other neighbors.

II Kings 24:2, which notes the involvement of Ammon and Moab in Nebuchadnezzar's conquest, omits Edom. In *Obadiah* 1:11, there is only a hint of its participation, where the prophet castigates Edom for 'standing from afar' on the day of Jerusalem's fall. *Yalkut* (there) reports:

When Nebuchadnezzar besieged Jerusalem, Esau (Edom) came and stood at some distance and killed all the people who had managed to escape ... Now this fight was not Edom's but Babylon's [Edom's time was yet to come at the destruction of the Second Temple (see *comm.* 21:24-27)] ... [but nevertheless] they wanted to be among the very first of the destroyers [of the Temple] ...

These events form the background of the prophecies in our chapter.

12. יַעַן עֲשׂוֹת אֱדוֹם בִּנְקֹם נָקָם — *Since Edom acted in wreaking vengeance.*

בִּנְקֹם נָקָם לְבֵית יְהוּדָה וַיֶּאְשְׁמוּ אָשׁוֹם
יג וְנִקְּמוּ בָהֶם׃ לָכֵן כֹּה אָמַר אֲדֹנָי יֱהֹוִה
וְנָטִתִי יָדִי עַל־אֱדוֹם וְהִכְרַתִּי מִמֶּנָּה
אָדָם וּבְהֵמָה וּנְתַתִּיהָ חָרְבָּה מִתֵּימָן
יד וּדְדָנֶה בַּחֶרֶב יִפֹּלוּ׃ וְנָתַתִּי אֶת־נִקְמָתִי
בֶּאֱדוֹם בְּיַד עַמִּי יִשְׂרָאֵל וְעָשׂוּ בֶאֱדוֹם
כְּאַפִּי וְכַחֲמָתִי וְיָדְעוּ אֶת־נִקְמָתִי נְאֻם
טו אֲדֹנָי יֱהֹוִה׃ כֹּה אָמַר אֲדֹנָי
יֱהֹוִה יַעַן עֲשׂוֹת פְּלִשְׁתִּים בִּנְקָמָה וַיִּנָּקְמוּ
נָקָם בִּשְׁאָט בְּנֶפֶשׁ לְמַשְׁחִית אֵיבַת עוֹלָם׃

Edom's participation in the Destruction is described as an act of vengeance. [נקם means *to avenge*. Although *Targum* generally translates פּוּרְעָנוּתָא, *punishment,* (for an exception see *Targum* to *Exodus* 21:20; *Nefesh HaGer* there), it is a punishment which contains an element of vengeance, since פּוּרְעָנוּת derives from פרע, *to pay,* or *repay*].

There is no indication of what offense Edom was avenging. *Radak* and other commentators view the word as a metaphor. Edom's actions were as fierce *as though* they were acts of vengeance.

Perhaps Edom was interested in avenging its conquest at the hands of Judah's king Amaziah which is reported in *II Kings* 14:7.

[It is also possible that Edom's desire for vengeance goes back to the very dawn of its history. *Amos* 1:11 described Edom as one who *guards his animosity eternally.* This 'animosity' is understood as the bearing of a grudge (see *Rambam, Hilchos Teshuvah* 3:10) and is interpreted by *Bereishis Rabbah* 77:9 as based on Esau's hatred of Jacob for depriving him of Isaac's blessings (see *Genesis* 27). From the very beginning of Edom's nationhood, its path through history was animated by a hatred of Israel and a thirst for vengeance.]

13. וּנְתַתִּיהָ חָרְבָּה מִתֵּימָן — *And I shall make it desolate from the south.*

We have translated תֵּימָן, as *south,* in accordance with *Targum.* Israel lies to the north of Edom, so the verse indicates that Edom's desolation will be complete. It will start from the south and extend northward until Israel's border *(Metzudos).*

Radak treats תֵּימָן, *Teman,* as a proper noun. Teman was Esau's grandson (*Genesis* 36:11) and his portion of Edom was named after him.

דְּדָנֶה — *Dedan.*

Dedan was a major Edomite city *(Radak).* See *Jeremiah* 49:8.

14. וְנָתַתִּי אֶת נִקְמָתִי בֶּאֱדוֹם בְּיַד עַמִּי יִשְׂרָאֵל — *And I shall take My vengeance from Edom by the hand of My people Israel.*

Israel will be the tool through which God will take His vengeance of Edom.

How will this come about?

If it means that Israel will actually punish Edom as implied by the next phrase, then the intent of the verse is to describe what will happen בְּאַחֲרִית הַיָּמִים, *in the End of Days.* Concerning that time *Obadiah* 1:18 says: *And the family of Jacob will be a fire, and the family of Joseph a flame, and the family of Esau shall be as chaff*

Radak suggests that Israel may have subjugated Edom during the period of

of Judah; and has committed great offense and taken
vengeance against them, 13 *therefore, thus says my*
Lord HASHEM/ELOHIM: I shall extend My hand
against Edom and cut off from it man and beast, and
I will make it desolate from the south, and the people
of Dedan will fall by the sword. 14 *And I shall take*
My vengeance from Edom by the hand of My people
Israel, and they shall act upon Edom in accordance
with My anger and My fury, and they shall know
My vengeance — the words of my Lord
HASHEM/ELOHIM.

15 *Thus says my Lord HASHEM/ELOHIM: Because*
the Philistines have acted with vengeance, and they
wreaked vengeance with the rashness of the soul to
destroy for everlasting hatred. 16 *Therefore, thus says*

the Second Temple, although we have no Biblical record of events of that era.

Another explanation of this verse is found in *Gittin* 56a. The Talmud tells of a Roman general who, as Jerusalem was about to fall to him, asked a Jewish child what verse he had studied that day. Upon hearing our verse, he suddenly realized the enormity of what he was about to do. He understood the verse to mean that God makes Edom the instrument of Israel's destruction and thereby causes Edom to be exposed to His wrathful vengeance. The general decided to give up all he had and to convert to Judaism. [According to this interpretation, by being made Edom's victim, Israel became the cause of God's ultimate vegeance against Edom, but we are not told when and how this revenge would come.]

15-17 During the early years of Israel's nationhood, there was constant war between them and the Philistines. Particularly the books of *Judges* and *Samuel* have many accounts of these conflicts. In *Kings*, however, all reference to wars with the Philistines cease and there are only sporadic references (cf. *II Chronicles* 28:18) to any kind of conflict. One must turn to *Joel* 4:4ff, for even a general reference to continuing tension. Nevertheless, from our passage it is obvious that the ancient enmity continued through the centuries. (In *Isaiah* 14:28-32 there is a prophecy against Philistia, but according to *Rashi* there, the prophecy concerned events which were current at the time of Isaiah.)

15. יַעַן עֲשׂוֹת פְּלִשְׁתִּים בִּנְקָמָה — *Because the Philistines have acted with vengeance.*

Once more the commentators explain that the ferocity with which the Philistines acted against Israel made it seem as though they had some wrongs to avenge. Normal hatred is not so intense.

בִּשְׁאָט בְּנֶפֶשׁ — *With the rashness of the soul.*

See *comm.* to *v.* 6.

לְמַשְׁחִית אֵיבַת עוֹלָם — *To destroy for everlasting hatred.*

They acted with the kind of destructiveness which would guarantee eternal hatred between them and Israel (*Radak);* or they behaved as though there had been hatred between them

כה טז-יז

טז לָכֵ֞ן כֹּ֤ה אָמַר֙ אֲדֹנָ֣י יֱהֹוִ֔ה הִנְנִ֤י נוֹטֶה֙
יָדִ֣י עַל־פְּלִשְׁתִּ֔ים וְהִכְרַתִּ֖י אֶת־כְּרֵתִ֑ים
וְהַ֣אֲבַדְתִּ֔י אֶת־שְׁאֵרִ֖ית ח֥וֹף הַיָּֽם׃
יז וְעָשִׂ֤יתִי בָם֙ נְקָמ֣וֹת גְּדֹל֔וֹת בְּתוֹכְח֖וֹת
חֵמָ֑ה וְיָֽדְעוּ֙ כִּֽי־אֲנִ֣י יְהוָ֔ה בְּתִתִּ֥י אֶת־
נִקְמָתִ֖י בָּֽם׃

כו א-ב

א וַיְהִ֛י בְּעַשְׁתֵּֽי־עֶשְׂרֵ֥ה שָׁנָ֖ה בְּאֶחָ֣ד לַחֹ֑דֶשׁ
ב הָיָ֥ה דְבַר־יְהוָ֖ה אֵלַ֥י לֵאמֹֽר׃ בֶּן־אָדָ֗ם יַ֩עַן֩

since the very beginning of time *(Metzudos).*

16. וְהִכְרַתִּי אֶת־כְּרֵתִים — *And I shall cut off the Kereisim.*

Targum takes כְּרֵתִים, *Kereisim,* as a common noun: *those who deserve to be cut off,* from כרת, *to cut off.* Our translation, however, follows *Rashi,* who points out that the Philistines are occasionally referred to as *Kereisim* (I *Samuel* 10:14; *Zephanyah* 2:5) and writes that this was the name of an area within Philistia.

אֶת שְׁאֵרִית חוֹף הַיָּם — *The remainder of those who dwell by the seashore.*

This refers to the Philistines, who lived in the southwest corner of Israel's boundary, on the shores of the Mediterranean Sea *(Rashi).*

XXVI

After the short, almost perfunctory prophecies concerning Israel's neighbors to the east and south, Yechezkel unexpectedly lavishes penetrating and detailed analysis on Tyre, the island state to Israel's north.[1]

*The lengthy condemnation of Tyre is all the more surprising when we consider that with the exception of one reference (*Psalms *83:8) there is no indication anywhere in Scripture that Tyre ever seemed to consider herself Israel's enemy. Quite the contrary appears to be true. Hiram, king of Tyre had friendly ties with David and Solomon (see e.g.,* I Kings *5:21), and from 27:17 it is clear that four centuries later the two countries were still commercial partners. Much later Tyre was active in the supply of materials needed for the building of the Second Temple (*Ezra *3:7).*

How had Tyre sinned, and what are we to learn from her fate?

Yechezkel answers these questions by peeling away the outer veneer of friendliness and revealing Tyre in her malicious joy, lusting for the gain which would come her way with the elimination of her competitor. אִמָּלְאָה הָחֳרָבָה, I shall be filled by the desolation!

Chapter 27 portrays Tyre's position in the ancient world. Untold wealth and lux-

1. We have identified Tyre as an island because throughout Scripture it is referred to as אִי, *an island.* The Tyre we know today became joined to the mainland over the centuries in a process which began during the thirteen year siege which Nebuchadnezzar established against Tyre. (See *Josephus, Antiquities* 10:11.) At that time he built a dam from the mainland in order to facilitate his troop movements. This dam was subsequently improved by Alexander during his Tyrian wars, and eventually became an indistinguishable part of the land. *(Tyrus in der Schilderung der Prophaten,* by *Rabbi Dr. Solomon Stein* in *v.* 7 of *Jahrbuch der Judisch-Literarischen Gesellschaft* 1909).

25
17
my Lord HASHEM/ELOHIM: *See, I extend My hand against the Philistines, and I shall cut off the Kereisim and destroy the remnant by the seashore.* 17 *And I shall execute great vengeance against them with rebukes of wrath, and they shall know that I am* HASHEM *when I shall place My vengeance upon them.*

26
1-2
It was in the eleventh year on the first of the month that the word of HASHEM *came to me saying:* 2 *Ben*

*uries poured into her coffers from every corner of the earth. Her merchants had established a new aristocracy of wealth (*Isaiah *23:8), and with wealth came power. The name of Tyre evoked the same kind of terror as the name of a military power like Egypt (27:5). (See* Hirsch, Gesammelte Schriften, *vol. 2 p. 190.) Judah represented only a tiny fraction of the trading activities, and the commercial gain which could accrue from the destruction of its competitor (see* v. *2) must have been minute when reckoned against her total capacities.*

R' Dessler (Michtav MeEliyahu, *vol. 1 p. 42, vol. 3, p. 182) describes a rapaciousness which can never be assuaged because its source does not lie in the object of the desire but in the inner need of the person to yearn for and grasp that which is beyond him. No fulfillment will ever quench that consuming thirst because every attainment serves only to mock the efforts expended in its acquisition by creating even greater desires for further gain.*

Tyre was a living example of this terrible sickness. Her lust befouled the friendly and positive relationship which she had had with Israel and turned her into the symbol of that evil which cannot be assimilated and sublimated by holiness (see comm., v. *2). Her philosophy of life stands in diametric opposition to the Torah's ideal of the fusion of the temporal and the Divine.*

1. בְּעַשְׁתֵּי־עֶשְׂרֵה שָׁנָה בְּאֶחָד לַחֹדֶשׁ — *In the eleventh year on the first of the month.*

The dating places this prophecy in the eleventh year of Zidkiyahu's reign — the year of the destruction of the Temple.

The prophecy came on the first of the month, but the month is not specified. *Rashi* (responsum to the Sages of Auxerres) assumes it to be the month of Tishri — the first month of the year.

Radak and *Metzudos* write that since the year is that of the Destruction, the month is Av, the month in which the Destruction took place.

Yerushalmi Taanis 4:5, however, offers an Aggadic interpretation. It contends that the first of Av cannot be meant since at that time the Destruction had not yet taken place and Tyre could not be castigated for her reaction to it (*v.* 2). On the other hand, it would not have taken until even the first of Elul for the news to reach Tyre, which was fairly close to Jerusalem. The *Yerushalmi* suggests that in reality the ninth of Av, the day of the Destruction, is meant. The dating on the *first* of the month is a קִלְקוּל חֶשְׁבּוֹנוֹת, *a mistaken reckoning. R' Yochanan* and *Reish Lakish* suggest a parable. While working on his accounts, a king was interrupted by the news that his son had been captured. In his agitation he made mistakes [in the dating of] his accounts, but said, 'Let this day be the beginning of a new reckoning.'

אֲשֶׁר־אָמְרָה צֹּר עַל־יְרוּשָׁלִַם הֶאָח
נִשְׁבְּרָה דַּלְתוֹת הָעַמִּים נָסֵבָּה אֵלָי
ג אִמָּלְאָה הָחֳרָבָה׃ לָכֵן כֹּה אָמַר אֲדֹנָי
יֱהֹוִה הִנְנִי עָלַיִךְ צֹר וְהַעֲלֵיתִי עָלַיִךְ גּוֹיִם
ד רַבִּים כְּהַעֲלוֹת הַיָּם לְגַלָּיו׃ וְשִׁחֲתוּ חֹמוֹת
צֹר וְהָרְסוּ מִגְדָּלֶיהָ וְסִחֵיתִי עֲפָרָהּ מִמֶּנָּה
ה וְנָתַתִּי אוֹתָהּ לִצְחִיחַ סָלַע׃ מִשְׁטַח
חֲרָמִים תִּהְיֶה בְּתוֹךְ הַיָּם כִּי אֲנִי דִבַּרְתִּי
נְאֻם אֲדֹנָי יֱהֹוִה וְהָיְתָה לְבַז לַגּוֹיִם׃
ו וּבְנוֹתֶיהָ אֲשֶׁר בַּשָּׂדֶה בַּחֶרֶב תֵּהָרַגְנָה
ז וְיָדְעוּ כִּי־אֲנִי יְהֹוָה׃ כִּי

In the view of the *Yerushalmi*, then, the dating calls attention to two aspects of this terrible day. It points to the agitation which the events brought on; but it also indicates to the prophet that with the Destruction, an entirely new phase of his activities was to start. In that sense, what was really the ninth of Av could rightly be called the first *(R' Breuer).*

It is profoundly significant that this prophecy against Tyre reached the prophet on the very day of the Destruction. (See *comm., v.* 2.)

2. נִשְׁבְּרָה דַּלְתוֹת הָעַמִּים — *The gateway of the nations has been broken.*

The nations had been accustomed to pour into Jerusalem to do business *(Radak).*

נָסֵבָּה אֵלָי — *It is directed toward me.*

Jerusalem's income will now be directed to me.

Ammon's hatred of Israel (25:3) had been three-pronged (*comm.* 25:3). They hated not only the land, but also the people and their God. No such considerations animated Tyre's feelings. If Jerusalem had not been a business competitor, Tyre could have lived in complete amity with the people and their religion *(R' Breuer).*

אִמָּלְאָה הָחֳרָבָה — *The destruction will make me filled.*

Tyre's complete fulfillment can only be built on Jerusalem's destruction.

Based on this verse, the Sages teach in *Megillah* 6a, that if a person were to hear that Caesarea and Jerusalem are both flourishing or both sinking, he should not believe it. One of them must always be ascendant, while the other would be subjugated by it.

The *Talmud* proceeds to say that the same thought is expressed in *Genesis* 25:23, where Rebecca was told that there would never be equality between the twins, Jacob and Esau, whom she was carrying. One or the other would always be the stronger *Hirsch* (there) writes. The one state would build its greatness on spirit and morals, on the humane in humans, the other would seek its greatness through cunning and physical strength. Spirit and physical strength, morality and violence oppose each other ... The scales will constantly sway from one to the other ... The whole of history is nothing but a struggle as to whether the spirit or the sword, i.e., Jerusalem or Caesarea, is to be ascendant.

In this context we can understand why this prophecy was given to Yechezkel on the very day of the Temple's destruction (see *comm., v.* 1). Jerusalem

Adam, because Tyre has said of Jerusalem: Hurrah! The gateway of the nations has been broken; it is directed toward me, the destruction will make me filled.

3 *Therefore, thus says my Lord* HASHEM/ELOHIM: *Behold! I oppose you, Tyre, and I shall bring up many nations against you, as the sea brings up its waves.* 4 *And they shall destroy the walls of Tyre, and break down her towers, and I shall scrape her earth from her and turn her into a bare rock.* 5 *A spreading-place for nets shall she be in the midst of the sea, for I have spoken — the words of my Lord* HASHEM/ELOHIM. *She shall become a spoil for the nations,* 6 *and her daughter-cities in the field shall be killed by the sword. Then they shall know that I am* HASHEM.

had fallen. It was Caesarea's turn to flourish. It was imperative to proclaim that this would not last. The day will come when Tyre will fall.[1]

3. כְּהַעֲלוֹת הַיָּם לְגַלָּיו — *As the sea brings up its waves.*

The prophet chooses his similes and metaphors from the sea, its produce, and its travelers. This is natural since Tyre was the greatest seafaring nation of the ancient world.

4. וְסִחֵיתִי עֲפָרָהּ מִמֶּנָּה — *And I will scrape her earth from her.*

The word צֹר, *Tyre,* is derived from צוּר, *rock.* Tyre was built on a rock which was covered by a layer of earth making it habitable. The seas which would wash over the rock after Tyre's destruction would scrape away the covering of earth, leaving it a צְחִיחַ סֶלַע, *high, dry rock (Radak).*

Metzudos writes that the *earth* in this passage refers to the clay which held the stones of the buildings together. When this would be removed, the buildings would collapse and the streets would be filled with dry stones from the fallen buildings.

5. מִשְׁטַח חֲרָמִים — *A spreading-place for nets.*

After the seas have washed over it, it will remain high and dry, suitable for the spreading of the fishermen's nets *(Radak).* In contrast to its present when Tyre was filled with multitudes of people, it would be desolate with only a few fishermen there who would use the rock to dry their nets *(Metzudas David).*

6. וּבְנוֹתֶיהָ אֲשֶׁר בַּשָּׂדֶה — *And her daughter-cities* [lit. *daughters*] *in the field.*

The surrounding villages which were her suburbs would fall by the sword.

1. Caesarea is a Judean city built on the coast of the Mediterranean by Herod. In order to curry favor with his Roman sponsors and the more easily to wipe out all vestiges of Torah from Judea, that country to whose customs and mores he was not only foreign but actively antagonistic, Herod rebuilt this coastal town in vulgar and ostentatious splendor. It was to replace Jerusalem as capital, and would be a monument to his reign. (For details, see *Doros HaRishonim* vol. 1 ch. 3). Because of all that it represented, this city was roundly hated by the Jewish people and eventually became a symbol of everything worldly and gross. In that sense the Talmud uses it as the symbol of all foreign cultures, Tyre's included.

כו
ח־יב

כֹּה אָמַר אֲדֹנָי יֱהוִה הִנְנִי מֵבִיא אֶל־
צֹר נְבוּכַדְרֶאצַּר מֶלֶךְ־בָּבֶל מִצָּפוֹן
מֶלֶךְ מְלָכִים בְּסוּס וּבְרֶכֶב וּבְפָרָשִׁים
ח וְקָהָל וְעַם־רָב׃ בְּנוֹתַיִךְ בַּשָּׂדֶה בַּחֶרֶב
יַהֲרֹג וְנָתַן עָלַיִךְ דָּיֵק וְשָׁפַךְ עָלַיִךְ סֹלְלָה
ט וְהֵקִים עָלַיִךְ צִנָּה׃ וּמְחִי קָבָלּוֹ יִתֵּן
בְּחֹמוֹתָיִךְ וּמִגְדְּלֹתַיִךְ יִתֹּץ בְּחַרְבוֹתָיו׃
י מִשִּׁפְעַת סוּסָיו יְכַסֵּךְ אֲבָקָם מִקּוֹל פָּרַשׁ
וְגַלְגַּל וָרֶכֶב תִּרְעַשְׁנָה חוֹמוֹתַיִךְ בְּבֹאוֹ
יא בִּשְׁעָרַיִךְ כִּמְבוֹאֵי עִיר מְבֻקָּעָה׃ בְּפַרְסוֹת
סוּסָיו יִרְמֹס אֶת־כָּל־חוּצוֹתָיִךְ עַמֵּךְ
בַּחֶרֶב יַהֲרֹג וּמַצְּבוֹת עֻזֵּךְ לָאָרֶץ תֵּרֵד׃
יב וְשָׁלְלוּ חֵילֵךְ וּבָזְזוּ רְכֻלָּתֵךְ וְהָרְסוּ
חוֹמוֹתַיִךְ וּבָתֵּי חֶמְדָּתֵךְ יִתֹּצוּ וַאֲבָנַיִךְ

[The suburbs are the בָּנוֹת, *daughters* of the main city because they derive much of their income from it, as a child is fed by its mother. In this sense a large city is called אֵם, mother. (See *II Samuel* 20:19 and *Metzudos* there.]

7-14 [These verses seem to form a separate prophecy. According to the Masorah, they are a פָּרָשָׁה, *division*, by themselves. Furthermore, they address Tyre in the second person whereas verses 1-6 were in the third person. Verse 7 (כִּי כֹה אָמַר ...) and verse 14 (כִּי אֲנִי ה׳ ...) are introductory and concluding statements, respectively.

This explains the almost verbatim repetition of a number of phrases (*v.* 8 parallels *v.* 6; *v.* 12 parallels *v.* 4; and *v.* 14 parallels *vs.* 4-5); this new prophecy, directed *at* Tyre, utilized many of the thoughts expressed in the earlier prophecy *about* Tyre.

The word כִּי, *for,* which introduces this passage would imply that this second prophecy is an explanation and elaboration of the first.[1]

1. The dating of the prophecy at the beginning of the chapter need not deter us from assuming that verses 7-14 constitute a separate prophecy. If, indeed, this *is* all a single chapter, logic would indicate that the entire contents of the chapter should be regarded as a single prophecy given to Yechezkel on the date found in verse 1. Such, however, is not necessarily the case.

The division of Scripture into chapters has no basis in the Masorah and is not even of Jewish origin. It is commonly assumed to have been introduced by Stephen Langton, Archbishop of Canterbury, in the beginning of the thirteenth century. Jewish scholars, such as R' Yitzchak ben Nassan and R' Eliyahu Bachur, began to make use of the system during the fifteenth century, and it appeared in printed bibles towards the beginning of the sixteenth century. (For details see *Masores HaTorah VeHaNeviim*, Pesach Funfer, Vilna 1906.)

The chapter divisions are not the only work of non-Jewish origin which has crept into common usage. The numbering of verses (though not their division which is, of course, Masoretic) was first used in the middle of the sixteenth century in Bomberg's Great Bible. The

[7] *For thus says my Lord HASHEM/ELOHIM: Behold*
I shall bring against Tyre, Nebuchadnezzar king of
Babylon, from the north, a king of kings, with
horses, chariots and riders, a company and many
people. [8] *Your daughter-cities in the field, he will kill*
by the sword; he will set up a fort against you and
pour a mound against you and set up shields against
you. [9] *His catapult he shall set against your walls,*
and your towers he will dismantle with his swords.
[10] *From the abundance of his horses, their dust will*
cover you. From the noise of rider, wheel, and
chariot, your walls will tremble, when he enters your
gates as one enters a breached city. [11] *With the hoofs*
of his horses he will trample all your streets; your
people he will kill by the sword; and the pillars of
your strength will go down to the ground. [12] *Then*
they shall plunder your accumulation and despoil
your merchandise; they will break down your walls,
and the houses of your delight they will dismantle;

8. דָּיֵק ... סֹלְלָה — *Fort ... mound.*
See 4:2.

צִנָּה — *Shields* [lit. *a shield*].
Targum renders *men bearing shields.*

9. וּמְחִי קָבָלוֹ — *A catapult.*
Radak explains that מְחִי is Aramaic for *strike*, and קָבֵל is Aramaic for *towards;* hence, that which strikes towards — a *catapult.*

10. מִשִּׁפְעַת סוּסָיו — *From the abundance of his horses.*
שפע means *to flow abundantly:* שֶׁפַע is *abundance;* so is שִׁפְעָה.

עִיר מְבֻקָּעָה — *A breached city.*
The enemy will enter Tyre's gates without any real resistance as easily as one would enter a city whose walls had already been breached.

12. ... וְשָׁלְלוּ — *Then they shall plunder.*
Up to this sentence the subject was

division of *Samuel, Kings, Chronicles,* and *Ezra-Nehemiah* into two books each, also originated in the non-Jewish bible. The Talmud lists them respectively as single books.

It is one of the ironies of history that these systems, which were forced upon us mainly in order to make possible the public debates to which the Church subjected our Sages of the Middle Ages, have come to be universally accepted.

Particularly pernicious are the chapter divisions, which often are in direct conflict with the *parshios sesumos* or *pesuchos*, the *closed* or *open divisions* which the Masorah recognizes. (According to *Funfer* these conflicts occur in *Ezekiel* in the following instances: Chs. 11, 14, and 20 each begin one verse before a *parsha sesumah.* In addition to these flagrant contradictions, *Funfer* finds many other instances in *Ezekiel* in which the commonly accepted chapter divisions seem to interrupt prophecies or narratives which seem logically to belong together. (See ch. 3, which, while it begins at a *parshah sesumah*, nevertheless appears to be a continuation of the earlier narrative).

Thus, it is clear that the date at the beginning of the chapter can in no way influence our passage.

וְעֵצַיִךְ וַעֲפָרֵךְ בְּתוֹךְ מַיִם יָשִׂימוּ׃
יג וְהִשְׁבַּתִּי הֲמוֹן שִׁירָיִךְ וְקוֹל כִּנּוֹרַיִךְ
יד לֹא יִשָּׁמַע עוֹד׃ וּנְתַתִּיךְ לִצְחִיחַ סֶלַע
מִשְׁטַח חֲרָמִים תִּהְיֶה לֹא תִבָּנֶה
עוֹד כִּי אֲנִי יהוה דִּבַּרְתִּי נְאֻם אֲדֹנָי
טו יֱהֹוִה׃ כֹּה אָמַר אֲדֹנָי יֱהֹוִה
לְצוֹר הֲלֹא | מִקּוֹל מַפַּלְתֵּךְ בֶּאֱנֹק חָלָל
טז בֵּהָרֵג הֶרֶג בְּתוֹכֵךְ יִרְעֲשׁוּ הָאִיִּים׃ וְיָרְדוּ
מֵעַל כִּסְאוֹתָם כֹּל נְשִׂיאֵי הַיָּם וְהֵסִירוּ
אֶת־מְעִילֵיהֶם וְאֶת־בִּגְדֵי רִקְמָתָם יִפְשֹׁטוּ
חֲרָדוֹת | יִלְבָּשׁוּ עַל־הָאָרֶץ יֵשֵׁבוּ וְחָרְדוּ
יז לִרְגָעִים וְשָׁמְמוּ עָלָיִךְ׃ וְנָשְׂאוּ עָלַיִךְ
קִינָה וְאָמְרוּ לָךְ אֵיךְ אָבַדְתְּ נוֹשֶׁבֶת
מִיַּמִּים הָעִיר הַהֻלָּלָה אֲשֶׁר הָיְתָה חֲזָקָה
בַיָּם הִיא וְיֹשְׁבֶיהָ אֲשֶׁר־נָתְנוּ חִתִּיתָם

the *king of kings* (Nebuchadnezzar) of *v.* 7.

A new subject, *they,* is introduced here. The despoiling will be done by his armies *(R' Breuer).*

13. Isaiah (23:7) had called Tyre עַלִּיזָה, *a happy* city. Her joy would now be stilled *(R' Breuer).*

14. See verses 4 and 5.

15-18 This passage constitutes a separate פָּרָשָׁה, *division,* and may well have been a different prophecy. (See *comm.,* footnote 7-14 above.)

During the thirteen-year siege of Tyre (see Josephus, quoted in pref.), when this comparatively tiny city-state frustrated every effort of mighty Babylon to subdue it, Yechezkel may well have felt called upon to prophesy repeatedly to reassure Israel that Tyre's resistance would eventually be worn down and she would indeed fall.

The prophecy describes the effect which Tyre's fall will have on all the people who regarded her as the central power (see pref.). In a sense they were all יוֹשְׁבֶיהָ, *her inhabitants (v.* 17), and they sensed their own fall in her destruction.

15. בֶּאֱנֹק חָלָל — *Like the groan of the slain.*

The root אנק is dscussed in *comm.,* 24:17.

יִרְעֲשׁוּ הָאִיִּים — *The islands will tremble.*

אִי is commonly translated a *island.* However, according to *Radak (Sefer HaShorashim),* Jerusalem is sometimes referred to as אִי (*Isaiah* 20:6; but see *Radak* and other commentators there), which indicates that it can be used to describe any area of land.

Hirsch to *Genesis* 10:5 derives the word from אַיֵּה, *where?* He writes that it describes any far-off, little-known place (see also *Isaiah* 66:19) concerning which one might ask: Where is it? (See further *ArtScroll Bereishis* 10:5).

In our verse the meaning would then

26
13-17

and your stones, your wood and your dust, they will
place into the midst of the water. 13 *I shall abolish the*
multitude of your songs, and the sound of your harps
will be heard no more. 14 *Then I shall make you into a*
bare rock. You shall become a spreading-place for
nets, nevermore to be rebuilt, for I, HASHEM, have
spoken — the words of my Lord HASHEM/ELOHIM.
15 *Thus says my Lord HASHEM/ELOHIM to Tyre:*
From the noise of your downfall, like the groan of the
slain, as slaughter is perpetrated in your midst — will
not the islands tremble? 16 *Then all the princes of the*
sea will descend from their throne, remove their
robes, and strip their garments. With trembling they
will garb themselves, upon the ground they will sit,
they will tremble constantly and be desolate because
of you. 17 *They shall take up a lament for you and say*
about you:

How have you been lost,
Who were established by the seas!
The lauded city
That was mighty in the sea.
She and her inhabitants,
Who had inspired terror

be that even landlocked nations far away from Tyre would be shaken to their very foundations by the downfall of this all-important city.

16. וְחָרְדוּ לִרְגָעִים — *They will tremble constantly* [lit. *by the second*].

The translation follows *Metzudos. Targum,* followed by *Rashi* renders: *They will tremble in fear of destruction.* He translates the root רגע as it is used in *Job* 26:12.

17. נוֹשֶׁבֶת מִיַּמִּים — *Who were established by the seas* [lit. *made to be dwelt in by the seas*].

Life in Tyre was safe and secure because it was protected by the seas *(Rashi).*

The wealth which made her secure and established came to her by way of many seas *(Radak).*

הִיא וְיֹשְׁבֶיהָ ... לְכָל־יוֹשְׁבֶיהָ — *She and her inhabitants ... upon all its inhabitants.*

According to *Radak* and *Metzudos,* the first יֹשְׁבֶיהָ, *her inhabitants,* refers to Tyre, and the second one to the sea; therefore we have rendered the second word *its* [i.e., the sea's] inhabitants. Tyre and her inhabitants were the strongest of all nations of the sea. All other sea-going nations feared Tyre's superiority.

R' Breuer writes that both refer to Tyre: יֹשְׁבֶיהָ, *her inhabitants,* are the people of Tyre. כָּל יוֹשְׁבֶיהָ, *all her dwellers,* are the people of all the other

יח לְכָל־יוֹשְׁבֶיהָ׃ עַתָּה יֶחֶרְדוּ הָאִיִּן יוֹם
מַפַּלְתֵּךְ וְנִבְהֲלוּ הָאִיִּים אֲשֶׁר־בַּיָּם
יט מִצֵּאתֵךְ׃ כִּי כֹה אָמַר אֲדֹנָי
יֱהֹוִה בְּתִתִּי אֹתָךְ עִיר נֶחֱרֶבֶת כֶּעָרִים
אֲשֶׁר לֹא־נוֹשָׁבוּ בְּהַעֲלוֹת עָלַיִךְ אֶת־
כ תְּהוֹם וְכִסּוּךְ הַמַּיִם הָרַבִּים׃ וְהוֹרַדְתִּיךְ
אֶת־יוֹרְדֵי בוֹר אֶל־עַם עוֹלָם וְהוֹשַׁבְתִּיךְ
בְּאֶרֶץ תַּחְתִּיּוֹת כֶּחֳרָבוֹת מֵעוֹלָם אֶת־
יוֹרְדֵי בוֹר לְמַעַן לֹא תֵשֵׁבִי וְנָתַתִּי
כא צְבִי בְּאֶרֶץ חַיִּים׃ בַּלָּהוֹת אֶתְּנֵךְ וְאֵינֵךְ
וּתְבֻקְשִׁי וְלֹא־תִמָּצְאִי עוֹד לְעוֹלָם נְאֻם
כז
א אֲדֹנָי יֱהֹוִה׃ וַיְהִי דְבַר־יְהֹוָה

countries who, because their economies depended on Tyre, were considered her inhabitants.

18. הָאִיִּים ... הָאִיִּן — *The open places ... the islands.*

The translation follows *Targum,* who differentiates between the two expressions in order to avoid redundancy.

מִצֵּאתֵךְ — *By your departure.*

The islands will be confounded by your departure into exile *(Targum).*

19. וְכִסּוּךְ הַמַּיִם הָרַבִּים — *And the abundant waters cover you up.*

The island was to be covered by water, which would wash away the layer of earth that made the rock habitable. The island would be left hard and dry (see *v.* 4).

Metzudos interprets this as a reference to the many nations who will attack Tyre and inundate it.

20. A contrast is made between Jerusalem and Tyre. Their respective fates would always be influenced by one another (see *comm., v.* 2). Only one could ever be ascendant at a time. Now, with exquisite drama, the ultimate picture is presented.

Jerusalem was lying in ruins. Tyre was pulsating with life. Jerusalem seemed condemned to oblivion. The future seemed to lie at Tyre's feet.

Yet the prohetic eye sees quite a different truth. God's gift of beauty (וְנָתַתִּי צְבִי) will, at a point in the future, be bestowed upon Jerusalem, that death-defying place (אֶרֶץ חַיִּים), in which true life will flourish. By contrast, the seemingly invincible Tyre is fated to sink into *the nether depths* to join יוֹרְדֵי בוֹר, *the many nations who descend to the pit;* see 32:22ff.) who have been there since eternity (עַם עוֹלָם), testifying to the essential emptiness of lives which had once seemed so meaningful.

עַם עוֹלָם — *The ancient people* [lit. *people of eternity*].

According to most commentators, this refers to the people who have been in the nether depths for ages.

In *R' Breuer's* view, the expression describes the illusion of permanence with which these nations deluded themselves, as Tyre had. All thought that nothing would ever change; all learned their lesson fully when the בּוֹר, *pit of death* — or, according to *Midrash Tanchuma, Genesis 7, Gehinnom,* closed over them.

Upon all its inhabitants.
18 *Now the open places will tremble*
On the day of your downfall
And the islands of the sea will be confounded
By your departure.
19 *For thus says my Lord HASHEM/ELOHIM: When*
I make you a devastated city, like cities that were
never inhabited, when I raise the depths upon you
and the abundant waters cover you, 20 *then I shall*
bring you down with those who descend to the pit, to
the ancient people, and I shall settle you in the nether
depths like the cities destroyed in antiquity, with
those who descend to the pit, so that you shall no
more be inhabited; but I shall bestow beauty upon
the land of life. 21 *A desolation I shall make you and*
you shall be no more; you will be sought but never
more be found forever — the words of my Lord
HASHEM/ELOHIM.

אֶרֶץ חַיִּים — *The land of life.*

Targum translates אֶרֶץ חַיִּים as *the Land of Israel.* According to the Sages, quoted by *Radak*, it is so called because it is there that תְּחִיַּת הַמֵּתִים, *the resurrection of the dead,* will take place.

This is in contrast to אֶרֶץ תַּחְתִּיּוֹת, *the nether depths* [lit., *the nether land*].

21. בַּלָּהוֹת — *Desolation.*

Our translation follows *Rashi* who cites *Targum's* rendering of the word as a contraction כְּדְלָא הֲוֵית, *as though you had not existed. Metzudos* writes that the root בלה may be the same as בהל with the letters inverted. Then, like בֶּהָלָה, the word would mean *confusion.*

XXVII

The kinnah, lamentation, *which Yechezkel is commanded to take up for Tyre in this chapter, places the admonitions of the previous chapter and indeed all the prophecies against the nations, in correct perspective.*

'See the difference between Israel's prophets and those of the nations ... All the [Jewish] prophets were mercifully inclined towards both Jew and non-Jew [as we see in] Yechezkel: Ben Adam, take up a lamentation for Tyre, *but this cruel [Balaam] wanted to destroy a whole nation for no good reason' (*Bamidbar Rabbah *20:1).*

The tragic futility of the might and beauty which had been Tyre and was now dragged into the dust was to move Yechezkel to a soul-shattering lament, no less than the downfall of Israel's princes (see 19:1, comm.*) had done. His was no chauvinistic love for Israel to the exclusion of the rest of mankind. Israel's prophets are filled with love and mercy for every man, a truth reflected in their admonitions no less than in their dirges: 'The prophets of Israel are merciful people and ad-*

כז
ב־ז

ב אֵלַי לֵאמֹר׃ וְאַתָּה בֶן־אָדָם שָׂא עַל־צֹר
ג קִינָה׃ וְאָמַרְתָּ לְצוֹר °הישבתי עַל־ °הַיֹּשֶׁבֶת ק׳
מְבוֹאֹת יָם רֹכֶלֶת הָעַמִּים אֶל־אִיִּים רַבִּים
כֹּה אָמַר אֲדֹנָי יֱהֹוִה צוֹר אַתְּ אָמַרְתְּ אֲנִי
ד כְּלִילַת יֹפִי׃ בְּלֵב יַמִּים גְּבוּלָיִךְ בֹּנַיִךְ כָּלְלוּ
ה יָפְיֵךְ׃ בְּרוֹשִׁים מִשְּׂנִיר בָּנוּ לָךְ אֵת כָּל־
לֻחֹתָיִם אֶרֶז מִלְּבָנוֹן לָקָחוּ לַעֲשׂוֹת תֹּרֶן
ו עָלָיִךְ׃ אַלּוֹנִים מִבָּשָׁן עָשׂוּ מִשּׁוֹטָיִךְ
קַרְשֵׁךְ עָשׂוּ־שֵׁן בַּת־אֲשֻׁרִים מֵאִיֵּי כִּתִּיִּם׃
ז שֵׁשׁ בְּרִקְמָה מִמִּצְרַיִם הָיָה מִפְרָשֵׂךְ

*monish the foreign nations to forsake their evil ways, for God stretches forth His hand to the evil as well as to the good' (*Rashi; Psalms *2:10).*

*Yechezkel passes before his prophetic eye the proud galley which so aptly symbolizes this great marine power. As it glides through the waters, manned by experts and loaded with a great variety of goods, it seems as solid and indestructible as the 'rock' (*צוֹר*) which it represented. When the waters finally close over her, a terrible wailing arises from among the people for whom it had been the focus of hope and ambition.*

Yechezkel is to join that wailing — though surely from a different perspective. These bounties from God need not have been wasted. The blessing which God bestows can be used in His service; indeed, God 'hid' some of Tyre's wealth for the future use of the righteous (see beginning of ch. 28). It is the misuse of these divine gifts that evokes Yechezkel's tears (based on R' Breuer).

3. עַל מְבוֹאֹת יָם — *At the entry of the sea.*

I.e., a harbor *(Rashi).* Many coastal towns do not have a harbor, but Tyre was blessed with one, which enabled ships to enter from the sea.

רֹכֶלֶת הָעַמִּים — *Merchant for the nations.*

The custom was that merchants who came to Tyre were not allowed to do business with one another. The townspeople would buy from one and sell to the other *(Rashi).*

Generally the term רוֹכֵל refers to a peddler who brings the wholesaler's wares to the various customers (see *v.* 13). In that sense he is subordinate to the סֹחֵר, *wholesale merchant;* however, where Tyre is described in all her splendor, רֹכֶלֶת cannot have that subordinate meaning. Rather, it describes Tyre as the pivot of world trade. The centrality of its location made it the natural conduit for the flow of goods אֶל אִיִּים רַבִּים, *to far-flung lands.*

For אִיִּים, see *comm.* 26:15.

אֲנִי כְּלִילַת יֹפִי — *I am perfection in beauty.*

Until now all had said that Jerusalem was *the perfection of beauty, joy of all the earth (Lamentations* 2:15). Now you, Tyre, are priding yourself that you have usurped this position *(Rashi).*

Midrash Tehillim (48) points out that whereas in the case of Jerusalem, the other nations had testified that she was כְּלִילַת יֹפִי, *the perfection of beauty,* it was Tyre who made the claim concerning herself. The *Midrash* quotes a proverb: 'Not as the mother says, but as the neighbors say!'

27 *The word of HASHEM came to me, saying:*
1-7 *² Now you, Ben Adam, take up a lament for*
Tyre; ³ and say to Tyre, which dwells at the entry of
the sea, merchant for the nations to far-flung lands:
Thus says my Lord HASHEM/ELOHIM:

Tyre, you have said:
I am perfection in beauty.

⁴ In the heart of the seas were your boundaries
Your builders perfected your beauty.

⁵ Of cypress wood from Senir
did they fashion you
all the planks.
They took cedar from the Lebanon
to make a mast upon you.

⁶ Of oaks from Bashan
did they make you oars.
Your rudder did they make
of ivory-inlaid ebony
from the isles of Kettites.

⁷ Finely embroidered Egyptian linen
was your sail,

4. בְּלֵב יַמִּים גְּבוּלָיִךְ — *In the heart of the seas were your boundaries.*

Tyre was an island *(Radak).* See pref., ch. 26.

בֹּנַיִךְ כָּלְלוּ יָפְיֵךְ — *Your builders perfected your beauty.*

This begins the description of the boat.

5. בְּרוֹשִׁים מִשְּׂנִיר בָּנוּ לָךְ — *Of cypress wood from Senir.*

According to *Deuteronomy* 3:9, Senir is another name for Mount Hermon. The fact that it is mentioned together with Hermon in *Shir HaShirim* (4:8) makes it likely that a part of Hermon was called Senir *(R' D. Z. Hoffman).*

אֵת כָּל לֻחֹתָיִם — *All the planks.*

The suffix ַיִם indicates a pair, rather than an ordinary plural. This form may be used with regard to a ship to indicate its two sides *(Radak).*

6. אַלּוֹנִים מִבָּשָׁן — *Of oaks from Bashan.*

Bashan lies east of the Jordan (*Deut.* 3:10-14) and was famous for its oaks (see *Zecharyah* 11:2).

קַרְשֵׁךְ עָשׂוּ־שֵׁן בַּת־אֲשֻׁרִים — *Your rudder did they make of ivory-inlaid ebony.*

Rashi writes that this refers to the rudder that is opposite the mast (תֹּרֶן of *v.* 5), by which the helmsman steers the boat. He reads בַּת־אֲשֻׁרִים as one word [בִּתְאַשֻּׁרִים] and interprets it as in תְּאַשּׁוּר, *boxwood* or *ebony (Isaiah* 41:19 and 60:13). The rudder was made from

לִהְי֥וֹת לָ֖ךְ לְנֵ֑ס תְּכֵ֧לֶת וְאַרְגָּמָ֛ן מֵאִיֵּ֥
ח אֱלִישָׁ֖ה הָיָ֥ה מְכַסֵּֽךְ׃ יֹשְׁבֵ֤י צִידוֹן֙ וְאַרְוַ֔ד
הָי֥וּ שָׁטִ֖ים לָ֑ךְ חֲכָמַ֤יִךְ צוֹר֙ הָ֣יוּ בָ֔ךְ הֵ֖מָּה
ט חֹבְלָֽיִךְ׃ זִקְנֵ֨י גְבַ֤ל וַחֲכָמֶ֙יהָ֙ הָ֣יוּ בָ֔ךְ
מַחֲזִיקֵ֖י בִּדְקֵ֑ךְ כָּל־אֳנִיּ֨וֹת הַיָּ֤ם וּמַלָּֽחֵיהֶם֙
י הָ֣יוּ בָ֔ךְ לַעֲרֹ֖ב מַעֲרָבֵֽךְ׃ פָּרַ֨ס וְל֤וּד וּפוּט֙
הָי֣וּ בְחֵילֵ֔ךְ אַנְשֵׁ֖י מִלְחַמְתֵּ֑ךְ מָגֵ֤ן וְכוֹבַע֙
יא תִּלּוּ־בָ֔ךְ הֵ֖מָּה נָתְנ֥וּ הֲדָרֵֽךְ׃ בְּנֵ֧י אַרְוַ֣ד
וְחֵילֵ֗ךְ עַל־חוֹמוֹתַ֙יִךְ֙ סָבִ֔יב וְגַ֨מָּדִ֔ים

ebony inlaid with ivory. [Presumably he rejects the translation *ivory fashioned by Assyrians* (see *Radak*) since the rudder must be made out of wood.]

7. לִהְיוֹת לָךְ לְנֵס — *To be your ensign.*

The brightly embroidered sails served as a sign by which the ship could be recognized. This translation follows *Targum* who renders נֵס as אָת, meaning *a sign.*

Isaiah 33:23 indicates that נֵס is a part of the ship associated with the mast. *Rashi* renders: to spread on your mast. I.e., the *sail* of the first part of the verse is to be hoisted on to the mast.

אִיֵּי אֱלִישָׁה — *The isles of Elishah.*

[Elishah is listed in *Genesis* (10:4) as a son of יָוָן, who is usually identified as *Greece.* Hence the meaning might be Greek islands.] *Targum* renders: *from the country of Italia.*

מְכַסֵּךְ — *Your awning.*

I.e., a canopy spanning the whole ship *(Rashi).*

8. יֹשְׁבֵי צִידוֹן וְאַרְוַד — *The dwellers of Sidon and Arvad.*

Sidon and Arvad are listed in *Genesis* 10:15 and 18 as descendants of Canaan. They were both coastal towns whose people were presumably expert sailors. (See ArtScroll *Bereishis* 10.)

חֹבְלָיִךְ — *Your sailors.*

חֹבְלָיִךְ refers to one of the three different functionaries on a boat (see *v.* 9.]

The word is derived from חֶבֶל, *rope,* associated with the sails *(Metzudos).*

9. זִקְנֵי גְבַל וַחֲכָמֶיהָ — *The elders of Geval and its wise men.*

The people of Geval were skilled workmen, ideally suited to be the ship's carpenters. *I Kings* 5:32 reports that they were among the artisans employed in building Solomon's Temple *(Rashi).*

וּמַלָּחֵיהֶם — *And their mariners.*

מַלָּח is another term for sailor. *Rashi (Exodus* 30:35) writes that the root מלח means *to mix.* The sailors who man the oars are called מַלָּחִים because they churn up the water. *Ramban* (there) disagrees. He identifies three categories of workers on the ship. שָׁטִים (*v.* 8) are the people who row. The מַלָּחִים are the older, more experienced sailors who can taste the מֶלַח, *salt* content of the waters to determine what effect it might have on shipping. The third category is that of the חוֹבְלִים, *sailriggers (v.* 8).

לַעֲרֹב מַעֲרָבֵךְ — *To provide your merchandise.*

This follows *Targum* who renders: *to bring merchandise into you.*

The root ערב, which means *to guarantee,* is used to describe merchandise either because property is the guarantee of life *(Rashi)* or because merchants when doing business with one another guarantee their purchases *(Radak).* (See *v.* 13).

to be your ensign.
Blue and purple from the isles of Elishah
was your awning.

8 *The dwellers of Sidon and Arvad*
were your oarsmen.
Your wise men, O Tyre, were within you —
they were your sailors.

9 *The elders of Geval and its wise men*
were within you —
caulkers of your cracks.
All the ships of the sea and their mariners
were within you
to provide your merchandise.

10 *Persia, Lud, and Put were in your army —*
your warriors.
They hung shield and helmet in you;
they provided your beauty.

11 *The sons of Arvad and your army*
were on your walls roundabout.

10-25 The metaphor of the ship is set aside. The following description centers on Tyre itself. The story of the ship is resumed once more in *v.* 26.

According to *Maharal,* poetry often lacks strict sequence because it arises from the turmoil of a soul deeply moved *(Nesivos Olam, Nesiv HaAvodah* 12; see footnote 7:2).

[The preceding descriptive verses conjured up the memory of Tyre's beauty and wealth, causing the prophet to break off in the middle of the metaphor to elaborate upon it.]

10. פָּרַס וְלוּד וּפוּט הָיוּ בְחֵילֵךְ — *Persia, Lud, and Put were in your army.*

When Tyre had to wage war, there was no shortage of trained soldiers who would pour into the city to help *(Radak).*

Since Put is a brother of *Mitzraim,* [Egypt] *(Genesis* 10:6), it is likely that Lud mentioned with him here is the son of *Mitzraim (Genesis* 10:13), not the Lud who was a son of Shem *(Genesis* 10:22). The import of our verse is then that these soldiers poured in from the East (Persia) and from the West (Egypt) *(R' Breuer).*

הֵמָּה נָתְנוּ הֲדָרֵךְ — *They provided your beauty.*

The weapons and armor hanging in the city gave it a festive air *(Radak).*

11. בְּנֵי אַרְוַד וְחֵילֵךְ — *The sons of Arvad and your army.*

For Arvad, see *v.* 8. The commentators interpolate *together with the rest of your army* — although the construction is awkward. *Eliezer of Beaugency* writes that חֵילֵךְ is the name of a nation in Asia Minor. This, although in the

בְּמִגְדְּלוֹתַיִךְ הָיוּ שִׁלְטֵיהֶם תִּלּוּ עַל־
חוֹמוֹתַיִךְ סָבִיב הֵמָּה כָּלְלוּ יָפְיֵךְ׃
יב תַּרְשִׁישׁ סֹחַרְתֵּךְ מֵרֹב כָּל־הוֹן בְּכֶסֶף
יג בַּרְזֶל בְּדִיל וְעוֹפֶרֶת נָתְנוּ עִזְבוֹנָיִךְ׃ יָוָן
תּוּבַל וָמֶשֶׁךְ הֵמָּה רֹכְלָיִךְ בְּנֶפֶשׁ אָדָם
יד וּכְלֵי נְחֹשֶׁת נָתְנוּ מַעֲרָבֵךְ׃ מִבֵּית
תּוֹגַרְמָה סוּסִים וּפָרָשִׁים וּפְרָדִים נָתְנוּ

previous verse he renders the same word, *army*.

וְגַמָּדִים בְּמִגְדְּלוֹתַיִךְ הָיוּ — *And dwarfs were upon your towers.*

גֹּמֶד is an ancient measure somewhere in the range of a cubit (see *Judges* 3:16). Thus the word came to have the meaning of *dwarf* who might only be a cubit tall. Most commentators take it to have this meaning in our verse. *Metzudos* explains that dwarfs were idealy suited to act as lookouts in the towers since they would not be noticed by the enemy.

Others however write that גַּמָּדִים also is the name of a nation *(Mahari MiTrani)* and *Targum* identifies them as the people of Cappadocia (a district in Asia Minor). *Rashi* suggests that they were called גַּמָּדִים from the word גֹּמֶד, a word indicating an ancient measurement, because they were deep sea-divers who descended into the waters to *measure* (גמד) their depth.

12. תַּרְשִׁישׁ — *Tarshish.*

תַּרְשִׁישׁ is thought to be Tartessus which lies on the southwest coast of the Iberian peninsula near the mouth of the Guadala River. It was certainly a coastal city with sea-faring people. *Targum* simply renders: *from the sea.*

סֹחַרְתֵּךְ — *Your merchant.*

סֹחֵר is a merchant (*Genesis* 23:16). The feminine form is used here to stress that although Tarshish was a great maritime power in her own right, compared to Tyre she was weak. The feminine form is used to denote weakness throughout this chapter *(R' Breuer).*

נָתְנוּ עִזְבוֹנָיִךְ — *They provided your wares.*

Tarshish was richly endowed with the natural resources mentioned in our verses. It exported these materials to Tyre, which, in turn, processed them and became wealthy selling them throughout the world *(Metzudos).*

The use of the root עזב to describe merchandise is unique to *Ezekiel* (according to some commentators the exception is *Deuteronomy* 32:36).

The association of עזב, *to forsake,* with merchandise is variously explained by the commentators:

— *Ibn Janach (Sefer HaShorashim)* writes that one *forsakes* his merchandise in the country to which it is exported.

— *Eliezer of Beaugency* writes that the idea derives from the practice of selling merchandise cheaply (to 'forsake' some of its value) in order to attract customers.

— *Malbim* says that it refers specifically to merchandise stored *(forsaken)* in barns or storehouse [*Targum* renders: *storage houses.*]

— *HaKesav VeHaKaballah (Deuteronomy* 32:36) writes that any article that is sold can be described as עִזָּבוֹן since the seller is *forsaking* it to the buyer.

[This explanation has the advantage of not being limited to one particular aspect (e.g., exporting, pricing, or storing) of the merchandise. The use of עזב in this sense is

And dwarfs were upon your towers,
They hung their shields upon
your walls roundabout.
They perfected your beauty.

12 *Tarshish was your merchant*
because of the multitude of every richness.
With silver, iron, tin, and lead
they provided your wares.

13 *Yavan, Tuval, and Meshech —*
they are your peddlers.
With human slaves and brazen vessels
they guaranteed your merchandise.

14 *From Bais Togarmah came*
horses, riders, and mules —
they provided your wares.

analagous to the use of the verb לקח, *to take* to describe the act of giving. (See for example *Exodus* 25:2.) The giver or seller permits the other to *take* the property, or, as *Ibn Ezra* (there) explains, he *takes* from himself to give to another. Either way it expresses the loss of the seller. This is the precise idea expressed by עִזָּבוֹן. The more precious the object, the more difficult it is for the seller to part from it (see *Berachos* 5a, כִּי לֶקַח טוֹב). Thus merchandise is called עִזָּבוֹן to stress its excellent quality. The seller considers himself forced to part with it.]

13. יָוָן תּוּבַל וָמֶשֶׁךְ — *Yavan, Tuval, and Meshech.*

These are identified in *Genesis* (10:2) as descendants of Noach's son Japheth. (See ArtScroll there for closer identification.) Tuval and Meshech are assumed to lie at the Black Sea.

רֹכְלָיִךְ — *Your peddlers.*

Malbim contrasts the רוֹכֵל, *peddler*, with the סוֹחֵר, *merchant*, of *v.* 12. The latter are wholesalers; the former, middlemen who bring the merchandise to the customers.

In *Malbim's* view, the term עִזָּבוֹן *of v.* 12 refers to merchandise stored in barns or storehouse מַעֲרָב at the end of our verse refers to the surety which the רוֹכֵל, *peddler*, must leave behind in order to guarantee that he will not steal the goods which he is supposed to sell (*comm., v.* 9). Verses 12 and 13 are related in the following manner.

Tarshish was the great wholesaler which deposited precious metals in Tyre's warehouses. Yavan, Tuval, and Meshech, as middlemen, were then charged with the duty of selling these metals to Tyre's customers. To guarantee payment for their merchandise, these peddler states were required to deposit slaves and brass vessels with Tyre.

בְּנֶפֶשׁ אָדָם — *With human slaves* [lit. *people*].

This refers to male and female slaves for sale *(Rashi).*

14. בֵּית תּוֹגַרְמָה— *Bais Togarmah.*

According to *Kesses HaSofer*, this is Armenia. (See ArtScroll *Bereishis* 10:13.)

°וְהָבְנִים ק׳

טו עִזְבוֹנָיִךְ׃ בְּנֵי דְדָן רֹכְלַיִךְ אִיִּים רַבִּים
סְחֹרַת יָדֵךְ קַרְנוֹת שֵׁן °והובנים הֵשִׁיבוּ
טז אֶשְׁכָּרֵךְ׃ אֲרָם סֹחַרְתֵּךְ מֵרֹב מַעֲשָׂיִךְ
בְּנֹפֶךְ אַרְגָּמָן וְרִקְמָה וּבוּץ וְרָאמֹת
יז וְכַדְכֹּד נָתְנוּ בְּעִזְבוֹנָיִךְ׃ יְהוּדָה וְאֶרֶץ
יִשְׂרָאֵל הֵמָּה רֹכְלָיִךְ בְּחִטֵּי מִנִּית וּפַנַּג
יח וּדְבַשׁ וָשֶׁמֶן וָצֹרִי נָתְנוּ מַעֲרָבֵךְ׃ דַּמֶּשֶׂק
סֹחַרְתֵּךְ בְּרֹב מַעֲשַׂיִךְ מֵרֹב כָּל־הוֹן בְּיֵין
יט חֶלְבּוֹן וְצֶמֶר צָחַר׃ וְדָן וְיָוָן מְאוּזָּל
בְּעִזְבוֹנַיִךְ נָתָנוּ בַּרְזֶל עָשׁוֹת קִדָּה וְקָנֶה

15. בְּנֵי דְדָן— *The men of Dedan.*

This name is repeated in *v.* 20 among the Arab nations, but the people mentioned in our verse must have been from a different nation. The name occurs in *Genesis* among the descendants of Yavan (10:4), Kush (10:7), and Keturah (5:3).

סְחֹרַת יָדֵךְ — *Your local merchants.*

This phrase parallels the one in *v.* 21 where the more usual form סֹחֲרֵי is used. The word יָד with the meaning *place (Rashi)* is quite common in Scripture. (See *Deut.* 23:13).

וְהָבְנִים — *And peacocks.*

The translation follows *Targum* and *Rashi. Radak* identifies the term as referring to a certain type of wood. (The similarity in sound may indicate ebony.)

אֶשְׁכָּרֵךְ — *Your tribute.*

The word is obscure. The meaning of *tribute* (see commentators) can be deduced from *Psalms* 72:10.

16. מַעֲשָׂיִךְ — *Wealth.*

The translation follows *Targum,* who renders עוּתְרִיךְ, *your wealth.* In a similar context (*Jeremiah* 38:7) he renders: *storage houses.* [Perhaps the word indicates a *business* or *pursuit* as in *Genesis* 46:33, or *manufactured goods* as in *Exodus* 26:1].

נֹפֶךְ — *Nofech.*

Nofech is mentioned in *Exodus* 28:18 as one of the precious stones on the clothes of the High Priest. Its exact meaning is unknown. *Targum* renders *clothing.*

17. חִטֵּי מִנִּית — *Wheat from Minis.*

Most commentators assume Minis to be the name of a town, also mentioned in *Judges* 11:33. Perhaps it was particularly rich in high quality wheat.

Rashi quotes a *Midrash* which relates the word to מִנְיָן, *number.* The wheat was of such high quality that it was traded by number of kernels rather than by volume.

Targum renders רִיחוּשׁ. *Radak* declares ignorance of the meaning of this word. According to *Rashi* it means a kind [of wheat] which is bought and stored in great quantities.

פַּנַּג — *Balsam oil.*

Rashi quotes *Joseph ben Gurion* as the source of this rendering.

Targum renders קוּלְיָא, which according to *Radak* is a kind of vegetable.

Radak writes that פַּנַּג is a place name. The phrase means *wheat from Minis and Panag.*

18. דַּמֶּשֶׂק — *Damascus.*

Damascus was the capital of Aram which was mentioned in *v.* 16. (See *Isaiah* 7:8).

27
15-19

[15] *The men of Dedan were your peddlers.*
Many far-flung lands became your local merchants.
Ivory tusks and peacocks
they brought back as your tribute.

[16] *Aram became your merchant*
because of your great wealth.
With nofech, *purple wool, embroidery,*
fine linen, coral, and kadkod
which they provided for your wares.

[17] *Judah and the Land of Israel —*
they were your peddlers.
With wheat from Minis, balsam oil,
honey, oil, and balm
they guaranteed your merchandise.

[18] *Damascus became your merchant*
because of your great wealth, because of the multitude of every richness,
with wine from Chelbon and white wool.

[19] *Vedan and Yavan*
provided your wares with yarn.
Iron fashioned into bars, cassia, and calamus

יֵין חֶלְבּוֹן — *Wine from Chelbon.*

Radak and *Metzudos* write that Chelbon is the name of a place.

Rashi based on *Targum* translates *white wine which is cooked.* [*The word* חֶלְבּוֹן is derived from חָלָב, *milk.*] *Rashi* also quotes *Menachem* who traces חֶלְבּוֹן to חֵלֶב, meaning *fat,* often used to denote the best. Accordingly, יֵין חֶלְבּוֹן means *the very best of wine.*

צָחַר — *White.*

See *Judges* 5:10.

19. וְדָן וְיָוָן — *Vedan and Yavan.*

The *vav* of וְדָן, *Vedan,* is not a conjuctive prefix meaning *and,* but part of the country's name.

מְאוּזָּל — *Yarn.*

The punctuation (מְאוּזָּל rather than מֵאוּזָּל) precludes the possibility of taking מֵ as the prefix *from* and אוּזָּל as a place name (see *Genesis* 10:27).

Rashi takes the word to mean thread or yarn. He does not explain the reasoning behind this. [Perhaps he relates it to the Aramaic root עזל (*ayin* instead of *aleph*) which means *to spin.*]

Radak and *Metzudos* base their translation on *Targum.* In his view, the word is formed from אזל, *to go* or *move.* מְאוּזָּל means *caravans* or *merchants* who travel from place to place in pursuit of their business.

בַּרְזֶל עָשׁוֹת — *Iron fashioned into bars.*

The translation follows *Rashi* who explains: עָשׂוּי כְּעֶשָׁשִׁיּוֹת, which were

כ בְּמַעֲרָבֵךְ הָיָה: דְּדָן רֹכַלְתֵּךְ בְּבִגְדֵי־חֹפֶשׁ
כא לְרִכְבָּה: עֲרַב וְכָל־נְשִׂיאֵי קֵדָר הֵמָּה
סֹחֲרֵי יָדֵךְ בְּכָרִים וְאֵילִם וְעַתּוּדִים
כב בָּם סֹחֲרָיִךְ: רֹכְלֵי שְׁבָא וְרַעְמָה הֵמָּה
רֹכְלָיִךְ בְּרֹאשׁ כָּל־בֹּשֶׂם וּבְכָל־אֶבֶן יְקָרָה
כג וְזָהָב נָתְנוּ עִזְבוֹנָיִךְ: חָרָן וְכַנֵּה וָעֶדֶן
כד רֹכְלֵי שְׁבָא אַשּׁוּר כִּלְמַד רֹכַלְתֵּךְ: הֵמָּה
רֹכְלַיִךְ בְמַכְלֻלִים בִּגְלוֹמֵי תְּכֵלֶת וְרִקְמָה
וּבְגִנְזֵי בְּרֹמִים בַּחֲבָלִים חֲבֻשִׁים וַאֲרֻזִים

made like *metal bars.*

Radak and *Metzudos* render *smooth* or *shining iron,* as in *Jeremiah* 5:28, where it means *to be sleek.*

קִדָּה וְקָנֶה — *Cassia and calamus.*

קִדָּה and קָנֶה are spices mentioned in *Exodus* 30:23-24.

20. דְּדָן — *Dedan.*

See *comm., v.* 15.

רֹכַלְתֵּךְ — *Your peddler.*

The feminine possessive form (as opposed to רֹכְלַיִךְ in previous verses) is explained by *R' Breuer* as an expression of weakness. Dedan did indeed trade with Tyre, but only in a small way. It did not have much to offer.

בִּגְדֵי חֹפֶשׁ — *Luxurious clothes.*

חֹפֶשׁ is *freedom.* They were luxurious clothes such as would be worn by a free man rather than a slave *(Metzudos).*

21. קֵדָר — *Kedar.*

Kedar is a son of Ishmael (*Genesis* 25:13). *Isaiah* 60:7 shows that the land occupied by his descendants was famous for its flocks.

בְּכָרִים — *With fat sheep.*

Rashi translates *sheep. Metzudos* adds *'fat' sheep. Targum* translates *oxen.*

22. שְׁבָא וְרַעְמָה — *Sheba and Raamah.*

שְׁבָא and רַעְמָה are grandson and son, respectively, of Canaan's son Cush (see ArtScroll *Bereishis* 10:17 for closer identification).

Even proud Sheba, itself the center for many dealers (*v.* 23), was not above considering herself simply a peddler (רֹכֵל) of Tyre *(R' Breuer).*

23. חָרָן וְכַנֵּה וָעֶדֶן — *Charan, Caneh, and Eden.*

Charan is mentioned in the narrative of *Genesis* 11 and 28. [Caneh does not recur but could be identical with Calneh in *Genesis* 10:10.] Eden lies on the banks of the Euphrates and is mentioned in *Isaiah* 37:12.

רֹכְלֵי שְׁבָא — *The peddlers of Sheba.*

R' Breuer notes that in relation to Sheba, all the nations are described in the masculine, indicating that they were powerful and important compared to Sheba. In doing business with bustling, internationally-respected Tyre, however they are described with the feminine רֹכַלְתֵּךְ, indicating a lack of relative strength. Only after they became Tyre's trading partners did they regain their confidence and become רֹכְלִים (masculine, suggesting power) once more.

כִּלְמַד — *Media.*

Targum identifies כִּלְמַד (which does not recur in Scripture) as Media.

Radak suggests that it is derived from למד, which can be rendered *accustomed: Ashur was accustomed* to trading with you.

were among your merchandise.

20 *Dedan was your peddler,*
with luxurious clothes for riding.

21 *Arabia and all Kedar's princes—*
They are your local merchants.
With fat sheep, rams, and goats —
with these they were your merchants.

22 *The peddlers of Sheba and Raamah —*
they are your peddlers.
With the best of every spice,
and every precious stone and gold,
they provided your wares.

23 *Charan, Caneh, and Eden,*
the peddlers of Sheba,
Asher, and Media,
were your peddlers.

24 *They are your peddlers in perfect objects*
in wraps of blue wool and embroidery;
in treasures kept in chests, fastened with bands
and cedar-boxed, for your wares.

24. בְּמַכְלֻלִים — *In perfect objects.*

מַכְלֻלִים, from כלל, *to be complete* or *perfect,* are objects of perfection. The word itself gives no indication of the type of object. The verse proceeds to explain *(Rashi).*

בִּגְלוֹמֵי תְּכֵלֶת וְרִקְמָה — *In wraps of blue wool and embroidery.*

The מַכְלֻלִים, wholly beautiful objects, are *wraps* (טַלִּיתוֹת — *Rashi)* of embroidered blue wool. According to *Metzudos,* גְּלוֹמִים are *bundles* rather than wraps.

וּבְגִנְזֵי בְּרֹמִים — *In treasures kept in chests.*

Targum, followed by *Rashi* and *Metzudos,* translates בְּרוֹם as *a chest.* Since גנז means *to hide* or *store away,* the phrase must be rendered: Treasures or objects sufficiently valuable to be stored in chests. Based on the Arabic, *Radak* translate בְּרוֹמִים as *precious clothes,* but agrees that גִּנְזֵי indicates storage, hence: *robes kept in chests.*

בַּחֲבָלִים חֲבֻשִׁים — *Fastened with bands.*

The chests were fastened with linen bands for ornamentation *(Rashi).*

וַאֲרֻזִים — *Cedar-boxed.*

Targum, followed by *Rashi,* derives the word from אֶרֶז, *cedar.* The chests containing the embroidered wraps were placed in larger cedar boxes for additional protection.

Metzudos writes that אֲרֻזִים has the same meaning as חֲרָזִים (the letters אחה״ע are interchangeable) which derives from חרז, *to bead a string. Accordingly,* אֲרוּזִים are *necklaces.*

כה בְּמַרְכֻלְתֵּךְ: אֳנִיּוֹת תַּרְשִׁישׁ שָׁרוֹתַיִךְ
מַעֲרָבֵךְ וַתִּמָּלְאִי וַתִּכְבְּדִי מְאֹד בְּלֵב
כו יַמִּים: בְּמַיִם רַבִּים הֱבִאוּךְ הַשָּׁטִים אֹתָךְ
כז רוּחַ הַקָּדִים שְׁבָרֵךְ בְּלֵב יַמִּים: הוֹנֵךְ
וְעִזְבוֹנַיִךְ מַעֲרָבֵךְ מַלָּחַיִךְ וְחֹבְלָיִךְ
מַחֲזִיקֵי בִדְקֵךְ וְעֹרְבֵי מַעֲרָבֵךְ וְכָל־אַנְשֵׁי
מִלְחַמְתֵּךְ אֲשֶׁר־בָּךְ וּבְכָל־קְהָלֵךְ אֲשֶׁר
בְּתוֹכֵךְ יִפְּלוּ בְּלֵב יַמִּים בְּיוֹם מַפַּלְתֵּךְ:
כח לְקוֹל זַעֲקַת חֹבְלָיִךְ יִרְעֲשׁוּ מִגְרֹשׁוֹת:
כט וְיָרְדוּ מֵאָנִיּוֹתֵיהֶם כֹּל תֹּפְשֵׂי מָשׁוֹט
מַלָּחִים כֹּל חֹבְלֵי הַיָּם אֶל־הָאָרֶץ
ל יַעֲמֹדוּ: וְהִשְׁמִיעוּ עָלַיִךְ בְּקוֹלָם וְיִזְעֲקוּ
מָרָה וְיַעֲלוּ עָפָר עַל־רָאשֵׁיהֶם בָּאֵפֶר
לא יִתְפַּלָּשׁוּ: וְהִקְרִיחוּ אֵלַיִךְ קָרְחָה וְחָגְרוּ
שַׂקִּים וּבָכוּ אֵלַיִךְ בְּמַר־נֶפֶשׁ מִסְפֵּד מָר:

25. אֳנִיּוֹת תַּרְשִׁישׁ שָׁרוֹתַיִךְ — *The ships of Tarshish were your caravans.*

This translation follows *Radak* and *Metzudos* who relate שָׁרוֹתַיִךְ to שַׁיָּרָה, *caravan. Rashi* relates it to מִישׁוֹר, from ישר meaning a *straight, well trodden road.* The translation would be: *The ships of Tarshish beat a path to your door.*

26. The theme of the ship (*v.* 9) is resumed. (See *comm., vs.* 10-25). The proud galley is suddenly smashed by an east wind in the midst of the ocean.

A less heavily laden boat might have survived, but the ship of Tyre was heavy with wealth, a condition that guaranteed its sinking *(Rashi).*

The metaphor was closely related to the reality. After Nebuchadnezzar finally captured Tyre, the sea rose and swamped the whole island *(Radak).*

28. יִרְעֲשׁוּ מִגְרֹשׁוֹת — *The surrounding areas will tremble.*

The area surrounding a city is called מִגְרָשׁ *(Numbers* 35:2) because it is as though the area had been *expelled* (גרש) from within the city's walls *(Metzudos).*

29-31 In 26:16 ff. the *princes of the sea* would leave their thrones to lament Tyre's tragedy. Here it is the sailors who sing the dirge. They leave their ships to stand on the land, for, as *Rashi* points out, once Tyre has disappeared their ships are of no more use to them. They have nowhere to go.

Their desperation expresses itself in all the outward forms of mourning.

27
25-31

25 *The ships of Tarshish were your caravan*
for your merchandise;
so you were filled and made very heavy
in the heart of the seas.

26 *Into many waters*
your oarsmen brought you.
The east wind has broken you
in the heart of the seas.

27 *Your riches, your wares, and your merchandise;*
your mariners and your sailors;
the caulkers of your cracks
and your guarantors,
and all the men of war
who were within you
and with your entire company
which was in your midst —
these will fall in the heart of the seas
on the day of your downfall.

28 *To the sound of your sailors' cries*
the surrounding areas will tremble;

29 *and from their boats will descend*
everyone who grasps an oar,
the mariners and all the seafarers —
and stand upon the ground.

30 *They shall cause their voice*
to be heard because of you
and cry out bitterly,
put dust upon their heads
and roll themselves in ashes.

31 *They shall tear out all their hair*
for you
and gird themselves in sack-cloth
and cry about you in bitterness of soul
with bitter lamentation.

כז
לב-לו

לב וְנָשְׂאוּ אֵלַיִךְ בְּנִיהֶם קִינָה וְקוֹנְנוּ עָלָיִךְ
לג מִי כְצוֹר כְּדֻמָה בְּתוֹךְ הַיָּם: בְּצֵאת
עִזְבוֹנַיִךְ מִיַּמִּים הִשְׂבַּעַתְּ עַמִּים רַבִּים
בְּרֹב הוֹנַיִךְ וּמַעֲרָבַיִךְ הֶעֱשַׁרְתְּ מַלְכֵי־
לד אָרֶץ: עֵת נִשְׁבֶּרֶת מִיַּמִּים בְּמַעֲמַקֵּי־מָיִם
לה מַעֲרָבֵךְ וְכָל־קְהָלֵךְ בְּתוֹכֵךְ נָפָלוּ: כֹּל
יֹשְׁבֵי הָאִיִּים שָׁמְמוּ עָלָיִךְ וּמַלְכֵיהֶם
לו שָׂעֲרוּ שַׂעַר רָעֲמוּ פָּנִים: סֹחֲרִים בָּעַמִּים
שָׁרְקוּ עָלָיִךְ בַּלָּהוֹת הָיִית וְאֵינֵךְ עַד־
כח
א
א עוֹלָם: וַיְהִי דְבַר־יְהוָה אֵלַי לֵאמֹר:

32. בְּנִיהֶם — *In their wailing.*

The root is נהה, meaning *to wail* (*Rashi*).

כְּדֻמָה בְּתוֹךְ הַיָּם — *Like she who is cut off in the midst of the sea.*

The translation follows *Radak* and *Metzudos*. Who is like Tyre in her greatness, and who is like her in the hour of her destruction!

Rashi writes that דֻמָה is the name of an Edomite city (*Isaiah* 21:1). [Perhaps it was a particularly well known metropolis.] *Who can be compared to Tyre, the Dumah of the sea!*

Targum derives the word from the root דמה, *to compare. Who in the midst of the sea can be compared to her.*

R' Breuer derives the word from דמם, *to be silent:* the one who was doomed to silence in the midst of the sea.

35. וּמַלְכֵיהֶם שָׂעֲרוּ שַׂעַר — *And their kings shook with trembling.*

Ibn Janach (Sefer HaShorashim) explains that שַׂעַר with a *sin* has the same meaning as סַעַר with a *samech,* which is *a storm;* hence the meaning of shaking and trembling.

Others trace it to the root שֵׂעָר, meaning *hair. The hair of the kings bristled with horror.*

רָעֲמוּ פָּנִים — *Their faces looked thunderstruck.*

Ibn Janach (Sefer HaShorashim) explains that the root of רָעֲמוּ is the same as רַעַם, *thunder.* It describes a person who is severely upset.

36. סֹחֲרִים בָּעַמִּים שָׁרְקוּ עָלָיִךְ — *The merchants of the nations hissed against you.*

R' Breuer detects one of the great ironies of history in this verse. The initial shock of Tyre's destruction did indeed evoke wailing and dirges from her former trading partners (סֹחֲרֵי יָדֵךְ and סֹחַרְתֵּךְ). However, once the initial shock had passed, they very quickly become independent — סֹחֲרִים בָּעַמִּים, *merchants of the nations* — quite happy to be ride of their domineering partner and even hissing at her in derision. Their fickleness was a true reflection of Tyre's own attitude to Jerusalem's destruction. She, too, had rejoiced all too quickly at the downfall of her former friend (see 26:2).

בַּלָּהוֹת — *Desolation.*

See 26:21.

XXVIII

Although history records Ithabeal II as ruler of Tyre during the years of Nebuchadnezzar's siege, the Sages (Bereishis Rabbah *85:4) identify this king as the same*

27
32-36

[32] *In their wailing, they shall take up*
a lament for you,
and lament over you,
'Who is like Tyre! Cut off like
her in the midst of the sea!'

[33] *When your wares went forth*
from the seas
you satiated many nations.
With your abundant wealth and merchandise,
you enriched the kings of the earth.

[34] *Now that you are broken by the seas*
in the depth of the water,
your merchandise and all your company
collapsed in your midst.

[35] *All inhabitants of far-flung islands*
were desolate concerning you
and their kings shook with trembling.
Their faces looked thunderstruck.

[36] *The merchants of the nations*
hissed against you.
You became a desolation
and shall be no more.

Hiram of Tyre who had befriended David and Solomon (I Kings *5:15). According-ly, he lived close to 500 years. Another opinion in the* Midrash *identifies him with Chirah, the friend of Judah* (Genesis *38:1). According to this view, he lived approx-imately 1200 years.*[1]

Yechezkel is to take up a lamentation for this great king, and just for this king there was much for Yechezkel to lament.

There had been so much to hope for. Through his close friendship with King David (I Kings *5:15), which carried over to Solomon* (v. *21), it might have been ex-*

1. Not infrequently, the Sages teach that people who lived many years apart were really one and the same man. See, for example, *Sanhedrin* 101b, where the *Talmud* identifies Nevat who lived at the time of David and Solomon with Michah who lived when Israel was in Egypt. *Yad Ramah* (there) in fact queries how it is possible for a wicked person to have lived so long. *Margalios HaYam (there)* quotes *Ein Eliyahu* that in many instances when the Sages make such a claim they do not mean it literally, but rather wish to point out similar character traits or activities which are shared by the various people. (See also *Tzvi Hirsch Chayos, Mavo HaTalmud* ch. 21).

Applying this theory here, the Sages may be teaching us that all the kings of Tyre from

כח ב בֶּן־אָדָם אֱמֹר לִנְגִיד צֹר כֹּה־אָמַר | אֲדֹנָי
ב יֱהוִה יַעַן גָּבַהּ לִבְּךָ וַתֹּאמֶר אֵל אָנִי
מוֹשַׁב אֱלֹהִים יָשַׁבְתִּי בְּלֵב יַמִּים וְאַתָּה

*pected that Israel's destiny as witness to the nations (*Isaiah *55:4) would become fulfilled. Surely the echo of Hiram's cry* (II Chronicles *2:11):* Blessed be God, Lord of Israel, Who created heaven and earth ... , *would continue to reverberate throughout the gentile world, awakening the people to be receptive to the Torah and the word of God which, with the erection of the Temple, were about to emanate from Zion and Jerusalem.*

Hiram stinted with nothing. His enormous wealth and wisdom were placed at the service of the Temple. Men and goods poured south in unbelievable quantities with the sole purpose of helping Solomon build the House of God.

Hiram did not go unrewarded. He was granted longevity far beyond his expectations. As his ships plowed every known sea route, wealth poured into his coffers, resulting not only in his own enrichment but also in propelling Tyre to the very peak of political eminence. He attained a unique combination of health, wealth, and power.

Initially his worldly success was equaled by his moral growth. Surprisingly, Derech Eretz Zutah 1 *counts him among the nine people who entered* גַּן עֵדֶן, paradise, *during their lifetime.*

This very greatness carried a danger within itself. There is a tendency for spiritually inclined people to use every gift of power and wealth as an additional stimulant towards modesty and self-abnegation. However, one whose tendency is towards the crassly materialistic will use every new gift as a source of pride and self-aggrandizement. This, in Maharal's *view, is the meaning of the Sages in* Chullin 89a *where they teach: 'God said to Israel: I love you because even when I grant you greatness you make yourselves small ... but the idol worshipers are not like that ...' Of the later category Hiram is quoted as a prime example.*

The enormity of his accomplishments crazed him and deluded him into self-deification. Where before he had been inspired by recognition of the God of Israel, Who had created heaven and earth; his glance now turned only towards himself and, in preposterous myopia, he saw only his own wealth and power.

This man, who in his lifetime, had tasted Eden's pinnacle of holiness (Derech Eretz Zuta *1), died, degraded and tortured at Nebuchadnezzar's hands* (Yalkut Yechezkel *367).*

This personal and universal tragedy inspires Yechezkel's dirge in this chapter.

2. נְגִיד צֹר — *Prince of Tyre.*

נָגִיד stems from נגד, *to be in front of,* hence is a leader to whom all turn for their needs *(Ibn Janach* and *Radak)* or

earliest antiquity shared the characteristics which were to prove both the source of their greatness and that of their downfall.

Those Sages who felt that Chirah the Adulmaite was identical with Hiram of Tyre may have based their thinking on the seemingly insignificant role which Chirah plays in the narrative in *Genesis*. Superficially it would seem that the whole drama of Judah and Tamar could have been told without mentioning, and certainly without identifying by name, the Adulamite with whom Judah struck up his friendship. His mention would be significant only if it enabled us to relate him to other personalities or events otherwise known to us. But if Chirah is indeed Hiram it is eminently logical that he should appear at this particular point in Jewish history.

The story of Judah and Tamar seems to interrupt the narrative of Joseph's descent into

28 The word of HASHEM came to me, saying: 2 Ben
2 Adam! say to the prince of Tyre: Thus says my
Lord HASHEM/ELOHIM: Because your heart was
proud and you said, 'I am a god. I sat in the seat of
God in the midst of the seas.' But you are a man and

for an example *(R' Breuer)*. The word is often used in Scripture to describe a prince.

R' Breuer writes that in our context the use of this word is particularly apt. Hiram was indeed an example which his people, together with all the nations, would have done well to follow (see pref.). This verse castigates him for allowing himself to lose that high moral standing.

יַעַן גָּבַהּ לִבְּךָ — *Because you heart was proud.*

Hiram was proud because he sent cedars for the building of the Temple. So God said, 'I shall destroy My house so that Hiram shall no longer pride himself' *(Yalkut Shimoni, Ezekiel,* 367).

The *Midrash* goes on to quote Hiram: 'Am I a mortal? Surely I will live forever ... Many kings have died and I have outlived them: twenty-one kings from David's descendants and twenty-one kings of Israel, five prophets and ten high priests. I have buried them all and I am alive!' (See further below).

אֵל אָנִי מוֹשַׁב אֱלֹהִים יָשַׁבְתִּי בְּלֵב יַמִּים — *I am a god. I sat in the seat of God in the midst of the seas.*

Radak and *Metzudos* explain *seat of God* metaphorically. I am as invincible as though I were a god. My island fortress is impregnable. I am in danger from no one.

[The word אֵל is used frequently in Yechezkel to describe human rather than godly strength. See, for example, 17:13; 31:11; 32:21. The term אֱלֹהִים also, is used throughout Scripture to describe human beings who wield power. Some examples are *Genesis* 6:2 (see *Targum); Exodus* 4:16; 21:6.

Thus the first part of our verse can be understood without an implication of self-deification.

However, the second half of the verse: וְאַתָּה אָדָם וְלֹא אֵל, *but you are a man and no god,* seems to imply that אֵל is used in the meaning of *a god.*]

However, the *Midrash (Yalkut Shimoni,* here) understands the words literally; Hiram declares that his palace is worthy of description as a *seat of God.* In vivid and graphic detail, the *Midrash* describes the fantastic structure which Hiram built out of all kinds of precious metals. It had seven levels to parallel the seven firmaments (see *Chagigah* 12b), and the contents of each level were formed into an exact replica of the cosmos as it was understood by him. Our verse refers to that structure when it says: מוֹשַׁב אֱלֹהִים יָשַׁבְתִּי בְּלֵב

Egypt, completely breaking the continuity. The Sages *(Bereishis Rabbah* 85:2) address themselves to this problem. They explain the juxtaposition of these two episodes in the following way: Joseph's descent into Egypt was the first Jewish step into exile. Before God allowed this to happen, He ensured that the seed for the ultimate redeemer from Exile was sown. The Messiah will be descended from Peretz, the child born of Judah's union with Tamar.

Thus Chirah/Hiram stands, as it were, at the cradle of Israel's redeemer.

We shall see how Hiram, the king, was to be the prototype of the non-Jew who places his all at the service of God in harmonious cooperation with His chosen people. We shall learn how this was his greatness, but, through a fatal flaw in character, it was also to be the cause of his doom.

However, that still lay far in the future. In Judah's day, Chirah/Hiram was his friend and support at that most pivotal point in Jewish history.

כח אָדָם֙ וְלֹא־אֵ֔ל וַתִּתֵּ֥ן לִבְּךָ֖ כְּלֵ֥ב אֱלֹהִֽים׃
ג־ו °מִדָּנִיֵּאל ק׳ ג הִנֵּ֥ה חָכָ֛ם אַתָּ֖ה °מדנאל כָּל־סָת֖וּם לֹ֥א
ד עֲמָמֽוּךָ׃ בְּחָכְמָֽתְךָ֙ וּבִתְב֣וּנָתְךָ֔ עָשִׂ֥יתָ לְּךָ֖
ה חָ֑יִל וַתַּ֤עַשׂ זָהָב֙ וָכֶ֔סֶף בְּאוֹצְרוֹתֶֽיךָ׃ בְּרֹ֤ב
חָכְמָֽתְךָ֙ בִּרְכֻלָּ֣תְךָ֔ הִרְבִּ֖יתָ חֵילֶ֑ךָ וַיִּגְבַּ֥הּ
ו לְבָבְךָ֖ בְּחֵילֶֽךָ׃ לָכֵ֕ן כֹּ֥ה
אָמַ֖ר אֲדֹנָ֣י יֱהֹוִ֑ה יַ֛עַן תִּתְּךָ֥ אֶת־לְבָבְךָ֖

יַמִּים, *I sat in the seat of God in the midst of the seas.*[1]

When it was built, Hiram went and sat upon the highest of the seven levels and said אֵל אָנִי, *I am a god.*

וְאַתָּה אָדָם וְלֹא אֵל — *But you are a man, and no god.*

See footnote.

3. הִנֵּה חָכָם אַתָּה מִדָּנִאֵל — *Behold! Are you wiser than Daniel?*

The question is rhetorical. It is meant sarcastically *(Rashi).*

Nebuchadnezzar had wanted to

1. No attempt is made here to fathom the exact meaning of this Midrash. The building and its implications belong, together with so much else which the Sages teach about Hiram, to the secrets of the Torah into which we have no permission to delve.

[It is, however, of profound significance that the Midrash ends by saying that after Hiram's downfall, God caused the earth to open and to swallow the structure, in order to store it for the righteous people in the World to Come, גְּנָזָם לַצַּדִּיקִים לֶעָתִיד לָבוֹא. The implication is clear. Somehow, this structure stands for the ultimate dominion which can be exercised by man over the physical world. Hiram mistakenly arrogated this to himself, but such dominion is not for mortal man in his present state. The time will come when it will be possible, but that will be a time when the tendency to evil will have been removed, and the pride which caused Hiram's downfall will no longer be a danger.]

A friend of David and Solomon was no fool. How could this great king have deluded himself into self-deification?

It is probable that אֵל אָנִי should be understood as *I am an angel* (i.e., a superhuman, non-physical being) rather than *a god.* This seems indicated not only because it is patently ridiculous for Hiram to have considered himself God in the sense of creator of heaven and earth, but also from a parallel passage. The end of our verse reads: וְאַתָּה אָדָם וְלֹא אֵל, which recalls *Psalms* 82:6-7: אֲנִי אָמַרְתִּי אֱלֹהִים אַתֶּם וּבְנֵי עֶלְיוֹן כֻּלְּכֶם אָכֵן כְּאָדָם תְּמוּתוּן, *I had thought you to be* ELOHIM *... but you shall die like man.* In this verse it is God Who is speaking, and He had surely never seen man as a God. The meaning of that passage as rendered by *Targum* (כְּמַלְאֲכַיָּא) and explained by the commentators is that man, if he had chosen, could have been immortal like the angels.

In Midrashic literature, the idea of immortality is often bracketed with the absence of a need to defecate. The *Talmud (Bava Basrah* 75a) teaches in connection with Hiram (based on *v.* 13, see below): God said to Hiram, king of Tyre, 'I had you in mind when I created orifices in man [that is, it was to curb your crazed pride that I made man dependent upon his digestive system].' Others say: He said, 'I had you in mind when I decreed death over Adam.'

Bamidbar Rabbah 7:4 explicates *Psalms* 82:6-7 in connection with the manna (see further below): When God brought down the manna, many miracles occurred. Our Rabbis said it should not have been necessary to defecate as humans need to do, for God said: How can I call them אֱלֹהִים if they have such needs? Rather just as angels have no such needs, so they shall not have them.

Again, we find *Midrash Tanchuma, (Va'eira* 14) explaining *Exodus* 7:15 where Moses was told to meet Pharaoh as he goes out to the water: Why did he go out to the water? That wicked Pharaoh pretended to be a god, not needing to defecate. He went out to the water in the early

no god, though you considered your heart like the
heart of God. 3 *Behold! are you wiser than Daniel?*
Does no hidden thing perplex you? 4 *Through your*
wisdom and discernment you have accumulated
property for yourself and gathered gold and silver in
your storage houses. 5 *Through your wisdom and*
your commerce you have increased your wealth; and
your heart became proud through your wealth.
6 *Therefore, thus says my Lord HASHEM/ELOHIM:*
Because you have set your heart like the heart of

proclaim Daniel a god and to bow down to him (*Daniel* 2:46), but Daniel refused to be deified *(Rashi).*

כָּל סָתוּם לֹא עֲמָמוּךָ — *Does no hidden thing perplex you?*

This is a play on Nebuchadnezzar's description of Daniel *(Daniel* 4:6): *no secret is hidden from you (Rashi).*

עמם is *to shroud*, or *place in the dark.*

4. חָיִל — *Property* [lit. *might*].

Targum, quoted by *Rashi,* equates this with property.

וַתַּעַשׂ זָהָב וָכֶסֶף — *And gathered gold and silver.*

Targum, quoted by *Rashi,* renders: *And have gathered.*

morning before anyone else awoke so that people should not be able to detect him and suspect his mortality.

Concerning this same Pharaoh, *Yalkut Shimoni (Exodus* 181) tells that when he saw Moses and Aharon ... in appearance like the ministering angels, tall like the cedars of Lebanon, their eyes flashing like the sun ... and the shine on their face like the sun ... at that moment Pharaoh felt the need to defecate ...

Yomah 75b teaches that the manna which sustained Israel during their desert wanderings was absorbed in their limbs and not digested in the normal way.

Now it is precisely at this crassly physical function that the nature of man as a being with the potential for the spiritual becomes significant. The Sages ordained a blessing to be recited when this function is performed which ends with the words that God is מַפְלִיא לַעֲשׂוֹת, *wondrous in His actions.* According to *Rama, (Orach Chayim* 6:1), the *wonder* referred to is the miracle of the fusion of the essentially physical with the spiritual. The body is wholly physical but nonetheless, has a wholly spiritual soul within it.

It is just this coexistence between body and soul which defines man vis-a-vis an angel. It describes his limitations, but also prescribes his greatness. Death is a function of the body — not of the soul (see *Ramban, Genesis* 2:17), and as long as a body functions in its own right, it will be subject to bodily needs. At the same time, the soul which God planted so miraculously within the body calls man to the unique challenge of sanctifying this physical existence.

An angel is a being of the soul. It does not know the limitations of the body and does not have the duty of sanctifying it. A man who becomes an 'angel' would be one in whom the body does not coexist with the soul but is completely subordinate to it. It relates to the soul as a garment to a body, and has no existence of its own. In such a state man would be immortal (see *Ramban, Genesis* 2:17, *Leviticus* 18:4) and his food would sustain only the soul (see *Vilna Gaon* to the wording of the blessing mentioned above). The needs of the body would be non-existent.

Hiram and Pharaoh deluded themselves into thinking that they had attained such a level of being. In Hiram's case, his great age and moral stature made him think that perhaps indeed he had shed the limitations of the body. God had him in mind when He ordained death and the body's physical needs (see above). They would keep him constantly aware of the true nature of his being.

When he allowed himself to forget, he forged his own ruin.

כח
ז־יב

ז כְּלֵב אֱלֹהִים: לָכֵן הִנְנִי מֵבִיא עָלֶיךָ זָרִים
עָרִיצֵי גּוֹיִם וְהֵרִיקוּ חַרְבוֹתָם עַל־יְפִי
ח חָכְמָתֶךָ וְחִלְּלוּ יִפְעָתֶךָ: לַשַּׁחַת יוֹרִדוּךָ
ט וָמַתָּה מְמוֹתֵי חָלָל בְּלֵב יַמִּים: הֶאָמֹר
תֹּאמַר אֱלֹהִים אָנִי לִפְנֵי הֹרְגֶךָ וְאַתָּה
י אָדָם וְלֹא־אֵל בְּיַד מְחַלְלֶיךָ: מוֹתֵי עֲרֵלִים
תָּמוּת בְּיַד זָרִים כִּי אֲנִי דִבַּרְתִּי נְאֻם
יא אֲדֹנָי יֱהֹוִה: וַיְהִי דְבַר־
יב יְהוָה אֵלַי לֵאמֹר: בֶּן־אָדָם שָׂא קִינָה
עַל־מֶלֶךְ צוֹר וְאָמַרְתָּ לּוֹ כֹּה אָמַר
אֲדֹנָי יֱהֹוִה אַתָּה חוֹתֵם תָּכְנִית מָלֵא

7. עָרִיצֵי גּוֹיִם — *The strong of the nations.*

This is a term favored by Yechezkel when talking about Nebuchadnezzar and Babylon. See 30:11; 31:12; 32:12.

וְהֵרִיקוּ חַרְבוֹתָם — *And they shall draw their swords.*

When used in the Hiphil, *causative,* the root ריק, *empty,* means *to empty out* and is usually used in connection with the object which is being emptied. For example, in *Genesis* 42:35 we find *they emptied their sacks.* The causative word there refers to the sacks which were made empty, rather than the merchandise which was taken from them. Thus, in our verse, the use of *sword* as the object of the verb is unexpected, for the *scabbard* was made empty, not the sword. However, *Rashi* to *Exodus* 15:9 (based on *Mechilta* there) explains that it is also correct to use the causative form with reference to an object taken from its container.

The Sages (*Yalkut Shimoni, Exodus* 15:9, quoted in *Rashi* here) note that, in line with the more commonly used form, if the object is the sword then the verb should have been יִתְּנוּ, *they will set* [their sword], instead of הֵרִיקוּ, literally *emptied.* They conclude that the expression is a euphemism for sexual molestation. The Babylonian soldiers would abuse Tyre's army sexually. *Midrash Torah* to *Va'eira* states: Four deemed themselves god-like and were molested like women: Pharaoh, Hiram, Yoash, and Nebuchadnezzar. (For a discussion of Yoash or Yehoash, see footnote to 21:28.)

יְפִי חָכְמָתֶךָ — *The beauty of your wisdom.*

I.e., the beautiful products of your wisdom *(Malbim).* Even those symbols of your significant achievements will not help to save you from the onslaught of the enemy *(Metzudos).*

יִפְעָתֶךָ — *Your brightness.*

יפע means *to shine.*

8. בְּלֵב יַמִּים — *In the heart of the seas.*

Metzudos explains: In spite of the fact that you feel safe in the heart of the seas.

9. Your self-delusions will not help you to escape from your enemies.

10. מוֹתֵי עֲרֵלִים — *The death of the wicked* [lit. *uncircumscribed*].

Targum renders: רַשִׁיעִין, *the wicked ones.* The word עֲרֵלִים is used in the sense of עַרְלֵי לֵב (44:7, 9; *Jeremiah* 9:25), *the obtuse of heart (Radak).* Wicked people die at the hands of

28
7-12

God, 7 therefore behold! I shall bring strangers upon
you, the strong of the nations, and they shall draw
their swords against the beauty of your wisdom, and
they shall desecrate your brightness. 8 They shall
bring you down to the grave, and you shall die the
death of those that are slain, in the heart of the seas.
9 Will you then say before your murderer, 'I am a
god?' But you are a man and no god in the hand of
your desecrators. 10 You will die the death of the
wicked by the hand of strangers, for I have spoken —
the words of my Lord HASHEM/ELOHIM.
11 The word of HASHEM came to me, saying. 12 Ben
Adam, take up a lamentation over the king of Tyre.
Say to him: Thus says my Lord HASHEM/ELOHIM:
You are one who engraves images, full of wisdom,

strangers (בְּיַד זָרִים), not on their beds *(Metzudos).*

Eliezer of Beaugency takes עֲרֵלִים as a term denoting derision. Your death will not be a dignified one. You will die naked and ashamed.

12. מֶלֶךְ צוֹר — *King of Tyre.*

[The change from נְגִיד צֹר (*v.* 2), *prince of Tyre, to* מֶלֶךְ צוֹר, *king of Tyre,* is noted by *Abarbanel* and *Malbim.* They suggest that, in deference to Hiram's memory, no new king was appointed after his death, but the affairs of state were in the hands of a governor (נָגִיד). [In connection with this view, we may note the interpretation cited in the preface to this chapter that it was only symbolically that the Sages spoke of Hiram as living for so many centuries.] *Abarbanel* writes that after Tyre's defeat at Nebuchadnezzar's hands, a king was appointed, and from that time until Tyre's conquest by Alexander, kings once more ruled the land. In his view, the first dirge deals with the Babylonian war and therefore addresses itself to the נָגִיד, *governor,* but the subject of the second dirge is the war with Macedonia and is addressed to a מֶלֶךְ, *king. Malbim* suggests that although the administration of the country was in the hands of a *governor,* the memory of Hiram was kept alive by an engraving (or perhaps even a living actor) depicting that great king ensconced in גַּן עֵדֶן *paradise,* to which, in the tradition of the Sages, he had been admitted during his lifetime (see pref.). Thus Tyre had both a נָגִיד, *governor,* and a מֶלֶךְ, *king.* The latter dirge is addressed to that 'king'.

[It should be noted that most commentators do not make this distinction and assume both dirges to have been directed at Hiram].

אַתָּה חוֹתֵם תָּכְנִית — *You are one who engraves images.*

The phrase is obscure.

Rashi writes: You possess the wisdom to seal and give form to all likenesses and images.

[*Rashi* takes חוֹתֵם in the sense of a die from which coins are cast. It is used in this sense in *Sanhedrin* 37a:

A man strikes several coins from one die. All are identical with one another. But God 'struck' all men from Adam's die and not one of them is identical with another.

Thus חוֹתֵם is the die which gives shape and form to an image. *Rashi* further gives the French equivalent to תָּכְנִית as *peinture* which

יג חָכְמָה וּכְלִיל יֹפִי: בְּעֵדֶן גַּן־אֱלֹהִים הָיִיתָ
כָּל־אֶבֶן יְקָרָה מְסֻכָתֶךָ אֹדֶם פִּטְדָה
וְיָהֲלֹם תַּרְשִׁישׁ שֹׁהַם וְיָשְׁפֵה סַפִּיר נֹפֶךְ
וּבָרְקַת וְזָהָב מְלֶאכֶת תֻּפֶּיךָ וּנְקָבֶיךָ בָּךְ
יד בְּיוֹם הִבָּרַאֲךָ כּוֹנָנוּ: אַתְּ־כְּרוּב מִמְשַׁח
הַסּוֹכֵךְ וּנְתַתִּיךָ בְּהַר קֹדֶשׁ אֱלֹהִים

is a *picture* or *painting*. In this he follows *Targum* who renders צַרְתָא.

We have gone to some length to explain *Rashi* because his rendering of the phrase is the same as that of the Sages in its essentials though not in detail.]

Koheles Rabbah 8:2 states that חוֹתֵם תָּכְנִית refers to אָדָם הָרִאשׁוֹן, *Adam. Mahari MiTrani* on our verse explains this reference on the basis of *Sanhedrin* 37a quoted above. Adam was the die from which mankind was cast. According to this interpretation, the phrase should be rendered as a question *(Mahari MiTrani): Do you think yourself as great as Adam, mankind's die? He was full of wisdom and perfect in beauty* and still did not proclaim himself a god. [This same structure must be assumed through *v.* 14. The verses describe Adam and mock Hiram for his pretensions.]

[See *Mahari Karo* for a rendering similar to *Rashi's.*]

Radak renders חוֹתֵם in the sense of bringing something to completion (as in *Berachos* 1:4). *All proportion or symmetry is at the peak of perfection in you.*

[The word תָּכְנִית is not easy to define. Considering that the word is unique to Yechezkel and occurs only twice in the book, it seems likely that it has the same meaning in both places. In 43:10 the word certainly describes the symmetry of the Temple's proportions. *R' Breuer* adduces the same meaning and reads the phrase as a reference to the help which Hiram gave Solomon in building the Temple.

This context fits in with *Radak's* translation of חוֹתֵם, *bring to perfection or completion.* Hiram had brought Solomon's initiative to perfection by helping to build God's dwelling place on earth.

The precise harmony between Israel and the nations, which God had desired (see pref.; *Sforno, Exodus* 19:6 where Israel is described as a *kingdom of priests,* that is, a nation charged with bringing the whole of mankind closer to the service of God) came about through Hiram's deep perception of Solomon's purpose. Solomon had indeed brought the Divine Presence down to dwell among man, but that Presence would have lacked perfection without the finishing touch of Hiram's cooperation. Only through that did God's house become: *a house of prayer to all the nations (Isaiah* 56:7).]

13. בְּעֵדֶן גַּן אֱלֹהִים הָיִיתָ — *You were in Eden, garden of God.*

Targum renders this metaphorically. Tyre was a paradise for its king. As the earth willingly yielded its bounties, there was no physical indulgence which was beyond his means.

Bava Basra 75a reads the verse as a description of Adam in the Garden of Eden. The precious stones which are enumerated formed canopies over his head. [See *Maharal, Chidushei Aggadah* there for an elaboration of the idea of the חוּפָּה, *canopy,* as a reward for the righteous.] In context this would require reading the passage as a question, as *Mahari MiTrani* did the previous verse: Can you compare yourself to Adam? *Were you in Eden protected by the canopies?*

Derech Eretz Zutah 1, which lists Hiram among those who entered Paradise during their lives (see above), would read the passage simply as describing Hiram in Eden.

מְסֻכָתֶךָ — *Your covering.*

According to the Midrashic sources quoted above, this term refers to the 'canopies' in the Garden of Eden.

Targum renders: *your clothes.* The precious stones were in settings of gold (that is the meaning of וְזָהָב, *gold,*

perfect in beauty. 13 *You were in Eden, garden of*
God, your covering was of every precious stone:
Odem, Pitedah, and Yahalom; Tarshish, Shoham,
and Yoshfeh; Sapir, Nofech, and Borakas, and gold.
The manufacture of your drums and wind instru-
ments were within you. From the day of your crea-
tion they were established. 14 *You are a great protec-*
tive cheruv. Such I granted you because you were

among the precious stones) and affixed to the king's garments.

Radak renders: *your wall* (as in *Isaiah* 5:5). The king's 'Garden of Eden' was protected by walls made from precious stones.

מְלֶאכֶת תֻּפֶּיךָ וּנְקָבֶיךָ בָּךְ — *The manufacture of your drums and wind instruments were within you.*

Only the very rich have the means of producing complicated musical instruments and the leisure to enjoy the music *(Mahari Karo).*

The prophet tells of the sweet music which could be heard in Tyre, in consonance with the metaphor of the bird which he uses in the next verse. The sound of music like the sweet singing of a bird, was prevalent in Tyre *(Eliezer of Beaugency).*

In their translation (with which most commentators concur), בְּיוֹם הִבָּרַאֲךָ, *from the day of your creation,* would mean that your skill in making instruments, or your musical ability, was bred into you at the moment of your birth.

The Sages (*Bava Basra* 75a) interpret the phrase as referring to man's digestive system. תֻּפֶּיךָ, *your drums,* describes stomach and intestines which are roughly shaped like a drum, and נְקָבֶיךָ are the body's *orifices* used in eliminating wastes. God tells Hiram that from the moment of creation, He decided to put a digestive system into man with Hiram in mind. It was meant to counteract his pride. (See footnote to *v.* 2.)

14. אַתְּ כְּרוּב מִמְשַׁח הַסּוֹכֵךְ — *You are a great protective cheruv.*

[The translation of this extremely obscure phrase is in accordance with most commentators, although it differs from the cantillation, which indicates a pause after אַתְּ כְּרוּב, *you are a cheruv,* and then reads מִמְשַׁח הַסּוֹכֵךְ, together. See further below.]

The feminine form אַתְּ for the masculine occurs twice more in Scripture, at *Numbers* 11:15 and *Deuteronomy* 5:24. See below.]

Most commentators take כְּרוּב as a *cherub.* Hiram had reached heights which took him beyond the merely human. מִמְשַׁח derives from the Hebrew root משח, *to anoint,* but is used in a borrowed sense to mean *exalted.* Just as *Exodus* 25:20 describes כְּרוּבִים as סֹכְכִים, *protecting* the lid of the Ark, so the *exalted cheruv,* Hiram, is seen as הַסּוֹכֵךְ, *the protector,* of his land or his people.

Rashi, however, translates כְּרוּב as *a bird.* See also *Eliezer of Beaugency, comm., v.* 13. [Although Scripture depicts *cheruvim* as having wings, they are never described as birds. The only verses where a similar meaning might be intended are *II Samuel* 22:11 and *Psalms* 18:11, where God is depicted as riding and flying upon a *cheruv.* These verses are quoted here by *Mahari MiTrani.* However, considering that the Sages interpret the word כְּרוּב as כְּרַבְיָא, *childlike (Chagigah* 13b), referring to the human face of the *cheruvim* on the Ark, it is difficult to see why Rashi translates כְּרוּב as *bird.*]

For מִמְשַׁח *Rashi* goes to the Aramaic root מְשַׁח which means to be *spread wide.* According to *Rashi,* the entire phrase means: *Your are like a bird with wide protecting wings.*

The cantillation, which separates

טו הָיִיתָ בְּתוֹךְ אַבְנֵי־אֵשׁ הִתְהַלָּכְתָּ: תָּמִים
אַתָּה בִּדְרָכֶיךָ מִיּוֹם הִבָּרְאָךְ עַד־נִמְצָא
טז עַוְלָתָה בָּךְ: בְּרֹב רְכֻלָּתְךָ מָלוּ תוֹכְךָ
חָמָס וַתֶּחֱטָא וָאֲחַלֶּלְךָ מֵהַר אֱלֹהִים
וָאַבֶּדְךָ כְּרוּב הַסֹּכֵךְ מִתּוֹךְ אַבְנֵי־אֵשׁ:
יז גָּבַהּ לִבְּךָ בְּיָפְיֶךָ שִׁחַתָּ חָכְמָתְךָ עַל־

מִמְשַׁח from כְּרוּב, precludes its being an adjective and therefore contradicts both the above interpretations.

Hirsch (Gesammelte Schriften vol. 3 p. 400) translates in accordance with the cantillation: *You are a cheruv!* You were *anointed* (therefore appointed) *to be a protector.*

[*Hirsch* (ibid.; *Exodus* 25:20) shows in detail that *cheruvim* in Scripture are depicted as having a dual function. They are guardians and protectors as in *Genesis* 3:24 and bearers of God's Glory as in the Merkavah visions in Yechezkel.]

וּנְתַתִּיךָ בְּהַר קֹדֶשׁ אֱלֹהִים הָיִיתָ — [*Such*] *I granted you* [*because*] *you were upon the holy mountain of God.*

From his vantage point on God's holy mountain (בְּהַר קֹדֶשׁ אֱלֹהִים הָיִיתָ) when he helped Solomon to build the Temple *(Rashi; Radak)*, he had become a repository for, and guardian of, all that is best and most desirable in the development of a non-Jewish nation *(Hirsch, Exodus* 25:20). All the goodness and beauty with which God had endowed His world seemed safe and protected under the guardianship of this enlightened man.

According to *Hirsch's* interpretation the verse is singing Hiram's praises. In that context *R' Breuer* writes that the use of the feminine אַתְּ in place of אַתָּה indicates the completeness of Hiram's self-abnegation. He knew himself to be completely dependent upon God.

All this I gave to you because you had once been on God's holy mountain, when you supplied the cedars for Solomon's Temple *(Metzudos)*.

Most commentators are in essential agreement with this interpretation, although the syntax (וּנְתַתִּיךָ ... הָיִיתָ) *I granted you ... you were* is extremely awkward.

R' Breuer reads the passage as two separate phrases. וּנְתַתִּיךָ בְּהַר קֹדֶשׁ, *I have placed you upon a holy mountain,* and אֱלֹהִים הָיִיתָ, *you were a god,* meaning that you were so exalted as to be angelic. This latter statement is in the sense of *Psalms* 82:6: אֲנִי אָמַרְתִּי אֱלֹהִים אַתֶּם, *I had thought you to be as a god* (see footnote, *v. 2*).

בְּתוֹךְ אַבְנֵי אֵשׁ הִתְהַלָּכְתָּ — *In the midst of fiery stones have you walked.*

A number of explanations are offered for this extremely obscure phrase.

Targum translates: *You had thought to rule over a holy nation.* Thus, אַבְנֵי אֵשׁ is rendered as *holy nation.* There is no explanation for the actual meaning of the term, nor why such stones are an apt metaphor for a holy nation.

Rashi translates: *You acquired a name for yourself among Israel's kings who are like the ministering angels.* Once more there is no indication of what אַבְנֵי אֵשׁ really are, nor why they describe Israel's kings. Furthermore, *v.* 16, which talks of Tyre's king being wiped out from among the אַבְנֵי אֵשׁ, *fiery stones,* needs explanation. Israel's kings no longer existed if, with the rest of the prophecies against Tyre in the preceding chapters, this dirge was sung after the Destruction. *Rashi* to *v.* 16 offers: *You will not receive reward together with the righteous people.*

Radak offers three explanations. אַבְנֵי אֵשׁ could be a description of Israel, a holy people; it could mean some kind of heavenly fire and brimstone; or it

28
15-17

upon the holy mountain of God. In the midst of fiery
stones have you walked. 15 *You are perfect in your*
ways, from the day you were created, until wrongdo-
ing was found in you. 16 *Because of your abundant*
commerce, your midst was full of violence and you
sinned; so I desecrated you from the mountain of
God and destroyed you, O protective cheruv, from
among the fiery stones. 17 *Your heart became proud*
because of your beauty; you have corrupted your

could describe diamonds and precious stones which flash like fire.

[In the absence of corroborating evidence, since the expression אַבְנֵי אֵשׁ is unique to this passage, we look for associations within the passage which shed light upon the actual meaning of the words. None of the ideas contained in the dirge such as, הַר קֹדֶשׁ, כְּרוּב, עֵדֶן גַּן אֱלֹהִים, חוֹתֵם תָּכְנִית suggest an association with אַבְנֵי אֵשׁ. (Of course, according to *Radak's* interpretation of *precious stones*, the association is in *v.* 13).

Perhaps the exact meaning can be determined by taking the words at their most literal. A fire-stone would be a *flintstone*, which can be used to make fire when struck with iron.

Flint is a precise metaphor for something which contains immense powers of destruction, but hides those powers within itself and will harm none except those who abuse it.

Perhaps the concept of flint as a metaphor for *a holy people (Targum)* and *the righteous kings of Israel (Rashi)* can be found in Talmudic literature. The *talmid chacham* [*Torah scholar*] is described as one whose total being is fire (*Chagigah* 27a), but this is a fire which spreads beneficial warmth and will not scorch anyone who relates to him in an appropriate manner. However, one who oversteps the bounds of propriety will be severely burned (*Mishnah, Avos* 2:10). Verse 18 seems to support this interpretation. Hiram's punishment is that God will *bring forth fire from within you,* and *it will consume you.* In his contact with the righteous ones of Israel, Hiram had avoided being scorched by their fire. In the days of his greatness, that fire had burned within him. That very fire would be brought forth from him, as fire is extracted from flint, and bring about his destruction.]

15. מִיּוֹם הִבָּרַאֲךָ — *From the day you were created.*

This must be taken as poetic hyperbole *(Metzudas David),* unless we take it to mean *from the day you became a responsible person (Radak).*

עַד נִמְצָא עַוְלָתָה בָּךְ — *Until wrongdoing was found in you.*

When you said I am a god (*v.* 2) *(Rashi),* or when you were inordinately proud against God's people and rejoiced in their destruction *(Radak),* wrongdoing was found in you.

16. מָלוּ — *Was full.*

Since the word מָלוּ is from מלא, *to be full,* it should be written מָלְאוּ *(Radak).* However, it is not infrequent that a silent aleph is dropped completely. An example for this root is *Job* 32:18.

The people of Tyre subjected those who dealt with them to violence and theft. Their economic situation was so strong that their business associates could not afford to protest.

This evildoing is seen as a sin of the king (וַתֶּחֱטָא, *you sinned*), because he had the power to forbid such behavior.

וָאַבֶּדְךָ — *And (I) destroyed you.*

This word, too, is a case of a silent root letter being omitted. Since the root is אבד, the complete word should be וָאֲאַבֶּדְךָ *(Rashi).* This omission of an *aleph* occurs sometimes in the *Piel — the intensified form.* See *II Samuel* 22:40 et. al.

For the meaning of the whole phrase, see *comm., v.* 14.

17. שִׁחַתָּ חָכְמָתְךָ — *You have corrupted your wisdom.*

יִפְעָתֶךָ עַל־אֶרֶץ הִשְׁלַכְתִּיךָ לִפְנֵי מְלָכִים
יח נְתַתִּיךָ לְרַאֲוָה בָךְ׃ מֵרֹב עֲוֺנֶיךָ בְּעֶוֶל
רְכֻלָּתְךָ חִלַּלְתָּ מִקְדָּשֶׁיךָ וָאוֹצִא־אֵשׁ
מִתּוֹכְךָ הִיא אֲכָלַתְךָ וָאֶתֶּנְךָ לְאֵפֶר עַל־
יט הָאָרֶץ לְעֵינֵי כָּל־רֹאֶיךָ׃ כָּל־יוֹדְעֶיךָ
בָּעַמִּים שָׁמְמוּ עָלֶיךָ בַּלָּהוֹת הָיִיתָ וְאֵינְךָ
כ עַד־עוֹלָם׃ וַיְהִי דְבַר־יְהוָה אֵלַי
כא לֵאמֹר׃ בֶּן־אָדָם שִׂים פָּנֶיךָ אֶל־צִידוֹן
כב וְהִנָּבֵא עָלֶיהָ׃ וְאָמַרְתָּ כֹּה אָמַר אֲדֹנָי

The translation is in accordance with *Metzudos'* interpretation. Pride erodes wisdom. If wisdom is to be maintained it must be accompanied by a sense of modesty.

In *Radak's* view the phrase more nearly attempts to demonstrate that Hiram's was no true wisdom. A truly wise man will not pride himself on worldly accomplishments.[1]

עַל יִפְעָתֶךָ — *Because of your brightness.*

You corrupted your wisdom because you were proud of your brightness (*Rashi*). See *v.* 7.

Metzudos renders עַל as *together with:* You corrupted your wisdom together with the brightness [of your understanding].

לְרַאֲוָה — *So that they may gaze.*

רַאֲוָה, *to look upon,* is formed from ראה, *to see,* as גַּאֲוָה, *conceit* is formed from גאה, *to be proud.*

18. חִלַּלְתָּ מִקְדָּשֶׁיךָ — *You have desecrated your sanctuary.*

You have desecrated your holiness (*Rashi*).

[Hiram could have been a sanctuary, a repository for all that is holy and good, just as Israel is, in itself, a sanctuary for God (See *Leviticus* 20:3, *Rashi*). That sanctuary could have risen up upon the *holy mountain* (*v.* 14) which was Tyre, a veritable *Eden* (*v.* 13) lying in tranquility and repose under the protective wings of its cherublike king (*v.* 14).

That, ultimately, is the tragedy which Yechezkel's dirge bemoans. Hiram as *Elohim* (*v.* 14), a being of the spirit (see footnote to *v.* 2) which absorbs all earthly existence into the fiery core (אַבְנֵי אֵשׁ, *fiery stones*) of holiness which defines his essence (see *v.* 14), could have nurtured Tyre's wealth into a mighty edifice testifying to the boundless goodness which God showers upon man.

However, that same edifice could never protect Hiram the אָדָם, *man* (contrasted to אֱלֹהִים as in *Psalms* 82:6, see above), who had rejected the promise of his earlier years. With the *holy mountain* desecrated, Eden disappeared from earth. No cherub wings hovered over the great metropolis; and

1. That wisdom and pride cannot coexist, is an often repeated theme in Scripture.

For one example among many see *Proverbs* 11:2: וְאֶת צְנוּעִים חָכְמָה, *Wisdom is to be found with the modest, retiring person. Vilna Gaon* remarks: True wisdom lies with modest people who will not project themselves by voicing their own opinions but instead, will listen to their teachers. For when a person speaks it gives him nothing, but wisdom comes through listening. The proverb says: The advantage of speech is never to oneself; the advantage of silence is to no other. For this reason man has two eyes and two ears but only one mouth.

See further in *Vilna Gaon, Proverbs* 12:15.

wisdom because of your beauty; you have corrupted
your wisdom because of your brightness. To the
ground, have I thrown you, before kings have I set
you, that they may gaze upon you. 18 *Because of the*
multitude of your sins, because of the iniquity of
your commerce, you have desecrated your sanctuary.
Therefore I will withdraw fire from within you — it
will consume you, and I shall make you into ashes
upon the earth, in the eyes of all that see you. 19 *All*
who knew you among the nations were appalled at
you; you were a terror, and you shall be nevermore.
20 *The word of HASHEM came to me, saying:* 21 *Ben*
Adam, set your face against Sidon and prophesy
against it, 22 *and you shall say: Thus says my Lord*

unprotected, it crumbled before Babylon's onslaught (Based on *R' Breuer).*

From *v.* 17 onwards, Tyre's fate is given in the past tense, as though it had already happened. *Radak* points out that prophets often talk of future occurences in the past tense to indicate the certainty of the prophet that they would indeed come about. (See footnote, 7:2).]

וְאוֹצִא אֵשׁ מִתּוֹכֵךְ — *Therefore I will withdraw fire from within you.*

The fire is a metaphor for either Hiram's sin *(Radak)* or his pride *(Metzudas David).* It will be brought out from within him and make him into אֵפֶר, *ashes,* upon the ground.

For a discussion see *comm., v.* 14.

The Midrash *(Vayikra Rabbah* 18:2) tells of a tradition that Hiram was Nebuchadnezzar's father. Thus the fire (Nebuchadnezzar) which is to consume him (Hiram, since Babylon destroyed Tyre) came from within himself.

20-23 These verses contain a prophecy against Sidon. Except for a passing reference in *Zechariah* 9:2 where the meaning is far from clear, Sidon is nowhere among the nations against whom prophecies were given.

Indeed, even in this passage no particular sin is ascribed to Sidon. In contrast to the four nations mentioned in ch. 25 and to Tyre, all of whom are blamed for their vindictive gloating at Israel's downfall, no such accusation is made against Sidon.

Sidon had intimate commercial ties with Tyre (*Isaiah* 23:2) and 27:8 indicates that Sidonian sailors manned Tyre's navy. Possibly there was an exchange of ideas and attitudes together with the traffic between the two peoples.

An explanation of Sidon's crime is contained in a fragment of the commentary of *R' Menachem ben Chelbo* which has been preserved. (*Pisroney Rabbi Menachem bar Chelbo, ed. Poznanski, Warsaw* 1904).

He raises the question: Why does the prophecy against Tyre which was said in the eleventh year (26:1) precede that against Egypt which was in the tenth year (29:1; see below)?

He explains that the prophecies against Tyre belong together with those against the nations mentioned in ch. 25 since, according to *Jeremiah* 27:3 and *Eichah Rabbah* 2:18 (see also *comm.,* 17:5), Zidkiyahu had been given

יֱהֹוִה הִנְנִי עָלַיִךְ צִידוֹן וְנִכְבַּדְתִּי
בְּתוֹכֵךְ וְיָדְעוּ כִּי־אֲנִי יהוה בַּעֲשׂוֹתִי
כג בָהּ שְׁפָטִים וְנִקְדַּשְׁתִּי בָהּ: וְשִׁלַּחְתִּי־בָהּ
דֶּבֶר וָדָם בְּחוּצוֹתֶיהָ וְנִפְלַל חָלָל בְּתוֹכָהּ
בְּחֶרֶב עָלֶיהָ מִסָּבִיב וְיָדְעוּ כִּי־אֲנִי יְהֹוָה:
כד וְלֹא־יִהְיֶה עוֹד לְבֵית יִשְׂרָאֵל סִלּוֹן
מַמְאִיר וְקוֹץ מַכְאִב מִכֹּל סְבִיבֹתָם
הַשָּׁאטִים אוֹתָם וְיָדְעוּ כִּי אֲנִי אֲדֹנָי
כה יְהֹוִה: כֹּה־אָמַר אֲדֹנָי יֱהֹוִה
בְּקַבְּצִי | אֶת־בֵּית יִשְׂרָאֵל מִן־הָעַמִּים
אֲשֶׁר נָפֹצוּ בָם וְנִקְדַּשְׁתִּי בָם לְעֵינֵי הַגּוֹיִם
וְיָשְׁבוּ עַל־אַדְמָתָם אֲשֶׁר נָתַתִּי לְעַבְדִּי
כו לְיַעֲקֹב: וְיָשְׁבוּ עָלֶיהָ לָבֶטַח וּבָנוּ בָתִּים
וְנָטְעוּ כְרָמִים וְיָשְׁבוּ לָבֶטַח בַּעֲשׂוֹתִי

dominion over the five nations: Edom, Moab, Ammon, Tyre, and Sidon. Since Edom, Moab, and Amon are mentioned in ch. 25, it is logical to place the prophecies against Tyre and Sidon next to them.

In the course of his discussion, *R' Menachem* reports that all those five nations together betrayed Zidkiyahu to Nebuchadnezzar (הלשינו יחד לנבוכדנצר על צדקיהו). Sidon was part of this betrayal. [Some Midrashic source for this assertion of *R' Menachem*, although not known, must be assumed.]

22. וְנִכְבַּדְתִּי בְּתוֹכֵךְ – *And I shall be glorified within you.*

See *Exodus* 14:4: *And I shall be glorified through Pharaoh. Rashi* comments: When God takes vengeance against the wicked, His name becomes exalted and glorified.

וְיָדְעוּ ... וְנִקְדַּשְׁתִּי – *And they shall know ... and shall be sanctified.*

See 38:22-23, and above.

23. וְנִפְלַל חָלָל בְּתוֹכָהּ – *And the corpses will fall within her.*

The translation follows *Radak* and *Metzudos* who derive this unusual form from נפל, *to fall. Metzudos* explains the doubled lamed as a strengthening of the implication perhaps, *fall in heaps.*

Rashi derives the word from פלל, *to anticipate* or *judge* (although this root is nowhere else found in the *niphal, passive)* and renders: *They will expect themselves to become corpses within it.*

Eliezer of Beaugency derives the word from the same root. *They will have judgments rendered against them and therefore fall as corpses.*

R' Breuer writes that the word is a combination of the two roots נפל and פלל (for an analogy, see מִשְׁתַּחֲוִיתֶם in 8:16). *They will fall as corpses and* only then *recognize themselves as having been judged and condemned to death.*

24. סִלּוֹן מַמְאִיר – *A malignant briar.*

Rashi interprets this verse as referring back to all the nations which have been condemned in the last four chapters. Once all Israel's neighbors are punished, none will remain to be a painful thorn in Israel's side.

*HASHEM/ELOHIM: Behold! I am against you, Sidon,
and shall be glorified within you; and they shall
know that I am HASHEM when I execute judgments
upon her and shall be sanctified through her;* 23 *and I
shall send against her pestilence and blood in her
streets, and the corpses will fall within her through
the sword which comes upon her from all around,
and they shall know that I am HASHEM.* 24 *Then
there shall no more be for the Family of Israel a
malignant briar and painful thorn, among all their
surroundings, who disdain them; and they shall
know that I am my Lord HASHEM/ELOHIM.*
25 *Thus says my Lord HASHEM/ELOHIM: when I
gather in the family of Israel from the people among
whom they were scattered, and shall be hallowed by
them in the eyes of the nations, and they shall dwell
on their land which I gave to My servant Jacob,*
26 *then they shall dwell upon it securely and build
houses and plant vineyards and dwell securely —*

מַמְאִיר is from מאר, *to be painful* or *irritated*, as in *Leviticus* 13:51.

R' Breuer detects a progression between סִלּוֹן מַמְאִיר and קוֹץ מַכְאִב. According to *Toras Kohanim (Leviticus* 13:51), מַמְאִיר implies a malignancy which 'curses' (תן בו מאירה ולא תהנו בו) and wastes away whatever it touches. (See *Hirsch* there.) The gentile neighbors of Israel had been just that to Israel. By blandishing the delights of their idol worship, they slowly eroded Israel's loyalty to God. A cancerous growth of national assimilation began to eat away at Israel.

In contrast to the early years of Solomon' s reign, when relations with the neighbors had been peaceful and constructive because of the awe which an Israel true to its destiny inspired in them, a period now began in which the nations proved to be קוֹץ מַכְאִיב, *a painful splinter*, a constant irritant. Israel had become just another people, and as such became subject to all the political and military ambitions and maneuvers of its neighbors.

With their passing, all this would cease.

הַשָּׁאטִים — *Who disdain.*
See 16:57.

25-26. The passage ends with a glimpse into the distant future. Nebuchadnezzar's seemingly invincible might had now been clearly demonstrated. All the countries with which Israel came into contact would be crushed by him. What would become of Israel? Would this sadly splintered and exiled people be lost in the turmoil of a world history dominated by military giants such as Babylon, with whom they could no longer hope to compete?

To the terrifying doubts raised by these questions, these verses give the answer. The time will come when the purpose of all this historical movement

שֹׁפְטִים בְּכֹל הַשָּׁאטִים אֹתָם מִסְּבִיבוֹתָם
א וְיָדְעוּ כִּי אֲנִי יהוה אֱלֹהֵיהֶם׃ בַּשָּׁנָה
הָעֲשִׂרִית בָּעֲשִׂרִי בִּשְׁנֵים עָשָׂר לַחֹדֶשׁ
ב הָיָה דְבַר־יהוה אֵלַי לֵאמֹר׃ בֶּן־אָדָם
שִׂים פָּנֶיךָ עַל־פַּרְעֹה מֶלֶךְ מִצְרָיִם וְהִנָּבֵא
ג עָלָיו וְעַל־מִצְרַיִם כֻּלָּהּ׃ דַּבֵּר וְאָמַרְתָּ

will become clear. Fired in the crucible of exile, Israel will once more become receptive to God's holiness, which will find a welcome place within them (וְנִקְדַּשְׁתִּי בָם). Having rediscovered their essential being, they will once more, as true descendants of their forefather Jacob (אֲשֶׁר נָתַתִּי לְעַבְדִּי לְיַעֲקֹב), be settled in their land. They will live there securely (לָבֶטַח), no longer fearing that the land would vomit them forth (*Leviticus* 18:25) as it did in the past. In the end they will know that HASHEM is their God (based on *R' Breuer*).

⊲§ Prefatory Remarks to Chapters 29-32

The next four chapters are devoted to prophecies against Egypt. They contain a number of different prophecies, and altogether six different dates are assigned. With one exception, the dating is relative to Yehoyachin's exile (as in most of the dating throughout the book, e.g., 1:2) and is in chronological order. The exception is the second prophecy which is dated by the years of Nebuchadnezzar's reign and does not follow the chronological order.

[*Nebuchadnezzar ascended his throne in the fourth year of Yehoyakim (*Jeremiah *25:1). This places the destruction in the 19th year of his reign (*Jeremiah *52:12; see* Appendix II).][1]

XXIX

1. בַּשָּׁנָה הָעֲשִׂרִית — *In the tenth year.*

This prophecy came to Yechezkel in the tenth year of Zidkiyahu's reign and Yehoyachin's exile. See pref.

בָּעֲשִׂרִי — *In the tenth month.*

The month is *Teves.*

2. *Sotah* 9a tells of three cups of punishment which Egypt was destined to drink in the course of its history: one in the time of Moses, one in the days of Pharaoh Necho, and one in Messianic times. This seems to identify the Pharaoh who fell to Nebuchadnezzar as Pharaoh Necho.

Pharaoh Necho is mentioned in *Jeremiah* 46:2. Nebuchadnezzar waged a campaign against him during Yehoyakim's reign. However, *Jeremiah* 44:30 seems to identify the Pharaoh who ultimately fell to Babylon as Pharaoh Chofra (חָפְרַע). But, according to some commentators there, חָפְרַע may not be a proper noun at all. (See *Targum*

1. See *Megillah* 11b for an explanation of why *Jeremiah* 52:29 dates the Destruction in Nebuchadnezzar's eighteenth rather than nineteenth year.

There seems, however, to have been a tradition among historians that the correct dating is the eighteenth year. See, for example *Josephus Neged Apyon* 1:21.

According to *Rosh HaShanah* 3a, the years of Jewish kings are counted uniformly from Nissan, and those of gentile kings, from Tishrei. If we postulate that Nebuchadnezzar ascended the throne between Nissan and Tishrei of Yehoyakim's fourth year, then Scripture would begin counting his second year in Tishrei of that year. Av, eighteen years later, would be his nineteenth year.

29
1-2

when I execute judgments upon all who disdain them roundabout them — then they shall know that I am HASHEM, their God.

In the tenth year in the tenth month on the twelfth of the month, the word of HASHEM came to me, saying: 2 Ben Adam, set your face against Pharaoh, king of Egypt, and prophesy against him and against all Egypt.

there, who translates חֲפְרַע as תְּבִירָא, *broken* or *lame)* in which case the reference would indeed be to Pharaoh Necho, who was a cripple.

If Josephus counted Nebuchadnezzar's years from the date of his ascension, that might well explain the discrepancy.

The six dates are as follows:

(all years are counted from Yehoyachin's exile except where indicated)			
	Year	**Day/month**	**Relation to the Destruction**
29:1	**10th**	**12th of Tevet**	**7 months before**
29:17	**27th (of Nebuchadnezzar)**	**1st of Nissan (or Tishrei, s.fn.)**	**8 years after**
30:20	**11th**	**7th of Nissan**	**5 months before**
31:1	**11th**	**1st of Sivan**	**3 months before**
32:1	**12th**	**1st of Adar**	**19 months after**
32:17	**12th**	**15th of the month (probably also Adar)**	**19 months after**

The following highlights of Egyptian history in the period of the Destruction are recounted in Scripture:

(a) Zidkiyahu seeks an alliance with Egypt against Babylon's forces (see 17:7)

(b) Egypt unsuccessfuly attempts to help Israel in response to Zidkiyahu's initiative (*Jeremiah* 37:5-7)

(c) Yochanan ben Kareach persuades the Jews who remained in Jerusalem after the Destruction to flee to Egypt in defiance of Jeremiah's prophecy (*Jeremiah* ch. 43).

(d) Egypt falls to Nebuchadnezzar.

Seder Olam dates these events as follows:

(a) Seventh year. [The date mentioned immediately prior to this event is the fifth month of the seventh year. However, there are divergent readings in the *Seder Olam*. Reading באותה שעה, lit., *in that hour,* would place this event in the fifth month. However, if the correct reading is באותה שנה, *in that year,* we know the year but not the month.]

(b) Ninth year

(c) Eleventh year. [This is not explicitly recorded; but *Seder Olam* dates Gedaliah's assassination fifty-two days after the Destruction, and immediately afterwards states that the remainder of the Jews went down to Egypt.]

(d) Twenty-seventh year of Nebuchadnezzar. (See *Rashi, Jeremiah* 46:13.)

In attempting to correlate the prophecies with the events, one discovers that with the exception of the second prophecy, said in the same year that Babylon subdued Egypt, there is nothing which would explain the timing. The earliest prophecy seems too long removed from

כט
ד־ה

כֹּה־אָמַר ׀ אֲדֹנָי יֱהֹוִה הִנְנִי עָלֶיךָ פַּרְעֹה
מֶלֶךְ־מִצְרַיִם הַתַּנִּים הַגָּדוֹל הָרֹבֵץ בְּתוֹךְ
יְאֹרָיו אֲשֶׁר אָמַר לִי יְאֹרִי וַאֲנִי עֲשִׂיתִנִי׃
ד °הַחִים ק׳ וְנָתַתִּי °חחיים בִּלְחָיֶיךָ וְהִדְבַּקְתִּי דְגַת־
יְאֹרֶיךָ בְּקַשְׂקְשֹׂתֶיךָ וְהַעֲלִיתִיךָ מִתּוֹךְ
יְאֹרֶיךָ וְאֵת כָּל־דְּגַת יְאֹרֶיךָ בְּקַשְׂקְשֹׂתֶיךָ
ה תִּדְבָּק׃ וּנְטַשְׁתִּיךָ הַמִּדְבָּרָה אוֹתְךָ וְאֵת

3-5. When Jacob blessed Pharaoh in *Genesis* 47:10, he prayed that: 'the waters of the Nile would rise up to meet Pharaoh' (*Rashi* based on *Tanchuma Nasso* 26). The history and well-being of Egypt has always been bound up with the life-dispensing waters of the overflowing Nile. Because the river was the source of their prosperity, the Egyptians worshiped it as a god (*Tanchuma Va'eirah* 13).

Thus water in general and the sea in particular (see *Bereishis Rabbah, Noah* 8), are a natural metaphor used often in Scripture for the Egyptians.

This is the background for these three verses.

3. הַתַּנִּים הַגָּדוֹל הָרֹבֵץ בְּתוֹךְ יְאֹרָיו — *The great sea-monster that crouches within its rivers.*

When Moses was sent to bring God's word to Pharaoh, he was given signs by which to authenticate his Divine mission. *Exodus* 4:2-4 tells how God told him to throw his stick upon the ground where it turned into a snake. As Moses ran away in fear, God told him to take hold of the snake's tail. When he did so, the snake turned once more into a stick.

Shemos Rabbah (3;17; 9:2) explains the significance of this sign. Egypt's Pharaohs were *sea-monsters (Hirsch* translates: *crocodiles)* who, protected by the deep waters within which they dwelt, controlled their surroundings completely. Moses was to show first the Israelites and then Pharaoh himself that this awesome might was only an illusion. The mighty crocodile became a dry, impotent stick upon God's command. Far from controlling anything at all, it was completely controlled by God's decree. Verse 4 describes this impotence.

This crocodile is described as dwelling in many rivers (יְאֹרָיו is in the plural) rather than just in the Nile River. An ingenious system of canals spread the Nile's bounty over huge areas which the mother river by itself could never have reached.

It was the construction of these canals which goaded the Pharaohs into

the events of the ninth year to have been influenced by them, and the fourth and fifth prophecy take place a year and a half after the flight to Egypt, preceding Egypts' fall by several years.

Why, then, was Yechezkel preoccupied with Egypt in those terrible months immediately preceding the Destruction? One would surely have supposed that at that time Yechezkel's thoughts would be riveted on Jerusalem, with no room for the seemingly peripheral fate of Egypt.

The role which Egypt plays in Israel's history is discussed in footnote 23:8 and *comm.* 23:19-21. There remains yet another dimension in this relationship.

The אַרְבַּע מַלְכֻיּוֹת, *Four Kingdoms,* which struggle on the stage of world history to extinguish the light of Godliness that Israel is to project upon earth, are discussed in *comm.* 21:24-27. At the moment that Nebuchadnezzar destroyed the Temple and drove Israel into exile, mankind became shrouded in the cosmic darkness which will not be relieved until the coming of the Messiah.

29
3-5

[3] *Speak and say: Thus says my Lord HASHEM/ ELOHIM: Behold! I am against you, Pharaoh, king of Egypt, the great sea-monster that crouches within its rivers, who said, 'Mine is the river, and I have made myself.'* [4] *Now, I will attach hooks to your cheeks and I shall cause the fish of your rivers to cleave to your scales, and I shall draw you out from within your rivers, and all the fish of your rivers shall stick to your scales;* [5] *and I shall cast you into the*

the grandiose claim that אֲנִי עֲשִׂיתִנִי, *I have enriched myself* (see below). They did indeed have a hand in the production of Egypts' fabulous wealth *(R' Breuer).*

לִי יְאֹרִי *Mine is the river.*

I do not need Divine help, for my river can dispense all my needs *(Rashi).*

In contrast to the land of Israel which *drinks water from the rain of heaven (Deut.* 11:11) and which consequently depends constantly upon God's direct Providence. Egypt had an inexhaustible supply of water which was always at its diposal. In Egypt it was hard to feel the need for God's constant good-will. (See *Ramban, Deut.* 11:11.)

וַאֲנִי עֲשִׂיתִנִי – *And I have made myself.*

With my ability and wisdom, I built up my greatness and authority. The expression is a metaphor; Pharaoh had not really 'made' (that is, created) himself, but had enriched himself *(Rashi).*

The Sages (*Shemos Rabbah* 8:3), however, interpret the phrase literally. They quote our verse to prove that Pharaoh, like Hiram and Nebuchadnezzar, thought himself divine: *I have 'created' myself.* See *comm., footnote* 28:2 for an exhaustive analysis of this concept.

4. וְנָתַתִּי חַחִים בִּלְחָיֶיךָ – *Now I will attach hooks to your cheeks.*

This picture of complete impotence contrasts with the illusion of invulnerability described in the previous verse *(R' Breuer).* This metaphor is particularly apt because Pharaoh had been compared to a sea monster which can be caught by a hook *(Radak),* but it is not limited to this situation. Yechezkel uses the same picture of hooks in cheeks in connection with Gog (38:4), although Gog was not compared to a sea creature.

וְהִדְבַּקְתִּי דְּגַת יְאֹרֶיךָ בְּקַשְׂקְשֹׂתֶיךָ – *And I shall cause the fish of your rivers to cleave to your scales.*

I will inspire all your warriors to go out to war with you, that they may fall *(Rashi).* [This interpretation implies that the previous phrase *I will draw you out...* means that Pharaoh will be lured

Abraham was apprised of Israel's subjugation to these four nations at the בְּרִית בֵּין הַבְּתָרִים, *Covenant between the Parts,* at the same time that Israel's bondage in Egypt was announced to him.

This was no coincidence. Rather, it indicates that Egypt was the precursor of these four nations. Egypt strove mightily to prevent the birth of God's People. In this it was the forerunner of those later nations whose ambition would be to eliminate God's People from among mankind. (For elaboration, and for functions of Egypt and Amalek in Israel's development, see *Pachad Yitzchak, Pessach* 21:1 ff., 53:7].

Perhaps this is the explanation of the dating of these prophecies. As twilight came and darkness began to descend, Yechezkel's mind returned to the roots of this development. Perhaps just these prophecies imbued this section of the Book with its element of comfort. (See footnote to pref., ch. 24, and pref., chs. 25-32.) If Egypt meets its just fate, the four nations will surely be no different. In time, they, too, will disappear from the stage of history.

כָּל־דְּגַת יְאֹרֶיךָ עַל־פְּנֵי הַשָּׂדֶה תִּפּוֹל
לֹא תֵאָסֵף וְלֹא תִקָּבֵץ לְחַיַּת הָאָרֶץ
ו וּלְעוֹף הַשָּׁמַיִם נְתַתִּיךָ לְאָכְלָה: וְיָדְעוּ
כָּל־יֹשְׁבֵי מִצְרַיִם כִּי אֲנִי יהוה יַעַן
הֱיוֹתָם מִשְׁעֶנֶת קָנֶה לְבֵית יִשְׂרָאֵל:
ז °בַכַּף ק׳ בְּתָפְשָׂם בְּךָ °בככפך תֵּרוֹץ וּבָקַעְתָּ
לָהֶם כָּל־כָּתֵף וּבְהִשָּׁעֲנָם עָלֶיךָ תִּשָּׁבֵר
ח וְהַעֲמַדְתָּ לָהֶם כָּל־מָתְנָיִם: לָכֵן
כֹּה אָמַר אֲדֹנָי יֱהוִה הִנְנִי מֵבִיא עָלַיִךְ
ט חֶרֶב וְהִכְרַתִּי מִמֵּךְ אָדָם וּבְהֵמָה: וְהָיְתָה

from the safety of his homeland into a battle that will result in his destruction.]

Myriads of fish had felt themselves safe in the protection of the sea monster. Now they will be sucked up together with him to share his fate *(R' Breuer)*.

5. הַמִּדְבָּרָה ... עַל פְּנֵי הַשָּׂדֶה — *Into the wilderness ... upon the face of the field.*

The dry, arid desert spells certain death for the creatures of the sea *(Rashi)*. The field is the location of the battle, indicating that the 'dry' field of battle will result in the death of the giant 'sea monster' *(Radak)*.

These interpretations explain the individual ideas portrayed by these words but leave the use of them in our metaphor unexplained. *R' Breuer* suggests: Even a fertile field will turn into an arid desert for you.

לֹא תֵאָסֵף וְלֹא תִקָּבֵץ — *Not to be brought in nor gathered together.*

Radak (Sefer HaShorashim, to פאר and קבץ) contrasts the root אסף with קבץ. The former describes the act of bringing something in to its former status or eminence (see *Genesis* 25:8; 49:33), while the latter is used for gathering things that are scattered. Thus, לֹא תֵאָסֵף expresses the idea that nothing will occur to restore Egypt to its former glory, while לֹא תִקָּבֵץ means that its scattered people would not be gathered together (at least for the present. See *v.* 13.)

Targum does not differentiate between אסף and קבץ. He translates both (as also the roots כנס, קהל, and קוה) as כנש (see *Targum* to *v.* 13). To avoid redundancy in our verse, he translates וְלֹא תִקָּבֵץ to mean *you will not be buried.*

6. מִשְׁעֶנֶת קָנֶה — *A reed-like support.*

Israel relied upon Egypt many times in the days of Sennacherib and in the days of Nebuchadnezzar, but they were of no help, just like a reed which is soft and does not support one who leans upon it *(Rashi)*. (See *footnote* 17:7; *comm.* 23:8).

Radak writes that the phrase assumes an implied adjective, as though it were written מִשְׁעֶנֶת קָנֶה [רָצוּץ], *a support of [crushed (*or splintered*)] reed,* as in *II Kings* 18:21 and *Isaiah* 36:6. [See next verse.] This implies that Egypt was worse than a mere absence of support. By promising help, they had lulled Israel into a sense of security and encouraged them to rebel against Nebuchadnezzar. Then when Egypt abjectly retreated to its land (see *Jeremiah* 37:5-7), Israel remained unprotected to face the brunt of Nebuchadnezzar's fury. Thus Egypt was a *splintered reed* which

wilderness, you and all the fish of your rivers. Upon
the face of the field you shall fall, not to be brought
in, nor gathered together. To the wild beasts of the
land and to the birds of the heavens have I given you
as food. 6 *Then all the dwellers of Egypt shall know*
that I am HASHEM because they were a reed-like
support for the family of Israel. 7 *When they grasp*
you with the hand, you are broken and pierce their
every shoulder, and where they lean upon you, you
will be broken and will cause their loins to stand up.
8 *Therefore, thus says my Lord HASHEM/ELOHIM:*
Behold! I shall bring the sword against you and cut
off from you man and beast; 9 *and Egypt shall be*

not only gives no support but even pierces the shoulder of the person who attempts to lean on it.

7. בְּתָפְשָׂם בְּךָ בַכַּף... — *When they grasp you with the hand...*

God continues to address Egypt with the metaphor of the frail reed to which Egypt is likened. When a falling victim — Israel — clutches a reed it breaks, with the result that he falls into its splintered remains, which pierce his shoulder. Not only does he fail to receive support, he is even injured *(Rashi).*

וְהַעֲמַדְתָּ לָהֶם כָּל מָתְנָיִם — *And will cause their loins to stand up.*

By not providing support to those who rely on you, you cause them to support themselves upon their own loins *(Rashi). Targum* also renders: *You will no longer be a support for them.*

Radak suggests that the word is an inverted form of וְהִמְעַדְתָּ from מעד, *to totter: You will cause their loins to totter.* (See *Psalms* 69:24.)

8-12. These verses describe the desolation which is to overtake the once fertile land of Egypt.

The passage is divided into two sections. Verses 8-9 deal with the immediate conquest. God will bring the *sword* against Egypt to *cut off... man and beast (v.* 8), and as a result of this *the land shall be desolate (v.* 9). The desolation is not a direct act of God. Rather it results from the slaughter to be perpetrated by Nebuchadnezzar's forces.

Verse 10 introduces a new *destruction,* this one directly caused by God (וְנָתַתִּי אֶת אֶרֶץ מִצְרַיִם לְחָרְבוֹת). This must be read together with *vs.* 11-12 and predicts the fact that not only would Egypt be *laid* waste by Babylon, but it would *remain* desolate for forty years. This duration of Egypt's desolation is ascribed to direct intervention by God.

This interpretation could form the basis for the view of the Sages (quoted in *Rashi;* based on *Bereishis Rabbah* 89:11) that the forty years of Egypt's desolation were 'owed' from Joseph's time. In that view Joseph predicted forty-two years of famine. [Pharaoh had two dreams. One concerning the cows and the other concerning the sheaves, each of which predicted a seven-year famine. We encounter these dreams three times: when Pharaoh dreamed; when he told them to Joseph and when Joseph repeated them for the purpose of his interpretation. The thrice repeated fourteen years yield forty-two years.] However, only two years of

אֶרֶץ־מִצְרַיִם לִשְׁמָמָה וְחָרְבָּה וְיָדְעוּ כִּי־
אֲנִי יְהוָה יַעַן אָמַר יְאֹר לִי וַאֲנִי עָשִׂיתִי׃
י לָכֵן הִנְנִי אֵלֶיךָ וְאֶל־יְאֹרֶיךָ וְנָתַתִּי אֶת־
אֶרֶץ מִצְרַיִם לְחָרְבוֹת חֹרֶב שְׁמָמָה
יא מִמִּגְדֹּל סְוֵנֵה וְעַד־גְּבוּל כּוּשׁ׃ לֹא תַעֲבָר־
בָּהּ רֶגֶל אָדָם וְרֶגֶל בְּהֵמָה לֹא תַעֲבָר־
יב בָּהּ וְלֹא תֵשֵׁב אַרְבָּעִים שָׁנָה׃ וְנָתַתִּי
אֶת־אֶרֶץ מִצְרַיִם שְׁמָמָה בְּתוֹךְ |
אֲרָצוֹת נְשַׁמּוֹת וְעָרֶיהָ בְּתוֹךְ עָרִים
מָחֳרָבוֹת תִּהְיֶיןָ שְׁמָמָה אַרְבָּעִים שָׁנָה
וַהֲפִצֹתִי אֶת־מִצְרַיִם בַּגּוֹיִם וְזֵרִיתִים
יג בָּאֲרָצוֹת׃ כִּי כֹּה אָמַר אֲדֹנָי
יֱהוִה מִקֵּץ אַרְבָּעִים שָׁנָה אֲקַבֵּץ אֶת־
מִצְרַיִם מִן־הָעַמִּים אֲשֶׁר נָפֹצוּ שָׁמָּה׃
יד וְשַׁבְתִּי אֶת־שְׁבוּת מִצְרַיִם וַהֲשִׁבֹתִי אֹתָם
אֶרֶץ פַּתְרוֹס עַל־אֶרֶץ מְכוּרָתָם וְהָיוּ שָׁם
טו מַמְלָכָה שְׁפָלָה׃ מִן־הַמַּמְלָכוֹת תִּהְיֶה

famine actually occurred, because when Jacob descended to Egypt after the second year, the famine ceased. To repay the remaining forty years, God intervened to assure Egypt's desolation for the full forty years.

9. לִשְׁמָמָה וְחָרְבָּה — *Desolate and waste.*

The roots שמם and חרב recur throughout these verses. *Malbim* suggests two differences between them: שמם refers to the land in general, while חרב is used more in connection with the cities (based on *v.* 12; 30:7); and שמם describes a greater degree of desolation than חרב (based on *v.* 10; 36:4).

[*Targum* seems to see the two roots as very close in meaning. Although he makes use of both חרב and שמם in his translation, he nevertheless introduces the root צדה to translate both terms where he finds it necessary to avoid the appearance of redundancy. Thus in *v.* 10 he renders חֹרֶב as צָדוּ, and in *v.* 12 he uses the same translation for שְׁמָמָה.]

10. הִנְנִי אֵלֶיךָ — *Behold! I am against you.*

I shall send My anger against you (*Targum*).

וְאֶל יְאֹרֶיךָ — *And against your rivers.*

Targum interprets: *against your king.* [In *v.* 4, *Targum* renders וְהַעֲלִיתִיךָ מִתּוֹךְ יְאֹרֶיךָ as *I will terminate your kingship.*]

Your rivers is mentioned as the Egyptian deity (*R' Breuer*). *Rashi* (*Exodus* 7:17) states: 'The Egyptians served the Nile. Therefore he smote their deity and only then smote them .

[The rivers might be mentioned especially since they were the source of Egypt s wealth. See above *vs.* 3-5.]

desolate and waste and they shall know that I am
HASHEM, for he said, 'The river is mine and I have
created.' 10 *Therefore, behold! I am against you and*
your rivers and I shall make the land of Egypt into a
destruction, wasted and desolate, from Migdol to
Seveneh, even to the border of Kush. 11 *The feet of*
man shall not pass through it, and the feet of beasts
shall not pass through it, and it shall not be inhabited
for forty years, 12 *and I shall make the land of Egypt*
desolate among desolate lands, and its cities shall be
desolate among waste cities for forty years; and I
shall scatter Egypt among the nations and disperse
them through the countries.
13 *For thus says my Lord HASHEM/ELOHIM: At the*
end of forty years I will gather Egypt from the na-
tions where they were scattered; 14 *and I will return*
the captivity of Egypt and bring them back to the
land of Pasros, upon the land of their dwelling, and
they shall be a lowly kingdom. 15 *Among the*

לְחָרְבוֹת חֹרֶב שְׁמָמָה — *A destruction, waste and desolate.*

חֹרֶב and שְׁמָמָה, *wasted* and *desolate* modify חָרְבוֹת, *destruction (Radak; Metzudos).*

[*Targum* here renders חֹרֶב as צְדוּ in order to avoid the appearance of redundancy.]

Eliezer of Beaugency renders חֹרֶב as *dry* (cf. *Genesis* 8:13), because the threat is leveled not only against the land but also against the rivers (see above).

מִמִּגְדֹּל סְוֵנֵה וְעַד גְּבוּל כּוּשׁ — *From Migdol to Seveneh, even to the border of Kush.*

If the translation were: *the tower of Seveneh,* the phrase would read מִגְדַּל in the construct form. Therefore מִגְדֹּל must be the place mentioned several times in Scripture (cf. *Exodus* 14:2; *Numbers* 33:7), and the verse means *from Migdol* (in the north) *till Seveneh* (the modern Assonan) in the south *even up to the border of Ethiopia (R' Breuer).*

11. וְלֹא תֵשֵׁב אַרְבָּעִים שָׁנָה — *It shall not be inhabited for forty years.*

See introductory remarks to these verses above. See also *comm. v.* 21.

12. While the land lies in desolation, its people will be scattered amongst the nations of the world.

13-15. Egypt's might will have been smashed forever. It will never again be in a position to attract Israel's misguided confidence. Its people will be brought back to the land (אֲקַבֵּץ, *I will gather, v.* 13), but not to their former greatness. (There will be no אֲסִיפָה, *bringing in;* see *comm., v.* 5.)

14. אֶרֶץ מְכוּרָתָם — *The land of their dwelling.*

See *comm.* 16:3.

15. *Mechilta (Exodus* 15:7) tells that the Roman emperor Antoninus asked R' Yehudah HaNassi whether he had anything to fear in his campaign against

כט
טז־יח

שְׁפָלָה וְלֹא־תִתְנַשֵּׂא עוֹד עַל־הַגּוֹיִם
טז וְהִמְעַטְתִּים לְבִלְתִּי רְדוֹת בַּגּוֹיִם׃ וְלֹא
יִהְיֶה־עוֹד לְבֵית יִשְׂרָאֵל לְמִבְטָח מַזְכִּיר
עָוֺן בִּפְנוֹתָם אַחֲרֵיהֶם וְיָדְעוּ כִּי אֲנִי אֲדֹנָי
יז יֱהֹוִה׃ וַיְהִי בְּעֶשְׂרִים
וָשֶׁבַע שָׁנָה בָּרִאשׁוֹן בְּאֶחָד לַחֹדֶשׁ
יח הָיָה דְבַר־יְהוָה אֵלַי לֵאמֹר׃ בֶּן־אָדָם
נְבוּכַדְרֶאצַּר מֶלֶךְ בָּבֶל הֶעֱבִיד אֶת־חֵילוֹ
עֲבֹדָה גְדוֹלָה אֶל־צֹר כָּל־רֹאשׁ מֻקְרָח
וְכָל־כָּתֵף מְרוּטָה וְשָׂכָר לֹא־הָיָה לוֹ

Egypt. Based on this verse, the sage answered him that no significant king or general would ever emerge from Egypt again. He would face no real opposition.

16. לְמִבְטָח מַזְכִּיר עָוֺן — *A guarantor* [lit. *source of trust*] *recalling sin.*

By placing its faith in Egypt which guaranteed its safety, Israel brought sin upon itself.

The sin recalled is the prohibition mentioned in *Exodus* 14:3: *As you have seen Egypt this day, you shall not see her again ever (Rashi).* See footnote 23:8.

Israel would not have put its trust in Egypt if it had not first turned away from God. The passage recalls *Chovos HaLevavos, Sha'ar HaBitachon:* For he who does not trust God trusts another; and one who trusts someone other than God, from him God will withhold His providence and forsake him for the one in whom he trusted.[1]

In this sense, the destruction of Egypt at Nebuchadnezzar's hands could be a seminal point in Israel's history. Freed from its debilitating dependence on Egypt, Israel would once more be able to turn to God, thereby sowing the seeds of a future regeneration.

Whether Israel would make use of this opportunity depended upon its perception of the event. If Babylon's ascendancy were seen as a result of political or military happenstance, God would remain hidden from the people. If, on the other hand, Nebuchadnezzar were perceived as a tool in God's hand in the execution of a Divine plan, then there would be hope that Israel could be galvanized into a true confrontation with its soul and destiny. See further below.

17-21. The prophecy contained in these verses is the only one of the six prophecies against Egypt which is not in its correct chronological place (pref., chs. 29-32). The previous section can explain the irregularity.

This prophecy was said in the year of Egypt's destruction (see pref., 29-32). In it the prophet places these events in their true perspective. In his campaign

1. The obligation to trust in God does not free man from trying to help himself (הִשְׁתַּדְּלוּת). However, the means by which man may avail himself in his attempts at self-help are defined and limited by the obligation of trust in God (בִּטָּחוֹן). Thus, an action which is unlikely to bring about results but is undertaken out of desperation is precluded. A בַּעַל בִּטָּחוֹן, *one who truly trusts in God,* will not 'clutch at a straw' (*Chazon Ish, Emunah Ubitachon* 2:6).

Egypt had always proved to be an unreliable ally (see *comm., v.* 6; footnote 17:7; *comm.* 23:8). Under such circumstances, it was sinful for Israel to place its trust in Egypt.

kingdoms it shall be the lowest, and it shall no more exalt itself above the nations; and I shall diminish them that they shall not rule over the nations; [16] *and they shall no more be for the Family of Israel a guarantor, of trust recalling sin, as they turn after them, and they shall know that I am my Lord HASHEM/ELOHIM.*

[17] *It was in the twenty-seventh year in the first month on the first of the month. The word of HASHEM came to me, saying:* [18] *Ben Adam, Nebuchadrezzar, king of Babylon, caused his army to perform a great service against Tyre. Every head is bald, every shoulder peeled; and he and his army had no reward from Tyre for the service which he had performed against her.* [19] *Therefore, thus says my Lord*

against Tyre, Nebuchadnezzar was doing God's *work*. His victory over Egypt is granted him as *reward* for his *service*. (See below, particularly *comm.* to אֲשֶׁר עָשׂוּ לִי, *v.* 20.) The mighty forces of history are reduced to their correct dimension; its heroes are revealed as personally impotent — unless they act as tools of God's purpose. This prophecy and no other must follow the previous one if Egypt's downfall is to have its hoped-for effect. (*R' Breuer;* see particularly *comm. v.* 21.)

17. בְּעֶשְׂרִים וְשֶׁבַע שָׁנָה... — *In the twenty-seventh year.*

See pref. chs. 29:32.

Abarbanel offers the following explanation for why this prophecy is dated according to Nebuchadnezzar's reign rather than according to the years of Zidkiyahu and Yehoyachin's exile as are the other events in the Book.

Verse 11 teaches that Egypt would lie desolate for forty years. What period does this cover? By placing the beginning of Egypt's exile in the twenty-seventh year of Nebuchadnezzar, Scripture informs us that the forty years ended in the first year of Persia's ascendancy over Babylon. [See *Megillah* 11b: Nebuchadnezzar reigned forty-five years and his son Evil Merodach reigned thirty-two years. By counting the year of Nebuchadnezzar's death and Evil Merodach's ascension to the throne twice, once for each king, we have the year of Belshazzar's ascension to the throne as exactly forty years after Egypt's fall. It was in that year that Daniel saw visions of Persia's rise to power (*Daniel* 7:1 ff.). As the balance of world power passed to Persia, Babylon lost its grip on Egypt, and the dispersed Egyptians managed to return to their land.

18. הֶעֱבִיד אֶת חֵילוֹ עֲבֹדָה גְדֹלָה אֶל צוֹר — *Caused his army to perform* [lit. *serve*] *a great service against Tyre.*

Nebuchadnezzar's campaign against Tyre is described as a *service* because he fought against them at God's 'command' (*Rashi, v.* 20). *Jeremiah* 43:10 describes Nebuchadnezzar as God's *servant,* and Yechezkel 30:24 talks of God placing His sword in Nebuchadnezzar's hand. See also *Habbakuk* 1:12; Intro. 21:24-27; *comm., v.* 24.

כָּל רֹאשׁ מֻקְרָח וְכָל כָּתֵף מְרוּטָה — *Every head is bald, every shoulder peeled.*

These are the effects of the heavy

כט וּלְחֵילוֹ מִצֹּר עַל־הָעֲבֹדָה אֲשֶׁר־עָבַד
יט־כא יט עָלֶיהָ: לָכֵן כֹּה אָמַר אֲדֹנָי
יֱהֹוִה הִנְנִי נֹתֵן לִנְבוּכַדְרֶאצַּר מֶלֶךְ־בָּבֶל
אֶת־אֶרֶץ מִצְרָיִם וְנָשָׂא הֲמֹנָהּ וְשָׁלַל
שְׁלָלָהּ וּבָזַז בִּזָּהּ וְהָיְתָה שָׂכָר לְחֵילוֹ:
כ פְּעֻלָּתוֹ אֲשֶׁר־עָבַד בָּהּ נָתַתִּי לוֹ אֶת־אֶרֶץ
מִצְרָיִם אֲשֶׁר עָשׂוּ לִי נְאֻם אֲדֹנָי יֱהֹוִה:
כא בַּיּוֹם הַהוּא אַצְמִיחַ קֶרֶן לְבֵית יִשְׂרָאֵל
וּלְךָ אֶתֵּן פִּתְחוֹן־פֶּה בְּתוֹכָם וְיָדְעוּ כִּי־
ל א אֲנִי יהוה: וַיְהִי דְבַר־יהוה אֵלַי
א־ב ב לֵאמֹר: בֶּן־אָדָם הִנָּבֵא וְאָמַרְתָּ כֹּה אָמַר

burden which the soldiers had to carry in order to sustain an effective siege *(Rashi).*

וְשָׂכָר לֹא הָיָה לוֹ וּלְחֵילוֹ מִצֹּר — *But there was no reward for him or for his army from Tyre.*

Before Nebuchadnezzar was able to despoil Tyre, it was inundated by water which swept away its wealth *(Rashi.* See 26:4, 19.)

20. אֲשֶׁר עָשׂוּ לִי — *For what they had done to Me.*

The translation follows *Targum* and *Rashi.* לִי is translated: *to Me,* and the phrase refers to the evil which Egypt had done by promising support to Israel and then reneging. The clear implication is that an evil done to Israel is considered to have been done to God Himself.

However, *Eliezer of Beaugency* and *Mahari MiTrani* render לִי: *for Me.* The phrase refers to Babylon, which deserved to be rewarded because it acted for God in its campaign against Tyre. This interpretation puts the phrase in consonance with the thrust of the whole passage (see *comm., v.* 18).

21. בַּיּוֹם הַהוּא — *On that day.*

This verse asserts that בַּיּוֹם הַהוּא, *on that day,* there will be a flowering of Israel's strength. If *that day* is the day of Egypt's downfall, the meaning seems obscure. How can Israel, which had been destroyed eight years earlier, be said to flower anew as a result of Egypt's fall?

In answer to this problem, *Rashi* suggests *that day* refers back to *v.* 11, where Egypt's forty-year exile is foretold. The end of the exile which corresponds to the first year of Belshazzar's reign (*comm., v.* 17), can be seen as the beginning of Israel's regeneration, because it was then that Daniel saw the visions which presaged Persia's ascendancy. It was Persia's king Cyrus who initiated the beginnings of Israel's return and the rebuilding of the Temple.

Radak interprets בַּיּוֹם הַהוּא as *at that time* rather than *on that day.* During the period of Babylonian empire, the revival of Israel's honor will begin with the birth of Cyrus, whom Isaiah describes as God's anointed.

Eliezer of Beaugency has a completely different approach. *That day* is the day of Egypt's destruction. The flowering of Israel's strength describes the small group of exiles from Israel who had settled in Egypt (see *Jeremiah,* chs. 42-44). They were not completely wiped out together with the Egyptians. A new

29 20-21 *HASHEM/ELOHIM: Behold! I will give the land of Egypt to Nebuchadrezzar, king of Babylon, and he will carry off her abundance and take her spoil and take her prey — that shall be a reward for his army.*
20 *For his work which he performed in her I have given him the land of Egypt for what they had done to Me — the words of my Lord HASHEM/ELOHIM.*
21 *On that day I will cause the strength of the family of Israel to flower, and to you I will grant an opening of the mouth in their midst; and they shall know that I am HASHEM.*

30 1-2 *The word of HASHEM came to me, saying.*
2 *Ben Adam, prophesy and say: Thus says my*

community was to grow from the few who remained.

[Although this seems to be contradicted by *Jeremiah* 42:17 which threatened this group with total extinction, it finds confirmation in *Rashi* to *Jeremiah* 46:27. According to that *Rashi* the righteous among them, who had not wanted to go down to Egypt in disregard of Jeremiah's exhortation but were forced to join their fellows, were saved. *Jeremiah* 42:17 refers only to those who went down of their own volition.]

Eliezer of Beaugency uses this interpretation to explain the seeming irregularity of this prophecy in the otherwise chronological sequence of the prophecies against Egypt. (See intro., *vs.* 17-21.) The earlier prophecy had ended with the prediction that Egypt would no longer be a false support for Israel (*v.* 16). This left open the question of what would happen to Israel once its ally was destroyed. Would it also fall or would it, on the contrary, be spared for a future regeneration? This second prophecy is the answer. Israel would not be pulled down in the wake of Egypt's destruction. It would live and go on to a glorious future.

R' Breuer also interprets our verse with *v.* 16 in mind. The flowering of Israel's might would take place on the day of Egypt's fall. Israel can only flourish under the blessing of God's providence. As long as Israel's trust in Egypt placed a barrier between them and God, there could be no development or growth. With the elimination of that obstacle, the road became clear for the flowering of Israel's true destiny.

וּלְךָ אֶתֵּן פִּתְחוֹן פֶּה בְּתוֹכָם — *And to you I will grant an opening of the mouth in their midst.*

The march of events would confirm the authenticity of Yechezkel's prophecy. Henceforth, the people would listen to him willingly thus, in effect, allowing him to 'open his mouth' to a receptive audience (*Rashi;* see 24:26-27).

XXX

The prophecies that begin this chapter (vs. 1-20) are undated. In Radak's *view, they continue the preceding prophecy (29:17-21), and were said in the year of Egypt's destruction. His proof is the expression* קָרוֹב יוֹם, the day [*of Egypt's destruction*] is close, *in* v. *3.* Malbim, *too, agrees that the prophecy refers to Egypt,*

ל
ג־ט

ג אֲדֹנָי יֱהוִה הֵילִילוּ הָהּ לַיּוֹם׃ כִּי־קָרוֹב
יוֹם וְקָרוֹב יוֹם לַיהוָה יוֹם עָנָן עֵת גּוֹיִם
ד יִהְיֶה׃ וּבָאָה חֶרֶב בְּמִצְרַיִם וְהָיְתָה
חַלְחָלָה בְּכוּשׁ בִּנְפֹל חָלָל בְּמִצְרָיִם
ה וְלָקְחוּ הֲמוֹנָהּ וְנֶהֶרְסוּ יְסוֹדוֹתֶיהָ׃ כּוּשׁ
וּפוּט וְלוּד וְכָל־הָעֶרֶב וְכוּב וּבְנֵי אֶרֶץ
ו הַבְּרִית אִתָּם בַּחֶרֶב יִפֹּלוּ׃ כֹּה־
אָמַר יהוה וְנָפְלוּ סֹמְכֵי מִצְרַיִם וְיָרַד
גְּאוֹן עֻזָּהּ מִמִּגְדֹּל סְוֵנֵה בַּחֶרֶב יִפְּלוּ־בָהּ
ז נְאֻם אֲדֹנָי יֱהוִה׃ וְנָשַׁמּוּ בְּתוֹךְ אֲרָצוֹת
נְשַׁמּוֹת וְעָרָיו בְּתוֹךְ־עָרִים נַחֲרָבוֹת
ח תִּהְיֶינָה׃ וְיָדְעוּ כִּי־אֲנִי יהוה בְּתִתִּי־אֵשׁ
ט בְּמִצְרַיִם וְנִשְׁבְּרוּ כָּל־עֹזְרֶיהָ׃ בַּיּוֹם הַהוּא
יֵצְאוּ מַלְאָכִים מִלְּפָנַי בַּצִּים לְהַחֲרִיד
אֶת־כּוּשׁ בֶּטַח וְהָיְתָה חַלְחָלָה בָהֶם כְּיוֹם

but he holds that the preceding prophecy (29:17-21) is a self-contained insert (see comm. *29:17,21), while this chapter continues the prophecies of* the tenth year *(29:1-16).*

2. הָהּ — *Woe.*

הָהּ is an expression of distress, similar to אֲהָהּ (cf. 4:14).

לַיּוֹם — *For the day.*

Lament in anticipation of the day of destruction *(Rashi).*

3. כִּי קָרוֹב יוֹם — *For the day is close.*

This prophecy was said in the year of Egypt's destruction *(Radak;* see pref.).

וְקָרוֹב יוֹם לַה׳ — *The day of HASHEM is close.*

The day described as *close* is not a time when a haphazard, coincidental event will take place. Rather, the destruction of Egypt is willed by Him as part of His plan *(Metzudos).*

עֵת גּוֹיִם יִהְיֶה — *A time for the nations it shall be.*

It will be a time for the breaking of the nations *(Targum);* a time when their ascendancies will come to an end *(Metzudos).*

4. וְהָיְתָה חַלְחָלָה בְּכוּשׁ — *And a trembling will be in Kush.*

Kush is Egypt's neighbor to the south (see 29:10). (Both Kush and Egypt were sons of Ham, the son of Noah. See *Genesis* 10:6.) As Egypt, the buffer state between Kush and Babylon, falls, the Kushites will begin to fear for their own fate.

בִּנְפֹל חָלָל בְּמִצְרָיִם — *When the slain shall fall in Egypt.*

The singular חָלָל is used in place of the plural חֲלָלִים *(Radak).*

5. וּפוּט וְלוּד — *And Put and Lud.*

See *comm.* 27:10.

וְכָל הָעֶרֶב — *All the motley* [lit. *people*].

Lord HASHEM/ELOHIM: Wail: woe for the day! 3 *For*
the day is close, the day of HASHEM is close — a
murky day. It will be a time for the nations. 4 *Then a*
sword will come against Egypt, and a trembling will
be in Kush, when the slain shall fall in Egypt, when
they shall take her multitude and her foundation will
be broken. 5 *Kush and Put and Lud and all the motley*
people, and Kuv and the inhabitants of the allied
land, will fall with them by the sword. 6 *Thus says*
HASHEM: The supporters of Egypt shall fall and the
pride of her power shall come down. From Migdol to
Seveneh — by the sword they will fall in her — the
words of my Lord HASHEM/ELOHIM. 7 *They shall be*
desolated among desolate lands; and her cities,
among destroyed cities they will be. 8 *They shall*
know that I am HASHEM when I set fire in Egypt and
all her helpers are smashed. 9 *On that day messengers*
will go out from Me in ships, to frighten sanguine
Kush, and there will be a trembling among them like

The translation follows most commentators who take the word in the same sense in which it is used in *Exodus* 12:38 where the motley groups that attached themselves to Israel at the Exodus are described as עֶרֶב רַב, *large mixture* [of people]. Here, it refers to the various peoples who were clustered around Egypt and saw that land as their protector.

However, *Targum* renders סוּמְכָוָתָא from סמך, to support. (See *Nahum* 3:9 where he renders כּוּשׁ עָצְמָה as סוּמְכְתָהָא). *Rashi* quotes *Targum* and relates the word to עָרֵב, a *co-signer* on a loan, from the root ערב, *to pledge* or *guarantee, as in Genesis* 44:32.

וְכוּב — *And Kuv.*

Kuv does not recur in Scripture.

וּבְנֵי אֶרֶץ הַבְּרִית — *And the inhabitants of the allied land.*

These are the lands which had pacts with Egypt to come to her aid *(Rashi).*

6. מִמִּגְדֹּל סְוֵנֵה — *From Migdol to Seveneh.*

See *comm.* 29:10.

8. בְּתִתִּי אֵשׁ — *When I set fire.*

My anger burns like fire *(Rashi).*

9. מַלְאָכִים — *Messengers.*

Groups of regiments will travel at My behest to convulse the sanguine Kush *(Rashi).*

The Babylonian army is projected as being God's messengers in the execution of His plans. (See *comm.* 29:17.)

בַּצִּים — *In ships.*

The translation follows *Radak* and *Metzudos. Rashi* to *Numbers* 24:24 also renders צִים as *ships.*

However, *Rashi* here quotes *Targum,* who translates לִגְיוֹן, which means *a legion* or *company.* In *Numbers* (24:24). *Onkelos* renders סִיעַן, which means a *crowd of people.*

Targum Yerushalmi there renders

י מִצְרַיִם כִּי הִנֵּה בָּאָה׃ כֹּה אָמַר
אֲדֹנָי יֱהוִה וְהִשְׁבַּתִּי אֶת־הֲמוֹן מִצְרַיִם
יא בְּיַד נְבוּכַדְרֶאצַּר מֶלֶךְ־בָּבֶל׃ הוּא וְעַמּוֹ
אִתּוֹ עָרִיצֵי גוֹיִם מוּבָאִים לְשַׁחֵת הָאָרֶץ
וְהֵרִיקוּ חַרְבוֹתָם עַל־מִצְרַיִם וּמָלְאוּ
יב אֶת־הָאָרֶץ חָלָל׃ וְנָתַתִּי יְאֹרִים חָרָבָה
וּמָכַרְתִּי אֶת־הָאָרֶץ בְּיַד־רָעִים וַהֲשִׁמֹּתִי
אֶרֶץ וּמְלֹאָהּ בְּיַד־זָרִים אֲנִי יְהוָה
יג דִּבַּרְתִּי׃ כֹּה־אָמַר אֲדֹנָי יֱהוִה
וְהַאֲבַדְתִּי גִלּוּלִים וְהִשְׁבַּתִּי אֱלִילִים מִנֹּף
וְנָשִׂיא מֵאֶרֶץ־מִצְרַיִם לֹא יִהְיֶה־עוֹד
יד וְנָתַתִּי יִרְאָה בְּאֶרֶץ מִצְרָיִם׃ וַהֲשִׁמֹּתִי
אֶת־פַּתְרוֹס וְנָתַתִּי אֵשׁ בְּצֹעַן וְעָשִׂיתִי
טו שְׁפָטִים בְּנֹא׃ וְשָׁפַכְתִּי חֲמָתִי עַל־סִין

אוּכְלוּסִין סַגְיָין בִּלְבְרָנַיָא, *great crowds in ships,* thus encompassing both ideas.

כְּיוֹם מִצְרַיִם — *Like the day of Egypt.*

Verse 4 tells how Kush trembled on the day of Egypt's fall. Its fears are now confirmed. The time has come for Kush to tremble on its own account *(Radak).*

10. וְהִשְׁבַּתִּי — *I will cause to cease.*

The *hiphil, causative* voice, of שבת, *to rest,* is used often by Yechezkel. God is said to be מַשְׁבִּית [*cause to cease* or bring an end to] pride (7:24), proverbs (12:23), harlotry (16:41), promiscuity (23:27, 48), music (26:13), multitudes of Egypt (here), idols (*v.* 13), shepherds from tending their flock (34:10), and wild animals (34:25).

[From this list it is obvious that the word does not imply complete destruction. It can also be used in the sense of inhibiting, sapping something of its power.

[The classic application of these two possibilities is found in *Toras Kohanim (Leviticus* 26:6). One of the promises which God makes concerning Messianic times is: וְהִשְׁבַּתִּי חַיָּה רָעָה מִן הָאָרֶץ, *I will cause evil beasts to cease from the land.* To this *Toras Kohanim* comments: Rabbi Yehudah said, 'He will wipe them off the face of the earth.' Rabbi Shimon said, 'He will stop them from doing any harm.'

[Thus, this verse does not imply that Egypt will be totally wiped out, since this is contradicted by previous verses which predict an exile and an ultimate return (29:12-16). Rather it means the erosion of Egypt's political and military stature as a result of Babylon's victory. This reflects the ideas expressed in 29:15.]

11. וְהֵרִיקוּ חַרְבוֹתָם — *They will draw their swords.*

See *comm.* 28:7.

12. יְאֹרִים — *Rivers.*

This refers to Egypt which, because of its many irrigation canals distributing water from the Nile, is called a land of rivers *(Rashi).*

וּמָכַרְתִּי אֶת הָאָרֶץ — *And (I shall) transfer the land.*

Rashi quotes *Targum* who renders: וְאִימְסַר, *I will give over.* The root מכר is

the day of Egypt, for behold it is come!
10 *For thus says my Lord HASHEM/ELOHIM: I will*
cause the multitude of Egypt to cease, by the hand of
Nebuchadrezzar, king of Babylon. 11 *He and his peo-*
ple with him, the strongest of the nations, are
brought to destroy the land; they shall draw their
swords against Egypt and fill the land with slain.
12 *Then I shall dry the rivers and transfer the land*
into the hand of evil ones, and I shall desolate the
land and its fullness by the hand of strangers. I,
HASHEM, have spoken.
13 *Thus says my Lord HASHEM/ELOHIM: And I will*
destroy idols and cause the nothingnesses to cease
from Nof; and a king from the land of Egypt will be
no more and I will set fear over the land of Egypt;
14 *and I will desolate Pasros and set a fire in Zoan,*
and I will execute punishments in No; 15 *and I shall*

used in this sense throughout Scripture (cf. *Deuteronomy* 32:30), although in Talmudic usage it is used exclusively to mean selling. *Ibn Ezra* there explains that this 'giving over' is like a sale (מכר) because God transfers Israel's land to its enemies as a consequence of its sinful deeds, just as a seller gives his property to a purchaser in return for value received.

13. וְהַאֲבַדְתִּי גִלּוּלִים — *And I will destroy idols.*

Obviously, idols have no meaningful existence. Why, then, must they be destroyed? *Radak* answers that the idols must be destroyed in order to educate the people who believed and trusted in them. *Metzudos* simply interprets the phrase to mean that idolatry will cease. *Targum* renders: *I will destroy idol worshipers.*

נֹף — *Nof.*

Nof is an Egyptian city that is also mentioned by Isaiah and Jeremiah.

וְנָשִׂיא מֵאֶרֶץ־מִצְרַיִם לֹא יִהְיֶה עוֹד — *And a king from the land of Egypt will be no more.*

Since ch. 29 predicted that Egypt's desolation would last only forty years, both *Radak* and *Metzudas David* suggest that this phrase is an exaggeration. It means that for a long time there would be no king, or, at any rate, no signifcant king. Egypt would at best be a lowly kingdom (29:15), and its king would have little power.

וְנָתַתִּי יִרְאָה בְּאֶרֶץ מִצְרָיִם — *And I will set fear into the land of Egypt.*

While *Mahari MiTrani* interprets this as the fear of Nebuchadnezzar, most commentators perceive a wider meaning in the phrase. Egypt would never feel safe again. It would always fear its neighbors.

Eliezer of Beaugeney compares *Isaiah* 19:17: *The land of Judah will be a terror to Egypt.*

See *comm.* 29:15.

14. פַּתְרוֹס ... צֹעַן ... נֹא — *Pasros ... Zoan ... No.*

These are places in Egypt. *Targum* identifies נֹא as Alexandria.

15. סִין — *Sin.*

מָעוֹז מִצְרָיִם וְהִכְרַתִּי אֶת־הֲמוֹן נֹא:
טז וְנָתַתִּי אֵשׁ בְּמִצְרַיִם חוּל °תחיל סִין וְנֹא °תָּחוּל ק׳
יז תִּהְיֶה לְהִבָּקֵעַ וְנֹף צָרֵי יוֹמָם: בַּחוּרֵי אָוֶן
וּפִי־בֶסֶת בַּחֶרֶב יִפֹּלוּ וְהֵנָּה בַּשְּׁבִי
יח תֵּלַכְנָה: וּבִתְחַפְנְחֵס חָשַׂךְ הַיּוֹם בְּשִׁבְרִי־
שָׁם אֶת־מֹטוֹת מִצְרַיִם וְנִשְׁבַּת־בָּהּ גְּאוֹן
עֻזָּהּ הִיא עָנָן יְכַסֶּנָּה וּבְנוֹתֶיהָ בַּשְּׁבִי
יט תֵּלַכְנָה: וְעָשִׂיתִי שְׁפָטִים בְּמִצְרָיִם וְיָדְעוּ
כ כִּי־אֲנִי יהוה: וַיְהִי
בְּאַחַת עֶשְׂרֵה שָׁנָה בָּרִאשׁוֹן בְּשִׁבְעָה
לַחֹדֶשׁ הָיָה דְבַר־יהוה אֵלַי לֵאמֹר:

This is an Egyptian city not mentioned again in Scripture.

16. לְהִבָּקַע — *To split asunder.*
Its wall will split open *(Rashi).*

צָרֵי יוֹמָם — [*Beset by*] *daily enemies.*
Enemies will descend upon it daily *(Targum,* quoted by *Rashi).*

17. אָוֶן וּפִי־בֶסֶת — *Aven and Pi-Beses.*
These are Egyptian cities.

וְהֵנָּה — *And they.*
וְהֵנָּה (feminine form) could refer to these two cities but might also refer to the women of the cities. The *young men* were to fall by the sword; their wives be taken captive *(Radak).*

18. חָשַׂךְ יוֹם — *The day will withdraw.*
It will withhold its light *(Rashi).* (The word derives from חשך with a שׂ, sin, as in *Genesis* 22:12).

Targum renders: *Darkness* (חֹשֶׁךְ) *will come by day.* Perhaps *Targum* had the reading חָשַׁךְ (שׁ, *shin)* rather than חָשַׂךְ (שׂ, *sin).*] (See footnote 14:8).

[Perhaps *Targum* had our reading (שׂ, *sin)* but *Ibn Janach (Sefer HaShorashim)* thinks that such inversions (תְּמוּרָה) are possible and that Scripture could write חָשַׂךְ and mean חָשַׁךְ.] However, this is a controversial issue. *Ibn Ezra (Sefer Tzachos)* calls the proponent of such an idea מַהְבִיל, *one who asserts something groundless,* and *Radak (Sefer HaShorashim)* also claims that such an inversion does not exist in Hebrew.

מֹטוֹת מִצְרַיִם — *The rods of Egypt.*
Radak comments that these rods are the yokes by which Egypt subjugated its neighboring states.

Targum translates: *the strength of Egypt.*

וְנִשְׁבַּת בָּהּ גְּאוֹן עֻזָּהּ — *And the pride of her power will cease in her.*
This phrase recalls 7:24, where a similar expression is used with reference to Israel.

הִיא עָנָן יְכַסֶּנָּה — *And a cloud will cover her.*
The Babylonian King and his army will cover Techafneches like a cloud which covers the earth *(Targum).*

20-26. A scant two months after the first prophecy against Egypt, Yechezkel is granted another vision.

Some eighteen years earlier, in the fourth year of Yehoyakim's reign, Pharaoh Necho had suffered a great defeat at Nebuchadnezzar's hands (*Jeremiah* 46:1 ff.). It had permanently crippled Egypt's might and had made it impossible for Pharaoh to venture out of his country on military campaigns (*II Kings* 24:7), but her losses had been

30
16-20

and I will cut off the multitude of No; 16 *and I shall*
set a fire in Egypt. Sin shall tremble greatly and No
shall be split asunder and Nof beset by daily enemies.
17 *The young men of Aven and Pi-Beses will fall by*
the sword and they shall go into captivity; 18 *and in*
Techafneches, the day will withdraw when I will
break the rods of Egypt there, and the pride of her
power will cease in her. And a cloud will cover her,
and her daughters will go into captivity; 19 *I shall ex-*
ecute punishments in Egypt, then they shall know
that I am HASHEM.
20 *It was in the eleventh year in the first month on*
the seventh of the month The word of HASHEM came

limited to her western possessions (*II Kings* 24:7). Inside Egypt proper, Pharaoh still wielded a mighty scepter *(Mahari Karo).*

Now Yechezkel is told that Egypt's humiliation would not end with its first defeat. Egypt proper, too, would fall to Nebuchadnezzar. Nothing would remain except the lowly kingdom which was promised in 29:15.[1]

1. What does this prophecy, which came just two months after the earlier one, add to what is already known? What are we to learn from the juxtaposition of Nebuchadnezzar's two campaigns against Pharaoh (duplicated in *Jeremiah* 46, where verses 1-12 deal with the first campaign and from verse 13 on the second campaign is described)? What is the significance of verse 22, which implies that even the *arm* which had already been broken in the first campaign (*v.* 21) would be broken once more?

We suggest the following solution.

Babylon had two scores to settle with Egypt. When Jeremiah was ordered to pass the cup of destruction to all the nations who were to fall to Babylon, Egypt was included among them (*Jeremiah* 25:15 ff.).

Long before, at the very dawn of Egypt's relations with Israel, there had been another cup. *Sotah* 9a and *Chullin* 92a teach that the three times which the *cup of Pharaoh* was mentioned in the butler's dream (*Genesis* 40:9 ff.) symbolized the three humiliations which Egypt was to endure in the course of its history: the first, in the days of Moses; the second in the days of Pharaoh Necho; and the final one, in Messianic days.

Chapter 25 of *Jeremiah,* in which world conquest was granted to Nebuchadnezzar, is not concerned with the various nations as individual units. As *Chagigah* 13b teaches (see pref., ch. 1), it was ordained that Nebuchadnezzar should be a world conqueror so that it might not be said that Israel fell to a lowly nation. Within that framework, Egypt was not different from any other people. By contrast, the cups of the butler's dream seem to indicate a fate specific to Egypt itself.

Perhaps the first campaign (which took place in Nebuchadnezzar's first year; see the computations in pref., chs. 29-32) was the one hinted at in the butler's dream. The rise of the Babylonian kingdom (see *comm.* 21:24-27) was to spell the end of Egypt's supremacy. This was accomplished by crippling Egypt in such a way that it could no longer be regarded as a world power.

Egypt would be exposed to yet another defeat, this time as part of Nebuchadnezzar's world conquest, in fulfillment of Jeremiah's vision.

This dual fate is the subject of the two-stage prophecy contained in these verses.

כא בֶּן־אָדָם אֶת־זְרוֹעַ פַּרְעֹה מֶלֶךְ־מִצְרַיִם
שָׁבָרְתִּי וְהִנֵּה לֹא־חֻבְּשָׁה לָתֵת רְפָאוֹת
לָשׂוּם חִתּוּל לְחָבְשָׁהּ לְחָזְקָהּ לִתְפֹּשׂ
כב בֶּחָרֶב: לָכֵן כֹּה־אָמַר | אֲדֹנָי
יֱהוִֹה הִנְנִי אֶל־פַּרְעֹה מֶלֶךְ־מִצְרַיִם
וְשָׁבַרְתִּי אֶת־זְרֹעֹתָיו אֶת־הַחֲזָקָה וְאֶת־
הַנִּשְׁבָּרֶת וְהִפַּלְתִּי אֶת־הַחֶרֶב מִיָּדוֹ:
כג וַהֲפִיצוֹתִי אֶת־מִצְרַיִם בַּגּוֹיִם וְזֵרִיתִם
כד בָּאֲרָצוֹת: וְחִזַּקְתִּי אֶת־זְרֹעוֹת מֶלֶךְ בָּבֶל
וְנָתַתִּי אֶת־חַרְבִּי בְּיָדוֹ וְשָׁבַרְתִּי אֶת־
זְרֹעוֹת פַּרְעֹה וְנָאַק נַאֲקוֹת חָלָל לְפָנָיו:
כה וְהַחֲזַקְתִּי אֶת־זְרֹעוֹת מֶלֶךְ בָּבֶל וּזְרֹעוֹת
פַּרְעֹה תִּפֹּלְנָה וְיָדְעוּ כִּי־אֲנִי יהוה בְּתִתִּי
חַרְבִּי בְּיַד מֶלֶךְ־בָּבֶל וְנָטָה אוֹתָהּ אֶל־
כו אֶרֶץ מִצְרָיִם: וַהֲפִצוֹתִי אֶת־מִצְרַיִם
בַּגּוֹיִם וְזֵרִיתִי אוֹתָם בָּאֲרָצוֹת וְיָדְעוּ כִּי־
א אֲנִי יְהוָֹה: וַיְהִי בְּאַחַת עֶשְׂרֵה

21. אֶת זְרוֹעַ פַּרְעֹה מֶלֶךְ־מִצְרַיִם שָׁבָרְתִּי *— The arm of Pharaoh, king of Egypt, I broke.*

According to *Rashi,* this refers to Nebuchadnezzar's defeat of Pharaoh Necho at Karkemish on the Euphrates, which took place in the fourth year of Yehoyakim's reign (*Jeremiah* 46:1 ff.; see above). In contrast to verse 22, which speaks of the breaking of both arms, here only one is broken. Pharaoh had been disabled as far as foreign campaigns were concerned, but he remained a strong ruler within his land (*II Kings* 24:7).

וְהִנֵּה לֹא־חֻבְּשָׁה *— And behold! it has not been bound.*

חבש describes the binding of a broken limb *(Rashi).* The broken arm was never healed in the sense that Pharaoh could never again wage an effective foreign campaign *(Rashi).*

Rashi points out that this same idea is expressed in *Jeremiah* 46:11.

לשום חתול *— To place a bandage.*

The root חתל occurs in 16:4, where it refers to swaddling clothes.

לִתְפֹּשׂ בֶּחָרֶב *— To hold a sword.*

The arm was never healed sufficiently to enable it to hold a sword.

22. Nevertheless, the other arm was still healthy and able to wield the sword. But in the coming war, both arms would be broken so that Egypt would not be able to hold a sword at all.

23. This verse repeats part of 29:12. See *comm., v. 26.*

to me, saying: 21 *Ben Adam, the arm of Pharaoh, king*
of Egypt, I broke — and behold! it has not been
bound, to give medicines, to place a bandage, to bind
it, to strengthen it, to hold a sword. 22 *Therefore, thus*
says my Lord HASHEM/ELOHIM: *Behold! I am*
against Pharaoh, king of Egypt, and I shall break his
arms, the strong with the broken one, and I shall
make the sword fall from his hand; 23 *and I shall scat-*
ter Egypt among the nations and disperse them
among the lands; 24 *and I shall strengthen the arms of*
the king of Babylon and put My sword in his hand;
and I shall break the arms of Pharaoh and he shall
groan the groaning of a slain man before him.
25 *And I shall support the arms of the king of*
Babylon, but the arms of Pharaoh will drop, and they
shall know that I am HASHEM *when I put My sword*
in the hand of Babylon's king and he shall stretch it
over the land of Egypt. 26 *I shall scatter Egypt among*
the nations and disperse them among the lands; and
they shall know that I am HASHEM.

24. וְנָתַתִּי אֶת חַרְבִּי בְּיָדוֹ — *And (I shall) put My sword in his hand.*

See intro. 29:17-21.

וְנָאַק נַאֲקוֹת חָלָל — *And he shall groan the groaning of a slain man.*

Radak defines נְאָקָה as the *death rattle,* as he renders בֶּאֱנֹק חָלָל at 26:15, although the words derive from two different roots: the former from נאק, the latter from אנק.

Targum also translates both terms with the same expression: נהם.

25. וְהַחֲזַקְתִּי אֶת זְרֹעוֹת מֶלֶךְ בָּבֶל — *And I shall support the arms of the king of Babylon.*

Rashi points out that, in contrast to וְחִזַּקְתִּי in *v.* 24, which means *I will strengthen,* the word in our verse has the meaning *I will support.* This is borne out by the end of the verse *but the arms of Pharaoh will fall.* This will happen because they are not supported by God.

וְנָטָה אוֹתָהּ — *And he will stretch it.*

The use of נטה, *stretch,* with the object חֶרֶב, *sword,* is unique.

The root נטה is usually used to describe the symbolic stretching out of a hand (cf. *Exodus* 8:1) or weapon (cf. *Joshua* 8:18) over a place which is destined to be destroyed. It does not describe the actual destruction.

Nebuchadnezzar, God's messenger, need only stretch out his hand against Egypt. After that, Egypt will crumble by itself under the onslaught of God's fury *(R' Breuer).*

26. This verse is almost a repetition of *v.* 23.

[Perhaps *vs.* 24-26 must be seen as commentary to *vs.* 22-23. At first no mention is made of Nebuchadnezzar or

לא ב־ד

שָׁנָה בַּשְּׁלִישִׁי בְּאֶחָד לַחֹדֶשׁ הָיָה דְבַר־
ב יְהוָה אֵלַי לֵאמֹר: בֶּן־אָדָם אֱמֹר אֶל־
פַּרְעֹה מֶלֶךְ־מִצְרַיִם וְאֶל־הֲמוֹנוֹ אֶל־מִי
ג דָּמִיתָ בְגָדְלֶךָ: הִנֵּה אַשּׁוּר אֶרֶז בַּלְּבָנוֹן
יְפֵה עָנָף וְחֹרֶשׁ מֵצַל וּגְבַהּ קוֹמָה וּבֵין
ד עֲבֹתִים הָיְתָה צַמַּרְתּוֹ: מַיִם גִּדְּלוּהוּ
תְּהוֹם רֹמְמָתְהוּ אֶת־נַהֲרֹתֶיהָ הֹלֵךְ
סְבִיבוֹת מַטָּעָהּ וְאֶת־תְּעָלֹתֶיהָ שִׁלְּחָה

Babylon. It is God who is against Egypt. He breaks Pharaoh's arms and forces him to drop his sword, with the intention of driving Egypt into exile (*v.* 23).

The last three verses explain how this will be accomplished. Nebuchadnezzar and Babylon are to be God's agents in the execution of His plan. It is through them that God's purpose (*v.* 26) will be brought about.]

XXXI

Pharaoh is exhorted to learn a lesson from history. If mighty Assyria, which in its heyday had been absolute ruler over the whole civilized world, had fallen to Nebuchadnezzar, then Pharaoh ought not to delude himself that Egypt could escape that fate.

Some historical background is in order.

*Assyria (*אַשּׁוּר*) achieved world empire under Sennacherib. Concerning him,* Yadayim *4:4 reports that he 'moved the inhabitants of the whole world around.' He completed the destruction of the kingdom of Israel and all but conquered the kingdom of Judah as well. (See* II Kings *18:9 ff. According to* Sanhedrin *94a, Shalmaneser and Sennacherib were one and the same man). His army was wiped out miraculously at the gates of Jerusalem (*II Kings *19:35).*

*This blow effectively eliminated Assyria as a world power, but it continued as an independent nation until it fell to Nebuchadnezzar in the first year of his reign (*Megillah *11b). (See* Seder Olam *20: 'From the time that the kings of Assyria fell in Chizkiyahu's time, they never again put up a king'. However not only is this contradicted by historical records which list later Assyrian kings, it also robs the lesson for Egypt of any meaning since Pharaoh could hardly draw a lesson from the conquest of an enfeebled nation. Logic dictates, therefore, that even then Assyria was a powerful monarchy, although perhaps not as strong as it had once been. There are other readings to* Seder Olam*, according to which Assyria 'never again put up a king over the whole world,' which would eliminate this problem).*

It is from this conquest that Pharaoh is to draw his lesson. One may surmise that the lesson from Assyria's fall was particularly effective since Egypt itself had been one of Sennacherib's victims. (See Seder Olam *23;* Tosafos Sotah *9a). Egypt had learned of Assyria's strength firsthand and would surely be able to draw the required conclusion from Assyria's defeat.*

1. בַּשְּׁלִישִׁי — *In the third month.*

This is Sivan, just two months before the destruction of Jerusalem in Av. Immediately prior to Israel's downfall, Yechezkel's prophecy turns once more towards Egypt. (See pref., chs. 29-32.)

2. אֶל מִי דָּמִיתָ בְגָדְלֶךָ — *To whom are you likened in your greatness?*

Rashi translates גָּדְלֶךָ as *self-*

1 It was in the eleventh year in the third month on
the first of the month that the word of HASHEM came
to me, saying:
2 Ben Adam, say to Pharaoh, king of Egypt, and to
his multitude: to whom are you likened in your
greatness? 3 Behold! Assyria was a cedar in the
Lebanon, beautiful of branch, a shade-casting thicket
and tall of stature, and its crown was among the interwoven branches. 4 Water made it grow, the depths
elevated it. Its rivers ran around its bed, and it sent

aggrandizement. To whom did you compare yourself when you claimed greatness before Me? [Presumably *Rashi* is referring to Pharaoh's claim to divinity — see 29:3.]

Other commentators take the word simply to mean *power.* To whose might is your power comparable? You are surely no stronger than Assyria (*v.* 3).

3-17. This section is a description of the might and subsequent downfall of Assyria. As he did in ch. 17 where the subject was the royal house of Judah, Yechezkel uses the metaphor of the cedar to describe Assyria in the days of its flowering. Many of his terms here are familiar from that chapter.

3. הִנֵּה אַשּׁוּר אֶרֶז בַּלְּבָנוֹן — *Behold! Assyria was a cedar in the Lebanon.*

The cedar is the loftiest tree in the great forest of Lebanon *(Metzudos).*

יְפֵה עָנָף — *Beautiful of branch.*

In addition, it was blessed with exceptional beauty *(Metzudos).*

וְחֹרֶשׁ מֵצַל — *A shade-casting thicket.*

The Hebrew חֹרֶשׁ occurs rarely and never in a context with an unambiguous meaning. Commentators assume it to mean *forest* which is certainly the meaning of the Aramaic חוּרְשָׁא (which *Targum* uses throughout to translate the Hebrew יַעַר).

The cedar in this verse is certainly an individual tree, not a forest. The meaning must be that its branches are so thick that they cast a forestlike shadow.

וּבֵין עֲבֹתִים הָיְתָה צַמַּרְתּוֹ — *And its crown was among the interwoven branches.*

For עֲבֹתִים, see *comm.* to 19:11. For צַמֶּרֶת, see *comm.* 17:3,

In contrast to his comment to 19:11, where *Rashi* interprets עֲבֹתִים as *trees with many branches,* here he comments: *fresh trees.*

The meaning of the phrase seems to be that this particular cedar had its place among the choicest trees of the Lebanon.

The Sages (quoted in *Rashi*) offer a different interpretation. *Genesis* 10:11 tells how Ashur (after whom Assyria is named) left the land in which plans were being laid for the building of the tower which was to be a sign of rebellion against God. (See *ArtScroll* edition *Genesis* 10:11). He had the courage to leave his home and seek a new life when he saw his sons falling under the pernicious influence of Nimrod. (See *Rashi* there.) It was as a reward for that courageous action that his subsequent rise to world dominion took place. This verse refers to that incident. The crown of the cedar remained separate from the interwoven branches which surrounded it.

4. מַיִם גִּדְּלוּהוּ תְּהוֹם רֹמְמָתְהוּ — *Water made it grow, the depths elevated it.*

The cedar was richly watered and flourished accordingly.

Once more the Sages offer a different interpretation. Assyria's growth was due to *water* and *the depths.* Reference

לא
ה־י

ה אֶל כָּל־עֲצֵי הַשָּׂדֶה׃ עַל־כֵּן גָּבְהָא קֹמָתוֹ
מִכֹּל עֲצֵי הַשָּׂדֶה וַתִּרְבֶּינָה סַרְעַפֹּתָיו
וַתֶּאֱרַכְנָה פֹארֹתָו מִמַּיִם רַבִּים בְּשַׁלְּחוֹ׃
ו בִּסְעַפֹּתָיו קָנְנוּ כָּל־עוֹף הַשָּׁמַיִם וְתַחַת
פֹּארֹתָיו יָלְדוּ כֹּל חַיַּת הַשָּׂדֶה וּבְצִלּוֹ
ז יֵשְׁבוּ כֹּל גּוֹיִם רַבִּים׃ וַיְּיִף בְּגָדְלוֹ בְּאֹרֶךְ
דָּלִיּוֹתָיו כִּי־הָיָה שָׁרְשׁוֹ אֶל־מַיִם רַבִּים׃
ח אֲרָזִים לֹא־עֲמָמֻהוּ בְּגַן־אֱלֹהִים בְּרוֹשִׁים
לֹא דָמוּ אֶל־סְעַפֹּתָיו וְעַרְמֹנִים לֹא־
הָיוּ כְּפֹארֹתָיו כָּל־עֵץ בְּגַן־אֱלֹהִים לֹא־
ט דָמָה אֵלָיו בְּיָפְיוֹ׃ יָפֶה עֲשִׂיתִיו בְּרֹב
דָּלִיּוֹתָיו וַיְקַנְאֻהוּ כָּל־עֲצֵי־עֵדֶן אֲשֶׁר בְּגַן
י הָאֱלֹהִים׃ לָכֵן כֹּה אָמַר אֲדֹנָי
יֱהֹוִה יַעַן אֲשֶׁר גָּבַהְתָּ בְּקוֹמָה וַיִּתֵּן

is to the time when Nineveh, the capital city of Assyria (see *Genesis* 10:11), repented on its sins upon the urging of the prophet Jonah, who had come up from *the depths.* This merit also contributed to Assyria's growth.

וְאֵת תְּעָלֹתֶיהָ שִׁלְחָה אֶל כָּל עֲצֵי הַשָּׂדֶה — *And it sent forth its streams to all the trees of the field.*

Targum renders: She appointed her own rulers over all the lands of the earth. [In *Targum's* view, the subject of the sentence seems to be the cedar, the metaphor for Assyria. This ignores the feminine form of the verbs which would indicate that the subject is תְּהוֹם, *the depth,* which can be both masculine and feminine — see *Radak.*]

5. וַתִּרְבֶּינָה סַרְעַפֹּתָו — *And its boughs multiplied.*

In verses 6 and 8 a bough is called סְעַפָּה (without the ר).

Metzudos points out that because of the frequent interchange between ס and שׂ, סַרְעַפָּה could be the same word as שַׂרְעַף, *anxious thought (Psalms* 94:19). The same association is found in סעף (without the ר), which has the meaning of *bough (vs.* 6 and 8) and also of *thought* (as in *Psalms* 119:113). *Radak* in *Sefer HaShorashim* suggests that the basic meaning of the words could be *that which grows out of something else.* Thought is to the mind what the bough is to the tree.]

מִמַּיִם רַבִּים בְּשַׁלְּחוֹ... — *When she sent it forth because of the abundant waters.*

The expression וְתִשַׁלַּח פֹּארוֹת, *and sent out boughs,* in 17:6 is similar to our phrase which describes the expansion of these branches as a result of a generous water supply. The idea of the phrase, as expressed in *Targum,* is that Assyria expanded its influence over many nations.

6. בִּסְעַפֹּתָיו ... וְתַחַת פֹּארֹתָיו — *In its branches ... and under its boughs.*

See *comm.* to *v.* 5.

Metzudos writes that פֹּארֹת, *boughs* are the lower branches of the tree; hence the wild beasts bear their young under them rather than under the branches.

The metaphor continues the description of Assyria's far-flung influence.

7. וַיְּיִף בְּגָדְלוֹ — *It became beautiful in its greatness.*

The word derives from יפה, *to be*

forth its streams to all the trees of the field.
5 *Therefore its height surpassed all the trees of the*
field; and its boughs multiplied, and its branches grew
long when she sent it forth, because of the abun-
dant waters. 6 *In its boughs nested all the fowl of*
heaven, and under its branches all the beasts of the
fields gave birth, and in its shadow dwelt all the
many nations. 7 *It became beautiful in its greatness,*
in the length of its tendrils, for its roots were upon
abundant waters. 8 *Cedars could not obscure it in*
God's garden, the cypresses could not compare to its
boughs, and the plane trees were not like its
branches. No tree in God's garden was like it in its
beauty. 9 *I made it so beautiful with its abundant*
tendrils that it was envied by all the trees of Eden in
God's garden.
10 *Therefore, thus says my Lord HASHEM/*
ELOHIM: Because you grew tall in height and put its

beautiful. The first י, is the prefix denoting the third person future (*Radak*).

דָּלִיּוֹתָיו — *Its tendrils.*

The translation follows *Rashi*. According to *Radak* the word derives from דלה, *to raise up* and means the highest branches.

8. עֲמָמֻהוּ — *Cedars could not* [lit. *did not*] *obscure it.*

None of the mighty trees in *God's garden* could eclipse the grandeur of this cedar. עמם means *to darken* or *make dim* (see *Eichah* 4:1). At 28:3 we translated *perplexed* in context. Literally it would be translated: *No secret would keep you in the dark.)*

Ibn Ezra in *Yesod Dikduk* writes that עֲמָמֻהוּ derives from עִם, *with.* He translates: *cedars were not with him* — he was so much greater than other trees that they could not be considered in the same category.

9. יָפֶה עֲשִׂיתִיו — *I made it* [*so*] *beautiful.*

Sennacherib, Assyria's king, had said: 'By the strength of my hand have I done it and by my wisdom, for I am full of understanding' (*Isaiah* 10:13). By contrast, God tells Assyria, 'It is I Who made you beautiful (*Radak*).

10. As so many nations had done and were yet to do (see *Chullin* 89a), Assyria ascribed its success to its own prowess (see *v.* 9). Far from recognizing God as the source of his greatness, Sennacherib, through his general Ravshakeh, hurled the insolent challenge at Him: *Who among the gods of all the lands was able to save his land from me that* [*one should suppose that*] *God* [*can*] *save Jerusalem from my hand!* (*II Kings* 18:35; see *Chullin* 89a).

This pride will bring about his downfall.

גָּבַהְתָּ ... וַיִּתֵּן — *You grew tall ... and put ...*

Both the second person (you) and the third person (it) refer to Assyria. *Radak*

צַמַּרְתּוֹ אֶל־בֵּין עֲבוֹתִים וְרָם לְבָבוֹ
יא בְּגָבְהוֹ׃ וְאֶתְּנֵהוּ בְּיַד אֵיל גּוֹיִם עָשׂוֹ
יב יַעֲשֶׂה לוֹ כְּרִשְׁעוֹ גֵּרַשְׁתִּיהוּ׃ וַיִּכְרְתֻהוּ
זָרִים עָרִיצֵי גוֹיִם וַיִּטְּשֻׁהוּ אֶל־הֶהָרִים
וּבְכָל־גֵּאָיוֹת נָפְלוּ דָלִיּוֹתָיו וַתִּשָּׁבַרְנָה
פֹּרֹאתָיו בְּכָל־אֲפִיקֵי הָאָרֶץ וַיֵּרְדוּ מִצִּלּוֹ
יג כָּל־עַמֵּי הָאָרֶץ וַיִּטְּשֻׁהוּ׃ עַל־מַפַּלְתּוֹ
יִשְׁכְּנוּ כָּל־עוֹף הַשָּׁמָיִם וְאֶל־פֹּרֹאתָיו הָיוּ
יד כֹּל חַיַּת הַשָּׂדֶה׃ לְמַעַן אֲשֶׁר לֹא־יִגְבְּהוּ
בְקוֹמָתָם כָּל־עֲצֵי־מַיִם וְלֹא־יִתְּנוּ אֶת־
צַמַּרְתָּם אֶל־בֵּין עֲבֹתִים וְלֹא־יַעַמְדוּ
אֲלֵיהֶם בְּגָבְהָם כָּל־שֹׁתֵי מָיִם כִּי כֻלָּם
נִתְּנוּ לַמָּוֶת אֶל־אֶרֶץ תַּחְתִּית בְּתוֹךְ בְּנֵי
טו אָדָם אֶל־יוֹרְדֵי בוֹר׃ כֹּה־אָמַר

points out that such changes in person are not infrequent.

11. אֵל גּוֹיִם — *The strongest of nations.*

This refers to Babylon. In the first year of Nebuchadnezzar's reign he conquered Nineveh, capital of Assyria *(Megillah* 11b cited in *Rashi).*

עָשׂוֹ יַעֲשֶׂה לוֹ — *He shall deal freely with him.*

The doubling of the verb indicates that Nebuchadnezzar will be in complete control of Assyria. Nothing will prevent him from doing whatever he wishes *(Rashi).*

כְּרִשְׁעוֹ גֵּרַשְׁתִּיהוּ — *Commensurate with his wickedness I have driven him out.*

Once more the stress is on God's involvement in Assyria's destruction. Nebuchadnezzar is the agent, but it is God Who wills his actions.

This treatment of the verse follows the cantillation. However, *Radak* points out that כְּרִשְׁעוֹ can instead be read together with the foregoing: *He shall act toward him in accordance with his wickedness.*

12. וַיִּטְּשֻׁהוּ — *They abandoned him.*

This expression appears twice in this verse. *Targum* translates both: רטש, which he uses consistently to translate נטש (cf. *Exodus* 23:11), *to abandon.*

Rashi translates the first expression: *and they threw it upon the ground.*

[*Rashi* gives as reference *Numbers* 11:31; but there he himself translates *and it spread out.*]

Rashi is silent concerning the second expression. The context indicates, *and they will forsake it* (See 29:5).

Metzudos translates the first *and they scattered* [*its branches*], *but he translates the second like Rashi.*

[One can readily see that the concepts abandoning, spreading, and scattering are all related. See *Sefer HaShorashim* of *Ibn Janach* to נטש.]

13. עַל מַפַּלְתּוֹ — *Upon its ruins.*

Within the context of the metaphor and taking verse 6 into consideration, one would assume that מַפֶּלֶת is *a ruin,* that is, *something that was thrown down,* (from נפל, *to fall*) and that the birds who used to nest in the crown of

31
11-15 *crown among the interwoven branches, and its heart became proud because of its height,* [11] *so I put him in the hand of the strongest of nations, he shall deal freely with him; commensurate with his wickedness I have driven him out.* [12] *Strangers cut it down, the mighty among the nations, and they abandoned him. Upon the mountains and in all the valleys its tendrils fell, and its boughs broke in all the channels of the earth, and all the nations of the earth descended from its shadow and forsook him.* [13] *Upon its ruins rested all the birds of heaven, and upon its branches were all the beasts of the field.* [14] *In order that none of the water-trees shall be haughty with their stature and will not place their crowns among the interwoven branches, nor will their mighty ones endure in their height — all that drink water — for they are all given over to death into the nether earth into the midst of men, among those that descend to the pit.*

[15] *Thus says my Lord HASHEM/ELOHIM: On the*

the lofty cedar (*v.* 6) now dwell among the shattered limbs of the fallen giant.

However, *Targum,* renders: *on the carcass of the slain.* It is, of course, possible that *Targum* offers the explanation rather than the translation; but it is also possible that he translates מַפֶּלֶת as *carcass* since that is its meaning in *Judges* 14:8. This is also the opinion of *Eliezer of Beaugency* who explains that מַפֶּלֶת is used for *carcass* since it *falls down.*

14. לְמַעַן — *In order that.*

Assyria's fate is to be a lesson to other nations. They are to take note of the results of misplaced pride.

עֲצֵי־מַיִם — *Water—trees.*

Most commentators take עֲצֵ־מַיִם as a generic term which includes the cedar upon which the whole metaphor (*v.* 3 ff.) is based. Other cedars which draw their might from plentiful water as this one had done (*v.* 4) would be held back from making the same mistakes.

Rashi, however, takes עֲצֵי־מַיִם in a much more limited sense. *Water trees* are trees which grow tall and have long tendrils because of the abundance of available water, but which lack the inner strength of the real cedar. It appears that the *cedar* of verse 3 was not a true cedar at all. Its pride prevented it from recognizing the truth about itself, and that was the cause of its downfall.

אֵלֵיהֶם — *Their mighty ones.*

The translation follows *Metzudos.* אֵל is used in the same sense as in verse 11.

Radak writes that אֵלָה is the name of a tree, as in *Isaiah* 6:13. (See also 6:13).

כִּי כֻלָּם נִתְּנוּ לַמָּוֶת ... — *For they are all given over to death ...*

This is part of the lesson meant for the kings who are to learn from Assyria's downfall. The realization that they, like everyone else, are destined for the grave will help them to control their pride.

לא
טז־יח

אֲדֹנָי יֱהֹוִה בְּיוֹם רִדְתּוֹ שְׁאֹלָה הֶאֱבַלְתִּי
כִּסֵּתִי עָלָיו אֶת־תְּהוֹם וָאֶמְנַע נַהֲרוֹתֶיהָ
וַיִּכָּלְאוּ מַיִם רַבִּים וָאַקְדִּר עָלָיו לְבָנוֹן
טז וְכָל־עֲצֵי הַשָּׂדֶה עָלָיו עֻלְפֶּה׃ מִקּוֹל
מַפַּלְתּוֹ הִרְעַשְׁתִּי גוֹיִם בְּהוֹרִדִי אֹתוֹ
שְׁאֹלָה אֶת־יוֹרְדֵי בוֹר וַיִּנָּחֲמוּ בְּאֶרֶץ
תַּחְתִּית כָּל־עֲצֵי־עֵדֶן מִבְחַר וְטוֹב־לְבָנוֹן
יז כָּל־שֹׁתֵי מָיִם׃ גַּם־הֵם אִתּוֹ יָרְדוּ שְׁאֹלָה
אֶל־חַלְלֵי־חָרֶב וּזְרֹעוֹ יָשְׁבוּ בְצִלּוֹ בְּתוֹךְ
יח גּוֹיִם׃ אֶל־מִי דָמִיתָ כָּכָה בְּכָבוֹד וּבְגֹדֶל
בַּעֲצֵי־עֵדֶן וְהוּרַדְתָּ אֶת־עֲצֵי־עֵדֶן אֶל־
אֶרֶץ תַּחְתִּית בְּתוֹךְ עֲרֵלִים תִּשְׁכַּב אֶת־
חַלְלֵי־חֶרֶב הוּא פַרְעֹה וְכָל־הֲמוֹנֹה נְאֻם

לב
א

א אֲדֹנָי יֱהֹוִה׃ וַיְהִי בִּשְׁתֵּי עֶשְׂרֵה

15. הֶאֱבַלְתִּי — *I caused mourning.*

According to *Rashi* there is an implied object: *I caused* [*mourners*] *to mourn.*

Radak reads the word with the following phrase. *I have caused the depths to mourn over him* [the cedar whom they had nourished (*v.* 4)] *and covered them in mourning.*

Radak's interpretation ignores the cantillation, which makes a break between הֶאֱבַלְתִּי and the following phrase.

It is not infrequent that commentators interpret in opposition to the cantillation (cf. *Rashi, Isaiah* 1:9, *Jeremiah* 6:29).

כִּסֵּתִי עָלָיו אֶת תְּהוֹם — *I have covered the depths against it.*

I have prevented the depths from rising up to water it as they had done in the past, so that they should not extinguish the fire which was consuming it *(Rashi).*

Radak and *Metzudos* render: *I have covered the depths in mourning clothes.*

וָאֶמְנַע נַהֲרוֹתֶיהָ — *And* [*I have*] *withheld its rivers.*

These are the rivers which used to surround the bed in which the cedar was planted *(Rashi).* For an explanation of the feminine form, see *comm., v.* 4.

וַיִּכָּלְאוּ מַיִם רַבִּים — *And the abundant waters ceased.*

These are the waters which had made its branches grow (*v.* 5) *(Rashi).*

וְכָל עֲצֵי הַשָּׂדֶה עָלָיו עֻלְפֶּה — *And all the trees of the field grew faint because of it.*

Verse 4 tells how *the depths* had sent their streams to all the trees to water and invigorate them. As the depths are *covered,* these streams disappear and the trees grow *faint* with the loss of water *(Rashi).*

16. וַיִּנָּחֲמוּ בְּאֶרֶץ תַּחְתִּית כָּל־עֲצֵי־עֵדֶן — *Then were comforted in the nether earth all the trees of Eden.*

The mighty kings who are already in *Gehinnom* will become reconciled to their fate when they see that it is shared by the mighty Assyrian king *(Rashi).*

31
16-18

day that he descended to the grave I caused mourning; I have covered the depths against it and withheld her rivers and the abundant waters ceased. I have darkened the Lebanon because of it, and all the trees of the field grew faint because of it.
16 *From the sound of its fall I made the nations tremble, when I brought him down to the grave with those that descend to the pit. Then were comforted in the nether earth all the trees of Eden, the choicest and best of the Lebanon, all that drink water.*
17 *They too descended with him to the grave, to those slain by the sword, — his supporters who had lived under his protection among the nations.*
18 *To whom did you thus liken yourself, in glory and size among Eden's trees? Now you were brought down with Eden's trees into the nether earth. Among the uncircumcised you will lay with the slain of the sword. This is Pharaoh and all his multitude — the words of my Lord* HASHEM/ELOHIM.

17. אֶל־חַלְלֵי־חָרֶב — *To those slain by the sword.*

32:17 ff. expands on this theme.

וּזְרֹעוֹ יָשְׁבוּ בְצִלּוֹ בְּתוֹךְ גּוֹיִם — *His supporters* [lit. *his arm*] *who had lived under his protection among the nations.*

His arm is a metaphor for those who had helped Assyria. Many nations had lived under Assyria's protection *(in its shade)* and had at the same time supplied forces for its armies *(Rashi).* These allies and supporters would descend with Assyria into *Gehinnom.*

18. אֶל מִי דָמִיתָ כָּכָה — *To whom did you thus liken yourself.*

The verse turns back to Pharaoh and exhorts him to learn the needed lesson from Assyria's fall. Dare he compare himself to mighty Assyria? Yet even Assyria was destroyed; surely Pharaoh has no right to consider himself immune to punishment for his misdeeds.

בְּתוֹךְ עֲרֵלִים — *Among the uncircumcised.*

See *comm.* 28:10.

XXXII

In the kinnah, *the* lament *which Yechezkel sang over Tyre's king, (pref. ch. 27) we recognized the true greatness of Israel's prophets, who mourned the downfall of the gentile nations with the same hot tears which they shed over their own (see pref., ch. 17).*

In the case of Tyre, this was less surprising than in the case of Egypt. Tyre, at least overtly, had always been a good friend of the Jewish people (see intro., chs. 26-28). Its king had been a man of vast potential, and one can readily understand why Yechezkel would be moved to lament when he succumbed to his baser nature.

שָׁנָה בִּשְׁנֵי־עָשָׂר חֹדֶשׁ בְּאֶחָד לַחֹדֶשׁ
ב הָיָה דְבַר־יְהוָה אֵלַי לֵאמֹר׃ בֶּן־אָדָם שָׂא
קִינָה עַל־פַּרְעֹה מֶלֶךְ־מִצְרַיִם וְאָמַרְתָּ
אֵלָיו כְּפִיר גּוֹיִם נִדְמֵיתָ וְאַתָּה כַּתַּנִּים
בַּיַּמִּים וַתָּגַח בְּנַהֲרוֹתֶיךָ וַתִּדְלַח־מַיִם
ג בְּרַגְלֶיךָ וַתִּרְפֹּס נַהֲרוֹתָם׃ כֹּה
אָמַר אֲדֹנָי יֱהוִה וּפָרַשְׂתִּי עָלֶיךָ אֶת־
רִשְׁתִּי בִּקְהַל עַמִּים רַבִּים וְהֶעֱלוּךָ
ד בְחֶרְמִי׃ וּנְטַשְׁתִּיךָ בָאָרֶץ עַל־פְּנֵי הַשָּׂדֶה
אֲטִילֶךָ וְהִשְׁכַּנְתִּי עָלֶיךָ כָּל־עוֹף הַשָּׁמַיִם
ה וְהִשְׂבַּעְתִּי מִמְּךָ חַיַּת כָּל־הָאָרֶץ׃ וְנָתַתִּי
אֶת־בְּשָׂרְךָ עַל־הֶהָרִים וּמִלֵּאתִי הַגֵּאָיוֹת

Egypt's, however, had been quite a different record. Egypt had never had Israel's good at heart, and time and again proved a bitter disappointment to them (see footnote 23:8). Most recently, a scant three years before the date of this chapter, Pharaoh had let Israel down at the most crucial point of their confrontation with Babylon (Jeremiah *37:5-7). It would have been understandable for Israel, if not to gloat at Egypt's downfall, at least to view it with quiet satisfaction.*

Yechezkel is taught differently. Just one year after the Temple's destruction he is to take up a kinnah over Pharaoh.

1. The prophecy takes place in Adar of the twelfth year, that is, some twenty months after the destruction.

2. כְּפִיר גּוֹיִם נִדְמֵיתָ — *To a young lion among the nations were you likened.*

See 19:2 for כְּפִיר.

The translation follows *Radak* and *Metzudos* and is borne out by *Targum,* who renders: *You were mighty among the nations.*

However, this translation ignores the fact that elsewhere when Yechezkel uses דמה in the sense *to be similar to,* he uses it in the *kal, active,* rather than in the *niphal, passive* in which it occurs here (cf. 31:21).

Perhaps because of this consideration, *Rashi* reads this phrase together with the next one and renders as follows: *You, who should simply have been a sea monster in the waters, pretended* (not דומה, *to be similar,* but נדמה, *to act as though similar*) *to be a lion among the nations.* Because of your pride, you went beyond that which was rightfully yours.

Eliezer of Beaugency agrees with *Rashi* and adds the thought that the sea-monster has his every need at hand in the water, while the lion is occasionally forced to leave his natural habitat to hunt for food. Pharaoh's expansionary campaign had no real justification. He could have filled his needs within his own country.

R' Breuer takes דמה in its meaning *to cease,* thus נדמה means *to be made to cease.* He renders: *You who were a roaring lion among the nations were silenced* (made to cease your roaring).

וַתָּגַח בְּנַהֲרוֹתֶיךָ — *And you burst forth with your rivers.*

It was in the twelfth year, in the twelfth month on
the first of the month; the word of HASHEM came to
me, saying:

Ben Adam, take up a lament for Pharaoh, king of
Egypt, and say to him: To a young lion among the
nations, were you likened, but you are like a monster
in the seas and you burst forth with your rivers and
you churned water with your feet and fouled their
rivers. 3 Thus says my Lord HASHEM/ELOHIM: I will
spread My net over you with the company of many
nations, and they will raise you in My destructive
net; 4 and I shall abandon you upon the earth; upon
the open field will I hurl you, and I will cause to settle
upon you all the fowl of heaven, and I will sate with
you the beasts of the land; 5 and I will lay your flesh
upon the mountains and fill the valleys with your

גיח means *to burst forth* (for example, the baby from its mother's womb, *Psalms* 22:10). The sea monster burst forth with his rivers (his armies — *Radak*) beyond his normal boundaries *(Rashi).*

Metzudos derives וַתָּגַח from נגח, *to push* or *gore*, and the phrase means *You gored among your rivers* (that is, within your country).

וַתִּדְלַח מַיִם בְּרַגְלֶיךָ — *And you churned water with your feet.*

דלח (and רפס in the next phrase) combines the ideas of churning the water and of dirtying it with the mud that is swirled around in it.

The sea monster, Egypt, did not really have legs but God made legs for it so that it could pass through the waters of the nations and foul their rivers *(Rashi).* [The fouling of the river is a metaphor for Egypt's conquests of the neighboring lands.]

According to *Targum*, the verse describes Egypt's campaigns into foreign lands and the havoc which they wreaked there.

3. בִּקְהַל עַמִּים רַבִּים — *With the company of many nations.*

This describes the armies which were to be brought by Nebuchadnezzar in his invasion of Egypt *(Metzudos).*

בְּחֶרְמִי — *In My destructive net.*

Though all commentators agree that רֶשֶׁת and חֶרֶם are synonymous for *net*, *Radak* adds that use of the word חֶרֶם adds the further implication of *destruction*, the other meaning of חרם.

4. וּנְטַשְׁתִּיךָ בָאָרֶץ — *And I shall abandon you upon the earth.*

See *comm.* 31:12.

The corpses of the Egyptians will lie unburied on the open fields, where the birds and animals will feed on them *(Metzudos).*

5. עַל הֶהָרִים — *Upon the mountains.*

Radak writes that the mountains are mentioned because the Egyptians would flee there, thinking to escape from the invading armies. Alternatively, he suggests that the birds might carry the flesh of the corpses into the mountains.

רָמוּתֶךָ — *With your decay.*

The translation follows one of *Rashi's* suggestions. [רָמוּתֶךָ stems from

ו רָמוּתֶךָ: וְהִשְׁקֵיתִי אֶרֶץ צָפָתְךָ מִדָּמְךָ
אֶל־הֶהָרִים וַאֲפִקִים יִמָּלְאוּן מִמֶּךָּ:
ז וְכִסֵּיתִי בְכַבּוֹתְךָ שָׁמַיִם וְהִקְדַּרְתִּי אֶת־
כֹּכְבֵיהֶם שֶׁמֶשׁ בֶּעָנָן אֲכַסֶּנּוּ וְיָרֵחַ לֹא־
ח יָאִיר אוֹרוֹ: כָּל־מְאוֹרֵי אוֹר בַּשָּׁמַיִם
אַקְדִּירֵם עָלֶיךָ וְנָתַתִּי חֹשֶׁךְ עַל־אַרְצְךָ
ט נְאֻם אֲדֹנָי יֱהֹוִה: וְהִכְעַסְתִּי לֵב עַמִּים
רַבִּים בַּהֲבִיאִי שִׁבְרְךָ בַּגּוֹיִם עַל־אֲרָצוֹת
י אֲשֶׁר לֹא־יְדַעְתָּם: וַהֲשִׁמּוֹתִי עָלֶיךָ עַמִּים
רַבִּים וּמַלְכֵיהֶם יִשְׂעֲרוּ עָלֶיךָ שַׂעַר
בְּעוֹפְפִי חַרְבִּי עַל־פְּנֵיהֶם וְחָרְדוּ לִרְגָעִים
יא אִישׁ לְנַפְשׁוֹ בְּיוֹם מַפַּלְתֶּךָ: כִּי
כֹּה אָמַר אֲדֹנָי יֱהֹוִה חֶרֶב מֶלֶךְ־בָּבֶל
יב תְּבוֹאֶךָ: בְּחַרְבוֹת גִּבּוֹרִים אַפִּיל הֲמוֹנֶךָ

רמה, *to grow rotten* or *decay.*] The alternative which *Rashi* offers is that the word derives from רמה, *to cast out,* and means: *that part of you which is cast out* [the corpses].

Metzudos derives the word from רום, *to be high.* The meaning is *your former pride.*

6. אֶרֶץ צָפָתְךָ — *The land where you swam.*

צָפָתְךָ is derived from צוף, *to flow* or *float.*

The commentators offer various translations of this phrase: the land within which you (the sea monster) *swam (Rashi);* the land which is normally covered with water *(Radak; Metzudos);* the land which you inundated with your thrashings (וַתָּגַח בְּנַהֲרוֹתֶיךָ, *v.* 2) *(Eliezer of Beaugency).*

וַאֲפִקִים יִמָּלְאוּן מִמֶּךָּ — *And the channels shall be filled from you.*

The channels which flowed with water will be fillled with your blood *(Radak; Metzudos).*

7. בְּכַבּוֹתְךָ — *With your smoke* [lit. *extinguishing*].

כַּבּוֹתְךָ derives from כבה, *to extinguish.* The smoke that rises after your fire has been *extinguished* will cover the heavens. Your downfall will sadden all who hear of it as they realize that they may also, one day, share your fate *(Rashi).*

וְהִקְדַּרְתִּי אֶת־כֹּכְבֵיהֶם — *And I shall darken their stars.*

The entire verse, speaking of the darkening of the heavens, reflects the feelings of a victim of tragedy. When a person suffers disaster, the whole world seems dark to him *(Metzudos).*

8. כָּל־מְאוֹרֵי אוֹר בַּשָּׁמַיִם — *All the bright lights of heaven.*

These are the heavenly powers who interceded with God in Egypt's behalf *(Rashi).*

9. וְהִכְעַסְתִּי לֵב עַמִּים רַבִּים — *Then I shall vex the heart of many nations.*

Although כַּעַס usually means *anger,* it is used here in the sense of *fear* or *con-*

decay. 6 *I will inundate the land where you swam*
with blood until the mountaintops, — and the chan-
nels shall be filled from you; 7 *and with your smoke I*
will cover the heavens, and I shall darken their stars.
Then I will cover with a cloud and the moon shall not
shed its light. 8 *All the bright lights of heaven — I will*
darken them because of you, and I shall cast darkness
upon your land — the words of my Lord
HASHEM/ELOHIM.

9 *Then I shall vex the heart of many nations, when*
I bring your destruction among the peoples, into
lands which you did not know; 10 *and I will appall*
many nations because of you, and their kings will
shake with trembling concerning you when I bran-
dish My sword upon their faces; and they will trem-
ble constantly, each man for his own sake, upon the
day of your downfall.

11 *For thus says my Lord HASHEM/ELOHIM: The*
sword of Babylon's king will come upon you. 12 *By*
the swords of the mighty I shall topple your mul-

---

sternation. Targum renders זוע, which the *Targumim* generally use for words like פַּחַד, *fear (I Samuel* 11:7) or חֲרָדָה, *trembling (Jeremiah* 30:5).

בַּהֲבִיאִי שִׁבְרְךָ בַּגּוֹיִם — *When I bring your destruction among the peoples.*

This will be when the nations see your wounded and crippled remnants *(Targum);* or, as *Radak* suggests, when news of your destruction reaches the nations.

10. וּמַלְכֵיהֶם יִשְׂעֲרוּ עָלֶיךָ שַׂעַר — *And their kings will shake with trembling concerning you.*

See *comm.* 27:35.

בְּעוֹפְפִי חַרְבִּי עַל פְּנֵיהֶם — *When I brandish My sword upon their faces.*

עוף suggests flying and movement. It is used in a borrowed sense to picture the brandished sword *(Metzudos).*

My sword [חַרְבִּי] refers to Nebuchadnezzar. He is described as God's sword because he is God's agent in the execution of His plans *(Metzudos).* See intro., 29:17-21; 30:23.

וְחָרְדוּ לִרְגָעִים — *And they will tremble constantly.*

See *comm.* 2:16.

אִישׁ לְנַפְשׁוֹ — *Each man for his own sake.*

Each man will fear that Pharaoh's fate might overtake him *(Metzudos).*

13-15 In *Rashi's* view, the next three verses tell of the curtailment of Egyptian activities outside its own border. The beginning of this chapter describes Egypt's incursions into foreign lands. These will now cease.

Radak writes that reference is to the desolation which will come about within Egypt's own borders. Its busy waterways will become quiet and unused while the people will be in exile.

עָרִיצֵי גוֹיִם כֻּלָּם וְשָׁדְדוּ אֶת־גְּאוֹן מִצְרַיִם
יג וְנִשְׁמַד כָּל־הֲמוֹנָהּ׃ וְהַאֲבַדְתִּי אֶת־כָּל־
בְּהֶמְתָּהּ מֵעַל מַיִם רַבִּים וְלֹא תִדְלָחֵם
רֶגֶל־אָדָם עוֹד וּפַרְסוֹת בְּהֵמָה לֹא
יד תִדְלָחֵם׃ אָז אַשְׁקִיעַ מֵימֵיהֶם וְנַהֲרוֹתָם
טו כַּשֶּׁמֶן אוֹלִיךְ נְאֻם אֲדֹנָי יֱהֹוִה׃ בְּתִתִּי
אֶת־אֶרֶץ מִצְרַיִם שְׁמָמָה וּנְשַׁמָּה אֶרֶץ
מִמְּלֹאָהּ בְּהַכּוֹתִי אֶת־כָּל־יוֹשְׁבֵי בָהּ
טז וְיָדְעוּ כִּי־אֲנִי יְהוָה׃ קִינָה הִיא וְקוֹנְנוּהָ
בְּנוֹת הַגּוֹיִם תְּקוֹנֵנָּה אוֹתָהּ עַל־מִצְרַיִם
וְעַל־כָּל־הֲמוֹנָהּ תְּקוֹנֵנָּה אוֹתָהּ נְאֻם
אֲדֹנָי יֱהֹוִה׃
יז וַיְהִי בִּשְׁתֵּי עֶשְׂרֵה שָׁנָה בַּחֲמִשָּׁה עָשָׂר
לַחֹדֶשׁ הָיָה דְבַר־יְהוָה אֵלַי לֵאמֹר׃

13. עוֹד — *Again.*

According to *Rashi,* that reference is to Egypt's foreign conquests, 'again' is meant literally. Egypt would be so weakened by Nebuchadnezzar's victory that she would never again be a conqueror beyond her own borders.

In *Radak's* view this describes the land of Egypt while its people are in exile. Accordingly, עוֹד can only mean *for a long time.* The desolation of the land will last for a long time until the people return from their exile (see 29:11).

14. אָז אַשְׁקִיעַ מֵימֵיהֶם — *Then I shall make their waters settle.*

שקע means to *sink.* Waters which are constantly churned by the passage of man and beast become dirty. With the defeat of Egypt, however, these waters will be quite still. All the mud will sink to the bottom *(Rashi).*

וְנַהֲרוֹתָם כַּשֶּׁמֶן אוֹלִיךְ — *And cause their rivers to run like oil.*

This repeats the thought of the earlier phrase. The rivers will run as smoothly as oil because no mud will be churned up in them *(Rashi).*

15. אֶרֶץ מִמְּלֹאָהּ — *The land from its fullness.*

Egypt will be transformed from its present fullness and prosperity to utter desolation *(Rashi).*

17-32. The prophetic eye moves from the present to the distant future of אַחֲרִית הַיָּמִים, *the End of Days (Metzudos). (*See also *Abarbanel* and *Malbim.)*

Sotah 9a speaks of three cups [of defeat and suffering] which Egypt was destined to drink in the course of its history. The first had been in Moses' days, the second was Egypt's defeat at Babylonian hands and the third will be the one which Egypt will drink together with her fellow nations (עם חברותיה) in Messianic times. (See *comm.* 29:2.)

It seems likely that this final prophecy against Egypt describes that third 'cup' of punishment.

In his vision, Yechezkel is to consign Pharaoh and his hordes to the אֶרֶץ תַּחְתִּיּוֹת, *nethermost earth,* together with all יוֹרְדֵי בוֹר, *those that descend into the pit.* That pit, in *Targum's* words, is בֵּית

32
13-17

titudes; the strong ones of the nations are they all, and they shall despoil the pride of Egypt, and all her multitude shall be destroyed; [13] *and I shall destroy all her beasts from beside abundant waters, nor shall the foot of man trouble them again, and the hooves of beasts shall not trouble them.* [14] *Then I shall make their waters settle and cause their rivers to run like oil — the words of my Lord HASHEM/ELOHIM.* [15] *When I make the land of Egypt desolate and waste — the land from its fullness — when I smite all that dwell in it, then shall they know that I am HASHEM.* [16] *It is a lamentation and they shall lament it, the daughters of the nations shall lament with it — upon Egypt and upon all her multitude they will lament the words of my Lord HASHEM/ELOHIM.*

[17] *It was in the twelfth year on the fifteenth of the month, the word of HASHEM came to me, saying:*

אֲבַדּוֹנָא, *the place of ultimate and unrelieved loss — Gehinnom.*

If we are to understand this extremely obscure passage we must be guided by the key phrases, which, by their constant repetition, lend form and substance to the picture which the prophet paints for us.

The inhabitants of this *Gehinnom* are described ten times as עֲרֵלִים, *uncircumcised ones.* The fault which condemned them to their fate was that *they spread terror over the Land of Life.*

The term עֲרֵלִים is discussed in *comm.* 28:10. Its constant use in our passage necessitates a reexamination of its meaning.

The term עָרֵל generally refers to *an uncircumcised male,* but it also has two other definitions. It describes the state of a fruit tree during its first three years, when it is forbidden to eat its fruits (*Leviticus* 19:23); and when used in tandem with לֵב, *heart,* [עֲרַל לֵב], it describes one whose heart is obtuse and unreceptive to spiritual stimuli (*Deuteronomy* 10:16).

Rashi (Leviticus 19:23) defines עָרֵל as a synonym of אטם, *to be closed off.*

One of the promises which God made to the Jewish people about the Messianic age is that He will *circumcise your hearts (Deuteronomy* 30:6). *Ramban* (there) explains that this circumcision of the heart means a return to the state of innocence and rectitude (יְשָׁרוּת) that had been Adam's nature before he sinned. Sin 'closes off' the heart, making it unreceptive to the apprehension of Godliness. The hallmark of the Messianic era will be the openness and receptiveness of mankind's hearts to God.

The inhabitants of the *Gehinnom* to which Pharaoh finds himself consigned are עֲרֵלִים. Their lives were lived in a way which precluded the possibility of their ever becoming fit for the kind of existence which the Messianic era requires. Their עָרְלַת הַלֵּב, *closing off of the heart,* was such that it would forever shut out the light of the Divine.

Throughout the passage *Targum* renders אֶרֶץ חַיִּים (lit. *land of life*) as *the*

יח בֶּן־אָדָם נְהֵה עַל־הֲמוֹן מִצְרַיִם וְהוֹרִדֵהוּ
אוֹתָהּ וּבְנוֹת גּוֹיִם אַדִּרִם אֶל־אֶרֶץ
יט תַּחְתִּיּוֹת אֶת־יוֹרְדֵי בוֹר: מִמִּי נָעָמְתָּ רְדָה
כ וְהָשְׁכְּבָה אֶת־עֲרֵלִים: בְּתוֹךְ חַלְלֵי־חֶרֶב
יִפֹּלוּ חֶרֶב נִתָּנָה מָשְׁכוּ אוֹתָהּ וְכָל־
כא הֲמוֹנֶיהָ: יְדַבְּרוּ־לוֹ אֵלֵי גִבּוֹרִים מִתּוֹךְ
שְׁאוֹל אֶת־עֹזְרָיו יָרְדוּ שָׁכְבוּ הָעֲרֵלִים
כב חַלְלֵי חָרֶב: שָׁם אַשּׁוּר וְכָל־קְהָלָהּ

land of Israel (see *commm.* 26:20). The term אֶרֶץ חַיִּים, *land of life,* is used in contrast with אֶרֶץ תַּחְתִּיּוֹת, *nethermost earth,* and בּוֹר, *pit,* which describe *Gehinnom.* Thus, where the latter are בֵּית אַבְדָנָא, *the place of ultimate hopelessness* where no growth or development is possible, אֶרֶץ חַיִּים would be *the land* where true *life,* in its sense of growth, can flourish. (For a discussion of the land of Israel as the ideal location for spiritual growth, see *comm.* 20:6.)

These kings had spread terror over the אֶרֶץ חַיִּים, *land of life.* As Israel fell under foreign dominion, beginning with the Assyrian conquest, and especially during the centuries of darkness which started with Babylon's ascendancy (see *comm.* 21:24-27), spiritual 'life' had gradually been choked out of the *land of life.* God had willed that the land of Israel should be that place on earth where man could actualize his spiritual strivings, and these kings had tried to frustrate God's will.

If history is the story of man's groping for, and ultimate attainment of Godliness, then these kings are its true villains. They had imposed their עֲרֵלוּת, *closing off of the heart,* upon the land. That is the true *terror* to which the land of Israel had been subjected.

However, the ultimate mover of history is God Himself. Verse 32 teaches how this *terror* became the forerunner of God's purpose in creation. In the end it will be the fear of God which fills the land.

[These prefatory remarks assume *Rashi's* interpretation (see below) that this passage is a description of what is to take place in *Gehinnom.* In *Metzudos'* view the description is not of *Gehinnom* but of the communal grave in which will be buried the soldiers who will fall in the great war which is to come at the end of days (see chs. 38 and 39). See further below.]

17. The verse makes no mention of the month in which this vision took place. It is assumed to be the twelfth month as in verse 1 *(Radak).*

18. נְהֵה עַל הֲמוֹן מִצְרַיִם — *Wail for the multitude of Egypt.*

See the prefatory remarks to ch. 27 for a discussion of the laments which Jewish prophets took up for the non-Jewish nations. Unlike the Midrash quoted there, *Radak* to this verse writes that these laments were meant as texts for the use of gentile nations. The Jewish prophet, on the contrary, would rejoice at the downfall of God's enemies.

וְהוֹרִדֵהוּ — *And cast it down.*

The prophet did not lower Pharaoh into the pit. He only predicted his fate *(Metzudos).* [Nevertheless, since God's word is bound to come true, it is as though Yechezkel himself consigned Pharaoh to the pit].

וּבְנוֹת גּוֹיִם אַדִּרִם — *And the daughters of mighty nations.*

R' Breuer comments that אַדִּירִים, *mighty,* is written אַדִּרִם, missing two

[18] *Ben Adam, wail for the multitude of Egypt and cast
it down, her and the daughters of mighty nations to
the nether world, together with those that descend to
the pit.* [19] *Whom have you surpassed in beauty? Go
down and be laid with the uncircumcised.* [20] *They
shall fall amid those slain by the sword; to the sword
they are delivered. Drag her and all her multitudes.*
[21] *From the nether world, the strong among the
mighty will speak about him and his helpers, 'They
have descended, lain among the uncircumcised victims of the sword.'* [22] *Assyria is there and all her mul-*

letters, to point out how puny these seemingly mighty nations were to the prophetic eye.

אֶל אֶרֶץ תַּחְתִּיּוֹת אֶת יוֹרְדֵי בוֹר — *To the nether world, together with those that descend to the pit.*

The 'nether world' is *Gehinnom* according to *Rashi.* According to *Metzudos* it is a communal grave for the fallen in the wars of Gog and Magog (Chs. 38 and 39).

19. מִמִּי נָעָמְתָּ — *Whom have you surpassed in beauty?*

Are you better than any of the other nations? You also will go down to the pit and be laid to rest with them *(Rashi).*

20. The seeming redundancy of phrases here is explained by *Metzudos* as prophetic idiom which tolerates [or perhaps requires] a manifold repetition of the same thought.

21. יְדַבְּרוּ לוֹ — *Will speak about him.*

The translation follows *Rashi* who quotes the rule that words like לִי [lit. *to me*] and לוֹ [lit. *to him*] after the verb דבר, *to speak* are to be translated *about* rather than *to.*

The complete subject of the sentence is: *The strong among the mighty from the nether world.* They will speak *about* Pharaoh (לוֹ) *and his helpers,* saying: *They have descended ...*

Radak differs from *Rashi* in two points. He renders לוֹ, *'to' him* and he treats the last words of the sentence ... יָרְדוּ שָׁכְבוּ as a description of *his helpers.* The sentence is to be read as follows: *From the nether world the strong among the mighty will speak to Pharaoh and to his helpers who had gone down.* The verse does not report what they will say. Their words are left to the imagination of the reader.

מִתּוֹךְ שְׁאוֹל — *From the nether world.*

The translation follows *Rashi* who, as noted in verse 18, interprets this passage as a description of the events happening in *Gehinnom.* According to *Metzudos* שְׁאוֹל is to be translated, *grave.*

22. Throughout this and the following verses *Rashi* and *Metzudos* continue to interpret in accordance with their respective approaches to the entire passage. According to *Rashi* we have a description of *Gehinnom.* According to *Metzudos,* of the mass grave for the fallen in the war of the end of days.

Wherever there are substantive differences between the two opinions we will first interpret according to *Rashi,* then according to *Metzudos.*

שָׁם אַשּׁוּר וְכָל־קְהָלָהּ — *Assyria is there and all her multitude.*

When Egypt descends into *Gehinnom* it will find itself awaited by Assyria and her multitudes. [Assyria had presumably been in *Gehinnom* from the

סְבִיבוֹתָיו קִבְרֹתָיו כֻּלָּם חֲלָלִים הַנֹּפְלִים
כג בֶּחָרֶב: אֲשֶׁר־נִתְּנוּ קִבְרֹתֶיהָ בְּיַרְכְּתֵי־בוֹר
וַיְהִי קְהָלָהּ סְבִיבוֹת קְבֻרָתָהּ כֻּלָּם חֲלָלִים
נֹפְלִים בַּחֶרֶב אֲשֶׁר־נָתְנוּ חִתִּית בְּאֶרֶץ
כד חַיִּים: שָׁם עֵילָם וְכָל־הֲמוֹנָהּ סְבִיבוֹת
קְבֻרָתָהּ כֻּלָּם חֲלָלִים הַנֹּפְלִים בַּחֶרֶב
אֲשֶׁר־יָרְדוּ עֲרֵלִים | אֶל־אֶרֶץ תַּחְתִּיּוֹת
אֲשֶׁר נָתְנוּ חִתִּיתָם בְּאֶרֶץ חַיִּים וַיִּשְׂאוּ
כה כְלִמָּתָם אֶת־יוֹרְדֵי בוֹר: בְּתוֹךְ חֲלָלִים
נָתְנוּ מִשְׁכָּב לָהּ בְּכָל־הֲמוֹנָהּ סְבִיבוֹתָיו
קִבְרֹתֶהָ כֻּלָּם עֲרֵלִים חַלְלֵי־חֶרֶב כִּי־
נִתַּן חִתִּיתָם בְּאֶרֶץ חַיִּים וַיִּשְׂאוּ כְלִמָּתָם
אֶת־יוֹרְדֵי בוֹר בְּתוֹךְ חֲלָלִים נִתָּן:

time of its miraculous destruction during Chizkiyahu's reign. See Appendix II for approximate dates.

סְבִיבוֹתָיו קִבְרֹתָיו — *His surroundings are his graves.*

It is to remain within the confines of *Gehinnom,* without ever being brought to burial in a normal grave *(Rashi).*

[It is not clear whether this refers to Assyria, the earlier subject of the verse, or to Egypt, the subject of the previous verse. The change from the feminine (קְהָלָהּ) to the masculine (קִבְרוֹתָיו סְבִיבוֹתָיו) is striking. Since Egypt had been described in the masculine in the previous verse (לוֹ ... עֹזְרָיו), the obvious assumption would seem to be that our verse has returned to that subject. However, a careful reading of the whole passage will show that whenever the *nation* is the subject the feminine is used, but that the text changes to the masculine when the discussion shifts to individual people. As a result, the subject of סְבִיבוֹתָיו קִבְרֹתָיו could well be the individual soldiers of Assyria.]

Metzudos renders as follows: During the [final] war Assyria will [also] fall. Their graves will surround Egypt's graves.

23. אֲשֶׁר נִתְּנוּ קִבְרֹתֶיהָ בְּיַרְכְּתֵי בוֹר — *Whose graves are placed at the depths of the pit.*

Rashi does not offer an explanation for this phrase. Presumably *graves* should be taken metaphorically as in סְבִיבוֹתָיו קִבְרֹתָיו, *his surroundings are his graves,* in the previous verse. Their travail in *Gehinnom* is to take the place of the normal resting in a grave.

According to *Metzudos* the phrase is a direct continuation of the previous verse. Because they all fell by the sword, they will all be buried together in a communal grave. They are not to be buried in individual graves as would be the case had they died a peaceful death.

וַיְהִי קְהָלָהּ סְבִיבוֹת קְבֻרָתָהּ — *And whose company was around her grave.*

In her place in *Gehinnom* Assyria will be surrounded by her company *(Rashi).*

In *Metzudos'* view the phrase follows from the beginning of the verse. Since they are all to be buried in a communal

titude; his surroundings are his graves; all of them slain, who fall by the sword, [23] *whose graves are placed at the depths of the pit, and whose company was around her grave, all of them slain who fall by the sword because they spread terror in the land of life.* [24] *There is Elam and all her multitude around her grave, all of them slain who fall by the sword, who descended uncircumcised to the nethermost earth, because they spread their terror in the land of life and bore their shame with those that descend to the pit.* [25] *Among the slain they placed a bed for her with all her multitude, surrounding him are her graves; all of them uncircumcised, slain by the sword; for their terror was spread in the land of life; and they bore their shame with those that descend to the pit. Among the*

grave it is not surprising that Assyria's soldiers will be lying near those of Egypt. In war time not many graves are dug and soldiers from different armies are often buried together.

אֲשֶׁר־נָתְנוּ חִתִּית בְּאֶרֶץ חַיִּים — *Because they spread terror in the land of life* [i.e., *Eretz Yisrael*].

The translation חִתִּית, *terror,* follows the Sages in *Rosh HaShanah* 17a. *Radak* also translates it in this way.

Rashi and *Metzudos* render שֶׁבֶר, *destruction, breakage.* [They may have chosen this translation, rather than that of the Sages, because of the contextual use of this same word in *v.* 30. See *comm.* below.]

Targum offers: *because they ruled* (שלט) *over the land of Israel.* [שלט is taken here to mean *to rule* because that is its most common usage. It should, however, be noted that Targum also uses שלט to translate פגע when it is used in the sense of *killing.* Apparently, murder is the ultimate domination of a person; the murderer allows himself to decide whether or not his victim should live. See *II Samuel* 1:15; *I Kings* 2:25,34, 46.]

24. עֵילָם — *Elam.*

Elam is also among the fallen countries who await Egypt's descent into the pit.

Elam is identified in *Daniel* 8:2 as the area in which th city of Shushan was located. (See ArtScroll *Daniel* for closer identification.) According to the Sages (*Sanhedrin* 89a), it was allied with Babylon in the latter's attacks against the Jews. Except for this passage in *Ezekiel,* only *Jeremiah* contains prophecies against this nation. He includes Elam in ch. 25 among the people who were to drink the cup of anger symbolizing their conquest by Babylon, and in ch. 49 he predicts Elam's fall. Isaiah (21:2) saw it allied with Media against Babylon.

וַיִּשְׂאוּ כְלִמָּתָם — *And bore their shame.*

Shame is the feeling engendered when they compare the depths to which they have sunk to the peaks of power and prosperity which they once enjoyed *(Radak).*

25. נָתְנוּ מִשְׁכָּב לָהּ — *They placed a bed for her.*

The bed is for Elam *(Rashi).*

לב
כו־לא

כו שָׁם מֶשֶׁךְ תֻּבַל וְכָל־הֲמוֹנָהּ סְבִיבוֹתָיו
קִבְרוֹתֶיהָ כֻּלָּם עֲרֵלִים מְחֻלְלֵי חֶרֶב
כז כִּי־נָתְנוּ חִתִּיתָם בְּאֶרֶץ חַיִּים׃ וְלֹא
יִשְׁכְּבוּ אֶת־גִּבּוֹרִים נֹפְלִים מֵעֲרֵלִים
אֲשֶׁר יָרְדוּ־שְׁאוֹל בִּכְלֵי־מִלְחַמְתָּם וַיִּתְּנוּ
אֶת־חַרְבוֹתָם תַּחַת רָאשֵׁיהֶם וַתְּהִי
עֲוֹנוֹתָם עַל־עַצְמוֹתָם כִּי־חִתִּית גִּבּוֹרִים
כח בְּאֶרֶץ חַיִּים׃ וְאַתָּה בְּתוֹךְ עֲרֵלִים
כט תִּשָּׁבַר וְתִשְׁכַּב אֶת־חַלְלֵי־חָרֶב׃ שָׁמָּה
אֱדוֹם מְלָכֶיהָ וְכָל־נְשִׂיאֶיהָ אֲשֶׁר־נִתְּנוּ
בִגְבוּרָתָם אֶת־חַלְלֵי־חָרֶב הֵמָּה אֶת־
ל עֲרֵלִים יִשְׁכָּבוּ וְאֶת־יֹרְדֵי בוֹר׃ שָׁמָּה
נְסִיכֵי צָפוֹן כֻּלָּם וְכָל־צִדֹנִי אֲשֶׁר־יָרְדוּ
אֶת־חֲלָלִים בְּחִתִּיתָם מִגְּבוּרָתָם בּוֹשִׁים
וַיִּשְׁכְּבוּ עֲרֵלִים אֶת־חַלְלֵי־חֶרֶב וַיִּשְׂאוּ
לא כְלִמָּתָם אֶת־יוֹרְדֵי בוֹר׃ אוֹתָם יִרְאֶה
פַרְעֹה וְנִחַם עַל־כָּל־הֲמוֹנֹה חַלְלֵי־חֶרֶב

26. See 27:13 for *Meshech* and *Tuval.*

27. Most commentators read the verse as meaning that Meshech and Tuval will be buried ignominiously and will not be honored in death as are other warrriors.

There are several ways in which the words may be translated, yielding this meaning. *Rashi* is followed here.

וְלֹא יִשְׁכְּבוּ אֶת־גִּבּוֹרִים — *They shall not lie with the mighty.*

The warriors of Meshech and Tuval will not be buried with honors like those of undefeated soldiers who die a natural death.

נֹפְלִים מֵעֲרֵלִים — *They are inferior to the* [*other*] *uncircumcised ones.*

These other warriors are buried together with their weapons which are placed under their heads as a symbol of their heroism. Meshech and Tuval will have no such honors.

נפל is used in the sense of being less worthy, as in *Job* 12:3 and 13:2.

וַתְּהִי עֲוֹנוֹתָם עַל־עַצְמוֹתָם — *Their sins (shall) remain upon them.*

Their death will not have atoned for their sins. They will carry to the gravetheir sin of spreading terror over the Land of Life.

28. וְאַתָּה — *And as for you.*

The prophet turns back to Pharoah *(Rashi).*

אֶת חַלְלֵי חָרֶב — *With the victims of* [lit. *those slain by*] *the sword.*

You will not be with those that died a natural death *(Rashi).*

32 *slain it is placed.* 26 *There, Meshech, Tuval, and all*
26-31 *her multitudes, surrounding him are her graves, all of*
them uncircumcised, slain by the sword, for they
spread their terror in the land of life. 27 *They shall not*
lie with the mighty; they are inferior to the uncir-
cumcised, who have descended to the netherworld
with their weapons and they placed their swords
beneath their heads. Their sins remain upon them;
for the terror of the mighty is in the land of life.
28 *And as for you — you shall be broken among the*
uncircumcised and lie with the victims of the sword.
29 *There is Edom, her kings and all her princes, which*
were placed, despite their might, with the victims of
the sword. With the uncircumcised they will lie
together with those that descend to the pit. 30 *There*
are the princes of the North, all of them, and the
Sidonians who descended with the slain, ashamed as
they are broken from their might; and they lie uncir-
cumcised with the victims of the sword and bear their
shame with those that descend to the pit. 31 *Them will*
Pharaoh see, and find comfort for all his multitude,
the victims of Pharaoh's sword and all his army — the

29. אֲשֶׁר־נִתְּנוּ בִגְבוּרָתָם — *Which were placed, despite their might.*

The translation follows *Metzudos.*

אֱדוֹם — *Edom.*

For a discussion of Edom, see 25:12-14 and ch. 35.

30. נְסִיכֵי צָפוֹן — *The princes of the North.*

According to *Radak* these are the kings of Babylon. (See 21:1 for a discussion of Babylon as the 'Northern' power.)

צִדֹנִי — *Sidonians* [lit. *Sidonian*].

This must be understood as though it were written צִדֹנִים, the *Sidonians.* (For a discussion of the role Sidon played in Israel's history, see *comm.* 28:20-23.)

בְּחִתִּיתָם מִגְּבוּרָתָם בּוֹשִׁים — *Ashamed as they are broken from their might.*

The translation follows *Rashi* and *Metzudos.* It is the simplest way to render this obscure phrase and may have been the cause for *Rashi* and *Metzudos* to take חִתִּית as *breakage* rather than as *terror* throughout this chapter. (See *comm., v.* 23.)

Eliezer of Beaugency renders: They are ashamed of having spread terror by virtue of their strength.

31. A person tends to find comfort for his troubles when he sees them shared by others. When Pharaoh will see all these nations who accompany him to *Gehinnom* or to the grave (see *comm., v.* 22), he will feel comforted concerning his and his people's fate.

לב לב פַּרְעֹה וְכָל־חֵילוֹ נְאֻם אֲדֹנָי יֱהֹוִה׃ כִּֽי־
לב °חִתִּיתִי ק׳ נָתַתִּי אֶת־°חתיתו בְּאֶרֶץ חַיִּים וְהֻשְׁכַּב
בְּתוֹךְ עֲרֵלִים אֶת־חַלְלֵי־חֶרֶב פַּרְעֹה
לג א וְכָל־הֲמוֹנֹה נְאֻם אֲדֹנָי יֱהֹוִה׃ וַיְהִי
א־ב ב דְבַר־יְהוָה אֵלַי לֵאמֹר׃ בֶּן־אָדָם דַּבֵּר

32. כִּי־נָתַתִּי אֶת־חִתִּיתִי בְּאֶרֶץ חַיִּים — *For I have spread My terror in the land of life.*

This verse predicts that in place of the terror which Pharaoh had once spread over Israel, God will cause Himself to be feared there (*Rashi.* In this verse *Rashi* reverts to the more usual meaning of חִתִּית as *fear* rather than *breakage.*)

R' Breuer points out that, although we read חִתִּיתִי, *My terror* (referring to God), the spelling is חִתִּיתוֹ, *his fear* (referring to Pharaoh). This expresses the idea that it is Pharaoh's terror which, in the end, will bring about the fear of God. The power which had been granted him is a step in the gradual educating of Israel towards attaining its spiritual maturity.

XXXIII

This chapter can be divided into four distinct sections:

[There is no significance whatever to the fact that these four sections are all included in one chapter; the division into chapters is merely a convenient expedient. For a discussion of the chapter division of Scripture, see footnote 26:7-14.] The four sections are:

A. the duties of the צֹפֶה, sentinel, *reminiscent of 3:7-21;*

B. explication of God's justice as it relates to wicked people who repent their wickedness, reminiscent of parts of ch. 18;

C. the coming of the פָּלִיט, the fugitive, *foretold in 24:25-27;*

D. several prophecies of rebuke, similar to those in the first half of the Book.

These sections are followed by ch. 34, which is the first of the great consolation prophecies with which Yechezkel closes his book.

The following is a possible rationalization for this structure.

*Concerning the structure of the Book of Ezekiel, the Sages (*Bava Basra *14b) stated,* רֵישֵׁיה חוּרְבְּנָא וְסֵיפֵיה נֶחֱמְתָא, Its beginning [tells of] destruction and its conclusion [tells of] consolation. *In introducing ch. 24 we noted that it might be the last of the destruction prophecies, and that the self-contained group of prophecies concerning the nations (chs. 25-32) might be the bridge between the two sections of the book. [The 'consolation' aspect of these prophecies is discussed in pref., chs. 25-32.] If, indeed, ch. 34 is the true beginning of the 'consolation' prophecies, this would explain the repetition in ch. 33 of the* צֹפֶה, sentinel, *metaphor used in ch. 3, since a new era of prophecy is being ushered in. Although the final section of this chapter seems to fit in much better with the destruction prophecies, this problem is eliminated by* Metzudos' *interpretation that the section refers to events after the destruction.*

A careful analysis of 3:17-27 on the one hand and chs. 24 and 33 on the other hand, will yield further insights.

In 3:17-21 Yechezkel was informed of his צֹפֶה, sentinel, *status. In* vs. *3:25-27 he was told that for the time being he was not to be an* אִישׁ מוֹכִיחַ, a reprover, *since the people were not yet ready to accept his teachings. Thus his sentinel status was held in abeyance until the people would be more receptive. Chapter 24 (vs. 26-27)*

32 *words of my Lord* HASHEM/ELOHIM; 32 *for I have*
32 *spread My terror in the land of life; and he will have*
been laid amid the uncircumcised with those slain by
the sword of Pharaoh and all his multitude — the
words of my Lord HASHEM/ELOHIM.

33 *The word of* HASHEM *came to me, saying:*
1-2 2 *Ben Adam, speak to the children of your peo-*

defines that time as the day of the coming of the פָּלִיט, fugitive. *As* Rashi *(24:27) points out, the dreadful events which the fugitive is to announce would be an unambiguous vindication of the prophet and the people would now accept his every word.*

Considering that ch. 33 begins with the sentinel metaphor and continues (vs. *21, 22) with an account of the coming of the fugitive predicted at the end of ch. 24, the conclusion is inescapable that ch. 33 is a direct continuation of ch. 24. The intervening chapters (25-32) must be viewed as an interruption in the sequence which was inserted for a specific reason. [Perhaps the introduction of the fugitive idea (at the end of ch. 24) was the cause of the insertion. In* comm. *24:26, the fugitive is identified as the angel Michael, and the significance of his escape from Nebuchadnezzar's clutches is discussed. It meant that the essential holiness of Israel had become a fugitive, but had not fallen victim to Babylonian ascendancy. The tragedy of defeat was only a way station on the road of Israel's regeneration, and the very day of the Temple's burning would one day become a day of rejoicing* (Zechariah *8:19). In contrast to this, there was to be no* פָּלִיט, fugitive *for the other nations which fell to Babylon. Theirs was to be a complete fall.*]

Thus the sequence of the prophecies is clearly evident. Chapter 24 (vs. 26-27) announces the eventual coming of the fugitive with its attendant change in Yechezkel's function. His mouth is finally to be 'opened'. The people will be receptive to his teachings. He is to introduce himself to them as a צֹפֶה, sentinel, *and spell out to them the duties and implications of that office (33:1-9). (This repetition was also necessary for Yechezkel himself, although he had already been apprised of the sentinel responsibilities in ch. 3, in accordance with the dictum of the Sages* (Mechilta, Yisro): A man is to be encouraged to do his duty at the time that it is to be performed [even though] he was already encouraged to do it at a time when it was still theoretical.)

But the coming of the fugitive would involve Yechezkel in another duty besides that of the sentinel. It was to be anticipated that the news of Jerusalem's fall would completely break the spirit of the people. They would think of themselves as borne down by the weight of their sins and as utterly beyond redemption. It would devolve upon Yechezkel to open their eyes to the gift of תְּשׁוּבָה, repentance, *and to encourage them to face life once more (33:10-20).*

These prophecies (33:1-20) were all said on the tenth of Teves of the ninth year (24:1; see comm., *ch. 24). Then 33:21-22 jumps ahead to the twelfth year, when the predicted events actually took place. The destruction prophecies in the last part of our chapter (vs. 23-33) could have been said before this last date, probably in the ninth year, together with ch. 24.* [Ramban (Exodus *12:43;* Numbers *7:1, and elsewhere) points out that there is a tendency in Scripture to ignore chronology in favor of completing a given unit. Therefore, Scripture will often jump ahead to*

אֶל־בְּנֵי־עַמְּךָ וְאָמַרְתָּ אֲלֵיהֶם אֶרֶץ כִּי־
אָבִיא עָלֶיהָ חָרֶב וְלָקְחוּ עַם־הָאָרֶץ אִישׁ
אֶחָד מִקְצֵיהֶם וְנָתְנוּ אֹתוֹ לָהֶם לְצֹפֶה׃
ג וְרָאָה אֶת־הַחֶרֶב בָּאָה עַל־הָאָרֶץ וְתָקַע
ד בַּשּׁוֹפָר וְהִזְהִיר אֶת־הָעָם׃ וְשָׁמַע הַשֹּׁמֵעַ
אֶת־קוֹל הַשּׁוֹפָר וְלֹא נִזְהָר וַתָּבוֹא חֶרֶב
ה וַתִּקָּחֵהוּ דָּמוֹ בְרֹאשׁוֹ יִהְיֶה׃ אֵת קוֹל
הַשּׁוֹפָר שָׁמַע וְלֹא נִזְהָר דָּמוֹ בּוֹ יִהְיֶה
ו וְהוּא נִזְהָר נַפְשׁוֹ מִלֵּט׃ וְהַצֹּפֶה כִּי־יִרְאֶה
אֶת־הַחֶרֶב בָּאָה וְלֹא־תָקַע בַּשּׁוֹפָר וְהָעָם
לֹא־נִזְהָר וַתָּבוֹא חֶרֶב וַתִּקַּח מֵהֶם נָפֶשׁ
הוּא בַּעֲוֺנוֹ נִלְקָח וְדָמוֹ מִיַּד־הַצֹּפֶה
ז אֶדְרֹשׁ׃ וְאַתָּה בֶן־אָדָם
צֹפֶה נְתַתִּיךָ לְבֵית יִשְׂרָאֵל וְשָׁמַעְתָּ
ח מִפִּי דָּבָר וְהִזְהַרְתָּ אֹתָם מִמֶּנִּי׃ בְּאָמְרִי
לָרָשָׁע רָשָׁע מוֹת תָּמוּת וְלֹא דִבַּרְתָּ

events which rightfully belong to the subject under discussion, and then go back to the intervening events.]

In summary, the consolation prophecies of Yechezkel begin with ch. 34; the last of the destruction prophecies are contained in ch. 24. Ch. 33 is a continuation from the latter part of ch. 24. Chapters 25-32 bridge the two parts of the Book.

2-9. Verses 2-6 contain the parable of the צֹפֶה, *sentinel.* This parable is then explicated in verses 7-9. (See *comm.,* footnote 21:4 for a discussion of the use of parable and metaphor in Scripture.) While we have given צֹפֶה its literal rendering of *sentinel,* the sense of the word is captured by *Targum* who renders it in the parable as *one who warns,* and in the explication as *teacher.*

2. דַּבֵּר אֶל־בְּנֵי־עַמְּךָ — *Speak to the children of your people.*

The time had come for Yechezkel to let the people know about his sentinel status. In ch. 3, he was told that God had made him a צֹפֶה, *sentinel,* but he was not told to share this knowledge with the people. Their obduracy would not permit him to exercise that office (see *comm.* 3:17-21). With the coming of the fugitive, this would change. The people would thirst for guidance from him *(R' Breuer).*

Radak writes that בְּנֵי עַמְּךָ, *the children of your people,* is used in this sentence to contrast it to the prophecies in the previous chapters addressed to the foreign nations.

וְלָקְחוּ עַם־הָאָרֶץ — *And the people of the land take.*

In this point, the parable differs from

33
3-8

ple and say to them: When I bring a sword upon a
land, and the people of the land take one man from
among them and set him as their sentinel; 3 *and he*
sees the sword coming upon the land, he blows the
horn and warns the people, 4 *and a listener heard the*
sound of the horn but did not heed the warning and
the sword came and took him; his blood shall be
upon his head. 5 *He heard the sound of the horn but*
did not heed the warning; His blood shall be upon
him. Had he heeded the warning, he would have
saved his life. 6 *But the sentry, if he saw the sword*
coming and he did not blow the horn, and the people
were not warned, and the sword came and took a life
from them — he was taken for his sin — but his blood
I will seek from the sentry's hand. 7 *Now you, Ben*
Adam — I have made you a sentry for the family of
Israel, and when you hear a matter from My mouth,
warn them for Me. 8 *When I say of the wicked one,*
'Wicked one, you shall surely die,' and you did not

the explication. In the parable, it is the people who are under attack who appoint the sentry. In the explication, God, Who brings the attacker, is also the One who appoints the sentry (*v.* 7: צֹפֶה נְתַתִּיךָ).

The implication of this change is obvious. God wishes His people to be saved. He would rather that the suffering He brings upon them could be avoided *(R' Breuer).*

According to the formula of עִמּוֹ אָנֹכִי בְצָרָה, *I* [*God*] *am with him* [*Israel*] *in his distress* (*Psalms* 91:15) God regards Himself, as it were, as one of the citizens under attack. In His role as King — albeit, king of a rebellious people — He is required to provide sentinels for His city.

3. הַחֶרֶב — *The sword.*

Targum renders: *those who kill with the sword.*

This refers to the armies *(Rashi).*

4. דָּמוֹ בְּרֹאשׁוֹ יִהְיֶה — *His blood shall be upon his head.*

He will be punished for having been careless of his own life *(Rashi).*

5. וְהוּא נִזְהָר נַפְשׁוֹ מִלֵּט — *Had he heeded the warning, he would have saved his life.*

The translation follows *Rashi.*

6. הוּא בַּעֲוֹנוֹ נִלְקָח — *He was taken for his sin.*

The sentry had been negligent in his duty, and the people were unwarned and therefore unable to protect themselves. Of course, none would be killed who did not deserve to die. The victims must have been guilty of some sin. However, this does not exonerate the negligent sentry. He is held responsible for the bloodshed.

7-9. See 3:17-19.

לְהַזְהִיר רָשָׁע מִדַּרְכּוֹ הוּא רָשָׁע בַּעֲוֺנוֹ
ט יָמוּת וְדָמוֹ מִיָּדְךָ אֲבַקֵּשׁ׃ וְאַתָּה כִּֽי־
הִזְהַרְתָּ רָשָׁע מִדַּרְכּוֹ לָשׁוּב מִמֶּנָּה וְלֹא־
שָׁב מִדַּרְכּוֹ הוּא בַּעֲוֺנוֹ יָמוּת וְאַתָּה
י נַפְשְׁךָ הִצַּלְתָּ׃ וְאַתָּה בֶן־אָדָם
אֱמֹר אֶל־בֵּית יִשְׂרָאֵל כֵּן אֲמַרְתֶּם לֵאמֹר
כִּֽי־פְשָׁעֵינוּ וְחַטֹּאתֵינוּ עָלֵינוּ וּבָם אֲנַחְנוּ
יא נְמַקִּים וְאֵיךְ נִחְיֶה׃ אֱמֹר אֲלֵיהֶם חַי־אָנִי ׀
נְאֻם ׀ אֲדֹנָי יֱהֹוִה אִם־אֶחְפֹּץ בְּמוֹת
הָרָשָׁע כִּי אִם־בְּשׁוּב רָשָׁע מִדַּרְכּוֹ וְחָיָה
שׁוּבוּ שׁוּבוּ מִדַּרְכֵיכֶם הָרָעִים וְלָמָּה
יב תָמוּתוּ בֵּית יִשְׂרָאֵל׃ וְאַתָּה
בֶן־אָדָם אֱמֹר אֶל־בְּנֵֽי־עַמְּךָ צִדְקַת

10-20. The coming of the fugitive with his awesome news would once and for all destroy the edifice of pride and arrogance with which Jerusalem's inhabitants had insulated themselves from God's word. (See *comm.,* 11:3,15.) In a complete about-face, they who had thought that their sins would automatically be forgiven because of the Temple in their midst (*Jeremiah* 7:9-10) suddenly lost all hope of forgiveness. They felt that they would pine away in their wickedness with no prospect of regeneration.

It is Yechezkel's duty to guide these broken spirits to an understanding of תְּשׁוּבָה [*teshuvah*], *repentance,* that greatest of all of God's mercies. (See *comm.,* 18:21-32.) There is no need for the family of Israel to die (*v.* 11). (This background follows *Rashi.* See *comm., v.* 10.)

10. כֵּן אֲמַרְתֶּם — *Thus have you said.*

The translation follows the apparent intent of *Rashi.* Yechezkel tells the people that they have erroneously claimed that it is too late for repentance. Yechezkel has previously used the phrase in this sense in 11:5. [Perhaps Yechezkel uses the expression here with that passage in mind. There the people had arrogantly asserted that Jerusalem could never be conquered (11:3). To this Yechezkel had reacted (11:5): כֵּן אֲמַרְתֶּם — *Thus have you said.* Now, in claiming that they are doomed, the people are making the opposite mistake.]

Radak translates כֵּן as *true,* as in *Exodus* 10:29 and *Numbers* 27:7. You have said the truth. In his view, the verse means: It is good that you say you are suffering because of your sins, since that awareness is the first step in *teshuvah.*

וּבָם אֲנַחְנוּ נְמַקִּים — *And through them we pine away.*

The root of נְמַקִּים, is מקק, which means *to waste* or *pine away.*

The people do not believe that *teshuvah, repentance,* can help them, and therefore do not wish to repent (*Rashi*).[1]

What is the reason for their disbelief? Perhaps it was part of the same misconception which had lulled them into a

speak up to warn the wicked one concerning his evil
ways, he, the wicked one, shall die for his sin — but I
shall demand his blood from you hand; 9 but you — if
you did warn the wicked one concerning his way that
he should repent of it, and he did not repent of his
way, he shall die for his sin. And as for you — you
have saved your soul.

10 Now you, Ben Adam, say to the family of Israel:
Thus have you said, saying: 'For our iniquities and
sins are upon us, and through them we pine away —
so how can we live?' 11 Say to them: 'As I live, the
words of my Lord HASHEM/ELOHIM, I do not desire
the death of the wicked one, but the wicked one's
return from his way that he will live. Repent, repent
from your evil ways; why should you die, O family
of Israel?'

12 Now you Ben Adam, speak to the children of
your people: The righteousness of the righteous one

sense of security as long as the Temple had stood among them. If the Temple in their midst frees them of responsibility for their sins, then surely its destruction would leave them completely unprotected.

According to *R' Yitzchok Blaser (Kochvei Ohr,* 3), the reality of the destruction finally shocked them into an awareness of the enormity of their sins. The guilt of having driven God's Presence from their midst appeared so enormous to them that they could not conceive of a mercy great enough to pardon their sin.

This seems borne out by *Tanna De'Bei Eliyahu* which tells that Yechezkel told the elders of Israel to repent, but they would not do so because they were ashamed.

11. God calls for repentance and affirms that, far from desiring the death of the wicked, He yearns for their return to Him. This verse is an echo of 18:21-23, 30-32. See *comm.* there.

1. In *Leviticus* 26:39, the Torah predicts that exile will be followed by a state in which *those that are left of you will pine away because of your sins, in the lands of your enemies, and also because of the sins of their fathers with them will they pine away.* The commentators do not explain the exact meaning of the word, but *R' David Tzvi Hoffman* writes: The sinner who is not aroused to *teshuvah* sinks deeper into the morass of sin until he becomes irrational. He has no escape from ultimate destruction and it will be all the same to him if he continues to sin or not. Thus, in the moral and ethical sense, he passes from the world as misdemeanor accumulates upon brazen sin. This seems to be the way *Rashi* understands our verse. However, we find this same term used earlier in *Ezekiel* (4:17; 24:23) where it clearly denotes a physical decline. It is perhaps for that reason that *Radak* adopts his interpretation.

Radak interprets: It is good that you say you are pining away (suffering) because of your sins, because awareness is the first step in *teshuvah.*

See *Metzudos* for a possible combination of the two opinions.

הַצַּדִּיק לֹא תַצִּילֶנּוּ בְּיוֹם פִּשְׁעוֹ וְרִשְׁעַת
הָרָשָׁע לֹא־יִכָּשֶׁל בָּהּ בְּיוֹם שׁוּבוֹ מֵרִשְׁעוֹ
וְצַדִּיק לֹא יוּכַל לִחְיוֹת בָּהּ בְּיוֹם חֲטֹאתוֹ׃
יג בְּאָמְרִי לַצַּדִּיק חָיֹה יִחְיֶה וְהוּא־בָטַח עַל־
צִדְקָתוֹ וְעָשָׂה עָוֶל כָּל־צִדְקֹתָו לֹא
תִזָּכַרְנָה וּבְעַוְלוֹ אֲשֶׁר־עָשָׂה בּוֹ יָמוּת׃
יד וּבְאָמְרִי לָרָשָׁע מוֹת תָּמוּת וְשָׁב
טו מֵחַטָּאתוֹ וְעָשָׂה מִשְׁפָּט וּצְדָקָה׃ חֲבֹל
יָשִׁיב רָשָׁע גְּזֵלָה יְשַׁלֵּם בְּחֻקּוֹת הַחַיִּים
הָלַךְ לְבִלְתִּי עֲשׂוֹת עָוֶל חָיוֹ יִחְיֶה

12. צִדְקַת הַצַּדִּיק לֹא תַצִּילֶנּוּ בְּיוֹם פִּשְׁעוֹ — *The righteousness of the righteous one shall not save him on the day of iniquity.*

In *Kiddushin* 40b, R' Shimon bar Yochai derives from this verse that even if a person was a צַדִּיק גָּמוּר, *perfectly righteous man,* all his life but rebelled against God in the end, he forfeits his earlier good deeds. The Talmud explains that this is true only if he regrets having done the good deeds which he had performed before his rebellion (תּוֹהֵא עַל הָרִאשׁוֹנוֹת). (See *comm.,* 3:20; 18:24.)

[R'Shimon's interpretation is difficult. First, why does he not interpret the verse, (as does *Metzudos)* to mean simply that his earlier good deeds would not protect the righteous man from punishment for his sin. Conceivably the justice of God might have permitted the 'trading' of a good deed for a sin. For example, if a man did ten good deeds and one sin, it would be possible to free him from punishment for the sin which he had done and reward him for only *nine* of his good deeds. The verse tells us that this will not happen. He will be punished for the sin, despite his many *mitzvos.* (See *Rambam, Avos* 4:22; *Ramban, Deuteronomy* 10:17; at *Sotah* 21a עֲבֵירָה מְכַבָּה מִצְוָה, *Maharal, Derech Chayim, Avos* 4:22.) Perhaps the answer is that R' Shimon interprets the first part of the verse to parallel the second. Certainly when the verse says that a wicked man who repents will not stumble over his former sins, the meaning is that these sins will be wiped out completely. In the same way, the first part of the verse must mean that the earlier merits of the *tzaddik* who became a sinner are completely lost. This would be true only if he regrets his previous good deeds.

Secondly, the implication of R' Shimon's interpretation is that had he not regretted his former good deeds, they would have saved him on the day of his iniquity. How is this possible since, as discussed above, God will not 'trade' a merit for a sin?

This problem may be solved in the light of *Sotah* 21a, where the Sages teach us that besides the reward which accrues for the performance of a *mitzvah,* the *mitzvah* also has the property of 'protecting' (אֲגוּנֵי מַגְנָא) the person from the results of his sins, at least temporarily. Our verse means that had he not regretted his earlier *mitzvos,* his merits would have afforded him temporary protection from the results of his iniquity.]

וְרִשְׁעַת הָרָשָׁע לֹא־יִכָּשֶׁל בָּהּ בְּיוֹם שׁוּבוֹ מֵרִשְׁעוֹ — *And the wickedness of the wicked one — he shall not stumble over it on the day of his return from his wickedness.*

R' Shimon (*Kiddushin* 40b) further derives from this verse that even if a person who has been wicked all his life repents on his dying day, his wickedness is not held against him.

וְצַדִּיק לֹא יוּכַל לִחְיוֹת בָּהּ בְּיוֹם חֲטֹאתוֹ — *But the righteous one cannot survive* [lit. *live*] *through it on the day of his sin.*

The word בָּהּ, *through it, lends* itself

33
13-15

shall not save him on the day of his iniquity and the
wickedness of the wicked one — he shall not stumble
over it on the day of his return from his wickedness;
but the righteous one cannot survive through it on
the day of his sin. 13 *When I say to the righteous one,*
'You shall surely live,' and he relied on his
righteousness and did evil, all his righteousness will
not be recalled; and through the evil he did — for it he
shall die. 14 *Now when I say to the wicked one: 'You*
shall surely die,' and he repented from his sin and
practiced justice and charity — 15 *the wicked one*
returns a pledge, repays a robbery, walks in the laws
of life not practicing evil — he will surely live; he will

to two interpretations. To *Rashi,* בָּהּ refers to the *tzaddik's* righteousness, which will not keep him alive (i.e., protect him from punishment) on the day of his sin. To *Metzudos,* בָּהּ refers to the wickedness of the *tzaddik* after he begins to sin, which will prevent him from living (unpunished) in spite of the many merits which he had accumulated before he became a sinner.

The apparent redundancy of this phrase is explained by *Rashi* in his responsum to the men of Auxerres. The beginning of the verse states that the *tzaddik's* former righteousness would not save him, but does not indicate from what he needed to be saved. The phrase לֹא יוּכַל לִחְיוֹת, *[he] cannot live,* shows that the death penalty is meant.

13-16. These verses are explanations of *v.* 12. Verse 13 discusses the *tzaddik,* and verses 14-16, the *wicked one.*

Metzudos prefaces his explanation of *v.* 13 with the word לָכֵן, *therefore* to show that these verses complement v. 12.

13. כָּל־צִדְקֹתָיו לֹא תִזָּכַרְנָה — *All his good deeds will not be recalled.*

They will not save him from being punished for his present sin *(Rashi).*

God will not balance a sin against a good deed. Each will be dealt with on its own merit.

Assuming that *Rashi* agrees with *Metzudos* that this verse explains verse 12, this would be his understanding of the last clause of the previous verse as well. Although the Sages in *Kiddushin* 40b rejected this interpretation of *v.* 12 (see *comm.* above), *Rashi* is explaining the verses according to their simple meaning (פשט) without reference to the exegesis of the Sages (דרש). *Metzudos* does the same.

It is also possible that *Rashi* interprets *v.* 13 as a new lesson rather than as an explanation of *v.* 12. Verse 12 teaches about regretting past *mitzvos.* This is also the view of the Sages. Verse 13 teaches another aspect of God's justice: *mitzvos* cannot offset sins.

The latter seems the more likely considering that at 3:20 and 18:24 *Rashi* interprets similar phrases to apply when the *tzaddik* regrets his good deeds. Evidently, the reason *Rashi* does not do so here is that the lesson was already taught in *v.* 12.

14-15. Verse 12 taught that a wicked person would not 'stumble' on his former sins on the day of his repentance. Verses 14 and 15 define the requirements of *teshuvah.* It consists of embarking on a new path of justice and charity (*v.* 14), and divesting oneself of the gains of his former sins (*v.* 15).

טז לֹא יָמוּת: כׇּל־חַטֹּאתָו אֲשֶׁר חָטָא לֹא
תִזָּכַרְנָה לוֹ מִשְׁפָּט וּצְדָקָה עָשָׂה חָיוֹ
יז יִחְיֶה: וְאָמְרוּ בְּנֵי עַמְּךָ לֹא יִתָּכֵן דֶּרֶךְ
יח אֲדֹנָי וְהֵמָּה דַּרְכָּם לֹא־יִתָּכֵן: בְּשׁוּב־
צַדִּיק מִצִּדְקָתוֹ וְעָשָׂה עָוֶל וּמֵת בָּהֶם:
יט וּבְשׁוּב רָשָׁע מֵרִשְׁעָתוֹ וְעָשָׂה מִשְׁפָּט
כ וּצְדָקָה עֲלֵיהֶם הוּא יִחְיֶה: וַאֲמַרְתֶּם לֹא
יִתָּכֵן דֶּרֶךְ אֲדֹנָי אִישׁ כִּדְרָכָיו אֶשְׁפּוֹט
כא אֶתְכֶם בֵּית יִשְׂרָאֵל: וַיְהִי בִּשְׁתֵּי
עֶשְׂרֵה שָׁנָה בָּעֲשִׂרִי בַּחֲמִשָּׁה לַחֹדֶשׁ
לְגָלוּתֵנוּ בָּא־אֵלַי הַפָּלִיט מִירוּשָׁלַםִ
כב לֵאמֹר הֻכְּתָה הָעִיר: וְיַד־יהוה הָיְתָה

16. כׇּל חַטֹּאתָיו ... לֹא תִזָּכַרְנָה — *All his sins will not be remembered.*

After repentance, the sinner begins life with a clear state.

[The formulation *will not be remembered* is used in verse 13 to describe the *tzaddik's* good deeds. There, also, the meaning must be that all his former deeds will be wiped out, which is only true if he regrets them. This seems to disagree with *Rashi.* (See analysis of *Rashi* in *comm., v.* 13.)]

17-20. Both the idea of *teshuvah* and the concept that a person may lose the merit of his deeds if he regrets having done them were difficult for the people of Israel to accept. For a discussion of the people's thinking, see *comm.*, ch. 18, particularly 18:25.

20. אִישׁ כִּדְרָכָיו — *Each man according to his ways.*

Each person is judged according to his present ways *(Metzudos).* This is an affirmation of God's justice as it relates both to *teshuvah* and to the doctrine of תוֹהֶא עַל הָרִאשׁוֹנוֹת, *regretting one's earlier good deeds. See comm. v.* 12.

21-22. At last the pivotal moment in Yechezkel's relationship with the people has come. The imposed silence that had weighed upon him so heavily for six years (since the fifth year of the exile when the people had 'put ropes upon him' — see 3:25-27) is to be lifted. God 'opens his mouth and he will never have to be dumb again. His prophecy has found bitter vindication.

21. Since Teves of the ninth year (24:1), Yechezkel had known that one day a fugitive would come to him with the news of the destruction (24:25-27). (See pref. to this chapter for the place of this section in the structure of the Book.)

The dating of the fugitive's coming is difficult. Throughout Scripture it is made abundantly clear that the destruction took place in the fifth month, Av, of the eleventh year of Zidkiyahu's reign (which is also the eleventh year of Yehoyachin's exile). (See *Jeremiah* 39:2.) This would make the tenth month of the twelfth year, the date given here for the coming of the fugitive, a full seventeen months after the event, (since according to *Rosh HaShanah* 3a, the years of Jewish kings are counted uniformly from Nissan). It is inconceivable that there should have

not die. 16 All the sins which he sinned will not be remembered for him. He practiced justice and charity, so he shall surely live.

17 Now the children of your people say, 'Incorrect are the ways of the Lord,' but it is they whose ways are incorrect. 18 Upon a righteous man's return from his righteousness and he does evil, he shall die for them; 19 but upon a wicked man's return from his wickedness and he practices justice and charity, for them he shall live. 20 Yet you say, 'The way of the Lord is incorrect!' Each man according to his ways I will judge you, family of Israel.

21 It was in the twelfth year, in the tenth, on the fifth of the month from our exile. The fugitive came to me from Jerusalem, saying, 'The city has been smitten.' 22 Now the hand of HASHEM had been upon

been a lapse of so much time before the news of the destruction reached Babylon. (See *Rashi, Rosh Hashanah* 18b).

Rashi, in his responsum to the men of Auxerres (Appendix IX), refers to the problem and offers a solution, but the available texts are incomplete and the passage is obscure.

Metzudos and *Mahari MiTrani* write that in contrast to the years of the Jewish kings which are counted from Nissan, the years of the exile are counted from Tishrei. If so, the twelfth year of exile started two months after the destruction. The tenth month however is counted from Nissan. This would make a time lapse of five months until the news reached Babylon.

[This interpretation assumes that the method of counting the exile years is subject to the same system as the counting of the years of a given reign, that is, that a new year always begins on a specific date — in this case the first of Tishrei — even if a full twelve months have not elapsed.

In this system, much of the analysis of the dates of the prophecies against Egypt (pref., chs. 29-32) needs revision. For example, the prophecy in 29:1, dated the twelfth of Teves in the tenth year, was assumed to have occurred seven months before the destruction. In the new system it would be nineteen months before. A similar revision would have to be made for 32:1 (first of Adar, twelfth year) and 32:17 (fifteenth of Adar, twelfth year.)]

R' Breuer suggests a completely novel approach. In 26:1 it was noted that a קִלְקוּל חֶשְׁבּוֹנוֹת, *mistaken reckoning,* had taken place at the moment of the destruction. The events which took place on the Ninth of Av were registered in the mind of the prophet as though they had occurred on the first of the month. There had been a new beginning (see *comm.* there). It is conceivable that a new 'prophetic' year started at that point also. Thus the fugitive came in the twelfth year לְגָלוּתֵנוּ, *of our exile.* It was not really the twelfth calendar year, but relative to 'our exile' which began a new counting, for us, on the Ninth of Av, it was indeed the twelfth year. (The tenth month of the twelfth year is really the tenth month of the eleventh [calendar] year).

22. This is the fulfillment of the prophecy of 24:27.

אֵלַי בָּעֶרֶב לִפְנֵי בּוֹא הַפָּלִיט וַיִּפְתַּח אֶת־
פִּי עַד־בּוֹא אֵלַי בַּבֹּקֶר וַיִּפָּתַח פִּי וְלֹא
כג נֶאֱלַמְתִּי עוֹד׃ וַיְהִי דְבַר־יְהוָה
כד אֵלַי לֵאמֹר׃ בֶּן־אָדָם יֹשְׁבֵי הֶחֳרָבוֹת
הָאֵלֶּה עַל־אַדְמַת יִשְׂרָאֵל אֹמְרִים
לֵאמֹר אֶחָד הָיָה אַבְרָהָם וַיִּירַשׁ אֶת־
הָאָרֶץ וַאֲנַחְנוּ רַבִּים לָנוּ נִתְּנָה הָאָרֶץ
כה לְמוֹרָשָׁה׃ לָכֵן אֱמֹר אֲלֵיהֶם
כֹּה־אָמַר | אֲדֹנָי יֱהוִה עַל־הַדָּם | תֹּאכֵלוּ
וְעֵינֵכֶם תִּשְׂאוּ אֶל־גִּלּוּלֵיכֶם וְדָם תִּשְׁפֹּכוּ
כו וְהָאָרֶץ תִּירָשׁוּ׃ עֲמַדְתֶּם עַל־חַרְבְּכֶם
עֲשִׂיתֶן תּוֹעֵבָה וְאִישׁ אֶת־אֵשֶׁת רֵעֵהוּ

23-29. This passage describes the thinking which was prevalent in Jerusalem before the Destruction *(Radak;* see *pref.).*

However, since verses 21-22 describe events which took place at least several months later, many commentators assume this passage, too, to refer to that period. They understand it to be addressed to the pitiful remnant which remained in Jerusalem under Gedaliah ben Achikom. Even after the Destruction, they had not learned their lesson.

24. הֶחֳרָבוֹת הָאֵלֶּה — *These ruins.*

Although this prophecy is directed to Jerusalem during Zidkiyahu's reign, the expression is still apt since much of the Southern Kingdom had already been laid waste *(Radak).*

Metzudos and others, however, refer this to the period after the Destruction. According to them, the phrase refers quite literally to the ruins left by Nebuchadnezzar's army.

אֶחָד הָיָה אַבְרָהָם — *Abraham was alone* [lit. *one*].

Superficially it is easy to understand the reasoning of the people. Relative to the heyday of Israel's might, the remnant was small and abject; but relative to Abraham, who had entered the Land of Canaan accompanied only by his family, they were still a force with which to reckon. They felt that in time, they would once more establish themselves securely in the land. They had forgotten that not Abraham, the mighty warrior, had captured the land, but that it had been granted to Abraham, the man who walked before God. This is the rebuttal to their argument in verses 25-29 *(Metzudos).*

Both *Rashi* and *Radak* quote *Sifri,* where a dispute is recorded between R' Akiva and R' Shimon bar Yochai. R' Akiva explained the reasoning in our verse as follows: If Abraham who served only one God was given the land, we who have served many gods should certainly receive the land. (See footnote, 8:12 for a discussion of this strange idea.) R' Shimon bar Yochai said: If Abraham who had only one commandment (circumcision) inherited the land, we, who have many commandments, should surely inherit the land.

[Perhaps the Sages chose an interpretation which seems far removed from the simple meaning of the phrase because, translated literally, the logic seems flawed. Abraham as an individual

33
23-26

me in the evening before the coming of the fugitive,
and He opened my mouth before his coming to me in
the morning; my mouth was opened and I was dumb
no more.
23 *The word of HASHEM came to me, saying:* 24 *Ben*
Adam! The inhabitants of these ruins upon the ground of Israel speak, saying, 'Abraham was alone, yet he inherited the land, but we are many — to us the land is given as an inheritance.'
25 *Therefore say to*
them: Thus says my Lord HASHEM/ELOHIM: You eat over the blood, and raise your eyes to your idols and shed blood — yet you inherit the land?
26 *You stood*
upon your sword; you committed abominations; each of you has defiled his neighbor's wife — yet you in-

never really owned the land; God promised that He would give the land to Abraham's descendants. Therefore, the people could not have referred to owning the land, but to meriting it. (For an analysis of God's promises to Abraham, see *Ramban, Genesis* 15:18. For Abraham's individual rights to the land see *Rashi, Genesis* 13:7, 23:4; *Mizrachi; Gur Aryeh* there; *Pardes Yosef, Genesis).*

25. עַל הַדָּם תֹּאכֵלוּ – *You eat over the blood.*

The delicacies with which you indulge yourselves are obtained by killing people and taking their money *(Rashi).* This interpretation is confirmed by *Targum* who injects the adjective זַכַּאי, *innocent,* to qualify דָּם, *blood.*

Radak and *Metzudos* interpret this as a form of idolatry which, as indicated by the context of *Leviticus* 19:26, involves sorcery whereby evil spirits were invited to partake of a meal of blood (see *Ramban* there).

The next phrase, *raise your eyes to your idols,* recalls 18:6. Eating *upon the blood* parallels eating *upon the mountains* indicating that the subject here is a forbidden ritual rather than murder and thievery *(R' Breuer).*

וְעֵינֵכֶם תִּשְׂאוּ אֶל גִּלּוּלֵיכֶם – *And raise your eyes to your idols.*

See comm. 18:6.

The folly of their thinking is spelled out. It is in the Land of Israel, the place on earth closest to God (see comm. to 20:6), that you practice idol worship and sorcery, and shed innocent blood. This reveals your insensitivity to man's innate holiness (see *comm.* to 22:3). Can you really expect to inherit the land? The litany of sins continues in the next verse.

26. עֲמַדְתֶּם עַל חַרְבְּכֶם – *You stood upon your sword.*

You placed your trust in your sword *(Rashi).*

The very climate of Israel is designed to turn the trust of its inhabitants to God because the lack of natural irrigation forces the people to pray for rain, thus making them ever cognizant of their dependence on His mercy (*Ramban Deuteronomy* 11:10; *comm.* 20:6). How little affinity they had for the land which they so arrogantly claimed!

עֲשִׂיתֶן תּוֹעֵבָה – *You committed abomination.*

You have practised homosexuality *(Rashi).* This, together with adultery, represents the sexual abominations

כז טִמֵּאתֶם וְהָאָרֶץ תִּירָשׁוּ: כֹּה־תֹאמַר
אֲלֵהֶם כֹּה־אָמַר אֲדֹנָי יֱהֹוִה חַי־אָנִי אִם־
לֹא אֲשֶׁר בֶּחֳרָבוֹת בַּחֶרֶב יִפֹּלוּ וַאֲשֶׁר
עַל־פְּנֵי הַשָּׂדֶה לַחַיָּה נְתַתִּיו לְאָכְלוֹ
וַאֲשֶׁר בַּמְּצָדוֹת וּבַמְּעָרוֹת בַּדֶּבֶר יָמוּתוּ:
כח וְנָתַתִּי אֶת־הָאָרֶץ שְׁמָמָה וּמְשַׁמָּה
וְנִשְׁבַּת גְּאוֹן עֻזָּהּ וְשָׁמְמוּ הָרֵי יִשְׂרָאֵל
כט מֵאֵין עוֹבֵר: וְיָדְעוּ כִּי־אֲנִי יהוה בְּתִתִּי
אֶת־הָאָרֶץ שְׁמָמָה וּמְשַׁמָּה עַל כָּל־
ל תּוֹעֲבֹתָם אֲשֶׁר עָשׂוּ: וְאַתָּה
בֶן־אָדָם בְּנֵי עַמְּךָ הַנִּדְבָּרִים בְּךָ אֵצֶל
הַקִּירוֹת וּבְפִתְחֵי הַבָּתִּים וְדִבֶּר־חַד
אֶת־אַחַד אִישׁ אֶת־אָחִיו לֵאמֹר בֹּאוּ־
נָא וְשִׁמְעוּ מָה הַדָּבָר הַיּוֹצֵא מֵאֵת
לא יהוה: וְיָבוֹאוּ אֵלֶיךָ כִּמְבוֹא־עָם וְיֵשְׁבוּ

which, according to *Leviticus* 18:27-28, defile the land and cause it to vomit forth its inhabitants.

27. אִם לֹא — *Surely* [lit. *if not*].

This phrase always implies an oath. God is swearing that the land will be lost.

אֲשֶׁר בֶּחֳרָבוֹת — *Those that are in the ruins.*

The ruins refers to the fortified cities which are destined to become ruins *(Rashi).* Apparently *Rashi* agrees with those commentators (*intro., vs.* 23-29) who place this prophecy before the Destruction. *Metzudos* who places it after the Destruction, interprets literally: The people who still dwelt in the ruins of the cities would be killed.

28. וְשָׁמְמוּ הָרֵי יִשְׂרָאֵל — *And the mountains of Israel shall be desolate.*

The mountains of Israel are a focus of many of Yechezkel's visions, both those of destruction (6:1ff) and those of comfort (36:ff).

30-33. The shattering news from the Land of Israel will once and for all confirm Yechezkel as the true prophet, of God (*v.* 33): The source of God's word, the organ through which His spirit speaks to men *(v.* 33; see footnote 2:5). For many years, the words: *'Let us go and hear what is this matter which comes forth from HASHEM' (v.* 30), spoken when people came to visit Yechezkel, had a ring of derision. The people felt themselves privy to God's true message through the medium of the false prophets (ch. 13) who flatteringly assured them that all would be well. Yechezkel's prophecies were entertaining because of the sublime music of their powerful poetry, but were not seen as binding the people in any way (*vs.* 31; 32). All this would now change.

30. בְּנֵי עַמְּךָ — *The children of your people.*

33
27-31

herit the land? [27] *Thus shall you say to them: Thus*
says my Lord HASHEM/ELOHIM: As I live! Surely
those that are in the ruins shall fall by the sword; and
those that are on the face of the field, to the wild
beasts I have presented him their food; and those that
are in the strongholds and the caves — by the plague
they shall die; [28] *and I shall make the land a desolate*
waste, and her prideful power shall cease, and the
mountains of Israel shall be desolate without a pas-
serby. [29] *Then they shall know that I am HASHEM*
when I make the land a desolate waste because of all
the abominations which they committed. [30] *Now*
you, Ben Adam — the children of your people who
talk against you near the walls and in the doorways
of the houses, and they speak to one another, each
man to his brother, saying: Come now and hear what
this matter is that comes forth from HASHEM. [31] *And*
they come to you as a people comes and they shall sit

The exact connotation of this expression is discussed in *comm.* 13:17. God may mean to exclude Himself: 'They are *your people,* not Mine!' The expression could also be designed to evoke Yechezkel's love for them: 'Do not forget that with all their depravity, they are still *your people.'*

What is the meaning in our verse?

The word עַם is used twice more in this section (*v.* 31), once without inflection in the phrase כִּמְבוֹא עָם, *as a people comes,* and once inflected עַמִּי, *My people.*

Surely this repetition is no coincidence. See *comm.* 13:17 where it was noted that in *Exodus* ch. 32, at the incident of the Golden Calf, the Torah uses different inflections of the word עַם to highlight the tensions of that narrative. Perhaps, as in the rest of the chapter, the expression in this verse is one of endearment. God exhorts Yechezkel to be patient and to recognize his fellow exiles as *your people,* although they scorn his message. To teach Yechezkel this lesson, God reminds him that they are עַמִּי, *My people;* God does not spurn them in spite of their disloyalty. Yechezkel should find it easier to practice forbearance, since he can look at them neutrally as עָם, *a people;* their offense to Yechezkel is not as great as it is to God. Yechezkel is to have patience. In the end, they will recognize that he is the prophet of God.

הַנִּדְבָּרִים בְּךָ — *Who talk against you.*

They ridicule you *(Rashi).*

The *nifal* (נִדְבָּרִים) is used to intensify. They are constantly talking. The prefix ב (בְּךָ) together with דבר indicates talking *against (Radak).*

אֵצֶל הַקִּירוֹת — *Near the walls.*

Instead of talking on the street, they talk near the walls and at the doors of the houses for greater privacy *(Radak).*

31. כִּמְבוֹא־עָם — *As a people comes.*

See *comm.,* verse 30. *Targum* renders: *as pupils come.* They pretend to be interested in his message.

לג
לב־לג

לְפָנֶיךָ עַמִּי וְשָׁמְעוּ אֶת־דְּבָרֶיךָ וְאוֹתָם
לֹא יַעֲשׂוּ כִּי־עֲגָבִים בְּפִיהֶם הֵמָּה
לב עֹשִׂים אַחֲרֵי בִּצְעָם לִבָּם הֹלֵךְ: וְהִנְּךָ
לָהֶם כְּשִׁיר עֲגָבִים יְפֵה קוֹל וּמֵטִב
נַגֵּן וְשָׁמְעוּ אֶת־דְּבָרֶיךָ וְעֹשִׂים אֵינָם
לג אוֹתָם: וּבְבֹאָהּ הִנֵּה בָאָה וְיָדְעוּ כִּי נָבִיא
א הָיָה בְתוֹכָם: וַיְהִי דְבַר־יהוה
ב אֵלַי לֵאמֹר: בֶּן־אָדָם הִנָּבֵא עַל־רוֹעֵי
יִשְׂרָאֵל הִנָּבֵא וְאָמַרְתָּ אֲלֵיהֶם לָרֹעִים

לד
א־ב

וְיֵשְׁבוּ לְפָנֶיךָ עַמִּי — *And they shall sit before you — My people.*

See *comm.*, verse 30. Commentators render: *as though they were My people.* There is nothing to distinguish them from people who honestly seek God's word; but it is all a matter of appearances, for, although they sit before you with feigned seriousness, they do not act upon your words *(Rashi).*

כִּי עֲגָבִים בְּפִיהֶם הֵמָּה עֹשִׂים — *For they relegate* [lit. *make*] *them to verbal* [lit. *with their mouths*] *ridicule.*

The commentators follow *Targum* who explains that your words become a topic for them to speak of with ridicule.

[The use of בְּפִיהֶם, literally *with their mouths* may indicate that the people viewed Yechezkel's message superficially; they repeated his words, but did not take them to heart. The result was that his eloquent words were ridiculed as meaningless rhetoric. Alternatively, they may have mimicked his words and delivery *with their mouths,* thus making him a subject of *verbal ridicule.*]

אַחֲרֵי בִצְעָם — *After their spoils.*

They ignore Yechezkel's message because they are concerned only with the potential profits of their thievery, rather than with the content of your message.

Metzudos renders *after their lust;* they care only for the pleasure of mocking you.

32. כְּשִׁיר עֲגָבִים — *As a love song.*

The translation follows *Radak* who derives the word from עגב, *sexual desire* (see 23:5).

Yechezkel's prophecies were couched in beautiful language. It was an aesthetic delight to listen to him (see footnote, 7:2); but he was not taken seriously. The people would not allow him to change their ways.

Rashi follows *Targum* who renders: *the song of a harp.* [Perhaps he does not mean a literal translation. A love song might be played on a harp.]

33. וּבְבֹאָה — *But when it comes.*

When the evil finally comes, they will know that הִנֵּה בָאָה, *see, it* [his prophecy] *has come.* They will realize that his words were not a joke after all.

XXXIV

True regeneration becomes possible only once the past is understood. Yechezkel begins his prophecies of נֶחָמָה, comfort, *by placing the tragedy in its true perspective.*

What had gone wrong?

Yechezkel places the blame on Israel's shepherds — its kings who had interposed themselves between God and His people. King David had taught (Psalms 100:3)

33 *before you — My people — and they shall hear your*
32-33 *words, but will not perform them, for they relegate*
them to verbal ridicule; their heart follows after their
spoils. 32 *And behold! you are to them as a love song,*
a pleasant voice, and skillful musician and they hear
your words, but do not perform them. 33 *But when it*
comes, it will have come! Then they shall know that a
prophet was among them.

34 *The word of HASHEM came to me saying:*
1-2 2 *Ben Adam, prophesy against Israel's*
shepherds; prophesy and say to them, to the

that Israel's nationhood could be defined only in terms of a flock tended by its Divine Shepherd (עַמּוֹ וְצֹאן מַרְעִיתוֹ; Yalkut there), and Yechezkel will conclude this chapter (v. 31) with the affirmation that Israel can attain its 'Adam' destiny (see Overview IV) only as God's sheep.

In this perspective it can readily be seen that a self-serving monarchy is an aberration and a terrible distortion of Israel's true nature. Even while pining in exile, Israel would have the comfort of knowing that its corrupted monarchical period lay in the past; henceforth the nation would be directly in God's hands. Until the time when God establishes a king over it (v. 24) who, as God's servant (v. 23), will be a true shepherd (ibid.) *in His stead, Israel would look only to God.*[1]

2. עַל־רוֹעֵי יִשְׂרָאֵל — *Against Israel's shepherds.*

Targum renders פַּרְנָסֵי יִשְׂרָאֵל, *the providers of Israel;* so does *Rashi.*

Radak writes: These are the kings, for if Israel is compared to sheep, its kings are shepherds.

Rambam (Hilchos Melachim 2:6),

1. We have interpreted the chapter as an indictment of the monarchy and a promise of its abolition, in favor of God's direct stewardship, until the establishment of the Davidic dynasty in Messianic times, because that seems to be the simple meaning of the passage. If, as the commentators explain, the *shepherds* who are to be shunted aside are Israel's kings, then the description of God's personal shepherding assumedly refers to a period during which there would be no kings.

Nevertheless the author of this commentary could not have committed himself to an interpretation that blames the monarchy for the entire tragedy of the period of the First Temple if this were not borne out by Scriptural and Rabbinic sources.

A short survey of the Torah's view of the period of the monarchy follows.

In *Devarim Rabbah* 5:11, the Rabbis taught: God said, 'In This World you requested kings, and kings came and caused you to fall by the sword. Saul made you fall on Mount Gilboa ... David brought about a plague ... Ahab brought a drought ... and Zidkiyahu destroyed the Temple.' When Israel saw what their kings had brought about, all of them began to cry, 'We do not want a king. We want our first King, *for God is our Judge; God is our Lawgiver; God is our King; He will save us (Isaiah* 33:22),' so God said to them, 'Truly that is what I shall do, as it is written (*Zechariah* 14:9); *And God will be King over the whole land.'*

From the very beginning, Scripture viewed the establishment of the monarchy as a rejection of God. When the elders of Israel demanded that Samuel appoint a king (*I Samuel* 8:4ff), God told him to accede to their request: *'For they have not rejected you; but they have rejected Me from ruling over them.'*

As the commentators explain, it was not the request for a king in itself which contravened

לד
ג־ו

כֹּה־אָמַר | אֲדֹנָי יֱהֹוִה הוֹי רֹעֵי יִשְׂרָאֵל
אֲשֶׁר הָיוּ רֹעִים אוֹתָם הֲלוֹא הַצֹּאן יִרְעוּ
ג הָרֹעִים׃ אֶת־הַחֵלֶב תֹּאכֵלוּ וְאֶת־הַצֶּמֶר
תִּלְבָּשׁוּ הַבְּרִיאָה תִּזְבָּחוּ הַצֹּאן לֹא
ד תִרְעוּ׃ אֶת־הַנַּחְלוֹת לֹא חִזַּקְתֶּם וְאֶת־
הַחוֹלָה לֹא־רִפֵּאתֶם וְלַנִּשְׁבֶּרֶת לֹא
חֲבַשְׁתֶּם וְאֶת־הַנִּדַּחַת לֹא הֲשֵׁבֹתֶם וְאֶת־
הָאֹבֶדֶת לֹא בִקַּשְׁתֶּם וּבְחָזְקָה רְדִיתֶם
ה אֹתָם וּבְפָרֶךְ׃ וַתְּפוּצֶינָה מִבְּלִי רֹעֶה
וַתִּהְיֶינָה לְאָכְלָה לְכָל־חַיַּת הַשָּׂדֶה
ו וַתְּפוּצֶינָה׃ יִשְׁגּוּ צֹאנִי בְּכָל־הֶהָרִים וְעַל

describing the selflessness required of a Jewish king, writes: Scripture calls him a shepherd, as it is written: *To shepherd his people Jacob (Psalms* 78:71) and a shepherd's bearing is described in Scripture (*Isaiah* 40:11): *As a shepherd tends his flock, gathering lambs into his arms, and leading the little ones.*

Thus the shepherd is the prototype of selfless caring for one's charges. How great is the distortion when the shepherds care only for themselves (*vs.* 3-4)!

אֲשֶׁר הָיוּ רֹעִים אוֹתָם — *Who have shepherded themselves.*

They were indulging themselves with the property of their subjects *(Rashi).*

God's wishes. The Torah provides for the institution of monarchy, and *Rambam (Hilchos Melochim* 1:1) counts the appointment of a king among the 613 commandments of the Torah. In Isaiah's visions of the Messianic era, it is Israel's king who becomes focus of humanity's aspirations (*Isaiah* 11:10), the Prince of Peace whose throne upholds universal justice and charity *(Isaiah* 9:5,6).

Such a king must be totally imbued with the fear of God, a bearer of the spirit of God, wisdom, knowledge, understanding, resourcefulness and strength *(Isaiah* 11:2,3). Such a man will never stand as an *alternative* to God's rule; rather, he will be the conduit through which the light of Godliness shines upon His people.

Had the people wanted *such* a king, no stigma would have been attached to their request. It is what God had wanted for them. However, as the commentators demonstrate, both the timing of their demands and the terms in which they couched them showed that the people had a quite different king in mind. The monarchy envisaged by them, rather than serving as a conduit for Godliness, would interpose itself between the people and God. Their demand constituted a rejection of God's rule.

Therefore, although God granted their wish, it was not an agreement born of good will. *I have given you a king in My anger; and taken, in My fury (Hosea* 13:11). In one of *Radak's* interpretations, this refers to the entire institution of monarchy: *I have given you a king in My anger* — that is Saul. *And taken, in My fury* — that is Zidkiyahu. See also *Pesikta Rabbasi* 33). The monarchy began on the wrong footing — and ended in tragedy. (See *Hosea* 13:9.)

Therefore, it is appropriate that Yechezkel should see the downfall of the monarchy as the point where God will once more be in direct touch with His people. God's Providence made sure that David's royal seed would survive for a different era (see introd. 17:22-24), but until then, Israel would have no more kings. (See *Ramban, Genesis* 49:10, for his view concerning the Hasmonean dynasty.) God Himself would be their shepherd until the reign of the ideal Jewish king, the Messiah.

*shepherds: Thus says my Lord HASHEM/ELOHIM:
Woe! shepherds of Israel who have shepherded
themselves! Should it not be the sheep whom the
shepherds tend?* 3 *Should you eat the fat, should you
don the wool, should you slaughter the choicest —
but not tend the sheep!* 4 *The frail you have not
strengthened; the ill, you have not cured; the broken,
you have not bound; the banished, you have not
retrieved; the lost, you have not sought — but with
force you have subjugated them and with rigor.*
5 *Thus they were scattered, without a shepherd, and
they became food for all the beasts of the field, and
they were scattered further.* 6 *My sheep wander*

When an action is described as being done to oneself, we expect the *nifal* or *hispa'el* conjugation rather than the *kal* with the accusative אֶת. [The word אוֹתָם is a contraction of אֶת הֵם.] However, here (as in *Jeremiah* 7:19) the sharp contrast between caring for themselves and caring for the sheep could best be expressed by retaining the same voice. (See *Gesenius* 57 §4).

הֲלוֹא הַצֹּאן יִרְעוּ הָרֹעִים — *Should it not be the sheep whom the shepherds tend?*

Is it not the duty of the shepherds to tend the sheep rather than to tend themselves *(Rashi)?*

The kings had the obligation to guide the people in their quest for spiritual growth. This they could do by establishing educational facilities to teach the people Torah and by encouraging justice and righteousness throughout the land *(Radak).*

3. Rather than do these things, they used their power to enrich themselves at the people's expense.

4. אֶת־הַנַּחְלוֹת — *The frail.*

Those that are weak *(Rashi)* or hurt in one of their limbs and require strengthening *(Radak; Metzudos).*

Five different categories of needy sheep are mentioned in this verse. [*Rambam* (introd. to *Moreh Nevuchim)* holds that in come types of parable it is not necessary to interpret every single detail. Often it is the total picture, rather than its individual components, which is significant. Nevertheless, the exact counting of the various types of need assumedly lends color to the picture. Each individual sheep is different, each needs to be dealt with in its own way. This is the duty of the conscientious shepherd, and this is expected of a Jewish king.][1]

5. וַתְּפוּצֶינָה — *Thus they were scattered.*

Metzudos explains the twice repeated word as follows: Unwatched by their shepherd, the sheep scattered from their central pasture. In their new location they became endangered by the marauding wild animals. They fled with the result that they strayed even further away.

6. יִשְׁגּוּ צֹאנִי — *My sheep wander.*

They went straying over the moun-

1. In *Berachos* 4a, David is reported as contrasting his sense of duty to his people with that of all the kings of east and west. While other kings sat together in groups basking in their power and pomposity, David describes himself as unselfishly ignoring his personal comfort for the sake of the people. His hands were soiled with menstrual blood and afterbirths which he always made himself available to examine in order to determine whether wives were ritually pure and permitted to their husbands.

כָּל־גִּבְעָה רָמָה וְעַל כָּל־פְּנֵי הָאָרֶץ נָפֹצוּ
ז צֹאנִי וְאֵין דּוֹרֵשׁ וְאֵין מְבַקֵּשׁ: לָכֵן רֹעִים
ח שִׁמְעוּ אֶת־דְּבַר יהוה: חַי־אָנִי נְאֻם | אֲדֹנָי
יֱהוִה אִם־לֹא יַעַן הֱיוֹת־צֹאנִי | לָבַז
וַתִּהְיֶינָה צֹאנִי לְאָכְלָה לְכָל־חַיַּת הַשָּׂדֶה
מֵאֵין רֹעֶה וְלֹא־דָרְשׁוּ רֹעַי אֶת־צֹאנִי
וַיִּרְעוּ הָרֹעִים אוֹתָם וְאֶת־צֹאנִי לֹא רָעוּ:
ט־י לָכֵן הָרֹעִים שִׁמְעוּ דְּבַר־יהוה: כֹּה־
אָמַר אֲדֹנָי יֱהוִה הִנְנִי אֶל־הָרֹעִים
וְדָרַשְׁתִּי אֶת־צֹאנִי מִיָּדָם וְהִשְׁבַּתִּים
מֵרְעוֹת צֹאן וְלֹא־יִרְעוּ עוֹד הָרֹעִים
אוֹתָם וְהִצַּלְתִּי צֹאנִי מִפִּיהֶם וְלֹא־תִהְיֶיןָ
יא לָהֶם לְאָכְלָה: כִּי כֹּה אָמַר
אֲדֹנָי יֱהוִה הִנְנִי־אָנִי וְדָרַשְׁתִּי אֶת־
יב צֹאנִי וּבִקַּרְתִּים: כְּבַקָּרַת רֹעֶה עֶדְרוֹ
בְּיוֹם־הֱיוֹתוֹ בְתוֹךְ־צֹאנוֹ נִפְרָשׁוֹת כֵּן
אֲבַקֵּר אֶת־צֹאנִי וְהִצַּלְתִּי אֶתְהֶם מִכָּל־
הַמְּקוֹמֹת אֲשֶׁר נָפֹצוּ שָׁם בְּיוֹם עָנָן
יג וַעֲרָפֶל: וְהוֹצֵאתִים מִן־הָעַמִּים וְקִבַּצְתִּים

tains. This means that the people were left to their own devices; each man doing as he wanted. The leaders did not exhort the people to better their ways, nor did they encourage social justice *(Rashi)*.

7-10. The monarchy has failed (see pref.). Far from acting as a unifying force through which Israel could develop its genius, it had left the people in spiritual shambles [and had invariably been the source of all the spiritual malaise in the country.] The people as a whole remained true to the Torah throughout most of the period of the monarchy (a change for the worse took place in Menashe's reign), thus the chastisements of the prophets were aimed mainly at the royal house and its immediate sphere of influence. [See *Doros HaRishonim, Tekufas HaMikrah.*] God will remove those selfish shepherds and be reunited with His sheep.

9. שִׁמְעוּ דְּבַר־ה׳ — *Listen to the word of HASHEM.*

Verse 9 repeats verse 7 because the flow was interrupted by the long parenthetical passage in verse 8 *(Metzudos)*.

Targum renders: Therefore, wicked providers, return to the Torah and I shall have mercy upon you. Listen to the teachings of the Torah and accept

through all the mountains and upon every high hill;
and upon the whole face of the earth have My sheep
scattered. And no one searches or seeks.
7 *Therefore, shepherds, listen to the word of*
HASHEM. 8 *As I live — the words of my Lord*
HASHEM/ELOHIM — surely because My sheep
became a prey, and My sheep became food for all the
beasts of the field without a shepherd, and My
shepherds sought not My sheep, and the shepherds
tended themselves, but My sheep they did not tend,
9 *therefore, shepherds, listen to the word of HASHEM.*
10 *Thus says my Lord HASHEM/ELOHIM: Behold! I*
am against the shepherds, and I will seek My sheep
from their hands, and I will cause them to cease
shepherding sheep, so the shepherds will no longer
tend themselves. Thus I will rescue My sheep from
their mouths, and no more will they be food for
them; 11 *for thus says my Lord HASHEM/ELOHIM:*
Behold! I am here, and I shall seek out My sheep, and
I will investigate them. 12 *As a shepherd tends his*
flock on the day that he is among his scattered sheep,
so I will investigate My sheep and rescue them from
all the places where they were scattered on the day of
clouds and darkness.
13 *I shall bring them out from the nations and*

the word of God.

11. וּבִקַּרְתִּים — *And I will investigate them.*

I will analyze their needs *(Metzudos).*

Hirsch (Leviticus 19:20) demonstrates that בקר denotes *differentiating,* thus, *treating something according to its special requirements.* The good shepherd gives each sheep the individual treatment that it requires (see *comm., v.* 4).

12. נִפְרָשׁוֹת — *Scattered* [lit. *set aside, separated*].

נִפְרָשׁוֹת means *separated,* therefore *scattered.* Sheep which scattered and got lost on a dark, cloudy day need the special attention of the shepherd. Each one must be searched out and returned to the fold.[1]

13-16. These verses describe God's guardianship of His people.

The two words רעה and רבץ which

1. Though it is never explicated here, one imagines that the shepherd motif of our chapter would carry connotations of comfort for the exiles.

Exile, the *valley overshadowed by death* (see *Targum, Psalms* 23:4), holds no terrors for one who recognizes God as his Shepherd (*Psalms* 23:1). It is in His capacity of ever-caring shepherd that God is close even when He seems very far.

מִן־הָֽאֲרָצ֔וֹת וַהֲבִיאוֹתִ֖ים אֶל־אַדְמָתָ֑ם
וּרְעִיתִים֙ אֶל־הָרֵ֣י יִשְׂרָאֵ֔ל בָּאֲפִיקִ֕ים
יד וּבְכֹ֖ל מוֹשְׁבֵ֥י הָאָֽרֶץ׃ בְּמִרְעֶה־טּוֹב֙
אֶרְעֶ֣ה אֹתָ֔ם וּבְהָרֵ֥י מְרוֹם־יִשְׂרָאֵ֖ל יִהְיֶ֣ה
נְוֵהֶ֑ם שָׁ֤ם תִּרְבַּ֙צְנָה֙ בְּנָ֣וֶה טּ֔וֹב וּמִרְעֶ֥ה
טו שָׁמֵ֛ן תִּרְעֶ֖ינָה אֶל־הָרֵ֥י יִשְׂרָאֵֽל׃ אֲנִ֞י
אֶרְעֶ֤ה צֹאנִי֙ וַאֲנִ֣י אַרְבִּיצֵ֔ם נְאֻ֖ם אֲדֹנָ֥י
טז יֱהֹוִֽה׃ אֶת־הָאֹבֶ֤דֶת אֲבַקֵּשׁ֙ וְאֶת־הַנִּדַּ֣חַת
אָשִׁ֔יב וְלַנִּשְׁבֶּ֣רֶת אֲחַבֵּ֔שׁ וְאֶת־הַחוֹלָ֖ה
אֲחַזֵּ֑ק וְאֶת־הַשְּׁמֵנָ֧ה וְאֶת־הַחֲזָקָ֛ה אַשְׁמִ֖יד
יז אֶרְעֶ֥נָּה בְמִשְׁפָּֽט׃ וְאַתֵּ֣נָה צֹאנִ֔י כֹּ֥ה אָמַ֖ר
אֲדֹנָ֣י יֱהֹוִ֑ה הִנְנִ֤י שֹׁפֵט֙ בֵּין־שֶׂ֣ה לָשֶׂ֔ה
יח לָאֵילִ֖ים וְלָעַתּוּדִֽים׃ הַמְעַ֣ט מִכֶּ֗ם הַמִּרְעֶ֤ה
הַטּוֹב֙ תִּרְע֔וּ וְיֶ֨תֶר֙ מִרְעֵיכֶ֔ם תִּרְמְס֖וּ
בְּרַגְלֵיכֶ֑ם וּמִשְׁקַע־מַ֣יִם תִּשְׁתּ֔וּ וְאֵת֙
יט הַנּ֣וֹתָרִ֔ים בְּרַגְלֵיכֶ֖ם תִּרְפֹּשֽׂוּן׃ וְצֹאנִ֑י
מִרְמַ֤ס רַגְלֵיכֶם֙ תִּרְעֶ֔ינָה וּמִרְפַּ֥שׂ רַגְלֵיכֶ֖ם
כ תִּשְׁתֶּֽינָה׃ לָכֵ֗ן כֹּ֥ה אָמַ֛ר אֲדֹנָ֥י
יֱהֹוִ֖ה אֲלֵיהֶ֑ם הִנְנִי־אָ֕נִי וְשָׁפַטְתִּי֙ בֵּין־שֶׂ֣ה
כא בִרְיָ֔ה וּבֵ֥ין שֶׂ֖ה רָזָֽה׃ יַ֗עַן בְּצַ֤ד וּבְכָתֵף֙

recur in these verses describe two different aspects in the care of a flock of sheep. רעה is the active shepherding where each sheep receives individual care; while רבץ describes the state of rest in which the flock lies during the heat of day, at which time the shepherd sits at a distance, protecting the flock as a whole but not concerning himself with each sheep individually.

Malbim (*Shir HaShirim* 1:7) writes that both these aspects are reflected in the way God extends His providence over His people. When Israel is deserving, God's Providence extends over every aspect of each individual's life. God alone watches over him; the cause-and-effect relations of nature play no role at all. This relationship is described as רעה.

However, when Israel is not deserving, God relates to it as a shepherd relates to his flock when they are *resting* in the heat of the day. While He will always assure that the nation will never be destroyed, His direct Providence is denied to the individual. The laws of nature hold sway.

Our passage should be read with these two meanings in mind.

gather them from the lands and bring them to their
ground, and tend them upon Israel's mountains, by
the streams and in all the earth's habitations. 14 *Upon*
good pasture I will shepherd them, and upon the
heights of Israel's mountains their fold will be. There
they will lie down in a good fold and upon fat
pastures they will graze on the mountains of Israel.
15 *I will tend My sheep, and lay them down — The*
words of my Lord HASHEM/ELOHIM. 16 *The lost, I*
will seek out; and the banished, I will retrieve; the
broken, I will bind; and the frail, I will strengthen.
But the fat one and the strong one, I will destroy. I
will shepherd them with justice.

17 *Now you, My sheep, thus says my Lord*
HASHEM/ELOHIM: *See, I will judge between one*
sheep and another, between rams and he-goats. 18 *Is*
it not enough for you that you graze in good
pastures; that the rest of your pasture you trample
underfoot; that you drink settled waters, that the rest
you befoul with your feet? 19 *And My sheep —*
should they graze at the tramplings of your feet and
drink the befoulment of your feet? 20 *Therefore, thus*
says my Lord HASHEM/ELOHIM *to them: Behold! I*
am here! — and I shall judge between the robust
sheep and the famished sheep. 21 *Because, with flank*

16. וְאֶת הַשְּׁמֵנָה וְאֶת הַחֲזָקָה — *But the fat one and the strong one.*

Targum renders: *the sinners and the guilty ones. Rashi* explains that this refers to those who take advantage of the weak and defenseless.

17. בֵּין־שֶׂה לָשֶׂה — *Between one sheep and another.*

Rashi explains between violent men and weak men.

לָאֵילִים וְלָעַתּוּדִים — *Between rams and he-goats.*

Targum renders this and the preceding phrase: *between man and man, sinners and guilty ones.*

18-22 Under God's direct guardianship, no self-serving aristocracy would be allowed to flourish. Under the monarchy, the rich and the powerful had often ignored the needs of their poorer and weaker brothers. Isaiah (5:8) chastised the people who *touched house to house, brought field close to field*, expanding their possessions by ruthlessly squeezing out the common people. Yechezkel now cries out in outrage against the selfish, powerful ones who

תֶּהְדֹּפוּ וּבְקַרְנֵיכֶם תְּנַגְּחוּ כָּל־הַנַּחְלוֹת
עַד אֲשֶׁר הֲפִיצוֹתֶם אוֹתָנָה אֶל־הַחוּצָה׃
כב וְהוֹשַׁעְתִּי לְצֹאנִי וְלֹא־תִהְיֶינָה עוֹד לָבַז
כג וְשָׁפַטְתִּי בֵּין שֶׂה לָשֶׂה׃ וַהֲקִמֹתִי עֲלֵיהֶם
רֹעֶה אֶחָד וְרָעָה אֶתְהֶן אֵת עַבְדִּי דָוִיד
הוּא יִרְעֶה אֹתָם וְהוּא יִהְיֶה לָהֶן לְרֹעֶה׃
כד וַאֲנִי יהוה אֶהְיֶה לָהֶם לֵאלֹהִים וְעַבְדִּי
דָוִד נָשִׂיא בְתוֹכָם אֲנִי יהוה דִּבַּרְתִּי׃
כה וְכָרַתִּי לָהֶם בְּרִית שָׁלוֹם וְהִשְׁבַּתִּי חַיָּה־
רָעָה מִן־הָאָרֶץ וְיָשְׁבוּ בַמִּדְבָּר לָבֶטַח
כו וְיָשְׁנוּ °ביעורים׃ וְנָתַתִּי אוֹתָם וּסְבִיבוֹת
גִּבְעָתִי בְּרָכָה וְהוֹרַדְתִּי הַגֶּשֶׁם בְּעִתּוֹ
כז גִּשְׁמֵי בְרָכָה יִהְיוּ׃ וְנָתַן עֵץ הַשָּׂדֶה אֶת־
פִּרְיוֹ וְהָאָרֶץ תִּתֵּן יְבוּלָהּ וְהָיוּ עַל־

°בַּיְּעָרִים ק׳

are not content with their own advantages; they go so far as to deprive the poor of opportunities that are legitimately theirs.

23. The time will come when it is possible for God to tend His sheep through the agency of a human shepherd. As David himself had once been taken *from the sheep pens, from among the young sheep, to shepherd Jacob, His people, and Israel, His inheritance (Psalms* 78:71-72), so his descendant — the Messiah — will become God's shepherd over His people (see *Rashi).*

24. וְעַבְדִּי דָוִד נָשִׂיא בְּתוֹכָם — *And My servant David, a prince among them.*

HASHEM will be God to His people when His servant David is a *prince* among them. The expression נָשִׂיא, *nassi*, for Israel's princes describes the entirely selfless ruler who draws from the populace only in order that, like a cloud, he may return what he has taken and thus become a blessing to them *(comm.* 22:6). The Davidic Messiah will be such a king. His subjects will never have to reject God in order to recognize him as king. On the contrary, in him his people will apprehend the peaks of Godliness to which the human spirit can strive.

The term *nassi* here sharpens the contrast between the Messianic king and the self-serving monarchs of the past.

25-30. This vision of the peace and harmony of Messianic times is based on *Leviticus* 26:3-13. See Appendix IV.

25. וְהִשְׁבַּתִּי חַיָּה־רָעָה מִן־הָאָרֶץ — *And cause the evil beasts to cease from the land.*

If the prophet is still using the parable of the sheep, then this phrase stands for the nations who despoiled Israel. However, verse 28 speaks separately of the nations and wild animals; moreover, this phrase is taken from *Leviticus* 26:6, which surely means wild beasts. Therefore, this is not a parable, but a promise that wild beasts will present no danger in Messianic times. The covenant of peace which is

34
22-27

and shoulder you push, and with your horns you
gore all the sickly ones until you have scattered them
abroad; 22 *so I will save My sheep, and they shall no*
more be for spoil, and I will judge between sheep and
sheep; 23 *and I will appoint over them a single*
shepherd, and he shall tend you — My servant
David. He shall tend them and he shall be a shepherd
to them; 24 *and I, HASHEM, will be God to them, and*
My servant David, a prince among them. I, HASHEM,
have spoken.

25 *Then I shall make a covenant of peace with them*
and cause the evil beasts to cease from the land, and
they shall dwell in the wilderness securely and sleep
in the woods. 26 *Then I shall make them and the sur-*
roundings of My hill, a blessing, and I shall bring
down the rain in its time; showers of blessing will
they be. 27 *And the tree of the field will yield its fruit,*
and the earth will yield its produce, and they shall re-

the hallmark of the Messiah will extend even to the animal world.

[The Sages in *Toras Kohanim* disagree as to the meaning of the phrase *I will cause to cease.* R' Yehudah says that they will cease to exist; R' Shimon maintains that they will indeed exist but will not do any damage.

Ramban (Leviticus 26:6) explains R' Shimon's view. The wild beast's power to kill lies not in its nature, but in man's sinfulness: The serpent does not kill; sin does (*Berachos* 33a). In God's plan of creation, even the wild beasts were to be herbivorous (*Genesis* 1:30). It was only as part of the general degeneration of the world which resulted from man's sin that fighting and killing became part of animal nature. The Messianic era will see a return to the ideal world which existed in Eden before Adam's sin; strife and killing will become a thing of the past. This same vision of peaceful coexistence between man and wild beast was seen by Isaiah in his vision of the future (*Isaiah* 11:6-9).]

26. גִּבְעָתִי — *My hill.*

According to *Targum* this refers to the Temple. According to *Metzudos*, to the land of Israel.

27. וְנָתַן עֵץ הַשָּׂדֶה אֶת־פִּרְיוֹ — *And the tree of the field will yield its fruit.*

See *Leviticus* 26:4. According to *Toras Kohanim* (quoted by *Rashi* there) עֵץ הַשָּׂדֶה is a barren tree. Even it will bear fruit in Messianic times.

Toras Kohanim views the Messianic era as a time of return to Eden, as it was before Adam's sin (*comm. v.* 25): *The tree of the field will yield its fruit* — not as it does now, but as it did in the time of Adam ... the tree will bear fruit on the day on which it is planted ... the wood of the tree will also be edible ... even barren trees will bear fruit.

It is a return to the time when the earth had not yet been cursed because of Adam's sin, but yielded its bounty openhandedly to man.

וְהָיוּ עַל אַדְמָתָם לָבֶטַח — *And they shall remain securely upon their ground.*

The association between לָבֶטַח, *securely*, and אַדְמָתָם, *their ground*, is no coincidence. *Leviticus* 26:5 reads וישבתם לָבֶטַח בְּאַרְצְכֶם, *you shall dwell*

אַדְמָתָם לָבֶטַח וְיָדְעוּ כִּי־אֲנִי יְהוָה
בְּשִׁבְרִי אֶת־מֹטוֹת עֻלָּם וְהִצַּלְתִּים מִיַּד
כח הָעֹבְדִים בָּהֶם׃ וְלֹא־יִהְיוּ עוֹד בַּז לַגּוֹיִם
וְחַיַּת הָאָרֶץ לֹא תֹאכְלֵם וְיָשְׁבוּ לָבֶטַח
כט וְאֵין מַחֲרִיד׃ וַהֲקִמֹתִי לָהֶם מַטָּע לְשֵׁם
וְלֹא־יִהְיוּ עוֹד אֲסֻפֵי רָעָב בָּאָרֶץ וְלֹא־
ל יִשְׂאוּ עוֹד כְּלִמַּת הַגּוֹיִם׃ וְיָדְעוּ כִּי־אֲנִי
יְהוָה אֱלֹהֵיהֶם אִתָּם וְהֵמָּה עַמִּי בֵּית
לא יִשְׂרָאֵל נְאֻם אֲדֹנָי יֱהוִה׃ וְאַתֵּן צֹאנִי צֹאן
מַרְעִיתִי אָדָם אַתֶּם אֲנִי אֱלֹהֵיכֶם נְאֻם
לה
א אֲדֹנָי יֱהוִה׃ וַיְהִי דְבַר־יְהוָה

securely in Your land, to which *Toras Kohanim* remarks: In *your* land you will live securely — but never outside it.

בְּשִׁבְרִי אֶת־מֹטוֹת עֻלָּם — *When I break the bars of their yoke.*

Toras Kohanim (Leviticus 26:13) comments: This is comparable to a farmer who owned a cow and lent it to a certain man to plow with. This man had ten sons. The first, the second, and the others came to plow with it until the cow became exhausted. The owner came and, without waiting for excuses from the borrower, smashed the yoke and tore the ropes. So it was with Israel. In This World, power after power imposed their yoke upon them and the furrow is very long. When the time comes God will not enter into discussion with the nations, but will smash the yoke and tear the ropes asunder.

28. וְחַיַּת הָאָרֶץ — *The beasts of the field.*

This refers to the gentile nations *(Radak).*

29. מַטָּע לְשֵׁם — *A plantation of renown.*

A pleasing and beautiful plant which will be famed throughout the nations *(Metzudos).*

The prophets use the metaphor of the plant to picture Israel's growth in its own land *(Amos* 9:15) *(Radak).*

אֲסֻפֵי רָעָב — *Gathered in by famine.*

The translation follows *Rashi* who comments that people who suffer the embarrassment of famine and poverty tend to *gather* themselves into the privacy of their homes because they are ashamed to face people.

Radak and *Metzudos* render: *destroyed by famine.* (אסף is used as in *Jeremiah* 8:13).

31. וְאַתֵּן צֹאנִי צֹאן מַרְעִיתִי אָדָם אַתֶּם — *Now you My sheep, sheep of My pasture — you are Adam.*

You are not like animals in My eyes *(Rashi),* see below.

When you are the sheep of My flock, meaning that you are *worthy* of My attention, then I will tend you, giving you knowledge, understanding and wisdom, then you shall be called Adam and not sheep or animal. When a person permits himself to be drawn to the desires of This World, he is called animal — not man — since man and animal have similar physical functions. However, when the earth is filled with the knowledge of God, and man loves God

34
28-31

main securely upon their ground. Then shall they know that I am HASHEM, when I break the bars of their yoke and save them from the hands of those who enslave them. 28 *Then they shall no longer be for spoil to the nations, and the beasts of the field will not devour them, and they will dwell securely, and none shall frighten them;* 29 *and I shall establish for them a plantation of renown, and they shall no more be gathered in by famine in the land, and they shall no more bear the shame of the nations.* 30 *Then they shall know that I HASHEM, their God, am with them, and they are My people, the Family of Israel — the words of my Lord HASHEM/ELOHIM.* 31 *Now you My sheep, sheep of My pasture — you are Adam. I am your God — The words of my Lord HASHEM/ELOHIM.*

and serves Him with all his heart, that man is worthy of the supreme title, *Adam (Radak).* [See *Overview IV.*]

[The Midrash to *Psalms* 100:3: עַמּוֹ וְצֹאן מַרְעִיתוֹ remarks: When are we His people? When we are the sheep of His flock, as it is written: *Now you are My sheep, the sheep of My flock.* But when you are like lions ...

Perhaps our verse is also meant in that way: When are you truly Adam? When you relate to God as His sheep.

The sheep is the symbol of absolute dependence. It is completely in the hands of the shepherd. One might have supposed that such dependence erodes one's manliness, and that sheep cannot be Adam. Yechezkel teaches that the opposite is true. The true *Adam-Hadom* (see *Overview IV)* can only be one who feels himself a sheep in God's hands. Absolute dependence upon God is the *sine qua non* of true independence. *Bava Kamma* 16a contains a cryptic teaching of the Sages: The punishment for not bowing down at the blessing of *Modim* is that the spine turns into a snake. *Maharal* (there) explains. Man's upright stance is a symbol of his kingship. A true king must be able to bow before a greater power. If man, the king, cannot bring himself to bow before God, then his spine — symbol of his royalty — turns into a snake — that other 'king' among the animals who lost his stature because of his unwillingness to submit to God's will.]

The relationship between true dependence upon God on the one hand and true independence and manhood on the other is detected by *R' Breuer* in the constant change of gender in *v.* 23 (עֲלֵיהֶם, אֶתְהֶן, אוֹתָם, לָהֶן). By establishing His Messianic shepherd over them, God nurtures Israel into true manhood (masculine); but this is predicated upon their complete dependence (feminine) upon the shepherd.

Targum renders: *Now you are My people, the people known by My name. You are the Family of Israel.* This accords with the teaching of the Sages (e.g., *Yevamos* 61a): You are called Adam but the nations of the world are not called Adam. This idea (discussed in detail in Overview IV) is a fitting finale to the first of the chapters of נֶחָמָה, *comfort,* which define God's relationship to His people in order to restore the broken courage of the exiles.

ב אֵלַי לֵאמֹר: בֶּן־אָדָם שִׂים פָּנֶיךָ עַל־הַר
ג שֵׂעִיר וְהִנָּבֵא עָלָיו: וְאָמַרְתָּ לּוֹ כֹּה אָמַר
אֲדֹנָי יֱהֹוִה הִנְנִי אֵלֶיךָ הַר־שֵׂעִיר וְנָטִיתִי
ד יָדִי עָלֶיךָ וּנְתַתִּיךָ שְׁמָמָה וּמְשַׁמָּה: עָרֶיךָ
חָרְבָּה אָשִׂים וְאַתָּה שְׁמָמָה תִהְיֶה וְיָדַעְתָּ
ה כִּי־אֲנִי יהוה: יַעַן הֱיוֹת לְךָ אֵיבַת עוֹלָם
וַתַּגֵּר אֶת־בְּנֵי־יִשְׂרָאֵל עַל־יְדֵי חָרֶב בְּעֵת

XXXV

Mount Seir, against which this prophecy is directed, was the home of the Edomites, descendants of Jacob's brother Esau (Genesis 36:1, 8, 9).

This is Yechezkel's second prophesy against them; they were the subject of his visions in 25:8, 12-14. The mere fact of a second prophecy is not unusual, both Tyre (chs. 26-28) and Egypt (chs. 29-32) were the subject of more than one vision. However, those prophecies appear as a group and are part of the self-contained and cohesive unit (chs. 25-32) dealing with prophecies against the nations (see pref. chs. 25-32), but this vision against Mount Seir is unexpectedly placed among the chapters of נֶחָמָה, comfort, *rather than among the visions against the nations of which it seems to be a part.*

Perhaps this chapter views the Edomites from a different perspective than does the prophecy in ch. 25. A small country to the south of Israel, it had joined Israel's other neighbors in displaying its ethical bankruptcy by rejoicing at the Babylonian victory. In this context it is no different from its sister nations, and chapter 25 tells of the punishments which would overtake it for its vindictive hatred.

There is another dimension to Edom, one that carries it beyond its territorial boundaries and places it squarely at the center of world history. Edom is the last, and most vicious, of the Four Monarchies destined to subjugate Israel in its road through history. (See comm. 21:24-27; Overview, *The Four Monarchies, Bereishis ArtScroll ed., Vol. II, p. 417.) It destroyed the Second Temple, in its exile Israel has languished for close to 2000 years, and from its hands Israel will be redeemed by the Messiah.* [*Both the destruction of the Temple and the subsequent exile are ascribed to Edom. See Ramban, Sefer HaGeulah Ch. 3, p. 284.*]

It is no coincidence that Edom plays this pivotal role in Israel's history. At the very dawn of Israel's beginnings, God had decreed that it whom He was to love (Malachi 1:2) would, until the End of Days, have its fate intertwined with a balancing force of evil which would embody everything hateful to God (Malachi 1:3). Two nations were within Rebecca's womb, and two irreconcilable world views of peoplehood were to diverge from within her (Genesis 25:23). Never would these two be able to coexist. One would always be in the ascendant; the other, in decline (Rashi, there, based on Pesachim 42b, Megillah 6a).

Throughout its history, as Israel fulfilled its destiny as God's chosen people, it subjugated Edom. But when Israel lost its perspective, forgot its own unique character, and foundered on its road to holiness, Edom's star would rise as Israel's fell. (See Derashos HaRan, D'rush 2 for a detailed tracing of these events).[1]

Israel's nadir was reached when the Second Temple fell to Rome's legions. That was the moment at which the final and darkest of all the exiles came upon it. This

1. The relationship between the twin brothers, Jacob and Esau, and between their descendants is one of the great themes of the *Aggadah*. There is hardly an aspect of Jewish experience

The word of HASHEM came to me, saying:
[2] Ben Adam, set your face against Mount Seir
and prophesy against it; [3] and say to it: Thus says my
Lord HASHEM/ELOHIM: Behold! I am against you,
Mount Seir, and I shall stretch out My hand against
you and make you desolate and empty. [4] Your cities I
will lay waste, and you will be desolate; then you
shall know that I am HASHEM. [5] Because you have
eternal hatred, and you have caused the Children of
Israel to stream forth, by the sword at the moment of

was Edom's moment in history, and the two millenia of suffering which its ascendancy brought upon mankind will not be relieved until the coming of the Messiah. At that time saviors will go up on Mount Zion to punish Mount Esau. Then kingship will be God's *(Obadiah v. 21).*

The prophecy against Edom in this chapter is to be understood from this perspective. Edom as a nation neighboring upon Israel's borders belongs with the other nations and is dealt with in chs. 25-32; but Edom as the *force of evil in the world whose downfall will herald the Messianic age must be dealt with among Yechezkel's prophecies of comfort.*

2. שִׂים פָּנֶיךָ עַל הַר־שֵׂעִיר — *Set your face against Mount Seir.*

The prophecy against Seir follows the prophecy of Israel's redemption in the previous chapter, because Edom will fall at the time of that redemption (*Radak*, based on *Obadiah v.* 21, quoted in pref.)

5. אֵיבַת עוֹלָם — *Eternal hatred.*

Eternal is in the sense of *irreconcilable (R' Breuer).* Israel and Edom represent two utterly opposing world views. Already in their mother's wombs they had contended with one another for ascendancy in both this world and the next (*Midrash Avkir;* see *Rashi, Genesis* 25:22). Jacob had been granted the World to Come, Esau had won This World (see *Maharal, Netzach Yisrael* 15 and *Derush Naeh LeShabbas HaGadol*). A terrible hatred grew up between them. R' Shimon bar Yochai said, 'It is an immutable law (הֲלָכָה) that Esau hates Jacob' (*Sifri, Numbers* 9:10). (See *comm.* 25:12-14; *The Four Monarchies, Bereishis,* ibid).

וַתַּגֵּר אֶת בְּנֵי יִשְׂרָאֵל עַל יְדֵי חָרֶב — *And you have caused the Children of Israel to stream forth, by the sword.*

נגר in the הִפְעִיל, *causative,* means *to cause* or *allow something to flow forth. Rashi* stretches this meaning to include casting something down. The Edomites had hurled down the fleeing Jews in front of their enemies (see 25:12-14). Scripture uses the word in this sense in *Michah* (1:6.)

According to *Radak* and *Metzudos,* the word refers to Israel's blood which was shed (made to flow) by the Edomite sword.

which remains untouched by it. See, for example, *Maharal's Netzach Yisrael,* much of which is devoted to a detailed explication of this theme. Our Sages explain God's motive in creating such a balance between the forces of good and evil.

Yalkut to (*Psalms* 17:13) refers to Esau as: *'God's sword with which He subdues the world.' Yalkut (Psalms* 10:14) points out that when Isaac gave Esau the blessing of the sword (*Genesis* 27:40), it must have been God's own wish, for it was He who granted Isaac the Divine inspiration which enabled him to confer that gift. *Ramban (Genesis* 27:4) even suggests that Rebecca's puzzling silence in not revealing to Isaac that she had been told that the younger of her two sons would be the greater, was a result of God's direct intervention. God wanted to insure

ו אֵידָ֔ם בְּעֵ֖ת עֲוֺ֥ן קֵֽץ׃ לָכֵ֣ן חַי־אָ֗נִי נְאֻם֙
אֲדֹנָ֣י יֱהֹוִ֔ה כִּֽי־לְדָ֥ם אֶעֶשְׂךָ֖ וְדָ֣ם יִרְדֲּפֶ֑ךָּ
ז אִם־לֹ֥א דָ֛ם שָׂנֵ֖אתָ וְדָ֥ם יִרְדֲּפֶֽךָּ׃ וְנָתַתִּי֙
אֶת־הַ֣ר שֵׂעִ֔יר לְשִׁמְמָ֖ה וּשְׁמָמָ֑ה וְהִכְרַתִּ֥י
ח מִמֶּ֖נּוּ עֹבֵ֥ר וָשָֽׁב׃ וּמִלֵּאתִ֥י אֶת־הָרָ֖יו
חֲלָלָ֑יו גִּבְעוֹתֶ֨יךָ וְגֵאוֹתֶ֜יךָ וְכָל־אֲפִיקֶ֗יךָ
ט חַלְלֵי־חֶ֖רֶב יִפְּל֥וּ בָהֶֽם׃ שִׁמְמ֤וֹת עוֹלָם֙
אֶתֶּנְךָ֔ וְעָרֶ֖יךָ לֹ֣א °תישבנה וִֽידַעְתֶּ֖ם כִּֽי־ °תָּשֹׁבְנָה ק׳
י אֲנִ֥י יְהוָֽה׃ יַ֣עַן אֲ֠מָרְךָ אֶת־שְׁנֵ֨י הַגּוֹיִ֜ם
וְאֶת־שְׁתֵּ֧י הָאֲרָצ֛וֹת לִ֥י תִהְיֶ֖ינָה וִֽירַשְׁנ֑וּהָ

בְּעֵת אֵידָם — *At the moment of their disaster.*

The word אֵיד occurs once in *Ezekiel* but some twenty times throughout Scripture. The word 'disaster' seems to come close to the intended meaning. *Targum* renders: *shattering. Rashi* comments: at the time when I delivered them to the hands of their enemies. [There is no indication in the text whether a specific disaster is meant, or whether Edom was involved whenever there was a time of suffering for the Jews.]

עֲוֺן קֵץ — *The climactic sin.*

This expression is unique to *Ezekiel.* See *comm.* 21:30.

6. לְדָם אֶעֶשְׂךָ וְדָם יִרְדֲּפֶךָּ — *I will turn you to blood, and blood shall pursue you.*

The second דָּם, *blood,* is to be understood as *shedders of blood (Radak).* The phrase means: I shall set you up for slaughter, and you will be pursued by people intent upon your murder.

אִם לֹא דָם שָׂנֵאתָ וְדָם יִרְדֲּפֶךָּ — *Surely though you have hated blood, blood shall pursue you.*

Radak continues to interpret דָּם as *shedders of blood.* God tells Esau: 'You have lived in hateful fear of those who sought your blood. Your attempts to protect yourself will fail. Those whom you fear will pursue and catch you.'

Rashi, however, interprets דָּם, literally as *blood;* Esau is described as one who hates blood. The expression *you have hated blood* is particularly striking as a description of Esau and his descendants, the Edomites. *Genesis* 25:25 had described Esau as אַדְמוֹנִי, *ruddy,* to which the Midrash (*Bereishis Rabbah* 63:11) remarks that he looked as though he was a murderer. Isaac knew well the nature of his son and predicted that he would *live by* [*his*] *sword (Genesis* 27:40). This being so, why would Esau who represents bloodlust, be described as one who hates blood?

The Midrash (*Bereishis Rabbah* 63:18, quoted in part by *Rashi)* raises the question. The Sages answer that the blood which Esau hated was not the blood of slaughtered people. Such blood disturbed him not at all. It was part and parcel of his daily life. The blood which he hated was the blood of the sacrifices, with which he would have been

that Esau would receive the blessing of the sword.

Thus it is Jacob's need which places the sword in Esau's hand. Without the power granted to Esau, a time might come in which Jacob would forget its holy destiny and assimilate with the other nations. Esau's sword is an eternal guarantee that this will not happen. As Israel sinks, Edom rises — an implacable foe who will not let God's people forget its identity.

their disaster — at the moment of the climactic sin —
6 *therefore, as I live — the words of my Lord HASHEM/ELOHIM — I will turn you to blood, and blood shall pursue you. Surely though you have hated blood, blood shall pursue you;*
7 *and I shall make Mount Seir desolate and empty and cut off from it anyone who passes through or returns;*
8 *and I shall fill his mountains with his slain. Your hills, your valleys, and all your streams — the victims of the sword shall fall there.*
9 *For eternal desolation I shall make you that your cities shall not be settled. Then you shall know that I am HASHEM.*
10 *Because you said: The two nations and the two lands will be mine and we shall inherit them! But*

splashed had he retained his birthright and shouldered the priestly duties which were among the privileges of the first-born. In addition, it was the blood of circumcision which he rejected by disfiguring himself in order to deny that the mark of God's covenant had ever been placed upon him. Esau's portion was the physical world, and he hated anything that had the power to sanctify it (see *comm., v.* 5). Thereby he forfeited his right to live. He would be pursued by the sword.[1]

8. הָרָיו ... גְּבְעוֹתֶיךָ — *His mountains ... your hills.*

The change from third person to second person is irregular, but similar switches are not unusual in Scripture *(Radak).*

10. אֶת־שְׁנֵי הַגּוֹיִם וְאֶת־שְׁתֵּי הָאֲרָצוֹת — *The two nations and the two lands.*

These are Israel and Judah *(Rashi).*

Edom's gleeful anticipation at taking over Israel's land is understandable. It is less clear why Edom stresses the fact that there are *two* nations and *two* lands. The commentators do not discuss this question.

A solution may be found by considering that the northern kingdom is iden-

1. Esau's hatred of sacrifices and circumcision can be readily understood. Both introduce sanctity into the realm of the otherwise purely physical, and Esau, the man of עוֹלָם הַזֶּה, *This World,* hates all that is holy. Less obvious is why this hatred is expressed in terms of *blood.* In the words of the Midrash, Esau does not want to be 'dirtied' by the blood of the sacrifices, and the *blood* of circumcision offends him. It is surprising that Esau, the killer, would be offended by blood.

However, the Torah teaches that contact between the spiritual and the physical is established in the blood: *Blood is the soul (Deuteronomy* 12:23; see footnote 21:2 on שְׁפִיכַת דָּם, *bloodshed).*

It is perhaps for this reason that blood plays such a central role not only in the Halachic structure of the sacrificial service, but also in its philosophical aspects. (See *Pesachim* 65b: It is praiseworthy for ... the priests to walk in [the sacrificial] blood up to their knees.) *Ramban (Leviticus* 17:11) explains the use of blood in sacrifice in terms of its being the seat of the נֶפֶשׁ, *soul.* The significance of blood in circumcision is discussed in *comm.* 16:6. The covenant of circumcision is symbolic of Israel's willingness to lay down its life for God. It is written *(Psalms* 44:23): *For You are we killed all day.* R' Shimon ben Menasya says: 'Is it possible for a man to be killed every day? This must refer to circumcision. Esau is repelled by this aspect of blood — its symbolism as the ennobling process which elevates that animal creature of creation' *(Sifri, Deuteronomy* 6:5).

יא וַיהוָה שָׁם הָיָה: לָכֵן חַי־אָנִי נְאֻם אֲדֹנָי
יֱהוִה וְעָשִׂיתִי כְּאַפֵּךְ וּכְקִנְאָתֵךְ אֲשֶׁר
עָשִׂיתָה מִשִּׂנְאָתַיִךְ בָּם וְנוֹדַעְתִּי בָם
יב כַּאֲשֶׁר אֶשְׁפְּטֵךְ: וְיָדַעְתָּ כִּי אֲנִי יְהוָה
שָׁמַעְתִּי | אֶת־כָּל־נָאָצוֹתֶיךָ אֲשֶׁר אָמַרְתָּ
עַל־הָרֵי יִשְׂרָאֵל לֵאמֹר | °שממה (°שָׁמֵמוּ ק׳)
יג לָנוּ נִתְּנוּ לְאָכְלָה: וַתַּגְדִּילוּ עָלַי
בְּפִיכֶם וְהַעְתַּרְתֶּם עָלַי דִּבְרֵיכֶם אֲנִי
יד שָׁמָעְתִּי: כֹּה אָמַר אֲדֹנָי יֱהוִה
כִּשְׂמֹחַ כָּל־הָאָרֶץ שְׁמָמָה אֶעֱשֶׂה־לָּךְ:
טו כְּשִׂמְחָתְךָ לְנַחֲלַת בֵּית־יִשְׂרָאֵל עַל
אֲשֶׁר־שָׁמֵמָה כֵּן אֶעֱשֶׂה־לָּךְ שְׁמָמָה
תִהְיֶה הַר־שֵׂעִיר וְכָל־אֱדוֹם כֻּלָּהּ וְיָדְעוּ

לו
א כִּי־אֲנִי יְהוָה: וְאַתָּה בֶן־אָדָם

tified with the descendants of Jacob's wife Rachel, while the southern kingdom, although it included Benjamin was called Judah because it remained the seat of the Davidic dynasty and is therefore associated with the descendants of Leah (see *comm.* 23:3).

According to *Bava Basrah* 123b, Rachel's descendants are the implacable antagonists of Esau. Joseph is to be the flame which will consume the straw which is Esau. Israel never won a victory over Edom unless its army contained contingents from Joseph's family. Edom had enjoyed military successes against Judah (*II Kings* 8:20, 22), but trembled at the thought of the northern tribes.

Assyria's conquest of Shomron must have been a moment of great exultation for Edom; henceforth it would have nothing more to fear from Israel.

This provides the background for understanding our verse. Edom rejoices at its power, for not only Judah, but even the hated and feared northern kingdom lie defenseless before it.

וַה׳ שָׁם הָיָה — *But HASHEM was there.*

He knew your thoughts *(Rashi).*

11. וְעָשִׂיתִי כְּאַפֵּךְ — *And I shall act according to your anger.*

In accordance with the anger which you showed Israel I shall do to you *(Rashi).*

וְנוֹדַעְתִּי בָם — *Then I shall be acknowledged among them.*

When I punish you (Edom) then they will recognize My might *(Rashi).*

Since I will punish you for the sake of Israel, I will become recognized by them as He Who chose them and [made them] My people *(Radak).*

12. כָּל־נָאָצוֹתֶיךָ — *All your provocations.*

Targum renders אַרְגָּזוּתָךְ, *that which makes angry.* (See *Targum,* 20:28.) *Rashi* to *Exodus* 14:11 seems to agree to this translation. However *Rashi* to *Psalms* 10:3 quotes *Menachem* who translates נאץ as *blasphemy.*

13. וְהַעְתַּרְתֶּם עָלַי דִּבְרֵיכֶם — *And multiplied your words against Me.*

The root עתר means: *to be abundant,* as in 8:11 *(Rashi).*

HASHEM was there. 11 *Therefore, as I live — the*
words of my Lord HASHEM/ELOHIM — and I shall act
according to your anger and your jealousy, as you
have done because of your hatred against them. Then
I shall be acknowledged among them when I judge
you. 12 *Then you shall know that I am HASHEM. I*
have heard all your provocations that you have ut-
tered about Israel's hills, saying 'They are desolate;
they are given to us to devour;' 13 *and you have*
magnified yourselves against Me with your mouth
and multiplied your words against Me. I have heard.
14 *Thus says my Lord HASHEM/ELOHIM: When all*
the world rejoices, I will make you desolate. 15 *As you*
rejoiced over the heritage of the Family of Israel
because it was desolate, so shall I do to you. Desolate
will you be, Mount Seir, and every bit of Edom. Then
they shall know that I am HASHEM.

14. כְּשְׂמֹחַ כָּל־הָאָרֶץ — *When all the world rejoices.*

When I establish My kingship, the whole world will rejoice, as it is written (*Psalms* 97:1): *God has ruled. Let the earth jubilate (Rashi).*

This clearly refers to Messianic times (see pref.). The world will rejoice when history will have run its course and the darkness of the ascendancy of the Four Monarchies will have been lifted to make room for the רוּחַ אֱלֹהִים, *Divine Presence (Genesis* 1:2), that will rest on the Messiah (see *comm.* 21:24-27). That era, when Jacob-Israel will have been vindicated finally, spells Esau-Edom's doom. His power derived from Jacob's weakness (*Genesis* 27:40). He cannot share in Israel's greatness.[1]

XXXVI

This chapter is an extension of the previous one. In contrast to Seir's mountains, whose desolation will bear mute testimony to that proud nation's final downfall, Israel's hills will burst forth with a profusion of God's bounty, welcoming a reborn Israel to its eternal home.

The theme of the chapter is renewal: *renewal of the people, as a new heart and a new spirit are implanted in them (v. 26), and renewal of the land, as its once barren soil turns into a Garden of Eden (v. 35; Maharal, Netsach Yisrael 39). Thus the prophet brings us face to face with one of the great mysteries of Jewish experience — the bond between land and people which has never weakened despite centuries of exile from one another.*

This unity of fate was predicted in the Torah. When Israel's destiny of exile was pronounced in the תּוֹכָחָה, rebuke, *of* בְּחֻקֹּתַי *(Leviticus, ch. 26), it was accompanied*

1. [For analysis or this concept, see *Pachad Yitzchak, Purim,* ch. 1, where the inevitability of Esau's downfall in the Messianic era is shown to be predicted by *Numbers* 24:20 and is discussed in depth.]

לו
ב־ה

הִנָּבֵא אֶל־הָרֵי יִשְׂרָאֵל וְאָמַרְתָּ הָרֵי
ב יִשְׂרָאֵל שִׁמְעוּ דְּבַר־יְהוָה׃ כֹּה אָמַר אֲדֹנָי
יֱהוִה יַעַן אָמַר הָאוֹיֵב עֲלֵיכֶם הֶאָח
ג וּבָמוֹת עוֹלָם לְמוֹרָשָׁה הָיְתָה לָּנוּ׃ לָכֵן
הִנָּבֵא וְאָמַרְתָּ כֹּה אָמַר אֲדֹנָי יֱהוִה יַעַן
בְּיַעַן שַׁמּוֹת וְשָׁאֹף אֶתְכֶם מִסָּבִיב
לִהְיוֹתְכֶם מוֹרָשָׁה לִשְׁאֵרִית הַגּוֹיִם
ד וַתֵּעֲלוּ עַל־שְׂפַת לָשׁוֹן וְדִבַּת־עָם׃ לָכֵן
הָרֵי יִשְׂרָאֵל שִׁמְעוּ דְּבַר־אֲדֹנָי יֱהוִה כֹּה־
אָמַר אֲדֹנָי יֱהוִה לֶהָרִים וְלַגְּבָעוֹת
לָאֲפִיקִים וְלַגֵּאָיוֹת וְלֶחֳרָבוֹת הַשֹּׁמְמוֹת
וְלֶעָרִים הַנֶּעֱזָבוֹת אֲשֶׁר הָיוּ לְבַז וּלְלַעַג
ה לִשְׁאֵרִית הַגּוֹיִם אֲשֶׁר מִסָּבִיב׃ לָכֵן

by a comforting clause (Ramban, Leviticus 26:16). Israel would leave the land, driven from it by the mighty empire builders of antiquity, but its conquerors would never find the land hospitable. Your enemies who dwell upon it will be desolate *(Leviticus 26:32). Over the centuries many a people attempted to strike roots in the country which seemed to have so much to offer. It rejected them all, preferring to reflect the desolation of exiled Israel's heart in the desolation of its once fertile mountains and valleys.*

But its desolation was not to be a permanent one. Always the land lay ready to yield an open-handed bounty at the moment of Israel's return.

This loyalty of the land to its people is reflected in our prayers. In the ninth blessing of the Shemoneh Esrei, *we pray that God may shower His blessings on the earth and satisfy us with His goodness. This we immediately follow with the tenth blessing — an entreaty for the ingathering of the exiles — for, as Megillah 17b (based on v. 8 of our chapter) teaches, it is inconceivable that the blessings of the land would be granted except at the time of Israel's return.*

R' Abba taught (Sanhedrin 98a): There is no more obvious sign of the ultimate redemption (אין לך קץ מגולה) than the flowering of Israel's hills. If Israel's land ceases its mourning it must be because the children are returning to their home *(Jeremiah 31:16).*

The second half of our chapter (vs. 16-37) deals more specifically with the renewal of the people, the new heart and the new spirit with which they will experience in the Messianic era. Because this revitalization is expressed in terms of טוּמְאָה *and* טָהֳרָה, contamination *and* cleansing, *this passage was chosen as the Haftarah* for *Parshas Parah* (see intro. *vs.* 16-37).

1. הָרֵי יִשְׂרָאֵל — *Mountains of Israel.*

The same mountains of Israel upon which Yechezkel had poured out the bitter denunciations of ch. 6 now become the focus of his visions of renewal.

The comforting message of renewal addressed to the mountains of Israel

36
1-4

Now you, Ben Adam, prophesy to the mountains
of Israel and say: Mountains of Israel! Hear the
word of HASHEM. 2 *Thus says my Lord* HASHEM/
ELOHIM: *Because the enemy has said against you:*
'Hurrah — the heights of the world have become an
inheritance for us;' 3 *Therefore, prophesy and say:*
Thus says my Lord HASHEM/ELOHIM: *Because, and*
again because, they were astounded and craved you
from all around, for you to become an inheritance for
the rest of the nations, and you were raised upon the
lips of the nations, and became a topic of peoples,
4 *therefore, mountains of Israel, hear the word of my*
Lord HASHEM/ELOHIM! *Thus says my Lord*
HASHEM / ELOHIM *to the mountains and to the hills,*
to the streams and to the valleys, to the desolate
wastes and to the forlorn cities, which became prey
and derision for the rest of the nations all around —

contrasts with the vision of the disasters which are to befall Mount Seir in the previous chapter *(Radak).*

2. הָאוֹיֵב — *The enemy.*

The enemy of this verse is identified as Edom by *Mechilta* to *Exodus* 15:6. Thus this chapter is a direct continuation of the previous one.

וּבָמוֹת עוֹלָם — *The heights of the world.*

This refers to the land of Israel, which is the high point and beauty of the world *(Rashi).*

3. יַעַן בְּיַעַן — *Because, and again because.*

The double expression is intended to lend strong emphasis to the following point *(Radak; Metzudos).*

Targum tends to ascribe separate meanings to such double expressions. Here *Targum* renders: *Because you have prided yourself and because you planned to destroy* ... [*See comm.* 13:10 for discussion.]

שַׁמּוֹת וְשָׁאֹף אֶתְכֶם מִסָּבִיב — *They were astounded and craved you from all around.*

שַׁמּוֹת is derived from שמם, which can mean *to be astounded* or *appalled,* or *to be desolate.* שאף means either *to crave* or *yearn,* or *to inhale* or *swallow.*

Rashi, using the first meanings for both words, comments: Because they have been watching your destruction in shocked silence, eagerly awaiting your downfall so that they could take over your land...

Radak, using the second meaning for both words, comments: Because they plotted your desolation and planned to swallow you up so that you would become their inheritance...

וַתֵּעֲלוּ עַל שְׂפַת לָשׁוֹן וְדִבַּת עָם — *And you were raised upon the lips of the nations, and became a topic of peoples.*

Scripture often uses לָשׁוֹן, *tongue,* or *language,* as a synonym for *nation* since different nations speak different languages *(Metzudos, Isaiah* 66:18).

דִּבָּה from לדבב, *to move gently,* describes that which people discuss (move their lips) or whisper about. It is generally used in the sense of *defamation (Metzudos).*

4. Compare 6:3.

כֹּה־אָמַר אֲדֹנָי יֱהֹוִה אִם־לֹא בְּאֵשׁ
קִנְאָתִי דִבַּרְתִּי עַל־שְׁאֵרִית הַגּוֹיִם וְעַל־
אֱדוֹם כֻּלָּא אֲשֶׁר נָתְנוּ־אֶת־אַרְצִי ׀ לָהֶם
לְמוֹרָשָׁה בְּשִׂמְחַת כָּל־לֵבָב בִּשְׁאָט נֶפֶשׁ
ו לְמַעַן מִגְרָשָׁהּ לָבַז׃ לָכֵן הִנָּבֵא עַל־
אַדְמַת יִשְׂרָאֵל וְאָמַרְתָּ לֶהָרִים וְלַגְּבָעוֹת
לָאֲפִיקִים וְלַגֵּאָיוֹת כֹּה־אָמַר ׀ אֲדֹנָי יֱהֹוִה
הִנְנִי בְקִנְאָתִי וּבַחֲמָתִי דִּבַּרְתִּי יַעַן כְּלִמַּת
ז גּוֹיִם נְשָׂאתֶם׃ לָכֵן כֹּה אָמַר אֲדֹנָי יֱהֹוִה
אֲנִי נָשָׂאתִי אֶת־יָדִי אִם־לֹא הַגּוֹיִם אֲשֶׁר
ח לָכֶם מִסָּבִיב הֵמָּה כְּלִמָּתָם יִשָּׂאוּ׃ וְאַתֶּם
הָרֵי יִשְׂרָאֵל עַנְפְּכֶם תִּתֵּנוּ וּפֶרְיְכֶם
ט תִּשְׂאוּ לְעַמִּי יִשְׂרָאֵל כִּי קֵרְבוּ לָבוֹא׃ כִּי
הִנְנִי אֲלֵיכֶם וּפָנִיתִי אֲלֵיכֶם וְנֶעֱבַדְתֶּם
י וְנִזְרַעְתֶּם׃ וְהִרְבֵּיתִי עֲלֵיכֶם אָדָם כָּל־בֵּית
יִשְׂרָאֵל כֻּלֹּה וְנֹשְׁבוּ הֶעָרִים וְהֶחֳרָבוֹת
יא תִּבָּנֶינָה׃ וְהִרְבֵּיתִי עֲלֵיכֶם אָדָם וּבְהֵמָה
וְרָבוּ וּפָרוּ וְהוֹשַׁבְתִּי אֶתְכֶם כְּקַדְמוֹתֵיכֶם
וְהֵיטִבֹתִי מֵרִאשֹׁתֵיכֶם וִידַעְתֶּם כִּי־אֲנִי

5. בִּשְׁאָט נֶפֶשׁ — *With a rashness of soul.*

See *comm.* 16:57.

לְמַעַן מִגְרָשָׁהּ לָבַז — *Because her expulsion was for plunder.*

Rashi translates לְמַעַן as *because* (rather than as *in order to.* See *comm.* 4:17). The nations regarded Israel's expulsion from its land as nothing more than an opportunity for them to plunder (בַּז from לבוז, *to plunder) her abandoned land.*

Metzudos renders: in order that her expulsion might be turned into an embarrassment (בַּז from לבוז, *to despise.)*

8. Israel reserves its bounty for its people (see pref.).

Megillah 17b explains the connection between the ninth and tenth blessing of the *Amidah* on the basis of this verse (see pref.).

9. וּפָנִיתִי אֲלֵיכֶם — *And I shall turn to you.*

This promise, addressed to הָרֵי יִשְׂרָאֵל, *mountains of Israel (v.* 8), recalls 6:2, where Yechezkel was told *set your face* [שִׂים פָּנֶיךָ] against these same mountains. (See *comm. v.* 1). The outpouring of love in these prophecies of נֶחָמָה, *comfort,* is in striking contrast to the earlier visions of חוּרְבָּן, *destruction.*

10. וְהִרְבֵּתִי עֲלֵיכֶם אָדָם — *And I will multiply men upon you.*

[5] therefore thus says my Lord HASHEM/ELOHIM:
Surely in the fire of My jealousy I have spoken
against the rest of the nations and against all Edom,
who have arrogated My land to themselves as an in-
heritance with the joy of all their heart, with a
rashness of soul — because her expulsion was for
plunder.

[6] Therefore prophesy about the land of Israel and
say to the mountains and to the hills, to the streams
and to the valleys: Thus says my Lord HASHEM/
ELOHIM: *Behold! In My jealousy and in My anger I*
have spoken, because the shame of the nations you
have borne. [7] Therefore, thus says my Lord
HASHEM/ELOHIM: *I have lifted My hand in an oath.*
Surely the nations which surround you — they will
bear their shame, [8] but you, mountains of Israel —
you shall shoot forth your branches and bear your
fruit for My people Israel, when they are about to
come; [9] for behold! — I am for you, and I shall turn to
you; then you shall be tilled and sown; [10] and I will
multiply men upon you, the entire family of Israel —
all of it. Then the cities will be inhabited and the
ruins will be built up. [11] Then I will multiply men and
animals upon you, and they shall increase and be
fruitful, and I shall cause you to be inhabited in your
earlier times, and I shall bring greater benefit than at
your beginnings, and you shall know that I am

As the rest of the verse makes clear, these *men* are the family of Israel. By referring to them as אָדָם, *man,* Yechezkel reinforces the lesson which he taught at 34:31. (See *comm.* there.)

כָּל בֵּית יִשְׂרָאֵל כֻּלֹּה — ***The entire family of Israel — all of it.***

In the view of *Radak* and *Metzudos,* the phrase alludes to the return of the ten tribes. (See *comm., footnote* 11:15). This idea is discussed further in *comm.* 37:15-28.

11. וְהֵיטִבֹתִי מֵרִאשֹׁתֵיכֶם — ***And I shall bring greater benefit than at your beginnings.***

The wording recalls *Deuteronomy* 30:5, which promises that upon Israel's return to the land, God will *do good to you and increase you more than your fathers.*

Yerushalmi Kiddushin 1:8 quotes R' Elazar who is of the opinion that reference is to Messianic times, when their situation will be an improvement

לו
יב־יז

יב יְהוָה׃ וְהוֹלַכְתִּי עֲלֵיכֶם אָדָם אֶת־עַמִּי
יִשְׂרָאֵל וִירֵשׁוּךָ וְהָיִיתָ לָהֶם לְנַחֲלָה
יג וְלֹא־תוֹסִף עוֹד לְשַׁכְּלָם׃ כֹּה
אָמַר אֲדֹנָי יֱהוִה יַעַן אֹמְרִים לָכֶם אֹכֶלֶת
°אָתְּ/גּוֹיַיִךְ ק׳ יד אָדָם °אתי וּמְשַׁכֶּלֶת °גויך הָיִית׃ לָכֵן
°וְגוֹיַיִךְ ק׳ אָדָם לֹא־תֹאכְלִי עוֹד °וגויך לֹא
תְשַׁכְּלִי ק׳ טו °תכשלי־עוֹד נְאֻם אֲדֹנָי יֱהוִה׃ וְלֹא־
אַשְׁמִיעַ אֵלַיִךְ עוֹד כְּלִמַּת הַגּוֹיִם וְחֶרְפַּת
°וְגוֹיַיִךְ ק׳ עַמִּים לֹא תִשְׂאִי־עוֹד °וגויך לֹא־תַכְשִׁלִי
טז עוֹד נְאֻם אֲדֹנָי יֱהוִה׃ וַיְהִי
יז דְבַר־יְהוָה אֵלַי לֵאמֹר׃ בֶּן־אָדָם בֵּית

and an 'increase' over that of their fathers. Originally, Israel occupied the land of only seven out of the ten nations which had been promised to Abraham (*Genesis* 15:19-21), whereas in Messianic times it will occupy all ten.

Perhaps our verse has a similar meaning.

13-15. Over the centuries *Eretz Yisrael* would come to be known as an inhospitable land. Neither the early Canaanite settlers nor the Jewish people were able to remain there for long. The Canaanites had been driven out by Joshua; the Jewish people by successive invasions at the hands of Assyria, Babylon, and Rome. In the following centuries many attempts were made to settle the land, none of them achieving any permanence. The land became an object of derision; it seemed to consume its inhabitants, to be unable to hold its people.

The cause for this historical phenomenon lies in the land's unique status of being *God's portion* on earth (*Deuteronomy* 32:9). As such it cannot and will not tolerate sin within its boundaries (*Ramban, Leviticus* 18:25), and the Torah predicts (*Leviticus* 18:25, 28) that it will *vomit out* all those who defile its sanctity. No people had been able to rise to this challenge to holiness for any length of time. Time and again the land had to preserve its sanctity by evicting the nations that had defiled it.

The promise of this section is that the future will be different. No more will the land have to defend itself against desecration. It will be settled by people who will heed its call to greatness.

16-37. Every year, on one of the Sabbaths between Purim and Pesach, *Parshas Parah* [*the Chapter of the Red Cow*] (*Numbers* 19:1-22) is read in the synagogue. The passage deals with the טוּמְאָה, *spiritual contamination,* which is caused by contact with a dead body, and the means by which טָהֳרָה, *ritual purity,* may be achieved. Central to the cleansing process was the פָּרָה אֲדֻמָּה, *red cow,* whose ashes, mixed with water, were sprinkled upon the person who had become טָמֵא, *contaminated.*

Megillah 30a specifies our section as the *Haftarah* to be read on that occasion. This is based on *v.* 25, where God promises to cleanse Israel of sin by (metaphorically) sprinkling pure water upon them.

Verse 25 is only one among several in our passage which draws parallels between the ideas of sin and *contamination,* and of atonement and *purity.*

HASHEM, 12 *and I shall cause men to walk upon you*
— My people Israel — and they shall inherit you.
Then you shall be theirs for an inheritance and you
shall no longer be bereaved of them.
13 *Thus says my Lord HASHEM/ELOHIM: Because*
they say of you, 'A devourer of men are you, and one
bereaved of your nations, have you become'.
14 *Therefore — men, you shall never again devour,*
and of your nations, you shall never again be
bereaved — the words of my Lord HASHEM/ELOHIM
— 15 *and I shall no longer cause the derision of na-*
tions to be heard about you, and the shame of the
peoples you shall no longer bear, of your nations you
shall never again be bereaved — the words of my Lord
HASHEM/ELOHIM.
16 *The word of HASHEM came to me, saying:* 17 *Ben*

The connection between sin and (spiritual) death is found in *Deuteronomy* 30:15-19, which equates *good* with *life* and *evil* with *death*. However, the metaphor in our passage deals not with sin as death, but rather as a cause of contamination similar to that caused by contact with death. Atonement is projected as a cleansing process which frees man from contamination.

In the view of *R' Hirsch* bolstered by proofs from the Midrashic and Talmud, these conditions have their source in the moral, rather than the ritual, sphere. Contamination occurs, and cleansing becomes necessary, when man is exposed to a situation inimical to Torah morality.

Freedom of will in moral matters is the first and irreplaceable condition for living one's life on the higher plane demanded by the Torah. Belief in man's freedom of action, however, is endangered by the fact that man cannot avoid death and that he is subject to the superficial limitations imposed by the forces of nature. This belief is particularly shaken by the sight of a dead human being. If the whole human being has succumbed to death, overpowered by physical forces — if man, like all other organic beings, cannot escape the spell of an overpowering force — then there is no room for the moral 'you shall' next to the physical 'you must'. Moral freedom of will would then be an illusion, and the Divine law of morality with its demand for total, free-willed devotion to the illuminating, purifying fire of its Sanctuary, would be incomprehensible (*Hirsch, Numbers* 19:22).

Thus, sin is related not only to death, but also to contamination, which is closely associated with death. Because the sinner is shackled by his desires, he loses spiritual control of his actions. He is swept along by the physical lusts which have overpowered his spiritual self. Thus, the most meaningful part of his life, the spiritual, has been killed.

For this reason, when God forgives man's sin and grants him a new heart and a new spirit, he is imbuing him with טָהֳרָה, *purity*, the state in which man is the sole master of his actions. A living, and therefore a pure person uses his body as he wills; it is his tool to use as

יִשְׂרָאֵל יֹשְׁבִים עַל־אַדְמָתָם וַיְטַמְּאוּ
אוֹתָהּ בְּדַרְכָּם וּבַעֲלִילוֹתָם כְּטֻמְאַת
יח הַנִּדָּה הָיְתָה דַרְכָּם לְפָנָי׃ וָאֶשְׁפֹּךְ חֲמָתִי
עֲלֵיהֶם עַל־הַדָּם אֲשֶׁר־שָׁפְכוּ עַל־הָאָרֶץ
יט וּבְגִלּוּלֵיהֶם טִמְּאוּהָ׃ וָאָפִיץ אֹתָם בַּגּוֹיִם
וַיִּזָּרוּ בָּאֲרָצוֹת כְּדַרְכָּם וְכַעֲלִילוֹתָם
כ שְׁפַטְתִּים׃ וַיָּבוֹא אֶל־הַגּוֹיִם אֲשֶׁר־בָּאוּ
שָׁם וַיְחַלְּלוּ אֶת־שֵׁם קָדְשִׁי בֶּאֱמֹר לָהֶם
כא עַם־יהוה אֵלֶּה וּמֵאַרְצוֹ יָצָאוּ׃ וָאֶחְמֹל
עַל־שֵׁם קָדְשִׁי אֲשֶׁר חִלְּלֻהוּ בֵּית יִשְׂרָאֵל
כב בַּגּוֹיִם אֲשֶׁר־בָּאוּ שָׁמָּה׃ לָכֵן

he sees fit. The regenerate sinner, upon returning to the state of purity, joins once more the ranks of the living — and the free *(Chazon HaMikrah).*

17. וַיְטַמְּאוּ אוֹתָהּ — *And contaminate it.*

From *Rashi, Joshua* 22:19 (see also *Ramban, Numbers* 21:21) it would seem that the land is considered טָמֵא, *contaminated,* when there is no Divine Presence there. Jewish sins had driven the Divine Presence from Jerusalem (see pref., ch. 1) and thus caused the city's contamination.

כְּטֻמְאַת הַנִּדָּה — *Like the contamination of a menstruous women.*

With exquisite compassion the prophet tempers his harsh judgment. Israel had defiled the land, but it was a defilement comparable to that of a woman in the days of her impurity. Her husband waits anxiously for the contamination to pass, yearning for the time when he may come close to her once more *(Rashi).*

The *Midrash* quoted in *Yalkut* reads somewhat differently. It offers two explanations why the illustration of the *niddah,* a *menstruous woman,* is chosen. First, her impurity is transitory and she can be purified (while a dead body remains permanently contaminated). Secondly, even the High Priest may enter a *niddah's* home and sit in close proximity to her, while no priest is allowed in a house which contains a dead body. Thus even in the period of Israel's impurity, God remains with her; as it is written: *Who dwells among them in the midst of their contamination (Leviticus* 16:16).

The *Midrash,* which stresses that Israel's contamination is compared to that of a *niddah* rather than to that of a dead body, seems to contradict the ideas spelled in the introduction to this section. However, the choice of this section for the *Haftarah* of *Parshas Parah* seems to confirm the comparison to the contamination of the dead body (see also *Rashi* to v. 25).

We must concludes that Israel's contamination is indeed comparable to that of a dead body. Nevertheless, God, in His compassion, views the contamination as no more than that of a menstruous woman. In God's infinite mercy the harsh nature of the contamination is mitigated.

20. Another dimension of the problem of גָּלוּת, *exile,* is introduced. When Israel is forced from its land, God's Name is desecrated (חִלּוּל הַשֵּׁם). He seems impotent against the foes of His people.

וַיָּבוֹא — *And they* [lit. *he*] *came.*

Minchas Shai to 23:44 lists all the places in Scripture where the singular יָבוֹא is used instead of the expected plural form. (See *comm.* there).

*Adam, the family of Israel dwell on their land and
contaminate it, by their way and their actions. Like
the contamination of a menstruous woman was their
way before Me.* 18 *So I poured My anger upon them
because of the blood which they poured upon the
earth — and they had defiled it with their idols —* 19 *so
I scattered them among the nations and they were
dispersed among the lands. According to their ways
and their doings did I judge them;* 20 *and they came to
the nations to which they came, and they desecrated
My holy Name when it was said of them, 'These are
HASHEM's people but they departed His land;'* 21 *but
I pitied My holy Name which the family of Israel
desecrated among the nations to which they came.*

Rashi suggests that the singular form is used because it goes back to the subject בֵּית יִשְׂרָאֵל, *family of Israel (v.* 17), but this fails to explain why all other verses in the section are in the plural.

The *Midrash (Eichah Rabbah, Pesichtah* 15, quoted by *Rashi*) offers its own explanation. וַיָּבוֹא is in the singular because it refers not to the people, but to God. Because God, as it were, accompanies Israel in its exile, *He* also *came* among the nations. There He heard the captors talking among themselves and saying that their success proved His impotence to prevent His people from being forced from their land. This is the חִלּוּל הַשֵּׁם, *desecration of the Name,* referred to in our verse.[1]

Yomah 86a seems to understand this desecration of the Name differently. After describing the behavior of a person who wanted to cause God's Name to become beloved by people, the Talmud goes on to describe one whose actions have the opposite effect: Someone who learned Scripture, Mishnah, and Talmud, and is dishonest in his business dealings, and is unpleasant in his relationships — what do people say about him? Woe to him who learned Torah; woe to his father who taught him Torah; woe to his teacher who taught him Torah. This person who has learned Torah — see how imperfect are his actions, how ugly are his dealings. Concerning him our verse says: *These are HASHEM's people but have left His land.*

Thus the desecration of the Name is seen as deriving from Israel's sins. For a people who claimed to be God's special and chosen nation to act in a way that caused the land to spew them forth is the greatest possible desecration.

21-23. God will gather Israel's scattered exiles, not because they deserve it, but so that the desecration of exile may turn into a קִדּוּשׁ הַשֵּׁם, *sanctification of the Name.* (See *comm.,* footnote, 20:9).

1. It was by pointing out the potential of a similar desecration of the Name that Moses achieved God's forgiveness when He threatened to wipe out the Jewish people in connection with the sending of the spies (*Numbers* 14:16, 20; see *Rashi).*

The implications of Moses' argument and God's willingness to accept it are discussed in footnote to 20:9. The conclusions drawn there are of great relevance to this section of our chapter which repeats many of the ideas mentioned in ch. 20.

אֱמֹר לְבֵית־יִשְׂרָאֵל כֹּה אָמַר אֲדֹנָי יֱהֹוִה
לֹא לְמַעַנְכֶם אֲנִי עֹשֶׂה בֵּית יִשְׂרָאֵל כִּי
אִם־לְשֵׁם־קָדְשִׁי אֲשֶׁר חִלַּלְתֶּם בַּגּוֹיִם
כג אֲשֶׁר־בָּאתֶם שָׁם: וְקִדַּשְׁתִּי אֶת־שְׁמִי
הַגָּדוֹל הַמְחֻלָּל בַּגּוֹיִם אֲשֶׁר חִלַּלְתֶּם
בְּתוֹכָם וְיָדְעוּ הַגּוֹיִם כִּי־אֲנִי יהוה נְאֻם
אֲדֹנָי יֱהֹוִה בְּהִקָּדְשִׁי בָכֶם לְעֵינֵיהֶם:
כד וְלָקַחְתִּי אֶתְכֶם מִן־הַגּוֹיִם וְקִבַּצְתִּי
אֶתְכֶם מִכָּל־הָאֲרָצוֹת וְהֵבֵאתִי אֶתְכֶם
כה אֶל־אַדְמַתְכֶם: וְזָרַקְתִּי עֲלֵיכֶם מַיִם
טְהוֹרִים וּטְהַרְתֶּם מִכֹּל טֻמְאוֹתֵיכֶם
כו וּמִכָּל־גִּלּוּלֵיכֶם אֲטַהֵר אֶתְכֶם: וְנָתַתִּי
לָכֶם לֵב חָדָשׁ וְרוּחַ חֲדָשָׁה אֶתֵּן

24. God's Name will be sanctified when He brings scattered Israel back to its land.

Israel's dispersal meant much more than the loosening of national bonds. Much that was alien to the Jewish spirit entered into Jewish hearts as they mingled with the nations with whom they came in contact (*Psalms* 106:35). A major cleansing would be required. This is described in the next verse.

[The קִבּוּץ גָּלֻיּוֹת, *ingathering of exiles,* described in our chapter forms an element of the ninth blessing of *Shemoneh Esrei* (see pref.).

We begin that blessing with the prayer that God 'blow the great horn (שׁוֹפָר גָּדוֹל) for our deliverance' (based on *Isaiah* 27:13). The blowing of this great *shofar* is understood by our Sages (*Yerushalmi* quoted by *Aruch* under ערב, but unknown in our *Yerushalmi;* see also *Tosafos, Rosh Hashanah* 16b) to signal the moment when the forces of evil will finally be wiped out.

This is one more aspect of the sanctification of God's Name which accompanies the ingathering of the exiles.]

25. וְזָרַקְתִּי עֲלֵיכֶם מַיִם טְהוֹרִים וּטְהַרְתֶּם — *And I shall sprinkle pure water upon you, that you be cleansed.*

I shall cleanse you and remove your impurity by sprinkling the cleansing waters [of the red cow] which remove the contamination caused by contact with a dead body *(Rashi).*

R' Akiva said: Happy are you, O Israel! Before Whom you are cleansed, and Who it is that cleanses you? Your Father in Heaven, as it is written: *And I shall sprinkle pure water upon you and you shall be cleansed;* and it also says: *God is Israel's* mikvah.

Just as a *mikvah* cleanses those who have become defiled, so God cleanses Israel *(Yoma* 85b).

[This is a play on words. The simple meaning of the phrase is that God is Israel's source of hope (קוה, *to hope).* The Mishnah takes מִקְוֵה [*Mikvah*] to mean *a gathering of water* (from לקוה, *to gather).*]

Millenia of גָּלוּת, *exile,* will have left their mark. A stultifying contamination will have infected mind and heart of many of Israel's sons and daughters. Yet not one will have become so filthied but that God Himself, with loving and personal concern, will help him to remove that taint.

The picture of God Himself washing

36
22-26

[22] Therefore say to the family of Israel: Thus says
my Lord HASHEM/ELOHIM: Not for your sake do I
act, family of Israel, but for My holy Name which
you have desecrated among the nations to which you
came; [23] so I will sanctify My great Name which is
desecrated among the nations, which you have
desecrated among them. Then the nations shall know
that I am HASHEM — the words of my Lord
HASHEM/ELOHIM — when I become sanctified
through you in their sight; [24] and I shall take you
from the nations and gather you in from all the
countries, and I shall bring you to your land; [25] and I
shall sprinkle pure water upon you, that you be
cleansed. From all your contamination and from all
your filth I will cleanse you; [26] and I shall give you a
new heart and a new spirit I will put within you; I

away the marks of defilement is not unique to our Book (see also *Isaiah* 4:4).[1]

Within Yechezkel's prophecies, it awakens a special association. It recalls the vivid imagery of ch. 16, where the benefactor refused to be repulsed by the filth caking the infant child whom he had found forsaken and neglected in the fields. There, too, he was able to see through the surface grime to the royal soul underneath.

The passage of centuries will have done nothing to change God's love for His people. The same ardor which welcomed the young bride out of Egypt (*Jeremiah* 2:2) will be there to greet the unfaithful wife when she finally returns to her husband (*Jeremiah* 3:1). The long periods of seeming estrangement were of Israel's making, never of God's. In constant faithfulness, He waits for Israel to become ready for the new heart and spirit which He will implant in it.

26. Having been cleansed by God, Israel is ready for a true rejuvenation.

In Yechezkel's view, this rejuvenation will consist of replacing a *heart of stone* with a *heart of flesh.*

Yechezkel was the first of Israel's teachers who described the evil within man with the metaphor of the stone. According to *Succah* 52a, the יֵצֶר הָרַע, *evil inclination,* in man has seven names. Before Yechezkel it had been called: *evil, foreskin, contamination, enemy,* and *stumbling block.* Later it was called *the hidden one.* Yechezkel described it as *stone.*

The five descriptions which preceeded Yechezkel all see the evil inclination as actively antagonistic to man. Man is thought of as intrinsically good while the evil inclination opposes that goodness with evil or impurity. The *stone,* on the other hand, is passive. Yechezkel's vision of evil is not as an outside force which wishes to mislead man, but rather as the intractable ir-

1. *Tomer Devorah* (1:3) discusses the concept of God, Himself, cleansing the sinner rather than doing so through the agency of an intermediary.

He concludes: A man should be ashamed to repeat a sin for he will cause the King Himself to wash the filth off his clothes.

בְּקִרְבְּכֶם וַהֲסִרֹתִי אֶת־לֵב הָאֶבֶן
כז מִבְּשַׂרְכֶם וְנָתַתִּי לָכֶם לֵב בָּשָׂר: וְאֶת־
רוּחִי אֶתֵּן בְּקִרְבְּכֶם וְעָשִׂיתִי אֵת אֲשֶׁר־
בְּחֻקַּי תֵּלֵכוּ וּמִשְׁפָּטַי תִּשְׁמְרוּ וַעֲשִׂיתֶם:
כח וִישַׁבְתֶּם בָּאָרֶץ אֲשֶׁר נָתַתִּי לַאֲבֹתֵיכֶם
וִהְיִיתֶם לִי לְעָם וְאָנֹכִי אֶהְיֶה לָכֶם
כט לֵאלֹהִים: וְהוֹשַׁעְתִּי אֶתְכֶם מִכֹּל
טֻמְאוֹתֵיכֶם וְקָרָאתִי אֶל־הַדָּגָן וְהִרְבֵּיתִי
ל אֹתוֹ וְלֹא־אֶתֵּן עֲלֵיכֶם רָעָב: וְהִרְבֵּיתִי
אֶת־פְּרִי הָעֵץ וּתְנוּבַת הַשָּׂדֶה לְמַעַן
אֲשֶׁר לֹא תִקְחוּ עוֹד חֶרְפַּת רָעָב
לא בַּגּוֹיִם: וּזְכַרְתֶּם אֶת־דַּרְכֵיכֶם הָרָעִים
וּמַעַלְלֵיכֶם אֲשֶׁר לֹא־טוֹבִים וּנְקֹטֹתֶם
בִּפְנֵיכֶם עַל עֲוֺנֹתֵיכֶם וְעַל תּוֹעֲבוֹתֵיכֶם:

responsive lethargy which weighs him down and makes him unreceptive to the stimulation of the spirit (see *Maharal, Nesivos Olam, Nesiv HaYetzer).*

God proposes to exchange this *heart of stone* with *a heart of flesh* — a heart that is pliant and ready to submit *(Rashi,* 11:19; see *comm.* there).

Besides this change from the heart of stone to one of flesh, Yechezkel also speaks of a לֵב חָדָשׁ, *new heart,* and a רוּחַ חֲדָשָׁה, *new spirit,* which God will implant in Israel. According to *v.* 27, this *new spirit* will ensure that henceforth Israel follow in God's decrees and guard His social laws.

What is meant by *a new heart* and *a new spirit?*

In *Deuteronomy* 30:6, God promises that the day will come when He will *circumcise* the hearts of Israel. *Ramban* explains this 'circumcision' as follows: In Messianic times, the 'foreskin of the heart' which drives man to follow his physical cravings will be excised, and man's nature will become wholly good. Then, the gift of בְּחִירָה, *freedom of choice between good and evil,* which God granted man in order that he might earn his just reward, will be removed (see *comm., vs.* 21-23). In *Ramban's* view, this critical point of man's existence is described in our verse. The לֵב, *heart,* is man's *nature.* The רוּחַ, *spirit,* is his *craving.* Both of these will be entirely new and different from what they were in the past. The new *heart* and the new *spirit* will insure that, by his very nature, man will want nothing but to walk in God's ways.[1]

29. וְהוֹשַׁעְתִּי אֶתְכֶם מִכֹּל טֻמְאוֹתֵיכֶם — *And I shall save you from all your contaminations.*

The idea of being 'saved' from defilement is novel. One usually thinks in

1. *Meiri* in *Chibur HaTeshuvah* 1:9 offers a different explanation.

A truly and sincerely penitent sinner is considered a בַּעַל תְּשׁוּבָה, *repentant,* even if he subsequently commits his old sins once more. In order for the תְּשׁוּבָה [*teshuvah*], *penitence,* to be acceptable to God, it is not necessary to change his nature so drastically as to make it un-

shall remove the heart of stone from your flesh and
give you a heart of flesh; 27 *and My spirit I will put*
within you, and I will cause that you will go by My
decrees and guard My laws and perform them; 28 *and*
you will dwell in the land which I gave your fathers;
and you will be to Me a people, and I shall be your
God; 29 *and I shall save you from all your contamina-*
tions, and I shall summon the grain and increase it,
and I shall not place famine upon you; 30 *and I shall*
increase the fruit of the tree and the produce of the
field so that you no longer accept the shame of
hunger among the nations. 31 *Then you will*
remember your evil ways and your doings which
were not good, and you shall loathe yourselves in
your own sight because of your sins and your

terms of being cleansed from impurity rather than being saved.

However, in the thinking of the Torah, salvation is indeed an apt term for the process of being freed from the shackles of sin. The Sages speak of Yom Kippur as the day upon which God relates to us as a Savior(*Vayikra Rabbah* 21:3 to *Psalms* 27:1). God is אוֹרִי, *my light,* on Rosh Hashanah; יִשְׁעִי, *my Savior,* on Yom Kippur. (See ArtScroll *Tehillim, there),* and they associate תְּשׁוּבָה, *repentance,* with the idea of גְּאוּלָּה, *redemption (Yoma* 86b).

וְקָרָאתִי אֶל הַדָּגָן — *And I shall summon the grain.*

The connection between Israel's redemption and the fertility of the land which is stated in our verse and in some of the subsequent verses has been discussed in the pref. and at verse 8.

30. לֹא תִקְחוּ עוֹד חֶרְפַּת רָעָב בַּגּוֹיִם — *So that you no longer accept the shame of hunger among the nations.*

Radak points out that *Eretz Yisrael's* dependence on rain makes it prone to famine, as is seen from the many famines reported in Scripture. (See *comm.*, 20:7.) It is embarrassing when people must leave their country because of hunger. God promises that in the future this will not happen.

31. וּנְקֹטֹתֶם בִּפְנֵיכֶם — *And you shall loathe yourselves in your own sight.*

The use of the root קוט in this context is discussed in *comm.*, 6:9.

Yechezkel's insistence that Israel must react to God's love with an

thinkable that he would transgress again. It is sufficient that at the time of his *teshuvah* he was firmly determined to better his ways.

Nevertheless a person who does not really change as a result of his *teshuvah* but slips into his old ways cannot be admired. Indeed, if this happens often, his very *teshuvah* becomes suspect. Rather than concentrate on cessation of evil deeds, it would be much better for such a man to take himself in hand energetically and attempt seriously to rid himself of those character traits which *cause* him to sin.

This is God's promise in our verse. Verse 25 described God's forgiveness — but God's love does not stop there. He will implant new heart and spirit in the people in order to guarantee that they will not repeat their mistakes.

לב לֹא לְמַעַנְכֶם אֲנִי־עֹשֶׂה נְאֻם אֲדֹנָי יֱהֹוִה
יִוָּדַע לָכֶם בּוֹשׁוּ וְהִכָּלְמוּ מִדַּרְכֵיכֶם בֵּית
יִשְׂרָאֵל׃
לג כֹּה אָמַר אֲדֹנָי יֱהֹוִה בְּיוֹם טַהֲרִי אֶתְכֶם
מִכֹּל עֲוֹנוֹתֵיכֶם וְהוֹשַׁבְתִּי אֶת־הֶעָרִים
לד וְנִבְנוּ הֶחֳרָבוֹת׃ וְהָאָרֶץ הַנְּשַׁמָּה תֵּעָבֵד
תַּחַת אֲשֶׁר הָיְתָה שְׁמָמָה לְעֵינֵי כָּל־
לה עוֹבֵר׃ וְאָמְרוּ הָאָרֶץ הַלֵּזוּ הַנְּשַׁמָּה הָיְתָה
כְּגַן־עֵדֶן וְהֶעָרִים הֶחֳרֵבוֹת וְהַנְשַׁמּוֹת
לו וְהַנֶּהֱרָסוֹת בְּצוּרוֹת יָשָׁבוּ׃ וְיָדְעוּ הַגּוֹיִם
אֲשֶׁר יִשָּׁאֲרוּ סְבִיבוֹתֵיכֶם כִּי ׀ אֲנִי יהוה
בָּנִיתִי הַנֶּהֱרָסוֹת נָטַעְתִּי הַנְּשַׁמָּה אֲנִי
לז יהוה דִּבַּרְתִּי וְעָשִׂיתִי׃ כֹּה
אָמַר אֲדֹנָי יֱהֹוִה עוֹד זֹאת אִדָּרֵשׁ
לְבֵית־יִשְׂרָאֵל לַעֲשׂוֹת לָהֶם אַרְבֶּה

overwhelming feeling of shame is discussed in *comm.* 16:61 and 20:43.

32. This is one of the many verses in Scripture, and in particular in the book of *Ezekiel,* which imply that Israel's merit plays no part in its salvation. God will always help Israel, and its ultimate redemption is assured for the sanctification of His Name, not because Israel will deserve it. (See *comm.*, footnote 20:9.)

However, there are many verses in Scripture which indicate that Israel's repentance will bring the ultimate redemption.

Radak (Isaiah 59:16) shows that the same kind of ambivalence exists in Talmudic sources. Sometimes the final redemption is attributed to Israel's repentance and merit, sometimes it is seen as coming despite their lack.

Radak resolves the conflict. God will send the first signs of the Messiah's coming even while Israel is as yet undeserving. The End of Days must come because it is required by the historical process which may be described as the sanctification of God's Name. Once the footsteps of the Messiah are heard, the majority of Jews will be galvanized into repenting, and the final stages of the redemption will come in the merit of *teshuvah.*[1]

33-36. In a prophetic vision, Yechezkel sees a new Israel. Fortified cities bustling with people will rise up where now there are only ruins. (See

1. One of the Talmudic sources quoted by *Radak* is *Sanhedrin* 97b, where R' Eliezer and R' Yehoshuah argue over this question. *Margolios HaYam* (there) provides a wealth of material concerning this issue. Based on *Yomah* 86b he suggests that the *teshuvah* of some individuals might be enough to save the whole of Israel. This could solve the apparent conflict between the sources: For many people the redemption will come without their own repentance because the *teshuvah* of a few will bring the Messiah for everyone.

36
32-37
abominations. 32 *Not for your sake do I act — the*
words of my Lord HASHEM/ELOHIM *— let it be*
known to you. Be ashamed and embarrassed because
of your ways, family of Israel.
33 *Thus says my Lord* HASHEM/ELOHIM: *On the*
day when I cleanse you from all your sins, and cause
the cities to be inhabited, and the ruins to be built,
34 *and the desolated land to be tilled instead of*
remaining desolate in the eyes of every passerby;
35 *then they shall say, 'This very land which was*
desolate has become a Garden of Eden; and the cities
which were destroyed, and were desolate and ruined
shall be fortified — inhabited! 36 *And the nations that*
will remain around you will know that I am
HASHEM. *I will have rebuilt the ruins, replanted the*
wasteland. I, HASHEM, *have spoken and acted.*
37 *Thus says my Lord* HASHEM/ELOHIM:
Furthermore I will make Myself accessible to the
family of Israel to act for them. I shall increase them

Psalms 48, *Yalkut Shimoni,* for a vivid description of Israel's love for the walls, towers, and buildings of Jerusalem.). A Garden of Eden bursting forth with God's bounty will replace the desolate and deserted fields.

God's hand will be visible in this rebirth. The surrounding nations who had known the land only as an arid waste will recognize the new Israel as fulfillment of God's promise.

37. אִדָּרֵשׁ — *I will make Myself accessible.*

I will allow Myself to be persuaded by their prayers *(Rashi).* (See *comm.,* 20:1: According to *Ramban,* the root דרש, when used in connection with God, invariably refers to *prayer.)*

Commentary 20:31 quoted *Midrash Tanchuma,* which understands God's promise to make Himself accessible to the family of Israel (אִדָּרֵשׁ) as a reversal of His refusal to be accessible to the elders (אִם אִדָּרֵשׁ), recorded in 20:3 and 31. The prophet uses the same expression in both places in order to highlight the contrast between the two situations. (See *Rambam, Hilchos Teshuvah* 7:6). A permanent estrangement between God and Israel is inconceivable.

אַרְבֶּה אֹתָם כַּצֹּאן אָדָם — *I shall increase them — the men — like sheep.*

The translation follows *Rashi* and is based on the cantillation, which separates כַּצֹּאן, *like sheep,* from אָדָם, *men.* According to this interpretation, our verse teaches that man will be increased like sheep, and verse 38 explains what type of sheep is meant.

In *Mahari Karo's* view, verse 38 adds that the flock of sheep of our verse is not one of ordinary size, but like the huge masses of sheep which filled Jerusalem on the holy days when all of

לו לח אֹתָ֖ם כַּצֹּ֥אן אָדָֽם׃ כְּצֹ֣אן קָֽדָשִׁ֗ים
לח כְּצֹ֣אן יְרוּשָׁלַ֘͏ִם֮ בְּמוֹעֲדֶ֒יהָ֒ כֵּ֤ן תִּֽהְיֶ֙ינָה֙
הֶעָרִ֣ים הֶחֳרֵב֔וֹת מְלֵא֖וֹת צֹ֣אן אָדָ֑ם
וְיָדְע֖וּ כִּֽי־אֲנִ֥י יהוֽה׃

Israel gathered there and offered untold masses of sheep on the altar.[1]

The syntax is simpler if צֹאן אָדָם is read as a single term: *sheep-men* — as the cantillation indicates in verse 38. (See *comm.* 31:15.) This is how *Mahari Karo* reads our verse.

The expression צֹאן אָדָם, *sheep-man*, can be understood in the light of *comm.* 34:31.

Adam, the peak of God's creation, the Divine הֲדוֹם, *footstool*, on earth (see Overview IV), attains his most splendid grandeur as צֹאן, *sheep*, of God. He is truly free, stands truly straight, only when he knows that he is completely in God's hands; when he knows that God is his Shepherd.

Yechezkel's vision of a new, pulsating, reborn Israel would be distorted if it were occupied by any but צֹאן אָדָם, *sheep-man*. Only this unique combination guarantees that in that land *they will know that I am HASHEM* (*v.* 38).

38. כְּצֹאן קָדָשִׁים כְּצֹאן יְרוּשָׁלַיִם בְּמוֹעֲדֶיהָ — *Like the sheep for Divine service, like the sheep of Jerusalem on her festivals.*

According to *Rashi*, our verse explains what type of sheep Israel is compared to in the preceding verse. Rather than ordinary sheep, these are צֹאן קָדָשִׁים, *sheep for Divine service,* the עוֹלוֹת, *burnt offerings,* which were burned on the altar in their entirety. The multitudes of Israel, like burnt offerings, will be entirely sanctified for God's service.

צֹאן יְרוּשָׁלַיִם בְּמוֹעֲדֶיהָ, *sheep of Jerusalem on her festivals,* refers to שְׁלָמִים, *peace offerings,* through which the people rejoiced before God. Israel's dedication to God will likewise be joyous *(Malbim).*

XXXVII

Yechezkel is led into a valley where, by means of Divine prophecy, he is to bring life to a multitude of dried out human bones which are scattered there.

Sanhedrin ***92b quotes R' Yehudah that the entire account is*** a parable (מָשָׁל הָיָה), ***and there was no actual resurrection. However, the general thrust of the Talmud in*** Sanhedrin, ***and that of most Midrashic allusions to the incident is in accord with the opinion of R' Elazar (there) that our chapter describes an actual event. Both opinions are referred to in the commentary.***

Rambam ***in*** Moreh Nevuchim ***2:46 assumes the event to have been perceived in***

1. The description of Israel as God's sheep carries many implications. Some of these are discussed in *comm., 34:31. Tanchuma (Buber)* to *Exodus* 15:22 suggests a number of them.

R' Berechya said: See how beloved Israel is by God, Who called them שֶׂה, *sheep* (in the singular) (*Jeremiah* 50:17); for if someone has one sheep he feeds it and waters it in its right time [without trouble], since he has only one; but if he has many sheep he has no time to look after them properly but must exhaust himself for their sake.

The implication is that although there are so many people, God nevertheless cares for each one individually, just as a shepherd of a great flock expends much effort to give each sheep its due.

36 *— the men — like sheep.* [38] *Like the sheep for Divine*
38 *service, like the sheep of Jerusalem on her festivals,*
so shall the destroyed cities be filled by sheep-men —
and they shall know that I am HASHEM.

prophetic vision rather than to have occurred physically. This is in line with his opinion concerning other symbolic actions recounted in our Book. (See comm. *to 2:8; 5:1-4; footnote 4:4.)*

By its position in the Book, we judge this section to belong among Yechezkel's Messianic visions. It is preceded by the picture of a blooming land whose deserts have burst forth into lush fields in anticipation of Israel's return. It is followed by the promise of a reunited nation, encompassing all of its twelve tribes, welcoming God's eternal Presence into its midst under the benign rulership of one Davidic king (vs. 15-28). *Surely then, the vision of the dried bones should be interpreted within this context.*

Indeed, could we have conceived of a Messianic era if the lessons of our chapter had not been firmly planted in Israel's consciousness? Is it not true that by any measure of the laws of history, millenia of harsh and hopeless exile should have extinguished any spark of hope from Israel's breast? If today, in defiance of any logic, Israel's ears are attuned to the עִקְבְתָא דִמְשִׁיחָא, the Messianic footfalls, *as they become audible upon the stage of history, it is because Yechezkel taught that no skeleton can be so hopelessly scattered, but that the spirit emanating from God can join its members into one viable whole; that no bone can be so dried out, but that a spark remains within it, waiting to be wafted into life by Divine inspiration.*

Both Rashi *and* Radak *offer this interpretation as one possibility and it certainly was in this sense that our passage inspired thinkers like* R' Yehudah HaLevi *as they grappled with the philosophical implication of the exile experience (see* Kuzari *2:29-30, 34).*

The other possibility offered by Radak *is found in various Talmudic and Midrashic sources (see* Pirkei DeRabbi Eliezer *33, quoted in* Yalkut; Tana DeBei Eliyahu Rabbah *5;* Bereishis Rabbah *13:4;* Vayikra Rabbah *27:4;* Tanchuma Vayeitzei *16;* Emunos VeDeos *of* R' Saadiah Gaon *7:4). It interprets our chapter as a lesson designed to reinforce belief in the doctrine of* תְּחִיַּת הַמֵּתִים, the resurrection of the dead, *which is the thirteenth of Rambam's* Thirteen Principles of Faith. (See Rambam *to* Mishnah Sanhedrin *10:1).* Radak *explains that with the prospect of a seemingly endless exile before them, it was likely that those people who were destined to die on foreign ground would feel eternally excluded from sharing in the experience of Israel's ultimate salvation. Yechezkel demonstrated to them graphically that they were not lost to their people. The time will come when they will rise from their graves.*

According to Megillah *31a, our passage is read as the* Haftarah *on the Sabbath of* Chol HaMoed Pesach. Rashi *explains why (according to one opinion — see* comm., v. *1). The dried bones belonged to the Ephraimites who anticipated the Exodus by thirty years and were killed in the wilderness. The passage is therefore topical on Pesach.*

However, Nimukei Yosef *to* Megillah *quotes* R' Hai Gaon, *that the practice is based on a tradition that* תְּחִיַּת הַמֵּתִים, the resurrection of the dead, *will take place in the month of Nissan.*

If, however, the point of the prophecy was to encourage a belief in an ultimate redemption in spite of the seemingly endless exile (see above), the prophecy would certainly be apt for Pesach, the festival of redemption (Kuzari).

א הָיְתָה עָלַי יַד־יהוה וַיּוֹצִאֵנִי בְרוּחַ יהוה
וַיְנִיחֵנִי בְּתוֹךְ הַבִּקְעָה וְהִיא מְלֵאָה
ב עֲצָמוֹת: וְהֶעֱבִירַנִי עֲלֵיהֶם סָבִיב | סָבִיב

1. הָיְתָה עָלַי יַד־ה׳ — *Upon me was the hand of HASHEM.*

This expression denotes force. The prophetic spirit took him by force, as though he were in a trance (*Rashi*, see *comm.* 1:2).

בְּרוּחַ ה׳ — *By the spirit of HASHEM.*

Yechezkel uses רוּחַ in two senses. Sometimes it means *wind*, sometimes, *spirit* (see *comm.* 3:12). Here *Targum* renders: *a spirit of prophecy.*

בְּתוֹךְ הַבִּקְעָה — *In the valley.*

The definite article implies a known valley. *Radak* identifies this as the valley of 3:22.

וְהִיא מְלֵאָה עֲצָמוֹת — *Now it was full of bones.*

As stated by *Targum*, and as clearly indicated by later verses, these were human bones, but whose were they? *Sanhedrin* 92b brings the following opinions:

— They were Ephraimites who erred in computing the time for the redemption (from Egypt). They left on their own, prematurely, and were killed.[1]

— They were people who denied the doctrine of תְּחִיַּת הַמֵּתִים, *the ultimate resurrection of the dead.*

— They lacked the life force which comes by keeping God's commandments (לחלוחית שֶׁל מִצְוָה). [Like dry bones, their lives were shriveled and meaningless.]

— They were the people who had engraved the idolatrous images upon the Temple walls (see 8:10-12).

— They were the victims of the massacre at the Valley of Durah.[2]

Pirkei d'Rabbi Eliezer (33) has a different tradition. When Nebuchadnezzar erected the statue (see *Daniel* ch. 3; 20:1) and demanded that everyone bow down to it, many Jews complied. Chananiah, Mishael, and Azariah were the exceptions and preferred to be thrown into the fiery furnace rather than submit to this order. They were miraculously saved. When Nebuchadnezzar saw that he was powerless to harm them, he became furious with the other Jews, the ones who had complied with his decree. How could they have been disloyal to such a mighty God? Immediately, he ordered the execution of all the people who had bowed down to his statue. These people were the ones whom Yechezkel resurrected some twenty years later.[3]

2. סָבִיב סָבִיב — *All around.*

God led him around the valley but

1. According to *Pirkei D'Rabbi Eliezer* 48, *Genon*, a descendant of Ephraim, claimed that he had been sent by God to take the Jews out of Egypt. His tribesmen, who were proud because they knew themselves to be of royal blood (they were destined to rule over the northern kingdom of Israel) and therefore chafed particularly under the Egyptian domination (see *Radal there)*, followed him, and 200,000 of their number anticipated the redemption by thirty years *(Rashi, Sanhedrin* 92b and *Ramban* to *Exodus* 12:40 explain how they reached their conclusion) thereby contraverting the oath which the brothers had made to Joseph (see *Mechilta* to *BeShalach*). They were killed as they came to Philistia, and their bones remained scattered where they had fallen. According to *Mechilta* there, it was to avoid the sight of their fallen brothers that God later led the Jews through the wilderness rather than taking them to the Promised Land by the shortest route which lay through Philistia.

2. *Sanhedrin* 92b tells the following: When Nebuchadnezzar exiled the Jews, there were young boys among them who eclipsed the sun by their beauty. When the Chaldean women saw them, their sensual lust would be stimulated. They told their husbands who told the king. He had the boys killed. However, the women still lusted for them (because even in death they were exceptionally beautiful), so the king had them trampled into the ground.

37
1-2

Upon me was the hand of HASHEM. It took me out by the spirit of HASHEM and set me down in the valley. Now it was full of bones. 2 He led me all around and behold! they were very abundant upon

not through it, among the bones, because Yechezkel, as a *Kohen* (1:3),was forbidden to come in direct contact with human remains *(Rashi).*

Radak argues that this contradicts verse 1 that Yechezkel was placed *in the valley. Radak* maintains that this is a prophetic vision rather than an actual

3. *Sanhedrin* 92b associates the account of the dry bones with that of Chananiah, Mishael, and Azariah. In that tradition the two miracles occured on the same day. At the same time that the three were being saved from the furnace, Yechezkel was resurrecting the bones in the valley.

We may surmise the following connection.

Chananiah, Mishael, and Azariah's heroism had implications far beyond the determination of three people to lay down their lives for קִדּוּשׁ הַשֵּׁם, *the sanctification of God's Name.* According to *Sanhedrin* 93a, God would have destroyed the whole world had it not been for the steadfast loyalty of these three men.

When Nebuchadnezzar erected the statue and commanded all his subjects to bow before it, it was no ordinary act of arrogance perpetrated by a man crazed by self-importance. Nebuchadnezzar was king of the first of the Four Kingdoms who were to stand for the negation of all that is good and holy in the world — in direct opposition to Israel, the bearers of God's Presence on earth (see *comm.* 21:24-27). A statue erected in his honor was a symbol of the victory of evil over good, of the expulsion of the Divine from the affairs of man. The order that all people bow down to it was an order that all of mankind was to submit to the new order implicit in Babylon's ascendancy. (See *Maharal,* Introduction to *Ohr Chadash.)*

Small wonder that, when the whole of Israel was prepared to obey the king's decree, God wanted to destroy His world! An Israel bowing to Nebuchadnezzar's statue is an Israel cut completely loose from the anchorage of its own destiny, affirming that its own role in history is past. God has been effectively driven out of His world, and the representative of evil rules supreme. (According to *Pesikta Rabbasi* the dimensions of the statue were such that it could not possibly stand. It fell repeatedly until all the gold and silver which the Babylonians had captured from Jerusalem was melted down to make a base for it. [The implication is that the existence of the statue depended upon Israel's defection from God, as a result of which their wealth was placed in Babylon's hands.])

Chananiah, Mishael, and Azariah saved the day. Their decision to stand firm had not been based on wisdom (Daniel had refused to advise them) nor on prophecy (Yechezkel, at God's direction, had repulsed them) but on the תְּמִימוּת, *perfect faith,* which strengthened their deep inner conviction that they had intuited the correct Jewish reaction to the situation (footnote 20:1).

Perhaps the Sages mean to teach us that the justification for תְּחִיַּת הַמֵּתִים, *the resurrection of the dead,* is basic, uncompromising Jewishness. All the outer trappings of Jewishness may indeed disapppear. Wisdom and prophecy and much more may be lost in the travail of exile and persecution. The Jewish people may come to resemble the dried bones which seem to have lost all hope of viability. Chananiah, Mishael, and Azariah taught that a spark will always remain which can be coaxed back into life.

Thus, when Nebuchadnezzar threw Chananiah, Mishael, and Azariah into the furnace, the statue toppled over (*Sanhedrin* 92b). In fact, the very wind which threw over the statue was the wind (*v.* 9) which Yechezkel commanded to blow life into the dead bones (*Shir HaShirim Rabbah* 7:14).

Shir HaShirim Rabbah (7:14) also reports that all these events took place on *Yom Kippur,* that day upon which all the outer layers of sin and impurity are wiped away, and Israel learns of its true essence, that inner core of holiness which can never be touched by sin. Yom Kippur is the appropriate day to discover the spark of life within the dry bones. [See *Overview* to ArtScroll *Daniel.*]

וְהִנֵּה רַבּוֹת מְאֹד עַל־פְּנֵי הַבִּקְעָה וְהִנֵּה
ג יְבֵשׁוֹת מְאֹד׃ וַיֹּאמֶר אֵלַי בֶּן־אָדָם
הֲתִחְיֶינָה הָעֲצָמוֹת הָאֵלֶּה וָאֹמַר אֲדֹנָי
ד יֱהֹוִה אַתָּה יָדָעְתָּ׃ וַיֹּאמֶר אֵלַי הִנָּבֵא
עַל־הָעֲצָמוֹת הָאֵלֶּה וְאָמַרְתָּ אֲלֵיהֶם
ה הָעֲצָמוֹת הַיְבֵשׁוֹת שִׁמְעוּ דְּבַר־יהוָה׃ כֹּה
אָמַר אֲדֹנָי יֱהֹוִה לָעֲצָמוֹת הָאֵלֶּה הִנֵּה
ו אֲנִי מֵבִיא בָכֶם רוּחַ וִחְיִיתֶם׃ וְנָתַתִּי
עֲלֵיכֶם גִּידִים וְהַעֲלֵתִי עֲלֵיכֶם בָּשָׂר
וְקָרַמְתִּי עֲלֵיכֶם עוֹר וְנָתַתִּי בָכֶם רוּחַ
ז וִחְיִיתֶם וִידַעְתֶּם כִּי־אֲנִי יהוָה׃ וְנִבֵּאתִי
כַּאֲשֶׁר צֻוֵּיתִי וַיְהִי־קוֹל כְּהִנָּבְאִי וְהִנֵּה־
רַעַשׁ וַתִּקְרְבוּ עֲצָמוֹת עֶצֶם אֶל־עַצְמוֹ׃

occurrence (see *pref.)* and therefore Yechezkel's priesthood is of no significance. In *Radak's* view, the expression simply conveys that God led Yechezkel through the entire valley so that he should be thoroughly acquainted with the whole situation.

[According to *Rashi*, verse 1 would mean that Yechezkel was placed *in the valley*, but not at the exact location of the bones. When approaching them, he was told to walk around them.]

3. אַתָּה יָדָעְתָּ — *You know.*

By natural law there is no way for these bones to come alive, but if it is Your will that they should live, they will surely live. Only You know whether it is Your will that they will live *(Metzudos).*

Was this the answer expected from Yechezkel? *Pirkei d'Rabbi Eliezer* (33) writes that Yechezkel answered as though he did not believe. Therefore his bones were not buried in the Land of Israel. In explanation of this apparent condemnation of the prophet, *Radal* suggests that Yechezkel understood God's question: 'Can these bones live?' to mean 'Do you feel that they deserve to live? Do they have enough merit?' Instead of stating the obvious, that he did not know, Yechezkel should have reminded God of His inexhaustible mercy which could surely transcend any lack of merit. He was faulted for not doing so. Thus, Yechezkel's reply was regarded as a 'sin' only in relation to his greatness.

On the other hand, *Bereishis Rabbah* (19:20) praises Yechezkel for his answer: In contrast to Adam, Cain, Balaam, and Chizkiyahu, each of whom had not reacted correctly when God addressed them, Yechezkel rose to the challenge. The matter is comparable to a hunter holding a bird in his hands. The hunter asked a passerby, 'Is this bird in my hand alive or dead?' He answered, 'It is as you wish. It is alive if you wish it, dead if you wish it.'

4. Yechezkel is to be the instrument through which the bones will be infused with life. Because he was a צַדִּיק, *righteous man*, and the times required it, he was given the 'key' to תְּחִיַּת הַמֵּתִים, *the resurrection of the dead* (see *Taanis*

the surface of the valley, and behold! they were very
dry. 3 *Then He said to me: Ben Adam, can these*
bones live? And I said, My Lord HASHEM / ELOHIM,
You know.
4 *And he said to me: Prophesy over these bones*
and say to them: O dry bones, hear the word of
HASHEM. 5 *Thus says my Lord HASHEM / ELOHIM to*
these bones: Behold! I bring spirit into you and you
shall live. 6 *I shall put sinews upon you and bring*
flesh upon you and draw skin over you. Then I shall
put spirit into you and you shall live; and you shall
know that I am HASHEM.
7 *And I prophesied as I had been commanded, and*
there was a noise while I prophesied, and behold! a
rattling and the bones drew near, bone to matching

2a), which God normally reserves only for Himself *(Tanchuma, Vayeitzei* 16).

According to *Eliyahu Rabbah* (5), Yechezkel's special merit was that he felt a complete sense of identity with Israel. He made himself one with them (הסתפח יחזקאל על ישראל).

שִׁמְעוּ דְּבַר־ה׳ – *Hear the word of HASHEM.*

The *Midrash* (*Tanchuma Yisro* 4) points out the irony. These same words had been ignored by the people when Jeremiah (2:4) had implored them to pay heed. The dried bones would be more receptive to his call than living Israel had been.

5-6. The spirit with which the bodies will be imbued is mentioned (*v.* 5) before the sinews, flesh, and skin (*v.* 6) although, as the resurrection took place, the physical components of the body (*v.* 8) preceded the coming of the spirit *(v.* 10) *(Radak).*

An analogy is found in *Exodus* 25:10 where the Ark is mentioned at the very beginning of God's commands concerning the building of the Tabernacle, although in practice the boards, sockets, and curtains were made first. *Ramban (there)* explains that in giving the command, God began with the *purpose:* God wanted a sanctuary for the Ark containing the Tablets of the Law — therefore, there had to be a Tabernacle. Here, too, the *purpose* of life is the spirit with which bodies are imbued. Sinews, flesh, and skin are there only to serve the spirit. Therefore, the spirit is mentioned first.

Metzudos offers a different solution. The רוּחַ, *spirit,* of verse 5 is not the same as that of verse 6. Verse 5 refers to an initial life force which is just enough to stimulate the bones to find each other and join into complete skeletons. Verse 6 describes the spirit which enabled the newly born people to live.

7. וַיְהִי־קוֹל ... וְהִנֵּה־רַעַשׁ – *And there was a noise ... a rattling.*

In the course of time, many of the bones had been separated from their skeletons and strewn over a huge area. There was a great clattering noise as the bones banged against each other and rejoined their skeletons.

ח וְרָאִיתִי וְהִנֵּה־עֲלֵיהֶם גִּדִים וּבָשָׂר עָלָה
וַיִּקְרַם עֲלֵיהֶם עוֹר מִלְמָעְלָה וְרוּחַ אֵין
ט בָּהֶם׃ וַיֹּאמֶר אֵלַי הִנָּבֵא אֶל־הָרוּחַ הִנָּבֵא
בֶן־אָדָם וְאָמַרְתָּ אֶל־הָרוּחַ כֹּה־אָמַר |
אֲדֹנָי יֱהֹוִה מֵאַרְבַּע רוּחוֹת בֹּאִי הָרוּחַ
י וּפְחִי בַּהֲרוּגִים הָאֵלֶּה וְיִחְיוּ׃ וְהִנַּבֵּאתִי
כַּאֲשֶׁר צִוָּנִי וַתָּבוֹא בָהֶם הָרוּחַ וַיִּחְיוּ
וַיַּעַמְדוּ עַל־רַגְלֵיהֶם חַיִל גָּדוֹל מְאֹד

8. Sinews, flesh, and skin obey the prophetic exhortation and give human appearance to the newly formed skeletons. However, the spirit which had been promised in verses 5 and 6 does not come. Not until another, specific prophecy (*vs.* 9, 10) does the spirit enter the bodies, enabling them to stand on their feet and live.

What is the significance of this tarrying of the spirit?

Abarbanel and *Malbim* offer an explanation which solves the problem if the episode is to be understood as a reassurance to the people concerning the doctrine of the resurrection of the dead (see *pref.*). The prophet had the power to form the bodies; it lies in the realm of the physical, and, with Divine inspiration, it can be performed by a human being. The spirit — the soul — is for God alone. To bring the spirit into the bodies, a new prophecy was required — specifically relaying God's commands that it enter the newly formed body (*v.* 9). In this matter the prophet acted only as a direct agent of God's purpose.

If the episode is a מָשָׁל, *parable*, for the ultimate redemption, do these verses not permit us a glimpse at the historical developments through which God will bring about our redemption? Are we justified in concluding from our verses that the Messianic dawn, when the spirit of God will finally imbue mankind, will be preceded by a twilight period of a physical redemption which, while having the physical appurtenances of nationhood, is nevertheless like a dead body as long as the spirit of God is absent from it?

Before discussing this question, and, indeed, as an indispensable preface to the rest of our chapter and the next two chapters, which deal so palpably with events leading up to the Messianic era, we quote *Rambam, Hilchos Melachim* 12:2. Having discussed some aspects of the Messianic era in chapters 11 and 12, *Rambam* writes:

> No one can know just how [these matters] happen until they take place, for they are unclear in the Prophets, and ... the Sages have no tradition [concerning them]. Therefore there are disagreements [about] these matters. Certainly the sequence of events and the details concerning them are not principles of faith. A person should never delve into Aggadic material and should not spend much time studying the *Midrashim* which deal with these and similar matters, and should not consider them of great importance, for they bring neither to fear of God nor to His love.

Thus, it would be idle to attempt to interpret specific historic events in the light of our verses or indeed of any reference in Scripture or in Rabbinic sources.

Nevertheless, throughout the ages, there have been attempts to fathom, at least in general terms, what the sequence of events leading up to the redemption might be. [Indeed, in the light of *Megillah* 14a that Scripture contains only such prophecies as are of im-

bone. 8 *Then I looked, and behold! — sinews were*
upon them, and flesh had come up and skin had been
drawn over them; but spirit was not in them. 9 *Then*
He said to me: Prophesy to the spirit, prophesy, Ben
Adam, and say to the spirit: Thus says my Lord
HASHEM / ELOHIM: From the four directions come,
O spirit, and blow into these slain ones that they may
live. 10 *I prophesied as I had been commanded. The*
spirit entered into them and they lived and they stood
upon their feet — a very, very vast multitude.

port for all generations, it could be argued that such attempts must be made if we are not to ignore large portions of Scripture.]

One example is *Yerushalmi, Berachos* 1:1, which compares the process of redemption to the breaking of day. Just as night gives way slowly to the morning light, so the redemption will come stage by stage [קימעא קימעא]. This theme recurs in various forms in many Midrashic sources (cf. *Shir HaShirim Rabbah* 6:10; *Midrash Tehillim, Psalm* 18; *Tanchuma, Devarim* 1).

(See *Malbim, Michah* 4:8; R' Nosson Friedlander in *Yosef Chen*, Warsaw, 1878. References are from *HaTekufah Hagedolah.)*

The concept of a gradually developing redemption may well be the matrix within which the tradition of two Messiahs — one descended from Joseph, one from Judah through King David — (see *Succah* 52b) is grounded.

We have at least two detailed descriptions of how events leading from the one Messiah to the next are destined to unfold: that of *R' Saadiah Gaon* in his *Emunos VeDeos* (8:2, 5) and *Ramban* in commentary to *Shir HaShirim* (8:13).(In *R' Saadiah's* view, this developmental process will only come about if the redemption takes place at the קֵץ, *predetermined time,* meaning that it was not precipitated by universal repentance. Were such a repentance to take place, the Davidic Messiah would come immediately without the prerequisite of a preparatory period.)

The common thread which runs through the reconstructions of both *R' Saadiah* and *Ramban* is that initially there will be a Messiah descended from Joseph who will bring about a degree of independence in a rebuilt Jerusalem where many of the former exiles will have gathered. However, this Messiah is destined to be killed in battle and only after that will the events be set in motion which will culminate in the rule of the Davidic Messiah.

Shmuel in *Berachos* 34b states: There is no difference between the Messianic era and our times except that then we shall not be subjugated by the Nations. Many commentators (e.g., *R' Yonosan Eibeshutz, Yaaros Devash,* Part 2; reference is from *HaTekufoh HaGedoloh)* see Shmuel's words as a description of an initial stage of redemption. In later stages, all the many visions contained in Scripture which imply a radically different, purer world will become reality.

Any of these initial stages might well be to the ultimate redemption as a lifeless body is to a vibrant human being. We assume that our verse hints at the type of developing redemption alluded to in the writings of our Sages.

9. מֵאַרְבַּע רוּחוֹת — *From the four directions.*

From wherever their souls went to hover in the four directions of the world ... let them gather and come *(Rashi).*

10. מְאֹד מְאֹד — *Very, very.*

From the similarity of expression

יא מְאֹד׃ וַיֹּאמֶר אֵלַי בֶּן־אָדָם הָעֲצָמוֹת
הָאֵלֶּה כָּל־בֵּית יִשְׂרָאֵל הֵמָּה הִנֵּה
אֹמְרִים יָבְשׁוּ עַצְמוֹתֵינוּ וְאָבְדָה תִקְוָתֵנוּ
יב נִגְזַרְנוּ לָנוּ׃ לָכֵן הִנָּבֵא וְאָמַרְתָּ אֲלֵיהֶם
כֹּה־אָמַר אֲדֹנָי יֱהֹוִה הִנֵּה אֲנִי פֹתֵחַ אֶת־
קִבְרוֹתֵיכֶם וְהַעֲלֵיתִי אֶתְכֶם מִקִּבְרוֹתֵיכֶם
עַמִּי וְהֵבֵאתִי אֶתְכֶם אֶל־אַדְמַת יִשְׂרָאֵל׃
יג וִידַעְתֶּם כִּי־אֲנִי יְהֹוָה בְּפִתְחִי אֶת־
קִבְרוֹתֵיכֶם וּבְהַעֲלוֹתִי אֶתְכֶם
יד מִקִּבְרוֹתֵיכֶם עַמִּי׃ וְנָתַתִּי רוּחִי בָכֶם
וִחְיִיתֶם וְהִנַּחְתִּי אֶתְכֶם עַל־אַדְמַתְכֶם
וִידַעְתֶּם כִּי אֲנִי יְהֹוָה דִּבַּרְתִּי וְעָשִׂיתִי
טו נְאֻם־יְהֹוָה׃ וַיְהִי דְבַר־יְהֹוָה

between this verse and *Exodus* 1:6, *Pirkei DeRabbi Eliezer* (33) deduces that the number of resurrected people was 600,000.

Pirkei DeRabbi Eliezer (33) proceeds to say that one of the people whose bones had been scattered in the valley did not come alive. His livelihood had been from the interest which he had charged people for loans. In the tradition of the Sages (*Shmos Rabbah* 30:6), one who lends for interest has no share in the world to come.

What happened to the people who were resurrected by Yechezkel?

Three opinions are recorded in *Sanhedrin* 92b:

— R' Elazar said, '[They] stood up on their feet, said שִׁירָה, *a song of jubilation to God,* and immediately died.[1]

— R' Yose HaGallili said, '[They] went up to the Land of Israel, married, and bore children.' [Then] R' Yehudah ben Besairah stood up and said, 'I am descended from them and these are the *tefillin* which my grandfather bequeathed to me from them'.

— R' Yehudah said, 'Truly the whole episode was a parable; [i.e., it did not really happen; rather, Yechezkel perceived it in prophetic vision. See *pref.*][2]

11-14 These verses contain the explanation of the foregoing. If the event actually took place with the pur-

1. *Maharal (Chiddushei Aggadah* there) explains: The sole purpose of the resurrection was to demonstrate God's power. To accomplish this it was sufficient that they live for a short time only ... God sent a נִיצוֹץ, *spark,* of the true תְּחִיַּת הַמֵּתִים, *resurrection,* which will one day take place. The short life span allotted to these people is analagous to that of angels whom God creates for the sole purpose of saying *shirah,* [*a song of praise*] and who, having done so, immediately cease to exist. These people, too, said *shirah,* thereby fulfilling the purpose of their creation.

2. The opinion discussed in the Prefatory Remarks — that the purpose of the episode was to comfort the people and reassure them that no exile would ever be so hopeless but that God would one day redeem them — is based on R' Yehudah's statement *(Radak).* If it was a parable, this comfort was its purpose.

37
11-14

[11] *And He said to me: Ben Adam, These bones —
they are the whole family of Israel ... Behold! they
say, 'Our bones have dried and our hope is lost. We
are doomed.'* [12] *Therefore, prophesy and say to them:
Thus says my Lord HASHEM / ELOHIM: Behold! I
open your graves and raise you up from your graves,
O My people, and I shall bring you to the soil of
Israel.* [13] *Then you shall know that I am HASHEM,
when I open your graves and when I raise you up
from your graves, O My people;* [14] *and I shall put
My spirit into you, and you shall live, and I shall set
you on your soil, and you shall know that I,
HASHEM, have spoken and done — the words of
HASHEM.*

pose of demonstrating the truth of the doctrine of תְּחִיַּת הַמֵּתִים, *the resurrection of the dead,* then our verses explain why this was necessary. If it was a parable [מָשָׁל] for the ultimate redemption, our verses supply the interpretation of the parable [נִמְשָׁל].

Pirkei DeRabbi Eliezer (33) gives the background for the former opinion: The [exiled] Jews were crying and saying, 'We had hoped to be gathered in [from the Babylonian exile] with the rest of Israel — now we are cut off; we had hoped for light — and darkness came; we had hoped to stand up with the rest of Israel when the dead are to be resurrected — but now our hope is lost.' *(Yalkut's* reading, which is more detailed than the extant version of *Pirkei DeRabbi Eliezer.)*[1]

Evidently people thought that there would be no resurrection outside the boundaries of the Land of Israel. [Indeed there was some justification for this thinking. According to R' Elazar in *Kesubos* 111a, people who die outside the boundaries of Eretz Yisrael would not come alive were it not that God will make 'tunnels' for them in the earth through which they will make their way to Eretz Yisrael, there to be resurrected.] Through Yechezkel's actions the people would be reassured that they too would one day share in Israel's destiny.

If our passage is a parable for the redemption from exile, then the graves which God will open to release their corpses are a metaphor for the countries of Israel's exile.

Indeed, exile has been a grave to untold numbers of Israel's sons and daughters — a grave for the bodies of the millions who were murdered at the whim of bloodthirsty host nations and a grave for the spirits of many more who, in times when there was less physical persecution, lost touch with their inner being, their holy destiny, and fell prey to the grasp of assimilation.

You will be lost among the nations, and the land of your enemies will devour you (Leviticus 26:38). This is the awesome judgment which the Torah passes over exile existence. Rav said

1. *Eliezer of Beaugency* offers a novel insight into the reason for the despair expressed in our verses. The people who died in exile bemoaned their fate because 'woe to us that we die in [the evil circumstances [of exile]. We had hoped all our lives to die on the battlefield and thus be killed for the sanctification of His Name.'

לז
טז

טז אֵלַי לֵאמֹר: וְאַתָּה בֶן־אָדָם קַח־לְךָ עֵץ
אֶחָד וּכְתֹב עָלָיו לִיהוּדָה וְלִבְנֵי יִשְׂרָאֵל
חֲבֵרָו וּלְקַח עֵץ אֶחָד וּכְתוֹב עָלָיו לְיוֹסֵף
עֵץ אֶפְרַיִם וְכָל־בֵּית יִשְׂרָאֵל חֲבֵרָו:

(*Makkos* 24a), 'This verse frightens me.' This was the fear which gripped Yechezkel's fellow exiles. Rav, too, had to be reassured.

Perhaps *lost* does not mean completely lost, but is rather in the sense of a lost object which the owner attempts to find. Perhaps *consumed* does not mean utterly consumed but is rather as in the case of cucumbers and pumpkins [which grow so fast that they constantly replenish themselves after they are harvested]. (*Makkos* there.)

This same message of comfort is the one which Yechezkel conveyed to his listeners.

15-22 Yechezkel is to perform another symbolic act. He is to take two wooden tablets, one of them inscribed with the words *For Judah and the children of Israel his comrades* (the tribe of Benjamin), and the other inscribed with the words *For Joseph, Ephraim's tablet, and all the family of Israel his comrades* (the ten tribes) and join them together so that the two tablets become one in his hands.

When people ask him to explain the significance of his actions, he is to say that they symbolize the unity of Israel after God gathers the exiles. Where formerly there had been two kingdoms, the Messianic era will see a single unified nation, never more to be divided, under the rule of one Davidic king.

The presence of the ten tribes, who had been driven into exile by Assyria some 140 years before the Destruction, is an indispensible component of Yechezkel's projection of the Messianic era (see 11:15, 36:10).

From Israel's earliest beginnings, it was destined to comprise exactly twelve tribes (see *Rashi, Genesis* 29:21, 34). This is by no means an arbitrary number, but parallels the twelve heavenly constellations and the twelve months of the year (*Ramban, Deuteronomy* 33:6) and appears consistently unchanged in Scripture. (When the tribes are listed, either Joseph is counted as one tribe, or if for some reason Ephraim and Menashe (the sons of Joseph), are counted separately, Levi is omitted — *Ramban,* there.)]

Our passage and ch. 48, in which Yechezkel delineates the division of the land among the tribes in the Messianic era, clearly demonstrate that this will never change. Israel has always been and will always be defined in terms of its twelve tribes. [See *Bava Basra* 115b: It is a tradition (גמירי) that no tribe will ever be wiped out.]

Ramban in *Sefer HaGeulah, Sha'ar* I, brings at least eight proofs besides the two cited here that Scripture assumes a return of the ten tribes. (See also *Maharal* in *Gur Aryeh* to *Genesis* 45:14. When Joseph and Benjamin were reunited, they fell upon each other's neck and cried. *Maharal* explains that these were tears of joy. They recognized that their reunion symbolized the eventual reunion between the ten tribes (Joseph) and the two (Benjamin who remained with the Davidic dynasty).

The question must be asked: Where will the ten tribes, which have been lost since their dispersal, come from? The Mishnah, in *Sanhedrin* 110b records a dispute between R' Akiva and R' Elazar. In R' Akiva's opinion the ten tribes are not destined to return (see also *Toras Kohanim, Leviticus* 26:38). R' Elazar holds that 'just as the day darkens and then becomes light, so the darkness which befell the ten tribes will one day be changed into light.'

Although *Rambam,* in his commentary to the Mishnah, writes that in a dis-

[15] *The word of HASHEM came to me, saying:* [16] *Now you, Ben Adam, take yourself one wooden tablet and write upon it: 'For Judah and the children of Israel his comrades, and take another wooden tablet and write upon it: 'For Joseph, Ephraim's tablet, and all the family of Israel his comrades.'*

agreement such as this it is meaningless to establish a halachah since it has no practical applications, it is nevertheless of interest to understand the argument in the light of the many passages in Scripture which seem to assume the presence of all twelve tribes.

Rashi to *Sanhedrin* 110b suggests that the argument in the Mishnah refers only to the generation which was exiled. They were wicked and unrepentant and, in R' Akiva's opinion, were lost forever. However, even R' Akiva agrees that their descendants will share fully in Israel's destiny. *R' David Bonfils* (a pupil of *Ramban*) in his commentary to *Sanhedrin*, elaborates on *Rashi*. In his opinion, there were a measurable number among the exiled tribes who remained loyal servants of God, and in the course of time these would grow into a large community. The prophecies in Scripture refer to these people. (This opinion is also shared by the *Tosafos Yom Tov* in *Tzuras HaBayis*. He demonstrates how this opinion would clarify several points in *Sanhedrin* 110b.)

In this opinion, the many Midrashim which describe in detail where the ten tribes are located and the form which their redemption will take (e.g., *Pesikta Rabbasi* 31; *Yerushalmi Sanhedrin* 10:6; *Bamidbar Rabbah* 16:15;) are consistent with both R' Elazar's and R' Akiva's views.

However, the plain meaning of *Toras Kohanim* seems to imply that the ten tribes will be entirely 'consumed' in the lands of their exile (see also *Yevamos* 16b, 17a) and this leads us to explore another possibility.

According to *Megillah* 14b, a portion of the ten tribes returned to their homeland during Yoshiyahu's reign. (*Rashi* to *Sanhedrin* 110b writes that not many returned at that time, but *Tiferes Yisrael* there demonstrates that probably most of the ten tribes returned then.) *Tosafos* to *Gittin* 36a concludes from this tradition that during the period of the second Temple there were representatives of all twelve tribes in Israel. (*Ramban, Gittin* 36a, disagrees, maintaining that though they came back as stated in the Talmud, they never shared the Babylonian exile, but returned to the lands to which the ten tribes had been exiled when Jerusalem fell to Nebuchadnezzar.)

Thus it is possible that even if we interpret R' Akiva's opinion to be that the exiled ten tribes will not return (and assume that all the Midrashic allusions to their return are based on R' Elazar's opinion), it is still possible that in Messianic times all twelve tribes will be represented. From the time of Yoshiyahu onwards they blended with the two southern tribes. However, they will be identified by the Messiah and take their rightful place in Israel.

16. לִיהוּדָה וְלִבְנֵי יִשְׂרָאֵל חֲבֵרָו — *For Judah and the children of Israel his comrades.*

He is to write these four words onto the wooden tablet to indicate that it stands for Judah and the tribe of Benjamin who is joined to Judah *(Rashi).* [The tribe of Benjamin had its portion of the land adjacent to Judah's and was always part of the southern kingdom.]

לְיוֹסֵף עֵץ אֶפְרַיִם וְכָל־בֵּית יִשְׂרָאֵל חֲבֵרָו — *For Joseph, Ephraim's tablet, and all the family of Israel his comrades.*

The second tablet was to be inscribed with these seven words: *For Joseph* [i.e.,

יז וְקָרַב אֹתָם אֶחָד אֶל־אֶחָד לְךָ לְעֵץ אֶחָד
יח וְהָיוּ לַאֲחָדִים בְּיָדֶךָ׃ וְכַאֲשֶׁר יֹאמְרוּ
אֵלֶיךָ בְּנֵי עַמְּךָ לֵאמֹר הֲלוֹא־תַגִּיד לָנוּ
יט מָה־אֵלֶּה לָּךְ׃ דַּבֵּר אֲלֵהֶם כֹּה־אָמַר אֲדֹנָי
יֱהֹוִה הִנֵּה אֲנִי לֹקֵחַ אֶת־עֵץ יוֹסֵף אֲשֶׁר
בְּיַד־אֶפְרַיִם וְשִׁבְטֵי יִשְׂרָאֵל חֲבֵרָו וְנָתַתִּי
אוֹתָם עָלָיו אֶת־עֵץ יְהוּדָה וַעֲשִׂיתִם לְעֵץ
כ אֶחָד וְהָיוּ אֶחָד בְּיָדִי׃ וְהָיוּ הָעֵצִים אֲשֶׁר־
כא תִּכְתֹּב עֲלֵיהֶם בְּיָדְךָ לְעֵינֵיהֶם׃ וְדַבֵּר
אֲלֵיהֶם כֹּה־אָמַר אֲדֹנָי יֱהֹוִה הִנֵּה אֲנִי
לֹקֵחַ אֶת־בְּנֵי יִשְׂרָאֵל מִבֵּין הַגּוֹיִם אֲשֶׁר
הָלְכוּ־שָׁם וְקִבַּצְתִּי אֹתָם מִסָּבִיב וְהֵבֵאתִי
כב אוֹתָם אֶל־אַדְמָתָם׃ וְעָשִׂיתִי אֹתָם לְגוֹי
אֶחָד בָּאָרֶץ בְּהָרֵי יִשְׂרָאֵל וּמֶלֶךְ אֶחָד
°יִהְיוּ ק׳ יִהְיֶה לְכֻלָּם לְמֶלֶךְ וְלֹא °יהיה־עוֹד לִשְׁנֵי
גוֹיִם וְלֹא יֵחָצוּ עוֹד לִשְׁתֵּי מַמְלָכוֹת עוֹד׃
כג וְלֹא יִטַּמְּאוּ עוֹד בְּגִלּוּלֵיהֶם וּבְשִׁקּוּצֵיהֶם
וּבְכֹל פִּשְׁעֵיהֶם וְהוֹשַׁעְתִּי אֹתָם מִכֹּל
מוֹשְׁבֹתֵיהֶם אֲשֶׁר חָטְאוּ בָהֶם וְטִהַרְתִּי
אוֹתָם וְהָיוּ־לִי לְעָם וַאֲנִי אֶהְיֶה לָהֶם

this tablet represents Joseph as embodied by his major son], *the tablet of Ephraim* ... The founder of the secessionist nation of the ten tribes was Jeraboam ben Nebat, an Ephraimite *(Rashi).*

17. וְהָיוּ לַאֲחָדִים בְּיָדֶךָ — *And they shall become one in your hand.*

Metzudos understands the phrase to mean that the two tablets will actually fuse miraculously into one to indicate the absolute unity of the two parts of Israel.

19. וְנָתַתִּי אוֹתָם עָלָיו — *And shall place them with him.*

אוֹתָם, *them,* refers to the tribes of Israel which are *his comrades.* עָלָיו, *with him,* refers to Ephraim. The nine tribes together with Ephraim will be joined to Judah (Radak).

אֶת־עֵץ יְהוּדָה — [*Together*] *with Judah's wooden tablet.*

אֶת, *with,* is used rather than אֶל, *to.* The latter would indicate *bringing them towards.* This would, at the very most, describe the moment of contact. אֶת, *with,* expresses a complete reconciliation which brings about a permanent union *(R' Mendel Hirsch).*

17 *And bring them close to yourself, one to the other,*
like a single wooden tablet, and they shall become
one in your hand. 18 *Now when the children of your*
people say to you: Will you not tell us what those are
to you? 19 *Speak to them: Thus says my Lord*
HASHEM / ELOHIM: See! I take Joseph's wooden
tablet which is in Ephraim's hand, and the tribes of
Israel his comrades, and shall place them with him
together with Judah's wooden tablet, and I will make
them one wooden tablet, and they shall become one
in My hand, 20 *and the wooden tablets upon which*
you will write shall be in your hand, in their sight.
21 *Then speak to them: Thus says my Lord*
HASHEM/ELOHIM: Behold! I take the Children of
Israel from among the nations to which they went,
and I shall gather them from around and I shall bring
them to their soil; 22 *and I shall make them into a*
single nation in the land upon Israel's hills, and a
single king shall be for them all as king; and they
shall no longer be two nations, no longer divided into
two kingdoms again; 23 *and they will no longer be*
contaminated with their idols and their abhorrent
things and with all their sins; and I shall save them
from all their habitations in which they sinned, and I
shall purify them, and they shall be a nation for Me,

22. לְגוֹי אֶחָד בָּאָרֶץ – *A single nation in the land.*

The phrase recalls *I Chronicles* 17:21: *Who is like your people Israel, a single nation in the land!* which, in the Sabbath afternoon *Shmoneh Esrei,* is juxtaposed to the phrase: *'You [God] are one and your Name is one'* (based on *Zechariah* 14:9). The latter phrase describes our perception of God in the Messianic era (See *Pesachim* 50a) since – until the time when the knowledge of God will cover the earth *as the sea covers its bed* – our perception of God remains imperfect. The juxtaposition of the two phrases thus makes the concept of Israel as *a single nation in the land* a hallmark of Messianic times.

Indeed, this unity of Israel was never achieved in history except for the relatively short period of David's reign. In Solomon's reign, the seeds of discord which led to the split in Rehaboam's reign were already sown. (See *Maharal, Netzach Yisrael,* ch. 33.)

23. וְטִהַרְתִּי אוֹתָם – *And I shall purify them.*

See 36:25.

לז
כד־כח

כד לֵֽאלֹהִֽים׃ וְעַבְדִּ֤י דָוִד֙ מֶ֣לֶךְ עֲלֵיהֶ֔ם וְרוֹעֶ֥ה
אֶחָ֖ד יִהְיֶ֣ה לְכֻלָּ֑ם וּבְמִשְׁפָּטַ֣י יֵלֵ֔כוּ וְחֻקֹּתַ֥י
כה יִשְׁמְר֖וּ וְעָשׂ֥וּ אוֹתָֽם׃ וְיָשְׁב֣וּ עַל־הָאָ֗רֶץ
אֲשֶׁ֤ר נָתַ֙תִּי֙ לְעַבְדִּ֣י לְיַעֲקֹ֔ב אֲשֶׁ֥ר יָֽשְׁבוּ־
בָ֖הּ אֲבֽוֹתֵיכֶ֑ם וְיָשְׁב֣וּ עָ֠לֶיהָ הֵ֨מָּה וּבְנֵיהֶ֜ם
וּבְנֵ֤י בְנֵיהֶם֙ עַד־עוֹלָ֔ם וְדָוִ֣ד עַבְדִּ֔י נָשִׂ֥יא
כו לָהֶ֖ם לְעוֹלָֽם׃ וְכָרַתִּ֤י לָהֶם֙ בְּרִ֣ית שָׁל֔וֹם
בְּרִ֥ית עוֹלָ֖ם יִהְיֶ֣ה אוֹתָ֑ם וּנְתַתִּים֙
וְהִרְבֵּיתִ֣י אוֹתָ֔ם וְנָתַתִּ֧י אֶת־מִקְדָּשִׁ֛י
כז בְּתוֹכָ֖ם לְעוֹלָֽם׃ וְהָיָ֤ה מִשְׁכָּנִי֙ עֲלֵיהֶ֔ם
וְהָיִ֥יתִי לָהֶ֖ם לֵֽאלֹהִ֑ים וְהֵ֖מָּה יִֽהְיוּ־לִ֥י
כח לְעָֽם׃ וְיָֽדְעוּ֙ הַגּוֹיִ֔ם כִּ֚י אֲנִ֣י יהוה מְקַדֵּ֖שׁ
אֶת־יִשְׂרָאֵ֑ל בִּֽהְי֧וֹת מִקְדָּשִׁ֛י בְּתוֹכָ֖ם

לח
א

א לְעוֹלָֽם׃ וַיְהִ֥י דְבַר־יְהוָ֖ה אֵלַ֥י

24. רוֹעֶה — *Shepherd.*

See 34:13ff. for a description of the king as a shepherd.

25. וְיָשְׁבוּ עַל־הָאָרֶץ ... אֲשֶׁר יָשְׁבוּ־בָהּ אֲבוֹתֵיכֶם — *And they shall dwell upon the land within which your fathers dwelt.*

R' Mendel Hirsch notes that Israel is described as dwelling *upon* while the fathers are described as dwelling *within* it. According to R' S.R. Hirsch to *Leviticus* 25:18, the expression עַל הָאָרֶץ, *upon the land,* indicates that the land supports the people, and thus serves them. This is in contrast to the situation described in *Leviticus* 18:28 where the land controls the inhabitants, vomiting them forth when they defile it.

Our verse promises that in contrast to their fathers who lived *within* [the control] of the land, they, the sons, will live *upon* it.

לְעַבְדִּי לְיַעֲקֹב — *To My servant, to Jacob.*

Jacob is chosen from among the fathers because to him the land was promised without any limitation at all. When the land was promised to Abraham (*Genesis* 13:17) and to Isaac (26:3), boundaries were assigned to it. But when it was promised to Jacob (28:14), he was told that his offspring would spread out powerfully in all directions *(Rashi).*

נָשִׂיא — *A prince.*

See 22:6 and 34:24.

26. וּנְתַתִּים — *And I shall emplace them.*

This obscure phrase is a shortened form of *I shall place them in their land (Radak; Metzudos)* or: *I shall place them* in a state of being blessed *(Radak).*

Targum renders *And I shall bless them.*

27. וְהָיָה מִשְׁכָּנִי עֲלֵיהֶם — *And My dwelling place will be upon them.*

God's purpose in bringing Israel out of Egypt had been that He might dwell among them. (*Exodus* 29:46, *Ramban;* see footnote 20:9). In the Messianic era this purpose will finally be accomplished. For all eternity Israel will bear the Presence of God in its midst.

37
24-28

and I will be God for them, [24] *with My servant David*
king over them, and a single shepherd will be for all
of them. In my ordinance they will go and My
decrees they will guard, and perform them, [25] *and*
they shall dwell on the land which I gave to My ser-
vant Jacob within which your fathers dwelt; and they
shall dwell upon it — they, their children and their
children's children forever, and My servant David
will be prince for them, forever.
[26] *And I shall seal a covenant of peace with them;*
an eternal covenant shall it be with them; and I shall
emplace them, and I shall increase them, and I shall
place My Sanctuary among them forever; [27] *and My*
dwelling place will be upon them, and I shall be God
for them, and they will be My people. [28] *Then the na-*
tions shall know that I am HASHEM who hallows
Israel, when My Sanctuary is among them for
always.

The unusual form עֲלֵיהֶם, *upon them,* rather than בְּתוֹכָם, *among them,* is noted by *Radak.* The phrase promises that the Presence of God will be *among them (Targum),* and the fear of God will be *upon them.*

XXXVIII

Yechezkel is to address a prophecy to Gog of the land of Magog. He is to describe three things: Gog's plans to thrust his military might against a defenseless Israel, the utter annihilation which God will inflict upon Gog in the Holy Land, and the aftermath of that holocaust as Israel spends seven months cleansing the land.

Rambam (Hilchos Melochim *12:2) advises against a detailed study of the events which lead to the coming of the Messiah. Knowledge of these matters, he teaches, leads neither to fear not to love of God. We will understand the exact meaning of the many obscure passages in Scripture with the occurrence of the events which they describe. In the meantime, we need know no more than the general picture which the sources yield. The details are in no way principles of faith.*

Among the many mysteries which surround the advent of the Messianic era, מִלְחֶמֶת גּוֹג וּמָגוֹג, the War of Gog and Magog, *plays a major role. Following* Rambam's *directive, we shall not attempt an exact delineation of the events which are to happen. Rather we will offer a very general outline and a short analysis of the meaning of these wars.*

Dark days are to precede the coming of the Messiah. Sanhedrin *98b quotes a number of our Sages who prayed that they might be spared the terrible experience of the time.* Rashi (Sanhedrin *98b) explains the very term* חֶבְלוֹ שֶׁל מָשִׁיחַ the pain of the pre-Messianic period, *as describing the fear which these armies will inspire.*

Who is this Gog around whom history's climactic events are to occur? Which is the land of Magog? Who are Gog's allies? Above all, what motive will he have to wage the war which will prove to be his undoing? Why does the nation of Israel, dwelling peacefully within its boundaries, inspire the hatred which drags Gog inexorably to his doom?

In attempting some answers to these questions, we will resist the temptation to relate the prophecies concerning Gog and Magog to contemporary events. We live in momentous times, and there is no doubt that we are witnessing the fulfillment of much that is contained in the prophetic books. Nevetheless, it is beyond the scope of this commentary to attempt to interpret specific historical figures and places in prophetic terms. [The interested reader is referred to Chevlei Mashiach BiZemaneinu *by* Refoel HaLevi Eisenberg (Jerusalem *5730). Written between the two great seminal wars of 1967 and 1973, its purpose was to collect all Scriptural, Talmudic, and Rabbinic sources which seem to have a bearing on contemporary times. It was published with the approbation of many* Gedolei Yisroel *and makes an important contribution to the understanding of the turbulent times in which we live.]*

Midrash Tanchuma *to* Korach *points out that the numerical value of* גוֹג וּמָגוֹג, Gog and Magog, *is seventy, which alludes to the seventy nations of the world. The wars of Gog and Magog are thus projected as battles which all the seventy nations of the world will wage against Israel. [According to* Yalkut Shimoni *1:76, the* Four Kingdoms *(see* comm. *21:24-27), who had subjugated Israel separately, will now come against her in unison.]*

The Sages speak of three separate wars which are to be fought (see Midrash Tehillim *to* Psalms *118). According to* Malbim, *the first two of these are the subject of our chapters in* Ezekiel. *The final war when Gog will actually break into Jerusalem, is described in* Zechariah *14. [References to the wars of Gog and Magog abound in Scripture, overtly in the prophets and, according to the* Targumim *and* Midrashim, *by allusion in the Torah. However, the longest, most detailed, and most specific accounts are contained in the books of* Ezekiel, Zechariah, Joel, *and* Daniel.]

*Yechezkel portrays Israel at the time of Gog's attack as a of people recently gathered from exile, living peacefully within their boundaries, following agricultural and commercal pursuits, and prospering (*vs. *8, 11-12). It is an economically viable community, wealthy enough to be an attractive target for Gog and his cohorts who are interested in spoils (*v. *12) of silver, gold, and livestock (*v. *13).*

Such a description seems to assume Messianic times and, indeed, according to most sources the wars of Gog and Magog will take place after the first steps of the redemption — which are to be initiated by Mashiach ben Yosef, the Messiah descended from Ephraim, who is to precede the Davidic Messiah — will already have taken place.[1]

1. The tradition concerning *Mashiach ben Yosef* is mentioned at 23:3, 4 and 37:7. Although brief mention of such a Messiah is made in the Talmud *(Succah* 52a), detailed discussions are to be found mainly in *Kabbalah* literature such as the *Zohar* and in the *Midrashim* (e.g., *Pirkei Heichalos Rabbasi* 39:1). It is a subject of profound depth and mystery which figures prominently in the writings of *ARIzal, Vilna Gaon,* and *Luzzatto.* Our Sages see this Messiah as preparing the way for the Davidic Messiah (see *R' Saadiah Gaon, Emunos VeDeos, Maamar* 8: *He will be like a representative [of the Davidic Messiah] preparing the people and smoothing the path) by being active in* קִבּוּץ גָּלֻיּוֹת, *ingathering of the exiles (Ramban, Sefer HaGeulah, Shaar* 4) and in cleansing Israel of sin (*Emunos VeDeos,* 8).

Pirkei Mashiach (Beis HaMedrash Part 3) describes *Mashiach ben Yosef* in the following way: *'Mashiach ben Yosef* will take them up to Jerusalem, build the Temple, and bring sacrifices, whereupon a fire will come down from heaven and consume their sacrifices.' Pirkei Heichalos (39:1) writes: *'Forty years before the Davidic Messiah ... Mashiach ben Yosef will*

Thus we learn that the might of the earth's seventy nations is to be thrown against an Israel enjoying the first stages of its ultimate redemption.

What is the deeper meaning of this epic battle?

Sanhedrin *95b describes the exact numbers of Sennacherib's toops when he moved against the Northern Kingdom. This, the Talmud states, was the same number of soldiers who fought against Abraham (in his war against the four kings* [Rashi]*) and who were destined to accompany Gog in his campaign against Israel.*

Maharal, (Chiddushei Aggadah), *explains the connection between these three wars as follows: Israel was chosen from among the nations of the world. Any choice must, by definition, imply a rejection of the ones who were not chosen. These then react to this implied rejection by an all-consuming drive to destroy its cause; hence, the unrelieved animosity of the nations of the world to Israel. This animosity expressed itself in overt battle on two occasions, and will do so once more in the future.*

It was Abraham with whom the singularization of Israel began. Immediately, the nations of the world [the Sages teach that the four kings who fought against Abraham symbolized the Four Kingdoms, who were destined to subjugate Israel] gathered together for an attack designed to frustrate that choice.

In the waning years of the Northern Kingdom, Israel reached the nadir of its existence. Ten of the twelve tribes were to be lost to their people. This seemed the ideal moment for an all out war which would strike Israel when it was weakest. Once more the nations, led by Sennacherib, gathered for the attack.

With the advent of the Davidic Messiah, the choice of Israel will have been finally vindicated. If the nations are to destroy Israel, it must be before that point in history. At the beginning of the end, when Mashiach ben Yosef *will have begun the process which with culminate in the final and everlasting establishment of Israel, the nations will gather once more in a vain attempt to prevent the final bursting forth of the Messianic light.*

At that moment God's anger will be kindled against the nations (v. *18). As He comes forth to smite Israel's enemies, who, in the final analysis, are His enemies, the Sanctification of His Name — the ultimate goal of all historic developments (see* footnote *20:9) — will finally have been accomplished* (v. *23).*[1]

come and stand in Jerusalem, and all Israel will gather around him, each man with his family, and the Family of Israel will bring sacrifices which will be pleasant to God, and all of Israel will be identified by their correct families.'

According to tradition, *Mashiach ben Yosef* will be killed during the wars of Gog and Magog. (See *Succah* 52a.)

The picture of Israel painted in our chapter reflects the stage of redemption associated with *Mashiach ben Yosef.*

1. That the enemies of Israel are really God's enemies, and that their attacks against Israel are challenges to God Himself, is one of the great themes of Aggadic literature. It is brought out with great clarity in the Midrash to *Psalms* 2. This psalm is interpreted by the Sages to refer to the wars of Gog and Magog. Verse 2 describes how the kings and princes of the world gather together *against God and against his anointed one.* To this the Midrash *(Vayikra Rabbah* 27:11) remarks: 'Cursed are the wicked ones who plot against Israel. Each one claims that his strategy is better than the other.

Esau said, 'Cain was a fool for killing Abel during Adam's lifetime. Did he not know that Adam would have another son? I shall not make the same mistake, but wait till my father dies.'

Pharaoh said, 'Esau was a fool. Did he not know that Jacob would have children during their father's lifetime?'

Haman said, 'Pharaoh was a fool when he planned to drown the baby boys. Did he not know that the girls would marry men?'

Gog and Magog will one day say, 'The earlier ones were fools for plotting against Israel. Did they not know that Israel has a Defender in heaven? I shall not make the same mistake. First I shall join battle with the Defender, and then I shall tackle Israel.'

לח ב
ב לֵאמֹר: בֶּן־אָדָם שִׂים פָּנֶיךָ אֶל־גּוֹג אֶרֶץ הַמָּגוֹג נְשִׂיא רֹאשׁ מֶשֶׁךְ וְתֻבָל וְהִנָּבֵא

A portion of our two chapters (37:18-39:16) is the Haftarah *of the Intermediate Sabbath of Succos (see* Megillah *31a). According to* Rashi, *the reason is that the wars of Gog and Magog are also the subject of* Zechariah *12, which is the Haftarah of the first day of Succos and which, in* Rashi's *view, was chosen because of the prediction contained in it that those nations who would survive the wars would join Israel every year in celebrating the Succos festival.*

Nimukei Yosef *to* Megillah *quotes a tradition from* R' Hai Gaon *that the victory over Gog and Magog will take place in the month of* Tishrei, *the same month within which Succos occurs.*

These explanations do not deal with the inner connection between Gog and Magog and Succos. R' Hirsch (Numbers *29:13) discusses the profound implications of this subject. Following is a free translation of his thesis:*

In the name גוֹג, Gog, *one recognizes the word* גַּג, roof, *and thereby at once sees the contrast to* succah, *the weak, unstable covering of foliage. Actually, the whole history of mankind consists of this contrast. Just as people have the power to make [themselves] safe and secure against their earthly contemporaries by* דְּפָנוֹת, strongly built walls, *so do they imagine that they have power to make themselves safe and sure against that which comes from above — against God and ... His power to direct matters. They think that they can find security in the protection of their own might, take their fate in their own hands, and crown the building up of human greatness with gabled roofs, rendering them independent of God.*

[The war of Gog and Magog] is the battle of גַּג, roof, *against* סוּכָּה, succah, *the fight of the 'roof' illusion of human greatness which never allows ... rest, against the 'succah' truth of cheerful confidence and serenity which comes of placing one's trust in God's protection.*

[R' Hirsch's *exposition of the Gog-Magog relationship bases itself on the Hebrew grammatical rule that the prefix* מ, mem, *expresses the idea of projecting something. For example,* אוֹר *is* light; מָאוֹר, luminary, *is a heavenly body which projects light. So too,* גַּג means *roof* — in *R' Hirsch's* view, it represents the philosophy that man can insulate himself against the heavenly power of God — מָגוֹג is the attempt to project this philosophy on earth.]

2. גּוֹג אֶרֶץ הַמָּגוֹג — *Gog of the land of Magog.*

The identity of Gog, a personality who will live at a far-off time defined by the prophet as אַחֲרִית הַשָּׁנִים, *the end of years (v.* 8), must remain shrouded in mystery. Indeed, in *Malbim's* view this very point is expressed in *v.* 17: *Are you the one concerning whom I spoke?* Only when Gog actually comes will he be identified as the king who was the subject of centuries-old prophecies. Nevertheless we will have some remarks to make about Gog. These will gain in significance after we have identified the land of Magog more closely.

It would seem that Magog was a known place in Yechezkel's time, and, therefore, we should be able to identify it with reasonable accuracy. Our chapter offers a hint by telling that Gog will come from יַרְכְּתֵי צָפוֹן, *the farthest north (v.* 15). In Torah symbolism the north is viewed as the seat of the forces of evil (see *comm.* 21:1). Thus it is not surprising that Gog, like Babylon in its time, is to come from the north. Still the יַרְכְּתֵי צָפוֹן, *farthest north,* is surely also meant to define a geographic location. Thus, Magog must lie in what was the northernmost extremity of the then civilized world.

The various traditions concerning the identity of Magog, who in *Genesis* 10:2

The word of HASHEM came to me, saying: Ben Adam, set your face towards Gog of the land of Magog, prince, leader of Meshech and Tubal and

is listed among the sons of Noah's son Japheth, tend to place the land of Magog in what today is southeastern Russia — the Caucasian region, which lies between the Black and Caspian seas.

Josephus (Antiquities 1:6) identifies the descendants of מָגוֹג, *Magog,* as the Scythians, who, some centuries before the common era, branched out eastward and westward from the region somewhat north of the Black Sea. This is in agreement with *Yerushalmi Megillah* 3:9, which renders Magog as גוטיָא (or גותיָא — see *Aruch* on גְרַמְמַיָא), *the Goths,* a group of nomadic tribes who destroyed the Scythians and made their homes in Scythian territory.

Considering that the Goths were a Germanic people, the identification of Magog's descendants as the Goths is in accord with *Targum Yonasan* to *Genesis* 10:2, who renders מָגוֹג as גְרַמְמַיָא, *Geramemaia,* which in *Bereishis Rabbah* 37:1, is given as גֵירְמַנְיָא, *Germaniah.* Reference seems to be to the nomads who settled in the Caucasion regions.

[*Yomah* 10a offers קנדיא *(possibly a Greek part of the island of Crete) for Magog. However, there are many divergent readings. For a discussion, see Aruch HaShalem* to אַפְרִיקִי.]

Thus אֶרֶץ הַמָּגוֹג, *land of Magog,* is located in a region aptly described as יַרְכְּתֵי צָפוֹן, *the farthest north.*[1]

Our identification of Magog as Caucasia, which was at one time inhabited by the Goths, is based on the assumption that the land of Magog is named after Japheth's son. Indeed this seems likely since some of Gog's allies have names identical to, or strikingly similar to, offspring of Japheth. Meshech and Tubal *(v.* 2), are names of Japheth's sons; פָּרַס, *Persia (v.* 5) is identified with Japheth's son Teras, and Togarmah *(v.* 6) is a grandson of Japheth.

From this it seems that when, finally, the forces of evil are to be pitted against Israel, the Japhethic tribes will be in the forefront of the battle. A closer identification of some of Gog's other allies who are not of Japhethic descent will be attempted. Nevertheless the identification of the king as coming from the land of Magog and his title נְשִׂיא רֹאשׁ מֶשֶׁךְ וְתֻבָל, *prince, leader of Meshech and Tuval,* surely indicate that the Japhethic peoples are to be the main components of his army.]

This forces us to consider the identity of Gog himself more closely. For, surely, it is not Japheth but Edom, who, throughout the Torah, is identified as the epitome of evil and the one irreconcilable enemy of Israel. (For a detailed discussion, see pref. ch. 35). Indeed, *Tanchuma Bo* (4) constantly refers to Gog and Magog as Edom.

Chevlei Mashiach BiZemaneinu brings much source material which indicates that although Gog's land is Japhethic, he himself is a descendant of Esau. In Midrashic literature (cf. *Yonasan ben Uziel, Isaiah* 11:4), Gog is often referred to as אַרְמִילוּס which is a variant of Romulus, founder of Rome (see *Aruch* under ארמילוס). This name is also quoted in later sources (e.g., *R' Saadiah Gaon, Emunos VeDeos* 8:2) and seems to have been generally ac-

1. If we have located אֶרֶץ הַמָּגוֹג, *land of Magog,* correctly, then the *island dwellers* mentioned in 39:6 (but see *comm.* 26:15) would be the inhabitants of the many islands scattered around the Aegean Sea.

In this light, one may understand an oral tradition passed down from the *Vilna Gaon* (see *Chevlei Mashiach BiZemaneinu* p. 134), that when the Russian navy passes through the Bosporus (that is, on the way to the Mediterranian through the Dardanelles) it will be time to put on Sabbath clothes [in anticipation of the coming of *Mashiach.*]

ג עָלָיו: וְאָמַרְתָּ כֹּה אָמַר אֲדֹנָי יֱהֹוִה הִנְנִי
אֵלֶיךָ גּוֹג נְשִׂיא רֹאשׁ מֶשֶׁךְ וְתֻבָל:
ד וְשֹׁובַבְתִּיךָ וְנָתַתִּי חַחִים בִּלְחָיֶיךָ
וְהוֹצֵאתִי אוֹתְךָ וְאֶת־כָּל־חֵילֶךָ סוּסִים
וּפָרָשִׁים לְבֻשֵׁי מִכְלוֹל כֻּלָּם קָהָל רָב צִנָּה
ה וּמָגֵן תֹּפְשֵׂי חֲרָבוֹת כֻּלָּם: פָּרַס כּוּשׁ וּפוּט
ו אִתָּם כֻּלָּם מָגֵן וְכוֹבָע: גֹּמֶר וְכָל־אֲגַפֶּיהָ

cepted. The implication is that the Messiah will be pitted against a king not of the same nationality as the nation over which he is to rule.

The same conclusion seems to be yielded by *Bereishis Rabbah* 76:5 where the Midrash comments on Daniel's visions of the four beasts (*Daniel* ch. 7) symbolizing the Four Kingdoms which are to subjugate Israel. The fourth and most terrible beast has ten horns from which an eleventh is seen to sprout. The Midrash comments that these ten horns symbolize ten kings of the Fourth Kingdom, and the eleventh horn is the final king whom Israel will confront. All these kings, the *Midrash* stresses, are to be descendants of Esau.

The implication is that the king and initiator of the campaign against Israel will be from Esau-Edom. The fighting force, however, will be drawn from the ranks of Japheth and Ham (*v.* 5) and from Ishmael's descendants.

This picture of Esau-Edom instigating other nations to fight Israel is entirely in consonance with the teachings of our Sages concerning the Fourth Kingdom. Its very essence, which distinguishes it from the other Kingdoms, is its ability to spread the poison of its hatred to other nations. (See *Ramban*, to *Genesis* 14:1; *Pachad Yitzchak, Purim* ch. 2; ArtScroll *Bereishis* vol. 2, *The Four Monarchies* p. 417). So it was in Esther's time, when the Amalekite Haman (descended from Esau) was the instigating force in the Persian (Japhethic) court, and so it will be in the wars of Gog and Magog, when the Edomite king Gog will lead the Japhethic nations to war.[1]

2. ... נְשִׂיא רֹאשׁ — *Prince, leader.*

Apparently the phrase is to be understood as though there were two phrases, נְשִׂיא מֶשֶׁךְ, *prince of Meshech*, and רֹאשׁ מֶשֶׁךְ, *leader of Meshech. Radak* and *Metzudos* quote analagous passages in which almost synonymous terms, both in the construct form, follow one another. (The cantillation, which separates נְשִׂיא from רֹאשׁ, precludes a translation such as *chief prince.)*

מֶשֶׁךְ וְתֻבָל — *Meshech and Tubal.*

Both Meshech and Tubal are listed in *Genesis* 10:2 as sons of Japheth. Tubal

1. We have drawn an analogy between Purim and the wars of Gog and Magog. In both cases Esau-Edom instigates another nation to fight against Israel. It is significant that in both cases it is a Japhethic people that is drawn into Edom's net.

This is entirely in consonance with what the Sages teach about Japheth.

In *Genesis* 9:20-27, we learn how Japheth helped his brother Shem to safeguard Noah's dignity. On that occasion the initiative lay entirely with Shem who took the garment with which to cover their father's nakedness. Japheth allowed himself to be drawn into this meritorious act (see *Rashi, Gur Aryeh* there).

Our Sages teach that Japheth's role in history is as the precursor of man's sense of the esthetic. All appreciation of the arts, drama, poetry, music, athletics, and philosophy has its roots in Japheth the forerunner of Greece. (See *Overview, Shem and Japheth* in ArtScroll *Bereishis* vol. 1, p. 216). These gifts are tools which God granted man. However, as *Hirsch*

prophesy against him, 3 *and say: Thus says my Lord*
HASHEM/ELOHIM: Behold! I turn to you Gog,
prince, leader of Meshech and Tubal. 4 *I shall lead*
you astray and I shall affix hooks to your cheeks and
lead you out with all your army, horses and riders, all
of them clothed in splendor, a vast assembly with
buckler and shield, all of them wielding swords.
5 *Persia, Cush, and Put with them, all of them with*
shield and helmet; 6 *Gomer and all her cohorts, Bais*

is identified as Beth Unyaki, and Meshech as Mysia in *Yomah* 10a. *Yerushalmi* reads Bithynia instead of Beth Unyaki and, according to *Torah Temimah* to *Genesis* 10:2, there is a province of that name in the Black Sea region. Mysia is also located in Asia Minor. [*Chevlei Mashiach BiZemaneinu* quotes a letter which *R' Chisdai Ibn Shaprut* wrote to the king of Khazaria [a Caucasian kingdom which converted to Judaism in the eighth century C.E.] in which he addresses the king as נְשִׂיא רֹאשׁ מֶשֶׁךְ וְתֻבָל, *prince, leader of Meshech and Tubal.* This salutation, drawn from our verse, indicates that the *Gaonim* had a tradition that these countries were indeed located in Russia.

3. הִנְנִי אֵלֶיךָ — *Behold! I turn to you.*

I turn My attention towards you *(Metzudos).*

4. וְשׁוֹבַבְתִּיךָ — *I shall lead you astray.*

The translation follows *Rashi* and *Metzudos. Radak* renders *I will splinter your heart,* [i.e., what you will do will not be because of your own wishes, but because I will draw you to your fate.]

At the very moment when his military might assembles, Gog is reminded that he is no more than a tool in God's hand *(R' Breuer).*

The control which God wields over the minds of kings is discussed in *comm.* and footnote 21:24.

וְנָתַתִּי חַחִים בִּלְחָיֶיךָ — *And I shall affix hooks to your cheeks.*

This symbolizes Gog's complete impotence in the face of God's decree. See *comm.* 29:4.

5. פָּרַס כּוּשׁ וּפוּט — *Persia, Cush, and Put.*

Gog's forces will be augmented by other armies. The Japhethic Persia will converge on Israel from the east, while the Hammite Cush, and Put will come from the south.

Persia [פָּרַס] is the modern Iran. *Yoma* 10a identifies it with תִּירָס, *Tiras,* another son of Japheth (*Genesis* 10:2).

Cush lies to the south of Egypt between the southern Nile Valley and the Red Sea. It probably spread over the area which today is the eastern part of

writes, 'The seeker of beauty, the artist, is receptive to external stimuli.' Japheth is pliable. He can place his gifts at Edom's feet as readily as he can subordinate them to Shem's striving for the Divine. Therefore, throughout history, we find Japheth fluctuating between the poles of true spirituality and the grossest sensuality.

The same Japheth who allowed himself to be turned to holiness by his brother Shem was able, centuries later, to allow a Haman to control his empire, and attempt to wipe out Shem's descendants. When Gog will seek supporters in his final war against holiness and Godliness, he will turn to the pliable Japheth.

This provides insight into another aspect of the wars of Gog and Magog. In the final struggle, Japheth — representative of all the worldly culture of which the human race is capable — will be ranged with Edom. Man will have shown himself incapable of using these gifts in the service of holiness.

לח
ז־י

בֵּית תּוֹגַרְמָה יַרְכְּתֵי צָפוֹן וְאֶת־כָּל־
ז אֲגַפָּיו עַמִּים רַבִּים אִתָּךְ׃ הִכֹּן וְהָכֵן לְךָ
אַתָּה וְכָל־קְהָלֶךָ הַנִּקְהָלִים עָלֶיךָ וְהָיִיתָ
ח לָהֶם לְמִשְׁמָר׃ מִיָּמִים רַבִּים תִּפָּקֵד
בְּאַחֲרִית הַשָּׁנִים תָּבוֹא | אֶל־אֶרֶץ |
מְשׁוֹבֶבֶת מֵחֶרֶב מְקֻבֶּצֶת מֵעַמִּים רַבִּים
עַל הָרֵי יִשְׂרָאֵל אֲשֶׁר־הָיוּ לְחָרְבָּה תָּמִיד
וְהִיא מֵעַמִּים הוּצָאָה וְיָשְׁבוּ לָבֶטַח כֻּלָּם׃
ט וְעָלִיתָ כַּשֹּׁאָה תָבוֹא כֶּעָנָן לְכַסּוֹת
הָאָרֶץ תִּהְיֶה אַתָּה וְכָל־אֲגַפֶּיךָ וְעַמִּים
י רַבִּים אוֹתָךְ׃ כֹּה אָמַר אֲדֹנָי

the Sudan, Ethiopia, and Eritrea.

Put, according to *Josephus (Antiquities* 1:6) is Libya. *Nahum* 3:9 mentions פוט and לובים together, which suggests that Put is only a part of Libya.

6. תּוֹגַרְמָה ... גֹּמֶר — *Gomer ... Togarmah.*

גֹּמֶר and תּוֹגַרְמָה are son and grandson of Japheth, respectively. It is difficult to identify גֹּמֶר with any certainty. (See ArtScroll *Bereishis* vol. 1, p. 310). *Josephus (History of the Jews,* ch. 1) identifies בְּנֵי גֹּמֶר, *children of Gomer,* as the 'Franks who live in France on the River Seine' (see ArtScroll *Bereishis* vol. 1, p. 312).

[Our passage lists six Japhethite and two Hammite nations among Gog's armies. No Arab nation (that is, Shemite people descended from Abraham's son Ishmael) are mentioned. However, there is much source material which indicates that the Arab nations will play a major role in the wars of Gog and Magog. See *Chevlei Mashiach BiZemaneinu* p. 149 ff.]

7. הִכֹּן וְהָכֵן לְךָ — *Prepare and make ready for yourself.*

Prepare yourself and make others ready to join you to embark on the purpose set forth below *(Rashi). Targum* renders: *spur yourself on.*

וְהָיִיתָ לָהֶם לְמִשְׁמָר — *And be a guardian for them.*

We have translated *guardian* rather than *guard* in order to convey the far-reaching duties of a general upon whom devolves the entire management of the army in all its complexities. All aspects of the soldiers' well-being are his responsibility.

8. מִיָּמִים רַבִּים תִּפָּקֵד — *From ancient times* [lit. *from many days*] *you are to be recalled.*

In the *nifal,* פקד [*passive*] usually means that one is recalled with the purpose of subjecting him to his predestined fate, good or bad.

Rashi sees the wars of *Mashiach ben Yosef* as a time of reckoning for all the evils which the nations had perpetrated against Israel over the centuries. He renders, *You are to be recalled* (that is, punished) for sins which were committed *long ago.* In this view our phrase is connected with the next one ... (בְּאַחֲרִית הַשָּׁנִים) by an implied *'therefore':* You are to be punished; therefore — in order to facilitate your punishment — you will come in the end of years ...

Considering that אַחֲרִית הַיָּמִים *(v.* 16) is not so much the End of Days as the end result, the culmination, the legacy of days (see *Hirsch, Genesis* 49:1) — another interpretation is possible. God's פְּקִידָה, *consideration,* of Gog goes back

Togarmah, in the farthest north, and all its cohorts, many peoples with you.

[7] *Prepare and make ready for yourself, you and all the battalions mustered about you, and be a guardian for them.* [8] *From ancient times you are to be recalled. In the end of years you shall come to a land restored from the sword, gathered from many nations, upon the hills of Israel which had lain desolate continuously — and she had been liberated from the nations, all of them dwelling confidently. —* [9] *But you shall advance; like a storm you will come. Like a cloud covering the earth you will be, you and all your cohorts, and the many nations with you.* [10] *Thus says my*

into antiquity. This final confrontation had been planned all along. It is the culmination of all of world history which was inexorably flowing towards this point; although we could not understand how while the events were taking place *(R' Breuer).*

אֶל אֶרֶץ מְשׁוֹבֶבֶת מֵחֶרֶב — *To a land restored from the sword.*

Gog plans to attack a land whose inhabitants had returned [מְשׁוֹבֶבֶת from שוב, *to return*] from the exile into which they had been driven by the sword *(Rashi).*

Alternatively, one could translate *to a land* [whose people had been] *snatched* [מְשׁוֹבֶבֶת from לשבה, *to take captive*] *from the sword (R' Breuer).* The Jews who had returned to *Eretz Yisrael* are described as people rescued from *the sword* because exile can destroy a people (*Leviticus* 26:38). Those who will have returned to Israel could easily have succumbed to the sword which is the constant companion of a homeless people.

עַל הָרֵי יִשְׂרָאֵל אֲשֶׁר־הָיוּ לְחָרְבָּה תָּמִיד — *Upon the hills of Israel which had lain desolate continuously.*

The memory of *Eretz Yisrael's* desolation is still alive. For centuries it had been an arid wilderness, yearning for the return of its children. As they gradually came back, pouring into their home from the many countries of their exile, Israel's hills began to bloom (see pref., ch. 36).

Upon these newly blossoming hills, Gog's armies will march.

וְהִיא מֵעַמִּים הוּצָאָה — *And she had been liberated from the nations.*

We cannot know how God will bring about the initial ingathering of the exiles. Perhaps, as in the time of Cyrus when the Persian king encouraged the return of the Jews to Israel to build the Second Temple, international political considerations will cause the nations of the world to help and encourage a return of the Jews to their land. (See *Ramban, Shir HaShirim* 8:13; *Chofetz Chayim, Shem Olam* ch. 4; [see source material in *HaTekufah HaGedolah,* p. 96 ff). By whichever way they return, it is God who brings them there. The outward appearance may be that they come by their own volition, but in reality they are *liberated from the nations.*

On this basis, *Rashi* comments: It should have occurred to you, Gog, that He Who took them out from among the other nations of their exile would not forsake them in your hands.

וְיָשְׁבוּ לָבֶטַח כֻּלָּם — *All of them dwelling confidently.*

The returning Jews will live on their

יֱהֹוִה וְהָיָה | בַּיּוֹם הַהוּא יַעֲלוּ דְבָרִים עַל־
יא לְבָבֶךָ וְחָשַׁבְתָּ מַחֲשֶׁבֶת רָעָה: וְאָמַרְתָּ
אֶעֱלֶה עַל־אֶרֶץ פְּרָזוֹת אָבוֹא הַשֹּׁקְטִים
יֹשְׁבֵי לָבֶטַח כֻּלָּם יֹשְׁבִים בְּאֵין חוֹמָה
יב וּבְרִיחַ וּדְלָתַיִם אֵין לָהֶם: לִשְׁלֹל שָׁלָל
וְלָבֹז בַּז לְהָשִׁיב יָדְךָ עַל־חֳרָבוֹת נוֹשָׁבֹת
וְאֶל־עַם מְאֻסָּף מִגּוֹיִם עֹשֶׂה מִקְנֶה וְקִנְיָן
יג יֹשְׁבֵי עַל־טַבּוּר הָאָרֶץ: שְׁבָא וּדְדָן
וְסֹחֲרֵי תַרְשִׁישׁ וְכָל־כְּפִירֶיהָ יֹאמְרוּ לְךָ
הֲלִשְׁלֹל שָׁלָל אַתָּה בָא הֲלָבֹז בַּז הִקְהַלְתָּ
קְהָלֶךָ לָשֵׂאת | כֶּסֶף וְזָהָב לָקַחַת מִקְנֶה
יד וְקִנְיָן לִשְׁלֹל שָׁלָל גָּדוֹל: לָכֵן
הִנָּבֵא בֶן־אָדָם וְאָמַרְתָּ לְגוֹג כֹּה
אָמַר אֲדֹנָי יֱהֹוִה הֲלוֹא | בַּיּוֹם הַהוּא
טו בְּשֶׁבֶת עַמִּי יִשְׂרָאֵל לָבֶטַח תֵּדָע: וּבָאתָ
מִמְּקוֹמְךָ מִיַּרְכְּתֵי צָפוֹן אַתָּה וְעַמִּים
רַבִּים אִתָּךְ רֹכְבֵי סוּסִים כֻּלָּם קָהָל
טז גָּדוֹל וְחַיִל רָב: וְעָלִיתָ עַל־עַמִּי יִשְׂרָאֵל
כֶּעָנָן לְכַסּוֹת הָאָרֶץ בְּאַחֲרִית הַיָּמִים

land without fear *(Metzudos)*, and without aggressive designs against any neighbor *(Malbim)*.

11. אֶרֶץ פְּרָזוֹת — *A land of open towns.*

Many of the people live in undefended villages, feeling so secure from attack that they do not bother to seek refuge in the walled cities (*Rashi*; see *v.* 14).

12. לְהָשִׁיב יָדְךָ עַל־חֳרָבוֹת נוֹשָׁבוֹת — *To turn your hand against repopulated wastes.*

You wish to destroy again these cities which had been laid waste before and which had been repopulated only now *(Rashi)*.

עֹשֶׂה מִקְנֶה וְקִנְיָן — *Acquiring livestock and possessions.*

Metzudos points out that עשה, usually translated *to make*, can mean, *to acquire*, as in *Genesis* 12:5.

יֹשְׁבֵי עַל־טַבּוּר הָאָרֶץ — *Dwelling upon the navel of the land.*

They dwell on the highest and strongest part of the land, just as the navel is the center from which the rest of the body slopes down on all sides (when in a supine position) *(Rashi)*.

13. שְׁבָא וּדְדָן — *Sheba and Dedan.*

The name Sheba appears as a grandson of Cush, but also among the children of Yaktan and of Keturah.

38
11-16

Lord HASHEM/ELOHIM: On that day thoughts will
occur to you, and you will conceive a wicked design;
11 *and you will say: 'I will advance against a land of*
open towns, I will come against the tranquil ones,
dwelling confidently, all of them living without a
wall — no bar or gates are theirs — 12 *seize spoil and*
plunder booty, to turn your hand against
repopulated wastes, against a people gathered from
the nations, acquiring livestock and possessions,
dwelling upon the navel of the land. 13 *Sheba, Dedan,*
and the merchants of Tarshish and all her magnates
will say to you, 'Have you come to seize spoils? Is it
to plunder booty that you assembled your hordes, to
carry off silver and gold, to make off with livestock
and goods, to seize immense spoils?
14 *Therefore, prophesy, Ben Adam, and say to*
Gog: Thus said my Lord HASHEM/ELOHIM: Surely
on that day, when My people Israel dwells confident-
ly, you shall come to know, 15 *and you will come*
from your place in the farthest north — you and
many peoples with you, riding horses all of them, a
vast horde, a mighty army — 16 *and you will advance*
against My people Israel like a cloud covering the
earth. At the End of Days it will happen, that I shall

Sheba was a wealthy nation of Arab traders, which comprised many tribes and occupied many lands. Dedan is also mentioned among the sons of Keturah, and here, too, it refers to a wealthy Arab nation of traders (*R' David Tzvi Hoffman, Genesis* 10:7).

תַּרְשִׁישׁ — *Tarshish.*
See 27:12.

וְכָל־כְּפִירֶיהָ — *And all her magnates.*
כְּפִיר means a young lion. Aggressive, sharp traders are called כְּפִירִים because they too roam near and far in pursuit of their business *(Rashi).*

14. בַּיּוֹם הַהוּא ... תֵּדָע — *On that day ... you shall [come to] know.*
You shall learn Who is their Supporter and Protector *(Rashi).*
[Gog had seen their apparent disregard of danger when he observed them dwelling in open towns without the protection of a wall. Thinking that they trusted in their own strength, Gog felt strong enough to challenge them. He was to learn that their trust was not in themselves but in God. Before Him, Gog's mighty armies would prove to be impotent.]

16. בְּאַחֲרִית הַיָּמִים — *At the End of Days.*
see *comm., v.* 8.

תִּהְיֶה וַהֲבִאוֹתִיךָ עַל־אַרְצִי לְמַעַן
דַּעַת הַגּוֹיִם אֹתִי בְּהִקָּדְשִׁי בְךָ לְעֵינֵיהֶם
יז גּוֹג׃ כֹּה־אָמַר אֲדֹנָי יֱהוִֹה
הַאַתָּה־הוּא אֲשֶׁר־דִּבַּרְתִּי בְּיָמִים
קַדְמוֹנִים בְּיַד עֲבָדַי נְבִיאֵי יִשְׂרָאֵל
הַנִּבְּאִים בַּיָּמִים הָהֵם שָׁנִים לְהָבִיא אֹתְךָ
יח עֲלֵיהֶם׃ וְהָיָה | בַּיּוֹם הַהוּא

בְּהִקָּדְשִׁי בְךָ — *When I am sanctified through you.*

Verse 23 teaches that through the holocaust which will befall Gog's armies, God will manifest His greatness and holiness and make Himself known among all the nations.

This recalls *Exodus* 14:4, where God tells Moses that He would be *honored through Pharaoh* when the Egyptians drowned in the sea. *Rashi* there comments: When God takes vengeance from His enemies, His Name becomes exalted and sanctified.

God will become honored and sanctified when evil is finally wiped from the earth because then His essential goodness — which had become obscured by the pain and suffering brought by man's sins — will be recognized.[1]

17. הַאַתָּה הוּא — *Are you the one...?*

The question form of our verse (albeit a rhetorical one) makes it seem as though the identity of Gog is unknown. This indicates that the identity of Gog is to be shrouded in mystery until the time when he actually comes (*Malbim;* see *comm., v.* 2).

בְּיַד עֲבָדַי נְבִיאֵי יִשְׂרָאֵל — *Through My servants, the prophets of Israel.*

The *prophets* are Yechezkel and Zechariah, who also prophesied concerning Gog and Magog *(Rashi).*

Midrashically *Sanhedrin* 17a teaches that the *prophets* are Eldad and Medad, the two prophets mentioned in *Numbers* 11:27. [According to this interpretation, שָׁנִים in the next phrase is read as though it were written שְׁנַיִם, *two*, that is, which was said by the two prophets who are mentioned together.] According to the tradition of the Sages, the subject of their prophecy was the wars of Gog and Magog.[2]

1. These thoughts touch upon the great theme of יחוד, *the indivisible Oneness of God,* which precludes the possibility of any independent place for evil in the scheme of existence. That this theme be understood and acknowledged is the ultimate purpose of creation and the goal toward which all events lead. This concept is analyzed in great depth in *Ramchal's Daas Tevunos.* The following is an excerpt:

> God, Himself, testifies and makes known that [the purpose of] all that can be understood from all the major forces which direct history, is the revelation of His יחוד, *His complete Oneness,* as it is written *(Deuteronomy* 32:39): *See now that I, I Am He, and there is no other God with Me.* Now this verse was said after all events had been described which would ever occur in world history — for all is alluded to in *Haazinu,* as its contents imply — and the ending of it all is: *See now that I, I Am He ...*

2. *Maharal, Chiddushei Aggadah* there, explains why a prophecy concerning Gog and Magog was apt at that particular moment. God had just commanded Moses to appoint *seventy* elders to help him with the burden of governing the people. Therefore, this was the time to talk about Gog and Magog, who represent all the *seventy* nations of the world (see pref.).

We may understand this *Maharal* in the light of *Ramban* to *Numbers* 11:16. According to *Ramban* the fact that the Sanhedrin is composed of seventy members is based on the existence

bring you to My land so that the nations shall know Me, when I am sanctified through you before their eyes, Gog!

17 *Thus says my Lord HASHEM/ELOHIM: Are you the one about whom I spoke in ancient days through My servants, the prophets of Israel, who prophesied in those days many years ago that I would bring you against them?* 18 *And it shall be on that day, on the*

18-20 These verses describe a shattering physical upheaval which is to come about when Gog and his hordes descend upon the land. In *Joel* (ch. 4), there are hints that such an upheaval will take place and *Zechariah* (ch. 14) describes it in greater detail.

Metzudos writes that these verses are only a metaphor for the general fear and panic which will prevail in those terrible days. *Rashi* and *Radak* seem to interpret the verses literally.[1]

18. בַּיּוֹם הַהוּא — *On that day.*

יוֹם, *day*, does not necessarily mean a period of twenty-four hours. It can be used to describe a period of much longer duration. (See *Doros HaRishonim*, vol. 3, p. 322.) Thus, it is possible that the רַעַשׁ, *earthquake*, will occur during the

of seventy nations. The meaning of seventy nations is that there are seventy different qualities of human nature, each of which is represented by one nation (see *Ramchal, Derech HaShem* part 2, ch. 4). Thus, the number seventy encompasses all [possible] opinions since it encompasses all [possible] qualities.' The *Sanhedrin* is to be composed of seventy members, so that 'nothing can remain hidden from them.'

Thus Israel, by virtue of its seventy-member *Sanhedrin*, encompasses within itself all qualities of mankind which are scattered among the seventy nations. To use *Ramchal's* expression, Israel is 'mankind in its more exalted form,' while the nations of the world in their totality represent 'mankind in its less exalted form.'

In the framework of these thoughts, the ultimate defense of Israel against attack by the seventy nations is assured. Therefore the moment in which Israel was granted its seventy member Sanhedrin was the moment that Eldad and Medad were granted the prophecy concerning Gog and Magog.

1. *Mechilta* to *BeShalach* compares Pharaoh's empty boasts at the Sea to those of Gog and Magog:

This is comparable to a robber who stands [impotently] beside the palace walls and threatens that if he could get hold of the king's son, he would torture him to death. Thus did Pharaoh stand and boast in Egypt, *I will pursue, I will overtake and divide the spoils;* but the Heavenly Spirit mocks him and says, *'You* [*God*] *have blown with your breath and the sea covered them;* and so also it is written [*Psalms* 2, in connection with Gog and Magog]: *'Why do the peoples gather ... ?' He who sits in heaven will laugh;* and so it says [in our chapter]: *'Have you come to take spoils?' ... and it shall be on that day, on the day that Gog comes on the soil of Israel ... 'The fish of the sea, the birds of the sky, the beasts of the field, all creeping things that move on the ground, and every human being on earth shall quake before Me. Mountains shall be overthrown, cliffs shall topple ...*

This *Mechilta* draws a parallel between Pharaoh's destruction at the Red Sea and the רַעַשׁ, *earthquake*, of our chapter. The idea which seems to bind the two instances together is first, the self-delusion of the attackers who imagine themselves in control of a situation which, in reality, is completely beyond them, and second, the picture of a mocking, laughing God who destroys them.

God's 'laughter' at Gog's destruction is discussed in *Avodah Zarah* 3b. The *Gemara* main-

בְּיוֹם בּוֹא גוֹג עַל־אַדְמַת יִשְׂרָאֵל נְאֻם
יט אֲדֹנָי יֱהֹוִה תַּעֲלֶה חֲמָתִי בְּאַפִּי: וּבְקִנְאָתִי
בְאֵשׁ־עֶבְרָתִי דִּבַּרְתִּי אִם־לֹא | בַּיּוֹם
הַהוּא יִהְיֶה רַעַשׁ גָּדוֹל עַל אַדְמַת
כ יִשְׂרָאֵל: וְרָעֲשׁוּ מִפָּנַי דְּגֵי הַיָּם וְעוֹף
הַשָּׁמַיִם וְחַיַּת הַשָּׂדֶה וְכָל־הָרֶמֶשׂ הָרֹמֵשׂ
עַל־הָאֲדָמָה וְכֹל הָאָדָם אֲשֶׁר עַל־פְּנֵי
הָאֲדָמָה וְנֶהֶרְסוּ הֶהָרִים וְנָפְלוּ הַמַּדְרֵגוֹת
כא וְכָל־חוֹמָה לָאָרֶץ תִּפּוֹל: וְקָרָאתִי עָלָיו
לְכָל־הָרַי חֶרֶב נְאֻם אֲדֹנָי יֱהֹוִה חֶרֶב
כב אִישׁ בְּאָחִיו תִּהְיֶה: וְנִשְׁפַּטְתִּי אִתּוֹ בְּדֶבֶר
וּבְדָם וְגֶשֶׁם שׁוֹטֵף וְאַבְנֵי אֶלְגָּבִישׁ אֵשׁ
וְגָפְרִית אַמְטִיר עָלָיו וְעַל־אֲגַפָּיו וְעַל־

general period of the wars, not necessarily on any particular day.

תַּעֲלֶה חֲמָתִי בְּאַפִּי — *My raging anger shall flare up* [lit. *My anger will come up in My nose*].

Fierce anger is characterized by heavy breathing and a flaring of the nostrils. Therefore, the 'nose' is commonly used in Scripture to denote anger.

21. וְקָרָאתִי עָלָיו לְכָל־הָרַי חֶרֶב — *I will summon the sword against him to all My mountains.*

The sword which God will summon is one of internecine slaughter. In the terror of God's wrath, Gog's soldiers will turn against each other, thus bringing about their own destruction.

22. There is a wealth of Midrashic literature which relates the plague, blood, hailstones, etc. mentioned in this verse to similar disasters which befell

tains that this is a unique occurrence. Never throughout history would God laugh at His creatures, save only on that one day — the day of Gog's destruction.

What is the meaning of God's laughter, and what new light do these teachings of the Sages shed upon מִלְחֶמֶת גּוֹג וּמָגוֹג, *the war of Gog and Magog?*

Mocking laughter is a reaction to the superiority one feels upon observing another person in an absurd, futile, or incongruent situation. (See *Sefer HaIkkarim* 2:16). Mockery is that faculty with which man finds, or tries to find, the inner bankruptcy behind an imposing facade (see *Pachad Yitzchak, Purim ch. 1).*

The king, safely ensconced behind his palace walls, laughs at the impotent threats of the robber outside. They are absurd, futile, and — since the robber is a thinking being who should be in touch with reality — incongruous. He mocks the robber's bragging because he recognizes its true nature — an empty posturing not based on any real ability.

So God, who needs only to 'release His breath' for the seas to come crashing down around Pharaoh's forces, mocks his foolish plans. And so God will one day laugh as the nations *gather and ... talk in vain ... take their stand ... and conspire against HASHEM and against His anointed.* It is futile for them to marshal their forces when it requires nothing more than God's anger to rise within Him for the very earth on which they stand to quake and shake so that *mountains fall and cliffs topple.*

day that Gog comes on the soil of Israel — the words
of my Lord HASHEM/ELOHIM — My raging anger
shall flare up; 19 *For in My indignation and in My*
blazing wrath I have spoken: I take an oath that on
that day a great earthquake shall come upon the soil
of Israel. 20 *And there shall quake before Me the fish*
of the sea, the birds of the sky, the beasts of the field,
all creeping things that move on the ground, and
every human being on the face of the earth. Moun-
tains shall be overthrown, cliffs shall topple, and
every wall shall topple to the ground. 21 *I will sum-*
mon the sword against him to all My mountains —
the words of my Lord HASHEM / ELOHIM. Every
man's sword shall be against his brother. 22 *I will*
punish him with pestilence and with blood. Torren-
tial rain, hailstones, and sulfurous fire I will rain
upon him and his cohorts and the many peoples that

the Egyptians (see *Tanchuma Bo* 4). In fact, *Tanchuma (VaEirah* 22) teaches that when Moses prayed that the plague of the hailstones stop, the stones which were then falling remained suspended in the air until the time they would fall upon Gog's army.

Apparently, the Sages wish to draw our attention to the thread which, spanning the centuries, ties Gog to Egypt. Pharaoh attempted to squash the new nation before it ever achieved an independent existence. Gog, in one last gigantic effort, throws the might of the nations against a people whose resilience had been tested over the centuries, but who now seemed vulnerable to attack. Egypt, at the beginning of history, and Gog, at its end, share a hatred against the bearers of Divine Glory on earth. Both are smashed by the furious forces of nature, which God chooses as the agent with which He establishes His nation.

There is yet another dimension to this laughter. *Midrash Tanchuma (Noah* 18) uses the description in *Psalms* 2 of God 'laughing,' to understand God's actions when mankind decided to build the Tower of Babel to defy Him. The *Midrash* explains why God did not prevent the building of the tower in the first place. Had he done so the people might always have thought that if only they could have gone through with their project they could indeed have 'gone up to heaven.' Therefore God allowed them to do as much as they could. When they failed — He 'laughed.'

This, too, is God's 'laughter' when the quaking earth will have finally destroyed Gog's pretensions. God has allowed man thousands of years to build his own 'tower.' The ebb and flow of history has witnessed man's struggle to 'go up to heaven' without God's guidance. The גַּג, *roof,* philosophy of Gog (see pref. to this chapter) was given ample opportunity to prove itself. The falling of the hills and toppling of the cliffs at the moment of the רַעַשׁ, *earthquake,* will bury those false hopes in the rubble of destruction.

At that moment God will be exalted, sanctified, and made known to many nations (*v.* 23). Mankind will have come to recognize true indivisible Oneness of God [יִחוּד (see footnote, *v.* 16) בַּיּוֹם הַהוּא, *on that day,* when [when the realization that] *God will be One and His Name One* [will have been achieved].

כג עַמִּים רַבִּים אֲשֶׁר אִתּוֹ׃ וְהִתְגַּדִּלְתִּי
וְהִתְקַדִּשְׁתִּי וְנוֹדַעְתִּי לְעֵינֵי גּוֹיִם רַבִּים
א וְיָדְעוּ כִּי־אֲנִי יְהוָה׃ וְאַתָּה בֶן־
אָדָם הִנָּבֵא עַל־גּוֹג וְאָמַרְתָּ כֹּה אָמַר
אֲדֹנָי יֱהוִה הִנְנִי אֵלֶיךָ גּוֹג נְשִׂיא רֹאשׁ
ב מֶשֶׁךְ וְתֻבָל׃ וְשֹׁבַבְתִּיךָ וְשִׁשֵּׁאתִיךָ
וְהַעֲלִיתִיךָ מִיַּרְכְּתֵי צָפוֹן וַהֲבִאוֹתִיךָ עַל־
ג הָרֵי יִשְׂרָאֵל׃ וְהִכֵּיתִי קַשְׁתְּךָ מִיַּד
ד שְׂמֹאולֶךָ וְחִצֶּיךָ מִיַּד יְמִינְךָ אַפִּיל׃ עַל־
הָרֵי יִשְׂרָאֵל תִּפּוֹל אַתָּה וְכָל־אֲגַפֶּיךָ
וְעַמִּים אֲשֶׁר אִתָּךְ לְעֵיט צִפּוֹר כָּל־כָּנָף
ה וְחַיַּת הַשָּׂדֶה נְתַתִּיךָ לְאָכְלָה׃ עַל־פְּנֵי
הַשָּׂדֶה תִּפּוֹל כִּי אֲנִי דִבַּרְתִּי נְאֻם אֲדֹנָי
ו יֱהוִה׃ וְשִׁלַּחְתִּי־אֵשׁ בְּמָגוֹג וּבְיֹשְׁבֵי
ז הָאִיִּים לָבֶטַח וְיָדְעוּ כִּי־אֲנִי יְהוָה׃ וְאֶת־
שֵׁם קָדְשִׁי אוֹדִיעַ בְּתוֹךְ עַמִּי יִשְׂרָאֵל

23. וְהִתְגַּדִּלְתִּי וְהִתְקַדִּשְׁתִּי — *Thus will I be exalted and sanctified.*

The one purpose of creation, the one aim of history, is the sanctification of God's Name (see Overview X, *The Book of Triumph).* Throughout the Book, Yechezkel teaches that it is this imperative and none other which shapes Israel's destiny (see *comm.,* footnote 20:9); and this will have been attained with Gog's downfall (see footnote, *vs.* 18-20). God's Name will be exalted, hallowed, and made known because Israel, the bearers of that Glory, will have been vindicated by the annihilation of their enemies.

The form וְהִתְגַּדִּלְתִּי וְהִתְקַדִּשְׁתִּי instead of וְהִתְגַּדַּלְתִּי וְהִתְקַדַּשְׁתִּי is unusual but not unique. See *Leviticus* 11:44.

XXXIX

Gog is to wage three separate campaigns against Israel (see pref., chs. 38-39). Malbim *writes that ch. 38 deals with the first of these three wars, while our chapter deals with the second. In this way he explains the introduction which implies that Yechezkel was being charged with a new prophecy, in addition to that of ch. 38. Yechezkel had not been the first one to predict the campaign described in the previous chapter. As 38:17 clearly states, it had been the subject of many earlier prophecies. However, the subject of this chapter, the second of the three wars, had not been foretold by anyone else.*

Another indication that our chapter deals with a new campaign is that in ch. 38 the earthquake which annihilates Gog's forces comes on the very day that Gog sets foot upon Israel's soil (v. 18, but see comm. *there), while our chapter sees him com-*

38 *are with him.* [23] *Thus will I be exalted and sanctified,*
23 *and I will become known in the eyes of many na-*
tions, and; they shall know that I am HASHEM.

39 **A***nd you, Ben Adam, prophesy against Gog and*
1-7 *say: Thus says my Lord* HASHEM/ELOHIM: *See I am*
against you Gog, prince, leader of Meshech and
Tubal. [2] *I shall lead you astray and seduce you, and I*
shall cause you to advance from the farthest north and
bring you to the mountains of Israel, [3] *and I will*
strike your bow from your left hand, and your ar-
rows from your right hand I will cast down. [4] *Upon*
Israel's mountains shall you fall, you and all your
cohorts and the nations that are with you; as carrion
for every winged bird and beast of the field I will give
you. [5] *Upon the open field you will fall, for I have*
spoken — the words of my Lord HASHEM/ELOHIM.
[6] *I will dispatch a fire against Magog and against*
those who dwell confidently in the islands, and they
shall know that I am HASHEM; [7] *and My holy Name*
I will make known among My people Israel, and I

ing all the way to the hills of Israel, a destination Gog could not have reached immediately. (In Malbim's *view, the third and most terrible of the wars of Gog, in which half of Jerusalem actually falls to him, is the subject of Zechariah's prophecy in* Zechariah *14.)*

2. וְשֹׁבַבְתִּיךָ — *I shall lead you astray.*
See 38:4.

וְשִׁשֵּׁאתִיךָ — *And* [*I shall*] *seduce you.*
This word does not recur in Scripture. *Rashi* and *Metzudos* relate it to the root נשא which, in the *hiphil* (השיא), means to *seduce* or *persuade.* God will seduce Gog into accepting the foolish notion that he can wage a successful war against Israel.

Unless the word is completely irregular, we suppose its root to be be ששא (and it is so classified by *Ibn Janach* and *Radak*). However, there is no known meaning for this root. From the context *Radak* suggests that it means *to destroy,* or that it is related to שֵׁשׁ, *six: I will reduce you to a sixth* [of your population], *or I will punish you with the six forces* [of nature mentioned in 38:22].

4. צִפּוֹר כָּל־כָּנָף — *Every winged bird.*
See 17:23. The thought in this verse is expanded at verse 17.

5. עַל פְּנֵי הַשָּׂדֶה — *Upon the open field.*
Besides falling on the hills (*v.* 4) they will also fall on the open field *(Radak).*

6. יֹשְׁבֵי הָאִיִּים — *Those who dwell in the islands.*
See footnote 38:2.

וְלֹא־אַחֵל אֶת־שֵׁם־קָדְשִׁי עוֹד וְיָדְעוּ
ח הַגּוֹיִם כִּי־אֲנִי יהוה קָדוֹשׁ בְּיִשְׂרָאֵל׃ הִנֵּה
בָאָה וְנִהְיָתָה נְאֻם אֲדֹנָי יֱהֹוִה הוּא הַיּוֹם
ט אֲשֶׁר דִּבַּרְתִּי׃ וְיָצְאוּ יֹשְׁבֵי | עָרֵי יִשְׂרָאֵל
וּבִעֲרוּ וְהִשִּׂיקוּ בְּנֶשֶׁק וּמָגֵן וְצִנָּה בְּקֶשֶׁת
וּבְחִצִּים וּבְמַקֵּל יָד וּבְרֹמַח וּבִעֲרוּ בָהֶם
י אֵשׁ שֶׁבַע שָׁנִים׃ וְלֹא־יִשְׂאוּ עֵצִים
מִן־הַשָּׂדֶה וְלֹא יַחְטְבוּ מִן־הַיְּעָרִים
כִּי בַנֶּשֶׁק יְבַעֲרוּ־אֵשׁ וְשָׁלְלוּ אֶת־
שֹׁלְלֵיהֶם וּבָזְזוּ אֶת־בֹּזְזֵיהֶם נְאֻם אֲדֹנָי
יא יֱהֹוִה׃ וְהָיָה בַיּוֹם הַהוּא אֶתֵּן
לְגוֹג | מְקוֹם־שָׁם קֶבֶר בְּיִשְׂרָאֵל גֵּי

7. וְלֹא־אַחֵל אֶת־שֵׁם־קָדְשִׁי עוֹד — *And I will desecrate My holy Name nevermore.*

Israel's humiliation is a desecration of God's Name, for it appears that He cannot help them (*Rashi.* See *comm.*, footnote 36:20).

ה׳ קָדוֹשׁ בְּיִשְׂרָאֵל — *That I am HASHEM, the holy, in Israel.*

All will know that the holy God rests his Presence only upon His people (*Metzudos; Malbim*).

8. הִנֵּה בָאָה וְנִהְיָתָה — *Behold! it has come and happened.*

The pronoun *it* refers to the implied subject עֵת יְשׁוּעָה, *the time of salvation* (*Radak*). God's promised salvation has come about.

9-10 After Gog's defeat there will be no more wars. The only purpose of the weapons will be to fuel Israel's fires. For seven years there will be no need for the people of Israel to gather firewood. Instead, they will use the abundance of abandoned weapons lying around all over the land.

The euphoria of the people of Israel during those first years of their final vindication is described in *Yerushalmi Sheviis* 4:8: 'He who dies during the seven years of Gog will have no share in the World to Come. The commentators offer various explanations: The joy of those years will be so great that it will be sufficient reward in itself (*Matnos Kehunah* to *Vayikra Rabbah, Shimini* 2). One who dies during that wonderful time and is thus denied the ability to take part in its joys must be undeserving and surely will not merit any reward in his afterlife (*Anaf Yosef* there. See commentators to the Yerushalmi for other explanations).

11-16 For months after the holocaust, the remains of the soldiers of Gog's army (which were left over by the feasting beasts — see 17-20) are to be buried and the land cleansed from its defilement. The first seven months are to be devoted to burying the corpses lying in the open, and after that special cadres will be dispatched to make sure that no stray bones have been overlooked.

The care which the Jewish people will expend on the burial of their mortal enemies will spread their fame among the nations (*v.* 13). A special quality of mercy is required to show such concern

39
8-11

will desecrate My holy Name nevermore; and the na-
tions shall know that I am HASHEM, the holy, in
Israel.
8 *Behold! it has come and happened — the words of*
my Lord HASHEM/ELOHIM. This is that day of which
I have spoken. 9 *Then the inhabitants of Israel's cities*
will go out and make fires and feed them with
weapons, shields and buckles, with bow and with ar-
rows, with hand-club and spear — and shall fuel fire
with them for seven years; 10 *and they shall not carry*
wood from the field, nor cut it from the forests, for
with weapons they shall feed the fires. They shall
despoil those who despoiled them and plunder those
who plundered them — the words of my Lord
HASHEM/ELOHIM.
11 *On that day I shall assign to Gog a burial site*

for the very people who had tried to annihilate them. (See *Rashi, v.* 13. But see *Radak* quoted in *comm., v.* 13.)

The significance of our passage goes beyond the insight which it gives us into the innate רַחֲמָנוּת, *mercifulness,* of the Jewish character. It has its antecedents in earliest antiquity when Japheth, forefather of Gog's armies, allowed himself to be persuaded by his brother Shem to safeguard Noah's honor by covering his nakedness. According to the Sages, both Shem and Japheth were rewarded. Shem's reward was that his descendants, Israel, would one day be given the commandment of *tzitzis, fringes,* affixed to the four corners of garments; since he had used a garment to honor his father, he would be given the privilege of using a garment to serve God. Japheth's reward was that his descendants (Gog's armies) would be buried and would not lie in shame on the open fields; the respect which he showed for his father's dignity assured that the dignity of his progeny would be safeguarded.

Maharal (*Gur Aryeh* to *Genesis* 9:23) explains: Both Shem and Japheth displayed sensitivity to the כָּבוֹד, *human dignity,* which was being compromised by Noah's exposure. Therefore they would be rewarded in kind with an enhancement of their dignity. However, Shem, who initiated the good deed (see footnote 38:2) and thereby displayed a greatness of spirit, was rewarded in spiritual kind — with the mitzvah of *tzitzis* — while Japheth, who played the passive, submissive role of the body serving the spirit, was rewarded with a gesture of honor towards his body — the burial of his descendants. [In *Maharal's* works, the רוּחַ, *spiritual aspect of man,* is always portrayed as the active, driving force which influences the passive, pliant גּוּף, *body.*]

Thus we are taught to view the burial of Gog's soldiers as a note of grace by which Japheth's debacle is alleviated. Japheth, in throwing in his lot with God's enemies, had failed in his historic task (ch. 28). The 'beauty of Japheth' which could have been placed in God's service will, instead, have been ranged with Amalek's forces. Japheth's actions will have condemned him to the gruesome fate described in verses 17-20, but these actions cannot obscure the basic decency which is the hallmark of Japheth's pliant nature. Even in the mo-

הָעֹבְרִים קִדְמַת הַיָּם וְחֹסֶמֶת הִיא אֶת־
הָעֹבְרִים וְקָבְרוּ שָׁם אֶת־גּוֹג וְאֶת־כָּל־
יב הֲמוֹנֹה וְקָרְאוּ גֵּיא הֲמוֹן גּוֹג׃ וּקְבָרוּם
בֵּית יִשְׂרָאֵל לְמַעַן טַהֵר אֶת־הָאָרֶץ
יג שִׁבְעָה חֳדָשִׁים׃ וְקָבְרוּ כָּל־עַם הָאָרֶץ
וְהָיָה לָהֶם לְשֵׁם יוֹם הִכָּבְדִי נְאֻם אֲדֹנָי
יד יֱהֹוִה׃ וְאַנְשֵׁי תָמִיד יַבְדִּילוּ עֹבְרִים
בָּאָרֶץ מְקַבְּרִים אֶת־הָעֹבְרִים אֶת־
הַנּוֹתָרִים עַל־פְּנֵי הָאָרֶץ לְטַהֲרָהּ מִקְצֵה
טו שִׁבְעָה־חֳדָשִׁים יַחְקֹרוּ׃ וְעָבְרוּ הָעֹבְרִים
בָּאָרֶץ וְרָאָה עֶצֶם אָדָם וּבָנָה אֶצְלוֹ צִיּוּן
עַד קָבְרוּ אֹתוֹ הַמְקַבְּרִים אֶל־גֵּיא הֲמוֹן
טז גּוֹג׃ וְגַם שֶׁם־עִיר הֲמוֹנָה וְטִהֲרוּ
יז הָאָרֶץ׃ וְאַתָּה בֶן־אָדָם כֹּה־
אָמַר | אֲדֹנָי יֱהֹוִה אֱמֹר לְצִפּוֹר כָּל־כָּנָף

ment of his greatest degradation, the positive aspects of this tragic character are not overlooked.

11. גֵּי הָעֹבְרִים קִדְמַת הַיָּם — *The valley of the travelers, east of the sea.*

Targum identifies this sea as יַם גִּינוֹסַר, *the Sea of Ginossar;* we know it as יַם כִּנֶּרֶת, *the Sea of Galilee (Radak).* The travelers used to cross the sea in order to import fruit from Ginossar, a place that was known for its luscious produce. According to *Bereishis Rabbah* 98, the name Ginossar is a contraction of the two words גַּנֵּי שָׂרִים, *royal gardens.* Only the very rich could afford to buy land there.

וְחֹסֶמֶת הִיא אֶת־הָעֹבְרִים — *It shall block the travelers.*

The corpses will be piled so densely that the path of the travelers will be blocked *(Rashi).* Alternatively the stench of the decaying bodies will cause the travelers to cover (block off) their noses as they pass *(Rashi; Radak).*

וְקָבְרוּ שָׁם אֶת גּוֹג — *And there they will bury Gog.*

The implication is that Gog will be killed in this campaign. This seems to contradict *Malbim* that this passage describes the second of three projected campaigns. Perhaps *Malbim* assumes that Gog is not a single person but is the name given to whichever king will lead the campaign against Israel. See Pref. to Chs. 38 and 39.

וְאֶת־כָּל־הֲמוֹנֹה — *And all his horde.*

The unexpected ה ending is unique to *Ezekiel.* (See 31:18; 32:31; 32.) Perhaps the use of the feminine form is intended to emphasize the essential weakness and impotence of all these seemingly invincible forces (see *v.* 15).

12. לְמַעַן טַהֵר אֶת־הָאָרֶץ — *In order to cleanse the land.*

The presence of the corpses lying unburied is an offense against the holiness and purity of the land (see *Deuteronomy* 21:23). According to

39
12-17

there in Israel — the valley of the travelers, east of the
sea. It shall block the travelers — and there they will
bury Gog and all his horde, and call it the Valley of
Gog's Horde; 12 *and the family of Israel shall bury*
them for seven months, in order to cleanse the land.
13 *All the people of the land shall bury, and it shall*
cause them renown; the day I manifest My Glory —
the words of my Lord HASHEM/ELOHIM — 14 *and*
they shall designate permanent officials passing
through the land, burying, with passersby, those that
remain upon the open field in order to cleanse it.
After seven months, they are to seek out; 15 *and as*
the passersby traverse the land and see a human
bone, then they shall build a marker near it, till the
time that the buriers bury it in the Valley of Gog's
Horde. 16 *There shall also be a city called Hamona.*
Thus will they cleanse the land.
17 *Now you, Ben Adam! Thus says my Lord*
HASHEM/ELOHIM: *Say to every winged bird and to*

Ramban (there) this is the reason that Joshua buried the Canaanite kings the same day he executed them (*Joshua* 10:26,27). (See *Radak.)*

13. Israel's purpose in burying the dead is to cleanse the land (*v.* 12). But the nations will perceive it as an act of magnanimity towards their fallen enemies *(Radak).*

14. עֹבְרִים ... הָעֹבְרִים — *Passing ... passersby.*

Rashi explains that the word עֹבְרִים, which occurs twice in this sentence, is to be translated in two different ways. The first is a verb describing the function of the *permanent officials.* They are to pass through the land to arrange for the burial of the many corpses strewn about everywhere. The second עֹבְרִים is a noun, *passersby;* they are travelers who will assist in the burial work as needed.

אֶת־הַנּוֹתָרִים עַל־פְּנֵי הָאָרֶץ — *Those that remain upon the open field.*

This phrase refers to those corpses which do not lie in the path of the travelers mentioned in verse 11 *(Rashi).*

מִקְצֵה שִׁבְעָה חֳדָשִׁים יַחְקֹרוּ — *After seven months, they are to seek out.*

Burial of the visible corpses will be completed in seven months. Thereafter, the officials are to begin seeking isolated, unnoticed remains *(Rashi).*

16. וְגַם שֶׁם הָעִיר הֲמוֹנָה — *There shall also be a city called Hamona.*

Verse 11 spoke of the valley which was to be called גֵּיא הֲמוֹן גּוֹג, *the Valley of Gog's Horde.* Our verse teaches that the city near the valley should also be given by a name which recalls Gog's hordes (הֲמוֹן means *multitude).* (For an explanation of the feminine form, see *comm., v.* 11). In this way the land would be easily cleansed from any defilement, because people would be aware that because so many people were buried in the valley it is the place to

וּלְכֹ֣ל | חַיַּ֣ת הַשָּׂדֶ֗ה הִקָּבְצ֤וּ וָבֹ֙אוּ֙ הֵאָסְפ֣וּ
מִסָּבִ֔יב עַל־זִבְחִ֗י אֲשֶׁ֨ר אֲנִ֜י זֹבֵ֤חַ לָכֶם֙ זֶ֣בַח
גָּד֔וֹל עַ֖ל הָרֵ֣י יִשְׂרָאֵ֑ל וַאֲכַלְתֶּ֥ם בָּשָׂ֖ר
יח וּשְׁתִ֥יתֶם דָּֽם׃ בְּשַׂ֤ר גִּבּוֹרִים֙ תֹּאכֵ֔לוּ וְדַם־
נְשִׂיאֵ֥י הָאָ֖רֶץ תִּשְׁתּ֑וּ אֵילִ֨ים כָּרִ֤ים
וְעַתּוּדִים֙ פָּרִ֔ים מְרִיאֵ֥י בָשָׁ֖ן כֻּלָּֽם׃
יט וַאֲכַלְתֶּם־חֵ֙לֶב֙ לְשָׂבְעָ֔ה וּשְׁתִ֥יתֶם דָּ֖ם
לְשִׁכָּר֑וֹן מִזִּבְחִ֖י אֲשֶׁר־זָבַ֥חְתִּי לָכֶֽם׃
כ וּשְׂבַעְתֶּ֤ם עַל־שֻׁלְחָנִי֙ ס֣וּס וָרֶ֔כֶב גִּבּ֖וֹר
וְכָל־אִ֣ישׁ מִלְחָמָ֑ה נְאֻ֖ם אֲדֹנָ֥י יֱהֹוִֽה׃
כא וְנָתַתִּ֥י אֶת־כְּבוֹדִ֖י בַּגּוֹיִ֑ם וְרָא֣וּ כָל־הַגּוֹיִ֗ם
אֶת־מִשְׁפָּטִי֙ אֲשֶׁ֣ר עָשִׂ֔יתִי וְאֶת־יָדִ֖י
כב אֲשֶׁר־שַׂ֥מְתִּי בָהֶֽם׃ וְיָדְעוּ֙ בֵּ֣ית יִשְׂרָאֵ֔ל כִּ֛י
אֲנִ֥י יְהֹוָ֖ה אֱלֹהֵיהֶ֑ם מִן־הַיּ֥וֹם הַה֖וּא
כג וָהָֽלְאָה׃ וְיָדְע֣וּ הַ֠גּוֹיִם כִּ֣י בַעֲוֺנָ֞ם גָּל֣וּ בֵית־

bring anything טָמֵא, *spiritually contaminated.*

17-20 Nowhere else do we find God exulting over the fall of His enemies. Yechezkel himself had taught that God finds no pleasure in the death of the wicked (18:23) but, on the contrary, craves their repentance. Yet, there is no denying the tone of exultation in this call to the birds and beasts to come and gorge themselves on the flesh and blood of Gog's fallen army.

We suggest that the joy expressed in this passage relates to the final eradication of evil rather than the horrible fate of the evildoers. God's exultant call to the beasts of the wild is to teach us how the whole of nature is to rise up and, in one final unambiguous gesture, repudiate once and for all man's crazed pretensions to an independence which allows him to pit himself against his God.

For centuries heaven and earth had observed man's depravity. Moses had called upon them to bear witness to the truths of the Torah (*Deuteronomy* 32:1). The Psalmist had pictured the heavens as proclaiming God's glory (19:2), and Isaiah (6:3) had spoken of the earth as being filled by His honor. As Gog and Magog, the embodiment of all that can be evil in Man, lie prostrate, the moment of testimony will have come. As the raging heavens pour torrential rain, hailstones, fire, and sulfur over Gog's hapless forces, as the earth by its quaking tosses mountains and topples cliffs in its fury, the animal world, with gruesome gluttony, throws itself upon the corpses. The physical world has no place for purely physical man. Bereft of the spiritual grandeur which Godliness would have granted him, he becomes utterly worthless, and nature will not tolerate him among its myriad forms.

It is surely no coincidence that just Yechezkel was granted this vision of man at his nadir; for it was Yechezkel

*every beast of the field: Assemble and come, gather
together from all around for My feast which I
slaughter for you, a great feast upon Israel's mountains — you shall eat flesh and drink blood!* 18 *The
flesh of warriors you will eat and the blood of the
earth's princes you will drink: like rams, lambs, he-
goats, and bulls — fatlings of Bashan, all of them.*
19 *You shall eat fat to satiety and drink blood to in-
toxication from My feast which I have slaughtered
for you;* 20 *and you shall sate yourselves at My table
with horses and riders, warriors and all men of war —
the words of my Lord HASHEM/ELOHIM.*
21 *Thus will I manifest My glory among the nations, and all the nations shall see My punishment
which I have executed and My hand which I have
placed upon them.* 22 *Then the family of Israel shall
know that I am HASHEM, their God, from that day
onward.* 23 *Then shall the nations know that because*

whose prophetic eye had apprehended Man at his greatest. The idea of Man as the sheep of God, finding his manhood in complete submission and dependence (see *comm.* 34:31 36:37), permeates the whole Book. Indeed the very name, Ben Adam, by which God addresses him, bears witness to his soaring vision of the Adam-Hadom pinnacle of God's creation (see Overview IV). That vision would have been incomplete and Yechezkel's mission unfulfilled, if that picture had not been brought into sharp focus by the understanding of the alternative. Yechezkel is unsparing in the lurid horror with which he paints the fate of Gog's armies because we need to perceive the true nature of evil, with all mitigating masks torn away, if we are to know man, bearer of God's Glory on earth.

Radak points out that this call to the animals does not contradict the plans for burial mentioned earlier. There would be time for the animals to feast before the burial could take place.

18. ... אֵילִים, *Rams ...*

These animals are metaphors for the officers of Gog's army *(Targum).*

20. — [*With*] *horses and riders.*

The birds and beasts will gorge themselves on the carcasses of corpses of those fallen in Gog's defeat *(Metzudos).*

21. See *comm.* to 38:23.

מִשְׁפָּטִי — *My punishment.*

As in much of *Ezekiel,* מִשְׁפָּט in this verse is translated as *punishment* rather than justice *(Targum; Rashi).*

23. וְיָדְעוּ הַגּוֹיִם — *Then shall the nations know.*

Gog's defeat is to be a vindication of God's power in the eyes of the nations. It will have become obvious that Israel had been exiled not because God lacked the power to save them, but because their sins had driven them from their land *(Rashi).* (See *comm.,* footnote 36:20).

יִשְׂרָאֵל עַל אֲשֶׁר מָעֲלוּ־בִי וָאַסְתִּר פָּנַי
מֵהֶם וָאֶתְּנֵם בְּיַד צָרֵיהֶם וַיִּפְּלוּ בַחֶרֶב
כד כֻּלָּם׃ כְּטֻמְאָתָם וּכְפִשְׁעֵיהֶם עָשִׂיתִי אֹתָם
כה וָאַסְתִּר פָּנַי מֵהֶם׃ לָכֵן כֹּה
°שְׁבוּת ק׳ אָמַר אֲדֹנָי יֱהֹוִה עַתָּה אָשִׁיב אֶת־°שְׁבִית
יַעֲקֹב וְרִחַמְתִּי כָּל־בֵּית יִשְׂרָאֵל וְקִנֵּאתִי
כו לְשֵׁם קָדְשִׁי׃ וְנָשׂוּ אֶת־כְּלִמָּתָם וְאֶת־
כָּל־מַעֲלָם אֲשֶׁר מָעֲלוּ־בִי בְּשִׁבְתָּם
עַל־אַדְמָתָם לָבֶטַח וְאֵין מַחֲרִיד׃
כז בְּשׁוֹבְבִי אוֹתָם מִן־הָעַמִּים וְקִבַּצְתִּי אֹתָם
מֵאַרְצוֹת אֹיְבֵיהֶם וְנִקְדַּשְׁתִּי בָם לְעֵינֵי
כח הַגּוֹיִם רַבִּים׃ וְיָדְעוּ כִּי אֲנִי יהוה
אֱלֹהֵיהֶם בְּהַגְלוֹתִי אֹתָם אֶל־הַגּוֹיִם
וְכִנַּסְתִּים אֶל־אַדְמָתָם וְלֹא־אוֹתִיר עוֹד
כט מֵהֶם שָׁם׃ וְלֹא־אַסְתִּיר עוֹד פָּנַי מֵהֶם
אֲשֶׁר שָׁפַכְתִּי אֶת־רוּחִי עַל־בֵּית יִשְׂרָאֵל
נְאֻם אֲדֹנָי יֱהֹוִה׃

23. וָאַסְתִּר פָּנַי מֵהֶם — *And I hid My Face from them.*

In *Deuteronomy* 31:17-18, exile and suffering are associated with הֶסְתֵּר פָּנִים, *the hiding of God's Face*. In its initial stage, הֶסְתֵּר פָּנִים means that God acts 'as though He does not see their suffering,' thus making it possible for Israel's enemies to overpower them (*Rashi* there). Even after the exile begins to have its desired cleansing effect and the people begin to grope towards true repentance, God's Face continues to 'be hidden' in the sense that the time for their redemption remains concealed from them. They have only their trust and hope in God to sustain them in a seemingly endless exile (*Ramban* there).

24. כְּטֻמְאָתָם — *According to their contamination.*

See *comm.* to 36:16-37.

25. שְׁבוּת יַעֲקֹב — *Jacob's captivity.*

Israel's return is associated more closely with Jacob than with the other two Patriarchs. Thus *Jeremiah* 30:18 talks of returning the captivity of *Jacob's tents* [a formulation used in the Selichah prayer זְכוֹר בְּרִית אַבְרָהָם of the day before *Rosh Hashanah*]. Midrashim assign a number of causes for Jacob's singularity. *Tanchuma (Bober) (Toldos* 2) ascribes it to his merit for being יוֹשֵׁב אֹהָלִים, *a dweller in tents* [*of Torah*] *(Genesis* 25:27), while *Shocher Tov (Psalm* 81) points out the uniform righteousness of his children, in contrast to Abraham and Isaac, each of whom bore a son who has no place among God's people.

לְשֵׁם קָדְשִׁי — *For My holy Name.*

The prefix ל means *for the sake of*. *I will be zealous for the sake of My holy*

of their sins was the family of Israel exiled — because they betrayed Me — and I hid My Face from them and delivered them into the hand of their enemies so that they all fell by the sword. 24 *According to their contamination and their transgressions did I deal with them, so I hid My Face from them.*

25 *Therefore, thus says my Lord HASHEM/ELOHIM: Now I will bring back Jacob's captivity and show mercy to all the family of Israel and be zealous for My holy Name.* 26 *They shall bear their shame and all their betrayal — which they committed against Me when they dwelt upon their soil, confidently with none to frighten them —* 27 *when I have brought them back from among the nations and gathered them in from the land of their enemies; and I will manifest My holiness through them in the eyes of many nations.*

28 *Then they shall know that I am HASHEM, their God, for I will have exiled them to the nations, but I will have brought them in to their soil and I will have left none of them.* 29 *Then I shall no more hide My face from them for I will have poured out My spirit upon the family of Israel. The words of my Lord HASHEM/ELOHIM.*

Name (see 38:19).

26. וְנָשׂוּ אֶת־כְּלִמָּתָם — *They shall bear their shame.*

When I am good to them and do not deal with them in accordance with their evil deeds — then they shall feel truly ashamed *(Rashi).* (See *comm.* 16:61 for a discussion of shame as an indispensable component of *teshuvah.)*

According to this interpretation, וְנָשׂוּ is irregular since it would be derived from the root נשא, *to bear,* and there is no grammatical reason for the letter א to be omitted.

Because of this irregularity, *Rashi* quotes *Menachem,* who translates וְנָשׂוּ אֶת־כְּלִמָּתָם, *and their shame will be forgiven.* This interpretation treats וְנָשׂוּ as a form similar to אַשְׁרֵי נְשׂוּי פֶּשַׁע, which he would translate, *praiseworthy is one whose trangression is forgiven (Psalms* 32:1). [*Menachem* either assumes that there exists a root נשה meaning to forgive (although such a root is not found anywhere else) or he agrees with other grammarians that the phrase נְשׂוּי פֶּשַׁע also derives from נשא, but demonstrates that נשא in its meaning of forgiveness is occasionally treated as a ל־ה verb in which the final root-letter is dropped in certain cases. (See *Radak* in *Sefer HaMichlol,* נשא and *Ibn Ezra, Psalms* 32:1.) For a full treatment of this

subject see Gesenius Hebrew Grammar §75qq.

28. וְלֹא־אוֹתִיר עוֹד מֵהֶם — *And I will have left none of them.*

I will not leave even a single one of them in exile *(Rashi).*

[The word עוֹד, literally *more, again,* or *still* is rendered as *none;* if even one were left behind it could be said that there is עוֹד, *still* one in exile, and the redemption is incomplete].

29. אֲשֶׁר שָׁפַכְתִּי אֶת־רוּחִי — *For I will have poured out My spirit.*

Eichah Rabbasi 2:11 notes that the root שפך, *to pour out,* is used in Scripture four times with a happy connotation (as in our verse) and four times to describe the outpouring of God's wrath. One of the four latter is also in *Ezekiel* (9:8). We surmise that Yechezkel uses this expression in this final verse before beginning his visions of the Third Temple, to contrast his present prophecy with the earlier one. There he had fallen on his face in despair, crying out in anguish, as he thought that God meant to destroy Israel completely in the *outpouring* of His wrath. Here he is comforted as he sees God *pouring out* His spirit with unstinting love upon His regenerated people.

◆§ *Chapters 40-48*

The Third Temple

The contents of the last nine chapters of the Book are unique in prophetic literature. The usual visions of the Messianic era are couched in the most general terms, describing the peace and harmony which will reign then between man and his world, between man and his fellow-man, and finally between man and God. These chapters, however, are unprecedented. They offer detailed laws which are to govern Temple and Kohanim, *king and subjects, land and people, when the final redemption will have come about. An entire blueprint of a regenerated society rises up before the prophet's eye — at a time when the very idea of such a society must have seemed utterly remote.*

*Our Sages have taught (*Bava Basra *14b) that* Ezekiel *ends on a note of comfort. (See Overview; footnote to pref. ch. 24; pref. chs. 25-32; pref. to ch. 33; pref. ch. 34). We could hardly conceive of a more exquisitely designed message of consolation than these final nine chapters of Yechezkel's prophecy, for they contain much more than the promise of a brighter future. They taught the exiles — who had viewed themselves as 'dry bones' with no share in Israel's future (see ch. 37); abandoned by God, cut off from the sources of holiness (see comm., 6:8-9, 20:1) — that, on the contrary, they and no other generation were the repository of Israel's future.*

*Babylon's exiles were weeping — because they were tied by memories to a glorious Zion of the past (*Psalms *137:1). We can imagine how this prophecy galvanized them into a state of hope as it directed their thoughts to the glorious Zion of the future. Boundaries of time and space melt away in the ecstasy of prophecy. As before their eyes a new and everlasting Jerusalem rose up, the exiles sitting near Babylon's rivers learned that the 'Song of God' need not be completely stilled, even while they were still on foreign soil (see* Psalms *137:4).*

Master Diagram of the Third Temple

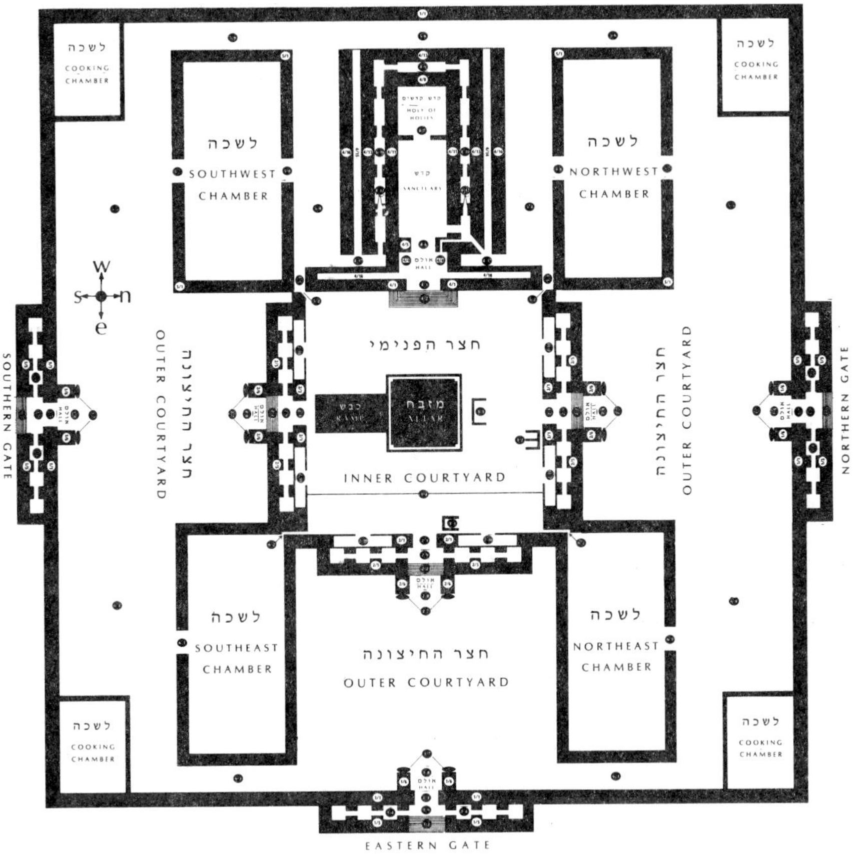

☙ Prefatory Remarks to 40:1-43:17

As the focus of the new Jerusalem, the בֵּית הַמִּקְדָּשׁ [Beis HaMikdash], Holy Temple, *is the first institution towards which Yechezkel directs his vision.*

The new city is to be called ה׳ שָׁמָּה, HASHEM Is There *(48:35). The locus of the* הַשְׁרָאַת הַשְּׁכִינָה, Resting of the Divine Presence, *implied in this name is the* Beis HaMikdash. *God wills that there be a new Jerusalem only because He wills that there be a place of welcome for the Divine Presence. [See the fourteenth blessing in the* Amidah: O return to Jerusalem in Your mercy and dwell in it as You have spoken.] *Because of this centrality to the Divine plan, it is logical that the Temple should be the very first of the institutions discussed. (See* Ramban, *to* Exodus *25: in his second explanation of why the Ark is mentioned in* Terumah *before any of the other vessels.)*

In loving detail, the new building and the altar which will stand within it, are passed before the prophet's eye. God's love for these institutions is underscored by the great care which the Torah lavished upon the description of מִשְׁכָּן, Tabernacle in the wilderness, *and* מִקְדָּשׁ, Temple. [*See* Ramban, Exodus *36:8, in his explanation of why the Torah repeats all the directions for the building of the Tabernacle no less than five times. The same degree of repetition is used in the description of Solomon's Temple (I Kings 6:15-7:51).*]

This Temple is to become throne and footstool for the Divine Presence (43:7) and, in contrast to the two previous Temples which became defiled — and subsequently destroyed — through Israel's sins, this one is to stand inviolate. God is to dwell in it, never to depart (43:7).

While the basic components of this Temple are to be essentially similar to those of the previous ones, there are nevertheless to be significant differences in the details of the design.[1] *We will try to explore the implications of these changes in light of the history and halachah of the Temple.*

The Torah commands us to erect a house for God for the purpose of bringing sacrifices and serving as focus for the celebrations which were to take place three times a year [on Pesach, Shavuos, *and* Succos]. *In the centuries preceding Solomon's ascension to the throne, tabernacles were erected at various locations, to comply with this commandment. Once Solomon built his Temple on Mount Moriah in Jerusalem it became the permanent and sole acceptable site for the* Beis HaMikdash (Rambam, Beis HaBechirah *1:1-3).*

Solomon's Temple was destroyed by Nebuchadnezzar 410 years after it was built. When, under Cyrus, the Jews returned from the Babylonian exile and set about building a new Temple, they found themselves in a quandary. Yechezkel's prophecies had already been received but the specifications contained in them were

---

1. The fact that Yechezkel's Temple is to be different from the previous ones poses a halachic problem. Based on *I Chronicles* 28:19, the Sages have a tradition that the general design and dimensions of the original Temple were given to King David in writing, either by the prophet Samuel (*Yerushalmi Megillah* 1:1) or by Gad the Seer and Nathan the Prophet (*Rashi, Succah* 51). According to *Midrash Shmuel* 15, these instructions had originally been given to Moses by God and were then handed down through the generations.

These written instructions are considered by the *Talmud* (see *Succah* 51b) to be binding. No leeway was left for any changes. Nevertheless the Second Temple was significantly different from the one built by Solomon and Yechezkel's Temple is to be different from both of them. What halachic justifications exist for these changes?

Chasam Sofer addresses this problem and suggests that the verse, *in accordance with all that I shall show you (Exodus* 25:9) which was said as part of the instructions for building the Tabernacle in the wilderness, indicates an allowance for future revelations in connection with the form that God's dwelling on earth is to take *(Responsa, Orach Chaim* 20 and *Yoreh Deah* 236).

מ
א   א בְּעֶשְׂרִים וְחָמֵשׁ שָׁנָה לְגָלוּתֵנוּ
בְּרֹאשׁ הַשָּׁנָה בֶּעָשׂוֹר לַחֹדֶשׁ בְּאַרְבַּע
עֶשְׂרֵה שָׁנָה אַחַר אֲשֶׁר הֻכְּתָה הָעִיר
בְּעֶצֶם | הַיּוֹם הַזֶּה הָיְתָה עָלַי יַד־יהוה

'not clear nor explicit' (ibid. *1:4). They were therefore unable to build the Temple according to Yechezkel's directions. Instead they 'built it according to the plans of Solomon's Temple, but included some modifications based on the Book of* Ezekiel' (Rambam *1:4).*

Tosafos Yom Tov *(introduction,* Tzuras HaBayis*) suggests the following explanation for this phenomenon. The true interpretation of Yechezkel's directions was withheld from the returning exiles because it is a design which is meant only for the ultimate* Beis HaMikdash *which is never to be destroyed. The second Temple from the very beginning was destined to fall, and therefore could not be built according to these specifications.* Tosafos Yom Tov *explains this in light of a* Midrash *quoted by* Rashi *at 43:11.*

According to this Midrash, Yechezkel's Temple could indeed have been built by the returning exiles — if they had deserved it. Had the Babylonian community really risen to the challenge of exile, had they wiped out their sinful past with true repentance, their return to Zion could have ushered in the Messianic era (for a discussion, see comm., 11:17-20). However they fell short of the ideal and the opportunity was lost. The Temple which they were allowed to build had to be one which was not yet perfect. It was not to last forever. Nevertheless, they incorporated some details from Yechezkel's design — to remind themselves of what might have been.

A description of this Second Temple is preserved in Tractate Middos. Rambam, *in his commentary to the* Mishnah, *points out that this description has importance beyond its historical interest because 'when [the* Beis HaMikdash] *will be built, speedily in our days, it will be incumbent upon us to preserve the [former] design and dimensions, because they [were given] through the spirit of prophecy.'*

Thus, the future Temple will be similar to the Second Temple (which already contained elements of Yechezkel's Temple), but will — in accordance with its status as a permanent, indestructible abode for the Divine Presence — contain other changes which are indicated in the Book of Ezekiel, *but have remained hidden from previous generations. When the time comes, God will grant us the insight required to understand the prophecy in all its details.*[1]

The study of Yechezkel's vision of the Temple is difficult. Volumes have been written in an attempt to fathom its complexities. Our commentary is based on Rashi, *as his opinion is explicated by* Tosafos Yom Tov. *Our efforts to understand that which will tax our faculties to the utmost should be informed by the words of our Sages:*

> *When God showed Yechezkel the form of the House ... Yechezkel said to Him, 'O God! We are now in exile in the land of our enemies and you tell me to go and tell Israel the form of the House ... is there anything that they can do about it? [Would it not be better to] leave them until they go back to the*

---

1. The commentary implies that this third and final *Beis HaMikdash* will be a structure built by human hands, in accordance with *Rambam's* language in his commentary to the *Mishnah.* This is in complete agreement with *Rambam's* opinion (*Maaseh HaKorbanos* 2:14, *Melachim* 11:1) that *Mashiach* [*Messiah*] is to build the third *Beis HaMikdash.*

However, *Rashi (Succah* 41a, *Rosh Hashanah* 30a) and *Tosafos (Shavuos* 15b) write that the Temple will be made of fire and descend miraculously from heaven, already built.

According to this opinion it would seem that the directions contained in the Book of *Ezekiel*

40
1 *In the twenty-fifth year of our exile, on the New Year on the tenth of the month in the fourteenth year after the city had fallen, on that very day the hand of HASHEM came upon me, and He brought me*

land and then I will tell them?'

God answered Yechezkel, 'Is it right that because My children are in exile that the building of My Temple should be ignored?' So God said to him, 'The study [of the Temple structure] in the Torah is considered as [being of equal merit to] its building. Go, tell them to study the Temple structure and as a reward I will consider their study as though they were actually building the Beis HaMikdash' (Tanchuma, Tzav *14, see* R' Bachya, *end of* VaYakhel).

XL

1. בְּעֶשְׂרִים וְחָמֵשׁ שָׁנָה לְגָלוּתֵנוּ — *In the twenty-fifth year of our exile.*

This is twenty years after Yechezkel's first prophecy (1:2). Since that earlier prophecy took place in the thirtieth year of the יוֹבֵל [*yovel*], *jubilee*, cycle *(comm.* 1:1), this places the visions of our chapter in the year which would have been the *yovel* year had the exile not intervened *(Rashi).*

בְּרֹאשׁ הַשָּׁנָה בֶּעָשׂוֹר לַחֹדֶשׁ — *On the New Year, the tenth of the month.*

Arachin 12a remarks: [Only] the *yovel* year has its Rosh HaShanah, on the tenth of the month [Yom Kippur, the tenth of Tishrei.] That day is considered the Rosh HaShanah of the *yovel* because it was then that the special laws of the year, such as the freeing of the slaves and the returning of fields to their original owners, take effect.

בְּאַרְבַּע עֶשְׂרֵה שָׁנָה אַחַר אֲשֶׁר הֻכְּתָה הָעִיר — *In the fourteenth year after the city had fallen* [lit. *was smitten*].

The word לְגָלוּתֵנוּ, *of our exile*, in the previous phrase refers to the exile of Yehoyachin, after he had reigned only three months (see *comm.* 1:2; Time Line, Appendix II). He was succeeded by his uncle Zidkiyahu, who reigned eleven years, until the Destruction of the Temple. Thus the Temple was destroyed in the eleventh year of Yehoyachin's exile, and the twenty-fifth year of the exile was fourteen years later.

בְּעֶצֶם הַיּוֹם הַזֶּה — *On that very day.*

This expression is used when the day, by its nature, is particularly suited to the events which happened on it *(comm.* 24:2).

Indeed, no more suitable day than the Yom Kippur of a *yovel* year could have been chosen for showing Yechezkel the Jerusalem of the future. *Yovel* is the year of universal freedom: *You shall proclaim liberty throughout the land (Leviticus* 25:10). Yom Kippur is the day God cleanses Israel of its sins. True freedom growing out of a state of spiritual purity is the hallmark of the Messianic era. On this of all days, Israel was ready to perceive its destiny. [See *Radak.*]

יַד־ה׳ — *The hand of HASHEM.*

He placed upon me the weight of His

---

will never concern us directly since the Temple will not be built by human hands.

[This opinion would imply that the Torah's command to build a *Beis HaMikdash* will never again have a practical application. However, there is no indication anywhere that this command will not be binding in the future. *Maharil Diskin* (quoted in *Siddur HaGra*) suggests a solution. The building which will descend from heaven will have certain indispensible parts missing. It will be our obligation to add these components and this will be our way of fulfilling the command to build the *Beis HaMikdash.* This theory explains the seeming redundancy in our *Yom Tov* prayers. We say, 'Grant that we may see it in its rebuilding and rejoice in its

ב וַיָּבֵא אֹתִי שָׁמָּה: בְּמַרְאוֹת אֱלֹהִים
הֱבִיאַנִי אֶל־אֶרֶץ יִשְׂרָאֵל וַיְנִיחֵנִי אֶל־הַר
גָּבֹהַּ מְאֹד וְעָלָיו כְּמִבְנֵה־עִיר מִנֶּגֶב:
ג וַיָּבֵיא אוֹתִי שָׁמָּה וְהִנֵּה־אִישׁ מַרְאֵהוּ
כְּמַרְאֵה נְחֹשֶׁת וּפְתִיל־פִּשְׁתִּים בְּיָדוֹ
ד וּקְנֵה הַמִּדָּה וְהוּא עֹמֵד בַּשָּׁעַר: וַיְדַבֵּר
אֵלַי הָאִישׁ בֶּן־אָדָם רְאֵה בְעֵינֶיךָ
וּבְאָזְנֶיךָ שְּׁמָע וְשִׂים לִבְּךָ לְכֹל אֲשֶׁר־אֲנִי
מַרְאֶה אוֹתָךְ כִּי לְמַעַן הַרְאוֹתְכָה
הֻבָאתָה הֵנָּה הַגֵּד אֶת־כָּל־אֲשֶׁר־אַתָּה
ה רֹאֶה לְבֵית יִשְׂרָאֵל: וְהִנֵּה חוֹמָה מִחוּץ
לַבַּיִת סָבִיב | סָבִיב וּבְיַד הָאִישׁ קְנֵה
הַמִּדָּה שֵׁשׁ־אַמּוֹת בָּאַמָּה וָטֹפַח וַיָּמָד אֶת־

might, to force me into my mission *(Rashi).*

שָׁמָּה — *There.*

Yechezkel was taken to the smitten city, Jerusalem. It was in that year that God showed him the future Temple *(Rashi).*

2. בְּמַרְאוֹת אֱלֹהִים — *In visions of God.*

Yechezkel was not taken physically to Jerusalem. It was only in prophetic vision that he came there *(Rashi).*

הַר גָּבֹהַּ מְאֹד — *A very high mountain.*

In Messianic times the Temple Mount will be very high (*Rashi,* based on *Isaiah* 2:2).

וְעָלָיו — *And near it.*

Although usually translated *upon,* עָלָיו is often used as *near* or *next to.* Near the Temple Mount upon which Yechezkel was placed in his vision was the rebuilt city of Jerusalem (Radak).

כְּמִבְנֵה־עִיר מִנֶּגֶב — *The appearance of a built city to the south.*

Rebuilt Jerusalem is to lie to the south of the Temple Mount. [See *pref.* ch. 48.]

3. וַיָּבֵיא אוֹתִי שָׁמָּה — *Now He brought me there.*

This phrase is to be understood as though it were written: *And as He brought me there (Metzudos).* It refers back to הֱבִיאַנִי, *He brought me,* of the previous verse.

וְהִנֵּה־אִישׁ — *And behold! A man.*

A heavenly messenger in human form *(Radak)* was sent to show the Temple to Yechezkel.

מַרְאֵהוּ כְּמַרְאֵה נְחֹשֶׁת — *Whose appear-*

---

perfecting.' The 'rebuilding' would refer to the building descending from heaven. The 'perfecting' would be the finishing touches which we are to provide (see further below).]

Both the opinions of *Rashi* and *Tosafos* on the one hand and *Rambam* on the other can be justified on the basis of Talmudic and Midrashic sources.

Another complicated issue is the question of whether the command to build a *Beis HaMikdash* is binding upon us even before the coming of the Messiah. (See *Yerushalmi, Maaser Sheni* 5:2.) A detailed presentation of all the sources and opinions is beyond the scope of this commentary. The interested reader is directed to *R' Tukotzinski's* עִיר הַקֹּדֶשׁ וְהַמִּקְדָּשׁ vol. 3 part 5, and the קוּנְטְרֵס בִּנְיַן בֵּית הַמִּקְדָּשׁ קוֹדֶם לְמַלְכוּת בֵּית דָּוִד by *R' Frank* in הַמַּעְיָן, 5730.

there.
2 *In visions of God He brought me to the Land*
of Israel and set me down on a very high mountain
and near it was the appearance of a built city to the
south.
3 *Now He brought me there and behold! A*
man whose appearance was like that of copper with a
linen cord in his hand and a measuring rod, as he
stood by the gate.
4 *Then the man spoke to me: 'Ben Adam, look with*
your eyes and with your ears listen, and apply
yourself to all that I show you, for in order to show
you have you been brought here. Relate all that you
see to the family of Israel.
5 *And behold! There was a*
wall outside the House, surrounding it. And in the
man's hand was a measuring rod of six cubits — each
of a cubit and a handbreadth — and he measured the

ance was like that of copper.

He glittered like burnished copper. The angels of the *Merkavah* vision (1:7) are similarly described *(Rashi).*

פְּתִיל־פִּשְׁתִּים ... קְנֵה הַמִּדָּה — *A linen cord ... a measuring rod.*

The former was needed for measuring the ground, and for that the linen cord is best. The latter was for measuring the depth of the walls and the length and width of the gates *(Rashi).*

בַּשָּׁעַר — *By the gate.*

This gate led to the Temple Mount *(Metzudos),* see below).

4. לְכֹל אֲשֶׁר אֲנִי מַרְאֶה אוֹתָךְ — *To all that I show you.*

The expression implies that Yechezkel actually saw the Temple in his prophetic vision. For a mere verbal description the term *that I show you* is inappropriate (*Rashbam, Exodus* 25:9).

Yechezkel is exhorted to pass his vision on to the people. It is necessary that they be made aware of God's undying love for them, in order that they be stimulated to a true repentance. This idea is amplified at 43:10-11.

5. חוֹמָה — *A wall.*

The Temple Mount was surrounded by the חוֹמַת הַר הַבַּיִת, *outermost wall of the Temple Complex* [see 42:20]. This wall is described in our verse. [Note that the Temple Mount is not indicated on the Master Diagram due to its large size, which makes it impossible to scale down in the available space.]

מִחוּץ לַבַּיִת סָבִיב סָבִיב — *Outside the House, surrounding it.*

Chapter 45 (*vs.* 1-4) describes a piece of land which is to be set aside as a gift sacred to God to the north of the city. In its exact center lies a piece of land, measuring 500 rods by 500 rods, that is to be called the הַר הַבַּיִת, *Temple Mount.* At six cubits to the rod, this gives us an area of 9,000,000 square cubits. By contrast the Temple Mount of the Second Temple was only 250,000 square cubits, as recorded in *Middos* 2:1.

[We have used the term Temple Mount in its broadest sense to incorporate the whole of the mountain on which the Temple stood. The term is occasionally used in the Mishnah in a narrower sense to describe the outermost part of the Temple Complex.]

שֵׁשׁ־אַמּוֹת בָּאַמָּה וָטֹפַח — *Of six cubits — each of a cubit and a handbreadth.*

Scripture speaks of two different size

מ
ה

רֹחַב הַבִּנְיָן קָנֶה אֶחָד וְקוֹמָה קָנֶה אֶחָד׃

אַמּוֹת, *cubits*: one of five טְפָחִים, *handbreadths*, and one of six *(Kelim* 7:10, *Menachos* 97a).

Yechezkel's guide held a measuring rod of six cubits. The phrase goes on to specify that the cubit to be used was one of *six* handbreadths, that is, as our verse describes it: a cubit (of only five handbreadths), plus an additional handbreadth, for a total of six *(Rashi,* based on *Targum).* [N.B. This rod should not be confused with the present day surveyor's rod which measures 16½ feet. Yechezkel's rod is somewhat shorter than this.]

וַיָּמָד אֶת־רֹחַב הַבִּנְיָן קָנֶה אֶחָד — *And he measured the width of the building, one rod.*

Width in this context means *the thickness.* The wall referred to here as בִּנְיָן, *building,* was one rod (that is, six cubits) thick *(Rashi).*

וְקוֹמָה קָנֶה אֶחָד — *And the height, one rod.*

The wall was 6 cubits high. The text appears to imply that the wall was of the same height on all four sides. However, *Rashi,* based on *Middos* 2:4, explains that the measurement of one rod was true only of the eastern side of the wall. The other three sides were much higher.

According to *Middos* 2:3, all the gates in the Temple were 50 cubits high. Since the walls were taller than the gates, this would make the walls considerably higher than 50 cubits. The eastern part of the outermost wall of the Temple Complex was the sole exception. It was built lower than the others in order not to obscure the vision of the *kohen* whose duty it was to sprinkle the blood of the פָּרָה אֲדֻמָּה, *red cow,* in the direction of the Temple. He did this while standing on הַר הַזֵּתִים, *Mount of Olives,* which lies to the east of the Temple.

Since this purpose could be accomplished

Fig. 1

Eastern Gate Structure and its Cells

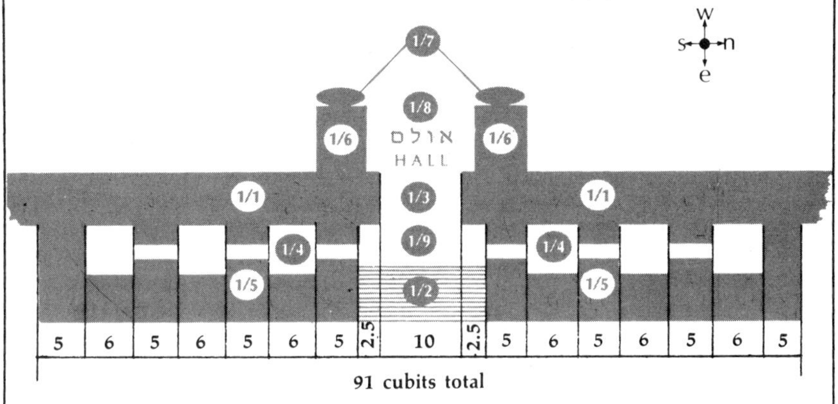

1/1 — Wall of outer courtyard (6 cubits).
1/2 — 12 steps (½ cubit each) leading up towards the outer courtyard.
1/3 — Gateway (10 cubits wide).
1/4 — Cells: three on each side (each cell 6 cubits by 6 cubits).
1/5 — Outer walls of the cell complex (5 cubits wide); also the walls between cells.
Note: The width and exact placement of the entrances to the cell are by conjecture only.
1/9 — Vestibule (15 cubits wide).

40
5 *width of the building, one rod; and the height, one*

by lowering only the eastern wall, the Mishnah assumes that the other three walls were of normal height. *Rashi* learns that this will be the case in the Third Temple, although from the text one might think that all four walls would be the same height. See further in *Abarbanel.*]

6-16. Situated within the 9,000,000 square cubit Temple Complex, there was another walled-in area which the prophet calls חָצֵר הַחִיצוֹנָה, *outer courtyard (v.* 17). [This designation differentiates it from the חָצֵר הַפְּנִימִי, *inner courtyard,* which was contained within it.]

The outer courtyard was 312 cubits from north to south and 317 cubits from east to west. These measurements are not explicated in the text, but we arrive at them by computing the various measurements which are given. (See *comm.* vs. 19, 23 and 42:9).

These eleven verses describe the eastern wall (1/1) of the outer courtyard (Figs. 1 and 2). The description in these verses concerns itself only with the gateway in this wall, and the portion of the wall immediately surrounding it. Figure 1 is limited to that portion of the wall.

This wall was reached by twelve steps (1/2) which went up from the Temple Mount (v. 6; see *Middos* 2:3).

[Since the Temple was built on the slope of Mount Moriah *(Rambam, Bais HaBechirah* 6:1), several stairways were needed throughout the structure to get from one level to the next. In the Second Temple, the steps leading up to the women's courtyard (עֶזְרַת נָשִׁים), which is the equivalent of our outer courtyard, led up from a section known as the חֵיל[*chail*]. This was a piece of ground ten cubits wide, just before the women's courtyard. There is no mention of the *chail* in *Ezekiel,* although we assume that there will be one as there was in the Second Temple.]

The eastern wall of the outer courtyard had a thickness of one rod, or six cubits. In the center there was a gateway (1/3) which (like all the gateways) had a width of ten cubits. The doors (not shown) of this gateway had a height of fifty cubits. On the outside of this wall there were six cells (1/4), each with an inside area of six cubits square. They were separated from one another by walls which were five cubits thick, as was also their eastern wall (1/5) *(Metzudos).* In the west, no special wall was necessary since these cells were built up against the wall of the outer courtyard (1/1).

The walls of the cells that were closest to the entrance created the effect of a vestibule (1/9) as one entered the gate. There was an entrance from the vestibule into the cells on either side (Fig. 3) and a passageway from one cell to the next. There were windows from the two inner cells facing the vestibule

Fig. 2

Eastern Entrance to Outer Courtyard

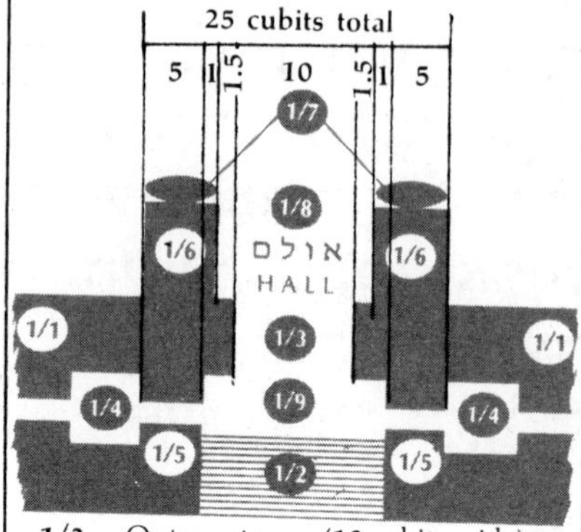

1/3 – Outer gateway (10 cubits wide).
1/4 – Cells.
1/5 – Outer wall of cell complex (5 cubits wide).
1/6 – The hall walls (6 cubits wide).
1/7 – Pillars (oval shaped; 5 cubits wide by 2 cubits deep).
1/8 – Inner gateway created by hall walls.
1/9 – Vestibule (15 cubits wide).
Note: The beginning of the two inner cells correspond exactly to the outer side of the hall walls.

מ
ו־י

ו וַיָּבוֹא אֶל־שַׁעַר אֲשֶׁר פָּנָיו דֶּרֶךְ הַקָּדִימָה
וַיַּעַל בְּמַעֲלֹתָו וַיָּמָד | אֶת־סַף הַשַּׁעַר קָנֶה
אֶחָד רֹחַב וְאֵת סַף אֶחָד קָנֶה אֶחָד רֹחַב׃
ז וְהַתָּא קָנֶה אֶחָד אֹרֶךְ וְקָנֶה אֶחָד רֹחַב
וּבֵין הַתָּאִים חָמֵשׁ אַמּוֹת וְסַף הַשַּׁעַר
מֵאֵצֶל אֻלָם הַשַּׁעַר מֵהַבַּיִת קָנֶה אֶחָד׃
ח וַיָּמָד אֶת־אֻלָם הַשַּׁעַר מֵהַבַּיִת קָנֶה אֶחָד׃
ט וַיָּמָד אֶת־אֻלָם הַשַּׁעַר שְׁמֹנֶה אַמּוֹת
וְאֵילָו שְׁתַּיִם אַמּוֹת וְאֻלָם הַשַּׁעַר
י מֵהַבָּיִת׃ וְתָאֵי הַשַּׁעַר דֶּרֶךְ הַקָּדִים

(Fig. 3) and also from all the cells facing the outer courtyard. The cell structure began 2½ cubits from the gateway so that there were exactly 25 cubits between the beginning of the innermost cell on the south and the beginning of the innermost cell on the north (which coincide with the outer walls of the halls; see below). The measurements are as follows: five cubit wall, 2½ cubit space, ten cubit gateway, 2½ cubit space, and five cubit wall.

Within the eastern wall of the outer courtyard was another vestibule called the אוּלָם, *hall*, which was formed by two walls (1/6), each fifty cubits high and six cubits thick. These walls each began 1½ cubits from the gateway. Hence their outer wall coincided with the inner wall of each innermost cell (1½+6=2½+5). Both were 7½ cubits from the gateway. The walls extended eight cubits into the outer courtyard. At the end of each of these walls was an oval pillar (1/7) two cubits in depth, making the total depth of the hall into the outer courtyard ten cubits. These pillars were sixty cubits high and were decorated with a palm-like motif. This structure created another gateway (1/8) into the outer courtyard. As was the case from the cells, there were windows opening from the hall onto the outer courtyard.

This description of the eastern gateway follows *Rashi* as explicated by *Tosafos Yom Tov.* The individual verses which make up this description do not always seem to yield this picture. There are many other views among the commentators. *Rambam* (see above) writes that the descriptions in *Ezekiel* are by no means clear and unambiguous.

6. שַׁעַר אֲשֶׁר פָּנָיו דֶּרֶךְ הַקָּדִימָה — *The gate which faced eastward.*

He entered the Temple Mount compound and came to the gate of the women's courtyard [עֶזְרַת נָשִׁים] *(Rashi).*

Rashi's use of the term women's courtyard [a term used for the courtyard of the Second Temple] is justified because the Halachic status of the outer courtyard was indeed equivalent to that of the women's courtyard. (See *Keilim* 1:8 for a delineation of the various levels of sanctity that applied within the Temple area.)

However, the outer courtyard of *Ezekiel* is built quite differently from the women's courtyard of the Second Temple. The latter was a 135 cubits square area which lay in front of the *Azarah* (equivalent to the inner courtyard of *Ezekiel)* but did not surround it *(Middos* 2:5; see Fig. 12), while the outer courtyard measured 312 cubits by 317 cubits (see *comm.* above and further below) and completely surrounded it (see below).

וַיַּעַל בְּמַעֲלֹתָו — *And went up its steps.*

rod. 6 *And he came to the gate which faced eastward and went up its steps; and he measured the doorpost of the gate, one rod deep; and the other doorpost; one rod deep.* 7 *And the cell was one rod in length and one rod in width; and between the cells, five cubits. And the doorpost of the gate, from the hall of the gate inward, one rod.* 8 *And he measured the hall of the gate inward, one rod.* 9 *Then he measured the hall of the gate, eight cubits; and its pillars, two cubits. Now this hall extended inward.* 10 *Now the cells of*

Rashi quotes *Middos* 2:3 that there were twelve steps (1/2) leading up from the *chail* (see pref. 6-16) to the women's courtyard in the Second Temple. These steps will be in Yechezkel's Temple also.

וַיָּמָד אֶת־סַף הַשַּׁעַר...וְאֵת סַף אֶחָד — *And he measured the doorpost of the gate...and the other doorpost.*

The two ends of the wall which framed the gateway were the doorposts for the fifty cubit high doors which led into the outer courtyard. The thickness of the wall was one rod (six cubits).

7. וְהַתָּא — *And the cell.*

The first part of this verse describes the תָּאִים, *cells,* which ran along the outside of the walls. They were one rod square, separated from one another by walls (1/5) with a five cubit thickness. *Metzudos* notes that their eastern wall was also five cubits thick.

אֻלָם — *Hall.*

The second part of the verse moves to the אֻלָם, *hall,* which extends into the outer courtyard on the other side of the wall. The ends of its two walls (which are described as מֵהַבָּיִת, *inward,* because they face inwards to the outer courtyard) had doorposts for the second set of 50 cubit high doors (see *v.* 15) which led into the outer courtyard through the two walls of the hall. These doorposts (which corresponded to the thickness of the walls of the hall — see next verse) were also one rod thick.

8. אֻלָם הַשַּׁעַר — *The hall of the gate.*

These are the two walls (1/6) upon which the hall rested *(Rashi).* [It appears from *Rashi* that there was a roof of some kind over this vestibule, but this is nowhere explicated in the text. Perhaps it is implied by the name אֻלָם, *hall.*]

מֵהַבָּיִת — *Inward.*

They are so described because they extend inward (see below).

קָנֶה אֶחָד — *One rod.*

Their thickness was one rod.

9. In this verse, the depth of the two walls of the hall are measured. They extended eight cubits into the outer courtyard. Together with the two-cubit diameter of the pillars (1/7) at their ends, this gave the entire vestibule a depth of ten cubits.

וְאֵילָו — *And its pillars.*

These pillars (1/7) were called אֵילִים, *elim,* because in appearance they were similar to the אֵלָה [*elah*], *terebinth (Rashi).*

וְאֻלָם הַשַּׁעַר מֵהַבָּיִת — *Now this hall extended inward.*

In contrast to the hall of the inner courtyard, which extended *outward* from that courtyard (see Fig. 8), this hall of the outer courtyard extended *inward,* into the courtyard. In this way, the two halls faced each other, which was aesthetically pleasing *(Rashi).*

10. The first part of the verse states

שְׁלֹשָׁה מִפֹּה וּשְׁלֹשָׁה מִפֹּה מִדָּה אַחַת
לִשְׁלָשְׁתָּם וּמִדָּה אַחַת לָאֵילִם מִפֹּה
יא וּמִפּוֹ: וַיָּמָד אֶת־רֹחַב פֶּתַח־הַשַּׁעַר עֶשֶׂר
אַמּוֹת אֹרֶךְ הַשַּׁעַר שְׁלוֹשׁ עֶשְׂרֵה אַמּוֹת:
יב וּגְבוּל לִפְנֵי הַתָּאוֹת אַמָּה אֶחָת וְאַמָּה־
אַחַת גְּבוּל מִפֹּה וְהַתָּא שֵׁשׁ־אַמּוֹת מִפּוֹ
יג וְשֵׁשׁ אַמּוֹת מִפּוֹ: וַיָּמָד אֶת־הַשַּׁעַר מִגַּג
הַתָּא לְגַגּוֹ רֹחַב עֶשְׂרִים וְחָמֵשׁ אַמּוֹת
יד פֶּתַח נֶגֶד פָּתַח: וַיַּעַשׂ אֶת־אֵילִים שִׁשִּׁים
אַמָּה וְאֶל־אֵיל הֶחָצֵר הַשַּׁעַר סָבִיב ׀
טו סָבִיב: וְעַל־פְּנֵי הַשַּׁעַר °היאתון עַל־

°הָאִיתוֹן ק׳ טו

that all the six cells were of the same size.

The second part of the verse says the same for the two pillars. They were each 2 cubits deep *(Rashi).*

11. The hall was thirteen cubits wide: the gateway was ten cubits, and its walls were built 1½ cubits away from the gateway, (towards north and south, respectively).

רֹחַב...אֹרֶךְ — *Width...length.*

The text uses רֹחַב, *width,* for the gateway but אֹרֶךְ, *length,* for the hall, because the latter is always used for the biggest dimension. In the case of the gateway, the height of the doors (fifty cubits) would be considered the אֹרֶךְ, *length,* therefore the width is called the רֹחַב. However, the depth of the hall was only ten cubits in contrast with its width which was thirteen cubits. Hence the width is called אֹרֶךְ, *length (Rashi).*

12. The inner walls of the two sets of cells were built 2½ cubits away from the gateway to the north and south, respectively. The *one cubit* mentioned in our verse means that they were removed one cubit more than the inner walls of the hall which began 1½ cubits from the gateway *(v.* 11). [The width of the outer vestibule was thus fifteen cubits, in contrast to the width of the hall, which was thirteen cubits see Fig. 2).]

Rashi points out that the result of this arrangement was that the beginning of the two inner cells corresponded exactly with the outer side of the walls of the hall. (2½+5=1½+6; see Fig. 2.)

וְהַתָּא שֵׁשׁ־אַמּוֹת מִפּוֹ — *And the cell was six cubits from this side.*

If the cell wall began one cubit away from the beginning of the hall wall, then the cell itself was six cubits distant from that point (since the cell wall was five cubits). *Metzudos* suggests that the verse tells us this in order to make clear that the walls of the cells closest to the vestibule (1/9) were also five cubits. Verse 7 only stated this explicitly concerning the walls that separated the cells from one another.

13. גַּג הַתָּא — *One roof of the cell.*

The cells (1/4) had roofs (not shown) over them. These roofs covered the actual rooms but did not extend over the dividing walls. Therefore, the distance between the northernmost roof of the southern group of cells and the southernmost roof of the northern group was 25 cubits (5+2½+10+2½+5=25).

the eastern gate — three on this side and three on that
side, the same size for all three. So, also, the same size
for the pillars on either side. 11 *Then he measured the*
width of the gate, ten cubits; the length of the gate,
thirteen cubits. 12 *Now there was a space before the*
cells, one cubit; and one cubit space from the other
side. And the cell was six cubits from this side and six
cubits from the other side. 13 *Then he measured the*
gate from one roof of the cell to the next, a width of
twenty five cubits; one door opposite the other door.
14 *Then he made the pillars, sixty cubits, thus each*
pillar of the courtyard's gates all around. 15 *And con-*
cerning the height of the entry gate as also the height

פֶּתַח נֶגֶד פָּתַח — *One door opposite the other door.*

Entry into the cells (1/4) was through the vestibule (1/9; pref., *vs.* 6-16). Therefore the door leading into the northernmost cell of the southern group was opposite the door leading into the southernmost cell of the northern group (Fig. 3).

14. אֵילִים — *Pillars.*

After this verse tells us that the pillars (1/7) at the end of the two hall walls were sixty cubits high, it proceeds to say that all the pillars *round* about the outer courtyard had the same height. (The northern and southern walls of the outer courtyard had gate structures which were identical to those of the eastern wall. See Master Diagram where all pillars along the outer walls are numbered 1/7.)

15. פְּנֵי הַשַּׁעַר — *The height* [lit. *face*] *of the gate.*

Rashi's explanation of this phrase is difficult. He explains his interpretation of פְּנֵי הַשַּׁעַר as the *height of the gate,* as being derived from the height of all the other gates mentioned in this description which is fifty cubits. *Radak* points out that nowhere in the entire description is there any mention of a height of fifty cubits for any gates. The gates in

Fig. 3

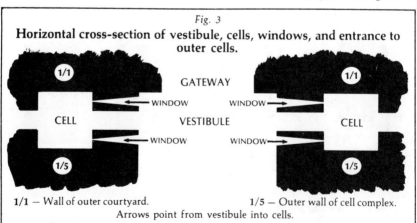

Horizontal cross-section of vestibule, cells, windows, and entrance to outer cells.

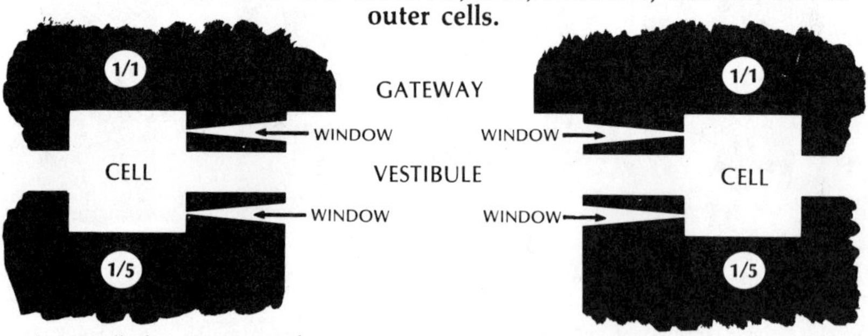

1/1 — Wall of outer courtyard. 1/5 — Outer wall of cell complex.
Arrows point from vestibule into cells.

מ
טז־יז

לִפְנֵי אֻלָם הַשַּׁעַר הַפְּנִימִי חֲמִשִּׁים אַמָּה׃
טז וְחַלּוֹנוֹת אֲטֻמוֹת אֶל־הַתָּאִים וְאֶל
אֵלֵיהֵמָה לִפְנִימָה לַשַּׁעַר סָבִיב | סָבִיב
וְכֵן לָאֵלַמּוֹת וְחַלּוֹנוֹת סָבִיב | סָבִיב
יז לִפְנִימָה וְאֶל־אַיִל תִּמֹרִים׃ וַיְבִיאֵנִי אֶל־
הֶחָצֵר הַחִיצוֹנָה וְהִנֵּה לְשָׁכוֹת וְרִצְפָה
עָשׂוּי לֶחָצֵר סָבִיב | סָבִיב שְׁלֹשִׁים

the Second Temple were fifty cubits (*Middos* 2:3) and there seems no reason to suppose that the gates in Yechezkel's Temple were to be any different.

Abarbanel and *Tosafos Yom Tov* discuss this difficulty, but conclude that *Rashi's* explanation of the verse is more acceptable than any of the alternatives.

Thus, the translation follows *Rashi*, who interprets this verse to mean that both the outer gate (1/3) and the inner gate (1/8) were fifty cubits high.

הָאִיתוֹן — *The entry.*

Rashi explains that this is the outer gate (1/3) of the courtyard wall. It was called שַׁעַר הָאִיתוֹן — from the Aramaic root אתא, *to come* — because it was the main entry gate into the Temple.

16. חַלּוֹנוֹת אֲטֻמוֹת — *Narrowing windows.*

There were windows at various points of the gate structure (pref., *vs.* 6-16). These windows are described as אֲטֻמוֹת, *narrowing*, because they were narrower on the inside than on the outside (see Fig. 4).

Yalkut Shimoni to *I Kings* 6:4 explains the reason for this strange structure. We would expect *narrowing windows* to be wider towards the *inside* so that the incoming sunlight would be spread as far as possible in the dark interior. The design of these windows, however, symbolized that the Temple needed no light from the outside. On the contrary, the *outside* world required the spiritual light that emanated from the Temple.Therefore the windows widened towards the outside.

The verse places windows at several locations.

Fig. 4

The Narrowing Windows

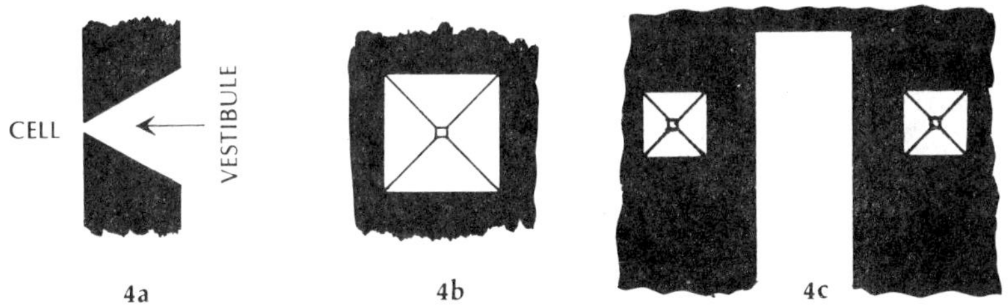

4a 4b 4c

4a — cross-section of window. Arrow points from vestibule into cell.
4b — Head-on view of window.
4c — A head-on view of entrance and windows to cells as it would appear to someone standing in the vestibule.

of the inner gate of the hall, fifty cubits. [16] *And narrowing windows in the cells, and in their pillars inward of the gate all around, and also for the halls there were windows all around, inward. And each pillar had a crown of date leaves.*

[17] *Then he brought me into the outer courtyard, and behold! chambers and a balcony were provided for the courtyard all around, thirty chambers on the*

אֶל־הַתָּאִים וְאֶל אֵלֵיהֵמָּה לִפְנִימָה — *In the cells, and in their pillars inward.*

There were doors leading from the vestibule into the cells. The walls on either side of these doors can be considered *pillars* of the door. There were windows in these two *pillars* looking out onto the vestibule. (See Fig. 3.)

In this context לִפְנִימָה, *inward,* is used to indicate that these windows looked towards the 'inside' of the gate, that is, the vestibule (1/9 in Fig. 2) formed by the two sets of cells.

סָבִיב סָבִיב — *All around.*

All the vestibules around the outer courtyard, that is, including those on the northern and southern walls, had these windows.

וְכֵן לָאֵלַמּוֹת — *And also for the halls.*

The word is an unusual form of אוּלָמּוֹת, *halls.* The walls of the hall also had windows looking out upon the outer courtyard (not shown).

וְחַלּוֹנוֹת סָבִיב סָבִיב לִפְנִימָה — *(And) there were windows all around inward.*

In the back wall of each cell there were windows looking into the outer courtyard.

וְאֶל־אַיִל תִּמֹרִים — *And each pillar had a crown of date leaves.*

On top of each sixty cubit high pillar (Fig. 1, 1/7), there was a crownlike decoration in the form of a date palm.

17-18. High up, along the inside of the wall of the outer courtyard, ran a balcony (Fig. 5). The bottom of this balcony was flush with the top of the gate, which, according to *Rashi,* was fifty cubits high. It ran along all four sides of the outer courtyard, but there were breaks in it where it would have crossed over the gateways and also at the corners of the outer courtyard where the cooking chambers (46:22-23) were situated.

There were thirty chambers (לְשָׁכוֹת) arranged around this balcony (not shown). There is no indication of the exact arrangement of these elevated chambers nor of the number of chambers on each side of the outer courtyard.

17. וַיְבִיאֵנִי אֶל־הֶחָצֵר הַחִיצוֹנָה — *Then he brought me into the outer courtyard.*

Until now he had been standing on the Temple Mount, outside the wall, in order to observe the arrangements of the gate structure from the outside. Now he enters the outer courtyard.

רִצְפָה — *A balcony.*

רִצְפָה, literally, is *a pavement (Esther* 1:6). *Rashi* deduces from the next verse that this pavement was not on the floor of the outer courtyard, but ran along the wall, overhanging the floor, at a height of fifty cubits.

[Although some editions of *Ezekiel* contain a *dagesh* in the פ — רִצְפָּה — our text follows the authoritative *Minchas Shai* who omits the *dagesh.*]

עָשׂוּ לֶחָצֵר סָבִיב סָבִיב — *Were provided for the courtyard all around.*

This expression implies that the balcony ran on all sides of the outer

יח לְשָׁכוֹת אֶל־הָרִצְפָּה׃ וְהָרִצְפָּה אֶל־כֶּתֶף
הַשְּׁעָרִים לְעֻמַּת אֹרֶךְ הַשְּׁעָרִים הָרִצְפָּה
יט הַתַּחְתּוֹנָה׃ וַיָּמָד רֹחַב מִלִּפְנֵי הַשַּׁעַר

courtyard. In ch. 42, the balcony is mentioned for the north and south sides. It is nowhere mentioned for the west side but *Tosafos Yom Tov deduces from our verse that it ran on that side also.*

18. וְהָרִצְפָּה אֶל־כֶּתֶף הַשְּׁעָרִים — *Now the balcony ran until the side of the gates.*

Rashi deduces from this phrase that the balcony did not extend over the gateway, nor did the balcony run above the cooking chambers which lay at all four corners of the outer courtyard (pref., *vs.* 17-18, Fig. 5). This is not stated by *Rashi* but by *R' Shemayah, Rashi's* student, in his commentary to *Middos.*

לְעֻמַּת אֹרֶךְ הַשְּׁעָרִים — *Flush with the top* [lit. *length*] *of the gates.*

This is at a height of fifty cubits. (*Rashi.* See *comm., vs.* 11, 15).

הַתַּחְתּוֹנָה — *The lower* [*part of the balcony*].

Rashi points out that this word denotes not a 'lower balcony' [meaning that there were two balconies], but *the lower part* of the balcony.

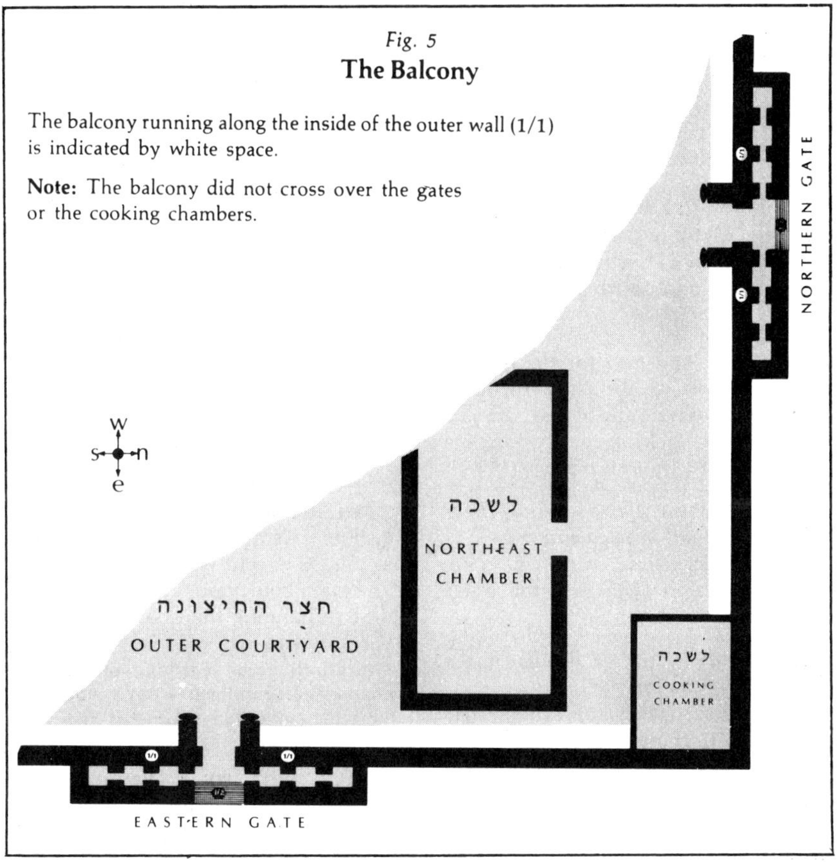

Fig. 5
The Balcony

The balcony running along the inside of the outer wall (1/1) is indicated by white space.

Note: The balcony did not cross over the gates or the cooking chambers.

40
18-19
balcony. [18] *Now the balcony ran until the side of the*
gates. The lower part of the balcony was flush with
the top of the gates. [19] *Then he measured the width*

19. In contrast to the Second Temple, in which the women's courtyard was in front of the *azarah*, but did not surround it, (see Fig. 12, p. 631) the outer courtyard (which in Yechezkel's Temple is the equivalent of the women's courtyard) did surround the inner courtyard on all four sides.

Our verse describes the width of the outer courtyard (see Fig. 6).

The walls of the inner courtyard (2/1) were a hundred cubits removed from the eastern, southern, and northern walls of the outer courtyard.

Tosafos Yom Tov points out that according to our verse, the entire width

Fig. 6

The Width of the Outer Courtyard

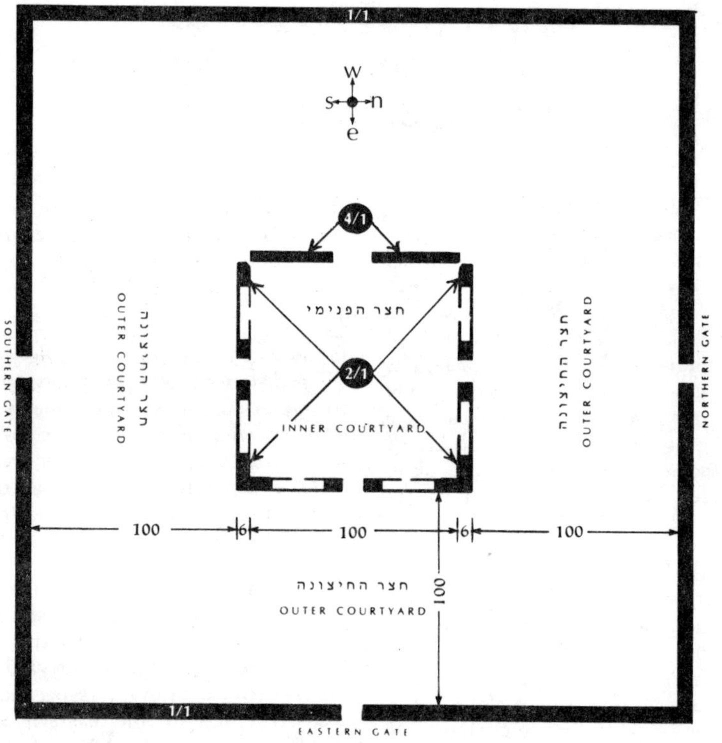

1/1 – The wall surrounding the outer courtyard on all four sides.
2/1 – The wall surrounding the inner courtyard on the eastern, northern, and southern sides.
4/1 – The wall around the entrance to the Temple complex.
Note: To avoid confusion, only the components that are necessary to the understanding of this diagram are shown.

הַתַּחְתּוֹנָה לִפְנֵי הֶחָצֵר הַפְּנִימִי מִחוּץ
כ מֵאָה אַמָּה הַקָּדִים וְהַצָּפוֹן׃ וְהַשַּׁעַר אֲשֶׁר
פָּנָיו דֶּרֶךְ הַצָּפוֹן לֶחָצֵר הַחִיצוֹנָה מָדַד
כא אָרְכּוֹ וְרָחְבּוֹ׃ וְתָאָו שְׁלוֹשָׁה מִפּוֹ
וּשְׁלֹשָׁה מִפּוֹ וְאֵילָו וְאֵלַמָּו הָיָה כְּמִדַּת
הַשַּׁעַר הָרִאשׁוֹן חֲמִשִּׁים אַמָּה אָרְכּוֹ
כב וְרֹחַב חָמֵשׁ וְעֶשְׂרִים בָּאַמָּה׃ וְחַלּוֹנָו
וְאֵילַמָּו וְתִמֹרָו כְּמִדַּת הַשַּׁעַר אֲשֶׁר פָּנָיו
דֶּרֶךְ הַקָּדִים וּבְמַעֲלוֹת שֶׁבַע יַעֲלוּ־בוֹ
כג וְאֵילַמָּו לִפְנֵיהֶם׃ וְשַׁעַר לֶחָצֵר הַפְּנִימִי
נֶגֶד הַשַּׁעַר לַצָּפוֹן וְלַקָּדִים וַיָּמָד מִשַּׁעַר
כד אֶל־שַׁעַר מֵאָה אַמָּה׃ וַיּוֹלִכֵנִי דֶּרֶךְ
הַדָּרוֹם וְהִנֵּה־שַׁעַר דֶּרֶךְ הַדָּרוֹם וּמָדַד

of the outer courtyard was 312 cubits. The distances from the northern and southern walls respectively to the inner courtyard were each a hundred cubits, and the inner courtyard itself was a hundred cubits (40:47), for a total of three hundred cubits of floor space. The thickness of the walls of the inner courtyard, although not explicated in the text, is assumed to be six cubits each, as were the walls of the outer courtyard. (See *Rashi* 42:5 and *Tzuras HaBayis* 22).

The gateway in the wall surrounding the outer courtyard is called שַׁעַר הַתַּחְתּוֹנָה, *lower gate* (Fig. 1, 1/3), relative to the inner courtyard, because it was on a lower part of the mountain's slope. As noted above (pref., *vs.* 6-16), the Temple was built on a slope and it was necessary to climb eight steps to reach the gate of the inner courtyard (Fig. 8, 2/3; *v.* 34). Again this is a change from the Second Temple, where there were fifteen steps between the women's courtyard and the inner courtyard (*Middos* 2:5).

רֹחַב — *Width.*

The width measured here is the distance between the eastern wall of the outer courtyard (1/1) and the eastern wall of the inner courtyard (2/1; see Fig. 6).

הַקָּדִים וְהַצָּפוֹן — *As the east, so the north.*

The distance (100 cubits) between the two eastern walls was the same as that between the two northern walls. *Metzudos* assumes that the same distance separated the two southern walls, although this is not indicated in the text.

20-26 These verses describe the gate structures of the northern and southern walls of the outer courtyard and their distance from the inner courtyard. All this is identical in every respect to the gate structure of the eastern wall, described in verses 6-16, and to its relation to the inner courtyard, described in verse 19.

The only difference between the eastern approach and those of the north and south was in the number of steps leading up from the Temple Mount to the outer courtyard. The number of

from before the lower gate to the outside of the inner courtyard, one hundred cubits; as the east, so the north.

20 *Now the gate of the outer courtyard which faced north, he measured its height and width.* 21 *Its cells were three to this side and three to that side, its pillars and halls were the same dimension as those of the first gate. A height of fifty cubits. A width of twenty-five cubits.*

22 *Now its windows, halls and date leaf crown — all were exactly like those of the gate facing east. Up seven steps they would ascend to it, as its halls are before them.* 23 *And there was a gate to the inner courtyard opposite this gate. To the north as to the east. And he measured from gate to gate, one hundred cubits.*

24 *Then he took me towards the south and behold! — a gate to the south. And he measured its pillars and*

these steps is not given in connection with the eastern gate, but *Rashi* to verse 6 writes that there were twelve, as there had been in the Second Temple. In contrast, the text (*vs.* 22, 26) is explicit that from the northern and southern approaches there were only seven steps leading up to the outer courtyard. *Tosafos Yom Tov* explains that the mountain may have been steeper on the east than on the other sides.

21. אָרְכּוֹ — *Height.*

This follows *Rashi* who translates אֹרֶךְ as *height* rather than the more common translation of *length.* See *comm., v.* 18.

וְרֹחַב חָמֵשׁ וְעֶשְׂרִים בָּאַמָּה — *A width of twenty-five cubits.*

This measurement is the over-all width of the hall structure. See Fig. 2 above. See *v.* 13.

22. וּבְמַעֲלוֹת שֶׁבַע יַעֲלוּ־בוֹ — *Up seven steps they would ascend to it.*

See *comm.*, 20-27.

וְאֵילַמָּו לִפְנֵיהֶם — *As its halls are before them.*

As people came up these stairs they saw the אוּלָם, *hall, of the gate before them.*

23. This verse repeats what was already learned in verse 19: That just as in the east there were a hundred cubits between the gates of the outer courtyard and inner courtyard which were directly opposite one another, so it was in the north. [Perhaps this information is repeated in order to stress the point made by *Metzudos* that in order for the two northern gates to be opposite one another, we must postulate that the northern gate of the outer courtyard was not in the center of the northern wall. This was in contrast to the eastern gate, which was in the precise center of the eastern wall. This difference came about because, as Figure 7 shows, while the length of the walls from north to south was 312 cubits (see *comm., v.* 18),

כה אֵילָו וְאֵילַמָּו כַּמִּדּוֹת הָאֵלֶּה: וְחַלּוֹנִים לוֹ
וּלְאֵילַמָּו סָבִיב | סָבִיב כְּהַחַלֹּנוֹת הָאֵלֶּה
חֲמִשִּׁים אַמָּה אֹרֶךְ וְרֹחַב חָמֵשׁ וְעֶשְׂרִים
כו אַמָּה: וּמַעֲלוֹת שִׁבְעָה עֹלוֹתָו וְאֵלַמָּו
לִפְנֵיהֶם וְתִמֹרִים לוֹ אֶחָד מִפּוֹ וְאֶחָד
כז מִפּוֹ אֶל־אֵילָו: וְשַׁעַר לֶחָצֵר הַפְּנִימִי דֶּרֶךְ
הַדָּרוֹם וַיָּמָד מִשַּׁעַר אֶל־הַשַּׁעַר דֶּרֶךְ

Fig. 7

The Length of the Outer Courtyard

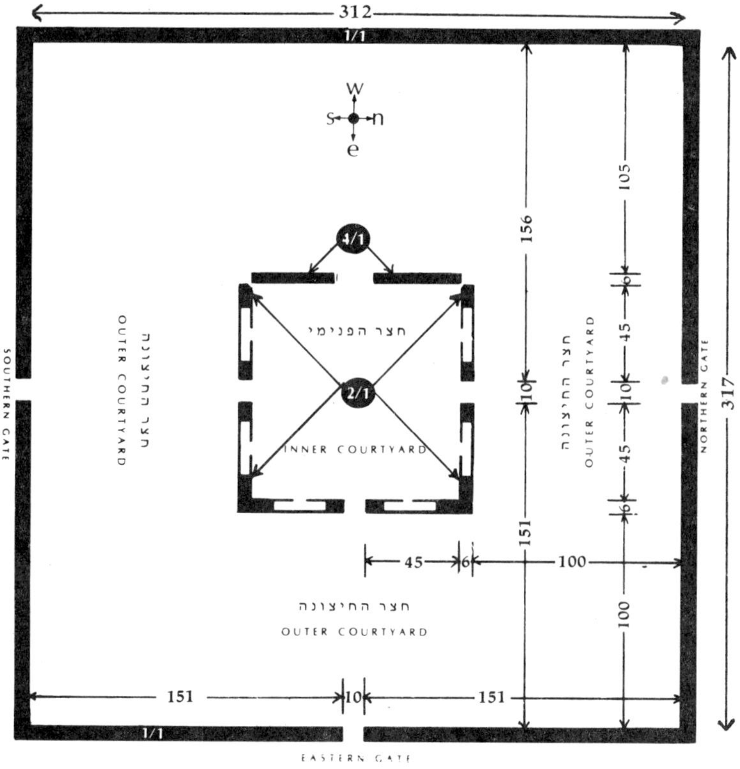

1/1 – The wall surrounding the outer courtyard on all four sides.
2/1 – The wall surrounding the inner courtyard on the eastern, northern, and southern sides.
4/1 – The wall around the entrance to the Temple complex.
Note: To avoid confusion, only the components that are necessary to the understanding of this diagram are shown.

halls, the same measurement as these. 25 *There were*
windows for it and its halls all around, like these win-
dows. A height of fifty cubits. A width of twenty-
five cubits. 26 *And seven steps were its stairs and its*
hall was before them. It had date leaf crowns, one to
this side and one to that side of its pillars. 27 *And*
there was a gate to the inner courtyard toward the
south. And he measured from gate to gate in the
south, one hundred cubits.

the length of the northern and southern walls was 317 cubits (see *comm.* 42:9).

Fig. 8

The Halls at the Gateways to the Outer and Inner Courtyards

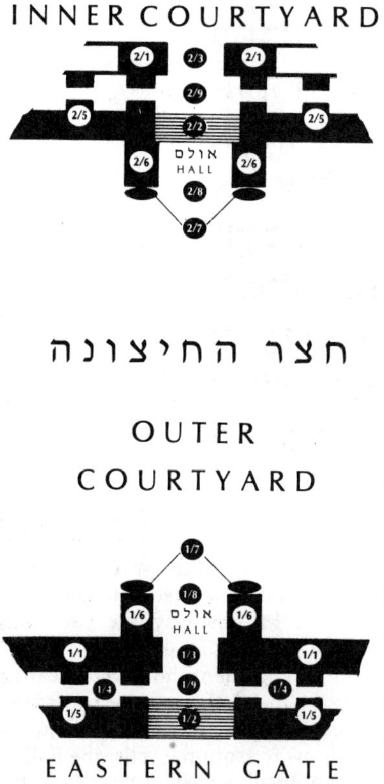

Note: Both halls faced into the outer courtyard.

24-26 These verses repeat for the southern side everything that had been taught for the northern side.

27-37 In this passage the prophet is shown the southern, eastern, and northern walls (Master Diagram, see 2/1) and gateways (2/3 and 2/8) of the inner courtyard which was the equivalent of the *azarah* of the Second Temple.

[There was no western wall to this courtyard. Instead, the הֵיכָל, *Temple Building,* stood in the west.]

All three walls under discussion had gate structures at their center facing the gates in the wall of the outer courtyard. Except for one detail these gateways were identical with those described in 6-16 (see Master Diagram). The one difference was that their אוּלָם, *hall,* did not jut inwards as did that of the outer courtyard, but was placed in front of the cells (2/4), jutting outward into the outer courtyard, directly opposite the halls of the outer wall. (See Fig. 8.) This enhanced the beauty of the structure.

Each of the three walls under discussion also had two halls (2/10) of 25 cubits×5 cubits, built into their thickness, one on each side of their respective gateways. These halls had no equivalent in the walls of the outer courtyard.

Eight steps (2/2) had to be climbed in order to go from the outer to the inner courtyard. There was a set of such steps before each of the three gates discussed above.

כח הַדָּרוֹם מֵאָה אַמּוֹת׃ וַיְבִיאֵנִי אֶל־חָצֵר
הַפְּנִימִי בְּשַׁעַר הַדָּרוֹם וַיָּמָד אֶת־הַשַּׁעַר
כט הַדָּרוֹם כַּמִּדּוֹת הָאֵלֶּה׃ וְתָאָו וְאֵלָו
וְאֵלַמָּו כַּמִּדּוֹת הָאֵלֶּה וְחַלּוֹנוֹת לוֹ
וּלְאֵלַמָּו סָבִיב ׀ סָבִיב חֲמִשִּׁים אַמָּה אֹרֶךְ
ל וְרֹחַב עֶשְׂרִים וְחָמֵשׁ אַמּוֹת׃ וְאֵלַמּוֹת
סָבִיב ׀ סָבִיב אֹרֶךְ חָמֵשׁ וְעֶשְׂרִים אַמָּה
לא וְרֹחַב חָמֵשׁ אַמּוֹת׃ וְאֵילַמָּו אֶל־חָצֵר
הַחִצוֹנָה וְתִמֹרִים אֶל־אֵילָו וּמַעֲלוֹת
לב שְׁמוֹנֶה מַעֲלָו׃ וַיְבִיאֵנִי אֶל־הֶחָצֵר
הַפְּנִימִי דֶּרֶךְ הַקָּדִים וַיָּמָד אֶת־הַשַּׁעַר
לג כַּמִּדּוֹת הָאֵלֶּה׃ וְתָאָו וְאֵלָו וְאֵלַמָּו
כַּמִּדּוֹת הָאֵלֶּה וְחַלּוֹנוֹת לוֹ סָבִיב ׀ סָבִיב
אֹרֶךְ חֲמִשִּׁים אַמָּה וְרֹחַב חָמֵשׁ וְעֶשְׂרִים
לד אַמָּה׃ וְאֵלַמָּו לֶחָצֵר הַחִיצוֹנָה וְתִמֹרִים
אֶל־אֵילָו מִפּוֹ וּמִפּוֹ וּשְׁמֹנֶה מַעֲלוֹת
לה מַעֲלָו׃ וַיְבִיאֵנִי אֶל־שַׁעַר הַצָּפוֹן וּמָדַד
לו כַּמִּדּוֹת הָאֵלֶּה׃ תָּאָו אֵלָו וְאֵלַמָּו וְחַלּוֹנוֹת
לוֹ סָבִיב ׀ סָבִיב אֹרֶךְ חֲמִשִּׁים אַמָּה וְרֹחַב
לז חָמֵשׁ וְעֶשְׂרִים אַמָּה׃ וְאֵילָו לֶחָצֵר
הַחִיצוֹנָה וְתִמֹרִים אֶל־אֵילָו מִפּוֹ וּמִפּוֹ

30. וְאֵלַמּוֹת סָבִיב סָבִיב — *Halls were all around.*

These are the two halls (2/10), one on each side of the gateway, which were described above (pref., *vs.* 27-37).

While the text does not specify that there was one on each side of the gateway, *Tosafos Yom Tov* shows that no other arrangement was possible. Since on each side of the gateway there were only 45 cubits (see Fig. 7) and these halls were 25 cubits in length, it follows that there was room for only one on each side of the doorway.

31. וְאֵילַמָּיו אֶל חָצֵר הַחִצוֹנָה — *And its halls were toward the outer courtyard.*

This is similar to the way the hall of the outer wall projected into the outer courtyard. In this way the two halls faced each other. See Fig. 8.

This arrangement, however, meant a change in the design of the two gates. Whereas the hall of outer wall jutted inward, away from the cells, the hall of the inner wall jutted outward on the same side as the cells (see pref., *vs.* 27-37).

Otherwise descriptions of the gates of

28 *Then he brought me to the inner courtyard at*
the southern gate and he measured the southern gate.
It had the same measurements. There were windows
for it and its halls all around. 29 *Its cells, its pillars and*
its halls had the same size measurements. There were
windows for it and its halls around. A height of fifty
cubits. A width of twenty-five cubits. 30 *Halls were*
all around, a length of twenty-five cubits and a width
of five cubits. 31 *And its halls were toward the outer*
courtyard. Date leaf crowns were on its pillars. Eight
stairs were its steps. 32 *Then he brought me to the in-*
ner courtyard through the east and he measured the
gate. It had these same measurements. 33 *Its cells, its*
pillars, its halls had these same measurements. There
were windows for it and its halls all around. A height
of fifty cubits, a width of twenty-five cubits. 34 *Its*
halls were toward the outer courtyard. There were
date leaf crowns on its pillars to this side and that,
and eight stairs were its steps.

35 *Then he brought me to the northern gate and*
measured by these same measurements. 36 *Its cells, its*
pillars, and its halls. It had windows all around. A
height of fifty cubits, a width of twenty-five cubits.
37 *Its pillars were in the outer courtyard and a date*
leaf crown was on its pillars to this side and that.

the inner wall are identical in every detail with those of the outer wall and the description of those gates (*vs.* 6-16) should be consulted for commentary up to verse 37. Again in these verses, *Rashi* takes אֹרֶךְ, which usually means *length,* to mean the height of the gates, and the measurement of 25 cubits (*vs.* 29, 33, 36) is the distance between the two inner cells. See Fig. 2, pref. *vs.* 6-16.

34. וּשְׁמֹנֶה מַעֲלוֹת מַעֲלָיו — *And eight stairs were its steps.*

These eight steps led from the outer to the inner courtyard. In the Second Temple, fifteen steps led from the women's courtyard to the *azarah* (*Middos* 2:5) which corresponded to the fifteen Songs of Ascents in *Psalms* 120-134. [These psalms were recited by the Levites while they stood on these steps during the ceremony of the שִׂמְחַת בֵּית הַשּׁוֹאֵבָה, *Rejoicing at the Drawing of the Water,* on Succos.] In the Second Temple these fifteen steps were rounded in the shape of a semi-circle (*Middos,* there) in order to make more room for the choristers.

Since there are to be eight rather than fifteen steps in Ezekiel's Temple, we

לח וּשְׁמֹנֶה מַעֲלוֹת מַעֲלָו: וְלִשְׁכָּה וּפִתְחָהּ
בְּאֵילִים הַשְּׁעָרִים שָׁם יָדִיחוּ אֶת־הָעֹלָה:
לט וּבְאֻלָם הַשַּׁעַר שְׁנַיִם שֻׁלְחָנוֹת מִפּוֹ
וּשְׁנַיִם שֻׁלְחָנוֹת מִפֹּה לִשְׁחוֹט אֲלֵיהֶם
מ הָעוֹלָה וְהַחַטָּאת וְהָאָשָׁם: וְאֶל־הַכָּתֵף

would not be justified in drawing a parallel and making these steps circular. In the absence of any contrary indication, we have shown them straight in the Main Diagram.

38. This verse, together with 42 and 43, describes a לִשְׁכָּה, *chamber,* (3/1) on the north side of the inner courtyard (see Fig. 9). No dimensions are given for this chamber, and the only direction that is given for its construction is that it is to be open towards the gate of the inner courtyard (that is, northward), and its doorposts (that is, the eastern and western wall ends)are to be opposite the sides of the gate in the northern wall. Therefore, we may assume that the inner width of this chamber corresponds to that of the gate (2/3), ten cubits.

In this chamber they washed the flesh of sacrifices which were slaughtered at the northern side of the inner courtyard (see *Zevachim,* ch. 2). It was equipped with hooks on which the animals were hung during the skinning process *(v.* 43) and tables on which knives and other implements were laid out.

Tosafos Yom Tov identifies this chamber with the בֵּית הַמִּטְבָּחַיִם, *butchering area,* of the Second Temple (*Middos* 3:5; but see *Tiferes Yisrael* there that the word בַּיִת in that context describes an open area, rather than a house enclosed by walls). He suggests two possible reasons why this building opened up to the north, that is, away from the main area of the inner courtyard. This could be either in order that the people in the courtyard (between the altar and this chamber) not see the animals being butchered, or to provide privacy for the people who brought the sacrifices and, as part of the act of sacrifice, confessed their sins [וִדּוּי].

Fig. 9

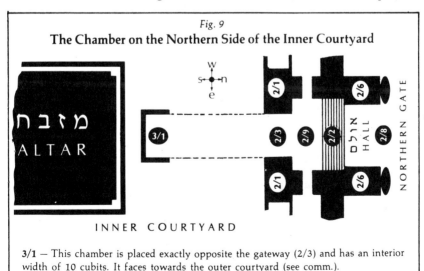

The Chamber on the Northern Side of the Inner Courtyard

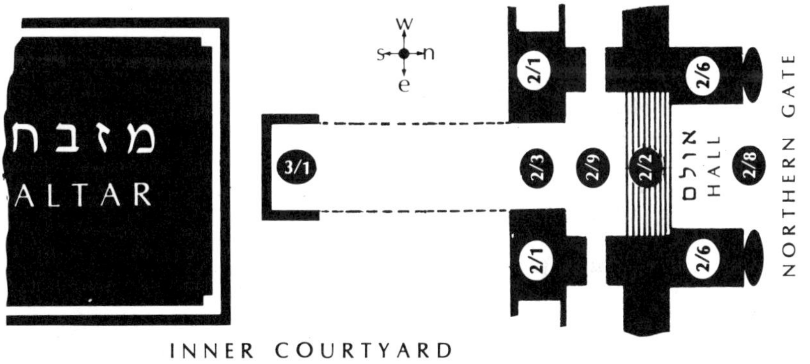

3/1 — This chamber is placed exactly opposite the gateway (2/3) and has an interior width of 10 cubits. It faces towards the outer courtyard (see comm.).

40
38-40

Eight stairs were its steps. 38 *And a chamber whose*
opening was opposite the sides of the gate. There
they washed the burnt offering.

39 *Now in the hall of the gate there were two tables*
on one side and two tables on the other side, near
which to slaughter the burnt offering, the sin offer-
ing and the guilt offering. 40 *And by the recess for*

בְּאֵילִים הַשְּׁעָרִים – *Sides of the gate.* Although the word אֵילִים has generally been used in our chapter to mean *pillars, Rashi* points out that it can also mean *sides,* as in our verse and verse 16.

39-41. Eight tables were positioned in the gate structure of the northern wall (see Fig. 10): two each on either side of the hall [אוּלָם] and another four in the vestibule formed by the inner walls (2/9) of the cells.

Fig. 10

The Northern Entrance to the Inner Courtyard

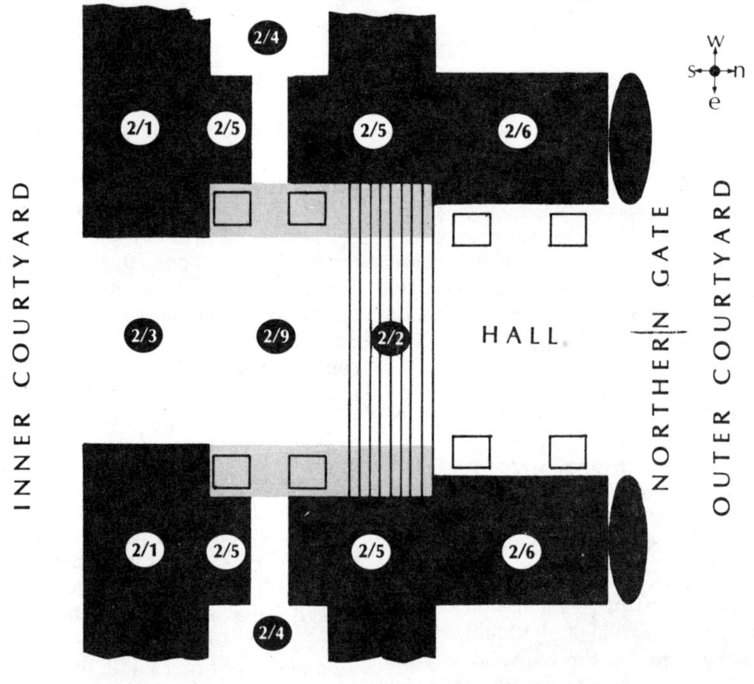

The width of the gate (2/3) formed by the walls of the inner courtyard (2/1) is 10 cubits; the width of the hall formed by its walls (2/6) is 13 cubits. Since the width of the vestibule (2/9) formed by the outer walls of the cells (2/5) is 15 cubits, two recesses (shaded areas) are formed on either side of the vestibule (2/9).

Two tables are placed in each of these recesses and two tables alongside each of the hall walls (2/6).

מִחוּצָה לָעוֹלֶה לְפֶתַח הַשַּׁעַר הַצָּפוֹנָה
שְׁנַיִם שֻׁלְחָנוֹת וְאֶל־הַכָּתֵף הָאַחֶרֶת
אֲשֶׁר לְאֻלָם הַשַּׁעַר שְׁנַיִם שֻׁלְחָנוֹת׃
מא אַרְבָּעָה שֻׁלְחָנוֹת מִפֹּה וְאַרְבָּעָה
שֻׁלְחָנוֹת מִפֹּה לְכֶתֶף הַשָּׁעַר שְׁמוֹנָה
מב שֻׁלְחָנוֹת אֲלֵיהֶם יִשְׁחָטוּ׃ וְאַרְבָּעָה
שֻׁלְחָנוֹת לָעוֹלָה אַבְנֵי גָזִית אֹרֶךְ אַמָּה
אַחַת וָחֵצִי וְרֹחַב אַמָּה אַחַת וָחֵצִי וְגֹבַהּ
אַמָּה אֶחָת אֲלֵיהֶם וְיַנִּיחוּ אֶת־הַכֵּלִים
אֲשֶׁר יִשְׁחֲטוּ אֶת־הָעוֹלָה בָּם וְהַזָּבַח׃
מג וְהַשְׁפַתַּיִם טֹפַח אֶחָד מוּכָנִים בַּבַּיִת
סָבִיב | סָבִיב וְאֶל־הַשֻּׁלְחָנוֹת בְּשַׂר

40. הַכָּתֵף — *The recess.*

The walls of the cells (2/5) began 2½ cubits from the gate; the walls of the אולם, *hall* (2/6) began 1½ cubits from the gate (see Fig. 10; pref. *vs.* 6-16). Thus two recesses were formed just outside the gate. These recesses are called the כְּתֵפוֹת [lit. *shoulders*] in our verse. The four tables in the vestibule (2/9; see pref., *vs.* 39-41) were arranged in pairs within these two recesses.

לָעוֹלֶה לְפֶתַח הַשַּׁעַר הַצָּפוֹנָה — *For someone ascending to the opening of the northern gate.*

The two כְּתֵפוֹת, *recesses* [lit. *shoulders*], had the effect of a 'shoulder' for someone ascending the eight steps leading up from the outer courtyard.

41. שְׁמוֹנָה שֻׁלְחָנוֹת — *Eight tables.*

There was a total of eight tables in the gateway: four in the hall and another four in the recesses of the vestibule (see Fig. 10).

42. This verse and the next resume the description of the לִשְׁכָּה, *chamber,* described in verse 38. It contained four stone tables. On them, the knives and receptacles for the sacrifice lay ready. In addition, the tables were used to wash the organs of the slaughtered animals. Stone was well suited to this purpose, as marble had been in the Second Temple (*Middos* 3:5), since both materials are cold and help preserve the freshness of the meat (*Tos. Yom Tov*). According to *Shekalim* 6:4, there were eight marble tables in the slaughtering area of the Second Temple. That this chamber contained only four tables must be listed among the differences between the Second Temple and Yechezkel's Temple.

43. שְׁפַתַּיִם — *Hooks.*

These hooks are the אוּנְקְלִיוֹת שֶׁל בַּרְזֶל, *iron hooks*, of *Middos* 3:5. These were inserted in עַמּוּדִים נַנָּסִים, *low pillars,* eight of which stood in the slaughtering area and in the surrounding walls. On these the slaughtered animals were hung while they were being skinned.

44-46 This passage describes three chambers (3/2; 3/3) which were situated in the inner courtyard. Two (3/2) were at the כָּתֵף, *shoulder*, that is, *the side* of the northern gate and opened

someone ascending to the opening of the northern
gate there were two tables, and to the other side of the
gate's hall were two tables. 41 *Four tables to this side*
and four tables to that side for the recess of the gate.
Eight tables near which they will slaughter.
42 *And there were four tables for the burnt offer-*
ing, made of hewn stone, with a length of one and a
half cubits, and a width of one and a half cubits, and
a height of one cubit. Upon them they will store the
implements with which they will slaughter the burnt
offering and the sacrifice. 43 *And the hooks were one*
handsbreadth — set up in the House all around.

southward; the other (3/3) was closer to the eastern gate, with its opening towards the north. The two nearer the northern gate (3/2) were for the use of the Levites (see *v.* 44); the other nearer the east (3/3) was for the *Kohanim.* [Any diagram of these chambers must be based on conjecture since the text specifies neither the exact dimensions nor the exact position.]

Fig. 11

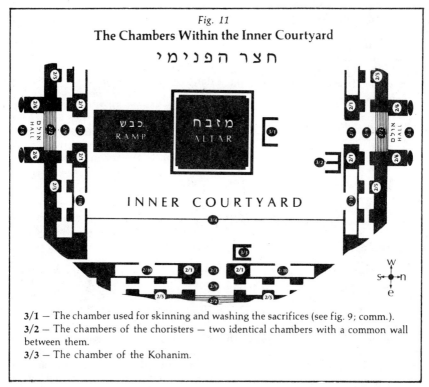

The Chambers Within the Inner Courtyard

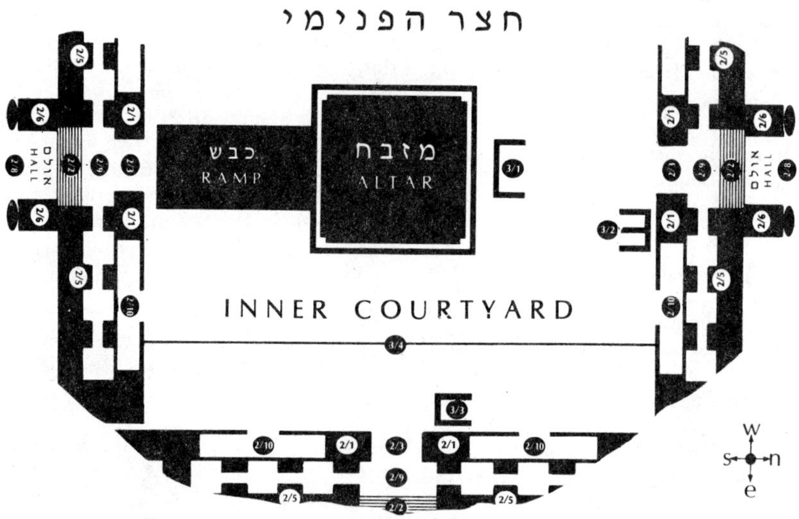

3/1 — The chamber used for skinning and washing the sacrifices (see fig. 9; comm.).
3/2 — The chambers of the choristers — two identical chambers with a common wall between them.
3/3 — The chamber of the Kohanim.

מד הַקָּרְבָּן: וּמִחוּצָה לַשַּׁעַר הַפְּנִימִי לִשְׁכוֹת
שָׁרִים בֶּחָצֵר הַפְּנִימִי אֲשֶׁר אֶל־כֶּתֶף
שַׁעַר הַצָּפוֹן וּפְנֵיהֶם דֶּרֶךְ הַדָּרוֹם אֶחָד
אֶל־כֶּתֶף שַׁעַר הַקָּדִים פְּנֵי דֶּרֶךְ הַצָּפֹן:
מה וַיְדַבֵּר אֵלַי זֹה הַלִּשְׁכָּה אֲשֶׁר פָּנֶיהָ דֶּרֶךְ
הַדָּרוֹם לַכֹּהֲנִים שֹׁמְרֵי מִשְׁמֶרֶת הַבָּיִת:
מו וְהַלִּשְׁכָּה אֲשֶׁר פָּנֶיהָ דֶּרֶךְ הַצָּפוֹן
לַכֹּהֲנִים שֹׁמְרֵי מִשְׁמֶרֶת הַמִּזְבֵּחַ הֵמָּה
בְנֵי־צָדוֹק הַקְּרֵבִים מִבְּנֵי־לֵוִי אֶל־יהוה
מז לְשָׁרְתוֹ: וַיָּמָד אֶת־הֶחָצֵר אֹרֶךְ | מֵאָה
אַמָּה וְרֹחַב מֵאָה אַמָּה מְרֻבָּעַת וְהַמִּזְבֵּחַ

44. לִשְׁכוֹת שָׁרִים — *Chambers of the choristers.*

These chambers (3/2) were for the Levites who sang *(Rashi;* according to *Succah* 51a, שִׁירָה denotes *choral music). Tosafos Yom Tov* points out that according to *Middos* 2:6, there were chambers in the Second Temple which opened from the *Azarah* into the Women's Courtyard in which the Levites kept the musical instruments with which they accompanied their songs. This suggests that the chambers mentioned in our verse serve a similar purpose.

45. לַכֹּהֲנִים שֹׁמְרֵי מִשְׁמֶרֶת הַבָּיִת — *For the ministrants, the protectors of the charge of the House.*

A chamber opening to the south was used by the *Kohanim.* However, since no mention of such a chamber has been made (the two chambers of *v.* 44, opening to the south, were for the use of the Levites), *Rashi* concludes that the *Kohanim* in our phrase refers to the Levites, and this *chamber* is, the same as those referred to in the previous verse.

Abarbanel points out that the verb לְכַהֵן means *to serve.* Thus, it can be used for Levites as well as for *Kohanim.*

Radak assumes the presence of an additional chamber that also opened to the south.

46. שֹׁמְרֵי מִשְׁמֶרֶת הַמִּזְבֵּחַ — *Protectors of the charge of the altar.*

The single *chamber* (3/3) mentioned at the end of verse 44 was for the use of the *Kohanim* whose duties centered on the מִזְבֵּחַ, *altar.* No specific function is assigned for this chamber but *Tosafos Yom Tov* assumes that its purpose was similar to that of the two chambers *(Middos* 1:4) which were built on either side of the שַׁעַר נִקָּנוֹר, *eastern gate,* of the *azarah* in the Second Temple. One was used for storing the priestly vestments, the other for preparing the חֲבִיתִּין, daily *meal offering* of the *kohen gadol.*

הֵמָּה בְנֵי־צָדוֹק — *They, the descendants of Tzadok.*

The duties of those *kohanim* who descended from Tzadok, the first high priest in Solomon's Temple, will be centered on the altar *(I Chronicles* 29:22). See further at 44:9-16.

47. הֶחָצֵר — *The courtyard.*

According to the Mishnah *Kelim* 1:8-9, the Temple area contained several levels of sanctity. The women's court-

44 And outside of the inner gate were chambers for
the choristers in the inner courtyard to the side of the
northern gate, facing towards the south. One was to
the side of the eastern gate facing the north.
45 Then he spoke to me: 'This chamber which faces
south is for the ministrants, protectors of the charge
of the House. 46 And the chamber which faced north
is for the Kohanim, *protectors of the charge of the*
altar. They, the descendants of Tzadok, are those
drawn close from among the Levites, to HASHEM, *to*
serve Him.'
47 Then he measured the courtyard. A length of
one hundred cubits and a width of one hundred
cubits, a square. And the altar was before the House.

yard was of a lower level of sanctity than the עֶזְרַת יִשְׂרָאֵל, *courtyard of Israelites* (the outer part of the *Azarah),* which, in turn, was less holy than the *courtyard of kohanim* (the inner part of the *azarah*; see Fig. 12). In general, the holier a particular area, the more restricted the entry into it. See the Mishnah for the halachic implications of the various areas. In this hierarchy of sanctity, the inner courtyard of Yechezkel is the equivalent of the *azarah* (comprised of the courtyards of the Israelites and of the *kohanim*) of the Second Temple.

Nevertheless, the dimensions of the inner courtyard are to be quite different from those of the *azarah* of the Second Temple, and, in an even more radical departure, its relation to the הֵיכָל, *Temple building,* is to undergo a complete change.

In the Second Temple, the Temple building was within the *azarah,* which surrounded it on all four sides. (Figure 12 is based on *Middos* 5:1-2; the interested reader is directed there for a thorough understanding.)

By contrast, the inner courtyard of Yechezkel's Temple lay completely before the Temple building, which, in fact, formed its western wall. The building itself lay within the outer courtyard, which surrounded it on its northern, western, and southern sides. (See Master Diagram, and Fig. 6.)

Fig. 12
Layout of the Second Temple

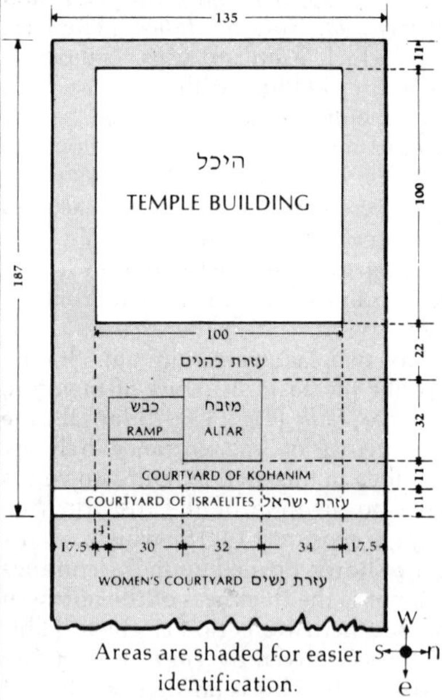

Areas are shaded for easier identification.

מח לִפְנֵי הַבָּיִת: וַיְבִאֵנִי אֶל־אֻלָם הַבַּיִת וַיָּמָד
אֵל אֻלָם חָמֵשׁ אַמּוֹת מִפֹּה וְחָמֵשׁ אַמּוֹת
מִפֹּה וְרֹחַב הַשַּׁעַר שָׁלֹשׁ אַמּוֹת מִפּוֹ
מט וְשָׁלֹשׁ אַמּוֹת מִפּוֹ: אֹרֶךְ הָאֻלָם עֶשְׂרִים
אַמָּה וְרֹחַב עַשְׁתֵּי עֶשְׂרֵה אַמָּה
וּבַמַּעֲלוֹת אֲשֶׁר יַעֲלוּ אֵלָיו וְעַמֻּדִים אֶל־

Our verse teaches that the length and width of this inner courtyard were a hundred cubits each. See Fig. 6 and 7 above.

וְהַמִּזְבֵּחַ לִפְנֵי הַבָּיִת — *And the altar was before the House.*

Precisely centered *(Metzudos)*. This is R' Yehudah's view (*Yoma* 16a; *comm.* 43:13-17). Its thirty-two cubits lay along the Hall and its two walls (4/11) which had a combined width of thirty-two cubits.

48-49. The Temple building [הֵיכָל], to which Yechezkel now turns his attention, was comprised of three basic (עִקָּר) components *(Rambam, Beis HaBechirah* 1:5): the אוּלָם, *entrance hall;* the קֹדֶשׁ, *Sanctuary* [lit. *holy*] and קֹדֶשׁ הַקֳּדָשִׁים, *Holy of Holies.* (The term הֵיכָל, which *Rambam* uses to describe the entire building with its three main components, is generally used as the specific name of the middle section, the קֹדֶשׁ, *Sanctuary.*) In addition to these, there were various chambers, cells, and passageways which extended the building to a hundred cubits in length by a hundred cubits in width at its widest point.

The two last verses in our chapter describe the basic structure of the אוּלָם, *entrance hall* (Fig. 13). [Not all the components of the entrance hall are described in this section. Our two verses make no mention of the בֵּית הַחֲלִיפוֹת, *Knife Depository* (4/18) which, as the figure shows, opened upon the entrance hall, nor is the thickness of the northern and southern walls (4/11) given. [This thickness is given by *Tosafos Yom Tov* as six cubits. This is nowhere explicated in the text, but, as the computations at 41:9 show, must be assumed (according to the interpretation of מוּנָח, *open space,* which we have chosen [see 41:9]) in order to attain a width of seventy cubits for the whole building. [See there.]

48. אֵל אֻלָם — *The doorposts of the hall.*

This verse contains two measurements (see Fig. 13). The first five cubits on either side, refers to אֵל אֻלָם which *Rashi* interprets as the *ends of the eastern wall of the hall* (4/1) which was also the western wall of the inner courtyard. The wall was five cubits thick, and this gave the gateway of the hall (4/3) a depth of five cubits.

The second measurement is for רֹחַב הַשַּׁעַר, *width of the gate,* and is given as three cubits on either side. In *Rashi's* view, this refers to the part of the wall (4/1) which extended three cubits past the northern and southern inner walls (4/11) of the Temple. The north to south measurement of the hall is given in the next verse as 20 cubits; but the gateway (4/3) was only fourteen cubits wide. Three cubits on each side were filled by these extensions of the wall. [This is in contrast to the gate of the hall in the Second Temple, which was open completely, that is, it measured the full cubit size of the hall *(Middos* 3:7).]

49. אֹרֶךְ הָאֻלָם — *The length of the hall.*

The twenty cubit measurement refers to the size of the hall from north to south. *Rashi* to verse 11 pointed out that the word אֹרֶךְ, *length* is used for the longest dimension even if we would normally have referred to it as width.

40
48-49

[48] *Then he brought me to the hall of the House and*
he measured the doorposts of the hall, five cubits
from this side and five cubits from that side. And as
for the width of the gate — three cubits from this side
and three cubits from that side. [49] *The length of the*
hall, twenty cubits; and the width, eleven cubits; and
also the steps by which they ascend to it. And there

וְרֹחַב עַשְׁתֵּי עֶשְׂרֵה אַמָּה — *And the width, eleven cubits.*

This measurement begins from the inside of the eastern hall wall (4/1) and extends to the beginning of the wall of the Sanctuary (4/15).

וּבַמַּעֲלוֹת אֲשֶׁר יַעֲלוּ אֵלָיו — *And also the steps by which they ascend to it.*

According to *Middos* 3:6, there were twelve steps leading from the *azarah* to the hall. Each of these steps had a height of one-half cubit and a depth of one cubit.

There are different opinions among the commentators concerning the arrangement of these twelve steps. (See *Middos,* there). In *Tiferes Yisrael's*

Fig. 13

Entrance Hall to the Temple Complex

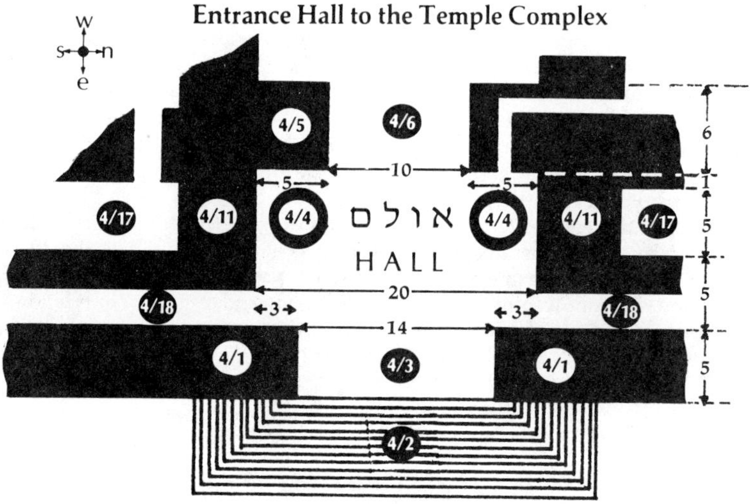

4/1 — Outside wall of the Temple structure (5 cubits thick).
4/2 — Steps leading into Hall (number, size, and placement of steps are by conjecture only).
4/3 — Gateway (14 cubits wide).
4/4 — Round pillars (size and precise placement by conjecture only).
4/5 — Walls forming gateway into Sanctuary (5 cubits wide by 6 cubits thick).
4/6 — Gateway into Sanctuary (10 cubits wide).
4/11 — Inner wall of Temple on the northern and southern sides.
4/17 — מוּנָח, *open space* (5 cubits).
4/18 — בֵּית הַחֲלִיפוֹת, *knife depository* (5 cubits thick combined with its western wall.)
Note: Only the combined width is known to total 5 cubits. However, the exact width of the inner space or of the wall is not known.

א הָאֵילִים אֶחָד מִפֹּה וְאֶחָד מִפֹּה׃ וַיְבִיאֵנִי
אֶל־הַהֵיכָל וַיָּמָד אֶת־הָאֵילִים שֵׁשׁ־
אַמּוֹת רֹחַב מִפּוֹ וְשֵׁשׁ־אַמּוֹת רֹחַב־מִפּוֹ
ב רֹחַב הָאֹהֶל׃ וְרֹחַב הַפֶּתַח עֶשֶׂר אַמּוֹת
וְכִתְפוֹת הַפֶּתַח חָמֵשׁ אַמּוֹת מִפּוֹ וְחָמֵשׁ
אַמּוֹת מִפּוֹ וַיָּמָד אָרְכּוֹ אַרְבָּעִים אַמָּה
ג וְרֹחַב עֶשְׂרִים אַמָּה׃ וּבָא לִפְנִימָה וַיָּמָד
אֵיל־הַפֶּתַח שְׁתַּיִם אַמּוֹת וְהַפֶּתַח שֵׁשׁ
ד אַמּוֹת וְרֹחַב הַפֶּתַח שֶׁבַע אַמּוֹת׃ וַיָּמָד
אֶת־אָרְכּוֹ עֶשְׂרִים אַמָּה וְרֹחַב עֶשְׂרִים
אַמָּה אֶל־פְּנֵי הַהֵיכָל וַיֹּאמֶר אֵלַי זֶה
ה קֹדֶשׁ הַקֳּדָשִׁים׃ וַיָּמָד קִיר־הַבַּיִת שֵׁשׁ

וְעַמֻּדִים אֶל הָאֵילִים — *And pillars for the doorposts.*

In Solomon's Temple, there were two pillars called יָכִין, *Yachin*, and בֹּעַז, *Boaz* (*I Kings* 7:21). Yechezkel's Temple is to have two pillars (4/4) corresponding to the ones in Solomon's Temple.

According to *Metzudos*, these names were given to bring a blessing to the Temple: יָכִין stems from כון, *to be established*, and בֹּעַז is a contraction of two words בּוֹ עוֹז, [*may there be*] *strength in it.*

discussion of the Second Temple, he shows the steps as taking up the entire twenty-two cubit area from the altar to the entrance hall. In the Third Temple, however, that area will be thirty-four cubits long. Thus, in any case, the arrangement would not be the same as that in the Second Temple. *R' Moshe Ivier* in his diagram (Appendix VIII) indicates no special arrangements for these steps and we follow him in this. The arrangement which we offer is based on conjecture.

XLI

1-2. The prophet, led by his angelic guide (40:3), progresses through the Temple building from east to west. In the last two verses of the previous chapter he described the אולם, *entrance hall.* He now turns his attention to the קודש, *Sanctuary.* [In *comm.* 40:48-49 we noted that the word הֵיכָל, which occasionally describes the complete Temple building, is generally used, as it is in our verse, for the קוֹדֶשׁ, *Sanctuary*, which lay between the entrance hall and the קֹדֶשׁ הַקֳּדָשִׁים, *Holy of Holies.*]

The inner dimensions of the Sanctuary (Figs. 13,14) were forty cubits long from east to west by twenty cubits wide from north to south (*v.* 2). It was entered by a gateway (4/6) ten cubits wide (*v.* 2), leaving room for doorposts on each side of five cubits measured from north to south (*v.* 2). These two doorposts, together with the ten cubit gap between them, served as the western wall of the entrance hall and the eastern wall of the Sanctuary. The doorposts were six cubits thick (*v.* 1). [These two verses do not tell us anything about the thickness of the northern and

were pillars for the doorposts, one to this side and one to that side.

Then he brought me to the Sanctuary and he measured the doorposts. A six-cubit width from this side and a six cubit width from that side, the width of the structure. 2 *The width of the gateway was ten cubits and the shoulders of the gateway five cubits from this side and five cubits from that side. He measured its length, forty cubits; and a width of twenty cubits.* 3 *Then he came to the inner [sanctum] and he measured the doorposts of the door — two cubits and the door was six cubits [high] and its width was seven cubits.* 4 *He measured its length, twenty cubits; and a width of twenty cubits along the width of the Sanctuary. And he said to me: 'This is the Holy of Holies.'*

5 *Then he measured the wall of the House, six*

southern walls (that is, the walls running from east to west). These will be dealt with later].

1. וַיָּמָד אֶת הָאֵילִים — *And he measured the doorposts.*

In the previous chapter we found the word אַיִל used in three different ways. In the description of the various gateways leading into the two courtyards, the אֵילִים were the oval pillars (1/7; 2/7) which were part of the hall walls. In verses 16 and 38 the word described the walls of the sides of the gates, and in verse 48 it meant *doorposts.* Here it refers to the two parts of the wall (4/5) which separated the hall from the Sanctuary. Their thickness is given as six cubits *(Rashi,* according to *Levushei Serad).*

רֹחַב הָאֹהֶל — *The width of the structure.*

In connection with the hall, רֹחַב, *width,* refers to the east-west dimension since that is shorter than the north-south dimension (see 40:11). This confirms *Rashi's* interpretation of the beginning of the verse-viz., the thickness (i.e., east-west) of wall 4/5 is given in this verse (Fig. 14).

3-4. We now come to the קֹדֶשׁ הַקֳּדָשִׁים, *the Holy of Holies* (see Fig. 14). It was separated from the Sanctuary by a wall (4/7) two cubits thick.

It extended six and a half cubits from each side, leaving a gateway of seven cubits. It had a door which was six cubits high (*v.* 3).[The two-cubit thickness of the wall contrasts with both Solomon's Temple, and the Second Temple. In Solomon's Temple a wall with a thickness of one cubit separated the Sanctuary from the Holy of Holies, and in the Second Temple the wall was replaced by two curtains separated from one another by a space of one cubit. See *Yomah* 51b.]

Inside, the Holy of Holies was an area twenty cubits square (*v.* 4).

This description brings us to the in-

ner surface of the western wall of the Holy of Holies.

3. אֵיל הַפֶּתַח – *The doorposts of the door.*

See *comm.* to *v.* 1.

וְהַפֶּתַח שֵׁשׁ אַמּוֹת – *And the door was six cubits [high].*

Rashi points out that this can only refer to the height of the door. Since our verse gives the opening of the doorways as seven cubits, the north-south measurement of the two sections (4/7) of the eastern wall of the Holy of Holies (or the western wall of the Sanctuary) must have been six and a half cubits (20-6½-6½=7).

Fig. 14

Inner Dimensions of Sanctuary and Holy of Holies

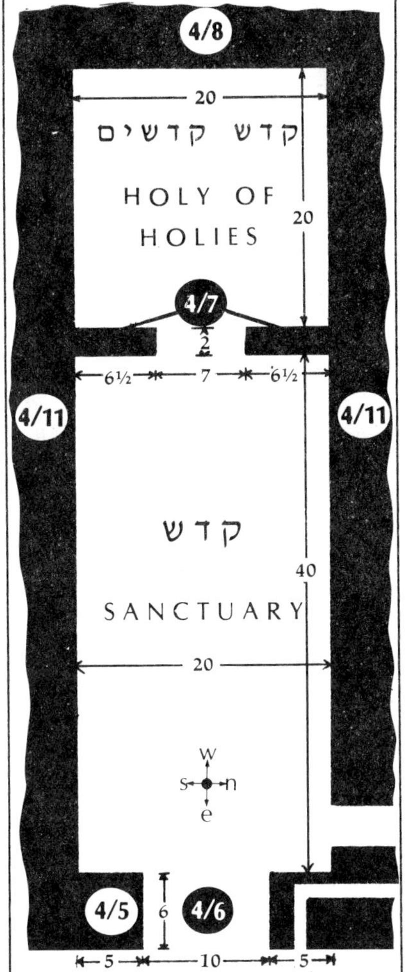

Combined inner dimensions: 62 cubits by 20 cubits.

4. אֶל פְּנֵי הַהֵיכָל – *Along the width of the Sanctuary.*

The width of the Holy of Holies was twenty cubits, identical with the width of the Sanctuary.

5-15 This passage deals with the cells, walls and passages which were attached to the Sanctuary at its western, northern, and southern sides.

There is no unanimity among the commentators concerning the exact arrangement of this part of the Sanctuary. The text is obscure and the printed version of *Rashi* extremely corrupt, with numerous ambiguities and inconsistencies. As a result, there is no way to determine exactly what *Rashi's* opinion was. [*HaMikdash HaShelishi* is an excellent compendium of the various possibilities of explaining *Rashi.*]

For the purpose of the *comm.* a choice had to be made. We decided upon the system illustrated in the Master Diagram for the following reasons: (1) It is the way that *Rashi's* student, *R' Shemaya,* interprets his master's opinion in his commentary to *Middos.* Since, according to *Rashi's* own testimony in his responsum to the *Rabbis of Auxerres (Appendix IX)* he discussed his commentary to Yechezkel's Temple with *R' Shemaya,* we can assume that the latter's interpretation is correct. (2) It is closest to the text of *Rashi's* commentary to *Ezekiel* as offered by *Abraham J. Levy* in his critical edition *Rashi's Commentary on Ezekiel 40-48;* (edited on the basis of eleven manuscripts), *Philadelphia* 1931. This volume, represents a fine attempt to present *Rashi* to these chapters in an unadulterated form and deserves consideration as, at the very least, a close approximation of *Rashi's* intent. [We offer the text of the relevant sections in Appendix VII. A

Fig. 15

Dimensions of the Temple Structure

Total Width: 70 cubits

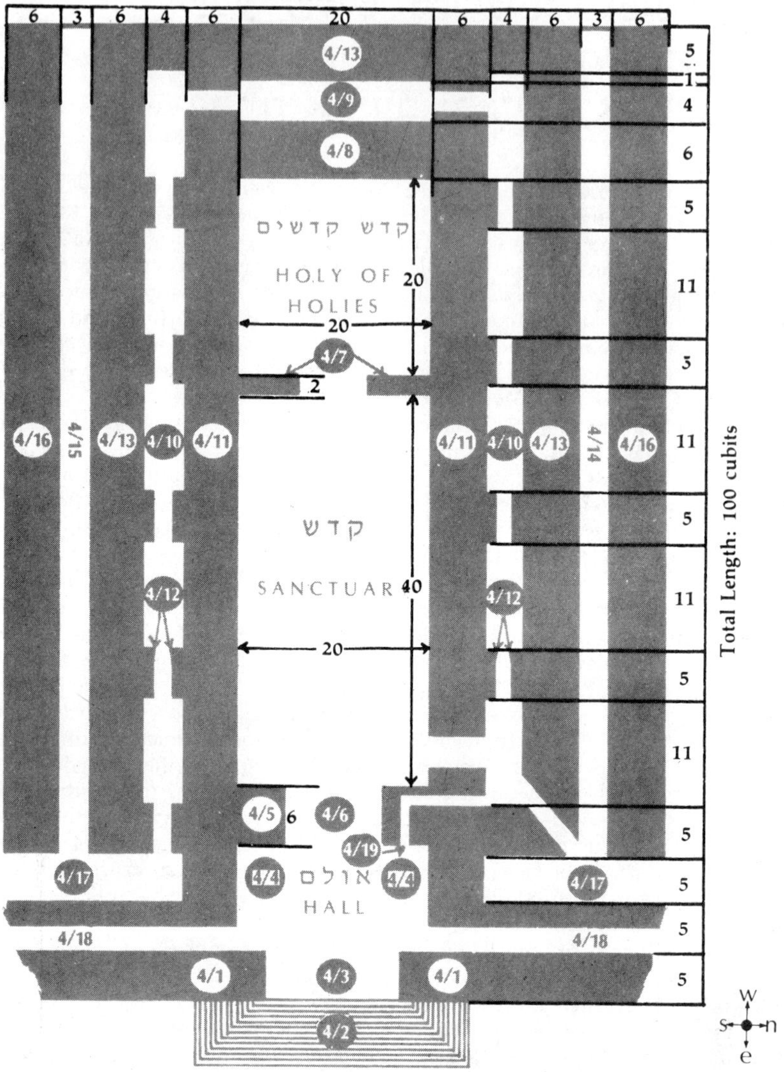

4/1 — Outer wall of the Temple structure on the eastern side; **4/2** — Steps leading from the inner courtyard to the Temple structure; **4/3** — Gateway to the hall; **4/4** — Pillars; **4/5** — Walls creating gateway from hall to Sanctuary; **4/6** — Gateway to Sanctuary; **4/7** — Walls between Sanctuary and Holy of Holies; **4/8** — Western inner wall of the Holy of Holies; **4/9** — Cell behind Holy of Holies; **4/10** — Cells along the northern and southern sides of the Temple; **4/11** — Northern and southern inner walls of the Temple; **4/12** — Walls between cells; **4/13** — Outer wall of the cell complex; **4/14** — Ramp leading upwards from east to west; **4/15** — Water drain from roof leading down from west to east; **4/16** — Outer walls of the Temple structure on the northern and southern sides; **4/17** — Open space; **4/18** — Knife depository; **4/19** — Northern wicket.

מא
אַמּוֹת וְרֹחַב הַצֵּלָע אַרְבַּע אַמּוֹת סָבִיב | ו
סָבִיב לַבַּיִת סָבִיב׃ וְהַצְּלָעוֹת צֵלָע אֶל־
צֵלָע שָׁלוֹשׁ וּשְׁלֹשִׁים פְּעָמִים וּבָאוֹת
בַּקִּיר אֲשֶׁר־לַבַּיִת לַצְּלָעוֹת סָבִיב | סָבִיב
לִהְיוֹת אֲחוּזִים וְלֹא־יִהְיוּ אֲחוּזִים בְּקִיר

cursory comparison with the printed text of *Rashi* will show the extent of the corruptions.] (3) It comes closest to the system used in the Second Temple. Although there are major differences in the two structures as we have seen, there are sufficient similarities to favor a system which is not radically different.

In spite of these reasons, we can by no means exclude the other possibilities. Grave difficulties remain according to the system which we have chosen, and an alternative diagram is presented in Appendix VIII.

Thirty-three cells (4/9 and 4/10) surrounded the building on three sides. (See Fig. 15.) Fifteen of them ran along both the northern and southern sides arranged in three levels of five cells (4/10) laying atop one another. Each cell of the lowest level was eleven cubits long (see *comm. v.* 9) and four cubits wide. The second level cells were each five cubits wide, the third level cells, were each six cubits wide (see Fig. 16). Their height, though not specified in the text, is assumed to be five cubits for each level (see *comm., v.* 8). The inner wall of these cells was the wall (4/11) of the Sanctuary and of the Holy of Holies; their outer wall (4/13) was five cubits thick, but rested on a base six cubits thick. (It is therefore counted as six cubits in the total measurements, see *comm., v.* 12). Each cell was separated from the next one in its row by a wall five cubits long (4/12), through which ran a narrow passageway.

The remaining three cells (4/9) were large ones, each twenty cubits long, running along the western wall of the Holy of Holies. These were also on three levels; that is, they lay one on top of the other. Their eastern wall was the western wall (4/8) of the Holy of Holies; their western wall (4/13) was six cubits thick, and they had walls at both ends which were six cubits wide. These walls served as passageways to the cells (4/10) along the northern and southern sides. The widths of these cells were graduated like those of the other two sides.

Beyond the outer walls of the cells (4/13) lay two ramps, one on the north and one on the south (4/14 and 4/15, respectively). These ramps started out on the eastern side and rose upwards towards the western wall. The one on the northern side (4/14) called מְסִיבָּה, *the winding passage*, was used for access to the higher levels of the building. The one on the southern side (4/15) was called בֵּית הוֹרָדַת הַמַּיִם, *the drainage ramp*, and allowed water to run off the Sanctuary roofs, which may have been slightly slanted in that direction. Each of these ramps was three cubits wide. On the outside of each ramp there was a wall five cubits thick on a six-cubit base. In the overall measurement of the Sanctuary's length this wall is counted as six cubits because of its base.

[The two ramps (4/14 and 4/15) and their outer walls (4/16) are not mentioned in the text. However verse 12 gives the width of the building (excluding the knife depository (4/18) which extended to a width of a hundred cubits; see figure 18 below) as seventy cubits. If we compute the width without the ramps, the result is far less than seventy (6+4+6+20+6+4+6=52). The difference is made up by two ramps (3+3=6) and two outer walls (6+6=12), which supply the missing eighteen cubits. The justification for assuming that these ramps (4/14 and

41
6

cubits. The width of the cell was four cubits all around the sides of the House. [6] *Now the cells, a cell next to a cell, thirty-three times and they rested upon the inner wall of the cells round about that they might be tight, yet not fastened to the wall of the*

4/15) and their outer walls (4/16) are to be part of the building is based on *Middos* 4:5, which reports such ramps in the Second Temple.

The assumption that such a major part of the structure finds no mention in the text poses a problem. The difference of opinion between the commentators comes to a head on this issue. We have chosen the opinion described here for the reasons given above. Other commentators arrive at the total of seventy cubits by assuming a passageway of five cubits width between the Sanctuary and the cells. This in turn necessitates the inclusion of another wall, five cubits wide, on the side of these cells. (See Appendix VIII.) The seventy cubits width for the building is computed on the assumption that five-cubit walls resting on a six-cubit base are counted as five cubits (as opposed to the system we use in which they are counted as six cubits). The computation would then be as follows: 5+4+5+5+6+20+6+5+5+4+5=70. The basis for this opinion is discussed in *comm., v.* 9.]

5. וַיָּמָד קִיר הַבַּיִת — *Then he measured the wall of the House.*

This is the western wall of the Holy of Holies (4/8).

וְרֹחַב הַצֵּלָע — *The width of the cell.*

This refers to the cell (4/9) behind the western wall, but the words סָבִיב סָבִיב, *all around,* indicate that the cells on the northern and southern sides (4/10) were also four cubits wide.

Bava Basra 61a points out that the words: יָצִיעַ *(I Kings* 6:5), צֵלָע (in our verse), and תָּא (40:7) all have the same meaning. They describe a small chamber next to a larger house.

The cells described here are two cubits narrower than those of the Second Temple which were six cubits wide (*Middos* 4:4). *Rashi* indicates that this was necessary to compensate for the extra thickness of the wall (4/7) between the Sanctuary and the Holy of Holies. In the Second Temple, this wall had a thickness of one cubit and this, together with the six cubits of the cell and the five of the outer wall (*Middos* 4:6), yielded twelve cubits of the total length. In Yechezkel's Temple, the separating wall (4/7) was two cubits and the outer wall (4/13) was six cubits. Thus the cell could be no wider than four cubits if the overall size of the building was to remain the same (2+4+6=12).

6. וְהַצְּלָעוֹת צֵלָע אֶל צֵלָע שָׁלוֹשׁ וּשְׁלֹשִׁים פְּעָמִים — *Now the cells, a cell next to a cell, thirty-three times.*

Altogether, there were three levels, each with eleven cells: five cells in the north, one in the west, and five in the south (5+1+5=11), for a total of thirty-three cells. (See *Rashi* ms., Appendix VII.)

וּבָאוֹת בַּקִּיר...לִהְיוֹת אֲחוּזִים ...וְלֹא יִהְיוּ אֲחוּזִים — *They rested upon the inner wall ... that they might be tight ... yet not fastened.*

From Figure 15 it can be seen that the inner wall (4/11) of the cells which were ranged from east to west on the northern and southern sides was at the same time the wall of the Sanctuary. We have already learned that there were three levels of cells, one above the other. The ceiling of the lowest was the floor of the middle one, and, in turn, its ceiling was the floor of the highest. Some accommodation had to be made for the beams which were needed for these floors. In order to avoid making holes in the Sanctuary wall (4/11), this wall was indented one cubit at each level so that the beams could rest on the wall without piercing it. (See Fig. 16.)

ז הַבָּיִת: וְרָחֲבָה וְנָסְבָה לְמַעְלָה לְמַעְלָה
לַצְּלָעוֹת כִּי מוּסַב־הַבַּיִת לְמַעְלָה
לְמַעְלָה סָבִיב | סָבִיב לַבַּיִת עַל־כֵּן רֹחַב־
לַבַּיִת לְמָעְלָה וְכֵן הַתַּחְתּוֹנָה יַעֲלֶה עַל־
ח הָעֶלְיוֹנָה לַתִּיכוֹנָה: וְרָאִיתִי לַבַּיִת גֹּבַהּ
סָבִיב | סָבִיב °מיסדות הַצְּלָעוֹת מְלוֹ °מוּסדות ק׳
ט הַקָּנֶה שֵׁשׁ אַמּוֹת אַצִּילָה: רֹחַב הַקִּיר
אֲשֶׁר־לַצֵּלָע אֶל־הַחוּץ חָמֵשׁ אַמּוֹת

This method of indentation was first used in Solomon's Temple (*I Kings* 6:6) and was also incorporated into the building of the Second Temple (*Middos* 4:3, 4; see also *Tosafos, Yoma* 52a).

Fig. 16

The Three Levels of the Cells

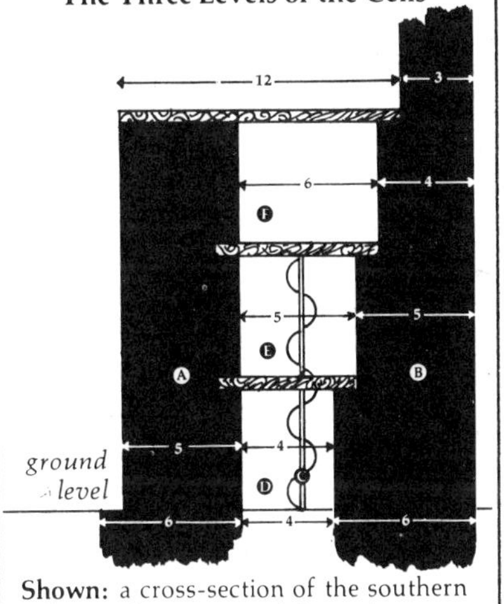

Shown: a cross-section of the southern cell complex as viewed from the east

A — Outer wall of cell (4/13 in main diagram).
B — Inner wall of cell (4/11 in main diagram).
C — Spiral staircase.
D — Bottom cell (4 cubits wide; 5 cubits high).
E — Middle cell (5 cubits wide; 5 cubits high).
F — Top cell (6 cubits wide; 5 cubits high).

The meaning of our verse is now clear: וּבָאוֹת בַּקִּיר means that the floor beams *rested on the* [*Sanctuary*] *wall.* לִהְיוֹת אֲחוּזִים, *that they might be tight,* explains that some accommodation for these beams was necessary to make sure that they were firmly anchored. וְלֹא יִהְיוּ אֲחוּזִים, *yet not fastened,* explains that the need for the indentation was to avoid piercing the wall.

[The need for this indentation seems to argue in favor of the system which we have chosen for the purpose of the *comm.*, against that illustrated in Appendix VIII. According to the latter system, the cells did not share a wall with the Sanctuary at all. Consequently there was no need to protect the inner wall of the cells any more than the outer wall. If we assume that in that system both walls were, in fact, indented a half-cubit each, then the system will be quite different from that in use in Solomon's Temple, but *Rashi* compares the two in his commentary. See further in *Levushei Srad* in *HaBayis HaShlishi;* a full discussion also appears in *Bais HaBechirah,* Moshe Weis, Jerusalem, 5706.]

7. וְרָחֲבָה — *And a widening.*

Rashi explains this word as an extension of the previous verse. Because the Sanctuary wall was indented to accommodate the beams, there was *a widening* in the size of the cells.

וְנָסְבָה לְמַעְלָה לְמַעְלָה לַצְּלָעוֹת — *And a winding passage went upwards to the cells.*

It would be attractive to assume the interpretation of *Metzudos,* that this phrase refers to the ramp (4/14) which

House, 7 and a widening. And a winding passage went upwards to the cells, for the encompassing of the House ascended upward all around the House. So the House's width was above. So, too, the lowest ascended to the highest one by way of the middle one. 8 And I saw the height of the House all around. The foundations of the cells were a full rod. Six cubits space. 9 The width of the wall toward the out-

led to the upper cells. This would avoid the problems raised in *pref.* 5-15, for if the ramp is meant then it is explicated in the text.

Rashi, however, does not agree with this interpretation. He clearly describes a *spiral staircase* which led from cell to cell within the cells. His reference to *I Kings* 6:8 leaves no doubt about this (see *Rashi* there).

כִּי מוּסַב הַבַּיִת... — *For the encompassing of the House* ...

This phrase explains the first word in the verse: וְרָחֲבָה, *Widening* [of the cells], took place, *because the encompassing of the House* — that is, its indentations led ever higher up the side of the house; עַל כֵּן רֹחַב לַבַּיִת לְמָעְלָה, *so the House's width was on top*, meaning that the widest part of the cell structure was the uppermost of the three levels (*Metzudos;* see Fig. 16).

וְכֵן הַתַּחְתּוֹנָה — *So, too, the lowest.*

This phrase explains the second word in the verse: וְנָסְבָה. There was a *winding passage* [a spiral staircase] and *thus* [by means of this spiral staircase] *the lower* [cell] *ascended to the highest* [cell] *by way of the middle* [cell].

8. וְרָאִיתִי לַבַּיִת גֹּבַהּ סָבִיב סָבִיב — *And I saw the height of the House all around.*

His contemplation of the cell complex led his gaze up the sides of the Sanctuary so that from the size of the cell complex he was able to estimate the height of the whole building *(R' Breuer).*

The text gives no measurements for either the height of the building as a whole or for the height of the cells.

For the height of the building we must turn to *Middos* 4:6, which gives one hundred cubits as the height of the Sanctuary in the Second Temple *(Rashi).*

For the cells we must go back to *I Kings* 6:10, where the height of each יָצִיעַ, *cell,* is given as five cubits. The assumption is that in the Second Temple and Yechezkel's Temple this measurement would have been preserved (see *HaMikdash HaShlishi).*

מוּסְדוֹת הַצְּלָעוֹת מְלוֹ הַקָּנֶה — *The foundations of the cells were a full rod.*

Verse 9 assigns a width of five cubits to the outer wall (4/13) of the cells. Our verse teaches that this wall stood on a six-cubit wide foundation (see 40:5 for the length of a rod). *Rashi* explains that this foundation wall was buried in the earth. [Nevertheless the extra cubit of the foundation must be counted into the overall dimension of the width of the Sanctuary if we are to obtain a total of seventy cubits. See *pref.* 5-15.]

שֵׁשׁ אַמּוֹת אַצִּילָה — *Six cubits space.*

אַצִּילָה is obscure. Our translation follows *Rashi* based on *Targum,* but it is unclear how the root אצל yields רֶוַח, *space.*

Ibn Janach interprets אצל: *to remove,* and therefore אַצִּיל יָד is *the armpit* (see 13:18), because it is a part of the body that is 'removed' from sight. אַצִּילָה becomes *a cubit,* that is, a measure taken from the fingertips till the armpit (see also *Radak).*

9. רֹחַב הַקִּיר — *The width of the wall.*

The outer wall of the cells (4/13). See *comm.* to previous verse.

מא
י־יא

י וַאֲשֶׁר מֻנָּח בֵּית צְלָעוֹת אֲשֶׁר לַבָּיִת: וּבֵין
הַלְּשָׁכוֹת רֹחַב עֶשְׂרִים אַמָּה סָבִיב לַבַּיִת
יא סָבִיב | סָבִיב: וּפֶתַח הַצֵּלָע לַמֻּנָּח פֶּתַח

וַאֲשֶׁר מֻנָּח בֵּית צְלָעוֹת אֲשֶׁר לַבָּיִת — *So also the open space of the cell complex which belonged to the House.*

We have followed *R' Breuer* in his translation of this difficult passage.

The מֻנָּח, *open space*, mentioned in this verse is the focus of much of the controversy which exists concerning the exact structure of the Sanctuary complex. In the Master Diagram the מֻנָּח (4/17) is a five cubit open space which lies between the end of the cells (4/10) and the knife depository (4/18). In the diagram pictured in Appendix VIII, the מֻנָּח is the open space which runs east to west along the whole length of the Sanctuary between the Sanctuary wall and the cells.

The printed *Rashi* brings this latter interpretation as a דָּבָר אַחֵר, *an alternative explanation*. However, this interpretation is missing entirely from *Rashi* ms. (see Appendix VII). There are many indications that *Rashi*, throughout his explanation of the Sanctuary, assumed the former interpretation exclusively. [Thus also *R' Shemaya* to *Middos*.]

The *comm.* is based on the former (and, in the manuscript, the only) interpretation.[1]

The open space mentioned in our verse lay between the ends of the cells and the knife depository (4/18). Its size is given as five cubits (*v.* 11).

Our knowledge that there was an open space [the purpose of which was to allow access to the cells; see *v.* 11] allows us to compute the size of the cells and their walls which are nowhere given in the text.

The knife depository (4/18), including both its eastern and western walls, had a ten-cubit width, leaving ninety cubits for the east-west dimension of the Sanctuary (see *vs.* 12, 13). As we have seen, there was then an open space of five cubits, leaving eighty-five cubits for five cells (4/10) and six walls (4/12). Thus, yielding eleven cubits for the width of the cells and five cubits for the walls [(5×11)+(6×5)=85]. According to the system pictured in Appendix VIII, which eliminates the open space along the eastern dimension, each cell must have been twelve cubits long [(5×12)+(6×5)=90].

10. וּבֵין הַלְּשָׁכוֹת — *Until* [lit. *between*] *the chambers.*

At the begining of ch. 42 we shall learn of the presence of two huge לְשָׁכוֹת, *chambers*, which lay to the north and south of the Sanctuary building (see Master Diagram). Our verse teaches that there was a distance of twenty cubits (5/4) between them and the outer wall (4/16) of the Sanctuary (see Fig. 23, p. 658).

11. וּפֶתַח הַצֵּלָע לַמֻּנָּח — *Now the gate of the cell opened upon the open space.*

The only access to the cells was through the first cell and from there to the other ones through the passageways leading from one to the other (see Figs. 15 and 17).

[*Middos* 4:3 discusses the number of passageways which led from the various cells of the Second Temple. Each of the inner cells had three passageways: one each to the cell on either side, and a trap

1. There is, however, a complicating factor. In the manuscript version there are two references to an open space at the *western* side of the Sanctuary. It is difficult to see how this can be a correct reading, and, from this point of view, the text of the printed *Rashi* — to the extent that it deals with the former interpretation — is to be preferred. [Some manuscripts, however, have alternative readings which eliminate reference to the western side.]

Thus, we base our commentary on the manuscripts which eliminate the second explanation of *Rashi*, while omitting the reference to the western wall.

side was five cubits. So also the open space of the cell complex which belonged to the House.
[10] *Until the chambers, there was a width of twenty cubits all around the House, round about the House.*
[11] *Now the gate of the cell opened upon the open*

door or skylight leading to the cell immediately above or below.

The eastern cell on the north side had five passageways. To understand their disposition some background is necessary.

According to *Middos* 4:2 the gate leading from the entrance hall into the Sanctuary had two wickets (פִּשְׁפָּשִׁים). *Aruch* defines a פִּשְׁפָּשׁ as a small gate within a larger gate. [The wicket here must have been *near* the gate rather than *within* it — see Fig. 17. This can be demonstrated from Rabbi Yehuda's opinion in the Mishnah in *Middos*.] One wicket to the north, the other to the south. The southern one was kept permanently locked (see 44:2). The northern one was used for access to the Sanctuary as follows:

When the main gates were to be opened in the morning, the person unlocking them would enter through the northern wicket and proceed to the easternmost cell of the northern group. From there he would enter the Sanctuary and unlock the large gates from the inside. (See note in Fig. 17).

Fig. 17

The Passageways of the Northeastern Cell

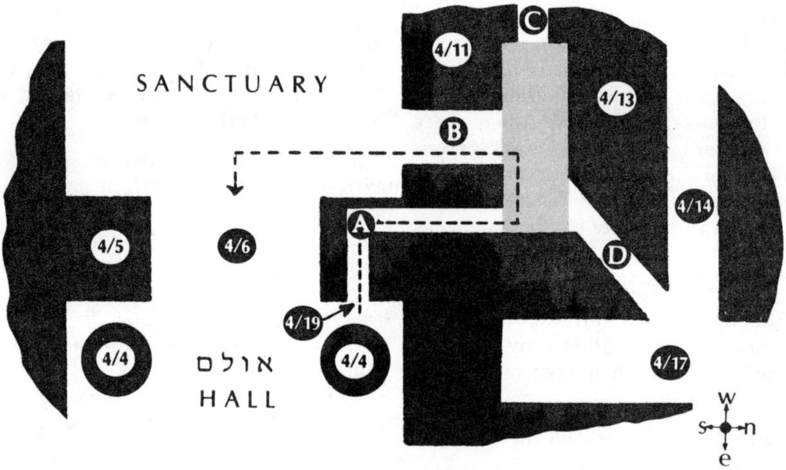

Shaded area indicates northeastern cell.

4/19 — פִּשְׁפָּשׁ, *wicket* (opening from hall into passageway to cell).
A — Passageway from wicket into cell.
B — Passageway from cell into Sanctuary.
C — Passageway from northeastern cell into the next cell on its western side.
D — Passageway from cell into both the open space (4/17) and the ramp (4/14).
Note: Broken line and arrow indicates path followed by the one opening the gates (4/6) each morning.

אֶחָד֙ דֶּ֣רֶךְ הַצָּפ֔וֹן וּפֶ֥תַח אֶחָ֖ד לַדָּר֑וֹם
וְרֹ֙חַב֙ מְק֣וֹם הַמֻּנָּ֔ח חָמֵ֥שׁ אַמּ֖וֹת סָבִ֥יב ׀
יב סָבִֽיב׃ וְהַבִּנְיָ֗ן אֲשֶׁר֙ אֶל־פְּנֵ֣י הַגִּזְרָ֔ה פְּאַ֣ת
דֶּֽרֶךְ־הַיָּם֮ רֹ֣חַב שִׁבְעִ֣ים אַמָּה֒ וְקִ֣יר הַבִּנְיָ֗ן
חָמֵשׁ־אַמּ֥וֹת רֹ֖חַב סָבִ֣יב ׀ סָבִ֑יב וְאָרְכּ֖וֹ
יג תִּשְׁעִ֥ים אַמָּֽה׃ וּמָדַ֥ד אֶת־הַבַּ֖יִת אֹ֣רֶךְ

Consequently there must have been some means of access from the wicket to the cell and from the cell to the Sanctuary. *R' Shemaya* to *Middos* describes the dispositions which can be seen in Fig. 17.

Now, the Mishnah assigns the following five passageways to the outer cell in the northeast: one each to the neighboring cell, the cell above it, the ramp 4:14, the wicket, and the Sanctuary.

There seems to be no provision for a passageway into the open space (4/17); this seems to contradict our verse, which assigns a passageway leading from the cell into the open space.

R' Shemaya's solution is to suggest that the passageway to the ramp (4/14) and the passageway to the open space (4/17) were really one passageway which cut diagonally across the northeastern corner of the cell. Thus, there were in fact only five passageways to the cell.]

פֶּתַח אֶחָד ... — *One gate ...*

The text points out that both the northern and the southern rows of cells opened up upon their respective open spaces.

וְרֹחַב מְקוֹם הַמֻּנָּח ... — *And the width of the open space ...*

We discussed the five cubit size of the open space in *comm.* to *v.* 9.

12. After having described the individual components of the Temple structure, we now turn to the cumulative dimensions. In this verse, the tall and imposing hundred-cubit high Sanctuary building (see *comm.* to *v.* 8) is contrasted with the much lower fifteen-cubit tall cell cluster at its base (see *comm.* to *v.* 8). The Temple itself is referred to by a new term גִּזְרָה, which *Rashi* explains as the 'main building.' We translate the word *fortress*, following *Targum* who renders בְּצוּרְתָּא, *fortified building. Metzudos* explains that in the idiom of Scripture, the concepts of height and fortification go together. Therefore the soaring Sanctuary is called *fortress* in contrast to the low (15 cubit height — see *comm., v.* 8) cell cluster around its base. The cell complex is referred to as בִּנְיָן which we translate conventionally as *structure*. See Fig. 15.

[The term *'fortress'* for the Sanctuary may be understood in the extended, figurative sense of the word. Thus, the Temple served as the protector of Israel's spiritual greatness.]

פְּאַת דֶּרֶךְ הַיָּם רֹחַב שִׁבְעִים אַמָּה — *On the extremity to the west, a width of seventy cubits.*

The computation in the printed *Rashi* text does not appear in any of the eleven manuscripts. It is based on that system which we picture in Appendix VIII. In the *comm.* system, the computation is as follows:

The two outer walls (4/16) are each six cubits (measured at the foundation — see above); the two ramps (4/14) and 4/15) are each three cubits, the outer walls (4/13) of the cells (at the foundation) are each six cubits, the cells (4/10) are four each; the walls of the Sanctuary (4/11) are six each; and the Sanctuary and Holy of Holies are twenty. Thus: 6+3+6+4+6+20+6+4+6+3+6=70. (See Fig. 15.)

This measurement is given for the western extremity, because in the east

space; one gate to the north and one gate to the
south, and the width of the open space was five
cubits all around. 12 *The structure which ran along*
the fortress on the extremity to the west, a width of
seventy cubits. And the wall of the structure had a
five-cubit width all around. And its length was
ninety cubits. 13 *Now he measured the House, a*

the knife depository and its walls extended the width of the building to a hundred cubits (see below *v.* 14).

וְקִיר הַבִּנְיָן חָמֵשׁ אַמּוֹת רֹחַב — *And the wall of the structure had a five-cubit width.*

Rashi comments that this refers to the walls between the cells (4/12). However, this dimension was already given in verse 9. It is easier to understand this phrase if it refers to the outer walls (4/13) whose dimensions have not yet been given (thus, *Metzudos).* [It is important to give this dimension here because, as we pointed out in the first part of this verse, it was necessary to assign a width of six cubits to those two walls in order to reach the sum of seventy cubits. This was done by measuring the foundation wall at six cubits. For this reason the verse stresses that above ground the wall was five cubits.]

וְאָרְכּוֹ תִּשְׁעִים אַמָּה — *And its length was ninety cubits.*

The ninety cubits are measured from the exterior of the westernmost wall until the knife depository (4/18). Although the depository has the sacred status of the Sanctuary, it is excluded from this measurement because it protruded from the rectangular shape of the Sanctuary northward and southward, fifteen cubits in each direction. Therefore, the knife depository can be regarded as a separate structure. However, in the next verse, the ten-cubit width of the depository *is* included in computing the hundred-cubit total length of the Sanctuary. (See Fig. 18).

We compute as follows (see Fig. 15 above): The outer wall in the west (4/13) was six cubits; the westernmost cell (4/9) four; the wall of the Holy of Holies (4/8), six; the Holy of Holies, twenty; the dividing wall (4/7), two; the Sanctuary, forty; its outside wall (4/5), six, and the entrance hall, eleven. But of these last eleven cubits, five are part of the knife depository (4/18) and are therefore not included in the ninety cubits. We subtract these five and are left with a remainder of six for the entrance hall. Thus: 6+4+6+20+2+40+6+11-5=90.

We can also compute the total by measuring the northern and southern cells: There were five cells of eleven

Fig. 18
Overall Dimensions of the Temple Structure

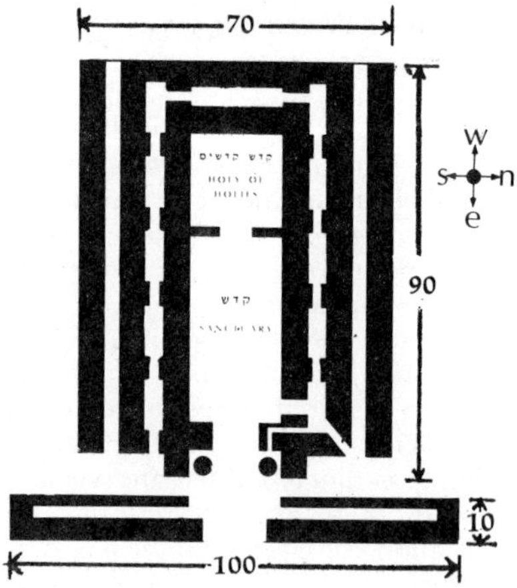

Shown: The main structure and knife depository as separate units.

מֵאָה אַמָּה וְהַגִּזְרָה וְהַבִּנְיָה וְקִירוֹתֶיהָ
יד אֹרֶךְ מֵאָה אַמָּה׃ וְרֹחַב פְּנֵי הַבַּיִת
טו וְהַגִּזְרָה לַקָּדִים מֵאָה אַמָּה׃ וּמָדַד אֹרֶךְ־
הַבִּנְיָן אֶל־פְּנֵי הַגִּזְרָה אֲשֶׁר עַל־אַחֲרֶיהָ
°ואתוקידהא מִפּוֹ וּמִפּוֹ מֵאָה אַמָּה °וְאַתִּיקֶיהָ ק׳
טז וְהַהֵיכָל הַפְּנִימִי וְאֻלַמֵּי הֶחָצֵר׃ הַסִּפִּים
וְהַחַלּוֹנִים הָאֲטֻמוֹת וְהָאַתִּיקִים | סָבִיב

cubits each and six walls of five cubits each for a combined total of eight-five. The מְנַח, *open space* was five, for a total of ninety.

13. This verse gives the total length from east to west, including the knife depository and its walls (4/18), as one-hundred cubits. The ten cubits of the knife depository are made up of five cubits for its eastern wall (4/1) and five for the combined passage and western wall of the depository (4/18).

... וְהַגִּזְרָה — *And the fortress...*

The second part of the verse is an explanation of the first half. The one hundred cubits are made up of the main building, cell structure, and wall.

[It should be noted that the knife depository is never mentioned by name in the text. We know of its existence and general structure only from *Middos* 4:7.

In the *pref.* 5-15 we noted the difficulty of assuming the existence of ramps which are never actually mentioned in the text. This problem seems just as perplexing in connection with the knife depository.

However, in the case of the knife depository there are hints in the text that such a structure must have existed. Thus, verse 12 gives the length of the building as ninety cubits, and verse 13 gives it as a hundred cubits. The implication is clear that a ten cubit structure which was not an actual part of the Sanctuary must have existed. See further אַתִּיקֶיהָ in verse 15.]

14. וְרֹחַב פְּנֵי הַבַּיִת וְהַגִּזְרָה — *And the width of the front of the structure and the fortress.*

Verse 12 gave the width of the building at its western extremity as only seventy cubits. Now the measurement is made in the east. Here the width is a full hundred cubits, because the knife depository extended fifteen cubits in each direction, adding thirty cubits to the seventy of the rest of the building. Thus Yechezkel's Temple was like the Second Temple which *Middos* 4:7 compares to a crouching lion — narrow in the back, broader in the front.

Our verse uses *structure* for the two extensions and *fortress* for the hall which was part of the main building. The hall together with the extensions measured one hundred cubits *(Metzudos).*

15. The dimension of one hundred cubits mentioned in this verse is the length of the building from east to west. This dimension was already given in verse 13. However, it is repeated here because the measurement in verse 13 was taken along the northern side, while this one was taken along the southern side *(Metzudos).*

[Verse 12 described the measurement of the western extremity. This measurement was taken, so to speak, by walking along the western wall from south to north. Verse 13 then gave the length of the building, which was measured by walking from west to east along the northern wall. He then turned right and

length of one hundred cubits. And the fortress, and the structure and its walls, a length of one hundred cubits. 14 *And the width of the front of the structure and the fortress to the east, one hundred cubits.* 15 *He*
measured the length of the structure, toward the front of the fortress, which was on his way back and [the width of] its corners from this side and from that, one hundred cubits. Now the Sanctuary, the inner [chamber], and the entrance hall from the courtyard — 16 *all three of them had the doorposts, closed*
windows, and pillars all around.

walked along the eastern wall from north to south to take that measure (*v.* 14) and now makes a final right turn to measure the east-west dimension along the southern side. This is the meaning of the words אֲשֶׁר עַל אַחֲרֶיהָ, *which was on his way back.* He retraced, along the southern side, the path which he had previously followed on the northern side *(Metzudos).*]

The verse states that the measurement included: בִּנְיָן, *structure,* which, as we have seen, refers to the cells, and אַתִּיקֶיהָ, which *Targum* renders as זִיוְיָתָהָא, meaning *corners.* [*Ibn Janach* derives the word from the root נתק, *to be pulled aside*]. This, according to *Rashi,* refers to the knife depository, the width of which was included in the 100 cubits. וּמָדַד ... (ו)אַתִּיקֶיהָא מִפּוֹ וּמִפּוֹ should be translated: *And he measured ... the* [*width of the*] *corner section which* [*on the eastern side, extended*] *in both directions.*

וְהַהֵיכָל הַפְּנִימִי — *Now the Sanctuary (and) the inner* [*chamber*].

This phrase is to be taken together with the next verse *(Rashi).* All the places mentioned in this verse shared the three features — *doorposts, covered windows* and *pillars* — which are mentioned in the next. The next verse talks of שְׁלָשְׁתָּם, *all three* [*places*], so our verse must refer to three places. This forces us to interpret וְהַהֵיכָל הַפְּנִימִי as though it were written וְהַהֵיכָל [וְ]הַפְּנִימִי, *the Sanctuary* [*and*] *the inner* [*chamber*] *(Rashi).*

The translation reflects *Rashi's* interpretation. (See Appendix for the accurate version of this *Rashi.* The printed version is inaccurate at this point).

וְאֻלַמֵּי הֶחָצֵר — *And the entrance hall from the courtyard.*

These are the halls which were contained within the thickness of the walls (2:6) of the inner courtyard [(40:30)] *(Rashi).* [See *Metzudos.*]

16-20 This passage describes the cedar paneling which covered the inside of the stone walls throughout the building. It was necessary to have such paneling because the inside walls are to be covered with gold plating which require a wooden base, since gold does not adhere well to stone.

As noted above, verse 16 starts with a list of three features common to all three locations — Sanctuary, Holy of Holies and courtyard halls — mentioned in the previous verse.

16. הַסִּפִּים — *Doorposts.*

סַף is used throughout these chapters for *doorpost.*

וְהַחַלּוֹנִים הָאֲטֻמוֹת — [*And the*] *closed windows.*

Rashi explains that even the windows were covered with wood paneling on the inside of the building — thus they were

לִשְׁלָשְׁתָּם נֶגֶד הַסַּף שְׂחִיף עֵץ סָבִיב |
סָבִיב וְהָאָרֶץ עַד־הַחַלֹּנוֹת וְהַחַלֹּנוֹת
יז מְכֻסּוֹת׃ עַל־מֵעַל הַפֶּתַח וְעַד־הַבַּיִת
הַפְּנִימִי וְלַחוּץ וְאֶל־כָּל־הַקִּיר סָבִיב |
יח סָבִיב בַּפְּנִימִי וּבַחִיצוֹן מִדּוֹת׃ וְעָשׂוּי
כְּרוּבִים וְתִמֹרִים וְתִמֹרָה בֵּין־כְּרוּב
יט לִכְרוּב וּשְׁנַיִם פָּנִים לַכְּרוּב׃ וּפְנֵי אָדָם
אֶל־הַתִּמֹרָה מִפּוֹ וּפְנֵי־כְפִיר אֶל־
הַתִּמֹרָה מִפּוֹ עָשׂוּי אֶל־כָּל־הַבַּיִת סָבִיב |
כ סָבִיב׃ מֵהָאָרֶץ עַד־מֵעַל הַפֶּתַח
הַכְּרוּבִים וְהַתִּמֹרִים עֲשׂוּיִם וְקִיר
כא הַהֵיכָל׃ הַהֵיכָל מְזוּזַת רְבֻעָה וּפְנֵי הַקֹּדֶשׁ

'closed.' It is difficult to understand the point of having 'windows' which were entirely covered. *Metzudos* explains that they were 'closed' by some transparent, clear material (glass?), that is, they were not just open holes.

וְהָאַתִּיקִים — *And [the] pillars.*

Rashi (to *v.* 15) confesses ignorance of the exact meaning of אַתִּיקִים in our context but surmises that they were *square wooden blocks* which projected from the walls and were needed to reinforce the structure.

Metzudos defines them as cone-like pillars near the walls.

נֶגֶד הַסַּף שְׂחִיף עֵץ סָבִיב סָבִיב — *By the doorpost there was wood paneling all around.*

Here the verse begins to describe the places which were covered by the wood paneling. All the doorposts were covered *around* the whole door.

וְהָאָרֶץ עַד הַחַלּוֹנוֹת — *From the ground to the windows.*

All this expanse was covered by the paneling.

וְהַחַלּוֹנוֹת מְכֻסּוֹת — *Even the windows were covered.*

We follow *Rashi,* who learns that the wood paneling covered the windows from the inside. According to *Metzudos,* the windows were covered with transparent material.

17. The description of the areas covered by the paneling continues. It reached above the doorways; it was used in the בַּיִת הַפְּנִימִי, *the Inner House;* the Holy of Holies, and חוּץ, *outside* in the Sanctuary. All around, both in the Holy of Holies and in the Sanctuary, they used the same paneling, which is described as מִדּוֹת, *of uniform size.*

18. וְעָשׂוּי — *And they were decorated.*

The wood paneling had figures on it in relief in such a way that when the gold panels were hammered over the wood paneling, these figures stood out in gold *(Metzudos).*

The figures were cheruvim — human bodies with two heads: one *of* a man and one of a lion (*v.* 19) — and palm trees. These alternated with one another in such a way that there was always one palm tree between two cheruvim.

19. Since the cherubs had a man's head and a lion's head, each palm tree throughout the House had a human head facing it on one side and lion's head on the other.

By the doorpost there was wood paneling all around from the ground to the windows — even the windows were covered.
17 *Until above the gates, until the inner chamber and outward, and upon the entire wall all around, inside and outside was of uniform size.*
18 *And they were decorated with cheruvim and palm trees — one palm tree between two cheruvim. Each cheruv had two faces.*
19 *A human's visage faced the palm tree from one side and a lion's visage faced the palm tree from the other side. So it was for the entire House all around.*
20 *From the ground until above the door were the cheruvim and palm trees carved. Thus was the wall of the Sanctuary.*
21 *The Sanctuary had a square doorpost and from the Holy [of Holies] — an appearance like the appearance ...!*

20. These figures covered the whole height of the wall, including the space above the doors. This was also true in the Sanctuary.

Radak is puzzled as to why the Sanctuary should be singled out for special mention. Surely we must assume that it was included in כָל הַבַּיִת, *the entire House* of the previous verse. A solution based on *Middos* 4:1 suggests itself. There we learn that the inner set of doors leading into the Sanctuary opened *into* the Sanctuary and were folded back to lie against the inner wall thus covering it completely (see Fig. 19). Since the five cubits on either side of the gateway were never visible, there was no need to cover them with gold.(See below, *v.* 24, for a description of these doors.) The Mishnah mentions only that there was no gold on these two parts of the wall. No mention is made of the wood paneling. Two possibilities must be considered: Either paneling was applied even where there was to be no gold, and this is the lesson of our verse; or no paneling was affixed to those parts, in which case we must be told that the *rest* of the Sanctuary walls must have the paneling and figures.

[There are dots on the word הַהֵיכָל, *the Sanctuary.* Such symbols usually have a limiting function — see *Deuteronomy* 29:28. Perhaps they indicate the latter of the above possibilities: part of the Sanctuary wall, but not all of it, was paneled.

However, this solution will not hold good according to R' Yehudah in *Middos.* He learns that the doors opened into the thickness of the gateway (Fig. 20), and consequently the whole inner wall was visible and, hence, covered with gold.]

21. הַהֵיכָל מְזוּזַת רְבֻעָה — *The Sanctuary had a square doorpost.*

This verse seems to stand alone, unconnected to the previous section. According to *Rashi* it teaches that the doorposts supporting the doors of the Sanctuary were square rather than round. מְזוּזַת [usually rendered in the construct form, *doorpost 'of'*] is rendered as though it were written מְזוּזָה, *doorpost.* It is not uncommon for a ת to replace a ה *(Radak).*

כב הַמַּרְאֶה כַּמַּרְאֶה: הַמִּזְבֵּחַ עֵץ שָׁלוֹשׁ
אַמּוֹת גָּבֹהַּ וְאָרְכּוֹ שְׁתַּיִם־אַמּוֹת
וּמִקְצֹעוֹתָיו לוֹ וְאָרְכּוֹ וְקִירֹתָיו עֵץ וַיְדַבֵּר
כג אֵלַי זֶה הַשֻּׁלְחָן אֲשֶׁר לִפְנֵי יהוה: וּשְׁתַּיִם

Rashi and *Metzudos*, however, seem to read מְזוּזוֹת, in the plural.

וּפְנֵי הַקֹּדֶשׁ הַמַּרְאֶה כַּמַּרְאֶה — *And from the Holy [of Holies] — an appearance like the appearance ...!*

The prophet catches a glimpse of a shine of Glory emanating from the Holy of Holies (*Rashi* based on *Targum).* Perhaps this first inkling of the return of the Divine Glory takes him by surprise. This would explain the strange formulation. It is as though the prophet asks himself whether this is indeed the Divine Presence Whose departure he had witnessed in the early days of his prophecy. Filled with yearning to know it to be true, yet not daring to confirm it to himself, he leaves the sentence dangling in the middle *(R' Breuer).*

22. הַמִּזְבֵּחַ — *The altar.*

The following problems require solutions if we are to understand this verse correctly:

1) At the end of the verse the prophet is told: *'This is the table* (הַשֻּׁלְחָן) *before HASHEM.'* Why is the altar described as a table?

2) No other object in the Sanctuary is shown to the prophet. He sees neither the מְנוֹרָה, *candelabrum,* nor the שֻׁלְחָן, *table for the showbread,* nor, in the Holy of Holies, is he shown the אָרוֹן, *ark.* Why is he shown this altar?

3) Why should the description of the altar interrupt the account of the decorative paneling which, after this verse, continues until the end of this chapter?

4) We know of two altars which served in the Tabernacle and, later, in the two Temples: The large outer altar (מִזְבַּח הָעוֹלָה) which stood in the courtyard and was used for most sacrifices, and the smaller golden altar (מִזְבַּח הַזָּהָב) which stood in the Sanctuary and was used mainly for the daily קְטוֹרֶת, *incense offering.* Of the two, the outer altar cannot be meant here since that is described later (43:13 ff.). Nor can the golden altar be meant, since the dimensions in our verse are different from those given in the Torah (*Exodus* 30:1 ff.) for that golden altar. Also, it is described as a block of wood with no reference to the golden covering.

(1) The first question is raised in the Talmud (*Berachos* 55a): The verse begins with *altar* and ends with *table* to teach you that as long as the Temple stood, the altar atoned for Israel, but now a person's table atones for him [because it gives him the opportunity to practice charity by sharing his food. See *Berachos* 55a]

Does this mean that the word מִזְבֵּחַ in our verse is to be translated as *table?* We think not. It seems likely that the Sages simply found a support for their homily in the unexpected change of expression from altar to table. In the first place, there is no real problem in describing the altar as a *table,* since we see in *Malachi* 1:12 that this is correct prophetic idiom. (See further in *Radak* and *Metzudos* 44:16.) Second, there seems little logic in Scripture teaching us the atoning qualities of charity in the middle of a description of the Third Temple. It seems much more likely that we are dealing with a דְּרָשָׁה, *homiletic device,* grounded in an irregularity of expression rather than in the actual meaning of the verse. (See remarks on a similar problem in Appendix VI.) Nevertheless, *Targum* (quoted by *Rashi*) renders: *table,* and this seems also to be the assumption of the *Talmud* in *Menachos* (96b, 97a).

However, translating *table* does not help in answering the other questions and many commentators do in fact

22 *The altar — a wooden block three cubits high, its length was two cubits and its ends were part of it. Its surface and its walls were of wood. And he spoke to me: 'This is the table before HASHEM.'* 23 *Now there*

translate מִזְבֵּחַ as *altar* (see *Ramban, Toras HaShem Temimah; Tosafos, Menachos* 97a.)

(2) The Torah itself treats the golden altar differently than the other holy vessels. The Tabernacle, with all its components and vessels, is described in *Terumah;* not so the golden altar, which is dealt with separately at the end of *Tetzaveh.* This is so because it had a unique function. While the Temple service as a whole had the purpose of bringing the Divine Presence down to dwell among Man, the incense burnt at the inner altar was brought to pay homage to the Divine Presence after it had come to rest in the Temple (*Sforno* to *Exodus* 30:1; see also *Ramban* there). The Torah discusses it only after 28:45, in which the Divine Presence is already assumed. Thus, Yechezkel isolates this altar from all the other vessels, which he had not described, in reflection of a truth already taught in the Torah.

(3) The answer to the third question follows from the answer to the second. Yechezkel had suddenly become aware of a Divine light emanating from the Holy of Holies (*v.* 21). In the overwhelming rapture of that moment, his mind was torn away from the detailed description of the Temple structure and he was filled with a burning desire to pay homage to the *Shechinah,* which had finally returned to its rightful abode. In recognition of this ecstasy, God showed him the inner altar. This is to be the *table before HASHEM.* The incense burnt on this altar is to be the expression of Man's adoration.

(4) We should not be surprised that the dimensions of this altar are different from those enumerated in *Exodus.* We have already noticed many changes in the Third Temple and we can assume that the larger size of the golden altar is part of the general enlarging of the Temple structure.

Again, we should not be surprised that no mention is made of the golden covering. The altar in our verse is not treated differently from the rest of the Sanctuary. All the inner surface of the Sanctuary was, as we have learned, to be covered with a gold plating but no mention is made of this in the text. We must assume that God's purpose was to show Yechezkel the underlying structure of the Temple rather than the finished, shining edifice. (See *Malbim).*

From the fact that the altar is referred to as *wood,* the Sages in *Menachos* (96b, 97a) derive a *halachah* concerning the laws of ritual purity and impurity: Since there is a rule that, concerning these laws, the status of an object is determined by the material from which it is made, our verse indicates that the status is dependent on an object's substance, not its plating. Therefore, the gold-plated altar is treated as if it were all wood.

וּמִקְצוֹעֹתָיו לוֹ — *And its ends were part of it.*

Rashi, who follows *Targum* in interpreting the מִזְבֵּחַ as *table,* explains that מִקְצוֹעֹתָיו means the *legs of the table. Metzudos* explains that the legs of the table were carved from the same block as the rest of the table. They were not made separately and then connected. אָרְכּוֹ, which literally means *its length,* is the *surface of the table* and קִרֹתָיו, *its walls,* are the מִסְגֶּרֶת, *rim,* which according to *Exodus* 25:5, surrounded the table.

If the altar is meant we must follow *Malbim* in interpreting מִקְצוֹעֹתָיו as the *horns* [protrusions at the upper corners] of the altar, אָרְכּוֹ as *the upper surface,* and קִירֹתָיו, as its *walls.* Both *horns* and *walls* are mentioned in *Exodus* 30:2, 3.

כד דְּלָתוֹת לַהֵיכָל וְלַקֹּדֶשׁ: וּשְׁתַּיִם דְּלָתוֹת
לַדְּלָתוֹת שְׁתַּיִם מוּסַבּוֹת דְּלָתוֹת שְׁתַּיִם
לְדֶלֶת אֶחָת וּשְׁתֵּי דְלָתוֹת לָאַחֶרֶת:
כה וַעֲשׂוּיָה אֲלֵיהֶן אֶל־דַּלְתוֹת הַהֵיכָל
כְּרוּבִים וְתִמֹרִים כַּאֲשֶׁר עֲשׂוּיִם לַקִּירוֹת
וְעָב עֵץ אֶל־פְּנֵי הָאוּלָם מֵהַחוּץ:

23-24. These two verses describe the doors of the gateway which led into the Sanctuary (see Fig. 19).

The thickness of the wall (4/5) was six cubits. There were two sets of doors within this thickness. The eastern set was fixed near the front, one cubit westward; the other, at the very back. The gateway (4/6) was ten cubits wide, so each door in the two sets was five cubits. As they swung open, the doors near the front opened 90° inwards and covered the inner five cubits of the thickness of the wall; the back door swung 180° into the Sanctuary and covered the five cubits on either side of the gate. These ten cubits of the wall required no gold plating, for they were not visible when the doors were opened against them. (See *comm., v.* 20.)

This is the first opinion in *Middos* 4:1. However, R' Yehudah maintains that both sets of doors opened into the thickness of the gateway. Each door was hinged at its center in such a way that it folded in half as it was opened. Each door was hinged to the wall one half cubit from the outer edge. Thus when all the doors were opened the inner five cubits of the gateway were covered.

23. וּשְׁתַּיִם דְּלָתוֹת לַהֵיכָל וְלַקֹּדֶשׁ — *Now*

Fig. 19

The Two Sets of Doors Between the Sanctuary and the Hall

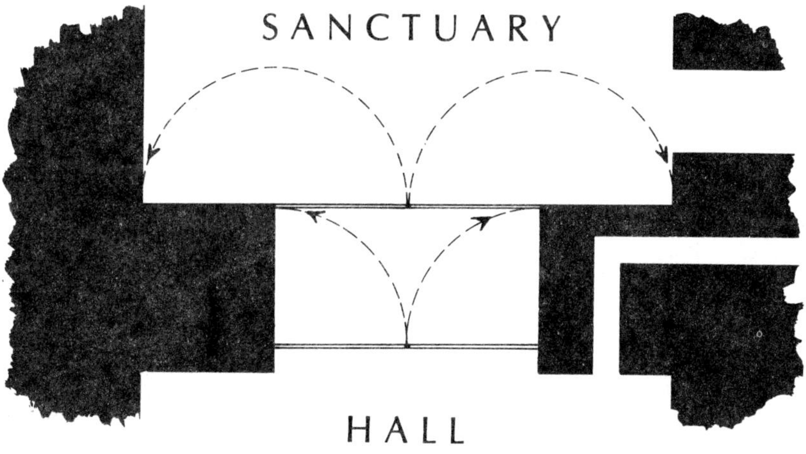

Both sets of doors open westward. The outer (eastern) doors open to 90° and cover the walls on the right and left sides of the gateway. The inner (western) doors open to 180° and cover the eastern wall of the Sanctuary on either side of the gate.

were two [sets of] doors to the Sanctuary and the
Holy [of Holies]. 24 *Two doors for each set of doors;*
two swinging doors. Two for the one set of doors and
two doors for the other. 25 *Now upon them — upon*
the doors of the the Sanctuary — cheruv and palm
trees were carved just as they were carved on the
walls. And wooden beams led to the front of the

there were two [sets of] doors [leading] to the Sanctuary and the Holy of Holies.

Rashi explains that this sentence refers to the northern and southern doors of each of the two sets of doors. He does not make clear how he translates the next verse.

It is easier to account for all the words in the two verses if we take this earlier one to refer to the sets rather than the individual doors: *There were two [sets of] doors.* The individual (northern and southern) doors are described in the next verse (*Metzudos*).

24. וּשְׁתַּיִם דְּלָתוֹת לַדְּלָתוֹת — *Two doors for each set of doors.*

See *comm.* to previous verse.

שְׁתַּיִם מוּסַבּוֹת דְּלָתוֹת — *Two swinging doors.*

This would be the correct translation according to the first opinion in *Middos* 4:1 (see above). R' Yehudah would translate: *two hinged doors.*

25. The doors leading to the Sanctuary were paneled and decorated in precisely the same way as the inner walls were.

וְעָב עֵץ אֶל פְּנֵי הָאוּלָם מֵהַחוּץ — *And wooden beams led to the front of the entrance hall from the outside.*

The enormous height of the buildings (see *comm., v.* 8) made it necessary to

Fig. 20

The Doors to the Sanctuary According to R' Yehudah

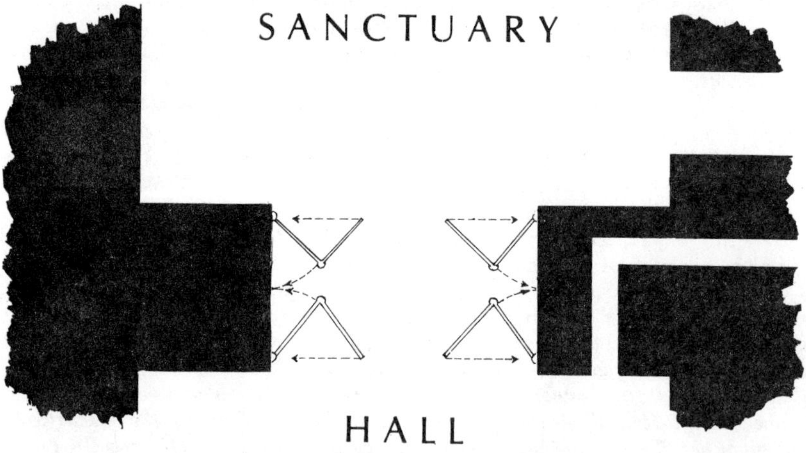

Each set of doors actually consists of 4 doors (each door 2½ cubits wide. 4×2½=10 — the width of the gateway.) The doors attached to the wall had hinges on both sides (one set of hinges attached to the wall and another set to a second door). Each set of doors open towards the gateway walls.

מא כו וְחַלּוֹנִים אֲטֻמוֹת וְתִמֹרִים מִפֹּו וּמִפּוֹ אֶל־ כו
כִּתְפוֹת הָאוּלָם וְצַלְעוֹת הַבַּיִת וְהָעֻבִּים׃
מב א וַיּוֹצִיאֵנִי אֶל־הֶחָצֵר הַחִיצוֹנָה הַדֶּרֶךְ
א דֶּרֶךְ הַצָּפוֹן וַיְבִאֵנִי אֶל־הַלִּשְׁכָּה אֲשֶׁר

have reinforcing beams running from the walls of the entrance hall *(Rashi).*

26. כִּתְפוֹת הָאוּלָם — *On the shoulders of the entrance hall.*

These are the walls on either side of the gate leading into the entrance hall [that is, the three cubit extension of the outer wall (4/1) which extended inward beyond the end of the knife depository (4/18); see *comm.* on 40:48]. These also had closed windows (see *comm.* 16-20) and palm decorations.

וְצַלְעוֹת הַבַּיִת וְהָעֻבִּים — *And the casings of the House and the beams.*

The translation follows *Bava Kama* 67a. צַלְעוֹת are wooden frames which surround windows and doors and act as *casings* for the עֻבִּים, *beams,* which are to rest there.

XLII

◆§ Prefatory Remarks to Verses 1-12

*These verses describe the location and the dimensions of four huge chambers (*לְשָׁכוֹת*) within the outer courtyard.*

[For this section we cannot adhere to the principle which has guided us throughout the commentary to Yechezkel's Temple, which has been to follow Rashi's *opinion consistently, for* Rashi *confesses that he is unable to unravel some of the complexities of the verses concerning these chambers, exclaiming in verse 6 [in the printed* Rashi *this appears at end of v. 3]: 'As for me, I had neither teacher nor helper for [the understanding of] this building; only what I was shown by Heaven.' (See* Rashi *to vs. 3 and 5 and see* Radak *to v. 5: '...this section must wait for elucidation by Elijah the prophet'), Since much of this section is intimately connected with three verses concerning which* Rashi *offers no explanation, we will, for this section, follow* Metzudos, *who offers a cohesive and readily understandable commentary to all twelve verses. His explanations concerning the two western chambers are identical with those of* Rashi *(except as they pertain to the three verses which* Rashi *does not explain), but his description of the two eastern chambers must be considered entirely his own since according to* Rashi *(v. 9) there may have been no such chambers in the east, and whatever explanation* Rashi *does offer for verses 9-12 seems to be quite incompatible with that of* Metzudos.

Verses 1-8 deal with the chamber which lay directly north of the Temple building, and make no mention of such a chamber on its southern side. However, as Rashi *points out in verse 12, there is a clear indication from the expression* סָבִיב לַבַּיִת סָבִיב סָבִיב, all around the House, *(41:10) that there was another chamber to the south (Fig. 21), and we assume that its dimensions and its location relative to the Temple were identical with the northern one.*

Earlier, in 41:10, we were taught that there was a space of twenty cubits (5/4) between the outer wall (4/16) of the Temple building and the southern wall (5/1) of this chamber. This information is augmented by verse 2, which gives the distance from the northern wall of the outer courtyard (1/1) to the northwest chamber as fifty cubits (5/5), and by verse 7, which gives the width of the chamber (from north to south) as fifty cubits. With these three measurements we are able to locate the chamber exactly along the north-south line. As yet we know nothing concerning its location along the east-west line.

41 *entrance hall from the outside.* [26] *And there were*
26 *closed windows and palm trees from this side and*
that on the shoulders of the entrance hall, and the
casings of the House and the beams.

42 *Then he brought me to the outer courtyard — the*
1 *path was the northern way — and he brought me*

Verse 2 teaches that the length of the chamber (from east to west) was one hundred cubits, but this is still not enough information to locate it exactly. Verse 8 fixes the location with complete accuracy.

To understand v. 8, *we work out the measurements. The total width of the entire Temple complex was 312 cubits (40:19), and the width of the Temple building [excluding the knife depository (4/18)] was seventy cubits (41:12). (See Fig. 18.) Since the Temple building was exactly centered between north and south, this leaves exactly 121 cubits on either side [(312-70)÷2=121]. The space between the chamber and the Temple building (5/4) was twenty cubits, and between the chamber and the outer wall of the courtyard (5/5) was fifty cubits. This leaves fifty-one cubits for the width of the chamber [(121-20-50=51)]. Why then does verse 8 give the width of the chamber as only fifty cubits?*

The explanation is that Yechezkel was looking at the chamber from the eastern side of the outer courtyard as indicated by verses 1-3 and as will be elucidated in the commentary. From that point he saw the eastern wall of the chamber where it met the wall of the inner courtyard. As illustrated in Fig. 22, the northern wall of the inner courtyard (2/1) met and covered one cubit of the chamber's eastern wall. The wall of the inner courtyard began exactly a hundred cubits from the outer courtyard wall (1/1; see 40:27) while the southern wall of the chamber extended 101 cubits from the courtyard wall. Thus, the last cubit of the chamber wall was covered and all that could be seen from Yechezkel's vantage point were fifty-cubits of the chamber's wall.

The above computations dictate that the eastern end of the chamber started at the exact point where the northern wall (2/1) of the inner courtyard ended. We have therefore located the exact point on the east-west line at which the chamber began. The 100 cubits of its length ran exactly alongside of the 100 cubit length of the building.

This explains why it was necessary to build a gap (5/2) as a passageway between the two walls, (4/1) and (2/1) [see details in verse 4]. Without such an opening, there would have been no direct access from the inner courtyard to (5/4) the space between the Temple and the chamber. (See Fig. 23, p. 658.)

1. וַיּוֹצִאֵנִי אֶל הֶחָצֵר הַחִיצוֹנָה — *Then he brought me to the outer courtyard.*

The prophet is to be shown the לִשְׁכָּה, *chamber,* which lay to the north of the Temple building. The verse continues that, to reach this chamber, he went out of the inner courtyard by way of the northern gate.

[The printed *Rashi* contains a passage which explains why he had to use the center gate on the north side. There was simply no other way to get to the chamber since the front of the Temple, which was hundred cubits wide, closed off the entire width of the inner courtyard, which was also exactly a hundred cubits.

This passage seems to be a later addition to the text of *Rashi* and does not appear in the manuscripts (see Appendix VII).

However, from *Rashi's* responsum to the *Rabbis of Auxerres* (Appendix IX) it appears that this was indeed part of the original text but, on discussion with his student *Shemaya, Rashi* removed it. He recognized that on the basis of *v.* 4 there must have been a gap (5/2)

נֶגֶד הַגִּזְרָה וַאֲשֶׁר־נֶגֶד הַבִּנְיָן אֶל־הַצָּפוֹן׃
ב אֶל־פְּנֵי אֹרֶךְ אַמּוֹת הַמֵּאָה פֶּתַח הַצָּפוֹן
ג וְהָרֹחַב חֲמִשִּׁים אַמּוֹת׃ נֶגֶד הָעֶשְׂרִים
אֲשֶׁר לֶחָצֵר הַפְּנִימִי וְנֶגֶד רִצְפָּה אֲשֶׁר
לֶחָצֵר הַחִיצוֹנָה אַתִּיק אֶל־פְּנֵי־אַתִּיק
ד בַּשְּׁלִשִׁים׃ וְלִפְנֵי הַלְּשָׁכוֹת מַהֲלַךְ עֶשֶׂר

between the eastern wall of the building (4/1) and the northern wall (2/1) of the inner court (see above), and therefore Yechezkel could have reached the chamber by way of the gap.

Given this possibility, the route through the northern gate was not the only possible way to reach the chamber.]

נֶגֶד הַגִּזְרָה ... נֶגֶד הַבִּנְיָן — *Along the fortress and the structure.*

At 41:12 we explained that the Temple building was called the *fortress,* and the cell complex was called the *structure.* See fig. 21 and pref. remarks above, where we demonstrated that the hundred cubits of the chamber were exactly opposite the hundred cubits of the Temple building.

2. This verse is to be understood in the following manner: [He brought him] to the northern gate (5/6) [of the chamber] from which he could see the hundred-cubit length of the chamber from east to west, and a fifty-cubit wide area (5/5) between the chamber and the northern wall of the outer courtyard.

3. This verse helps us locate the chamber along the north-south line. It is to be understood as follows: The southern wall of the chamber ran along the twenty-cubit space (5/4) between the chamber and the Temple. The northern wall of the chamber faced the balcony which ran along the wall (1/1) of the outer courtyard (see 40:18 and fig. 5).

אַתִּיק אֶל פְּנֵי אַתִּיק בַּשְּׁלִישִׁים — *Pillar faced pillar because of the three floors.*

Fig. 21

Placement of the Western Chambers

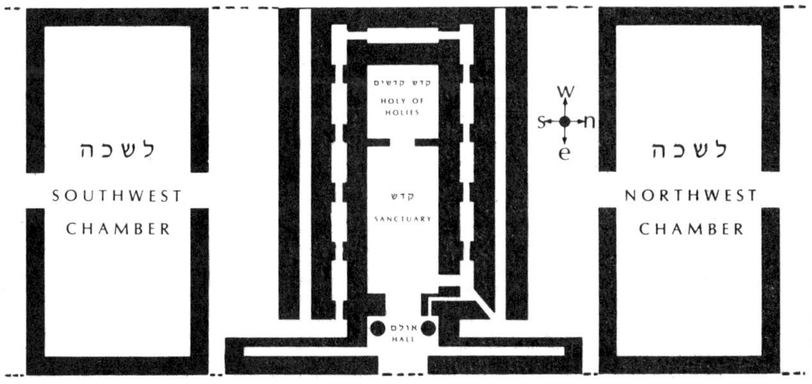

Note: Dotted lines show that both chambers lined up with the Temple Complex from east to west: 100 cubits.

to the chamber which ran along the fortress and the structure to the north; [2] *facing the hundred-cubit length by the northern gate and the fifty-cubit width.* [3] *It was opposite the twenty cubits of the inner courtyard and opposite the balcony. Pillar faced pillar because of the three floors.* [4] *In front of the chambers*

Rashi is baffled by the expression אַתִּיק, (which we translate *pillar)* in this verse: What was its function? What bearing has it on the three floors? Why did the pillars cause a narrowing of the floors, as set forth in verse 5?

Metzudos explains as follows: As in 41:16, אַתִּיק is to be understood as *pillar.* The chamber described in these verses had three stories [בַּשְׁלִישִׁים]. Such a high structure required supporting pillars. In contrast to simple walls in a courtyard *(v.* 6), which do not require more than one supporting pillar, a structure this heavy would require two, one on the outside another on the inside. This arrangement would affect the appearance of the structure as described in verse 5. See *comm.* there.

4. וְלִפְנֵי הַלְּשָׁכוֹת — *In front of the chambers.*

This refers to the twenty cubit space (5/4) between the Temple and the chamber. It could be reached by a ten-cubit walkway (5/3) leading westward between the knife depository (4/18) and the chamber.

[Going from east to west, the knife depository (4/18) together with its outer wall (4/1) was ten cubits wide; these ten cubits were the *length* of the walkway.

Fig. 22

North-South Placement of Northwest Chamber

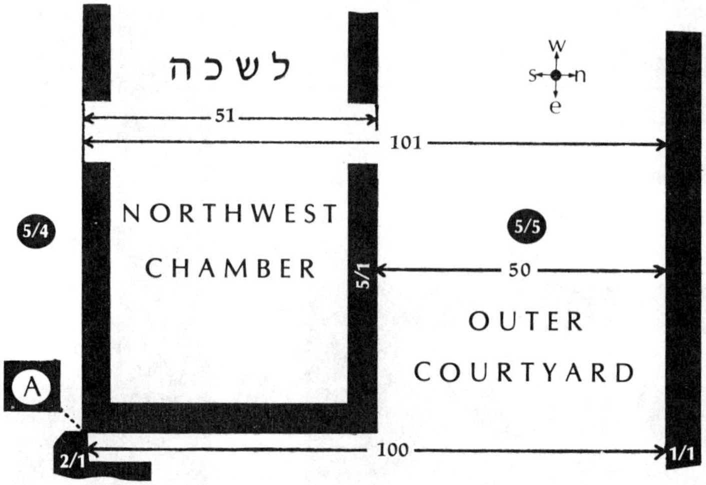

Note: The distance between the outer wall of the outer courtyard (1/1) and the northern wall of the chamber is 50 cubits. The width of the chamber is 51 cubits for a combined width of 101 cubits. Since the width of the outer courtyard (1/1 to 2/1) is 100 cubits, there was an overlay of 1 cubit at point A.

אַמּוֹת רֹחַב אֶל־הַפְּנִימִית דֶּרֶךְ אַמָּה
ה אַחַת וּפִתְחֵיהֶם לַצָּפוֹן׃ וְהַלְּשָׁכוֹת
הָעֶלְיוֹנֹת קְצֻרוֹת כִּי־יוֹכְלוּ אַתִּיקִים
ו מֵהֵנָּה מֵהַתַּחְתֹּנוֹת וּמֵהַתִּיכֹנוֹת בִּנְיָן׃ כִּי
מְשֻׁלָּשׁוֹת הֵנָּה וְאֵין לָהֶן עַמּוּדִים

Fig. 23
Access to the Western Chamber from the Inner Courtyard

Note: 1 cubit since 5/2 leads from courtyard to 5×10 cubits passageway (5/3), from where the *kohen* was able to enter the chamber through gateway 5/1.

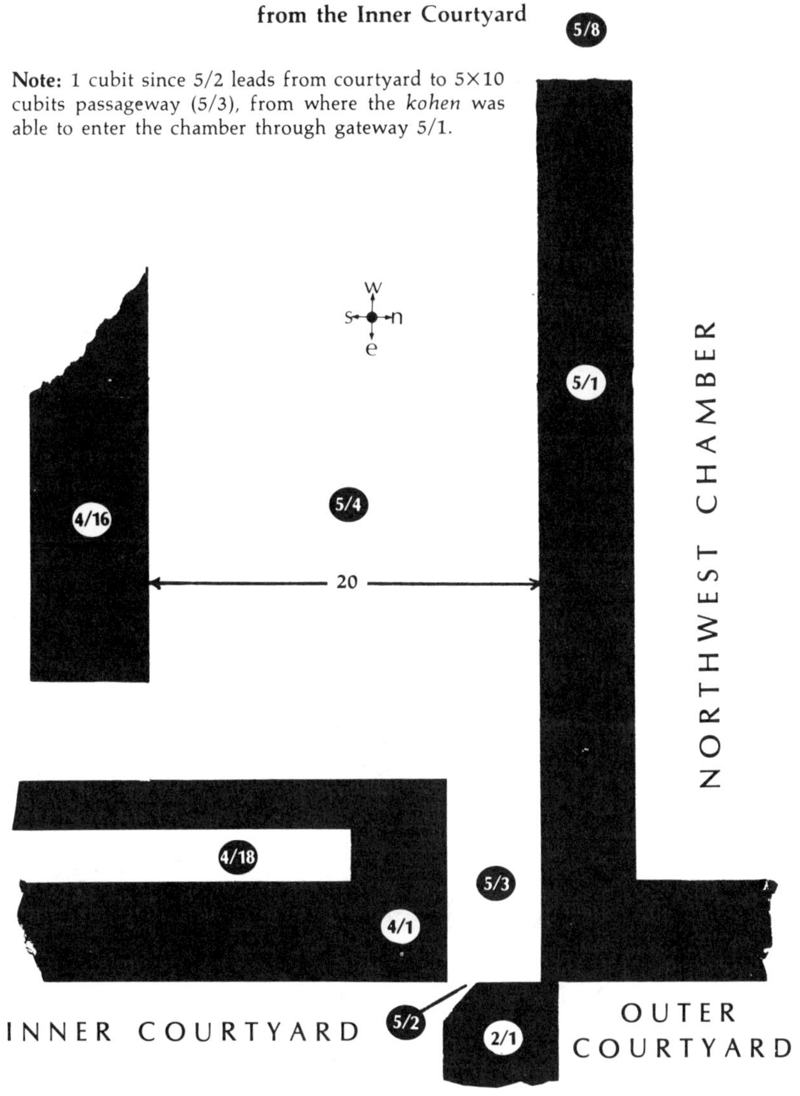

there was a walkway ten cubits wide leading to the
inner space through a path of one cubit. Their gate
faced northward. 5 *The upper chambers were nar-*
rowed because the pillars consumed space from
them, from the lower and middle floor of the
building. 6 *For they were three-storied, and unsuited*
for them were pillars like the pillars of courtyards,

By means of the following computation, we learn that the walkway was five cubits wide: The knife depository extended fifteen cubits beyond the width of the Sanctuary (see 41:14). The chamber was twenty cubits from the Sanctuary (see 41:10); 20-15=5.

דֶּרֶךְ אַמָּה אֶחָת — *Through a path of one cubit.*

The walkway was reached through a 1 cubit gap (5/2) between the northeastern extremity of the knife depository and the northern wall (2/1) of the inner courtyard. This gap was obtained by shortening the latter by 1 cubit.

וּפִתְחֵיהֶם לַצָּפוֹן — *Their gate faced northward.*

This refers to the opening (5/6) in the northern wall of the chamber which had already been mentioned in verse 2.

[No explanation is offered why the plural (הַלְּשָׁכוֹת, וּפִתְחֵיהֶם) is used in this verse, when Yechezkel was shown *one* gate and *one* chamber. Perhaps it hints at the existence of the northeast chamber which, as we shall see below, lay to the east of and was identical to this chamber.]

5. וְהַלְּשָׁכוֹת הָעֶלְיוֹנֹת קְצֻרוֹת — *The upper chambers were narrowed.*

Verse 6 teaches that the chambers were three-tiered. One of *Rashi's* difficulties with verses 6 and 7 is the question of why the highest of the three floors should be narrower than the lower two (see *comm.* to *v.* 3).

Metzudos offers a solution which allows him to interpret verses 5 and 6 quite simply. The term עֶלְיוֹנוֹת, *upper,* in our phrase does not refer to the third floor of a single structure, but to the two chambers at the western end of the courtyard. Those chambers — parallel to the Sanctuary, one to its north and one to its south — are described as עֶלְיוֹנוֹת, *higher,* relative to the two identical chambers which, as we shall see, lay at the eastern end of the outer courtyard. Since the Temple area sloped upwards from east to west, and the level of the Temple building was twelve steps higher than the courtyards in front of it, these chambers are correctly described as 'upper' chambers.

The reason why these 'upper' chambers — and also, of course, the lower (eastern) ones (but see comm. to *v.* 11) — were 'narrow' is explained in the rest of our verse and in the next verse. Verse 3 had introduced us to the need of two pillars to support the weight of the three-story chamber structure. Our verse explains that these pillars, inside the chamber, 'consumed' (יוּכְלוּ like יֹאכְלוּ, *to eat)* space from the lower floor and the middle floor. They took no space from the upper story — which was consequently broader than the other two — because it could rest on the pillars. The weight of the third story's roof was not great enough to require extra support. Verse 6 explains that because of the height of these three story [מְשֻׁלָּשׁוֹת], structures, it was impossible to support it with the normal one pillar support which would have been appropriate for the support of courtyard walls [וְאֵין לָהֶן עַמּוּדִים כְּעַמּוּדֵי הַחֲצֵרוֹת]: therefore space from the lower and middle levels was lost.

7-8. Together, these two verses yield the position of the chamber on the east-west line. The *pref. remarks* to verses 1-12 examine them in detail and explains

כְּעַמּוּדֵי הַחֲצֵרוֹת עַל־כֵּן נֶאֱצַל
ז מֵהַתַּחְתֹּנוֹת וּמֵהַתִּיכֹנוֹת מֵהָאָרֶץ: וְגָדֵר
אֲשֶׁר־לַחוּץ לְעֻמַּת הַלְּשָׁכוֹת דֶּרֶךְ הֶחָצֵר
הַחִצוֹנָה אֶל־פְּנֵי הַלְּשָׁכוֹת אָרְכּוֹ חֲמִשִּׁים
ח אַמָּה: כִּי־אֹרֶךְ הַלְּשָׁכוֹת אֲשֶׁר לֶחָצֵר
הַחִצוֹנָה חֲמִשִּׁים אַמָּה וְהִנֵּה עַל־פְּנֵי
ט הַהֵיכָל מֵאָה אַמָּה: °ומתחתה לשכות
הָאֵלֶּה °המבוא מֵהַקָּדִים בְּבֹאוֹ לָהֵנָּה

°וּמִתַּחַת הַלְּשָׁכוֹת ט
°הַמֵּבִיא ק׳

why the latter part of verse 8 — telling that the hundred-cubit length of the chamber ran exactly parallel to the length of the building — follows logically upon the first part.

9. וּמִתַּחַת הַלְּשָׁכוֹת הָאֵלֶּה — *And for those below these chambers.*

Rashi is uncertain whether this indicates some kind of subterranean chamber or whether it refers to the eastern chambers which were on the downward slope of the mountain.

Metzudos — who understood עֶלְיוֹנֹת, *upper,* in verse 5 as describing the two chambers in the western part of the courtyard because they were higher up on the slope — quite consistently interprets this phrase as a reference to two more chambers which lay towards the eastern (and therefore lower) end of the outer courtyard.

As *Metzudos* interprets the next few verses, we learn that these eastern chambers had the same dimensions and occupied the same positions (relative to the walls of the outer courtyard) as the western chambers. However, while the entire length of the western ones ran along the building and did not protrude toward the east or west, this was not so in the case of the eastern ones. This will become clearer below, as we locate these chambers, first along the east-west line and then along the north-south line (Fig. 24).

הַמֵּבִיא מֵהַקָּדִים — *An approach from the east.*

There is an approach along the courtyard's eastern wall (6/3) for a person coming to the chambers from the outer courtyard. According to *Metzudos,* this *approach* is a path, eleven cubits wide, between the eastern walls of the outer courtyard (1/1) and the eastern wall of the chamber.

Metzudos assumes that the distance of these eastern chambers from the outer courtyard wall (1/1) should be the same as that of the western chambers from the western wall. Therefore, he gives the distance to the east as eleven cubits. (See Fig. 24.)

[The measurement for the western path (5/6) is also not given in the text but is assumed on the basis of *Middos* 4:7, which reports an eleven-cubit space for the Second Temple. See *comm.* 40:22.]

Given this distance between the chambers and the eastern wall, the hundred-cubit length of these chambers must have protruded into the space alongside the inner courtyard as shown in the Master Diagram and relevant figures.

This, in turn, means that the chamber cut off half a cubit from the cell wall (2/5) located on the eastern extremity of the cell complex on the north wall of the inner courtyard. This happened as follows:

The entire northern wall of the inner courtyard (2/1) was a hundred cubits long (40:47). Allowing ten cubits for the central gate (2/3) (40:11), this leaves forty-five cubits on either side [(100-10)÷2=45]. The cells structure built

hence, the lower and middle stories were deprived of
floor space. 7 *The outer wall in front of the chambers,*
from the direction of the outer courtyard facing the
chambers — it's length was fifty cubits. 8 *For the*
length of the chambers which was toward the outer
courtyard was fifty cubits, and behold! they paral-
leled the Temple, a hundred cubits. 9 *And for those*
below these chambers there was an approach from
the east, for entering them from the outer courtyard.

Fig. 24

The Northeast Chamber

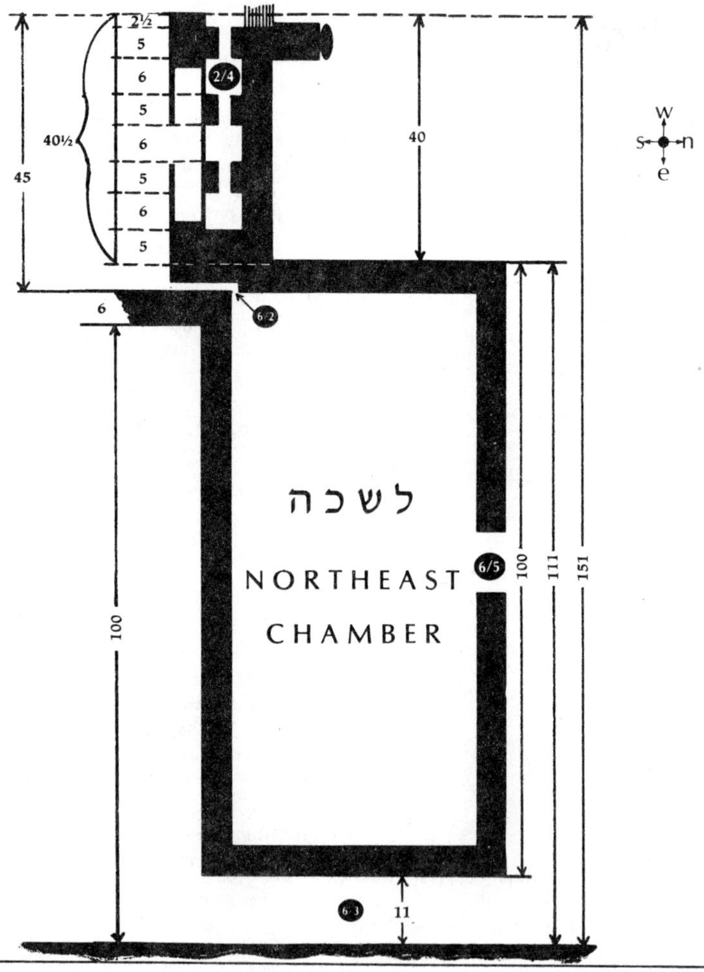

י מֵהֶחָצֵר הַחִצֹנָה: בְּרֹחַב | גֶּדֶר הֶחָצֵר
דֶּרֶךְ הַקָּדִים אֶל־פְּנֵי הַגִּזְרָה וְאֶל־פְּנֵי
יא הַבִּנְיָן לְשָׁכוֹת: וְדֶרֶךְ לִפְנֵיהֶם כְּמַרְאֵה
הַלְּשָׁכוֹת אֲשֶׁר דֶּרֶךְ הַצָּפוֹן כְּאָרְכָּן כֵּן
רָחְבָּן וְכֹל מוֹצָאֵיהֶן וּכְמִשְׁפְּטֵיהֶן
יב וּכְפִתְחֵיהֶן: וּכְפִתְחֵי הַלְּשָׁכוֹת אֲשֶׁר דֶּרֶךְ
הַדָּרוֹם פֶּתַח בְּרֹאשׁ דָּרֶךְ דֶּרֶךְ בִּפְנֵי

outside the wall began 2½ cubits from the gateway (*comm.* 40:12); each of the three cells was six cubits wide (40:7), and the walls were each five cubits (40:7). This gives the entire cell structure a length of 40½ cubits (Fig. 24) [2½+5+6+5+6+5+6+5=40½]. If we add the remaining 4½ cubits to the six cubit thickness of the eastern wall of the inner courtyard (2/1) we find that the eastern extremity of the cell complex was 10½ cubits distant from the eastern edge of the northern wall of the inner courtyard. Since the chamber extended 11 cubits past the eastern wall, ½ cubit of the cell complex was cut off.

Along the north-south line, we are told that just as in the case of the western chambers, there was space of fifty cubits between the northern wall of the outer courtyard and the beginning of the chamber. The chamber itself was fifty-one cubits wide (see *comm.* 1-12) and must therefore have encroached one cubit along the northern edges of walls (2/1). This encroachment of one cubit was duplicated in the western chambers, as noted in *comm.* 1-12.

10. This verse continues the description of the chamber's location. It is essentially an elaboration of the previous verse. Relative to the רֹחַב גֶּדֶר הֶחָצֵר דֶּרֶךְ הַקָּדִים, *the width of the eastward courtyard wall* (1/1), the chambers were closer to the Temple building [the Fortress], the [cell] structure, (see 41:12) and the western chambers, i.e., there was a space between the eastern chambers and the outer courtyard's eastern wall (6/3). [From the *comm.* to the previous verse we know that this space was eleven cubits.]

11. וְדֶרֶךְ לִפְנֵיהֶם — *And there was a passage before them.*

This refers to the fifty cubit space (6/4) between the northern wall of the chamber and the northern wall of the outer courtyard.

The rest of the verse affirms that in all structural details these eastern chambers were identical with the western ones. The western chambers are here referred to as *northern* following the pattern of the earlier verses *(Rashi; Metzudos).* [However, nothing is said concerning the three stories. Perhaps these eastern chambers had only one story, which would eliminate the need for supportive pillars. See *comm.* to הַלְּשָׁכוֹת הָעֶלְיוֹנֹת in *v.* 5.]

12. וּכְפִתְחֵי הַלְּשָׁכוֹת אֲשֶׁר דֶּרֶךְ הַדָּרוֹם — *And like the gates of the chambers which lay to the south.*

Metzudos explains that although the text had thus far described only the northwest and northeast chambers, there were identical chambers to the southwest and southeast. [He deduces this from the words סָבִיב, *all around,* in 41:10]. Whereas the gates of the northern chambers opened to the north, those of the southern chambers opened to the south. Thus, the southern chambers were mirror images of the northern ones.

פֶּתַח בְּרֹאשׁ דָּרֶךְ — *There was also a gate at the main approach.*

In addition to the abovementioned

10 *Along the width of the eastward courtyard wall*
over toward the Fortress and toward the structure
were the chambers. 11 *And there was a passage be-*
fore them. They were identical to the northward
chambers, like their length, like their width; at all
their gateways, like their measurements, and like
their number of doors, 12 *and like the gates of the*
chambers which lay to the south. There was also a
gate at the main approach, an approach facing the

gates which all the chambers had in common, there was another gate which only the lower one had. This one led to the *main approach.* This description is then expanded: דֶּרֶךְ בִּפְנֵי הַגְּדֶרֶת הֲגִינָה, *an approach facing the platform of the singers.* This translation based on *Targum,* refers to the stone, fence-like platform [הַגְּדֶרֶת from גֶּדֶר, *fence*] (3/4) upon which the Levites stood when they sang and played musical accompaniment to the sacrificial service. The same platform was mounted by the *Kohanim* when they blessed the people *(Rashi; Metzudos).*

Alternatively, *Metzudos* renders הֲגִינָה as *worthy,* meaning that the platform was built like a sturdy 'worthy' fence.

The verse concludes by explaining that this platform faced the people as they entered the courtyard from an easterly direction.

According to *Middos* 2:6 this platform (3/4) was situated between the Israelite courtyard and the priestly courtyard, that is halfway between the beginning of the Azarah (which comprised both the courtyard of the Kohanim and the courtyard of the Israelites — see *Rambam, Beis HaBechirah* 5:12) and the altar (see Fig. 12). In Yechezkel's Temple it would lie exactly centered between the beginning of the inner courtyard and the altar. (See Master Diagram.) Since the platform could be approached from any part of the eastern section of the courtyard which lay before it, this whole section of the courtyard is considered as a *way* leading to the platform. In effect, our verse is saying that the eastern chambers had a gate (6/2) leading into the front part of the inner courtyard, which was the *way* leading to the platform.

[*Metzudos* learns that this entrance lay in the five cubits which the chamber encroached upon the inside of the inner courtyard (that is, beyond the thickness of wall 2/1). We have assumed a thickness of five cubits for the walls of the chamber although this is nowhere stated. If we are correct then the entrance must lie through the wall of the chamber. See Fig. 25. It is, of course, possible that the wall of the chamber was much narrower, in which case our diagram would be inaccurate to that degree.]

Fig. 25
Passageway from Inner Courtyard to the Northeast Chamber

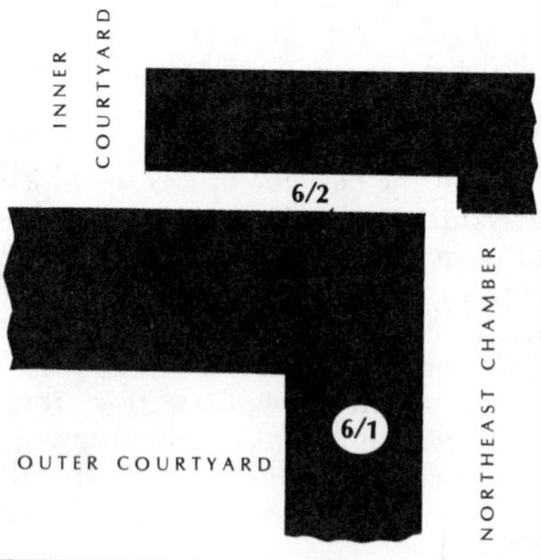

הַגְּדֶרֶת הַגִּינָה דֶּרֶךְ הַקָּדִים בְּבוֹאָן:
יג וַיֹּאמֶר אֵלַי לִשְׁכוֹת הַצָּפוֹן לִשְׁכוֹת
הַדָּרוֹם אֲשֶׁר אֶל־פְּנֵי הַגִּזְרָה הֵנָּה |
לִשְׁכוֹת הַקֹּדֶשׁ אֲשֶׁר יֹאכְלוּ־שָׁם הַכֹּהֲנִים
אֲשֶׁר־קְרוֹבִים לַיהוָה קָדְשֵׁי הַקֳּדָשִׁים
שָׁם יַנִּיחוּ | קָדְשֵׁי הַקֳּדָשִׁים וְהַמִּנְחָה
וְהַחַטָּאת וְהָאָשָׁם כִּי הַמָּקוֹם קָדֹשׁ:
יד בְּבֹאָם הַכֹּהֲנִים וְלֹא־יֵצְאוּ מֵהַקֹּדֶשׁ אֶל־
הֶחָצֵר הַחִיצוֹנָה וְשָׁם יַנִּיחוּ בִגְדֵיהֶם

13-15. Various levels of sanctity existed in the Temple (see *Keilim* 1:8; *comm.* 40:6). The courtyard which Yechezkel's calls the outer courtyard was the equivalent of the women's courtyard of the Second Temple, and what Yechezkel's calls inner courtyard was the equivalent of the *azarah* which itself can be divided into three levels: the Israelites' courtyard, the priestly courtyard and the area between the entrance hall and the altar (see fig. 12). See *Keilim* 1:8 for the exact halachic properties of those division.

There are also various levels of sanctity which attach to the sacrifices which, for our purposes, we can divide into two general groups: קָדְשֵׁי קָדָשִׁים, *Holy of Holies,* a group which comprises: עוֹלָה, מִנְחָה, חַטָּאת, אָשָׁם, *burnt, meal, sin and guilt offerings,* (as also שַׁלְמֵי צִבּוּר, *communal peace offerings,* which are in a separate category — see below) and the קָדָשִׁים קַלִּים, *sacrifices of lesser holiness,* comprising all other sacrifices.

One of the halachic properties which differentiates the inner courtyard/*azarah* from the outer/women's courtyard concerns the Holy of Holies group of sacrifices. These may never be taken out of the inner courtyard. Their status of special sanctity requires that they always remain in a place possessing the level of sanctity of the inner courtyard.

This is the background to our two verses.

The four chambers which have been described in our chapter lay within the outer courtyard (see above, and Main Diagram). It should necessarily follow that they would be disqualified for anything connected with the most holy offerings, which, as we have learned, require the sanctity of the inner courtyard. Nevertheless our two verses teach that the function of these chambers was to provide space for the *kohanim* to eat their portion of the most holy offerings. This implies that these chambers possessed the inner courtyard's level of sanctity, that is, although they were located *outside* the inner courtyard they were nevertheless considered part of it.

This is simply understood in connection with the eastern chambers which, as we saw in verse 12, had an entrance (6/2) straight into the inner courtyard. However, a glance at the Master Diagram will show that there was no direct access from the western chambers to the inner courtyard. How, then, could the most holy offerings get to them without being taken through the outer courtyard?

This can only be understood in connection with 46:20, which teaches that not only the chambers themselves but also the twenty-cubit space (5/4) between them and the Sanctuary had the status of the inner courtyard. Therefore it was possible to take the most holy offerings through the gap

platform of the singers, the easterly path as they entered.
13 *Then he said to me: The northern chambers and southern chambers which are by the fortress, they are holy chambers where the Kohanim who come close to HASHEM may eat the most holy. There they may leave the most holy, the meal offering, the sin offering, and the guilt offering, for the place is holy.*
14 *The kohanim having arrived there, they are not to leave the holy place for the outer chamber, rather they must leave the garments in which they minister*

and walkway (5/2 and 5/3) which led from the inner courtyard to those open spaces. Of course, this assumes that there must have been an entrance into the chambers from the twenty-cubit space. Indeed *Rashi* to 46:19 states that there *was* such an entrance (5/8), although it is nowhere specified in the text.

13. אֲשֶׁר אֶל פְּנֵי הַגִּזְרָה — *Which are by the fortress.*

This accurately describes the western chambers which were very close to the Temple. However, as *Metzudos* points out, this description can also apply to the eastern chambers since they were moved up eleven cubits from the eastern wall towards the main building (see *v.* 10).

לִשְׁכוֹת הַקֹּדֶשׁ אֲשֶׁר יֹאכְלוּ שָׁם...קָדְשֵׁי הַקֳּדָשִׁים— *The holy chambers where the...may eat the most holy.*

Although these chambers lay outside the inner courtyard, they are still described as possessing the requisite degree of holiness for the eating of the most holy offerings (see above).

הַכֹּהֲנִים אֲשֶׁר קְרוֹבִים לַה׳ — *The kohanim who come close to HASHEM.*

The descendants of Tzadok (see 40:46 and 44:9-16).

שָׁם יַנִּיחוּ קָדְשֵׁי הַקֳּדָשִׁים — *There they may leave the most holy.*

Since these chambers have the character of the inner courtyard, the most holy offerings may be left there in readiness to be eaten.

All personal sacrifices which are most holy offerings are listed specifically in our verse מִנְחָה, חַטָּאת, אָשָׁם, *meal, sin,* and *guilt offerings); עוֹלָה, burnt offering,* cannot be meant since our verse discusses only sacrifices that were *eaten.* Therefore, this seemingly superfluous term *the most holy* can refer only to שַׁלְמֵי צִבּוּר, *communal peace offerings.* [These are a unique category since all שְׁלָמִים, *peace offerings,* when offered by individuals belong to the category of sacrifices of lesser holiness. Only communal peace offerings are considered to be most holy offerings.]

14. These chambers were also used to store בִּגְדֵי כְּהוּנָּה, *priestly garments.* While wearing such garments, the *kohanim* were not allowed to mingle with other people because, by Rabbinic decree, physical contact with clothes not having the sanctity of priestly garments caused the priestly garments to become contaminated. [See *Chagigah* 2:7.]

Normally the *kohanim* would wear their priestly garments when they entered the chambers to eat the most holy offerings. Before leaving to mingle with the people, they would put on their ordinary clothes.

15-20. For the moment, Yechezkel's guide has finished his description of the

מב °וְלָבְשׁוּ ק׳ אֲשֶׁר־יְשָׁרְתוּ בָהֶן כִּי־קֹדֶשׁ הֵנָּה °ילבשו
טו־כ בְּגָדִים אֲחֵרִים וְקָרְבוּ אֶל־אֲשֶׁר לָעָם׃
טו וְכִלָּה אֶת־מִדּוֹת הַבַּיִת הַפְּנִימִי וְהוֹצִיאַנִי
דֶּרֶךְ הַשַּׁעַר אֲשֶׁר פָּנָיו דֶּרֶךְ הַקָּדִים
טז וּמְדָדוֹ סָבִיב | סָבִיב׃ מָדַד רוּחַ הַקָּדִים
°מֵאוֹת ק׳ בִּקְנֵה הַמִּדָּה חֲמֵשׁ־°אמות קָנִים בִּקְנֵה
יז הַמִּדָּה סָבִיב׃ מָדַד רוּחַ הַצָּפוֹן חֲמֵשׁ־
יח מֵאוֹת קָנִים בִּקְנֵה הַמִּדָּה סָבִיב׃ אֵת רוּחַ
הַדָּרוֹם מָדָד חֲמֵשׁ־מֵאוֹת קָנִים בִּקְנֵה
יט הַמִּדָּה׃ סָבַב אֶל־רוּחַ הַיָּם מָדַד חֲמֵשׁ־
כ מֵאוֹת קָנִים בִּקְנֵה הַמִּדָּה׃ לְאַרְבַּע
רוּחוֹת מְדָדוֹ חוֹמָה לוֹ סָבִיב | סָבִיב אֹרֶךְ
מג חֲמֵשׁ מֵאוֹת וְרֹחַב חֲמֵשׁ מֵאוֹת לְהַבְדִּיל
א א בֵּין הַקֹּדֶשׁ לְחֹל׃ וַיּוֹלִכֵנִי אֶל־הַשָּׁעַר

Temple buildings. He will resume it once more at 46:21. Now he returns to the point of departure from which he began his description at 40:5, the חוֹמַת הַר הַבַּיִת, *wall of the Temple Mount.* There he began his description by measuring the height and depth of this wall. Now he measures the length.

Each wall measured five hundred rods (see 40:3) which, at six cubits to the rod (40:5), yields an area of nine million square cubits. *Rashi* points out that this is an increase by a factor of thirty-six over the area of the Temple Complex in the Second Temple, which, with sides of five hundred cubits (*Middos* 2:1), yielded an area of two-hundred fifty thousand square cubits (9,000,000÷250,000=36).

15. The measurement was to include all four sides of the outer wall.

16. סָבִיב — *All around.*

This term in our verse is hard to understand. The measurement was for only one dimension of the wall. Why would this be described as *all around?*

Metzudos renders: From one end to the other.

Levushei Serad (in *HaMikdash HaShlishi)* suggests the following solution. He points out that the term is used in our verse only to describe the eastern side, and in the next verse, to describe the northern side. It is omitted completely in verse 18, which describes the measurement of the southern side and appears in a slightly different form in verse 19 in connection with the western side.

In his view, *all around* describes the *guide's* progress around the wall. Logically he would have started at the east wall and gone around by way of the north to the west and then back to the east wall along the south wall. For reasons which we cannot fathom he did not do so. After measuring the north wall, he doubled back to the south and only then went on to the west.

Verse 16, which describes the measurement of the east wall, uses סָבִיב,

for they are holy; they are to don other clothes and
then approach the domain of the nation.
15 *When he finished the measurements of the inner*
House, he took me out through the gate which faced
eastward and measured it all around. 16 *He measured*
the eastern side with the measuring rod, five hundred
rods with the measuring rod all around. 17 *He*
measured the northern side, five hundred rods with
the measuring rod all around. 18 *The southern side he*
measured, five hundred rods with the measuring rod.
19 *He circled around to the western side; he measured*
five hundred rods with the measuring rod. 20 *On four*
sides he measured it, its wall all around, a length of
five hundred and a width of five hundred — to
separate between the holy and the ordinary.

all around — he was going around the building in a logical fashion; so also verse 17 in connection with the north wall. But verse 18 began a new measurement of the south side after he had doubled back from the northwest corner and *all around* would have been out of place. The measurement of the west wall (*v.* 19) once more followed a 'surrounding' of the wall, albeit in a different direction than the original one.

20. לְהַבְדִּיל בֵּין הַקֹּדֶשׁ לְחֹל — *To separate between the holy and the ordinary.*

Although the Temple Mount complex, the section immediately outside the outer wall, (in its narrower sense — see *comm.* 40:5), lay inside an area which was also sacred (see 40:5), it is nevertheless described as חֹל, *ordinary*, relative to the Temple complex contained within the outer wall, which had a greater level of sanctity.

XLIII

Yechezkel is brought back to the eastern gate to witness the high drama of the Shechinah's *return. The book began with the tragedy of the* Shechinah's *withdrawal from the Temple, leaving it an empty shell; and concludes by reversing the process. Yechezkel had been shown the majesty of the rebuilt Temple, but the beautiful building which he had now examined in such loving detail would be devoid of meaning were it not to house the Divine Presence within itself.*

Twenty years earlier a majestic Temple had towered over the same mountain on which, in his vision, he was now standing. At the foot of that mountain lay a city teeming with proud and self-sufficient people, secure in their strength, confident in their future. Six years later the Temple was a smoldering ruin, the city, a desolate wilderness. Yechezkel knew the secret behind that catastrophe. He had witnessed the agonized withdrawal of the Shechinah *from home; he had seen the soul leaving the body. Before his prophetic eye the mighty building had become a spiritless mockery of its former grandeur,a meaningless pile, willing fuel for Nebuchadnezzar's eager flames (Chs. 8-11).*

The Shechinah *had left the Temple — but not the people. At the very moment of*

ב שַׁעַר אֲשֶׁר פֹּנֶה דֶּרֶךְ הַקָּדִים: וְהִנֵּה כְּבוֹד
אֱלֹהֵי יִשְׂרָאֵל בָּא מִדֶּרֶךְ הַקָּדִים וְקוֹלוֹ
כְּקוֹל מַיִם רַבִּים וְהָאָרֶץ הֵאִירָה מִכְּבֹדוֹ:
ג וּכְמַרְאֵה הַמַּרְאֶה אֲשֶׁר רָאִיתִי כַּמַּרְאֶה
אֲשֶׁר־רָאִיתִי בְּבֹאִי לְשַׁחֵת אֶת־הָעִיר
וּמַרְאוֹת כַּמַּרְאֶה אֲשֶׁר רָאִיתִי אֶל־נְהַר
ד כְּבָר וָאֶפֹּל אֶל־פָּנָי: וּכְבוֹד יְהוָה בָּא אֶל־
הַבָּיִת דֶּרֶךְ שַׁעַר אֲשֶׁר פָּנָיו דֶּרֶךְ הַקָּדִים:
ה וַתִּשָּׂאֵנִי רוּחַ וַתְּבִאֵנִי אֶל־הֶחָצֵר הַפְּנִימִי
ו וְהִנֵּה מָלֵא כְבוֹד־יְהוָה הַבָּיִת: וָאֶשְׁמַע
מִדַּבֵּר אֵלַי מֵהַבָּיִת וְאִישׁ הָיָה עֹמֵד
ז אֶצְלִי: וַיֹּאמֶר אֵלַי בֶּן־אָדָם אֶת־מְקוֹם

the destruction God and Israel were locked in an embrace of surpassing tenderness (footnote to 7:4) — witness to the indestructibility of the love which joined them. And on the banks of the River Kevar, in the darkest night of Babylonian exile, the Merkavah *hovered over Israel in silent testimony to the essential holiness the nation retains even in its degradation (ch. 1).*

The two Merkavah *visions of chapters 1 and 8 are the links which hold together the myriad parts of Yechezkel's prophetic edifice. The permanence of the bond between God and people informs his view of history that all events flow inexorably towards an ultimate* קִדּוּשׁ שֵׁם שָׁמַיִם, a sanctification of the Heavenly Name *(see footnote to 20:9). The ultimate goal of history is this sanctification; Israel's acquisition of homeland and construction of Temple are milestones along the way, not the end of the journey. Therefore, the nation could be stripped of these precious treasures temporarily, but not be deterred from its pursuit of the one overriding goal. This concept of the transience of Israel's bond to land, city, and Temple is an indispensable basis of the unsparing and unflinching predictions of exile and destruction which form such a major part of his prophetic activity.*

And now, a third encounter with the Merkavah *is to crown the earlier two. History will have run its course; lessons will have been learned from centuries of exile (see* comm. *and footnote to 6:8-9); and the bond to land, city, and Temple will be seen to be permanent after all. They were transient only in a relative sense. They are an ideal; not a condition. But the inspiration of history is that that ideal will be achieved. Now, as a logical outgrowth of his life's work, Yechezkel is granted a vision of the fulfillment of that achievement.*

1. כְּבוֹד אֱלֹהֵי יִשְׂרָאֵל — *The Glory of the God of Israel.*

Nineteen years earlier the Glory of the God of Israel had awaited Yechezkel in the Temple Courtyard (8:4). It had shown him the dreadful defilement of the Temple's sanctity (ch. 8), then been lifted out of the city upon wings of *cheruvim* (11:22) which would henceforth be its bearers (*comm.* 10:20). Now that same *Glory of the God of Israel* is about to reenter the Temple from the east, the direction of its departure (see 11:23).

*Then he led me to the gate, the gate which opens to
the east.* ² *And behold! — the Glory of the God of
Israel came from the east, with a sound like the sound
of great waters, and the earth shone with His Glory.*
³ *And the vision was like [the] vision that I had seen:
like the vision that I had seen when I came to destroy
the city, and visions like the vision that I had seen at
the River Kevar. Then I fell upon my face.* ⁴ *The
Glory of* HASHEM *entered the House through the
gate which opened to the east.* ⁵ *Then a wind lifted
me up and brought me into the inner courtyard; and
behold! — the Glory of* HASHEM *filled the House.*
⁶ *I heard Him addressing Himself to me from the
House. A man was standing near me.* ⁷ *And He said
to me: Ben Adam! This is the site of My throne, this*

2. כְּקוֹל מַיִם רַבִּים — *Like the sound of great waters.*

I.e., torrential waters. The expression is not meant literally, but to give some idea of the crescendo accompanying the *Shechinah's* return *(Metzudos).*

וְהָאָרֶץ הֵאִירָה מִכְּבֹדוֹ — *And the earth shone with His Glory.*

God's Divine Presence is the source of all light. *Bereishis Rabbah* 3:4 teaches that it was from the מְקוֹם בֵּית הַמִּקְדָּשׁ, *the site of the Temple,* that God fashioned the light of creation.

In *comm.* 21:24-27, we discussed the terrible and fearsome darkness which fell upon Abraham when he saw a world subjugated by the Four Kingdoms under whom the agony of Israel's exile was to drag out. We saw that this darkness was an extension of the primeval darkness which covered the depths at the time of creation, waiting to be dispelled by the 'Spirit of God' which was to express itself with the coming of the Messiah. Yechezkel now sees that darkness lifting. With God's return to His Temple the earth will once more shine with the light which reflects its true nature.

3. וּכְמַרְאֵה הַמַּרְאֶה אֲשֶׁר רָאִיתִי — *And the vision was like the vision that I had seen.*

Yechezkel refers to the *Merkavah* visions of his previous experience. He then proceeds to enumerate them in our verse. See *pref.*

וָאֶפֹּל אֶל פָּנָי — *Then I fell upon my face.*

He falls in veneration before God *(Metzudos).*

4. The *Shechinah* enters the הֵיכָל, *the Temple building,* by way of the eastern entrance of the outer courtyard *(Metzudos).*

5. Yechezkel had been standing at the eastern gate of the Temple Mount. The wind carries him to the inner courtyard.

6. וָאֶשְׁמַע מִדַּבֵּר אֵלַי — *I heard Him addressing Himself to me.*

The voice was that of God. His speaking is described in the reflexive voice as if to say: *He spoke to Himself,* and I listened. This displays respect for God; He does not lower Himself to address man directly. See footnote to 2:2 for an explanation of this rarely found construction.

וְאִישׁ הָיָה עֹמֵד אֶצְלִי — *A man was standing near me.*

This may have been the angelic guide

מג
ח

כִּסְאִי וְאֶת־מְקוֹם כַּפּוֹת רַגְלַי אֲשֶׁר
אֶשְׁכָּן־שָׁם בְּתוֹךְ בְּנֵי־יִשְׂרָאֵל לְעוֹלָם
וְלֹא יְטַמְּאוּ עוֹד בֵּית־יִשְׂרָאֵל שֵׁם קָדְשִׁי
הֵמָּה וּמַלְכֵיהֶם בִּזְנוּתָם וּבְפִגְרֵי מַלְכֵיהֶם
ח בָּמוֹתָם׃ בְּתִתָּם סִפָּם אֶת־סִפִּי וּמְזוּזָתָם
אֵצֶל מְזוּזָתִי וְהַקִּיר בֵּינִי וּבֵינֵיהֶם וְטִמְּאוּ |
אֶת־שֵׁם קָדְשִׁי בְּתוֹעֲבוֹתָם אֲשֶׁר עָשׂוּ

who had led him through the Temple in the previous chapters, or it may have been a different angel *(Radak)*.

Although the angel still accompanies Yechezkel, he no longer speaks. The voice emanates from the Holy of Holies *(Malbim)*.

7. אֶת מְקוֹם כִּסְאִי וְאֶת מְקוֹם כַּפּוֹת רַגְלַי — *This is the site of My Throne, this is the side of My footstool.*

Radak comments out that אֶת in this verse is to be rendered, *this*, as though it were written: זֶה.

In *Radak's* view, כִּסְאִי, *My Throne* refers to the כִּסֵּא הַכָּבוֹד, *the Divine Throne*, seat of God's Glory in the heavens. To the Divine Throne, the Temple relates as a footstool. The physical building in Jerusalem is 'opposite' the spiritual 'throne' in the heavens. [The situation is analagous to Jerusalem. According to *Taanis* 5a the physical Jerusalem is 'opposite' a heavenly, spiritual city. See Prefatory Remarks to Ch. 22.]

When we recall that in *Jeremiah* 17:12 the Temple itself is described as כִּסֵּא כָבוֹד, *a Throne of Glory*, another explanation suggests itself for our verse. Yechezkel teaches that the true 'Throne' of God is the footstool. It is not God's desire that his *Shechinah* should be located in the heavens but that He should dwell among men. If Israel will welcome God to its midst, it will have turned the footstool into the Throne (see *Radak;* see also *Isaiah* 66:1).

וְלֹא יְטַמְּאוּ...הֵמָּה וּמַלְכֵיהֶם בִּזְנוּתָם וּפִגְרֵי מַלְכֵיהֶם — *Let...no more contaminate...they and their kings, with their promiscuity and with the corpses of their kings.*

Taking this phrase and the next two verses together the following picture emerges: In earlier times it had been the custom of the kings to build their palaces next to the Temple (see *II Chronicles* 9:4). Because of this proximity, some of the excesses that took place in the palaces were considered a direct offense against the sanctity of the Temple; in particular, the practice of burying kings in the palace grounds caused a contamination of the surroundings.

The Temple foretold in these prophecies will be immune from similar encroachments upon its sanctity. The disposition of the new city will be such that the portion assigned to the king will be far removed from the Temple grounds (see 45:7 for details). Under these new conditions there will be nothing to prevent the *Shechinah* from abiding permanently in the Temple.[1]

בִּזְנוּתָם — *With their promiscuity.*

By the idol worship which was occasionally practiced *(Metzudos)*.

1. The injection of this apparently minor issue into the account of the *Shechinah's* return seems incongruous. Again and again Yechezkel had castigated the people for the sins which had driven the *Shechinah* from their midst. No detail seems to have escaped his stricture. Yet, nowhere do we find even a hint that the proximity of the palace to the Temple was in any way a contributing factor. The elimination of this problem would seem more pertinent to 45:7

43
8

is the site of My footstool where I will dwell amid the children of Israel forever. Let the family of Israel no more contaminate My holy Name, they and their kings, with their promiscuity and with the corpses of their kings — their high places. [8] *When they place their thresholds near My threshold and their doorposts near My doorposts with but a wall between Me and them, whereby they defiled My holy Name by the abominations which they committed, so I*

וּבְפִגְרֵי מַלְכֵיהֶם בָּמוֹתָם — *And with the corpses of their kings—their high places.*

The kings were occasionally buried in the gardens of their palaces *(Rashi)* and because of the close proximity to the Temple this was considered a contamination. Once buried, the custom was to establish an altar for idol worship (בָּמָה) near the grave *(Metzudos).*

8-9. See commentary and footnote to *v. 7.*

where the new disposition of the land is described; that it is mentioned at this point seems to underline its significance.

We suggest the following solution to this problem. Although the command to build a Temple is addressed to the people rather than to the king (see *Ramban, Numbers* 16:21), the very nature of the vast communal resources needed for such an effort required the involvement of the executive powers of the monarchy. The First Temple was built by Solomon, after David's longing to do so had been frustrated. Scripture also records many instances when necessary upkeep and repair was undertaken only upon the initiative of righteous kings (see *HaMelech VeHaMikdash; Chazon HaMikrah* by *R' Yissachor Jacobson,* Tel Aviv 5722). We may surmise that this close association between the monarchy and the Temple gave rise to a certain sense of proprietorship, and that such an attitude was reinforced by the close proximity of the palace to the Temple grounds.

Against this background some kings may well have had the urge to obliterate the boundaries between the monarchy and the priesthood and to arrogate to themselves the right of divine service in the Temple. There was precedent for such a combination of the two functions. Malchizedek was both *King of Salem* and *Priest to God the Most High (Genesis* 14:18). Even within Israel, such a combination had been envisaged for Jacob's son Reuben, who would have been both king and *kohen* if he had not sinned *(Rashi, Genesis* 49:3). Nevertheless, for reasons which need not concern us here, the Torah forbade such a combination. *Yerushalmi Horios* 3b expressly disqualifies a *kohen* from the monarchy (see *Ramban Genesis* 41:10) and Scripture often stresses that the two functions are entirely separate from one another (cf. *Jeremiah* 33:24 and *Zechariah* 4:14).

A case can be made that the first intimation of an ultimate destruction of the Temple, the first tremors of the earthquake which would ultimately topple the whole structure, came when this division was forgotten. *Isaiah* 6 describes how the prophet saw God on a 'high and uplifted throne' with [only] the 'edge of His garment filling the Sanctuary.' Since the *Shechinah* rightfully dwells upon the *cheruvim* whose wings were spread over the Ark, *R' Hirsch (Gesammelte Schriften* v. 2, Frankfort 1904, p. 162) deduces that the *Shechinah* had begun the process of withdrawal at that moment. The date given for this vision is the year when King Uzziahu dies. The Sages teach that it was not the year of his death, but the year when he was stricken with leprosy and forced to relinquish the throne. We learn the background to this story in *II Chronicles* 26:16.

Drunk by the successes with which his rule had been crowned, Uzziahu entered the Temple with the intention of burning incense before God, an act of service which must be done by a *kohen.* But Uzziahu was from the tribe of Judah. According to the commentator to *Chronicles,*

ט וָאֲכַל אוֹתָם בְּאַפִּי׃ עַתָּה יְרַחֲקוּ אֶת־
זְנוּתָם וּפִגְרֵי מַלְכֵיהֶם מִמֶּנִּי וְשָׁכַנְתִּי
י בְתוֹכָם לְעוֹלָם׃ אַתָּה בֶן־אָדָם
הַגֵּד אֶת־בֵּית־יִשְׂרָאֵל אֶת־הַבַּיִת וְיִכָּלְמוּ
יא מֵעֲוֺנוֹתֵיהֶם וּמָדְדוּ אֶת־תָּכְנִית׃ וְאִם־
נִכְלְמוּ מִכֹּל אֲשֶׁר־עָשׂוּ צוּרַת הַבַּיִת
וּתְכוּנָתוֹ וּמוֹצָאָיו וּמוֹבָאָיו | וְכָל־צוּרֹתָו
וְאֵת כָּל־חֻקֹּתָיו וְכָל־צוּרֹתָו וְכָל־תּוֹרֹתָו
הוֹדַע אוֹתָם וּכְתֹב לְעֵינֵיהֶם וְיִשְׁמְרוּ
אֶת־כָּל־צוּרָתוֹ וְאֶת־כָּל־חֻקֹּתָיו וְעָשׂוּ
יב אוֹתָם׃ זֹאת תּוֹרַת הַבָּיִת עַל־רֹאשׁ הָהָר
כָּל־גְּבֻלוֹ סָבִיב | סָבִיב קֹדֶשׁ קָדָשִׁים הִנֵּה־

10-11. Yechezkel is to pass on his visions of the Temple to the people. In *pref.* to 40:1-43:17 we cited the Midrash which has Yechezkel inquiring about the purpose of teaching the people the details of the Temple while they were still in exile with no prospect of escaping it. God had answered that He would consider the study of the Temple's design to be as meritorious as the actual building.

According to *Radak* our section goes even further. He explains the last phrase in verse 11, *That they may remember its form and its decrees and perform them,* as follows. If they do indeed study all the details of the structure and make an effort to remember them, then they will indeed be among those who will build it — at the resurrection of the dead. Accordingly, this passage is a guarantee that תְּחִיַּת הַמֵּתִים, *the resurrection of the dead,* will take place.

10. וְיִכָּלְמוּ מֵעֲוֺנוֹתֵיהֶם — *And let them be ashamed of their sins.*

They will feel ashamed when I show them that I do not forsake them despite their sins *(Rashi).*

Alternatively, when they realize that the first Temple was destroyed because of them, they will be ashamed of their sins *(Radak).*

וּמָדְדוּ אֶת תָּכְנִית — *And measure the design.*

From *Radak* it seems that they were to make a three-dimensional model to symbolize that eventually they would build the actual Temple (see commentary 10-11). *Tosafos Yom Tov* in his

he reasoned that it is fitting for a human king to serve the Almighty King. When the high priest and the *kohanim* explained to him that this constituted an encroachment upon the rights of priesthood he would have defied them. At that moment leprosy appeared on his forehead, and simultaneously a terrible earthquake shook the land (*Zechariah* 14:5) causing the portals of the Temple to tremble (*Isaiah* 6:4). Plainly, when the boundaries between the monarchy and the priesthood were endangered the foundations of the nation were shaken, for it was then that the *Shechinah* began the withdrawal which would culminate in the ultimate destruction. The very structure of Israel, bearers of Divine Glory on Earth, had been compromised.

If our analysis is correct we can understand the central importance which Yechezkel assigns to the new disposition of the palace and the Temple grounds. It would safeguard the division which was so vital to maintain the presence of the *Shechinah* in Israel.

destroyed them in My anger. 9 *Now let them distance*
their promiscuity and the corpses of their kings from
Me, that I may dwell among them, forever.
10 *You Ben Adam! Tell the family of Israel of the*
Temple and let them be ashamed of their sins, and
measure the design. 11 *And if they are ashamed — the*
form of the House and its design, its exits and
entrances, and all its appearance, its laws, all its
decoration, and all its regulations make known to
them and write it down before their eyes, that they
may remember its form and its decrees and perform
them. 12 *This is the teaching of the House; the moun-*
tain, its entire boundaries all around, is most holy.

Introduction to *Tzuras HaBayis* also maintains that the people were expected to make a model of the Temple. He deduces this from the seemingly redundant word צוּרֹתָיו, literally *its forms,* in verse 11 (but see below for another explanation of the word).

11. וְאִם נִכְלְמוּ — *And if they are ashamed.*

Metzudos understands this as a precondition. Only if you see true shame and repentance, should you continue telling them all the details enumerated later in the verse. If on the other hand, they seem unaffected there will be no point in continuing.

We follow *Metzudos* in his interpretation of the following words:

צוּרַת הַבַּיִת — *The form of the House.*

This is a general statement that the Temple is to consist of a Holy of Holies, a Sanctuary, a hall, various cells and halls, and all the other components.

וּתְכוּנָתוֹ — *And its design.*

An exact floor plan of where each component is to be. The Holy of Holies in the west, and so on.

מוֹצָאָיו וּמוֹבָאָיו — *Its exits and entrances.*

The dimensions of the gateways by which one goes out and in.

וְכָל צוּרֹתָיו — *And all its appearance.*

The appearance of each individual room.

וְאֵת כָּל חֻקֹּתָיו — *Its laws* [lit. *and all its laws*].

The function of each individual room.

וְכָל צוּרוֹתָיו — *All its decorations.*

A description of the decorative palm trees and *cheruvim* which were carved on the wooden panels and beaten out on the golden veneer.

וְכָל תּוֹרֹתָיו — *And all its regulations.*

Which parts are more holy than the others, where only *kohanim* are allowed to go and which parts are open to everybody.

וּכְתֹב לְעֵינֵיהֶם — *And write it down before their eyes.*

Yechezkel was to write down all these details so that everyone could study them.

For the interpretation of the rest of the verse see commentary to 10-11.

12. זֹאת תּוֹרַת הַבַּיִת — *This is the teaching of the House.*

Our translation follows *Metzudos* who renders: All the details in the previous verse are the teachings concerning the Temple which the people are expected to learn.

כָּל גְּבֻלוֹ ... קֹדֶשׁ קָדָשִׁים — *Its entire boundaries around is most holy.*

מג יג זֹאת תּוֹרַת הַבָּיִת: וְאֵלֶּה מִדּוֹת הַמִּזְבֵּחַ
יג בָּאַמּוֹת אַמָּה אַמָּה וָטֹפַח וְחֵיק הָאַמָּה

The expression קֹדֶשׁ קָדָשִׁים, *most holy,* in this verse is not synonymous with that in 41:4. There, it refers to the Inner Sanctuary which was called קֹדֶשׁ קָדָשִׁים, *Holy of Holies,* because it stood highest in the hierarchy of sanctity. In our verse the term is used to describe the Temple Mount's status relative to the much larger area in which it was set (see 40:5). The entire area is described in 45:1 as *holy* since it was set aside as a תְּרוּמָה לַה׳, *a gift for HASHEM, but its* קְדוּשָׁה, *sanctity,* has no halachic standing, for טֻמְאָה, *contamination,* is not prohibited there. Relative to this status, the Temple Mount which *does* have halachic strictures, is described as *most holy (Metzudos).*

13-17. These four verses deal with the dimensions of the מִזְבַּח הָעוֹלָה, *the altar of the burnt offering,* or, as it is also called, the מִזְבֵּחַ הַחִיצוֹן, *the outer altar,* which stood in the inner courtyard.

At 41:22 we noted that since Yechezkel was not shown any of the implements used in the Divine service, an explanation is required for the fact that he was shown the מִזְבֵּחַ הַזָּהָב, *the Golden [inner] Altar.* This question need not disturb us concerning the outer altar. It was a solid building, attached to the ground, and should be considered a part of the Temple structure together with all the other parts of the building which the prophet had been shown.

We may, however, ask why the altar is described separately rather than in the general description of the past few chapters. *Malbim* offers the following answer: According to *Rambam (Beis HaBechirah* 2:3), the altar in the second Temple was built according to Yechezkel's directions (except for the height of the יְסוֹד, *base* — see below). The rest of Yechezkel's instruction, however, apply only to the future Temple. [We have discussed the reason for this in the *pref. remarks* to 40:1 — 43:17.] For this reason the two descriptions were separated from one another; one was applicable immediately, while the other would be used only in Messianic times.

Before we study the dimensions of the altar, a word is in place concerning its exact location in the courtyard.

As explained by *Rambam (Beis HaBechirah* Ch. 2) the altar's location is of vital significance: The location of the altar is pinpointed with extreme precision and it may never be moved to another place ... (for) we have a universally recognized tradition that the place upon which David and Solomon built the altar ... is the exact place upon which Abraham built the altar and bound Isaac upon it, and it is in that place that Noah built an altar when he left the Ark. It is the same altar upon which Cain and Abel sacrificed, and upon it Adam sacrificed when he was created.

The Talmud records a number of opinions. [For a discussion, see *Tosafos Yom Tov* to *Middos* 2:1, also in the section of the altar in his *Tzuras HaBayis.*] In accordance with *comm.* 40:47 (see there) we shall assume the opinion of R' Yehudah (*Yoma* 16a and *Zevachim* 58b) that the altar was precisely centered in the inner courtyard. Since the inner courtyard was exactly one hundred cubits by one hundred cubits and the altar was thirty-four cubits from east to west (see below) and sixty-two cubits (including the ramp) from north to south (see below), we get the following: On the east-west line the altar was removed exactly thirty-four cubits from both the eastern wall and the אוּלָם, *Hall* (34+34+32=100). On the north-south line it began thirty-four cubits from the north wall, extended thirty-two cubits toward the south, and its ramp another thirty cubits, leaving a space of nineteen cubits betwen the foot of the ramp and the southern wall (34+32+30+4=100).

The Talmud (*Eruvin* 4a and *Menachos* 97b) discusses the structure of the altar in some detail. The description is considerably complicated by the fact that אַמּוֹת, *cubits,* of two different lengths are used: one of six טְפָחִים, *handbreadths,* and one of five. As we shall see below, some of the measurements use the shorter cubits and some, the longer. *Rambam* and *Rashi* disagree about the correct interpretation of the Talmudic discussion and, consequently, about the exact description of the altar. As we have done throughout the description of Yechezkel's Temple, we shall base the commentary on *Rashi's* opinion.

Middos 3:1 describes the altar of the Second Temple which, as we have seen

43 *Behold! this is the teaching of the House.*
13 [13] *Now these are the dimensions of the altar in*
cubits; each cubit, a cubit and a handbreadth. But
the base is to be a cubit as is the cubit of the width;

above, was modeled on the one described here. The Mishnah will help us in the understanding of our verse.

The altar comprised four basic components:

1. The יְסוֹד, *base.* In our text, it is called חֵיק. The top surface of the base is referred to as עֲזָרָה הַתַּחְתּוֹנָה or עֲזָרָה הַקְּטַנָּה, *the lower* or *smaller azarah* [lit. *courtyard*].

2. סוֹבֵב, *the surround.* The top surface of its indentation is called the עֲזָרָה הַגְּדוֹלָה, literally, *the large courtyard.*

3. The גַּג הַמִּזְבֵּחַ, *roof* (or top) *of the altar.* In the text, it is called הַרְאֵל, *har'el* [lit. *God's mountain*]. The very top of the altar is the מְקוֹם הַמַּעֲרָכָה, *the location of the woodpile,* i.e., the place where the fires burned. It is called אֲרִיאֵל, *ari'el* [lit. *God's lion*], in the text.

4. The קְרָנוֹת, *horns,* at the four corners of the altar are called גְּבוּל in the text.

[For a precise description of the מִזְבֵּחַ, *altar,* and the method by which it was built, the reader is directed to the Mishnah and commentators in *Middos.* For the purpose of our commentary to the text in *Ezekiel* the accompanying diagrams make the disposition sufficiently clear.]

13. [The exact meaning of this verse is discussed at *Eruvin* 4a. *Rashi* there explains the verse differently than he does here. His explanation here is based on a gloss to his commentary in *Eruvin* which states that his original explanation had been the one taught by his teacher *R' Yaakov ben Yakar,* but that *Rashi* abandoned it when he realized that it stood in conflict with *Targum.* Our commentary is based on *Rashi's* final choice.]

וְאֵלֶּה מִדּוֹת הַמִּזְבֵּחַ בָּאַמּוֹת — *Now these are the dimensions of the altar in cubits.*

The next phrase **אַמָּה אַמָּה וָטֹפַח**, *each cubit, a cubit and a handbreadth,* is taken as an explanation of the first phrase. The meaning is that the dimensions of the altar are to be given in cubits, which are to be six handbreadths long. [The basic cubit is five handbreadths, so **אַמָּה וָטֹפַח**, *a cubit and a handbreadth* implies a unit of measurement — one handbreadth longer than the basic cubit. See *comm.* to 20:5.]

Fig. 26

The Altar *(a side view)*

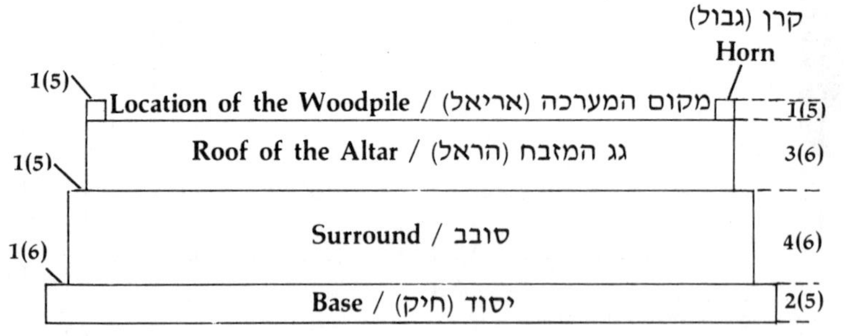

The number in parenthesis indicates whether the cubit measured 5 or 6 handbreadths

מג וְאַמָּה־רֹחַב וּגְבוּלָהּ אֶל־שְׂפָתָהּ סָבִיב
יד זֶרֶת הָאֶחָד וְזֶה גַּב הַמִּזְבֵּחַ: וּמֵחֵיק
הָאָרֶץ עַד־הָעֲזָרָה הַתַּחְתּוֹנָה שְׁתַּיִם

Now the second part of our verse lists a number of dimensions which were to be measured in cubits of *five* handbreadths, rather than of *six*. Therefore *Rashi* explains that וְאֵלֶּה, *and these*, refers not to the second half of our verse but to the measurements mentioned in the next three verses (14-16).

וְחֵיק הָאַמָּה — *But the base is to be a cubit.*

This is the standard handbreadth of five cubits. Each of the succeeding measures of this verse is likewise in cubits of five handbreadths.

We have translated חֵיק as *base* in accordance with *Eruvin* 4a. [Perhaps from חקק, *that which is dug out*, or *formed*. See *Rashi* to *Eruvin* and here, and *Ibn Janach* to חקק].

According to *Menachos* 97b this specification does not refer to the length of the base which, as we shall see, was thirty-two cubits, nor to its indentation which was one cubit (see *Mishnah, Middos*). Both of these were to be measured in cubits of six handbreadths. Reference is to the height of the base which verse 14 gives as two cubits. These two cubits (or perhaps

Fig. 27
The Altar *(viewed from above)*

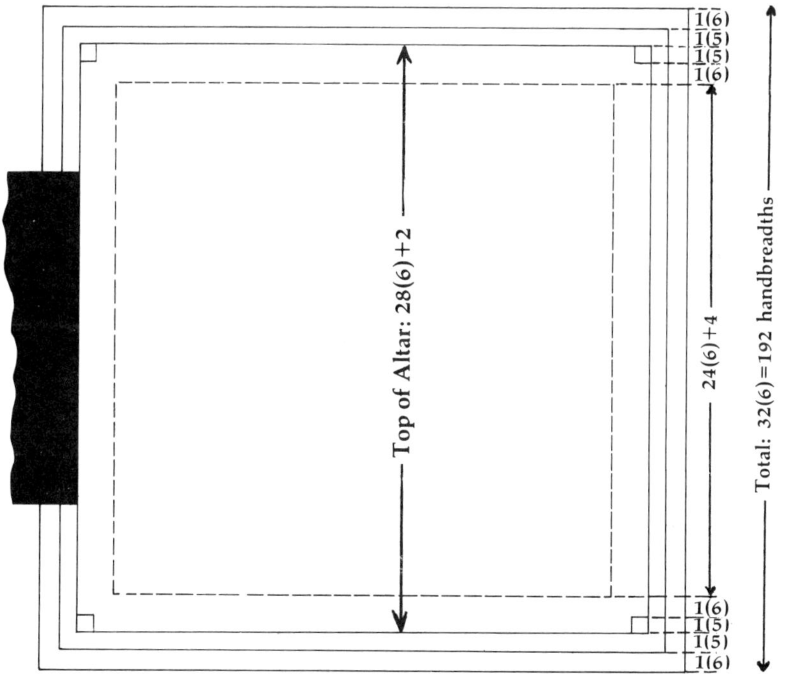

The number in parenthesis indicates whether the cubit measured 5 or 6 handbreadths

43 *and its boundary upon its edge all around is half a*
14 *cubit each. Similarly the top of the altar.* 14 *Now from*
the base upon the ground up to the lower azarah, two

only one of them — see below) were to be measured in a cubit of five handbreadths.

וְאַמָּה רֹחַב — *As is the cubit of the width.*

This refers to the indentation of the סוֹבֵב, *surround.* It, like the height of the base, was to be a cubit of five handbreadths.

[According to the above, some of the dimensions mentioned in *Middos* are rounded out. The length of the יְסוֹד, *base,* is given as thirty-two cubits (see below) of six handbreadths. This is exact, as is the thirty cubit length given for the סוֹבֵב, *surround.* However, the twenty-eight cubit measure given for the top of the altar is inexact. Since the indentation of the surround is measured in five handbreadth cubits, the top was twenty-eight cubits *plus,* as follows: After deducting the indentation of the base, the altar was thirty-cubits wide. Since the indentation of the surround was *five* handbreadths on all sides, thus the thirty cubit was reduced by ten handbreadths, or 1 2/3 cubits. The top of the altar was, therefore 28 1/3 cubits, which the Mishnah rounded out to twenty-eight.]

וּגְבוּלָהּ אֶל שְׂפָתָהּ סָבִיב זֶרֶת הָאֶחָד — *And its boundary upon its edge all around is half a cubit each.*

This refers to the קְרָנוֹת, *horns.* They were square extensions of the altar that protruded at the altar's top, at each of its four corners. These 'horns' played an essential part in the service of the holiest sacrifices, such as guilt and sin offerings. The horns are to measure half a cubit (זֶרֶת) measured from their center to each side. That is to say that they are to measure one cubit square. These cubits are to measure five handbreadths.

[The commentary has followed the simple meaning of *Rashi* to our text — that the five handbreadth implication in our verse refers to the one cubit by one cubit area of the horns rather than to their height. If this is correct then we assume that the *height* of the horns would be measured by a cubit of six handbreadths. (See below to *v.* 15). It should however be noted that *Menachos* 97b (and see *Rashi* 98a) assumes our verse to refer to the *height* of the horns, in which case they would be only five handbreadths high. According to the Talmud there is no clear direction concerning the width. The text could be read either way.]

[Once more this forces us to see some of the measurements given in *Middos* as approximations.

The measurements for the top of the altar are given as follows: Based on the round number that the top of the altar is twenty-eight cubits by twenty-eight (although, as shown above, it was actually 28 1/3 handbreadths) the Mishnah computes that since each 'horn' took a space of one cubit, there are twenty-six cubits between the 'horns'. Since the 'horns' were measured in cubits of five handbreadths, this free space was actually two handbreadths *more* than twenty-six cubits: 28 1/3 cubits=170 handbreadths. Since the horns on either side took up five handbreadths, we are left with 160, which, divided by six, yields 26 2/3 cubits. Thus, the Mishnah, which says twenty-six cubits rounds out to the nearest *full* cubit.]

וְזֶה גַּב הַמִּזְבֵּחַ — *Similarly the top of the altar.*

According to *Menachos* 97b this phrase does not refer to the outer altar. It is a reference to the מִזְבַּח הַזָּהָב, *the golden* [*inner*] *altar,* whose total area was one cubit by one cubit (*Exodus* 30:2). These were to be the lesser cubits of five handbreadths.

14. The height of the base is to be two cubits and its indentation one cubit. The two cubit height is a change from the Second Temple in which the base was one cubit. However the overall ten-cubit height of the altar was not altered since the סוֹבֵב, *surround,* was five cubits high in the Second Temple, while in Yechezkel's Temple, as the latter part of our verse indicates, it was only four cubits high.

מג
טו־יז

אַמּוֹת וְרֹחַב אַמָּה אֶחָת וּמֵהָעֲזָרָה
הַקְּטַנָּה עַד־הָעֲזָרָה הַגְּדוֹלָה אַרְבַּע
טו אַמּוֹת וְרֹחַב הָאַמָּה׃ וְהַהַרְאֵל אַרְבַּע
אַמּוֹת וּמֵהָאֲרִאֵיל וּלְמַעְלָה הַקְּרָנוֹת
טז אַרְבַּע׃ וְהָאֲרִאֵיל שְׁתֵּים עֶשְׂרֵה אֹרֶךְ
בִּשְׁתֵּים עֶשְׂרֵה רֹחַב רָבוּעַ אֶל אַרְבַּעַת
יז רְבָעָיו׃ וְהָעֲזָרָה אַרְבַּע עֶשְׂרֵה אֹרֶךְ
בְּאַרְבַּע עֶשְׂרֵה רֹחַב אֶל אַרְבַּעַת רְבָעֶיהָ
וְהַגְּבוּל סָבִיב אוֹתָהּ חֲצִי הָאַמָּה וְהַחֵיק־

מֵהָעֲזָרָה הַקְּטַנָּה...הָעֲזָרָה הַגְּדוֹלָה — *From the small azarah...the large azarah.*

The top of the base is called the small *azarah* because it was only two cubits above the floor. The top of the surround was called the large *azarah* because it was six cubits above the floor *(Metzudos).*

15. וְהַהַרְאֵל אַרְבַּע אַמּוֹת — *Now the har'el was four cubits.*

[We have pointed out above that the various components of the מִזְבֵּחַ carry different names in *Ezekiel* than those to which we are accustomed in Mishnah and Talmud. One supposes that these names relate to the symbolic significance of the altar but there are no Midrashic sources to help us to plumb their depths. The reader is directed to *R' Hirsch's* commentary to *Exodus* 27:8 where an attempt is made to understand the symbolism of the altar on the basis of our text.]

Har'el refers to the height of the section of the altar from the top of its surround to its roof. As the verse says, this was four cubits, in contrast to the *har'el* of the Second Temple which was only three cubits *(Rashi).* Thus, according to *Rashi* (based on *Middos* 3:1), we have a total of eleven cubits to the top of the קְרָנוֹת, *horns* [2+4+4+1=11]. This seems to be in conflict with *Zevachim* 59b which ascribes a height of ten cubits to the altar (see also *Menachos* 97b).

Indeed *Zevachim* 53a interprets our verse quite differently. Contrary to *Rashi's* view, the גַּג הַמִּזְבֵּחַ, *roof of the altar* [the section from the surround to the roof], is assumed to be three cubits. The meaning of our verse is that the top four cubits of the altar (excluding the קְרָנוֹת) are considered to be 'within the jurisdiction,' so to speak, of the קְרָנוֹת (רשות קרנות ד׳).

Following is the background for the interpretation of the Sages: As part of the sacrificial service, blood had to be sprinkled upon the altar. This requirement was fulfilled in different ways, depending on the particular sacrifice. Some had their blood sprinkled on the upper part of the altar, some on the lower. To accommodate these requirements a חוּט הַסִּיקְרָא, *red band,* was painted around the waist of the altar, surrounding it at the halfway mark. Since the altar had a height of ten cubits (including the horns), the red band circled the altar four cubits from the altar's top, that is one cubit beneath the top of the surround. Thus, since together with the single cubit height of the horns these four cubits constitute the upper half of the altar, it is true to say that the upper four cubits of the altar belong together with the horns. According to the Sages, this is the meaning of our verse. [Figure 26 is based on this interpretation and assumes a height of three cubits for the גַּג הַמִּזְבֵּחַ, *roof of the altar,* from the top of the surround to the top of the altar (excluding the horns). According to *Rashi's* interpretation of our verse, however, this section has a height of four cubits].

We have located the red band one cubit below the top of the surround and this is expressly stated in *Menachos* 97b. This forces us to reevaluate some of the assumptions of our text.

We have noted that in the Second Temple

cubits with a width of one cubit. From the small azarah up the large azarah, four cubits with a width of one cubit. 15 *Now the har'el was four cubits; and from the ari'el and up — four horns.*

16 *The ari'el is twelve cubits long by twelve cubits wide, squared toward its four quarters.* 17 *And the azarah is fourteen cubits long by fourteen cubits wide toward its four quarters. The boundary surrounding it is half a cubit, its base is a cubit all*

the height of the base was a single five handbreadth cubit. According to *Menachos* 97b the single cubit height of the horns was also a five handbreadth cubit. All the other measurements of the height of the altar are given in six handbreadth cubits. This yields a height of fifty-eight handbreadths for the complete altar. [5+30+18+5=58]. The half way mark (29 handbreadths) is thus six handbreadths (one cubit) below the top of the surround. [The horns, five handbreadths; the roof, 3×6=18, the surrounding, six (5+18+6=29).]

However, in Yechezkel's altar the base was two cubits high (*v.* 14). If *both* of those cubits are to be measured in cubits of five handbreadths, then the total height of the altar is lowered by one handbreadth. This would locate the halfway mark at 28½ handbreadths rather than twenty-nine, which would be 5½ handbreadths beneath the top of the surround.

To solve this dilemma we must assume (with *Tosafos Yom Tov)* that only the *lower* cubit of the base was a five handbreadth cubit, but the upper cubit was indeed six; if so, the center of the altar's height would have coincided precisely with that in the Second Temple. Alternatively, in Yechezkel's altar the height of the horns was measured in a cubit of six handbreadths in which case the total handbreadths would once more be fifty-eight; in this case the twenty-nine handbreadth mark would fall five handbreadths below the top of the surround which could still be considered one cubit. (The top of the surround would be 6+6+6+6=24 handbreadths from the top and 5+5+6+6+6+6=34 handbreadths from the bottom.)

וּמֵהָאֲרִיאֵל וּלְמַעְלָה הַקְּרָנוֹת אַרְבַּע — *And from the ari'el and up—four horns.*

The *ari'el* is the מְקוֹם הַמַּעֲרָכָה, *site of the fire,* the area on the top of the altar where sacrifices were burned (see below *v.* 16). Above it, 'four horns' rose at the four corners of the altar.

16. **אֶל אַרְבַּעַת רְבָעָיו** — *Squared toward its four quarters.*

This phrase allows us to understand the first part of the sentence correctly. It teaches that the *ari'el,* the site of the fire atop the altar, should be visualized as comprised of four quarters, each one to measure twelve cubits square. Thus, the measurement given earlier in the verse does *not* refer to the complete *ari'el* — which was twenty-four cubits by twenty-four cubits — but to each of its quadrants. In other words, the measurement is taken from the center of the *ari'el* (See *comm.* and diagram to *v.* 13).

17. In this verse הָעֲזָרָה, *the azarah* [lit. *courtyard*], refers to the top surface of the altar. Whereas the previous verse described the site of the fire as four twelve cubit squares [i.e., 24×24, see *comm. v.* 16] our verse gives the sides of each quadrant as fourteen cubits. Of these additional two cubits for each quadrant, one cubit was at the very edge of the altar (which is actually 28×28) from horn to horn, and the second cubit was for the passageway of the *kohanim* (see *comm.* to *v.* 13 and fig. 27).

וְהַגְּבוּל סָבִיב אוֹתָהּ חֲצִי הָאַמָּה — *The boundary surrounding it is half a cubit.*

This *boundary* refers to the קְרָנוֹת, *horns.* As above in verse 13 (see *comm.* there) the measurement is given as *half*

לָהּ אַמָּה סָבִיב וּמַעֲלֹתֵהוּ פְּנוֹת קָדִים׃
יח וַיֹּאמֶר אֵלַי בֶּן־אָדָם כֹּה אָמַר אֲדֹנָי יֱהֹוִה
אֵלֶּה חֻקּוֹת הַמִּזְבֵּחַ בְּיוֹם הֵעָשׂוֹתוֹ
לְהַעֲלוֹת עָלָיו עוֹלָה וְלִזְרֹק עָלָיו דָּם׃
יט וְנָתַתָּה אֶל־הַכֹּהֲנִים הַלְוִיִּם אֲשֶׁר הֵם
מִזֶּרַע צָדוֹק הַקְּרֹבִים אֵלַי נְאֻם אֲדֹנָי
יֱהֹוִה לְשָׁרְתֵנִי פַּר בֶּן־בָּקָר לְחַטָּאת׃
כ וְלָקַחְתָּ מִדָּמוֹ וְנָתַתָּה עַל־אַרְבַּע קַרְנֹתָיו
וְאֶל־אַרְבַּע פִּנּוֹת הָעֲזָרָה וְאֶל־הַגְּבוּל

a cubit, measured from the center of each horn, but the full horn measured one cubit square.

וְהַחֵיק לָהּ אַמָּה סָבִיב — *Its base is a cubit all around.*

As noted above (*pref.* to *v.* 13) Yechezkel refers to the יְסוֹד, *base*, as חֵיק, *cheik*. Verse 13 had dealt only with the *height* of the base, but said nothing of its indentation.

וּמַעֲלֹתֵהוּ פְּנוֹת קָדִים — *And its ramp turned eastward.*

Because the *kohanim* who mounted the altar were to make all turns towards the right, the ramp had to be positioned so that a *kohen* getting off it and turning right would face east. Therefore, the ramp had to be placed on the south side of the altar.

Middos 3:3 gives the dimensions of the ramp as thirty-two cubits long and sixteen cubits wide. Although it was thirty-two cubits long it took up only thirty cubits of floor space in the courtyard (*Middos* 5:2). [See *Zevachim* 62b for a discussion.]

18-27. These verses prescribe a series of sacrifices which must be brought in order to 'cleanse' the altar, and to ready it for its permanent functions.

Such a 'cleansing' was also prescribed during the שִׁבְעַת יְמֵי הַמִּלּוּאִים, *seven days of Consecration* during which the מִשְׁכָּן, *Tabernacle* in the wilderness, was made fit for Divine service (see *Exodus* 29:1-46 and *Leviticus* 8:1-36, particularly *Exodus* 29:36-37 and *Leviticus* 8:14 for details of that consecration). It is not unexpected, therefore, that a series of similar sacrifices was prescribed for the consecration of the Temple. By their very nature such מִלּוּאִים, *consecration*, sacrifices — because they serve a special function and are not part of the normal sacrificial service — may have laws of their own that are different not only from regular sacrifices, but also from the consecration sacrifices of *Exodus*.

[We shall point out the various irregularities in the course of the commentary. For an analysis of the idea of a consecration service and an explanation for their invariably unique laws, see *Pachad Yitzchak* to *Chanukah* ch. 12. His analysis is based on *Rashi* to *Shir HaShirim* 5:1. We direct the interested reader to that *Rashi* for a Midrashic approach to the concept of a consecration service.]

The text does not give a specific date for this cleansing. However, *Rashi* to 45:18 thinks that the bullock mentioned in verse 19 of our chapter is identical with the one mentioned in 45:18; this would place the date of the 'cleansing' on *Rosh Chodesh Nissan* (see there). This identification creates some problems since the locations given in our section for the sprinkling of the blood seem different from those mentioned in ch. 45 (see *Tosafos, Menachos* 45a). *Malbim* suggests that our passage

around, and its ramp turned eastward.
18 *Then He said to me: Ben Adam! Thus says my*
Lord HASHEM/ELOHIM: These are the requirements
of the altar upon the day that it is made, so that burnt
offerings may be brought upon it and blood may be
sprinkled on it:
19 *Give to the kohanim, the Levites,*
from the tribe of Levi, who are the seed of Tzadok,
and approach Me — the words of my Lord
HASHEM/ELOHIM — to serve Me, a bullock from the
herd for a cleansing offering.
20 *Take some of its*
blood and place it upon its four horns and upon the
four corners of the azarah and upon its boundary all

may refer to cleansing rites which were to take place on the twenty-third of *Adar,* a week before *Rosh Chodesh Nissan.* This would coincide with the procedure followed in the wilderness where a seven-day consecration service preceded the inauguration of the Tabernacle on *Rosh Chodesh Nissan.* In this way, the eighth day day (see vs. 25 and 26) would coincide with *Rosh Chodesh Nissan* at which time the rites prescribed in ch. 45 will take place. Besides the fact that this arrangement avoids the difficulties which we have noted with *Rashi's* opinion (see above), it has the advantage of duplicating the dates of the consecration in *Exodus.* See further below and in ch. 45.

18. אֵלֶּה חֻקּוֹת הַמִּזְבֵּחַ — *These are the requirements* [lit. *decrees*] *of the altar.*

These rites are needed to inaugurate the altar on the day of its completion so that it should be eligible for the sacrifice of burnt offerings and for the sprinkling of blood *(Metzudos).*

19. וְנָתַתָּה אֶל הַכֹּהֲנִים הַלְוִיִּם — *Give to the kohanim, the Levites.*

The *kohanim,* as the elite of the tribe of Levi, are those who have been selected to perform the Temple service.

Since this command is addressed to Yechezkel personally, [*you* shall give], *Radak* deduces from here a guarantee for תְּחִיַּת הַמֵּתִים, *the resurrection of the dead:* Yechezkel the *kohen* (1:3) will be involved personally in this 'cleansing' rite.

אֲשֶׁר הֵם מִזֶּרַע צָדוֹק — *Who are of the seed of Tzadok.*

See 40:46 and 44:15.

פַּר בֶּן בָּקָר לְחַטָּאת — *A bullock from the herd for a cleansing offering.*

We have translated: *cleansing offering* rather than *sin offering,* which is the usual translation of חַטָּאת, because the function of this sacrifice was to cleanse the altar rather than to atone for sin. The root חטא also has the meaning of *to cleanse,* and it is used in that sense in verse 20.

In the Consecration sacrifices of *Exodus* as well, a bullock was used for the cleansing of the altar (*Exodus* 29:1 and 36). However as the next verse shows the prescriptions for the עֲבוֹדַת הַדָּם, *the service of the blood,* are not exactly the same as those of *Exodus.*

20. The blood of this cleansing offering is to be sprinkled onto the four horns of the altar in exactly the same way as that of the bullock in *Exodus* (29:12), and indeed as is the case with every sin offering *(Rambam Ma'aseh HaKorbonos* 5:7). However, here, some additional sprinkling which finds no parallel elsewhere is required. Blood is to be sprinkled on the אַרְבַּע פִּנּוֹת הָעֲזָרָה,

כא סָבִיב וְחִטֵּאתָ אוֹתוֹ וְכִפַּרְתָּהוּ: וְלָקַחְתָּ
אֵת הַפָּר הַחַטָּאת וּשְׂרָפוֹ בְּמִפְקַד הַבַּיִת
כב מִחוּץ לַמִּקְדָּשׁ: וּבַיּוֹם הַשֵּׁנִי תַּקְרִיב
שְׂעִיר־עִזִּים תָּמִים לְחַטָּאת וְחִטְּאוּ אֶת־
כג הַמִּזְבֵּחַ כַּאֲשֶׁר חִטְּאוּ בַּפָּר: בְּכַלּוֹתְךָ
מֵחַטֵּא תַּקְרִיב פַּר בֶּן־בָּקָר תָּמִים וְאַיִל
כד מִן־הַצֹּאן תָּמִים: וְהִקְרַבְתָּם לִפְנֵי יהוה
וְהִשְׁלִיכוּ הַכֹּהֲנִים עֲלֵיהֶם מֶלַח וְהֶעֱלוּ
כה אוֹתָם עֹלָה לַיהוה: שִׁבְעַת יָמִים
תַּעֲשֶׂה שְׂעִיר־חַטָּאת לַיּוֹם וּפַר בֶּן־
בָּקָר וְאַיִל מִן־הַצֹּאן תְּמִימִים יַעֲשׂוּ:

the four corners of the azarah, which *Rashi* (on the strength of v. 17) takes to mean the four corners of the altar's top. Then, blood had to be placed upon the גְּבוּל, *boundary*. *Rashi* offers no interpretation. However, *Metzudos* points out that probably the *boundary*, in this case, refers to the *base*, which 'bounds' the bottom of the altar.

This is in contrast to the use of גבול throughout this chapter where it describes the horns. In our verse, however, where the horns are mentioned specifically, we are forced to assign a different meaning. While the type of service to be performed on the base is not specified, we may perhaps assume that it is the pouring of the remainder of the blood onto the base, a service which was common to all sin offerings (see *Rambam* ibid.).

וְכִפַּרְתָּהוּ — *And purify it.*

Elevate it from its neutral status and sanctify it so that henceforth it may be used to bring about atonement (כַּפָּרָה) [through the bringing of sacrifices] *(Rashi).*

21. וּשְׂרָפוֹ בְּמִפְקַד הַבַּיִת — *And burn it in the designated place of the House.*

There was a designated place, outside the Temple grounds, where the meat of this and similar offerings was burned. As will be explained below, there were classes of offerings whose meat (unlike that of burnt offerings) was not burned on the altar, but (unlike the meat of ordinary sin offerings) was not to be eaten. Such meat was burned outside the Temple grounds in this specially designated place.

We have followed *Malbim* in his translation of the obscure term מִפְקָד. He derives it from the root פקד, *to appoint* or *designate*. *Rashi* and *Metzudos* take פקד in the sense of *something withheld*. Hence the מִפְקָד is of a place 'withheld' from the House, that is, outside the house.

The intent of the term is the same according to both interpretations. The meat of this bullock was not to be eaten but was to be burned in a designated area outside the Temple.

[This is an irregularity. There are two kinds of חַטָּאוֹת, *sin offerings*. The common ones are known as חַטָּאוֹת חִצוֹנִיּוֹת, *outside sin offerings*, because their blood was sprinkled only on the *outside* altar; the meat of these offerings was eaten by the *kohanim*. A second category of special sin offerings, had as חַטָּאוֹת פְּנִימִיּוֹת, *inside sin offerings*, had their blood sprinkled upon the *inside* altar; their meat was not eaten but burned outside the Temple. (For details see *Rambam, Ma'aseh HaKorbonos* 1:16 and ch. 7). Our offering is irregular, because it was an *outside* one, and nevertheless had its meat burned.

around. Cleanse it and purify it. 21 *Then take this*
bullock which is a cleansing offering and burn it in
the designated place of the House — outside the Temple. 22 *Then, on the second day you are to bring near*
a perfect he-goat for a cleansing offering; and let them cleanse the altar as they had cleansed with the bullock.

23 *When you have finished the cleansing, bring close a perfect bullock from the herd and a perfect ram from the flock,*
24 *and bring them close before HASHEM and let the kohanim throw salt upon them and bring them up as a burnt offering to HASHEM.*
25 *For seven days, prepare a he-goat every day, and a perfect bullock from the herd and a ram from the flock. They are to prepare.*
26 *For seven days let them*

In the context of the consecration offerings, this is not surprising since other parts of consecration proceedings also share this dual requirement. See *Exodus* 29:14; *Leviticus* 9:11 and *Numbers* 8:8. See *Rashi*).]

22. On the next day a goat is substituted for the bullock. *Rashi* points out that there is no parallel for this in the consecration of *Exodus*, where a bullock was used for the full seven days.

23-24. In addition to this goat a bullock and a ram were to be brought as burnt offerings. [In the consecration of *Exodus*, the bullock was accompanied by two rams: one to be a burnt offering and one a peace offering.]

24. וְהִשְׁלִיכוּ הַכֹּהֲנִים עֲלֵיהֶם מֶלַח — *And let the kohanim throw salt upon them.*

There is some confusion concerning the question of whether the salting of sacrifices requires a *kohen* or whether it may be done by anyone. [See *Rambam, Bi'as HaMikdash* 9:5 and *P'sulei HaMukdoshin* 11:7].

Our verse which implies that the *kohanim* are to throw the salt need have no bearing on this issue. In the first place we have already noted that the laws of the consecration sacrifices place them in a unique category, and secondly our verse need not be interpreted to insist that the salting must be done by *kohanim* and none other. It is quite possible that anyone would qualify but that the privilege is to be reserved for *kohanim* in their honor. Such a practice was not unusual. See, for example, Mishnah, *Yomah* 66a which states that part of the *Yom Kippur* service could have been performed by any *kohen* but was nevertheless reserved for the *kohen gadol (R' Shimon Krasner).*

23-24. A goat with an accompanying bullock and ram were to be brought for seven days. The text does not make clear whether these seven days include the first day, when a bullock was brought instead of a goat — one day for the bullock and six days for the goat — or whether seven days of ram sacrifices are called for, in addition to the day of the bullock.

[Both options pose difficulties. Since verse 26 says that cleansing of the altar was to last seven days, that would imply that there were only seven days altogether and that these included the one day of the bullock. On the other hand, verse 25 prescribes seven full days for the bringing of goat, which seems to postulate an eight day cleansing period.]

מג
כו־כז

כו שִׁבְעַת יָמִים יְכַפְּרוּ אֶת־הַמִּזְבֵּחַ וְטִהֲרוּ
כז אֹתוֹ וּמִלְאוּ יָדָו: וִיכַלּוּ אֶת־הַיָּמִים
וְהָיָה בַיּוֹם הַשְּׁמִינִי וָהָלְאָה יַעֲשׂוּ
הַכֹּהֲנִים עַל־הַמִּזְבֵּחַ אֶת־עוֹלוֹתֵיכֶם
וְאֶת־שַׁלְמֵיכֶם וְרָצָאתִי אֶתְכֶם נְאֻם
מד א אֲדֹנָי יֱהֹוִה: וַיָּשֶׁב אֹתִי דֶּרֶךְ
א שַׁעַר הַמִּקְדָּשׁ הַחִיצוֹן הַפֹּנֶה קָדִים וְהוּא

We pointed out above that *Malbim* opts for the latter interpretation. Accordingly, the consecration period would duplicate that of *Exodus* which also consisted of an eight-day period: the seven days beginning with the twenty-third of Adar, described in *Exodus* 29 and *Leviticus* 8, and *Rosh Chodesh Nissan*, the שְׁמִינִי לַמִּלוּאִים, *eighth day of consecration*, described in *Leviticus* 9.

[The function of the sacrifices on the eighth day was different from that of the sacrifices of the earlier seven days. For an analysis, see *Ramban, Leviticus* 9:2. We shall come back to these two functions in various sections of the commentary, see below.]

Our eight days also began on the twenty-third of *Adar* and led into *Rosh Chodesh Nissan*. On that day a new series of sacrifices began which are described at 48:18 ff.

26. וּמִלְאוּ יָדָיו — *And consecrate it* [lit. *and they shall fill its hands*].

See *Rashi* to *Exodus* 28:41, where he explains that this is an idiom for consecration. The sense of the expression is that one places a responsibility into someone's 'hands', thereby consecrating him to the task.

27. This verse states that the rites described here were required in order to cleanse the altar and make it fit for sacrifice. There is no implication that these were the only consecration offerings. As we shall see in chapter 45, numerous other sacrifices were identified by the Sages as consecration offerings, but we shall find that they had functions other than the cleansing of the altar, the purpose served by the offerings of our chapter.

XLIV

1-3. Two trends are followed by the commentators on the first three verses on this chapter.

Rashi, Radak, and *Metzudos* follow the explanation of the Sages in *Middos* 4:2.

Abarbanel and *Malbim*, on the other hand, offer interpretations that seem much closer to the פְּשָׁט, *plain meaning*, of the verses. In their view, the interpretation in the *Mishnah* was not meant to supplant the simple meaning of the verses, but to augment it.[1]

1. שַׁעַר הַמִּקְדָּשׁ הַחִיצוֹן הַפֹּנֶה קָדִים — *The outer gate of the Sanctuary which faces eastward.*

Rashi translates: *the eastern gate of*

1. A short discussion is required to explain our contention that the criteria used in determining פְּשָׁט, *the plain meaning*, yield a different interpretation than that of the Sages.

While it is difficult to set forth exact criteria for determining the plain meaning of a scriptural section, it may be said that such an interpretation should fulfill the following three conditions:

(1) The interpretation must fit the words of the passage from the point of view of: (a) lexicology, the meaning of the word or combination of words; (b) grammar; and (c) syn-

43
27 *purify the altar, cleanse it and consecrate it.* [27] *And when the days will have passed, it shall be from the eighth day onward that the kohanim may prepare on the altar their burnt offerings and their peace offerings, and I shall find favor in them. The words of my Lord* HASHEM/ELOHIM.

44
1 *Then he brought me back toward the outer gate of the Sanctuary which faces eastward, and it was*

the outer Sanctuary.

According to *Rashi*, this *gate* is the southern wicket (see 41:11) at the side of the great gate (4/5) leading into the Sanctuary which is the *outer* and *eastern* of the two chambers of the Temple *(Metzudos)*. This southern wicket is to be closed.

Abarbanel translates: *the eastern gate* (1/3) *of the outer courtyard.*

tax, the way in which the verse is put together.

(2) It must fit the context in terms of subject matter.

(3) It must not contradict any other passage in Scripture.

[These criteria are suggested by *Menachem ben Yashar* in his review of פְּשׁוּטוֹ שֶׁל מִקְרָא by *Rabbi Shimon Kasher* in the journal *HaMa'ayan, Teves* 5725.]

The assertion of the Sages, that the שַׁעַר הַמִּקְדָּשׁ הַחִיצוֹן הַפֹּנֶה קָדִים of our verse is the wicket at the southern side of the entrance gate of the הֵיכָל (see *comm.)* stands up under the first and third of our criteria, but it does not fit the context for the following reasons: (1) Although *Middos* 4:1 states that there were wickets on the northern and southern sides of the Temple gate, these wickets have not been mentioned in *Ezekiel;* therefore the text could not assume our knowledge of them. (2) Throughout *Ezekiel* the term מִקְדָּשׁ is used to describe the whole Temple complex (e.g., in 43:21); the Temple *building* [הֵיכָל] alone is referred to as בַּיִת. (3) All commentators assume that the virtually identical phrase: שַׁעַר אֲשֶׁר פֹּנֶה דֶּרֶךְ קָדִים of 43:1 is the eastern gate of the outer courtyard. The addition of the term הַחִיצוֹן, *the outer,* in our verse would surely point to an identical meaning since that term has been used consistently in this series of chapters to describe the outer courtyard. (4) If the reference were to the gate of the הֵיכָל, *Temple,* the description: הַפֹּנֶה קָדִים, *which faces eastward,* would be redundant since this was the only gate which led into the Temple. (See *Metzudos* to 43:4 who takes an identical description to refer to the eastern gate of the חָצֵר הַחִיצוֹנָה, *outer courtyard,* although the context would have pointed to the Temple gate.)

For all these reasons it seems clear that the interpretation according to the plain meaning demands that we assume the gate in *v.* 1 to be the eastern gate of the courtyard as it is interpreted by *Abarbanel* and *Malbim* (see *comm.).* Therefore, there must be other criteria compelling the Sages to interpret it as the wicket on the southern side of the Temple gate. However, unless this was a קַבָּלָה, *an oral tradition,* it is difficult to see why this assertion was necessary.

When we recall that the Mishnah in *Middos* is describing the Second Temple, the following explanation seems possible:

The builders of the Second Temple knew that their Temple was not to be the ultimate one described by Yechezkel [see pref., ch. 40]. Therefore as *Rambam* taught, their building was designed like Solomon's, incorporating only some features of Yechezkel's Temple as a reminder that a more glorious future lay ahead.

According to *Abarbanel* and *Malbim* that the outer gate of the outer courtyard was to be kept closed permanently to symbolize that God's Glory would never depart (see *comm.),* then this feature would be most unsuited to the Second Temple which was destined to be destroyed. However, a 'closed door' *somewhere in the* Temple would have been an inspiring allusion to the future reality it symbolized.

For this reason they decided to have a permanently closed door, but not at the eastern

מד
ב־ד

ב סָגוּר: וַיֹּאמֶר אֵלַי יהוה הַשַּׁעַר הַזֶּה
סָגוּר יִהְיֶה לֹא יִפָּתֵחַ וְאִישׁ לֹא־יָבֹא בוֹ
כִּי יהוה אֱלֹהֵי־יִשְׂרָאֵל בָּא בוֹ וְהָיָה
ג סָגוּר: אֶת־הַנָּשִׂיא נָשִׂיא הוּא יֵשֶׁב־בּוֹ
°לאכול־לֶחֶם לִפְנֵי יהוה מִדֶּרֶךְ אוּלָם °לֶאֱכָל ק׳
ד הַשַּׁעַר יָבוֹא וּמִדַּרְכּוֹ יֵצֵא: וַיְבִיאֵנִי דֶּרֶךְ־
שַׁעַר הַצָּפוֹן אֶל־פְּנֵי הַבַּיִת וָאֵרֶא וְהִנֵּה

Yechezkel's guide leads him to the eastern gate of the outer courtyard which he finds closed. Yechezkel is astounded because he had seen this very gate open in order to admit the Glory of the God of Israel which was returning to the Temple from the east (43:1-4). The explanation for this change is given in the next verse.

2. כִּי ה׳...בָּא בוֹ — *Because HASHEM...entered by it.*

Rashi continues that this southern wicket is to remain closed and unused because it is there that the Divine Presence manifests Itself. [See *Moreh Nevuchim* 1:22 for a description of the development of the root בוא, *to come,* from a simple description of the act of a physical 'coming' to a descriptive term for הַשְׁרָאַת הַשְּׁכִינָה, *the manifestation of the Divine Presence.*]

It is not entirely clear what Godly Presence is associated with that particular wicket since we know that the Presence is 'between the two Cherubim [on the Ark]'. However, *Pirkei deRabbi Eliezer* 51 states that when the future Temple is built, its gates will open by themselves on the Sabbath and on *Rosh Chodesh* (see further at 46:1 ff). Thereupon the people will become aware that the *Shechinah* is at the wicket and will prostrate themselves towards it. Many *Midrashim* (e.g., *Tanchumah Ki Sisa* 15) also point out the humility of God Who confines Himself to the small wicket rather than to the large, main gates.

According to *Abarbanel,* בָּא is in the past tense: *entered.* Because *God had entered* through this gate, it was to remain locked — never to be opened again. This would symbolize that the Divine Presence, once in the Temple, would never depart again. The gate through which God had entered is closed. He cannot depart, so to speak.

3. הַנָּשִׂיא — *For the prince.*

Radak (following *Targum)* explains that the אֶת is to be rendered like אֶל, *to* or *for,* and joined to the end of the previous verse. The gate is to be closed and reserved *for* the use of the prince.

The term נָשִׂיא, [*nassi*], *prince,* will

entrance gate, because that would have implied a condition which had not yet been attained. Instead, they closed one of the small wickets at the side of the Temple gate, thereby assuring that its symbolism would be understood correctly: it expressed a hope and a prayer rather than a reality.

If this thesis is acceptable then the meaning of the Mishnah in *Middos* is clear. The closed wicket of the Third Temple was indeed to be that leading to the eastern gate of the *outer courtyard,* as the plain meaning of our verse would imply. That the wicket of the Second Temple building was closed, as stated in the Mishnah, was meant to symbolize the condition of Yechezkel's future Temple. The verse from *Ezekiel* is quoted because the laws assigned to the wicket had their source and justification in that verse.

We hesitate to recommend this thesis as more than a possibility, because none of the commentators suggest such an interpretation for the Mishnah in *Middos* and because the expression used in the Mishnah: עָלָיו הוּא מְפוֹרָשׁ עַל יְדֵי יְחֶזְקֵאל, *and this* [*the Temple wicket*] *is specified in Ezekiel,* indicates a stronger dependence than has been suggested.

closed. [2] *Then HASHEM said to me: This gate shall remain closed, not to be opened, that no man may enter by it. Because HASHEM, God of Israel entered by it, it shall remain closed* [3] *for the prince. He is a prince — he shall sit within it to eat food before HASHEM. Through the hall of the gate he is to come, and depart that way.* [4] *Then He brought me in the direction of the northern gate to the front of the*

recur many times in these final chapters. *Rashi* holds that it refers to the כֹּהֵן גָּדוֹל [*kohen gadol*], *high priest,* who is called *nassi* because of his preeminence among the *kohanim.* All other commentators, based on 34:24 and the usual meaning of the word, assume that it refers to the king — and specifically to the מֶלֶךְ הַמָּשִׁיחַ, *the King Messiah.* [See 22:6 and 34:24 for our understanding of the term *nassi.*]

נָשִׂיא הוּא יֵשֶׁב בּוֹ לֶאֱכָל לֶחֶם — *He is a prince — he shall sit within it to eat food.*

According to *Rashi,* the *nassi* [*high priest*] is to eat his portion of the sacrifices there.

Radak continues: and because he is a prince it is fitting that a special place should be assigned to him for eating. For him to eat together with commoners would be improper.

[*Rashi* states that the wicket will be opened for him, but this seems to be an addition and does not appear in the manuscript *Rashi* (which ends *Rashi's comm.* to this verse with the words פעמים רבות). It would certainly seem to contravene the implication of verse 2 that it is never to be opened. (However, see further at 46:1ff.) Another problem arises in the description of the *nassi* as 'sitting' to eat 'bread'. The halachah is explicit that only 'kings from the house of David' are allowed to sit in the inner courtyard (*Yoma* 28a). As we have seen, however, *Rashi* interprets *nassi* as the high priest rather than the king; if so, he would be forbidden to sit there. For a discussion see *Raavad* to *Tamid* 3:7.]

According to *Abarbanel,* when the prince sits in the outer courtyard in order to eat his portion of the sacrifices he is to sit within the gateway. [That is, despite the fact that the door itself would remain permanently closed, there would be room for him to sit in the doorway.] *R' Breuer* suggests that the reason for choosing this particular location was so that the *nassi* would contemplate the closed door while he was eating, and thus become aware of his responsibility to make sure that there be no cause for the *Shechinah* ever to depart again.

מִדֶּרֶךְ אוּלָם הַשַּׁעַר יָבוֹא — *Through the hall of the gate he is to come.*

As he goes to his place to the southern wicket he is to enter from the eastern gate of the inner courtyard. This is the main entrance and the one most fitting for the prince *(Rashi).*

וּמִדַּרְכּוֹ יֵצֵא — *And depart that way.*

This is an unrelated thought. In contrast to the common people who are not permitted to exit the courtyard by the same way through which they have entered (see 46:9), the prince leaves the same way he has entered. [This applies only when he comes alone. When he comes together with others, he, too, is required to exit by a different gate — see 46:9 and 10.]

[The first three verses of ch. 46 are closely related to these three. All should be studied as one unit.]

4. שַׁעַר הַצָּפוֹן אֶל פְּנֵי הַבַּיִת — *The northern gate to the front of the House.*

Metzudos (who follows *Rashi's* in-

ה מָלֵא כְבוֹד־יְהוָה אֶת־בֵּית יְהוָה וָאֶפֹּל
אֶל־פָּנָי: וַיֹּאמֶר אֵלַי יהוה בֶּן־אָדָם שִׂים
לִבְּךָ וּרְאֵה בְעֵינֶיךָ וּבְאָזְנֶיךָ שְּׁמָע אֵת
כָּל־אֲשֶׁר אֲנִי מְדַבֵּר אֹתָךְ לְכָל־חֻקּוֹת
בֵּית־יְהוָה וּלְכָל־תּוֹרֹתָו וְשַׂמְתָּ לִבְּךָ
ו לִמְבוֹא הַבַּיִת בְּכֹל מוֹצָאֵי הַמִּקְדָּשׁ:
וְאָמַרְתָּ אֶל־מֶרִי אֶל־בֵּית יִשְׂרָאֵל כֹּה
אָמַר אֲדֹנָי יֱהֹוִה רַב־לָכֶם מִכָּל־

terpretation of *v.* 1) understands this verse to refer to the northern wicket (4/19).

If, however, verse 1 referred to the gate of the outer courtyard (see *Abarbanel* to *v.* 1), this verse would probably mean the northern gate of the inner courtyard (2/3). On entering this gate he would be *in the front of the House.*

At the northern entrance to the outer courtyard, Yechezkel had been brought face to face with the depth of degradation to which his people had sunk (8:3). It was there that the leering, jealousy-provoking statue had been raised. It was fitting that the overwhelming realization that the Glory of God was now filling the House should come to him just on that same northern side *(R' Breuer).*

5. לִמְבֹא הַבַּיִת ... מוֹצָאֵי הַמִּקְדָּשׁ — *The entrance to the House ... the exits from the Sanctuary.*

R' Breuer thinks that the change of terms from House to Sanctuary has a lesson to teach us. Whether the Temple is to be a 'House' or a 'Sanctuary' to the person who comes there can only be known when he leaves. If as a result of his visit he carries sanctity with him into his daily life, then, indeed he had been in God's *Sanctuary.* If his life does not change, if he himself, in a small way, does not become bearer of God's Glory, then it was a *house* that he visited. God's *Sanctuary* remained hidden from him.

6-31. This section concerns the *kohanim* who are to serve in God's new Temple. It defines categories of disqualification which do not appear in the Torah; denies the privilege of serving at the altar to those priestly families which had succumbed to idol worship, and confines those privileges to descendants of Tzadok; spells out laws which are to govern the lives of the *kohanim,* including many laws which seem different from those required in the Torah; and, finally, delineates the obligations and rights which define the relationship of the *kohanim* with the rest of the people.

6-8. These verses introduce verse 9, which formalizes the disqualification from Divine service of the עֶרֶל לֵב, *uncircumcized spirit,* and the עֶרֶל בָּשָׂר, *uncircumcized body.* The former are *kohanim* who had been involved in idol worship, the latter, kohanim who had not been circumcised [even in cases where the halachah relieved them of that obligation as, for example, when two brothers had previously died as a result of a circumcision] (see below).

The verses are couched in a tone of stricture and the people are addressed as מֶרִי, *Rebellion* (that is, *Rebellion personified,* see *comm.* 2:7), in a style reminiscent of the earlier parts of the book which had been devoted to chastisement.

These verses seem to describe condi-

House and I beheld, and see! The Glory of HASHEM
filled the house of HASHEM. So I fell upon my face.
5 *And HASHEM said to me: Ben Adam, Consider!*
See with your eyes and hear with your ears all that I
shall speak with you about all the laws of the House
of HASHEM and all its teachings. Consider the
entrance to the House — all the exits from the Sanc-
tuary. 6 *Then say to 'Rebellion,' to the family of*
Israel: Thus says my Lord HASHEM/ELOHIM: You

tions which existed before the destruction, when the Temple service had reached a nadir, when idol worship was rife, and when (as *Eichah Rabbasi* 1:36 reports about Zidkiyahu's time) all the *kohanim* were uncircumcised.[1]

1. Even granting the historical background, it seems incongruous that these failings should be brought up during the description of the Temple and service of Messianic times. Furthermore, considering that the whole tenor of the latter part of the book is one of conciliation and comfort, the strictures of our passage call for an explanation.

We may find an answer by considering the history of the Second Temple. Thirty-three years after this prophecy, the Jews returned to Zion under Cyrus (see table; dates are taken from *Anvil of Sinai*, R' Zechariah Fendel, New York 1977).

TABLE

Event	**Year**		
Destruction	3338	Darius permits resumption of construction (seventy years after Destruction)	3408
Prophecies of *Ezekiel* 40-48	3357	Temple completed	3412
Cyrus permits building of Second Temple	3390	Ezra comes to Jerusalem	3413
		Nehemiah comes	3426
Ahasuerus halts construction	3392	Beginning of the *nassi — av beis din* 'partnership'	3550

The early years of the return to Zion were troubled times. The mood of the people rose and fell from the euphoria of once more having a Temple and the possibility of again serving God in the way He had prescribed, to the utter dejection which came about because of their abject poverty and the tremendous obstacles which lay in their path.

While much of the inspired leadership which encouraged their superhuman efforts came from the *kohanim* — Yehoshua, the *kohen gadol* who began the work with Zerubavel, and Ezra, who came at one of the lowest moments in their spiritual lives and galvanized them to repentance — it is nevertheless true that the *kohanim*, as a group, were also in the vanguard of those who succumbed to the terrible pressures and became disloyal to many of the Torah's precepts.

Malachi (one of the three prophets who were then in Jerusalem) had held out high hopes for the benign leadership role which the *kohanim* would be able to fill. They were to be the מַלְאָכִים, *representatives*, of the Divine among the people, whose unquestioned integrity,

ז תּוֹעֲבוֹתֵיכֶם בֵּית יִשְׂרָאֵל: בַּהֲבִיאֲכֶם
בְּנֵי־נֵכָר עַרְלֵי־לֵב וְעַרְלֵי בָשָׂר לִהְיוֹת
בְּמִקְדָּשִׁי לְחַלְּלוֹ אֶת־בֵּיתִי בְּהַקְרִיבְכֶם
אֶת־לַחְמִי חֵלֶב וָדָם וַיָּפֵרוּ אֶת־בְּרִיתִי
ח ח אֶל כָּל־תּוֹעֲבוֹתֵיכֶם: וְלֹא שְׁמַרְתֶּם
מִשְׁמֶרֶת קָדָשָׁי וַתְּשִׂימוּן לְשֹׁמְרֵי
ט מִשְׁמַרְתִּי בְּמִקְדָּשִׁי לָכֶם: כֹּה־
אָמַר אֲדֹנָי יֱהֹוִה כָּל־בֶּן־נֵכָר עֶרֶל לֵב

7. בְּנֵי־נֵכָר — *Strangers.*

This refers to people who, through their deeds, have become estranged from their Father in Heaven *(Rashi).*

עַרְלֵי לֵב — *Of uncircumcised spirit* [lit. *heart*].

This phrase explains the foregoing בְּנֵי נֵכָר, *strangers.* The priests who had been entrusted with God's service were alien to His ways; their heart, or spirit, was uncircumcised.

Ramban in his glosses to *Sefer HaMitzvos (Shoresh* 4) defines the *uncircumcised in spirit* as someone who ascribes corporeality to God and believes in the efficacy of idol worship. *Aruch HaShulchan (Hilchos Bias Mikdash* 48:6) broadens the definition to include a heretic or one who does not believe in the Oral Law; or one who serves idols, or desecrated the Sabbath in public; or one who transgresses the majority of the Torah's laws — even if he does so because of lust, not because he denies their binding authority.

לְחַלְּלוֹ אֶת־בֵּיתִי — *And to defile My House.*

This verse is the background to verse 9 which states formally that the uncircumcised of spirit is not to *come* to God's Sanctuary, meaning that he is disqualified from serving there in a priestly capacity. The word לְחַלְּלוֹ, *to defile* in our verse is the basis for the halachah that if the uncircumcised of spirit *did* perform a priestly service in contravention of this disqualification, that service is invalid. He has profaned the service, thereby invalidating it. (See *Aruch HaShulchan, Bias Mikdash* 45:1).

וְעַרְלֵי בָשָׂר — *And uncircumcised body* (lit. *flesh).*

Rashi points out this includes even someone who is relieved of the obligation to be circumcised because two of his brothers had previously died as a result of circumcision. Nevertheless, his own lack of circumcision is considered disgusting and disqualifies him from

wisdom, and love of fellow-man would make them the ideal teachers and guarantors of a God-fearing harmonious community (*Malachi* 2:5-7).

Instead, the *kohanim* became objects of derision among the people (*Malachi* 2:9), defilers of their priesthood (*Nechemiah* 13:29), and a stumbling block to the whole community (*Malachi* 2:8).

They, who of all the people, should have been guardians of Israel's sanctity, were among the worst offenders in the vicious practice of intermarrying with their gentile neighbors (*Ezra* 10:18 ff). This crime is particularly vicious because of their motives. The Sages (see *Rashi, Malachi* 2:13) explain that the formerly beloved Jewish wives had become 'black and ugly' from the terrible hunger and deprivation which stalked the heroic few who had returned to Zion. These Jewish women were then confined to the house and neglected by their husbands who flaunted their well fed, beautiful gentile wives.

Even the Temple service, which was the direct charge and responsibility of the *kohanim,* was performed without love or reverence. The sacrificial service, which should have uplifted

44
7-9

have indulged too much in all your abominations, O
family of Israel. [7] *When you bring strangers of uncir-*
cumcised spirit and uncircumcised body to be in My
Sanctuary, and to defile My House; when you bring
My food — fat and blood — and contravening My
convenant by all your abominations. [8] *You did not*
safeguard the charge of My holy places, and you ap-
pointed as guardians of My charge in My Sanctuary
whomever you pleased.
[9] *Thus says my Lord HASHEM/ELOHIM: No*
estranged person of uncircumcised spirit or uncir-

service. (See *Zevachim* 22b, *Tosafos).*

8. וְלֹא שְׁמַרְתֶּם מִשְׁמֶרֶת קָדָשָׁי — *You did not safeguard the charge of My holy places.*

Numbers 18:5 commands: *And you shall safeguard the charge of the Sanctuary and the charge of the altar.* According to *Sifri,* this command is addressed to the *Sanhedrin* [*high court,* as agent of the nation] which is to ensure that the priests perform the rites correctly because properly performed service prevents suffering from coming upon the world. Our verse blames the community for not having discharged that obligation *(R' Breuer).*

וַתְּשִׂימוּן לְשֹׁמְרֵי מִשְׁמַרְתִּי בְּמִקְדָּשִׁי לָכֶם — *And you appointed as guardians of My charge in My sanctuary whomever you pleased* [lit. *for yourselves*].

To serve as *kohanim* in the Temple, you freely appointed priests who had formerly performed services for idols *(Radak; Metzudos).*

9. כָּל־בֶּן־נֵכָר — *No estranged person* [lit. *stranger*].

Radak and *Metzudos* explain that the last phrase of the verse clarifies the subject. The injunction refers not to a non-Jew — the more common use of בֶּן נֵכָר, *stranger* — but to a Jew who is tantamount to a stranger because of his heretical practices or lack of circumcision. [*Exodus* 12:43 excludes the בֶּן נֵכָר from partaking of the Pesach sacrifice. *Mechilta* there defines the term בֶּן נֵכָר as alluding to both the *estranged Israelite* and the *gentile;* and bases its definition on our verse.] Therefore we have translated *estranged person* which carries the implication of a Jew who has *become* a stranger though he was not born one.

the spirits of the poor and broken community, was regarded with contempt. No effort was made to beautify the rites, or to instruct the people about the kind of animals fitting for tribute to God (*Malachi* 1:14). Stolen, lame, and sick animals were accepted indiscriminately (*Malachi* 1:13). The respect paid to God was less than the courtesy shown to a local governor (*Malachi* 1:8).

We can only surmise the cause of the disintegration of the priestly standards. Perhaps they recalled the glories of Solomon's Temple and could not accept the modest building put up by the returned exiles (*Chaggai* 2:3). Even its main gate told the sad story of Jewish subjugation to a foreign people for, by royal decree, it bore an engraving of the city Shushan (*Rambam, Middos* 1:3). Perhaps the absence of the five elements (ark, cover, cheruvim, heavenly fire, and *Shechinah* — see *Yoma* 21b) which had been an integral part of the First Temple seemed to rob this Second Temple of any real significance. [For a description of the times as projected by the Sages see *Toldos Am Olam,* R' Shlomo Rottenberg, Brooklyn 5277, Part 7.]

In addition, with the abolition of the monarchy a leadership vacuum occurred which, for

מד
י־יג

וְעֶרֶל בָּשָׂר לֹא יָבוֹא אֶל־מִקְדָּשִׁי לְכָל־
י בֶּן־נֵכָר אֲשֶׁר בְּתוֹךְ בְּנֵי יִשְׂרָאֵל׃ כִּי אִם־
הַלְוִיִּם אֲשֶׁר רָחֲקוּ מֵעָלַי בִּתְעוֹת יִשְׂרָאֵל
אֲשֶׁר תָּעוּ מֵעָלַי אַחֲרֵי גִּלּוּלֵיהֶם וְנָשְׂאוּ
יא עֲוֺנָם׃ וְהָיוּ בְמִקְדָּשִׁי מְשָׁרְתִים פְּקֻדּוֹת
אֶל־שַׁעֲרֵי הַבַּיִת וּמְשָׁרְתִים אֶת־הַבָּיִת
הֵמָּה יִשְׁחֲטוּ אֶת־הָעֹלָה וְאֶת־הַזֶּבַח
יב לָעָם וְהֵמָּה יַעַמְדוּ לִפְנֵיהֶם לְשָׁרְתָם׃ יַעַן
אֲשֶׁר יְשָׁרְתוּ אוֹתָם לִפְנֵי גִלּוּלֵיהֶם וְהָיוּ
לְבֵית־יִשְׂרָאֵל לְמִכְשׁוֹל עָוֺן עַל־כֵּן
נָשָׂאתִי יָדִי עֲלֵיהֶם נְאֻם אֲדֹנָי יֱהֹוִה
יג וְנָשְׂאוּ עֲוֺנָם׃ וְלֹא־יִגְּשׁוּ אֵלַי לְכַהֵן לִי
וְלָגֶשֶׁת עַל־כָּל־קָדָשַׁי אֶל־קָדְשֵׁי
הַקְּדָשִׁים וְנָשְׂאוּ כְּלִמָּתָם וְתוֹעֲבוֹתָם

עֶרֶל לֵב וְעֶרֶל בָּשָׂר — *Of uncircumcised spirit or uncircumcised body.*

These terms are defined in *comm.* to *v. 7.*

The disqualification of these two categories from Divine service is not mentioned in the Torah. The Talmud (*Yoma* 71b) explains that these disqualifications had been part of the Oral Law from the time of Moses. Yechezkel did not legislate a new halachah; he merely committed an oral law to writing.

10-14 The priestly families which had succumbed to idol worship — but had now repented *(Rashi)* — would be demoted. They would be allowed to serve in the Temple as watchmen but — with the exception of the *shechitah* [slaughtering] of sacrifices, which does not require a *kohen* — they would not be permitted to perform the sacrificial service.

It is significant that these priestly families are called לְוִיִּם, *Levites,* in this context. *R' D. Z. Hoffmann* on *Deuteronomy* (17:9) demonstrates that the expression הַכֹּהֲנִים הַלְוִיִּם, *the Levite-kohanim,* which occurs frequently in *Deuteronomy,* is used exclusively where the *kohanim* appear as spiritual leaders of the community rather than in their role of bringing sacrifices in the

about two hundred years, until the establishment of the 'partnership' between *nassi* and *av beis din* [head of the court] in the time of Yose ben Yoezer, was to be filled by the *kohen gadol, high priest.* [For background of the period and an analysis of the changes which took place in the leadership of the people in those days, see *Doros HaRishonim, HaTekufah HaEmtzais.*] This situation thrust a mantle of political leadership upon the priesthood which may well have taken its toll from the spiritual standing of later *kohanim* who lacked the stature of such great leaders as Ezra and Shimon HaTzaddik.

We may surmise that Yechezkel, himself a *kohen* (1:3) and well aware of both the strengths and weaknesses of his tribe, was looking forward with his prophetic eye to this disappointing period in the history of the priesthood. Within this framework we understand the seemingly incongruous insertion of these fierce strictures amidst the prophecies of consolation.

cumcised body shall enter My Sanctuary: no es-
tranged person among the children of Israel.
10 Rather — those Levites who became remote from
Me with Israel's deviation when they strayed from
Me after their abominations, they shall bear their sin.
11 They may be attendants in My Sanctuary,
delegated to the gates of the House, serving the
House; they may slaughter the burnt offering and
the sacrifice for the people, and they may stand
before them to serve them. 12 For they served them
before their idols, and became for the family of Israel
a block of sin. Therefore I have raised My hand
against them, the words of my Lord HASHEM/
ELOHIM, that they shall bear their sin. 13 But let them
not approach Me to serve Me and to approach My
holy places — the Holy of Holies. Let them bear their
shame and their abominations which they commit-

Temple. Since the tribe of Levi was given the function of being Israel's teachers (*Deuteronomy* 33:10), the *kohanim* are referred to as Levites when that aspect of their duties is significant. *R' Hoffmann* bases his interpretation on *Deuteronomy* 31:9 which teaches that after Moses had written the Torah he handed it to the כֹּהֲנִים בְּנֵי לֵוִי, *kohanim descendants of Levi.* To this *Ibn Ezra* comments, [those] who are the teachers of the Torah. It is significant that in verse 25 of that chapter these same *kohanim,* who are to carry the ark, are referred to as Levites (without the word *kohanim)* exactly as they are in our verse.

By referring to the formerly idolatrous *kohanim* as Levites, Yechezkel means to imply that they had been untrue to their calling as Levites.

10. כִּי אִם הַלְוִיִּם — *Rather-those Levites.*

The phrase is foreshortened. It should be understood thus: Rather, the unfaithful, and therefore disqualified, Levite-*kohanim* shall be dealt with in this manner ... *(Rashi).*

Radak comments that the term כִּי אִם may be interpreted as an oath; God swears that these wayward *kohanim* will be extremely limited in the service they may perform.

11. וְהֵמָּה יַעַמְדוּ לִפְנֵיהֶם לְשָׁרְתָם — *And they may stand before them to serve them.*

These *kohanim* may stand ready to assist the people who bring offerings *(Metzudos).*

12. ... יַעַן — *For ...*

The reason these *kohanim* must serve the Israelites who bring offerings is in measure-for-measure retribution for their earlier sin: They served those who sacrificed to idols; let them now serve those who sacrifice to God.

נָשָׂאתִי יָדִי — *I have raised My hand.*

I.e., in an oath *(Metzudos).*

13. לְכַהֵן לִי — *To serve Me.*

They are to be disqualified from serving me in those capacities which require a *kohen (Metzudos).*

יד אֲשֶׁר עָשׂוּ׃ וְנָתַתִּי אוֹתָם שֹׁמְרֵי מִשְׁמֶרֶת
הַבָּיִת לְכֹל עֲבֹדָתוֹ וּלְכֹל אֲשֶׁר יֵעָשֶׂה
טו בּוֹ׃ וְהַכֹּהֲנִים
הַלְוִיִּם בְּנֵי צָדוֹק אֲשֶׁר שָׁמְרוּ אֶת־
מִשְׁמֶרֶת מִקְדָּשִׁי בִּתְעוֹת בְּנֵי־יִשְׂרָאֵל
מֵעָלַי הֵמָּה יִקְרְבוּ אֵלַי לְשָׁרְתֵנִי וְעָמְדוּ
לְפָנַי לְהַקְרִיב לִי חֵלֶב וָדָם נְאֻם אֲדֹנָי
טז יֱהֹוִה׃ הֵמָּה יָבֹאוּ אֶל־מִקְדָּשִׁי וְהֵמָּה
יִקְרְבוּ אֶל־שֻׁלְחָנִי לְשָׁרְתֵנִי וְשָׁמְרוּ אֶת־
יז מִשְׁמַרְתִּי׃ וְהָיָה בְּבוֹאָם אֶל־שַׁעֲרֵי
הֶחָצֵר הַפְּנִימִית בִּגְדֵי פִשְׁתִּים יִלְבָּשׁוּ

15. When we recall the significance of the title, Levite (see *comm., v.* 10), it is not surprising that the one family of *kohanim* which had remained completely loyal and which was therefore to be entrusted with the service of the future are called the *Levite-kohanim.*

The *kohanim* of the future are to be the descendants of Tzadok, the high priest during David's reign (*II Samuel* 8:17). The unique status of this family can be seen from the fact that in the book of *Chronicles,* its line of descent is the only one from among the *kohanim* which is traced (*I Chronicles* 5:30-41). This line of descent traces the family from Aaron's son Elazar through Tzadok, to Yehotzadok who was one of the exiles to Babylon. In the view of the Sages (*Shir HaShirim Rabbah* 5:6), this Yehotzadok seems to have been the last high priest in Solomon's Temple (although his father Seraya was still alive at the destruction and was among those whom Nebuchadnezzar killed at Rivlah — see *Jeremiah* 52:24 ff. See *Toldos HaKohanim HaGedolim* by R' Yekusiel Greenwald, New York 5693, for discussion).

The line of descent is then taken up by Nechemiah, who traces the family from Yehotzadok's son Yeshua, the high priest, through Yadua, the last of the *kohanim gedolim* mentioned in Scripture. This Yadua, the high priest at the time of Alexander, was a grandfather of Shimon HaTzadik. (See *Doros HaRishonim, HaTekufa HaEmtzais* ch. 12).

Thus we see that the line of *kohanim gedolim* was indeed that of Tzadok the *kohen.*

16. וְהֵמָּה יִקְרְבוּ אֶל שֻׁלְחָנִי — *And they shall approach My table.*

The golden table in the Sanctuary upon which the לֶחֶם הַפָּנִים, *showbread,* was displayed *(Radak; Metzudos).*

17. This is the first of a series of verses which, at first glance, seem to contradict the halachah as revealed in the Torah. The commentators on this difficult section follow two basic approaches represented by *Rashi* and *Radak. Rashi* interprets the verses in light of the halachah, even when the literal meaning seems different. *Radak* (and *Malbim),* on the other hand, interprets according to the apparent, literal meaning. He assumes that the greater sanctity of the future Temple will be reflected in higher standards imposed on the *kohanim* and that the ordinary *kohanim* would come closer to the spiritual level of the *kohen gadol.* As a result, they would be bound

44
14-17 *ted.* 14 *Therefore I will appoint them guardians of the House — for all its service and everything done in it.*

15 *But the Levite-kohanim — descendants of Tzadok who safeguarded the charge of My Sanctuary when the children of Israel strayed from Me — let them draw near Me to serve Me; let them stand before Me to offer Me fat and blood, the words of my Lord HASHEM/ELOHIM.* 16 *They shall come to My Sanctuary and they shall approach My table to serve Me and they shall safeguard My charge.*

17 *Now when they come to the gates of the inner area they are to wear linen clothes. Let no wool be*

by some of the laws hitherto applicable only to him. In his commentary to 45:18, *Malbim* buttresses this interpretation with R' Yochanan's opinion (*Berachos* 34b. See further in footnote) that the Messianic era will be a period of spiritual eminence beyond our present comprehension.[1]

1. **Rashi's Approach**

In the commentary we noted that, whenever the simple meaning of a passage in *Ezekiel* seems to contradict a known halachah, *Rashi* interprets the verse in accordance with the halachah as we know it, even though the interpretation may not accord with the פְּשָׁט [*p'shat*], *simple meaning*. In doing so, *Rashi* will often quote the Sages [cf. 45:15]; at other times, he will give his own interpretation [cf. 45:24 ff]. However, *Rashi* leaves the *p'shat* of significant parts of these chapters unexplained. When we recall how *Rashi* in his commentary to the Torah stresses repeatedly how central the *p'shat* is to his perception of his commentary we must attempt a closer understanding of *Rashi's* system in *Ezekiel*.

It is true, of course, that *Rashi's* conception of פְּשׁוּטוֹ שֶׁל מִקְרָא, *the plain meaning of Scripture*, goes beyond that of *Ibn Ezra* [in *Safah Berurah*]; nevertheless, with very rare exceptions (cf. the argument of *Rashi* and *Ramban* to *Leviticus* 14:44), *Rashi* cites only interpretations that do not contradict the *p'shat*, but augment it. For example, though *Rashi* cites the exegesis that the word בְּרֵאשִׁית [*Genesis* 1:1] should be understood to teach that the world was created for the sake of Israel he has no intention of prejudicing the *p'shat* interpretation of *In the beginning*. Rather, he means to offer an *added* dimension to the simple meaning. In these chapters of *Ezekiel*, however, *Rashi* uses the interpretation of the Sages not to augment the *p'shat* but to replace it. Since the simple meaning contradicts the halachah as we know it, another interpretation must be offered, even though the *p'shat* may remain unexplained.

We find that some parts of Scripture were not intended to be understood literally. The Sages taught (*Vayikrah Rabbah* 1:3 — See Appendix I) that in the book of *Chronicles* there is no *p'shat* in the usual sense of the word, but that all the verses are to be seen as vehicles for דְּרָשׁ, *aggadic exegesis*. So, too, in our chapters, *p'shat* which appears to contradict halachah cannot be understood as the intent of the prophet's message. Instead, the verses were intended only to convey such exegetical interpretations as those cited by *Rashi*.

The explanation for this would be as follows:

Maharal (Gevuros HaShem 17) teaches an important rule of Scriptural exegesis. The Torah communicates events which happened in the physical world by means of *p'shat*, the use of words in their literal meaning. Truths of a spiritual, non-tangible level are conveyed by means of allegorical or exegetical interpretation [דְּרָשׁ or רֶמֶז]. For example, by means of such interpretation, the Sages [*Sotah* 12b] derive that the handmaidens of Pharaoh's daughter died because they opposed her decision to save the infant Moses [*Exodus* 2:5]. *Maharal* explains

וְלֹא־יַעֲלֶה עֲלֵיהֶם צֶמֶר בְּשָׁרְתָם בְּשַׁעֲרֵי
יח הֶחָצֵר הַפְּנִימִית וָבָיְתָה: פַּאֲרֵי פִשְׁתִּים
יִהְיוּ עַל־רֹאשָׁם וּמִכְנְסֵי פִשְׁתִּים יִהְיוּ
יט עַל־מָתְנֵיהֶם לֹא יַחְגְּרוּ בַּיָּזַע: וּבְצֵאתָם
אֶל־הֶחָצֵר הַחִיצוֹנָה אֶל־הֶחָצֵר

וְלֹא יַעֲלֶה עֲלֵיהֶם צֶמֶר — *Let no wool be upon them.*

According to *Rashi,* our verse refers to the Yom Kippur vestments of the *kohen gadol,* when he wore linen garments (in which there was no wool at all) for parts of the service. It cannot refer to the ordinary *kohen,* for he wore a belt (אַבְנֵט; *Exodus* 28:40) woven with strands of wool (*Rambam, Klei Mikdash* 8:1).

According to *Radak,* however, this verse applies to all *kohanim.* In this respect, *Malbim* explains, all will be elevated to a level of sanctity previously associated only with the *kohen gadol* on Yom Kippur.

הֶחָצֵר הַפְּנִימִית — *The inner area.*

Rashi interprets this as the inner sanctum of the Temple — the Holy of Holies — which the *kohen gadol* entered only on Yom Kippur.

Radak, however, interprets this [the way it is used throughout the book] as the inner courtyard.

Our translation, *the inner area,* is purposely ambiguous to allow for either interpretation.

18. לֹא יַחְגְּרוּ בַּיָּזַע — *Let them not gird*

that the women did *not* die in the literal sense; they are considered to have 'died' because God removed their power to influence the princess and hence, the course of events. Having been stripped of their power, they could be described as dead in terms of their significance.

Thus we learn that the *p'shat,* the open 'tangible' meaning of the verse is reserved for tangible physical events, while spiritual truths are conveyed by other levels of interpretation.

Yechezkel, in contrast to the other prophets who talk of the Messianic era in general terms, uses vivid details to discuss the laws of the priesthood and the sacrificial service of the End of Days. But that era is shrouded in mystery, its secrets locked in God's heart לִבָּא לְפוּמָא לֹא גַלְיָא, *the heart does not communicate* [*its secrets*] *to the mouth* [*Koheles Rabbah* 12:10]). *P'shat,* which deals with tangibles of our experience, cannot deal with those times except in generalities. Therefore, the *p'shat* meaning of those sections must indeed remain hidden from us until — in the words of R' Yochanan in *Menachos* 45a — Elijah the prophet will come and reveal it to us.

Radak's Approach

The idea of *any* change in the *mitzvos* seems surprising in light of the ninth of *Rambam's* Thirteen Principles of Faith which, in the form found in the *Siddur,* reads: I believe with perfect faith that this Torah will not be exchanged and that no other Torah will [come to us] from the Creator, Blessed be His Name.

A careful reading of *Radak's* approach to the difficulties in the next few chapters of *Ezekiel* will show that never once does he suggest that a given *mitzvah* will ח״ו be eliminated from the Torah. Rather, as we state in the commentary, he holds that the drastically heightened spiritual level of the Messianic era will be reflected in elevated standards.

It is true that some Talmudic passages seem to imply that there will be changes in the observance of *mitzvos* as we know them [*Maharatz Chayos* in his gloss to *Niddah* 61b lists most of the sources]. However, *Rashba* [*Berachos* 12b in *Ein Yaakov*] gives a lengthy exposition to show that such an understanding of the sources is erroneous. His concluding words illustrate the need for care in this delicate area:

> I have explained these matters at length to refute those who argue against us with deception, [misinterpreting the words of the Sages] to claim that the commandments of

upon them when they serve in the gates of the inner area and within. [18] *Linen turbans shall be on their heads and linen trousers shall be on their loins. Let them not gird themselves where one perspires.* [19] *Now when they leave for the outer courtyard, to*

themselves where one perspires [lit. *with sweat*].

Rashi's interpretation is based on *Zevachim* 18b: The *kohanim* are to wear their belts at elbow level, an area of the body relatively free of perspiration. The purpose of the injunction is to avoid soiling the priestly garments (*Metzudos*).

Rashi offers a second interpretation: *Let them not gird themselves with something that causes sweat,* that is wool. In this view, the verse now explains that the reason the *kohanim* are not to wear wool (*v.* 17) is to avoid perspiring.

19. וּבְצֵאתָם אֶל הֶחָצֵר הַחִיצוֹנָה — *Now when they leave for the outer courtyard.*

Yoma 35b teaches that our verse, like *v.* 17, gives directions concerning the garments worn by the *kohen gadol* during the Yom Kippur services.

After completing the Yom Kippur services, the high priest goes to the outer courtyard (called *women's courtyard* during the period of the Second Temple) where he must remove the linen garments in which he had performed the service in the Holy of Holies, and leave them in one of the sanctified chambers. This is in accord-

> the Torah are not eternal... They further claim that if the Sages reveal that the commandments depend on some particular time and can be annulled at some [future] time, then any claimant can argue that they are null and void at *any* time in This World [i.e., before the coming of Messiah]...

Only in one instance does *Rashba* hold that an observance will change, and even there he explains that the intent of the *mitzvah* requires the change. That particular instance refers to Ben Zoma's view that following the final Redemption, the command to remember the miracles accompanying it will supersede the command to remember the miracles of the Exodus [*Berachos* 12b]. *Rashba* explains that the commandment to recall the Exodus is, in essence, a requirement upon Israel never to forget God's Providence and miraculous intervention on our behalf. Throughout our history, this phenomenon has been illustrated by the Exodus; in the World to Come it will be even better illustrated by the final Redemption. Thus, the commandment *does,* in fact, remain essentially unchanged.

We feel that this very same thought underlies *Radak's* interpretation of our chapters. The *mitzvos* are indeed eternal; Yechezkel simply reveals that the implication of certain details will conform to the new circumstances of greater sanctity.

This, we think, is the proper understanding of R' Yochanan's view in *Menachos* 45a. There, R' Yochanan notes that the sacrifices listed in *Ezekiel* 45:18ff are quite different from those described by the Torah. R' Yochanan offers no explanation to justify the apparent discrepancy. He states: 'This passage will be elucidated by the prophet Elijah.' R' Yochanan was faced with two seemingly irreconcilable facts. On the one hand, the eternal and immutable Torah says one thing. On the other hand, Yechezkel — God's true prophet — gives directions which seem to assume a different set of laws. Both sources are of Divine origin, both command our absolute allegiance, and we know that the 'discrepancies' are a product of our own lack of knowledge. The resolution must lie with Elijah. He will show how Yechezkel's directions do not stand in contradiction to the Torah's requirements at all, and how the Torah's intention will be attainable through Yechezkel's directions. [Note R' Yochanan's opinion from *Berachos* 34b (quoted in comm.) that the Messianic era will be a period of spiritual eminence beyond our present comprehension. *Malbim* suggests that R' Yochanan's view in *Menachos* is based on his statement in *Berachos*.]

הַחִיצוֹנָה אֶל־הָעָם יִפְשְׁטוּ אֶת־בִּגְדֵיהֶם
אֲשֶׁר־הֵמָּה מְשָׁרְתִם בָּם וְהִנִּיחוּ אוֹתָם
בְּלִשְׁכֹת הַקֹּדֶשׁ וְלָבְשׁוּ בְּגָדִים אֲחֵרִים
וְלֹא־יְקַדְּשׁוּ אֶת־הָעָם בְּבִגְדֵיהֶם׃ וְרֹאשָׁם כ
לֹא יְגַלֵּחוּ וּפֶרַע לֹא יְשַׁלֵּחוּ כָּסוֹם יִכְסְמוּ
אֶת־רָאשֵׁיהֶם׃ וְיַיִן לֹא־יִשְׁתּוּ כָּל־כֹּהֵן כא
בְּבוֹאָם אֶל־הֶחָצֵר הַפְּנִימִית׃ וְאַלְמָנָה כב
וּגְרוּשָׁה לֹא־יִקְחוּ לָהֶם לְנָשִׁים כִּי אִם־
בְּתוּלֹת מִזֶּרַע בֵּית יִשְׂרָאֵל וְהָאַלְמָנָה
אֲשֶׁר־תִּהְיֶה אַלְמָנָה מִכֹּהֵן יִקָּחוּ׃ וְאֶת־ כג

ance with *Leviticus* 16:23 which provides that the garments which were used one Yom Kippur could not be used again, but had to be concealed permanently [טְעוּנִין גְּנִיזָה].

אֶל הֶחָצֵר הַחִיצוֹנָה אֶל הָעָם — *To the outer* [*most*] *courtyard to the people.*

The repetition of the phrase *outer courtyard* indicates that the *kohen gadol* went to the outer*most* courtyard: the עֶזְרַת נָשִׁים, *courtyard of women (Rashi).*

וְלָבְשׁוּ בְּגָדִים אֲחֵרִים — *Let them don other garments.*

Yoma 35a-b interprets this as a command to the *kohen gadol* that when he returns to the Holy of Holies for the *second* time during the Yom Kippur service, he is to wear a new set of vestments. *Rashi* (ibid.) explains that this had been an oral tradition stemming from Moses, but had only now been committed to Scriptural writing.

וְלֹא יְקַדְּשׁוּ אֶת הָעָם בְּבִגְדֵיהֶם — *And let them not mingle with the people in their clothes.*

This phrase is unrelated to the rest of the verse, since it does not deal solely with the Yom Kippur service (*Rashi* to *Yoma* 35b). It teaches the same lesson as 42:14, namely that priestly garments were not to be worn when mingling with the crowds since the garments could become defiled upon contact with the unsanctified clothes of the people (see commentary to 42:14).

Radak, however, follows his line of interpretation as explained above. In his understanding of verse 17 no mention had been made of *kohen gadol* or of Yom Kippur, therefore this verse 19 cannot be limited to that subject. This verse repeats the exhortation of 42:14 that *kohanim* are not to wear their priestly garments once they leave the area of holy service and go out to the people. Our verse repeats the prohibition in order to give it reason:

If the people were allowed to come into contact with the priestly garments, it would imply that the people are on the same level of sanctity as the *kohanim* [and this might erode the sanctity of the priesthood].

20. The simple meaning of this verse is that both extremes — that of shaving the head completely and that of allowing the hair to grow wild — are forbidden to *kohanim.* What is required is a medium between these two extremes.

וּפֶרַע לֹא יְשַׁלֵּחוּ — *Nor a wild growth may they permit.*

Sanhedrin 22b, defines פֶּרַע as a hair growth of thirty days. Our verse forbids ordinary priests to go thirty days without a haircut (*Rambam, Bias Mikdash* 1:11). [By contrast, the *kohen gadol* had to cut his hair every

the outer courtyard to the people, let them remove the clothes in which they minister and leave them in the holy chambers. Let them don other garments and let them not mingle with the people in their clothes. 20 *Their heads they may not shear nor a wild growth may they permit. They are to keep their heads trimmed.* 21 *Let no kohen drink wine when he enters the inner courtyard.* 22 *Neither widow nor divorcee may they take themselves for wives, only a virgin from the offspring of the family of Israel. But a widow who shall only be widowed, some kohanim*

Friday (*Rambam, Klei HaMikdash* 5:6).]

כָּסוֹם יִכְסְמוּ אֶת רָאשֵׁיהֶם — *They are to keep their heads trimmed.*

The expression is obscure.

Rashi cites an opinion that the term derives from כּוּסֶמֶת, *spelt;* the hair should be cut so that the individual hairs lie in relation to one another like ears of spelt growing together. According to *Sanhedrin* 22b, this is defined as: the tip of one [hair] next to the root of the other. Apparently this effect was extremely difficult to attain and the *Gemara* tells of a certain Ben El'asha who spent huge sums of money to learn the exact method for cutting the hair in this way.

[The Talmud (ibid) seems to require this special hair style only for the *kohen gadol.* The only requirement for the ordinary *kohen* is that he not leave his hair uncut for more than thirty days. Although *Rashi* does not mention the *kohen gadol* in his commentary to our verse, it may well be that *Rashi* found it unnecessary to mention him since this entire series of verses refers to the *kohen gadol.*

Once more the problem arises that our verse seems to deal with all *kohanim* and imposes identical requirements upon them. *Yad Ramah* to *Sanhedrin* (ad. loc.) thinks that this would seem to indicate that service in the Messianic Temple would require the same hair style for ordinary *kohanim* as had previously been required for the *kohen gadol.* Thus he seems in agreement with *Radak* in his general approach to our chapter.]

21. וְיַיִן לֹא יִשְׁתּוּ כָּל כֹּהֵן בְּבוֹאָם — *Let no kohen drink wine* [lit. *any kohen should not drink*] *when he enters* [lit. *when they enter*].

A *kohen* who is qualified to perform the Divine service is forbidden by Scriptural prohibition to enter the area west of the altar if he has drunk a sufficient amount of wine to be considered שִׁכּוֹר, *intoxicated,* as the halachah defines that term. (See *Rambam, Bias Mikdash* ch. 1 and *Aruch HaShulchan Bias Mikdash* ch. 33 for details.)

This verse is apparently no more than a repetition of the Scriptural injunction of *Leviticus* 10:9.

Malbim suggests that there may be an expansion of the halachah here. Whereas in previous Temples only those *kohanim* who were qualified to serve were included in the prohibition against drunkenness, the expression כָּל כֹּהֵן, *any kohen,* in our verse includes all *kohanim,* even those unqualified to serve.

22. וְאַלְמָנָה וּגְרוּשָׁה לֹא יִקְחוּ — *Neither widow nor divorcee may they take.*

Rashi, following the interpretation of *Kiddushin* 78b, comments that this part of our verse refers only to the *kohen gadol;* thus, it reiterates the Scriptural limitation that he may marry only a virgin (*Leviticus* 21:7, 13-14).

וְהָאַלְמָנָה אֲשֶׁר תִּהְיֶה אַלְמָנָה מִכֹּהֵן יִקָּחוּ — *But a widow who shall only be widowed, some kohanim may take.*

עַמִּי יוֹרוּ בֵּין קֹדֶשׁ לְחֹל וּבֵין־טָמֵא
כד לְטָהוֹר יוֹדִיעֻם׃ וְעַל־רִיב הֵמָּה יַעַמְדוּ
°לשפט בְּמִשְׁפָּטַי °ושפטהו וְאֶת־תּוֹרֹתַי °לְמִשְׁפָּט | יִשְׁפְּטֻהוּ
וְאֶת־חֻקֹּתַי בְּכָל־מוֹעֲדַי יִשְׁמֹרוּ וְאֶת־
כה שַׁבְּתוֹתַי יְקַדֵּשׁוּ׃ וְאֶל־מֵת אָדָם לֹא יָבוֹא
לְטָמְאָה כִּי אִם־לְאָב וּלְאֵם וּלְבֵן וּלְבַת
לְאָח וּלְאָחוֹת אֲשֶׁר־לֹא־הָיְתָה לְאִישׁ
כו יִטַּמָּאוּ׃ וְאַחֲרֵי טָהֳרָתוֹ שִׁבְעַת יָמִים

Rashi, following *Kiddushin* 78b, explains that the verse now reverts from *kohen gadol* to ordinary *kohanim.* They may marry women who have been widowed, provided they have not been divorced or been released from a levirate obligation [זִיקַת יְבָמָה] through *chalitzah.* [Although the disqualification of *chalitzah* was ordained by Rabbinic decree — Yechezkel here hints to that future prohibition *(Metzudos).*] אַלְמָנָה מִכֹּהֵן יִקָּחוּ means: [*some*] *of the kohanim may marry widows.* Only ordinary priests, but not the high priests, may marry widows.

Radak, consistent with his ideas above, interprets the verse as referring to ordinary *kohanim.* Although the Torah permits the ordinary *kohanim* to marry widows, in the future they will be forbidden to marry widows whose previous husbands had not been *kohanim.* This is a reflection of a new standard of sanctity which will be imposed even upon ordinary *kohanim.*

23. וְאֶת עַמִּי יוֹרוּ — *They are to instruct My people.*

The *kohanim* are assigned the responsibility of guiding the people in the complexities of the halachic division's between holy and ordinary, ritually clean and contaminated *(Metzudos;* see also *Leviticus* 10:10).

יוֹדִיעֻם — *Let them inform them.*

Malbim notes that holiness is the primary province of the *kohanim;* hence: *They are to 'instruct' My people concerning the holy.* However the entire nation is equally responsible for the laws and observance of the differentiation between the ritually clean and contaminated. Therefore, the *kohanim* are merely to *inform* the general population when such contamination has taken place.

24. הֵמָּה יַעַמְדוּ לְמִשְׁפָּט — *Let them stand in judgment.*

The *kohen's* active participation in civil litigations is discussed in *Deuteronomy* 17:9, from which *Sifri* derives that, if possible, a court should contain *kohanim* and Levites among its members (see *Rambam, Sanhedrin* 2:2; *R' Hoffman* on *Deuteronomy).*

וְאֶת־תּוֹרֹתַי ... יִשְׁמֹרוּ — *My teachings ... they are to protect.*

We have previously met the *kohen* as teacher of Torah (7:26) and as guardian of the sacred and the ritually clean (22:26). These functions of the priesthood derive from *Leviticus* 10:10-11 and from *Deuteronomy* 33:10.

25. וְאֶל מֵת אָדָם — *To a human corpse.*

A *kohen* may not allow himself to become contaminated through contact with a dead body — but this prohibition is lifted in regard to his close relatives, as specified in *Leviticus* 21:2-3. He is permitted — indeed, required — to participate in their burial although he will thereby become טָמֵא, *contaminated.*

כִּי אִם — *Except for.*

We can understand why Yechezkel found it necessary to state laws already

44
23-26 *may take.* 23 *They are to instruct My people concerning the differences between holy and ordinary. Let them inform them of the difference between contaminated and clean.* 24 *Concerning a grievance, let them stand in judgment, and according to my laws are they are to be adjudicate it. My teachings and decrees regarding My appointed times they are to protect, and My Sabbaths they are to sanctify.* 25 *To a human corpse they are not to come to become contaminated, except for father and mother, son and daughter, brother and sister who had never been married to a man they may become contaminated.*
26 *After his cleansing, let them count seven days for*

known from the Torah if we recall that in *Radak* and *Malbim's* interpretations there would be ways in which the status of the ordinary *kohen* would be elevated to that of the *kohen gadol* in earlier times. One might have supposed that in regard to defilement by a dead body this would also be true and that just as a *kohen gadol* was not allowed to defile himself even for his close relatives (*Leviticus* 21:10ff), so too, the ordinary *kohen* in Messianic times would not be permitted to do so. Our verse teaches otherwise.

Why does Yechezkel not mention the *kohen's* wife? The exceptions to the law of defilement in *Leviticus* 21:2 begin with שְׁאֵרוֹ, which according to the Sages, means *his wife.* Thus, it is clear that a *kohen* is allowed to defile himself for his dead wife. Why does Yechezkel make no mention of this?

A simple solution is suggested by *Radak's* comm. to verse 22. There he points out that there is no attempt in *Ezekiel* to give a complete list of all the laws affecting the *kohanim.* Just as verse 22 does not list all the categories of women which are forbidden to the *kohen*, so, too, our verse omits the wife in the list of relatives.

[Our question assumes that the *kohen* is obliged to defile himself for his wife by Torah law. However *Rambam* (*Ovel* 2:7), holds that although the Torah *permits* a kohen to take part in his wife's burial, the *obligation* to do so is of Rabbinic origin. Accordingly, the omission of his wife from our verse presents no difficulty, for Yechezkel is discussing only obligations under Torah law.]

Ibn Ezra (Lev. 21:2; Exodus 21:8) feels that the Sages' statement that the word שְׁאֵרוֹ refers to his wife is only a mnemonic device. The Sages had an oral tradition that defilement for the wife is permitted. They read this into the word שְׁאֵרוֹ as a memorv aid (but see *Ritva* to *Rosh Hashannah* 16a) without meaning that this is the actual translation. The true meaning of שְׁאֵרוֹ is *his relative* and the phrase is to be understood as a general statement explained by the six exceptions which are then listed. Thus the *p'shat* of the passage in *Leviticus* does not yield that a *kohen* may contaminate himself for his wife.In his *Safah Berurah, Ibn Ezra* proves this point from our passage in *Ezekiel.* Since Yechezkel does not list the wife, it is obvious that he did not view the permission to become defiled by her as being explicit in the *p'shat* of *Levitic*

26. וְאַחֲרֵי טָהֳרָתוֹ — *After his cleansing.*

According to *Moed Kattan* 15b cited by *Rashi,* this verse is in exact accordance with the halachah as we know it. The cleansing process to remove the contamination of a dead body requires a

כז יִסְפְּרוּ־לוֹ: וּבְיוֹם בֹּאוֹ אֶל־הַקֹּדֶשׁ אֶל־
הֶחָצֵר הַפְּנִימִית לְשָׁרֵת בַּקֹּדֶשׁ יַקְרִיב
כח חַטָּאתוֹ נְאֻם אֲדֹנָי יֱהֹוִה: וְהָיְתָה לָהֶם
לְנַחֲלָה אֲנִי נַחֲלָתָם וַאֲחֻזָּה לֹא־תִתְּנוּ
כט לָהֶם בְּיִשְׂרָאֵל אֲנִי אֲחֻזָּתָם: הַמִּנְחָה
וְהַחַטָּאת וְהָאָשָׁם הֵמָּה יֹאכְלוּם וְכָל־
ל חֵרֶם בְּיִשְׂרָאֵל לָהֶם יִהְיֶה: וְרֵאשִׁית כָּל־
בִּכּוּרֵי כֹל וְכָל־תְּרוּמַת כֹּל מִכֹּל
תְּרוּמֹתֵיכֶם לַכֹּהֲנִים יִהְיֶה וְרֵאשִׁית

seven-day period. Accordingly, our verse refers to the *beginning* of the cleansing process, i.e., *after his cleansing* process has begun. Thus, the seven days mentioned here are the normal seven-day period required (*Numbers* 19:11) for the cleansing of someone who came into contact with a dead body.

Radak, in accordance with his approach throughout this chapter, translates: *after he becomes cleansed*, i.e., after the initial seven days, when he is *already* cleansed. But, he suggests, in the future an extra seven days may be required for *kohanim* after the initial seven-day period ordained by the Torah.

27. יַקְרִיב חַטָּאתוֹ — *Let him bring his sin offering.*

According to *Moed Kattan* 15b, cited by *Rashi*, this verse is not a continuation of the previous one.

It teaches that any *kohen* who has never served in the Temple before must bring an offering as a consecration sacrifice (מִנְחַת חִנּוּךְ) before he begins to serve. This is in accordance with the halachah as we know it. (See *Rambam, Klei HaMikdash* 5:16.)

Malbim wonders why it would be necessary for Yechezkel to repeat this well known requirement. He suggests that our verse teaches that when the Second Temple was built even those *kohanim* who had served in the earlier Temple and had outlived the exile would be required to bring a sacrifice. Their service was to be considered as a fresh start. Similarly, in the future Temple, a sacrifice would be required even from *kohanim* who had served before.

Radak views this verse as a continuation of the previous one. After he is cleansed of his contamination, the *kohen* must bring a sin offering. Once again, this law is not found in the Torah but will be an effect of the increased sanctity of the Third Temple.

28. וְהָיְתָה לָהֶם לְנַחֲלָה — *And it shall be an inheritance for them.*

The inheritance is the priesthood (*Rashi*).

אֲנִי נַחֲלָתָם — *I am their inheritance.*

This phrase echoes *Numbers* 18:20, where God told Aaron that his descendants would not have a portion of the Land of Israel as would the other tribes. God is to be their portion; they are to be His legions (*Deut.* 33:11; see further *Rambam, Shemitah VeYovel* 13:12).

וַאֲחֻזָּה לֹא תִתְּנוּ לָהֶם — *Give them no possession.*

They were not to get a portion of the Land (see above). [In ch. 48 we shall learn that the Land was to be divided into thirteen strips, twelve were to be given to the twelve tribes (Joseph is counted as two — Menashe and

44 27-30 *him.* 27 *Now on the day of his entry into the Sanc-*
tuary, to the inner courtyard, to minister in the Sanc-
tuary, let him bring his sin offering. The words of my
Lord HASHEM/ELOHIM.
28 *And it shall be an inheritance for them; I am*
their inheritance. Give them no possession in Israel. I
am their possession. 29 *They shall eat the meal offer-*
ing, the sin offering, and the guilt offering. Any
cherem-vow in Israel shall be for them. 30 *All the*
choice first fruits of every kind and all terumah of
any kind — of all your terumah *gifts — shall go to the*
kohanim. You shall give the first yield of your dough

Ephraim — and Levi is not included) and the thirteenth is given to the *nassi.* In the middle of the Land which belongs to the *nassi,* a tract of Land is set aside in which the Temple Mount will rise up and in which the future Jerusalem will lie. (See chs. 45 and 48 for a full description.) Within this tract, areas are to be set aside for housing the *kohanim* and the Levites. These areas cannot be considered as an 'inheritance' in the Land. Rather they are the equivalent of the cities which had been scattered around the Land, reserved for the Levites (see *Numbers* 35:1-8), and which never contradicted the exhortation of the Torah that the Levites were not to receive a portion in the Land (*Deut.* 18:1-2).

Our verse seems perfectly clear and the matter would not require further elaboration were it not that a number of commentators assume that in Messianic times the Levites will indeed receive a portion of the Land (see *Malbim,* here). This is the opinion of *Smag, Lo Saaseh* 276 and *Rashbam* to *Bava Basra* 122a. That opinion is based on *Bava Basra* 122a which seems to imply that Levi will, in fact, have the same portion as every other tribe.

However, as we have shown, whole passages in *Ezekiel* stand in outright contradiction to this assumption. Both *Ran,* cited in *Shitah Mekubetzes,* and *Rashash* (there) demonstrate in great detail that the Talmud cannot possibly have meant such a thing. *Rashash* goes so far as to suggest that the text of the whole passage is erroneous and offers a reading which would in no way imply that the Levites will have a portion in the division of the Land in Messianic times. (See further at 48:31.)

[For further sources which deal with this complex issue the interested reader is directed to *Nachlas Shimon,* R' Shimon Krasner, Baltimore, 1978 3:5.]

29-30 These verses list some of the twenty-four מַתְּנוֹת כְּהוּנָה, *gifts for the kohanim,* most of which are enumerated in *Numbers* 18:8-20.

הַמִּנְחָה וְהַחַטָּאת וְהָאָשָׁם — *The meal offering, the sin offering, and the guilt offering.*

The *kohanim* received a portion of these offerings to eat.

חֵרֶם — *Cherem-vow.*

When a person declares a possession to be *cherem,* its use becomes forbidden and it reverts to the ownership of God, Who, in turn, presents it as a gift to the *kohanim. (See Lev.* 27:21 and *Numbers* 18:14.)

תְּרוּמָה — *Terumah.*

Literally, תְּרוּמָה means *that which is elevated.* It refers to a portion of the

מד
לא

עֲרִיסוֹתֵיכֶם תִּתְּנוּ לַכֹּהֵן לְהָנִיחַ
לא בְּרָכָה אֶל־בֵּיתֶךָ: כָּל־נְבֵלָה וּטְרֵפָה
מִן־הָעוֹף וּמִן־הַבְּהֵמָה לֹא יֹאכְלוּ
הַכֹּהֲנִים:

מה
א־ב

א וּבְהַפִּילְכֶם אֶת־
הָאָרֶץ בְּנַחֲלָה תָּרִימוּ תְרוּמָה לַיהוָה ׀
קֹדֶשׁ מִן־הָאָרֶץ אֹרֶךְ חֲמִשָּׁה וְעֶשְׂרִים
אֶלֶף אֹרֶךְ וְרֹחַב עֲשָׂרָה אָלֶף קֹדֶשׁ־הוּא
ב בְּכָל־גְּבוּלָהּ סָבִיב: יִהְיֶה מִזֶּה אֶל־הַקֹּדֶשׁ

produce which must be given to the *kohen.*

וְרֵאשִׁית עֲרִיסֹתֵיכֶם — *The first yield of your dough.*

This refers to חַלָּה, *challah*, a portion of the dough given to the *kohen.* [Details of these gifts fo the *kohanim* can be found in *Rambam, Arachin VeCharomim; Maaseh HaKorbonos.*]

31. נְבֵלָה וּטְרֵפָה — *Carcass or torn animal.*

נְבֵלָה, *Neveilah,* is an animal which died without proper *shechitah* [*ritual slaughter*]. טְרֵפָה, *treifah,* is an animal which is *torn* — injured internally or externally — in a way that makes it halachically unfit for eating.

לֹא יֹאכְלוּ הַכֹּהֲנִים — *The kohanim may not eat.*

Why is it necessary to explicate these prohibitions for the *kohanim* when they apply equally to all Jews?

Menachos 45a explains. The prohibition against *neveilah* was waived for *kohanim* in the instance of a bird brought for a sin offering, חַטָּאת הָעוֹף. The manner of ritual slaughter in that instance, מְלִיקָה, was of a nature that would render a bird *neveilah* in *non*-sacrificial circumstances. Nevertheless, *kohanim* were permitted to eat from it. Since the prohibition against *neveilah* was waived in this instance it might have been thought that *kohanim* were not bound by these prohibitions at all. For this reason the prohibition is repeated here, specifically mentioning the *kohanim (Rashi).*

XLV

◆§ Prefatory Remarks to Verses 1-8

The commentary to 40:5 gave a brief outline of the position of the Temple Mount within the larger area which surrounded it. The description was taken from vs. *1-4 of our chapter.*

In the future, the Land would be divided into thirteen portions, twelve of them for the tribes and the thirteenth to contain a portion known as the Terumah, *which would include the Temple area and its needs; with the remainder belonging to the* Nassi. *Each tribe will receive a strip of land 25,000 rods (i.e., 150,000 cubits) wide from north to south. These strips would run across the whole width of Eretz Yisrael from east to west. The northern seven strips and the southern five strips will be given to the twelve tribes (ch. 48). From north to south, the respective shares are in the following order:*

44 to the kohen to make a blessing rest upon your home.
31 [31] Any carcass or torn animal of fowl or livestock, the
kohanim may not eat.

45 When you allot the Land as an inheritance you are
1-2 to set aside a Terumah sacred to HASHEM from
the Land, a length twenty-five thousand, and a width
of ten thousand. It shall be holy around its entire
boundary. [2] From this shall be dedicated to the Sanc-

Fig. 28

Yechezkel's Division of the Land

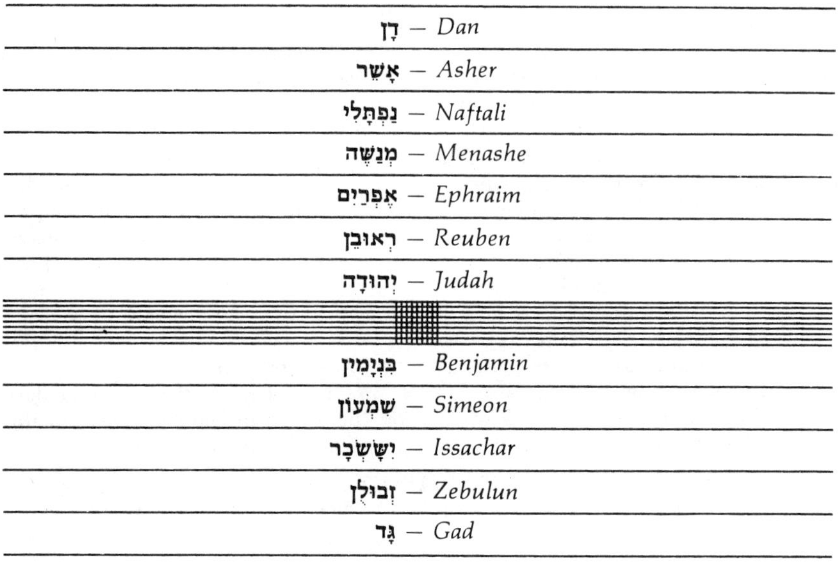

The middle strip is to be divided into three parts. The two outer sections are to be the property of the nassi *[prince], who, with such a generous portion of the land under his control, will feel no need to encroach upon those tracts which are not assigned to him* (v. 8)*. The inner section, which is to measure 25,000 rods square, is to be divided into three portions and utilized as follows:*

The northern portion, measuring 25,000 rods (from east to west) by 10,000 rods (from north to south) is to contain the Temple Mount (measuring 500 rods by 500 rods square) at its center. The rest of the area is to be used for housing for the kohanim.

South of this there is to be another portion, also measuring 25,000 rods by 10,000 rods, to be set aside for the Levites. Twenty chambers are to be situated in this area.

Finally, to the south of that portion there is to be another one, measuring 25,000 rods by 5000 rods. In the center of this portion, the city (measuring 4500 rods by 4500 rods), which has already been mentioned at 40:2, is to be situated. [Concerning this city, see further at 48:35]. The remaining space is to be common property for the people of all the tribes.

חֲמֵשׁ מֵאוֹת בַּחֲמֵשׁ מֵאוֹת מְרֻבָּע סָבִיב
ג וַחֲמִשִּׁים אַמָּה מִגְרָשׁ לוֹ סָבִיב׃ וּמִן־
הַמִּדָּה הַזֹּאת תָּמוֹד אֹרֶךְ חֲמֵשׁ וְעֶשְׂרִים
אֶלֶף וְרֹחַב עֲשֶׂרֶת אֲלָפִים וּבוֹ־יִהְיֶה
ד הַמִּקְדָּשׁ קֹדֶשׁ קָדָשִׁים׃ קֹדֶשׁ מִן־הָאָרֶץ
הוּא לַכֹּהֲנִים מְשָׁרְתֵי הַמִּקְדָּשׁ יִהְיֶה
הַקְּרֵבִים לְשָׁרֵת אֶת־יהוה וְהָיָה לָהֶם
ה מָקוֹם לְבָתִּים וּמִקְדָּשׁ לַמִּקְדָּשׁ׃ וַחֲמִשָּׁה
וְעֶשְׂרִים אֶלֶף אֹרֶךְ וַעֲשֶׂרֶת אֲלָפִים רֹחַב

1. וּבְהַפִּילְכֶם אֶת הָאָרֶץ בְּנַחֲלָה — *When you allot the Land as an inheritance.*

The text makes use of the verb לנפל, *to fall,* in the *Hiphil* [*causative*], to describe the division of the Land. This verb, the use of which is apt when a division of land is done by drawing lots, seems inappropriate here since the exact positions of each of the tribes is assigned. *Metzudos* holds that this root was used because in most cases land is divided by lots and so it came to be associated with the division of land irrespective of the method used.

Rashi points out that the division of the Land envisioned here is quite different from that which was undertaken in Joshua's time. At that time, the Land was assigned on the basis of the number of people in each tribe. Larger tribes received larger portions of the Land [but see *Ramban, Numbers* 26:54, who disagrees, maintaining that even Joshua's division was based on equal portions of the Land.] The division of the future will assign an equal share to each tribe.[1]

תְּרוּמָה — *Terumah.*

We follow *R' Hirsch's* commentary on the Torah in leaving this word untranslated for want of an exact

1. There is much in which the disposition of Land, Temple, and city described in *Ezekiel* differs from what had been previously taught in Scripture. We note some changes:

(A) At 47:18, we shall see that the entire area of the Land envisaged by Yechezkel lies west of the Jordan. [There we will discuss the problems that arise in connection with God's promise to Abraham (*Genesis* 15:19-21) that *Eretz Yisrael* will embrace both sides of the Jordan.] All twelve tribes are to have their portions in that part of the land, including Reuben, Gad, and part of Menashe whose portion had previously been located east of the Jordan.

(B) Simeon is to get a portion which is exactly equal to that of all the other tribes. In the previous division, his portion was not in one place but scattered in many different areas. (For a discussion of how Simeon had his land apportioned in the previous division see *Nachalas Shimon,* ch. 47).

(C) The Temple and Temple Mount are not in the city, but lie to the north of it (40:2). Previously, the position of the Temple was described as lying within Jerusalem (see *Rambam, Beis HaBechirah* 1:3, see further at 48:35).

(D) Jerusalem of old lay partly in the portion of Judah and partly in the portion of Benjamin, so that the Temple stood in both of these portions. [See *Yomah* 12a; *Zevachim* 53b, 54b. For a detailed discussion, see *Nachalas Shimon,* ch. 46]. In the disposition of the Land according to Yechezkel's vision, the entire complex of Temple and city lay between, but not in, the portions of Judah and Benjamin.

tuary a square five hundred by five hundred roun-
dabout, with fifty cubits of open space around it.
3 *Now by this same measure you shall measure a*
length of twenty-five thousand and a width of ten
thousand; within it shall be the Sanctuary — Holy of
Holies. 4 *It is to be a sacred portion from the land, for*
the kohanim, ministrants of the Sanctuary, it is to be
— those who approach to minister before HASHEM. It
shall afford them space for houses as well as holy
ground for the Sanctuary.
5 *Another twenty-five thousand long and ten*

equivalent in the vernacular. *Terumah* represents a portion of one's wealth that is separated and dedicated to a holy purpose.

לַה׳ קֹדֶשׁ מִן־הָאָרֶץ — *Sacred to HASHEM from the Land.*

God's bounty to Israel must be acknowledged. *From the land* which they had received in such generous measure, a part had to be made holy *(Metzudos).* This part was called *Terumah for HASHEM,* similar to the *terumah* given the *kohen* from all produce (see 44:30) as a testimonial to the essential holiness with which one must imbue his property. By sanctifying a part, one acknowledges the inner sanctity of the whole *(R' Breuer).*

This 'sacred *terumah'* is the northernmost strip of this portion within which the Temple was built *(Rashi).*

אֹרֶךְ...וְרֹחַב... — *A length...and a width...*

See fig. 28. Verse 3 specifies that these measurements are in rods.

2. מִגְרָשׁ — *Of open space.*

We already knew these dimensions from 42:15-20. The repetition of these measurements tells us that we are dealing with rods rather than cubits (see there). Our verse further adds the information that the Temple Mount was to have around it a מִגְרָשׁ, *an open space,* for beautification (see *Numbers* 35:2).

3. וּמִן הַמִּדָּה הַזֹּאת תָּמוֹד — *Now by this same measure you shall measure.*

Verse 1 did not indicate whether the measurements were given in rods (each of which was 6 cubits — see 40:5) or in cubits; but 42:15-20 taught that the Temple Mount area was to be measured in rods. Our phrase indicates that the 25,000 of verse 1 was to be measured by the same unit. Since a rod contains six cubits, the size of the *Terumah* was 150,000 cubits × 60,000 cubits *(Rashi).* [See further at 48:1.]

Radak translates מִן as *from* or *out of,* i.e., the 500 square area of the Temple Mount is to come from within the 25,000×10,000 area. Thus, the Temple Mount area was to be included in this tract, not separate from it.

[According to *Radak's* interpretation, unlike *Rashi's,* our verse is not meant to define the *unit* of measurement. Accordingly, it is possible that the 25,000×10,000 is to be measured in cubits rather than rods — a difference in a factor of 6. See further at 48:1.]

4. מָקוֹם לְבָתִּים וּמִקְדָּשׁ לַמִּקְדָּשׁ — *Space for houses as well as holy ground for the Sanctuary.*

Radak comments that the fifty cubit מִגְרָשׁ, *open space,* was included in the area designated for housing for the *kohanim,* although no houses could be built there.

מה
ו־ח

°יִהְיֶה לַלְוִיִּם מְשָׁרְתֵי הַבַּיִת לָהֶם °וְהָיָה ק׳
ו לַאֲחֻזָּה עֶשְׂרִים לְשָׁכֹת: וַאֲחֻזַּת הָעִיר
תִּתְּנוּ חֲמֵשֶׁת אֲלָפִים רֹחַב וְאֹרֶךְ חֲמִשָּׁה
וְעֶשְׂרִים אֶלֶף לְעֻמַּת תְּרוּמַת הַקֹּדֶשׁ
ז לְכָל־בֵּית יִשְׂרָאֵל יִהְיֶה: וְלַנָּשִׂיא מִזֶּה
וּמִזֶּה לִתְרוּמַת הַקֹּדֶשׁ וְלַאֲחֻזַּת הָעִיר
אֶל־פְּנֵי תְרוּמַת־הַקֹּדֶשׁ וְאֶל־פְּנֵי אֲחֻזַּת
הָעִיר מִפְּאַת יָם יָמָּה וּמִפְּאַת קֵדְמָה
קָדִימָה וְאֹרֶךְ לְעֻמּוֹת אַחַד הַחֲלָקִים
ח מִגְּבוּל יָם אֶל־גְּבוּל קָדִימָה: לָאָרֶץ יִהְיֶה־
לּוֹ לַאֲחֻזָּה בְּיִשְׂרָאֵל וְלֹא־יוֹנוּ עוֹד נְשִׂיאַי
אֶת־עַמִּי וְהָאָרֶץ יִתְּנוּ לְבֵית־יִשְׂרָאֵל

5. וְהָיָה לַלְוִיִּם — *Shall be for the Levites.*

The section assigned to the Levites lay to the south of the one just described. This is not explicated here, but can be derived clearly from ch. 48. There, the division of the Land is described going from north to south and the section for the *kohanim* is described (*v.* 8) before that of the Levites (*v.* 13).

לְשָׁכֹת — *Chambers.*

The twenty chambers mentioned in this verse are left unexplained. Neither their dimensions, nor their locations, nor, indeed, their function, is given. *Rashi* and *Radak* suggest that they were grouped close to the Temple Mount so that those Levites whose duty it was to guard the Temple could be close by.

6. וַאֲחֻזַּת הָעִיר — *As the property of the city.*

The entire 25,000×5000 area is described as the property of the city although the city itself occupied an area of only 4500×4500 (48:16). The rest of the area was used as follows:

The city was surrounded on all sides by an open space, measuring 250 rods, giving the city with its open space an area of 5000×5000 rods (48:17). The remaining 10,000 rods in either direction [(25,000-5000)÷2=10,000] was used to produce food for the city's inhabitants (48:18).

The whole 25,000×5000 area is described as חוֹל, *ordinary* (48:15), in contrast to the two other sections which lay to its north [25,000×10,000 for the Temple Mount and the *kohanim*; 25,000×10,000 for the Levites] which are considered קֹדֶשׁ, *sanctified*, because they served the Temple directly by providing living space for the *kohanim* and the Levites.

7. וְלַנָּשִׂיא — *And for the prince.*

Each of the other twelve strips ran along the entire width of the Land; the width of the three sections just described was only 25,000 rods. This left the whole width of the strip east and west of these sections. The outer areas were assigned to the *nassi, prince.* Verse 8 explains that the purpose of assigning such large tracts of land to the *nassi* was to discourage him from oppressing the people in an attempt to enlarge his holdings.

8. לָאָרֶץ יִהְיֶה לוֹ לַאֲחֻזָּה בְּיִשְׂרָאֵל — *For the country's sake, it shall be his as a possession in Israel.*

The translation follows *R' Breuer* whose interpretation is as follows: The *inheritance* of the *nassi* really belongs *to*

45
6-8

thousand wide shall be for the Levites, the servants of
the House, as their possession — twenty chambers.
6 *As the property of the city, you are to set aside five thousand wide by twenty-five thousand long alongside the sacred terumah: it shall belong to the entire family of Israel.*
7 *And for the prince, on either side of the sacred terumah and the property of the city, facing the sacred terumah and facing the property of the city, on the west extending westward and on the east extending eastward — equal to a single tribal portion extending from the western border to the eastern*
border. 8 *For the country's sake, it shall be his as a possession in Israel, that My princes will no longer defraud My people but give the land to the family of*

Fig. 29
The Sacred Terumah

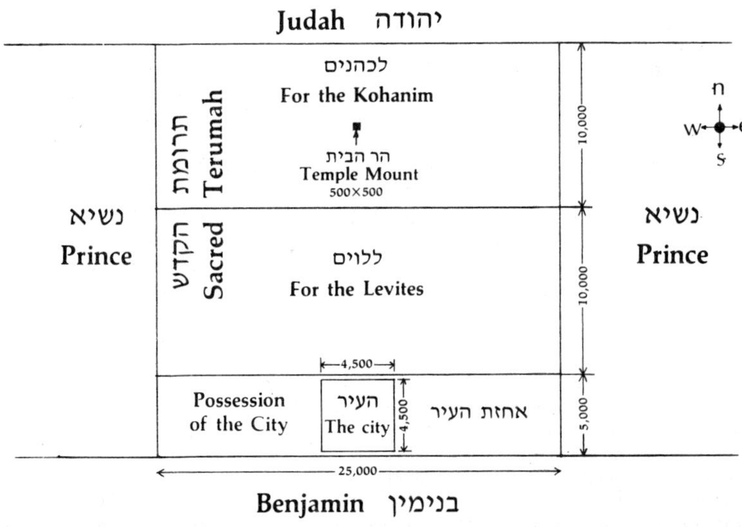

the whole *land*. The word נָשִׂיא also means cloud (see *comm.* to 22:6)]. As a cloud which takes moisture from the land and returns it as rain, the *nassi* takes his wealth from the people only so that he may then restore it to them like beneficent rain. The land assigned to the *nassi* is not lost to the people. It is *their* land, for the *nassi* embodies their nationhood within himself.[1]

1. At this point we must re-examine the monarchy in general and the kingship of the *nassi, the Messianic king* (except according to *Rashi*, see 44:3) in particular. Much of the final

ט לִשְׁבְטֵיהֶם: כֹּה־אָמַר אֲדֹנָי
יֱהֹוִה רַב־לָכֶם נְשִׂיאֵי יִשְׂרָאֵל חָמָס וָשֹׁד
הָסִירוּ וּמִשְׁפָּט וּצְדָקָה עֲשׂוּ הָרִימוּ
גְרֻשֹׁתֵיכֶם מֵעַל עַמִּי נְאֻם אֲדֹנָי יֱהֹוִה:
י מֹאזְנֵי־צֶדֶק וְאֵיפַת־צֶדֶק וּבַת־צֶדֶק יְהִי
יא לָכֶם: הָאֵיפָה וְהַבַּת תֹּכֶן אֶחָד יִהְיֶה
לָשֵׂאת מַעְשַׂר הַחֹמֶר הַבָּת וַעֲשִׂירִת
הַחֹמֶר הָאֵיפָה אֶל־הַחֹמֶר יִהְיֶה
יב מַתְכֻּנְתּוֹ: וְהַשֶּׁקֶל עֶשְׂרִים גֵּרָה עֶשְׂרִים

9. רַב לָכֶם נְשִׂיאֵי יִשְׂרָאֵל — *Enough for you, princes of Israel!*

This is a call to the former kings of Judah, who have now been demoted to the level of princes by the Babylonian conquerors. The robbery and rapine which you have practiced in the past must cease; instead, you must practice justice and righteousness *(Metzudos).*

Malbim offers an interpretation which looks to the future: You will have ample property, *O princes of Israel* (see *v.* 8). There is no need for you to practice robbery and rapine. My dispositions are such that you can practice justice and righteousness.

הָרִימוּ גְרֻשֹׁתֵיכֶם מֵעַל עַמִּי — *Desist from your evictions of My people* [lit. *remove your evictions from My people*].

Stop evicting My people from their properties *(Rashi).*

Radak and *Metzudos* hold that גרש can mean *to throw* or *to impose.* The meaning is: Desist from imposing [unfair] taxes upon My people.

10-12 These verses charge the nassi with the responsibility of overseeing the

chapters of the Book are concerned with this *nassi*, and we should try to picture his standing and function from the information we are given about him.

In many cases the monarchy as it had then existed had come to be a disaster to the Jewish people (see pref., ch. 34), but a radical change was envisioned for the future. In contrast to the kings of the past, who had been a block between God and His people, the kings of the future would serve as a conduit for God's direct stewardship (see footnote 43:7).

The dispositions in our section may serve to teach how the future monarchy is planned to guarantee the correct posture of the *nassi* in his relations to God and people, and how it is to avoid the pitfalls of the past.

A careful reading of ch. 48 (see also *comm.* 48:21-22) will show that the sacred *terumah* is part and parcel of the portion of the *nassi.* [That is, we are not to view the division of the strip as three different pieces, two belonging to the *nassi* and one being devoted to the sacred *terumah.* Rather, the whole strip from east to west is assigned to the *nassi.* From this portion he is to separate a given area for the sacred *Terumah.*]

Thus understood, the disposition of the land is highly significant. It is in the territory of the *nassi* that the *Shechinah* chooses to rest; the city whose name is to be ה' שָׁמָּה, *HASHEM is there,* (see 48:35) in recognition of its complete oneness with the Divine (see Prefatory Remarks to ch. 22) is specifically situated in the *nassi's* portion of the land. Surely this identifies him unambiguously in the role of conduit for the Divine Presence to rest in Israel. But the matter does not rest there.

In *Malbim's* view, verses 13-17 describe a permanent arrangement which will be inaugurated with the coming of Messianic times. [This contrasts with *Radak* who interprets the section as dealing with a one-time consecration rite.] According to this interpretation all the communal sacrifices which are brought daily and in celebration of special days will be brought

Israel according to their tribes. 9 *Thus says my Lord*
HASHEM/ELOHIM: Enough for you, princes of Israel!
Set aside lawlessness and rapine. Do justice and
righteousness. Desist from your evictions of My peo-
ple. The words of my Lord HASHEM/ELOHIM.
10 *Honest balances, an honest* ephah, *and an*
honest bas are you to have. 11 *The ephah and bas*
shall comprise the same volume, the bas shall contain
a tenth of a chomer and the ephah shall contain a
tenth of a chomer. Relative to the chomer is their
capacity to remain. 12 *The shekel shall be twenty ger-*

weights and measures which are to be used. *Bava Basra* 89a teaches that it was the duty of the community to appoint commissioners to check scales and weights against any possible abuse. These appointments are presumably the duty of the nassi who is to wield the executive power within the new state *(Malbim).*

[We may surmise that the centrality of Yechezkel's concern with this particular duty of the *nassi* reflects the teaching of the Sages in *Toras Kohanim* to *Leviticus* 19:35: ... for he who measures [for the purpose of a sale] is like a judge and if he is deceitful ... he causes five things: He defiles the Land, desecrates God's Name; causes the *Shechinah* to depart; causes Israel to fall by the sword; and causes them to be exiled from their land. Foremost in Yechezkel's mind is the need to safeguard the community from such abuses which bring these five results in their wake. (For discussion of the seriousness with which the Sages view dishonest weights and measures, see *Maharal, Gevuros HaShem,* ch. 45).]

10. וְאֵיפַת צֶדֶק וּבַת צֶדֶק — *An honest ephah and an honest bas.*

The *ephah* is a dry measure. The *bas* (which has the same volume — see *v.* 11) is a liquid measure *(Rashi).*

11. הַחֹמֶר — *The chomer.*

The *chomer* is both a dry and a liquid measure. It contains 30 סְאִין, *s'ahs* [see *Menachos* 77a]. Both the *ephah* and the *bas* of the previous verse are 1/10 *chomer,* that is 3 *s'ahs.*

אֶל הַחֹמֶר יִהְיֶה מַתְכֻּנְתּוֹ — *Relative to the chomer is their capacity to remain.*

The ratio of the *ephah* and the *bas* to the *chomer* is always one to ten. If the

by the *nassi* from his own property (*v.* 17). So that he can be enabled to fulfill these obligations, all the people are to be taxed in the amounts specified in verses 13-16. The halachah is quite clear, however, that communal sacrifices may not be brought by an individual [*Menachos* 65a and *Rambam, Shekalim* 4:1]. If, nevertheless, the *nassi* is designated to bring these sacrifices, this can only mean that his property, since it derives from the taxes of the community, is considered communal property.

Thus, it is clear that not only is the *nassi* the conduit through which the Divine Presence is to rest among the people; he is also the conduit through which the people pay homage to God through the communal sacrifices. [Hence comes the uncompromising insistence that the roles of king and *kohen* are not to be confused (footnote 43:7). If the king is to represent the people *vis-a-vis* God in their communal sacrifice, then he himself cannot be the *kohen* who, as it were, mediates between the people and God.]

We now have an entirely new picture of the Messianic king. He is, on the one hand, to embody Israel's nationhood, as their representative in the Temple service, bringing the communal sacrifices from the property which becomes his by way of the people. On the other hand, he brings Godliness to the people, as the Divine Presence rests in his portion of the Land.

שְׁקָלִים חֲמִשָּׁה וְעֶשְׂרִים שְׁקָלִים עֲשָׂרָה
יג וַחֲמִשָּׁה שֶׁקֶל הַמָּנֶה יִהְיֶה לָכֶם׃ זֹאת
הַתְּרוּמָה אֲשֶׁר תָּרִימוּ שִׁשִּׁית הָאֵיפָה
מֵחֹמֶר הַחִטִּים וְשִׁשִּׁיתֶם הָאֵיפָה מֵחֹמֶר
יד הַשְּׂעֹרִים׃ וְחֹק הַשֶּׁמֶן הַבַּת הַשֶּׁמֶן
מַעְשַׂר הַבַּת מִן־הַכֹּר עֲשֶׂרֶת הַבַּתִּים
טו חֹמֶר כִּי־עֲשֶׂרֶת הַבַּתִּים חֹמֶר׃ וְשֶׂה־
אַחַת מִן־הַצֹּאן מִן־הַמָּאתַיִם מִמַּשְׁקֵה

chomer increases or decreases in size, so will the *ephah* and the *bas (Rashi).*

12. עֶשְׂרִים שְׁקָלִים חֲמִשָּׁה וְעֶשְׂרִים שְׁקָלִים עֲשָׂרָה וַחֲמִשָּׁה שֶׁקֶל — *Twenty shekels, twenty-five shekels, and fifteen shekels.*

The combination of the three shekel denominations: a 20-shekel piece, a 25-shekel piece, and a 15-shekel piece (60 shekels total) is equivalent to 1 *mannah.*

This would seem to contradict the value of a *mannah* as it is given throughout the Talmud. A *shekel* contains four *zuz,* thus the sixty shekels of our verse would total 240 *zuz,* but the Talmud identifies a *mannah* as 100 *zuz.*

From this question the Sages (*Bava Basra* 90a) postulate that (a) A *mannah* used for the purposes of the Temple (מָנָה שֶׁל קוֹדֶשׁ) was double the size of an ordinary *mannah* [200 *zuz,* rather than 100]. (b) Since the total of 240 *zuz* is twenty percent more than 200, we infer that it is permissible to increase the value of a *mannah* by that amount, a course that was adopted in Yechezkel's time.

13-15 There are three different approaches to this section: *Rashi's, Radak's,* and *Malbim's.*

As in ch. 44, *Rashi* interprets these verses in accordance with the halachah as we know it. (See *footnotes* to 44:1-3,17).

Radak and *Malbim* both comment that the passage deals with new laws which will apply in the Messianic era. However, they differ in their interpretations. In *Radak's* view the gifts enumerated here were a one-time levy for the מִלוּאִים, *consecration rites,* for the new Temple.

Malbim thinks that we are dealing with a permanent tax to be paid the *nassi.* (See further at *v.* 17).

13. זאת הַתְּרוּמָה...שִׁשִּׁית הָאֵיפָה מֵחֹמֶר — *This is the terumah ... a sixth of an ephah from a chomer.*

Numbers 18:12 provides for a gift, a *terumah,* to be given to the *kohanim* from the grain, wine, and oil produced in the Land. The Torah does not specify any amount to be given, and indeed, the Sages teach that 'one kernel can fulfill the obligation for a whole pile of wheat.' However, while the Sages ordained that an average person should give 1/50 of his produce, they praise as generous one who gives 1/40 and specify that no one may give less than 1/60 as a *terumah.* The minimum of 1/60 is derived from our verse: since an *ephah* is 1/10 of a *chomer (v.* 11), the 1/6 of an *ephah* which is given as *terumah* would be 1/60 of the entire *chomer (Yerushalmi, Terumos* 4:3).

Rashi cites this *Yerushalmi* in his commentary, thus indicating that in his view our verse deals with the halachah of *terumah* which is specified in the Torah.

Radak (v. 15) objects on two counts. Since the Torah law of *terumah* applies to grain, wine, and oil equally, why should wheat and barley be mentioned separately in our verse, and why should oil be mentioned in a separate category

ah. Twenty shekels, twenty-five shekels, and fifteen
shekels shall be a mannah for you.
13 *This is the terumah which you shall separate: a*
sixth of an ephah from a chomer of wheat and you
are to take a sixth of an ephah from a chomer of
barley. 14 *Now, the due from the oil — the bas being*
the measure for oil — the bas is to be the tithe of the
kor for there are ten bas to the chomer since ten bas
constitute a chomer.
15 *A singular sheep from the flock from among two*

in the next verse? Moreover, why would Yechezkel mention only the least generous category of giving (1/60)? Would one not have expected him to recommend the most generous gift (1/40)?

For these reasons, *Radak* thinks the *Yerushalmi* must be viewed as a רֶמֶז, *allusion,* to the later Rabbinic decision to require a minimum gift of 1/60, but that the simple meaning of the verse is unrelated to the Torah law of *terumah.* [*Radak* here only deals with the section of the *Yerushalmi* cited by *Rashi.* According to one opinion, Shmuel's, in the *Yerushalmi,* the generous 1/40 designation is also derived from this verse — indeed, his view is based upon the separation of species.] *Radak* sees our verse as referring to a one-time levy which was to be made in connection with the consecration sacrifices. This tax was for 1/60 of the total wheat and barley harvest.

Malbim believes that our verse describes a permanent tax to be paid to the prince.

14. וְחֹק הַשֶּׁמֶן — *The due from the oil.*

According to *Rashi,* the verse is referring to the מַעֲשֵׂר, *tithe,*which the Torah gives the Levite from grain, wine, and oil *(Numbers* 18:-21-24).

According to *Radak,* the verse refers to a one-time levy for the consecration rites.

הַבַּת הַשֶּׁמֶן — *The bas being the measure for oil.*

Above we noted that *ephah* is a dry measure while *bas* is a liquid measure. This information derives from this verse where we learn that the *bas* is the measurement for oil.

מַעְשַׂר הַבַּת מִן הַכֹּר — *The bas is to be the tithe of the kor.*

The translation follows *Rashi.* A *bas* which is 1/10 of a *kor* is the correct amount for the tithe of oil.

Radak translates: The due from the oil is a tenth of a *bas* to be separated from the *kor.* This is to be a one time levy of 1/100 of the *chomer/kor* for the consecration rites.

כִּי עֲשֶׂרֶת הַבַּתִּים חֹמֶר — *Since ten bas constitute a chomer.*

Chomer is synonymous with *kor.* There are ten *bas* in a *chomer* or *kor.*

According to *Rashi (Menachos* 77a) the verse teaches that the *bas* is the correct fraction (a tenth) to separate as the tithe from a *chomer/kor.* It is essentially a repetition of the earlier part of the verse. This is not unusual in prophetic language.

According to *Radak,* our phrase teaches that these measurements are meaningful for the Messianic era because just as now there are 10 *bas* to a *chomer,* so will there be in Messianic times.

15. וְשֶׂה אַחַת מִן הַצֹּאן — *A singular sheep from the flock.*

Your offering should be from the very best sheep which you own,a sheep

יִשְׂרָאֵל לְמִנְחָה וּלְעוֹלָה וְלִשְׁלָמִים
טז לְכַפֵּר עֲלֵיהֶם נְאֻם אֲדֹנָי יֱהֹוִה׃ כֹּל
הָעָם הָאָרֶץ יִהְיוּ אֶל־הַתְּרוּמָה הַזֹּאת
יז לַנָּשִׂיא בְּיִשְׂרָאֵל׃ וְעַל־הַנָּשִׂיא יִהְיֶה
הָעוֹלוֹת וְהַמִּנְחָה וְהַנֵּסֶךְ בַּחַגִּים
וּבֶחֳדָשִׁים וּבַשַּׁבָּתוֹת בְּכָל־מוֹעֲדֵי בֵּית
יִשְׂרָאֵל הוּא־יַעֲשֶׂה אֶת־הַחַטָּאת וְאֶת־
הַמִּנְחָה וְאֶת־הָעוֹלָה וְאֶת־הַשְּׁלָמִים
יח לְכַפֵּר בְּעַד בֵּית־יִשְׂרָאֵל׃ כֹּה־
אָמַר אֲדֹנָי יֱהֹוִה בָּרִאשׁוֹן בְּאֶחָד לַחֹדֶשׁ

singular in its perfection *(Rashi).*

מִן הַמָּאתַיִם — *From among two hundred.*

According to *Rashi* based on *Pesachim* 47b, this refers to a particular circumstance regarding the נְסָכִים, *libations,* which are to accompany the sacrifice of a burnt or peace offering (see *Numbers* 15:1-16). If wine which was made from עָרְלָה, *grapes which grew during the first three years of the vine's life,* which is forbidden, fell into wine which was suitable for libations, the problem arises whether the mixture is rendered unfit for libations. The halachah permits the mixture to be used if there was at least 200 times as much permitted wine as there was forbidden wine. This is derived from our verse. The libations for the burnt or peace offerings are halachically acceptable if they come *from the two hundred.*

Radak, as in the previous two verses, explains our verse as describing a one-time gift to be used for the consecration rites. He reads this phrase together with the preceding one: From every Israelite's flock, *one sheep out of every two hundred* is to be donated for the consecration sacrifices.

מִמַּשְׁקֵה יִשְׂרָאֵל — *From Israel's festive banquet* [lit. *drink*].

According to *Rashi,* מַשְׁקֶה, literally *drink,* is used to describe a festive meal, since a banquet normally includes a beverage. Accordingly, the meaning of the phrase is: Sacrifices must be brought from such materials as could be described as *Israel's* (halachically permitted) *meals.* No sacrifice may be brought from anything which is forbidden to be eaten by the Torah.

Radak (as *Targum)* translates מִמַּשְׁקֶה as *from the fattest:* The sheep brought as sacrifices were to be of the very best quality.

16. הַתְּרוּמָה הַזֹּאת — *This Terumah.*

According to *Rashi,* this verse refers to the *Terumah* or gift of land which the whole of Israel is to give the *nassi (vs.* 7-8). The gift is to be made with the approbation of all the people.

According to *Radak,* the meaning of our verse is as follows: The consecration gifts described above are to be given by the people only, and the *nassi* is not obliged to contribute towards them. In spite of the fact that he does not contribute to them, he is still to have a share in the communal sacrifice. The next verse will describe the responsibility of the *nassi* toward the people in return for this privilege.

In *Malbim's* view, the verse means that all the gifts mentioned in *vs.* 13-15 are meant for the *nassi.* All the people are to be taxed in the amounts specified. See following verse.

hundred, from Israel's festive banquet for a meal offering, burnt offering and peace offering to atone for you. The words of my Lord, HASHEM/ELOHIM.
16 *The entire population of the land must join in this Terumah with the prince in Israel.*

17 *The prince's responsibility shall be the burnt offerings, the meal offerings and the libations on the festive days, the New Moons, and the Sabbaths — all festivals — of the family of Israel. He shall make the sin offering, the meal offering, the burnt offering, and the peace offering to atone for the family of Israel.*

18 *Thus says my Lord HASHEM/ELOHIM: In the first month on the first of the month you shall take a*

17. וְעַל־הַנָּשִׂיא — *The prince's responsibility.*

Rashi repeats his opinion (see 44:2) that the *nassi* mentioned here is the כֹּהֵן גָּדוֹל, *high priest,* meaning that he must officiate at the sacrificial service of these offerings. [*Rashi* does not explain why the high priest must perform the sacrificial rites on the occasions specified here. Whatever the reason, his view is not in accord with the halachah, which does not require the high priest's personal participation in sacrifices except for certain of the services of Yom Kippur. (See further at *v.* 22).]

Radak notes that whereas the consecration gifts are to be given by the people for themselves and the *nassi (v.* 16), the festival sacrifices mentioned in our verse are to be provided by the *nassi* for the entire community (see footnote to *v.* 7).

According to *Malbim,* since all the possessions of the *nassi* come to him from the people, his is a communal ownership and the obligation to bring the communal sacrifices for the occasions specified in our verse devolves upon him (see *footnote* to *v.* 7.]

18-24 Some of the sacrifices mentioned in this section have been mentioned in 43:18-27 (see also *comm., v.* 27). The two sections complement each other and should be studied as one unit.

The book of *Ezekiel* posed many problems to the Sages. In *Shabbos* 13b (see also *Chagigah* 13a; *Menachos* 45a) we read, 'R' Judah said in Rav's name: In truth, ... Chananiah ben Chizkiyahu ... is to be remembered for a blessing: but for him, the book of *Ezekiel* would have been withdrawn (נִגְנָז), for its words [seem to] contradict the Torah. What did he do? Three hundred barrels of oil [to maintain his lamp] were taken up to him, and he sat in an upper chamber and reconciled the contradictions.'

Even if we allow for hyperbole, (see *Rashbam, Pesachim* 119a; *Maharitz Chayos, Mavo HaTalmud* ch. 30) the story still indicates a prodigious amount of work that was invested in trying to find solutions to the problem posed by the book.

Nowhere are the problems with which Chananiah ben Chizkiyahu grappled identified.. *Chagigah* 13a quotes the story in connection with the sections of the book dealing with the *Merkavah* and *Menachos* 45a brings it in connection with the problems of the

תִּקַּח פַּר־בֶּן־בָּקָר תָּמִים וְחִטֵּאתָ אֶת־
יט הַמִּקְדָּשׁ: וְלָקַח הַכֹּהֵן מִדַּם הַחַטָּאת וְנָתַן
אֶל־מְזוּזַת הַבַּיִת וְאֶל־אַרְבַּע פִּנּוֹת
הָעֲזָרָה לַמִּזְבֵּחַ וְעַל־מְזוּזַת שַׁעַר הֶחָצֵר
כ הַפְּנִימִית: וְכֵן תַּעֲשֶׂה בְּשִׁבְעָה בַחֹדֶשׁ

sacrifices in our section. Thus, it seems that these two issues were the ones with which he dealt.

There is also no record of the explanations which he found. *Rashi* bemoans this fact in his commentary to verse 22: 'Because of our sins, we cannot know how he explained these sacrifices ... '

However, *Rashi* does interpret these passages and our translation follows him.

Later *Amoraim* once more grappled with these issues. The bullock to be brought on the first day of Nissan (*v.* 18) was the subject of the controversy in *Menachos* 45a discussed at 44:17.

R' Yochanan felt that the matter must be left to Elijah the prophet, who would explain this verse at some future date. In *Malbim's* view (see *comm.* 44:17) this means that R' Yochanan anticipated a new world order for Messianic times, when a new halachah would apply to the circumstances of heightened spirituality. *Radak* bases much of his commentary on this assumption, and his approach to the sacrifices in the following verses is consistent with that opinion.

R' Ashi does not accept this premise and explains the irregularity of the bullock in verse 18 by identifying it as a consecration sacrifice [which by its very nature had unique laws which need not conform to those of regular offerings.]

Would R' Ashi's solution for the bullock of *v.* 18 be valid for all the irregular sacrifices mentioned in this and the next chapter?

Rambam, Maasseh HaKorbanos 2:14, answers in the affirmative. 'All the amounts of the libations mentioned in the book of *Ezekiel*, the number of the sacrifices, and the order of the service described there — all are consecration sacrifices and have no permanent application ...

This raises the question of how long the consecration of the Third Temple was to last. Verse 21 tells of an irregular sacrifice to be brought on the fourteenth of Nissan, and verse 23 speaks of irregular sacrifices for Succos. If all these are consecration sacrifices, we must postulate that the consecration rites lasted more than six months, in sharp contrast to the consecration periods of Moses' Tabernacle and Solomon's Temple, each of which lasted seven days. Indeed, *Malbim* explains that, in accordance with the added sanctity of the new Temple, a greatly extended period of consecration will be required.

18. פַּר — *A bull.*

[The normal *Rosh Chodesh* offerings are prescribed at *Numbers* 28:11-15. A bullock for a חַטָּאת is not part of those requirements.]

This bullock is identical with the one mentioned at 43:19-20. Our verse adds that this consecration rite [R' Ashi's opinion in *Menachos* 45a] took place on the first day of Nissan *(Rashi).*

Rashi, who interprets that the two bullocks are identical, must identify the sprinkling of the blood here in verse 19 with that described in 43:20. *Tosafos (Menachos* 45a) objects that the simple meaning of the two verses clearly indicates that different orders of sprinkling were required, therefore it is clear that our verse and 43:19-20 refer to different offerings. Since our verse describes the function of the bullock mentioned here as being needed to cleanse the Sanctuary, whereas the one

45 *bull of the herd without blemish, and you shall*
19-20 *cleanse the Sanctuary.* 19 *And the kohen shall take*
from the blood of the sin offering and apply it to the
doorposts of the house and in the four corners of the
altar's courtyard and on the doorposts of the gate of
the inner courtyard. 20 *And so you shall do for a week*

in 43:20 was to cleanse the altar, it is simpler to assume that they were indeed two separate sacrifices.

Malbim maintains (see *comm.* 43:18-27) that the rites described in ch. 43 are to start on the twenty-third of Adar and continue until the first day of Nissan, lasting seven days exactly like the consecration in Moses' time. Then, on the first day of Nissan, a new series (see *vs.* 20-21) of sacrifices is to start, whose purpose is to cleanse the Sanctuary (rather than the altar). On the fourteenth day of Nissan, yet another series is to start (see *v.* 21).

19. מִדַּם הַחַטָּאת – *From the blood of the sin offering.*

The blood offering described in this verse is unique. Nowhere else do we find blood being placed on either the *doorposts of the Temple Building* or on the *doorposts of the inner courtyard.* As we have seen in verse 18, the purpose of these blood offerings was to cleanse the Sanctuary, thus possibly accounting for these novel offerings.

הָעֲזָרָה לַמִּזְבֵּחַ – *The altar's courtyard.*

Metzudos and the commentators cited in 43:20 understand this to mean the altar's roof. *Radak*, however, interprets this as the area of the courtyard in proximity to the altar. (See 43:20).

20. וְכֵן תַּעֲשֶׂה בְּשִׁבְעָה בַּחֹדֶשׁ – *And so you shall do for a week* [lit. *for seven*] *in the month.*

The translation follows *Rashi.* The verse repeats the information given in 43:25 that the cleansing rites were to take seven days.[1]

Rashi also notes the interpretation of the Sages in *Menachos* 45a: The halachah prescribes that if the Sanhedrin mistakenly permitted an act which is Scripturally prohibited and punishable by *kores* [*excision of the soul*], and the majority of the community acted upon this incorrect decision, the Sanhedrin is obliged to bring as a sin offering פַּר הֶעְלֵם דָּבָר שֶׁל צִבּוּר, *a bull for a matter that was concealed from the congregation.*

While it was clear that the offering was required only if a 'majority' of the nation sinned, the definition of 'majority' was in question: was it a majority of the population, or were seven of the twelve tribes sufficient even if they constituted less than half the population? The Sages find the solution in our verse. They interpret: וְכֵן תַּעֲשֶׂה, *And so shall you do* [i.e., just as the consecration offerings are burned in their entirety, so shall you do with the Sanhedrin's sin offering which is completely burned] בְּשִׁבְעָה, *for seven tribes* [i.e., it must be brought even if seven *tribes*, but not a majority of the people, sin] בַּחֹדֶשׁ is interpreted as if it were vocalized בֶּחָדָשׁ, *for something new* [i.e., if the Sanhedrin issued a novel, but incorrect, ruling in the event the sin was] מֵאִישׁ שֹׁגֶה וּמִפֶּתִי *committed by an unwitting or ig-*

1. *Rashi* is hesitant about offering this explanation, he prefaces it with the words, 'Perhaps the meaning is ...

Why did *Rashi* and the Sages in *Menachos* 45a (see *Tosafos* there) not translate simply: *And so you shall do on the seventh of the month* – that is, the same offering prescribed for the first of the month should also be brought on the seventh.

As shown in the comm. below, none of the 'simple' solutions offered by the commentators are without problems. According to *Radak* and *Malbim* a sacrifice is postulated for the seventh of Nissan, a day wholly without any special significance. *R' D.Z. Hoffman's* suggestion has no source in any Rabbinical teaching.

Perhaps for this reason *Rashi* preferred his solution which has the merit of postulating consecration rites which are similar to others mentioned in the Torah.

מֵאִ֥ישׁ שֹׁגֶ֖ה וּמִפֶּ֑תִי וְכִפַּרְתֶּ֖ם אֶת־הַבָּֽיִת׃
כא בָּרִאשׁ֡וֹן בְּאַרְבָּעָה֩ עָשָׂ֨ר י֜וֹם לַחֹ֗דֶשׁ יִהְיֶ֥ה
לָכֶ֖ם הַפָּ֑סַח חָ֕ג שְׁבֻע֣וֹת יָמִ֔ים מַצּ֖וֹת
כב יֵאָכֵֽל׃ וְעָשָׂ֤ה הַנָּשִׂיא֙ בַּיּ֣וֹם הַה֔וּא בַּעֲד֕וֹ
כג וּבְעַ֖ד כָּל־עַ֣ם הָאָ֑רֶץ פַּ֖ר חַטָּֽאת׃ וְשִׁבְעַ֨ת

norant person [i.e., the sin permitted by the Sanhedrin was not committed willfully, but in the mistaken belief that it was permissible.]

Malbim translates: *On the seventh of the month.*

The identical sacrifice which was brought on *Rosh Chodesh* [*the first of the month of*] Nissan in order to purify the Sanctuary was to be brought once more on the seventh day. The second offering was to cleanse the Sanctuary from contamination caused unwittingly, whereas the earlier one was meant to deal with impurities which had been caused intentionally.

Radak shares *Malbim's* view, adding that this sacrifice is an innovation for the consecration of the Messianic era. The difficulty with this view is that the seventh of Nissan seems an unlikely day for special sacrificial service. Nowhere else do we find any particular significance attached to it.

R' D.Z. Hoffman (Sefer Vayikra, Jerusalem 5714, p. 130) is troubled by this idea. To him it is inconceivable that such cleansing rites should be fixed for a day that has no other significance.

He further points out that throughout *Ezekiel* (including the very next verse), dates of months are given with the prefix ל — לַחֹדֶשׁ, never בַּחֹדֶשׁ. The first word in verse 21 בָּרִאשׁוֹן, *in the first month,* is redundant if our verse meant the seventh day of Nissan, the first month. Just as our verse gives the seventh of the month without repeating the name of the month, we should not expect the name of the month to be mentioned in the next verse either.

For these reasons he suggests a different translation for our verse (which is borne out by the reading of the *Septuagint).* בְּשִׁבְעָה is the *seventh month,* and בַּחֹדֶשׁ means on *Rosh Chodesh* (as in *Psalms* 81:4). The meaning is that the same rites prescribed for *Rosh Chodesh* Nissan were to be repeated on *Rosh Chodesh* Tishrei, *Rosh HaShanah.* The Sanctuary was to be purified twice a year, in preparation for the major holidays which fall in Nissan and Tishrei.

21-25 There are three opinions concerning the sacrifices in these verses.

Rashi interprets each verse in keeping with the halachah. Our translation is based on *Rashi.*

Radak, who throughout these chapters, envisages a new set of practices to apply to the new Temple, continues with the application of this concept. All the seemingly irregular sacrifices are innovations for the Messianic era.

Rambam (Maaseh HaKorbanos 2:14) writes that all the apparently irregular sacrifices in the book of *Ezekiel* are consecration rites, and *Malbim* bases his commentary on that assumption.

In *Malbim's* view, the consecration rites consisted of three distinct groups. The first series, described in ch. 43, would cleanse the altar. This series lasted eight days, from the twenty-third of Adar to *Rosh Chodesh* Nissan.

The second series, which was to cleanse the Sanctuary, consisted of a special sacrifice to be brought on *Rosh Chodesh* Nissan and on the seventh day of Nissan. This was described in *vs.* 18-20.

This third series is to begin on the fourteenth of Nissan and continue through the end of Succos. Our chapter prescribes the particular sacrifices which are to be brought during the two

in the month — from uncleanliness caused by an unwitting or ignorant person, you shall cleanse the House. 21 *In the first month on the fourteenth day of the month you shall have the Pesach, a festival of seven days. Unleavened bread shall be eaten.* 22 *The prince shall make on that day, for himself and for the entire population, a bull for a sin offering.* 23 *During*

holiday periods (Pesach and Succos) [as part of the consecration rites, in addition to the regular sacrifices prescribed by the Torah], while ch. 46 describes the special rites to be performed on regular days during that period.

The altar and Sanctuary have already been cleansed in the first two series. The third series is meant to atone for the *nassi* and the entire people.

21. בָּרִאשׁוֹן — *In the first* [*month*].

The translation follows *Targum.*

Malbim, however, translates: *On the first* [*day*] of the third consecration series.

יִהְיֶה לָכֶם הַפָּסַח — *You shall have the Pesach.*

According to *Malbim,* this verse teaches that the consecration sacrifices of the next verse do not replace the regular obligations of the month. On the fourteenth day, the Pesach offering is to be brought as it is in other years, and, as on every other Pesach, matzah must be eaten for seven days. The requirements listed in the next verse are to be in addition to these.

שְׁבֻעוֹת יָמִים — *Seven* [lit. *weeks of*] *days.*

This expression is irregular. Most commentators simply take it as equivalent to שִׁבְעַת יָמִים, *seven days. Rashi* explains that it is used to allude to the seven *weeks* which are to be counted, starting from Pesach.

22. *Rashi* holds that our verse is one of those which caused the Sages to wish to withdraw the book of *Ezekiel* from circulation because the Torah mentions no such sin offering as that described here. *Rashi* bemoans the loss of Chananiah ben Chizkiyahu's solution to the problem which it poses. *Rashi* offers his own solution.

Radak and *Malbim* find no difficulty with this verse. According to *Radak,* it is a new sacrifice to be brought in the Messianic era, and according to *Malbim,* it is the beginning of the third consecration series.

וְעָשָׂה הַנָּשִׂיא...חַטָּאת — *The prince shall make ... a sin offering.*

As noted before, *Rashi's* opinion is that the *nassi* mentioned in our chapter is the *kohen gadol.* According to verse 17, it was to be his obligation to bring the holiday sacrifices. Now, from *Leviticus* ch. 9, we learn that on the eighth day of the consecration rites, Aaron was obliged to bring a calf in order to become consecrated to the priesthood. *Rashi* assumes that this same consecration sacrifice would be required for the new *kohen gadol* who serves in the Third Temple, and that he was to bring this on the eighth day of the consecration rites [which in *Rashi's* view would be the eighth day of Nissan — see vs. 18-20]. Our verse teaches that if he did not bring it then, he would have to bring it on the fourteenth of Nissan, the day before Pesach, so that he would be able to bring the holiday sacrifices — as was his duty — the next day.

Malbim agrees that our verse refers only to the first year, but interprets it as dealing with a formal consecration sacrifice.

יְמֵי־הֶחָג יַעֲשֶׂה עוֹלָה לַיהוה שִׁבְעַת
פָּרִים וְשִׁבְעַת אֵילִים תְּמִימִם לַיּוֹם
שִׁבְעַת הַיָּמִים וְחַטָּאת שְׂעִיר עִזִּים לַיּוֹם:
כד וּמִנְחָה אֵיפָה לַפָּר וְאֵיפָה לָאַיִל יַעֲשֶׂה
כה וְשֶׁמֶן הִין לָאֵיפָה: בַּשְּׁבִיעִי בַּחֲמִשָּׁה
עָשָׂר יוֹם לַחֹדֶשׁ בֶּחָג יַעֲשֶׂה כָאֵלֶּה
שִׁבְעַת הַיָּמִים כַּחַטָּאת כָּעֹלָה וְכַמִּנְחָה
מו א וְכַשָּׁמֶן: כֹּה־אָמַר אֲדֹנָי יֱהוִֹה
שַׁעַר הֶחָצֵר הַפְּנִימִית הַפֹּנֶה קָדִים יִהְיֶה

23. שִׁבְעַת פָּרִים וְשִׁבְעַת אֵילִים...לַיּוֹם — *Seven bullocks and seven rams...daily.*

Numbers 28:19 teaches that two bullocks and one ram were sacrificed as a burnt offering each of the seven days of Pesach. According to *Rashi*, our verse teaches that even if for the total of seven days only seven bullocks and seven rams are available (instead of fourteen bullocks and seven rams) it is still permitted to bring the sacrifices. One sacrifice is not dependent on the other; even if all the animals are not available, those that are available should still be sacrificed. The phrase is translated: *The combined daily sacrifices* [of the seven days] *may be seven bullocks and seven rams.*

[*Rashi* notes that *Menachos* 45a affirms this halachah, but derives it from 46:6 rather than from our verse. Nevertheless, he holds that our verse, too, teaches us this halachah.]

According to *Radak* and *Malbim*, our verse implies that seven bullocks and seven rams are to be brought daily in addition to the goat which is to be the sin offering. *Radak* again sees these as new sacrifices to be brought in the Messianic era, and *Malbim* views them as the beginning of the third series of consecration rites.

24. וּמִנְחָה — *And a meal offering.*

Numbers 15:1 ff. specifies that burnt offerings were to be accompanied by מִנְחַת נְסָכִים, *a flour offering mixed with oil.* The amounts required vary with the type of animal which is brought.

אֵיפָה לַפָּר — *An ephah for the bullock.*

Numbers (ch. 15) specifies three *esronim,* or 3/10 *ephah* of flour. (An *esaron* is 1/10 *ephah* — see *vs.* 10-11).

Rashi suggests the following explanation. According to the Talmud's specifications, the flour used for these sacrifices should be ground so fine that an *ephah* (ten *esronim)* of coarse flour would yield only two *esronim* of refined flour. Our verse teaches that if there is not enough flour, it may be made slightly more coarse, so that the three *esronim* required will be produced from one *ephah.*

וְאֵיפָה לָאַיִל — *And an ephah for the ram.*

Numbers specifies that a ram requires two *esronim* of flour.

One *ephah* for the ram is the ideal refinement of flour; the *ephah* of coarse flour will yield two *esronim* of fine flour *(Rashi).*

וְשֶׁמֶן הִין לָאֵיפָה — *And a hin of oil for each ephah.*

Numbers specifies 1/2 *hin* of oil for a bull and 1/3 *hin* for a ram.

Rashi suggests that here reference is not to the required amount of oil, but to a vessel which holds one *hin.* These vessels were used as measuring cups and were marked so that they readily dispensed the fractions of a *hin* which were required for the various sacrifices.

45
24-25
the seven days of the festival he shall bring a burnt
offering for HASHEM: seven bullocks and seven rams
without a blemish daily for seven days and as a sin
offering a goat daily; 24 *and a meal offering: an*
ephah for the bullock and an ephah for the ram he is
to bring; and a hin of oil for each ephah. 25 *In the*
seventh month on the fifteenth day of the month on
the festival, let him bring the same for the seven
days. Like the sin offering, like the burnt offering,
like the meal offering and like the oil.

46
1
Thus says my Lord HASHEM/ELOHIM: The gate of
the inner courtyard which faces eastward shall be

According to *Radak* these are new specifications which will come into use in the Third Temple. According to *Malbim* these specifications are limited to the consecration rites.

25. יַעֲשֶׂה כָאֵלֶּה — *Let him bring the same.*

Identical sacrifices were to be brought during the Succos holiday (see *comm., v.* 24).

The festivals of Shavuos, Rosh HaShanah, and Yom Kippur are not mentioned because no special consecration sacrifices were ordained for those days [but see 46:11]. The consecration ended on the last day of Succos, so there was no occasion to mention Shemini Atzeres *(Metzudos).*

XLVI

The three different approaches represented by Rashi, Radak *and* Malbim *which we traced in the last two chapters will continue through much of this one.*

Rashi *interprets these verses to correspond to the laws of the Torah as they were applied in the Second Temple, although the* p'shat [*simple meaning*] *would seem to indicate different laws.*

Radak *and* Malbim *follow the* p'shat, *and therefore interpret the laws of this chapter as different from those of the Torah.* Radak *maintains that there will be innovations in the service of the Third Temple, while* Malbim *regards any previously unknown sacrifices mentioned here as special consecration sacrifices, but not part of the regular ritual.*

The above applies to the bulk of this chapter, but not to verses 1-3. The disagreement concerning these verses is independent of that controversy.

1-3 Because the meaning of our three verses depends to some extent on the meaning of 44:1-3, the two sections should be considered as one unit. We have discussed 44:1-3 in the commentary above.

Our commentary to these three verses follows *Rashi.* At the end of commentary to verse 3 we shall note the opinions of *Radak* and *Malbim.*

1. שַׁעַר הֶחָצֵר הַפְּנִימִי — *The gate of the inner courtyard.*

We quote *Pirkei d'Rabbi Eliezer* ch. 51

R' Eliezer said: One day the Temple

סָגוּר שֵׁשֶׁת יְמֵי הַמַּעֲשֶׂה וּבְיוֹם הַשַּׁבָּת
ב יִפָּתֵחַ וּבְיוֹם הַחֹדֶשׁ יִפָּתֵחַ: וּבָא הַנָּשִׂיא
דֶּרֶךְ אוּלָם הַשַּׁעַר מִחוּץ וְעָמַד עַל־מְזוּזַת
הַשַּׁעַר וְעָשׂוּ הַכֹּהֲנִים אֶת־עוֹלָתוֹ וְאֶת־
שְׁלָמָיו וְהִשְׁתַּחֲוָה עַל־מִפְתַּן הַשַּׁעַר
וְיָצָא וְהַשַּׁעַר לֹא־יִסָּגֵר עַד־הָעָרֶב:
ג וְהִשְׁתַּחֲווּ עַם־הָאָרֶץ פֶּתַח הַשַּׁעַר הַהוּא

will rise up and be renewed ... and the gates which had sunk into the earth will rise up and be renewed each one in its correct place; and the gate of the inner courtyard which faces eastwards will be closed during the six weekdays but on the Sabath they will open by themselves as it is written [in our verse] *the gate ... shall be closed during the six days of labor but shall be opened on the Sabbath.*

R' Yehudah said: On the Sabbath and on *Rosh Chodesh* the people stood there and saw the gates opening by themselves and they would realize that the Sabbath had come and they would sanctify it. So also on *Rosh Chodesh* the people would see the gates opening by themselves and they would realize that the new moon had been born and they would hallow the new moon ... and as they stood there and saw the gates open they realized that the *Shechinah* of God was there as it is written ... *He said to me; This gate shall be closed* ... (44:2) and immediately they would prostrate themselves and bow down before their God ...

R' Yonasan asked: Is it not written, *'There is nothing new under the sun?*

He answered him: The righteous and all that happens to them will be renewed but the wicked will not experience anything new. [There will be nothing new for people who live *under the sun;* that is, for those people (the wicked) who consider themselves to be subject only to the natural laws of material existence, which are symbolized by the sun. But the righteous, who lift themselves above the ordinary, will indeed be renewed *(Radal).*]

Since *Pirkei d'Rabbi Eliezer* brings our verse together with 44:2 it appears that *the gate of the inner courtyard* of our verse is identical with *the outer gate of the Sanctuary* of 44:1.

Rashi seems to share this view. Therefore, the *gate of the inner courtyard* is the southern wicket which was part of the gate structure leading into the Sanctuary. (See *Rashi* to 44:1).[1]

1. In the commentary we note that *Rashi* 'seems' to interpret our verse as does *Pirkei d'Rabbi Eliezer.* The qualification is necessary because *Rashi* is not explicit and it is possible that *Rashi* in fact interprets our verse as referring to the *northern* rather than the *southern* wicket.

If this were the case, two difficulties would be avoided:

(a) How can the same wicket be described in Ch. 44 as *the outer gate of the Sanctuary* and in our verse as *the gate of the inner courtyard?*

(b) 44:2 is explicit that the southern wicket is never to be opened, while according to our verse *the gate of the inner courtyard* is to be opened on the Sabbath and on *Rosh Chodesh.*

Nonetheless, a careful reading of *Rashi* seems to yield the opinion which we assumed in the commentary and which, as seen from the quote from *Pirkei d'Rabbi Eliezer,* seems to have been the opinion of the Sages.

The general tone of this passage in the *Pirkei d'Rabbi Eliezer* can be viewed as the background for a better understanding of *Radak's* view that, with the new Temple, a new era will unfold that will include halachic implications.

closed during the six days of labor, but on the day of
Sabbath it shall be opened, and on the day of the new
moon it shall be opened. 2 *Then the prince shall enter*
by way of the hall of the gate outward and stand by
the doorpost of the gate which the kohanim bring his
burnt offering and his peace offerings. He shall then
worship at the threshold of the gate and depart, and
the gate shall not be closed until the evening. 3 *And*
the people of the land shall worship at the entrance of

According to 44:2 it was at that southern wicket that the *Shechinah* rested and accordingly, it was there that the *nassi* (*v.* 2) and the people (*v.* 3) made their obeisance.

וּבְיוֹם הַשַּׁבָּת יִפָּתֵחַ וּבְיוֹם הַחֹדֶשׁ יִפָּתֵחַ — *But on the day of Sabath it shall be opened and on the day of the new moon it shall be opened.*

These were the days when the people customarily visited the Temple *(Metzudos).*

2. דֶּרֶךְ אוּלָם הַשַּׁעַר מִחוּץ — *By way of the hall of the gate outward.*

This refers to the eastern gate of the inner courtyard (2/3). The hall (אוּלָם) is described as *outward* since the hall and cell structure of the inner courtyard jutted outwards into the outer courtyard. (See Master Diagram.)

עַל מְזוּזַת הַשַּׁעַר — *At the doorpost of the gate.*

This gate is the wicket referred to in verse 1.

אֶת עוֹלָתוֹ וְאֶת שְׁלָמָיו — *His burnt offering and his peace offerings.*

No private burnt offerings or peace offerings could be brought on the Sabbath. Therefore *Rashi* deduces that *Sabbath* in verse 1 refers to *Yom Tov* rather than to the seventh day. The burnt offering is the sacrifice required of every individual who came to the Temple on *Yom Tov* 'to be seen' (עוֹלַת רְאִיָּה) and the peace offerings are the שַׁלְמֵי חֲגִיגָה, *the peace offerings of celebration,* which were also brought in connection with *Yom Tov.*

The *nassi* stood by the wicket while his sacrifices were being brought because it is fitting that a man should be present while the service of his offerings is performed *(Rashi).*

וְהִשְׁתַּחֲוָה — *And he shall worship* [lit. *bow*].

According to *Berachos* 34b this term implies complete prostration with hands and feet outstretched.

וְהַשַּׁעַר לֹא יִסָּגֵר עַד־הָעָרֶב — *And the gate shall not be closed until the evening.*

Rashi explains that this phrase is to be read together with the next verse. The gate is to remain open all day to allow time for all the people to make their obeisances before the *Shechinah* at the wicket. [See *v.* 12 that if the *nassi* came on an ordinary day where no crowds were expected, the wicket was closed immediately after he had finished his service.]

3. וְהִשְׁתַּחֲווּ עַם־הָאָרֶץ ... — *And the people* [*of the land*] *shall worship ...*

Since the gate was to be kept open the whole day there would be ample time for everyone to make his obeisance.

Radak agreed with *Rashi* at 44:1 that the gate which was to be permanently closed was the southern wicket, but he rejects the possibility that our verse modifies that injunction and limits it to weekdays. In his view our verse teaches another of the many innovations which will be instituted in the new Temple.

ד בַּשַּׁבָּתוֹת וּבֶחֳדָשִׁים לִפְנֵי יְהוָה: וְהָעֹלָה
אֲשֶׁר־יַקְרִב הַנָּשִׂיא לַיהוָה בְּיוֹם הַשַּׁבָּת
שִׁשָּׁה כְבָשִׂים תְּמִימִם וְאַיִל תָּמִים:
ה וּמִנְחָה אֵיפָה לָאַיִל וְלַכְּבָשִׂים מִנְחָה
ו מַתַּת יָדוֹ וְשֶׁמֶן הִין לָאֵיפָה: וּבְיוֹם
הַחֹדֶשׁ פַּר בֶּן־בָּקָר תְּמִימִם וְשֵׁשֶׁת
ז כְּבָשִׂים וָאַיִל תְּמִימִם יִהְיוּ: וְאֵיפָה לַפָּר

The eastern gate which leads into the inner courtyard is to be closed during the week and opened only on the special days indicated. On these days the *nassi* is to enter by that gate in order to be present when his sacrifices are offered and in order to make his obeisance at the southern wicket. [That is the meaning of וְהִשְׁתַּחֲוָה עַל מִפְתַּן הַשַּׁעַר, *and he shall worship at the threshold of the gate.*] This eastern gate of the inner courtyard is to remain open all day in order to allow all the people to follow the same rite.

In *Radak's* view the burnt offering mentioned in verse 2 is explicated in verse 4 and is another of the future sacrifices which find no parallel in the Torah (see below). He makes no attempt to explain the peace offering of verse 2. Since peace offerings are not mentioned among the new sacrifices ordained by Yechezkel in these chapters, one must assume that these peace offerings are voluntary ones which surely may not be brought on the Sabbath (when only the obligatory sacrifices are brought) and the reference to peace offerings must apply to *Rosh Chodesh (Metzudos).*

In our commentary to Ch. 44 we follow *Malbim* (based on *Abarbanel)* that the southern wicket is not mentioned at all. Rather, the gate which was to be permanently closed is the eastern gate of the outer courtyard.

Here we are taught the laws governing the entrance of the *nassi* during the מִלּוּאִים, *consecration* period, which, according to *Malbim,* was to last through *Succos* of the first year.

The consecration sacrifices for the *Yom Tov* days were specified in the previous chapter. Our chapter deals with the Sabbath and weekday sacrifices of the period (see below).

While the eastern gate of the *outer* courtyard was to remain permanently closed for the reason specified in Ch. 44, no such restriction applied to the eastern gate of the *inner* courtyard. Still, unless required by the *nassi* (see *v.* 12), this gate, too, was to remain closed during the week and was to be opened for longer periods only on the Sabbath and *Rosh Chodesh* which, according to *Isaiah* 66:23 were days when people were expected to come to *be seen by HASHEM* in the Temple.

The *nassi* was to make his entrance into the inner courtyard through this eastern gate (whose hall jutted to the *outside,* hence מחוץ, see above), bring his sacrifices, make his obeisance, and then exit (see *v.* 8). The gate would then remain open for the rest of the day for the benefit of the people.

The consecration sacrifices of the Sabbath and *Rosh Chodesh* are specified below. [*Malbim* does not explain the peace offering in verse 2 — see above for *Metzudos'* explanation.]

4-5 These two verses, like much of the remainder of the chapter, detail sacrifices which, at least on the surface, differ from those specified by the Torah. In dealing with the apparent discrepancies, *Rashi, Radak,* and *Malbim* continue with their respective approaches which we traced in the previous chapter. *Rashi* interprets the verses in line with the halachah as we

that gate — on Sabbaths and on new moons — before
HASHEM.
4 *This is the burnt offering which the prince shall*
bring: on the Sabbath, six sheep without blemish and
a ram without blemish. 5 *with a meal offering of one*
ephah for the ram, and for the sheep, a meal offering
according to what his hand can give, and a hin of oil
for each ephah. 6 *And on the new moon a bullock*
from the herd without a blemish and six sheep and a
ram. They shall be without a blemish. 7 *An ephah for*

know it, *Radak* assumes the sacrifices to be innovations consonant with the higher degree of sanctity that will prevail in the future, and *Malbim* interprets them as special inaugural sacrifices.

Our verse deals with the special Sabbath offerings for which the Torah (*Numbers* 28:9-10) specifies two sheep to be brought as burnt offerings. What, then, are the six sheep and one ram mentioned here? According to *Radak* they are an innovation for the future; according to *Malbim* they are inaugural sacrifices to be brought in addition to the regular ones (see *comm., v.* 2).

Rashi offers the following solution: the term *Sabbath* used in our verse is to be understood as a synonym for *festival* [a similar usage may be found in *Leviticus* 23:15]. The festival sacrifice specified in *Numbers* ch. 28 consists of seven sheep (except for *Succos,* when there are fourteen) and one ram (except for *Succos,* when there are two). [There are other sacrifices besides these, but Yechezkel does not discuss them.] The Talmud deals with the question of what should be done if less than the required number of animals are available. Our verse teaches that when, for example, only six sheep sheep are available, they may be brought in place of the seven; and if only one ram is available, it may be brought in place of the two. (See above at 45:23.)

5. *Rashi* has solved the problem of the *ephah* and *hin* at 45:24; see *comm.* there. He proposes that מַתַּת יָדוֹ in our verse means *according to what his hand can give,* which teaches that the meal offerings do not depend on one another. If one is missing the others may still be brought.

Radak explains מַתַּת יָדוֹ as follows: In the future, new laws will govern the meal offerings which accompany sacrifices. The ram will require an *ephah,* while the meal offering accompanying sheep will be left to the owner's discretion. He may bring as much or as little as he sees fit.

Malbim comments that the meal offering of the *nassi's* inaugural sheep is to be 1/6th *ephah.* This amount, is explicated in verse 14, and is exactly equal to the gift of 1/6th of an *ephah* from every *chomer* of wheat which the *nassi* is to receive from the population [see *Malbim's* view in *comm.* 45:13-15]. Thus מַתַּת יָדוֹ would be rendered *the amount that is placed in his hand* by the people.

6-7 The Torah (*Numbers* 28:11-15) specifies two bullocks, one ram, and seven sheep for the special *Rosh Chodesh* sacrifices. *Menachos* 45a, noting that our verse gives different specifications, interprets it to teach that even if the full number of animals is not available, as many should be brought as can be. [This is the solution which *Rashi* offered at 45:23 and *v.* 4 of our chapter. *Menachos* 45a does not discuss these other verses and uses its explanation only for the irregular *Rosh Chodesh* sacrifices.]

וְאֵיפָה לָאַיִל יַעֲשֶׂה מִנְחָה וְלַכְּבָשִׂים
כַּאֲשֶׁר תַּשִּׂיג יָדוֹ וְשֶׁמֶן הִין לָאֵיפָה׃
ח וּבְבוֹא הַנָּשִׂיא דֶּרֶךְ אוּלָם הַשַּׁעַר יָבוֹא
ט וּבְדַרְכּוֹ יֵצֵא׃ וּבְבוֹא עַם־הָאָרֶץ לִפְנֵי
יְהוָה בַּמּוֹעֲדִים הַבָּא דֶּרֶךְ שַׁעַר צָפוֹן
לְהִשְׁתַּחֲוֹת יֵצֵא דֶּרֶךְ־שַׁעַר נֶגֶב וְהַבָּא
דֶּרֶךְ־שַׁעַר נֶגֶב יֵצֵא דֶּרֶךְ־שַׁעַר צָפוֹנָה
לֹא יָשׁוּב דֶּרֶךְ הַשַּׁעַר אֲשֶׁר־בָּא בוֹ כִּי
יֵצֵא ק׳ י נִכְחוֹ °יצאו׃ וְהַנָּשִׂיא בְּתוֹכָם בְּבוֹאָם
יא יָבוֹא וּבְצֵאתָם יֵצֵאוּ׃ וּבַחַגִּים וּבַמּוֹעֲדִים
תִּהְיֶה הַמִּנְחָה אֵיפָה לַפָּר וְאֵיפָה
לָאַיִל וְלַכְּבָשִׂים מַתַּת יָדוֹ וְשֶׁמֶן הִין
יב לָאֵיפָה׃ וְכִי־יַעֲשֶׂה

Radak and *Malbim*, of course, find no problem in this verse.

7. *Rashi's* solution at 45:24 will be adequate for our verse too. His explanation of מַתַּת יָדוֹ in verse 5, [that the *nassi* should bring as many offerings as he can, even if the fully required amount is not available], will serve for כַּאֲשֶׁר תַּשִּׂיג יָדוֹ, *according to his means* of our verse.[1]

8-10 Three times every year, on the pilgrimage festivals, Israel's men must come up to the Temple to be *seen before HASHEM* (*Deuteronomy* 16:16). On these occasions they are to enter the courtyard by one gate and leave by the opposite gate (*v.* 9). [In effect this means that they have to enter by either the northern or southern gate since there is no gate opposite the eastern gate.]

Rashi explains that this is required because the command 'to be seen' is an implication that one is to be *well* seen. This is best accomplished by crossing the whole length of the courtyard. In *Rashi's* view, this explains why the *nassi*, when he came into the Temple on other occasions, was not bound by this requirement (*v.* 8). It is part of the command 'to be seen' and is therefore not applicable on any other occasion.

However, *Berachos* 62b derives from this requirement that anyone entering a synagogue to pray should leave by the far door (see *Shulchan Aruch, Orach Chayim* 152:5). This seems to indicate that the requirement is not so much a part of the command 'to be seen' but is, as the commentators explain (see *Mishneh Berurah*), to emphasize the person's love for the Temple or the synagogue by demonstrating that he delays his leavetaking

1. *Tosafos* to *Menachos* 45a quotes a *Sifri* which may contain the only recorded example of a solution which Chananiah ben Chizkiyahu found for a problem raised by these sections of *Ezekiel* [see 45:18-24]. The *Sifri* asks: Is the meal offering required for a bullock the same as that for a ram (see 45:24)? R' Chananiah ben Chizkiyahu ben Goron answered: This teaches us that *ephah* is the name for a cup with which flour was measured. There were larger and smaller measures, all of them called *ephah*.[This is similar to *Rashi's* solution for *hin* in 45:24).] There was a larger one containing three *esronim* for the bullock, and a smaller one containing two *esronim* for the ram. Both these vessels were called *ephah*. Thus, the amount of flour actually used for the offering was entirely consistent with established halachah.

the bullock and ephah for the ram he is to make
as the meal offering; and for the sheep, according to
his means. And one hin of oil for an ephah.
8 *Now when the prince enters, by way of the hall*
of the gate is he to enter, and by the same way he is to
leave. 9 *But when the people of the land come before*
HASHEM, on the appointed days, whoever enters by
way of the northern gate to worship is to leave by
way of the southern gate. And whoever enters by
way of the southern gate shall leave by way of the
northern gate. He should withdraw by the gate
through which he entered, rather he is to leave
through the opposite one. 10 *And as for the prince —*
among them, as they shall enter, is he to enter, and as
they leave is he to leave. 11 *And on the festivals and*
the appointed times, the meal offering shall be an
ephah for the bullock and an ephah for the ram. And
for the sheep, according to what his hand can give
and a hin of oil for each ephah. 12 *Now when the*

as much as he can. However, according to this reason it is not apparent why the *nassi* should not be bound by this same requirement when he enters the Temple on days when the command 'to be seen' does not apply.

During pilgrimage festivals, this rule was also binding on the *nassi*. When he entered with the people (that is, on those occasions when it was incumbent on the people to come) he was to leave with the people (that is, by the opposite door; *v.* 10).

However verse 8 teaches that on those days when there was no command for the people to appear, this rule did not bind the *nassi*. He was to be allowed to leave by the same door through which he had entered.

11. וּבַחַגִּים וּבַמּוֹעֲדִים — *And on the festivals and the appointed times.*

Rashi leaves this verse unexplained. Indeed it seems no more than a repetition of what was said in earlier verses (see 45:24).

Metzudos explains that חַגִּים refers to Shavuos (which was not mentioned above); and מוֹעֲדִים to *Rosh Hashanah* and *Yom Kippur*. Our verse points out that although these days were not to have special inaugural sacrifices (as had *Pesach* and *Succos* — see *comm.* 45:25), nevertheless the meal offering which accompanied the burnt offerings of those days *was* to be special. During the inaugural period, they were to consist of the amounts specified in our verse, rather than the usual amounts (see 45:24).

Malbim agrees with *Metzudos* that *Shavuos*, and *Rosh HaShanah*, and *Yom Kippur* are meant. However, in his opinion they *did* have special inaugural sacrifices. They were to be exactly the same as those of *Rosh Chodesh (vs.* 6-7). There is no need to specify this since *Rosh HaShanah* which occurs on the

הַנָּשִׂיא נְדָבָה עוֹלָה אוֹ־שְׁלָמִים נְדָבָה
לַיהוה וּפָתַח לוֹ אֶת־הַשַּׁעַר הַפֹּנֶה קָדִים
וְעָשָׂה אֶת־עֹלָתוֹ וְאֶת־שְׁלָמָיו כַּאֲשֶׁר
יַעֲשֶׂה בְּיוֹם הַשַּׁבָּת וְיָצָא וְסָגַר אֶת־
יג הַשַּׁעַר אַחֲרֵי צֵאתוֹ: וְכֶבֶשׂ בֶּן־שְׁנָתוֹ
תָּמִים תַּעֲשֶׂה עוֹלָה לַיּוֹם לַיהוה בַּבֹּקֶר
יד בַּבֹּקֶר תַּעֲשֶׂה אֹתוֹ: וּמִנְחָה תַעֲשֶׂה עָלָיו
בַּבֹּקֶר בַּבֹּקֶר שִׁשִּׁית הָאֵיפָה וְשֶׁמֶן
שְׁלִישִׁית הַהִין לָרֹס אֶת־הַסֹּלֶת מִנְחָה
טו לַיהוה חֻקּוֹת עוֹלָם תָּמִיד: °ועשו אֶת־ (יַעֲשׂוּ ק׳)
הַכֶּבֶשׂ וְאֶת־הַמִּנְחָה וְאֶת־הַשֶּׁמֶן בַּבֹּקֶר
טז בַּבֹּקֶר עוֹלַת תָּמִיד: כֹּה־אָמַר

first day of Tishrei is in fact *Rosh Chodesh,* and there is a presumption that the same sacrifices apply unless otherwise specified. If follows, also, that since this same verse alludes to *Shavuos* and *Yom Kippur,* they, too, have the same sacrifices as *Rosh HaShanah.*

12. הַשַּׁעַר הַפֹּנֶה קָדִים — *The gate facing eastward.*

According to *Rashi* reference is to the southern wicket, as it was in verse 1. This wicket is to be specially opened for the *nassi* to make his obeisance. Immediately afterwards it is to be closed once more. Verse 2 ordained that it should remain open on the Sabbath and *Rosh Chodesh* to enable all the people to pay homage. This was not necessary during the week since few people would be there *(Rashi).*

But *Radak* and *Malbim,* who argue with *Rashi's* interpretation to verse 1, explain this verse in accordance with their opinion there. On the *Sabbath* the people did not work and on *Rosh Chodesh,* because of the additional sacrifice, it was expected that there would be many people in the Temple. For this reason verse 2 specified that on those days the gate (2/3) was to remain open even after the *nassi* had departed because many others would want to come in. However, if the *nassi* decides to bring voluntary sacrifices at any other time, the gate would be opened for him to enter the courtyard, but it would be closed immediately upon his departure in accordance with verse 1, which ordained that this gate remain closed all week *(Radak, Malbim).*

13-15. בַּבֹּקֶר בַּבֹּקֶר — *Every morning.*

According to *Numbers* 28:1-8, the daily service in the Temple was to start and close with a burnt offering accompanied by a meal offering. These sacrifices were known as תָּמִיד שֶׁל שַׁחַר, *the morning continual offering* [*tamid*] and תָּמִיד שֶׁל בֵּין הָעַרְבַּיִם, *the evening tamid.*

Verses 13 and 14 seem to describe only the morning *tamid* but omit the evening one. *Rashi, Radak,* and *Malbim* interpret in a manner consistent with their earlier approaches. [However, here, for the first time, the simple meaning of the text seems inconsistent with the opinion of *Malbim* (and therefore, *Rambam* — see below).]

Radak's interpretation is the most

*prince offers a free will offering — a burnt offering or
a peace offering as a free will offering for HASHEM —
then one should open for him the gate facing
eastward. He is to make his burnt offering and his
peace offerings as he does on the Sabbath, then he
shall depart, and one is to close the gate after his
departure.*

13 *A yearling sheep without blemish you are to
make as a daily burnt offering for HASHEM. Every
morning you are to make it.*
14 *You are to bring a meal
offering with it every morning — one sixth of an
ephah and a third of a hin of oil with which to mix
the flour; a meal offering to HASHEM — an eternal
decree, continually.*
15 *And they shall make the sheep
and the meal offering and the oil every morning as a
continual burnt offering.*

consistent with the language of the verse. He maintains that in the future there will be only one *tamid* — the morning one — (*v.* 13), and the meal offering which is to accompany it is to have different measurements than those prescribed in the Torah (*v.* 14). [See *comm.* at the conclusion of ch. 44].

Malbim, who follows *Rambam* in interpreting all the irregularities in these past chapters as being caused by the fact that we are dealing with inaugural sacrifices, finds no difficulty with these two verses. They describe temporary sacrifices which are to be brought between *Pesach* and *Succos* during the first year, and are not a description of the regular *tamid sacrifice.* They are to be brought in addition to the regular *tamid.*

However, the last phrase in verse 14: מִנְחָה לַה' חֻקּוֹת עוֹלָם תָּמִיד, *a meal offering to HASHEM, an eternal decree, continually,* and in verse 15: עוֹלַת תָּמִיד, *a continual burnt offering,* indicate that we are dealing with a permanent, not a temporary sacrifice.

Malbim's solution is as follows: This phrase and the next verse, far from contradicting his assertion, confirm it. They are to be understood as follows. The inaugural offerings, which are purely temporary sacrifices, are not to replace the regular *tamid.* They are to be brought in *addition* to it. Verses 14-15 are translated thus: [*The above are only temporary but*] *there is to be a meal offering for HASHEM* [*which is*] *an eternal decree continually.* [*Even after the inaugural period is past you are to*] *bring the sheep, the meal offering, and the oil every morning as a permanent burnt offering.*

Rashi to verse 13 comments only that the verse refers to the morning *tamid,* but he ignores the omission of the evening *tamid.* [Perhaps he feels that this presents no more problem than the fact that not all women forbidden to the *kohanim* are mentioned in 44:22, or that the wife is not mentioned in the laws of inheritance at 44:25. See *comm.* there.]

He offers the following solution for the problem of the meal offering which is specified as a sixth of an *ephah* instead of the tenth of the *ephah* set by the Torah. The *ephah* mentioned here is an *ephah Yerushalmi* which was one

אֲדֹנָי יֱהוִֹה כִּי־יִתֵּן הַנָּשִׂיא מַתָּנָה לְאִישׁ
מִבָּנָיו נַחֲלָתוֹ הִיא לְבָנָיו תִּהְיֶה אֲחֻזָּתָם
יז הִיא בְּנַחֲלָה׃ וְכִי־יִתֵּן מַתָּנָה מִנַּחֲלָתוֹ
לְאַחַד מֵעֲבָדָיו וְהָיְתָה לּוֹ עַד־שְׁנַת
הַדְּרוֹר וְשָׁבַת לַנָּשִׂיא אַךְ נַחֲלָתוֹ בָּנָיו
יח לָהֶם תִּהְיֶה׃ וְלֹא־יִקַּח הַנָּשִׂיא מִנַּחֲלַת
הָעָם לְהוֹנֹתָם מֵאֲחֻזָּתָם מֵאֲחֻזָּתוֹ יַנְחִל
אֶת־בָּנָיו לְמַעַן אֲשֶׁר לֹא־יָפֻצוּ עַמִּי אִישׁ
יט מֵאֲחֻזָּתוֹ׃ וַיְבִיאֵנִי בַמָּבוֹא אֲשֶׁר עַל־כֶּתֶף
הַשַּׁעַר אֶל־הַלְּשָׁכוֹת הַקֹּדֶשׁ אֶל־הַכֹּהֲנִים

sixth larger than the ordinary *ephah.* Thus a sixth of the *ephah Yerushalmi* is equal to a fifth of the ordinary *ephah.* [See 45:12 for the explanation of this computation]. Since the ordinary *ephah* contains ten *esronim,* a fifth is two *esronim.* Of these, one *esaron* was for the meal offering of the *tamid* as specified by the Torah; the other was to be used for the מִנְחַת חֲבִתִּים, *the daily meal offering of the kohen gadol,* of which he brought half in the morning and half in the afternoon.

Rashi offers no explanation for the measurement of a third of a *hin* which is given for the oil in place of the *quarter hin* specified by the Torah. [The existence of a *Yerushalmi* measure cannot solve this problem since this could not account for an increase of one third.]

16-18 45:7-8 described the location of the huge tracts of land which were to be the property of the *nassi.* Verse 8 taught that he was given this land so that he would never feel the need to drive any of the people off their land in order to enrich himself.

Our section describes the nature of the control which he exercises over his portion of the land. We learn that if he wishes to give a gift to one of his sons during his own lifetime he may do so, and in that event, the son becomes permanent owner. If, instead, he chooses to make a gift to one of his servants, that gift remains valid only up to the *Yovel* [*Jubilee Year*]. At that time it reverts to the *nassi.* As a result of this provision, the land will never be depleted through gifts to anyone other than the *nassi's* children.

Abarbanel explains why Yechezkel had to stress that the *nassi* would be able to make gifts to his children from his property and that his property would eventually be inherited by his children (*v.* 16). We might have supposed that the *nassi's* property was vested in the *position* rather than the person, and that consequently his entire royal portion would fall only to the son who would succeed him as king. Therefore we are taught that all children of the *nassi* have a right to this inheritance, although, over the years, this will necessarily result in much smaller possessions for the succeeding princes.

16. אֲחֻזָּתָם הִיא בְּנַחֲלָה — *It is their holding by inheritance.*

Since they stand to inherit it at his death anyway, why should he not be able to make a permanent gift of it during his lifetime? *(Metzudos).*

17. וְשָׁבַת לַנָּשִׂיא — *It shall return to the prince.*

The substitution of the letter ת for ה (וְשָׁבָה instead of וְשָׁבַת) is irregular but not unique in Scripture *(Radak).*

אַךְ נַחֲלָתוֹ בָּנָיו לָהֶם יִהְיֶה — *His in-*

16 *Thus says my Lord HASHEM/ELOHIM: If the*
prince makes a gift to one of his sons — since it is his
heritage which will belong to his sons, it is their
holding by inheritance. 17 *But if he makes a gift from*
his inheritance to any of his subjects, it shall remain
his until the year of freedom; then it shall revert to
the prince. His inheritance must by all means pass
to his sons. 18 *So that the prince shall not take from*
the inheritance of the people to rob them of their
holdings. From his own property is he to endow his
sons in order that My people be not scattered, each
man from his holding.
19 *He led me through the passage which ran at the*
side of the gate to the sacred chambers of the

heritance must by all means pass on to his sons.

The gift reverts to him in the *Yovel* year so that the property of the *nassi* should not be permanently depleted through gifts to people other than his children *(Rashi).*

19-20 Yechezkel's guide had interrupted his description of the Temple at 43:17. After the measurements of the altar were completed, the text immediately turned to the provisions for the consecration of the altar and Sanctuary, which, with all the attendant details, continued to this point.

Now the description is resumed.

The implications of our passage are discussed in *comm.* 42:13-14. Those verses should be studied together with our section. Figure 23 is also helpful in understanding our passage.

In 42:4 (see also *comm.* 42:1), we learned that there was a one cubit gap (5/2) between the northern wall of the inner courtyard (2/1 north) and the wall of the knife depository (4/1). Through this gap, access was provided to the twenty-cubit space (5/4) which lay between the northern wall of the Temple building (4/16) and the chamber. The function of the chambers was to provide an area suitable for the *kohanim* to eat the most holy offerings (42:13), and it was therefore necessary to give them, as well as the space between them and the Temple building, the status of sanctity normally attached only to the inner courtyard. Without this, the most holy offerings would have been rendered unfit as soon as they left the inner courtyard (*comm.* 42:13-14).

Our passage is based on these assumptions.

This passage describes the location of a place set aside for the cooking and baking of most holy offerings (חַטָּאת אָשָׁם וּמִנְחָה, *sin, guilt, and meal offerings).* According to *Rashi* this place lay at the western end of the twenty cubit space (5/5).

19. While the altar was being described, the prophet had been standing in the inner courtyard. He is now taken out to the twenty cubit space (5/4) between the Temple building and the northern chamber.

בַּמָּבוֹא — *Through the passage.*

This is the one cubit passage (5/2) through which it was possible to reach the twenty cubit space *(Rashi).*

עַל כֶּתֶף הַשַּׁעַר — *At the side of the gate.*

This refers to the western side of the

הַפֹּנוֹת צָפוֹנָה וְהִנֵּה־שָׁם מָקוֹם
כ בירכתם° יָמָּה׃ וַיֹּאמֶר אֵלַי זֶה הַמָּקוֹם
אֲשֶׁר יְבַשְּׁלוּ־שָׁם הַכֹּהֲנִים אֶת־הָאָשָׁם
וְאֶת־הַחַטָּאת אֲשֶׁר יֹאפוּ אֶת־הַמִּנְחָה
לְבִלְתִּי הוֹצִיא אֶל־הֶחָצֵר הַחִיצוֹנָה
כא לְקַדֵּשׁ אֶת־הָעָם׃ וַיּוֹצִיאֵנִי אֶל־הֶחָצֵר
הַחִיצוֹנָה וַיַּעֲבִרֵנִי אֶל־אַרְבַּעַת מִקְצוֹעֵי
הֶחָצֵר וְהִנֵּה חָצֵר בְּמִקְצֹעַ הֶחָצֵר חָצֵר
כב בְּמִקְצֹעַ הֶחָצֵר׃ בְּאַרְבַּעַת מִקְצֹעוֹת
הֶחָצֵר חֲצֵרוֹת קְטֻרוֹת אַרְבָּעִים אֹרֶךְ
וּשְׁלֹשִׁים רֹחַב מִדָּה אַחַת לְאַרְבַּעְתָּם
כג מְהֻקְצָעוֹת׃ וְטוּר סָבִיב בָּהֶם סָבִיב
לְאַרְבַּעְתָּם וּמְבַשְּׁלוֹת עָשׂוּי מִתַּחַת
כד הַטִּירוֹת סָבִיב׃ וַיֹּאמֶר אֵלַי אֵלֶּה בֵּית
הַמְבַשְּׁלִים אֲשֶׁר יְבַשְּׁלוּ־שָׁם מְשָׁרְתֵי

° בַּיַּרְכָתַיִם ק׳

gate which led through the northern wall (1/1) of the outer courtyard. [This describes the northern chamber, which lay along the length of the western half of the northern wall of the outer courtyard. See Fig. 22.]

הַפֹּנוֹת צָפוֹנָה — *Opening northward.*
The northern chamber had an entrance (5/1 north) facing north (42:4). *Rashi* points out that there must have been a similar opening to the south (5/1 south) (leading into the twenty cubit space on the south) because otherwise there would have been no means by which the most holy offerings could have been brought into the southern chamber.

בַּיַּרְכָתַיִם יָמָּה — *At its western end.*
It is not clear whether this refers to the western end of the twenty cubit space (between the chamber and the Temple building) or the space between the western wall of the chamber and that of the outer courtyard (1/1 west). If the latter interpretation is correct we would have to assume that the eleven-cubit space between the chambers and the western wall of the outer courtyard (1/1 west) had the samel level of sanctity as the inner courtyard.

20. לְבִלְתִּי הוֹצִיא אֶל הֶחָצֵר הַחִיצוֹנָה — *So that it not be brought into the outer courtyard.*
See *comm.* to 42:13-14.
One of the properties which distinguishes the most holy offerings from other offerings is that the former must remain in an area which has the sanctity of the inner courtyard. The cooking area had to be located at the point designated in the previous verse because it could not have been assigned to the outer courtyard, a place where the most holy offerings could not be brought.

לְקַדֵּשׁ אֶת הָעָם — *To mingle with the people.*

*kohanim, opening northward. And behold! there was
a space at its western end.* 20 *Then he said to me:
This is the place where the kohanim are to cook the
guilt offering and the sin offering, where they are to
bake the meal offering so that it need not be brought
into the outer courtyard to mingle with the people.*
21 *Then he took me out into the outer courtyard
and led me past the four corners of the courtyard,
and behold! there was an enclosure at each corner of
the courtyard.* 22 *At the four corners of the courtyard
were open enclosures, forty in length and thirty in
width. The same measurements apply to all four
enclosures.* 23 *A platform ran around the four of
them and hearths were prepared beneath the platforms all around.* 24 *And he said to me: These are the
cooking places where the Temple ministrants are to
cook the sacrifices of the people.*

The translation follows *Targum*. See comm. to 42:14 and 44:19.

21-24 *Middos* 2:5 teaches that at the four corners of the women's courtyard (which corresponds to the outer courtyard of *Ezekiel*) there were four smaller courtyards which were open to the sky. These four enclosures are the ones which are described in our section — although the dimensions in *Middos* are not quite the same as those given in *Ezekiel*. The ones in the Second Temple were 40×40 cubits.

According to the Mishnah, these enclosures were used as follows: The southeastern one was used by the Nazirites to cook their peace offering; it was there that they burned their hair in the flames over which they cooked the meat of the sacrifices: The northeastern one was used to store wood; it was there that any wormy parts of the wood (which would have disqualified it from being burnt on the altar) were removed. The northwestern one was for the *mikvah* (ritual bath) in which the *metzoraim* [those stricken with the supernatural plague described in *Lev. 13-14*] immersed themselves on the day they were to become clean. The southwestern one was used for storing wine and oil.

22. חֲצֵרוֹת קְטֻרוֹת — *Open enclosures.*

According to *Metzudos*, קְטֻרוֹת comes from קטר, *to smoke*, and thus means *open enclosures*, from which the smoke can escape [see *v.* 23].

According to *Metzudos* the forty cubit length was from east to west; the thirty cubit width, from north to south.

23. Round the walls of these enclosures ran a low platform (טוּר) on which the meat of the holy offerings was cooked. The pots were placed on this platform over holes (מְבַשְּׁלוֹת) in which the burning coals were placed. [It was the smoke from this cooking which had to escape from these enclosures — see previous verse.]

24. מְשָׁרְתֵי הַבַּיִת — *The Temple ministrants.*

See 44:11.

XLVII

A paradise on earth unfolds before the prophetic eye. The painstaking detail of the past seven chapters gives way to the jubilant poetry — part factual, part allegorical — with which the prophet sings of a new world, unsullied by the mistakes of the past (see previous chapters) and, thus, unfettered in the profusion of its bounty.

Truly, Israel's soil is arid and desolate for the moment — its waters are too salty to coax life from the dead earth. Sulfur and salt, everything burned, no sowing is possible, no growth in sight, no blade of grass can struggle up; the chaos of Sodom and Gomorrah (Deuteronomy *29:22). But Israel can look to the future:* יִרְוְיֻן מִדֶּשֶׁן בֵּיתֶךָ וְנַחַל עֲדָנֶיךָ תַשְׁקֵם כִּי עִמְּךָ מְקוֹר חַיִּים, They will be sated from the abundance of Your house and from the stream of Your delights give them to drink, for with You is the source of life (Psalms *36:9-10). This* source *and this* stream *are to issue from God's Temple (cf.* Joel *4:18;* Zechariah *13:1, 14:8). They are to transform* your wilderness into a paradise, your desert into a garden of God (Isaiah *51:3) (R' Breuer).*

Let us examine the significance of this stream of water which is to have its source in the Holy of Holies of God's Temple. Middos *2:6 teaches that the most easterly of the four gates that ran along the southern wall of the* azarah *was called* שַׁעַר הַמַּיִם, the water gate.

The Mishnah explains: Why is it called the water gate? For it was through this gate that they brought in the bottle of water for the offering on Succos. [Normally, wine was used for the libations on the altar, but during Succos an offering of water was ordained. See Succah *48a ff. for details.] R' Eliezer ben Yaakov said: (And) through [this gate] the waters trickle and [they] are destined to issue forth from underneath the threshold of the house.*

R' Eliezer ben Yaakov's words leave room for two possible interpretations [reflected in variant readings in Tosefta Succah *ch. 3; see commentators there.] On the one hand, the phrase* וּבוֹ הַמַּיִם מְפַכִּים, and through it the waters trickle, *is clearly taken from* v. 2 *and implies that R' Eliezer means to teach that Yechezkel's prophecy concerning the trickling water will be fulfilled through that gate.*

On the other hand, the change in tense between the two halves of his statement ['the waters trickle' is in the present, 'and are destined to issue forth' is in the future] indicates that the earlier part of the statement refers to a situation that actually happened during the Second Temple era, when R' Eliezer lived.[1]

This appears to be the understanding of the Vilna Gaon (Middos *2:6), who renders: The water which, in the Second Temple, flowed out through the water gate*

---

1. A word is in place concerning the tractate *Middos* which we have quoted so frequently in these past chapters.

In contrast to the great majority of tractates comprising the Mishnah whose basic text goes back to the very beginning of the Second Temple, *Middos, Yoma, Tamid,* and some chapters of *Shekalim* and *Parah* were complied only after the destruction of the Temple. [For a wide-ranging discussion see *Doros HaRishonim* part I, vol. 5, ch. 21ff.] While the Temple stood, it had been unnecessary to make an exact recording of its components and dimensions. It was only after the destruction that it became vitally important to make a permanent record of what had been.

Therefore, as one of the very first priorities after the destruction, the sages who still remembered the glories of the Temple committed them to writing. It fell to R' Eliezer ben Yaakov to compile *Middos,* (see *Yoma* 16a). Even his prodigious memory failed him on two occasions *(Middos* 2:5, 5:4) but, these two lapses notwithstanding, it is to him that we owe our knowledge of the appearance of the Second Temple.

Thus, when we deduce from his use of the present tense that R' Eliezer ben Yaakov was describing events which were then occurring, this deduction must be qualified, for he made his statement when the Temple was already in ruins. Yet, his yearning for the glories he had experienced in the past might well have been reflected in his use of the present tense.

in a trickle, will one day have its source in the Holy of Holies and issue from under the threshold of the House.

Reference would seem to be to the stream of water which according to Pesachim (22a) used to flow through the azarah (Tiferes Yisrael). This stream had its source at עֵין עֵיטָם, Ein Etam (Yerushalmi, Yoma 3:8) and flowed through the azarah into the Kidron Valley (Pesachim 22a). [Ein Etam is assumed to lie south of Jerusalem in the general vicinity of Bethlehem.] Archaeologists have traced the aqueducts which run from there to the Temple Mount. The water seems to have entered through the Temple Mount on the northern part of the western wall. If we postulate that it entered the azarah from that general direction, then the lower southeastern corner would be a logical place for it to flow out to the Kidron Valley which lies to the south of the Temple Mount.]

R' Eliezer ben Yaakov, who teaches that at a future date this stream would be replaced by one coming out of the Holy of Holies, is not arguing with the Mishnah but adding to it. Thus, the water gate has two functions. It is there that the water of Succos was brought in, and it is from there that the stream flowing through the Temple flowed out. In Messianic times this small stream would become a mighty torrent of blessing for mankind.

What is the significance of the נִסּוּךְ הַמַּיִם, water libation, of Succos? When God divided the upper from the lower waters on the second day of creation, discord entered the world (Bereishis Rabbah 4:8). Henceforth a part of God's world would always fall short of pure Godliness — always striving upwards, but never quite attaining perfection. Already on the third day, the trees could not meet the challenge of the Divine call which beckoned them to be wholly good. the tree became עֵץ עֹשֶׂה פְּרִי, a tree producing fruit, but not עֵץ פְּרִי, a tree which is itself a food, which God had envisioned. This shortfall from the ideal became the hallmark of creation. Every fruit would have a husk to be discarded. Waste, death, and sterility would all claim a place in the scheme of nature. The realm above the firmament was effectively denied the lower waters (R' Bachya, Genesis 1:4).

The lower waters cried before God, 'We, too, want to share in the Divine.' Their distress, borne from a true yearning for holiness, was noted by God. For a moment each year the barrier would be removed. The water offering on Succos was to be the moment when the lower waters would rise above their limited status and be offered up on God's altar. (See R' Bachya, Leviticus 2:13. For an analysis of these profound teachings and an explanation of why the lower waters would come into their own just during Succos, see Pachad Yitzchak, Yom Kippur, ch. 10).

In Yechezkel's vision of the future, this division would be nullified. Water, the life force of God's creation, would have its source in that very Holy of Holies in which God Himself allows His Shechinah to rest. All life will derive from this holy source as the tiny trickle of water turns into a mighty river, and brings the healing touch of sanctity (vs. 8-12) to all the world's waterways.

Waste, sterility, and death retreat before the onslaught of holiness. Sanctuary waters (v. 12) not only produce unheard of bounties of fruit but even turn the once wasted leaf into a potent food (v. 12). Wilderness and desert will turn into gardens rich with vegetation (Isaiah 35:1) as water breaks through the hot, lifeless sands, and rivers crisscross the once arid wastes (Isaiah 35:6). Truly it is a well of salvation (Isaiah 12:3), from which we are bidden to draw water.

It is against the background of our passage that we must read Toras Kohanim to Leviticus 26:4.

> And the land will yield its produce. *Not as it does now but as it did in Adam's time. How do we know that the earth will be sown and will yield its fruits on the same day ... that a tree will be planted and bear fruits on that same day ... that the tree itself will serve as food ... that even a [formerly] barren tree will bear fruit...?*

א הַבַּיִת אֶת־זֶבַח הָעָם: וַיְשִׁבֵנִי אֶל־פֶּתַח
הַבַּיִת וְהִנֵּה־מַיִם יֹצְאִים מִתַּחַת מִפְתַּן
הַבַּיִת קָדִימָה כִּי־פְנֵי הַבַּיִת קָדִים וְהַמַּיִם
יֹרְדִים מִתַּחַת מִכֶּתֶף הַבַּיִת הַיְמָנִית
ב מִנֶּגֶב לַמִּזְבֵּחַ: וַיּוֹצִאֵנִי דֶּרֶךְ־שַׁעַר צָפוֹנָה
וַיְסִבֵּנִי דֶּרֶךְ חוּץ אֶל־שַׁעַר הַחוּץ דֶּרֶךְ
הַפּוֹנֶה קָדִים וְהִנֵּה־מַיִם מְפַכִּים מִן־
ג הַכָּתֵף הַיְמָנִית: בְּצֵאת־הָאִישׁ קָדִים וְקָו
בְּיָדוֹ וַיָּמָד אֶלֶף בָּאַמָּה וַיַּעֲבִרֵנִי בַמַּיִם מֵי
ד אָפְסָיִם: וַיָּמָד אֶלֶף וַיַּעֲבִרֵנִי בַמַּיִם מַיִם
בִּרְכָּיִם וַיָּמָד אֶלֶף וַיַּעֲבִרֵנִי מֵי מָתְנָיִם:

The shortcomings of the earth, inherent in the second day's division of upper and nether, will disappear. God's world will finally take the form which He had intended for it.

Thus, we see that the waters destined to gush from the water gate are really an extension of the modest bottle of water that had once been brought through there for the annual water offering. Small wonder that this water offering was the central point of the שִׂמְחַת בֵּית הַשּׁוֹאֵבָה, rejoicing at the drawing of the water, *the mighty celebration which took place during the last six days of Succos* (Rashi, Succah *50a). 'He who has not seen the rejoicing at the drawing of the water has never seen real joy in his life'. The Mishnah* (Succah *51a) teaches: For he has not experienced that intimation of pure Godliness which the water offering imparted to those who joined in its celebration.*

From its relationship to the rejoicing of the water drawing we can now find our way to the allegorical nature of Yechezkel's vision. The Succos celebration derived its name from Isaiah *12:3:* וּשְׁאַבְתֶּם מַיִם בְּשָׂשׂוֹן מִמַּעַיְנֵי הַיְשׁוּעָה, You shall draw water joyously from the wells of salvation. *But* Yerushalmi *teaches that it was not water that was to be drawn but* רוּחַ הַקּוֹדֶשׁ, God's holy spirit. *Perhaps the meaning of the* Yerushalmi *is that where the barrier between the upper and the nether waters disappears — even if only for a moment — God's holy spirit can find welcome.*

So it is in our passage. Surely it is a river of water that Yechezkel sees in this, his final, vision; but surely it is also a stream of Godliness that trickles out of the Holy of Holies to engulf the world.

1. Yechezkel had been in the outer courtyard to observe the four enclosures which were described at the end of the last chapter. He is now brought back into the inner courtyard to stand by the Temple building.

He observes water coming out on the south side of the Temple building near the center of the eastern wall (4/1), and from there bearing right in order to pass the altar on its southern side *(Rashi).*

[The flow is described as *descending* because the water flowed down the slope of the mountain.]

2. The prophet is taken out of the inner courtyard by its northern gate (2/3) and, once in the outer courtyard, circles to his right to the eastern gate of the

47
1-4

Then he returned me to the entrance of the House
and behold! Water was coming out from under
the threshold of the House to the east — for the
House faced east — and the water was descending under the right hand wall of the House, south of the
altar. 2 And he took me out through the northern gate
and led me around the outside to the outer gate in an
eastern direction and behold! water trickled from the
right wall. 3 As the man left to the east with the
measuring rod in his hand, he measured one thousand cubits. He led me through the water, ankle deep
water. 4 Then he measured one thousand and led me
through the water, knee deep water; then he
measured one thousand and led me through water,

outer courtyard (1/3). There he observes the water flowing to the south [since it was to the water gate in the south that it flowed after coming out of the inner courtyard — see pref.]

מַיִם מְפַכִּים — *Water trickled.*

פכך [derived from פַּךְ, *jug*] means: *to pour out from a jug.* מַיִם מְפַכִּים are waters in an amount which would be poured out of a bottle or jug.

Yoma 77b describes the flow of the water: The well flowing out from the Holy of Holies was the size of a locust's beak. By the time it reached the gates of the Temple building it had the thickness of a thread of a שְׁתִי, *warp* [lengthwise threads]. Once it reached the outer hall it became as thick as a thread of the עֵרֶב, *woof* [threads crossing the warp]. At the gate of the courtyard it had become the size of a small jug's mouth.

[This gradual widening of the stream continues to be reflected in *vs.* 3-5. The water gets deeper and deeper as it gets further from its source. If we equate our stream with the *well of salvation* (*Isaiah* 12:3) from which the holy spirit is to be drawn, this gradual growth of the stream need not surprise us. The further the distance from the source, the greater the need to spread the holiness of the Temple.]

3-5. The depth of the water increases with each thousand cubit distance from the Temple. [When we recall that the Temple complex lay within that part of the sacred *Terumah* which measured 25,000 rods×10,000 rods (see Fig. 29), it is evident that the three separate measurements of a thousand cubits all lay well within the sacred *Terumah.*]

However, *Pirkei d'Rabbi Eliezer* 51 has a different interpretation. Each of the thousand-cubit measurements ran in a different direction: 'The water of the well is destined to come up from beneath the threshold of the House, to gush forth, increase, and become twelve rivers to parallel the twelve tribes: three to the south with a depth up to the ankles, three to the west with a depth up to the knees, three to the north with a depth up to the hips, and three to the east with a depth up to the neck.[1]

מֵי אָפְסָיִם — *Ankle deep water.*

Ibn Janach traces the word to פַּס, meaning *hand* or *foot.* It was deep

1. *Radal* points out that *Pirkei d'Rabbi Eliezer* seems to identify Yechezkel's water with the well which is already known to us from the Torah, that is, Miriam's well, which accompanied the Israelites throughout their wandering in the desert; see also *Pirkei d'Rabbi Eliezer* 35.

ה וַיָּמָד אֶלֶף נַחַל אֲשֶׁר לֹא־אוּכַל לַעֲבֹר
כִּי־גָאוּ הַמַּיִם מֵי שָׂחוּ נַחַל אֲשֶׁר לֹא־
ו יֵעָבֵר׃ וַיֹּאמֶר אֵלַי הֲרָאִיתָ בֶן־אָדָם
ז וַיּוֹלִכֵנִי וַיְשִׁבֵנִי שְׂפַת הַנָּחַל׃ בְּשׁוּבֵנִי
וְהִנֵּה אֶל־שְׂפַת הַנַּחַל עֵץ רַב מְאֹד מִזֶּה
ח וּמִזֶּה׃ וַיֹּאמֶר אֵלַי הַמַּיִם הָאֵלֶּה יוֹצְאִים
אֶל־הַגְּלִילָה הַקַּדְמוֹנָה וְיָרְדוּ עַל־
הָעֲרָבָה וּבָאוּ הַיָּמָּה אֶל־הַיָּמָּה הַמּוּצָאִים
ט וְנִרְפְּאוּ הַמָּיִם׃ וְהָיָה כָל־נֶפֶשׁ חַיָּה |
אֲשֶׁר־יִשְׁרֹץ אֶל כָּל־אֲשֶׁר יָבוֹא שָׁם
נַחֲלַיִם יִחְיֶה וְהָיָה הַדָּגָה רַבָּה מְאֹד כִּי
בָאוּ שָׁמָּה הַמַּיִם הָאֵלֶּה וְיֵרָפְאוּ וָחָי כֹּל
י אֲשֶׁר־יָבוֹא שָׁמָּה הַנָּחַל׃ וְהָיָה °יעמדו (עָמְדוּ ק׳)
עָלָיו דַּוָּגִים מֵעֵין גֶּדִי וְעַד־עֵין עֶגְלַיִם
מִשְׁטוֹחַ לַחֲרָמִים יִהְיוּ לְמִינָה תִּהְיֶה
דְגָתָם כִּדְגַת הַיָּם הַגָּדוֹל רַבָּה מְאֹד׃

enough to cover the feet, that is, it reached the ankle (so also *Targum*). *Radak* in his *Sefer HaShorashim* derives the word from אֶפֶס, *nothing*, and translates *a negligible amount of water.*

5. כִּי גָאוּ הַמַּיִם — *For the water had swollen.*

From גאה, *to rise up.*

מֵי שָׂחוּ — *Water for swimming.*

The water was so deep that it could not be crossed except by swimming. The word is from שחה, *to swim* (see *Isaiah* 25:11).

6. וַיְשִׁבֵנִי עַל שְׂפַת הַנָּחַל — *And* [*he*] *returned me to the bank of the stream.*

Up to this point he had been walking in the water. Here it became too deep and it was necessary to follow it by walking along the bank *(Radak).*

7. וְהִנֵּה — *Behold!*

Rashi notes that הִנֵּה indicates surprise. The great profusion of trees had grown between the time he entered the river and the time he left it.

8. The river is to flow eastward (הַגְּלִילָה הַקַּדְמוֹנָה, *to the eastern region)* to the Sea of Galilee *(Yam Kineres)* and from there to the Dead Sea *(Yam HaMelach)* from which it would flow into the Mediterranean. Its healing touch would turn the salt water sweet.

There are divergent readings in the *Midrashim* concerning which phrase refers to which sea. *Rashi* identifies them as follows: וְיָרְדוּ עַל הָעֲרָבָה, *Sea of Galilee* [*Yam Ho'aravah*]; וּבָאוּ הַיָּמָּה, *Sea of Sodom* [the Dead Sea]; אֶל הַיָּמָּה הַמּוּצָאִים, *the Sea of Okeneanos* [ocean; that is, the Mediterranean].

הַיָּמָּה הַמּוּצָאִים וְנִרְפְּאוּ — *The spreading sea ... will become healthy.*

The translation follows *Metzudos.* The Mediterranean — and, by exten-

waist deep water. 5 *Then he measured one thousand*
— a stream through which I could not pass! For the
water had swollen, water for swimming, an im-
passable stream!
6 *He said to me: Have you seen, Ben Adam? And*
he led me and returned me to the bank of the stream.
7 *Upon my return, behold! on the bank of the stream*
was an exceedingly great profusion of trees on this
side and that. 8 *And he said to me: These waters go*
out to the eastern region, descend to the Arabah, and
come to the Sea, to the spreading sea — and the water
will become healthy. 9 *And it will be that every living*
thing that swarms, wherever these streams flow it
will live, and the fish will be exceedingly abundant;
for these waters came there and they became
wholesome, so they will live; everything wherever
the stream reaches. 10 *And it will be that by it will*
stand fishermen, from Ein Gedi to Ein Eglaim. There
will be a spreading place for nets. Their fish will be of
as many kinds as the fish of the Mediterranean, ex-

sion, the oceans — is called הַמּוּצָאִים because the waters spread *outwards* to encompass the whole world.

Alternatively, since verses 8 and 9 use the root רפא, *to cure,* to describe what the stream will accomplish, the implication is that they are presently polluted and unfit to sustain life. In this sense *R' Aryeh Carmel* suggests that the word הַמּוּצָאִים derives from צוֹאָה, *excrement* (similar to *II Kings* 10:27), and that the translation is *polluted sea.*

All these waters, salty or polluted, are to be sweetened by their contact with holy waters.

9. נַחֲלַיִם — *Streams* [lit. *pairs of streams*].

The word is in the plural because the stream is to split into many branches in order to spread its blessings in all directions.

וְהָיָה הַדָּגָה... — *The fish will be ...*

Many of the world's waters had been unable to accommodate fish because of their extreme saltiness. Now contact with this stream will cure them. Sweet and clear, they will be able to support a profusion of sealife.

10. וְהָיָה עָמְדוּ עָלָיו דַּוָּגִים — *And it will be that by it will stand fishermen.*

From Ein Gedi to Ein Eglaim fishermen will stand, eager to harvest the stream's bounty.

מִשְׁטוֹחַ לַחֲרָמִים — *A spreading place for nets.*

The entire area will be covered by the nets which they have laid out to dry.

לְמִינָה תִּהְיֶה דְגָתָם — *Their fish will be of [as] many kinds.*

There will be a profusion of different types of fish (the ה at the end of לְמִינָה [which is not the feminine possessive since it lacks the *mapik*] serves to turn

יא בִּצֹּאתָו וּגְבָאָיו וְלֹא יֵרָפְאוּ לְמֶלַח נִתָּנוּ׃
יב וְעַל־הַנַּחַל יַעֲלֶה עַל־שְׂפָתוֹ מִזֶּה | וּמִזֶּה |
כָּל־עֵץ־מַאֲכָל לֹא־יִבּוֹל עָלֵהוּ וְלֹא־יִתֹּם
פִּרְיוֹ לָחֳדָשָׁיו יְבַכֵּר כִּי מֵימָיו מִן־
וְהָיָה ק׳ הַמִּקְדָּשׁ הֵמָּה יוֹצְאִים °והיו פִרְיוֹ
יג לְמַאֲכָל וְעָלֵהוּ לִתְרוּפָה׃ כֹּה
אָמַר אֲדֹנָי יֱהֹוִה גֵּה גְבוּל אֲשֶׁר תִּתְנַחֲלוּ

the simple word מִין, *kind*, into one denoting many kinds). The stream will contain fish in numbers comparable to the swarms in the Mediterranean Sea.

11. Provision must be made to ensure a supply of salt after all the sea waters shall have been sweetened. For this reason the swamps (בִּצָּה) and pools (גֶּבֶא) will not become sweet *(Rashi).*

12. לָחֳדָשָׁיו יְבַכֵּר — *Every month it will yield new fruit.*

Such will be the fertility of the trees at the banks of the stream that they will yield a monthly harvest. [But see *Toras Kohanim (Lev.* 26:4), which speaks of a daily harvest].

וְעָלֵהוּ לִתְרוּפָה — *And its leaf for healing.*

לִתְרוּפָה stems from רפא, *to heal.* According to the Sages, the leaves will 'open the mouths of the dumb and the wombs of the barren' *(Rashi;* see *Sanhedrin* 100a).

This phrase announces the end of the curse which the 'discord' of the second day of creation injected into the world. The disobedience of the trees (on the third day) will be corrected, as every part of the tree will be edible. Nothing will be wasted. (See pref.)

13-20. These verses describe the boundaries of the future land of Israel. The verses are difficult to translate and lend themselves to widely divergent interpretations. Thus, while *Rashi* stresses repeatedly that the boundaries traced in our verses are identical with those given in *Numbers* 34:1-13, *Malbim* interprets that they circumscribe a vastly larger area (see *comm.* to יוֹסֵף חֲבָלִים in *v.* 13).

The *comm.* will be based on *Rashi.*

The most notable feature of this section, in *Rashi's* interpretation, is the total omission of any mention of עֵבֶר הַיַּרְדֵּן, *the land east of the Jordan River.* Since the conquest of this land described in *Numbers* 21:21ff, and its division among Reuben, Gad, and half of Menashe (see *Numbers* 32) it remained part of *Eretz Yisrael* both during the period of the First Temple and following the Babylonian exile. [For a discussion of the later assertion see *R' Joseph Lieberman, Beiur Gevulos HaAretz, Kerem Zion,* Jerusalem 5725]. It seems inconceivable that this part of the land should be missing in Messianic times, particularly since the east bank is the home of at least two of the three nations, (the Kenites, Kennizites and Kadmonites) whose lands had been promised to Abraham (*Genesis* 15:19) but withheld from his children until the coming of the Messiah. [See *Rashi,* who is of the opinion that this land was given to Edom, Ammon, and Moab until it would become part of the greater Israel of Messianic times.]

We suggest the following explanation.

Although the halachic status of the east bank seems to have been the same as that of *Eretz Yisrael* proper, its sanctity was nevertheless of a lower level. [For a discussion, see *Beiur Gevulos HaAretz* and *Nachalas Shimon* ch. 54.] *Tashbatz* 3:20 writes that the sanctity of *Eretz Yisrael* proper is superior to the east bank in that only it possesses the following virtues: burial in Israel is considered as burial 'beneath the altar'; the

ceedingly abundant. 11 *But the swamps and the pools*
will not become healthy. They will be set aside for
salt. 12 *By the stream there will rise up by its bank on*
this side and that every manner of food treee, its leaf will not wither nor will its fruit give out, every month it will yield new fruit, for its waters emanate from the Sanctuary. So its fruit will be for food and its leaf for healing.
13 *Thus says my Lord HASHEM/ELOHIM: This shall be the boundary by which you shall allot the*

ressurrection of the dead, can take place only in *Eretz Yisrael*; whoever lives outside the land of Israel is as one who has no God; a couple who are childless while they were outside the land can expect to be blessed with children through the merit of living in the land; whoever lives in *Eretz Yisrael* will have his sins forgiven; the 'air' of the land of Israel induces wisdom; and, finally, there is no prophecy outside *Eretz Yisrael.*

These differences derive from the assertion of the Sages *(Bamidbar Rabbah* 7:8, see also *Ramban, Numbers* 21:21) that in comparison to *Eretz Yisrael* proper, there is no *Shechinah* [Divine Presence] on the east bank (see *Rashi, Joshua* 22:19).

We may surmise that when Yechezkel defines the boundaries of the Land and describes its division among the twelve tribes (ch. 48), he is not thinking of the political boundaries. These may well have extended far to the east and encompassed the huge areas described by *Malbim.* [Indeed it seems unlikely that the land west of the Jordan, which at its widest point is no more than some fifty miles, would be big enough for the many millions of inhabitants which must be assumed for an Israel comprising all its twelve tribes.]

Rather, in consonance with the tenor of the last nine chapters of *Ezekiel,* it is the vision of people as bearers of God's Glory which engages the prophet's attention (see *footnote* to 45:7). The twelve tribes are to be ranged to the north and south of the *Sacred Terumah* where, through the conduit of the holy Temple in their midst, they become host to the *Shechinah,* which is to dwell there never to depart again. [See ch. 48 for *R' Breuer's* understanding of the pattern in which the tribes were arranged from north to south. The similarity to the pattern of the encampment in the wilderness seems to indicate that Israel is viewed here as the bearer of God's glory on earth as it had been in the wilderness.]

Therefore the prophet's description is limited to *Eretz Yisrael* proper. Only there, where the *Shechinah* can rest, can the people function as Its bearers. It is for this function that they were assigned the strips of land running from north to south, which are described in ch. 48. This in no way excludes the possibility that much land, in addition to that described here, lay at their disposal to the east of the Jordan.

Our suggestion has the merit of removing the seeming inequity of assigning land with a width of 25,000 rods (see ch. 48) to each of the twelve tribes. Apart from the fact that this ignores the needs of the more populous tribes (see *comm.* 45:1), it also seems to discriminate against those tribes whose portion fell along the narrower parts of the land. (Compare, for example, the dimensions of the land west of the Sea of Galilee with that west of the Dead Sea). However, if our contention is correct, this poses no problem. All inequities could be evened out through land east of the Jordan.

13. גֵה — *This.*

The substitution of a ג for a ז (גֵה in-

אֶת־הָאָרֶץ לִשְׁנֵי עָשָׂר שִׁבְטֵי יִשְׂרָאֵל
יד יוֹסֵף חֲבָלִים: וּנְחַלְתֶּם אוֹתָהּ אִישׁ כְּאָחִיו
אֲשֶׁר נָשָׂאתִי אֶת־יָדִי לְתִתָּהּ לַאֲבֹתֵיכֶם
טו וְנָפְלָה הָאָרֶץ הַזֹּאת לָכֶם בְּנַחֲלָה: וְזֶה
גְּבוּל הָאָרֶץ לִפְאַת צָפוֹנָה מִן־הַיָּם

stead of זֶה) is not unique. See 25:7 (בַּג instead of בַּז) *(Rashi).*

לִשְׁנֵי עָשָׂר שִׁבְטֵי יִשְׂרָאֵל — *To the twelve tribes of Israel.*

There is an unambiguous assumption that in Messianic times all the twelve tribes will be represented. (See pref. to 37:15-28). Since the tribe of Levi is not counted here [they are to receive their portion in the *Sacred Terumah* — see 45:5] the number twelve (see *Ramban, Deuteronomy* 33:6) must be made up by counting Joseph as two tribes — Ephraim and Menasheh. This, in *Rashi's* view, is the meaning of the next phrase: יוֹסֵף חֲבָלִים, *Joseph shall have two portions. Malbim,* who in contrast to *Rashi,* thinks that the boundaries described here are vastly expanded ones, has a different interpretation for this phrase: *portions will be added.*

14. אִישׁ כְּאָחִיו — *Each man like his brother.*

All portions are to be equal. Unlike the original division in which the number of people was taken into account, now all the tribes are to be equal and separate — as rows in a vineyard. From the eastern boundary to the Mediterranean, no two tribes will occupy one strip *(Rashi).*

אֲשֶׁר נָשָׂאתִי אֶת יָדִי לְתִתָּהּ לַאֲבֹתֵיכֶם — *Which I raised My hand in oath to give to your forefathers.*

In context (according to *Rashi's* interpretation) this refers to the land west of the Jordan. This would tend to confirm the opinion of many commentators that the east bank had not been promised to Abraham, but 'they conquered it on their own' *(Sifri, Deut.* 26:3. See also *Yerushalmi, Bikkurim* 1:8). [For a discussion see *Nachalas Shimon* ch. 54.]

The Northern Boundary.

15-17. In this description of the northern boundaries (and in *v.* 20 which identifies the northwestern point of the land as opposite *Levo Hamath*), we recognize a number of the names from the description of the northern boundary given in *Numbers* 34:7-9.

Besides the יָם הַגָּדוֹל [lit. *Great Sea*], *Mediterranean Sea,* the familiar names are Zedad, Hamath (but see *Eretz Yisrael BiSekufas HaMikrah* 24), and Hazar-enan.

According to *Rashi,* the boundaries delineated here are identical with those in *Numbers.* We must assume that Yechezkel used place names which were familiar, and therefore meaningful, to his listeners.

There is a vast literature which attempts to identify the place names used in the various passages in Scripture which describe the boundaries of the land. [For a useful compendium, see *Encyclopedia Talmudis* vol. 2 under *Eretz Yisrael.* More detailed studies can be found in *HaAretz LiGvuloseha,* R' Tukitzinski, end of vol. 3; and in Lieberman's article in *Kerem Zion.* See also ArtScroll *Joshua.*]

It would lie outside the scope of our commentary to attempt an accurate description of the boundaries. We will limit ourselves to a general description of the outline.

Rashi writes that Hor HaHar, Zedad, Hanal, Berothah, and Sibraim are all towns running along the northern boundary of the land. Since *Numbers* gives Hor HaHar as the northwestern tip of the land, we assume that the

47
14-15

land to the twelve tribes of Israel. Joseph shall have
two portions. 14 *And you shall inherit the land each*
man like his brother, as I raised My hand in an oath
to give it to your forefathers so shall this land fall to
you as an inheritance.
15 *Now this is the boundary of the land. On the*
north side: From the Mediterranean by way of

Fig. 30

Map of Eretz Yisrael and Its Surroundings

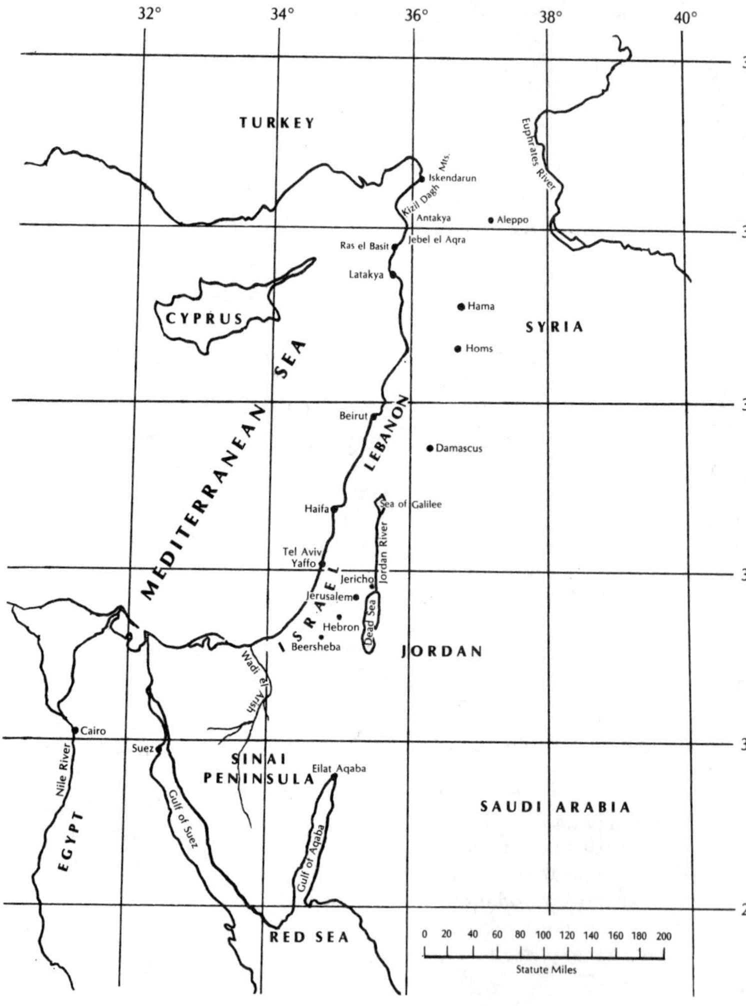

טז הַגָּדוֹל הַדֶּרֶךְ חֶתְלֹן לְבוֹא צְדָדָה: חֲמָת |
בֵּרוֹתָה סִבְרַיִם אֲשֶׁר בֵּין־גְּבוּל דַּמֶּשֶׂק
וּבֵין גְּבוּל חֲמָת חָצֵר הַתִּיכוֹן אֲשֶׁר אֶל־
יז גְּבוּל חַוְרָן: וְהָיָה גְבוּל מִן־הַיָּם חֲצַר
עֵינוֹן גְּבוּל דַּמֶּשֶׂק וְצָפוֹן | צָפוֹנָה וּגְבוּל
יח חֲמָת וְאֵת פְּאַת צָפוֹן: וּפְאַת קָדִים מִבֵּין
חַוְרָן וּמִבֵּין דַּמֶּשֶׂק וּמִבֵּין הַגִּלְעָד וּמִבֵּין
אֶרֶץ יִשְׂרָאֵל הַיַּרְדֵּן מִגְּבוּל עַל־הַיָּם
יט הַקַּדְמוֹנִי תָּמֹדּוּ וְאֵת פְּאַת קָדִימָה: וּפְאַת

phrase in our verse: מִן הַיָּם הַגָּדוֹל הַדֶּרֶךְ חֶתְלוֹן, *from the Mediterranean, by way of Cheslon,* describes a road which runs by Hor HaHar.

[The exact location of Hor HaHar is a matter of much conjecture. Opinions vary widely. Some place it in the general vicinity of the 36° latitude (*Kaftor VaFerach* identifies it as Jebel el Aqra in the vicinity of Ras el Basit — '... a half day's journey north of Latakia' in northern Syria; *R' Tukitzinski* places it slightly further north and identifies it as the Kizil Dagh mountains in the vicinity of Iskenderun [formerly Alexandrette] in southern Turkey); *Admas Kodesh* places it in the vicinity of Beirut, which lies below the 34° latitude. There is a difference of some 190 miles between these points. We shall return to this question in ch. 48, when we discuss the division of the land.]

The furthest point east on this northern border is Hazar-enan, as in *Numbers* (*v.* 9).

[In *R' Tukitzinski's* view, it lies on the banks of the Euphrates, that is, somewhat beyond the 38° longitude mark. This is much further east than any of the other opinions. *Kaftor VaFerach* has it just beyond the 37° longitude.]

Since *v.* 16 seems to give the outermost eastern point as Hazar HaTichon, it would seem that this is the same place as Hazar-enan. This would place Havran (*v.* 16) at the boundaries of Damesek (*v.* 17; see *comm.*) and *Rashi* to verse 16 states this explicitly.

16. חֲמָת — *Hamath.*

The *Targumim* render חֲמָת as *Antochia.* It seems likely that this would be Antakya (formerly (Antioch) in Syria, *Kaftor VaFerach* asserts that someone standing on Hor HaHar and facing east would see Hamath, which is difficult to understand since Anatakia lies well to the north of the Jebel el Aqra, which *Kaftor VaFerach* identifies as Hor HaHar (see *comm.* above and map).

There are some who identify this place with the Hama, which lies some 115 miles north of Damascus, well to the south of Anatakia.

אֲשֶׁר בֵּין גְּבוּל דַּמֶּשֶׂק וּבֵין גְּבוּל חֲמָת — *Which lie between the border of Damesek and the border of Hamath.*

This describes Berothah and Sivraim. They lie between Hamath to the west and Damesek to the east (*Metzudos*).

[We have not rendered *Damesek* as Damascus because today's city of that name lies far to the south of Hazar-enan of the *Kaftor VaFerach* — who claims that his explication of the boundaries agrees with *Rashi's*. Thus, it is difficult to see how Hazar-enan can be described as bordering on Damesek. *R' Tukitzinski* suggests that the name Damesek refers to the area known as Aram Damesek, well to the north of Damascus, rather than to the city.]

17. וְהָיָה גְבוּל מִן הַיָּם חֲצַר עֵינוֹן — *And the border shall be from the Sea to Hazar-enan.*

This sums up the northern border. It

47
16-18

Cheslon approaching Zedad. 16 *Hamath, Berothan*
and Sivraim, which lie between the border of
Damesek and the border of Hamath. Hazar
HaTichon which lies on the border of Havran. 17 *And*
the border shall be from the Sea till Hazar-enan by
the border of Damesek; and everything to the north
including the border of Hamath. This is the northern
side.

18 *As for the eastern side: Between Havran and*
Damesek; between Gilead and the Land of Israel —
the Jordan. From the border by the eastern sea you
shall measure. This is the eastern side.

is to run from the Mediterranean in the west to Hazar-enan in the east *(Rashi).*

וְצָפוֹן צָפוֹנָה וּגְבוּל חֲמָת — *And everything to the north including the border of Hamath.*

As stated at the beginning of the verse, the northern boundary is to run from the Mediterranean Sea up to Hazar-enan. The verse now adds that in this area, all the other northern points which are mentioned in the Torah are to be included.

Rashi renders וְאֵת פְּאַת צָפוֹן as: *This is the northern boundary.* (The same formulation is used in *vs.* 18 and 19.)

The Eastern Boundary.

18. מִבֵּין חַוְרָן בֵּין דַּמֶּשֶׂק — *Between Havran and Damesek.*

In *comm.* 15-17 we noted that Havran and Damesek seem to border one another. This is confirmed in our verse which describes the eastern border as starting out between these two points. The point from which it starts would be Hazar-enan and that is explicitly stated in *Numbers* 34:10.

וּמִבֵּין הַגִּלְעָד וּמִבֵּין אֶרֶץ יִשְׂרָאֵל הַיַּרְדֵּן — *Between Gilead and the Land of Israel — the Jordan.*

Gilead is familiar from *Numbers* 32:39. It is the area settled by the part of Menashe which decided to settle east of the Jordan.Thus, if the border runs *between Gilead and the Land of Israel,* that border must be the Jordan River. This is stated by *Rashi,* who notes that the east bank is not included in this boundary (see pref. 13-20).

.[Since the Jordan River runs north to south between the Sea of Galilee, and the Dead Sea at approximately 35° 36′, and according to even the most conservative opinion, Hazar-enan lies beyond the 36° longitudual line, we must postulate a major bulge eastward in the part of the country north of the Sea of Galilee.]

As indicated by the cantillation, the text makes this point by grouping *the Jordan* with the foregoing phrase (וּמִבֵּין הַגִּלְעָד וּמִבֵּין אֶרֶץ יִשְׂרָאֵל הַיַּרְדֵּן). However, *Rashi* groups *the Jordan* with the following phrase. He renders: *The Jordan* [which is the eastern boundary] *is to run* מִגְּבוּל, *from the* northeastern *boundary* [Hazar-enan] *up to the sea of the east* [the Dead Sea].

The Southern Boundary

19. For the eastern extremity *Numbers* 34:3 and *Joshua* 15:2 seem to yield a point south (and somewhat to the east — of the Dead Sea (see *Lieberman, Beiur Gevulos HaAretz).* There the western extremity is given as the נַחַל מִצְרַיִם, *stream of Egypt. Targum, Rashi, Radak,* and *Vilna Gaon (Yehoshua* 13:3) identify it with the Nile, but *R'*

מז
כ־כג

נֶגֶב תֵּימָנָה מִתָּמָר עַד־מֵי מְרִיבוֹת קָדֵשׁ
נַחֲלָה אֶל־הַיָּם הַגָּדוֹל וְאֵת פְּאַת־תֵּימָנָה
כ נֶגְבָּה: וּפְאַת־יָם הַיָּם הַגָּדוֹל מִגְּבוּל עַד־
כא נֹכַח לְבוֹא חֲמָת זֹאת פְּאַת־יָם: וְחִלַּקְתֶּם
אֶת־הָאָרֶץ הַזֹּאת לָכֶם לְשִׁבְטֵי יִשְׂרָאֵל:
כב וְהָיָה תַּפִּלוּ אוֹתָהּ בְּנַחֲלָה לָכֶם וּלְהַגֵּרִים
הַגָּרִים בְּתוֹכְכֶם אֲשֶׁר־הוֹלִדוּ בָנִים
בְּתוֹכְכֶם וְהָיוּ לָכֶם כְּאֶזְרָח בִּבְנֵי יִשְׂרָאֵל
אִתְּכֶם יִפְּלוּ בְנַחֲלָה בְּתוֹךְ שִׁבְטֵי
כג יִשְׂרָאֵל: וְהָיָה בַשֵּׁבֶט אֲשֶׁר־גָּר הַגֵּר
אִתּוֹ שָׁם תִּתְּנוּ נַחֲלָתוֹ נְאֻם אֲדֹנָי
מח
א יֱהֹוִה: וְאֵלֶּה שְׁמוֹת הַשְּׁבָטִים

Saadia Gaon and many other commentators believe it to be the Wadi El Arish in Sinai (see *Gevulos HaAretz*).

Between those two points the border certainly dips south. *Tevuas HaAretz* thinks of a very slight southern dip, while *R' Tukitzinski* believes that *R' Saadia Gaon's* rendering of מַעֲלֵה עַקְרַבִּים as Aqaba implies that the whole Negev up to and including Eilat lies within the boundaries.

מִתָּמָר — *From Tamar.*

Our verse is very unclear. *Rashi* (based on *Targum*) learns that תָּמָר [literally *date palm*] is Jericho which is frequently referred to in Scripture as עִיר הַתְּמָרִים, *City of Date Palms (Deut.* 34:13; *Judges* 1:16). However, since Jericho lies slightly north of the Dead Sea, this stands in conflict with the implication of *Numbers* and *Joshua* as we described them above (see *Malbim*).

מֵי מְרִיבוֹת קָדֵשׁ — *The waters of Merivos Kadesh.*

Merivos Kadesh is the place where Moses and Aaron sinned, as described in *Numbers* 20:1-14. *Numbers* 20:1 locates the occurrence in Midbar Tzin, and thus our verse agrees with *Numbers* 34:3, which gives Midbar Tzin as one of the points identifying the boundary.

נַחֲלָה — *By way of the stream.*

That is, נַחַל מִצְרַיִם, *the Stream of Egypt,* which is discussed above. The point at which this river flows into יָם הַגָּדוֹל, *the Mediterranean Sea,* is the western extremity of the boundary.

The Western Boundary.

20. As in the Torah, the western boundary is the Mediterranean Sea. The northern extremity lies opposite Levo Hamath, which is one of the points in the northern boundary (see above).

21. The exact division of the land among the twelve tribes will be described in the next chapter.

22-23. These verses seem to point to another difference between the future division of the land and that which took place in Joshua's time. (See *comm.* and footnote 45:1). Whereas proselytes were not given a portion of the land in the earlier division (see *Sifri, Numbers* 26:55), it would seem that they will share in the future division.

Abarbanel suggests that it is only right that converts, who threw in their lot with Israel in exile and suffered with them as Jews, should also be considered

19 As for the southern side in the south: From
Tamar till the waters of Merivos Kadesh by way of
the stream to the great sea. This the southern side to
the south.
20 As for the western side — the Mediterranean.
From the border up to the point opposite Levo
Chamos. This is the western side.
21 You are to divide this land among yourselves for
the tribes of Israel. 22 And thus shall be what you al-
lot as a heritage, for yourselves and for the strangers
who dwell among you, who bear children in your
midst. They shall be considered by you as citizens in
the family of Israel with you; they are to be allotted
an inheritance among the tribes of Israel. 23 And it
shall be that within the tribe among whom the
stranger settled, there you should allot his portion.
The words of my Lord HASHEM / ELOHIM.

part of Israel in the division of the land. This is the opinion of the Sages in *Koheles Rabbah* 1:8.

However, *Sifri* to *Numbers* 10:29 disagrees. The Torah seems explicit when it excludes converts from receiving any portion. What then is the meaning of our verses? They refer not to receiving a portion of the land because converts are excluded from such a right. Rather, the meaning is that the converts share in the atonement which comes to one who lives in *Eretz Yisrael* (see *Kesubos* 111a). Each tribe, depending on its closeness to God, has its own level of purity and atonement. The converts among each tribe will share in that Divine gift (*Netziv* to *Sifri*). Alternatively, *Sifri* suggests that our text might refer to burial in *Eretz Yisrael*. The converts who live among us will have the right to burial in the land although they have no portion in it.

23. The proselyte is to receive his portion with that tribe among whom he lived when he became a convert during the exile *(Rashi)*.

XLVIII

This final chapter of the Book deals with the division of the land among the tribes and contains a closer and more detailed description of the city which is to lie to the south of the Temple Mount.

In the absence of guidance from the Sages we cannot say with any certainty why the descriptions contained in these last nine chapters follow the particular sequence they do. Nevertheless we wonder why the return of the Shechinah *to the Temple, which is described at 43:1-5, was not left to the end to serve as the climax of the book. The departure of the* Shechinah *was so central to the beginning of Yechezkel's prophecy — the chapters of* חוּרְבְּנָא, destruction, *which began the Book (*Bava Basra *14b) so obviously focused on that tragedy — that we could well have expected that the triumphant culmination of the chapters of* נֶחָמְתָּא, consolation, *would be Its return.*

What can we learn from the fact that this return of the Shechinah *to the Temple was not emphasized, while the conspicuous final verse is reserved for the future name of the city —* ה׳ שָׁמָּה, HASHEM-is-there?

Commentary to 45:1-8 noted briefly how the land is to be divided among the twelve tribes. Verses 1-29 of our chapter explain the division in detail. According to Sifri, *quoted by* Rashi *in v. 1 each tribe is to receive a strip of land measuring 25,000 rods, or 150,000 cubits from north to south and running along the whole width of the land from east to west (see Fig. 28, p. 705).*

This system for the allotment of the land poses a difficulty. If we convert the 150,000 cubit width of each strip into miles we get a minimum of 42.6 miles to a strip [taking a cubit as 18" or 1.5 feet. Thus $150{,}000 \times 1.5 \div 5280 = 42.6$*]. Multiplied by 13 (the numbers of strips — 12 tribes plus the* Sacred Terumah*) this yields 553.8 miles. If we take a cubit as two feet, each strip would be 56.8 miles and all thirteen would be 739.4 miles. A glance at a map and the information contained in Appendix XI will show that this is much larger than even the most extended boundaries described in comm. 47:13-19.*

How, then, can such a division be implemented?.

In comm. to 47:13, we have laid the groundwork to our perception of the division of the land described here. The boundaries described in ch. 47 seem not to be the political boundaries of the land. Those would extend far to the east and possibly in other directions. Rather, the prophet was concerned with the holy land in which the Shechinah *could come to rest. His concern, in these chapters, is with Israel as the bearers of the Divine Glory.*

We will expand this theory now by considering the order in which our chapter prescribes that the land be divided among the tribes. Superficially it is difficult to perceive any system. However R' Breuer *thinks that essentially the system is the same as that used in* Numbers *ch. 2 to describe the encampment of the tribes of Israel around the Tabernacle in the desert.*

*We can best discern the similarity between the two systems by listing the sequence of the desert encampment (*Numbers *ch. 2) starting from the north and comparing it to the division of the land described here.*

	Listing of the Desert Encampment	**Division of the Land**	
North	דָּן — Dan	Dan — דָּן	*North*
	אָשֵׁר — Asher	Asher — אָשֵׁר	
	נַפְתָּלִי — Naftali	Naftali — נַפְתָּלִי	
West	אֶפְרַיִם — Ephraim	Menashe — מְנַשֶּׁה	
	מְנַשֶּׁה — Menashe	Ephraim — אֶפְרַיִם	
	בִּנְיָמִין — Benjamin	————	
South	רְאוּבֵן — Reuben	Reuben — רְאוּבֵן	
	————	Judah — יְהוּדָה	
	————	Sacred Terumah — תְּרוּמַת הַקֹּדֶשׁ	
	————	Benjamin — בִּנְיָמִין	
	שִׁמְעוֹן — Simeon	Simeon — שִׁמְעוֹן	
	גָּד — Gad	————	
East	יְהוּדָה — Judah	————	
	יִשָּׂשכָר — Issachar	Issachar — יִשָּׂשכָר	
	זְבוּלֻן — Zebulun	Zebulun — זְבוּלֻן	
	————	Gad — גָּד	*South*

The lists are the same except that Judah, Benjamin, and Gad are out of place (and Menashe and Ephraim are reversed). We suggest that Judah and Benjamin are ranged on either side of the Sacred Terumah, *either because they had never succumbed to idol worship as the Northern Kingdom had done, or because it was in their portion that the First and Second Temples had stood. For this reason we ex-*

pect to find them adjacent to the Third Temple.

For Gad we suggest the following explanation: Ramban *to* Numbers *2:2 explains the order in which the tribes camped around the Tabernacle. For the three tribes who were grouped on the south side (Reuben, Simeon, Gad) he offers the following explanation: Reuben is the* בַּעַל תְּשׁוּבָה, penitent, *the one who taught Israel how to repent a sin (see* Rashi *to* Genesis *37:29), Gad was blessed with strength (see* Genesis *49:19) Let 'repentance' and 'strength' be with Simeon so as to atone for him. [Reference is to events described in* Numbers 25:19ff. The tribe of Simeon were the worst offenders on that occasion.]

Thus we see that the close proximity of Gad to Simeon had its source in Simeon's need for atonement. Now, it is possible that in Messianic times Simeon will have been completely forgiven. [This can be seen from the fact that he is to receive a portion of land, equal in every way to that of the other tribes in contrast to the past when his portion had been scattered among Judah's lands (Rashi)]. *Since the combination of tribes in the southern camp in the wilderness had to be broken up, so that Judah and Benjamin could be ranged alongside the* Sacred Terumah, *it will be better to displace Gad also in order not to leave any residue of embarrassment for Simeon.*

But just what is the significance of the encampments? The desert encampments define Israel's pride in itself as a Godly nation more than any other aspect of its national existence. Bamidbar Rabbah *2:3 teaches: Holy and exalted were Israel in their encampment, and all the nations observed them with wonder and offered them all kinds of enticements to forsake their unique character. But Israel answered them: With what promises of greatness can you entice us? Can you duplicate the greatness with which God imbued us in the desert by designating us as the encampment of Judah; the encampment of Reuben; the encampment of Ephraim; the encampment of Dan?*

Surely the meaning of this Midrash is that Israel's true greatness lies in its character as bearers of God's Glory on earth. The encampment which defined in precise terms how each tribe related to the other and how they all, with God's Tabernacle in their midst, made one unified sanctified whole, was the vehicle by which this character became manifest.

This period at which Israel reached the very peak of its glory will be reenacted in the division of the land. Once more the encampments are activated. Once more Israel appears in that role in which it finds the pride and majesty of its existence. Once more, Israel has become the overt bearer of God's Glory on earth.

The perception of this new, or rather renewed, role which the Messianic age will thrust upon Israel may serve as the key to the understanding of the question raised above. How can the relatively small territory within the boundaries described in ch. 47 contain strips of land adding up to a total length of at least 553.8 miles?

Bava Basra *99a teaches: We have this tradition from our parents: The* אָרוֹן, ark, *and* כְּרוּבִים, cheruvim, *which stood in Solomon's Temple, are not part of the dimensions of the Holy of Holies. The Talmud goes on to demonstrate that miraculously, the Ark and the* cheruvim, *although they were physical presences in the Temple, nevertheless occupied no physical space. There was as much empty space in the Holy of Holies as would have been there had the Ark and the* cheruvim *not existed.*

The meaning of this difficult Aggadah may be as follows (see Maharal *ad. loc.): Both the Ark and the* cheruvim *are not of this world. The Ark is the repository of God's wisdom; the* cheruvim *are bearers of God's Glory. Such other-worldly objects are not limited by the spatial limitations of a physical world. They exist in our world but are not truly of it. They occupy no room in it.*

The cheruvim *of the future are to be the people of Israel themselves. Ranged about the* Sacred Terumah, *they are the* cheruvim *upon whom God allows His glory to become manifest. Limitations of space do not inhibit them. The sphere of their existence cannot be cramped by the physical limitations of the land.*

מח
ב־ג

מִקְצֵה צָפוֹנָה אֶל־יַד דֶּרֶךְ־חֶתְלֹן | לְבוֹא־
חֲמָת חֲצַר עֵינָן גְּבוּל דַּמֶּשֶׂק צָפוֹנָה אֶל־
יַד חֲמָת וְהָיוּ־לוֹ פְאַת־קָדִים הַיָּם דָּן
ב אֶחָד: וְעַל | גְּבוּל דָּן מִפְּאַת קָדִים עַד־
ג פְּאַת יָמָּה אָשֵׁר אֶחָד: וְעַל | גְּבוּל אָשֵׁר

We believe this thought to be expressed by Sifri *to* Deuteronomy *32:12. The verse reads:* ה׳ בָּדָד יַנְחֶנּוּ, God will [in the future] lead [Israel] in isolation. *To this,* Sifri *(according to the reading of* Vilna Gaon*), remarks: This [isolation] implies that in the future God will have Israel inherit from one end of the world to the other; as it is written* (v. *2 ff.):* Adjoining Dan's border, from the eastern end till the western end: for Asher — one portion. Adjoining Asher's border, from the eastern end till the western end: for Naftali — one portion. *Now why does it say:* Dan — one portion ... Asher — one portion ... Naftali — one portion? *To teach us that Israel will one day inherit strips from east to west with a width of 25,000 rods [which is only about 56.8 miles (see Appendix XI)].*

Sifri *begins with the assertion that Israel is to 'inherit from one end of the world to the other' and ends by limiting the possession to a strip of 25,000 rods. According to the above, the answer is as follows: Freed from the limitations of space, Israel's national Templehood will indeed be equal to 'one end of the world to the other.'*

We believe that this same concept explains the unexpected disposition of the Temple Mount in relation to the city. It is not situated within the city but lies some twenty-five miles to the north (10,000 rods for the Levites' portion + 4750 rods = 88,500 cubits = 132,750 ft. = 25.1 miles; fig. 29). As noted in footnote 45:1, we would expect to find the Temple Mount and the Temple in Jerusalem.

*Our Sages teach (*Sifri, Deuteronomy *1) that Jerusalem will one day grow and spread all the way to Damesek. How can this be reconciled with the relatively small dimensions assigned to the city by* Yechezkel*?* Sifri *asks a similar question: Is it not written (*Jeremiah *30:18):* And the city shall be built on its hill *(which implies that it will not spread beyond its normal boundaries)?*

Sifri *answers: The land of Israel will be like a fig tree which is narrow beneath but widens on top. This cryptic teaching of the Sages appears to indicate that Jerusalem and Israel will indeed lie within certain physical boundaries, but will not be limited by them. At a higher (or deeper) level, they will expand vastly.*

Thus the twenty-five mile distance between the Temple Mount and the City is not significant. The true Jerusalem expands to encompass not only the Temple Mount, but vast areas beyond it.

We have solved the difficulty but not yet explained the fact. What can be learned from the disposition laid down by Yechezkel? Why is the Temple Mount not to lie within the actual physical confines of the Holy City?

Perhaps the solution is as follows.

According to Sforno (Exodus *24:28) the idea of a Holy Temple, a central place of worship which alone is acceptable as an abode for the* Shechinah, *is not the ideal form for Divine worship. Immediately after God had given Moses the first tablets of stone, He promised,* In any place where I will cause My Name to be uttered, I will come and bless you (Exodus *20:21). This implies that no central location would be necessary. Any Jew, at any time, could turn to God with his sacrifice. It was only after Israel had sinned with the golden calf that an entirely new system of worship*

48
1-3
Now these are the names of the tribes:
At the northern end, near the Cheslon road toward
Levo Chamos, Hazar-enan, the border of Damesek
northward near Hamath: From the eastern border till
the Sea: for Dan — one portion.
2 *Adjoining Dan's*
border, from the eastern end till the western end: for
Asher — one portion.
3 *Adjoining Asher's border,*

had to be inaugurated. [This is not a universally accepted opinion. Ramban, *for example, disagrees and thinks that a Sanctuary was envisioned long before the people had sinned.*]

If the Temple and the Temple Mount had been situated within the city, and that city were called ה' שָׁמָּה, HASHEM-is-there, (v. *35), with its implication of a complete identification with Godliness (see pref. ch. 22), it would have seemed as though only through the Temple could the city aspire to Godliness. The fact that although the Temple stood far outside the physical environs of the city, the city was still designated as the home of the Presence of God, teaches unambiguously that the* Shechinah *truly rests with the hearts of the people rather than on Temple or Mount.*

Now we return to the question posed at the beginning of these remarks. Why does the Book not end with the return of the Shechinah *to the Temple, since that seems to be the crowning glory of the Messianic era? The answer is there would be an even greater moment. When the city would rise in the midst of the twelve tribes of Israel, ranged about as the new* cheruvim, *when that city would merit the name of HASHEM-is-there — that moment would be the point at which Israel will have attained its true glory.*

1. Only the northern boundary of Dan (in our verse) and the southern boundary of Gad (*v.* 28) needed to be defined [and are given exactly as in 47:15-17, 19]. The inside boundaries of all thirteen divisions are determined automatically by measuring the assigned width of the strips *(R' Breuer).*

וְהָיוּ לוֹ פְאַת קָדִים הַיָּם — *From the eastern border till the Sea.*

This is the equivalent of מִפְּאַת קָדִים עַד פְּאַת יָמָּה, *from the eastern end till the western end,* which is repeated with minor variations for each of the twelve tribes (*v.* 2 ff.). It means that the length of each strip ran the whole width of the land from east to west.

דָּן אֶחָד — *For Dan — one portion.*

The word אֶחָד, *one,* is repeated for each of the twelve tribes. From this *Sifri (Deut.* 1; *Rashi)* deduces that all these strips had the same width. This width is assumed to equal that of the *Sacred Terumah,* which is given (*v.* 8) as 25,000 rods. [The words in *v.* 8: כְּאַחַד הַחֲלָקִים, *equal to one of the portions,* are assumed to refer to both the length and the width.] Thus we have a width of 25,000 rods for each of the thirteen strips. [See pref. *comm.* 45:3 which showed that, according to *Radak,* it would be possible to assume a width of only 25,000 cubits for each strip. This would lessen the amount of land needed by a factor of six.]

2. See prefatory remarks for an explanation of the order in which the tribes received their allotment.

קָדִימָה — *East.*

The text repeatedly changes from קָדִים *(vs.* 1-2) to קָדִימָה *(vs.* 3-5) and back again *(vs.* 6-8). (See further *vs.* 23-27.)

מִפְּאַת קָדִימָה וְעַד־פְּאַת־יָמָּה נַפְתָּלִי
ד אֶחָד׃ וְעַל ׀ גְּבוּל נַפְתָּלִי מִפְּאַת קָדְמָה
ה עַד־פְּאַת יָמָּה מְנַשֶּׁה אֶחָד׃ וְעַל ׀ גְּבוּל
מְנַשֶּׁה מִפְּאַת קָדְמָה עַד־פְּאַת יָמָּה
ו אֶפְרַיִם אֶחָד׃ וְעַל ׀ גְּבוּל אֶפְרַיִם מִפְּאַת
ז קָדִים וְעַד־פְּאַת־יָמָּה רְאוּבֵן אֶחָד׃ וְעַל ׀
גְּבוּל רְאוּבֵן מִפְּאַת קָדִים עַד־פְּאַת יָמָּה
ח יְהוּדָה אֶחָד׃ וְעַל גְּבוּל יְהוּדָה מִפְּאַת
קָדִים עַד־פְּאַת יָמָּה תִּהְיֶה הַתְּרוּמָה
אֲשֶׁר־תָּרִימוּ חֲמִשָּׁה וְעֶשְׂרִים אֶלֶף רֹחַב
וְאֹרֶךְ כְּאַחַד הַחֲלָקִים מִפְּאַת קָדִימָה
עַד־פְּאַת־יָמָּה וְהָיָה הַמִּקְדָּשׁ בְּתוֹכוֹ׃
ט הַתְּרוּמָה אֲשֶׁר תָּרִימוּ לַיהוָה אֹרֶךְ
חֲמִשָּׁה וְעֶשְׂרִים אֶלֶף וְרֹחַב עֲשֶׂרֶת
י אֲלָפִים׃ וּלְאֵלֶּה תִּהְיֶה תְרוּמַת־הַקֹּדֶשׁ
לַכֹּהֲנִים צָפוֹנָה חֲמִשָּׁה וְעֶשְׂרִים אֶלֶף
וְיָמָּה רֹחַב עֲשֶׂרֶת אֲלָפִים וְקָדִימָה רֹחַב
עֲשֶׂרֶת אֲלָפִים וְנֶגְבָּה אֹרֶךְ חֲמִשָּׁה
וְעֶשְׂרִים אֶלֶף וְהָיָה מִקְדַּשׁ־יְהוָה בְּתוֹכוֹ׃
יא לַכֹּהֲנִים הַמְקֻדָּשׁ מִבְּנֵי צָדוֹק אֲשֶׁר שָׁמְרוּ

R' Breuer writes that the expression קָדִימָה, which literally means *towards the east* indicates that the territory expanded eastwards beyond the original borders of the land. (See *comm.* 47:13-20.)

7. In the original division of the land Judah and Benjamin were neighbors (*Joshua* 18:11). The Temple stood at the boundary between the two tribes so that part was in Judah's portion, and part in Benjamin's portion. (See *Yoma* 12a; and *Zevachim* 54b.) The new Temple is to be built in the Sacred *Terumah* — which lies in the portion of the *nassi* [*prince*], who represents the whole of Israel — rather than in any particular tribal territory (see footnote 45:7). Nevertheless Judah and Benjamin (*v.* 23) retain the privilege of bordering on the Sacred *Terumah*.

8. הַתְּרוּמָה – *The Terumah*.

The entire strip mentioned in our verse, running from the eastern boundary of the land to the western boundary, is characterized as Terumah. The word [which literally means *separation* or *setting aside*] has the connotation of a *gift* which is to be separated from general possessions and set aside for a

from the eastern end till the western end: for Naftali
— one portion. 4 *Adjoining Naftali's border, from the*
eastern end till the western end: for Menashe — one
portion. 5 *Adjoining Menashe's border, from the*
eastern end till the western end: for Ephraim — one
portion. 6 *Adjoining Menashe's border, from the*
eastern end till the western end: for Reuven — one
portion. 7 *Adjoining Reuven's border, from the*
eastern end till the western end: for Judah — one portion.

8 *Adjoining Judah's border from the eastern end*
till the western end shall be the Terumah which you
shall set aside, twenty-five thousand wide with a
length equal to one of the portions from the eastern
end till the western end. The Sanctuary shall be
within it. 9 *The Terumah which you set aside for*
HASHEM shall have a length of twenty-five thousand
and a width of ten thousand. 10 *To these the Sacred*
Terumah be apportioned: for the kohanim, to the
north twenty five thousand and to the west a width
of ten thousand and to the east a width of ten thousand and to the south a length of twenty-five thousand. And the Sanctuary of HASHEM shall be within
it. 11 *This hallowed place shall belong to the kohanim*
descended from Tzadok who guarded My charge, who

higher purpose. Within this strip, the Sacred *Terumah*, the portion used for the Temple, *kohanim*, Levites and the city runs only 25,000 rods from the east to west. This leaves room east and west of the Sacred *Terumah* for the portion of the *nassi* within the *Terumah (v.* 28).

Thus, the portion of the *nassi* is also a *Terumah* from the land, which is designated for sublime use. The portion is his only in a narrow sense. In a broader sense, he represents the whole people (see footnote 45:7).

9-12. These verses describe the northern portion of the Sacred *Terumah*. Measuring 10,000×25,000 rods *(v.* 9) it is to be given to the *kohanim*, in whose portion God's Temple is to stand (*v.* 10. See fig. 29). The verse stresses particularly that the Temple is to stand in the *kohanim's* portion so as to underline their responsibility of leading a life suited to close proximity to the *Shechinah*. This is the meaning of the words וּמִקְדָּשׁ לַמִּקְדָּשׁ (45:4): the portion of the *kohanim* is to be a *sanctuary for the Sanctuary* — an area where lives so holy are lead that the Sanctuary of God will be able to rise from its midst *(R' Breuer)*.

מִשְׁמַרְתִּ֑י אֲשֶׁ֣ר לֹא־תָע֗וּ בִּתְע֙וֹת בְּנֵ֣י
יב יִשְׂרָאֵ֔ל כַּאֲשֶׁ֥ר תָּע֖וּ הַלְוִיִּֽם׃ וְהָיְתָ֨ה לָהֶ֧ם
תְּרוּמִיָּ֛ה מִתְּרוּמַ֥ת הָאָ֖רֶץ קֹ֣דֶשׁ קָֽדָשִׁ֑ים
יג אֶל־גְּב֖וּל הַלְוִיִּֽם׃ וְהַלְוִיִּ֞ם לְעֻמַּ֣ת גְּב֣וּל
הַכֹּהֲנִ֗ים חֲמִשָּׁ֨ה וְעֶשְׂרִ֥ים אֶ֙לֶף֙ אֹ֔רֶךְ
וְרֹ֖חַב עֲשֶׂ֣רֶת אֲלָפִ֑ים כָּל־אֹ֗רֶךְ חֲמִשָּׁ֤ה
וְעֶשְׂרִים֙ אֶ֔לֶף וְרֹ֖חַב עֲשֶׂ֥רֶת אֲלָפִֽים׃
יַעֲבִיר ק׳ יד וְלֹֽא־יִמְכְּר֤וּ מִמֶּ֙נּוּ֙ וְלֹ֣א יָמֵ֔ר וְלֹ֥א °יעבור
טו רֵאשִׁ֣ית הָאָ֑רֶץ כִּי־קֹ֖דֶשׁ לַֽיהוָֽה׃ וַחֲמֵ֨שֶׁת
אֲלָפִ֜ים הַנּוֹתָ֣ר בָּרֹ֗חַב עַל־פְּנֵ֞י חֲמִשָּׁ֤ה
וְעֶשְׂרִים֙ אֶ֔לֶף חֹֽל־ה֥וּא לָעִ֛יר לְמוֹשָׁ֖ב
טז וּלְמִגְרָ֑שׁ וְהָיְתָ֥ה הָעִ֖יר בְּתוֹכֹֽה׃ וְאֵ֣לֶּה
מִדּוֹתֶ֗יהָ פְּאַ֨ת צָפ֜וֹן חֲמֵ֤שׁ מֵאוֹת֙
°כתיב ולא קרי וְאַרְבַּ֣עַת אֲלָפִ֔ים וּפְאַת־נֶ֗גֶב חֲמֵ֥שׁ °חמש
מֵא֖וֹת וְאַרְבַּ֣עַת אֲלָפִ֑ים וּמִפְּאַ֣ת קָדִ֗ים
חֲמֵ֤שׁ מֵאוֹת֙ וְאַרְבַּ֣עַת אֲלָפִ֔ים וּפְאַת־יָ֕מָּה
יז חֲמֵ֥שׁ מֵא֖וֹת וְאַרְבַּ֥עַת אֲלָפִֽים׃ וְהָיָ֤ה
מִגְרָשׁ֙ לָעִ֔יר צָפ֙וֹנָה֙ חֲמִשִּׁ֣ים וּמָאתָ֔יִם
וְנֶ֖גְבָּה חֲמִשִּׁ֣ים וּמָאתָ֑יִם וְקָ֙דִימָה֙ חֲמִשִּׁ֣ים
יח וּמָאתַ֔יִם וְיָ֖מָּה חֲמִשִּׁ֥ים וּמָאתָֽיִם׃ וְהַנּוֹתָ֨ר
בָּאֹ֜רֶךְ לְעֻמַּ֣ת ׀ תְּרוּמַ֣ת הַקֹּ֗דֶשׁ עֲשֶׂ֤רֶת

11. This piece of sanctified land shall be set aside for the *kohanim* descended from Tzadok, who remained steadfastly loyal to God when all the other *kohanim* had succumbed to idol worship (*v.* 11). [See *comm.* 44:1.]

הַלְוִיִּם — *The Levites.*

This phrase which literally means *the Levites* is used here to describe the *kohanim,* who are also descended from Levi *(Metzudos;* but see *comm.* 44:10-14).

12. תְּרוּמִיָּה מִתְּרוּמַת הָאָרֶץ — *A Terumah...from the land's Terumah.*

This northern strip of 10,000 rods is a *Terumah* from the 25,000 rod *Terumah.* It is called the *Terumah* of *Terumah* since it is the holiest part of the *Terumah.*

13-14 The middle portion of the Sacred *Terumah* is assigned to the Levites (Fig. 29). Their portion has the same dimensions as that of the *kohanim,* with one difference. Whereas the *kohanim* had to give up a part of their inheritance for the Temple Mount which stood in their midst, no such re-

did not stray when the family of Israel strayed — as
the Levites strayed. 12 *It shall be a Terumah for them*
from the land's Terumah, most holy by the border of
the Levites. 13 *Now for the Levites, along the border*
of the kohanim, twenty-five thousand in length and
a width of ten thousand, the entire length of twenty-
five thousand and width of ten thousand. 14 *They*
shall not sell from it, nor exchange nor transfer this
choicest of the land — for it is sacred to HASHEM.
15 *Now the five thousand remaining of the width*
along the twenty-five thousand shall be non-holy,
for the city — for dwellings and open space — and the
city shall be within it. 16 *Now these are its dimen-*
sions: On the northern side four thousand five
hundred and on the southern side four thousand five
hundred and on the eastern side four thousand five
hundred and on the western side four thousand five
hundred. 17 *And the city shall have an open space:*
To the north, two hundred and fifty; and to the
south, two hundred and fifty; and to the east, two
hundred and fifty; and to the west, two hundred and
fifty.
18 *Now the remainder of the length along the*

quirement was made of the Levites. Verse 13 emphasizes that the entire portion (כָּל אֹרֶךְ...) was set aside for their own use *(Metzudos).*

This possession of the Levites [and certainly that of the *kohanim (Radak)*] has the character of רֵאשִׁית — that which is *foremost* in standing (see *Numbers* 15:20; *Deut.* 18:4) and therefore holy. Its sacred character may never be eroded by being sold or traded (*v.* 14).

15-17. In the exact center of the lowest strip of the Sacred *Terumah,* 5000 rods wide along the whole 25,000 rod length of the *Terumah,* the city was to be located (Fig. 23).

It was to be 4,500 rods square (27,000 cubits=40,500 ft.=7.67 miles). On each side there was to be a מִגְרָשׁ, *open space,* of 250 rods (1500 cubits=2250 ft.=0.4 miles), so that the whole city complex measured 5000 rods by 5000 rods. This would take up the whole width of the strip from north to south and leave 10,000 rods on the eastern and western sides. This space is to be put to the use described in the next verses.

18. The entire length of the *Terumah* from east to west was 25,000 rods. When we subtract the 5000 rods taken up by the city and its open space, we are left with 20,000 rods, 10,000 on each side. These two pieces of land were to be used to produce food for עֹבְדֵי הָעִיר, *those that serve the city,* i.e., the city workers.

אֲלָפִים קָדִימָה וַעֲשֶׂרֶת אֲלָפִים יָמָּה
וְהָיָה לְעֻמַּת תְּרוּמַת הַקֹּדֶשׁ וְהָיְתָה
יט תְבוּאָתֹה לְלֶחֶם לְעֹבְדֵי הָעִיר׃ וְהָעֹבֵד
כ הָעִיר יַעַבְדוּהוּ מִכֹּל שִׁבְטֵי יִשְׂרָאֵל׃ כָּל־
הַתְּרוּמָה חֲמִשָּׁה וְעֶשְׂרִים אֶלֶף בַּחֲמִשָּׁה
וְעֶשְׂרִים אָלֶף רְבִיעִית תָּרִימוּ אֶת־
כא תְּרוּמַת הַקֹּדֶשׁ אֶל־אֲחֻזַּת הָעִיר׃ וְהַנּוֹתָר
לַנָּשִׂיא מִזֶּה ׀ וּמִזֶּה ׀ לִתְרוּמַת־הַקֹּדֶשׁ
וְלַאֲחֻזַּת הָעִיר אֶל־פְּנֵי חֲמִשָּׁה וְעֶשְׂרִים
אֶלֶף ׀ תְּרוּמָה עַד־גְּבוּל קָדִימָה וְיָמָּה עַל־
פְּנֵי חֲמִשָּׁה וְעֶשְׂרִים אֶלֶף עַל־גְּבוּל יָמָּה
לְעֻמַּת חֲלָקִים לַנָּשִׂיא וְהָיְתָה תְּרוּמַת
כב הַקֹּדֶשׁ וּמִקְדַּשׁ הַבַּיִת בְּתוֹכֹה׃ וּמֵאֲחֻזַּת

19. וְהָעֹבֵד הָעִיר — *(And) each* [lit. *the*] *worker of the city.*

Rashi quotes *R' Menachem ben Chelbo* that these city workers were the Gibeonites who had been condemned by Joshua to be *hewers of wood and drawers of water* for all eternity (*Joshua* 9:3-27). This opinion is confirmed by *Bereishis Rabbah* 20:5 which, on the basis of *v.* 19 of our chapter, declares the Gibeonites to be 'without a remedy.' They are cursed for all eternity. (See *Yevamos* 79a,b.) No explanation is offered of why the vast agricultural resources of these large tracts of land should be specifically assigned to the Gibeonites.

It is on this ground that *Radak* rejects the interpretation. It is inconceivable to him that the Gibeonites should be the dwellers of this most holy city. In addition, he argues, it is unlikely that the Gibeonites will exist as an identifiable entity in the Messianic age. He identifies the city's work force as its inhabitants since they, by their labors, support the city. These inhabitants of the city are to be drawn from all the tribes of Israel.

According to *Metzudos,* the sense of the verse is as follows: Each and every inhabitant, who may be called a *worker of the city* (עֹבֵד הָעִיר), has the right to be supported [יַעַבְדוּהוּ, i.e., *served* in turn] by all the tribes of Israel (מִכֹּל שִׁבְטֵי יִשְׂרָאֵל). Because they live in the city as representatives of the whole people they have the right to be supported by the produce of land which should really belong to the whole nation.

The Sages (*Bava Basra* 122a) have a different interpretation for our verse. The city worker is the *nassi* in whose territory the whole *Terumah* is situated (vs. 21, 24). The true king is a servant to the people (see *I Kings* 12:7). Accordingly, this verse is an introduction to the next section, which describes the rights of the *nassi.*

20. This verse sums up the total dimensions of the *Terumah* one final time. The total area is to be 25,000 [rods] by 25,000 [rods]. (See *comm.* 45:3.)

רְבִיעִית — *Square.*

The use of the word רְבִיעִית for square is irregular; the common word is

sacred Terumah, ten thousand to the east and ten thousand to the west — it shall be along the sacred Terumah. Its produce shall be food for those that serve the city. 19 Each worker of the city shall serve it on behalf of all the tribes of Israel.

20 The entire Terumah shall be twenty-five thousand by twenty-five thousand. Set aside a square — the sacred Terumah together with the property of the city.

21 And the remainder is the prince's, on either side of the sacred Terumah and the property of the city. Along the twenty-five thousand of the Terumah till the eastern border, and to the west, along the twenty-five thousand to the western border — corresponding to the tribal portions shall be the prince's. And the sacred Terumah and the Sanctuary of the Temple shall be within it. 22 As also the property of the

רָבוּעַ (see *Exodus* 28:16).

The cantillation separates רְבִיעִית, *square*, from the earlier phrase, thus indicating that the translation is not *25,000 rods by 25,000 rods, square.* Rather the word *square* is part of the following phrase.

The use of the word אֶל, literally *towards* or *for* in this connection is unexpected. *Metzudos* translates *together with*, and we have followed that rendering although this is clearly an irregular use of אֶל.

R' Breuer suggests that the word may be understood in its regular meaning. The sense of the verse is that all three components of the *Terumah* are to form a single unit or square. This unit is *for*, that is, it finds its focus and purpose in the city. The property of the city had been described as חוֹל, *non-holy* (*v.* 15), in contrast to the Sacred *Terumah*. However, that absence of intrinsic sanctity is in itself the crowning glory of the whole *Terumah* complex. The barrier between the holy and the ordinary becomes meaningless. Together, in a single unit, they become the *Terumah*, *gift*, which Israel separates from its own and dedicates to the service of God. (See Pref.)

21-22 The *nassi* is to receive the land which lies to the east and to the west of the Sacred *Terumah* [see Appendix XI].

Rambam (Hilchos Melachim 4:8) writes: 'The Messianic king gets one thirteenth of all lands which Israel conquers. This allotment is an eternal right for him and his children.' This halachah is based on the disposition of the land described in our chapter (see *Radvaz* ibid.) and on the statement cited in *Bava Basra* 122a: The land of Israel will one day be divided into thirteen strips. Who is to get the extra one [beyond the share of the twelve tribes]? Said R' Chisdah: The *nassi*.

From these sources it is clear that, although a huge area of twenty-two and a half billion square cubits (1814.8 square miles) is appropriated from his portion for the Sacred *Terumah*, the *nassi* receives a portion equal in area to

הַלְוִיִּם וּמֵאֲחֻזַּת הָעִיר בְּתוֹךְ אֲשֶׁר
לַנָּשִׂיא יִהְיֶה בֵּין | גְּבוּל יְהוּדָה וּבֵין גְּבוּל
כג בִּנְיָמִן לַנָּשִׂיא יִהְיֶה׃ וְיֶתֶר הַשְּׁבָטִים
מִפְּאַת קָדִימָה עַד־פְּאַת־יָמָּה בִּנְיָמִן
כד אֶחָד׃ וְעַל | גְּבוּל בִּנְיָמִן מִפְּאַת קָדִימָה
כה עַד־פְּאַת־יָמָּה שִׁמְעוֹן אֶחָד׃ וְעַל | גְּבוּל
שִׁמְעוֹן מִפְּאַת קָדִימָה עַד־פְּאַת־יָמָּה
כו יִשָּׂשכָר אֶחָד׃ וְעַל | גְּבוּל יִשָּׂשכָר מִפְּאַת
כז קָדִימָה עַד־פְּאַת־יָמָּה זְבוּלֻן אֶחָד׃ וְעַל |
גְּבוּל זְבוּלֻן מִפְּאַת קָדְמָה עַד־פְּאַת־יָמָּה
כח גָּד אֶחָד׃ וְעַל גְּבוּל גָּד אֶל־פְּאַת נֶגֶב
כט תֵּימָנָה וְהָיָה גְבוּל מִתָּמָר מֵי מְרִיבַת
קָדֵשׁ נַחֲלָה עַל־הַיָּם הַגָּדוֹל׃ זֹאת
הָאָרֶץ אֲשֶׁר־תַּפִּילוּ מִנַּחֲלָה לְשִׁבְטֵי
יִשְׂרָאֵל וְאֵלֶּה מַחְלְקוֹתָם נְאֻם אֲדֹנָי

that of each of the twelve tribes. Thus, the Sacred *Terumah* cannot be regarded as a separate entity but rather as a part of the property of the *nassi*, for it is he who serves as a conduit for bringing the *Shechinah* to rest in Israel (see footnote 45:7).

This thought seems to be expressed in our two verses which stress that both *the Sacred Terumah and the Sanctuary of the Temple (v.* 21) and *the property of the Levites and the property of the city (v.* 22) are to be בְּתוֹךְ, *within*, the portion of the *nassi.*

23-28 For the order in which these five tribes are to receive their allotment, see prefatory remarks.

29. נְאֻם ה׳ אֱלֹהִים — *The words of my Lord HASHEM/ELOHIM.*

The tribes are to receive their portion directly from God's hands. This is implied in the phrase: *and these are their divisions — the word of my Lord HASHEM/ELOHIM (Bava Basra* 122a).

[Although our phrase recurs often in the book, the Talmud attaches special significance to it here. Perhaps the Sages were struck by the contrast between our verse and 47:23. There, with reference to the stranger, the expression used is: שָׁם תִּתְּנוּ נַחֲלָתוֹ, *there 'you' shall allot his portion.* The portion is allotted by the people. An equivalent formulation, such as וְאֵלֶּה מַחְלְקֹתָם אֲשֶׁר תִּתְּנוּ, *these are their divisions 'which you shall allot';* is not used here. For this reason the phrase is to be understood: *And these are their divisions — (by) the word of my Lord HASHEM/ELOHIM.*]

30-35. The final glance of the prophet is directed not to the Temple but to the city (see Pref.). Within its walls, pure Godliness will find expression (*v.* 35), and it is there that Yechezkel's visions and aspirations will one day be realized.

We are told nothing of the life of this city. We know its dimensions and in our section we will learn, in addition, of the twelve gates that are to lead out (תוֹצָאוֹת from יצא, *to leave)* of it. As for the rest there is silence: no hint of what the

48
23-29

Levites and the property of the city shall be within
the prince's possessions. Between the border of Judah
and the border of Benjamin shall be the prince's.
23 *Now the rest of the tribes — from the eastern end*
till the western end: for Benjamin — one portion.
24 *Adjoining Benjamin's borders, from the eastern*
end till the western end: for Simeon — one portion.
25 *Adjoining Simeon's border, from the eastern end*
till the western end: for Issachar — one portion.
26 *Adjoining Issachar's border, from the eastern end*
till the western end: for Zebulun — one portion.
27 *Adjoining Zebulun's border from the eastern end*
till the western end: for Gad — one portion. 28 *Ad-*
joining Gad's border to the southern extreme the
boundary shall run from Tamar to the waters of
Merivas Kodesh, to the River to the Mediterranean
Sea. 29 *This is the land which you shall allot as a*
heritage to Israel's tribes and there are their portions
— the words of my Lord HASHEM / ELOHIM.

city's inhabitants will be doing; no indication of how the Presence of God implied in its name, ה׳ שָׁמָּה, *HASHEM-is-there* (*v.* 35), will make itself felt.

The Sages permit us a glimpse behind this curtain of mystery. Based on *v.* 35, which gives the perimeter of the city as 18,000 (rods). Rava teaches (*Succah* 45b; *Sanhedrin* 97b): There are to be 18,000 rows [of righteous men] before the Holy One Blessed be He [in the World to Come]. Thus, our city, which surely is a physical, tangible one situated on the site defined by the text, is seen as a symbol of God's closeness to the righteous people in the World to Come.[1]

It is, then, to be a city in which the close proximity of God is so pervasive that life there can be viewed as the earthly equivalent of the World to Come. The 18,000 rod perimeter defines the area where life is — in the most literal sense — lived before God. Small wonder that the details of such a life remain hidden from us!

What of the few details which we are taught? Of what significance are the walls which surround the city and the gates which lead from it?

1. *Rashi* to *Sanhedrin* (97b) remarks concerning *v.* 35: The verse at the end of *Ezekiel* deals with יְרוּשָׁלַיִם שֶׁל מַעְלָה, *the celestial Jerusalem.* This would seem to imply that the city described here is not a physically existing one at all, but rather some spiritual entity beyond our experience. However, *Tosafos Yom Tov* in his *Tzuras HaBayis* argues persuasively that this cannot be *Rashi's* meaning. [*Tosafos Yom Tov's* extreme concern to prove this point, which is evinced by the detailed and wide-ranging arguments which he offers, must be understood against the historic background of the times. Apparently this question was central to the religious polemic of the Middle Ages. Religions which posited that a Messiah had already come were forced to interpret Yechezkel's visions as referring to some other-wordly state,

ל יְהוָה׃ וְאֵלֶּה תּוֹצְאֹת הָעִיר מִפְּאַת
צָפוֹן חֲמֵשׁ מֵאוֹת וְאַרְבַּעַת אֲלָפִים מִדָּה׃
לא וְשַׁעֲרֵי הָעִיר עַל־שְׁמוֹת שִׁבְטֵי יִשְׂרָאֵל
שְׁעָרִים שְׁלוֹשָׁה צָפוֹנָה שַׁעַר רְאוּבֵן
אֶחָד שַׁעַר יְהוּדָה אֶחָד שַׁעַר לֵוִי אֶחָד׃
לב וְאֶל־פְּאַת קָדִימָה חֲמֵשׁ מֵאוֹת וְאַרְבַּעַת
אֲלָפִים וּשְׁעָרִים שְׁלֹשָׁה וְשַׁעַר יוֹסֵף
אֶחָד שַׁעַר בִּנְיָמִן אֶחָד שַׁעַר דָּן אֶחָד׃
לג וּפְאַת־נֶגְבָּה חֲמֵשׁ מֵאוֹת וְאַרְבַּעַת
אֲלָפִים מִדָּה וּשְׁעָרִים שְׁלֹשָׁה שַׁעַר
שִׁמְעוֹן אֶחָד שַׁעַר יִשָּׂשכָר אֶחָד שַׁעַר
לד זְבוּלֻן אֶחָד׃ פְּאַת־יָמָּה חֲמֵשׁ מֵאוֹת
וְאַרְבַּעַת אֲלָפִים שַׁעֲרֵיהֶם שְׁלֹשָׁה שַׁעַר
גָּד אֶחָד שַׁעַר אָשֵׁר אֶחָד שַׁעַר נַפְתָּלִי

We suggest that walls and gates have opposing functions. The walls enclose and protect; the gates permit egress and open the enclosed area to the world.

We are told the dimensions of the surrounding walls because it is the wall which makes the sanctity within the city viable [cf. קְלָטוּהוּ מְחִיצוֹת, *the walls have contained it,* in connection with the sanctity of Jerusalem relative to מַעֲשֵׂר שֵׁנִי, *the tithe that had to be eaten in Jerusalem (see Maccos* 20a)]. These walls bound the area in which the peak of mankind's aspirations will be attained.

We are also told that these walls have gates. The ecstasy of this immediate proximity to God must not remain within the city. Twelve exits are provided — one for each of Israel's twelve tribes. This is no coincidence.

Our Sages teach that these are twelve 'gates' to heaven, one for each of Israel's tribes, so that each with its particular and unique genius can approach God in a way fitting to its people (see *Magen Avraham, Orach Chayim* 68). These twelve heavenly gates are the self-same gates which are to lead out of this city of God. (*Maggid of Mezerich* in *Likutei Amarim;* See a detailed discussion in Introduction to Levant's *Shaar HaKollel.)* Each tribe according to its own nature will spread the experiences of the

since obviously they had not been realized on a physical level (see *Abarbanel).* Because of this it was of vital importance for Jewish commentators to demonstrate that, on the contrary, a real physical city was meant.] *Rashi* would be contradicting himself from his glosses to *Succah* 45b, where he writes: [This verse can teach us what is to be in the World to Come because] although this verse deals with the future Jerusalem [that is, the earthly city], it can at the same time teach me this: [for it implies that] wherever the *Shechinah* is, It will be surrounded by 18,000 — which are the righteous ones ...

Tosafos Yom Tov makes a number of suggestions for harmoninzing the two statements of *Rashi* with one another. The interested reader is directed to *Tzuras HaBayis* for a wide-ranging discussion.

[30] *Now these are the exits of the city, on the*
northern side, of four thousand five hundred
measures. [31] *And the gates of the city shall be ac-*
cording to the names of the tribes of Israel, three
gates to the north: the gate of Reuben — one; the gate
of Judah — one; the gate of Levi — one. [32] *And to the*
eastern end of four thousand and five hundred, with
three gates: Now the gate of Joseph — one; the gate
of Benjamin — one; the gate of Dan — one. [33] *And on*
the southern end of four thousand and five hundred
measures, with three gates: the gate of Simeon — one;
the gate of Issachar — one; the gate of Zebulun —
one. [34] *At the western end of four thousand and five*
hundred, their gates being three: the gate of Gad —
one; the gate of Asher — one; the gate of Naftali —
one.

city abroad.

This is the extent of what we may know about this Jerusalem of the future. There will be walls enclosing an area of sanctity which goes beyond anything we can conceptualize; but there will also be gates, means of allowing the whole land, perhaps the whole world, to bask in the light of God's Presence.

30. וְאֵלֶּה תּוֹצְאֹת הָעִיר — *Now these are the exits of the city.*

תּוֹצְאֹת stems from the root יצא, *to leave.* Gates have a dual function. They allow one to enter and to leave. It seems significant that these gates are described specifically as means of leaving the city. See *comm.* 30-35.

מִפְּאַת צָפוֹן חֲמֵשׁ מֵאוֹת ... — *On the northern side of five hundred ...*

Since we already know the dimensions of the city, the meaning of this phrase must be: *From the north side [where the measure is] five hundred ... (Metzudos).* We have attempted to convey this in the translation.

31. We learn in *Bava Basra* 122a: The division [of the land] in this world (Joshua's division) is not the same as that of the World to Come (Yechezkel's division). In this world a man may have a field for growing grain but may not have an orchard; he may have an orchard but no field. But in the World to Come there will not be anyone whose property does not extend over hills, valleys, and ravines; as it is written: *The gate of Reuben — one; the gate of Judah — one; the gate of Levi — one* [meaning that every tribal portion had all the combined characteristics of all the other portions.] This passage gave rise to those opinions (see *comm.* 44:28) that in the division of the future Levi (who is mentioned in our verse) is to receive a portion. However, the Levites did not, in fact, receive any of the thirteen strips of land described in our chapter and were only given part of the Sacred *Terumah,* which, as we have seen, was carved out of the *nassi's* portion.

Moreover, although the Talmud cites our verse to prove a point regarding the division of the land, it really has no bearing on the division, but deals exclusively with the gates leading out of the city.

לה אֶחָד׃ סָבִיב שְׁמֹנָה עָשָׂר אָלֶף וְשֵׁם־הָעִיר
מִיּוֹם יהוה | שָׁמָּה׃

Ran, cited in *Shitah Mekubetzes* to *Bava Basra* 122a, raises these questions (*comm.* 44:28). In his view, Levi did not receive a portion of the land, and the Talmud knows full well that our verse has no bearing on the issue of division of the land. Rather, the Sages derive this teaching in the apparently redundant word אֶחָד, *one*, repeated in connection with each of the twelve tribes. It implies that in addition to the gates, there was something else which they all had in common. That is assumed to be the topography of their various portions.

Because of these difficulties, *Rashash* (ad. loc.) suggests a different reading for the Gemara (*comm.* 44:28). The source for the Talmud's assertion that all the tribes were to have similar portions was, indeed, the word *one* — but not the *one* which is repeated in our verses. It is the *one* which is repeated for each of the twelve tribes in the earlier parts of the chapter, where the disposition of the thirteen strips is described.

35. It would seem unnecessary to give the measurement for the perimeter since that can be obtained simply by adding the four sides, given in verses 30-34. These superfluous words provided the Sages (*Succah* 45b; *Sanhedrin* 97b) with an insight into the special nature of the city, as discussed in *comm.* 30-35.

Tosafos Yom Tov (Tzuras HaBayis) suggests that the number 18,000 is given to allude to the 18,000 עוֹלָמוֹת, *worlds*, which, according to *Avodah*

35 *Round about [there shall be] eighteen thousand. And the name of the city from that day — HASHEM-is-there!*

Zarah 3b, are the total number of worlds under God's protection. (See *Maharal, Chiddushei Aggadah* there.) Again we have the lesson taught that this city is no ordinary one. Its tangible dimensions and location are only a small part of its true significance.

וְשֵׁם הָעִיר מִיּוֹם ה׳ שָׁמָּה — *And the name of the city, from that day, will be HASHEM-is-there.*

The phrase is obscure. *Rashi* quotes *Targum* and interprets his rendering: *The name of the city [— Jerusalem — will be the same as it was] from the day that HASHEM [first] appeared there.*

However, *Rashi* then offers the interpretation which most commentators prefer: From the day that this new city will be built up, its name is to be ה׳ שָׁמָּה, *HASHEM-is-there.*

Bava Basra 75b teaches that we should not read ה׳ שָׁמָּה, *HASHEM is there,* but ה׳ שְׁמָהּ, *its name is HASHEM.* (See pref., ch. 22, for detailed discussion.)

The essence of the new city — the rebuilt Jerusalem — is to be a total identification with all that is holy. A bond will have been forged between God and His people which will be pemanent. The *Merkavah,* that symbol of the 'mobility' of the *Shechinah* (see pref. ch. 1) will have finally come to rest. No more will God demonstrate His love by accompanying Israel into exile. He will remain firmly ensconced in the hearts of the people — the dwellers of the city, *HASHEM-is-there.*

APPENDIX I

The House of Yoshiyahu

The Identity of Zidkiyahu

We identify Zidkiyahu as a son of Yoshiyahu, and brother of Yehoachaz and Yehoyakim in accordance with *Horios* 11b, and *Kerisus* 5b. Although the Sages *(ibid.)* offer solutions to some of the problems posed by this identification, certain difficulties remain unanswered. Many commentators suggest identifications which, to a greater or lesser degree, differ from the Talmudic tradition. [See *Radak* to *II Kings* 23:30 for *Ibn Ezra's* and his own ideas, and *Abarbanel* to *II Kings* 24.]

We shall attempt to trace the thinking of the Sages, and to remove the seeming difficulties.

That King Zidkiyahu was a son of Yoshiyahu and not of Yehoyachin (whom he succeeded, and who, in fact did have a son, named Zidkiyahu — see I *Chron.* 3:16) is based on *II Kings* 24:17, where Zidkiyahu is called a דּוֹד, *an uncle,* of Yehoyachin. It is thus established that he was Yoshiyahu's son.

[However, *Abarbanel* ad. loc, suggests that the correct translation may be *'a friend'* (as דוד is always translated in Shir haShirim) i.e., Nebuchadnezzar appointed his (Nebuchadnezzar's) friend Zidkiyahu king.]

We thus have the following sequence for the last four kings of Judah:

1. Yehoachaz, son of Yoshiyahu *(II Kings* 23:30)
2. Yehoyakim, son of Yoshiyahu (23:34)
3. Yehoyachin, son of Yehoyakim and grandson of Yoshiyahu (24:6)
4. Zidkiyahu, uncle of Yehoyachin and son of Yoshiyahu (24:17).

The Unknown Shalum

A problem arises out of Jeremiah's prophecy *(Jeremiah* 22) in which he addresses three kings. The first is *'Shalum the son of Yoshiyahu ... who rules in the place of Yoshiyahu, his father' (v.* 11). The second is *Yehoyakim (v.* 18), and the third is Knoyahu (an obvious variant of Yehoyachin) *(v.* 24). Who is this *Shalum* of whom no mention is made in the book of *Kings?* The Sages *(Horios* loc. cit.) seem to address themselves to this problem in their interpretation to *I Chronicles* 3:15. That verse reads: *And the sons of Yoshiyahu: the first born, Yochanan; the second, Yehoyakim; the third Zidkiyahu; the fourth Shalum:*

Rabbi Yochanan taught: Yochanan is identical to Yehoachaz. He is called הַבְּכוֹר, *the first born* because he was the first to rule although he was, in fact younger than Yehoyakim [as evidenced by *II Kings* 23:31 and 36]. Zidkiyahu and Shalum are one and the same person. He is described as both the third and the fourth son because although he was the third of Yoshiyahu's sons, he was the fourth king after his father (since Yehoyachin the grandson of Yoshiyahu preceded him as king). Zidkiyahu is called Shalum either because he was 'perfect in his deeds' [שָׁלֵם=שָׁלוֹם, *perfect*] or, because 'the Davidic monarchy ceased in his days' [שָׁלֵם=שָׁלוֹם, *completed.*]

It would thus appear that the Shalum of *Jeremiah* 22, is, in fact, Zidkiyahu.

On the surface this seems to be the Talmudic tradition. However it leaves several problems:

1. It is at variance with the simple meaning of the verse in *Chronicles.*
2. The verse in *Jeremiah* 22:11: *'Shalum, the son of Yoshiyahu ... who rules in the place of Yoshiyahu, his father,'* implies that Shalum succeeded Yoshiyahu immediately after the latter's death. Surely this would equate Shalum with Yehoachaz, not with Zidkiyahu.

[If Shalum can be identified with Yehoachaz, then the sequence in the chapter would be eminently logical. The kings would be addressed in chronological sequence of their reigns: first Yehoachaz, then Yehoyakim,

then Yehoyachin. But if Shalum is Zidkiyahu then he is mentioned out of order.]

3. In *II Chronicles* 36:10, Zidkiyahu seems to be described as a brother of Yehoyachin rather than an uncle. (But see *Pseudo-Rashi* and *Metzudas David* ad. loc.).

Two Identities

We suggest that the Shalum of *Jeremiah* is, in fact, Yehoachaz. (But see *Rashi* and *Metzudas David* ad. loc.). Rabbi Yochanan's identification of Shalum with Zidkiyahu refers only to the Shalum mentioned in *Chronicles.*

According to *Vayikrah Rabbah* 1:3, *Chronicles* occupies a unique place in Scripture. Whereas in the rest of Scripture, דְּרָשָׁה, *the Aggadaic exegesis,* may never displace פְּשַׁט, *the simple meaning* (אֵין מִקְרָא יוֹצֵא מִידֵי פְּשׁוּטוֹ), *Chronicles* has no simple meaning in the usual sense of the word. The exegesis is always preeminent. [See *Rabbi Zvi Hirsch Chayes,* in *Mavoh Hatalmud Ch.* 22 for an analysis and elaboration of this concept.] Because of this rule, we need not be surprised to find an interpretation which cannot be justified according to normal interpretational usage.

The sequence in which the *'four'* sons of Yoshiyahu are listed in *Chronicles,* [with Shalum given last] could follow either chronological order, or the order in which they reigned. Neither of these criteria would permit the identification of Shalum with Yehoachaz. He was the first to reign, and he was older than Zidkiyahu. For this reason, Rabbi Yochanan preferred to identify Yehoachaz with the Yochanan of *Chronicles,* and to assume that the sequence was determined by the order in which they reigned.

This, however, would leave Shalum unidentified. [He could not be a son who never became king, because Jeremiah refers to Yehoachaz by the name Shalum (see above), and Yoshiyahu would not have had two sons with the same name.] Because of this difficulty (and licensed by the special character of *Chronicles)* Rabbi Yochanan explains that the Shalum mentioned there is not a fourth son at all, but that the name is added in order to lend an added dimension to the personality of Zidkiyahu, to indicate either his perfect righteousness or the tragic end of the Davidic dynasty which occurred in his days.

Why the Double Identity?

[It is not impossible that Zidkiyahu is pictured as 'two' people, in order to underline the essential duality of his character. Scripture describes him as a רָשָׁע, a wicked person (See especially (21:30), while the Sages teach that he was an entirely righteous man. (See *Overview*). We must deal with both aspects in order to understand all that we are taught about this king, and for this reason he is projected as two people.

Perhaps he is presented as 'two' people, for another reason. According to *II Kings* 24:17, it was Nebuchadnezzar who changed his name to Zidkiyahu. According to the Sages (loc. cit.) the purpose was to drive home the seriousness of the oath of loyalty which Nebuchadnezzar had exacted from him (see *comm.* to 17). Thus the name Zidkiyahu projects the Babylonian view of the king while Shalum teaches his significance from the Jewish standpoint.]

The Tradition of the Sages

Finally, *II Chronicles* 36:10 where Zidkiyahu is called Yehoyachin's 'brother', bears out the Sages' tradition. While we do find the word אָח used in the wider sense of *'relative'* (specifically for nephews: *Gen.* 14:16, 29:12; and *Lev.* 10:4), it is never used to describe a son. If Zidkiyahu the king, was Yehoyachin's son (based on *I Chronicles* 3:16) he would not have been called his *'brother'*. However, for an uncle the term is appropriate.

For the reader's convenience, we cite the Scriptural passages relevant to the above discussion:

II Kings 23:30-36.

וַיַּרְכִּבֻהוּ עֲבָדָיו מֵת מִמְּגִדּוֹ וַיְבִאֻהוּ יְרוּשָׁלַם
וַיִּקְבְּרֻהוּ בִּקְבֻרָתוֹ וַיִּקַּח עַם הָאָרֶץ אֶת יְהוֹאָחָז
בֶּן יֹאשִׁיָּהוּ וַיִּמְשְׁחוּ אֹתוֹ וַיַּמְלִיכוּ אֹתוֹ תַּחַת
אָבִיו. בֶּן עֶשְׂרִים וְשָׁלֹשׁ שָׁנָה יְהוֹאָחָז בְּמָלְכוֹ
וּשְׁלֹשָׁה חֳדָשִׁים מָלַךְ בִּירוּשָׁלָם וְשֵׁם אִמּוֹ
חֲמוּטַל בַּת יִרְמְיָהוּ מִלִּבְנָה. וַיַּעַשׂ הָרַע בְּעֵינֵי
יהוה כְּכֹל אֲשֶׁר עָשׂוּ אֲבֹתָיו. וַיַּאַסְרֵהוּ פַרְעֹה
נְכֹה בְרִבְלָה בְּאֶרֶץ חֲמָת בִּמְלֹךְ בִּירוּשָׁלָם וַיִּתֶּן
עֹנֶשׁ עַל הָאָרֶץ מֵאָה כִכַּר כֶּסֶף וְכִכַּר זָהָב.

וַיַּמְלֵךְ פַּרְעֹה נְכֹה אֶת אֶלְיָקִים בֶּן יֹאשִׁיָּהוּ תַּחַת יֹאשִׁיָּהוּ אָבִיו וַיַּסֵּב אֶת שְׁמוֹ יְהוֹיָקִים וְאֶת יְהוֹאָחָז לָקָח וַיָּבֹא מִצְרַיִם וַיָּמָת שָׁם. וְהַכֶּסֶף וְהַזָּהָב נָתַן יְהוֹיָקִים לְפַרְעֹה אַךְ הֶעֱרִיךְ אֶת הָאָרֶץ לָתֵת אֶת הַכֶּסֶף עַל פִּי פַרְעֹה אִישׁ כְּעֶרְכּוֹ נָגַשׂ אֶת הַכֶּסֶף וְאֶת הַזָּהָב אֶת עַם הָאָרֶץ לָתֵת לְפַרְעֹה נְכֹה. בֶּן עֶשְׂרִים וְחָמֵשׁ שָׁנָה יְהוֹיָקִים בְּמָלְכוֹ וְאַחַת עֶשְׂרֵה שָׁנָה מָלַךְ בִּירוּשָׁלָם וְשֵׁם אִמּוֹ זְבִידָּה בַת פְּדָיָה מִן רוּמָה.

Ibid. 24:6

וַיִּשְׁכַּב יְהוֹיָקִים עִם אֲבֹתָיו וַיִּמְלֹךְ יְהוֹיָכִין בְּנוֹ תַּחְתָּיו.

Ibid. 24:17

וַיַּמְלֵךְ מֶלֶךְ בָּבֶל אֶת מַתַּנְיָה דֹדוֹ תַּחְתָּיו וַיַּסֵּב אֶת שְׁמוֹ צִדְקִיָּהוּ.

Jeremiah 22:11

כִּי כֹה אָמַר ה׳ אֶל שַׁלֻּם בֶּן יֹאשִׁיָּהוּ מֶלֶךְ יְהוּדָה הַמֹּלֵךְ תַּחַת יֹאשִׁיָּהוּ אָבִיו אֲשֶׁר יָצָא מִן הַמָּקוֹם הַזֶּה לֹא יָשׁוּב שָׁם עוֹד.

Ibid. 22:18

לָכֵן כֹּה אָמַר ה׳ אֶל יְהוֹיָקִים בֶּן יֹאשִׁיָּהוּ מֶלֶךְ יְהוּדָה לֹא יִסְפְּדוּ לוֹ הוֹי אָחִי וְהוֹי אָחוֹת לֹא יִסְפְּדוּ לוֹ הוֹי אָדוֹן וְהוֹי הֹדֹה.

Ibid. 22:24

חַי אָנִי נְאֻם יהוה כִּי אִם יִהְיֶה כָּנְיָהוּ בֶּן יְהוֹיָקִים מֶלֶךְ יְהוּדָה חוֹתָם עַל יַד יְמִינִי כִּי מִשָּׁם אֶתְּקֶנְךָּ.

I Chronicles 3:15-16

וּבְנֵי יֹאשִׁיָּהוּ הַבְּכוֹר יוֹחָנָן הַשֵּׁנִי יְהוֹיָקִים הַשְּׁלִשִׁי צִדְקִיָּהוּ הָרְבִיעִי שַׁלּוּם. וּבְנֵי יְהוֹיָקִים יְכָנְיָה בְנוֹ צִדְקִיָּה בְנוֹ.

II Chronicles 36:9-10

בֶּן שְׁמוֹנֶה שָׁנִים יְהוֹיָכִין בְּמָלְכוֹ וּשְׁלֹשָׁה חֳדָשִׁים וַעֲשֶׂרֶת יָמִים מָלַךְ בִּירוּשָׁלָם וַיַּעַשׂ הָרַע בְּעֵינֵי ה׳. וְלִתְשׁוּבַת הַשָּׁנָה שָׁלַח הַמֶּלֶךְ נְבוּכַדְנֶאצַּר וַיְבִאֵהוּ בָבֶלָה עִם כְּלֵי חֶמְדַּת בֵּית יהוה וַיַּמְלֵךְ אֶת צִדְקִיָּהוּ אָחִיו עַל יְהוּדָה וִירוּשָׁלָם.

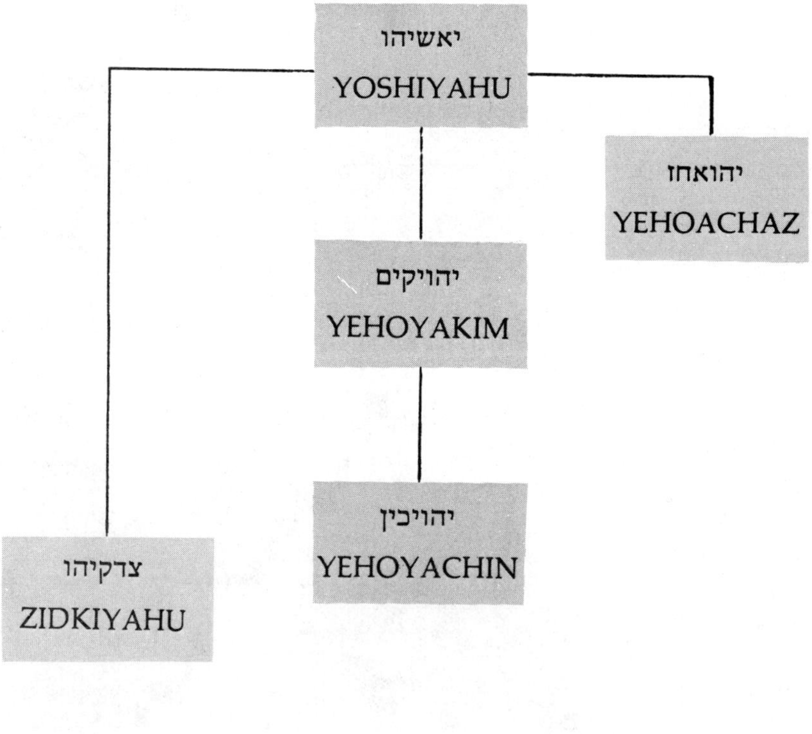

APPENDIX II

The Jewish Monarchy / A Time Line

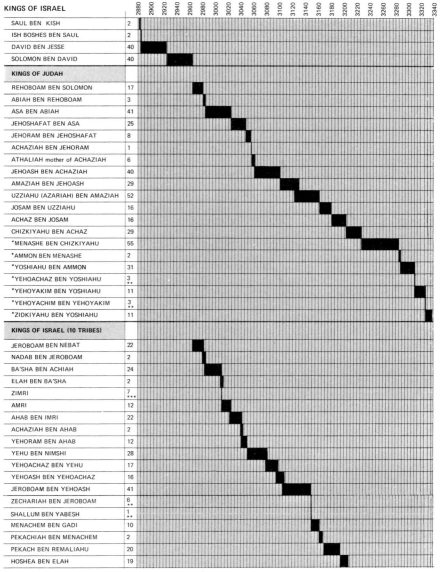

KINGS OF ISRAEL	
SAUL BEN KISH	2
ISH BOSHES BEN SAUL	2
DAVID BEN JESSE	40
SOLOMON BEN DAVID	40
KINGS OF JUDAH	
REHOBOAM BEN SOLOMON	17
ABIAH BEN REHOBOAM	3
ASA BEN ABIAH	41
JEHOSHAFAT BEN ASA	25
JEHORAM BEN JEHOSHAFAT	8
ACHAZIAH BEN JEHORAM	1
ATHALIAH mother of ACHAZIAH	6
JEHOASH BEN ACHAZIAH	40
AMAZIAH BEN JEHOASH	29
UZZIAHU (AZARIAH) BEN AMAZIAH	52
JOSAM BEN UZZIAHU	16
ACHAZ BEN JOSAM	16
CHIZKIYAHU BEN ACHAZ	29
*MENASHE BEN CHIZKIYAHU	55
*AMMON BEN MENASHE	2
*YOSHIAHU BEN AMMON	31
*YEHOACHAZ BEN YOSHIAHU	3 **
*YEHOYAKIM BEN YOSHIAHU	11
*YEHOYACHIM BEN YEHOYAKIM	3 **
*ZIDKIYAHU BEN YOSHIAHU	11
KINGS OF ISRAEL (10 TRIBES)	
JEROBOAM BEN NEBAT	22
NADAB BEN JEROBOAM	2
BA'SHA BEN ACHIAH	24
ELAH BEN BA'SHA	2
ZIMRI	7 ***
AMRI	12
AHAB BEN IMRI	22
ACHAZIAH BEN AHAB	2
YEHORAM BEN AHAB	12
YEHU BEN NIMSHI	28
YEHOACHAZ BEN YEHU	17
YEHOASH BEN YEHOACHAZ	16
JEROBOAM BEN YEHOASH	41
ZECHARIAH BEN JEROBOAM	6 **
SHALLUM BEN YABESH	1 **
MENACHEM BEN GADI	10
PEKACHIAH BEN MENACHEM	2
PEKACH BEN REMALIAHU	20
HOSHEA BEN ELAH	19

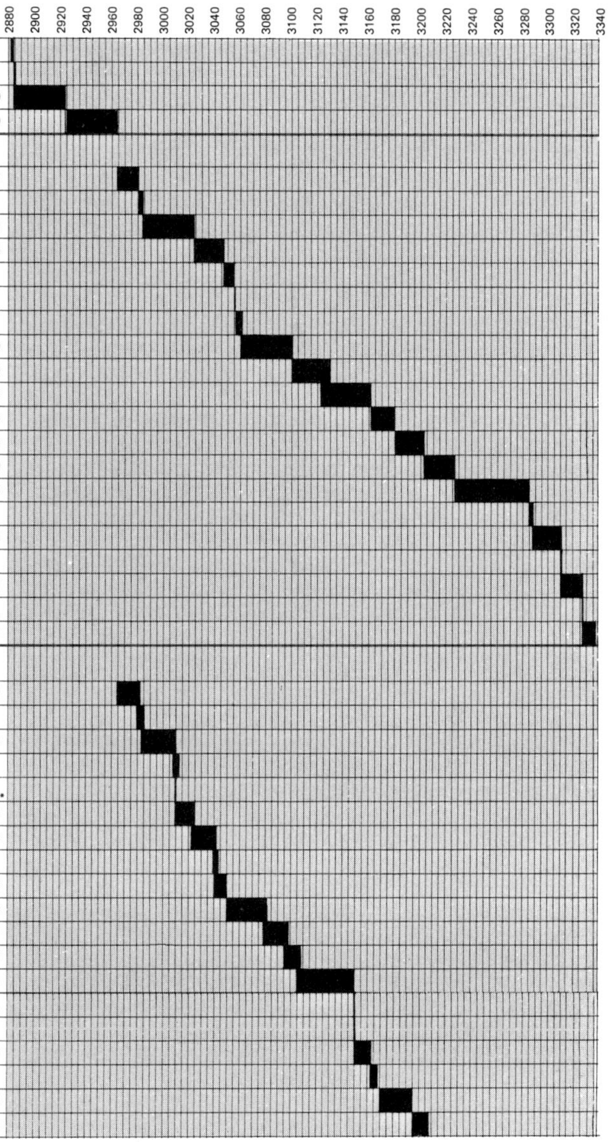

* The reigns of these kings are discussed in "Twilight of Monarchy", page lxii   ** Months   *** Days

APPENDIX III
Suffering of the Zaddik

The Mercy in Atonement

In *comm.* to 4:4 an attempt was made to explain how Yechezkel's suffering might serve to atone for the sins of his people. The thesis was advanced that the sight of the *Zaddik*'s agony, for which the people had been the cause, might inspire them to true repentance.

While this may be true, a careful analysis of the sources yields a more comprehensive picture.

Sanhedrin 39a relates that a מִין, *heretic,* said to Rabbi Abuha: 'Your God is a גַחֲכָן, *prankster,* in that he made Yechezkel lie on his left side and on his right side.'

The heretic saw the bizarre nature of these symbolic acts, as an opportunity to mock the Jewish belief in a wise and just God. The *Talmud* continues that just then a student came to Rabbi Abuha and asked him to explain the significance of the law of שְׁמִיטָה, the obligation to let fields lie fallow every seven years. Rabbi Abuha said: 'I will answer you both together. God commanded Israel to let its fields lie fallow every seventh year so that they should recognize that the earth is His. They did not do so and were driven into exile. When a country rebels against a mortal king, he will kill them all if he is cruel to them; if he is merciful he will kill half of them; if he is filled with mercy, he will cause the great ones among them to suffer. So also the Holy One, blessed be He, chastised Yechezkel in order to wipe out the sins of Israel.'

Communal Responsibility

The idea that the *Zaddik* suffers *in lieu* of the death of all or part of the community, is elaborated upon in *Sefer Chassidim* [ed. *Meikizei Nirdamim,* Berlin 1891] 115. The passage begins with a discussion of the communal responsibility which rests on the entire Jewish nation: כָּל יִשְׂרָאֵל עֲרֵבִים זֶה בָּזֶה, *All Israel are responsible one for another.* The sin of one is the sin of all. Thus, in his confession on *Yom Kippur,* the High Priest declares, 'I have sinned together with all Israel.' He says this whether or not he personally has sinned. This is in order that people come to feel a sense of love and responsibility for one another and learn to rebuke one another.

The Zaddik as Representative

Sefer Chassidim then cites Yechezkel's suffering as described in chapter 4, remarking: 'For this is [the way] before God. When something is decreed and they do not repent then punishment must come. Now if the *zaddik* is made to suffer, then הֲרֵי מִתְקַיְּים הַפּוּרְעָנוּת עָלָיו *that punishment has been borne by him.* Evil had been decreed in the sinful days of Menashe and Yehoyakim, but the people had merely been exiled — they had not suffered harsh physical punishment. The Attribute of Justice (מִדַּת הַדִּין) argued, 'Why should they be treated so leniently?' So God said to Yechezkel: 'Accept the suffering upon yourself so that the Attribute of Justice should not have a legitimate claim, for when he sees the suffering of the *Zaddik* who does not deserve to be punished, he will not press his claim.'

Thus, according to *Sefer Chassidim,* God's Attribute of Justice seeks a punishment for the entire community, *but is satisfied* when it is meted out only to the *Zaddik.*

The Oneness of Israel

To understand this concept we must once more revert to the idea which we have discussed throughout the commentary: the essential oneness of *Knesses Israel* (see *footnotes* to 3:18; 9:4; 14:12; 18:2). While every individual is created in the *'image of God'* and is in himself an עוֹלָם קָטָן, a *miniature world,* God's justice can nevertheless address Itself to the community of Israel (צִבּוּר), as a whole. [In the above mentioned places we examined this idea as it applied to the obligation of each individual to rebuke evildoers as part of his communal responsibility; to the situation where the 'innocent' are punished together with the guilty; to the ability of a righteous person to save the entire community in his merit; and to the possibility of a later generation being punished for the sins of an earlier one.]

Shared Guilt

When the entire community is considered an indivisible unit, then indeed every individual shares guilt for the sins of every other one. [See *Maharal Sanhedrin* loc. cit.: 'Although the Zaddik cannot be said to have sinned as an individual, nevertheless he can be said to have sinned as a part of the community'.] And by the same token the suffering of the one, can be seen as a suffering of the whole. [See *Maharal* loc. cit.: 'A merciful king punishes the great ones who are the צוּרָה, *form,* of the community, its worthiest part which is tantamount to the whole'. See also *Mesilas Yesharim* Ch. 4 who, in discussing the tension between God's Justice and His Mercy, mentions the possibility of Mercy tempering Justice to the extent that a 'partial' payment (i.e. punishment) may be accepted in lieu of the full severity of the appropriate chastisement.]

Thus Yechezkel 'atones' for his people, because the communal guilt is assuaged by the pain suffered *by the community* through one of its indivisible components.

The Seventh Year

The oneness of *Knesses Israel* upon which these concepts are predicated, exists only because of its essential holiness. It is 'one' because of its communal 'soul' which forges unity out of its many members. The law of the Seventh Year is crucial in fostering this perception because it teaches that even the ground is God's: if even the inanimate land must express its holiness as part of His creation, then surely live creatures have an essence of holiness (*Maharal* ad. loc.). A people who had forgotten the lessons of the 'seven year' cycle; who had forgotten that the land is His, and had seen themselves forsaken by God (8:12), would have had no understanding for this truth. Thus the explanation of the *Shemitah* law, and that of Yechezkel's suffering are essentially one, and were combined by Rabbi Abuha (see *Overview*).

APPENDIX IV

Similarities between Leviticus and Ezekiel

The following list is taken from *Rabbi David Zvi Hoffman's* commentary to *Lev. (Vol. II* p. 245-6, Hebrew ed. It is a compilation of the expressions of blessing and curse which the prophecies of Yechezkel draw from the Admonition of *Lev.* 26.

יחזקאל:	ויקרא כו:
וכרתי להם ברית שלום והשבתי חיה רעה מן הארץ (לד, כה).	ונתתי שלום בארץ . . . והשבתי חיה רעה מן הארץ (ו; השוה גם הושע ב, כ; במדבר כה, יב).
וישבו במדבר לבטח (לד, כה).	וישבתם לבטח בארצכם (ה).
והיו על אדמתם לבטח (לד, כז).	
וישבו לבטח ואין מחריד (לד, כח).	ושכבתם ואין מחריד (ו).
והורדתי הגשם בעתו (לד, כו).	ונתתי גשמיכם בעתם (ד).
ונתן עץ השדה את פריו והארץ תתן יבולה (לד ,כז).	ונתנה הארץ יבולה ועץ השדה יתן פריו (ד).
בשברי את מטות עֻלם (לד, כז).	ואשבור מטת עלכם (יג).
והצלתים מיד העבדים בהם (לד ,כז).	מהית להם עבדים (יג).
ואני ה׳ אהיה להם לאלהים (לד, כד).	והייתי לכם לאלהים (יב).
אני ה׳ אלהיהם (לד ,ל).	אני ה׳ אלהיכם (יג).
והמה עמי (לד ,ל).	ואתם תהיו לי לעם (יב).
בחקתי לכו ואת משפטי שמרו ועשו אותם (כ, יט).	אם בחקתי תלכו ואת מצותי תשמרו ועשיתם אתם (ג).
ופניתי אליכם . . . והרביתי (לו, ט־י).	ופניתי אליכם . . . והרביתי אתכם (ט).
חרב תעבר בארץ (יד, יז).	וחרב לא תעבר בארצכם (ו).
ונתתי את מקדשי בתוכם . . . משכני (לז,כו־כז).	ונתתי משכני בתוככם (יא).
הנני שבר מטה לחם . . . ואכלו לחם במשקל (ד, טז) (ה, טז) (יד, יג).	בשברי לכם מטה לחם . . . והשיבו לחמכם במשקל (כו).
ונמקו בעונם (ד, יז ועוד).	ימקו בעונם (לט).
ושלחתי . . . וחיה רעה ושכלך (ה, יז) (יד, טו).	והשלחתי . . . חית השדה ושכלה אתכם (כב).
והכרתי . . . ובהמה (יד, יג,יז).	והכריתה את בהמתכם (כב).
אני מביא עליכם חרב (ו, ג) (ה, יז) (יד, יז) (לג, ב).	והבאתי עליכם חרב (כה).
ואבדתי במותיכם ונשמו מזבחותיכם ונשברו חמניכם . . . ונתתי את פגרי . . . לפני גלוליהם (ו, ג־ה).	והשמדתי את במתיכם והכרתי את חמניכם ונתתי את פגריכם על פגרי גלוליכם (ל).
הערים תחרבנה והבמות תישמנה (ו, ו).	ונתתי את עריכם חרבה והשמותי את מקדשיכם (לא).
מעלו אשר מעל בי (יז, כ).	במעלם אשר מעלו בי (מ).
יען וביען (יג, י).	יען וביען (מג).
וחקותי מאסו (כ, כד).	ואם בחקתי תמאסו (טו).
ונתתי את הארץ שממה (לג, כח) (לה, ד).	והיתה ארצכם שממה (לג).
ונשבת גאון עזה (לג, כח) (ז, כד) (כד, כא).	ושברתי את גאון עזכם (יט).
מארצות איביהם (לט, כז).	בארצות איביהם (לו).
הפר את בריתו (יז, טז,יח־יט).	להפרכם את בריתי (טו).

APPENDIX V—
Hebrew Verb Patterns

Hebrew verb-patterns differ considerably from their English counterparts.

The main characteristic of the Hebrew verb is that inflections for *person* (I, you, he, ...), *tense* (past, present, and future) or *voice* (passive, causative, reflexive, ...) are indicated by the verb's vocalization and by prefixes and suffixes appended to the basic, three-letter root-word, rather than by additional words as is the case in English.

For example, the verb 'to wash' would, in English, be inflected for voice, by saying: he *was* washed (passive); he *caused* someone to be washed (causative); he washed *himself* (reflexive).

In Hebrew these inflections would be accomplished by slight changes in vocalization, and by adding different prefixes to the root-word רחץ, *to wash.* Thus: **נִרְחַץ** *(he was washed* — passive); **הִרְחִיץ** *(he caused someone to be washed* — causative); and **הִתְרַחֵץ** *(he washed himself* — reflexive).

Following, are the names of the seven voices of Hebrew grammar. [With the exception of קַל, *the simple form,* the names of the various voices are formed by taking the root-word פעל, *to act* (a word which is used to indicate that we deal with action-verbs) and changing it to accord with the particular voice which is being described.]

1. קַל, *the simple verb.* רָחַץ — He washed.

2. נִפְעַל, *passive of the* קַל. נִרְחַץ — He was washed.

3. פִּעֵל, *intensification of the* קַל. רִחֵץ — He cleansed (in the sense that he washed very thoroughly).

4. פֻּעַל, *passive of the* פִּעֵל. רֻחַץ — He was cleansed.

5. הִפְעִיל, *causative.* הִרְחִיץ — He bathed [someone] (i.e., he caused another to be washed).

6. הָפְעַל, *passive of* הִפְעִיל. הָרְחַץ — He was bathed.

7. הִתְפָּעֵל, *reflexive.* הִתְרַחֵץ — He washed himself.

There are, of course, many variations depending on tense, spelling and other factors. The above illustrations, however, serve to give a very basic understanding of the patterns which are referred to in the course of the commentary.

אציב בזה מצבת זכרון

להרב החסיד התמים

ר' חיים נחמן בן ר' משה ז"ל קובלסקי

שהלך לעולמו ביום כד' טבת תשל"ח

היה סמל חי לאמונה טהורה ולאהבת ישראל

ת נ צ ב ה

APPENDIX VI

We have translated the verse in *Deuteronomy* 28:63: *So HASHEM will rejoice over you* ... That is to say that we have treated the word יָשִׂישׂ which is in the *hiphil* (causative voice) [i.e., He will *cause* to rejoice] as though it were in the *kal* [i.e., He will rejoice]. This is in accordance with its usage throughout Scripture. (See *Isaiah* 62:5; *Zephaniah* 3:17; *Psalms* 19:6). [*Maharal* in *Gur Aryeh* to *Deuteronomy* ad. loc. explains that the *hiphil* is used even when the *kal* is meant, because joy is an emotion which a person brings upon himself. He allows himself to become aware of the happy situation and thereby opens himself up to joy.] This is also how the *Targum* (ad. loc.) translates (in contrast to *Targum Yonasan* – see below); and *Hirsch* and *Hoffman* whom we quoted in the comm. take the same view.

Rashi (based on *Megillah* 10b and *Sanhedrin* 39b) translates: *So I will cause your enemies to be happy* ... [see also *Targum Yonasan*].

The Talmud bases its interpretation on a theological consideration (God Himself is not happy when the wicked suffer) and proves it from a grammatical consideration (יָשִׂישׂ is in the *hiphil*. The *kal* would have had to read יָשׂוּשׂ).

The grammatical consideration is persuasive. Firstly because the beginning of the verse reads: כַּאֲשֶׁר שָׂשׂ ה׳, *as God rejoiced*, thus using the root שׂישׂ in the *kal*. We would have expected the end of the verse to parallel this usage. The use of the *hiphil* must be seen as an irregularity (see *Mizrachi* and *Gur Aryeh* ad. loc.) Secondly, in an almost identical formulation *Deuteronomy* 30:9 uses לָשׂוּשׂ (a gerund of the *kal*) in place of יָשִׂישׂ of our verse.

Nevertheless, great difficulties stand in the way of the assumption that the Sages meant their interpretation to be the simple meaning (פְּשָׁט) of the verse. Among them, if the verb is used transitively we would have expected the object (your enemies) to be mentioned. Furthermore, the introduction of an implied 'your enemies' does not fit smoothly into the context of the chapter.

Moreover the inner balance of the verse rejects the use of the causative: *As God rejoiced over you to benefit you ... so God will ... over you to make you lost,* requiring the translation *rejoice* rather than *cause to rejoice* in order to retain its inner logic.

It is therefore likely that the Sages did not offer their causative interpretation as the פְּשָׁט, the *simple meaning* of the sentence. Syntax and context demand the translation of the word in the *kal* (as in the rest of Scripture) and this presents no theological problem since it could well be that God is happy not at the destruction but at its results – the *Teshuvah* which it will bring about.

Nevertheless there is a jarring note in the verse because a literal translation of the words implies that God is happy with the actual destruction, which cannot be true because of the theological consideration. This is the problem to which the Sages address themselves and which they solve by showing that by its choice of words the Torah indicated that another translation (i.e., in the causative) is also hinted at in the text. And, *relative to the actual destruction,* the word is meant in that way; not that *God* rejoices, but that He causes the enemy to rejoice.

There are many analagous cases in which the Sages read certain meanings into Scripture because of grammatical considerations but did not mean to change the simple meaning of the verse, which must consider such aspects as syntax and context. One example among many is *Yevamos* 13b which proves that לֹא תִתְגֹּדְדוּ of *Deuteronomy* 14:1 includes the prohibition of having different halachic usages within one community (לֹא תַעֲשׂוּ אֲגוּדוֹת אֲגוּדוֹת) although the simple meaning remains the prohibition against wounding oneself in mourning for a dead person. (See *Rambam, Sefer Hamitzvos, Mitzvos Lo Sa'aseh* 45.)

We conclude that Scripture will occasionally introduce a grammatically irregular form in order to hint at something which is not explicated in the text, even though the actual simple meaning of the text remains unchanged.

APPENDIX VII

Contrast between standard printed text of *Rashi* and the text found in Biblical Ms.#82 in the Bodelian Library, Oxford, England.*

standard printed text

שלש ושלשים פעמים — ובית שני היו ל"ח. ט"ו בצפון וט"ו בדרום חמשה על חמשה וחמשה על גביהם. וח' במערב. הוא צלע הוא יציע הוא תא. ואומר אני שהתאים שבצפון ובדרום כך סדרן. שכל אחד ואחד ארכו י"ב אמה הרי ס' אמה לחמשה תאים. וה' כתלים של ה' ה' אמה הרי פ"ה. ורחב ה' אמות של המונח פירנסת ז' אמה של אורך הכותל. וכן לדרום. ושבמערב ח' ע"ג ח' ושלישי על גביהן. ואורכן על גביהן עשרים אמה כנגד רחב בית קדש הקדשים. הרי י"א בכל סדר. וכן ת"י חדא עסרי בסידרא.

ואשר מנח — ומקום פנוי היה מונח במקצעות הצפון והדרום שאצל המזרח והמערב שאין התאים מקיפין את כל הבית ולאותו מקום פנוי היו פתחי התאים שבמקצועות מזרחים כמו שאמור בענין ופתח הצלע למנח כי לא היו להם פתחים לתאים לא לצד החצר ולא לצד ההיכל אלא לאותן שבמקצוע מזרחית צפונית ומזרחית דרומית היה הפתח בכותל רחבו פתוח לאותו מקום המונח ובאותו פתח נכנסין לו וממנו לתא השני ומן השני אל השלישי וכן סביב שכן שנינו במסכת מדות שלש פתחים לכל אחד ואחד אחד לתא מן הימין ואחד לתא מן השמאל ואחד לתא שעל גביו ואף י"ת כן ואשר מונח ואתר שביק. ל' אחר ואשר מונח כלומר וכן אותן של צד פנים מן הצלעות לצד בית מונח מקום פנוי הָיה מונח בין התאים ובין הבית ובאותו מקום היו פתחי התאים כמו שמפרש בענין ופתח הצלע למונח ורחבו היה חמש אמות כמו שהוא אומר ורחב

manuscript text

(מא:ו) **שלש ושלשים פעמים** — צלע אל צלע. אחד עשר על גבי אחד עשר ואחד עשר על גביהן. כן תרגם יונתן. אחד עשר בסדרא. ובבית שני היו ל"ח. ט"ו בצפון וט"ו בדרום. חמשה על חמשה וחמשה על גביהן ושמנה במערב. הוא צלע. הוא יציע. הוא תא.

(מא:ט) **ואשר מנח** — מקום פנוי היה מונח במקצעות הצפון והדרום שאצל המזרח והמערב. שאין התאים מקיפין את כל הבית ולאותו מקום פנוי היו פתחי התאים שבמקצעות מזרחיים כמו שמפורש בענין ופתח הצלע למונח כי לא היו להם פתחים לתאים לא לצד ההיכל ולא לצד החצר אלא לאותן שבמקצוע מזרחית צפונית. ובמערבית דרומית היה פתח בכותל רחבו פתוח לאותו המונח ובאותו פתח נכנסין לו וממנו לתא השני ומן השני לשלישי. וכן סביב. שכן מצינו במסכת מדות שלשה לכל אחד ואחד. אחד לתא מהימין ואחד לתא מהשמאל ואחד לתא שעל גביו. ואף יונתן תרגם כן. ואשר מונח ואתר שביק.

* Published by Dr. Abraham J. Levy, Philadelphia, 1931.

manuscript text

standard printed text

מקום המונח חמש אמות כדפרישית לעיל שלא יהיו התאים סמוכים לבית כלל ואויר יהיה ביניהם והבית חמש אמות וכן ת"י ואתר שביק.

(מב:א) **ויבאני אל הלשכה אשר נגד** וגו' — אל אחת מהלשכות העומדות בצפון הבית המובדלות כ' אמה מן התאים. כמו שמוזכר למעלה. ובין הלשכות רחב עשרים אמה סביב לבית.

ויביאני אל הלשכה אשר נגד וגו' — אל אחת מהלשכות הראשונות אי נמי אל מקום הלשכות הם הלשכות העומדות בצפון הבית המובדלות עשרים אמה מן התאים כמ"ש למעלה ובין הלשכות רחב עשרים אמה סביב לבית ואין אדם יכול ליכנס לאותן לשכות ולא לאויר רחב העשרים שביניהם ובין התאים אלא דרך החצר החיצונה כמו שמפורש למטה בענין שהרי אמר שהחצר הפנימי מאה על מאה מרובע לפני הבית למזרח ואמר על רחב הבית לקדים מאה אמה נמלא רוחב הבית סותם את רוחב החצר הפנימית ואינו יכול ליכנס לפנים מצידי הלשכות לא לצפון ולא לדרום לכך הוצרך לבא לאותן הלשכות דרך החצר החיצונה הצפונית.

(מב:ו) **על כן נאצל** — תרגם יונתן דחיקן — ואני לא היה לי לא רב ולא עוזר לבנין הזה. אלא שהראוני מן השמים.

APPENDIX VIII

Alternative Diagram of Yechezkel's Temple

This diagram was drawn by the gaon R' Moshe Ivier (disciple of the Vilna Gaon) and appears in the Tosafos Yom Tov's *Tzuras HaBayis,* Grodno, 5548 (1788).

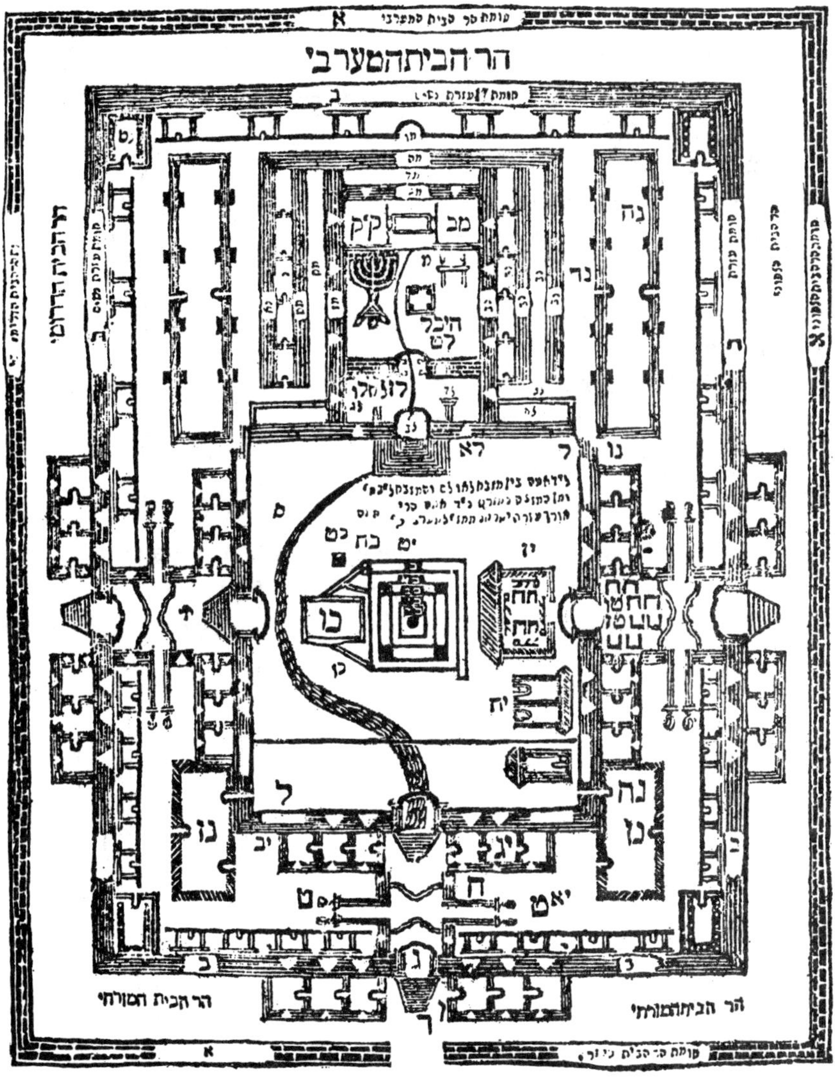

APPENDIX IX

Excerpts from *Rashi's* Responsum to the Rabbis of Auxerres which pertain to the Book of Ezekiel

בעשתי עשרה שנה באחד לחדש (כו:א) הואיל ולא פירש את החודש איזהו על כרחך הוא יום ראשון של שנה והחדש תשרי:

וששאל מאחר שכתב **צדקת הצדיק [לא תצילנו] ביום פשעו** (לג:יב) מהו שחזר וכתב וכפל בסוף המקרא **וצדיק לא יוכל לחיות בה ביום חטאתו?** בראש המקרא לא פירש מאיזה עונש לא תצילנה ולא הפורענות העתידה לבא עליו ופירש בסוף המקרא שהעונש עונש של מיתה:

וששאל **ויהי בשתי עשרה שנה בעשרי בחמשה לחדש לגלותנו** (לג:כא) מהו לגלותנו וכמה נשתהא ביאת הפליט אחר שהוכתה העיר ולאיזה חשבון מנה שתי עשרה? המקרא הזה מסורס הוא וכן פירושו ויהי (בעשתי) [בשתי] עשרה שנה לגלותנו בעשירי בחמשה לחדש ומהו לגלותנו הוא גלות יכניה שקדמה אחת עשרה שנה לחרבות ירושלים שגלה צדקיהו שהרי יחזקאל גלה עם החרש והמסגר שגלו עם יכניה כמו שנאמר בתחלת הספר שנדבר עמו בשנה החמישית לגלות המלך יהויכין ונגלה עליו בארץ כשדים על נהר כבר ועדיין היתה העיר קיימת וצדקיהו מלך בתוכה ובעשתי עשרה שנה לצדקיהו הוכתה העיר בתשעה באב משנת שתים עשרה לצדקיהו שהיא שנת שתים עשרה גם לגלות יהויכין בא הפליט שנה אחרי שהוכתה העיר ארבעה ימים, חשבון זה לא יכולתי לכוון:

וששאל לכן אחרי כן שכתב (לכם) **לכן רעים שמעו את דבר ה׳ חי אני** וכו׳ (לד:ז-ח) (לכם) **לכן הרעים שמעו** (לד:ט) (מה עונש אביא עליהם) בתחלה השמיעם על מה הוא כועס עליהם יען היות צאני לבז וכו׳ ולבסוף אמר **שמעו** מה עונש אביא עליהם **הנני אל הרועים... והשבתים** (לד:י) הנביא אין יכול לדבר אלא לפי רוח הקודש הנופלת בפיו:

כתוב בשאלתו **וימד משער אל שער מאה אמה** (מ:כג) והלא כבר מדד כל רחב עזרת נשים מזרח ומערב צפון ודרום כמו שכתוב למעלה **וימד רחב מלפני השער התחתונה לפני** (החיצונה והפנימית) **החצר הפנימי מחוץ מאה אמה הקדים והצפון** (מ:יט)? כאן לא דקדק חביבי בשאילתו והלא אין כתוב כאן הדרום והמערב אלא הקדים והצפון וכן היה לאחי לישאל והלא כבר מדד הקדים והצפון ולמה כשהוא עסוק בשער הצפון חזר ומדד משער עזרת הנשים אל שער עזרת הפנימית מאה אמה; ועוד תמיה חביבי על שכתב **ושער לחצר הפנימי נגד השער לצפון ולקדים** (מ:כג) וכי לא היה שער לפנימית אלא לצפון ולקדים? והלא אף לדרום כתוב לו בענין **השער הדרום** (מ:כח)? ועוד תמיה, עומד בחצר החיצונה ומונה שער הפנימית מכוונים כנגדם [מפני שעסוק היה בשערי החיצונה ופירש תפארת נוי שלהם ואף זו תפארתם שהיו שערי הפנימית] מכוונים כנגדם ואולם שער זה בולט בחצר כנגד שער אולם זה.

וששאל למה כפל וימד וימד בחלל הצפוני ומהו **ושער לחצר הפנימי** (וכו׳). **לצפון ולקדים** (מ:כג) והלא אף לדרום כן? יבין אחי בענין כשהראהו המלאך הכניסו בשער הקדים תחלה לתוך חצר החיצונה והראה לו שער הקדים ומדד רחב חצר החיצונה לקדים מאה אמה לחצר הפנימית ומשם סובב לצפון והראהו שער הצפון וכשבא להראותו שער הדרום לא הוליכו דרך המערב שהרי לא כתב רוח מערבית בכל בנין החצירות אלא החזירו על עקיביו כל רוח הצפון והקדים אל דרך הדרום לפיכך כשפירש הנביא מעשה שער הקדים של חיצונה והעיר על מדידת חלל רחב החצר פירש עמו את רחב הצפון והוסיף תיבה אחת בסוף המקרא וכתב הקדים והצפון לפי שמדידת הצפון היתה עם מדידת הקדים במהלך אחד קודם שהחזירו על עקיביו וכשחזר [ופירש את מעשה הצפון חזר והעיר על מדידת רחב חלל] צפוני של חצר החיצונה שהיא היתה שעת מדידתו

ובמדידה ראשונה לא מדד אלא לקדים ומה שכתוב כמדידה ראשונה [**הקדים והצפון**] לא שמדד לו רחב צפונית עם רחב הקדים אלא הנביא הוזקק להעיד על מדת הקדים ולפי שאף רחב חלל הצפון מדד לו באותו דרך עצמו קודם שהחזירו על עקיביו כתב הצפון אצל הקדים ומכל מקום לא מדדם יחד אלא כך היה הסדר, תחלה מדד שער הקדים ורחבו וגובהו ואח״כ רחב חלל החצר לקדים ואח״כ מדות שער הצפון בארכו ורחבו וגובהו ואולמיו ואח״כ חלל החצר לצפון וזהו שחזר וכתב וימד משער אל שער [ולפי שחזר שלא פירש מעשה שער הקדים של חיצונה שיהא שער חחצר הפנימי לצפון ולקדים].

ושכתב בשאילתו על לשכות החיצונות הצפונות (מ:יז) שאינו יכול להבין היכן מתחילות למערב וכמה אוכלות למזרח והיכן מתחילות לצד פנים וכמה אוכלות לחוץ? אינו יודע להוסיף על מה שפי׳ בקונטריס אך צורתם אצור ואשלח לו:

וששאל למה כתבתי שאין אדם יכול ליכנס אלא דרך חיצונה לא ידעתי מה שואל שהרי פ׳ לו שהאולם ובית חליפות עומדים עליו ט״ו אמות לצפון וט״ו אמות לדרום סתמו את כל רחב החצר הפנימי מן הצפון לדרום מכותל לכותל ואין אדם יכול לילך מן המזרח למערב משהוא מגיע לבית החלימות ומכל מקום אני טעיתי באותו פירוש כי דרך מבוא עשו לו אמה רחב בין בית החליפות לכותל צפוני של עזרה ששיפועו בעובי כותל הצפוני כלפי ראשו המגיע לבית החליפות וקיצרו את רחב עובי אמה ובו נכנסין לתוך אויר שבין הלשכות החיצונות לתאים הצפונים המחברים להיכל וכן פי׳ בסוף הענין וסתרו דברי זה את זה. ועתה עסקתי בה עם אחינו שמעיה והגהתיה. ויכול היה להכניסו דרך הפנימית דרך אותו מבוא הקטן וליכנס מן האויר שבין התאים והלשכות אל אחת מן הלשכות אף שבקש להראות לו פתחי הלשכות היאך הם פתוחים לחצר החיצונה ואת ארך האמה ורחב החמישים שלפניהם אבל הגהתי:

וששאל שאינו יכול להבין מהו הכותל המפסיק בין חצר הפנימי לחצר החיצונה לצפון והלא אינו בא מן המזרח למערב אלא מן הצפון לדרום? בדבר זה יש להפליא על שאילתו מאד וכי לא ראה לחצר הפנימי שער לצפון ושער לקדים ושער לדרום והיאך יהיה לו שער לצפון אם אין לו כותל צפוני מפסיק בינו לחצר החיצונה והיאך כותל צפוני בא אם לא ממזרח למערב וסופו כלה למאה אמה וזהו סמוך לזוית כל בית החליפות שהרי מדד חלל החצר הפנימי מאה על מאה מרובע והואיל ועוביו שש נמצא סותם כנגד אויר חמש אמות שבין זוית החליפות לזוית הלשכות החיצונות ואין דרך ליכנס בו לא מן החיצונה ולא דרך הפנימית אלא דרך ששיפועו כשיעור אמה רחב בעוביו של כותל בסופו אצל בית החליפות ליכנס בו אדם:

וששאל **ואם נכלמו** וכו׳ **ועשו אותם** (מג:יא) כלום צוה לעשות בנין זה בימי יחזקאל? אמת אם היתה תשובתם הוגנת על מנת שלא לחטוא היה בנין זה להם כשעלו מן הגולה וגאולת עולם בזרוע ולא על ידי כורש אלא שגרם החטא וכן שנינו בברכות עד יעבר עמך ה׳ זו ביאה ראשונה עד יעבר עם זו קנית זו ביאה שניה אמור מעתה ראויים היו ישראל ליעשות להם נס בימי עזרא כדץ שנעשה בימי יהושע אלא שגרם החטא:

נחלה (מז:יד) ואחוזה (מח:כב) שניהם שווין ודרך המקראות לכפל לשונם כמו כי עשית משפטי ודיני (תהלים ט:ה) הנה בשמים עדי וסהדי במרומים (איוב טז:יט) העירה והקיצה למשפטי (וריבי) לריבי (תהלים לה:כג):

APPENDIX X

◆§ The Master Diagram*

This Diagram is similar to, but not identical with, that of *R' Moshe Ivier* which is reproduced in *Tzuras HaBayis* and in *HaMikdash HaShlishi* and which we offer in Appendix VIII.[1]

It attempts to present the layout of Yechezkel's Temple as closely as possible (see comm. 42:1-12 and to *vs.* 3 and 5) to the way *Rashi* must have understood it. In addition to the printed *Rashi* which, in spite of the corrupt state of the text (see comm. 41:5-15) still yields many significant insights to *Rashi's* true opinion, it draws on three invaluable sources. *Levy's* critical edition of *Rashi* to the last nine chapters of *Ezekiel* (Appendix VII); *Rashi's* responsum to the *Sages of Auxerres* (Appendix IX); and the commentary to *Middos* of *Rashi's* pupil *R' Shemaya* (with whom, according to the above responsum, *Rashi* consulted in working out the details of his commentary).

These three additional sources were the basis for those instances in which we diverged from *R' Moshe Ivier's* diagram. The most significant of those deviations concerns the interpretation of the מוּנָּח, *open space* (41:9), and the consequently radically changed appearance of the whole Temple Building (see comm. there).

In addition, there are two important aspects in which our diagram differs from that of *R' Moshe Ivier.* To avoid confusion, our diagram is limited to the floor plan of the Temple (that is, it represents a bird's-eye view of the Temple as it would appear at ground level) omitting anything which appeared above ground level. Such above-ground details, when appropriate, are shown in small diagrams which accompany the text of the commentary. This comparative simplicity of the diagram made it easier to present the various components in their exact proportion to one another — which *R' Moshe Ivier* did not do.

In spite of the care taken to produce a faithful picture, we can make no claim to complete accuracy, and the diagram should be seen as no more than an aid to the understanding of the commentary. There are a number of components for which the sources do not offer accurate descriptions, and because of this some parts of the diagram are based on conjecture.

---

1. Many attempts have been made to grapple with the intricacies of the Third Temple. *HaMikdash HaShlishi* which is the most complete compendium of the various opinions, offers no fewer than four widely differing diagrams. Of these, the one which comes closest to ours is that of *R' Moshe Ivier* (which, according to the title page of the first edition of *Tzuras HaBayis*, Grodno 5548, is based on *Rashi* and *Rambam).*

It is interesting that *Malbim,* at the end of his commentary to *Ezekiel* is at complete odds with *R' Moshe Ivier* and presents a systematic, point by point, refutation of the latter's opinion.

* In most of its details this diagram is based on one painstakingly worked out by Mr. Gershon Goldman of Chicago. Reb Gershon kindly offered his labor of love to help us produce an accurate aid to the understanding of these difficult chapters. I consulted with Reb Gershon many times by letter and phone and his astounding mastery of this intricate subject helped me over many a difficulty.

The development and final execution of this and all the diagrams in the book are the product of R' Shea Brander's craftsmanship and several months of painstaking study and consultation. At every stage of the work he gave unstintingly of his interest and skill to produce a truly beautiful work. I am deeply grateful to both of these gentlemen for their unflagging interest and unfailing kindness. (M.E.).

Following is a list of such components [the exact degree of conjecture is given in the legend, the commentary, or the individual diagrams]: (1/5), (2/1), (2/10), (3/1), (3/2), (3/3), (4/2), (4/4), (4/10), (4/18), (5/2 south), (5/6), (5/8), (6/2), and the cooking chambers.

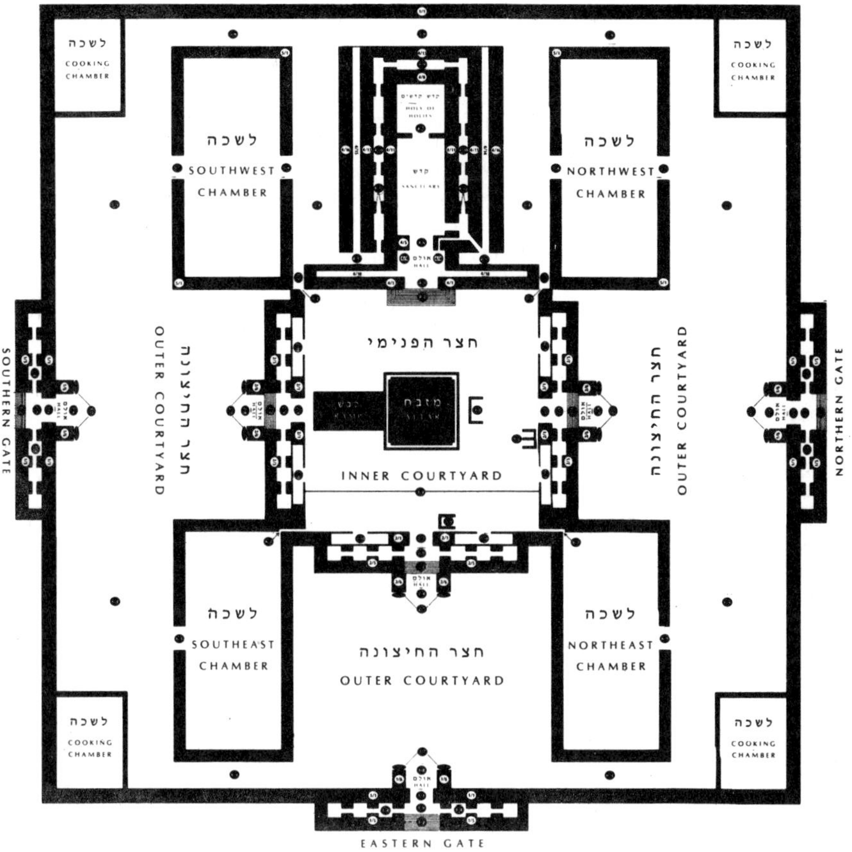

◆§ Legend

N.B. Numbers after each item refer to chapter and verse where mentioned (e.g. 1/1 is mentioned in chapter 40, verse 5).

1/x Outer Courtyard Gateway Complex
1/1 Wall surrounding the outer courtyard (40:5)
1/2 Steps leading to the outer courtyard (40:6)
1/3 Gateway to the outer courtyard (40:6, 16)
1/4 Cells (40:7, 10, 12, 13)
1/5 Walls between the cells and their outer wall (40:7 and see *Metzudos)*
1/6 Walls of the hall (40:8-9)
1/7 Pillars (40:9, 14, 16)
1/8 Inner (hall) gate (40:11, 16)
1/9 Vestibule (40:12)

N.B. A description of this whole gate complex can be found in comm. 40:6-16.
N.B. The sources here refer to the eastern gate complex. For the northern gate complex see 40:20-22 and for the southern one see 40:24-26.

2/x Inner Courtyard Gateway Complex
2/1 Wall surrounding the inner courtyard. (Not explicated in text. See *Rashi* 42:5 and *Tzuras HaBayis* 22)
2/2 Steps leading from the outer courtyard to the inner courtyard (40:31)
2/3 Gateway leading to the inner courtyard (40:28)
2/4 Cells (40:29)
2/5 Walls between the cells and the outer wall [implied in 40:29; see above at (1/5)]
2/6 Walls of the hall (40:29, 31)
2/7 Pillars (40:29, 31)
2/8 Outer hall gate (40:30)
2/9 Vestibule (40:39)
2/10 Chambers built into the walls of the inner courtyard (40:30)

N.B. A description of this whole gate structure can be found in comm. 40:27-37 which should be read together with comm. 40:6-16.
N.B. The sources here refer to the southern gate complex. For the eastern gate complex see 40:32-34 and for the northern one, see 40:35-37.

3/x Inner Courtyard
3/1 Chamber for skinning and washing the sacrifices (40:38, 42-43).
3/2 Two chambers for the choristers (40:44).
3/3 Chamber for the Tzadokite *kohanim* (40:44, 46)
3/4 Platform (42:12)

4/x Temple Structure
4/1 Eastern wall of the Temple structure (40:48)
4/2 Steps leading from the inner courtyard to the Temple structure (40:49)
4/3 Gateway to the entrance hall of the Sanctuary (41:1-2)
4/4 Pillars in the entrance hall (40:49)
4/5 Walls creating gateway from hall to Sanctuary (41:1-2)
4/6 Gateway from the hall into the Sanctuary (41:1-2)
4/7 Walls between Sanctuary and Holy of Holies (41:5)
4/8 Western wall of the Holy of Holies (41:5)
4/9 Cell in the west, behind Holy of Holies (41:5)
4/10 Cells on the northern and southern sides (41:6, 7, 8, 9, 11); [see further in comm. 41:9]
4/11 Northern and southern walls of the Temple. [The width of these walls is not explicated in the text — although the text assumes the existence of these walls (41:6). *Middos* 4:7 assigns a width of 6 cubits and that is implied in the measurements given at 41:12. See comm. there. Perhaps a width of 6 cubits is assumed since these two walls are one with the western wall (4/8) to which 41:5 assigns a width of 6 cubits.]
4/12 Walls between cells [These walls are not explicated in the text, but see comm. to 41:9.]
4/13 Northern, southern and western walls on the outside of the cells. [The northern and southern walls are described in 41:8-9. The western wall is not explicated in the text but *Rashi* to 41:13 assumes it to have the same dimensions as the northern and southern walls.]
4/14 Access ramp leading upward from east to west. [This ramp is not mentioned in the text but its existence is assumed at 41:12 (see comm. there and at 41:5-15). It is mentioned in *Middos* 4:5.]
4/15 Western drainage ramp leading down from west to east. [See 4/14 above].
4/16 Outer walls of the Temple on northern and southern sides. [See 4/14 above. *Middos* 4:7 assigns a thickness of 5 cubits to this wall. But 41:12 assumes a thickness of 6 cubits (see

comm. there). The assumption is that it was 6 cubits at ground level but 5 cubits above ground level (see comm. 41:8) and is therefore counted as 6 cubits (see comm. 41:12).]

4/17 Open space (41:9, 11).

4/18 The knife depository. [This is not explicated in the text but assumed at 41:14 (see comm. there). It is mentioned in *Middos* 4:7.]

4/19 Wicket for entry into cells (4/10) and access ramp (4/14) (41:11)

N.B. A description of the whole building complex can be found in comm. 40:48-49 and 41:5-15.

5/x Western Chambers

5/1 Walls of the northwestern and southwestern chambers (42:1-3)

5/2 Gap in wall (42:4)

5/3 Walkway (42:4)

5/4 Space between chamber and Sanctuary (41:10)

5/5 Space between chamber and northern [or southern] wall of outer courtyard (42:2)

5/6 Space between chamber and western wall of outer courtyard (42:9)

5/7 Gate to the north [or south] (42:2, 4)

5/8 Gate to the south [or north]. [This gate is not explicated in the text but is assumed by *Rashi* to 46:19. See comm. to 42:13-14.]

6/x Eastern Chambers

N.B. According to *Rashi* (42:9) these chambers may not have existed.

6/1 Walls of northeastern and southeastern chambers (42:9)

6/2 Gateway into inner courtyard toward the platform (3/4), (42:12)

6/3 Space between chamber and eastern wall of outer courtyard (42:9)

6/4 Space between chamber and northern [or southern] wall of outer courtyard (42:9)

6/5 Gate to the north [or south] (see 5/8 above)

N.B. A description of the eastern chambers can be found in comm. 42:7-8. This should be read with comm. 42:1-12.

Altar (43:13-17)
Ramp (43:18, see comm.)
Cooking Chambers (46:22-23)

APPENDIX XI

Calculations Concerning the Boundaries of the Land as Envisioned by Yechezkel

For a clearer picture of the division of the land (chs. 45 and 48) we offer the following computations. [In our computations we will assume a value of 1 cubit=1.5 ft. This, without intending any halachic connotation. (Opinions concerning the אַמָּה in halachah range from 18″ to 24″).]

The reader should familiarize himself with the following values:

1 rod=6 cubits (40.5)
2000 cubits=1 mil
4 mil=1 *parsah*
1 mile=5280 ft.
1 *parsah*=2.3 miles $[(2000 \times 4 \times 1.5) \div 5280 = 2.27]$.

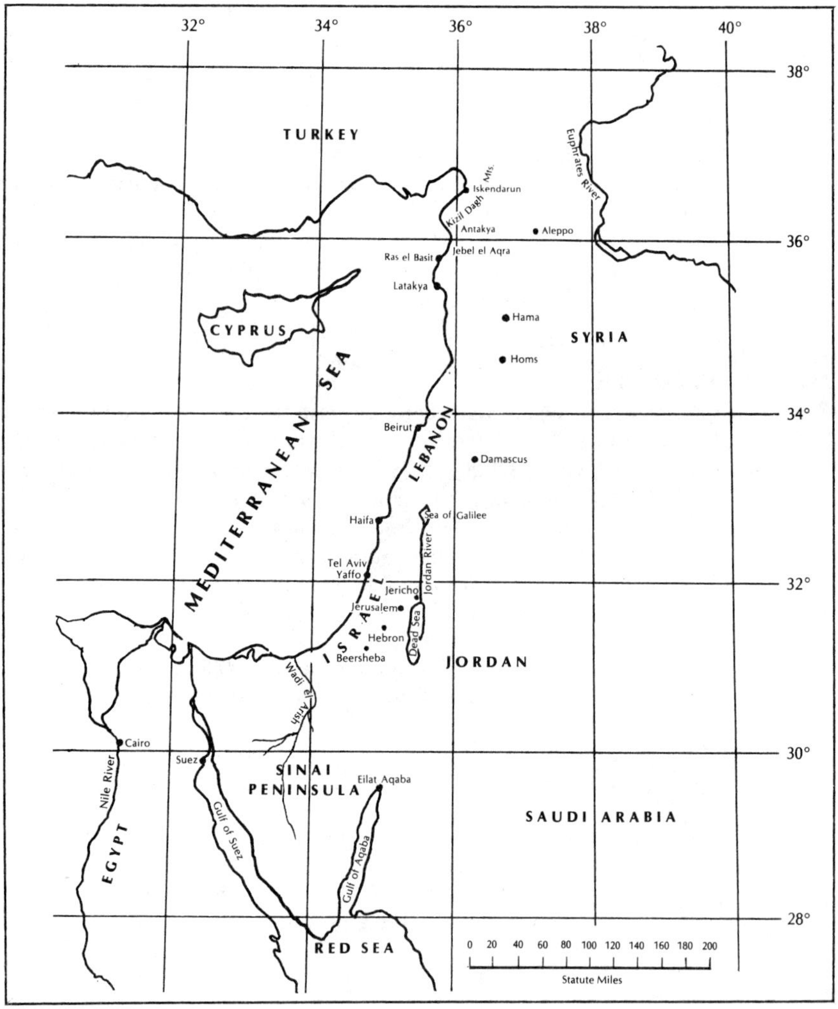

1) The strips described in ch. 48 were each 25,000 rods wide.
25,000 rods×6=150,000 cubits×1.5=225,000 ft.=42.6 miles.
There were 7 tribes north of the *Sacred Terumah* and 5 tribes south.

(a) 7×42.6=298.2
(b) 1×42.6= 42.6
(c) 5×42.6=213.0

553.8

The land is 553.8 miles from North to South.

2) 25,000 rods=150,000 cubits=75 mil=18.75 *parsah*

(a) 7×18.75=131.25
(b) 1×18.75= 18.75
(c) 5×18.75= 93.75

243.75

The land is 243.75 Parsah from North to South.

[243.75×2.27=553.31 miles. The small discrepancy of half a mile is due to the approximation of the decimal points.]

3) Our computations are confirmed by *Taanis* 10a and *Bava Metziah* 28a which assign 15 days walking between Jerusalem and the Euphrates. *Pesachim* 94a assumes that a man walks 10 *parsah* a day.

10 parsah=23 miles (10×2.27)

22.7×15=340.5 miles.

This yields a distance of 340.5 miles between Jerusalem and the Euphrates (and would tend to confirm *Kaftor Voferach* in his location of הֹר הָהָר — see Ch. 47).

Adding (1a) and (1b) yields 340.8 miles which closely approximates the distance measured above (340.5).miles, which is almost exactly the same.

[However, this takes the measurement from the southern tip of the city described in *Ezekiel*. But this city lies over 25 miles south of the Jerusalem of the בַּיִת שֵׁנִי.] If we assume the Temple Mount of Yechezkel to be at the same location as it was in previous times we have a distance of:

The *kohanim* portion south of the Temple Mount= 4750 rods
The Levites portion=10,000 rods

14,750 rods
14,750 rod=88,500 cubits=132,750 ft.=25.14 miles

If instead we measure from the Temple Mount we have a distance of only:

7 northern strips (1a) above=298.2 miles
4750 rods (north of Temple Mount)= 8.1 miles

306.3

This would be a distance covered in 306.3÷22.7=13.5 days. This problem can be solved by assuming that of the 15 days postulated for the trip the 2 Shabbos days must be eliminated. This leaves us with an actual traveling time of only 13 days. (But see *Tosafos Yom Tov* to *Taanis).*

4) Our computations yield that the portion of the *nassi* lying to the east of the Terumas HaKodesh (48:21) must have been very narrow.

According to *Beitzah* 5a there is a distance of 1 day's walk between Jerusalem and the Jordan.

In (3) we noted that this would approximate 22.7 miles.

If the Temple Mount was approximately centered in the Terumas HaKodesh which had a width (from east to west) of 42.6 miles (1) that would leave some 21.3 miles from the Temple Mount to the Jordan.

The strip available to the *nassi* would then be 1.4 miles in width with a North-South dimension of 42.6 miles. (But see commentary to 47:13-20 that the political boundaries of the land extended far to the East. This would make it possible to give the portion of the נָשִׂיא a more balanced form. However, no mention is made in the text concerning such an adjustment. See also *pref.* to Ch. 48).

5) In (1a) we have seen that the distance between the Temple Mount to the northern boundary of the land is approximately 300 miles. A glance at the map (**p. ???**) and at the commentary to 47:15-17 — *The Northern Boundary* will show that this approximates the distance postulated by *Kaftor VoFerach's* location of הֹר הָהָר (in southern Turkey) but is considerably more than the distance to the northern boundaries according to the other opinions quoted there.

To the south we see from (1c) that we need a distance of 213 miles. The distance, as the crow flies, between Jerusalem and Eilath is some 155 miles. Therefore, even if we assume with *Harav Tukizinski* (see *comm.)* that the southern border goes down to the gulf of Aqaba (see 47:19 — *The Southern Boundary)* There is a short fall of some 58 miles.

For a discussion of these questions see *pref.* to ch. 48.

Index

A part of this subject index was prepared by Mrs. Nechamah Frand. I am deeply grateful for the great effort which she expended to make this work as comprehensive as possible.

My son-in-law, R' Yitzchok Schwarz, spent many tedious hours checking and rechecking the sources. It was a labor of love which enhanced the usefulness of the index immeasurably.

Rabbi Moshe Eisemann

Bibliography
of Authorities Cited in the Commentary

Talmudic and Midrashic Sources

Aggados Bereishis

A collection of midrashim on parts of the Book of *Genesis*.

Avos d'Rabbi Nosson

Also called Mishnah, Tosefta, Aggadah, and Baraita d'Rabbi Nosson. it is the first of the 'small tractates' which are printed together with *Seder Nezikin* in standard editions of the Babylonian Talmud.

Derech Eretz Zuta

One of the 'small tractates'. See Avos d'Rabbi Nosson.

Eliyahu Rabbah and Zuta

Also known as Tanna d'Bei Eliyahu. A series of teachings revealed by Elijah the Prophet to the Amora R' Anan.

Josephus Flavius

The earliest Jewish historian whose works have reached us, Josephus lived from approximately 3800-3860 (40-100 C.E.). Born into an aristocratic family of *Kohanim,* he entered public life at a young age. When the war against Rome broke out, Josephus was appointed commander in the Galilee. According to his own account, it was the tanna R' Shimon ben Gameliel who recommended him for this appointment. After he was captured by the Romans following the siege of Jotapata, he managed to gain the favor of the Roman General Vespasian, at whose instruction he would go before the walls of Jerusalem, exhorting the inhabitants to surrender. When Vespasian was proclaimed emperor, he freed Josephus. In gratitude, Josephus assumed Vespasian's family name Flavius. Having been an eyewitness and an active participant in the war against Rome, he proceeded to write an account of it, *Wars of the Jews,* which has come down to us in Greek and has been translated into many languages. His other work, *Antiquities,* deals with Jewish History from the Creation to the destruction of the Second Temple.

Mechilta

Tannaic Midrash to *Exodus.*

Mechilta d'Rabbi Shimon bar Yochai

Tannaic Midrash.

Midrash Rabbah

Amoraic Midrash on the Torah and the five *Megillos.*

Midrash Tanchuma

Midrash on the Torah, ascribed to Rabbi Tanchuma.

Midrash Torah

A collection of Midrashim.

Pirkei d'Rabbi Eliezer

Ancient Aggadic work attributed to the first century tanna, R' Eliezer ben Hyrcanos.

Seder Olam

A history attributed to the tanna Rabbi Yose bar Chalafta.

Sefer HaBahir

A Kabbalistic work attributed to the tanna R' Nechunyah ben Hakana.

Sifri

Tannaic Midrash to *Numbers* and *Deuteronomy.*

Targum Onkelos

Aramaic interpretive translation of the Torah attributed to the proselyte Onkelos who lived during the tannaic period.

Targum Yerushalmi

Aramaic interpretive translation of the Torah.

Targum Yonasan

Aramaic interpretive translation of the Prophets, attributed to the tanna Yonasan ben Uziel.

Toras Kohanim

Halachic Midrash to *Leviticus,* as taught by the amora Rav [d. 243] and his school.

Tosefta

Lit. 'Addition'. A collection of teachings compiled by the early amora, Rav Chiya, to explain and expand upon the matters discussed in the Mishnah.

Yalkut Shimoni

Thirteenth century anthology of Talmudic and Midrashic comments on the Tanach. It is attributed to Rabbi Shimon HaDarshan of Frankfort who lived in the 13th century.

Zohar

The basic book of Kabbalah as transmitted by Rabbi Shimon bar Yochai to his disciples. It is arranged according to the portions of the Torah.

Rishonim / Earlier Rabbinic Sources

Abarbanel, R' Yitzchak

Celebrated philosopher and Biblical commentator at the time of the Spanish expulsion.

A scion of the Davidic royal family, he was born in Lisbon in 5197/1437. He was a disciple of R' Yosef Chayun. Alfonso V of Portugal recognized his great capabilities and appointed him minister of the treasury. He fled Portugal for Castile when the king suspected him of complicity in an insurrection against the throne. King Ferdinand of Castile appointed him minister of finance, a post which he held until the Jews of Spain were expelled from that country (9 Av 5252/1492). Abarbanel joined the refugees, despite the entreaties of the king and queen that he stay on. The title 'Don' was conferred on him when he served as a minister of finance in the Spanish government.

His major work is a voluminous commentary to Torah and Prophets. These and his many other works rank him among the classical Jewish Bible commentators and thinkers. Abarbanel attacks Christian theology in his writings, a feat which in his days was very dangerous. He died in Padua, Italy in 5268 (1508).

Aruch

Talmudic dictionary compiled by R' Nassan ben Yechiel of Rome (11th century).

Bachya ben Osher, R'

(Also pronounced Bechay or Bechie.)

Served as *dayyan* and rabbi in Saragossa, Spain, mid 13th century.

He was one of the foremost students of R' Shlomo ben Adaras *(Rashba)*. His most famous work is his commentary on the Torah, published in 1291.

Chovos HaLevavos by R' Bachya Ibn Pekuda

(Also pronounced Bechay or Bechie.) Second half of eleventh century. He was *dayyan* in Saragossa. Wrote *Toras Chovos HaLevavos* in Arabic. It was translated into Hebrew by R' Judah ibn Tibbon and became one of the most widely studied books of religious-ethical thought.

Dunash ben Labrat

Grammarian, exegete, and poet who flourished in the 10th century, he was a student of R' Saadiah Gaon and R' Chisdai ibn Shaprut. Dunash known mainly for his criticism of Menachem ben Saruk's grammar (see there).

Eleazar Kalir (or HaKalir).

The best known of the *payetannim (liturgical poets)*. He certainly predated R' Saadya Gaon who quotes him.

R' Eliyahu HaBachur

Called *R' Eliyahu HaBachur*, from the name of his book, *HaBachur*, he is also known as Elijah Levitas.

Grammarian and expert on the *Mesorah*, he was born in Neustadt, Bavaria in 5228/1488, but left his birthplace and settled in Italy, where he spent most of his adult life. In 5264/1504 he was in Padua, sustaining himself by teaching children. When Padua was sacked five years later, R' Eliyahu fled to Rome, where he was hired by Cardinal Egedio di Viterbo to be his Hebrew tutor. R' Eliyahu stayed at the cardinal's house for thirteen years writing many treatises, among them his *Sefer HaBachur*. He also copied many Hebrew manuscripts for the Cardinal, many of which are still extant.

Among his works are *Tishbi*, a short dictionary on Talmudic and Midrashic Aramaic; *Meturgeman*, a concordance and dictionary on Scripture and Targumic Aramaic; and *Mesoras HaMesorah* on the *Mesorah*.

Eliezer of Beaugency, R'

Bible commentator from the school of Rashi, who flourished in the north of France in the twelfth century. He may have been a student of the Rashbam.

His commentaries to *Ezekiel, Isaiah* and the *Twelve Prophets* are extant.

R' Hai ben R' Sherira Gaon

(939-1038).

Gaon in Pumbedisa. He was universally acknowledged to be one of the very greatest figures of the Gaonic era. Many of his works are still extant including many responsa and a commentary on parts of *Taharos*.

Ibn Ezra

R' Abraham ibn Ezra was born 1089 in Toledo. He was a famous poet, philosopher, grammarian, scientist, astronomer — and above all — Biblical commentator. In all his Bible commentaries he strived for the plain, literal meaning of the verse. His aim was to explain the etymology of difficult words within their grammatical context. Next to Rashi, his commentary on the Torah is most widely studied, and appears in almost all large editions of the Bible.

In France, he met R' Yaakov Tam [Rabbeinu Tam' — grandson of Rashi] and a deep friendship between the two followed. According to some, he married the daughter of R' Yehudah HaLevi, and had five sons. He traveled to many countries and endured much economic hardship until his death in 1164.

Legend had it that he once met the Rambam [Maimonides] and dedicated a poem to him that he wrote on the day of Rambam's death.

Ibn Janach, R' Yonah

He was born in Cordova c. 4750/990, and left it in 4772/1012 for Saragossa, where he was a prominent physician.

Ibn Janach published one of the first Biblical grammar books and dictionaries, the earliest to have come down to us in its entirety. It was originally written in Arabic and later translated

into Hebrew by R' Yehudah Ibn Tibbon. It is divided into two parts: *Sefer HaRikmah*, and *Sefer HaShorashim*.

He is often cited by such later Bible commentators and Hebraists as: Ibn Ezra (who sometimes refers to him as R' Merinus); Ibn Daud; Radak; Rambam; Mizrachi. The notable exception is Rashi, who seems to have been unacquainted with his work.

Kaftor VaFerach

R' Isaac ben Moses HaParchi, also known as Farhi Estori, was born in 1282 (prob. in France) and died in *Eretz Yisrael* in 1357.

He made it his life's work to identify the place names in Tanach, and his work *Kaftor VaFerach* is the classic presentation of the laws dealing with *Eretz Yisrael.*

Kara, R' Yosef

French Bible commentator, c. 1060-1130. [Not to be confused with R' Yosef Caro, 15th century author of *Shulchan Aruch*.

R' Yosef was the student of his illustrious uncle, R' Menachem Chelbo, whom he often cites in his commentary.

A resident of Troyes, he frequented Rashi's house, where he made the acquaintance of Rashi's grandson, *Rashbam*.

Rav Yosef wrote a commentary on Torah, based upon Rashi's commentary, which he enlarged and expanded. He also added glosses to Rashi's commentary, which Rashi later incorporated ito his own manuscript. Rav Yosef also wrote an independent commentary to most of Tanach, including *The Five Megillos*.

In his commentaries, he followed the general style of Rashi but was not as brief. He cared more for the sense of the whole sentence than for the grammatical dissection of a single word.

Kuzari

Rabbi Yehudah HaLevi (b. Toledo 1085 d. *Eretz Yisrael* ca. 1142).

Poet and philosopher. His most famous work is the Kuzari in which he lays down a far-ranging and consistent philosophy of Judaism.

Menachem ben Chelbo

Biblical exegete who flourished in northern France in the 11th century. His works, called *Pitronim*, are no longer extant although some fragments have survived.

Menachem ben Saruk

Spanish philologist who flourished in the 10th century. He wrote a grammatical dictionary called *Machberes*. It was against this dictionary that Dunash ben Labrat (see there) wrote. Menachem was a protege of R' Chasdai ibn Shaprut. Much of Rashi's grammar is based on Menachem's works.

Menachem ben Solomon Meiri

Flourished in Pespignan between 1248 and 1306. Famed talmudist who wrote voluminously on most of the Talmud. Many of his writings have been published from manuscripts fairly recently.

Nimukei Yosef

Gloss on Alfasi by Rabbi Yosef Chaviva. His teacher was a student of the Ritva.

Rabbeinu Tam

R' Yaakov ben Meir Tam was one of the greatest Tosafists. His father R' Meir ben Simcha was Rashi's son-in-law. Rabbeinu Tam was a disciple of his father and of his elder brother, R' Shmuel (Rashbam). His comments on the Talmud were collected by him and his disciples in *Sefer HaYashar* which also contains some of his responsa. Many of the greatest Tosafists were his disciples. He also wrote on Hebrew grammar and there is evidence that he wrote commentaries on the Bible. R' Tam also wrote *Piyutim* (liturgical poems) and *Selichos* (prayers). Died Tamus 4, 4931 (1171).

Radak

Commentary on much of Tanach by Rabbi David Kimchi who was born in Narbonne, 1160; died there in 1235.

His father, Rav Yosef, also a grammarian, died when Rav David was a child, and he studied under his brother, Rav Moshe, who had also published several volumes on grammar.

Radak's commentary on Prophets is profound, and is included in most large editions. Such was his influence that many applied to him the saying from *Pirkei Avos:* 'Without *kemach* ['flour' i.e. '*Kimchi*'], there is no Torah.

Unlike some of his contemporaries, he stressed the *p'shat,* the plain sense, wherever possible, striving for clarity and readibility.

His main work was the Michlol, the second edition of which came to be known independently as the *Sefer HaShorashim* (not to be confused with a work by the same name by Ibn Janach).

Ralbag

Commentary on much of Tanach by Rav Levi ben Gershom who was born in Bangols, France in 1288; died 1344.

One of the most important Bible commentators of his time, he was also a mathematician, astronomer, philosopher, and physician.

He wrote commentaries to the *Torah; Job,* the *Five Megillos, Former Prophets, Proverbs, Daniel,* and *Nehemiah.*

His Bible comments establish him as a profound philosopher. He also had great skill in textual analysis and in extracting the ethical and religious teachings of Scripture.

His commentary to *Job* was one of the first books printed in Hebrew (Ferrara, 1477).

Ramah

Rabbi Meir HaLevi ben Tudrus Abulaphia was a famed Talmudist who lived in Toledo at the end of the 12th century and the beginning of the

13th century. His most famous work is the *Yad Ramah*. He was also a student of the Masorah and composed a dictionary, *Masores S'yog LaTorah* on the spelling of the Biblical text.

Rambam

Rabbi Moshe ben Maimon was one of the most illustrious figures of post-Talmudic times. He was a rabbinic authority, codifier, philosopher, and court physician to the ruler of Egypt.

He was born in Cordova, Spain in 4895/1135. His father, the illustrious R' Maimon, was one of the major leaders of Spanish Jews. The family was forced to flee Spain to escape Christian persecution. Rambam wandered through North Africa and finally settled in Fostat, the old city of Cairo, Egypt.

At the age of 23 he began his *Commentary on the Mishnah,* which he wrote during his wanderings. His main work was *Mishnah Torah (Yad HaChazakah),* his codification of the full spectrum of Halachah up to his day. This was the only work he wrote in Hebrew; all his other works he composed in Arabic, a fact he said to have regretted later in life.

He is also known for his profound and philosophic *Moreh Nevuchim (Guide to the Perplexed),* and for his many works in the field of medicine, hygiene, astronomy, etc.

Rambam also wrote many short treatises in the form of letters, among them his famed *Iggeres Teman, (Letter* or *Epistle to Yemen),* which offers guidance and encouragement to the persecuted Yemenite Jews, who were seduced by a pseudo-Messiah, and were suffering serious persecution on his account. He died in 4964/1204 and is buried in Tiberias.

Ramban

Rabbi Moshe ben Nachman was the leading Bible and Talmud scholar in the generation following Rambam, and was also a renowned philosopher, poet, and physician.

Born in 4954/1194 to a famous rabbinic family, he is sometimes referred to as R' Moshe Gerondi, after his native town of Gerona, where he spent most of his life, supporting himself as a physician and exercising extensive influence over Jewish life. Ramban represented the Jewish community in debates against Christian scholars. Despite the risk of retaliation, he skillfully and courageously vanquished them, winning the respect of King James I in the process. By the age of 16, he had published works on Talmud and Halachah. Among his works are: *Milchamos Hashem,* in defense of Alfasi *(Rif)* against the arguments of R' Zerachiah HaLevi in his *Sefer HaMaor; Sefer HaZechus,* in response to the arguments of the *Ravad* against Alfasi *(Rif); Sefer HaMitzvos; Iggeres HaRamban; Iggeres HaKodesh;* and his profound and encyclopedic *Commentary on the Torah,* which is printed in all major editions of the *Chumash;* and many other writings which have been collected and published in *Kisvei HaRambam* ed. by Rabbi Ch. D. Chavel.

Ran

Rabbeinu Nissim Gerondi, a talmudist famous for his glosses on Alphasi, lived in Gerona 1340-1380. It is surmised that he is also the author of *Derashos HaRan,* a series of philosophical, homiletical, and ethical essays.

Rashba

R' Shlomo ben Aderes was the acknowledged leader of Spanish Jewry in his day. Rashba's commentary to many tractates of the Talmud is one of the classics of its genre. His halachic decisions were sought on all questions regarding Jewish life. They are collected in a multi-volume responsa work, *Teshuvos HaRashba,* which is one of the major authorative works of the period.

Rashbam

Rabbi Shmuel ben Meir, a Bible and Talmud commentator and Tosafist, was born in Northern France in 1080 to Rav Meir, one of the first Tosafists and disciples of Rashi. Rashbam's mother was Rashi's daughter, Yocheved.

Thus, he was a grandson of Rashi, the brother-in-law of the great Rabbeinu Tam, and a colleague of Rav Yosef Kara.

Rashbam studied under his father, but was influenced most by his grandfather. They spent much time together in legal and exegetical discussions. In many instances, it is noted that Rashi accepted his grandson's opinion in exegesis.

Rashbam lived a simple life. He would always pray that he might be privileged to perceive the truth and to love peace. His commentary to the Bible is characterized by his extreme devotion to *pshat.* He constantly refers to 'the profound literal meaning' of the text. In many ways, he considered his commentary as complementing that of Rashi.

As a Talmudic commentator he is best known for his writings on most of *Bava Basra* and the end of *Pesachim,* tractates where Rashi was unable to complete his own commentary.

Rashi

R' Shlomo ben Yitzchak is the leading commentator on the Bible and the Talmud. He was born in Troyes, France in 4800/1040, the year Rabbeinu Gershom Meor HaGolah died. According to tradition, Rashi's ancestry goes back to the tanna R' Yochanan HaSandlar and King David. *Rashi's* commentary on the Talmud — an encyclopedic and brilliant undertaking — has had an unequalled impact upon all who study Talmud. Rashi's commentary opened to all what otherwise would have remained a sealed book. Without his commentary it would be virtually impossible to navigate the 'Sea of Talmud'. Every word is precise and laden with inner meaning. *Rashi's* corrections of the Talmud text were so generally accepted that, for the most part, they were introduced into the standard editions and became the standard text.

His Commentary to the Bible had a similar impact — and virtually every printed Bible contains

his commentary which is distinguished by its conciseness and clarity.

Many Halachic works from the 'School of Rashi' have come down to us: *Sefer HaOrah; Sefer HaPardes; Machzor Vitry; Siddur Rashi;* and responsa.

Ravan

Rabbi Eliezer ben Nathan, a Talmudist who flourished in Mayence in the 12th century.

Ri Migash

R' Yoseph HaLevi ibn Migash was a Talmudist who flourished in Spain during the late 11th and early 12th centuries. He was a student of Alphasi (Rif) and teacher of Maimonides (Rambam).

Ri MiTrani

R' Yeshayah (b. Mali) of Trani, a great Talmudist and Biblical commentator in Southern Italy, is also called R' Yeshayah HaRishon [the first] or HaZaken [the Elder] to differentiate him from his grandson, R' Yeshayah b. Elijah of Trani. He was a disciple of R' Simchah of Verona who in turn was a disciple of Ri HaZaken. In spite of his great reverence for Rashi, whom he calls *HaMoreh,* the teacher, he does not hesitate to disagree with Rashi and other great commentators. Many unique views are to be found in his writings. He wrote voluminously on the Talmud (Tosafos Rid and Piskei Rid), and also wrote a commentary on Torah.

In our commentary to Yechezkel, he was referred to as *Mahari* MiTrani.

Saadiah Gaon, Rabbeinu

R' Saadiah ben Yosef Gaon, born in 4652/892 was Rosh Yeshiva of Sura and one of the most important figures of the illustrious Gaonic period. R' Saadiah was made Gaon (head of the academy) by the Resh Gelusa (Exilarch) David ben Zakkai in 928. The ancient academy in Sura, founded by Rav, then began a new period of brilliance.

A sage in every sphere of Torah knowledge, he had a full grasp of the secular knowledge of his time. A dynamic leader, he fought a valiant battle against the growing influence of Karaism.

He wrote in many areas: Halachah, responsa, philosophy, grammar, but most of his works are lost or scattered among the *genizos,* awaiting publication. Among the most important of R' Saadiah's surviving works are his *Tafsir,* a translation of the Bible from Hebrew into Arabic, which has remained the standard Bible for Yemenite Jews; his *Siddur; Sefer HaAgron,* on grammar; and his profound *Sefer Emunos V'Deos, (Book of Beliefs and Doctrines),* originally written in Arabic and translated into Hebrew by R' Yehudah ibn Tibbon. This major philosophical work is the earliest such book to have survived intact. Recently R' Y. Kafich has retranslated this book from manuscripts, showing that R' Saadiah later made many changes which are not found in the standard editions. R' Saadiah died 4702/942 and is credited with a rebirth of Torah study in North Africa.

Sefer Chassidim

Rabbi Yehudah HaChassid (c. 1150-1217), was one of the main teachers of the 'Chassidei Ashkenaz' and one of the most profound ethical teachers who ever lived.

He was the author-editor of *Sefer Chassidim,* a profound ethical/halachic treatise which has come down to us in two separate editions. The book has achieved great popularity and has been reprinted many times.

Rav Yehudah's father, Shmuel, was a saintly and renowned rosh yeshiva in Speyer, and Rav Yehudah studied under him.

His contemporaries said of him: 'Had he lived in the time of the prophets, he would have been a prophet; in the time of the tannaim, he would have been a tanna; in the time of the amoraim, an amora...'

Shemaya of Troyes, Rabbeinu

An 11th century French scholar, he was known to be one of Rashi's closest disciples and was probably related to him, either as his grandson or as father-in-law of Rashi's grandson, Rashbam.

He helped Rashi edit his commentary to Scripture and also his responsa. Rashi mentions that he consulted with R' Shemaya in the matter of Yechezkel's Temple.

S'MAG (Sefer Mitzvos Gadol)

R' Moshe ben Yaakov of Coucy was a French tosafist. He often traveled from town to town exhorting the people to be scrupulous in their observance of *mitzvos.* Upon receiving a Divine revelation to do the same in Spain, he went there and became a major influence in stemming a drift away from Torah observance.

S'MAG, his major work, is a voluminous treatment of all the Scriptural and Rabbinic *mitzvos* and, their laws. It is based on *Rambam's Mishneh Torah* which R' Moshe quotes virtually verbatim and elucidates.

Tosafos

A major school of commentators on all of the Talmud. Flourished in the 12th and 13th centuries in France and Germany.

Achronim / Later Rabbinic Sources

Aruch HaShulchan

One of the major halachic works of the last century, it is an encyclopedic compendium following the order of the four parts of the *Shulchan Aruch*. The author, R' Yechiel Michel Epstein (1829-1908), was *rav* of Novardak. In addition to his *Aruch HaShulchan* which deals, as does the *Shulchan Aruch*, with laws applying to Israel in exile, he also wrote *Aruch HaShulchan HaAsid* (of the *Future)*, a treatment of the halachah which will apply with the building of the Third Temple.

Aruch LeNer

Commentary to a number of tractates by R' Yaakov Ettinger, rabbi of Altona, Germany (19th century).

Daas Tevunos (Mesillas Yesharim, Derech Hashem)

Rabbi Moshe Chaim Luzzatto (1707-1746), Kabbalist, author of Mussar/ethical works, and poet, was born in Padua, Italy. He was regarded as a genius from childhood, having mastered Tanach, Midrash, and Talmud at an early age. He later went on to Kabbalistic and ethical studies.

He is most famous for his profound ethical treatise, *Mesillas Yesharim* ('The Path of the Upright'), which is regarded as a Mussar classic, alongside such works as the *Chovos HaLevavos* of R' Bachya ibn Pakuda and *Shaarei Teshuvah* of Rabbeinu Yonah.

Daas Tevunos is a Kabbalistic treatise which examines such subjects as the aim of Creation, the nature of Divinity, sin, and justice; and presents a general philosophy of history. Among his other Kabbalistic works were: *Razin Genizin, Megillas Sesarim, Maamar haGeulah,* and *Derech Hashem.*

In 1743, he emigrated to *Eretz Yisrael.* He lived a short time in Acre, and died there, with his family, in a plague.

Dov Ber of Mezeritch, R'

A disciple of the *Baal Shem Tov* and an interpreter of his teachings, R' Dov Ber, known as the *Maggid* (Preacher) of Mezeritch, was the leading figure in the Chassidic movement after the passing of the Besht. It was under him that the movement spread throughout Eastern Europe and took root in province after province.

After his passing in 5532/1772, Chassidim no longer had a single preeminent figure. His legacy passed to several great figures who founded the various dynasties and courts, most of which endure to this day. He lived in the Ukraine.

HaKesav VeHaKabbalah

Commentary to the Torah by R' Yaakov Zvi Mechlenburg, *Rav* of Koenigsberg, Germany (19th century).

The commentary attempts, with a novel etymological approach, to show how the Oral Law can be shown to derive directly from the Written Law.

Ivier, R' Moshe

A famous eighteenth century Talmudist (b. 1721 d. 1771), he was contempory with the Vilna Gaon and was considered one of his most brilliant students.

His diagram of Yechezkel's Temple was first published in *Yesod VeShoresh HaAvadah* by R' Alexander Ziskind of Grodno.

Kli Yakar

Commentary on many parts of Tanach by R' Samuel ben Abraham Laniado. He was born in Allepo, Syria and died in 1605. He is often referred to in books of Biblical commentary as the *Ba'al HaKeilim.*

Levush HaChur

Halachic work by R' Mordechai Jaffe (1535-1612) of Prague. He was a student of R' Shlomo Luria *(Maharshal)* and R' Moshe Isserles *(RaMa).*

When R' Yosef Caro's *Beis Yosef* appeared, R' Mordechai found it overlong, and so began to write his *Levush Malchus*. Later, the *Shulchan Aruch* appeared with the gloss of R' Moshe Isserles, and R' Mordechai put aside his work, only to reconsider many years later. He published his work, *The Levushim*, encompassing all of *Shulchan Aruch,* as well as a commentary on Rambam, Rashi, astronomy — "as a work that will be midway between the two extremes: the lengthy *Beis Yosef* of Rav Caro on the one hand, and on the other, Karo's *Shulchan Aruch* together with the *Mappah* of R' Isserles, which is too brief."

Magen Avraham

Commentary on *Shulchah Aruch Orach Chaim,* by R' Avraham of Kalish (1637-1683), universally accepted and printed in all complete editions of the *Shulchan Aruch.*

Maharal

R' Yehudah Loew ben Bezalel was one of the seminal figures in the last 500 years of Jewish thought. The year of R' Yehudah's birth is not known with certainty; he died in Prague in 1609. His genealogy can be traced to King David.

Although he was universally acknowledged as one of the rabbinic greats of the era, his life was not an easy one. He delayed his marriage for many years due to financial difficulties. He was chief rabbi of Moravia, residing in Nikolsburg for 20 years. In 1573, he transferred his yeshiva to Prague, the Torah metropolis of Europe. Upon two different occasions, he accepted the rabbinate of Posen. He was elected chief rabbi of Prague in 1598 as a very old man. It appears that the position had been denied him up to then because of his outspokenness in attacking social evils and religious laxity. His greatest con-

tribution was his formulation of a self-contained system of Jewish thought. His many books and lengthy sermons formed the basis for much of the significant writing of succeeding centuries. Among his many erudite works were: *Novellae* on *Shulchan Aruch Yoreh Deah; Gur Aryeh* on the Torah; *M'er haGolah Derech Chaim; Netzach Yisrael; Nesivos Olam*, etc.

Maharsha

Commentary on the Talmud by R' Shmuel Eliezer ben Yehudah HaLevi Eidels (1551-1631). His commentary is included in every standard edition of the Talmud. Born in Cracow, he moved to Posen in his youth. In 1614 he became *Rav* of Lublin, and in 1625 of Ostrog, where he founded a large yeshivah.

Metzudos

Commentary to the Prophets and Writings by the 18th century R' Yecheil Hillel ben David Altschuller.

The commentary consists of two parts: *Metzudas Zion*, which explains individual words; and *Metzudas David*, which provides a running commentary to the text. Due to their simple and concise language, the dual commentaries have become almost indispensible studyaids. They have attained great popularity and have been reprinted in nearly every edition of the Prophets.

Minchas Shai

R' Yedidiah Shlomo Raphael of Norzi, who was Rav in Mantua in 1585, consecrated the greater part of his life to authenticating the Masorah of the Bible by studying every previously printed Masorah text, comparing the various readings scattered through Talmudic and Midrashic literature, as well as in published and unpublished manuscripts. The resulting work was entitled *Goder Peretz*, but was published under the name *Minchas Shai*.

This work, which was as perfect as thorough learning and conscientious industry could make it, has become the most accepted work in establishing the Masorah. *Minchas Shai* is printed as an appendix to most large Bibles.

Mizrachi, R' Eliyahu

A commentary on *Rashi's* glosses on the Torah. R' Eliyahu ben Abraham Mizrachi (b. Constantinople 1455, died there 1526) was Chacham Bashi (chief rabbi) in Turkey, and wrote a large number of Talmudical, exegetical and mathematical books.

Nefesh HaChayim

R' Chaim of Volozhin (1749-1821) was one of the leading pupils of the Vilna Gaon and R' Aryeh Gunzberg *(Shaagas Aryeh)*, and the acknowledged spiritual leader of the non-Chassidic Russian Jewry of his day. In 1802, he founded the renowned Yeshiva of Volozhin which became the prototype and inspiration for nearly all Ashkenazic 'Litvisheh' yeshivos. Author of *Nefesh HaChaim* and *Ruach Chaim*.

Or HaChaim

Classic commentary on Torah by R' Chaim ibn Attar (born Sale, Morocco 1696 – died Jerusalem 1743). This commentary, which is printed in most standard editions of the *Chumash*, has had an extensive circulation in Germany and Poland, especially among Chassidim, and Sephardic Jewry.

Orach Chaim

One of the four sections of the *Shulchan Aruch*, the authorative Halachic work by R' Joseph Karo (b. Spain 1488, d. Safad 1575).

Rama

R' Moshe Isserles was *rav* of Cracow until his death in 1573, and one of the greatest halachic authorities. He authored many works and is best known for his glosses *Darchei Moshe* on the *Tur* and *HaMappah*, on the *Shulchan Aruch*, which emphasizes the Ashkenazic rite.

Rashash

R' Samuel ben Joseph Strashun (1794-1872) was a Lithuanian merchant and Talmudic scholar. He wrote glosses to every tractate in the Talmud.

Seder HaDoros

A history by R' Yechiel ben Solomon Heilprin who was a talmudic scholar and historian who flourished in Lithuania at the end of the 17th and the beginning of the 18th centuries.

Sforno

Commentary on the Torah by R' Ovadiah Sforno (1470-1550), who was one of the greatest Italian commentators and literary figures of the Renaissance Period. He studied medicine, the profession he followed. He settled in Bologna where he established a beis medrash which he headed until his death.

Tomer Devorah

R' Moshe Cordovero (1522-1570), known by his acronym: Ramak, was the leading Kabbalist in the period before the ARI. He lived in Safed and studied Torah from R' Yosef Karo, author of the *Shulchan Aruch*. He was one of the few who were ordained with the full *Semichah* reintroduced by R' Yaakov Berav.

Ramak was the brother-in-law of the Kabbalist R' Shlomo Alkabetz who initiated him into the mysteries of Kabbalah then being propagated in Safed. His stature was such that even the ARIzal referred to him as 'my master and mentor.'

One of Ramak's most important works was his *Pardes Rimonim*, elucidating the tenets of Kabbalah. He is also the author of *Tomer Devorah*, the famous *mussar* work which is widely studied even today.

Tzuras HaBayis

A description of Yechezkel's Temple by R' Yom Tov Lipman HaLevi Heller (b. 1579 in Wallustein, Bavaria), who is famous for *Tosafos Yom*

Tov, one of the classic commentaries to Mishnah.

Vilna Gaon (1720-1797)

The greatest Talmudist and Kabbalist of his age. R' Eliyahu of Vilna wrote extensively on both subjects. He is especially famous for his glosses on the *Shulchan Aruch*.

Yaaros Devash

R' Yonasan Eybeshuetz, born in 1690 in Cracow, served as Rosh Yeshivah in Prague. He was *rav* of the 'Three Communities,' Altona, Hamburg, and Wandsbech, until his death in 1796. Published extensively on Halachah and the Bible.

More Recent Rabbinic Sources

Admas Kodesh

A study of the boundaries and locations of *Eretz Yisrael*, Yitzchok ben Eliyahu Pessach Goldhor, who lived in *Eretz Yisrael* in the early 20th century.

Bloch, R' Avraham Yitzchak

Rav of Telshe in Lithuania and Rosh Yeshiva of the famous yeshivah which flourished there. He was killed in 1941 during the Holocaust.

Chazon HaMikrah

Discussions of topics in Tanach arranged according to the weekly *Haftaros*. R' Yissachar Jacobson, born in Germany, lived the later part of his life in *Eretz Yisrael* and published extensively on Jewish topics.

Chazon Ish

R' Avraham Yeshayah Karelitz (1878-1953), one of the foremost Torah scholars and leaders of the second quarter of this century. He was a disciple of his father who was Rav of Kossow (Lithuania).

At an early age, R' Karelitz decided to devote himself to learning Torah *Lishmah,* for its own sake; he never sought recognition. Even when he started publishing the first parts of his voluminous *Chazon Ish,* he remained virtually unknown since he published all his works anonymously. When he settled in *Eretz Yisrael* in 1933, he was immediately recognized as one of the Torah greats of his generation. From then on virtually nothing of importance was done in the religious community without consulting him.

His works, all entitled *Chazon Ish,* deal mainly with halachah. He also wrote a work (incomplete) on ethics: *Al Inyonei Emunah U'Vitachon V'Od.*

Der Neue Kusari (Messiaspuren, Moriah)

Dr. Isaac Breuer, a grandson of R' S.R. Hirsch, was one of the most eloquent transmitters of Hirschian teachings. Trained as a lawyer, he nevertheless wrote prolifically on Jewish philosophy. In the later part of his life he settled in *Eretz Yisrael* where he continued his eclectic writing until his death.

Die Drei Grosse Propheten

A major essay analyzing the works of the three major prophets, Isaiah, Jeremiah, and Ezekiel. R' Joseph Carlebach (1892-1942), a scion of a great rabbinic family, was a German *Rav* and educator. His father, R' Shlomo Carlebach, was rav of Lubech, Germany.

R' Carlebach wrote a commentary on *Shir HaShirim* and *Koheles* and a study of the *Ralbag*. Towards the end of his life, he was Chief Rabbi of Hamburg. He died in the Holocaust after refusing to desert his community to flee to safety.

Dikdukei Sofrim

A pioneering work by Rabbi Raphael Nathan Rabinowitz (1835-1888), providing variant readings for the greater part of the Babylonian Talmud.

Doros HaRishonim

A trail-blazing history of the period of the Second Temple and the development of the Mishnah, by R' Yitzchak Isaac HaLevy Rabinowitz (1847-1914) commonly referred to as HaLevy.

He was the first of the Torah greats of modern times to devote himself to the study of history. In an area which, by default, had become the exclusive province of Jews who had become estranged from Judaism, he succeeded in establishing a system, firmly grounded in the teachings of the Sages, which has become the indispensable basis for all further study in the field.

Hirsch, R' Samson Rafael

(1808-1888)

The father of modern German Orthodoxy, he was a fiery leader, brilliant writer, and profound educator. His greatness as a Talmudic scholar was obscured by his other monumental accomplishments. After becoming chief rabbi and member of Parliament in Bohemia and Moravia, he left to revitalize Torah Judaism in Frankfort-am-Main which he transformed into a Torah bastion.

His best known works are the classic six-volume *Commentary on Chumash,* noted for its

profound and brilliant philosophical approach to Biblical commentary, his similar *Commentary to Psalms*, and *Horeb*, a philosophical analysis of the *mitzvos*.

Hoffmann, R' David Tzvi

Talmudist and biblical scholar who was born in Hungary in 1844 and studied under Maharam Schick and R' Ezriel Hildesheimer.

He produced a vast body of writing in all areas of Jewish thought and his great erudition earned him recognition as one of the great Torah scholars of Germany where he went during the later part of his life to teach at the Rabbinical Seminary in Berlin.

Ir HaKodesh VeHaMikdash

An encyclopedic work by R' Yechiel Michael Tykucinsky concerning all aspects of Jerusalem in Halachah. R' Tykucinsky studied under R' Shmuel Salant, who was rav of Jerusalem for a full seventy years, and married R' Salant's granddaughter. He headed the famed Etz Chaim Yeshivah of Jerusalem, and was acknowledged as one of the Torah giants of his generation.

He died in 1956 leaving behind a vast body of work in all areas of Jewish thought and Halachah.

Kaplan, R' Avraham Eliyahu

(1890-1924)

Born in Keidan as the posthumous son of the famous 'Illuy of Rakow' of the same name who died at the early age of 33. The father belonged to the intimate circle of the Chofetz Chaim.

R' Avraham Eliyahu studied in Telshe under R' Eliezer Gordon and later in Slabodka, where, as a student of the famed Alter of Slobodka he came under the influence of the Mussar movement.

At the young age of 30 he was called to Berlin to assist the ailing R' David Zvi Hoffman in his duties as Rector of the Rabbinical Seminary and at the latter's death in 1921, he succeeded to that position. His impact upon the Orthodox German youth was phenomenal and many flocked to hear his lectures and to be warmed by the fire of his religious enthusiasm.

Tragically, he died only two years later. His writings have been collected in two volumes: *B'Ikvos HaYirah* and *Divrei Talmud*.

Kesses HaSofer

A work devoted to elucidating and identifying the place names in Scripture. R' Aaron Marcus (1843-1916) was a historian of Kabbalah and Chassidus.

Kronglass R' David

R' David was born in Kobrin, Poland, in 1910, where he was first educated, continuing on to the Yeshiva in Mir. Gaining recognition for his vast Torah knowledge and his great wisdom and perception in dealing with people, R' David was appointed *Mashgiach* of Yeshivas Ner Israel in America, a position that he could not fill for over eight years due to the outbreak of World War II. With the miraculous escape of the Mirrer Yeshiva, he fled to Shanghai, where under the most trying circumstances he wrote *Divrei David*, novellae on *Zeraim*.

Upon assuming his position in Baltimore, R' David conducted daily lectures on Talmud, and delivered his famous weekly *Mussar* talks. For over twenty-five years he was both teacher and father to his students. Through his guidance, and by setting a living example, R' David forged a link between the European *derech* (path) of Torah and *Mussar*, and his American talmidim. He died in 1972.

A series of his *mussar* lectures were published, entitled *Sichos Chochmoh U'Mussar*.

Levant, R' Avrohom Dovid

Talmid of R' Menachem Mendel of Lubavitch (the *Zemach Zedek*); rav of Nikolayev, Ukraine; authored many books including *Shaar HaKollel*.

Levovitz, R' Yerucham

Mashgiach Ruchani of the famed Mirrer Yeshivah in Europe, guide and mentor to thousands of students. Some of his writings have been published under the title: *Da'as Chochmah U'Mussar*.

Maharatz Chayes

Acronym for R' Zvi Hirsch Chayes (1805-1855), Galician rabbinic scholar. Author of *Mevo HaTalmud* (Introduction to Talmud), novellae to Talmud, and numerous treatments of historic and halachic topics. His glosses to the Talmud are printed in the larger standard editions.

Malbim, R' Meir Leibush

Rav and Biblical commentator (1809-1879), Malbim is an acronym of his name Meir Leibush ben Yechiel Michel.

He was born in Volhynia and was still a child when his father died. He studied in his native town until the age of 13. He then went to Warsaw where he was known as the 'iluy [prodigy] from Volhynia'. He was *rav* in several cities but he suffered much persecution because of his uncompromising stand against Reform, leading even to a brief imprisonment on a false accusation. He wandered much of his life, serving as *rav* in various cities for several years at a time — even serving for a short while as chief rabbi of Rumania.

His fame and immense popularity rests upon his widely esteemed commentary to the Bible. His first published commentary was on *Megillas Esther* (1845). His commentary to the remaining books of the Bible were published between then and 1876.

His commentary on the Bible [as the author sets forth in his introduction to *Isaiah*] is based upon three fixed principles: in the text of the Torah and the figurative language of the prophets there are no mere synonymous repetitions;

every word in a verse is essential to the meaning in accord with the rules of language; and every statement conveys a sublime thought and all metaphors are replete with wisdom, for they are the words of the living God.

Margolios, R' Reuven

Torah scholar in *Eretz Yisrael.* His prodigious knowledge in all areas of the Torah enabled him to publish basic research in many different fields.

Masores HaTorah VeHaNevi'im

R' Pesach Funfer (1830-1912) was a member of the Vilna rabbinate who did research on the division of Tanach into chapters and verses.

Mechokekei Yehudah

Commentary on *Ibn Ezra's* commentary to the Torah by R' Yehudah Leib Krinsky.

Michtav MeEliyahu

Essays on Jewish ethics by R' Eliyahu Eliezer Dessler (1891-1954), one of the outstanding personalities of the Mussar movement.

R' Dessler was born in Homel, Russia to one of Lithuania's distinguished Torah families. In 1929 he settled in London. He exercised a profound influence on the teaching of Mussar, not only because of the profundity of his ideas, but also on account of his personal, ethical conduct. In 1941 he became director of the Kollel of Gateshead Yeshiva in England.

In 1947, at the invitation of R' Yosef Kahaneman, he became *Mashgiach* of Ponovez Yeshiva in Bnei Brak, Israel, and remained there until his death.

His teachings are unique for their harmonious mixture of Mussar, Kabbalah, and Chassidus. Some of his ideas were published by his students in the three-volume *Michtav MeEliyahu.*

Nefesh HaGer

Commentary on *Targum Onkelos* by R' Mordechai Loevenstein.

Netziv

Acronym for R' Naftali Zvi Yehudah Berlin (1817-1893), who was one of the leading rabbis of his generation and Rosh Yeshivah of Volozhin for some 40 years. He was born at Mir, and was already known as a great Talmudic scholar in his early youth. In 1831 he married the daughter of R' Yitzchak of Volozhin — son of R' Chaim of Volozhin who was the head of the important yeshivah in that town.

When R' Chaim died in 1851 he was succeeded by his elder son-in-law, R' Eliezer Yitzchak. When the latter died in 1854, Netziv succeeded him, transforming the yeshivah into a spiritual center for the whole of Russian Jewry. For twenty-four hours a day, the sound of Torah learning could be heard resounding in the walls of the *beis midrash,* and Netziv's relationship with his students was one of father and son.

In his last years, he came into conflict with the Russian authorities as a result of their instructions to reduce the number of students at the yeshivah, and to introduce secular subjects into the curriculum. This resulted in a government decree to close the yeshiva in 1892, and to exile Netziv and his family. His health was so seriously affected by the closing, that he was unable to carry out his desire to settle in *Eretz Yisrael.* He died in Warsaw about 18 months after his departure from Volozhin.

Among Netziv's works were *Ha'amek She'eilah,* a comprehensive commentary to the *She'iltos* of R' Achai Gaon; *Ha'amek Davar,* commentary on the Torah; *Rinah Shel Torah,* commentary to *Shir HaShirim;* and his responsa *Meishiv Davar.*

Nevi'ei HaEmes

An analysis of prophecy and ten prophets by R' Avrohom Wolf, based on the writings of his father-in-law, R' Abraham Klein, the famed rav of Nuremberg.

R' Wolf, who died in 1979 was a well-known thinker and educator in *Eretz Yisrael,* headed the Beis Yaakov School for girls in Bnei Berak and educated thousands of girls in the traditional Jewish path.

Pardes Yosef

Commentary on *Rashi's* commentary to the Torah by R' Joseph Patsanovski in the early part of the 20th century.

Stein, R' Shlomo

Rav of Schweinfurt, Bayern (b. 1894, d. 1938) was a writer, thinker, and important Orthodox activist.

S'fas Emes

Posthumously published novellae on Talmud and chassidic discourses on Torah by R' Yehudah Aryeh Leib Alter (1847-1903), the Gerrer Rebbe. His father had died when he was only 12 years old, and he was raised and trained by his illustrious grandfather, the *Chiddushei HaRim.*

He was 19 years old when his grandfather died and, despite the pleas of the chassidim, insisted he was unwowrthy to become Gerrer Rebbe. Instead, he became a disciple of his grandfather's colleague and friend, R' Henach of Alexandrow. Several years later, after R' Henoch's death, he acceded to the wishes of the chassidim and molded Ger into the largest chassidus in Poland.

A prodigious and diligent scholar, he nevertheless found time to counsel many thousands of disciples every year and to become an effective leader in Torah causes.

Shem Olam

One of the numerous books by R' Yisroel Meir HaKohen (1838-1933), the famed Chofetz Chaim. From the small Polish town of Radin the

light generated by this saintly man spread throughout the Jewish world.

He became world renowned with the publication of his first book *Chofetz Chaim* on the laws of Lashon HaRa [slander and tale-bearing]; thereafter he became universally known by the name of that book. *Mishneh Berurah*, his monumental commentary to *Shulchan Aruch Orech' Chaim*, became a standard halachic reference even during his lifetime and there is hardly an aspect of Jewish life which was not touched by some product of his prolific pen.

Toldos HaKohanim HaGedolim

A historical sketch of all the High Priests. The author, R' Yekusiel Yehudah Greenwald (1889-1955), spent his most productive years as rav of Columbus, Ohio.

T'vuas Ha'aretz

An authoritative, meticulously researched work dealing with the boundaries and place names of *Eretz Yisrael*. Its author, Yehoseph Schwarz, was born in Germany in 1804 and emigrated to *Eretz Yisrael* in 1833. He died in 1865.

Yisrael Kedoshim

One of the many books on Jewish thought by the great Chassidic sage, R' Tzadok HaCohen Rabinowitz (1823-1900).

Born in Kreisburg, Latvia, young Tzadok attracted attention as a phenomenal genius. Orphaned at the age of six, he was raised by his uncle near Bialystok. Such was the child's reputation that R' Yitzchak Elchanan Spektor of Kovno made a point of testing him when he happened to be nearby. He prophecied that 'the boy will light a great torch of knowledge in Israel'.

In later years, R' Tzadok lived in Lublin where he became acquainted with R' Leibele Eiger, a disciple of R' Mordechai Yosef of Izhbica. R' Tzadok became their disciple, and with their passing, became Rebbe of the Chassidim of Izhbica. He became known far and wide as the 'Kohen of Lublin.' The breadth and depth of his thought is astonishing. Many considered him the greatest Torah scholar in all of Poland.

A very prolific writer, he left many unpublished manuscripts that were destroyed during World War II. Among his works are *Pri Tzaddik*, a major collection of discourses on Torah and the festivals, Responsa *Tiferes Zvi*,and *Resisei Layla*.

Contemporary Rabbinic Sources

Aley Shur

A book of guidance to the aspiring *ben Torah*. R' Shlomo Wolbe, Israel.

Anvil of Sinai

A comprehensive *hashkafah*/historical treatment of the chain of Torah tradition. R' Zecharia Fendel.

Bruer, R' Joseph

Formerly Rosh Yeshivah of Frankfort, author of *Der Prophet Jecheskel*. Great leader and founder of the German community which was transplanted to the Washington Heights neighborhood of New York.

Carmel, R' Aryeh

Torah scholar, writer and educator, Israel.

Da'as Sofrim

A commentary on Tanach. R' Chaim Dov Rabinowitz. America, Israel.

Darko Shel Rashi BeFeirusho LeTalmud Bavli

An examination of *Rashi's* methodology in his commentary to the Talmud. Yonah Frankel, Israel.

Forchheimer, Dr. Paul

Respected Hirschian scholar and writer.

HaMikdash HaShelishi

Encyclopedia on the Temple of Yechezkel. R' Shaul Schaefer, Israel.

HaTekufah HaGedolah

An examination of current events in the light of the teaching of the Sages. R' Menachem Kasher, Israel.

Lieberman, R' Joseph

Torah Scholar, Israel

Nachalas Shimon

An examination of halachic topics touched upon the Book of Joshua. R' Shimon Krasner, Kollel Ner Israel, Baltimore.

Pachad Yitzchak

A work on Jewish thought by one of the leading roshei hayeshivah of contemporary times. R' Yitzchak Hutner, Israel and New York.

Toldos Am Olam

Jewish history in the light of the teachings of the Sages. R' Shlomo Rottenberg, New York.